organisational
behaviour
third edition

marc buelens
herman van den broeck
karlien vanderheyden
robert kreitner
angelo kinicki

The McGraw·Hill Companies

London	Boston	Burr Ridge, IL	Dubuque, IA	Madison, WI	New York
San Francisco	St. Louis	Bangkok	Bogotá	Caracas	Kuala Lumpur
Lisbon	Madrid	Mexico City	Milan	Montreal	New Delhi
Santiago	Seoul	Singapore	Sydney	Taipei	Toronto

Organisational Behaviour, Third Edition
Marc Buelens, Herman Van den Broeck, Karlien Vanderheyden,
Robert Kreitner, Angelo Kinicki
ISBN-13: 978-0-07-710723-9
ISBN-10: 0-07-710723-3

 **Education**

Published by McGraw-Hill Education
Shoppenhangers Road
Maidenhead
Berkshire
SL6 2QL
Telephone: 44 (0) 1628 502 500
Fax: 44 (0) 1628 770 224
Website: www.mcgraw-hill.co.uk

British Library Cataloguing in Publication Data
A catalogue record for this book is available from the British Library

Library of Congress Cataloging in Publication Data
The Library of Congress data for this book has been applied for from the Library of Congress

Acquisitions Editor: Kirsty Reade
Development Editors: Catriona Watson and Emily Jefferson
Marketing Manager: Alice Duijser
Senior Production Editor: Eleanor Hayes
Editorial Assistant: Natalie Jacobs

Text Design by Jonathan Coleclough
Cover design by Fielding Design Ltd.
Printed and bound in Dubai by Oriental Press

The **McGraw-Hill** Companies

Authors

This book has been authored by a team at Ghent University. The following authors have all contributed to this book:

Dave Bouckenooghe

Marc Buelens

Eva Cools

Fannie Debussche

Geert Devos

Steven Mestdagh

Herman Van den Broeck

Karlien Vanderheyden

Dirk Van Poucke

Veronique Warmoes

Annick Willem

Brief table of contents

Detailed table of contents

detailed table of contents

Section 3: Group and social processes

Section 4: Organisational processes

Preface

When the authors were asked by McGraw-Hill to publish a third edition of *Organisational Behaviour*, they realised that this was a wonderful opportunity. This edition is a product of hard work and commitment from a team of 11 specialists in organisational behaviour.

Organisational Behaviour, Third Edition has become a fully European edition, as a result of feedback from users of the last edition. The first two editions focused primarily on the Europeanisation of organisational examples, exercises and cases. The focus of this edition was to introduce European theories to complement the European illustrative examples. This approach has allowed us to achieve a balance between American and European theories.

As we progressed through drafts of this edition, the text was continually updated to reflect recently published theories and examples. This enabled us to produce an up-to-date, relevant and interesting European text.

Structural improvements in the Third Edition

Section 1 contains one chapter providing an understanding of the foundations of organisational behaviour, followed by a Learning module on research methods in organisational behaviour. In Sections 2 to 4 the material flows from micro (individuals) to macro (groups and organisations) topics. We have tried to keep a balance between micro and macro topics and between a psychological and a sociological scope (also see 'Our approach'). As a guide for users of the previous edition, the following structural changes need to be noted:

- Section 1 covers an introductory chapter on organisational behaviour (Chapter 1) and a learning module.
- Section 2 contains six chapters. 'Personality dynamics' and 'Values, attitudes and emotions' are split up in two separate chapters (Chapters 2 and 3). Diversity is now treated in conjunction with stereotyping and perception in Chapter 4. Motivation still contains two chapters, but the themes are reshuffled: Chapter 5 treats content theories and Chapter 6 process theories. The chapter on feedback and organisational rewards from the previous edition is integrated in Chapter 6. Occupational stress is now considered as an individual process in Section 2 (Chapter 7).
- Section 3 covers six chapters. Teams and groups are two separate chapters as requested by reviewers (Chapters 9 and 10). Power, politics and conflict are combined in one single chapter (Chapter 13). Leadership, communication and decision making are the other group and social processes elaborated in Section 3.
- Section 4 covers five chapters. The first four chapters are completely reshuffled and renewed. 'Organisation structure and types' and 'Organisation design and effectiveness' are split up in two separate chapters (Chapters 14 and 15). International culture is placed in Chapter 16. It expands our treatment of culture. Knowledge management and learning are now clustered in Chapter 17, as an expansion of change. Section 4 ends with a totally new chapter on corporate social responsibility and ethics (Chapter 18).
- The Internet exercises have been moved to the end of the chapter exercises. All Internet links are centralised on one single webpage kept up to date by the editor, so as to avoid broken links.
- Each chapter contains at least one Activity to foster personal involvement and greater self-awareness. This results in 26 Activities in all.
- Each chapter contains at least one Snapshot, which cover OB topics in an international context. In total the book counts 21 Snapshots.

New and expanded coverage

Our readers and reviewers appreciate our efforts to keep this textbook up to date and relevant to a European context. This third edition is a huge step forward in the Europeanisation of the textbook. Each topic has been scrutinised as to its relevance for European lecturers and students. As described above a sound balance is kept between American and European approaches and between Anglo-Saxon and non-Anglo-Saxon visions. In addition, this edition includes the following new and improved topics.

- **Chapter 1** New part on European perspectives of OB, ideas and background information on the pioneers of OB, Morgan's organisational metaphors, update of the information on the Hawthorne studies
- **Learning module** Research methods in organisational behaviour: the research process and how to read a scientific journal article are covered
- **Chapter 2** Expansion of personality and abilities, new part on cognitive styles and learning styles
- **Chapter 3** New case study, new section on values, expansion of attitudes and emotions

- **Chapter 4** More attention to factors influencing perception, attribution is reconsidered and improved, stereotyping is expanded with diversity, the cross-generational workplace, updated demographic data
- **Chapter 5** New case study, critical view of Maslow, ERG theory, update of McClelland's theory, evaluation of job characteristics theory
- **Chapter 6** New case study, considerable update of research findings and practical implications of process theories, feedback and organisational rewards, new tables and more accessible figures
- **Chapter 7** Karasek's Job Demand-Control (JD-C) model
- **Chapter 8** Expansion of verbal and non-verbal communication, more attention to new technologies and gender differences
- **Chapter 9** New case study, considerable expansion of group theories including new figures: Homan, Sherif, sociometric assessment and sociogram, Belbin's theory and expanded coverage of homogeneous versus heterogeneous groups, updated research findings
- **Chapter 10** Update of research findings on different types of teams, focus only on teams and team work, while group-related aspects are shifted towards Chapter 9
- **Chapter 11** New European case study, supposed differences between 'weak' managers and 'real leaders', differences between 'sick' leaders and 'dedicated' managers, charismatic leadership as a mixed blessing
- **Chapter 12** Focus on ethical decision-making in group exercise, updated research findings
- **Chapter 13** New European case study, covers power, politics and conflict, Cialdini's six principles of influence and persuasion
- **Chapter 14** New European case study, updated and more European examples on the structure of Volvo, Agfa Gevaert, British Telecom and Atlas Copco, improved attention to European approach, Mintzberg, matrix organisation, new organisation types (network organisation, project organisation and platform organisation)
- **Chapter 15** New case study, European research on the effectiveness criteria (Boldwijn and Kumpe) and European examples (AT&T, Body Shop and Lego), broader view of organisational fit, chaos theory, systems theory, improved explanation of contingency approach, technology (Woodward, Thompson, Galbraith and Perrow), environment (Duncan and Daft, Lengel), strategy (Miles and Snow), strategy and structure, organisational diagnosis, the resource view, organisational effectiveness criteria
- **Chapter 16** New European case study, covers both organisational and international culture, new view of types of organisational cultures, European approach of international culture with European research findings and practical implications
- **Chapter 17** Theory E and O, challenges for understanding organisational change, considerable expansion of section on learning organisation and knowledge management
- **Chapter 18** New European case study, new chapter on social corporate responsibility and ethics

About the authors

Dave Bouckenooghe, Marc Buelens, Eva Cools, Fannie Debussche, Geert Devos, Steven Mestdagh, Herman Van den Broeck, Karlien Vanderheyden, Veronique Warmoes and Annick Willem have all contributed to this edition.

The authors all belong to the Vlerick Leuven Gent Management School, the Autonomous Management School of Ghent University and Katholieke Universiteit Leuven. The School possesses 3 important international accreditations, which makes the school 1 out of 21 worldwide to have been granted the AACSB, the AMBA and the EQUIS accreditations.

AACSB accreditation is a global quality assurance system for undergraduate, masters (including MBA), and doctoral education in business. It is administered by AACSB International – The Association to Advance Collegiate Schools of Business. AACSB International accreditation assures quality and promotes excellence and continuous improvement in undergraduate and graduate education for business administration and accounting by an external awarding body. Worldwide, there are 480 business schools accredited of which 62 are outside the United States (www.aacsb.edu).

**Accredited by
Association
of MBAs** The Association of MBAs currently accredits programmes at 91 leading international business schools. Vlerick Leuven Gent Management School has been awarded accreditation for its four MBA programmes. Programmes are assessed against a set of criteria developed by the Association's International Accreditation Advisory Board and criteria are monitored to reflect changes in business and management practice (www.mbaworld.com).

EQUIS
ACCREDITED EQUIS is the quality assurance scheme run by EFMD (European Foundation for Management Development) as a service to the management education profession worldwide. It is the leading international system of quality assessment, improvement and accreditation of higher education institutions in management and business administration. Currently 79 business schools are accredited by EQUIS worldwide (www.efmd.org). Twenty-seven countries are represented among EQUIS accredited schools: Australia, Belgium, Brazil, Canada, China, Colombia, Costa Rica, Denmark, Finland, France, Germany, Ireland, Italy, Mexico, the Netherlands, New Zealand, Norway, Philippines, Poland, Portugal, South Africa, Singapore, Spain, Sweden, Switzerland, United Kingdom, United States of America.

Our approach

Organisational behaviour is a multi- and interdisciplinary field. It finds its inspiration in a variety of social science disciplines such as (social) psychology, sociology, anthropology and economics. It is also influenced by disciplines such as (evolutionary) biology or mathematical theories of networks. One could make a distinction between micro and macro organisational behaviour.

In a micro organisational behaviour perspective, the way individuals interact with organisations is studied. Drawing primarily on psychology, this perspective deals with topics such as job attitudes and work motivation (Chapters 3, 5 and 6), emotions in the workplace (Chapter 3), stress (Chapter 7), group processes (Chapter 9), leadership (Chapter 11), decision making (Chapter 12), negotiation (Chapter 13), influence (Chapter 13) and learning (Chapters 2 and 17).

In a macro organisational behaviour perspective, one studies organisations as systems, and how organisations interact with their environments (including other organisations). Drawing primarily on sociology, this perspective deals with topics such as organisation structure and design (Chapters 14 and 15), culture (Chapter 16), organisational change (Chapter 17) and corporate social responsibility (Chapter 18).

We have thoroughly enjoyed working on this edition and we are sure you will enjoy the learning while using this OB book.

Marc Buelens
Herman Van den Broeck
Karlien Vanderheyden

Guided tour

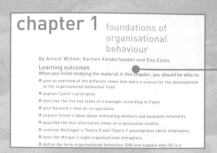

chapter 1 foundations of organisational behaviour

By Annick Willem, Karlien Vanderheyden and Eva Cools

Learning outcomes

When you finish studying the material in this chapter, you should be able to:

- give an overview of the different views that were a source for the development of the organisational behaviour field
- explain Taylor's principles
- describe the five key tasks of a manager according to Fayol
- give Barnard's view on co-operation
- explain Simon's ideas about motivating workers and bounded rationality
- describe the four alternative views on organisation studies
- contrast McGregor's Theory X and Theory Y assumptions about employees
- describe Morgan's eight organisational metaphors
- define the term organisational behaviour (OB) and explain why OB is a

Learning outcomes
Each chapter opens with a set of learning outcomes that pinpoint the key concepts introduced.

Management blasted at nuclear plant

A lack of 'people management skills' such as leadership, vision was at the core of the UK's Sellafield scandal, accord Inspectorate (NII), the national nuclear safety watchdog. Resources (HR) director, however, the process workers w Sellafield nuclear power plant and led to cancelled orders chief executive. What had happened at Sellafield?

An inspection at the plant revealed that workers had falsifi of an experimental, mixed plutonium and uranium fuel. The a Japanese customer, power company Kansai. Workers ha samples of each sample, se figures from previous batches. A major scandal broke out and

But this was not the end: a report by the NII discovered a improper management across the plant. 'In a plant with a caused the scandal could not have happened', one of the ins Leek admitted that there had 'probably not been enough in

Case study
Each chapter opens with an interesting and relevant case study to introduce and apply key theories in OB. Each case study contains questions to encourage discussion.

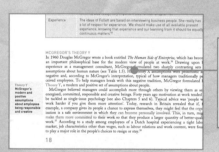

| Experience | The ideas of Follett are based on interviewing business people. She really has a lot of respect for experience. 'We should make use of all available present experience, knowing that experience and our learning from it should be equally continuous matters.' |

MCGREGOR'S THEORY Y

In 1960 Douglas McGregor wrote a book entitled *The Human Side of Enterprise*, which has becom an important philosophical base for the modern view of people at work. Drawing upon experience as a management consultant, McGregor formulated two sharply contrasting sets assumptions about human nature (see Table 1.5). His Theory X assumptions were pessimistic a negative and, according to McGregor's interpretation, typical of how managers traditionally pe ceived employees. To help managers break with this negative tradition, McGregor formulated Theory Y, a modern and positive set of assumptions about people.

McGregor believed managers could accomplish more through others by viewing them as se energised, committed, responsible and creative beings. Forty years ago motivation at work tended be tackled as single-issue psychology (see also Chapters 5 and 6). Typical advice was 'people work harder if you give them more attention'. Today, research in Britain revealed that if, example, a company gives its people a chance to express themselves, they might feel that the org iation is a safe environment in which they can become personally involved. This, in turn, mig make them more committed to their work so that they produce a larger quantity of better-qual work.' According to a study among employees of a Dutch hospital experiencing a tight labo market, job characteristics other than wages, such as labour relations and work content, were fou to play a major role in the people's choices to resign or stay.'

Theory Y
McGregor's modern and positive assumptions about employees being responsible and creative

18

Key terms
Each new term introduced in the book is highlighted in the text, and a margin box provides a concise definition to aid revision. A complete list of key terms is provided in the glossary at the end of the book.

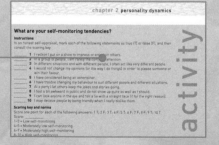

chapter 2 **personality dynamics**

What are your self-monitoring tendencies?

Instructions

In an honest self-appraisal, mark each of the following statements as true (T) or false (F), and then consult the scoring key.

1 I reckon I put on a show to impress or entertain others.
2 In a group of people, I am rarely the centre of attention.
3 In different situations and with different people, I often act like very different people.
4 I would not change my opinion for the way I do things) in order to please someone or with their favour.
5 I have considered being an entertainer.
6 I have trouble changing my behaviour to suit different people and different situations.
7 At a party I let others keep the jokes and stories going.
8 I feel a bit awkward in public and do not show up quite as well as I should.
9 I can look anyone in the eye and tell a lie with a straight face (if for the right reason).
10 I may deceive people by being friendly when I really dislike them.

Scoring key and norms
Score one point for each of the following answers: 1 T; 2 F; 3 T; 4 F; 5 T; 6 F; 7 F; 8 F; 9 T; 10 T
Score:
1–3 = Low self-monitoring
4–5 = Moderately low self-monitoring
6–7 = Moderately high self-monitoring
8–10 = High self-monitoring

Activity
Activities are interspersed throughout the text to encourage analytical thinking and to develop skills through interactive tasks.

Culture dictates the degree of self-disclosure in Japan and the United States

Survey research in Japan and the United States uncovered the following distinct contrasts in Japanese versus American self-disclosure:

- Americans disclosed nearly as much to strangers as the Japanese did to their own fathers.
- Americans reported two to three times greater physical contact with parents and twice greater contact with friends than the Japanese.
- The Japanese may be frightened at the prospect of being communicatively invaded (because of the unexpected spontaneity and bluntness of the American); the American is annoyed at the prospect of endless formalities and tangential replies.
- Americans emphasis on self-assertion and talkativeness cultivates a communicator who is highly self-oriented and expressive; the Japanese emphasis on 'reserve' and 'sensitivity' cultivates a communicator who is other-oriented (oriented toward the other person) and receptive.

American public and private self   Japanese public and private self

Private self

Snapshot
These snapshots provide examples from around the globe, focusing on the differences in perceptions, cultures and beliefs that affect behaviour in the workplace, providing relevant and interesting insights and an international outlook on OB.

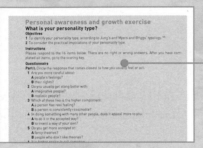

Learning outcomes: Summary of key terms
At the end of the chapter, a short recap reinforces and clarifies the chapter learning outcomes.

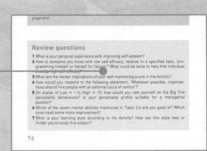

Review questions
These end of chapter exercises test understanding of core theories and can be used in class or as an assessment. As well as checking comprehension, the exercises require you to demonstrate your analytical abilities by citing examples and applications of the concepts in the chapter.

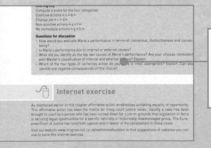

Personal awareness and growth exercise
An in-depth exercise illustrates decisions one might face in the workplace. These organisational problems aim to develop ethical awareness and transferable skills, for instance in communication, negotiation or dealing with conflict.

Group exercise
These exercises encourage group discussion and activity and are ideal for seminar study.

Internet exercise
Internet exercises make full use of the web as a research tool. The tasks are set to help develop online research skills through examining real organisations and companies.

Notes
A comprehensive list of references for each chapter can be found at the end of each chapter.

Technology to enhance learning and teaching

Visit www.mcgraw-hill.co.uk/textbooks/buelens **today**

Resources for lecturers

Online Learning Centre

Lecturers can find a range of resources and tools to support their teaching at the Online Learning Centre Website, including:

- Lecturer manual containing lecture outlines, exercises and more
- PowerPoints for lecture presentations and for handouts
- Discussion and essay questions
- Case study guide answers
- Artwork from the textbook

To access all of the Online Learning Centre lecturer resources, and to contact your McGraw-Hill representative, simply visit the website at www.mcgraw-hill.co.uk/textbooks/buelens and follow the instructions to register for a password.

For lecturers: Primis Content Centre

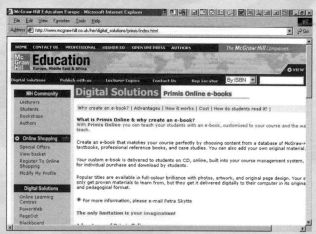

Can't find the perfect book for your course? If you need to supplement your course with additional cases or content, create a personalised e-Book for your students. Visit www.primiscontentcenter.com or e-mail primis_euro@mcgraw-hill.com for more information.

Online Learning Centre

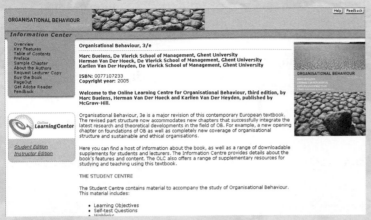

After completing each chapter, log on to the supporting Online Learning Centre website. Take advantage of the free study tools offered to reinforce the material you have read in the text, and to develop your knowledge of OB in a fun and effective way. A range of resources are offered providing revision tools and handy exam practice!

The new edition provides the complete package of materials for students of OB:

- Learning objectives
- Additional case studies
- New case study questions
- Internet exercises
- Interactive self-assessment questions
- Web links

Visit the OLC at www.mcgraw-hill.co.uk/textbooks/buelens for access to all these materials free with every student purchase of the textbook.

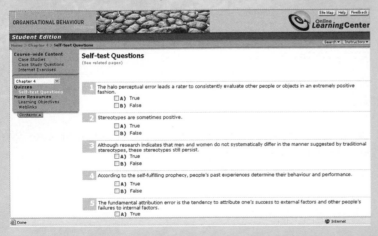

Study skills

Need help with exams, essays, assignments or research projects? Open University Press publishes guides to study, research and exam skills, to help undergraduate and postgraduate students through their university studies.

Visit www.openup.co.uk/ss/ to see the full selection.

Computing skills

If you'd like to brush up on your Computing skills, we have a range of titles covering MS Office applications such as Word, Excel, PowerPoint, Access and more.

Get a £2 discount off these titles by entering the promotional code **app** when ordering online at www.mcgraw-hill.co.uk/app

Acknowledgements

This book is the work of a great team. You will find the names of the contributors on page xi. But behind each team there is always the hard work of implementers and finishers, in our case Eva Cools and Fannie Debussche.

Thanks to Eva Cools' excellent 'expert' and 'planner' capacities the book resulted in one fluent text, both as to the content, style and lay-out. Fannie Debussche's experience with the two previous editions and her co-ordination skills resulted in on-time delivery. A special and warm thanks is going to Eva and Fannie!

Our thanks also go to the following reviewers for their comments at various stages in the text's development:

Brian Abbot, University of Kingston

Ray French, University of Portsmouth

Julie Gore, University of Surrey

Annie Hollings, University of Staffordshire

Mohammed Ishaq, University of Paisley

Ian Kirkpatrick, University of Leeds

Sarah MacCurtain, University of Limerick

Sarah Mackie, University of the West of England

Alma McCarthy, National University of Ireland, Galway

Caroline Ramsey, University of Northampton

Gwenny Ruel, University of Groningen

Herman Steensma, University of Leiden

Svenja Tams, University of Bath

Patrick Tissington, University of Aston

Daan van Knippenberg, University of Rotterdam

We would also like to thank the following companies for their permission to reproduce material within this textboook:

'Good Performer Track of a Performance' from Sims, 'The New Leadership Paradigm: Social Learning and Cognition', copyright by Sage Publications Inc. Reprinted with permission of Sage Publications Inc.

Adaptation from pages 62–69, from 'The Knowledge-creating Company: How Japanese Companies Create the Dynamics of Innovation' by Ikujiro Nonaka and Hirotaka Takeuchi, copyright © 1995 by Oxford University Press, Inc. Used by permission of Oxford University Press, Inc.

section

1

the world of OB

chapter 1 foundations of organisational behaviour

By Annick Willem, Karlien Vanderheyden and Eva Cools

Learning outcomes

When you finish studying the material in this chapter, you should be able to:

- give an overview of the different views that were a source for the development of the organisational behaviour field
- explain Taylor's principles
- describe the five key tasks of a manager according to Fayol
- give Barnard's view on co-operation
- explain Simon's ideas about motivating workers and bounded rationality
- describe the four alternative views on organisation studies
- contrast McGregor's Theory X and Theory Y assumptions about employees
- describe Morgan's eight organisational metaphors
- define the term organisational behaviour (OB) and explain why OB is a horizontal discipline

case study

Management blasted at nuclear plant

A lack of 'people management skills' such as leadership, communication, motivation and supervision was at the core of the UK's Sellafield scandal, according to the British Nuclear Installations Inspectorate (NII), the national nuclear safety watchdog. According to the company's Human Resources (HR) director, however, the process workers were to blame for the scandal that hit Sellafield nuclear power plant and led to cancelled orders and ultimately the resignation of the chief executive. What had happened at Sellafield?

An inspection at the plant revealed that workers had falsified some important quality control data of an experimental, mixed plutonium and uranium fuel. The falsified data involved a test ordered by a Japanese customer, power company Kansai. Workers had to check the diameters of random samples of fuel pellets. Instead of testing each sample, several workers had simply copied old figures from previous batches. A major scandal broke out and five workers were sacked.

But this was not the end: a report by the NII discovered a lack of high-quality safety systems and improper management across the plant. 'In a plant with a proper safety culture, the events that caused the scandal could not have happened', one of the inspectors said. While HR director Roger Leek admitted that there had 'probably not been enough investment in training', he insisted that operators, rather than senior managers, were responsible for practices that had jeopardised safety: 'You rely on the operators to do what is expected of them, rather than stand over them day and night. There are a lot of jobs in this industry that are rather technical, but people still do them', he said.

There had been a perception at the plant that nothing more than the dismissal of those process workers involved in the affair, along with a tightening-up of procedures, would be necessary. After it was revealed that they had falsified the quality check, many thought that it was only the process workers who would be criticised.

However, the report from the UK's nuclear watchdog sent shockwaves through the plant's senior management. It focused on how the nature of the job, lack of supervision and poor training had contributed largely to the procedural failures. The workers' actions were 'not at all surprising' given the 'tedious' nature of the tasks involved, the report said.

Trade unions were quick to blame the crisis on a lack of 'people skills' among middle managers. John Kane, site convenor for the GMB (General and Municipal Boilermakers) union, claimed that managers at the plant rarely talked to staff. 'We have this treacle layer of middle managers who, although highly qualified in certain tasks, have very few people-management skills', he said. But key figures in personnel believe the problem runs deeper.

The data check was part of a quality assurance inspection and had never been connected with safety, although the use of substandard pellets could have safety implications, according to recent press reports. However, the significance of the check, even for quality control, was not emphasised to staff. As a result, falsifying the data became a way of avoiding what was seen as a pointless task. The NII report warned that allowing this attitude towards dull and monotonous work to develop through a failure to explain its significance, could lead to more serious errors in future. Sellafield's initial response was simply to promise improvements, but the Government indicated that this was not enough and that more serious action was required.

The NII report criticised almost every aspect of Sellafield's management structure. It condemned reductions in staff numbers made in response to the Government's plans to prepare British Nuclear Fuels (BNFL) for partial privatisation, and warned that health and safety arrangements were unclear, with safety managers overworked and safety training poor.

There was no excuse for falsifying records, the report said, but 'inadequacies' in the working environment were a major factor. Because supervision of the inspection was 'virtually non-existent', managers had sent out 'entirely the wrong message regarding the importance of the task and acted as a demotivator'. Awareness training had been 'ineffective', leaving workers with no idea of the significance of their job. Consequently, staff were 'unlikely to appreciate the importance of the task or take ownership of it'.

The task itself had been poorly conceived, the report said. Other than the prospect of an eventual quality control stamp and payment for completing the work, there was no recognition of diligent performance. Other workstations at Sellafield, which employs 10 000 people, were also badly designed, according to the report.

Job structures would now be reviewed, Leek said, but the incident had created apprehension among managers about the security of their jobs. 'The ramification of a few people not following operating procedures has damaged this company. There comes a point where you train people, you give them responsibilities and you expect them to fulfil them correctly – even if the job is boring', he said.

Tom Cannon, chief executive of the Management and Enterprise National Training Organisation, also blamed the management at Sellafield. 'As a nation, we are deeply confused about technology. On the one hand, we are technophobes; on the other, we believe that technology will solve everything. There is an implication that, if you get the science right, the people will fit around it. But all the evidence shows that this simply isn't true,' he said. 'The Sellafield managers thought the maths would do the job – and that the more people acted like machines, the better. They didn't seem to be aware of the people-development strategies you'd expect to have in a company that's not short of money.'[1]

For discussion

Sellafield's HR director and the British Nuclear Installations Inspectorate have rather contrasting views on who is to blame for the nuclear scandal. What do you think caused the problems?

True or false? People are the key to success in today's highly competitive global economy. It is nearly a century since Henry Ford said: 'You can destroy my factories and offices, but give me my people and I will build the business right back up again.'[2] Every day, business magazines come up with new stories reporting famous chief executive officers' (CEOs) claims that their employees are their main source of competitive advantage. For example Virgin boss, Richard Branson, said:

> There is only one thing that keeps your company alive, that is: the people you work with. All the rest is secondary. You have to motivate people, and attract the best. Every single employee can make a difference. For instance, the girl who opened the best bridal boutique in Europe worked as a stewardess at the airline. She came to me with an idea and I encouraged her to put it into practice. She did, and so Virgin Bride was originated. Because she was free to prove herself, she has been able to use all her talents optimally. The people you hire are so important. If you support the idea that every operator can excel in what he's doing, then that will eventually happen. People often make mistakes but you need to give them space even for that. You have to confirm people in what they're doing and make sure they have fun doing their job. You have to make them feel their work is important and give them the chance to do the things they like. At Virgin, of course, we're lucky that there are so many different functions. Everybody can develop in whatever way he or she wants to. If people see a former stewardess running her own company, people become inspired. Some people who are now working on the Eurostar were also those who helped get the airline off the ground. Some of them are already dreaming of new projects and this keeps the work exciting. People are the essence of an organisation and nothing else.[3]

But wait a minute. Dilbert cartoonist Scott Adams, who humorously documents managerial lapses of sanity, sees it differently. Adams rates the oft-heard statement: 'Employees are our most valuable asset', as top of his list of Great Lies of Management.[4] This raises serious questions. Is Branson an exception, a manager who actually acts on the idea that people are the most valuable resource? Does the typical manager merely pay lip-service to the critical importance of people? If so, what are the implications of this hypocrisy for organisational productivity and employee well-being?

A number of recent studies have been enlightening. Generally, they show that there is a substantial and rapidly expanding body of evidence – some of it based on quite sophisticated methodology – of the strong connection between how firms manage their people and the economic results they achieve.[5]

Jean-Claude Larreche, Professor at Insead, France, investigated which were the most 'healthy' companies in 1998 and 1999. In both reports Hewlett-Packard, Unilever, Credit Suisse, L'Oreal and Whitbread came out as the five healthiest of the largest European and American organisations. Larreche analysed the companies with a system called 'Market Effectiveness Capabilities Assessment'. Over 800 senior managers from 263 organisations were to evaluate the competitiveness of their companies on 150 determinants, clustered in 12 fundamental capacities. It turned out that the healthiest companies differed from the rest in particular aspects such as organisational culture, customer orientation and human resources. On the other hand, according to Larreche, 'the most harmful thing for competitive organisations is that top managers are often unable to relate to their employees and customers'.[6]

A study by the University of Sheffield's Institute of Work Psychology, based on extensive examination of over 100 medium-sized manufacturing companies over a seven-year period, revealed that people management is not only critical to business performance. It also far outstrips emphasis on quality, technology, competitive strategy, and research and development in its influence on the bottom line. The study, known as the Sheffield Effectiveness Programme, also showed that half the firms have no individual in charge of human resources and that more than two-thirds have no written personnel strategy. One researcher said: 'Managers placed considerable emphasis on strategy and technology, but our research suggests that these areas account for only a small part of the differences in financial performance.'[7]

Jeffrey Pfeffer and his colleagues from Stanford University reviewed evidence from companies in both the United States and Germany that 'people-centred practices' were strongly associated with much higher profits and significantly lower employee turnover. Further analysis uncovered the following seven people-centred practices in successful companies:

- Job security (to eliminate fear of lay-offs).
- Careful hiring (emphasising a good fit with the company culture).
- Power to the people (via decentralisation and self-managed teams).
- Generous pay for performance.
- Lots of training.
- Less emphasis on status (to build a 'we' feeling).
- Trust-building (through the sharing of critical information).[8]

It is vital that these factors form a package deal – they need to be installed in a co-ordinated and systematic manner rather than in bits and pieces.

The dark side of this study is that Scott Adams's cynical assessment is too often true. Organisations tend to act counter to their declarations that people are their most important asset. Pfeffer and his colleagues blame a number of modern management trends and practices. For example, undue emphasis on short-term profit precludes long-term efforts to nurture human resources. Also, excessive lay-offs – when organisations view people as a cost rather than an asset – erode trust, commitment and loyalty.[9] 'Only 12 per cent of the organisations', according to Pfeffer, 'have the systematic approaches and persistence to qualify as true people-centred organisations, thus giving them a competitive advantage.'[10] The studies at Insead and the Sheffield Effectiveness Programme seem to confirm this.

To us, an 88 per cent shortfall in the quest for people-centred organisations represents a tragic loss, both to society and to the global economy. Toward that end, the aim of this book is to help increase the number of people-centred managers and organisations around the world in order to narrow the often found gap between what people say (e.g. people are our most important asset) and what people do (e.g. layoffs, no training . . .).

We start our journey in the organisational behaviour field with a look at the history of the field. This history began in the early years of the industrial revolution. The first steps in its development led to a rational-system view of organisations. Several alternative views were developed later. Attention on the human factor started as early as the late 1930s but it took several decades before the organisational behaviour field was fully developed. The different sequential and contemporary views have resulted in different ways of studying, evaluating and managing people and organisations. The historical overview of the OB field will reveal that there were very different ways of looking at human behaviour in organisations. Gareth Morgan, for instance, has emphasised the fact that there are numerous ways in which we can view organisations. He summarised these different views in eight 'lenses' or metaphors for looking at organisations. The chapter concludes by presenting the ways in which we can learn more about organisational behaviour. Also, a topical model for understanding and managing OB is introduced.

Sources of inspiration of organisation and organisational behaviour theories

A historical perspective of the study of people at work helps in studying organisational behaviour. According to a management history expert, this is important because it sharpens one's vision of the present rather than of the past.[11] In other words, we can better understand where the field of OB is today and where it appears to be aiming, by appreciating where it has been.

In the nineteenth century sociologists such as Karl Marx, Emile Durkheim and Max Weber studied the implications of a shift from feudalism to capitalism and from an agriculture-based society to an industrial one. Karl Marx[12] studied the development of the working class,[13] while Emile Durkheim studied the loss of solidarity in the new kind of society. Max Weber was the first to study the working of organisations and the behaviour of people within organisations.[14] He is especially known for his work on bureaucratic organisations (see Chapter 14). As a sociologist, he studied also the rise of rationality in the new society and the importance of legal authority and efficiency in industrial production in particular.

Organisation studies developed as separate studies with the birth of 'scientific management' (see further Frederick Taylor). This happened around the end and beginning of respectively the nineteenth and twentieth centuries with the founding of the first large corporations, such as Ford, General Motors and Esso. Scientific management offered a rational and efficient way to streamline production. It is called 'scientific management' because the recommendations to companies were based on exact scientific studies of individual situations. Within this field a system view on organisations is taken, meaning that organisations are seen as systems and combinations of technology with little attention paid to the people in the organisation. Those people are only elements in the production system. According to Burns this scientific approach to organisations developed in the second phase of industrialism.[15] In that phase the factory system expanded from simple manufacturing processes, such as textile, to more complex manufacturing ones, such as food, engineering and iron. These complex processes required complex organisational procedures, including control mechanisms, routinisation and, especially, intense specialisation. Profound scientific study of the processes was required to develop complex but also highly efficient, organisation structures (for more on organisation structures, see Chapters 14 and 15). As part of that evolution, the function of management and administrative tasks rose and expanded considerably in number.

However, the system view was already being criticised in its early days and alternative views on organisations were developed, such as the conflict theory, the chaos theory, symbolic interactionism and postmodernism. These perspectives on organisations and society in general did not pay much attention to the people working in the factories. As a reaction to the systemic view, the human relations view developed, which studied the life of the employees in the factory system. However, the system view still dominated the organisation, working and thinking of managers during the first half of the twentieth century. Organisational behaviour developed from this human relations view as a separate academic discipline. We will highlight the work of some of the major management thinkers and explain the different views on organisations. Figure 1.1 provides a schematic overview of the different sources of inspiration for the development of the organisational behaviour field.

A rational-system view of organisations

We successively focus on the works of Frederick Taylor, Henri Fayol, Chester Barnard and Herbert Simon.

FREDERICK TAYLOR

The founding father of Scientific management and one of the best-known researchers in the rational-system view on organisations is Frederick Taylor. He was born into a Quaker Philadelphia aristocratic family in 1856. At that time Philadelphia was an important industrial region in the United States with several engineering companies – hence, providing the ideal location for the development of scientific management. The breakthrough for Taylor came when he started to work in the Midvale Steel Company in 1878.[16]

Taylor's principles

Taylor made the work of labour men more efficient by increasing the speed of work and by organising the work differently. He studied each task by comparing how different workers performed the same task. Each of the studied tasks was divided into as many subtasks as possible. The next step was eliminating the unnecessary subtasks and timing the fastest performance of each task. The whole task with its subtasks was then described in detail and an optimal time was attached to each task. Workers were asked to do the task in exactly this manner and time. Hence, each task had only 'one best way' allowing no freedom for workers to choose 'how' to do their tasks. Making the work in factories more efficient was an obsession. Taylor accused workers of 'soldiering'. Part of the slow working was due to the fact that there was no management to control the workforce, who were left entirely to develop their own working methods and to use ineffective rules-of-thumb. Workers were also systematically soldiering so they could just take it easy. In fact, Taylor accused them of conspiring to work slower in order to hide how fast they really could work.

Applying the ideas of Taylor resulted in the following consequences for the factory owners and workers:

Scientific management a scientific approach to management in which all tasks in organisations are in-depth analysed, routinised, divided and standardised, instead of using rules-of-thumb

FIGURE 1.1 THE SOURCES OF INSPIRATION FOR THE ORGANISATIONAL BEHAVIOUR FIELD

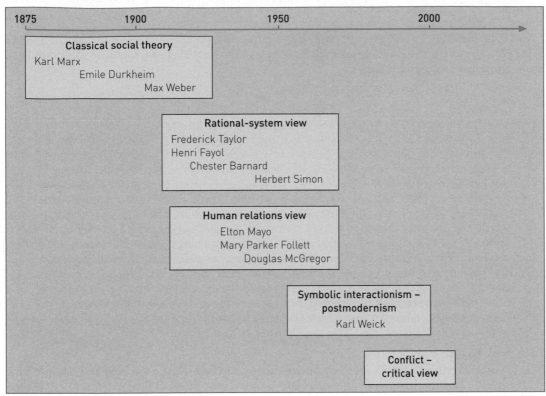

- Higher output.
- Standardisation.
- Control and predictability.
- The routine of the tasks allowed the replacement of skilled workers by non-skilled workers.
- Thinking is for the managers, workers only work.
- Optimisation of the tools for each worker (such as size and weight of the tools).

Taylor also analysed the work of foremen. Their jobs could also be divided into subtasks and greater efficiency could be reached if different foremen specialised only in one of the subtasks, such as controlling the speed, inspecting the quality or allocating the work.

Applying Taylor's ideas

One of the most famous examples of a factory that successfully applied Taylor's principles was Ford Motor Company. Many managers tried to implement time studies and other elements of Taylor's system but refused to pay the higher wages that are also part of Taylor's system. Ford Motor Company doubled the wages simultaneously with the implementation of assembly lines and scientific management. Henry Ford, the founder of Ford Motor Company, changed the production of automobiles from custom-made to a product for the mass. The Ford T, only available in black with no factory options at all, was the first car produced for the masses. This car was produced from 1908 until 1927 and 15 million cars of the same model were produced. There were so many cars sold because they were cheap enough to be affordable by the masses. This lower cost could only be reached by highly efficient production based on interchangeable parts (all pieces of the cars are the same for all cars), continuous flow (making use of an assembly line), division of labour (each worker is specialised in one very particular task) and eliminating unnecessary efforts (by applying motion studies). Low-skilled, and thus cheaper, workers could replace high-skilled workers through the use of more machinery and through specialisation. Frederick Taylor was asked to do time and motion

7

studies to eliminate all wasted efforts and to optimise each of the 48 steps in the production process. The combination of double wages and cheap cars made it possible for the workers to save for their own car. The higher wages were both compensation for the dull work and a way of creating customers for the cars.[17]

Car manufacturers, as well as many other factories, are still working according to many of Taylor's principles. Especially the work on assembly lines has hardly been changed. Consider the example of the German car manufacturer Opel:

> The production figures, the number of cars that are produced daily, are extremely important. Hence, the assembly line should move as fast as possible and stop as few times as possible. However, Opel Belgium now also strives for high quality. The assembly line must stop each time the smallest mistake is made. Diana Tremblay, plant director at Opel Belgium, explains that in the past quality was not such a major issue. Nothing was allowed to stop the murderous pace of the rolling assembly line but now the assembly line has to stop whenever a tiny nut is not well fixed. This required a change of mentality on the part of the employees. One of the workers explains: 'We have 54 seconds for attaching each back-door, 48 seconds to fix it well to the car and 6 seconds to return to our initial starting position for the next door because the line just rolls on.' Another worker says: 'I do not regret to work here, although I wanted to leave after the first two months because I almost got crazy knowing the line never stops.' Many of the employees complain about the high work pace but they are also proud to work in the high productivity plant. Every employee, even the director, has to work a few days on the assembly line to know what it means to do the work. Each job on that line is perfectly timed but this is discussed closely with the labour unions. There is no slack any more. Reducing tasks by two seconds would lead to a revolution.[18]

Critics of Taylor's principles

Many workers resisted Taylor's methods because they feared the harder working and because their skills became obsolete. Jobs were turned into non-skilled ones that could be done by anyone. Hence, workers lost their value as skilled employees. They also lost any decision-making power regarding their work. Taylor selected workers and foremen on the basis of other qualities than their skills and ability to think about their job. He chose them on the basis of their physical condition and their ability to learn and cope with the standard methods. Although the workers regarded Taylor and his principles as a threat, in his way Taylor respected them by paying them more when they followed his methods and increased productivity. Nonetheless, he mainly saw workers as people that could be

activity

Are Taylor's principles still alive?

Call centres are subject to tight control on call handling time with standardisation of the way customers' queries are handled. However, this should not be generalised for all call centres. Some focus on quantity and apply Taylor's principles to maximise the number of calls, while others focus on quality and allow more flexibility in time and manner of call handling. Nonetheless, most call centres are intensively monitoring their operators, even if this reduces staff motivation.

Questions

1 Do you agree that tight control and intensively monitoring are necessary at work in general?
2 Do you agree that tight control and intensively monitoring is necessary in an environment such as a call centre?
3 Will people work more if they are paid more?
4 What else than pay do people work for?

SOURCE: Based on studies of P. Bain, A. Watson, G. Mulvey, P. Taylor and G. Gall, 'Taylorism, Targets and the Pursuit of Quantity and Quality by Call Centre Management', *New Technology, Work and Employment*, November 2002, pp. 170–72; and P. Taylor and P. Bain, 'An Assembly Line in the Head: Work and Employee Relations in the Call Centre', *Industrial Relations Journal*, June 1999, pp. 101–17.

perfectly conditioned and trained. The application of Taylor's ideas in many factories led to resistance by the labour unions and even to a strike. On 21 August 1911 a special committee of the House of Representatives of the United States was assigned to the task of investigating the shop floor systems, including Taylor's system. There grew a general resistance towards Taylor's systems on grounds of inhumanity.

However, a recent study of UK call centres teaches us that the principles of scientific management and of Frederick Taylor are still alive (see Activity).[19]

Previous examples show that Taylor's principles and elements of the shop floor production methods of the Ford Motor Company are still used in mass production factories all over the world. His ideas are very useful in creating high levels of efficiency and productivity, not only for labour workers but also for office workers and in service industries. However, Taylor's ideas have been misinterpreted and misused, giving him a bad (but unfair) reputation for squeezing out workers by inhuman work methods and working speed to enrich management. Nonetheless, Taylor did neglect some important organisational behaviour aspects, such as the importance of job satisfaction (see Chapter 3), non-financial work incentives (see Chapter 6) or the positive role of groups and teams (see Chapters 9 and 10). Taylor saw groupings of workers as the basis of 'soldiering'. Furthermore, critics referred to the 'deskilling' of jobs because the systems and machinery replaced the craftsmen skills and destroyed work satisfaction. Deskilling was especially present in the Ford Motor Company's production systems, also called 'Fordism'. Taylor optimised productivity around existing tools and machinery but did not strive for maximum replacement of skilled labour by machinery. It was a combination of Taylor's principle on specialisation by dividing the tasks and the use of new machinery (Fordism) that led to deskilling. Many researchers in the organisational behaviour field have been reacting to this job deskilling, the alienation of the workers from their work and the product they are making and the negative human consequences of scientific management.

HENRI FAYOL

Henri Fayol[20] lived in the same period as Taylor but was born and lived in France where he worked as an engineer and manager in the mining industry. Fayol is known through his landmark work *General and Industrial Management* in which he described the basic principles of management. His management principles were proposed as general principles and based on rationality, in a similar way to Taylor, who also took a fundamental rational view on management. Fayol worked his whole career, first as engineer and later as manager, in the same company, namely the mining company Commentary Fourchamboult Décazeville. His famous management book summarised the lessons he learned during his work as manager in that company. The reason for its success is that Fayol was the first to describe management as a separate profession and activity in companies. It is said that Fayol 'invented' the concept of management. In fact, management is a very young profession and scientific discipline. This does not mean that companies had no leaders, directors or managers previously, but only that those management tasks were not studied until Fayol.

Fayol's principles

Henri Fayol made management visible by defining it and describing in a normative way what managers should do. There are a number of general principles that managers should follow and basic tasks that they should execute. Table 1.1 describes the five main management tasks, which are often abbreviated as POLCC.

To execute these five basic tasks of management well, 14 general management principles should be obeyed. These are:

1 Division of labour.
2 Authority and responsibility.
3 Discipline.
4 Unity of command.
5 Unity of direction.
6 Subordination of individual interest to the general interest.
7 Fair remuneration of personnel.
8 Centralisation.

TABLE 1.1 THE FIVE BASIC MANAGEMENT TASKS ACCORDING TO FAYOL

Planning	Predicting and drawing up a course of action to meet the planned goals. To plan is literally making written plans, for ten years, one year, one month, one week, one day and special plans. The ten-year, one year and special plans are the most important and form the general plan. The ten-year plan should be adapted slightly every year and totally reviewed every five years
Organising	This consists of allocating the materials and organising the people. Most organisations are very hierarchical but every employee and department can still take some initiative. Nonetheless, authority, discipline and control are major forces in the organisation. Fayol pays a lot of attention to the role of the Board of Directors, which is the hardest to compose and has the important task of selecting the general management
Leading (commanding)	Giving directions and orders to employees. Commanding consists of influencing and convincing others to make them accomplish the goals and plans. This involves not only giving orders but also motivating people
Co-ordinating	Co-ordinating mainly refers to meetings with the departmental heads to harmonise the different departments to one unit, working for the one general interest of the company. Liaison officers can help to tune radically different ideas and goals between two departments
Controlling	Controlling to what extent the goals were met and if everyone is following orders rigorously. This should be carried out by an independent and competent employee

SOURCE: Based on H. Fayol, *Administration Industrielle et Générale* (Paris: Dunol, 1916).

9 Hierarchy.
10 Order.
11 Equity.
12 Stability of tenure of personnel.
13 Initiative by every employee.
14 Unity among the employees.

These principles clearly include some aspects that we would now consider as organisation theory, organisational behaviour and human resource management. Authority cannot work without responsibility. Everyone needs to know his or her responsibilities and should be punished or rewarded by his or her boss. Discipline includes again sanctions when the rules are broken. Although Fayol puts the stress on centralisation in the organisation, he recognises that we should not overreact but find an optimal balance between centralisation and decentralisation. The same goes for hierarchy, which should not be too strict since it makes the organisation inflexible. Direct communication between two persons of the same hierarchical level but of different departments should be possible when they get the permission of their two direct bosses. Fayol took a very mechanistic view of management and a lot of what he considers management refers to organising and structuring organisations. In Chapter 14 you will notice that the four basic elements of the organisation structure, namely a common goal, division of labour, co-ordination and hierarchy of authority, parallel the managerial activities.

Management as separate discipline

Fayol's major concern was the lack of management teaching, although management is the most important task for directors. The lack of teaching had three causes. First, there was no management theory or management science and therefore this could not be taught like other sciences. Second, mathematics was considered for decades as the best and highest possible development for engineers who will run a company. Third, in France the most reputed schools were the schools that educate engineers. Accordingly, the smartest students were stimulated to choose engineering studies and so would learn more mathematics than writing and social skills. Specific knowledge, such as mathematics, is only one of the many skills a director needs. Fayol identifies six important skills a good manager or director needs. These are physical qualities, mental qualities, moral qualities, general education, specific education and experience.

Taylor versus Fayol

Fayol admired Taylor, although he disagreed on two very important aspects of Taylor's ideas. Fayol does not totally divide thinking and acting. Every employee has some management tasks and should be able to take initiatives within their responsibility and within the rules of the company. Unity of command (i.e. one employee should only receive orders from one boss – see Chapter 14) is a very important principle for Fayol but does not fit in with the principles of Taylor. According to Taylor there should be functional management instead of military management. Functional management refers to the specialisation of managers and departmental heads in certain management fields, such as time study, planning, the way the task should be performed, etc. Fayol accepts the importance of this daily guidance of the workers by specialised managers but this does not imply that the unity of command disappears. The very normative approach in his work is criticised. Not all organisation need to be very hierarchical, tightly controlled and mechanistically organised to be successful. In fact, applying such principles may even threaten the success of the organisation.

CHESTER BARNARD

Chester Barnard[21] is less well known than many of the other authors mentioned in this overview. However, his ideas are no less important. Barnard found that previous organisation theories had underestimated the variability of individual behaviour and its effects on organisational effectiveness. Chester Barnard was the president of the New Jersey Bell Telephone Company. He published his ideas in 1938 in the book *The Functions of the Executive*.

Barnard's principles

Barnard builds his theory and ideas on some general principles of co-operative systems. Co-operation involves individuals. He describes individuals as separate beings but not totally independent. They have individual behaviour and the power of choice but their freedom is bounded by two kinds of limitation, namely biological and physical. An individual has only limited possibilities when he acts alone because of his limited physical strength and because of his impact on his environment. Co-operative action in a formal organisation is therefore needed. However, co-operation is not obvious. There are several possible limitations to co-operative actions which Barnard categorises as either a lack of efficiency or a lack of effectiveness (see also Chapter 15). Efficiency exists here when there is a contribution of resources for the use of material and for human effort, in such a way that co-operation can be maintained. If the reward for one's efforts is too small one will resign from co-operation. Effectiveness exists, according to Barnard, when the (personal) goals of the co-operative action are achieved. Barnard identifies three necessary elements for co-operative actions, namely the willingness to co-operate, a common purpose and communication (see Table 1.2).

TABLE 1.2 NECESSARY CO-OPERATION ELEMENTS ACCORDING TO BARNARD

Willingness to co-operate	The will to co-operate is often very low. There are a lot of organisations and for only a few, people's willingness is large enough to co-operate
A common purpose	Goals differ for each person but there has to be some consensus between the individual and organisational goals
Communication about the actions	Communication should be interpreted very broadly; a signal can be enough but the communication needs to be clear

SOURCE: Based on C. I. Barnard, *The Functions of the Executive* (Cambridge, MA: Harvard University Press, 1948).

Besides the three basic elements there are some other important elements necessary for good co-operation in companies, namely specialisation, incentives, authority and decision making (see Table 1.3).

Informal organisations

Furthermore, Barnard explains that every organisation consists of smaller, less formal groups with their own goals. Management needs to align those goals with the overall organisational goal. An informal organisation exists within formal organisations and formal organisations cannot exist without the informal organisation. The informal organisation is more invisible and its existence is too often denied. Barnard made a major contribution by including individual choice, power and

TABLE 1.3 NECESSARY ELEMENTS FOR EFFICIENT CO-OPERATION

Specialisation	Specialisation refers to: the way things are done, which things are done, with which persons one has contact, at what places and in what time period. Organisations should try to find new ways of specialisation to make the work more efficient
Incentives	Incentives are necessary to persuade people to join co-operative actions and to reduce the burden of the work. There are many types of incentives, some are objective and some are subjective (also see Chapter 6). The incentives that increase the willingness to co-operate are: ■ material inducements (most used but in fact of minor importance) ■ personal non-material inducements (like prestige) ■ desirable physical conditions (better working conditions) ■ ideal benefactions (like pride and altruism). Negative effects on co-operation come from: ■ associatal attraction (e.g. racial incompatibility) ■ adaptation to unfamiliar habits ■ opportunities for enlarged participation (only in large companies do people feel they are useful) ■ conditions of commitment (like difficult social integration). These positive and negative incentives can be increased and decreased by: ■ coercion (forcing people or threatening with dismissal) ■ rationalisation of opportunities (convincing people of the opportunities the work offers and the moral benefits it gives) ■ inculcation of motives (educating children in the importance of working). Selection of employees on which the incentives are effective is important. Opportunities within the company and prestige are important. Therefore, organisations need to grow to offer these opportunities
Authority	Authority is: 'communication (to order) in a formal organisation by virtue of which it is accepted by a contributor of the organisation for governing the contributor's actions'. Authority does not work without the individual's will to accept the orders. Therefore the orders should cope with the following conditions: ■ They need to be given in the context of the organisation and its goals. ■ They need to be very clear. ■ They have to be in the contributor's personal interest, not a misuse in the interest of the ordering person. ■ The contributor must be able to execute the orders. ■ They should be given in a culture of acceptance of similar orders. ■ It must be in the zone of indifference.

TABLE 1.3 continued

	The latter condition refers to a zone where orders are expected and accepted. Someone who starts working in a company knows he or she has to work but not exactly which work and how to execute it. So, orders clarifying this will be accepted; they are in the zone of indifference. The authority must be objective, that is, they should be given by someone who has this authority because he or she takes a certain place in the line of communication, the hierarchy. Outside this line of communication there are some staff members who gather and analyse the information from the environment to help the executives. Managers can influence and control the behaviour of the organisational members by instilling a moral purpose, which helps individuals to set aside their personal goals to achieve the organisational goals. Each employee is driven by personal subjective interests and more objective factors
Decision making	Decision making is determining what has to be done in what way. There are individual and organisational decisions based on own initiatives or authority. The former should be limited. Opportunism is the counterpart of decision making. It is only a reaction to the environment. For every action there are some limitations in the environment. To perform the action the limiting factors must be removed, but doing this leads to new limitations. Constantly eliminating the limitations requires experience and experimenting

SOURCE: Based on C. I. Barnard, *The Functions of the Executive* (Cambridge, MA: Harvard University Press, 1948).

informal groups into organisation theory. Managers do not only need to 'pull' the formal organisation but have to manage also the informal aspects of the organisation (also see Chapters 8 and 9). This informal aspect of management and organisations is the major difference with scientific management that was still very popular when Barnard wrote his landmark book. Barnard also clearly rejected the idea that material incentives (wages) are sufficient to motivate workers.

HERBERT SIMON

The work of Herbert Simon[22] is far too comprehensive to be labelled only as a rational-system view of organisations and is also much broader than the work of Taylor and Fayol. He is also from a later period. Nonetheless, we categorise Herbert Simon under the rational view because of his rational approach to the working of organisations and because he tried to apply principles of the 'hard' sciences (such as physics and mathematics) to social sciences, in particular to administrative and decision-making processes.

Herbert Simon lived as son of German immigrants in Milwaukee, US. Unlike the previous organisation theorists, Simon had no working experience in factories, but had instead an academic career. From 1949 he worked at the Carnegie Mellon University. He started his career with research in administrative behaviour, but was also strongly interested in cognitive science and computer science. He did pioneering research in programming for computer applications. In his later years he was especially active in research in computer science. One of the most important highlights in his career was the Nobel prize for his pioneering research into the decision-making processes of organisations.

His famous work *Administrative Behavior*, first written in 1945, is the basis for many thoughts in organisation theory and organisational behaviour. The work describes the behaviour of managers and the process of decision making by managers and individuals in organisations. Simon explains that an organisation is characterised by its communications, relations and its decision-making processes. A major concern in Simon's book is how one can motivate an employee to work in the organisation.

Simon identifies three ways. The first one is the loyalty of the employee to the organisation because the employee identifies himself with the organisation (also see Chapter 3 for work-related attitudes). This seems to be the best reason to work for an organisation, but there is a danger that the employee puts the organisational goals above those of society. The organisational goals should not go against the goals of society, which are at a higher level. Second, training can help to teach the employee to work according to the organisational goals and it reduces the need for authority and control. The third aspect is coercion, further divided in authority (via persuasion, leadership, formal hierarchy or informal authority relations), advisory and information. In the last two situations the employee is not so much forced as convinced. Simon describes in depth the role of authority in organisation.

Simon is also very famous for challenging the idea that people always make decisions in a rational way. Rationality means taking into account all advantages and disadvantages and also aspects like time, future (uncertain) positive and negative effects. Humans are intentionally rational but are limited in the possibilities to be rational. Simon indicates this limitation as 'bounded rationality'. Limitations are both physiological (limited brain capacity and the physical ability to speak and read) and social (physiological limits are determined by social factors). Chapter 12 elaborates on the implications of bounded rationality in decision making in organisations. Most theories, especially in economics, were based on the idea that human beings would always make rational decisions. Nowadays, the bounded rationality concept is also taken into account in a number of economic theories.

Simon worked together with one of his former doctoral students, James March, on the rationality concepts. They published the book *Organisations* in 1958. March himself also became a famous writer in organisation theory. He wrote the book *A Behavioral Theory of the Firm* with Richard Cyert. Both books discuss decision-making processes in organisations and question the rational-economic view of the working of organisations. Bargaining, control and adjustment determine the objectives in the organisation. Bargaining occurs among all parties in the organisation. There are coalitions formed mostly with the owners and managers and not with the employees. Still, the latter have some bargaining power. March and Cyert further explain that decision making in organisations is not only a political process but also heavily influenced by the previous state and decision-making rules, which can be considered as the memory of the organisation. The authors create a more realistic model of decision making in organisations but are still trying to develop general applicable rules for decision making in a very scientific way, similar to the approaches of the other organisation theorists taking a rational-system view on organisations.

Alternative views on organisation studies

The rational-system view was – and still is – very dominant in organisation studies. However, there are other views as well, approaching the working of organisations from a less mathematic, more subjective and often more realistic view. Those alternative views are aimed less at developing general principles for all organisations but instead try to explain the variation in organisations, organisational forms and their working. We briefly discuss the alternative views of symbolic interactionism, postmodernism, conflict theory and critical theory.

SYMBOLIC INTERACTIONISM

Symbolic interactionism
subjective
interpretation of
the world around
us through
interacting in this
world

Symbolic interactionism is a stream within the field of organisation studies that is mainly concerned with analysing the individual's behaviour and interactions on a micro level. It studies our interaction and the symbols of this interaction, this communication and the meaning we give to the elements in the communication. One of the best-known theorists of symbolic interactionism within an organisational behaviour context is Karl Weick.

Karl Weick, an American psychologist, views organisations as sensemaking systems. People, and also managers and employees in organisations, make sense of their environment and are actually 'creating' a language to talk about their environment. Weick explains the enacted theory in his book *The Social Psychology of Organizing*, published in 1969. This theory states that we create a phenomenon, such as an organisation, by talking about it. Hence, our world is a world created or socially constructed by our minds. Therefore, the world is subjective and how the world and organisations look and work depends on our subjective reference frame. Peter Berger and Thomas Luckman are two German sociologists who explained in depth the idea of a socially constructed world.[23] Weick applied this to organisations. He explains among other things that organisational leaders are selectively absorbing information from the environment, interpreting this information and constructing, on the basis of that information, the environment in which they think they are operating. They then make decisions based on this constructed environment. The filtering is personal but heavily determined by the social and cultural context of individuals. Within a similar context, people can observe or interpret the environment equally and are convinced that they have an objective view of the environment. This enacted view is important because it explains why people can have very different reactions and make different decisions in similar situations. It also stresses the difficulty in developing general scientific and rational principles on the working of organisations.[24] Chapter 4 discusses in depth the concept of perception and the biases this might cause.

POSTMODERNISM

The postmodernist view on organisations takes an even stronger subjective approach to organisations and their working. The way individuals interpret their world is also the topic of study in **Postmodernism**. There are many authors taking a postmodernistic view on the world but there are not many who applied it to the organisation studies field. A well-known postmodernist thinker is the Frenchman Jean-François Lyotard.

Furthermore, there are no uniform concepts within the postmodernist field because that field specifically rejects uniform concepts, general principles or any other statement about the truth or the true world. There is no such thing as 'the' world or 'the' truth. Postmodernist thinkers also question traditional boundaries that are placed, as between work and private life, between the organisation and the outside world, between different cultures, groups, etc. They also agree on the fact that the boundaries of organisations, as far as boundaries exist or are interpreted by us as boundaries, will fade and that work will be more flexible, informal, decentralised and changing in an unpredictable way.

It was no coincidence that postmodernism developed in a period of change with new information and communication technology and globalisation changing the way organisations can and must work. Changes fitting within this postmodernist world are: just-in-time, global product and financial markets, despecialisation, flexible working forms (such as teleworking), virtual organisations, inter-organisational networks, temporary organisations and jobs, and many other new trends in working that seem to blur time and space in our work conditions (several of these changes are handled throughout the book). However, organisation theory and organisational behavioural theories will not help us much to predict and control these changes according to the postmodernist view.

Nonetheless, postmodernism provides us with a critical way of thinking and a deconstructive approach to organisational theories. Those theories should be deconstructed to their basic assumptions and analysed from the point of view or reference frame with which they are constructed. In fact, you need to clear your mind of all previously held assumptions when you want to study the working of organisations, allowing you to see things really differently. The lack of general principles in this view has, however, as a consequence that this view has minimal impact on the organisational behavioural theories.[25] Nevertheless, postmodernism deals with the new trends in the daily life of organisations and can therefore become more influential in the way we do research and the way we organise work.[26]

CONFLICT THEORY

Conflict theory states that all social structures and relationships are based on conflicts and changes. This contradicts the rational-system view, which sees organisations primarily as stable with a clear order. According to the system view change can occur but is simply a temporary phase between two periods of stability. According to conflict theory there is never stability. People in society and in organisations are always in a state of conflict because they have different goals and worldviews based on the different social, religious, ethnic, occupational or regional classes to which people belong. Scarce resources in combination with different objectives and views create conflicts that can never be fully resolved. Viewing organisations as based on conflicts between people has major consequences for organisation theories. Power, conflict and politicking will dominate the principles of organisation theory and organisational behaviour (see Chapter 13). Conflict is a source of change. Hence, conflict views on organisations are also used to explain transformations of societies and organisations. The roots of conflict theory can be found in conflicts between workers and company owners in the capitalistic economic model. The worker class and the capitalist class fight over control of resources and the distribution of profits. Karl Marx's theories are therefore an important foundation of the conflict theory.[27]

Postmodernism a very subjective and situational view on the world around us making it impossible to develop general applicable theories of this world

Conflict theory social structures and relationships in organisations are based on conflicts between groups and social classes

CRITICAL THEORY

The critical theory also has a very different point of view from the rational-system view, strongly criticising the functional perspective, control and efficiency orientedness of this view. Critical theory accuses many of the other organisation views as supporting capitalistic thinking. The field of critical theory is dispersed and broad and therefore, one definition or description of this view is difficult to find. However, all critical thinkers have in common the criticism of functionalism and capitalism. Critical theory is like conflict theory grounded in Karl Marx's theories. Also similar is the emphasis on power as the dominant system in organisations. Critical theory takes as its starting point in studying organisations that control over resources and the labour force is the major objective of owners, leaders and managers.

However, up till now the impact of both critical and conflict theories on established organisational behaviour theories has been limited. The functional view, originating from the rational-system view, is still dominant.[28]

The human relations movement

A unique combination of factors during the 1930s fostered the human relations movement. First, following legalisation of union–management collective bargaining in the United States in 1935, management began looking for new ways of handling employees. Second, behavioural scientists conducting on-the-job research started calling for more attention to be paid to the 'human' factor. Managers who had lost the battle to keep unions out of their factories heeded the call for better human relations and improved working conditions.

ELTON MAYO AND THE HAWTHORNE STUDIES

The connection between improving productivity and treating workers with respect is not new. Elton Mayo is one of the well-known human relations theorists who focused attention on employees. He did research at Western Electric's Hawthorne plant and these studies (known as the Hawthorne studies) gave rise to the profession of industrial psychology, focusing on the human factor in the organisations.[29]

To understand the value of the Hawthorne studies, it is important to describe the situation of the workers at that time. From 1900 till 1930 the scientific management approach of Taylor was the main theory. As explained, Frederick Taylor believed in time-and-motion studies as the most efficient way to improve performance. Piecework wage incentive was also introduced to motivate workers and to increase productivity.

At first the scientific management approach was very successful as it provided an answer to the chaotic business atmosphere. Later on concern arose about the disregarding of employees' needs. Trade unions rebelled against the principles and practices of scientific management. A federal investigation followed. Time-and-motion studies were no longer allowed in any federal work programmes and projects. The same was true for piecework rate systems and bonuses.

Until then there were not enough empirical data to justify paying more attention to human factors. The Hawthorne studies, however, provided concrete evidence. The experiments took place at the Hawthorne plant of the Western Electric Company, the manufacturing subsidiary of the American Telephone and Telegraph Company (AT&T).

Four different studies were conducted. The first took place between 1924 and 1927. This project was carried out by Western Electric and the National Research Council. The purpose of this study was to find a relationship between the environment and worker efficiency. The original hypothesis was that improved lighting would increase productivity. Tests were done in three different departments. Results indicated that productivity increased in all three departments. No relationship was found with the level of lighting. The conclusion of the researchers was that many different factors influence worker output.

The first study was a stimulus to study human factors in organisations. William J. Dickson, chief of employee relations for Western Electric, hired several Harvard faculty members for further research. Elton Mayo looked for new research methods and adapted the original hypotheses. Roethlisberger co-ordinated the project and was responsible for the daily operation. The second study, which took place between 1927 and 1933, is known as the Relay Assembly Test Room. Six women were put into a special test room. Researchers studied the influence of certain variables, like length of workday, temperature and lighting. After one year the researchers, however, had failed to find any correlation between working conditions and employee output. Researchers were convinced that not only money and working conditions had an influence on productivity. Increases in output of the six women were influenced by the motivating effect of the special status (being involved in the experiment), participation (they were consulted and informed by the experimenter), another type of supervision (they were not treated by their own supervisor but by an experimenter) and the support and mutual dependence within their working group.

On the basis of the results of the second study, the researchers decided to interview all employees at the Hawthorne plant. Researchers learned about workers' attitudes toward company policies and management practices. Also the existence of informal groups within the formal groups was revealed. The interviews provided workers with the opportunity to air grievances, but in the meantime they showed appreciation for management's interest in their output. Management really used the results of the interviews to change the way of working in the organisation to improve work conditions, supervisory techniques and employee relations.

The last study (1931–2) took place in the Bank Wiring Observation Room. Fourteen men were organised in three subgroups (of three wirers and one supervisor). Two inspectors moved between the three groups. The study revealed two important findings with regard to the social organisation of employees. First of all, two informal groups existed within the three formal groups. Members of an informal group did not always belong to the same formal group. Secondly, these informal groups developed their own rules of behaviour, their own norms. Workers were more responsive to the social forces of their peer group than to the controls and incentives of management.

THE HAWTHORNE LEGACY

Ironically, many of the Hawthorne findings have turned out to be more myth than fact. Interviews conducted decades later with three subjects of the Hawthorne studies, and a re-analysis of the original data using modern statistical techniques, do not support the initial conclusions about the positive effect of supportive supervision. Specifically, money, fear of unemployment during the Great Depression, managerial discipline and high-quality raw materials – not supportive supervision – turned out to be responsible for high output in the relay assembly test room experiments.[30] Nonetheless, the human relations movement gathered momentum through the 1950s, as academics and managers alike made stirring claims about the powerful effect that individual needs, supportive supervision and group dynamics apparently had on job performance.

MARY PARKER FOLLETT

Another human relations researcher reacting against the lack of attention for the human side in scientific management was Mary Parker Follet. She stressed the importance of human relations in organisations. Crucial to her was improving the relationship between management and employees. According to Follett this was very important for the effective functioning of an organisation. Mary Parker Follett was in favour of participatory decision making and a decentralised power base. The employees, the human elements of the organisations, were the key parts. Paying attention to the needs of the employees was the way to improve productivity.

Mary Parker Follett's view[31] on management was the integration of the individual and the organisation. She focused on both the interests and needs of the workers and of the managers. The self-development of employees was very important to her. The work of Mary Parker Follett was rather philosophical and idealistic. She had no experience with organisations but she observed business leaders and translated their ideas into useful management concepts. Several of the management concepts of today are based on her ideas. Important themes for today's managers that are discussed in Follett's work are dynamism, empowerment, participation, leadership, conflict and experience (several of these themes are addressed in further chapters). Table 1.4 gives an overview of these six concepts as explained by Mary Parker Follett.

Mary Parker Follett has received significant attention recently for her early insights into the very modern complexities of administration.[32] Her philosophical and managerial arguments were idiosyncratic in her time, injecting a humanistic element into the scientific and analytical approach to human relations.[33]

TABLE 1.4 MANAGEMENT CONCEPTS OF MARY PARKER FOLLETT

Dynamism	An organisation is a complex system of dynamic social relations. People influence each other and they react to each other. 'When we think we have solved a problem, well, by the very process of solving, new elements or forces come into the situation and you have a new problem on your hand to be solved'[34]
Empowerment	According to Mary Parker Follett there are two types of power: 'power-over' is coercive power; 'power-with' is the co-active, jointly developed power. According to Follett power is a self-developed capacity, not a 'pre-existing thing' given to someone. Power cannot be delegated but you have to give employees the opportunity to grow and develop their power. The concept of empowerment today is in accordance with Follett's ideas: employees are authorised to develop their power in the workplace (see further in Chapter 13)
Participation	Follett describes participation as the co-ordination of the contribution of each individual so that it becomes a working unit. The prerequisites for co-ordination are clear communication, openness and explicitness (see further in Chapter 12 about participative management)
Leadership	Follett does not see the leader as a commander but as someone who communicates and shares the vision of the organisation. A good leader inspires others to innovate and to achieve new goals (see further Chapter 11)
Conflict	According to Follett a conflict is neither good nor bad. Conflict shows the differences between people. Differences can be solved through domination, compromise or integration. No one likes to be dominated and a compromise feels as a loss. Follett's idea is that integration is the best solution. People can talk about the differences and reach a solution that is accepted by all parties. Integration is not always possible but it stimulates creative problem solving which is, also today, very important (see further Chapter 13)
Experience	The ideas of Follett are based on interviewing business people. She really has a lot of respect for experience. 'We should make use of all available present experience, knowing that experience and our learning from it should be equally continuous matters'[35]

MCGREGOR'S THEORY Y

In 1960 Douglas McGregor wrote a book entitled *The Human Side of Enterprise*, which has become an important philosophical base for the modern view of people at work.[36] Drawing upon his experience as a management consultant, McGregor formulated two sharply contrasting sets of assumptions about human nature (see Table 1.5). His Theory X assumptions were pessimistic and negative and, according to McGregor's interpretation, typical of how managers traditionally perceived employees. To help managers break with this negative tradition, McGregor formulated his **Theory Y**, a modern and positive set of assumptions about people.

Theory Y McGregor's modern and positive assumptions about employees being responsible and creative

McGregor believed managers could accomplish more through others by viewing them as self-energised, committed, responsible and creative beings. Forty years ago motivation at work tended to be tackled as single-issue psychology (see also Chapters 5 and 6). Typical advice was 'people will work harder if you give them more attention'. Today, research in Britain revealed that if, for example, a company gives its people a chance to express themselves, they might feel that the organisation is a safe environment in which they can become personally involved. This, in turn, might make them more committed to their work so that they produce a larger quantity of better-quality work.[37] According to a study among employees of a Dutch hospital experiencing a tight labour market, job characteristics other than wages, such as labour relations and work content, were found to play a major role in the people's choices to resign or stay.[38]

TABLE 1.5 McGREGOR'S THEORY X AND THEORY Y

Outdated (Theory X) assumptions about people at work	Modern (Theory Y) assumptions about people at work
1 Most people dislike work; they avoid it when they can	1 Work is a natural activity like play or rest
2 Most people must be coerced and threatened with punishment before they will work. People require close direction when they are working	2 People are capable of self-direction and self-control if they are committed to objectives
3 Most people actually prefer to be directed. They tend to avoid responsibility and exhibit little ambition. They are interested only in security	3 People generally become committed to organisational objectives if they are rewarded for doing so
	4 The typical employee can learn to accept and seek responsibility
	5 The typical member of the general population has imagination, ingenuity and creativity

SOURCE: Adapted from D. McGregor, *The Human Side of Enterprise* (New York: McGraw-Hill, 1960), Ch 4.

New assumptions about human nature

Unfortunately, unsophisticated behavioural research methods caused the human relations theorists to embrace some naive and misleading conclusions. For example, they believed in the axiom 'A satisfied employee is a hardworking employee'. Subsequent research, as discussed later in this book (Chapter 3), shows the satisfaction–performance linkage to be more complex than originally thought.

Despite its shortcomings, the human relations movement opened the door to more progressive thinking about human nature. Rather than continuing to view employees as passive economic beings, organisations began to see them as active social beings and took steps to create more humane work environments.

Morgan's organisational metaphors

Gareth Morgan, originally from Wales, lives and works in Canada where he is a professor at York University. Morgan is especially known for his creative view on organisations and for his famous book *Images of Organization*. In this book, he explains that each individual has a different 'image' of how organisations look in general. Each individual can view organisations through different lenses. Morgan explains that each lens or image only gives a partial view of how organisations work. The overview and evolution of views to organisation theory and organisational behaviour presented earlier in this chapter all take different lenses to organisations and therefore all take a partial view. Hence, if we want to understand organisations, we need to combine different lenses.

Gareth Morgan wrote another book together with Gibson Burrell, which preceded his bestseller *Images of Organization*, namely *Sociological Paradigms and Organizational Analysis*. This is a book well known among organisation theorists in which Burrell and Morgan categorise the different classical and new approaches to organisation theory. They explain how the different organisation theories and organisational behaviour theories are influenced by the specific views on the world of their writers.

In his more popular bestseller *Images of Organization*, Morgan identifies eight images of organisations grounded in the different theoretical views on organisation theories. His 'images' are highly recognisable metaphors (i.e. a figure of speech characterising an object in terms of another object, often a more everyday object that helps to explain a more complex object). We briefly describe the eight images of Morgan (see Table 1.6).[39]

Organisations as machines

The machine metaphor is very similar to how bureaucratic organisations (see Chapter 14) are described and the way the rational-system thinkers view organisations. Machines represent a

TABLE 1.6 MORGAN'S ORGANISATIONAL METAPHORS

Metaphor	Characterised by
Organisations as machines	Orderly relationships Clearly defined logical system with subsystems Predictability and controllability
Organisations as organisms	Adaptation to the environment Open system that transforms inputs in various outputs Dealing with survival
Organisations as brains	Think tanks, having information-processing capacity Strategy formulation, planning processes and management of the organisation Self-regulation of dispersed intelligence
Organisations as cultures	Constructed beliefs and interpretations Subjective reality Own language, shared values, norms and mental models
Organisations as political systems	Competition, conflict and influencing Power and politicking Own goals versus organisational goals
Organisations as physical prisons	Being controlled mentally by the organisation Constrained thinking Unconsciously getting trapped in web of own creation
Organisations as flux and transformation	Self-producing system Mutual causality Dialectic change
Organisations as instruments of domination	Ugly face External domination of environment and humans Dominating own people

SOURCE: Based on G. Morgan, *Images of Organization* (Thousand Oaks, CA: Sage Publications, 1986).

number of relationships between elements that work together harmoniously. Each element, each component in the machine, is crucial and must work exactly as intended or the whole machine malfunctions. The machine metaphor thus represents a system with subsystems but does not take the point of view of single individuals. In a machine view, there is no space for creativity, individual thinking or change unless the whole system changes. Concepts such as hierarchy, authority, line of command, departments, work allocation and organisation charts are all crucial elements in the machine view of organisations (these concepts are all explained more thoroughly in Chapters 14 and 15).

Machines are built for automating repetitive work and so are organisations which look like machines. Production lines, fast-food hamburger chains such as McDonald's and other kinds of organisations oriented towards efficiency and routine work can be viewed as machines. However, taking a machine view in the case of organisations that need to be creative will lead to the application of inappropriate principles. Furthermore, the machine metaphor is criticised for neglecting human aspects and for viewing people as instruments or parts of the machine. Nonetheless, many people still see organisations as logical systems with orderly relationships which are predictable and controllable.

Organisations as organisms

This metaphor compares organisations with the human body. Human beings need resources to survive. In biological sciences the survival of living beings through evolution and competition is an important topic. An organism metaphor thus considers that organisations must try to adapt to their environment to be able to survive. The organism model characterises the organisation as an open system that transforms inputs into various outputs. The outer boundary of the organisation is permeable. People, information, capital, goods and services move back and forth across this boundary. Feedback about such things as sales and customer satisfaction or dissatisfaction enables the organisation to self-adjust and survive despite uncertainty.

Adaptation is the key concept when we study organisations from this metaphor. Hence, principles of open systems (see Chapter 15), change (see Chapter 17) and life cycles fit within this view. Contrary to the machine, organisms thrive on change. Such a kind of metaphor is of particular interest when we study organisations that are in a highly turbulent and demanding environment, such as many e-business organisations today. Internally, the organisation is seen as flexible, open and creative with only loose structures. However, a disadvantage of this view is the over-strong emphasis on change, since organisations need some structure as backbone and cannot change infinitely.

In *Organizations in Action*, James D. Thompson explained the biological model of organisations in the following terms:

> Approached as a natural system, the complex organisation is a set of interdependent parts which together make up a whole because each contributes something and receives something from the whole, which in turn is interdependent with some larger environment. Survival of the system is taken to be the goal, and the parts and their relationships presumably are determined through evolutionary processes.
>
> Central to the natural-system approach is the concept of homeostasis, or self-stabilisation, which spontaneously, or naturally, governs the necessary relationships among parts and activities and thereby keeps the system viable in the face of disturbances stemming from the environment.[40]

Organisations as brains

Organisations learn, make decisions, process information, in other words they act and think like our brains do. For organisation theorists taking the brain view as dominant paradigm, the information-processing capacity is the most crucial aspect of the working of organisations. Our brains, however, do not process information in a linear cause-and-effect way or via a fixed set of relations between elements of our brains. Brains have a more complex and flexible way of processing information.

Considering organisations as brains, however, does not mean that we focus on the strategic decision-making unit, the planning processes or the management of the organisations. Viewing organisations as brains means that thinking is dispersed in organisations. Organisations can work because the dispersed intelligence in the organisation works together in a self-regulating manner. The learning capacity of organisations is crucial in this metaphor. Everyone in the organisation is able to learn and has valuable knowledge. Frederick von Hayek explains that every worker holds valuable knowledge and discusses how organisations work with the 'problem of utilisation of knowledge not given to anyone in its totality'.[41] Furthermore, such organisations are characterised by self-regulation (instead of structure), flexibility, autonomy, openness, horizontal co-operation and empowerment. In the machine view on organisations there is a clear task differentiation with a clear distinction between the decision and thinking tasks and the acting and operational tasks. Hence, such view clearly contradicts the brains metaphor.

This metaphor is described by the organisation theorists Richard Daft and Karl Weick as:

> This perspective represents a move away from mechanical and biological metaphors of organisations. Organisations are more than transformation processes or control systems. To survive, organisations must have mechanisms to interpret ambiguous events and to provide meaning and direction for participants. Organisations are meaning systems, and this distinguishes them from lower-level systems.
>
> Almost all outcomes in terms of organisation structure and design, whether caused by the environment, technology or size, depend on the interpretation of problems or opportunities by key decision makers. Once interpretation occurs, the organisation can formulate a response.[42]

In fact, the concept of the learning organisation, which will be discussed in detail in Chapter 17, is very popular in management circles these days and builds on the brains metaphor.

Organisations as cultures

Viewing organisations as cultures means that we emphasise the development of norms, language, shared values and mental models among people during their interactions. Hence, organisations are social groups that interact, build intersubjectively shared meanings and reinforce this meaning and interpretations through further co-operation and interacting. Important in this view is the fact that the members of the organisation construct their subjective reality. Thus, constructed beliefs and interpretations bound the organisational members.

The culture metaphor relates to the symbolic interactionism view of organisations. However, it is not the development of this organisational view that led to the culture metaphor but the impression that Japanese organisations were much more successful than Western organisations in the 1960s and 1970s. Researchers found that culture was the only factor that could explain the differences in success. Chapter 16 discusses in depth the importance of culture in organisations. However, many organisational behaviour researchers studying culture are looking at culture as an element of organisations besides other elements, such as formal structures, decision-making processes, co-ordination systems, etc. A few researchers study culture from the culture metaphor and consider the organisation as 'being culture', not as 'having culture'.[43] Gareth Morgan describes this as follow: 'Organisations are mini-societies with their own distinctive patterns of culture and subculture.'[44]

Organisations as political systems

The political metaphor is a model of competition. Organisations have scarce resources and everyone in the organisations takes part in the competition for these. Furthermore, each employee in the organisation has his or her own goals, which often do not match the organisational ones. Hence, politicking is used to achieve personal goals. This metaphor parallels the conflict view on organisations. Central values in such organisation are: power, conflict, coalitions, competition and influence. Politicking is actually the unjustified use of power. Power can originate from formal positions in the organisation (authority), expertise (the possession of unique knowledge), (charismatic) leadership, a position of control, having valuable information about the organisation (knowing how things work around here), dependency (hold-up positions) or from the personality of the powerful person.[45] Interest groups and pressure groups arise in the organisation, which try to influence decision making.

The strength of the metaphor is in the fact that politicking is not neglected as in many other organisational views. Many, if not all, organisations face some degree of politicking, although most like to hide or deny that fact. However, viewing organisations as only political is for most organisations highly inaccurate. An organisation that is dominantly political will suffer from large dysfunctionality and may have difficulty surviving. Power is used in organisations to achieve personal goals or to get control of more of the resources than is appropriate.[46] Hence, the achievement of organisational goals is at risk. Chapter 13 teaches us more about how to deal with conflict, power and politicking in organisations.

Organisations as psychic prisons

People can become trapped in the organisation as in a kind of psychic prison. We spend a great deal of our time working in organisations and our thinking can be dominated by that organisation, its rules and way of working. Our identification with the organisation can become so great that it starts to control us mentally. Our thinking becomes constrained by our life in the organisation. In fact, the organisation becomes a prison for our mind and body, not just from nine to five but also when we are outside the organisation. Organisations with a strong control system, requiring obedience to many rules and limiting individual creativity, for instance, will also limit our ability for creative thinking outside the organisation.

However, people themselves create the organisation, rules and social systems that become their prisons. Hence, people construct organisations based on their own beliefs shaped partly by their own personality, while the constructed organisation in turn shapes their beliefs and personality. As Morgan puts it: 'Human beings have a knack of getting trapped in webs of their own creation.'[47] Important in this metaphor is that the development of a psychic prison happens unconsciously. Hardly any organisational member is really aware of the impact that the organisation has on their life in general. Consider the following example:

> "Satoshi Hirata, a young auditor at one of Japan's top accountancy firms, committed suicide most probably because of the results of an audit at Resona. Resona is Japan's fifth biggest bank. Mr Hirata had just discovered together with the rest of the audit team that there was a big hole where Resona's capital ought to have been. The young auditor could not stand the pressure that went along with his job, namely deciding on the life or death of large companies and with this the jobs of many thousands. Such stories are not uncommon in Japan where workers and managers identify themselves very strongly with the company they work for. Often they work their whole lives for one company and start to live for the company. Managers and workers who risk shameful dismissal prefer to die rather than starting a new life outside the company.[48] "

Organisations as flux and transformation

The flux and transformation metaphor views organisations as being in a continuous change process. Morgan compares the organisation with all other aspects of our universe that are in constant evolution. The organisation is permanent in the sense that it can exist for a long time, but it is constantly changing inside. We observe permanence and order, but underneath there is a logic of change. Morgan further explains that 'the explicate reality of organisational life is formed and transformed by underlying processes with a logic of their own'.[49] He suggest three images of change to explain this underlying logic.

First, there is the logic of self-producing systems or autopoiesis systems. Such systems are closed and autonomously self-renewing. The organisation makes representations of its environment and organises this environment as part of itself. Note the similarity with the self-represented or constructed environment in the postmodernist view of organisations.

Second, there is the logic of mutual causality. There can be negative or positive feedback making the system change. The negative feedback loops prevent change and create stability, while the positive feedback loops result in exponential change. The organisation consists of numerous feedback loops based on causal relationships between its elements. To understand organisations, we need to understand these loops.

Third, there is the logic of dialectical change. All phenomena have their opposites: cold and hot, order and disorder, etc. The one cannot exist without the other, meaning that there is no use talking about wrong when there is no right. The same logic counts for organisations. An organisation exists because of its opposite, disorder. This also goes for any other aspect of organisations. The two sides often include conflict. Hence, many aspects of organisations are based on conflict. Think back on the conflict view on organisations previously mentioned in this chapter, for instance, the conflict between capital and labour.

Organisations as instruments of domination

Finally, organisations can also be seen as instruments of domination, what Morgan calls the 'ugly face'. He means that organisation are able to create many good things for the world but can also be very destructive for humans and the environment. Think of environmental pollution, social disasters when thousands of people are laid off at once, the health effects of cigarettes, the production of arms, child labour, etc. In fact, the organisation producing cigarettes obtains profits for its owners and creates jobs for its employees, but in the meantime destroys the health of many others. Hence, this organisation uses its dominance to gain benefits at the expense of others. It actually uses power, not internally as in the political organisation, but externally to dominate others in the environment. Think also of multinationals that escape control of local government or can even control these local governments. Hence, we view here again the conflict view of organisations with conflicts between different social classes.

However, the dominance of organisations, like the bureaucratic organisation forms (see Chapter 14), also has negative implications for the employees of these organisations. The fact that this is the dominant form of organisations forces many people to work in such organisations and suffer from the disadvantage of control and alienation. Furthermore, some people dedicate most of their lives to one organisation, spending all their energy and emotions in the organisation and sacrificing their private lives. They are voluntarily or involuntarily abused and dominated by that organisation. In 2002, 143 people committed suicide because of overwork in Japan. 'Japan is the only country in the world that has a specific word that means death by overwork: Karoshi.'[50] Many researchers also investigated the exploitation of blue- and also white-collar workers and the creation of organisation structures that favour workaholism. In Chapter 18, the ethical aspects of business are further discussed. This metaphor found support in the critical view on organisations, criticising the capitalistic system.

To make the eight metaphors of Morgan more concrete, consider the next Activity.

activity

Assessing your understanding of Morgan's organisational metaphors

Review Morgan's eight metaphors in Table 1.6. Think about an example that evokes for each of the images Morgan describes. It may help to use organisational characteristics such as:

■ a recent merger,
■ a strong mission statement,
■ a lot of contact with stakeholders,
■ strict internal procedures,
■ a high absenteeism and/or turnover rate,
■ a strong CEO.

Learning about OB from theory, research and practice

As a human being with years of interpersonal experience to draw upon, you already know a good deal about people at work. But more systematic and comprehensive understanding is possible and desirable. A working knowledge of current OB theory, research and practice can help you develop a tightly integrated understanding of why organisational contributors think and act as they do. In order for this to happen, however, prepare yourself for some intellectual surprises from theoretical models, research results or techniques that may run counter to your current thinking. For instance, one important reason why stress and satisfaction remain popular concepts is the belief that happy, satisfied workers are necessarily more productive workers (also see Chapters 3 and 7). Hence, improving the 'feel-good factor' is believed to produce improvements in work performance. This argument has great superficial appeal. But on closer inspection it makes less sense. For example, feeling particularly happy may make it difficult to concentrate on a complex task, while a person's performance in a repetitive, machine-paced job may not depend on how they feel. In addition, there is little research evidence that supports such links.[51]

Therefore, research surprises can not only make learning fun, they can also improve the quality of our lives both in and outside the workplace. Let us examine the dynamic relationship between, and the value of, OB theory, research and practice.

Figure 1.2 illustrates how theory, research and practice are related. Throughout the balance of this book, we focus primarily on the central portion, where all three areas overlap. Knowledge of why people behave as they do and what organisations can do to improve performance is greatest within this area of maximum overlap. For each major topic we build a foundation for understanding with generally accepted theory. This theoretical foundation is then tested and expanded by reviewing the latest relevant research findings. After interpreting the research, we discuss the nature and effectiveness of related practical applications.

Sometimes, depending on the subject matter, it is necessary to venture into the large areas outside the central portion of Figure 1.2. For example, an insightful theory supported by convincing research evidence might suggest an untried or different way of managing. In other instances, an innovative management technique might call for an explanatory theoretical model and exploratory research. Each area – theory, research and practice – supports and, in turn, is supported by the other two. Each area makes a valuable contribution to our understanding of, and ability to manage, organisational behaviour.

Learning from theory

Theory
a story defining key terms, providing a conceptual framework and explaining why something occurs

A respected behavioural scientist, Kurt Lewin, once said there is nothing as practical as a good theory. According to one management researcher, a **Theory** is a story that explains 'why'.[52] Another

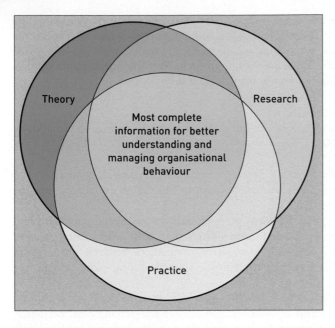

FIGURE 1.2 LEARNING ABOUT OB THROUGH A COMBINATION OF THEORY, RESEARCH AND PRACTICE HERE

calls well-constructed theories 'disciplined imagination'.[53] A good OB theory, then, is a story that effectively explains why individuals and groups behave as they do. Moreover, a good theoretical model:

- Defines key terms.
- Constructs a conceptual framework that explains how important factors are interrelated (graphic models are often used to achieve this end).
- Provides a departure point for research and practical application.

Indeed, good theories are a fundamental contributor to improved understanding and management of organisational behaviour.[54]

Learning from research

Because of unfamiliar jargon and complicated statistical procedures, many professionals are put off by behavioural research.[55] This is unfortunate because practical lessons can be learned as OB researchers steadily push back the frontier of knowledge. If you want to learn more about research methods in OB, the Learning module which is included after this chapter can be a good starting point. Let us examine the various sources and uses of OB research evidence.

FIVE SOURCES OF OB RESEARCH INSIGHTS

To enhance the instructional value of our coverage of major topics, we systematically cite 'hard' evidence from five different categories. Worthwhile evidence was obtained by drawing upon the prioritised research methodologies, namely meta-analyses, field studies, laboratory studies, sample surveys and case studies.

A **Meta-analysis** is a statistical pooling technique that permits behavioural scientists to draw general conclusions about certain variables from many different studies.[56] It typically encompasses a vast number of subjects, often reaching the thousands. Meta-analyses are instructive because they focus on general patterns of research evidence, not fragmented bits and pieces or isolated studies.[57]

In OB, a **Field study** probes individual or group processes in an organisational setting. Because field studies involve real-life situations, their results often have immediate and practical relevance for organisations.

In a **Laboratory study**, variables are manipulated and measured in contrived situations. College students are commonly used as subjects. The highly controlled nature of laboratory studies enhances research precision. But generalising the results to organisational contexts requires caution.[58]

Meta-analysis pools the results of many studies through statistical procedure

Field study examination of variables in real-life settings

Laboratory study manipulation and measurement of variables in contrived situations

Sample survey
questionnaire
responses from a
sample of people

Case study
in-depth study of
a single person,
group or
organisation

In a **Sample survey**, samples of people from specified populations respond to questionnaires. The researchers then draw conclusions about the relevant population. Generalisability of the results depends on the quality of the sampling and questioning techniques.

A **Case study** is an in-depth analysis of a single individual, group or organisation. Because of their limited scope, case studies yield realistic but not very generalisable results.[59]

THREE USES OF OB RESEARCH FINDINGS

Organisational scholars point out that organisations can put relevant research findings to use in three different ways.[60]

1 *Instrumental use*. This involves directly applying research findings to practical problems. For example, a professional experiencing high stress tries a relaxation technique after reading a research report about its effectiveness (see Chapter 7).
2 *Conceptual use*. Research is put to conceptual use when professionals derive general enlightenment from its findings. The effect here is less specific and more indirect than with instrumental use. For example, after reading a meta-analysis showing a negative correlation between absenteeism and age,[61] a manager might develop a more positive attitude towards hiring older people (see Chapter 4).
3 *Symbolic use*. Symbolic use occurs when research results are relied upon to verify or legitimise stances that are already held. Negative forms of symbolic use involve self-serving bias, prejudice, selective perception and distortion (see Chapter 4). For example, tobacco industry spokespeople routinely deny any link between smoking and lung cancer because researchers are largely, but not 100 per cent, in agreement about the negative effects of smoking. A positive example would be professionals maintaining their confidence in setting performance goals after reading a research report about the favourable impact of goal setting on job performance (see Chapter 6).

By systematically reviewing and interpreting research relevant to key topics, this book provides instructive insights about OB.

Learning from practice

Relative to learning more about how to effectively manage people at work, one might be tempted to ask, 'Why bother with theory and research; let's get right down to how to do it.' Scholars have wrestled for years with the problem of how best to apply the diverse and growing collection of management tools and techniques. Our answer lies in the **contingency approach**. The contingency approach calls for the use of management techniques or specific theoretical models in a situationally appropriate manner, instead of trying to rely on 'one best way'. According to a pair of contingency theorists:

Contingency approach
using tools and
techniques in a
situationally
appropriate
manner; avoiding
the one-best-way
mentality

> [Contingency theories] developed and their acceptance grew largely because they responded to criticisms that the classical theories advocated 'one best way' of organising and managing. Contingency theories, on the other hand, proposed that the appropriate organisational structure and management style were dependent upon a set of 'contingency' factors, usually the uncertainty and instability of the environment.[62]

The contingency approach encourages professionals to view organisational behaviour within a situational context. According to this modern perspective, evolving situations, not hard-and-fast rules, determine when and where various management techniques are appropriate. For example, as will be discussed in Chapter 11, contingency researchers have determined that there is no single best style of leadership. In Chapter 15, contingency theory is applied to organisation design. Also consider the next Snapshot as an example of the contingency approach.

Fortunately, systematic research is available that tests our 'commonsense' assumptions about what works where. Management 'cookbooks' that provide only how-to-do-it advice with no underlying theoretical models or supporting research virtually guarantee misapplication. As mentioned earlier, the three elements of theory, research and practice mutually reinforce one another.

snapshot

No one best way of managing organisations

One cross-cultural study of a large multinational corporation's employees working in 50 countries led the Dutch researcher Geert Hofstede to conclude that most made-in-America management theories and techniques are inappropriate in the context of other cultures.[63] Many, otherwise well-intentioned, performance improvement programmes based on American cultural values have failed in other cultures because of naive assumptions about transferability.

In France, the most common medical complaint is *crise de foie* (liver crisis) while in Germany it is *Herzinsufficienz* (heart insufficiency). Prescriptions to soothe the digestive system are higher in France, while in Germany digitalis is prescribed six times more frequently to stimulate the heart. These differences have been attributed to the French cultural obsession with food, and the German cultural quest for romanticism. In other words, different countries have very different approaches to medicine. If the practice of medicine is shaped by its cultural origins, why should the practice of management be any different?

SOURCE: Based on C. Schneider and J. L. Barsoux, *Managing across Cultures* (London: Prentice-Hall, 1997).

The theory → research → practice sequence discussed in this section will help you better to understand each of the major topics addressed later in the book. Attention now turns to a topical model that sets the stage for what lies ahead.

A topical model for understanding and managing OB

By definition, organisational behaviour is both research and application orientated. The three basic levels of analysis in OB are the individual, the group and the organisation. OB draws upon a diverse array of disciplines – including psychology, management, sociology, organisation theory, social psychology, statistics, anthropology, general systems theory, economics, information technology, political science, vocational counselling, human stress management, psychometrics, ergonomics, decision theory and ethics. This rich heritage has spawned many competing perspectives and theories about human work behaviour. By the mid-1980s one researcher had identified 110 distinct theories about behaviour within the field of OB.[64]

Organisational behaviour is an academic designation. With the exception of teaching and research positions, OB is not an everyday job category such as accounting, marketing or finance. Students of OB typically do not get jobs in organisational behaviour, *per se*. This reality in no way demeans OB or lessens its importance in effective organisational management. OB is a horizontal discipline that cuts across virtually every job category, business function and professional specialty. Anyone who plans to make a living in a large or small, public or private, organisation needs to study organisational behaviour. Moreover, according to a recent *Management Review* article, more and more CEOs have become 'self-made psychologists'.

Freudian disciples, they are not. But in their commonsense way, CEOs have turned their attention to issues of human behaviour and psychology. In coming down from the mountain, they have discarded the old reliance on organisation and process and become much more directly involved with people and psychological issues. They have adopted a strong 'show me' approach to employee behaviour. It is all very well to create mission statements and articulate corporate values, but CEOs want to see concrete evidence of behaviour that reflects those values. That is why we see IBM's Lou Gerstner spending more than a third of his time visiting and interacting with customers, and Heinrich von Pierer from Germany's Siemens stating that his most important task in directing a change programme was to stimulate people to think differently. The fact is, the previous generation of CEOs placed too high a priority on ivory tower [academic] strategising. Nowadays they spend much more time on people issues and learning as they go; in that sense they are getting into applied psychology.[65]

Figure 1.3 is a map for our journey through this book, indicating the topics through which we pass. Our destination is organisational effectiveness via continuous improvement. The study of OB can be a wandering and pointless trip if we overlook the need to translate OB lessons into effective and efficient organised endeavour.

At the far left of our 'topical road map' are managers, those who are responsible for accomplishing

> **Organisational behaviour** interdisciplinary field dedicated to better understanding of management of people at work

FIGURE 1.3 A TOPICAL MODEL FOR WHAT LIES AHEAD

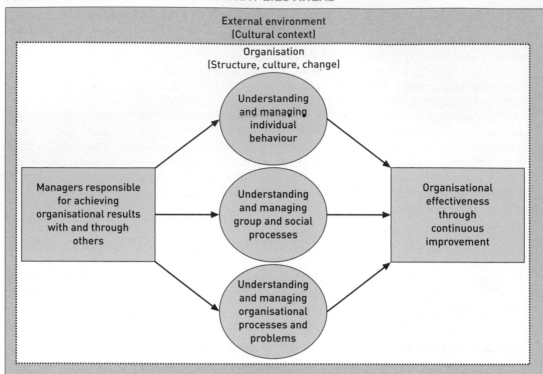

organisational results with and through others. The three circles at the centre of the map correspond to Parts Two, Three, and Four of this book. Logically, the flow of topical coverage in this book (following the introductory Part One) goes from individuals, to group processes, to organisational processes and problems. Around the core of our topical road map in Figure 1.3 is the organisation.

The broken line represents a permeable boundary between the organisation and its environment. Energy and influence flow both ways across this permeable boundary. Truly, no organisation is an island in today's highly interactive and interdependent world.

Learning outcomes: Summary of key terms

1 Give an overview of the different views that were a source for the development of the organisational behaviour field

First studies on organisational behaviour were made by the sociologists. However, studies of the working of organisations started at the very beginning of the twentieth century with the birth of scientific management in which a rational-system view of organisations is taken. The main researchers of this view were Taylor, Fayol, Barnard and Simon. Later, alternative views on the working of organisations developed, such as symbolic interactionism, postmodernism, conflict theory and critical theory. Around 1930 the Human Relations movement arose with more attention paid to the human factor in organisations. The Hawthorne studies, Mary Parker Follett and McGregor's Theory Y provided the most influential ideas in this movement.

2 Explain Taylor's principles

Taylor increased productivity by studying work methods. He divided tasks into many small sub-tasks for which he determined the most optimal time and manner to do the task. All tasks should be standardised, controlled and routinised. The management of the tasks and the execution of the tasks should be clearly separated.

3 Describe the five key tasks of a manager according to Fayol

The key tasks are: planning, organising, commanding, co-ordinating and controlling. Every person in the company has to do these tasks to some degrees but the higher in the hierarchy, the more time is spent on these five sequential tasks.

4 Give Barnard's view on co-operation

There are several conditions that need to be fulfilled to allow co-operation, such as a willingness to co-operate, a common purpose and communication. This needs to be accomplished with specialisation, incentives, authority and decision making to allow efficient co-operation in organisations. Managers need to create the conditions for efficient co-operation but have to pay attention to informal aspects as well, such as the existence of informal groups and power.

5 Explain Simon's ideas about motivating workers and bounded rationality

There are three ways in which employees can be motivated: identification with the organisation, training and coercion. To make the right decisions in organisations, we need to think rationally but humans are bounded, physically and socially, in their ability to process information and to be rational.

6 Describe the four alternative views of organisation studies

Symbolic interactionism explains that our world is subjectively created through interactions. Post-modernism questions the existence of any objective concept and principle. Conflict theory is based on the idea that all organisational structures are based on conflict. Critical theory reacts against the dominant capitalistic view of organisations, which is based on control over resources.

7 Contrast McGregor's Theory X and Theory Y assumptions about employees

Theory X employees, according to traditional thinking, dislike work, require close supervision and are primarily interested in security. According to the modern Theory Y, employees are capable of self-direction, seeking responsibility and being creative.

8 Describe Morgan's eight organisational metaphors

The eight metaphors are: machines (a system view on organisations), organisms (organisations are like human organisms), brains (dispersed information-processing and knowledge-creating capacity), culture (organisation is a culture), political system (competition is the core of organisations), psychic prison (our lives are completely dominated by the organisation), flux and transformation (there are fundamental change processes in organisations) and instruments of domination (organisations dominate their internal and external environment).

9 Define the term organisational behaviour (OB) and explain why OB is a horizontal discipline

Organisational behaviour (OB) is an interdisciplinary field dedicated to better understanding and managing people at work. It is both research and application oriented. Except for teaching and research positions, one does not normally get a job in OB. Rather, because OB is a horizontal discipline, its concepts and lessons are applicable to virtually every job category, business function and professional specialty.

Review questions

1 Why has Taylor been so strongly criticised?
2 What are the major differences between the ideas of Taylor, Fayol and Barnard?
3 What do you think are the functions of a manager?
4 Think of an important decision you had to make and discuss how your rational decision making was bounded.
5 Consider the alternative views and the rational view on organisations. Which of these views has according to your opinion the most realistic view on the working of organisations? Why?
6 Why look at the typical employee as a human resource?
7 Why is it said that Mary Parker Follett was ahead of her time?
8 What is your personal experience of Theory X and Theory Y managers (see Table 1.5)? Which did you prefer? Why?

Personal awareness and growth exercise

What is your view of today's employees?

Objective

To identify whether you have a rather modern or a rather conservative view of today's employees.

Introduction

How we look at employees influences our behaviour towards them. Douglas McGregor identified two contrasting sets of assumptions of people at work, as described in Table 1.5. The rather positive, modern view is called Theory Y, the contrasting, negative one Theory X.

Instructions

Respond to the items below as they apply to your view of people at work today. Upon completion, compute your total score by adding up your responses. In the scoring key, you will find the interpretation of your results.

5 = strongly agree
4 = agree
3 = neither agree nor disagree
2 = disagree
1 = strongly disagree

1 Work is distasteful to most employees.	5	4	3	2	1
2 People are mainly motivated by extrinsic rewards, such as bonuses.	5	4	3	2	1
3 Most people dislike working.	5	4	3	2	1
4 People prefer to avoid responsibility.	5	4	3	2	1
5 People working in large companies show no interest in organisational goals. They only have their own interests in mind.	5	4	3	2	1
6 Most people have little innovative capacity and do no efforts to help solving problems within their companies.	5	4	3	2	1
7 Most people desire to be directed.	5	4	3	2	1
8 Most people are not ambitious, prefer to stay where they are and do not want to work hard to get ahead in life.	5	4	3	2	1
9 Work is unnatural to most people.	5	4	3	2	1
10 Most employees show no interest in developing their full potential and abilities.	5	4	3	2	1

Your score: _____

Scoring key and norms

Once you have added up your responses, you get a total between 50 and 10.

A score below 20? You have a very positive view of employees and they certainly enjoy working under your supervision!

A score above 40? Your view of employees is outdated and you are probably convinced that close direction is the only way to lead. We have serious doubts about the atmosphere in your team. This should certainly change!

A score between 20 and 40? You are characterised by both Theory X and Y. Ask yourself which points of view should be altered to enhance the relationship with your employees!

The lower your score, the more positive your view of people at work is. You are convinced that people have a natural need to work and you will do everything to create a climate to meet that need. The higher your score, however, the more negative your view of modern employees is. You are convinced that people only come to work to earn an income. You also think that people are inherently lazy.

Group exercise

Timeless advice

Objectives

1 To get to know some of your fellow students.

2 To put the management of people into a lively and interesting historical context.

3 To begin to develop your teamwork skills.

Introduction

Your creative energy, willingness to see familiar things in unfamiliar ways, and ability to have fun while learning are keys to the success of this warm-up exercise. A 20-minute, small-group session will be followed by brief oral presentations and a general class discussion. Total time required is approximately 40 to 45 minutes.

Instructions

Your lecturer will divide your class randomly into groups of four to six people each. Acting as a team, with everyone offering ideas and one person serving as official recorder, each group will be responsible for writing a one-page memo to your current class. Subject matter of your group's memo will be 'My advice for managing people today is . . .'. The fun part of this exercise (and its creative element) involves writing the memo from the viewpoint of the person assigned to your group by your lecturer.

Among the memo viewpoints your lecturer may assign are the following:

- Henry Ford (the founder of Ford Motor Company).
- A Japanese bank manager requiring full dedication of its employees.
- Mary Parker Follett.
- Douglas McGregor.
- A Theory X supervisor of a construction crew.
- The manager of an extremely competitive organisation where everyone is competing to be perceived as the best.
- Henri Fayol.
- The manager of a company operating in a communistic world.
- Owner of a company that developed a totally new kind of fast airway transportation in 2030.
- A Japanese auto company executive.
- The head of the world's largest call centre.

Use your imagination, make sure everyone participates and try to be true to any historical facts you have encountered. Attempt to be as specific and realistic as possible. Remember, the idea is to provide advice about managing people from another point in time (or from a particular point of view at the present time).

Make sure you manage your 20-minute time limit carefully. A recommended approach is to spend 2 to 3 minutes putting the exercise into proper perspective. Next, take about 10 to 12 minutes brainstorming ideas for your memo, with your recorder jotting down key ideas and phrases. Have your recorder use the remaining time to write your group's one-page memo, with constructive comments and help from the others. Pick a spokesperson to read your group's memo to the class.

Questions for discussion

1 How can each of the views and lenses from the different researchers help us to improve the working in organisations?

2 Suppose you have to work for one of the managers from the above list, for which one would you like to work? Why?

3 Which of the views is most accurate for the situation in which organisations operate today? Are the ideas of Taylor and Barnard of almost a century ago still useful today? Why (not)?

4 Which of the different views in this chapter on how to motivate people will be most effective?

Internet exercise

The purpose of this exercise is to build bridges between what you've read in this chapter and what's going on in the world today. Thanks to the internet you have loads of current information at your fingertips to keep you up to date. Go to our website www.mcgraw-hill.co.uk/textbooks/buelens for further instructions.

Notes

1 C. Cooper, 'Management Blasted at Nuclear Plant', *People Management*, 16 March 2000.

2 P. Whiteley, 'Five Steps to Added Value', *The Times*, 19 October 2000.

3 Adapted and translated from D. Sheff, 'Richard Branson: Je mensen zijn het belangrijkst', *Vacature*, 28 June 1997.

4 Scott Adams, *The Dilbert Principle* (New York: HarperBusiness, 1996), p. 51. Also see A. Bryant, 'Make That Mr. Dilbert', *Newsweek*, 22 March 1999, pp. 46–7.

5 J. Pfeffer and J. F. Veiga, 'Putting People First for Organizational Success', *Academy of Management Executive*, May 1999, p. 37.

6 Adapted and translated from K. Weytjens, 'Fiere en geëngageerde werknemers', *Vacature*, 1 May 1999.

7 J. West and M. Patterson, 'Profitable Personnel', *People Management*, 8 January 1998.

8 Adapted from J. Pfeffer and J. F. Veiga, see note 5.

9 See the brief report on lay-offs in the United States in G. Koretz, 'Quick to Fire and Quick to Hire', *Business Week*, 31 May 1999, p. 34. For the case against lay-offs, see J. R. Morris, W. F. Cascio and C. E. Young, 'Downsizing After All These Years: Questions and Answers About Who Did It, How Many Did It, and Who Benefited from It', *Organizational Dynamics*, Winter 1999, pp. 78–87.

10 Data from J. Pfeffer and J. F. Veiga, 'Putting People First for Organizational Success', *Academy of Management Executive*, May 1999, p. 47.

11 B. S. Lawrence, 'Historical Perspective: Using the Past to Study the Present', *Academy of Management Review*, April 1984, p. 307.

12 K. Marx, *Economic and Philosophical Manuscripts of 1844* (New York: International Publishing, 1964).

13 E. Durkheim, *The Division of Labour in Society* (New York: Free Press, 1984 – first published in 1893).

14 M. Weber, *Gesammelte Aufsätze zur Soziologie und Sozialpolitik* (Tübingen: Mohr, 1924).

15 T. Burns, 'The Sociology of Industry', in *Society: Problems and Methods of Study*, eds A. T. Walford, M. Argyle, D. V. Glass and J. J. Morris (London: Routledge, 1962).

16 R. Kanigel, *The One Best Way: Frederick Winslow Taylor and the Enigma of Efficiency* (London: Little Brown and Company, 1997).

17 H. Ford and S. Crowther, *My Life and Work* (London: William Heinemann, 1924); and P. Collier and D. Horowitz, *The Fords: An American Epic* (London: Futura Collins, 1987).

18 Translated from B. Lenaerts, 'Foutenmarge nul bij Opel Belgium', *De Morgen*, 14 January 2004, p. 22.

19 See P. Bain, A. Watson, G. Mulvey, P. Taylor and G. Gall, 'Taylorism, Targets and the Pursuit of Quantity and Quality by Call Centre Management', *New Technology, Work and Employment*, November 2002, pp. 170–72; and P. Taylor and P. Bain, 'An Assembly Line in the Head: Work and Employee Relations in the Call Centre', *Industrial Relations Journal*, June 1999, pp. 101–17.

20 H. Fayol, *Administration Industrielle et Générale* (Paris: Dunol, 1916).

21 C. I. Barnard, *The Functions of the Executive* (Cambridge, MA: Harvard University Press, 1948).

22 H. A. Simon, *Administrative Behavior* (New York: The Free Press, 1945). Discussion of the life and work of Simon (translated), see M. Buelens, *Managementprofeten* (Amsterdam: Uitgeverij Nieuwezijds, 2000), pp. 34–41.

23 P. L. Berger and T. Luckmann, *The Social Construction of Reality: A Treatise in the Sociology of Knowledge* (Garden City, NY: Doubleday, 1966).

24 For an explanation of symbolic interactionism, see M. J. Hatch, *Organization Theory* (New York: Oxford University Press, 1997). The main works of Karl Weick on enacted theory are K. E. Weick, *The Social Psychology of Organizing* (Reading, MA: Addison-Wesley Publishing Company, 1969); and K. E. Weick, *Sensemaking in Organizations* (Thousand Oaks, CA: Sage Publications, 1995).

25 See M. J. Hatch, *Organization Theory* (Oxford: Oxford University Press, 1997), p. 387; and D. Jaffee, *Organization Theory* (New York: McGraw-Hill, 2001), p. 315. Also see S. R. Clegg, *Modern Organizations: Organization Studies in the Postmodern World* (Newbury Park, CA: Sage Publications, 1990); and D. Harvey, *The Conditions of Postmodernity* (Cambridge: Blackwell, 1989).

26 A. B. Thomas, *Controversies in Management, second edition* (London: Routledge, 2003), p. 260; and D. Jaffee, *Organization Theory: Tension and Change* (Boston, MA: McGraw-Hill, 2001), p. 315.

27 See G. Burrell and G. Morgan, *Sociological Paradigms and Organizational Analysis* (London: Heinemann, 1979); and D. Jaffee, *Organization Theory* (New York: McGraw-Hill, 2001), p. 315

28 J. Pfeffer, *New Directions for Organization Theory* (New York: Oxford University Press, 1997), p. 264.

29 Based on B. J. Rieger, 'Lessons in Productivity and People', *Training and Development*, October 1995, pp. 56–8.

30 Evidence indicating that the original conclusions of the famous Hawthorne studies were unjustified can be found in R. G. Greenwood, A. A. Bolton and R. A. Greenwood, 'Hawthorne a Half Century Later: Relay Assembly Participants Remember', *Journal of Management*, Fall–Winter 1983, pp. 217–31; and R. H. Franke and J. D. Kaul, 'The Hawthorne Experiments: First Statistical Interpretation', *American Sociological Review*, October 1978, pp. 623–43. For a positive interpretation of the Hawthorne studies, see J. A. Sonnenfeld, 'Shedding Light on the Hawthorne Studies', *Journal of Occupational Behaviour*, April 1985, pp. 111–30.

31 T. R. Miller and B. J. Vaughan, 'Messages from the Management Past: Classic Writers and Contemporary Problems', *S.A.M. Advanced Management Journal*, Winter 2001, pp. 4–12.

32 P. Graham, *Mary Parker Follett – Prophet of Management* (Boston, MA: Harvard Business School Press, 1995). Also see N. O. Morton and S. A. Lindquist, 'Revealing the Feminist in Mary Parker Follett', *Administration and Society*, no. 3, 1997, pp. 349–71.

33 R. L. Verstegen and M. A. Rutherford, 'Mary Parker Follett: Individualist or Collectivist? Or Both?', *Journal of Management History*, no. 5, 2000, pp. 207–23.

34 See L. F. Urwick, *The Elements of Administration* (New York: Harper & Row, 1944), quoting Follet, p. 102.

35 E. M. Fox and L. F. Urwick, *Dynamic Administration: The Collected Papers of Mary Parker Follett, second edition* (London: Pitman Publishing, 1973).

36 See D. McGregor, *The Human Side of Enterprise* (New York: McGraw-Hill, 1960).

37 R. McHenry, 'Spuring Stuff', *People Management*, 24 July 1997.

38 F. van de Looy and J. Benders, 'Not Just Money: Quality of Working Life as Employment Strategy', *Health Manpower Management*, no. 3, 1995, pp. 27–33.

39 G. Morgan, *Images of Organization* (Thousand Oaks, CA: Sage Publications, 1986).

40 J. D. Thompson, *Organizations in Action* (New York: McGraw-Hill, 1967), pp. 6–7. Also see A. C. Bluedorn, 'The Thompson Interdependence Demonstration', *Journal of Management Education*, November 1993, pp. 505–9.

41 F. von Hayek, 'The Use of Knowledge in Society', *American Economic Review*, no. 35, 1945, pp. 519–30.

42 R. L. Daft and K. E. Weick, 'Toward a Model of Organizations as Interpretation Systems', *Academy of Management Review*, April 1984, p. 293.

43 Articles in which the organisation is considered as being culture or in which the metaphor is discussed are, for instance, D. Meyerson and J. Martin, 'Cultural Change: An Integration of Three Different Views', *Journal of Management Studies*, November 1987, pp. 623–47; L. Smircich, 'Concepts of Culture and Organizational Analysis', *Administrative Science Quarterly*, September 1983, pp. 339–58; J. Walsh and G. R. Ungson, 'Organizational Memory', *Academy of Management Review*, January 1991, pp. 57–91; and K. E. Weick, *The Social Psychology of Organizing* (Reading, MA: Addison-Wesley Publishing Company, 1979).

44 G. Morgan, *Images of Organization* (Thousand Oaks, CA: Sage Publications, 1986), p. 121.

45 J. R. P. French and B. Raven, 'Bases of Social Power', in *Studies in Social Power*, ed. D. Cartwright (Ann Arbor, MI: University of Michigan, 1959); D. Krackhardt, 'Assessing the Political Landscape: Structure, Cognition, and Power in Organizations', *Administrative Science Quarterly*, June 1990, pp. 342–69; and J. Pfeffer, *Power in Organizations* (Cambridge, MA: Ballinger Publishing Company, 1981).

46 H. Mintzberg, *The Structuring of Organizations* (Englewood Cliffs, NJ: Prentice Hall, 1979).

47 G. Morgan, *Images of Organization* (Thousand Oaks, CA: Sage Publications, 1986), p. 199.

48 D. Pilling and M. Nakamoto, 'Resona Could Transform Role of Japanese Auditors', *Financial Times*, 12 June 2003.

49 G. Morgan, *Images of Organization* (Thousand Oaks, CA: Sage Publications, 1986), p. 235.

50 D. Ibison, 'Asia-Pacific: Overwork Kills Record Number of Japanese', *Financial Times*, 29 May 2002.

51 B. Briner, 'Feeling for the Facts', *People Management*, 9 January 1997.

52 See R. L. Daft, 'Learning the Craft of Organizational Research', *Academy of Management Review*, October 1983, pp. 539–46.

53 K. E. Weick, 'Theory Construction as Disciplined Imagination', *Academy of Management Review*, October 1989, pp. 516–31. Also see D. A. Whetten's article in the same issue, pp. 490–95.

54 Theory-focused versus problem-focused research is discussed in K. E. Weick, 'Agenda Setting in Organizational Behavior: A Theory-Focused Approach', *Journal of Management Inquiry*, September 1992, pp. 171–82. Also see K. J. Klein, H. Tosi and A. A. Cannella, Jr, 'Multilevel Theory Building: Benefits, Barriers, and New Developments', *Academy of Management Review*, April 1999, pp. 243–8. (Note: The special forum on multilevel theory building in the April 1999 issue of *Academy of Management Review* includes an additional five articles.)

55 For instance, see M. R. Buckley, G. R. Ferris, H. J. Bernardin and M. G. Harvey, 'The Disconnect between the Science and Practice of Management', *Business Horizons*, March–April 1998, pp. 31–8.

56 Complete discussion of this technique can be found in J. E. Hunter, F. L. Schmidt and G. B. Jackson, *Meta-Analysis. Cumulating Research Findings across Studies* (Beverly Hills, CA: Sage Publications, 1982); and J. E. Hunter and F. L. Schmidt, *Methods of Meta-Analysis: Correcting Error and Bias in Research Findings* (Newbury Park, CA: Sage Publications, 1990). Also see R. Hutter Epstein, 'The Number-Crunchers Drugmakers Fear and Love', *Business Week*, 22 August 1994, pp. 70–71.

57 Limitations of meta-analysis technique are discussed in P. Bobko and E. F. Stone-Romero, 'Meta-Analysis May Be Another Useful Tool, But It Is Not a Panacea', in *Research in Personnel and Human Resources Management, vol. 16*, ed. G. R. Ferris (Stamford, CT: JAI Press, 1998), pp. 359–97.

58 For an interesting debate about the use of students as subjects, see J. Greenberg, 'The College Sophomore as Guinea Pig: Setting the Record Straight', *Academy of Management Review*, January 1987, pp. 157–9; and M. E. Gordon, L. A. Slade and N. Schmitt, 'Student Guinea Pigs: Porcine Predictors and Particularistic Phenomena', *Academy of Management Review*, January 1987, pp. 160–63.

59 Good discussions of case studies can be found in A. S. Lee, 'Case Studies as Natural Experiments', *Human Relations*, February 1989, pp. 117–37; and K. M. Eisenhardt, 'Building Theories from Case Study Research', *Academy of Management Review*, October 1989, pp. 532–50. The case survey technique is discussed in R. Larsson, 'Case Survey Methodology: Analysis of Patterns across Case Studies', *Academy of Management Journal*, December 1993, pp. 1515–46.

60 Based on discussion found in J. M. Beyer and H. M. Trice, 'The Utilization Process: A Conceptual Framework and Synthesis of Empirical Findings', *Administrative Science Quarterly*, December 1982, pp. 591–622.

61 See J. J. Martocchio, 'Age-Related Differences in Employee Absenteeism: A Meta-Analysis', *Psychology & Aging*, December 1989, pp. 409–14.

62 H. L. Tosi, Jr, and J. W. Slocum, Jr, 'Contingency Theory: Some Suggested Directions', *Journal of Management*, Spring 1984, p. 9.

63 For complete details, see G. Hofstede, 'The Cultural Relativity of Organizational Practices and Theories', *Journal of International Business Studies*, Fall 1983. For related discussion, see G. Hofstede, 'Cultural Constraints in Management Theories', *Academy of Management Executive*, February 1993, pp. 81–94.

64 See J. B. Miner, 'The Validity and Usefulness of Theories in an Emerging Organizational Science', *Academy of Management Review*, April 1984, pp. 296–306.

65 G. W. Dauphinais and C. Price, 'The CEO as Psychologist', *Management Review*, September 1998. ©1998 American Management Association. Published by American Management Association International, New York, NY. Used with permission of the publisher. All rights reserved. http://www.amanet.org.

Appendix: Learning module

Research methods in organisational behaviour

As a future professional, you probably will be involved in developing and/or implementing programmes for solving business problems. You may also be asked to assess recommendations derived from in-house research reports or judge the usefulness of proposals from consultants. These tasks might entail reading and evaluating research findings presented both in scientific and professional journal articles. Thus, it is important for professionals to have a basic working knowledge of the research process. Moreover, such knowledge can help you critically evaluate research information encountered daily in newspaper, magazine and television reports.

One study revealed people cannot judge the difference between good and bad research.[1] So, how do they know what to believe about research results pertaining to organisational or societal problems? This Learning module presents a foundation for understanding the research process. Our purpose is not to make you a research scientist. The purpose is to make you a better consumer of research information.

The research process

Research on organisational behaviour is based on the scientific method. The scientific method is a formal process of using systematically gathered data to test hypotheses or to explain natural phenomena. To gain a better understanding of how to evaluate this process, we discuss a model of how research is conducted, explore how researchers measure organisationally relevant variables, highlight three ways to evaluate research methods and provide a framework for evaluating research conclusions. We also discuss how to read a research article.

A model of the research process

A flowchart of the research process is presented in Figure LM-1. Organisational research is conducted to solve problems. The problem may be one of current interest to an organisation, such as absenteeism or low motivation, or may be derived from published research studies. In either case, properly identifying and attempting to solve the problem necessitates a familiarity with previous research on the topic. This familiarity contributes background knowledge and insights for formulating a hypothesis to solve the problem. Students who have written formal library-research papers are well acquainted with this type of secondary research.

According to a respected researcher, 'A hypothesis is a conjectural statement of the relations between two or more variables. Hypotheses are always in declarative form, and they relate, either generally or specifically, variables to variables.[2] Regarding the problem of absenteeism, for instance, a manager might want to test the following hypothesis: 'Hourly employees who are dissatisfied with their pay are absent more often than those who are satisfied.' Hypothesis in hand, a researcher is prepared to design a study to test it.

There are two important, interrelated components to designing a study. The first consists of deciding how to measure independent and dependent variables. An independent variable is a variable that is hypothesised to affect or cause a certain state of events. For example, a study demonstrated that losing one's job led to lower self-esteem and greater depression.[3] In this case, losing one's job, the independent variable, produced lowel levels of self-esteem and higher levels of depression. A dependent variable is the variable being explained or predicted. Returning to the example, self-esteem and depression were the dependent variables (the variables being explained). In an everyday example, those who eat less (independent variable) are likely to lose weight (dependent variable). The second component of designing a study is to determine which research method to use. Criteria for evaluating the appropriateness of different research methods are discussed in a later section.

After a study is designed and completed, data are analysed to determine whether the hypothesis is supported. Researchers look for alternative explanations of results when a hypothesis is not supported.[4]

MEASUREMENT AND DATA COLLECTION

'In its broadest sense, measurement is the assignment of numerals to objects or events according to the rules.'[5] Organisational researchers measure variables. Job satisfaction, turnover, performance

FIGURE LM-1 MODEL OF THE RESEARCH PROCESS

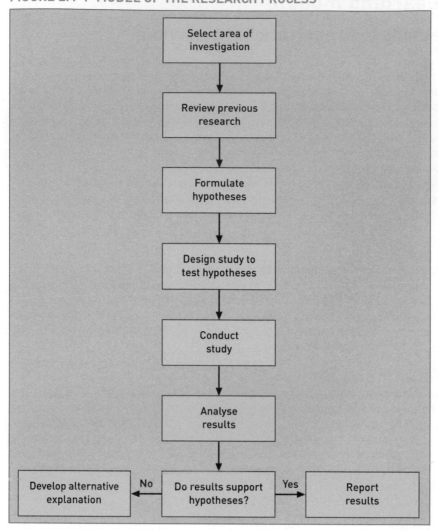

SOURCE: V. R. Boehm, 'Research in the "Real World": A Conceptual Model', *Personnel Psychology*, Autumn 1980, p. 496. Used with permission.

and perceived stress are variables typically measured in OB research. Valid measurement is one of the most critical components of any research study because research findings are open to conflicting interpretations when variables are poorly measured.[6] Poor management reduces the confidence one has in applying research findings. Four techniques are frequently used to collect data: (1) direct observation, (2) questionnaires, (3) interviews and (4) indirect methods.

1 *Observation.* This technique consists of recording the number of times a specified behaviour is exhibited. For example, psychologist Judith Komaki developed and validated an observational categorisation of supervisory behaviour. She then used the instrument to identify behaviour differences between effective and ineffective managers from a large medical insurance firm. Managerial effectiveness was based on superior ratings. Results indicated that effective managers spent more time monitoring their employees' performance than did ineffective managers. Komaki more recently applied the same instrument to examine the performance of sailboat captains competing a race. Similarly to her previous study, skippers finished higher in the overall race standings when they monitored and rewarded their crews.[7]

2 *Questionnaires*. Questionnaires ask respondents for their opinions or feelings about work-related issues. They generally contain previously developed and validated instruments and are self-administered. Given their impersonal nature, poorly designed questionnaires are susceptible to rate bias. Nevertheless, a well-developed survey can be an accurate and economical way to collect large quantities of data.[8]

3 *Interviews*. Interviews rely on either face-to-face or telephone interactions to ask respondents questions of interest. In a structured interview, interviewees are asked the same question in the same order. Unstructured interviews do not require interviewers to use the same questions or format. Unstructured interviews are more spontaneous. Structured interviews are the better of the two because they permit consistent comparisons between people. Accordingly, human resource management experts strongly recommend structured interviews during the hiring process to permit candidate-to-candidate comparisons.[9]

4 *Indirect methods*. These techniques obtain data without any direct contact with respondents. This approach may entail observing someone without his or her knowledge. Other examples include searching existing records, such as personnel files, for data on variables such as absenteeism, turnover and output. This method reduces rater error and is generally used in combination with one of the previously discussed techniques.

EVALUATING RESEARCH METHODS

All research methods can be evaluated from three perspectives: (1) generalisability, (2) precision in control and measurement, and (3) realism of the context.[10] Generalisability, which also is referred to as 'external validity', reflects the extent to which results from one study are generalisable to other individuals, groups or situations. Precision in control and measurement pertains to the level of accuracy in manipulating or measuring variables. A realistic context is one that naturally exists for the individuals participating in the research study. In other words, realism implies that the context is not an artificial situation contrived for purposes of conducting the study. Table LM.1 presents an evaluation of the five most frequently used research methods (see Chapter 1) in terms of these three perspectives.

In summary, there is no one best research method. Choosing a method depends on the purpose of the specific study.[11] For example, if high control is necessary, as in testing for potential radiation leaks in pipes that will be used in a nuclear power plant, a laboratory experiment is appropriate (see Table LM.1); in contrast, sample surveys would be useful if a company wanted to know the generalisable impact of a television commercial for light beer.

EVALUATING RESEARCH CONCLUSIONS

There are several issues to consider when evaluating the quality of a research study.[12] The first is whether results from the specific study are consistent with those from past research. If not, it is helpful to determine why discrepancies exist. For instance, it is insightful to compare the samples, research methods, measurement of variables, statistical analyses and general research procedures across the discrepant studies. Extreme differences suggest that future research may be needed to reconcile the inconsistent results. In the meantime, however, we need to be cautious in applying research findings from one study that are consistent with those from a larger number of studies.

TABLE LM.1 ASSESSMENT OF FREQUENTLY USED RESEARCH METHODS

Method	Generalisability	Precision in control and measurement	Realistic context
Case study	Low	Low	High
Sample survey	High	Low	Low
Field study	Moderate	Moderate	High
Laboratory experiment	Low	High	Low
Field experiment	Moderate	Moderate	Moderate

SOURCE: Adapted in part from J. E. McGrath, J. Martin, and R. A. Kulka, *Judgment Calls in Research* (Beverly Hills, CA: Sage Publications, 1982).

The type of research method used is the second consideration. Does the method have generalisability (see Table LM-1)? If not, check the characteristics of the sample. If the sample's characteristics are different from the characteristics of your work group, conclusions may not be relevant for your organisation. Sample characteristics are very important in evaluating results from both field studies and experiments.

The level of precision in control and measurement is the third factor to consider. It is important to determine whether valid measures were used in the study. This can be done by reading the original study and examining descriptions of how variables were measured. Variables have questionable validity when they are measured with one-item scales or 'ad hoc' instruments developed by the authors. In contrast, standardised scales tend to be more valid because they are typically developed and validated in previous research studies. We have more confidence in results when they are based on analyses using standardised scales. As a general rule, validity in measurement begets confidence in applying research findings.

Finally, it is helpful to brainstorm alternative explanations for the research results. This helps to identify potential problems with research procedures.

Reading a scientific journal article

Research is published in scientific journals and professional magazines. *Journal of Applied Psychology* and *Academy of Management Journal* are examples of scientific journals reporting OB research.

TABLE LM.2 A LIST OF HIGHLY REGARDED MANAGEMENT JOURNALS AND MAGAZINES

1 Administrative Science Quarterly	27 Public Administration Quarterly
2 Journal of Applied Psychology	28 Journal of Organizational Behavior
3 Organizational Behavior and Human	Management
Decision Processes	29 Organizational Dynamics
4 Academy of Management Journal	30 Monthly Labour Review
5 Psychological Bulletin	31 Journal of World Business
6 Industrial and Labor Relations Review	32 Journal of Business Research
7 Journal of Personality and Social	33 Group and Organization Management
Psychology	34 Human Resource Planning
8 Academy of Management Review	35 Journal of Management Studies
9 Industrial Relations	36 Administration and Society
10 Journal of Labor Economics	37 Negotiation Journal
11 Personnel Psychology	38 Arbitration Journal
12 American Psychologist	39 Compensation and Benefits Review
13 Journal of Labor Research	40 Journal of Collective Negotiations in
14 Journal of Vocational Behavior	the Public Sector
15 Journal of Applied Behavioral Science	41 Public Personnel Management
16 Occupational Psychology	42 Journal of Management Education*
17 Sloan Management Review	43 Review of Business and Economic
18 Journal of Conflict Resolution	Research
19 Human Relations	44 Personnel Journal
20 Journal of Human Resources	45 Journal of Small Business
21 Labor Law Journal	Management
22 Harvard Business Review	46 SAM Advanced Management Journal
23 Social Forces	47 Business Horizons
24 Journal of Management	48 Business and Public Affairs
25 California Management Review	49 HR Magazine**
26 Journal of Occupational Behavior	50 Training and Development***

*Formerly Organizational Behavior Teaching Review.
**Formerly Personnel Administrator.
***Formerly Training and Development Journal.

SOURCE: Adapted by permission from M. M. Extejt and J. E. Smith, 'The Behavior Sciences and Management: An Evaluation of Relevant Journals', *Journal of Management*, September 1990, p. 545.

Harvard Business Review and *HR Magazine* are professional magazines that sometimes report research findings in general terms. Table LM.2 contains a list of 50 highly regarded management journals and magazines. You may find this list to be a useful source of information when writing term papers.

Scientific journal articles report results from empirical research studies, overall reviews of research on a specific topic and theoretical articles. To help you obtain relevant information from scientific articles, let us consider the content and structure of these three types of articles.[13]

EMPIRICAL RESEARCH STUDIES

Reports of these studies contain summaries of original research. They typically comprise four distinct sections consistent with the logical steps of the research process model shown in Figure LM-1. These sections are as follows:

- *Introduction.* This section identifies the problem being investigated and the purpose of the study. Previous research pertaining to the problem is reviewed and sometimes critiqued.
- *Method.* This section discusses the method used to conduct the study. Characteristics of the sample or subjects, procedures followed, materials used, measurement of variables and analytic procedures typically are discussed.
- *Results.* A detailed description of the documented results is presented.
- *Discussion.* This section provides an interpretation, discussion and implications of results.

REVIEW ARTICLES

These articles, included meta-analyses, are critical evaluations of material that has already been published. By organising, integrating, and evaluating previously published materials, the author of a review article considers the progress of current research toward clarifying a problem.[14] Although the structure of these articles is not as clear-cut as reports of empirical studies, the general format is as follows:

- A statement of the problem.
- A summary or review of previous research that attempts to provide the reader with the state of current knowledge about the problem (meta-analysis frequently is used to summarise past research).
- Identification of shortcomings, limitations and inconsistencies in past research.
- Recommendations for future research to solve the problem.

THEORETICAL ARTICLES

These articles draw on past research to propose revisions to existing theoretical models or to develop new theories and models. The structure is similar to that of review articles.

Notes

1 This study is discussed in A. Finkbeiner, 'Some Science Is Baloney; Learn to Tell the Difference', *USA Today*, 11 September 1997, p. 15A.
2 F. N. Kerlinger, *Foundations of Behavioral Research* (New York: Holt, Rinehart & Winston, 1973), p. 18.
3 See A. H. Winefield and M. Tiggemann, 'Employment Status and Psychological Well-Being: A Longitudinal Study', *Journal of Applied Psychology*, August 1990, pp. 455–9.
4 See P. J. Frost and R. E. Stablein, eds, *Doing Exemplary Research* (Newbury Park, CA: Sage, 1992); and S. Begley, 'The Meaning of Junk', *Newsweek*, 22 March 1993, pp. 62–4.
5 S. S. Stevens, 'Mathematics, Measurement, and Psychophysics', in *Handbook of Experimental Psychology*, ed. S. S. Stevens (New York: John Wiley & Sons, 1951), p. 1.
6 A thorough discussion of the importance of measurement is provided by D. P. Schwab, 'Construct Validity in Organizational Behavior', in *Research in Organizational Behavior*, eds B. M. Staw and L. L. Cummings (Greenwich, CT: JAI Press, 1980), pp. 3–43.
7 See J. L. Komaki, 'Toward Effective Supervision: An Operant Analysis and Comparison of Managers at Work', *Journal of Applied Psychology*, May 1986, pp. 270–79. Results from the sailing study can be found in J. L. Komaki, M. L. Desselles, and E. D. Bowman, 'Definitely Not a Breeze: Extending an Operant Model of Effective Supervision to Teams', *Journal of Applied Psychology*, June 1989, pp. 522–9.
8 A thorough discussion of the pros and cons of using surveys or questionnaires is provided by J. A. Krosnick,

'Survey Research', in *Annual Review of Psychology*, eds J. T. Spence, J. M. Darley, and D. J. Foss (Palo Alto, CA: 1999); pp. 537–67.

9 See F. L. Schmidt and M. Rader, 'Exploring the Boundary Conditions for Interview Validity: Meta-Analytic Validity Findings for a New Interview Type', *Personnel Psychology*, Summer 1999, pp. 445–64; and M. A. McDaniel, D. Whetzel, F. L. Schmidt, and S. Maurer, 'Validity of Employment Interviews: a Comprehensive Review and Meta-Analysis', *Journal of Applied Psychology*, August 1994, pp. 599–616.

10 A complete discussion of the guidelines for conducting good research methods is provided by T. D. Cook and D. T. Campbell, *Quasi-Experimentation: Design & Analysis Issues for Field Settings* (Chicago: Rand McNally, 1979).

11 Ibid.

12 For a thorough discussion of the guidelines for conducting good research, see L. Wilkinson, 'Statistical Methods in Psychology Journals', *American Psychologist*, August 1999, pp. 594–604.

13 This discussion is based on material presented in the *Publication Manual of the American Psychological Association, fourth edition* (Washington, DC: American Psychological Association, 1994).

14 Ibid., p. 5.

section

2

individual
processes

chapter 2 personality dynamics

By Eva Cools and Herman Van den Broeck

Learning outcomes

When you finish studying the material in this chapter, you should be able to:

- explain what self-esteem is and how it can be improved

- define self-efficacy and explain its sources

- contrast high and low self-monitoring individuals and describe resulting problems each may have

- explain the difference between an internal and an external locus of control

- identify and describe the Big Five personality dimensions

- describe Jung's and Myers and Briggs' personality typology

- elaborate on cautions and tips concerning (personality) testing in the workplace

- describe the evolution of intelligence and abilities research

- describe the cognitive styles of Kirton and those of Riding

- focus on the learning styles of Kolb and those of Honey and Mumford

Character assignation at Liverpool Victoria

Introverts and extraverts have such different training needs that Liverpool Victoria, one of the UK's leading financial services companies, devised separate development programmes for them. Tony Miller (a former group training manager at Liverpool Victoria and currently an international consultant specialising in HR and business improvement) and Adrian Furnham (Professor of Psychology at London University) set up a study at the company's telephone call centre and discovered that personality crucially affects productivity. He therefore adapted the company's policies to match its findings.

'Most companies have clear policies about selection and training, believing that they know what they are doing – what to select for, how to train and, equally important, how to manage their employees. But their confidence may be misplaced', says Tony Miller. 'Few managers have done the research to back up their intuitions or, indeed, their prejudices. Such work can be expensive and time-consuming but if you want to examine the effects of training, you need sound information about people's behaviour and performance.'

Doing applied research is a way of gaining competitive advantage, Miller and Furnham found in their study at Liverpool Victoria. UK's call centre industry is continuing to grow (even though firms are transferring work to overseas countries), employing currently around 435 000 people. There is, however, significant evidence that call centres are experiencing serious problems in the recruitment, selection, motivation, productivity and retention of their employees. Companies that install the latest systems for handling telephone business can be seriously handicapped if they do not have properly trained, satisfied and confident staff.

Therefore, Miller and Furnham wanted more insight into the individual characteristics of the call centre employees. They looked at a number of personality factors, and matched these against people's performance. These personality factors were:

- *Extraversion or sociability:* Miller and Furnham thought that being an extravert could be a double-edged sword in telesales. Extraverts are more people-oriented. This is obviously desirable, but there are also sensation-seekers among them who are easily bored. The physical constraints of telesales might lead to greater productivity but also to greater absenteeism.
- *Negative affectivity or neuroticism:* unstable people tend to be more moody, have a lower job satisfaction and tend not to get on with their colleagues and supervisors.
- *Learning style:* this provides four measures of how people learn – people can be classified as activists, pragmatists, theorists and reflectors.

Performance was measured in two ways: first, by the researchers looking at ratings from supervisors and second, by measuring absenteeism caused by sickness.

'The results confirmed our prediction that extraversion is a mixed blessing for work in a call centre', Miller explains. 'The extraverts were absent more often but were given higher performance ratings. But they also received a lower developmental rating from their supervisors. It could be that the supervisors perceived extraverts as good "short-hire" staff who were too easily bored or ambitious for a long career in telesales. Introverts were seen as having more potential in the long term.'

The best and most consistent predictors of success in terms of both productivity and development were found to be the learning styles. Being a reflector – that is, thoughtful, thorough and methodical – was associated with poor performance, possibly because people with this learning style are averse to taking risks and tend to hold back from direct participation.

Being a theorist, however, was positively related to telesales success. These tend to be logical, rational, disciplined and objective. It may be their low tolerance of uncertainty, ambiguity and disorder which makes them good sales staff.

'What we were able to show was that personality variables and learning styles do statistically predict productivity at work', says Adrian Furnham. 'We are the first to admit that these are not the only factors that lead to productivity but one should not overlook the potential benefits this study has offered to Liverpool Victoria in understanding individual differences of their staff.'

The results of the study were indeed successfully fed back into recruitment, training and motivational programmes at Liverpool Victoria. The company developed a clear picture of the type of personality that would be suited to working in a call centre. This gave its recruitment process a clear focus. For jobs on the sales side, the personality profile favoured extraverts, while introverts were the preferred character type for customer service posts.

The company's approach to staff training was then extensively modified, with different programmes developed for extraverts and introverts, although both types learned the same skills.

Extraverts need to be continually stimulated and respond better to imaging and activity-based training. Accordingly, participation was actively encouraged in their development programmes, backed up by the use of picture-aided visual aids. Alternatively, introverts prefer to absorb the material by reading it, rather than making presentations and participating in group work. They also react better to text-based visual aids.[1]

For discussion

Do you think this type of extensive personality research will become common in organisations? What are the possible benefits and drawbacks of surveying all employees like this?

What makes you you? What characteristics do you share with others? Which ones set you apart? Perhaps you have a dynamic personality and dress accordingly, while a low-key friend dresses conservatively and avoids crowds. Some computer freaks would rather surf the Internet than eat; other people suffer from computer phobia. Sometimes students who skim their reading assignments at the last moment get higher grades than those who study for days. People standing patiently in a long queue watch an angry customer shout at a store clerk. One employee consistently does more than asked, while another equally skilled employee barely does the job. Thanks to a vast array of individual differences such as these, modern organisations have a rich and interesting human texture. On the other hand, dealing with all these individual differences makes organisational life endlessly challenging. Growing workforce diversity compels organisations to view individual differences in a fresh new way. Rather than limiting diversity, as in the past, today's organisations need to better understand and accommodate their employees' diversity and individual differences.[2]

Figure 2.1 is a conceptual model showing the relationship between self-concept (how you view yourself), personality (how you appear to others) and key forms of self-expression. Self-concept, personality, abilities and styles are elaborated in this chapter. In the next chapter, we look at values, attitudes and emotions. Considered as an integrated package, these individual differences provide a foundation for understanding each employee better as a unique and special individual.

FIGURE 2.1 A CONCEPTUAL MODEL FOR THE STUDY OF INDIVIDUAL DIFFERENCES IN OB

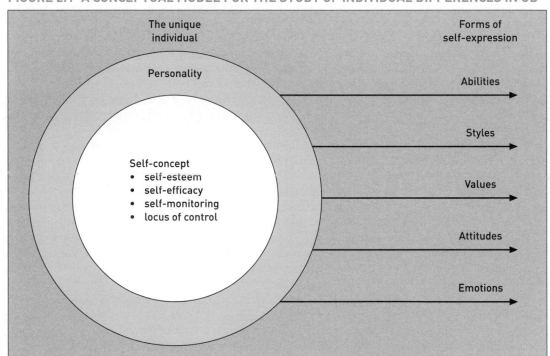

We first look at some often studied personality traits: self-esteem, self-efficacy, self-monitoring and locus of control. We put them into a different subsection (self-concept) from personality, because they cannot be directly integrated into one of the personality theories which are to be explained. Moreover, these traits have a substantial influence in organisations, so they need some more explanation. We then focus on personality, abilities and styles. Research into these concepts has always existed, although it intensified during the twentieth century. Several traditions and streams of research arose for each of these concepts. Gradually, more and more models and accompanying measurements were developed. Relationships between personality and abilities, personality and styles and abilities and styles, respectively, were also investigated.

Self-concept: the I and me in OB

Self is the core of one's conscious existence. Awareness of self, how you view yourself is referred to as one's self-concept. Sociologist Viktor Gecas defines **Self-concept** as 'the concept the individual has of himself as a physical, social, and spiritual or moral being'.[3] In other words, because you have a self-concept, you recognise yourself as a distinct human being. A self-concept would be impossible without the capacity to think. This brings us to the role of **Cognitions**. Cognitions represent 'any knowledge, opinion or belief about the environment, about oneself or about one's behaviour'.[4] Among the many different types of cognitions, those involving anticipation, planning, goal setting, evaluating and setting personal standards, are particularly relevant to OB.[5]

Several cognition-based topics are discussed in later chapters. Differing cognitive styles are introduced later on in this chapter and attitudes will be elaborated in Chapter 3. Cognitions play a central role in social perception, as will be discussed in Chapter 4. Also, as we will see in Chapters 5 and 6, modern motivation theories and techniques are powered by cognitions. Importantly, ideas of self and self-concept vary from one historical era to another, from one socio-economic class to another, and from culture to culture.[6] How well one detects and adjusts to different cultural notions of self can spell the difference between success and failure in international dealings.

Self-concept
a person's self-perception as a physical, social, spiritual being

Cognitions
a person's knowledge, opinions or beliefs

Culture dictates the degree of self-disclosure in Japan and the United States

Survey research in Japan and the United States uncovered the following distinct contrasts in Japanese versus American self-disclosure:

- Americans disclosed nearly as much to strangers as the Japanese did to their own fathers.
- Americans reported two to three times greater physical contact with parents and twice greater contact with friends than the Japanese.
- The Japanese may be frightened at the prospect of being communicatively invaded (because of the unexpected spontaneity and bluntness of the American); the American is annoyed at the prospect of endless formalities and tangential replies.
- American emphasis on self-assertion and talkativeness cultivates a communicator who is highly self-oriented and expressive; the Japanese emphasis on 'reserve' and 'sensitivity' cultivates a communicator who is other-oriented [oriented toward the other person] and receptive.

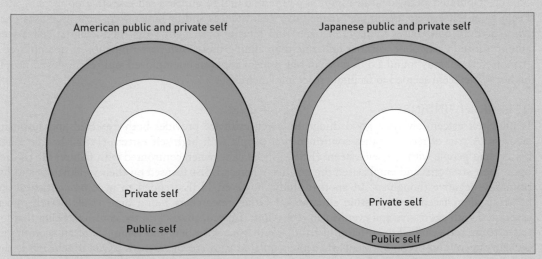

SOURCE: Adapted from D. C. Barnlund, 'Public and Private Self in Communicating with Japan', *Business Horizons*, March–April 1989, pp. 32–40.

snapshot

For example, as detailed in the Snapshot on page 45, Japanese–US communication and understanding is often hindered by significantly different degrees of self-disclosure. With a comparatively large public self, Americans pride themselves in being open, honest, candid and to the point [direct]. Meanwhile, Japanese people, who culturally discourage self-disclosure, typically view Americans as blunt, prying and insensitive to formalities. For their part, Americans tend to see Japanese as distant, cold and evasive.[7] One culture is not right and the other wrong, they are just different. A key difference involves culturally rooted conceptions of self and self-disclosure. Related to these cultural differences in self and self-disclosure are also cultural differences in emotional display rules and norms (also see Chapter 3). Keeping this cultural qualification in mind, let us explore four topics invariably mentioned when behavioural scientists discuss self-concept. They are self-esteem, self-efficacy, self-monitoring and locus of control.[8] Each of these areas deserves a closer look to better understand and effectively deal with people at work.

Self-esteem: a controversial topic

Self-esteem
belief about one's self-worth based on overall self-evaluation

Self-esteem is a belief about one's own self-worth based on an overall self-evaluation.[9] It refers to the degree to which people like or dislike themselves. People with high self-esteem see themselves as worthwhile, capable and acceptable. People with low self-esteem view themselves in negative terms. They do not feel good about themselves and are hampered by self-doubts.[10] The subject of self-esteem has generated a good deal of controversy in recent years, particularly among educators and those seeking to help the disadvantaged.[11] While both sides generally agree that positive self-esteem is a good thing for students and youngsters, disagreement rages over how to improve self-esteem. Consider the findings of a British study among students in sports schools on this matter.

> Sport seems to be a way out that can improve self-esteem. A British study of the Northumbria University compared the school career of pupils at sport schools with the school careers of pupils in other secondary schools. The study reveals that the self-esteem and self-image of students at the sport school was after a while higher than that of students in other secondary schools. Their study results increased as well. Moreover, adolescents at a sport school have a more positive image of their body, something that is very important for a teenager. These results are particularly found for boys, less for girls. A reason for this gender difference might be that boys are more sensitive for the way in which sport improves their image. Researcher Gordon Macfayden comments: 'Studying in a sport school has a positive influence on all aspects of boys' physical and psychological self-image. I even think that sport schools can be a remedy against antisocial behaviour. Sport is an outlet and a way to feel appreciated.'[12]

So, the elaborated study identifies sport as a potential tool to improve self-esteem among youngsters. Feelings of self-esteem are, in fact, shaped by circumstances and by how others treat us. Researchers who surveyed 654 young adults (192 male, 462 female) over eight years found higher self-esteem among those in school or working full-time than among those with part-time jobs or unemployed.[13] A more recent study found a difference in self-esteem between unemployed and re-employed people: higher self-esteem seemed to facilitate re-employment.[14]

RESEARCH FINDINGS

Is high self-esteem always a good thing? Research evidence provides both expected and surprising answers. A pair of recent studies confirmed that people with high self-esteem (HSE) handle failure better than people with low self-esteem (LSE). Specifically, when confronted with failure, HSEs drew upon their strengths and emphasised the positive whereas LSEs focused on their weaknesses and had primarily negative thoughts.[15] In another study, however, HSEs tended to become egotistical and boastful when faced with pressure situations.[16] Other researchers found high levels of self-esteem associated with aggressive and even violent behaviour. Indeed, contrary to the common belief that low self-esteem and criminality go hand in hand, youth gang members and criminals often score highly on self-esteem and become violent when their inflated egos are threatened.[17] Our conclusion is that high self-esteem can be a good thing, but only if – like many other human characteristics such as creativity, intelligence and persistence – it is nurtured and channelled in constructive and ethical ways. Otherwise, it can become antisocial and destructive.

From the organisation's point of view, high self-esteem can also be a mixed blessing. In non-downsizing organisations, employees with lower self-esteem tend to leave, but in downsizing organisations self-confidence and self-esteem have a positive direct effect on intent to leave.[18] Individuals with the capabilities and the confidence to perform well in other firms tend to leave first. In this way, of course, the downsizing companies are losing not the low performers, but those employees they hoped to retain.

Recently, the striking results of a 30-year longitudinal study in Britain were presented. Leon Fernstein and his team, of the Centre for Economic Performance at the London School of Economics, interviewed the parents of all babies born in the UK in the first week of April 1970. The children were subsequently questioned at ages 5, 10, 16, 26 and again as they reached their 30th birthday in April 2000. Self-esteem was monitored at the age of 10 by asking the children a series of questions. Fernstein found a very close correlation between childhood self-esteem and adult success. According to Fernstein, 'there is now clear evidence that children with higher self-esteem at age 10 get as much of a kick to their adult earning power as those with equivalent higher maths or reading ability. Childhood self-esteem can overwhelm academic disadvantage or social deprivation in determining future earnings power.'[19]

What are the cross-cultural implications of self-esteem, a concept that has been called uniquely Western? In a survey of 13 118 students from 31 countries worldwide, a moderate positive correlation was found between self-esteem and life satisfaction. However, the relationship was stronger in individualistic cultures (such as the United States, Canada, New Zealand and the Netherlands) than in collectivist cultures (such as Korea, Kenya and Japan). The researchers concluded that individualistic cultures socialise people to focus more on themselves, while people in collectivist cultures 'are socialised to fit into the community and to do their duty. Thus, how a collectivist feels about himself or herself is less relevant to … life satisfaction.'[20] Global organisations need to remember to de-emphasise self-esteem when doing business in collectivist ('we') cultures, as opposed to emphasising it in individualistic ('me') cultures (for more on organisational and international culture, see Chapter 16).

PRACTICAL IMPLICATIONS

Can self-esteem be improved? The short answer is yes (also see Table 2.1). A recent study led to the following conclusion: 'Low self-esteem can be raised more by having the person think of desirable characteristics possessed rather than of undesirable characteristics from which he or she is free.'[21] This approach can help neutralise the self-defeating negative thoughts of LSEs (see our related discussions of the self-fulfilling prophecy in Chapter 4).

According to a study by the Society for Human Resource Management, organisations can build employee self-esteem in four ways:

TABLE 2.1 BRANDEN'S SIX PILLARS OF SELF-ESTEEM

What nurtures and sustains self-esteem in grown-ups is not how others deal with us but how we ourselves operate in the face of life's challenges – the choices we make and the actions we take.

This leads us to the six pillars of self-esteem:

1 *Live consciously:* be actively and fully engaged in what you do and with whom you interact
2 *Be self-accepting:* don't be overly judgmental or critical of your thoughts and actions
3 *Take personal responsibility:* take full responsibility for your decisions and actions in life's journey
4 *Be self-assertive:* be authentic and willing to defend your beliefs when interacting with others, rather than bending to their will to be accepted or liked
5 *Live purposefully:* have clear near-term and long-term goals and realistic plans for achieving them to create a sense of control over your life
6 *Have personal integrity:* be true to your word and your values

Between self-esteem and the practices that support it, there is reciprocal causation. This means that the behaviours that generate good self-esteem are also expressions of good self-esteem.

SOURCE: Excerpted and adapted from N. Branden, *Self-Esteem at Work: How Confident People Make Powerful Companies* (San Francisco: Jossey-Bass, 1998), pp. 33–6.

■ Be supportive by showing concern for personal problems, interests, status and contributions.
■ Offer work involving variety, autonomy and challenges that suit the employee's values, skills and abilities (also see Chapters 5 and 6 on motivation).
■ Strive for supervisor–employee cohesiveness and build trust. Trust, an important teamwork element, is discussed in Chapter 10.
■ Have faith in each employee's self-management ability. Reward each success.[22]

Self-efficacy

Self-efficacy
belief in one's ability to accomplish a task successfully

Have you noticed how those who are confident about their ability tend to succeed, while those who are preoccupied with failing tend to fail? At the heart of this performance mismatch is a specific dimension of self-esteem called self-efficacy. Self-efficacy is a person's belief about his or her chances of successfully accomplishing a specific task. According to one OB writer, 'self-efficacy arises from the gradual acquisition of complex cognitive, social, linguistic and/or physical skills through experience'.[23] Self-efficacy refers to personal beliefs regarding your competencies, skills and abilities. To gain a better understanding of what this concept entails, carefully read the following example.

> " According to the Briton James Dyson, founder of Dyson Appliances: 'The key to success is failure. Not other people's failure, but how you respond to failure yourself. Everyone gets knocked back, no-one rises smoothly to the top without hindrance. The ones who succeed are the ones who say, right, let's give it another go. Who cares what others think? I believe in what I'm doing. I will never give up. Success is made up of 99 per cent failure. You galvanise yourself and you keep going.'[24] "

Learned helplessness
debilitating lack of faith in one's ability to control the situation

The relationship between self-efficacy and performance is a cyclical one. Efficacy → performance cycles can spiral upward toward success or downward toward failure.[25] Researchers have documented in naval cadets a strong linkage between high self-efficacy expectations and success in widely varied physical and mental tasks, anxiety reduction, addiction control, pain tolerance, illness recovery and avoidance of seasickness.[26] In contrast, those with low self-efficacy expectations tend to have low success rates. Chronically low self-efficacy is associated with a condition called Learned helplessness, the severely debilitating belief that one has no control over one's environment.[27] Although self-efficacy sounds like some sort of mental magic, it operates in a very straightforward manner.

WHAT ARE THE MECHANISMS OF SELF-EFFICACY?

A basic model of self-efficacy is displayed in Figure 2.2. It draws upon the work of the Stanford University psychologist Albert Bandura.[28] Let us explore this model with a simple illustrative task.[29] Imagine you have been told to prepare and deliver a 10-minute talk to an OB class of 50 students on the workings of the self-efficacy model in Figure 2.2. Your self-efficacy calculation would involve cognitive appraisal of the interaction between your perceived capability and the situational opportunities and obstacles.

As you begin to prepare for your presentation, the four sources of self-efficacy beliefs would come into play. Because prior experience is the most potent source, according to Bandura, it is listed first and connected to self-efficacy beliefs with a solid line.[30] Past success in public speaking would boost your self-efficacy. Bad experiences with delivering speeches, however, would foster low self-efficacy. Regarding behaviour models as a source of self-efficacy beliefs, the success or failure of your classmates in delivering similar talks will influence you. Their successes would tend to bolster you (or perhaps their failure would, if you are very competitive and have high self-esteem). Likewise, any supportive persuasion from your classmates that you will do a good job would enhance your self-efficacy. Physical and emotional factors might also affect your self-confidence. A sudden case of laryngitis or a bout of stage fright could cause your self-efficacy expectations to plunge. Your cognitive evaluation of the situation would then yield a self-efficacy belief – ranging from high to low expectations for success. Significantly, self-efficacy beliefs are not merely boastful statements based on bravado; they are deep convictions supported by experience.

Moving to the behavioural patterns portion of Figure 2.2, we see how self-efficacy beliefs are acted out. In short, if you have high self-efficacy about giving a 10-minute speech you will work harder, more creatively and longer when preparing for your talk than will your low self-efficacy classmates.

FIGURE 2.2 A MODEL OF HOW SELF-EFFICACY BELIEFS CAN PAVE THE WAY FOR SUCCESS OR FAILURE

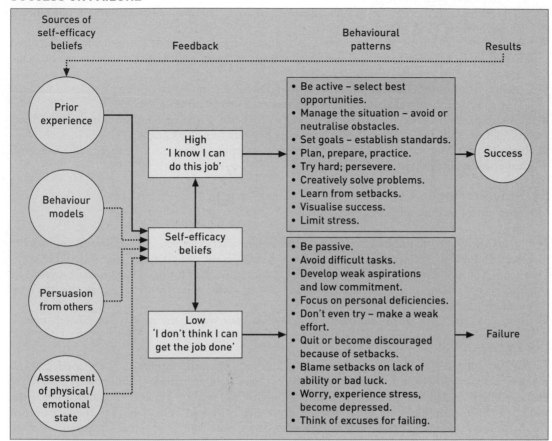

SOURCE: Adapted from discussion in A. Bandura, 'Regulation of Cognitive Processes through Perceived Self-Efficacy', *Developmental Psychology*, September 1989, pp. 729–35: and R. Wood and A. Bandura, 'Social Cognitive Theory of Organizational Management,' *Academy of Management Review*, July 1989, pp. 361–84.

The results would then take shape accordingly. People programme themselves for success or failure by enacting their self-efficacy expectations. Positive or negative results subsequently become feedback for one's base of personal experience.

RESEARCH FINDINGS AND PRACTICAL IMPLICATIONS

On-the-job research evidence encourages professionals to nurture self-efficacy, both in themselves and in others. In fact, a recent meta-analysis encompassing 21 616 participants found a significant positive correlation between self-efficacy and job performance.[31] Self-efficacy requires constructive action in each of the following eight organisational areas:

■ Recruiting/selection/job assignments: interview questions can be designed to probe job applicants' general self-efficacy as a basis for determining orientation and training needs. Pencil-and-paper tests for self-efficacy are not in an advanced stage of development and validation. Care needs to be taken not to hire solely on the basis of self-efficacy, because studies have detected below-average self-esteem and self-efficacy among women and protected minorities (also see the Group exercise at the end of this chapter).[32]

■ Job design: complex, challenging and autonomous jobs tend to enhance perceived self-efficacy.[33] Boring, tedious jobs generally do the opposite (see Chapter 5).

■ Training and development: employees' self-efficacy expectations for key tasks can be improved through guided experiences, mentoring and role modelling.[34] A recent study also found a positive influence of all kinds of group stimuli (like diversity, an open group climate and supportive leadership) on people's self-efficacy.[35]

■ Self-management: systematic self-management training involves enhancement of self-efficacy expectations (see also Chapter 10).[36]

■ Goal setting and quality improvement: goal difficulty needs to match the individual's perceived self-efficacy.[37] As self-efficacy and performance improve, goals and quality standards can be made more challenging (see also Chapter 6).

■ Coaching: those with low self-efficacy, and employees victimised by learned helplessness, need lots of constructive pointers and positive feedback (see also Chapters 6 and 11).[38]

■ Leadership: the necessary leadership talent surfaces when top management gives high self-efficacy professionals a chance to prove themselves under pressure (see also Chapter 11).[39]

■ Rewards: small successes need to be rewarded as stepping-stones to a stronger self-image and greater achievements (see also Chapter 6).

Self-monitoring

Consider the following contrasting scenarios:

■ You are rushing to an important meeting when a co-worker pulls you aside and starts to discuss a personal problem. You want to break off the conversation, so you glance at your watch. He keeps talking. You say, 'I'm late for a big meeting'. He continues. You turn and start to walk away. The person keeps talking as if he never received any of your verbal and non-verbal signals that the conversation was over.

■ Same situation. Only this time, when you glance at your watch, the person immediately says, 'I know, you've got to go. Sorry. We'll talk later.'

In the first, all-too-familiar scenario, you are talking to a 'low self-monitor'. The second scenario involves a 'high self-monitor'. But more is involved here than an irritating situation. A significant and measurable individual difference, called self-monitoring, is highlighted. **Self-monitoring** is the extent to which people observe their own self-expressive behaviour and adapt it to the demands of the situation. It refers to people's ability to adapt their behaviour to external, situational factors. Experts on the subject offer this explanation:

> Individuals high in self-monitoring are thought to regulate their expressive self-presentation for the sake of desired public appearances, and thus to be highly responsive to social and interpersonal cues of situationally appropriate performances. Individuals low in self-monitoring are thought to lack either the ability or the motivation to so regulate their expressive self-presentations. Their expressive behaviours, instead, are thought to functionally reflect their own enduring and momentary inner states, including their attitudes, traits and feelings.[40]

In organisational life, both high and low self-monitors are subject to criticism. High self-monitors are sometimes called chameleons, who readily adapt their self-presentation to their surroundings. Low self-monitors, on the other hand, are often criticised for being on their own planet and insensitive to others. Remember, within an OB context, self-monitoring is like any other individual difference, not a matter of right or wrong or good versus bad but rather a source of diversity that needs to be adequately understood to be effective in (organisation) life (see also Chapter 4).

A MATTER OF DEGREE

Self-monitoring is not an either–or proposition. It is a matter of degree; a matter of being relatively high or low in terms of related patterns of self-expression. The following Activity is designed to assess your self-monitoring tendencies. It can help you better understand yourself. Take a short break from your reading to complete the 10-item survey. Does your score surprise you in any way? Are you unhappy with the way you present yourself to others? What are the ethical implications of your score (particularly with regard to items 9 and 10) (see also Chapter 18 with regard to ethical behaviour)?[41]

Self-monitoring the extent to which a person adapts his/her behaviour to the situation

activity

What are your self-monitoring tendencies?

Instructions

In an honest self-appraisal, mark each of the following statements as true (T) or false (F), and then consult the scoring key.

_____ **1** I reckon I put on a show to impress or entertain others.

_____ **2** In a group of people, I am rarely the centre of attention.

_____ **3** In different situations and with different people, I often act like very different people.

_____ **4** I would not change my opinions (or the way I do things) in order to please someone or win their favour.

_____ **5** I have considered being an entertainer.

_____ **6** I have trouble changing my behaviour to suit different people and different situations.

_____ **7** At a party I let others keep the jokes and stories going.

_____ **8** I feel a bit awkward in public and do not show up quite as well as I should.

_____ **9** I can look anyone in the eye and tell a lie with a straight face (if for the right reason).

_____ **10** I may deceive people by being friendly when I really dislike them.

Scoring key and norms

Score one point for each of the following answers: 1 T; 2 F; 3 T; 4 F; 5 T; 6 F; 7 F; 8 F; 9 T; 10 T

Score: _____

1–3 = Low self-monitoring

4–5 = Moderately low self-monitoring

6–7 = Moderately high self-monitoring

8–10 = High self-monitoring

SOURCE: Excerpted and adapted from M. Snyder and S. Gangestad, 'On the Nature of Self-Monitoring: Matters of Assessment, Matters of Validity', *Journal of Personality and Social Psychology*, July 1986, p. 137.

RESEARCH FINDINGS AND PRACTICAL IMPLICATIONS

According to field research, there is a positive relationship between high self-monitoring and career success. Among 139 MBA graduates who were surveyed over five years, high self-monitors enjoyed more internal and external promotions than did their low self-monitoring classmates.[42] Another study of 147 managers and professionals found that high self-monitors had a better record of acquiring a mentor (someone to act as a personal career coach and professional sponsor).[43] These results mesh well with an earlier study that found managerial success (in terms of speed of promotion) tied to political savvy (knowing how to socialise, network and engage in organisational politics).[44] A study among 118 telecommunications employees and their colleagues investigated the moderating effects of self-monitoring on speaking-up behaviour. As predicted, low self-monitors, in comparison to high self-monitors, spoke up more often as internal locus of control, self-esteem, top management openness and trust in supervisor increased.[45] A recent meta-analysis including 23 191 people from 136 samples concluded that self-monitoring is a relevant and useful factor when dealing with job performance and emerging leaders.[46]

The foregoing evidence and practical experience leads us to make the following practical recommendations:

■ For high, moderate and low self-monitors: become more consciously aware of your self-image and how it affects others (the Activity is a good start).

■ For high self-monitors: don't overdo it by turning from a successful chameleon into someone who is widely perceived as insincere, dishonest, phoney and untrustworthy. You cannot be everything to everyone.

■ For low self-monitors: you can bend without breaking, so try to be a bit more accommodating while being true to your basic beliefs. Don't wear out your welcome when communicating. Practice reading and adjusting to non-verbal cues in various public situations. If your conversation partner is bored or distracted, stop – because they are not really listening.

Locus of control: self or environment?

Individuals vary in terms of how much personal responsibility they take for their behaviour and its consequences. Julian Rotter, a personality researcher, identified a dimension of personality he labelled **Locus of control** to explain these differences. He proposed that people tend to attribute the causes of their behaviour primarily either to themselves or to environmental factors.[47]

People who believe they control the events and consequences that affect their lives are said to possess an **Internal locus of control** ('internals'). Internals see themselves as active agents. They trust in their capacity to influence the environment and assume that they can control events in their lives by effort and skill. For example, an internal tends to attribute positive outcomes, such as passing an exam, to her or his abilities. Similarly, an 'internal' tends to blame negative events, such as failing an exam, on personal shortcomings (e.g. not studying hard enough). Many entrepreneurs eventually succeed because their internal locus of control helps them overcome setbacks and disappointments. They see themselves as masters of their own fate and not simply lucky.

On the other side of this personality dimension are those who believe their performance is the product of circumstances beyond their immediate control. These individuals are said to possess an **External locus of control** ('externals'). Externals see themselves as passive agents. They believe that events in their lives and things that they want to achieve are subject to uncontrollable forces, luck, chance and powerful others. Unlike someone with an internal locus of control, an 'external' would attribute a pass in an exam to something external (e.g. an easy test or a good day) and attribute a failing grade to an unfair test or problems at home. Recent studies suggest that locus of control beliefs may vary across situations. This means that locus of control beliefs at work may differ from locus of control beliefs in other life areas.[48]

RESEARCH FINDINGS

Locus of control is an important variable for the explanation of human behaviour in organisations. Both laboratory and field studies have established that the behaviour of internals and externals can differ across work-related situations. Let us focus on some relevant research findings for organisations.

Internals and externals have different information-processing capabilities and learning strategies. Internals are more inclined to search for relevant information than externals, and seem to learn more from feedback and past experiences than externals. Since internals are more concerned with self-direction, they pay more attention to information that is relevant for attaining their goals and they recognise the relevance of information for goal attainment more quickly than do externals. They will also process this information more actively. Externals, on the other hand, more readily accept dependency on a more competent other and thus have less need for information.[49]

Another study found that an internal locus of control was positively related to the initiative dimension of performance, which means that internals engaged more frequently in innovative and spontaneous performance that goes beyond basic job requirements. External locus of control was related to the compliant dimension of performance, which means behaviour that complies with given role requirements. This relationship between an internal locus of control and performance is explained by the stronger motivation of employees with an internal locus of control. They place a higher value to goal attainment and feel more in control to attain these goals. The differential impact of locus on control on different performance dimensions is explained by the fact that internals look at themselves for direction, while externals depend on outside factors such as a supervisor or company rules.[50]

Research also studied locus of control cross-culturally to know whether research findings can be generalised across cultures or that they are uniquely Western. More specifically, Western culture always placed a high value on personal autonomy, which implies that an internal locus of control is more favourable than an external locus of control. However, studies in other cultures found that they hold external locus of control beliefs more than Euro-Americans. These studies demonstrate that locus of control beliefs vary across cultures and that cultural and societal factors often account for the difference. Moreover, locus of control beliefs, like values and attitudes, tend to be formed early in life and are influenced by learning experiences, family and other sources (see Chapter 16 about socialisation). So, taking into account one's cultural identity can be important to interpret correctly one's locus of control.[51] In a recent study among 5185 managers from 24 countries, however, the relationship between locus of control and well-being was found to be universal (i.e. consistent among all

---

Locus of control degree to which a person takes responsibility for his/her behaviour and its consequences

Internal locus of control attributing outcomes to one's own actions

External locus of control attributing outcomes to circumstances beyond one's control

samples), although the researchers of this study also warn that further research is necessary to better understand the cross-cultural differences and similarities of locus of control beliefs. 'Beliefs about control and, presumably, perceptions of control at work must be culturally appropriate for the context in which people live, and exploring such context differences should be the next direction for international control research.'[52]

PRACTICAL IMPLICATIONS

The preceding summary of research findings on locus of control has important implications for organisations.

First, since internals have a tendency to believe they control the work environment through their behaviour, they will attempt to exert control over the work setting. This can be done by trying to influence work procedures, working conditions, task assignments or relationships with peers and supervisors. As these possibilities imply, internals may resist a boss's attempts to closely supervise their work. Accordingly, organisations may want to place internals in jobs requiring high initiative and low compliance. Internal employees seem to be more satisfied with supervision than external employees under a participative leadership style, whereas externals are more satisfied than internals under a directive style. Externals might be more amenable to highly structured jobs requiring greater compliance. Routine and clearly structured tasks are found to increase the motivation of externals, while they decrease motivation among internals. Direct participation can also bolster the attitudes and performance of externals. This conclusion comes from a field study of 85 computer system users in a wide variety of business and government organisations. Externals who had been significantly involved in designing their organisation's computer information system had more favourable attitudes toward the system than their external-locus co-workers who had not participated.[53]

Second, locus of control has implications for reward systems (also see Chapter 6). Given that internals have a greater belief that their effort leads to performance, internals would probably prefer, and respond more productively to, incentives such as merit pay or sales commissions. Externals on the other hand seem unresponsive to incentives. They want them, but will not necessarily work harder for them.[54]

Personality

Individuals have their own way of thinking and acting, their own unique style or personality. **Personality** is defined as the combination of stable physical and mental characteristics that give the individual his or her identity.[55] These characteristics or traits – including how one looks, thinks, acts and feels – are the product of interacting genetic (nature) and environmental (nurture) influences. Nature refers to genetic factors you inherited from your parents. Research on twins that were reared apart suggests that these genetic or hereditary factors may be responsible for half of the variation in personalities.[56] Nurture refers to external influences from culture, social class, work environment, family, peers, etc. Experiences, learning and socialisation in these different environments influence who we are. After a longstanding debate between researchers defending the nature argument (also known as part of the nomothetic approach) and the ones defending the nurture argument (also known as part of the ideographic approach), most researchers now believe that both kinds of influences determine our personality. If it was only the nature argument that was right (implying that our personality is completely determined by heredity), our personality would be fixed from birth and not adaptable by, for instance, experiences or other external influences. On the other hand, if only the nurture argument was right, no consideration would be given to the fact that a major part of personality is rather stable and consistent.

In this section we introduce two personality dimensions models (trait theories of personality) and two personality types models (type theories of personality) and look at how they can be useful in organisations. We conclude with some cautions and tips for workplace personality testing.

> **Personality**
> stable physical and mental characteristics responsible for a person's identity

Personality dimensions or traits

Personality is a concept that is used to refer to many characteristics of people. Characteristics of people that are shown in varying situations are called personality traits. Traits that are fairly consistent and that show up in many situations are important in describing someone's personality. Endless lists of personality dimensions and traits are identified and suggested by researchers (like Machiavellianism, authoritarianism, dogmatism, risk-taking propensity, type A and type B personality). Over the years, people have tried to reduce the number of dimensions and traits. The work of Hans Eysenck (who identified two dimensions on which personality varies: the extraversion–introversion or 'E' dimension and the neuroticism–stability or 'N' dimension),[57] for instance, stimulated other people to search for reduced models of personality. We focus on the two best-known attempts that distinguished central personality dimensions and traits: Cattell's 16 Personality Factors and the Big Five personality model.

CATTELL'S 16 PERSONALITY FACTORS

Raymond Cattell, a researcher who was inspired by Eysenck's work, attempted to define a set of traits that would cover the whole range of personality.[58] He identified 16 personality factors (or source traits) that can be used as a framework for personality testing. Table 2.2 lists these 16 personality factors (**16 PF model**).

Cattell developed the Sixteen Personality Inventory (16 PF) to measure these factors. He also used ratings by trained observers and observations collected in specific situation tests to collect data on these different factors. Both Cattell and Eysenck contributed to a lively debate among researchers on personality structure and how to measure personality, which stimulated the advancement of useful techniques for selection and other job-related decisions.[59]

BIG FIVE PERSONALITY MODEL

Another attempt to reduce the long list of personality dimensions and traits led to the identification of five dimensions. These dimensions, usually referred to as the '**Big Five**' personality dimensions (or just 'Big Five'), are assumed largely to describe human personality.[60] Let us briefly focus on each of them (see Figure 2.3).

Extraversion refers to people's comfort level with relationships. People scoring high on this dimension (extraverts) tend to be sociable, outgoing, assertive and talkative. They enjoy interacting with other people and are more open to establishing new relationships. People scoring low on this dimension (introverts) are rather reserved and quiet. They tend to be more reluctant to start new relationships. Introverts are more inclined to direct their interests to ideas than social events.

Agreeableness refers to people's ability to get along with others. High agreeable people are more forgiving, tolerant, co-operative, trusting, soft-hearted, understanding, gentle and good-natured in

16 PF model
16 traits or factors representing personality according to Cattell

Big Five
five dimensions largely representing human personality

Extraversion
personality dimension referring to a person's comfort level with relationships

Agreeableness
personality dimension referring to a person's ability to get along with others

TABLE 2.2 CATTELL'S 16 PERSONALITY FACTORS

Factor	High score description	Low score description
A	Outgoing	Reserved
B	More intelligent (abstract thinker)	Less intelligent (concrete thinker)
C	Emotionally stable	Emotionally unstable
E	Dominant (assertive)	Submissive (humble)
F	Optimistic	Pessimistic
G	Conscientious	Expedient
H	Adventurous	Timid
I	Tender-minded	Tough-minded
L	Suspicious	Trusting
M	Imaginative	Practical
N	Shrewd	Forthright
O	Apprehensive (insecure)	Self-assured
Q1	Experimenting	Conservative
Q2	Self-sufficient	Group-dependent
Q3	Controlled	Undisciplined (casual)
Q4	Tense (frustrated)	Relaxed (tranquil)

SOURCE: Based on Table 4.1 in R. B. Cattell and P. Kline, *The Scientific Analysis of Personality and Motivation* (London: Academic Press, 1977), pp. 44–5. Reprinted with permission from Elsevier.

FIGURE 2.3 THE BIG FIVE PERSONALITY DIMENSIONS

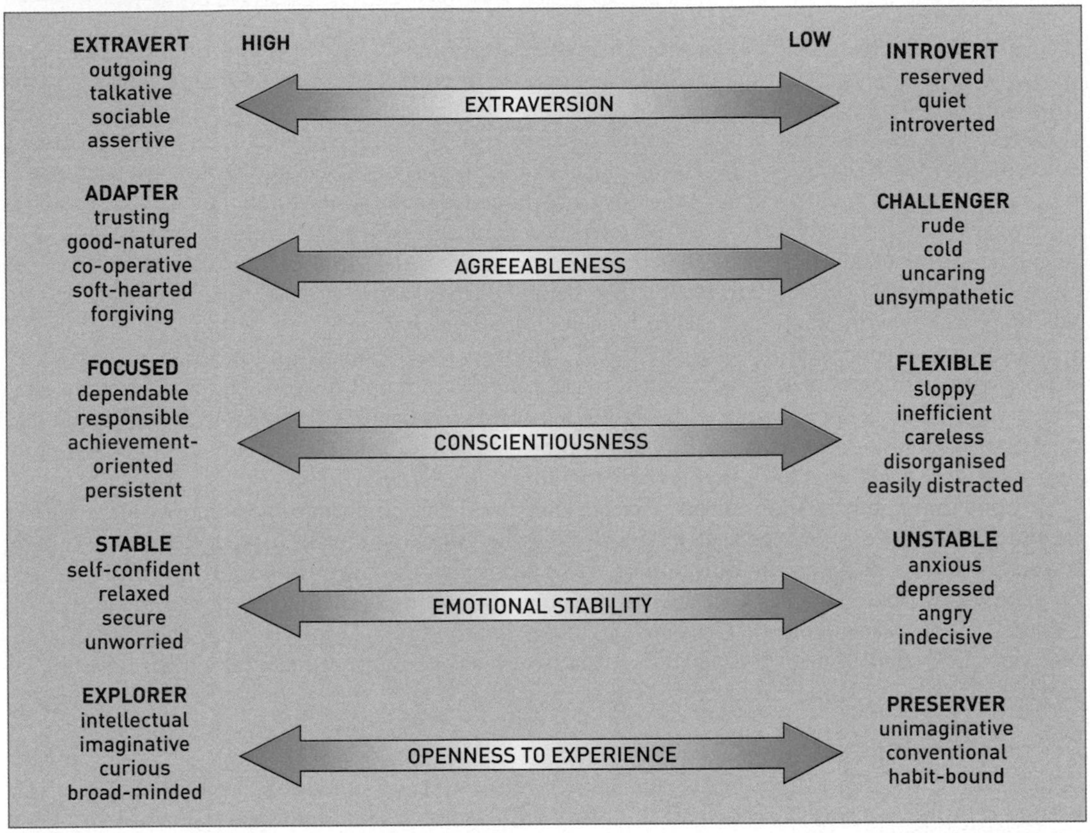

their interactions with others. People scoring low on this dimension are described as being rude, cold, uncaring, unsympathetic, irritable and unco-operative.

Conscientiousness refers to the extent that people are organised, careful, responsible, dependable and self-disciplined. A highly conscious person is dependable, responsible, achievement-oriented, reliable and persistent, while a low conscious person tend to be careless, sloppy, inefficient, disorganised, irresponsible and easily distracted.

Emotional stability refers to the extent people can cope with stress situations and experience positive emotional states. People with high emotional stability are fairly relaxed, secure, unworried and self-confident. They are expected to cope better with stress, pressure and tension. People with low emotional stability tend to be nervous, anxious, depressed, indecisive and subject to mood swings.

Openness to experience refers to the extent people are open to new experiences and have a broad interest and fascination with novelty. People who are open to experience are curious, broad-minded, intellectual and imaginative. People who score low on this dimension tend to be resistant to change, conventional, habit-bound, closed to new ideas and unimaginative.

Standardised personality tests determine how people score on each of these dimensions. A person's scores on the Big Five reveal a personality profile as unique as his or her fingerprints. Important to mention also is that each pole of these five dimensions has positive and negative sides. One pole is not more desirable than the other; everything depends on the situation and environment. For instance, as already stated in the case study in the beginning of this chapter, extraverts are sociable, assertive and talkative, but also easily bored with tasks that are uninteresting (to them) and time-consuming. This means, people with extravert traits will be more useful in sales jobs, while introverts will be better in, for instance, production management.

RESEARCH FINDINGS AND PRACTICAL IMPLICATIONS

Of course, organisations are interested in research linking these personality dimension models with organisational behaviour and job performance. Many studies, for instance, investigated the Big Five

---

Conscientiousness personality dimension referring to the extent a person is organised, careful, responsible and self-disciplined

Emotional stability personality dimension referring to the extent a person can cope with stress situations and experiences positive emotional states

Openness to experience personality dimension referring to the extent a person is open to new experiences

in an organisational context and found a link between personality dimensions, organisational behaviour and performance.[61]

Ideally, Big Five personality dimensions that correlate positively and strongly with job performance would be helpful in the selection, training and appraisal of employees. A meta-analysis of 117 studies involving 23 994 participants from many professions offers guidance. Among the Big Five, conscientiousness had the strongest positive correlation with job performance and training performance. According to the researchers, 'those individuals who exhibit traits associated with a strong sense of purpose, obligation and persistence generally perform better than those who do not'.[62] Also, extraversion was a stronger predictor of job performance than agreeableness, across all professions. The researchers concluded: 'It appears that being courteous, trusting, straightforward and soft-hearted has a smaller impact on job performance than being talkative, active and assertive.' Extraversion correlated positively with promotions, salary level and career satisfaction.[63]

Another study concluded that low emotional stability was associated with low career satisfaction.[64] People with high emotional stability, on the other hand, are found to work better in stressful situations than other people. People with high agreeableness, as well as the ones with high conscientiousness and emotional stability, tend to provide better customer services.[65] The Big Five dimensions are also found to be useful predictors for job search behaviour.[66]

Yet, one important question lingers. Are personality models ethnocentric or unique to the culture in which they were developed? At least as far as the Big Five model goes, recent cross-cultural research evidence points in the direction of 'no'. Specifically, the Big Five personality structure held up very well in several studies with men and women from different countries (for example, Russia, Canada, Hong Kong, Poland, Germany, Finland, South Korea, Great Britain, the Netherlands, Norway, Spain and France).[67] One study even reviewed and compared several studies covering 15 nations of the European Union.[68]

Personality types

Personality type
personality
description based
on common
patterns of
characteristics of
people

Whereas trait theories of personality aim to reduce the existing amount of personality traits in a smaller set of dimensions, a second stream of theories wants to identify different **Personality types** of people based on common patterns of characteristics between people. These theories are called 'type theories of personality'. The difference between these two approaches is that people belong to types, while traits belong to people. We focus here on the two most often mentioned type theories: Jung's typology and Myers and Briggs' personality typology.

JUNG'S PERSONALITY TYPES

Sensing
preference for
perceiving
directly through
the five senses

Intuiting
preference for
perceiving
indirectly through
the unconscious

Thinking
preference for
judging based on
a logical,
objective and
impersonal
process

Feeling
preference for
judging based on
a subjective and
personal process

Early in the twentieth century, the noted Swiss psychoanalyst Carl Gustav Jung worked on a personality typology.[69] He actually distinguished three dimensions: one related to how people perceive, one related to how people judge and one focusing on how people look at the world.

According to Jung, there are two ways of perceiving or taking in information: **Sensing** (S), by which we become aware of things directly through our five senses, and **Intuiting** (N), by which we comprehend ideas and associations indirectly, by way of the unconscious. Sensing types see things as they are and have great respect for facts. They have an enormous capacity for detail, seldom make errors and are good at close, demanding tasks. They typically want to focus on rules and regulations, standard operating procedures, step-by-step explanations and doing things the way they have always been done. People who prefer intuiting concentrate on possibilities. They are holistic in handling problems and impatient with details. They often 'intuit' solutions and fail to back them with data, having gone on to something else. Intuiting types tend to concentrate on outwitting rules and regulations, creating new procedures, supplying conceptual or theoretical explanations and trying new ways of doing things.

People do not only perceive differently, they also use different approaches to draw conclusions from their perceptions: based on thinking (T) or feeling (F). **Thinking** implies a logical process that attempts to be objective and impersonal, while **Feeling** is a process of appreciation that is subjective and personal. Thinking types are analytical, precise and logical. They are concerned with principles, laws and objective criteria. They may find it easy to critique the work and behaviour of others, but are often uncomfortable dealing with people's feelings. Thinking types prefer objective analysis and decisions based solely on standards and policies. Feeling types are interested in the feelings of others, dislike intellectual analysis and follow their own likes and dislikes. They enjoy working with people and want to maintain harmony in the workplace.

Jung also formulated two different ways people look at the world. People who get their energy from their environment, from interacting with people and things, are Extraverts (E). Others get their energy from time spent alone, focusing their attention internally, on concepts and ideas. They are Introverts (I). Extraverts tend to respond quickly to situations and are oriented toward action, rather than reflection and introspection. Introverts, on the other hand, respond slowly to situations or the demands of others, as they require time to integrate and assimilate outside information. When circumstances permit, extraverts prefer to direct perception and judgement outwards, while introverts like to base perception and judgement upon ideas.

According to Jung, thinking, feeling, sensing and intuiting are functional types, while extraversion and introversion are attitudinal orientations. Because functional types are considered to be most important in distinguishing one's personality type, Jung arrived at eight combined types based on these three dimensions. We will not elaborate further on Jung's types as the extension of his work by Myers and Briggs is mostly used now.

MYERS AND BRIGGS' PERSONALITY TYPOLOGY

Although Jung completed his landmark work on personality types in the 1920s, his ideas did not catch on in the research of personality until the 1940s. That was when the mother–daughter team of Katharine C. Briggs and Isabel Briggs Myers created the Myers–Briggs Type Indicator (MBTI),[70] a self-evaluation questionnaire that was developed to measure the dimensions identified in Jung's type theory. Today, the MBTI is a widely used (and abused) personal growth and development tool in further education and business. (The Personal awareness and growth exercise at the end of this chapter, patterned after the MBTI, will help you determine your personality type.)

'The MBTI is primarily concerned with the valuable differences in people that result from where they like to focus their attention, the way they like to take in information, the way they like to decide and the kind of lifestyle they adopt.'[71] Katharine Briggs and Isabel Briggs Myers added a fourth dimension to the work of Jung, referring to the choices people make on how to allocate time priorities: either gathering information (relates to the Perceiving dimension) or making decisions (relates to the Judging dimension). Some people want a lot of information (based on either sensing or intuiting) before they make a decision; these are called the perceptive type (P). Perceptive types enjoy searching new information, can tolerate ambiguity and are more concerned with understanding life than controlling it. They prefer to stay open to experience, enjoying and trusting their ability to adapt to the moment. Others make decisions quickly despite the fact that they may have little data. Their priority is to reach a decision. They are called the judging type (J). Judging types like clarity and order, dislike ambiguity and are concerned with resolving issues. They tend to live in a planned, orderly way and want to regulate life and control it.

The MBTI classifies people according to their combination of preferences along four dimensions: extraversion–introversion, sensing–intuiting, thinking–feeling and judging–perceiving. Each of the four dimensions is independent of the other three, which leads to sixteen personality types (see Figure 2.4).

To understand people's type better, often only the perceiving and judging dimensions are used and combined in four personality types or styles. An individual's personality type is then determined by the pairing of one's perceiving and judging tendencies. Characteristics of each type are presented in Table 2.3.

An individual belonging to an ST type uses senses for perception and rational thinking for judgement. The ST-type person uses facts and objective analysis and develops greater abilities in technical areas involving facts and objects. A successful bank manager could be expected to belong to this type. In contrast, a person belonging to an NT type focuses on possibilities rather than facts and displays abilities in areas involving theoretical or technical development. This type can, for instance, be found within research scientists. Although an SF person is likely to be interested in gathering facts, he or she tends to treat others with personal warmth, sympathy and friendliness. Successful counsellors or teachers probably belong to this type. Finally, an NF-type person tends to exhibit artistic flair while relying heavily on personal insights rather than objective facts.

Extravert
preference for directing perception and judgement outwardly

Introvert
preference for basing perception and judgement upon ideas

MBTI
measure to identify a person's personality typology based on four dimensions

Perceiving
preference for gathering a lot of information before making decisions

Judging
preference for making quick decisions

FIGURE 2.4 MYERS AND BRIGGS' TYPOLOGY

| | Sensing types | | Intuitive types | |
	With thinking	With feeling	With feeling	With thinking
Introverts – With judging	**ISTJ** Quiet, serious, earn success by thoroughness and dependability. Practical, matter-of-fact, realistic and responsible. Decide logically what should be done and work towards it steadily, regardless of distractions. Take pleasure in making everything orderly and organised – their work, their home, their life. Value traditions and loyalty.	**ISFJ** Quiet, friendly, responsible, and conscientious. Committed and steady in meeting their obligations. Thorough, painstaking and accurate. Loyal, considerate, notice and remember details about people who are important to them, concerned with how others feel. Strive to create an orderly and harmonious environment at work and at home.	**INFJ** Seek meaning and connection in ideas, relationships and material possessions. Want to understand what motivates people and are insightful about others. Conscientious and committed to their firm values. Develop a clear vision about how best to serve the common good. Organised and decisive in implementing their vision.	**INTJ** Have original minds and great drive for implementing their ideas and achieving their goals. Quickly see patterns in external events and develop long-range explanatory perspectives. When committed, organise a job and carry it through. Sceptical and independent, have high standards of competence and performance – for themselves and others.
Introverts – With perceiving	**ISTP** Tolerant and flexible, quiet observers until a problem appears, then act quickly to find workable solutions. Analyse what makes things work and readily get through large amounts of data to isolate the core of practical problems. Interested in cause and effect, organise facts using logical principles, value efficiency.	**ISFP** Quiet, friendly, sensitive and kind. Enjoy the here-and-now, what's going on around them. Like to have their own space and to work within their own time frame. Loyal and committed to their values and to people who are important to them. Dislike disagreements and conflicts, do not force their opinions or values on others.	**INFP** Idealistic, loyal to their values and to people who are important to them. Want an external life that is congruent to their values. Curious, quick to see possibilities, can be catalysts for implementing ideas. Seek to understand people and to help them fulfil their potential. Adaptable, flexible and accepting unless a value is threatened.	**INTP** Seek to develop logical explanations for everything that interests them. Theoretical and abstract, interested more in ideas than in social interaction. Quiet, contained, flexible and adaptable. Have unusual ability to focus in depth to solve problems in their area of interest. Sceptical, sometimes critical, always analytical.
Extraverts – With perceiving	**ESTP** Flexible and tolerant, they take a pragmatic approach focused on immediate results. Theories and conceptual explanations bore them – they want to act energetically to solve the problem. Focus on the here-and-now, spontaneous, enjoy each moment that they can be active with others. Enjoy material comforts and style. Learn best through doing.	**ESFP** Outgoing, friendly and accepting. Exuberant lovers of life, people and material comforts. Enjoy working with others to make things happen. Bring common sense and a realistic approach to their work, and make work fun. Flexible and spontaneous, adapt readily to new people and environments. Learn best by trying a new skill with other people.	**ENFP** Warmly enthusiastic and imaginative. See life as full of possibilities. Make connections between events and information very quickly and confidently proceed based on the patterns they see. Want a lot of affirmation from others and readily give appreciation and support. Spontaneous and flexible, often rely on their ability to improvise and their verbal fluency.	**ENTP** Quick, ingenious, stimulating, alert and outspoken. Resourceful in solving new and challenging problems. Adept at generating conceptual possibilities and then analysing them strategically. Good at reading other people. Bored by routine, will seldom do the same thing the same way, apt to turn to one new interest after another.
Extraverts – With judging	**ESTJ** Practical, realistic, matter-of-fact. Decisive, quickly move to implement decisions. Organise projects and people to get things done, focus on getting results in the most efficient way possible. Take care of routine details. Have a clear set of logical standards, systematically follow them and want others to also. Forceful in implementing their plans.	**ESFJ** Warmhearted, conscientious and cooperative. Want harmony in their environment, work with determination to establish it. Like to work with others to complete tasks accurately and on time. Loyal, follow through even in small matters. Notice what others need in their day-to-day lives and try to provide it. Want to be appreciated for who they are and for what they contribute.	**ENFJ** Warm, empathetic, responsive and responsible. Highly attuned to the emotions, needs and motivations of others. Find potential in everyone, want to help others fulfil their potential. May act as catalysts for individual and group growth. Loyal, responsive to praise and criticism. Sociable, facilitate others in a group, and provide inspiring leadership.	**ENTJ** Frank, decisive, assume leadership readily. Quickly see illogical and inefficient procedures and policies, develop and implement comprehensive systems to solve organisational problems. Enjoy long-term planning and goal setting. Usually well informed, well read, enjoy expanding their knowledge and passing it on to others. Forceful in presenting their ideas.

SOURCE: Adapted from I. Briggs-Myers, *Introduction to Type, sixth edition* (Palo Alto, CA: Consulting Psychologists Press, 1998).

TABLE 2.3 PERSONALITY TYPES BASED ON MYERS AND BRIGGS' PERSONALITY MODEL

	ST Types	NT Types	SF Types	NF Types
Preferences	Sensing + Thinking	Intuiting + Thinking	Sensing + Feeling	Intuiting + Feeling
Focus of attention	Realities	Possibilities	Realities	Possibilities
Way of handling things	Objective analysis	Objective analysis	Personal warmth	Personal warmth
Tendency to become	Practical and matter-of-fact	Logical and analytical	Sympathetic and friendly	Enthusiastic and insightful
Expression of abilities	Technical skills with objects and facts	Theoretical and technical developments	Practical help and services to people	Understanding and communicating with people
Representative occupations	Applied science Business Administration Banking Law enforcement Production Construction	Physical science Research Management Computers Law Engineering Technical work	Health care Community service Teaching Supervision Religious service Office work Sales	Behavioural science Research Literature Art & music Religious service Health care Teaching

SOURCE: Based on and adapted from I. Briggs-Myers, *A Description of the Theory and Applications of the Myers-Briggs Type Indicator* (California: Consulting Psychologists Press, 1990), p. 28.

RESEARCH FINDINGS AND PRACTICAL IMPLICATIONS

Many studies used Jung's typology and the MBTI to investigate the link between personality types and all kinds of organisational behaviour.[72] If the personality typologies are valid, then individuals who belong to different types should seek different kinds of information when making a decision. A study of 50 MBA students found that those belonging to different personality types did in fact use qualitatively different information while working on a strategic planning problem.[73] Findings have further shown that individuals who make judgements based on 'thinking' have higher work motivation and quality of work life than 'feeling' types. In addition, sensing individuals have higher job satisfaction than intuiting people. Small business owner and managers belonging to a 'thinking' type made more money than their 'feeling' counterparts. But no correlation was found between the four personality types and small business owner/manager success.[74]

The following conclusion from a recent exhaustive review of management-oriented MBTI studies makes us cautious about these findings: 'It is clear that efforts to detect simplistic linkages between type preferences and managerial effectiveness have been disappointing. Indeed, given the mixed quality of research and the inconsistent findings, no definitive conclusions regarding these relationships can be drawn.'[75] On balance, we believe Jung's typology and the MBTI are useful for diversity training and management development purposes but are inappropriate for making personnel decisions such as hiring and promoting.[76] Finally, following practical tips related to the previous personality typologies can be useful for organisations.

First, organisations can use the knowledge of these different types to enhance understanding between people and reduce miscommunication and conflicts. It is clear from the description of the different types that barriers and conflicts can easily arise given the big differences between them. For instance, thinking and feeling types may have difficulties in understanding each other's decision-making processes. Someone scoring high on thinking may have difficulty in understanding the lack of logic behind a decision of a feeling type. Someone scoring high on feeling may search for the opinion and values of a thinking type related to his/her logical decision.

Second, organisations can use these types to stimulate co-operation between people. Opposite types can complement each other. This makes it possible for everyone to use his or her own strengths and balance his or her weaknesses. For instance, when people approach a problem from opposite sides, they see things which are not visible to the other and tend to suggest different solutions. Someone scoring high on thinking, for instance, can help a feeling type to analyse a problem thoroughly, while a feeling type can help a thinker to forecast how the other will feel about a solution.

Important to keep in mind when using these models is that they measure preferences. People can act in opposition to their type if they have to, but they will not like it very much and they will not be that good at it. It is like being left- or right-handed: when you are, for instance, right-handed you can write with your left hand when you have to (e.g. a broken arm), but it is not that easy and natural. Similarly, no one is, for instance, totally introverted or extraverted: we all have the ability to behave either way at various times. However, we all have a preference to relate more in one way than the other.

Psychological tests in the workplace

The concept 'psychometrics' is used to refer to all kinds of measurements, assessments and tests that are used to assess one's intelligence, abilities and personality. Psychological tests can be divided into two categories: the ones measuring typical performance (personality tests are an example here) and the ones measuring maximum performance (intelligence tests are an example of this category). Tests on typical performance try to identify people's preferences in certain situations, which implies that there are no right or wrong answers. By contrast, tests on maximum performance assess people's abilities under standard conditions and performance here is judged as right or wrong. We specifically focus our discussion on personality tests. Of course, the provisos concerning personality assessment are also relevant for intelligence and other ability tests, which are elaborated further.

WHAT ABOUT PERSONALITY TESTING IN THE WORKPLACE?

Organisations administer all kinds of personality and psychological tests. However, personality testing as a tool for hiring applicants or for other job-related decisions can be questioned for three main reasons. First is the issue of predictive validity. Can personality tests actually predict job performance? In the Big Five meta-analysis discussed earlier, conscientiousness may have been the best predictor of job performance but it was not a strong predictor. Moreover, the most widely used personality test, the Minnesota Multiphasic Personality Inventory (MMPI), does not directly measure conscientiousness. It is no surprise that the MMPI and other popular personality tests have, historically, been poor predictors of job performance.[77]

Second is the issue of differential validity, relative to race. Do personality tests measure whites and other races differently? We still have no definitive answer to this important and difficult question. Respected Big Five researchers recently concluded: 'To date, the evidence indicates that differential validity is not typically associated with personality measures. Caution is required in interpreting this conclusion, however, in light of the small number of studies available.'[78] Meanwhile, personality testing remains a lightning rod for controversy in the workplace.

A third issue involves faking. Both those who are in favour of and the ones who disapprove of personality testing in the workplace generally agree that faking occurs. Faking involves intentionally misrepresenting one's true beliefs on a personality test. The crux of the faking issue is this: to what extent does faking alter a personality test's construct validity (this is the degree to which the test actually measures what it is supposed to measure)? Recent research suggests faking is a threat to the construct validity of personality tests.[79]

The practical tips in Table 2.4 can help organisations avoid abuses and costly discrimination law-suits when using personality and psychological testing for employment-related decisions.[80] Another alternative for employers is to eliminate personality testing altogether. The growing use of job-related skills testing and behavioural interviewing is an alternative to personality testing.[81]

WHY NOT JUST FORGET ABOUT PERSONALITY?

Personality testing problems and unethical applications do not automatically cancel out the under-lying concepts. Organisations need to know about personality traits and characteristics, despite the controversy over personality testing. Rightly or wrongly, the term 'personality' is routinely encoun-tered both inside and outside the workplace.[82]

TABLE 2.4 ADVICE AND WORDS OF CAUTION ABOUT PERSONALITY TESTING IN THE WORKPLACE

Researchers, test developers and organisations that administer personality assessments offer the following suggestions for getting started or for evaluating whether tests already in use are appropriate for forecasting job performance:

- Determine what you hope to accomplish. If you are looking to find the best fit of job and employee, analyse the aspects of the position that are most critical for it.
- Look for outside help to determine if a test exists or can be developed to screen employees for the traits that best fit the position. Psychologists, professional organisations and a number of Internet sites provide resources.
- Insist that any test recommended by a consultant or vendor be validated scientifically for the specific purpose that you have defined. Vendors should be able to cite some independent, credible research supporting a test's correlation with job performance.
- Ask the provider to document the legal basis for any assessment. Is it fair? Is it job-related? Is it biased against any racial or ethnic group? Does it violate an employee's right to privacy?
- Make sure that every person who will be administering tests or analysing results is educated about how to do so properly and keeps results confidential.
- Use the scores of personality tests in combination with other factors that you believe are essential to the job, such as skills or experience, to create a comprehensive evaluation of the merits of applicants for a job. Apply those criteria identically for every person.
- Do not make employment-related decisions strictly on the basis of personality test results. Supplement any personality test data with information from reference checks, personal interviews, ability tests and job performance records.

SOURCE: S. Bates, 'Personality Counts' *HR Magazine*, February 2003, p. 34.

The critical remarks and cautions concerning (personality) tests do not alter the fact that they can be useful for self-awareness and for awareness of individual differences. Learning their own styles, types and traits makes people stronger, in the sense that they are made more aware of their own and other people's strengths and weaknesses and can act accordingly. Of course, this implies that people complete these tests for their own benefit and development and not, for instance, in a rewarding or appraisal context.

Knowledge of the Big Five or other personality aspects encourages more precise understanding of the rich diversity among today's employees. Professionals are encouraged to take time to get to know each employee's unique combination of personality, abilities and potential and to create a productive and satisfying person–job fit based on that knowledge. Personality tests can help professionals to lead, motivate and manage their employees differently, through awareness of their unique traits and types.

Abilities and styles

Individual differences in abilities, styles and accompanying skills are a central concern for organisations because nothing can be accomplished without appropriately skilled personnel. **Ability** represents a broad and stable characteristic responsible for a person's maximum – as opposed to typical – performance on mental and physical tasks. A **Style** usually refers to a habitual pattern or preferred way of doing something. A **Skill**, on the other hand, is the specific capacity to manipulate objects physically. Consider this difference as you imagine yourself being the only passenger on a small commuter plane in which the pilot has just passed out. As the plane nosedives, your effort and abilities will not be enough to save yourself and the pilot if you do not possess flying skills. Successful performance (be it landing a plane or performing any other job) depends on the right combination of effort, ability, style and skill.

Abilities and skills are getting a good deal of attention in organisations these days. The more encompassing term 'competencies' is typically used. A **Competence** is 'an underlying characteristic of an individual which is causally related to effective or superior performances'.[83] In other words, a competence is any individual characteristic that differentiates between superior and average performers or between effective and ineffective performers. Spencer and colleagues identified 20 competencies that are mostly associated with success in technical and professional jobs, managerial jobs and senior executive jobs (see Table 2.5).[84]

Competencies are widely used in organisations, because they offer a common language to identify and describe the key attributes (be it skills, abilities, traits or styles) required for effective performance.[85] This common language makes it possible to use it in job advertisements, hiring and other job-related decisions (also see Chapter 15).

This section further explores important abilities, cognitive styles and learning styles. Having (mental) abilities is a prerequisite for survival in the world, while cognitive and learning styles refer to the different ways people survive in the world (in the sense of perceiving, understanding and processing information and make decisions based on this information). There is one main difference between abilities and styles.[86] The ability construct is defined as a 'unipolar' concept; this means that people can have more or less of an ability (e.g. verbal comprehension). Usually, having more of an ability is considered as being better in our society. The style construct, on the other hand, is usually defined as a 'bipolar' concept; this means that it represents a dimension that ranges from one extreme to another. The two extremes (poles) of various style dimensions present different preferences of people. No one style is inherently better than another style, they are just different. One researcher summarises it as follows: 'Both style and ability may affect performance on a given task. The basic distinction between them is that performance on all tasks will improve as ability increases, whereas the effect of style on performance for an individual will either be positive or negative depending on the nature of the task.'[87]

Intelligence and cognitive abilities

Although experts do not agree on a specific definition, **Intelligence** represents an individual's capacity for constructive thinking, reasoning and problem solving. A similar debate as in personality research can be found in the history of intelligence research: nature versus nurture. Historically, intelligence was believed to be an innate capacity, passed genetically from one generation to the next (nature).

Ability
stable characteristic responsible for a person's maximum physical or mental performance

Style
a preferred way or habitual pattern of doing something

Skill
specific capacity to manipulate objects

Competence
any individual characteristic that is related to effective and superior performance

Intelligence
capacity for constructive thinking, reasoning and problem solving

TABLE 2.5 TWENTY MOST WIDELY USED COMPETENCIES IN ORGANISATIONS

Competence	Technical/professional job	Managerial job	Executive job
Achievement orientation	X	X	X
Concern for quality and order	X	X	
Initiative	X	X	X
Interpersonal understanding	X	X	X
Customer-service orientation	X	X	
Impact and influence		X	X
Organisational awareness			X
Relationship building (networking)		X	X
Directiveness		X	
Teamwork and co-operation	X	X	X
Developing others		X	
Team leadership			X
Technical expertise	X		
Information seeking	X		
Analytical thinking	X	X	
Conceptual thinking	X	X	X
Self-control; stress resistance	X	X	X
Self-confidence		X	
Organisational commitment; 'business-mindedness'	X	X	X
Flexibility		X	X

SOURCE: L. M. Spencer, D. C. McClelland and S. M. Spencer, *Competency Assessment Methods: History and State of the Art* (Boston: Hay/Ber Research Press, 1994).

Research since has shown, however, that intelligence (like personality) is also a function of environmental influences (nurture). One researcher states it as follows: 'The empirical findings provide no support for the pessimistic conclusion that low intelligence and the problems associated with it are inevitable and unalterable.'[88] Organic factors have more recently been added to the formula as a result of mounting evidence of the connection between alcohol and drug abuse by pregnant women and intellectual development problems in their children.[89]

Mental abilities

Human intelligence has been studied predominantly through the empirical approach. By examining the relationship between measures of mental abilities and behaviour, researchers have statistically isolated major components of intelligence. Using this empirical procedure, pioneering psychologist Charles Spearman proposed that two types of ability determine all cognitive performance.[90] The first type is the general mental ability required for all cognitive tasks. This general factor, called 'g', permeates all intellectual activities and accounts for a large proportion of the variance in intelligence scores. The second type of ability is unique to the task at hand. So, although people who do well on one type of task (e.g. spatial, verbal, numerical, memory or other tasks) tend to do well on other tasks also, a certain amount of variance is specific to each task.[91] For example, an individual's ability to complete crossword puzzles is a function of his or her general mental ability as well as the specific ability to perceive patterns in partially completed words. Through the years much research has been devoted to developing and expanding Spearman's ideas on the relationship between cognitive abilities and intelligence. Vernon, for instance, created a model that places the general factor and specific abilities in a hierarchy.[92]

Several researchers also attempted to split the general factor g into a number of more specific abilities. Guilford listed 120 distinct mental abilities and structured them in a three-dimensional model (according to a content, operations and products dimension).[93] Other researchers came to a smaller list of different abilities. Table 2.6 contains definitions of the seven most frequently cited mental

TABLE 2.6 MENTAL ABILITIES UNDERLYING PERFORMANCE

Ability	Description
1 Verbal comprehension	The ability to understand what words mean and to readily comprehend what is read
2 Word fluency	The ability to produce isolated words that fulfil specific symbolic or structural requirements
3 Numerical reasoning	The ability to make quick and accurate arithmetic computations such as adding and subtracting
4 Spatial ability	Being able to perceive spatial patterns and to visualise how geometric shapes would look if transformed in shape or position
5 Memory	Having good rote memory for paired words, symbols, lists of numbers or other associated items
6 Perceptual speed	The ability to perceive figures, identify similarities and differences, and carry out tasks involving visual perception
7 Inductive reasoning	The ability to reason from specifics to general conclusions

SOURCE: Adapted from M. D. Dunnette, 'Aptitudes, Abilities, and Skills', in *Handbook of Industrial and Organizational Psychology*, ed. M. D. Dunnette (Skokie, IL: Rand McNally, 1976), pp. 478–83.

abilities.[94] Of these seven, personnel selection researchers have found verbal ability, numerical ability, spatial ability and inductive reasoning to be valid predictors of job performance for both minority and mainstream applicants.[95]

Gradually, more and more criticisms are levelled at the IQ concept. It would seem to be too narrowly focused and would fail to cover the full range of intellectual activity. So, researchers start to expand the meaning of intelligence beyond mental ability. Gardner suggests that there are multiple intelligences.[96] Practical intelligence, for instance, is one of the more recent concepts, referring to all kind of problem-solving strategies people use to arrive at solutions.[97] Another new, although already widely used, concept is emotional intelligence, which is further elaborated in Chapter 3.

Another recent study divides intelligence into four subparts: cognitive, social, emotional and cultural.[98] Cognitive intelligence refers to the mental abilities that are measured by the traditional intelligence tests. Social intelligence refers to the ability to relate effectively with others. Emotional intelligence refers to the ability to identify, understand and manage your own and other people's emotions. Cultural intelligence refers to the ability to recognise cross-cultural differences and to function effectively in cross-cultural situations. The theory of multiple intelligences is quite new, but seems to promise a better explanation of differences between people. For instance, it can explain why two people with the same cognitive intelligence are not equally successful in their work life.

RESEARCH FINDINGS AND PRACTICAL IMPLICATIONS

Researchers have produced some interesting findings about abilities and intelligence in recent years. Not all jobs demand the same level of intellectual ability. Jobs that demand more information processing will also require higher general intelligence and verbal abilities to perform successfully.[99] Other jobs require more routine and less of one's own intellectual input, so high intelligence may here be unrelated to job performance. A unique, five-year study documented the tendency of people to 'gravitate to jobs commensurate with their abilities'.[100] This prompts the vision of the job market acting as a giant sorting or sifting machine, with employees tumbling into various ability bins.

Meanwhile, a steady and significant rise in average intelligence among those in developed countries has been observed over the past 70 years (called the Flynn effect, after the psychologist James Flynn who first discovered this phenomenon in the 1980s).[101] Why? Experts at a recent conference concluded: 'Some combination of better schooling, improved socio-economic status, healthier nutrition and a more technologically complex society, might account for the gains in IQ scores.'[102] So if you think you're smarter than your parents and your teachers, you're probably right!

> " Recently, studies also found that the visual intelligence of children and their speed to process images and sounds seem to be higher than those of a lot of adults. Their visual intelligence increased by 20 per cent, while their processing speed increased by 30 per cent in comparison of children of 1980. On the contrary, children's numerical intelligence as well as their analytical abilities decreased by 20 per cent. An explanation for these findings lies in the different world we live in now. We are confronted with more images (e.g. television and Internet culture) and everything goes faster (e.g. cars instead of bikes in the past).[103] "

These findings indicate that intelligence is not a static concept, which implies that intelligence tests need to be adapted to measure correctly who scores below or above the mean. For instance, to correctly measure the visual intelligence of children nowadays those items scoring visual intelligence have to be more difficult than in the past, while those items measuring logical and analytical skills need to be easier. This also implies that the use of intelligence tests in the workplace needs to be evaluated and adapted when necessary. Significantly, our earlier cautions about on-the-job personality testing extend to ability, intelligence and competency testing.

Cognitive styles

Cognitive styles are extensively studied in domains like education or experimental psychology. However, they also gained prominence in organisational behaviour and management literature during the past decades. A **Cognitive style** is the way an individual perceives environmental stimuli, and organises and uses information. A cognitive style influences how people look at their environment for information, how they organise and interpret this information, and how they use these interpretations for guiding their actions.[104] Cognitive psychologists who did research on problem solving and perceptual and sensory functions developed the term 'cognitive style'.[105] Interest in cognitive styles origins from the disappointment with the traditional psychometric research on abilities and intelligence, because it failed to uncover the processes that generate individual differences in abilities and IQ.

We focus on two widely studied cognitive style theories: Kirton's Adaption–Innovation Model and Riding's cognitive styles model.

> **Cognitive style**
> an individual's preferred way of processing information

KIRTON'S ADAPTION–INNOVATION MODEL

The British researcher Michael Kirton observed that 'people characteristically produce qualitatively different solutions to seemingly similar problems'.[106] Some people typically adapt, while others typically innovate when searching for a solution. He developed a cognitive style model that situates these two styles on a continuum, with the ends labelled 'adaptive' and 'innovative', respectively.[107] He further explored the sort of behaviour that might be related to these two cognitive styles. Characteristics of adaptors and innovators can be found in Table 2.7.

According to Kirton, the Adaption–Innovation dimension is a basic dimension that is relevant to the analysis of organisational change, because it focuses on the interaction between people and their often changing work environment. It gives organisations new information on, and insight into, the individual's aspects of change in organisations.[108] Knowledge of each other's style may also lead to mutual appreciation and co-operation between people with differing cognitive styles. It is clear from Table 2.7 that people with an **Innovator** and **Adaptor** style are necessary and useful for organisations as they can complement each other's weaknesses.

Kirton developed the Kirton Adaption–Innovation Inventory (KAI), a self-report measure with 32 items to measure these cognitive styles.[109] Several language versions of the KAI exist. Research indicates that cognitive style differences seem to vary more by occupation and work function than by nation. The Kirton Adaption–Innovation dimension appears to be largely independent of national culture.[110]

> **Innovator**
> cognitive style characterised by doing things differently
>
> **Adaptor**
> cognitive style characterised by doing things better

RIDING'S COGNITIVE STYLES MODEL

The British researcher Richard Riding and colleagues developed another cognitive styles model, based on two dimensions. After reviewing various existing dimensions on cognitive styles, Riding and Cheema concluded that they can be grouped into two basic dimensions: the Wholist–Analytic

TABLE 2.7 KIRTON'S ADAPTION–INNOVATION MODEL

Adaptor	Innovator
In general: Characterised by precision, reliability, efficiency, prudence, discipline, conformity Seen as sound, conforming, safe, dependable Seems impervious to boredom, seems able to maintain high accuracy in long spells of detailed work Is an authority within given structures Challenges rules rarely, cautiously, when assured of strong support	*In general:* Seen as undisciplined, thinking, tangentially, approaching tasks from unsuspected angles Seen as unsound, impractical, often shocks his opposite Capable of detailed routine work for only short bursts Tends to take control in unstructured situations Often challenges rules, has little respect for past custom
For problem definition: Tends to accept the problems as defined and generates novel, creative ideas aimed at 'doing things better'. Immediate high efficiency is the keynote of high adaptors.	*For problem definition:* Tends to redefine generally agreed problems, breaking previously perceived restraints, generating solutions aimed at 'doing things differently'
For solution generation: Generates a few well-chosen and relevant solutions that the adaptor generally finds sufficient, but which sometimes fails to contain ideas needed to break the existing pattern completely	*For solution generation:* Produces numerous ideas, many of which may not be either obvious or acceptable to others. Such a pool often contains ideas, if they can be identified, that may crack hitherto intractable problems
For organisational 'fit': Essential to the ongoing functions, but in times of unexpected changes may have some difficulty moving out of his/her established role	*For organisational 'fit':* Essential in times of change or crisis, but may have trouble applying him/herself to ongoing organisational demands

SOURCE: Based on Table 1 from M. J. Kirton, *Adaptors and Innovators, Styles of Creativity and Problem Solving* (London: Routledge/KAI Distribution centre, 1994), p. 10; and Table 1 from M. J. Kirton, 'Adaptors and Innovators: A Description and Measure', *Journal of Applied Psychology*, October 1976, p. 623. Copyright © 1976 by the American Psychological Association. Adapted with permission.

Wholist
cognitive style characterised by processing information in a whole

Analytic
cognitive style characterised by processing information into its component parts

Verbaliser
cognitive style characterised by representing information through verbal thinking

Imager
cognitive style characterised by representing information in mental pictures

and the Verbal–Imagery dimension.[111] These two dimensions are independent of one another. This means that the position of people on one dimension of cognitive styles does not affect their position on the other dimension.

The Wholist–Analytic style dimension describes the habitual way in which people process information: some individuals retain a global or overall view of information ('wholists'), while others process information into its component parts ('analytics'). **Wholists** tend to see the whole of a situation, are able to have an overall perspective and to appreciate the total context. **Analytics** see the situation as a collection of parts and will often focus on one or two of these parts at a time, while excluding other parts. People in the middle of the continuum tend to use either mode of processing information; they are called 'intermediates'.

The Verbal–Imagery style dimension concerns people's preferred mode of representing information: whether they are inclined to represent information through verbal thinking ('verbalisers') or in mental pictures ('imagers'). **Verbalisers** read, listen to or consider information in words. When **Imagers** read, listen to or consider information they experience fluent, spontaneous and frequent mental pictures. People in the middle of the continuum tend to use either mode of representation; they are called 'bimodals'.

Riding developed the Cognitive Styles Analysis (CSA) to measure people's position on both the Wholist–Analytic and the Verbal–Imagery dimension.[112] People's score on the CSA is indicated by means of a ratio (that ranges from 0.4 through to 4.0 with a central value around 1.0). Although the two cognitive style dimensions are continua, they may be divided into groupings and given descriptive labels (see Figure 2.5: 9 different styles). These labels are only used for descriptive convenience and are not meant to imply that there are style 'types' in any absolute sense.[113]

Numbers in bold face in Figure 2.5 indicate the extent to which style combinations complement each other. It ranges from the wholist–verbalisers who have complementary possibilities to the analytic–imagers who also have complementary possibilities. The italic numbers refer to a rank order according to analytical possibilities of style combinations. Highest in this rank order are the analytic–verbalisers, lowest the wholist–imagers.[114]

According to Riding, his model shows potential practical applications in the areas of education and training, occupational guidance, career development and team building, and counselling and personal development.[115]

FIGURE 2.5 COGNITIVE STYLES ANALYSIS

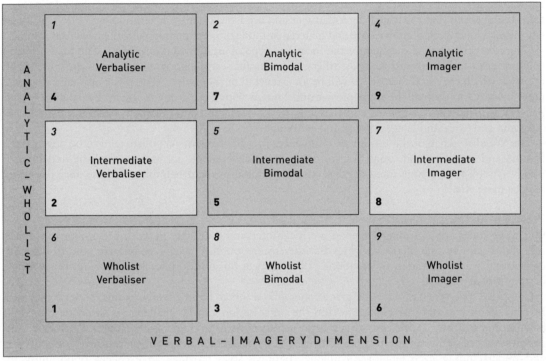

SOURCE: Reprinted from *Personality and Individual Differences*, Vol. 23, R. J. Riding and S. Wigley, 'The Relationship between Cognitive Style and Personality in Further Education Students', p. 380, Copyright 1997, with permission from Elsevier.

RESEARCH FINDINGS

Several studies looked at the models of Kirton and Riding in organisational contexts.

People within different occupations are inclined to have different cognitive styles. For instance, bankers, technical engineers and accountants tend to be more adaptive, while employees in R&D, personnel and marketing tend to be more innovative.[116] Of course, this does not mean that all people in these professions show these cognitive styles, but in comparison with the mean the chance to show a certain style in a certain occupation is greater.

Research also studied the link between Kirton's cognitive style model and personality models.[117] The innovator, for instance, is found to be more extravert, flexible, tolerant of ambiguity, risk-taking and self-confident, but less dogmatic and conservative than the adaptor. The tendency to solve problems using a more innovative than adaptive approach, as measured by the KAI, is positively correlated with MBTI preferences for extraversion, intuition, feeling and perception.[118] Innovators also tend to show higher self-esteem and higher self-confidence than adaptors. Adaptors tend to be more self-critical and doubtful about their abilities and skills. Research also found that adaptors are more likely to underrate themselves compared with others' ratings, unlike innovators.[119]

Kirton studied the link between his theory and the 'cognitive climate' in organisations; this is the collective preferred style of the group's majority. People who find themselves in a cognitive climate that is not suited to their own style are likely to be unhappy and tend to leave the group. They also feel more pressure to conform or to leave and they experience more stress. Interestingly, it seems that adaptors in non-fit situations may be under more pressure than corresponding innovators, because they are more concerned with being in consensus than innovators. Therefore, adaptors are more likely to feel the discomfort of not fitting.[120]

Riding's model is especially being studied in relation to children and students in school contexts. However, this does not make the results less useful and relevant in an organisational context. Research found that the Verbal–Imagery style dimension is related to performance on cognitive tasks, which can be relevant for training and development contexts.[121] For instance, it was found that imagers learned better from the pictorial presentation of material, while verbalisers learned better from the written material.[122] Imagers did best on the material that was highly descriptive and contained very few unfamiliar terms. Verbalisers were superior on the understanding and recall of the information from the material that contained the unfamiliar and acoustically difficult terminology.[123] When there is a mismatch between cognitive style and material or mode of presentation, performance is reduced.[124]

Cognitive styles will also influence the focus and type of an individual's activity. The focus of verbalisers tends to be outward towards others. They prefer a stimulating environment and the social group in which they find themselves will be an extension of themselves. The focus of imagers will be more inward and they will be more passive and content with a static environment. Social groups will be seen as distant to themselves and they may be less socially aware. Socially, verbalisers would be outgoing and lively and imagers polite and restrained.[125]

The Wholist–Analytic dimension also influences social behaviour. Wholists tend to be dependent, flexible and realistic, while analytics are rather more self-reliant, consistent, idealistic and organised.[126] Wholists also were rated as more assertive, humorous and helpful, while the analytics were seen as more shy.[127]

PRACTICAL IMPLICATIONS

Cognitive styles are increasingly seen as a critical intervening variable in work performance. Cognitive styles may be one of the variables that determine whether or not people are able to respond appropriately across a variety of situations.[128] Let us focus on some implications of cognitive styles for organisational practice.

Cognitive styles are useful for the practitioner who wants to build effective teams, because they can help to identify a cognitive climate within the organisation.[129] The challenge is to create the right balance and to foster tolerance between team members with varying cognitive styles. Differences in cognitive styles significantly affect one-on-one and team interactions in the workplace.[130] Identifying and understanding each employee's unique cognitive style provides an excellent opportunity to enhance individual and team performance and productivity.

Research indicates that cognitive styles may be used to inform and improve the quality of decision making in relation to personnel selection and placement, task and learning performance, internal communication, career guidance and counselling, fitting in with the organisation climate, task design, team composition, conflict management, team building, management style, and training and development.[131] Human resource practitioners have a crucial role in fostering individual versatility and in facilitating innovation through the effective management of differences in cognitive style.[132]

In other words, knowing employees' cognitive styles implies that they can be placed in jobs they like and in which they are likely to succeed. It can explain why people with the same abilities, knowledge and skills perform differently in the organisation. Research found that people effectively tend to choose professions that reward their own style.[133] People have different mental processes and different mental preferences and these affect their choice of work and activities. Knowing cognitive styles will also improve respect for diversity. People understand each other better when they know their own and others' cognitive style and they will be able to build on their strengths and to balance their weaknesses.

Learning styles

Research on learning has a long history, dating back to the beginning of the twentieth century, and has its roots in the history of psychology.[134] The early theories on learning focused on rather simple learning situations and led to a research stream called 'behaviourism' (e.g. the work of Watson, Pavlov, Thorndike and Skinner). A second stream of research, called 'cognitivism', considered more complex learning situations and tried to understand individual differences in learning (e.g. the work of Piaget, Tolman, Bruner, Ausubel and Vygotsky). The research on learning styles can be situated in this second stream of research.

The interest in learning styles arose at the end of the 1960s and the beginning of the 1970s. The style concept became popular among educators, because it was a useful concept to deal with individual differences in school contexts and classrooms.[135] The best-known researcher concerning learning styles is David Kolb. He defines a **Learning style** as 'the way people emphasise some learning abilities over others'.[136] It refers to people's preferences in acquiring and using information. Cognitive styles and learning styles are sometimes confused. Some researchers believe the two terms mean the same and use the terms interchangeably.[137] Others consider them to be different terms and attempt to define them as separate concepts.[138] Some authors regard a learning style as a subcategory of cognitive style.[139]

We focus here on two learning styles models: the well-known experiential learning cycle of Kolb and the learning styles model of Honey and Mumford.

Learning style
an individual's preferred use of learning abilities

KOLB'S EXPERIENTIAL LEARNING CYCLE

David Kolb developed an experiential learning model.[140] According to Kolb, in our fast changing society and work environments the ability to learn, this means to adapt to and master changing demands, is a prerequisite for success, which is even more important than having certain skills or knowledge. Kolb describes learning as a process whereby knowledge is created through the transformation of experience. Knowledge is continuously derived from and tested out in the experiences of the learner. This implies that all learning is actually relearning, in the sense that it is the forming and reforming of ideas through experiences. The job of a trainer is in this way not only passing on new ideas, but also modifying already present ideas. Learning involves a transaction between a person and the environment.[141]

The core of Kolb's experiential learning model is a learning cycle that describes four stages. As he describes it:

> Immediate concrete experience is the basis for observation and reflection. These observations are assimilated into a theory from which new implications for action can be deduced. These implications or hypotheses serve then as guides in acting to create new experiences.[142]

Effective learners need four different kinds of abilities:

- Concrete experience: involving yourself fully, openly and without bias in new experiences (e.g. experiencing what it is to use a computer)
- Reflective observation: reflecting on and observing these experiences from many perspectives (e.g. reflecting and thinking about what happens when you are using a computer program)
- Abstract conceptualisation: creating concepts that integrate these observations in logically sound theories (e.g. conceptualising principles that count when using a computer)
- Active experimentation: using these theories to make decisions and solve problems (e.g. applying these abstract computer principles in reality)

These abilities are situated on two independent dimensions (see Figure 2.6): Concrete Experience (CE)–Reflective Observation (RO) and Abstract Conceptualisation (AC)–Active Experimenting (AE).

Effective learners will be equally good in all these abilities. However, it reflectively (RO). like this. As a result of heredity, past experiences and d... ple's location four learning ing styles that emphasise some learning abiliti... style that has some strengths and some w... tion on both dimensions to determine ...
styles.

Divergers prefer to perceive ...

Diverger learning style preferring learning through feeling and watching

FIGURE 2.6 KOLB'S EXPERIENTIAL LEARNING CYCLE MODEL

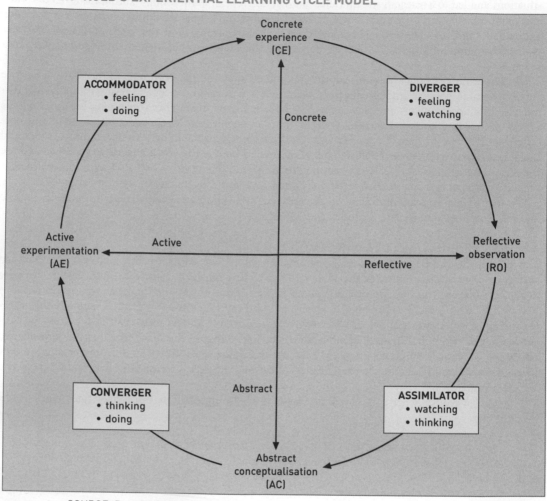

SOURCE: D. Kolb, *Experiential Learning: Experience as the Source of Learning and Development* © 1984. Adapted with the permission of Pearson Education, Inc. Upper Saddle River, NJ.

They learn by concrete information that is given to them by their senses (feeling) and by watching. They like sharing ideas, working in groups, brainstorming and reflecting on consequences of ideas. Their greatest strength lies in their imaginative abilities. They can easily look at concrete situations and ideas from many perspectives. A potential weakness of people with this style is that they can sometimes be hindered by too many alternatives and become indecisive. Divergers are interested in and concerned with people. They tend to be emotional and value harmony. They are imaginative and often have broad interests. These learners are called 'divergers', because they perform best in situations in which they have to generate many ideas or many perspectives on one idea.

Assimilators prefer to switch between reflection (RO) and conceptualisation (AC) and use inductive reasoning to develop new theory. They learn by watching and thinking. They value stability, order, accuracy, expert opinions, continuity, detailed information and certainty. They prefer to work alone. Their greatest strengths lie in the ability to create new theories. A potential weakness of people with this style is that they can be impractical and sometimes too cautious. Assimilators are concerned with abstract concepts than with the practical application of ideas. For them, it is that a theory is logically sound and precise. Assimilators are also less interested in are called 'assimilators', because they are good at assimilating different obser-

which means taking an idea (AC) and testing it out in practice These learners value practicality, productivity, efficiency and punctuality. Convergers do not like ambiguity, working in groups and wasting time. Their greatest strength is the practical application of ideas. A potential weakness is that they sometimes may act too quickly without having enough data or missing important implications. Convergers tend to be rather unemotional and impersonal and prefer to work with things rather than people. These learners are called 'convergers', because they do best in situations where they have to find a single correct answer or solution to a problem.

Accommodators prefer concrete experiences (CE) and active experimentation (AE). They learn by concrete information from their senses (feeling) and doing. They like to learn from talking with others and they also like to influence others. Accommodators do not like strict timetables, too many procedures and rules and too much structure. Accommodators tend to be more risk takers than the other three styles. The greatest strength of accommodators lies in doing things, in experimenting and carrying out plans. A potential weakness is that their plans may sometimes be impractical (because they tend to overlook theory when it conflicts with their own experience or their view of the facts) and they also do not complete work on time. Accommodators tend to be at ease with people, but they are sometimes seen as being impatient or 'pushy'. These learners are called 'accommodators', because they are good at adapting themselves to different circumstances and are good at applying knowledge in new situations.

> **Accommodator** learning style preferring learning through doing and feeling

Kolb developed the Learning Style Inventory (LSI) to measure people's learning styles.[143] It is a self-report instrument that forces people to rank four words for several items. Complete the next Activity, based on Kolb's LSI, to know your learning style.

HONEY AND MUMFORD'S LEARNING STYLES MODEL

The British researchers Peter Honey and Alan Mumford worked further on Kolb's experiential learning model.[144] They wanted a model that would be 'more readily acceptable to managers and which would provide us with a base from which we could more credibly develop ways of providing guidance on individual learning styles and associated learning behaviour'.[145] They kept the idea of learning as a four-stage process and also developed four learning styles, related to these four phases. The learning styles of Honey and Mumford are activist, reflector, theorist and pragmatist. Their four-stage process of learning starts with having an experience (best suited to the activist), then reviewing the experience (best suited to the reflector), afterwards concluding from the experience (best suited to the theorist) and ends with planning the next steps (best suited to the pragmatist).

Activists (linked with concrete experience) engage themselves fully and without biases in new experiences. They are open-minded and seem to be enthusiastic about anything new. They like brainstorming and jumping from one activity to another. Activists tend to act first and think about the consequences afterwards. They are bored with executing and implementing things and long-term consolidation. They like being involved with other people and, in doing so, seek to centre all activities on themselves.

> **Activist** learning style preferring learning by concrete experience

Questions activists may ask before they start learning activities:[146]

- Shall I learn something new?
- Will there be a wide variety of different activities?
- Shall I encounter some tough problems and challenges?
- Will there be other like-minded people to mix with?

Reflectors (linked with reflective observation) like to reflect on experiences from a distance and observe them from many perspectives. They tend to postpone definitive conclusions as long as possible, because they prefer to collect data from various sources and to analyse them thoroughly before concluding. Reflectors are thoughtful people who want to consider all possible perspectives and consequences before acting. In meetings and discussions they enjoy observing other people in action, listening and being at the background before making their own points.

> **Reflector** learning style preferring learning by reflective observation

Questions reflectors may ask before they start learning activities:

- Shall I get enough time to consider, assimilate and prepare?
- Will there be opportunities to assemble relevant information?
- Will there be opportunities to listen to other people's points of view?

activity

What is your learning style?

Instructions

Rank order each set of four words below (from 4 to 1). Give 4 to the word which best characterises your learning style, 1 for the word which least describes you as a learner.

1	Discriminating	Tentative	Involved	Practical
2	Receptive	Relevant	Analytical	Impartial
3	Feeling	Watching	Thinking	Doing
4	Accepting	Risk-taker	Evaluative	Aware
5	Intuitive	Productive	Logical	Questioning
6	Abstract	Observing	Concrete	Active
7	Present-oriented	Reflecting	Future-oriented	Pragmatic
8	Experience	Observation	Conceptualisation	Experimentation
9	Intense	Reserved	Rational	Responsible

Scoring key

Sum up your scores in column one for items 2, 3, 4, 5, 7, 8 = _____ CE
Sum up your scores in column two for items 1, 3, 6, 7, 8, 9 = _____ RO
Sum up your scores in column three for items 2, 3, 4, 5, 8, 9 = _____ AC
Sum up your scores in column one for items 1, 3, 6, 7, 8, 9 = _____ AE

Scoring norms

Comparative norms for Concrete Experience (CE):
6–11 = Low
12–15 = Moderate
16 and above = High
Comparative norms for Reflective Observation (RO):
6–10 = Low
11–14 = Moderate
15 and above = High
Comparative norms for Abstract Conceptualisation (AC):
6–15 = Low
16–20 = Moderate
21 and above = High
Comparative norms for Active Experimentation (AE):
6–14 = Low
15–17 = Moderate
18 and above = High

SOURCE: Based on and adapted from D. A. Kolb, I. M. Rubin and J. M. McIntyre, *Organizational Psychology: An Experiential Approach, second edition* (Englewood Cliffs, NJ: Prentice-Hall, 1974), pp. 23, 25, 27.

Theorists (linked with abstract conceptualisation) adapt and integrate observations in complex and logically sound theories. They like to analyse and to synthesise. They tend to be perfectionists who want everything to be tidy and to fit in a rational scheme. Theorists approach problems in a logical, step-by-step way and reject rigidly what does not fit in their approach. They prefer certainty and feel uncomfortable with subjective judgement, lateral thinking and ambiguity.

Questions theorists may ask before they start learning activities:

- Will there be lots of opportunities to question?
- Do the objectives and programme indicate a clear structure and purpose?
- Shall I encounter complex ideas and concepts that are likely to stretch me?
- Are the concepts and approaches to be explored sound and valid?

Pragmatists (linked with active experimentation) like to try out ideas, theories and techniques to see if they work in practice. They like to get on with things and act quickly with ideas that attract them. Their motto is: 'If it works, it is good.' Pragmatists are practical, realistic and down-to-earth people who want to solve problems and make practical decisions. They are straight to the point. They see problems and opportunities as a challenge. Pragmatists tend to be impatient with open-ended and slow discussions.

Questions pragmatists may ask before they start learning activities:

- Will there be ample opportunities to practise and experiment?
- Will there be lots of practical tips and techniques?
- Shall we address real problems and will it result in action plans to tackle some of my current problems?

The main difference between Honey and Mumford's model and that of Kolb lies in the instrument they developed to measure their styles and their emphasis on behaviour instead of psychological processes. Honey and Mumford attach more importance to giving advice to people on how they can use and modify their style instead of trying to explain the background of the style. In other words, they emphasise more the practical usefulness of their instrument and theory for people in organisations than its academic elaboration. Honey and Mumford's model is a widely used approach to learning style in the UK and is often used as an alternative to Kolb's model. Honey and Mumford developed the Learning Styles Questionnaire (LSQ) to measure their learning style model.[147] This is an 80-item (20 items for each style) self-report questionnaire that identifies people's relative strengths on each of Honey and Mumford's learning styles.

RESEARCH FINDINGS AND PRACTICAL IMPLICATIONS

The learning styles theories have been extensively studied in relation to other variables, such as learning strategies, performance outcomes, vocational choice, person–job fit and job satisfaction, problem solving and decision making.[148]

A study looked at the relationship between Kolb's learning styles and the MBTI.[149] People who score high on abstract conceptualisation (AC) also score high on thinking, while people who score high on concrete experience (CE) score high on feeling. People who score high on reflective observation (RO) tend to be introverts, while people who score high on active experimentation (AE) tend to be extraverts. The hypothesised relations between abstract conceptualisation (AC) and intuiting and between concrete experience (CE) and sensing were not confirmed in this study.

Research indicates that the learning styles can be linked with strengths in certain problem-solving aspects.[150] The problem-solving strengths of divergers lie in identifying possible problems and opportunities that exist in reality. Convergers are good at selecting solutions and evaluating the consequences of solutions. The problem-solving strengths of assimilators lie in building an abstract model that can help to identify the priority problem and alternative solutions. Accommodators are good at executing solutions and also at initiating problem finding based on some goal or model about how things should be. This research shows how people with different learning styles also perform better in different problem-solving phases.

Kolb's own research also shows that people's learning style indicates whether they perceive the

Theorist
learning style preferring learning by abstract conceptualisation

Pragmatist
learning style preferring learning by active experimentation

characteristics of the learning environment to be a help or a hindrance for learning. For instance, the learning of people who score high on concrete experience seemed to be enhanced by personalised feedback, sharing feelings, applying skills to real life problems and peer feedback. On the other hand, theoretical reading assignments hindered their learning.[151]

This finding shows the importance of taking into account people's learning style in organisations to enhance learning, for instance by matching people's learning style and the learning environment or intentionally mismatching them to promote people's abilities to learn from a variety of learning perspectives (stylistic versatility). A study investigated the effect of both approaches on learning performance, which fits in with the discussion whether learning styles are stable or not.[152] Empirical support was found in 12 of the 19 studies involved for the matching hypothesis. No empirical support was found so far for the mismatching hypothesis. However, some support suggests that it is possible to promote stylistic versatility through training.

The learning styles theories of Kolb and of Honey and Mumford can be very useful and relevant for organisations, certainly in our times where change and innovation are omnipresent and where organisations strive to be 'learning organisations' (see Chapter 17).[153] People's learning style determines how they prefer to perceive and process information. Moreover, we tend to send information in the same way as we wish to receive it. Differences in learning styles can cause misunderstandings and conflicts, when they are not addressed appropriately.

Tips to use learning styles effectively in an organisational context are:[154]

- Recognise the strengths and weaknesses of your own learning style.
- Respect other learning styles, as all styles are equal. The most effective learning environments are those which respect differences in perspective.
- Make use of the preferred style of others, for two reasons: to deliver your message quickly and easily and to avoid unnecessary misunderstanding.
- Develop teams in a smart way: mix or match different styles appropriately to capitalise on strengths and compensate for weaknesses.
- For trainers: send information in a variety of ways and make sure to use different assignments, material and presentation skills to address all learning styles, at least part of the time.

Learning outcomes: Summary of key terms

1 Explain what self-esteem is and how it can be improved

Self-esteem is a belief about one's own self-worth based on an overall self-evaluation. It refers to the degree to which people like or dislike themselves. People with high self-esteem see themselves as worthwhile, capable and acceptable. People with low self-esteem do not feel good about themselves and are hampered by self-doubts. Organisations can build employee's self-esteem in four ways, by: (1) being supportive and showing concern; (2) offering varying, autonomous and challenging work, related to one's abilities, values and skills; (3) striving for supervisor–employee cohesiveness and trust; and (4) having faith in one's self-management ability and rewarding successes.

2 Define self-efficacy and explain its sources

Self-efficacy involves one's belief about one's ability to accomplish specific tasks. Those extremely low in self-efficacy suffer from learned helplessness. Four sources of self-efficacy beliefs are prior experience, behaviour models, persuasion from others and assessment of one's physical and emotional states. High self-efficacy beliefs foster constructive and goal-oriented action, whereas low self-efficacy fosters passive, failure-prone activities and emotions.

3 Contrast high and low self-monitoring individuals and describe resulting problems each may have

A high self-monitor strives to make a good public impression by closely monitoring his or her behaviour and adapting it to the situation. Very high self-monitoring can create a 'chameleon' who is seen as insincere and dishonest. Low self-monitors do the opposite by acting out their momentary feelings, regardless of their surroundings. Very low self-monitoring can lead to a one-way communicator who seems to ignore verbal and non-verbal cues from others.

4 Explain the difference between an internal and an external locus of control

People with an internal locus of control ('internals') see themselves as active agents. They trust in their capacity to influence the environment and assume that they can control events in their lives by effort and skill. Internals see themselves as masters of their own fate. People with an external locus of control ('externals') see themselves as passive agents. They believe that events in their lives and things that they want to achieve are subject to uncontrollable forces, luck, chance and powerful others.

5 Identify and describe the Big Five personality dimensions

The Big Five personality model is one of the trait theories of personality. It identifies five dimensions that are assumed to largely describe human personality. These five dimensions are extraversion (people's comfort level with relationships); agreeableness (people's ability to get along with others); conscientiousness (the extent to which people are organised, careful, responsible, dependable and self-disciplined); emotional stability (the extent to which people can cope with stress situations and experience positive emotional states); and openness to experience (the extent to which people are open to new experiences and have a broad interest in and fascination with novelty).

6 Describe Jung's and Myers and Briggs' personality typology

Jung's personality typology is one of the type theories of personality. Jung identified three dimensions: one related to how people perceive and take in information (sensing versus intuiting), one related to how people judge and draw conclusions (thinking versus feeling) and one focusing on how people look at the world (extraversion versus introversion). Myers and Briggs' personality typology is an extension of Jung's work. The Myers–Briggs Type Indicator (MBTI), is primarily concerned with individual differences that result from where people like to focus their attention (extraversion–introversion), the way they like to take in information (sensing–intuiting), the way they like to decide (thinking–feeling) and the kind of lifestyle they adopt (judging–perceiving). The MBTI classifies people according to their combination of preferences along these four dimensions, which leads to sixteen personality types.

7 Elaborate on cautions and tips concerning (personality) testing in the workplace

Personality testing as a tool for hiring applicants or for other job-related decisions (like promotions) can be questioned for three main reasons. First is the issue of predictive validity. Can personality tests actually predict job performance? Second is the issue of differential validity, relative to race. Do personality tests measure whites and other races differently? A third issue involves faking (this is intentionally misrepresenting one's true beliefs on a personality test). To what extent does faking alter a personality test's construct validity (this is the degree to which the test actually measures what it is supposed to measure)? The critical remarks and cautions concerning (personality) tests do not alter the fact that (personality) tests can be useful for self-awareness and for awareness of individual differences. Of course, this implies that people complete these tests for their own benefit and development and not for instance in a rewarding or appraisal context.

8 Describe the evolution of intelligence and abilities research

Human intelligence has been studied predominantly through the empirical approach. By examining the relationship between measures of mental abilities and behaviour, researchers have statistically isolated major components of intelligence. Spearman proposed that two types of abilities determine all cognitive performance: a general mental ability required for all cognitive tasks and abilities unique to the tasks at hand. Over the years much research has been devoted to developing and expanding Spearman's ideas on the relationship between cognitive abilities and intelligence. Several researchers also attempted to split the general factor g in a number of more specific abilities. The seven most frequently cited mental abilities are verbal comprehension, word fluency, numerical reasoning, spatial ability, memory, perceptual speed and inductive reasoning. Gradually, more and more criticism has been levelled at the IQ concept. It would seem to be too narrow-focused and fails to cover the full range of intellectual activity. So, researchers start to expand the meaning of intelligence beyond mental abilities.

9 Describe the cognitive styles of Kirton and those of Riding

Kirton observed that some people typically adapt, while others typically innovate when searching for a solution. He developed a cognitive style model that situates these two styles on a continuum, with the ends labelled 'adaptive' and 'innovative', respectively. Characteristics of adaptors and innovators can be found in Table 2.7. Riding developed a cognitive style model based on two dimensions. The Wholist–Analytic style dimension describes the habitual way in which people process information: some individuals retain a global or overall view of information ('wholists'), while others process information into its component parts ('analytics'). The Verbal–Imagery style dimension concerns people's preferred mode of representing information: whether they are inclined to represent information through verbal thinking ('verbalisers') or in mental pictures ('imagers').

10 Focus on the learning styles of Kolb and those of Honey and Mumford

Kolb developed an experiential learning cycle that describes four stages, which each need other learning abilities. These abilities are situated on two independent dimensions: Concrete Experience (CE)–Reflective Observation (RO) and Abstract Conceptualisation (AC)–Active Experimentation (AE). People develop learning styles that emphasise some learning abilities over others. Kolb distinguishes between divergers, assimilators, convergers and accommodators. Honey and Mumford worked further on Kolb's experiential learning model. They kept the idea of learning as a four-stage process and also developed four learning styles, related to these four phases. The learning styles of Honey and Mumford are activist, reflector, theorist and pragmatist.

Review questions

1 What is your personal experience with improving self-esteem?

2 How is someone you know with low self-efficacy, relative to a specified task, 'programming himself or herself for failure'? What could be done to help that individual develop high self-efficacy?

3 What are the career implications of your self-monitoring score in the Activity?

4 How would you respond to the following statement: 'Whenever possible, organisations should hire people with an external locus of control'?

5 On scales of Low = 1 to High = 10, how would you rate yourself on the Big Five personality dimensions? Is your personality profile suitable for a managerial position?

6 Which of the seven mental abilities mentioned in Table 2.6 are you good at? Which ones need some more improvement?

7 What is your learning style according to the Activity? How can this style help or hinder you to study this subject?

Personal awareness and growth exercise
What is your personality type?
Objectives
1 To identify your personality type, according to Jung's and Myers and Briggs' typology.[155]
2 To consider the practical implications of your personality type.

Instructions
Please respond to the 16 items below. There are no right or wrong answers. After you have completed all items, go to the scoring key.

Questionnaire
Part I. Circle the response that comes closest to how you usually feel or act.

1 Are you more careful about:
  A people's feelings?
  B their rights?
2 Do you usually get along better with:
  A imaginative people?
  B realistic people?
3 Which of these two is the higher compliment:
  A a person has real feeling?
  B a person is consistently reasonable?
4 In doing something with many other people, does it appeal more to you:
  A to do it in the accepted way?
  B to invent a way of your own?
5 Do you get more annoyed at:
  A fancy theories?
  B people who don't like theories?
6 It is higher praise to call someone:
  A a person of vision?
  B a person of common sense?
7 Do you more often let:
  A your heart rule your head?
  B your head rule your heart?
8 Do you think it is worse:
  A to show too much warmth?
  B to be unsympathetic?
9 If you were a teacher, would you rather teach:
  A courses involving theory?
  B fact courses?

Part II. Which word in each of the following pairs appeals to you more? Circle A or B.
10 A compassion?
  B foresight?
11 A justice?
  B mercy?
12 A production?
  B design?
13 A gentle?
  B firm?
14 A uncritical?
  B critical?
15 A literal?
  B figurative?
16 A imaginative?
  B matter of fact?

Scoring key
To categorise your responses to the questionnaire, count one point for each response on the following four scales, and total the number of points recorded in each column. Instructions for classifying your scores are indicated below.

SENSING	INTUITING	THINKING	FEELING
2 B _____	2 A _____	1 B _____	1 A _____
4 A _____	4 B _____	3 B _____	3 A _____
5 A _____	5 B _____	7 B _____	7 A _____
6 B _____	6 A _____	8 A _____	8 B _____
9 B _____	9 A _____	10 B _____	10 A _____
12 A _____	12 B _____	11 A _____	11 B _____
15 A _____	15 B _____	13 B _____	13 A _____
16 B _____	16 A _____	14 B _____	14 A _____
Totals = _____	= _____	= _____	= _____

Classifying total scores
Write *intuiting* if your intuiting score is equal to or greater than your sensing score.
Write *sensing* if your sensing score is greater than your intuiting score.
Write *feeling* if feeling is greater than thinking.
Write *thinking* if thinking is greater than feeling.
When *thinking* equals feeling, you should write feeling if a male and thinking if a female.

Questions for discussion
1 What is your personality type?
   Sensing/Thinking (ST)
   Intuiting/Thinking (NT)
   Sensing/Feeling (SF)
   Intuiting/Feeling (NF)
2 Do you agree with this assessment? Why or why not?
3 Will your personality type, as determined in this exercise, help you achieve your career goal(s)?

Group exercise

Gender and self-efficacy

Objectives
1 To learn more about self-efficacy beliefs.
2 To think about possible ways organisations can increase people's – and especially women's – self-efficacy.

Introduction
Discussions about the leadership capacities and abilities of men and women, respectively, are centuries-old. Women are often viewed as less effective leaders, while men are viewed as better suited for decision-making tasks. Women would lack the necessary leadership abilities, so is the belief. Nowadays, progress has been made and women find their way to higher positions. However, progress is rather small. Inequity remains, especially in upper-level managerial and executive positions. This has led researchers to search for reasons other than the existence of sex-based stereotypes to explain this inequity (see case on next page). We will deal with this topic in a group exercise. A 20-minute, small-group session will be followed by brief oral presentations and a general class discussion. Total time required is approximately 45 minutes to an hour (depending on how many groups there are).

Instructions

Your lecturer will divide the class into groups of four to six. You should first read the following case. Once all group members are finished, try to answer the discussion questions below. When your discussion is over, prepare a short presentation with your answers to the class group. These short presentations can be followed by a general class discussion.

Case: self-limiting behaviour in women[156]

Could it be that women internalise negative beliefs (related to sex-based stereotypes) and as a result lack confidence in their ability to perform non-traditional tasks successfully? If women indeed have a low self-efficacy concerning leadership tasks, they will show self-limiting behaviour, for instance, avoiding leadership roles. This in turn would influence their career advancement. A recent study by Amy Dickerson and Mary Anne Taylor investigated this hypothesis. They first tested women's global self-esteem and their task-specific self-esteem (self-efficacy). In an experimental situation, women were then asked to choose between different tasks: a leadership task and a subordinate task.

The results of their study show that women with high self-efficacy (this means, women who believe they have the abilities needed to perform the leadership task) were more likely to choose this task and expressed more interest in performing it. However, women with low self-confidence in their leadership abilities (low self-efficacy) were more likely to self-select out of the leadership task and to choose the subordinate task. Global self-esteem measures were not useful to predict task choice.

These findings suggest that low self-efficacy may lead to self-limiting behaviour or self-selection out of leadership positions. This implicates that raising women's self-efficacy beliefs about leadership tasks may encourage women to take leadership roles. Useful tools hereto are modelling, mentoring, verbal persuasion, guided practice and feedback. Concretely, this means that women should have the opportunity to observe effective leaders and have the chance to talk with them about their strategies as leaders. Women should also be encouraged to accept leadership positions. Employing more women in leadership positions is a challenge for organisations, as diversity at all levels means enrichment and may lead to better results.

Questions for discussion

1 Do you agree with the findings of this study? Do you recognise forms of self-limiting behaviour of women in organisations? How can organisations become aware of this phenomenon?

2 Can the suggested solutions be effective ways to raise women's self-efficacy beliefs? Can you find some more useful tools to achieve the same result?

3 How can organisations stimulate people's self-efficacy beliefs in general?

Internet exercise

Lots of interactive questionnaires can be found on the Internet to help you learn more about yourself. These self-tests are for instructional and entertainment purposes only. They are not intended to replace rigorously validated and properly administered psychometric tests and should not be used to establish qualifications or make personnel decisions. Still, they can provide useful insights and stimulate discussion. The purpose of this exercise is to learn more about cognitive intelligence (IQ). On our website www.mcgraw-hill.co.uk/textbooks/buelens you will find a free IQ-test and further instructions and questions.

Notes

1   T. Miller and A. Furnham, 'Character Assignation', *People Management*, 2 April 1998.

2   See B. Filipczak *et al.* 'A Market Solution for Diversity?', *Training*, June 1998, p. 14; R. W. Thompson, 'Diversity among Managers Translates into Profitability', *HR Magazine*, April 1999, p. 10; J. Crockett, 'DIVERSITY as a Business Strategy', *Management Review*, May 1999, p. 62; and P. Dass and B. Parker, 'Strategies for Managing Human Resource Diversity: From Resistance to Learning', *Academy of Management Executive*, May 1999, pp. 68–80.

3   V. Gecas, 'The Self-Concept', in *Annual Review of Sociology, vol. 8*, eds R. H. Turner and J. F. Short, Jr (Palo Alto, CA: Annual Reviews, 1982), p. 3. Also see J. J. Sullivan, 'Self Theories and Employee Motivation', *Journal of Management*, June 1989, pp. 345–63; and L. Gaertner, C. Sedikides and K. Graetz, 'In Search of Self-Definition: Motivational Primacy of the Individual Self, Motivational Primacy of the Collective Self, or Contextual Primacy?', *Journal of Personality and Social Psychology*, January 1999, pp. 5–18.

4   L. Festinger, *A Theory of Cognitive Dissonance* (Stanford, CA: Stanford University Press, 1957), p. 3.

5   See J. Holt and D. M. Keats, 'Work Cognitions in Multicultural Interaction', *Journal of Cross-Cultural Psychology*, December 1992, pp. 421–43.

6   A Canadian versus Japanese comparison of self-concept can be found in J. D. Campbell, P. D. Trapnell, S. J. Heine, I. M. Katz, L. F. Lavallee and D. R. Lehman, 'Self-Concept Clarity: Measurement, Personality Correlates, and Cultural Boundaries', *Journal of Personality and Social Psychology*, January 1996, pp. 141–56.

7   See D. C. Barnlund, 'Public and Private Self in Communicating with Japan', *Business Horizons*, March–April 1989, pp. 32–40; and the section on 'Doing Business with Japan', in P. R. Harris and R. T. Moran, *Managing Cultural Differences, fourth edition* (Houston, TX: Gulf Publishing, 1996), pp. 267–76.

8   See T. A. Judge and J. E. Bono, 'Relationship of Core Self-Evaluations Traits – Self-Esteem, Generalized Self-Efficacy, Locus of Control, and Emotional Stability – with Job Satisfaction and Job Performance: A Meta-Analysis', *Journal of Applied Psychology*, February 2001, pp. 80–92; A. Erez and T. A. Judge, 'Relationship of Core Self-Evaluations to Goal Setting, Motivation, and Performance', *Journal of Applied Psychology*, December 2001, pp. 1207–79; F. Luthans, 'Positive Organizational Behavior: Developing and Managing Psychological Strengths', *Academy of Management Executive*, February 2002, pp. 57–72; and G. Chen, S. M. Gully and D. Eden, 'General Self-Efficacy and Self-Esteem: Toward Theoretical and Empirical Distinction between Correlated Self-Evaluations', *Journal of Organizational Behavior*, May 2004, pp. 375–95.

9   Based in part on a definition found in V. Gecas, 'The Self-Concept', in *Annual Review of Sociology, vol. 8*, eds R. H. Turner and J. F. Short, Jr (Palo Alto, CA: Annual Reviews Inc., 1982), p. 3. Also see N. Branden, *Self-Esteem at Work: How Confident People Make Powerful Companies* (San Francisco, CA: Jossey-Bass, 1998).

10 For related research, see R. C. Liden, L. Martin and C. K. Parsons, 'Interviewer and Applicant Behaviors in Employment Interviews', *Academy of Management Journal*, April 1993, pp. 372–86; M. B. Setterlund and P. M. Niedenthal, '"Who Am I? Why Am I Here?": Self-Esteem, Self-Clarity, and Prototype Matching', *Journal of Personality and Social Psychology*, October 1993, pp. 769–80; and G. J. Pool, W. Wood and K. Leck, 'The Self-Esteem Motive in Social Influence: Agreement with Valued Majorities and Disagreement with Derogated Minorities', *Journal of Personality and Social Psychology*, October 1998, pp. 967–75.

11 See S. J. Rowley, R. M. Sellers, T. M. Chavous and M. A. Smith, 'The Relationship between Racial Identity and Self-Esteem in African American College and High School Students', *Journal of Personality and Social Psychology*, March 1998, pp. 715–24.

12 'Sport "Improves Boys' Behaviour"', *BBC News*, 14 June 2004 (news.bbc.co.uk). Also see B. Debusschere, 'Uit het slop dankzij de sport', *De Morgen*, 16 June 2004, p. 33.

13 See J. A. Stein, M. D. Newcomb and P. M. Bentler, 'The Relative Influence of Vocational Behavior and Family Involvement on Self-Esteem: Longitudinal Analyses of Young Adult Women and Men', *Journal of Vocational Behavior*, June 1990, pp. 320–38.

14 L. E. Waters and K. A. Moore, 'Self-Esteem, Appraisal and Coping: A Comparison of Unemployed and Re-Employed People', *Journal of Organizational Behavior*, August 2002, pp. 593–604.

15 Based on P. G. Dodgson and J. V. Wood, 'Self-Esteem and the Cognitive Accessibility of Strengths and Weaknesses after Failure', *Journal of Personality and Social Psychology*, July 1998, pp. 178–97.

16 Details may be found in B. R. Schlenker, M. F. Weigold and J. R. Hallam, 'Self-Serving Attributions in Social Context: Effects of Self-Esteem and Social Pressure', *Journal of Personality and Social Psychology*, May 1990, pp. 855–63.

17 See R. F. Baumeister, L. Smart and J. M. Boden, 'Relation of Threatened Egotism to Violence and Aggression: The Dark Side of High Self-Esteem', *Psychological Review*, January 1996, pp. 5–33; and R. Vermunt, D. van Knippenberg, B. van Knippenberg and E. Blaauw, 'Self-Esteem and Outcome Fairness: Differential Importance of Procedural and Outcome Considerations', *Journal of Applied Psychology*, August 2001, pp. 621–8.

18 M. A. Mone, 'Relationships between Self-Concepts, Aspirations, Emotional Responses, and Intent to Leave a Downsizing Organization', *Human Resource Management*, Summer 1994, pp. 281–98.

19 T. Apter, 'Confidence Tricks', the *Guardian*, 27 September 2000.

20 E. Diener and M. Diener, 'Cross-Cultural Correlates of Life Satisfaction and Self-Esteem', *Journal of Personality and Social Psychology*, April 1995, p. 662. For cross-cultural evidence of a similar psychological process for self-esteem, see T. M. Singelis, M. H. Bond, W. F. Sharkey and C. S. Y. Lai, 'Unpackaging

Culture's Influence on Self-Esteem and Embarrassability', *Journal of Cross-Cultural Psychology*, May 1999, pp. 315–41.

21 W. J. McGuire and C. V. McGuire, 'Enhancing Self-Esteem by Directed-Thinking Tasks: Cognitive and Affective Positivity Asymmetries', *Journal of Personality and Social Psychology*, June 1996, p. 1124.

22 Adapted from discussion in J. K. Matejka and R. J. Dunsing, 'Great Expectations', *Management World*, January 1987, pp. 16–17. Also see P. Pascarella, 'It All Begins with Self-Esteem', *Management Review*, February 1999, pp. 60–61.

23 M. E. Gist, 'Self-Efficacy: Implications for Organizational Behavior and Human Resource Management', *Academy of Management Review*, July 1987, p. 472. Also see A. Bandura, 'Self-Efficacy: Toward a Unifying Theory of Behavioral Change', *Psychological Review*, March 1977, pp. 191–215; M. E. Gist and T. R. Mitchell, 'Self-Efficacy: A Theoretical Analysis of Its Determinants and Malleability', *Academy of Management Review*, April 1992, pp. 183–211; and S. L. Anderson and N. E. Betz, 'Sources of Social Self-Efficacy Expectations: Their Measurement and Relation to Career Development', *Journal of Vocational Behavior*, February 2001, pp. 98–117.

24 A. Davidson, 'The Andrew Davidson Interview: James Dyson', *Management Today*, July 1999.

25 Based on D. H. Lindsley, D. A. Brass and J. B. Thomas, 'Efficacy-Performance Spirals: A Multilevel Perspective', *Academy of Management Review*, July 1995, pp. 645–78.

26 See, for example, V. Gecas, 'The Social Psychology of Self-Efficacy', in *Annual Review of Sociology, vol. 15*, eds W. R. Scott and J. Blake (Palo Alto, CA: Annual Reviews, Inc., 1989), pp. 291–316; C. K. Stevens, A. G. Bavetta and M. E. Gist, 'Gender Differences in the Acquisition of Salary Negotiation Skills: The Role of Goals, Self-Efficacy, and Perceived Control', *Journal of Applied Psychology*, October 1993, pp. 723–35; D. Eden and Y. Zuk, 'Seasickness as a Self-Fulfilling Prophecy: Raising Self-Efficacy to Boost Performance at Sea', *Journal of Applied Psychology*, October 1995, pp. 628–35; and S. M. Jex, P. D. Bliese, S. Buzzell and J. Primeau, 'The Impact of Self-Efficacy on Stressor-Strain Relations: Coping Style as an Explanatory Mechanism', *Journal of Applied Psychology*, June 2001, pp. 401–9.

27 For more on learned helplessness, see M. J. Martinko and W. L. Gardner, 'Learned Helplessness: An Alternative Explanation for Performance Deficits', *Academy of Management Review*, April 1982, pp. 195–204; C. R. Campbell and M. J. Martinko, 'An Integrative Attributional Perspective of Empowerment and Learned Helplessness: A Multimethod Field Study', *Journal of Management*, March 1998, pp. 173–200; and S. B. Schepman and L. Richmond, 'Employee Expectations and Motivation: An Application from the "Learned Helplessness" Paradigm', *Journal of American Academy of Business*, September 2003, pp. 405–8.

28 A. Bandura, *Social Foundations of Thought and Action: A Social Cognitive Theory* (Englewood Cliffs, NJ: Prentice Hall, 1986); and A. Bandura, *Self-Efficacy: The Exercise of Control* (New York: W. H. Freeman, 1997).

29 A study on presentation self-efficacy can be found in M. L. Tucker and A. M. McCarthy, 'Presentation Self-Efficacy: Increasing Communication Skills through Service-Learning', *Journal of Managerial Issues*, Summer 2001, pp. 227–44.

30 Research on this connection is reported in R. B. Rubin, M. M. Martin, S. S. Bruning and D. E. Powers, 'Test of a Self-Efficacy Model of Interpersonal Communication Competence', *Communication Quarterly*, Spring 1993, pp. 210–20.

31 Data from A. D. Stajkovic and F. Luthans, 'Self-Efficacy and Work-Related Performance: A Meta-Analysis', *Psychological Bulletin*, September 1998, pp. 240–61.

32 Based in part on discussion in V. Gecas, 'The Social Psychology of Self-Efficacy', in *Annual Review of Sociology, vol. 15*, eds W. R. Scott and J. Blake (Palo Alto, CA: Annual Reviews, 1989), pp. 291–316.

33 See S. K. Parker, 'Enhancing Role Breadth Self-Efficacy: The Roles of Job Enrichment and Other Organizational Interventions', *Journal of Applied Psychology*, December 1998, pp. 835–52.

34 The positive relationship between self-efficacy and readiness for retraining is documented in L. A. Hill and J. Elias, 'Retraining Midcareer Managers: Career History and Self-Efficacy Beliefs', *Human Resource Management*, Summer 1990, pp. 197–217. Also see M. E. Gist, C. K. Stevens and A. G. Bavetta, 'Effects of Self-Efficacy and Post-Training Intervention on the Acquisition and Maintenance of Complex Interpersonal Skills', *Personnel Psychology*, Winter 1991, pp. 837–61; A. M. Saks, 'Longitudinal Field Investigation of the Moderating and Mediating Effects of Self-Efficacy on the Relationship between Training and Newcomer Adjustment', *Journal of Applied Psychology*, April 1995, pp. 211–25; and S. P. Brown, S. Ganesan and G. Challagalla, 'Self-Efficacy as a Moderator of Information-Seeking Effectiveness', *Journal of Applied Psychology*, October 2001, pp. 1043–51.

35 J. N. Choi, R. H. Price and A. D. Vinokur, 'Self-Efficacy Change in Groups: Effects of Diversity, Leadership, and Group Climate', *Journal of Organizational Behavior*, June 2003, pp. 357–72.

36 See A. D. Stajkovic and F. Luthans, 'Social Cognitive Theory and Self-Efficacy: Going Beyond Traditional Motivational and Behavioral Approaches', *Organizational Dynamics*, Spring 1998, pp. 62–74.

37 See P. C. Earley and T. R. Lituchy, 'Delineating Goal and Efficacy Effects: A Test of Three Models', *Journal of Applied Psychology*, February 1991, pp. 81–98; J. B. Vancouver, C. M. Thompson and A. A. Williams, 'The Changing Signs in the Relationships among Self-Efficacy, Personal Goals and Performance', *Journal of Applied Psychology*, August 2001, pp. 605–20; and A. Bandura and E. A. Locke, 'Negative Self-Efficacy and Goal Effects Revisited', *Journal of Applied Psychology*, February 2003, pp. 87–99.

38 See W. S. Silver, T. R. Mitchell and M. E. Gist, 'Response to Successful and Unsuccessful Performance: The Moderating Effect of Self-Efficacy on the Relationship between Performance and Attributions', *Organizational*

Behavior and Human Decision Processes, June 1995, pp. 286–99; R. Zemke, 'The Corporate Coach', *Training*, December 1996, pp. 24–8; J. P. Masciarelli, 'Less Lonely at the Top', *Management Review*, April 1999, pp. 58–61; and S. Berglas, 'The Very Real Dangers of Executive Coaching', *Harvard Business Review*, June 2002, pp. 89–92.

39 A model of 'leadership self-efficacy' can be found in L. L. Paglis and S. G. Green, 'Leadership Self-Efficacy and Managers' Motivation for Leading Change', *Journal of Organizational Behavior*, March 2002, pp. 215–35.

40 M. Snyder and S. Gangestad, 'On the Nature of Self-Monitoring: Matters of Assessment, Matters of Validity', *Journal of Personality and Social Psychology*, July 1986, p. 125. Also see M. Snyder, *Public Appearances/Private Realities: The Psychology of Self-Monitoring* (New York: W. H. Freeman, 1987).

41 For a recent longitudinal study on the relationship between self-monitoring and organisational citizenship behaviour, see C. L. Blakely, M. C. Andrews and J. Fullen, 'Are Chameleons Good Citizens? A Longitudinal Study of the Relationship between Self-Monitoring and Organizational Citizenship Behavior', *Journal of Business and Psychology*, Winter 2003, pp. 131–44.

42 Data from M. Kilduff and D. V. Day, 'Do Chameleons Get Ahead? The Effects of Self-Monitoring on Managerial Careers', *Academy of Management Journal*, August 1994, pp. 1047–60.

43 Data from D. B. Turban and T. W. Dougherty, 'Role of Protege Personality in Receipt of Mentoring and Career Success', *Academy of Management Journal*, June 1994, pp. 688–702.

44 See F. Luthans, 'Successful vs. Effective Managers', *Academy of Management Executive*, May 1988, pp. 127–32. Also see A. Mehra, M. Kilduff and D. J. Brass, 'The Social Networks of High and Low Self-Monitors: Implications for Workplace Performance', *Administrative Science Quarterly*, March 2001, pp. 121–46; and W. H. Turnley and M. C. Bolino, 'Achieving Desired Images while Avoiding Undesired Images: Exploring the Role of Self-Monitoring in Impression Management', *Journal of Applied Psychology*, April 2001, pp. 351–60.

45 S. F. Premeaux and A. G. Bedeian, 'Breaking the Silence: The Moderating Effects of Self-Monitoring in Predicting Speaking Up in the Workplace', *Journal of Management Studies*, September 2003, pp. 1537–62.

46 Data from D. V. Day, D. J. Schleicher, A. L. Unckless and N. J. Hiller, 'Self-Monitoring Personality at Work: A Meta-Analytic Investigation of Construct Validity', *Journal of Applied Psychology*, April 2002, pp. 390–401. Also see P. M. Caligiuri and D. V. Day, 'Effects of Self-Monitoring on Technical, Contextual, and Assignment-Specific Performance: A Study of Cross-National Work Performance Ratings', *Group & Organization Management*, June 2000, pp. 154–74; S. W. Gangestad and M. Snyder, 'Self-Monitoring: Appraisal and Reappraisal', *Psychological Bulletin*, July 2000, pp. 530–55; and I. M. Jawahar, 'Attitudes, Self-Monitoring and Appraisal Behaviors', *Journal of Applied Psychology*, October 2001, pp. 875–83.

47 For an instructive update, see J. B. Rotter, 'Internal versus External Control of Reinforcement: A Case History of a Variable', *American Psychologist*, April 1990, pp. 489–93. A critical review of locus of control and a call for a meta-analysis can be found in R. W. Renn and R. J. Vandenberg, 'Differences in Employee Attitudes and Behaviors Based on Rotter's (1966) Internal-External Locus of Control: Are They All Valid?', *Human Relations*, November 1991, pp. 1161–77.

48 See G. P. Hodgkinson, 'Development and Validation of the Strategic Locus of Control Scale', *Strategic Management Journal*, May 1992, pp. 311–18; and S. E. Hahn, 'The Effects of Locus of Control and Daily Exposure, Coping and Reactivity to Work Interpersonal Stressors: A Diary Study', *Personality and Individual Differences*, October 2000, pp. 729–48.

49 See P. E. Spector, 'Behavior in Organizations as a Function of Employee's Locus of Control', *Psychological Bulletin*, May 1982, pp. 482–97; and H. M. Lefcourt, *Locus of Control: Current Trends in Theory and Research*, second edition (Hillsdale, NJ: Lawrence Erlbaum Associates, 1982).

50 G. J. Blau, 'Testing the Relationship of Locus of Control to Different Performance Dimensions', *Journal of Occupational and Organizational Psychology*, June 1993, pp. 125–38.

51 See L. I. Marks, 'Deconstructing Locus of Control: Implications for Practitioners', *Journal of Counseling & Development*, Summer 1998, pp. 251–60.

52 See P. E. Spector, C. I. Cooper, J. I. Sanchez, M. O'Driscoll, K. Sparks *et al.*, 'Locus of Control and Well-Being at Work: How Generalizable are Western Findings?', *Academy of Management Journal*, April 2002, p. 462. For another cross-cultural study on locus of control, see P. B. Smith, F. Trompenaars and S. Dugan, 'The Rotter Locus of Control Scale in 43 Countries: A Test of Cultural Relativity', *International Journal of Psychology*, October 1995, pp. 377–400.

53 See S. R. Hawk, 'Locus of Control and Computer Attitude: The Effect of User Involvement', *Computers in Human Behavior*, no. 3, 1989, pp. 199–206. Also see A. S. Phillips and A. G. Bedeian, 'Leader-Follower Exchange Quality: The Role of Personal and Interpersonal Attributes', *Academy of Management Journal*, August 1994, pp. 990–1001; and S. S. K. Lam and J. Schaubroeck, 'The Role of Locus of Control in Reactions to Being Promoted and to Being Passed Over: A Quasi Experiment', *Academy of Management Journal*, February 2000, pp. 66–78.

54 These recommendations are from P. E. Spector, 'Behavior in Organizations as a Function of Employee's Locus of Control', *Psychological Bulletin*, May 1982, pp. 482–97.

55 For a good overview, see L. R. James and M. D. Mazerolle, *Personality in Work Organizations* (Thousand Oaks, CA: Sage Publications, 2002). For evidence on the stability of adult personality dimensions, see R. R. McCrae, 'Moderated Analyses of Longitudinal Personality Stability', *Journal of Personality and Social Psychology*,

September 1993, pp. 577–85. Adult personality changes are documented in L. Pulkkinen, M. Ohranen and A. Tolvanen, 'Personality Antecedents of Career Orientation and Stability among Women Compared to Men', *Journal of Vocational Behavior*, February 1999, pp. 37–58.

56 T. J. Bouchard, Sr, 'Genetic and Environmental Influences on Intelligence and Special Mental Abilities', *American Journal of Human Biology*, April 1998, pp. 253–75; L. Wright, *Twins: And What They Tell Us about What We Are* (New York: John Wiley, 1999).

57 H. J. Eysenck, *The Structure of Human Personality* (London: Methuen, 1960).

58 For more information on this model, see R. B. Cattell, H. W. Eber and M. M. Tatsouka, *Handbook for the Sixteen Personality Factor Questionnaire 16PF* (Champaign, IL: IPAT, 1970); and R. B. Cattell and P. Kline, *The Scientific Analysis of Personality and Motivation* (London: Academic Press, 1977).

59 E. Howarth, 'A Source of Independent Variation: Convergence and Divergence in the Work of Cattell and Eysenck', in *Multivariate Personality Research*, ed. R. M. Dreger (Baton Rouge, LA: Claitor, 1972), pp. 122–60.

60 The landmark report is J. M. Digman, 'Personality Structure: Emergence of the Five-Factor Model', in *Annual Review of Psychology, vol 41*, eds M. R. Rosenzweig and L. W. Porter (Palo Alto, CA: Annual Reviews, 1990), pp. 417–40. Also see R. R. McCrae, 'Special Issue: The Five-Factor Model: Issues and Applications', *Journal of Personality*, June 1992; M. R. Barrick and M. K. Mount, 'Autonomy as a Moderator of the Relationships between the Big Five Personality Dimensions and Job Performance', *Journal of Applied Psychology*, February 1993, pp. 111–18; and C. Viswesvaran and D. S. Ones, 'Measurement Error in "Big Five Factors" Personality Assessment: Reliability Generalization across Studies and Measures', *Educational and Psychological Measurement*, April 2000, pp. 224–35.

61 For research on the 'Big Five', see R. P. Tett, D. N. Jackson and M. Rothstein, 'Personality Measures as Predictors of Job Performance: A Meta-Analytic Review', *Personnel Psychology*, Winter 1991, pp. 703–42; P. H. Raymark, M. J. Schmidt and R. M. Guion, 'Identifying Potentially Useful Personality Constructs for Employee Selection', *Personnel Psychology*, Autumn 1997, pp. 723–42; G. M. Hurtz and J. J. Donavan, 'Personality and Job Performance: The Big Five Revisited', *Journal of Applied Psychology*, December 2000, pp. 869–79; D. B. Smith, P. J. Hanges and M. W. Dickson, 'Personnel Selection and the Five-Factor Model: Reexamining the Effects of Applicant's Frame of Reference', *Journal of Applied Psychology*, April 2001, pp. 304–15; and M. R. Barrick, G. L. Stewart and M. Piotrowski, 'Personality and Job Performance: Test of the Mediating Effects of Motivation among Sales Representatives', *Journal of Applied Psychology*, February 2002, pp. 43–51.

62 For more studies on the 'conscientiousness' dimension, see O. Behling, 'Employee Selection: Will Intelligence and Conscientiousness Do the Job?', *Academy of Management Executive*, February 1998, pp. 77–86; H. Moon, 'The Two Faces of Conscientiousness: Duty and Achievement Striving in Escalation of Commitment Dilemmas', *Journal of Applied Psychology*, June 2001, pp. 533–40; and L. A. Witt, L. A. Burke, M. R. Barrick and M. K. Mount, 'The Interactive Effects of Conscientiousness and Agreeableness on Job Performance', *Journal of Applied Psychology*, February 2002, pp. 164–9.

63 For the results of this study, see M. R. Barrick and M. K. Mount, 'The Big Five Personality Dimensions and Job Performance: A Meta-Analysis', *Personnel Psychology*, Spring 1991, pp. 1–26.

64 S. E. Seibert and M. L. Kraimer, 'The Five-Factor Model of Personality and Career Success', *Journal of Vocational Behavior*, February 2001, pp. 1–21.

65 M. Dalton and M. Wilson, 'The Relationship of the Five-Factor Model of Personality to Job Performance for a Group of Middle Eastern Expatriate Managers', *Journal of Cross-Cultural Psychology*, March 2000, pp. 250–58.

66 J. W. Boudreau, W. R. Boswell, T. A. Judge and R. D. Bretz, Jr, 'Personality and Cognitive Ability as Predictors of Job Search among Employed Managers', *Personnel Psychology*, Spring 2001, pp. 25–50.

67 For cross-cultural studies on the 'Big Five', see M. S. Katigbak, A. T. Church and T. X. Akamine, 'Cross-Cultural Generalizability of Personality Dimensions: Relating Indigenous and Imported Dimensions in Two Cultures', *Journal of Personality and Social Psychology*, January 1996, pp. 99–114; S. V. Paunonen *et al.*, 'The Structure of Personality in Six Cultures', *Journal of Cross-Cultural Psychology*, May 1996, pp. 339–53; V. Benet-Martinez and O. P. John, 'Los *Cinco Grandes* Across Cultures and Ethnic Groups: Multitrait Multimethod Analyses of the Big Five in Spanish and English', *Journal of Personality and Social Psychology*, September 1998, pp. 729–50; N. N. McCraw and P. T. Costa, 'A Big Five Factor Theory of Personality', in *Handbook of Personality, second edition*, eds L. A. Pervin and O. P. John (New York: Guilford, 1999), pp. 139–53; and K. Yoon, F. Schmidt and R. Ilies, 'Cross-Cultural Construct Validity of the Five-Factor Model of Personality among Korean Employees', *Journal of Cross-Cultural Psychology*, May 2002, pp. 217–35.

68 See J. F. Saldago, 'The Five Factor Model of Personality and Job Performance in the European Community', *Journal of Applied Psychology*, February 1997, pp. 30–43.

69 C. G. Jung, *The Collected Works of C. G. Jung, Vol 6: Psychological Types* (translated by H. G. Baynes, revised by R. F. Hull, originally published in 1921) (Princeton, NJ: Princeton University Press, 1971).

70 See I. Briggs Myers (with P. B. Myers), *Gifts Differing* (Palo Alto, CA: Consulting Psychologists Press, 1980); I. Briggs Myers and M. H. McCaully, *Manual: A Guide to the Development and Use of the Myers-Briggs Type Indicator* (Palo Alto, CA: Consulting Psychologists Press, 1985); and I. Briggs Myers, *A Description of the Theory and Applications of the Myers-Briggs Type Indicator* (Palo Alto, CA: Consulting Psychologists Press, 1990).

71 I. Briggs Myers, *A Description of the Theory and Applications of the Myers-Briggs Type Indicator* (Palo Alto, CA: Consulting Psychologists Press, 1990), p. 4.

72 See, for instance, A. Furnham and P. Stringfield, 'Personality and Occupational Behavior: Myers-Briggs Type Indicator Correlates of Managerial Practices in Two Cultures', *Human Relations*, July 1993, pp. 827–42; A. H. Church and J. Waclawski, 'The Effects of Personality Orientation and Executive Behavior on Subordinate Perceptions of Workgroup Enablement', *International Journal of Organizational Analysis*, January 1996, pp. 20–40; N. H. Leonard, R. W. Scholl and K. B. Kowalski, 'Information Processing Style and Decision Making', *Journal of Organizational Behavior*, May 1999, pp. 407–20; and S. A. Berr, A. H. Church and J. Waclawski, 'The Right Personality Is Everything: Linking Personality Preferences to Managerial Behaviors', *Human Resource Development Quarterly*, Summer 2000, pp. 133–57.

73 See B. K. Blaylock and L. P. Rees, 'Cognitive Style and the Usefulness of Information', *Decision Sciences*, Winter 1984, pp. 74–91. Also see D. E. Campbell and J. M. Kain, 'Personality Type and Mode of Information Presentation: Preference, Accuracy, and Efficiency in Problem Solving', *Journal of Psychological Type*, January 1990, pp. 47–51.

74 See G. H. Rice, Jr, and D. P. Lindecamp, 'Personality Types and Business Success of Small Retailers', *Journal of Occupational Psychology*, June 1989, pp. 177–82. Also see S. Goldman and W. M. Kahnweiler, 'A Collaborator Profile for Executives of Nonprofit Organizations', *Nonprofit Management and Leadership*, Summer 2000, pp. 435–50.

75 W. L. Gardner and M. J. Martinko, 'Using the Myers-Briggs Type Indicator to Study Managers: A Literature Review and Research Agenda', *Journal of Management*, January 1996, p. 77. Also see R. Zemke, 'Second Thoughts about the MBTI', *Training*, April 1992, pp. 42–7; and D. W. Salter and N. J. Evans, 'Test-Retest of the Myers-Briggs Type Indicator: An Examination of Dominant Functioning', *Educational and Psychological Measurement*, August 1997, pp. 590–97.

76 For example, see P. R. Lindsay, 'Counseling to Resolve a Clash of Cognitive Styles', *Technovation*, February 1985, pp. 57–67; M. J. Kirton and R. M. McCarthy, 'Cognitive Climate and Organizations', *Journal of Occupational Psychology*, June 1988, pp. 175–84; F. Ramsoomair, 'Relating Theoretical Concepts to Life in the Classroom: Applying the Myers-Briggs Type Indicator', *Journal of Management Education*, February 1994, pp. 111–16; B. McPherson, 'Re-Engineering Your Office Environment: Matching Careers and Personality via the Myers-Briggs Type Indicator', *Office Systems Research Journal*, Fall 1995, pp. 29–34; S. Shapiro and M. T. Spence, 'Managerial Intuition: A Conceptual and Operational Framework', *Business Horizons*, January–February 1997, pp. 63–8; and D. Leonard and S. Straus, 'Putting Your Company's Whole Brain to Work', *Harvard Business Review*, July–August 1997, pp. 111–21.

77 See the discussion in M. R. Barrick and M. K. Mount, 'The Big Five Personality Dimensions and Job Performance: A Meta-Analysis', *Personnel Psychology*, Spring 1991, pp. 21–2. Also see J. M. Cortina, M. L. Doherty, N. Schmitt, G. Kaufman and R. G. Smith, 'The "Big Five" Personality Factors in the IPI and MMPI: Predictors of Police Performance', *Personnel Psychology*, Spring 1992, pp. 119–40; M. J. Schmit and A. M. Ryan, 'The "Big Five" in Personnel Selection: Factor Structure in Applicant and Nonapplicant Populations', *Journal of Applied Psychology*, December 1993, pp. 966–74; and C. Caggiano, 'Psychopath', *Inc.*, July 1998, pp. 77–85.

78 M. K. Mount and M. R. Barrick, 'The Big Five Personality Dimensions: Implications for Research and Practice in Human Resources Management', in *Research in Personnel and Human Resources Management, vol. 13*, ed. G. R. Ferris (Greenwich, CT: JAI Press, 1995), p. 189. See J. M. Collins and D. H. Gleaves, 'Race, Job Applicants, and the Five-Factor Model of Personality: Implications for Black Psychology, Industrial/Organizational Psychology, and the Five-Factor Theory', *Journal of Applied Psychology*, August 1998, pp. 531–44.

79 See G. M. Alliger and S. A. Dwight, 'A Meta-Analytic Investigation of the Susceptibility of Integrity Tests to Faking and Coaching', *Educational and Psychological Measurement*, February 2000, pp. 59–72; and S. Stark, O. S. Chernyshenko, K. Chan, W. C. Lee and F. Drasgow, 'Effects of the Testing Situation on Item Responding: Cause for Concern', *Journal of Applied Psychology*, October 2001, pp. 943–53.

80 Other sources relating to Table 2.4 are D. Batram, 'Addressing the Abuse of Personality Test', *Personnel Management*, April 1991, pp. 34–9; C. Fletcher, 'Personality Tests: The Great Debate', *Personnel Management*, September 1991, pp. 38–42; R. Feltham, H. Baron and P. Smith, 'Developing Fair Tests', *The Psychologist*, January 1994, pp. 23–5; C. Jackson, *Understanding Psychological Testing* (Leicester: BPS Books, 1996); and B. Leonard, 'Reading Employees', *HR Magazine*, April 1999, pp. 67–73.

81 See J. C. McCune, 'Testing, Testing 1-2-3', *Management Review*, January 1996, pp. 50–52; and C. M. Solomon, 'Testing at Odds with Diversity Efforts?', *Personnel Journal*, April 1996, pp. 131–40.

82 For example, see J. C. Connor, 'The Paranoid Personality at Work', *HR Magazine*, March 1999, pp. 120–26; and 'Your Sleep Has a Personality', *Management Review*, May 1999, p. 9.

83 R. E. Boyatzis, *The Competent Manager: A Model for Effective Performance* (Chichester: Wiley, 1982).

84 L. M. Spencer, D. C. McClelland and S. M. Spencer, *Competency Assessment Methods: History and State of the Art* (London: Hay/McBer Research Press, 1994).

85 For interesting reading on competencies, see C. Woodruffe, *Assessment Centres: Identifying and Developing Competence, second edition* (London: IPM, 1993); and D. Dubois, *Competency-Based Performance Improvement: A Strategy for Organizational Change* (Amherst, MA: HRD Press, 1993).

86 See H. A. Witkin, C. A. Moore, D. R. Goodenough and P. W. Cox, 'Field-Dependent and Field-Independent Cognitive Styles and Their Educational Implications', *Review of Educational Research*, Winter 1977, pp. 1–64; J. P. Guilford, 'Cognitive Styles: What Are They?', *Educational and Psychological Measurement*, Fall 1980,

pp. 517–35; and S. Messick, 'The Nature of Cognitive Styles: Problems and Promises in Educational Practice', *Educational Psychologist*, Spring 1984, pp. 59–74.

87 R. J. Riding, *Cognitive Styles Analysis: Research Applications, revised edition* (Birmingham: Learning and Training Technology, 2000), p. 3.

88 M. J. A. Howe, 'Can IQ Change?', *The Psychologist*, February 1998, pp. 69–72.

89 For excellent works on intelligence, including definitional distinctions and a historical perspective of the IQ controversy, see S. J. Ceci, *On Intelligence* (London: Harvard University Press, 1996); M. J. A. Howe, *I.Q. in Question: The Truth about Intelligence* (London: Sage Publications, 1997); R. J. Sternberg and E. Grigorenko, *Intelligence, Heredity and Environment* (Cambridge: Cambridge University Press, 1997); and C. Cooper and V. Varma, *Intelligence and Abilities* (London: Routledge, 1999).

90 C. Spearman, *The Abilities of Man* (Oxford: Macmillan, 1927).

91 For related research, see M. J. Ree and J. A. Earles, 'Predicting Training Success: Not Much More Than g', *Personnel Psychology*, Summer 1991, pp. 321–32; and M. J. Ree, J. A. Earles and M. S. Teachout, 'Predicting Job Performance: Not Much More than g', *Journal of Applied Psychology*, August 1994, pp. 518–24.

92 P. E. Vernon, 'The Hierarchy of Abilities', in *Intelligence and Abilities, second edition*, ed. S. Wiseman (New York: Penguin, 1973).

93 J. P. Guilford, 'The Three Faces of Intellect', in *Intelligence and Abilities*, ed. S. Wiseman (New York: Penguin, 1959).

94 These seven abilities were first described by L. L. Thurstone, 'Primary Mental Abilities', *Psychometric Monographs* (no. 1, 1938).

95 See F. L. Schmidt and J. E. Hunter, 'Employment Testing: Old Theories and New Research Findings', *American Psychologist*, October 1981, p. 1128. Also see W. M. Coward and P. R. Sackett, 'Linearity of Ability–Performance Relationships: A Reconfirmation', *Journal of Applied Psychology*, June 1990, pp. 297–300; F. L. Schmidt and J. E. Hunter, 'The Validity and Utility of Selection Methods in Personnel Psychology: Practical and Theoretical Implications of 85 Years of Research Findings', *Psychological Bulletin*, September 1998, pp. 262–74; and Y. Ganzach, 'Intelligence and Job Satisfaction', *Academy of Management Journal*, October 1998, pp. 526–39.

96 See H. Gardner, *Frames of Mind: The Theory of Multiple Intelligences, second edition* (New York: Basic Books, 1993); H. Gardner, M. C. Kornhaber and W. K. Wake, *Intelligence: Multiple Perspectives* (London: Harcourt Brace, 1996); and H. Gardner, *Changing Minds: The Art and Science of Changing Our Own and Other People's Minds* (Boston, MA: Harvard Business School Press, 2004).

97 R. J. Sternberg and R. K. Wagner, *Practical Intelligence* (Cambridge: Cambridge University Press, 1986). Also see S. Fox and P. E. Spector, 'Relations of Emotional Intelligence, Practical Intelligence, General Intelligence, and Trait Affectivity with Interview Outcomes: It's Not all Just "g"', *Journal of Organizational Behavior*, April 2000, pp. 203–20.

98 See R. E. Riggio, S. E. Murphy and F. J. Pirozzolo, *Multiple Intelligences and Leadership* (Mahwah, NJ: Lawrence Erlbaum Associates, 2002).

99 D. Lubinski and R. V. Dawis, 'Aptitudes, Skills and Proficiencies', in *Handbook of Industrial and Organizational Psychology, vol. 3*, eds M. D. Dunnette and L. M. Hough (Palo Alto, CA: Consulting Psychologists Press, 1992), pp. 30–33.

100 S. L. Wilk, L. Burris Desmarais and P. R. Sackett, 'Gravitation to Jobs Commensurate with Ability: Longitudinal and Cross-Sectional Tests', *Journal of Applied Psychology*, February 1995, p. 79.

101 J. R. Flynn, 'The Mean IQ of Americans: Massive Gains 1932 to 1978', *Psychological Bulletin*, January 1984, pp. 29–51; J. R. Flynn, 'Massive IQ Gains in 14 Nations: What IQ Tests Really Measure', *Psychological Bulletin*, March 1987, pp. 171–91; and J. R. Flynn, 'Searching for Justice: The Discovery of IQ Gains over Time', *American Psychologist*, January 1999, pp. 5–20.

102 B. Azar, 'People Are Becoming Smarter – Why?', *APA Monitor*, June 1996, p. 20. Also see U. Neisser, 'Rising Scores on Intelligence Tests', *American Scientist*, September–October 1997, pp. 440–47; and U. Neisser, *The Rising Curve: Long Term Gains in IQ and Related Measures* (Washington, DC: American Psychological Association, 1998).

103 For data on this study, see R. Grimm, 'Is Sensory Overload Making Us Less Intelligent?', *Psycport*, 24 June 2000 (www.psycport.com). Also see B. Virole, *L'Enchantement Harry Potter. La Psychology de l'Enfant Nouveau* (Paris: Hachette Littérature, 2001).

104 J. Hayes and C. W. Allinson, 'Cognitive Style and the Theory and Practice of Individual and Collective Learning in Organizations', *Human Relations*, July 1998, pp. 847–71.

105 For more information on the origins of cognitive styles research, see E. L. Grigorenko and R. J. Sternberg, 'Thinking Styles', in *International Handbook of Personality and Intelligence*, eds D. H. Saklofske and M. Zeidner (New York: Plenum Press, 1995), pp. 205–29. For other review works on cognitive styles, see J. Hayes and C. W. Allinson, 'Cognitive Style and Its Relevance for Management Practice', *British Journal of Management*, March 1994, pp. 53–71; S. Rayner and R. J. Riding, 'Towards a Categorization of Cognitive Styles and Learning Styles', *Educational Psychology*, March–June 1997, pp. 5–27; R. J. Riding, 'On the Nature of Cognitive Style', *Educational Psychology*, March–June 1997, pp. 29–49.

106 M. Kirton, 'Adaptors and Innovators: A Description and Measure', *Journal of Applied Psychology*, October 1976, p. 622.

107 For more information on this model, see M. Kirton, 'Adaptors and Innovators: A Description and Measure', *Journal of Applied Psychology*, October 1976, pp. 622–9; M. Kirton, 'Adaptors and Innovators in Organizations', *Human Relations*, April 1980, pp. 213–24; and M. Kirton, *Adaptors and Innovators: Styles of Creativity and Problem Solving, second edition* (London: Routledge, 1994).

108 For more information on the organisational relevance of KAI, especially for change processes, see S. Mudd, 'Kirton Adaption-Innovation Theory: Organizational Implications', *Technovation*, April 1995, pp. 165–75; and A. D. Tullett, 'The Adaptive-Innovative (A-I) Cognitive Styles of Male and Female Project Managers: Some Implications for the Management of Change', *Journal of Occupational and Organizational Psychology*, December 1995, pp. 359–65.

109 M. J. Kirton, *KAI Manual, second edition* (Hatfield: Occuptional Research Centre, 1985).

110 A. D. Tullett, 'Cognitive Style: Not Culture's Consequence', *European Psychologist*, September 1997, pp. 258–67.

111 For more information on this model, see R. Riding and I. Cheema, 'Cognitive Styles: An Overview and Integration', *Educational Psychology*, September 1991, pp. 193–215; S. Rayner and R. Riding, 'Towards a Categorisation of Cognitive Styles and Learning Styles', *Educational Psychology*, March–June 1997, pp. 5–27; and R. Riding and S. Rayner, *Cognitive Styles and Learning Strategies* (London: David Fulton, 1998).

112 R. Riding, *Cognitive Styles Analysis Users' Guide* (Birmingham: Learning and Training Technology, 1991).

113 R. Riding, *Cognitive Styles Analysis: Research Applications* (Birmingham: Learning and Training Development, 2000), p. 12.

114 R. J. Riding and S. Wigley, 'The Relationship between Cognitive Style and Personality in Further Education Students', *Personality and Individual Differences*, September 1997, p. 380.

115 R. Riding, 'On the Nature of Cognitive Style', *Educational Psychology*, March–June 1997, pp. 29–49; and R. Riding and S. Rayner, *Cognitive Styles and Learning Strategies* (London: David Fulton, 1998).

116 G. R. Foxall, 'Managers in Transition: An Empirical Test of Kirton's Adaption-Innovation Theory and Its Implications for the Mid-Career MBA', *Technovation*, June 1986, pp. 219–32; I. G. R. Foxall, 'Managerial Orientations of Adaptors and Innovators', *Journal of Managerial Psychology*, 1986, no. 2, pp. 24–8; G. R. Foxall, 'An Empirical Analysis of Mid-Career Managers' Adaptive-Innovative Cognitive Styles and Task Orientations in Three Countries', *Psychological Reports*, December 1990, pp. 1115–24; and G. R. Foxall and P. M. W. Hackett, 'Styles of Managerial Creativity: A Comparison of Adaption-Innovation in the United Kingdom, Australia and the United States', *British Journal of Management*, June 1994, pp. 85–100.

117 M. J. Kirton and S. M. De Ciantis, 'Cognitive style and Personality: The Kirton Adaption-Innovation and Cattell's Sixteen Personality Factor Inventories', *Personality and Individual Differences*, February 1986, pp. 141–6. Also see R. E. Goldsmith, 'Creative Style and Personality Theory', in *Adaptors and Innovators: Styles of Creativity and Problem Solving, second edition*, ed. M. J. Kirton (London: Routledge, 1994), pp. 34–50.

118 C. M. Jacobson, 'Cognitive Styles of Creativity: Relations of Scores on the Kirton Adaption-Innovation Inventory and the Myers-Briggs Type Indicator among managers in the USA', *Psychological Reports*, December 1993, pp. 1131–8; and A. H. Church and J. Waclawski, 'The Effects of Personality Orientation and Executive Behavior on Subordinate Perceptions of Workgroup Enablement', *International Journal of Organizational Analysis*, January 1996, pp. 20–40.

119 E. H. Buttner, N. Gryskiewicz and S. C. Hidore, 'The Relationship between Styles of Creativity and Managerial Skills Assessment', *British Journal of Management*, September 1999, pp. 228–38.

120 M. J. Kirton and R. M. McCarthy, 'Cognitive Climate and Organizations', *Journal of Occupational Psychology*, June 1988, pp. 175–84. Also see K. M. McNeilly and R. E. Goldsmith, 'The Moderating Effect of Sales Managers' Approach to Problem Solving on the Salesperson Satisfaction/Intention to Leave Relationship', *Journal of Social Behavior and Personality*, March 1992, pp. 139–50.

121 R. Riding and M. Watts, 'The Effects of Cognitive Style on the Preferred Format of Instructional Material', *Educational Psychology*, March–June 1997, pp. 179–83; and E. Sadler-Smith and R. Riding, 'Cognitive Style and Instructional Preferences', *Instructional Science*, September 1999, pp. 355–71.

122 R. Riding and G. Douglas, 'The Effect of Cognitive Style and Mode of Presentation on Learning Performance', *British Journal of Educational Psychology*, September 1993, pp. 297–307.

123 R. Riding and L. Anstey, 'Verbal-Imagery Learning Style and Reading Attainment in Eight-Year-Old Children', *Journal of Research in Reading*, February 1982, pp. 57–66.

124 R. Riding and E. Sadler-Smith, 'Type of Instructional Material, Cognitive Style and Learning Performance', *Educational Studies*, November 1992, p. 329.

125 R. Riding, *Personal Style Awareness and Personal Development* (Birmingham: Learning and Training Development, 1994).

126 R. Riding, D. Burton, G. Rees and M. Sharratt, 'Cognitive Style and Personality in 12-Year-Old Children', *British Journal of Educational Psychology*, March 1995, pp. 113–24; R. Riding and O. Craig, 'Cognitive Style and Types of Problem Behaviour in Boys in Special Schools', *British Journal of Educational Psychology*, September 1999, pp. 307–22; and R. Riding and J. Al-Hajji, 'Cognitive Style and Behaviour in Secondary School Pupils in Kuwait', *Educational Research*, April 2000, pp. 29–42.

127 R. Riding and M. Wright, 'Cognitive Style, Personal Characteristics and Harmony in Student Flats', *Educational Psychology*, September 1995, pp. 337–49.

128 S. Streufert and G. Y. Nogami, 'Cognitive Style and Complexity: Implications for I/O Psychology', in *International Review of Industrial and Organizational Psychology*, eds C. L. Cooper and I. Robertson (Chichester: Wiley, 1989).

129 M. J. Kirton and R. M. McCarthy, 'Cognitive Climate and Organizations', *Journal of Occupational Psychology*, June 1988, pp. 175–84.

130 R. P. Talbot, 'Valuing Differences in Thinking Styles to Improve Individual and Team Performance', *National Productivity Review*, Winter 1989, pp. 35–50.

131 J. Hayes and C. W. Allinson, 'Cognitive Style and Its Relevance for Management Practice', *British Journal of Management*, March 1994, pp. 53–71.

132 E. Sadler-Smith and B. Badger, 'Cognitive Style, Learning and Innovation', *Technology Analysis & Strategic Management*, June 1998, pp. 247–65.

133 D. Leonard and S. Straus, 'Putting Your Company's Whole Brain to Work', *Harvard Business Review*, July–August 1997, pp. 111–21.

134 D. A. Bernstein, E. J. Roy, T. K. Srull and L. D. Wickens, *Psychology, second edition* (Boston, MA: Houghton Mifflin, 1991).

135 For more information on the origins of learning styles, see E. L. Grigorenko and R. J. Sternberg, 'Thinking Styles', in *International Handbook of Personality and Intelligence*, eds D. H. Saklofske and M. Zeidner (New York: Plenum Press, 1995), pp. 205–29. For other reviews on learning styles, see S. Rayner and R. J. Riding, 'Towards a Categorization of Cognitive Styles and Learning Styles', *Educational Psychology*, March–June 1997, pp. 5–27; E. Sadler-Smith, 'Learning Style: Frameworks and Instruments', *Educational Psychology*, March–June 1997, pp. 51–63.

136 D. A. Kolb, 'On Management and the Learning Process', in *Organizational Psychology: A Book of Readings, second edition*, eds D. A. Kolb, I. M. Rubin and J. M. McIntyre (Englewood Cliffs, NJ: Prentice-Hall, 1974), p. 29.

137 See, for instance, N. J. Entwistle, *Styles of Learning and Teaching* (Chichester: Wiley, 1981).

138 See, for instance, J. P. Das, 'Implications for School Learning', in *Learning Strategies and Learning Styles*, ed. R. R. Schmeck (New York: Plenum Press, 1988).

139 See, for instance, J. Hayes and C. W. Allinson, 'Cognitive Style and Its Relevance for Management Practice', *British Journal of Management*, March 1994, pp. 53–71; and J. Hayes and C. W. Allinson, 'Cognitive Style and the Theory and Practice of Individual and Collective Learning in Organizations', *Human Relations*, July 1998, pp. 847–71.

140 For more information on Kolb's model, see D. A. Kolb, I. M. Rubin and J. M. McIntyre, *Organizational Psychology: An Experiential Approach, second edition* (Englewood Cliffs, NJ: Prentice-Hall, 1974); and D. A. Kolb, *Experiential Learning: Experience as the Source of Learning and Development* (Englewood Cliffs, NJ: Prentice-Hall, 1984).

141 Characteristics of experiential learning are elaborated in D. A. Kolb, *Experiential Learning: Experience as the Source of Learning and Development* (Englewood Cliffs, NJ: Prentice-Hall, 1984), pp. 25–38.

142 D. A. Kolb, 'Management and the Learning Process', *California Management Review*, Spring 1976, p. 21.

143 D. A. Kolb, *LSI Learning Style Inventory: Self-Scoring Inventory and Interpretation Booklet, revised version* (Boston, MA: McBer, 1985); and D. M. Smith and D. Kolb, *User's Guide for the Learning Style Inventory: A Manual for Teachers and Trainers* (Boston, MA: McBer, 1986).

144 For more information on this model, see P. Honey and A. Mumford, *Using Your Learning Styles* (Maidenhead, Berkshire: Peter Honey, 1986); and P. Honey and A. Mumford, *The Manual of Learning Styles* (Maidenhead, Berkshire: Peter Honey, 1986).

145 P. Honey and A. Mumford, *The Manual of Learning Styles* (Maidenhead, Berkshire: Peter Honey, 1986), p. 4.

146 These questions are based on P. Honey and A. Mumford, *Using Your Learning Styles* (Maidenhead, Berkshire: Peter Honey, 1986), p. 14.

147 P. Honey and A. Mumford, *The Manual of Learning Styles, revised version* (Maidenhead, Berkshire: Peter Honey, 1992).

148 For references to these studies, see S. M. DeCiantis and M. J. Kirton, 'A Psychometric Re-Examination of Kolb's Experiential Learning Cycle Construct: A Separation of Level, Style and Process', *Educational and Psychological Measurement*, October 1996, p. 809.

149 N. H. Leonard, R. W. Scholl and K. B. Kowalski, 'Information Processing Style and Decision Making', *Journal of Organizational Behavior*, May 1999, pp. 407–20.

150 D. A. Kolb, 'Management and the Learning Process', *California Management Review*, Spring 1976, p. 26.

151 D. A. Kolb, *Experiential Learning: Experience as the Source of Learning and Development* (Englewood Cliffs, NJ: Prentice-Hall, 1984).

152 Both approaches are elaborated in J. Hayes and C. W. Allinson, 'The Implications of Learning Styles for Training and Development: A Discussion of the Matching Hypothesis', *British Journal of Management*, March 1996, pp. 63–73.

153 For works on the importance of learning and learning styles for organisations, see E. Sadler-Smith and B. Badger, 'Cognitive Style, Learning and Innovation', *Technology Analysis & Strategic Management*, June 1998, pp. 247–65; J. Hayes and C. W. Allinson, 'Cognitive Style and the Theory and Practice of Individual and Collective Learning in Organizations', *Human Relations*, July 1998, pp. 847–71; S. Gherardi, D. Nicolini and F. Odella, 'Toward a Social Understanding of How People Learn in Organisations', *Management Learning*, September 1998, pp. 273–97; and E. Sadler-Smith, C. W. Allinson and J. Hayes, 'Learning Preferences and Cognitive Style: Some Implications for Continuing Professional Development', *Management Learning*, June 2000, pp. 239–56.

154 Based on J. E. Sharp, 'Applying Kolb Learning Style Theory in the Communication Classroom', *Business Communication Quarterly*, June 1997, pp. 129–34.
155 The questionnaire and scoring key are excerpted from J. W. Slocum, Jr, and D. Hellriegel, 'A Look at How Managers Minds Work', *Business Horizons*, July–August 1983, pp. 58–68.
156 Based on A. Dickerson and M. A. Taylor, 'Self-Limiting Behavior in Women: Self-Esteem and Self-Efficacy as Predictors', *Group & Organization Management*, June 2000, pp. 191–210.

chapter 3 values, attitudes and emotions

By Eva Cools and Herman Van den Broeck

Learning outcomes

When you finish studying the material in this chapter, you should be able to:

- define values and explain their sources

- identify and describe Rokeach's instrumental and terminal values

- explain Schwartz's basic human values model and his related work values model

- explain how attitudes influence behaviour in terms of the model of planned behaviour

- describe three key work-related attitudes: organisational commitment, job involvement and job satisfaction

- discuss the determinants and consequences of job satisfaction

- distinguish between positive and negative emotions and explain how they can be judged

- define what emotional intelligence is and which components it implies

- focus on emotional contagion in the workplace

- describe what flow is and how it influences organisational behaviour

The greatest sources of satisfaction in the workplace are internal and emotional

It is scarcely big news in a full-employment economy that companies are desperately looking for ways to make themselves more alluring to employees. Employers are continuously undertaking different initiatives to deal with this critical need.

But there is one striking finding: the single most important variable in employee productivity and loyalty turns out to be not pay of perks or benefits or workplace environment. Rather, according to the Gallup Organization, it is the quality of the relationship between employees and their direct supervisors. More specifically, what people want most from their supervisors is the same thing that kids want most from their parents: someone who sets clear and consistent expectations, cares for them, values their unique qualities and encourages and supports their growth and development. Put another way, the greatest sources of satisfaction in the workplace are internal and emotional.

For the past 15 years, Marcus Buckingham and Curt Coffman have studied the connection between workplace performance and bottom-line results for many of Gallup's clients, including Toyota, Best Buy and Disney. Recently, Buckingham completed a Gallup study that helps to measure a culture's impact on company performance. For the study Buckingham first identified 12 core traits of a healthy work atmosphere (dubbed 'Q12'), such as workers feeling actively engaged

case study

in their work or whether workers have had the opportunity to learn and grow. Then, using more than 30 years of corporate data collected at Gallup, Buckingham measured how these factors contributed to a company's success.

On average, there is an inverse correlation between length of service and a positive Q12 score, according to the study. 'What it means is the longer you stay in your job with a company, the less engaged you become', Buckingham says. 'So [this study] makes it very specific. Despite all of the money that we are spending on leadership and management development, we actually depreciate our human capital.'

'We all say that human capital is one of the few assets that a company has that it can generally appreciate', he says. 'And yet, according to the humans within that human capital, over time they actually become less clear about their expectations, less cared about, less well-cast in their job.'

Job satisfaction at Best Buy

But how do you prove that these sorts of feelings translate across a company into higher profits and greater retention? One of Gallup's most comprehensive research projects was involved in the consumer-electronics specialty retailer Best Buy. Beginning in 1997, employees at 300 Best Buy stores were asked to answer the 12 Gallup questions, using a scale of one to five (with one signifying 'strongly disagree', and five 'strongly agree').

While the stores are designed to be nearly identical in design and operation, their employees had radically different experiences. The number of employees giving a 'five' to one of the 12 questions averaged as much as 60 percentage points higher at the most productive stores (those with the best retention rates, highest profits and so on) than the least productive stores. Indeed, employees at the most productive stores typically gave higher marks to all 12 questions than the employees at the least productive stores. This was true even in the case of the question about whether employees had the materials and the equipment that they needed. In the most productive Best Buy location, 45 per cent of employees strongly agreed that they had what they needed, compared with 11 per cent in the least productive location – even though both stores had exactly the same materials and equipment. In short, the subjective perception of employees outweighed the objective reality.

Buckingham hopes that his projects will be a call to arms for CEOs to begin actively measuring what really matters. 'What we are giving CEOs is a way for them to shine an accurate light within their company to say, "How strong is our culture? Where is it getting stronger? Where is it getting weaker? What's the range?".'

Buckingam says: 'If you want to build a stronger culture, you had better answered one question right: What is the best way to improve one's performance? If you can answer that question, it will inform everything that you do.'[1]

For discussion

What does an employer need to do to win your loyalty? What do you need to do to win an employer's loyalty?

As can be seen in the case study, people's feelings and emotions influence how they behave and perform in an organisation. Professionals who are aware of the importance of people's internal states can use this information to manage effectively the work environment and increase people's job satisfaction. In this second chapter on individual differences, we focus on three forms of self-expression (see Figure 2.1): values, attitudes and emotions. We put these concepts in another chapter, because they do not have the same history as the concepts elaborated in Chapter 2. Research on values, attitudes and emotions is more recent and is not characterised by the same research traditions as research on personality, abilities and styles. First, we focus on personal and work values and their impact on organisational behaviour and performance. Second, we define attitudes and take a closer look at some key work-related attitudes: organisational commitment, job involvement and job satisfaction. Finally, we elaborate on emotions, which is a rather recent stream of research that broadens the focus of traditional abilities research. It also balances some of the weaknesses of the other concepts. Research on emotions and emotional intelligence became important in the study of individual differences and organisational behaviour only a few decades ago.

Values

In our modern society characterised by individualisation and globalisation a person's values are of relevance for organisational behaviour. Individualisation is the process by which individuals increasingly become a point of reference in the shaping of values and attitudes.[2] In premodern times, values were based upon, and legitimised by, tradition and religion. In contemporary society, however, values are an object of personal autonomy and characterised by an ethic of personal fulfilment. Nevertheless, modern society is not only individualised, but also differentiated. This means that the different life areas became 'self-referential in terms of values'.[3] In contrast, premodern, traditional societies are described as integrated and non-differentiated. All life domains and their values were strongly connected, mainly by religion. As a consequence of the decreasing influence of religion, individuals are now freer to choose their values. 'Modernity confronts the individual with a diversity of choices and at the same time offers little help as to which options should be selected.'[4] The second trend that characterises modern society is globalisation. Individuals presently live in a 'global village'.[5] Information about different cultures is disseminated rapidly throughout the world, thereby confronting individuals with more alternatives. Accordingly, the likelihood that people select similar values is reduced. In addition, people are also increasingly influenced by foreign events, resulting in value fragmentation (i.e. increased diversity of individual value systems).

We first focus on what values are and then elaborate two different value models. We also look at work values. We conclude this section with research findings and practical implications. Organisational values are elaborated more thoroughly in the chapter on organisational culture (see Chapter 16). We confine our discussion here by focusing only on personal and work values (and not, for instance, on cultural or social values) and their relevance for organisational behaviour.

Defining values

Several different definitions of and views on values exist. Researchers, for instance, have likened values to beliefs, needs, goals, criteria for choosing goals and attitudes. Some authors tried to distinguish values from other constructs, while others did not. So, what are values then? Despite the abundance of definitions, most authors agree that **Values** are standards or criteria for choosing goals or guiding actions, and that they are relatively enduring and stable over time.[6] Even though values are relatively enduring and stable, they can change during our lifetime. Rokeach states it as follows: 'If values were completely stable, individual and social change would be impossible. If values were completely unstable, continuity of human personality and society would be impossible.'[7]

We can make a distinction between a content and an intensity aspect of values. People do not only vary in what values they find important (content aspect), they also differ in how important several values are (intensity aspect). An individual's values are not single entities; they can be ranked according to their intensity. In other words, values are integrated within a **Value system**, which is 'an enduring organisation of beliefs concerning preferable modes of conduct or end-states of existence along a continuum of relative importance'.[8]

Most researchers on values also propose, explicitly or implicitly, that values develop through the influence of personality, society and culture.[9] People are not born with an internal set of values (although a study[10] with twins reared apart concluded that 40 per cent of variance in work values can be attributed to genetic factors). Values are acquired throughout our life from diverse sources (parents, teachers, peers, work environment, national culture . . .), which is referred to as a process of socialisation (see Chapter 16 for organisational socialisation). The enduring nature of our values refers back to the way we acquire them initially.[11] Values are taught and learned initially in isolation from other values in an absolute, all-or-none manner. We are taught that it is always desirable to be honest and to strive for peace. We are not taught that it is desirable to be just a little bit honest or to strive for peace sometimes and not at other times. This absolute learning of values more or less guarantees their endurance and stability. As we grow older, we are exposed to several values from diverse sources that sometimes might be in conflict with each other. Gradually, we learn through a process of maturation

Values
standards or criteria for choosing goals and guiding actions that are relatively enduring and stable over time

Value system
a ranking of a person's values according to their intensity or importance

and experience to integrate the isolated, absolute values we acquired in different contexts into a hierarchically organised system wherein each value is ordered in importance relative to other values. This does not mean that values cannot change during our life. Certainly in the adolescence phase, values are questioned. This questioning process might lead to the conclusion that our values are no longer adequate. More often, however, this questioning leads to reinforcing the values we have.

Rokeach's instrumental and terminal values model

Milton Rokeach, the most cited author concerning values developed a model that distinguishes between instrumental and terminal values.[12] Instrumental values refer to desirable ways or modes of conduct to reach some kind of desirable goal. Terminal values refer to the desirable goals a person wants to reach during his or her life. Instrumental and terminal values are connected with each other and work together to help people reach their desirable goals through desirable ways of conduct. There is not necessarily a one-on-one correspondence between an instrumental and a terminal value. One way of conduct, for instance, may be instrumental in reaching several terminal goals or several modes of conduct may be instrumental in reaching one terminal value.

Rokeach developed the Rokeach Value Survey (RVS) to measure instrumental and terminal values. The RVS contains two sets of values (instrumental and terminal). Each set has 18 individual value items that were composed after several years of research (see Table 3.1: in capitals are the values, next to each value more explanation is given on the meaning of the value according to Rokeach). Respondents are instructed to arrange the instrumental and terminal values in order of importance, as guiding principles in their life.

Rokeach distinguishes between two kinds of instrumental values and two kinds of terminal values. Terminal values can be divided into personal and social ones. This means, terminal values may be self-centred, intrapersonal (e.g. inner harmony) or society-centred, interpersonal (e.g. a world at peace) in focus. Instrumental values are divided into moral and competence values. Moral values refer to those kinds of instrumental values that have an interpersonal focus and that lead to feelings

Instrumental values represent desirable ways or modes of conduct to achieve one's terminal goals

Terminal values represent desirable goals or end-states of existence a person wants to reach during his/her life

TABLE 3.1 ROKEACH'S INSTRUMENTAL AND TERMINAL VALUES

Instrumental values		Terminal values	
AMBITIOUS	Hard-working, aspiring	A COMFORTABLE LIFE	A prosperous life
BROADMINDED	Open-minded	AN EXCITING LIFE	A stimulating, active life
CAPABLE	Competent, effective	A SENSE OF ACCOMPLISHMENT	Lasting contribution
CHEERFU	Light-hearted, joyful		
CLEAN	Neat, tidy	A WORLD AT PEACE	Free of war and conflict
COURAGEOUS	Standing up for your beliefs	A WORLD OF BEAUTY	Beauty of nature and the arts
FORGIVING	Willing to pardon others	EQUALITY	Brotherhood, equal opportunity for all
HELPFUL	Working for the welfare of others	FAMILY SECURITY	Taking care of loved ones
HONEST	Sincere, truthful	FREEDOM	Independence, free choice
IMAGINATIVE	Daring, creative	HAPPINESS	Contentedness
INDEPENDENT	Self-reliant, self-sufficient	INNER HARMONY	Freedom from inner conflict
INTELLECTUAL	Intelligent, reflective		
LOGICAL	Consistent, rational	MATURE LOVE	Sexual and spiritual intimacy
LOVING	Affectionate, tender		
OBEDIENT	Dutiful, respectful	NATIONAL SECURITY	Protection from attack
POLITE	Courteous, well-mannered	PLEASURE	An enjoyable, leisurely life
		SALVATION	Saved, eternal life
RESPONSIBLE	Dependable, reliable	SELF-RESPECT	Self-esteem
SELF-CONTROLLED	Restrained, self-disciplined	SOCIAL RECOGNITION	Respect, admiration
		TRUE FRIENDSHIP	Close companionship
		WISDOM	A mature understanding of life

SOURCE: Based on Table 2.1 in M. Rokeach, *The Nature of Human Values* (New York: The Free Press, 1973), p. 28.

of guilt and wrongdoing when violated. Competence or self-actualisation values refer to intra-personal instrumental values, which lead to feelings of shame and personal inadequacy when violated. For instance, when behaving honestly or responsibly, you will feel that you behave morally, while behaving logically, intelligently or imaginatively, you will feel that you behave competently. People differ in the extent to which they value personal or social values, as well as moral or competence values.

Schwartz's basic human values model

Shalom Schwartz, another expert on value research, elaborated the model of Rokeach further and proposes a theory on basic human values based upon two components.[13] First, he distinguishes ten types of values that are recognised by members of most societies. Second, he shows how these values are connected dynamically with each other by specifying which values are compatible and mutually supportive, and which values are conflicting and opposed.

The ten value types of Schwartz are distinguished according to the type of motivational goal they express (see Table 3.2: the value type, its definition and the values used to measure the value type are

TABLE 3.2 SCHWARTZ'S MOTIVATIONAL TYPES OF VALUES

Value Type	Definition	Values
POWER	Social status and prestige, control and dominance over people and resources	Social power – Authority – Wealth
ACHIEVEMENT	Personal success through demonstrating competence according to social standards	Successful – Capable – Ambitious – Influential
HEDONISM	Pleasure and sensuous gratification for oneself	Pleasure – Enjoying life
STIMULATION	Excitement, novelty and challenge in life	Daring – A varied life – An exciting life
SELF-DIRECTION	Independent thought and action, seeking, creating, experimenting and exploring	Creativity – Freedom – Independent – Curious – Choosing own goals
UNIVERSALISM	Equality, tolerance and justice for all, and respect for nature	Broadminded – Wisdom – Social justice – Equality – A world at peace – A world of beauty – Unity with nature – Protecting the environment
BENEVOLENCE	Welfare for all, forgiveness, honesty, loyalty and responsibility	Helpful – Honest – Forgiving – Loyal – Responsible
TRADITION	Respect for traditional culture	Accepting one's portion in life – Humble – Devout – Respect for tradition – Moderate
CONFORMITY	Restraint for actions, inclinations and impulses likely to upset or harm others and violate societal expectations and norms	Self-discipline – Obedient – Politeness – Honouring parents and elders
SECURITY	Safety, security and stability in a stable society	Family security – National security – Social order – Clean – Reciprocation of favours

SOURCE: Based on Table 1 in S. H. Schwartz and G. Sagie, 'Value Consensus and Importance: A Cross-National Study', *Journal of Cross-Cultural Psychology*, July 2000, p. 468.

listed respectively). They are derived by reasoning that values represent, in the form of conscious goals, three universal requirements of human existence to which all individuals and societies have to be responsive: needs of individuals as biological organisms, requirements for co-ordinated social interaction, and survival and welfare needs of groups. In order to cope with reality in a social context, groups and individuals represent these requirements cognitively as specific values about which they can communicate. Schwartz started from and extended Rokeach's list of 36 values to determine his own basic human values model.

Schwartz also investigated the relationships between these value types. His value structure is based on the idea that every action to reach a value has psychological, practical and social consequences that can be in conflict or compatible with the pursuit of other values. It is, for instance, difficult to strive for achievement and for benevolence at the same time.[14] The dynamics between Schwartz's values can be situated on two underlying dimensions: self-transcendence versus self-enhancement and openness to change versus conservation (see Figure 3.1). The first dimension represents the tension between acceptance of others as equal and concern for their welfare (universalism and benevolence) versus the dominance over others and pursuit of own success (power and achievement). The second dimension opposes values that emphasise independent thought and action and readiness for change (self-direction and stimulation) to values of preserving traditional practices, protection of stability and submissive self-restriction (security, conformity and tradition).

FIGURE 3.1 SCHWARTZ'S BASIC HUMAN VALUES MODEL

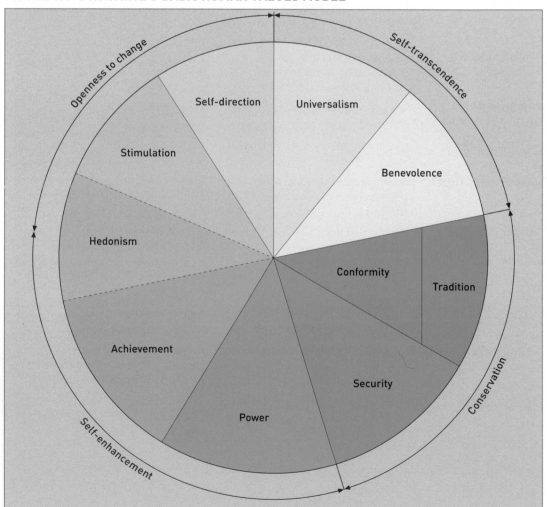

SOURCE: S. H. Schwartz, 'Are There Universals in the Structure and Contents of Human Values?', *Journal of Social Issues*, Winter 1994, p. 24.

Schwartz developed the Schwartz Value Survey (SVS), a 56-items test (30 terminal values and 26 instrumental values) that includes items from the ten value types described above. Respondents are first asked to choose the one value of most importance to them and the one most opposed to their values and then to rate each value according to the importance it has as a guiding principle in their life, on a 9-point scale. The difficulty in ranking large numbers of values led to the use of rating rather than ranking to measure value importance.[15] The SVS is available in a large number of languages. Schwartz found support for his model in 155 samples from 55 countries. Schwartz's research also permitted the assessment of the conceptual meaning of each single value in each single sample. The results of these analyses suggest that 45 of the values have cross-culturally consistent meanings.[16]

According to Schwartz, his theory adopts, with some modifications, the conceptualisation of values that is offered by Rokeach and builds further on Rokeach's methodology to measure values. The major innovations of the theory, however, are that it derives a comprehensive set of value contents and that it specifies the dynamic structures of relations among them. Schwartz's theory also provides the basis for fulfilling Rokeach's aim validly to compare values in one country with values in other countries.[17] As Schwartz puts it:

 The discovery of a parsimonious, well-defined and cross-culturally stable structure of values facilitates theorising about the relationships among values; between values and other personality variables; and between values and social psychological variables such as attitudes, beliefs and behavioural intentions.[18]

Work values

An important objective of research on values has been to study the link between individuals' value priorities and other aspects, such as social experiences and roles. A part of this research focused primarily on work.[19] Several authors attempted to create a model of work values and tried to link this with personal values.[20] We will only elaborate Schwartz's theory on work values.

Schwartz also adapted his basic values model to a work context.[21] According to Schwartz, **Work values** are expressions of basic values in the work setting. Like basic values, work values are ordered by their importance as guiding principles for evaluating work outcomes and settings, and for choosing among different work alternatives. Work values refer to what a person wants out of work in general, rather than to narrowly defined outcomes of particular jobs.

Work values refer to what a person wants out of work in general

Parallel to the basic values model, Schwartz tried to identify general types of work values. Most researchers on work values identify the same two or three types of work values (i.e. intrinsic or self-actualisation values; extrinsic, security or material values; and social or relational values).[22] According to Schwartz, however, there should be four general types of work values, related to the four poles of his two-dimensional basic human values model.

The four types of work values that Schwartz identifies are intrinsic, extrinsic, social and prestige values. Intrinsic values express openness to change values (e.g. the pursuit of autonomy, interest, growth and creativity in work). Extrinsic values refer to conservation values (e.g. job security, income). Social or interpersonal work values express self-transcendence values (e.g. work as a vehicle for positive social relations or contribution to society). The prestige or power values, a type added to the work values research by Schwartz, implies values related to the self-enhancement values (e.g. authority, influence and achievement in work).

Schwartz developed the Work Value Survey (WVS) to measure people's work values. The following Activity is based on the WVS. Which of the four work value types do you value most: intrinsic, extrinsic, social or prestige values?

Research findings and practical implications

A great deal of research on values exists, although the research field is very diverse. Some research investigates a single country or organisation, while other studies focus on a broader area. The European Value Study, for instance, investigates values of European citizens in several life domains on a longitudinal basis (see the next Snapshot).[23] Many value studies distinguish different values according to the life domains. However, a lot of these studies focus on only one life domain (e.g. work) and do not look at the interrelations between the values of several life domains (e.g. leisure time, private life, politics, family . . .). We summarise some relevant research findings for organisational behaviour.

Which work values are most important to you?

Instructions

Indicate for each of the following work values how important it is for you.

	Not at all important			Very important	
1 Good salary and work conditions	1	2	3	4	5
2 Job security (permanent job, pension)	1	2	3	4	5
3 Interesting and varied work	1	2	3	4	5
4 Work with people	1	2	3	4	5
5 Prestigious, highly valued work	1	2	3	4	5
6 Work in which you are your own boss	1	2	3	4	5
7 Contributing to people and society	1	2	3	4	5
8 Authority to make decisions over people	1	2	3	4	5
9 Social contact with co-workers	1	2	3	4	5
10 Opportunities for occupational advancement	1	2	3	4	5

Scoring key

Total your score:

Add questions 1 and 2 for the importance of extrinsic work values.

Add questions 3 and 6 for the importance of intrinsic work values.

Add questions 4, 7 and 9 for the importance of social work values.

Add questions 5 and 8 for the importance of prestige work values.

Scoring norms

Comparative norms for extrinsic, intrinsic and prestige work values:

2–4 = Low importance

5–7 = Moderate importance

8 and above = High importance

Comparative norms for social work values:

3–6 = Low importance

7–11 = Moderate importance

12 and above = High importance

SOURCE: Excerpted and adapted from M. Ros, S. H. Schwartz and S. Surkiss, 'Basic Individual Values, Work Values and the Meaning of Work', *Applied Psychology: An International Review*, January 1999, pp. 58–9.

Changing work values in Europe

The European Values Study investigates the values in several European countries on a longitudinal basis. Data from 12 countries are included in the analysis on work values: France, Great Britain, (former) West Germany, Italy, Spain, the Netherlands, Belgium, Denmark, Norway, Ireland, Northern Ireland and Iceland. Comparison of the survey data from 1981 and 1990 reveal that people's work values are evolving, although the changes are generally rather small (see Table). Which aspects of a job are valued most in Europe?

Data indicate that a good salary remains the most important aspect, although aspects related to the quality of the job are valued higher than before. This means that social aspects, like having nice colleagues or meeting people in your job, became more important. Aspects related to the content of the job and personal development (an interesting job, related to your capabilities, with responsibility, etc.) are also valued higher. Job certainty, on the other hand, has decreased in importance.

Work values	1990 (%)	1981 (%)
I Personal Development		
A responsible job	40	36
An interesting job	58	52
A job which encourages initiative	45	40
A job that corresponds to capabilities	54	47
A job with which you can achieve something	49	42
II Comfort and Status		
A respected job	37	31
Generous holidays	28	28
Good working hours	42	41
Not too much pressure	28	28
Reasonable promotion prospects	35	33
III Material Conditions		
Good wages	71	66
Job security	55	57
IV Social Aspects		
Nice colleagues	65	62
Meeting people	44	40

SOURCE: Based on discussion in S. Ashford and N. Timms, *What Europe Thinks: A Study of Western European Values* (Aldershot: Dartmouth, 1992); and R. de Moor, *Values in Western Societies* (Tilburg: Tilburg University Press, 1995).

Both Rokeach and Schwartz studied relationships between their values model and other individual differences, such as voting behaviour, readiness for outgroup social contact, interpersonal co-operation. Schwartz, for instance, concluded from a study with 90 participants (a mixed-motive experimental game) that power, achievement and hedonism were strong predictors for non-cooperation, while people who attach importance to value types like benevolence, universalism and conformity were more prone to co-operate.[24] Schwartz's basic human values model also proved to be a strong predictor of pro-environmental attitudes and behaviour.[25] Another study found a relationship between people's values and ethical decision and integrity.[26] Studies also investigated the relationship between values and personality,[27] and between values and cognitive styles.[28]

Many studies focus on the relationship between work values and several aspects of organisational behaviour (e.g. organisational commitment, motivation, performance, etc.).[29] One aspect of this research is, for instance, value congruence, which means the fit between people's work values and the job/organisation. Several studies found that people choose a job in accordance with their work values rather than the other way around.[30] Possible reasons for this finding are the fact that values have a relatively enduring and stable character and that many values are acquired very early in life.

Researchers also study cultural differences between work values. They want to know what the role of national culture is in the shaping of work values. A study of 2280 respondents from eight countries found differences in the rank order of the importance of certain work values.[31] For instance, job interest was the most important value for Western respondents from the United States, the Netherlands and Germany, while it was only of moderate importance for respondents from China and Hungary. Chinese respondents found contribution to society an important value, while it was the least important value for respondents from all other countries. Job security was only of marginal importance in China and Israel, while it was found to be the most important in Korea (also see Chapter 16 on international culture).

Individuals' values can explain a great deal regarding their interests and priorities, the choices they make and the goals for which they strive. Values are central to an individual because they serve as mechanisms that guide their life within society. The pervasive influence of values in all our life domains makes them an issue of utmost important for organisations to take into account. Values influence employees' perception, motivation and performance and play a role in decision making, ethics and evaluations. Differences in values can also cause conflicts and misunderstandings in organisations. Knowing, respecting and taking into account each other's values can be a good starting point for better co-operation and a nicer working sphere.

Attitudes and behaviour

Hardly a day goes by without the popular media reporting the results of another attitude survey. The idea is to take the pulse of public opinion. What do we think about euthanasia, the euro, the refugee problem, legalisation of soft drugs or abortion? Meanwhile, organisations conduct attitude surveys to monitor such things as job and pay satisfaction. All this attention to attitudes is based on the assumption that attitudes somehow influence behaviour such as voting for someone, working hard or quitting one's job. In this section, we examine the connection between attitudes and behaviour. We also look at job satisfaction as an important attitude that influences organisational behaviour.

Defining attitudes

Attitude
beliefs and feelings people have about specific ideas, situations and people, which influence their behaviour

An **Attitude** is defined as a 'learned predisposition to respond in a consistently favourable or unfavourable manner with respect to a given object'.[32] In other words, attitudes are beliefs and feelings people have about specific ideas, situations and people, which influence their behaviour. Attitudes are often confused with values, because both are social abstractions. Attitudes, however, affect behaviour at a different level from values. While values represent global beliefs that influence behaviour across all situations, attitudes relate only to behaviour directed toward specific objects, persons or situations.[33] Attitudes are more directed towards specific goals or situations, while values are more abstract. Individuals usually have more attitudes than values. Values and attitudes are generally, though not always, in harmony. An employee who strongly values helpful behaviour may have a negative attitude towards helping an unethical co-worker. The difference between attitudes and values can be clarified further with a description of the three components of attitudes: a cognitive (cognition), affective (affect) and behavioural (intention) one.[34]

Cognitive component of an attitude
beliefs, opinions, cognitions and knowledge someone has about a certain object, situation or person

The **Cognitive component of an attitude** refers to the beliefs, opinions, cognitions or knowledge someone has about a certain object, situation or person. For example, what is your opinion on mobbing at work? Do you believe this behaviour is completely unacceptable or do you think it is not your problem?

Affective component of an attitude
feelings, moods and emotions a person has about something or someone

The **Affective component of an attitude** refers to the feelings, moods, emotions a person has about something or someone. Applied to the same example, how do you feel about someone who nags another colleague in the organisation? If you feel angry or frustrated about it, you will express negative feelings towards people who pester other people. If you feel indifferent about mobbing, the affective component of your attitude is neutral.

Behavioural component of an attitude
how a person intends or expects to act towards something or someone

The **Behavioural component of an attitude** refers to how a person intends or expects to act towards something or someone. For example, how do you intend to react to someone who pesters another colleague? Will you say or do something? Will you defend the victim? Attitude theory states that your ultimate behaviour in a certain situation is a function of all three attitudinal components. You will defend a victim of mobbing at work if you feel angry about it (affective), if you believe mobbing is completely unacceptable (cognitive) and when you have an intention to do something about it (behavioural).

How stable are attitudes?

In one landmark study researchers found the job attitudes of 5000 middle-aged male employees to be very stable over a five-year period. Positive job attitudes remained positive; negative ones remained negative. Even those who changed jobs or occupations tended to maintain their prior job attitudes.[35] More recent research suggests the foregoing study may have overstated the stability of attitudes because it was restricted to a middle-aged sample. This time, researchers asked: 'What happens to attitudes over the entire span of adulthood?' General attitudes were found to be more susceptible to change during early and late adulthood than during middle adulthood. Three factors accounted for middle-age attitude stability: (1) greater personal certainty; (2) perceived abundance of knowledge; and (3) a need for strong attitudes. Thus, the conventional notion, that general attitudes become less likely to change as the person ages, was rejected. Elderly people, along with young adults, can and do change their general attitudes because they are more open and less self-assured.[36]

Like values, attitudes are acquired and formed during our life from diverse sources (family, peer group, work environment, etc.) and from our own experiences and personality through a socialisation process. Although attitudes are relatively stable, they can change. Gaining new information, for instance, can lead people to change their attitudes. When you hear a certain car has been recalled for defective brakes, your beliefs about the quality of that car may change. Attitudes can also change because the object of the attitude becomes less important or relevant to the person. You may, for instance, have a negative attitude towards your organisation's pension plans. When your private bank offers you a good pension plan, the attitude towards your organisation will be less negative because you no longer need to worry about it.

Another factor that might indicate attitudinal change is necessary is cognitive dissonance.[37] **Cognitive dissonance** refers to situations where different attitudes are in conflict with each other or where people behave in a way inconsistent with their attitudes. In these situations, people will feel tension and discomfort and accordingly try to reduce these feelings (called 'dissonance reduction'). People like consistency between their attitudes and behaviour or among their attitudes. Possible ways to solve situations of dissonance are changing your attitudes, altering your behaviour or perceptually viewing the situation differently (this means developing a rationalisation for the inconsistency) (also see equity theory in Chapter 6).

> **Cognitive dissonance** refers to situations of incompatibility between different attitudes or between attitudes and behaviour

Attitudes affect behaviour via intentions

Many researchers have studied the relationship between attitudes and behaviour.[38] Early research assumed a causal relationship between attitudes and behaviour, implying that your attitudes determine what you do (often referred to as the A–B relationship). However, gradually this relationship was criticised. Research found little or no relationship between attitudes and behaviour or that other aspects needed to be taken into account to explain the relationship between attitudes and behaviour.

Behavioural scientists, Martin Fishbein and Icek Ajzen, developed a comprehensive model of behavioural intentions used widely to explain attitude–behaviour relationships.[39] Over the years, they developed and refined this model that focuses on intentions as the key link between attitudes and actual behaviour.[40]

As depicted in Figure 3.2, an individual's intention to engage in a given behaviour is the best predictor of that behaviour. Intentions are indicators of how hard people are willing to try and of how much effort they are planning to exert to use a certain type of behaviour. For example, the quickest

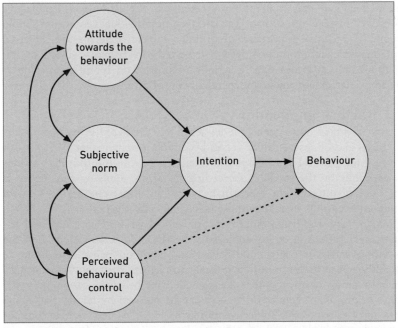

FIGURE 3.2 AJZEN'S THEORY OF PLANNED BEHAVIOUR

SOURCE: Based on Figure 1 in I. Ajzen, 'The Theory of Planned Behaviour,' *Organizational Behavior and Human Decision Processes*, December 1991, p. 182.

and possibly most accurate way of determining whether an individual will quit his or her job, is to have an objective third party ask if he or she intends to quit. A meta-analysis of 34 studies of employee turnover, involving more than 83 000 employees, validated this direct approach. The researchers found stated behavioural intentions to be a better predictor of employee turnover than job satisfaction, satisfaction with the work itself or organisational commitment.[41]

Although asking about intentions enables one to predict who will quit, it does not help explain why an individual would want to quit. Thus, to understand better why employees exhibit certain behaviours, such as quitting their jobs, one needs to consider their relevant attitudes and other related aspects. Three separate but interrelated determinants influence one's intention (planned behaviour) to do something (actual behaviour). As shown in Figure 3.2, behavioural intentions are influenced by one's attitude towards the behaviour, by perceived norms about exhibiting that behaviour and by perceived behavioural control.

The attitude towards the behaviour refers to the degree to which someone has a favourable or unfavourable evaluation or appraisal towards the behaviour in question. A person will have positive attitudes toward engaging in a given behaviour when he or she believes that it is associated with positive outcomes. An individual is more likely to quit a job when he or she believes it will result in a better position or in stress reduction. In contrast, negative attitudes toward quitting will be formed when a person believes quitting leads to negative outcomes, such as the loss of money and status.

The subjective norm refers to the perceived social pressure whether or not to engage in the behaviour. Subjective norms can exert a powerful influence on the behavioural intentions of those who are sensitive to the opinions of respected role models. This effect was observed in a laboratory study of students' intentions to apply for a job at companies that reportedly tested employees for drugs. The students generally had a negative attitude about companies that tested for drugs. However, positive statements from influential persons about the need for drug testing tended to strengthen intentions to apply to companies engaged in drug testing.[42]

The perceived behavioural control refers to the perceived ease or difficulty in performing the behaviour. It is assumed that the degree of perceived behavioural control reflects past experiences as well as anticipated impediments and obstacles (such as lacking the necessary resources, unavailable opportunities, etc.). Perceived behavioural control varies across situations and actions. The theory of planned behaviour is an extension of Fishbein and Ajzen's model of reasoned action, made necessary by the limitations of the original model in dealing with behaviours over which people have incomplete volitional control.

As a general rule, Ajzen and Fishbein state that the more favourable the attitude and subjective norm and the greater the perceived behavioural control, the stronger an individual's intention should be to perform certain behaviour. The relative importance of attitudes, subjective norms and perceived behavioural control in the prediction of intention is, however, expected to vary across situations and actions. For instance, sometimes only attitudes have a significant impact on intentions, while in another situation two or all three determinants make independent contributions.

Research findings and practical implications

Research has demonstrated that Fishbein and Ajzen's model accurately predicted intentions to buy consumer products, have children and choose a career versus becoming a homemaker. Weight loss intentions and behaviour, voting for political candidates and attending on-the-job training sessions have also been predicted successfully by the model.[43] According to Ajzen, applying the theory of planned behaviour provides a lot of information that can be useful in understanding all kind of behaviours or in implementing interventions to change those behaviours effectively.[44]

From an organisational point of view the behavioural intention model we have just reviewed has important implications. First, organisations need to appreciate the dynamic relationships between beliefs, attitudes, subjective norms, perceived control and behavioural intentions when attempting to foster productive behaviour. Although attitudes are often resistant to change, they can be influenced indirectly through education and training experiences that change underlying beliefs. A case in point is a study documenting how men's beliefs about gender differences can be reduced by taking a women's studies course.[45] Another tactic involves redirecting subjective norms through clear and credible communication, organisational culture values and role models. Finally, regular employee-attitude surveys can let professionals know whether their ideas and changes go with or against the grain of popular sentiment.

Key work-related attitudes

Three particular attitudes are mostly studied in relation to organisational behaviour. Those key work-related attitudes are organisational commitment, job involvement and job satisfaction. Before the explanation of these concepts, consider how Colruyt, a Belgian-based supermarket chain, stimulates the employees' work-related attitudes.

> In 2003, Colruyt employed 13 000 people of 37 different nationalities. Besides the low prices, Colruyt is known for its strong HR policy. This implies Colruyt received 35 000 applications in 2003, of which 2250 people were actually recruited. HR director Tony Verlinden: 'We start from the idea that people cannot be motivated, that is too superficial. People, however, have a natural tendency to contribute something. They will do this particularly when they feel involved and have the feeling they are necessary.' Colruyt has several strategies to create and stimulate this involvement. Employees receive as much information as possible on the company's strategy and they are encouraged to think about it themselves (e.g. work methods to improve efficiency). Every morning, all employees of the different stores are informed about the turnover of the previous day and they receive an explanation about the pricing and work strategy of the store. Degrees are not important in Colruyt. Every new employee starts at the lowest level and can climb up with the necessary effort. To help people in their careers, a large range of courses are available, from language courses to wine and IT lessons. Because of the many different nationalities among employees, regular workshops on cultural diversity and intercultural communication are provided to improve co-operation and team work. Every employee also gets courses in ergonomics and work simplification. All employees are polyvalent. Everybody has different tasks in a rotation system. This variety is motivating and counters boredom.[46]

Organisational commitment reflects the extent to which one identifies oneself with an organisation and is committed to its goals. It is an important work attitude because committed people are expected to display a willingness to work harder to achieve organisational goals and a greater desire to stay in an organisation. Research distinguishes between three different facets of organisational commitment: affective commitment (i.e. people's emotional attachment to, involvement in and identification with the organisation), continuance commitment (i.e. people's consideration of the benefits of organisational membership and the perceived costs of leaving) and normative commitment (i.e. people's commitment based on a sense of obligation to the organisation).[47] A meta-analysis of 68 studies and 35 282 individuals uncovered a significant and strong relationship between organisational commitment and satisfaction.[48] Organisations are advised to increase job satisfaction in order to elicit higher levels of commitment. In turn, higher organisational commitment can facilitate higher productivity.[49] Organisational commitment is also negatively related to absenteeism and turnover.[50] However, more commitment is not always better. For instance, very high commitment can lead to situations where people do not report unethical practices or, even worse, commit unethical and illegal acts themselves. Also, if low performers have very high organisational commitment, they will not easily leave the organisation.

Job involvement represents the extent to which an individual is personally involved with his or her work role. While organisational commitment refers to identification with one's organisation, job involvement refers to the extent one identifies with its specific job. A meta-analysis involving 27 925 individuals from 87 different studies demonstrated that job involvement was moderately related to job satisfaction.[51] High levels of job involvement also lead to lower absenteeism and turnover rates.[52] A recent study also found a positive relationship between job involvement and performance.[53] Organisations are thus encouraged to foster satisfying work environments in order to fuel employees' job involvement. However, overly high levels of job involvement may not always be desirable. 'Workaholics' neglect their family and private lives and may suffer from health problems.

Job satisfaction is an affective or emotional response toward various facets of one's job. It refers to the degree of fulfilment and pleasure one finds in one's job. In other words, job satisfaction is the general attitude one has towards one's job. Several factors may enhance job satisfaction (like need fulfilment, value attainment or met expectations). Job satisfaction in its turn influences several

Organisational commitment the extent to which one identifies oneself with an organisation and is committed to its goals

Job involvement the extent to which one is personally involved with his or her work role

Job satisfaction general attitude one has towards one's job

aspects of organisational life (like performance, motivation, organisational citizenship behaviour . . .). A lot of research and models on job satisfaction exists. We end this section on attitudes with elaborating further on job satisfaction as it is an important organisational variable and one of the most frequently studied attitudes by OB researchers.

Job satisfaction

The above description of job satisfaction already indicates that job satisfaction is a complex and multifaceted concept. A person can be relatively satisfied with one aspect of his or her job and dissatisfied with another. Different people are also satisfied or dissatisfied with different aspects of their jobs. It seems that there is no general, comprehensive theory that explains job satisfaction so far.

It is also difficult to measure job satisfaction objectively. Researchers do not agree whether job satisfaction contains one single dimension or several. Researchers at Cornell University in the US developed the Job Descriptive Index (JDI), the best-known scale to assess one's satisfaction, with the following job dimensions: work, pay, promotions, co-workers and supervision.[54] Researchers at the US University of Minnesota developed the Minnesota Satisfaction Questionnaire (MSQ) and concluded that there are 20 different dimensions underlying job satisfaction.[55] Other researchers use a single global rating to measure people's job satisfaction, like 'all elements included, how satisfied are you with your job?'. People are asked to indicate a number between one and five, ranging from 'very dissatisfied' to 'very satisfied'. Research indicates that both a questionnaire measuring several facets and one overall measure of job satisfaction seem to be valid and accurate.[56]

DETERMINANTS OF JOB SATISFACTION

Job satisfaction is influenced by a several individual, social, organisational and cultural variables. Five predominant models of job satisfaction specify its causes. The first four models support a situational perspective, which means they see job satisfaction largely as a function of environmental influences. The last model adheres to a dispositional perspective and sees job satisfaction as a function of individual factors. A brief review of these models will provide insight into the complexity of this seemingly simple concept:[57]

- *Need fulfilment.* These models propose that satisfaction is determined by the extent to which the characteristics of a job allow an individual to fulfil his or her needs (also see sources of motivation in Chapter 5). For example, a recent survey of 30 law firms revealed that 35 to 50 per cent of law-firm associates left their employers within three years of starting because the firms did not accommodate family needs. This example illustrates that unmet needs can affect both satisfaction and turnover.[58] Although these models generated a great degree of controversy, it is generally accepted that need fulfilment is correlated with job satisfaction.[59]
- *Discrepancies.* These models propose that satisfaction is a result of met expectations. Met expectations represent the difference between what an individual expects to receive from a job, such as good pay and promotional opportunities, and what he or she actually receives. When expectations are greater than what is received, a person will be dissatisfied. In contrast, this model predicts the individual will be satisfied when he or she attains outcomes above and beyond expectations. A meta-analysis of 31 studies, which included 17 241 people, demonstrated that met expectations were significantly related to job satisfaction.[60] Many companies use employee attitude or opinion surveys to assess employees' expectations and concerns.
- *Value attainment.* The idea underlying value attainment is that satisfaction results from the perception that a job allows for fulfilment of an individual's important work values.[61] In general, research consistently supports the prediction that value attainment is positively related to job satisfaction.[62] Organisations can thus enhance employee satisfaction by structuring the work environment and its associated rewards and recognition to reinforce employees' values.
- *Equity.* In this model, satisfaction is a function of how 'fairly' an individual is treated at work. Satisfaction results from one's perception that work outcomes, relative to inputs, compare favourably to those of a significant other. A meta-analysis involving 190 studies and 64 757 people supported this model. Employees' perceptions of being treated fairly at work related strongly to overall job satisfaction.[63] Chapter 6 explores this promising model in more detail (equity theory).

■ *Dispositional/genetic components.* Have you ever noticed that some of your co-workers or friends appear to be satisfied across a variety of job circumstances, whereas others always seem dissatisfied? This model of satisfaction attempts to explain this pattern.[64] Specifically, the dispositional/genetic model is based on the belief that job satisfaction is partly a function both of personal traits and genetic factors. It suggests that stable individual differences are just as important in explaining job satisfaction as characteristics of the work environment. Although only a few studies have tested these propositions, results support a positive, significant relationship between personal traits and job satisfaction over time periods ranging from 2 to 50 years.[65] Genetic factors were also found to be significant in predicting life satisfaction, well-being and general job satisfaction.[66] Overall, researchers estimate that 30 per cent of an individual's job satisfaction is associated with dispositional and genetic components.[67]

CONSEQUENCES OF JOB SATISFACTION

This area has significant practical implications because thousands of studies have examined the relationship between job satisfaction and other organisational variables. It is impossible, however, to examine them all, so we will consider a subset of the more important variables from the standpoint of practical relevance.

Table 3.3 summarises the pattern of results. The relationship between job satisfaction and these other variables is either positive or negative. The strength of the relationship ranges from weak to strong. Strong relationships imply that organisations can significantly influence that particular variable by increasing job satisfaction. Because of the complexity and broadness of the concept of job satisfaction, there is no one panacea for organisations to improve the job satisfaction of their employees. Rather, it is advised to make use of aspects in several chapters of this book to enhance facets of people's satisfaction (like feedback, rewards systems, participation, coaching, etc.).

TABLE 3.3 CORRELATES OF JOB SATISFACTION

Variables related with job satisfaction	Direction of relationship	Strength of relationship
Motivation	Positive	Moderate
Organisational citizenship behaviour	Positive	Moderate
Absenteeism	Negative	Weak
Tardiness	Negative	Weak
Withdrawal cognitions	Negative	Strong
Turnover	Negative	Moderate
Heart disease	Negative	Moderate
Perceived stress	Negative	Strong
Pro-union voting	Negative	Moderate
Job performance	Positive	Moderate
Life satisfaction	Positive	Moderate
Mental health	Positive	Moderate

Let us now consider some of the key correlates of job satisfaction. Throughout the book, more research on job satisfaction will be dealt with:

■ *Motivation.* A recent meta-analysis of nine studies and 2237 workers revealed a significant positive relationship between motivation and job satisfaction. Because satisfaction with supervision was also significantly correlated with motivation, supervisors are advised to consider how their behaviour affects employee satisfaction.[68] They can potentially enhance employees' motivation through various attempts to increase job satisfaction. Motivation theories are elaborated in Chapters 5 and 6.

■ *Absenteeism.* Absenteeism is costly and organisations are constantly on the lookout for ways to reduce it. One recommendation has been to increase job satisfaction. If this is a valid recommendation, there should be a strong negative relationship (or negative correlation) between satisfaction and absenteeism. In other words, as satisfaction increases, absenteeism should decrease.

A researcher investigated this prediction by synthesising three separate meta-analyses containing a total of 74 studies. Results revealed a weak negative relationship between satisfaction and absenteeism.[69] This result indicates that other factors also play an important role in explaining the relationship between absenteeism and job satisfaction. It is unlikely, therefore, that organisations will realise any significant decrease in absenteeism by increasing job satisfaction.

■ *Withdrawal cognitions.* Although some people quit their jobs impulsively or on a fit of anger, most go through a process of thinking about whether or not they should quit.[70] **Withdrawal cognitions** encapsulate this thought process by representing an individual's overall thoughts and feelings about quitting. What causes an individual to think about quitting his or her job? Job satisfaction is believed to be one of the most significant contributors. For example, a recent study of managers, salespeople and auto mechanics from a national automotive retail store chain demonstrated that job dissatisfaction caused employees to begin the process of thinking about quitting. In turn, withdrawal cognitions had a greater impact on employee turnover than job satisfaction in this sample.[71] Results from this study imply that organisations can indirectly try to reduce employee turnover by enhancing job satisfaction.

■ *Turnover.* Turnover is important to organisations because it both disrupts organisational continuity and is very costly. Although there are many things organisations can do to reduce employee turnover, many of them revolve around attempts to improve employees' job satisfaction.[72] This trend is supported by results from a meta-analysis of 67 studies covering 24 556 people. Job satisfaction obtained a moderate negative relationship with employee turnover.[73] Given the strength of this relationship, organisations are advised to try to reduce turnover by increasing employee job satisfaction. Other factors, however, also have a role in actually leaving an organisation, like labour-market conditions, expectations towards another job or organisational commitment.

■ *Job performance.* One of the biggest controversies within organisational research centres on the relationship between satisfaction and job performance. Although researchers have identified seven different ways in which these variables are related, the dominant beliefs are either that satisfaction causes performance or that performance causes satisfaction.[74] A team of researchers recently attempted to resolve this controversy through a meta-analysis of data from 312 samples involving 54 417 individuals.[75] First, job satisfaction and performance are moderately related. This is an important finding because it supports the belief that job satisfaction is a key work attitude organisations should consider when attempting to increase employees' job performance. Second, the relationship between job satisfaction and performance is much more complex than was originally thought. It is not as simple as satisfaction causing performance or performance causing satisfaction. Instead, researchers now believe both variables indirectly influence each other through a host of individual and work-environment characteristics.[76] There is one additional consideration to keep in mind regarding the relationship between job satisfaction and job performance.

Researchers believe that the relationship between satisfaction and performance is understated because of incomplete measures of individual-level performance. For example, if performance ratings used in past research did not reflect the actual interactions and interdependencies at work, inaccurate measures of performance served to lower the reported correlations between satisfaction and performance. Examining the relationship between aggregate measures of job satisfaction and organisational performance is one solution to correct this problem.[77] In support of these ideas, a team of researchers conducted a meta-analysis of 7939 business units in 36 companies. Results uncovered significant positive relationships between business-unit-level employee satisfaction and business-unit outcomes of customer satisfaction, productivity, profit, employee turnover and accidents.[78] It thus appears that organisations can positively affect a variety of important organisational outcomes, including performance, by increasing employee satisfaction.

Emotions

In the ideal world of organisation theory, employees pursue organisational goals in a logical and rational manner. Emotional behaviour seldom appears in the equation. The myth of rationality that reigned for long time in organisations caused emotions to be long banished in organisational life.[79]

Withdrawal cognitions overall thoughts and feelings about quitting a job

However, creating emotion-free organisations is not possible. Day-to-day organisational life shows us how prevalent and powerful emotions can be. Anger and jealousy, both potent emotions, often push aside logic and rationality in the workplace. Professionals use fear and other emotions both to motivate and to intimidate.[80]

In this final section, our examination of individual differences turns to emotions. Several related terms and conceptualisations on this matter exist, like emotions, moods and affect.[81] Emotions are usually feelings directed to something or someone, so they are object-specific. For instance, you are angry at someone or happy about something. By contrast, moods are not directed to a certain object and are less intense. They are context free, rather general affective states. Affect refers to the broad range of feelings people experience, covering both emotions and moods.

We first define emotions by reviewing a typology of 10 positive and negative emotions and focus then on emotional intelligence. We conclude with three themes that are particularly relevant to deal with in organisational behaviour: emotional influencing, flow and the management of anger.

Defining emotions

Richard Lazarus, a leading authority on the subject, defines **Emotions** as 'complex, patterned, organismic reactions to how we think we are doing in our lifelong efforts to survive and flourish and to achieve what we wish for ourselves'.[82] The word 'organismic' is appropriate because emotions involve the whole person – biological, psychological and social. Significantly, psychologists draw a distinction between felt and displayed emotions.[83] **Felt emotions** are people's actual or true emotions, while **Displayed emotions** refer to emotions that are organisationally desirable and appropriate in a given job. For example, a person might feel angry (felt emotion) at a rude co-worker but not make a nasty remark in return (displayed emotion). As will be discussed in Chapter 7, emotions play roles in both causing and adapting to stress and its associated biological and psychological problems. The destructive effect of emotional behaviour on social relationships is all too obvious in daily life.

Lazarus's definition of emotions centres on a person's goals. Accordingly, his distinction between positive and negative emotions is goal oriented. Some emotions are triggered by frustration and failure when pursuing one's goals. Lazarus calls these negative emotions. They are said to be goal incongruent. For example, which of the six negative emotions in Figure 3.3 are you likely to experience if you fail the final exam in a required course? Failing the exam would be incongruent with your goal of graduating on time. On the other hand, which of the four positive emotions in Figure 3.3 would you probably experience if you graduated on time and with honours? The emotions you would experience in this situation are positive because they are congruent (or consistent) with an important lifetime goal.

The individual's goals, it is important to note, may or may not be socially acceptable. Thus, a positive emotion, such as love/affection, may be undesirable if associated with sexual harassment (sexual harassment is discussed in Chapter 9). Conversely, slight pangs of guilt, anxiety and envy can motivate extra effort. On balance, the constructive or destructive nature of a particular emotion must be judged in terms of both its intensity and the person's relevant goal.

Quotes like 'he is a real optimist, he sees everything in a positive way' or 'she is always negative, she is a pessimist', indicate that emotions are not changing from day to day. Although short-term variations and fluctuations occur, people seem to have underlying stable, fairly constant and predictable moods and emotional states.[84] Some people have a higher degree of **Positive affectivity**, often referred to as optimists. These people are relatively optimistic and upbeat, see things usually in a positive light and have an overall sense of well-being. People with a higher degree of **Negative affectivity** are generally pessimistic and downbeat, usually see things in a negative way and seem to be in a bad mood all the time. Of course, negative events like being fired or missing a promotion may cause optimists to be in a bad mood. Or positive events like receiving positive feedback or being promoted may cause pessimists to be in a good mood. However, after the initial impact of these events, people generally seem to return to their normal positive or negative mood respectively.

People's moods and affectivity are expected to influence organisational behaviour and performance. Many studies, for instance, investigate the notion that happy workers are also productive workers. This means, they study the relationship between affective states and work-related outcomes.[85] Results of these studies are not very clear and unequivocal. A study among 132 civil service employees shows that people scoring highly on optimism tend to be in jobs characterised by high

Emotions
complex human reactions to personal achievements and setbacks

Felt emotion
a person's actual or true emotion

Displayed emotion
organisationally desirable and appropriate emotion in a given job or situation

Positive affectivity
tendency to experience positive emotional states

Negative affectivity
tendency to experience negative emotional states

FIGURE 3.3 POSITIVE AND NEGATIVE EMOTIONS

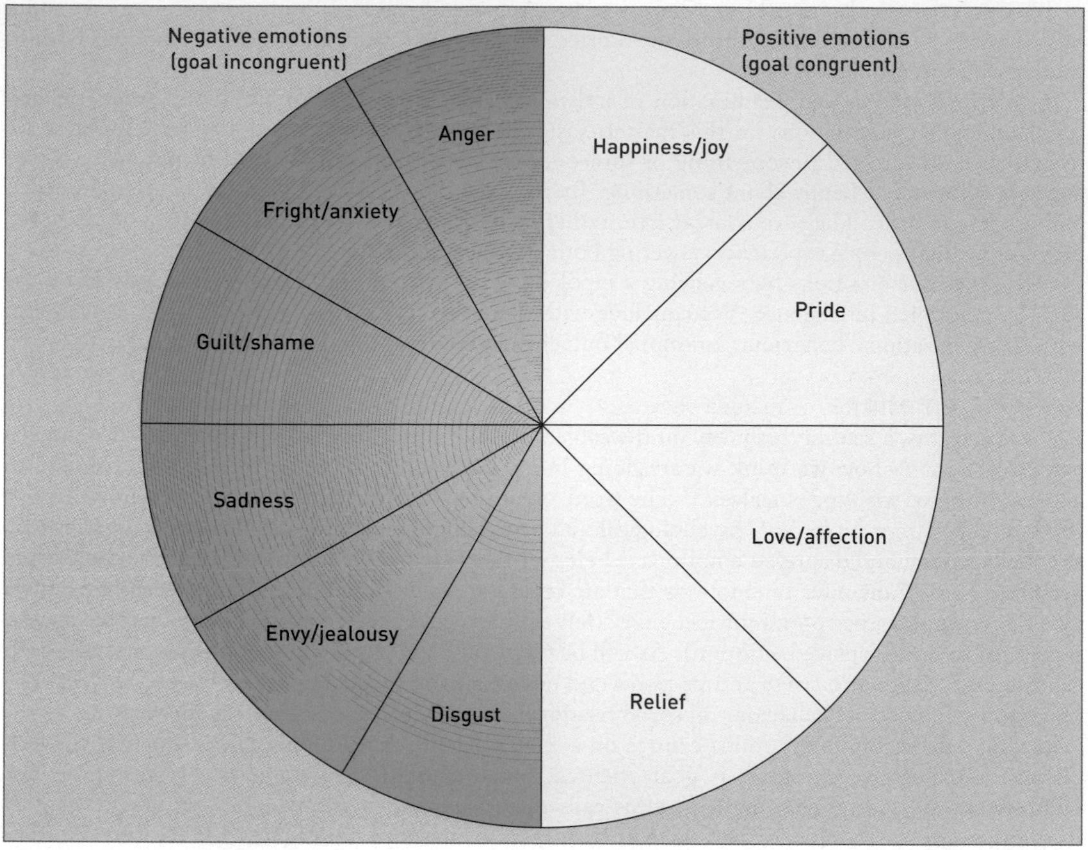

Negative emotions (goal incongruent): Anger, Fright/anxiety, Guilt/shame, Sadness, Envy/jealousy, Disgust

Positive emotions (goal congruent): Happiness/joy, Pride, Love/affection, Relief

SOURCE: Adapted from discussion in R. S. Lazarus, *Emotion and Adaptation* (New York: Oxford University Press, 1991).

levels of autonomy, variety, identity, feedback, significance and complexity.[86] People scoring highly on trait anxiety are found in jobs that have low levels of all these job characteristics. This indicates that people with certain personality traits can be found in certain types of jobs. The next Activity helps you to find out whether you are an optimist or rather a pessimist.

Emotional intelligence

When we discussed intelligence and mental abilities (Chapter 2), criticisms of the IQ concept were already being levelled. Traditional models of intelligence (IQ) were too narrow, because they failed to consider interpersonal competence. One of the expansions of intelligence research beyond mental abilities is the concept of emotional intelligence. Emotional intelligence has its roots in the concept of 'social intelligence', first defined by Thorndike in the 1920s. In 1995 Daniel Goleman, a psychologist, created a stir in education and management circles with the publication of his book *Emotional Intelligence*.[87] Hence, an obscure topic among psychologists has become a popular topic among the general public. Emotional intelligence (referred to as EQ or EI) is according to Goleman more important in understanding people than general intelligence. His broader approach (emotional intelligence) includes 'abilities such as being able to motivate oneself and persist in the face of frustrations; to control impulse and delay gratification; to regulate one's moods and keep distress from swamping the ability to think; to empathise and to hope'.[88] In other words, **Emotional intelligence** is the ability to manage your own emotions and those of others in mature and constructive ways. Emotional intelligence is said to have four key components: self-awareness, self-management, social awareness and relationship management. The first two components are referred to as 'personal'

Emotional intelligence ability to manage your own emotions and those of others in mature and constructive ways

106

Are you an optimist or a pessimist?

Instructions

Indicate for each of the following items to what extent you agree or disagree with them.

	Totally disagree			Totally agree	
1 In uncertain times, I usually expect the best.	1	2	3	4	5
2 It's easy for me to relax.	1	2	3	4	5
3 If something can go wrong for me, it will.	5	4	3	2	1
4 I always look on the bright side of things.	1	2	3	4	5
5 I'm always optimistic about my future.	1	2	3	4	5
6 I enjoy my friends a lot.	1	2	3	4	5
7 It's important for me to keep busy.	1	2	3	4	5
8 I hardly ever expect things to go my way.	5	4	3	2	1
9 Things never work out the way I want them to.	5	4	3	2	1
10 I don't get upset too easily.	1	2	3	4	5
11 I'm a believer in the idea that 'every cloud has a silver lining'.	1	2	3	4	5
12 I rarely count on good things happening to me.	5	4	3	2	1
13 Overall, I expect more good things to happen to me than bad.	1	2	3	4	5

Scoring key

Total your score:

Add the numbers you indicated for questions 1, 3, 4, 5, 8, 9, 11, 12 and 13.

Scoring norms

9–18 = Low optimism

19–35 = Moderate optimism

36 and above = High optimism

SOURCE: Excerpted and adapted from Table 1 of M. F. Scheier and C. S. Carver, 'Optimism, Coping, and Health: Assessment and Implications of Generalized Outcome Expectancies', *Health Psychology*, May 1985, p. 225; and Table 1 of M. F. Scheier, C. S. Carver and M. W. Bridges, 'Distinguishing Optimism from Neuroticism (and Trait Anxiety, Self-Mastery, and Self-Esteem): A Reevaluation of the Life Orientation Test', *Journal of Personality and Social Psychology*, December 1994, p. 1066. Copyright © 1994 by the American Psychological Association. Adapted with permission.

competence (those abilities that determine how we manage ourselves), while the last two are referred to as 'social' competence (those abilities that determine how we manage relationships) (see Table 3.4).

The components listed in Table 3.4 constitute a challenging self-development agenda for each of us.[89] Goleman[90] and other researchers[91] believe a greater emotional intelligence can boost individual, team and organisational effectiveness. Of course, stimulating and enhancing people's emotional intelligence needs intensive coaching, feedback and practice. Emotional intelligence usually increases with age, as part of a maturity process. Gradually, tests to measure emotional intelligence are also being developed.[92]

However, there are also some critical voices. Sometimes the validity and reliability of tests that are used to measure emotional intelligence are called into question.[93] Charles Woodruffe even questions the usefulness and newness of the emotional intelligence concept itself and states that its contribution to job performance has been exaggerated. He states that the concept 'emotional intelligence' is 'nothing more than a new brand name for a set of long-established competencies'.[94]

Although several theoretical models of emotional intelligence currently exist, Goleman's theory is the most widely known. Mayer and Salovey, for instance, developed another model of emotional intelligence.[95] They distinguish between four emotion-related abilities that move in their model from more basic toward more complex abilities: from perceiving and expressing emotion, to assimilating emotion in thought, to understanding emotions and finally reflectively regulating emotions.

TABLE 3.4 DEVELOPING PERSONAL AND SOCIAL COMPETENCE THROUGH EMOTIONAL INTELLIGENCE

Personal competence	Social competence
Self-awareness ■ *Emotional self-awareness*: Reading one's own emotions and recognising their impact; using 'gut sense' to guide decisions ■ *Accurate self-assessment*: Knowing one's strengths and limits ■ *Self-confidence*: A sound sense of one's self-worth and capabilities	**Social awareness** ■ *Empathy*: Sensing others' emotions, understanding their perspective and taking active interest in their concerns ■ *Organisational awareness*: Reading the currents, decision networks and politics at the organisational level ■ *Service*: Recognising and meeting follower, client or customer needs
Self-management ■ *Emotional self-control*: Keeping disruptive emotions and impulses under control ■ *Transparency*: Displaying honesty and integrity; trustworthiness ■ *Adaptability*: Flexibility in adapting to changing situations or overcoming obstacles ■ *Achievement*: The drive to improve performance to meet inner standards of excellence ■ *Initiative*: Readiness to act and seize opportunities ■ *Optimism*: Seeing the upside in events	**Relationship management** ■ *Inspirational leadership*: Guiding and motivating with a compelling vision ■ *Influence*: Wielding a range of tactics for persuasion ■ *Developing others*: Bolstering others' abilities through feedback and guidance ■ *Change catalyst*: Initiating, managing and leading in a new direction ■ *Conflict management*: Resolving disagreements ■ *Building bonds*: Cultivating and maintaining a web of relationships ■ *Teamwork and collaboration*: Co-operation and team building

SOURCE: Based on D. Goleman, R. Boyatzis and A. McKee, *Primal Leadership: Realizing the Power of Emotional Intelligence* (Boston, MA: Harvard Business School Press, 2002), p. 39.

We conclude this section on emotions by elaborating on some emotional processes that can be particularly relevant to organisations. We focus on how people's emotions influence each other (emotional contagion and emotional labour), on how people can have optimal experience in their job (flow) and on how organisations can manage anger in the workplace.

Emotional influencing

Coinciding with the start of more research on emotions, studies on how emotions play a role in organisational life began. We focus on two related concepts: emotional contagion and emotional labour.

EMOTIONAL CONTAGION

One process through which people influence each other (un)consciously in organisations is emotional contagion.[96] **Emotional contagion** is defined as 'the tendency to automatically mimic and synchronise facial expressions, vocalisations, postures and movements with those of another person and, consequently, to converge emotionally'.[97] We can, quite literally, catch other people's bad/good mood or displayed negative/positive emotions. An illustrative image to clarify what emotional contagion is, is 'the ripple effect'. As water ripples in a lake because of the wind, emotions can ripple through people, groups and organisations. Which mechanisms are involved in emotional contagion is not clearly known yet. Perceiving and (unconsciously) adopting other people's facial expressions seems to be important.[98] It seems that we, through the unconscious imitation of the facial expressions, gestures and other non-verbal signals of other people, internally also recreate the feelings they express. The person who expresses his or her emotion the strongest, influences the emotions of the other(s) in the interaction.

Emotional contagion emotional influencing process, by which people catch the feelings of others

More important than knowing how emotional contagion works exactly, is being aware that it exists and understanding its influence on organisational life. Several studies investigate the influence of emotional contagion in organisations.[99] A recent study among 131 bank tellers and 220 exit interviews with their customers revealed that tellers who expressed positive emotions tended to have more satisfied customers.[100] Two field studies with nurses and accountants found a strong linkage between the work group's collective mood and the individual's mood.[101] Research also found that spreading positive feelings improved co-operation, decreased conflict and increased task performance in group work.[102] These findings indicate the importance of using emotional contagion effectively to improve organisational behaviour and performance. Goleman elaborates five competencies in which the effective use of the emotions of other people (or the principle of emotional contagion) is essential:[103]

- *Influencing.* The effective use of influencing tactics is based on inducing certain feelings in other people – for instance, enthusiasm for a project or the passion to outdo a competitor (see further Chapter 13).
- *Communication.* Sending clear and convincing messages starts with the ability to know what others feel about something, how they will react and adapting your message accordingly (see Chapter 8).
- *Conflict management.*[104] Negotiating and solving conflicts is to a large extent a process of emotional influencing rather than a pure rational process (see further Chapter 13).
- *Leadership.*[105] Inspiring and coaching employees is based on the effective communication of feelings in a two-way direction (see Chapter 11).
- *Change management.*[106] The effective communication and implementation of change processes requires a high level of emotional appeal and influence to break down people's resistance (see Chapter 17).

EMOTIONAL LABOUR

Related to the study of emotional contagion is the recently developed research field dealing with how people manage their emotions in the workplace, known as 'emotional labour'.[107] The research on emotional labour first developed in relation to service jobs. **Emotional labour** refers to the effort, planning and control that are needed to express organisationally desired emotions during interpersonal interactions.[108] Emotional labour, for instance, implies expressing positive emotions, handling negative emotions, being sensitive to the emotions of clients and showing empathy. Organisations usually have certain (in)formal display rules. Display rules are norms that describe which emotions employees need to display and which emotions they need to withhold. Even when they feel bad, employees are told to 'smile, look happy for the customer'. This implies they sometimes have to fake and to mask their true feelings and emotions. Every employee has to undertake some emotional labour, for instance being friendly to co-workers. However, not all jobs require the same amount of emotional labour. People in jobs that require frequent and long durations of contact with clients, customers, suppliers, co-workers and others experience more emotional labour than others. Because of the importance of emotional labour for organisations, they provide their employees with training in expressing the appropriate, organisationally required emotions. Moreover, some organisations believe that the best way to support emotional labour is to hire people with the right attitude and skills (e.g. good customer service skills).

However, people still have difficulty in hiding their true or felt emotions all the time; this is particularly the case for anger. True emotions tend to leak out – for instance, as voice intonations or body movements. The conflict between felt (true) and displayed (required) emotions is called **Emotional dissonance**.[109] Of course, cultural differences exist concerning which emotions may or may not be displayed.[110] For instance, Japanese people think it is inappropriate to show emotions and to become emotional in business, while Americans are more likely to accept or tolerate people displaying their true emotions at work. Research did not find any gender differences in felt emotions, but women were found to be more emotionally expressive than men.[111]

Emotional labour
the effort, planning and control that is needed to express organisationally desired emotions during interpersonal interactions

Emotional dissonance
conflict between felt/actual and displayed/required emotions

Recently, the research lessons regarding emotional labour were summarised as follows:

> Emotional labour can be particularly detrimental to the employee performing the labour and can take its toll both psychologically and physically. Employees ... may bottle up feelings of frustration, resentment and anger; which are not appropriate to express. These feelings result, in part, from the constant requirement to monitor one's negative emotions and express positive ones. If not given a healthy expressive outlet, this emotional repression can lead to a syndrome of emotional exhaustion and burnout.[112]

A study among several groups of service workers (employees of service institutions, of the hotel business and call centres) led to the conclusion that the analysis of emotion work is a neglected area in organisational stress research that needs more attention in the future (also see Chapter 7). The data of the study suggest that emotion work is not *per se* either positive or negative. Rather, 'emotion display and sensitivity requirements are related to emotional exhaustion but also to personal accomplishment'.[113]

Flow in the workplace

Mihaly Csikszentmihalyi, an American psychologist of Hungarian origin, has studied the optimal experience for more than thirty years.[114] He is looking for the answer to the question: 'What makes some actions or activities worth pursuing for their own sake, even without any rational compensation?'. Csikszentmihalyi calls this optimal experience 'flow' (or 'autotelic enjoyment'). Research in sport contexts also calls this phenomenon 'peak performance'.[115]

According to Csikszentmihalyi, 'Flow is a subjective psychological state that occurs when one is totally involved in an activity. It is the state in which people are so involved in an activity that nothing else seems to matter. The experience itself is so enjoyable that people will do it even at great cost, for the sheer sake of doing it.'[116] Time seems to stop; hours pass by if it were only a few minutes.

Csikszentmihalyi studied people's flow experiences in order to understand more about their determinants and consequences. He developed the Experience Sampling Method (ESM) to measure people's quality of experience.[117] People receive an electronic pager (beeper) and a block of self-report forms with open-ended and scaled items (the Experience Sampling Form (ESF)). They keep this for a week and about 56 times at random intervals they are (by means of a signal) asked to describe their activity, feelings and experiences at that moment and to fill out some related questions. Csikszentmihalyi learned more about the characteristics of flow from people's descriptions. In interviews, people repeatedly mention certain key elements about their impressions of flow (Table 3.5).

A prerequisite to experience flow seems to be a match between people's perceived skills and the challenges they want to reach (i.e. attainable but challenging goals) (see also Chapter 6 on goal-setting theory).[118] In situations that are characterised by the simultaneous presence of high perceived challenges and high perceived skills, people may experience flow and the overall quality of the subjective experience is the highest. Challenges that are too low will lead to boredom and apathy, while too high challenges (in relation to people's perceived skills) may lead to stress and anxiety.

Flow is essentially a high level of concentration. The first step – being calm enough to start the activity – requires some discipline (think, for instance, about a top tennis-player who has to play an

Flow
a psychological state in which a person feels simultaneously cognitively efficient, motivated and happy

TABLE 3.5 CHARACTERISTICS OF FLOW

- There are clear goals every step of the way.
- There is immediate feedback to one's actions.
- There is a balance between challenges and skills.
- Action and awareness merge.
- Distractions are excluded from consciousness.
- There is no worry of failure.
- Self-consciousness disappears.
- The sense of time becomes distorted.
- The activity becomes an end in itself.

SOURCE: Based on M. Csikszentmihalyi, 'Happiness and Creativity', *The Futurist*, September–October 1997, pp. S8–S12.

important match or a professional who has to give an important presentation to the board of directors). Once the activity starts, attention tends to be focused and seems to take on a life on its own. For the moment people forget everything else going on in their lives and in the world and become totally involved in their current activity. Even if we started an activity with another intention, a characteristic of flow is that it becomes a goal in itself that intrinsically motivates us. That is why flow activities are also called autotelic activities ('auto' means self and 'telos' is the Greek word for goal). In an interview, the former Belgian tennis-player Dominique Van Roost-Monami (ex-Top 20) looks back on her career. The feelings described in the example clearly refer to a flow experience.

> Winning points is fantastic. There are matches where everything goes well; this really gives a 'kick'. You are in a kind of trance. It is only you and the ball, all the rest disappears. It does not even matter who is in front of you. You are calm, very concentrated and everything succeeds. Most of the times, you win such a match. It is a very addictive feeling. When you do not have this feeling when playing a match, you mostly lose. Over the years, you learn that the feeling will come back if you have enough faith in yourself.[119]

RESEARCH FINDINGS

Experiences of flow are found in studies with artists, musicians, mathematicians, athletes, rock climbers, surgeons, chess players, factory managers and workers, as well as in middle and high-level executives.[120] Flow seems to be a universal concept. It is found in all cultures, at all ages and in different social classes. People describe in a similar way how they felt during flow and also the reasons they give to explain their feelings are quite similar. Moreover, people's descriptions of flow during different kinds of activities seem to be fairly similar.

However, some people experience flow with a certain activity and others did not. Some people also experience more flow than others. Several researchers have studied the differences between people's flow experiences. They concluded that some people have characteristics or traits that stimulate the experience of flow, while others do not.[121] For instance, people who work primarily in order to be recognised and promoted will not experience flow. Paradoxically, people tend to do their best work and enjoy themselves in the process, when they forget about themselves and become involved in their current activity. People who do their job because they enjoy doing it, regardless of advancement, will be more likely to experience flow and achieve success. This is related to people's goal-orientation: people who have a task goal-orientation strive for learning and improvement, while people who have an ego goal-orientation emphasise winning, outperforming others and demonstrating ability.[122] People who are intrinsically motivated also seem to have a higher opportunity to experience flow than the ones who are more extrinsically motivated. Intrinsic motivation is related to a need for self-development and self-actualisation and to experiencing control over your own activities (see also Chapter 6).[123] Having a high perceived ability also seems to be related with experiencing flow.[124] Some people tend to feel confident about their skills and spend more time in flow, while others feel less confident and spend more time in stress and anxiety.

PRACTICAL IMPLICATIONS

Flow can be an important emotional process to stimulate in organisations as it has a positive influence on people's performance and well-being at work. Flow leads to higher productivity, motivation, creativity and satisfaction in people. People in flow also feel better at work and seem to be better 'equipped' to deal with stressful events (also see Chapter 7). Studies even found that flow might be contagious, so that people in flow pass this feeling through to others.[125]

Csikszentmihalyi formulates five 'C's' that are essential to maximise people's flow at the workplace:[126]

- *Clarity*. Make sure people have clear goals. This also means that people should know what they want to do and reach in their work and where they are already in relation to these goals. Formulating goals in terms of progress and outcomes and appropriate feedback methods are useful tools to enhance 'clarity'. In Chapter 6, more tips concerning goal setting and feedback are formulated.
- *Centre*. People should have an ability to focus. This means that they should be able to attend what needs to be the object of attention and what they need to do if they want to achieve a goal. People

should learn to focus only on the activity, on what they are doing here-and-now, and not, for instance, on themselves or what others might think of them.

■ *Choice*. People need to believe they control their life, that they have choices. This means they do not act as if they are victims of their environment. People should also trust in their strengths to reach their goals.

■ *Commitment*. This means that people should be able to commit themselves and their energy to whatever activity is needed to obtain their goals.

■ *Challenge*. As flow happens when there is a balance between people's skills and their challenges, people continuously and constantly need to seek new challenges and set new goals. People learn to match their challenges with their skills and also to develop the necessary skills to reach their challenges.

Every activity may lead to flow if the right elements are present (like clear goals, concentration, task-orientedness, commitment, challenges, focus and control). We can enhance the quality of our (work)life if we make sure the required conditions for flow are constantly present.

Managing anger

Of all the emotions in Figure 3.3, anger is the one most likely to be downright dangerous. It deserves special attention. Unchecked anger could be a key contributing factor to what one team of

TABLE 3.6 HOW TO MANAGE ANGER IN YOURSELF AND OTHERS

Reducing chronic anger [in Yourself]	Responding to angry provocation
Guides for action ■ Appreciate the potentially valuable lessons from anger ■ Use mistakes and slights to learn ■ Recognise that you and others can do well enough without being perfect ■ Trust that most people want to be caring, helpful family members and colleagues ■ Forgive others and yourself ■ Confront unrealistic, blame-oriented assumptions ■ Adopt constructive, learning-oriented assumptions	**Guides for action** ■ Expect angry people to exaggerate ■ Recognise the other's frustrations and pressures ■ Use the provocation to develop your abilities ■ Allow the other to let off steam ■ Begin to problem solve when the anger is at moderate levels ■ Congratulate yourself on turning an outburst into an opportunity to find solutions ■ Share successes with partners
Pitfalls to avoid ■ Assume every slight is a painful wound ■ Equate not getting what you want with catastrophe ■ See every mistake and slip as a transgression that must be a corrected immediately ■ Attack someone for you getting angry ■ Attack yourself for getting angry ■ Try to be and have things perfect ■ Suspect people's motives unless you have incontestable evidence that people can be trusted ■ Assume any attempt to change yourself is an admission of failure ■ Never forgive	**Pitfalls to avoid** ■ Take every word literally ■ Denounce the most extreme statements and ignore more moderate ones ■ Doubt yourself because the other does ■ Attack because you have been attacked ■ Forget the experience without learning from it

SOURCE: Reprinted with permission from D. Tjosvold, *Learning to Manage Conflict: Getting People to Work Together Productively*, pp. 127–9. Copyright © 1993 Dean Tjosvold. First published by Lexington Books.

researchers calls organisation-motivated aggression.[127] Worse, uncontrolled anger is certainly a contributor to workplace violence. As awareness of workplace violence increases, employers are installing various security systems and training employees to avoid or defuse incidents. The European Commission's definition of workplace violence includes 'incidents where persons are abused, threatened or assaulted in circumstances relating to their work, involving an explicit challenge to their safety, well-being and health'.[128] Anger-management training for all employees, based on the self-control tactics listed in Table 3.6, could make a positive contribution to reducing workplace violence and improving the general quality of work life.

Learning outcomes: Summary of key terms

1 Define values and explain their sources

Values are standards or criteria for choosing goals or guiding actions that are relatively enduring and stable over time. Although values are relatively enduring and stable, they can change during our life. Values develop through the influence of personality, society and culture. People are not born with an internal set of values. Values are acquired throughout our lives from diverse sources (e.g. parents, teachers, peers, work environment, national culture . . .).

2 Identify and describe Rokeach's instrumental and terminal values

Instrumental values refer to desirable ways or modes of conduct to reach some kind of desirable goal. Terminal values refer to the desirable goals a person wants to reach during his or her life. Instrumental and terminal values are connected with each other and work together to help people reach their desirable goals through desirable ways of conduct. Terminal values can be self-centred (personal) or society-centred (social). Instrumental values can be divided into moral and competence values. People differ in the extent to which they value personal or social values, as well as moral or competence values.

3 Explain Schwartz's basic human values model and his related work values model

Schwartz developed a theory of basic human values. He distinguishes ten types of values that are recognised by members of most societies and shows how these values are connected dynamically with each other by specifying which values are compatible and mutually supportive, and which values are conflicting and opposed. He situates the dynamics between these values in two underlying dimensions: self-transcendence versus self-enhancement and openness to change versus conservation. Parallel to the basic values model, Schwartz identified a model of work values. He distinguishes between intrinsic, extrinsic, social and prestige work values.

4 Explain how attitudes influence behaviour in terms of the model of planned behaviour

According to the model of planned behaviour, someone's intentions to engage in a given behaviour are the best predictor of that behaviour. Three separate but interrelated determinants influence one's intention (planned behaviour) to do something (actual behaviour). Behavioural intentions are influenced by one's attitude towards the behaviour, by perceived norms about exhibiting that behaviour and by perceived behavioural control. As a general rule, the more favourable the attitude and subjective norm and the greater the perceived behavioural control, the stronger an individual's intention to engage in certain behaviour. The relative importance of attitudes, subjective norms and perceived behavioural control in the prediction of intention is, however, expected to vary across situations and actions.

5 Describe three key work-related attitudes: organisational commitment, job involvement and job satisfaction

Organisational commitment reflects the extent to which an individual identifies oneself with an organisation and is committed to its goals. It is an important work attitude because committed people are expected to display a willingness to work harder to achieve organisational goals and a greater desire to stay in an organisation. Job involvement represents the extent to which an individual is personally involved with his or her work role. While organisational commitment refers to identification with one's organisation, job involvement refers to the extent one identifies with a specific job. Job satisfaction is an affective or emotional response toward various facets of one's job. It refers to the degree of fulfilment and pleasure one finds in his or her job. Job satisfaction is the general attitude one has towards one's job.

6 Discuss the determinants and consequences of job satisfaction
Five models specify the sources of job satisfaction. They are need fulfilment, discrepancy, value attainment, equity and trait/genetic components. Job satisfaction has been correlated with hundreds of consequences. Table 3.3 summarises the pattern of results found for a subset of the more important variables. Because of the complexity and broadness of the concept of job satisfaction, there is no one panacea for organisations to improve the job satisfaction of their employees. Rather, it is advisable to make use of several aspects to enhance facets of people's satisfaction (feedback, rewards systems, participation, coaching, etc.).

7 Distinguish between positive and negative emotions and explain how they can be judged
Positive emotions – happiness/joy, pride, love/affection and relief – are personal reactions to circumstances congruent with one's goals. Negative emotions – anger, fright/anxiety, guilt/shame, sadness, envy/jealousy and disgust – are personal reactions to circumstances incongruent with one's goals. Both types of emotions need to be judged in terms of intensity and the appropriateness of the person's relevant goal.

8 Define what emotional intelligence is and which components it implies
Emotional intelligence is the ability to manage your own emotions and those of others in mature and constructive ways. It includes such abilities as being able to motivate oneself and persist in the face of frustrations; to control impulse and delay gratification; to regulate one's moods and keep distress from swamping the ability to think; to empathise and to hope. Emotional intelligence has four key components: self-awareness, self-management, social awareness and relationship management. The first two components are referred to as 'personal' competence, while the last two are referred to as 'social' competence.

9 Focus on emotional contagion in the workplace
Emotional contagion refers to the process through which people catch the feelings of others. An illustrative image that clarifies what emotional contagion is, is 'the ripple effect'. As water ripples in a lake because of the wind, emotions can ripple through people, groups and organisations. Which mechanisms are involved in emotional contagion is not clearly known yet. Perceiving and (unconsciously) adopting other people's facial expressions seems to be important. Research findings indicate the importance of effectively using emotional contagion to improve organisational behaviour and performance.

10 Describe what flow is and how it influences organisational behaviour
Flow is a subjective psychological state that occurs when one is totally involved in an activity. It is the state in which people are so involved in an activity that nothing else seems to matter. The experience itself is so enjoyable that people will do it even at great cost, for the sheer sake of doing it. In situations that are characterised by the simultaneous presence of high perceived challenges and high perceived skills, people may experience flow. Flow can be an important emotional process to stimulate in organisations as it has a positive influence on people's performance and well-being at work. Flow leads to higher productivity, motivation, creativity and satisfaction in people. People in flow also seem to be better 'equipped' to deal with stressful events.

Review questions

1 Can you give an example of how your values influenced a choice you made?

2 How would you respond to a person who made this statement: 'I'm only interested in behaviour. I've never seen an attitude, so why be concerned with attitudes'?

3 Do you believe that job satisfaction is partly a function of both personal traits and genetic factors? Explain.

4 Do you think job satisfaction leads directly to better job performance? Explain.

5 What are your personal experiences of negative emotions being positive; and of positive emotions being negative?

6 What is your personal experience with emotions being contagious?

7 Have you ever experienced flow? In what situation(s)? How can you describe this experience?

Personal awareness and growth exercise

How satisfied are you with your present job?

Objectives

1 To assess your job satisfaction towards your present or last (student) job.

2 To stimulate reflection on your job satisfaction and how to enhance it.

Introduction

As mentioned in the text, researchers at the US University of Minnesota developed the Minnesota Satisfaction Questionnaire (MSQ) to measure job satisfaction. Selected Minnesota Satisfaction Questionnaire items – measuring satisfaction with recognition, compensation and supervision – are listed in this exercise.[129]

Instructions

Relative to your present or most recent job, indicate how satisfied you are with the following aspects.

	Very dissatisfied			Very satisfied	
1 The way I am noticed when I do a good job	1	2	3	4	5
2 The recognition I get for the work I do	1	2	3	4	5
3 The praise I get for doing a good job	1	2	3	4	5
4 How my pay compares with that for similar jobs in other companies	1	2	3	4	5
5 My pay and the amount of work I do	1	2	3	4	5
6 How my pay compares with that of other workers	1	2	3	4	5
7 The way my boss handles employees	1	2	3	4	5
8 The way my boss takes care of complaints brought to him/her by employees	1	2	3	4	5
9 The personal relationship between my boss and his/her employees	1	2	3	4	5

Scoring key

Total your score:

Add questions 1–3 for satisfaction with recognition.

Add questions 4–6 for satisfaction with compensation.

Add questions 7–9 for satisfaction with supervision.

Questions for discussion

1 Compare your scores with the following comparative norms for each dimension of job satisfaction:

3–6 = Low job satisfaction

7–11 = Moderate job satisfaction

12 and above = High job satisfaction

2 Do you recognise your score for each of the job satisfaction dimensions?

3 List possible solutions or ways to enhance your job satisfaction for each of the job satisfaction dimensions. Can you personally add a lot to increasing your job satisfaction or are you mainly dependent on your work environment?

Group exercise

Anger control role play

Objectives

1 To demonstrate that emotions can be managed.

2 To develop your interpersonal skills for managing both your own and someone else's anger.

Introduction

Personal experience and research tells us that anger begets anger. People do not make their best decisions when angry. Angry outbursts often inflict unintentional interpersonal damage by triggering other emotions (such as disgust in observers and subsequent guilt and shame in the angry person). Effective professionals know how to break the cycle of negative emotions by defusing anger in themselves and others. This is a role-playing exercise for groups of four. You will have a chance to play two different roles. All the roles are generic, so they can be played as either a woman or a man.

Instructions

Your lecturer will divide the class into groups of four. Everyone should read all five roles described. Members of each foursome will decide among themselves who will play which roles. All told, you will participate in two rounds of role playing (each round lasting no longer than 8 minutes). In the first round, one person will play Role 1 and another will play Role 3; the remaining two group members will play Role 5. In the second round, those who played Role 5 in the first round will play Roles 2 and 4. The other two will switch to Role 5.

ROLE 1: THE ANGRY (OUT-OF-CONTROL) SHIFT SUPERVISOR

You work for a leading electronics company that makes computer chips and other computer-related equipment. Your factory is responsible for assembling and testing the company's most profitable line of computer microprocessors. Business has been good, so your factory is working three shifts. The day shift, which you are now on, is the most desirable one. The night shift, from 11 p.m. to 7.30 a.m. is the least desirable and least productive. In fact, the night shift is such a mess that your boss, the factory manager, wants you to move to the night shift next week. Your boss just broke this bad news as the two of you are having lunch in the company cafeteria. You are shocked and angered because you are one of the most senior and highly rated shift supervisors in the factory. Thanks to your leadership, your shift has broken all production records during the past year. As the divorced single parent of a 10-year-old child, the radical schedule change would be a major lifestyle burden. Questions swirl through your head. 'Why me?' 'What kind of reliable child-care will be available when I sleep during the day and work at night?' 'Why should I be "punished" for being a top supervisor?' 'Why don't they hire someone for the position?' Your boss asks what you think.

When playing this role, be as realistic as possible without getting so loud that you disrupt the other groups. Also, if anyone in your group would be offended by foul language, please refrain from cursing during your angry outburst.

ROLE 2: THE ANGRY (UNDER-CONTROL) SHIFT SUPERVISOR
Although you will use the same situation as in Role 1, this role will require you to read and act according to the tips for reducing chronic anger in the left side of Table 3.6. You have plenty of reason to be frustrated and angry, but you realise the importance of maintaining a good working relationship with the factory manager.

ROLE 3: THE (HARD-DRIVING) FACTORY MANAGER
You have a reputation for having a 'short fuse'. When someone gets angry with you, you attack. When playing this role, be as realistic as possible. Remember, you are responsible for the entire factory with its 1200 employees and hundreds of millions of dollars of electronics products. A hiring freeze is in place, so you have to move one of your current supervisors. You have chosen your best supervisor because the night shift is your biggest threat to profitable operations. The night-shift supervisor gets a 10 per cent bonus. Ideally, the move will only be for six months.

ROLE 4: THE (MELLOW) FACTORY MANAGER
Although you will use the same general situation as in Role 3, this role will require you to read and act according to the tips for responding to angry provocation in the right side of Table 3.6. You have a reputation for being results-oriented but reasonable. You are good at taking a broad, strategic view of problems and are a good negotiator.

ROLE 5: SILENT OBSERVER
Follow the exchange between the shift supervisor and the factory manager without talking or getting actively involved. Jot down some notes (for later class discussion) as you observe whether or not the factory manager did a good job of managing the supervisor's anger.

Questions for discussion
1 Why is uncontrolled anger a sure road to failure?
2 Is it possible to express anger without insulting others? Explain.
3 Which is more difficult, controlling anger in yourself or defusing someone else's anger? Why?
4 What useful lessons have you learned from this role playing exercise?

 # Internet exercise

Lots of interactive questionnaires can be found on the internet to help you learn more about yourself. Note that these self-tests are for instructional and entertainment purposes only. They are not intended to replace rigorously validated and properly administered psychometric tests and should not be used to establish qualifications or make personnel decisions. Still, they can provide useful insights and stimulate discussion. The purpose of this exercise is to learn more about emotional intelligence (EQ). Go to our website www.mcgraw-hill.co.uk/textbooks/buelens, where you will find the homepage of an EQ test, further instructions and interpretation questions.

Notes

1 This case study is based on J. Schettler, 'Marcus Buckingham', *Training*, November 2001, p. 51; and T. Schwartz, 'The Greatest Sources of Satisfaction in the Workplace Are Internal and Emotional', *Fast Company*, November 2000.

2 L. Halman and T. Petterson, 'Individualization and Value Fragmentation', in *Values in Western Societies*, ed. R. De Moor (Tilburg: Tilburg University Press, 1995), pp. 297–316.

3 M. Waters, *Modern Sociological Theory* (London: Sage Publications, 1994), p. 309.

4 A. Giddens, *Modernity and Self-Identity* (Stanford, CA: Stanford University Press, 1991), p. 80.

5 R. Robertson, *Globalization: Social Theory and Global Culture* (London: Sage Publications, 1992), p. 8.

6 J. J. Dose, 'Work Values: An Integrative Framework and Illustrative Application to Organizational Socialization', *Journal of Occupational and Organizational Psychology*, September 1997, pp. 219–40.

7 M. Rokeach, *The Nature of Human Values* (New York: The Free Press, 1973), pp. 5–6.

8 M. Rokeach, *The Nature of Human Values* (New York: The Free Press, 1973), p. 5.

9 J. J. Dose, 'Work Values: An Integrative Framework and Illustrative Application to Organizational Socialization', *Journal of Occupational and Organizational Psychology*, September 1997, pp. 219–40.

10 L. M. Keller, T. J. Bouchard, Jr, R. D. Arvey, N. L. Segal and R. V. Dawis, 'Work Values: Genetic and Environmental Influences', *Journal of Applied Psychology*, February 1992, pp. 79–88.

11 For a description of this process, see M. Rokeach, *The Nature of Human Values* (New York: The Free Press, 1973), p. 6.

12 For more information on Rokeach's ideas and model, see M. Rokeach, *Beliefs, Attitudes and Values* (San Francisco, CA: Jossey-Bass, 1968); M. Rokeach, *The Nature of Human Values* (New York: The Free Press, 1973); and M. Rokeach, *Understanding Human Values* (New York: The Free Press, 1979).

13 For more information on this basic human values model and its origins, see S. H. Schwartz and W. Bilsky, 'Toward a Universal Psychological Structure of Human Values', *Journal of Personality and Social Psychology*, September 1987, pp. 550–62; S. H. Schwartz and W. Bilsky, 'Toward a Theory of the Universal Content and Structure of Values: Extensions and Cross-Cultural Replications', *Journal of Personality and Social Psychology*, May 1990, pp. 878–91; S. H. Schwartz, 'Universals in the Content and Structure of Values: Theoretical Advances and Tests in 20 Countries', in *Advances in Social Psychology, vol. 25*, ed. M. Zanna (Orlando, FL: Academic Press, 1992), pp. 1–65; S. H. Schwartz, 'Are There Universal Aspects in the Structure and Contents of Human Values?', *Journal of Social Issues*, Winter 1994, pp. 19–45; and S. H. Schwartz and L. Sagiv, 'Identifying Culture-Specifics in the Content and Structure of Values', *Journal of Cross-Cultural Psychology*, January 1995, pp. 92–116.

14 For extension on the shared orientations, see S. Schwartz, 'Value Priorities and Behavior: Applying a Theory of Integrated Value Systems', in *The Psychology of Values: The Ontario Symposium, vol. 8*, eds C. Seligman, J. M. Olson and M. P. Zanna (Mahwah, NJ: Lawrence Erlbaum Associates, 1996), p. 4. Also see S. H. Schwartz, 'Are There Universal Aspects in the Structure and Contents of Human Values?', *Journal of Social Issues*, Winter 1994, pp. 24–25.

15 For a more thorough discussion on the measurement models for values, see W. L. Rankin and J. W. Grube, 'A Comparison of Ranking and Rating Procedures for Value System Measurement', *European Journal of Social Psychology*, March 1980, pp. 233–46; S. H. Ng, 'Choosing between the Ranking and Rating Procedures for the Comparison of Values across Cultures', *European Journal of Social Psychology*, March 1982, pp. 169–72; D. F. Alwin and J. A. Krosnick, 'The Measurement of Values in Surveys: A Comparison of Ratings and Rankings', *Public Opinion Quarterly*, Winter 1985, pp. 535–52; and B. M. Meglino and E. C. Ravlin, 'Individual Values in Organizations: Concepts, Controversies, and Research', *Journal of Management*, May 1998, pp. 351–89.

16 M. Ros, S. H. Schwartz and S. Surkiss, 'Basic Individual Values, Work Values and the Meaning of Work', *Applied Psychology: An International Review*, January 1999, p. 54.

17 S. H. Schwartz, 'Are There Universal Aspects in the Structure and Contents of Human Values?', *Journal of Social Issues*, Winter 1994, p. 42.

18 P. C. Stern, T. Dietz and G. A. Guagnano, 'A Brief Inventory of Values', *Educational and Psychological Measurement*, December 1998, p. 985.

19 For more models on work values, see L. H. Lofquist and R. V. Dawis, 'Values as Second-Order Needs in the Theory of Work Adjustment', *Journal of Vocational Behavior*, February 1971, pp. 12–19; G. Hofstede, *Culture's Consequences: International Differences in Work-Related Values* (Beverly-Hills, CA: Sage Publications, 1980); G. Hofstede, *Culture and Organizations: Software of the Mind* (London: McGraw-Hill, 1991); D. Elizur, 'Facets of Work Values: A Structural Analysis of Life and Work Values', *Journal of Applied Psychology*, August 1984, pp. 379–89; B. M. Meglino, E. C. Ravlin and C. L. Adkins, 'A Work Value Approach to Corporate Culture: A Field Test of the Value Congruence Process and Its Relationship to Individual Outcomes', *Journal of Applied Psychology*, June 1989, pp. 424–32; D. Macnab and G. W. Fitzsimmons, 'A Multitrait-Multimethod Study of Work-Related Needs, Values, and Preferences', *Journal of Vocational Behavior*, August 1987, pp. 1–15; and D. E. Super and B. Sverko, *Life Roles, Values, and Careers: International Findings of the Work Importance Study* (San Francisco, CA: Jossey-Bass, 1995).

20 For studies that try to link work values and basic values, see D. Elizur, 'Work and Nonwork Relations: The

Conical Structure of Work and Home Life Relationship', *Journal of Organizational Behavior*, July 1991, pp. 313–22; R. A. Roe and P. Ester, 'Values and Work: Empirical Findings and Theoretical Perspective', *Applied Psychology: An International Review*, January 1999, pp. 1–21; M. Ros, S. H. Schwartz and S. Surkiss, 'Basic Individual Values, Work Values and the Meaning of Work', *Applied Psychology: An International Review*, January 1999, pp. 49–71; and D. Elizur and A. Sagie, 'Facets of Personal Values: A Structural Analysis of Life and Work Values', *Applied Psychology: An International Review*, January 1999, pp. 73–87.

21 For more details on Schwartz's work values model, see M. Ros, S. H. Schwartz and S. Surkiss, 'Basic Individual Values, Work Values and the Meaning of Work', *Applied Psychology: An International Review*, January 1999, pp. 49–71.

22 For examples of studies that identified two or three work values, see L. Dyer and D. Parker, 'Classifying Outcomes in Work Motivation Research: An Examination of the Intrinsic-Extrinsic Dichotomy', *Journal of Applied Psychology*, August 1975, pp. 455–8; D. Elizur, 'Facets of Work Values: A Structural Analysis of Life and Work Values', *Journal of Applied Psychology*, August 1984, pp. 379–89; and D. Elizur, I. Borg, R. Hunt and I. M. Beck, 'The Structure of Work Values: A Cross-Cultural Comparison', *Journal of Organizational Behavior*, January 1991, pp. 21–38.

23 Results of the 1990 European Value Study can be found in S. Ashford and N. Timms, *What Europe Thinks: A Study of Western European Values* (Aldershot: Dartmouth, 1992); and R. De Moor, *Values in Western Societies* (Tilburg: Tilburg University Press, 1995).

24 For more details on this study and other relevant research linking Schwartz's model with organisational behaviour, see S. Schwartz, 'Value Priorities and Behavior: Applying a Theory of Integrated Value Systems', in *The Psychology of Values: The Ontario Symposium, vol. 8*, eds C. Seligman, J. M. Olson and M. P. Zanna (Mahwah, NJ: Lawrence Erlbaum Associates, 1996), pp. 1–25.

25 For studies linking Schwartz's values model with pro-environmental behaviour, see P. C. Stern and T. Dietz, 'The Value Basis of Environmental Concern', *Journal of Social Issues*, Winter 1994, pp. 65–84; and D. G. Karp, 'Values and Their Effect on Pro-Environmental Behavior', *Environment and Behavior*, January 1996, pp. 111–33.

26 M. D. Mumford, W. B. Helton, B. P. Decker, M. S. Connelly and J. R. Van Doorn, 'Values and Beliefs Related to Ethical Decisions', *Teaching Business Ethics*, May 2003, pp. 139–70.

27 See, for instance, W. Bilsky and S. H. Schwartz, 'Values and Personality', *European Journal of Personality*, September 1994, pp. 163–81; and M. S. M. Yik and C. S. Tang, 'Linking Personality and Values: The Importance of a Culturally Relevant Personality Scale', *Personality and Individual Differences*, November 1996, pp. 767–74.

28 R. P. Claxton, R. P. McIntyre, K. E. Clow and J. E. Zemanek, Jr, 'Cognitive Style as a Potential Antecedent to Values', *Journal of Social Behavior and Personality*, March 1996, pp. 355–73.

29 For a more extensive overview of research linking work values with organisational behaviour aspects, see A. Sagie, D. Elizur and M. Kolowsky, 'Work Values: A Theoretical Overview and a Model of Their Effects', *Journal of Organizational Behavior*, December 1996, pp. 503–14; and B. M. Meglino and E. C. Ravlin, 'Individual Values in Organizations: Concepts, Controversies, and Research', *Journal of Management*, May 1998, pp. 351–89.

30 T. A. Judge and R. D. Bretz, 'Effects of Work Values on Job Choice Decisions', *Journal of Applied Psychology*, June 1992, pp. 261–71; and J. J. Dose, 'Work Values: An Integrative Framework and Illustrative Application to Organizational Socialization', *Journal of Occupational and Organizational Psychology*, September 1997, pp. 219–40.

31 D. Elizur, I. Borg, R. Hunt and I. M. Beck, 'The Structure of Work Values: A Cross-Cultural Comparison', *Journal of Organizational Behavior*, January 1991, pp. 21–38. For a recent study on cross-national differences in values, see T. Lenartowicz and J. P. Johnson, 'A Cross-National Assessment of the Values of Latin American Managers: Contrasting Hues or Shades of Gray?', *Journal of International Business Ethics*, May 2003, pp. 266–81.

32 M. Fishbein and I. Ajzen, *Belief, Attitude, Intention, and Behavior: An Introduction to Theory and Research* (Reading, MA: Addison-Wesley, 1975), p. 6.

33 For a discussion of the difference between values and attitudes, see M. Rokeach, *The Nature of Human Values* (New York: The Free Press, 1973).

34 For more information on the different aspects of attitudes, see A. P. Brief, *Attitudes In and Around Organizations* (Thousand Oaks, CA: Sage Publications, 1998), pp. 49–84.

35 See B. M. Staw and J. Ross, 'Stability in the Midst of Change: A Dispositional Approach to Job Attitudes', *Journal of Applied Psychology*, August 1985, pp. 469–80. Also see J. Schaubroeck, D. C. Ganster and B. Kemmerer, 'Does Trait Affect Promote Job Attitude Stability?', *Journal of Organizational Behavior*, March 1996, pp. 191–6.

36 Data from P. S. Visser and J. A. Krosnick, 'Development of Attitude Strength Over the Life Cycle: Surge and Decline', *Journal of Personality and Social Psychology*, December 1998, pp. 1389–410.

37 L. Festinger, *A Theory of Cognitive Dissonance* (Stanford, CA: Stanford University Press, 1957). See also A. J. Elliot and G. Devine, 'On the Motivational Nature of Cognitive Dissonance: Dissonance as Psychological Discomfort', *Journal of Personality and Social Psychology*, September 1994, pp. 382–94; B. Burnes and H. James, Culture, Cognitive Dissonance and the Management of Change', *International Journal of Operations and Production*, no. 8, 1995, pp. 14–33; E. Harmon-Jones and J. Mills, *Cognitive Dissonance Progress on a Pivotal Theory in Social Psychology* (Washington, DC: Braum Brumfield, 1999); and A. H. Goldsmith, S. Sedo, W. Darity,

Jr, and D. Hamilton, 'The Labor Supply Consequences of Perceptions of Employer Discrimination During Search and On-the-Job: Integrating Neoclassic Theory and Cognitive Dissonance', *Journal of Economic Psychology*, February 2004, pp. 15–39.

38 Several models and studies on the attitude–behaviour relationship exist, for instance S. J. Kraus, 'Attitudes and the Prediction of Behavior: A Meta-Analysis of the Empirical Literature', *Personality and Social Psychology Bulletin*, January 1995, pp. 58–75; M. Sverke and S. Kuruvilla, 'A New Conceptualization of Union Commitment: Development and Test of an Integrated Theory', *Journal of Organizational Behavior*, Special Issue 1995, pp. 505–32; and R. C. Thompson and J. G. Hunt, 'Inside the Black Box of Alpha, Beta and Gamma Change: Using a Cognitive Processing Model to Assess Attitude Structure', *Academy of Management Review*, July 1996, pp. 655–90.

39 For information on the previous model of Fishbein and Ajzen, see M. Fishbein and I. Ajzen, *Belief, Attitude, Intention, and Behavior: An Introduction to Theory and Research* (Reading, MA: Addison-Wesley, 1975); and I. Ajzen and M. Fishbein, *Understanding Attitudes and Predicting Social Behavior* (Englewood Cliffs, NJ: Prentice-Hall, 1980).

40 For a brief overview and update of the model, see I. Ajzen, 'The Theory of Planned Behaviour', *Organizational Behavior and Human Decision Processes*, December 1991, pp. 179–211; J. Doll and I. Ajzen, 'Accessibility and Stability of Predictors in the Theory of Planned Behavior', *Journal of Personality and Social Psychology*, November 1992, pp. 754–65; and I. Ajzen and M. Fishbein, 'Attitudes and the Attitude-Behavior Relation: Reasoned and Automatic Processes, in *European Review of Social Psychology*, eds W. Stroebe and M. Hewstone (New York: John Wiley, 2000), pp. 1–33.

41 See R. P. Steel and N. K. Ovalle II, 'A Review and Meta-Analysis of Research on the Relationship between Behavioral Intentions and Employee Turnover', *Journal of Applied Psychology*, November 1984, pp. 673–86. Also see J. A. Ouellette and W. Wood, 'Habit and Intention in Everyday Life: The Multiple Processes by Which Past Behavior Predicts Future Behavior', *Psychological Bulletin*, July 1998, pp. 54–74; R. J. Vandenberg and J. B. Nelson, 'Disaggregating the Motives Underlying Turnover Intentions: When Do Intentions Predict Turnover Behavior?', *Human Relations*, October 1999, pp. 1313–36; and A. Kirschenbaum and J. Weisberg, 'Employee's Turnover Intentions and Job Destination Choices', *Journal of Organizational Behavior*, February 2002, pp. 109–25.

42 Drawn from J. M. Grant and T. S. Bateman, 'An Experimental Test of the Impact of Drug-Testing Programs on Potential Job Applicants' Attitudes and Intentions', *Journal of Applied Psychology*, April 1990, pp. 127–31.

43 For data on attitude formation research, see I. Ajzen and M. Fishbein, *Understanding Attitudes and Predicting Social Behavior* (Englewood Cliffs, NJ: Prentice-Hall, 1980); and I. Ajzen, *Attitudes, Personality and Behaviour* (Chicago: Dorsey Press, 1988). Also see D. J. Canary and D. R. Seibold, *Attitudes and Behavior: An Annotated Bibliography* (New York: Praeger, 1984); S. Chaiken and C. Stangor, 'Attitudes and Attitude Change', in *Annual Review of Psychology*, eds M. R. Rosenzweig and L. W. Porter (Palo Alto, CA: Annual Reviews, 1987), pp. 575–630; and B. H. Sheppard, J. Hartwick and P. R. Warshaw, 'The Theory of Reasoned Action: A Meta-Analysis of Past Research with Recommendations for Modifications and Future Research', *Journal of Consumer Research*, December 1988, pp. 325–43.

44 See I. Ajzen, 'The Theory of Planned Behaviour', *Organizational Behavior and Human Decision Processes*, December 1991, p. 206. For research on the theory of planned behaviour, see for instance M. Fishbein and M. Stasson, 'The Role of Desires, Self-Predictions, and Perceived Control in the Prediction of Training Session Attendance', *Journal of Applied Social Psychology*, February 1990, pp. 173–98; I. Ajzen and B. L. Driver, 'Application of the Theory of Planned Behavior to Leisure Choice', *Journal of Leisure Research*, Third Quarter 1992, pp. 207–24; J. Reinecke, P. Schmidt and I. Ajzen, 'Application of the Theory of Planned Behavior to Adolescents' Condom Use: A Panel Study', *Journal of Applied Social Psychology*, May 1996, pp. 749–72; and K. A. Finlay, D. Trafimow and A. Villarreal, 'Predicting Exercise and Health Behavioral Intentions: Attitudes, Subjective Norms, and Other Behavioral Intentions', *Journal of Applied Social Psychology*, February 2002, pp. 342–58.

45 Based on evidence in C. J. Thomsen, A. M. Basu and M. Tippens Reinitz, 'Effects of Women's Studies Courses on Gender-Related Attitudes of Women and Men', *Psychology of Women Quarterly*, September 1995, pp. 419–26.

46 Based on and translated from V. Debruyne, 'Werken bij Colruyt: Fitness op roog niveau', *De Morgen*, 10 June 2004, p. 16.

47 J. P. Meyer and N. J. Allen, 'A Three-Component Conceptualization of Organizational Commitment', *Human Resource Management Review*, Spring 1991, pp. 61–89; and J. P. Meyer and N. L. Allen, *Commitment in the Workplace: Theory, Research, and Application* (Thousand Oaks, CA: Sage Publications, 1997).

48 See R. P. Tett and J. P. Meyer, 'Job Satisfaction, Organizational Commitment, Turnover Intention, and Turnover: Path Analysis Based on Meta-Analytic Findings', *Personnel Psychology*, Summer 1993, pp. 259–93.

49 See J. E. Mathieu and D. Zajac, 'A Review and Meta-Analysis of the Antecedents, Correlates, and Consequences of Organizational Commitment', *Psychological Bulletin*, September 1990, pp. 171–94; and M. Riketta, 'Attitudinal Organizational Commitment and Job Performance: A Meta-Analysis', *Journal of Organizational Behavior*, May 2002, pp. 257–66.

50 See R. T. Mowday, L. W. Porter and R. M. Steers, *Employee Organization Linkages: The Psychology of Commitment, Absenteeism, and Turnover* (New York: Academic Press, 1982); M. A. Huselid and N. E. Day, 'Organizational Commitment, Job Involvement, and Turnover: A Substantive and Methodological Analysis', *Journal of*

Applied Psychology, June 1991, pp. 380–91; M. J. Somers, 'Organizational Commitment, Turnover and Absenteeism: An Examination of Direct and Indirect Effects', *Journal of Organizational Behavior*, January 1995, pp. 49–58; M. Clugston, 'The Mediating Effects of Multidimensional Commitment on Job Satisfaction and Intent to Leave', *Journal of Organizational Behavior*, June 2000, pp. 477–86.

51 See S. P. Brown, 'A Meta-Analysis and Review of Organizational Research on Job Involvement', *Psychological Bulletin*, September 1996, pp. 235–55.

52 G. J. Blau and K. R. Boal, 'Conceptualizing How Job Involvement and Organizational Commitment Affect Turnover and Absenteeism', *Academy of Management Review*, April 1987, pp. 288–300; and A. Cohen, 'Organizational Commitment and Turnover: A Meta-Analysis', *Academy of Management Journal*, October 1993, pp. 1140–57.

53 M. Dieffendorp, D. J. Brown, A. M. Kamin and R. G. Lord, 'Examining the Roles of Job Involvement and Work Centrality in Predicting Organizational Citizenship Behaviors and Job Performance', *Journal of Organizational Behavior*, February 2002, pp. 93–108.

54 For a review of the development of the JDI, see P. C. Smith, L. M. Kendall and C. L. Hulin, *The Measurement of Satisfaction in Work and Retirement* (Skokie, IL: Rand McNally, 1969).

55 For norms on the MSQ, see D. J. Weiss, R. V. Dawis, G. W. England and L. H. Lofquist, *Manual for the Minnesota Satisfaction Questionnaire* (Minneapolis: Industrial Relations Center, University of Minnesota, 1967).

56 See J. Wanous, A. E. Reichers and M. J. Hudy, 'Overall Job Satisfaction: How Good Are Single-Item Measures?', *Journal of Applied Psychology*, April 1997, pp. 247–52; and T. Oshagbemi, 'Overall Job Satisfaction: How Good Are Single versus Multiple-Item Measures?', *Journal of Managerial Psychology*, October 1999, pp. 388–403.

57 For a review of these models, see A. P. Brief, *Attitudes In and Around Organizations* (Thousand Oaks, CA: Sage Publications, 1998).

58 See A. R. Karr, 'Work Week: A Special News Report about Life on the Job – And Trends Taking Shape There', *The Wall Street Journal*, 29 June 1999, p. A1.

59 For a review of need satisfaction models, see E. F. Stone, 'A Critical Analysis of Social Information Processing Models of Job Perceptions and Job Attitudes', in *Job Satisfaction: How People Feel about Their Jobs and How It Affects Their Performance*, eds C. J. Cranny, P. Cain Smith and E. F. Stone (New York: Lexington Books, 1992), pp. 21–52.

60 See J. P. Wanous, T. D. Poland, S. L. Premack and K. S. Davis, 'The Effects of Met Expectations on Newcomer Attitudes and Behaviors: A Review and Meta-Analysis', *Journal of Applied Psychology*, June 1992, pp. 288–97; P. G. Irving and J. P. Meyer, 'Re-Examination of the Met-Expectations Hypothesis: A Longitudinal Analysis', *Journal of Applied Psychology*, December 1994, pp. 937–49; P. W. Hom, R. W. Griffeth, L. E. Palich and J. S. Bracker, 'Revisiting Met Expectations as a Reason Why Realistic Job Previews Work', *Personnel Psychology*, Spring 1999, pp. 97–112; and W. H. Turnley and D. C. Feldman, 'Re-Examining the Effects of Psychological Contract Violations: Unmet Expectations and Job Satisfaction as Mediators', *Journal of Organizational Behavior*, January 2000, pp. 25–42.

61 A complete description of this model is provided by E. A. Locke, 'Job Satisfaction', in *Social Psychology and Organizational Behavior*, eds M. Gruneberg and T. Wall (New York: John Wiley, 1984), pp. 93–117.

62 For a test on value attainment, see W. A. Hochwarter, P. L. Perrewe, G. R. Ferris and R. A. Brymer, 'Job Satisfaction and Performance: The Moderating Effects of Value Attainment and Affective Disposition', *Journal of Vocational Behavior*, April 1999, pp. 296–313.

63 Results can be found in J. Cohen-Charash and P. E. Spector, 'The Role of Justice in Organizations: A Meta-Analysis', *Organizational Behavior and Human Decision Processes*, November 2001, pp. 278–321.

64 A thorough discussion of this model is provided by T. A. Judge and R. J. Larsen, 'Dispositional Affect and Job Satisfaction: A Review and Theoretical Extension', *Organizational Behavior and Human Decision Processes*, September 2001, pp. 67–98.

65 Supportive results can be found in B. M. Staw and J. Ross, 'Stability in the Midst of Change: A Dispositional Approach to Job Attitudes', *Journal of Applied Psychology*, August 1985, pp. 469–80; and R. P. Steel and J. R. Rentsch, 'The Dispositional Model of Job Attitudes Revisited: Findings of a 10-Year Study', *Journal of Applied Psychology*, December 1997, pp. 873–9.

66 See R. D. Arvey, T. J. Bouchard, Jr, N. L. Segal and L. M. Abraham, 'Job Satisfaction: Environmental and Genetic Components', *Journal of Applied Psychology*, April 1989, pp. 187–92; E. Diener and C. Diener, 'Most People Are Happy', *Psychological Science*, May 1996, pp. 181–5; and D. Lykken and A. Tellegen, 'Happiness Is a Stochastic Phenomenon', *Psychological Science*, May 1996, pp. 186–9.

67 C. Dormann and D. Zapf, 'Job Satisfaction: A Meta-Analysis of Stabilities', *Journal of Organizational Behavior*, August 2001, pp. 483–504.

68 Results can be found in A. J. Kinicki, F. M. McKee-Ryan, C. A. Schriesheim and K. P. Carson, 'Assessing the Construct Validity of the Job Descriptive Index: A Review and Meta-Analysis', *Journal of Applied Psychology*, February 2002, pp. 14–32.

69 See R. D. Hackett, 'Work Attitudes and Employee Absenteeism: A Synthesis of the Literature', *Journal of Occupational Psychology*, 1989, pp. 235–48; and R. Steel and J. R. Rentsch, 'Influence of Cumulation Strategies on the Long-Range Prediction of Absenteeism', *Academy of Management Journal*, December 1995, pp. 1616–34.

70 A thorough review of the various causes of turnover is provided by T. R. Mitchell and T. W. Lee, 'The Unfolding Model of Voluntary Turnover and Job Embeddedness: Foundations for a Comprehensive Theory of Attachment', in *Research in Organizational Behavior*, eds B. M. Staw and R. I. Sutton (New York: JAI Press, 2001), pp. 189–246.

71 Results can be found in P. W. Hom and A. J. Kinicki, 'Toward a Greater Understanding of How Dissatisfaction Drives Employee Turnover', *Academy of Management Journal*, October 2001, pp. 975–87.

72 Techniques for reducing employee turnover are thoroughly discussed by R. W. Griffith and P. W. Hom, *Retaining Valued Employees* (Thousand Oaks, CA: Sage Publications, 2001).

73 Results can be found in R. W. Griffeth, P. W. Hom and S. Gaertner, 'A Meta-Analysis of Antecedents and Correlates of Employee Turnover: Update, Moderator Tests, and Research Implications for the Next Millennium', *Journal of Management*, May 2000, pp. 463–88. Also see A. C. Glebbeek, 'Is High Employee Turnover Really Harmful? An Empirical Test Using Company Records', *Academy of Management Journal*, April 2004, pp. 277–86.

74 The various models are discussed by T. Judge, C. Thoresen, J. Bono and G. Patton, 'The Job Satisfaction–Job Performance Relationship: A Qualitative and Quantitative Review', *Psychological Bulletin*, May 2001, pp. 376–407.

75 Results can be found in T. Judge, C. Thoresen, J. Bono and G. Patton, 'The Job Satisfaction–Job Performance Relationship: A Qualitative and Quantitative Review', *Psychological Bulletin*, May 2001, pp. 376–407.

76 T. C. Murtha, R. Kanfer and P. L. Ackerman, 'Toward an Interactionist Taxonomy of Personality and Situations: An Integrative Situational-Dispositional Representation of Personality Traits', *Journal of Personality and Social Psychology*, July 1996, pp. 193–207; and T. Judge, C. Thoresen, J. Bono and G. Patton, 'The Job Satisfaction–Job Performance Relationship: A Qualitative and Quantitative Review', *Psychological Bulletin*, May 2001, pp. 376–407.

77 These issues are discussed by C. Ostroff, 'The Relationship between Satisfaction, Attitudes, and Performance: An Organizational Level Analysis', *Journal of Applied Psychology*, December 1992, pp. 963–74; and A. M. Ryan, M. J. Schmit and R. Johnson, 'Attitudes and Effectiveness: Examining Relations at an Organizational Level', *Personnel Psychology*, Winter 1996, pp. 853–82.

78 Results can be found in J. K. Harter, F. L. Schmidt and T. L. Hayes, 'Business-Unit-Level Relationship between Employee Satisfaction, Employee Engagement, and Business Outcomes: A Meta-Analysis', *Journal of Applied Psychology*, April 2002, pp. 268–79.

79 L. L. Putnam and D. K. Mumby, 'Organizations, Emotions and the Myth of Rationality', in *Emotion in Organizations*, ed. S. Fineman (Thousand Oaks, CA: Sage Publications, 1993), pp. 36–57; B. E. Ashforth and R. H. Humphrey, 'Emotion in the Workplace: A Reappraisal', *Human Relations*, February 1995, pp. 97–125; and J. M. Kidd, 'Emotion: An Absent Presence in Career Theory', *Journal of Vocational Behavior*, June 1998, pp. 275–88.

80 For works on emotions, see J. M. Jenkins, K. Oatley and N. L. Stein, eds, *Human Emotions: A Reader* (Malden, MA: Blackwell Publishers, 1998); T. A. Domagalski, 'Emotions in Organizations: Main Currents', *Human Relations*, June 1999, pp. 833–52; N. M. Ashkanasy, C. E. J. Härtel and C. S. Daus, 'Diversity and Emotion: The New Frontiers in Organizational Behavior Research', *Journal of Management*, May 2002, pp. 307–38; and F. Lelord and C. André, *La Force des Emotions* (Paris: Editions Odile Jacob, 2001).

81 See N. H. Frijda, 'Moods, Emotion Episodes and Emotions', in *Handbook of Emotions*, eds M. Lewis and J. M. Haviland (New York: Guilford Press, 1993), pp. 381–403; J. M. George, 'Trait and State Affect', in *Individual Differences and Behavior in Organizations*, ed. K. R. Murphy (San Francisco: Jossey-Bass, 1996); H. M. Weiss and R. Cropanzano, 'Affective Events Theory: A Theoretical Discussion of the Structure, Causes and Consequences of Affective Experiences at Work', in *Research in Organizational Behavior, vol. 18*, eds B. M. Staw and L. L. Cummings (Greenwich, CT: JAI Press, 1996), pp. 1–74; and R. Kelly and S. G. Barsade, 'Mood and Emotions in Small Groups and Work Teams', *Organizational Behavior and Human Decision Processes*, September 2001, pp. 99–130.

82 R. S. Lazarus, *Emotion and Adaptation* (New York: Oxford University Press, 1991), p. 6. Also see, D. Goleman, *Emotional Intelligence* (New York: Bantam Books, 1995), pp. 289–90; and J. A. Russell and L. F. Barrett, 'Core Affect, Prototypical Emotional Episodes, and Other Things Called Emotion: Dissecting the Elephant', *Journal of Personality and Social Psychology*, May 1999, pp. 805–19.

83 Based on discussion in R. D. Arvey, G. L. Renz and T. W. Watson, 'Emotionality and Job Performance: Implications for Personnel Selection', in *Research in Personnel and Human Resources Management, vol. 16*, ed. G. R. Ferris (Stamford, CT: JAI Press, 1998), pp. 103–47. Also see L. A. King, 'Ambivalence Over Emotional Expression and Reading Emotions', *Journal of Personality and Social Psychology*, March 1998, pp. 753–62; and S. Mann, *Hiding What We Feel, Faking What We Don't* (Shaftesbury, Dorset, UK: Element, 1999).

84 For research in this area, see J. M. George and G. R. Jones, 'The Experience of Mood and Turnover Intentions: Interactive Effects of Value Attainment, Job Satisfaction, and Positive Mood', *Journal of Applied Psychology*, June 1996, pp. 318–25; and A. P. Brief and H. M. Weiss, 'Organizational Behavior: Affect in the Workplace', in *Annual Review of Psychology, vol. 53*, ed. S. T. Fiske (Palo Alto, CA: Annual Reviews, 2002), pp. 279–307.

85 See, for instance, A. M. Isen and R. A. Baron, 'Positive Affect as a Factor in Organizational Behavior', in *Research in Organizational Behavior, vol. 13*, eds B. M. Staw and L. L. Cummings (Greenwich, CT: JAI Press, 1991), pp. 1–54; J. M. George and A. P. Brief, 'Feeling Good–Doing Good: A Conceptual Analysis of the Mood at Work-Organizational Spontaneity Relationships', *Psychological Bulletin*, September 1992, pp. 310–29;

R. Cropanzano, K. James and M. A. Konovsky, 'Dispositional Affectivity as a Predictor of Work Attitudes and Job Performance', *Journal of Organizational Behavior*, November 1993, pp. 595–606; B. M. Staw, R. I. Sutton and L. H. Pelled, 'Employee Positive Emotion and Favorable Outcomes at the Workplace', *Organization Science*, February 1994, pp. 51–71; T. A. Wright and B. M. Staw, 'Affect and Favorable Work Outcomes: Two Longitudinal Tests of the Happy-Productive Worker Thesis', *Journal of Organizational Behavior*, January 1999, pp. 1–23; and T. A. Judge and R. J. Larsen, 'Dispositional Affect and Job Satisfaction: A Review and Theoretical Extension', *Organizational Behavior and Human Decision Processes*, September 2001, pp. 67–98.

86 P. E. Spector, S. M. Jex and P. Y. Chen, 'Relations of Incumbent Affect-Related Personality Traits with Incumbent and Objective Measures of Characteristics of Jobs', *Journal of Organizational Behavior*, January 1995, pp. 59–65.

87 See D. Goleman, *Emotional Intelligence* (New York: Bantam Books, 1995); D. Goleman, *Working with Emotional Intelligence* (New York: Bantam Books, 1998); and D. Goleman, R. Boyatzis and A. McKee, *Primal Leadership. Realizing the Power of Emotional Intelligence* (Boston, MA: Harvard Business School Press, 2002).

88 D. Goleman, *Emotional Intelligence* (New York: Bantam Books, 1995), p. 34.

89 A useful and practical book that can help to stimulate emotional intelligence is P. McBride and S. Maitland, *The EI Advantage: Putting Emotional Intelligence into Practice* (London: McGraw-Hill, 2002).

90 D. Goleman, 'What Makes a Leader?', *Harvard Business Review*, November–December 1998, pp. 93–102; D. Goleman, 'Leadership That Gets Results', *Harvard Business Review*, March–April 2000, pp. 78–90; and D. Goleman, R. Boyatzis and A. McKee, 'Primal Leadership: The Hidden Driver of Great Performance', *Harvard Business Review*, Special Issue: Breakthrough Leadership, December 2001, pp. 43–51.

91 See V. Dulewicz, 'Emotional Intelligence: The Key to Future Successful Corporate Leadership?', *Journal of General Management*, Spring 2000, pp. 1–14; J. M. George, 'Emotions and Leadership: The Role of Emotional Intelligence', *Human Relations*, August 2000, pp. 1027–55; H. Weisinger, *Emotional Intelligence at Work* (San Francisco: Jossey-Bass, 2000); V. U. Druskat and S. B. Wolff, 'Building the Emotional Intelligence of Groups', *Harvard Business Review*, March 2001, pp. 80–90; G. Matthews, M. Zeidner and R. D. Roberts, *Emotional Intelligence: Science & Myths* (Cambridge, MA: The MIT Press, 2002); and R. J. Emmerling and C. Cherniss, 'Emotional Intelligence and the Career Choice Process', *Journal of Career Assessment*, May 2003, pp. 153–67.

92 See, for instance, J. D. Mayer, D. R. Caruso and P. Salovey, 'Selecting a Measure of Emotional Intelligence: The Case for Ability Scales', in *Handbook of Emotional Intelligence*, eds R. Bar-On and D. A. Parker (San Francisco: Jossey-Bass, 2000), pp. 320–42; and R. Bar-On, 'Emotional and Social Intelligence: Insights from the Emotional Quotient Inventory (EQ-I)', in *Handbook of Emotional Intelligence*, eds R. Bar-On and D. A. Parker (San-Francisco: Jossey-Bass, 2000), pp. 363–88.

93 M. Davies, L. Stankov and R. D. Roberts, 'Emotional Intelligence: In Search of an Elusive Construct', *Journal of Personality and Social Psychology*, October 1998, pp. 989–1015; J. V. Ciarrochi, A. Y. C. Chan and P. Caputi, 'A Critical Evaluation of the Emotional Intelligence Construct', *Personality and Individual Differences*, March 2000, pp. 539–61; and R. D. Roberts, M. Zeidner and G. Matthews, 'Does Emotional Intelligence Meet Traditional Standards for an Intelligence? Some New Data and Conclusions', *Emotion*, September 2001, pp. 196–231.

94 C. Woodruffe, 'Promotional Intelligence', *People Management*, 11 January 2001, pp. 26–9.

95 J. D. Mayer and P. Salovey, 'What is Emotional Intelligence?', in *Emotional Development and Emotional Intelligence: Implications for Educators*, eds P. Salovey and D. Sluyter (New York: Basic Books, 1997), pp. 3–34.

96 For recent reviews on emotional contagion, see R. Neumann and F. Strack, 'Mood Contagion: The Automatic Transfer of Mood between Persons', *Journal of Personality and Social Psychology*, 2000, pp. 211–23; R. Kelly and S. G. Barsade, 'Mood and Emotions in Small Groups and Work Teams', *Organizational Behavior and Human Decision Processes*, September 2001, pp. 99–130; and J. M. George, 'Affect Regulation in Groups and Teams', in *Emotions in the Workplace: Understanding the Structure and Role of Emotions in Organizational Behavior*, eds R. G. Lord, R. Klimoski and R. Kanfer (San Francisco: Jossey-Bass, 2002), pp. 183–217.

97 E. Hatfield, J. T. Cacioppo and R. L. Rapson, *Emotional Contagion* (New York: Cambridge University Press, 1994), p. 4.

98 The process of emotional contagion is explained more thoroughly in R. Kelly and S. G. Barsade, 'Mood and Emotions in Small Groups and Work Teams', *Organizational Behavior and Human Decision Processes*, September 2001, pp. 99–130.

99 See, for instance, R. W. Doherty, L. Orimoto, T. M. Singelis, E. Hatfield and J. Hebb, 'Emotional Contagion: Gender and Occupational Differences', *Psychology of Women Quarterly*, December 1995, pp. 355–71; C. D. Fisher, 'Mood and Emotions While Working: Missing Pieces of Job Satisfaction', *Journal of Organizational Behavior*, March 2000, pp. 185–202; and A. Singh-Manoux and C. Finkenauer, 'Cultural Variations in Social Sharing of Emotions: An Intercultural Perspective', *Journal of Cross-Cultural Psychology*, November 2001, pp. 647–61.

100 Data from S. D. Pugh, 'Service with a Smile: Emotional Contagion in the Service Encounter', *Academy of Management Journal*, October 2001, pp. 1018–27.

101 Data from P. Totterdell, S. Kellett, K. Teuchmann and R. B. Briner, 'Evidence of Mood Linkages in Work Groups', *Journal of Personality and Social Psychology*, June 1998, pp. 1504–15. Also see P. Totterdell, 'Catching Moods and Hitting Runs: Mood Linkage and Subjective Performance in Professional Sport Teams', *Journal of Applied Psychology*, December 2000, pp. 848–59.

102 S. G. Barsade, 'The Ripple Effect: Emotional Contagion and Its Influence on Group Behavior', *Administrative Science Quarterly*, December 2002, pp. 644–75. Also see C. A. Bartel and R. Saavedra, 'The Collective Construction of Work Group Moods', *Administrative Science Quarterly*, June 2000, pp. 197–231.

103 D. Goleman, *Working with Emotional Intelligence* (New York: Bantam Books, 1998), pp. 163–97.

104 For research on the role of emotional contagion in conflict management and negotiating, see R. Baron, 'Environmentally Induced Positive Affect: Its Impact on Self-Efficacy, Task Performance, Negotation and Conflict', *Journal of Applied Social Psychology*, March 1990, pp. 368–84; and J. P. Forgas, 'On Feeling Good and Getting Your Way: Mood Effects on Negotiator Cognition and Bargaining Strategies', *Journal of Personality and Social Psychology*, May 1998, pp. 565–77.

105 For research on the role of emotional contagion in leadership, see J. M. George, 'Leader Positive Mood and Group Performance: The Case of Customer Service', *Journal of Applied Social Psychology*, May 1995, pp. 778–94; and K. M. Lewis, 'When Leaders Display Emotion: How Followers Respond to Negative Emotional Expression of Male and Female Leaders', *Journal of Organizational Behavior*, March 2000, pp. 221–34.

106 For research on emotions and emotional contagion during change processes, see K. W. Mossholder, R. P. Settoon, A. A. Armenakis and S. G. Harris, 'Emotion during Organizational Transformations: An Interactive Model of Survivor Reactions', *Group & Organization Management*, September 2000, pp. 220–43; and S. Fox and Y. Amichai-Hamburger, 'The Power of Emotional Appeals in Promoting Organizational Change Programs', *Academy of Management Executive*, November 2001, pp. 84–94.

107 The first researcher who focuses on emotional labour is A. Hochschild, *The Managed Heart: Commercialization of Human Feeling* (Berkeley, CA: University of California Press, 1983).

108 J. A. Morris and D. C. Feldman, 'The Dimensions, Antecendents and Consequences of Emotional Labor', *Academy of Management Review*, October 1996, pp. 986–1010; J. A. Morris and D. C. Feldman, 'Managing Emotions in the Workplace', *Journal of Managerial Issues*, Fall 1997, pp. 257–74; and S. Mann, 'Emotion at Work: To What Extent Are We Expressing, Suppressing, or Faking It?', *European Journal of Work and Organizational Psychology*, September 1999, pp. 347–69.

109 R. Abraham, 'Emotional Dissonance in Organizations: Antecedents, Consequences and Moderators', *Genetic, Social and General Psychology Monographs*, 1998, pp. 229–46.

110 B. Mesquita and N. H. Frijda, 'Cultural Variations in Emotions: A Review', *Psychological Bulletin*, September 1992, pp. 179–204; and B. Mesquita, 'Emotions in Collectivist and Individualist Contexts', *Journal of Personality and Social Psychology*, September 2001, pp. 68–74.

111 See A. M. Kring and A. H. Gordon, 'Sex Differences in Emotions: Expression, Experience, and Physiology', *Journal of Personality and Social Psychology*, March 1998, pp. 686–703.

112 N. M. Ashkanasy and C. S. Daus, 'Emotion in the Workplace: The New Challenge for Managers', *Academy of Management Executive*, February 2002, p. 79. Also see K. Pugliesi, 'The Consequences of Emotional Labor: Effects on Work Stress, Job Satisfaction, and Well-Being', *Motivation and Emotion*, June 1999, pp. 125–54; and J. Schaubroeck and J. R. Jones, 'Antecedents of Workplace Emotional Labor Dimensions and Moderators of Their Effects on Physical Symptoms', *Journal of Organizational Behavior*, March 2000, pp. 163–83.

113 D. Zapf, C. Vogt, C. Seifert, H. Mertini and A. Isic, 'Emotion Work as a Source of Stress: The Concept and Development of an Instrument', *European Journal of Work and Organizational Psychology*, September 1999, p. 396.

114 For more information on flow, see M. Csikszentmihalyi, *Flow: The Psychology of Optimal Experience* (New York: HarperCollins, 1990); M. Csikszentmihalyi, *Creativity: Flow and the Psychology of Discovery and Invention* (New York: HarperPerennial, 1996); M. Csikszentmihalyi, *Finding Flow: The Psychology of Engagement with Everyday Life* (New York: Basic Books, 1997); and M. Csikszentmihalyi, *Good Business: Leadership, Flow and the Making of Business* (New York: Viking Books, 2003).

115 C. Gilson, *Peak Performance: Business Lessons from the World's Top Sporting Organisations* (London: HarperCollins, 2000).

116 M. Csikszentmihalyi, *Flow: The Psychology of Optimal Experience* (New York: HarperCollins, 1990).

117 M. Csikszentmihalyi and R. Larson, 'Validity and Reliability of the Experience Sampling Method', *Journal of Nervous and Mental Disease*, June 1987, pp. 526–36.

118 G. B. Moneta and M. Csikszentmihalyi, 'The Effect of Perceived Challenges and Skills on the Quality of Subjective Experience', *Journal of Personality*, June 1996, pp. 275–310.

119 Based on and translated from 'Betty Mellaerts praat met ex-tennisster Dominique Monami', *De Morgen*, 22 May 2004, p. 50.

120 E. J. Donner and M. Csikszentmihalyi, 'Transforming Stress to Flow', *Executive Excellence*, February 1992, p. 16.

121 For an overview, see S. A. Jackson, J. C. Kimiecik, S. K. Ford and H. W. Marsch, 'Psychological Correlates of Flow in Sport', *Journal of Sport and Exercise Psychology*, December 1998, pp. 358–78. Also see M. Csikszentmihalyi and I. Csikszentmihalyi, *Optimal Experience: Psychological Studies of Flow in Consciousness* (New York: Cambridge University Press, 1988).

122 See J. L. Duda, 'Motivation in Sport Settings: A Goal Perspective Approach', in *Motivation in Sport and Exercise*, ed. G. Roberts (Champaign, IL: Human Kinetics, 1992), pp. 57–72; and S. A. Jackson and G. C. Roberts, 'Positive Performance States of Athletes: Toward a Conceptual Understanding of Peak Performance', *The Sport Psychologist*, March 1992, pp. 156–80.

123 S. A. Jackson, 'Factors Influencing the Occurrence of Flow States in Elite Athletes', *Journal of Applied Sport Psychology*, March 1995, pp. 138–66. Also see M. Csikszentmihalyi and J. Nakamura, 'The Dynamics of Intrinsic Motivation: A Study of Adolescents', in *Research on Motivation in Education, vol. 3: Goals and Cognitions*, eds C. Ames and R. Ames (New York: Academic Press, 1989), pp. 45–71; and L. G. Pelletier, M. S. Fortier, R. J. Vallerand, K. M. Tuson, N. M. Briere and M. R. Blais, 'Toward a New Measure of Intrinsic Motivation, Extrinsic Motivation, and Amotivation in Sports: The Sport Motivation Scale (SMS)', *Journal of Sport and Exercise Psychology*, March 1995, pp. 35–53.

124 See, for instance, S. A. Jackson and G. C. Roberts, 'Positive Performance States of Athletes: Toward a Conceptual Understanding of Peak Performance', *The Sport Psychologist*, March 1992, pp. 156–80; S. A. Jackson, 'Factors Influencing the Occurrence of Flow States in Elite Athletes', *Journal of Applied Sport Psychology*, March 1995, pp. 138–66; and G. L. Stein, J. C. Kimiecik, J. Daniels and S. A. Jackson, 'Psychological Antecedents of Flow in Recreational Sport', *Personality and Social Psychology Bulletin*, March 1995, pp. 125–35.

125 See K. Scheeres and A. B. Bakker, 'Flow bij muziekdocenten en Run Peerlingen: de aanstekelijkheid van piekervaringen' [Flow among Music Teachers and Their Students: Transfer of Peak Performance], *Gedrag & Organisatie*, February 2003, pp. 23–38.

126 See M. Csikszentmihalyi, *Flow: The Psychology of Optimal Experience* (New York: HarperCollins, 1990). Also see H. L. Mills, 'Flow', 2001 (www.optimums.com).

127 See A. M. O'Leary, R. W. Griffin and D. J. Glew, 'Organization-Motivated Aggression: A Research Framework', *Academy of Management Review*, January 1996, pp. 225–53; R. A. Baron and J. H. Neuman, 'Workplace Violence and Workplace Aggression: Evidence on Their Relative Frequency and Potential Causes', *Aggressive Behavior*, June 1996, pp. 161–73; and J. Fitness, 'Anger in the Workplace: An Emotion Script Approach to Anger Episodes between Workers and their Superiors, Co-Workers and Subordinates', *Journal of Organizational Behavior*, March 2000, pp. 147–62.

128 E. Davies, 'How Violence at Work Can Hit Employers Hard', *People Management*, 12 September 1996, p. 50.

129 Adapted from D. J. Weiss, R. V. Dawis, G. W. England and L. H. Lofquist, *Manual for the Minnesota Satisfaction Questionnaire* (Minneapolis: Industrial Relations Center, University of Minnesota, 1967). Used with permission.

chapter 4 perception and diversity

By Dave Bouckenooghe, Fannie Debussche and Veronique Warmoes

Learning outcomes

When you finish studying the material in this chapter, you should be able to:

◼ recognise the antecedents influencing the perceptual process

◼ describe perception in terms of the social information processing model

◼ identify and briefly explain two implications of social perception

◼ explain Jones and Davis' correspondent inference theory

◼ explain, according to Kelley's model, how external and internal causal attributions are formulated

◼ review Weiner's model of attribution

◼ discuss how the self-fulfilling prophecy is created and how it can be used to improve individual and group productivity

◼ discuss stereotypes and the process of stereotype formation

◼ define diversity and give five reasons why managing diversity is a competitive advantage

◼ discuss the organisational practices used to effectively manage diversity

case study

Big brother? No, it's just another day at the office

You have one colleague who embarrassingly bursts into tears rather too often in your opinion. Another colleague withdraws from confrontation at every opportunity, something which eventually drives you crazy. And you're sick and tired of the good-looking smooth-talker from the accountancy department who tells tall tales and whose anti-gay talk the other day just confirmed everyone's suspicions that he might have something to hide. It's enough to make you think about giving in your notice.

But these tiresome acquaintances are not in your workplace. They are appearing almost nightly on various channels throughout Europe – including the UK, Belgium, Holland, Switzerland, Italy and Spain – in Big Brother, the programme where ten handsome young men and women have been locked up for two months in a house with one voted out each week.

When the show was launched, critics assumed it would be sex appeal that guaranteed its audience. In fact, we have been amazed to see the chilling way in which a randomly selected group of people sets about destroying one another under the gentle guise of mutual co-operation. Sounds familiar? It's probably a workplace near you.

The most frightening thing about the melodrama being played out in front of millions of people – and talked about by millions more than admit watching the programme – is its alarming similarity to the world in which we all live. Home, school, college and work are social environments in which we can often identify relatives, friends or colleagues whose embodiment we now see on our television screens.

This is the 'ambulance effect', explains Professor Cary Cooper, one of Britain's leading specialists in organisational and industrial psychology. 'You see potential disaster and you want to look. The biggest similarity of all, that Big Brother possesses, is to a workplace. After all, they are working, even if they don't do much, and also they are very competitive.

'Work is just like a game; some people get promotion, some people get rejected and some people who don't get promoted will leave. We're learning from Big Brother who is perceived by others to be worthwhile and who will be retained.

'That's just like the office. People chat at the coffee machine and talk about other people and their relationships. They make assumptions about colleagues and bosses. They wonder how they can make themselves more popular. They spread gossip. But this programme actually allows you to hear the rumours firsthand.'

However, in the Big Brother house – like too many workplaces – there is a much more sinister objective lurking beneath much of the residents' conversational veneer. Each is jockeying for someone else to be ditched but at the same they want to be liked.

'Big Brother shows us an environment where people are uncomfortable with their roles', said Angela Ishmael of the Industrial Society. 'It's exactly what's happening in lots of workplaces. When professionals aren't able to manage relationships in a team, team power takes over. It is a classic bullying scenario too, and it is becoming more and more common.'

'It's interesting how viewers form a certain picture of the people taking part in the programme. One person is marked as dishonest for not being open about plotting to get other people thrown out', said Ishmael. 'But he is quite genuine in terms of his feelings for his colleagues.'

'The simple truth is that he will look after himself more than everyone else. He's just more rehearsed that the rest of them at manipulating people. But another participant, who clearly isn't liked, will tell everyone exactly how he feels.'

'Even though that's quite aggressive, most people can identify with it. The sort of thing the second person will be accused of is not caring for other people's feelings. The sort of bullying the first one gets involved in is not as confrontational as the other approach but people do realise afterwards that they are being manipulated. That upsets them.'

'What the programme also picks up on vividly is an almost adolescent need for conformity', said Philip Hodson of the British Association for Counselling. 'It's that terrible fear of whether we're approved of, always worrying *does my bum look big in this?* So much of it is centred on trust, being liked and hanging up a positive picture of one's self. Do people say one thing to our face and another to our backs? Someone you think you trust is capable of damning you terribly.'

'At the heart of the programme is a focus on isolation', said Professor Cooper. 'This sort of environment is all about politics with a small "p", isolating certain people. They may be a threat to your promotion or they may be about to discover how incompetent you are. And you want to ensure their influence is minimal, so you spread rumours so that their position is undermined. Sometimes in this environment you will target someone by allying with a colleague, a third party, to put him down. That goes on in lots of organisations. It may be to undermine them or perhaps just because you don't like them.'

'When we watch Big Brother we're learning lessons at an unconscious level for use in our workplace. Is it any wonder that we're all entranced?'[1]

For discussion

We perceive every participant in 'Big Brother' in a certain way because of the behaviour we get to see on the screen. Do you think the producers of the programme can actually influence us – deliberately or not – to like certain individuals and dislike others?

In every social situation, we gather information on others. We form a certain picture of people based on the signals we receive from them. We encode and store this information and use it every time we interact with each other. In fact, we are constantly striving to make sense of our social surroundings, be it when watching a political conversation on TV or when having a romantic dinner.

The resulting knowledge influences our behaviour and helps us navigate our way through life. For example, think of the perceptual process that occurs when meeting someone for the first time. Your attention is drawn to the individual's physical appearance, mannerisms, actions and reactions to what you say and do. You ultimately arrive at conclusions based on your perceptions of this social inter-action. The brown-haired, green-eyed individual turns out to be friendly and fond of outdoor activities. You further conclude that you like this person and then ask him or her to go to a concert, calling the person by the name you stored in memory.

This reciprocal process of perception, interpretation and behavioural response also applies at work. A field study illustrates this relationship. Researchers wanted to know whether employees' perceptions of how much an organisation valued them affected their behaviour and attitudes. The researchers asked samples of high school teachers, brokerage-firm clerks, manufacturing workers, insurance representatives and police officers to indicate their perception of the extent to which their organisation valued their contributions and their well-being. Employees who perceived that their organisation cared about them reciprocated with reduced absenteeism, increased performance, innovation and positive work attitudes.[2] This study illustrates the importance of employees' perceptions. Also, many trainers in social skills increasingly emphasise the importance of perception in their seminars. For example, one trainer of a Dutch management consulting organisation, Multiplus, recently stated the following.

> Working with people requires both insights into others and into ourselves. If our self-concept doesn't match with the image others have of us, we can feel uncertain and conflicts can arise. By becoming conscious of what plays a role in our daily perceptions, we can appreciate the views of others. It is of great importance for everybody who has to work with people to learn the physiological, psychological and cultural factors that influence our perceptions and thereby limit our objectivity.[3]

Perception is not only vital for professionals; perception theories are also increasingly being applied in politics, the media, and recruitment advertisements and so on. For example, the London-based Institution of Chemical Engineers, which was suffering from a serious drop in its student numbers, hoped that by invoking the names of famous 'chemical engineers' such as Cindy Crawford and the Swedish actor Dolph Lundgren, it could tempt young people to take up the subject. By coupling the names of celebrities to it, the Institution tried to turn 'chemical engineering' into something 'cool' and appealing. Instead of perceiving the subject as boring, people could now say: 'Why not? Cindy Crawford and Dolph Lundgren did it!'[4]

In this chapter, we focus on the antecedents of perception, a social information processing model of perception, attribution, self-fulfilling prophecy, stereotypes and diversity.

Factors influencing perception

Perception cognitive process that enables us to interpret and understand our environment

Social perception process by which people come to understand one another

Perception is a cognitive process that enables us to interpret and understand our environment. It involves the way we view the world around us and adds meaning to the information gathered via the five senses. The study how people perceive one another is called social cognition. **Social perception** is the process by which people come to understand one another.[5] According to Fiske and Taylor 'social cognition is the study of how people make sense of other people and themselves. It focuses on how ordinary people think about people and how they think they think about people . . .'.[6]

We all perceive the world around us differently. These perceptions constitute our current and future demeanour. For instance, running four kilometres in 25 minutes is perceived as a piece of cake for somebody who is used to running marathons, while an untrained person is going to perceive it as a daunting task. If one person during a summer day perceives that it is thirsty weather, he is going to have an extra drink. If a person standing beside him does not share that impression, that person is probably not going to have an extra drink. Groups may also diverge in perceptions. For example, entrepreneurial-minded people have lower risk perceptions associated with starting up new ventures compared to less entrepreneurial people.[7] Human behaviour and thus organisational behaviour are a function of how we perceive our surroundings.

To improve our insights in other people's behaviour we need to understand how perceptions operate. Understanding and studying the perceptions of other people improves our ability to understand the meaning of our own behaviour. This is well demonstrated in a few studies. In a study about the perceived attractiveness of job ads, business students at Eastern Washington University were asked to analyse job descriptions. The results showed that the combination of perceived proximity of work to home with challenging job features were the most attractive job characteristics influencing the readiness to apply for a job. So, organisations wishing to attract strong candidates from this labour pool should mention these features when drawing up job ads.[8] A study of orientations to work and family among a wide range of youngsters aged between 18 and 30 years perceived that job insecurity appeared to be related to decreased trust in employers and reluctant compliance with organisational demands. Common reactions to the perceived job insecurity were: 'You have to do what management wants or you'll be out on your ear (man, white collar). You do the work they tell you or they get someone else. They're not bothered about your real life, they just want their profits. That's all they want nowadays, their profits. The world is now a profit margin (man, unemployed).'[9] The importance of knowing the perception process is also demonstrated by a survey study of 237 Singaporean managers. That study discovered a strong relationship between the perception of strong top management support for ethical behaviour and job satisfaction.[10]

In understanding the process of social perception we need first to learn which factors actually affect perception. These factors can be classified in three main categories as shown in Figure 4.1.

FIGURE 4.1 ANTECEDENTS INFLUENCING PERCEPTION

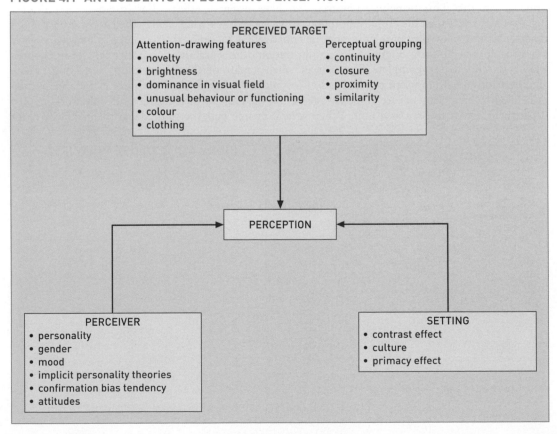

Features of perceived people, objects and events

The characteristics of perceived objects, people and events are of great importance in the formation of perceptions.[11] When a person looks at other people, objects or events, his interpretation is influenced by the features of the perceived target. For instance, a priest dressed as a biker and driving a Harley Davidson will draw more attention than the regular small-town priest. Even in 500 BC people used characteristics from the perceived target to form an impression about that target. First impressions about people are influenced in a subtle way by a person's skin colour, gender, hair colour, weight, clothes, etc.[12] For instance, the perception of people is often influenced by the colour of their clothes. An inquiry found that crime suspects were perceived as more violent and aggressive when dressed in black – a colour associated with demonic, evil sects and death – than when they wore lighter clothing.[13]

An important question regarding the impact of the perceived target is whether the mind perceives people, events, and ideas as a whole or rather as the sum of their features. This question was raised by the Gestalt theorists Wertheimer and von Ehrenfels.[14] The answer was that our minds perceive objects, people and ideas as organised and meaningful patterns rather than as separate bundles of data. Von Ehrenfels displayed this phenomenon in a music exemplar. When you play a melody of six tones and thereupon employ six new tones, you recognise the same melody despite the change in tones. So this scholar came to the conclusion that something else than the summation operator of the six tones, a seventh something, which is the *Gestaltqualität*, made it possible to recognise the melody despite the change. That objects are perceived as a whole instead as the summation of their constituents is well illustrated by the pictures in Figure 4.2 and Figure 4.3.

Even though the circle in the Figure 4.2 is not joined together we still perceive it as a circle. In Figure 4.3 we perceive a dog instead of a large number of spots.

Several Gestalt principles of perceptual grouping explain why we perceive objects as well-organised patterns rather than separate component parts. **Perceptual grouping** is the tendency to form individual stimuli into a meaningful pattern. The main factors that determine perceptual grouping are continuity, closure, proximity, and similarity.[15] **Continuity** is the tendency to perceive objects as continuous patterns. This principle, however, can have negative effects. For instance, an inflexible manager demands that his employees follow strict procedures when doing their jobs, even though random activity may solve problems more imaginatively. **Closure** is the tendency to perceive objects as a constant overall form. Figure 4.2 is an illustration of this organisation principle. Closure applies when we tend to see complete figures even when a part of the information is missing. These vital decisions are often taken on the basis of incomplete information. **Proximity** is the organisation principle in which elements are grouped together on the basis of their nearness. People working on a department are often seen as a unit. When several people quit the same department, however, for

Perceptual grouping
cognitive process to form individual stimuli into meaningful patterns

Continuity
tendency to perceive objects as continuous patterns

Closure
tendency to perceive objects as a constant overall form

Proximity
tendency to group elements based upon their nearness

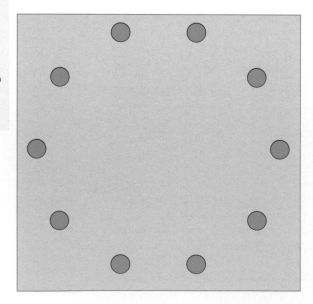

FIGURE 4.2 CLOSURE PRINCIPLE

FIGURE 4.3 PERCEPTION OF A TARGET AS A WHOLE

different unrelated reasons, the HR-department may still perceive it as a problem in that department and try to determine what the problem is. Similarity is the tendency to group objects, people and events that look alike. In some organisations each department has its own colour to visually define separate functions. For instance, the Sales Department has yellow painted doors, while the Marketing Department has green painted doors, so they are clearly distinct.

Similarity
tendency to group objects, people and events that look alike

The setting

The setting in which the interaction between perceiver and the perceived target (i.e. person, object or event) takes place, influences the perception. The Gestaltists advocate the idea that context is very important in perception. Some researchers state that the perception of things is affected by where they are and by what surrounds them.[16] So, because perceived targets are not looked at in isolation, the relationship of the target to its background or setting also influences perception.

A nice illustration of this phenomenon is the contrast effect. A Contrast effect is the tendency to perceive stimuli that differ from expectations as being even more different than they really are.[17] To illustrate, imagine that you have been presented with three iron plates – a cold, a warm and a plate at room temperature. After placing your left hand on the cold plate, and right hand on the hot plate, you place both hands simultaneously on the third plate. You can probably predict the outcome. Even though both hands are placed on the same plate, the right hand will feel cold while the left will sense a warmer feeling. Such a contrast effect often appears in a selection context. For instance, the admission of three applicants depends on their interview performance. The first and the last applicant are perceived as having performed excellently in the interview while the second one is assessed as weak because of the comparison with the first and the last applicant. However, when the applicants before and after the second applicant are assessed as weak performers, these same selection administrators perceive the second applicant as very good.

Contrast effect
tendency to perceive stimuli that differ from expectations as being even more different than they really are

Another significant situational characteristic refers to the impact of culture. In Japan, social context is very important. Business conversations after working hours or at lunch are taboo. If you try to talk business during these times, you may be perceived as crude.[18] In their work *Riding the Waves of Culture*, Trompenaars and Hampden-Turner underscore that differences in culture might induce distinct perceptions. For instance, jumping the lights, even when there is no traffic, won't be appreciated in a rule-based country such as Germany or Switzerland. In rule-based cultures – also labelled as universalist cultures – there is a strong tendency to oppose behaviour that deviates from the rule.

Such cultures are anxious for the reason that once you start to make exceptions for illegal behaviour the system will surely fail. In relationship-based cultures – also particularist societies – there exists a strong emphasis on the exceptional nature of present circumstances. When a person has done something wrong, that person will not be perceived as a citizen but as a friend, sister, husband, wife, and a person with unique importance to the perceiver. Consequently, when business is taking place between both societies, both will think each other corrupt. Universalists will perceive a particularist as lacking trustworthiness because they only help friends, while particularists perceive universalists as not trustworthy because of the perceived fact that universalists don't even help friends.[19] Culture is further discussed in Chapter 16.

A third contextual factor distorting perceptions is the primacy effect. If you meet an individual for the first time and he is accompanied by someone you admire, your judgement of that person will probably be positive. This perception will however be reversed when someone you dislike accompanies that person. So the **Primacy effect** is the effect by which the information first received often continues to colour later perceptions of individuals.[20]

The perceiver

Besides the influences of features of perceived objects and the setting of the formation of perceptions, a third group of relevant antecedents are the characteristics of the perceiver. Factors inherent to the perceiver are sometimes the underlying reason why the same event, person or object is perceived differently. Previous research found that when people are asked to describe a group of target individuals, there is typically more overlap between the various descriptions provided by the same perceiver than there is between those provided for the same target. For example, listening to a friend describing the personality of a mutual acquaintance may tell us more about our friend's personality than the personality of the person being described. Part of the reason for these differences among perceivers is that we tend to use ourselves as a standard in perceiving others.[21]

Research pointed out that field-dependent people tend to pay more attention to external cues, whereas field-independent people rely most of the time on internal, bodily sensations. This personality difference has some implications for organisational behaviour. The field-independent person interacts more independently with other people and seems to be more aware of important differences in other's roles, status and needs.[22]

Besides personality (also see Chapter 2), gender could also be responsible for differences in perception. For instance, a meta-analytic review of perceptions of sexual harassment showed that men and women had a different perception of social-sexual behaviours as harassment.[23] Another study displayed that compared to men women perceived greater gender inequity favouring males.[24] Gender differences are discussed at the end of this chapter. Sexual harassment is discussed in Chapter 9.

A perceiver's mood can also influence the impression formed about others. We think differently depending on whether we are in an optimistic or a pessimistic mood. When we are happy and an employee's task performance needs to be judged, we tend to assess this person's performance more positively than when we are in an unhappy state.[25]

People also seem to have implicit personality theories about which physical characteristics, personality traits and behaviours are related to others. **Implicit personality theories** are a network of assumptions that we hold about relationships among various types of people, traits and behaviours. Knowing that someone has one trait thus leads us to infer that they have other traits as well.[26] For example knowing that someone is an entrepreneur leads us to infer that this person is a risk-taker, recognises opportunities and is full of confidence.

Previous learning and experience might influence the impressions formed about objects, people or events. We sometimes see what we expect to see based on previous learning and experience. As a consequence, formed perceptions are very powerful and resistant to non-corroborating information. Thus, people have the tendency to seek and interpret information that verifies existing beliefs.[27] This tendency is called the **Confirmation bias tendency**.

Finally, we will discuss how the perceiver's attitudes affect social perception. Suppose you are rating the performance in your sales department, and you feel that females are better sales people than males. Your attitude will probably affect your perceptions about the female employees positively.

Primacy effect
effect by which the information first received often continues to colour later perceptions of individuals

Implicit personality theories
network of assumptions that we hold about relationships among various types of people, traits and behaviours

Confirmation bias tendency
tendency to seek and interpret information that verifies existing beliefs

The following example nicely illustrates that different factors might influence the perceptual process.

> A Finnish study tried to examine which antecedents contributed to the prediction of three types of perceived job insecurity (job uncertainty, the worry of job continuity and the probability of job related changes). By and large the perception of job insecurity differed for the private and the public sector. Employees working in the private sector were more worried about their job continuity than employees in the public sector, whereas the perception of the potential of job-related changes was higher among employees working in the public sector. Furthermore, female partners perceived more job insecurity compared to their male counterparts. Also psychosocial job and organisational features such as low job control and weak organisational communication had an important influence on the perceived job insecurity. Finally, it was found that personality factors such as high job involvement and low self-esteem best predicted the perceived emotional side of job insecurity.[28]

A social information-processing model of perception

In this section we elaborate on social information-processing model of perception. We first look at the four phases of this process and then focus on some practical implications.

Four-stage sequence and a working example

Social perception involves a four-stage information-processing sequence (hence, the label 'social information processing'). Figure 4.4 illustrates a basic social information-processing model. Three of the stages in this model – selective attention/comprehension, encoding and simplification, and storage and retention – describe how specific social information is observed and stored in memory. The fourth and final stage, retrieval and response, involves turning mental representations into real-world judgements and decisions.

FIGURE 4.4 SOCIAL PERCEPTION: A SOCIAL INFORMATION PROCESSING MODEL

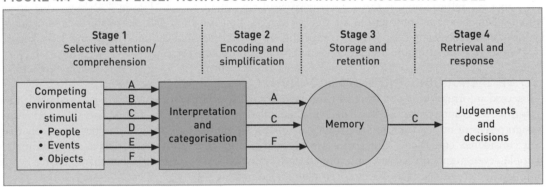

Keep the following everyday example in mind as you look at the four stages of social perception. Suppose you were thinking of taking a course in, say, personal finance. Three lecturers teach the same course, using different types of instruction and testing procedures. Through personal experience, you have come to prefer good lecturers who rely on the case method of instruction and essay tests. According to social perception theory, you would be most likely to arrive at a decision regarding which lecturer to select in the following way.

STAGE 1: SELECTIVE ATTENTION/COMPREHENSION

People are constantly bombarded by physical and social stimuli in the environment. Since they do not have the mental capacity to fully comprehend all this information, they selectively perceive subsets of environmental stimuli. This is where attention plays a role. **Attention** is the process of becoming consciously aware of something or someone. Attention can be focused on information either from the environment or from memory. In respect of the latter, if you sometimes find yourself thinking about totally unrelated events or people while reading a textbook, your memory is the focus of your attention. Research has shown that people tend to pay attention to salient stimuli.

Attention
being consciously aware of something or someone

Salient stimuli

Something is salient when it stands out from its context. For example, Youko Ahola, a 130 kg Finn and the winner of the 'World's Strongest Man' competition in 1999, would certainly be salient in a women's aerobics class, but not at the annual 'Viking Games' in Reykjavik. Social salience is determined by several factors (also see Figure 4.1), including being:

- Novel (the only person in a group of that race, gender, hair colour or age).
- Bright (wearing a yellow shirt).
- Unusual for that person (behaving in an unexpected way, such as a person with a fear of heights climbing a steep mountain).
- Unusual for a person's social category (such as a company president driving a motorcycle to work).
- Unusual for people in general (driving 30 km an hour in a 90 km an hour speed zone).
- Extremely positive (a noted celebrity) or negative (the victim of a bad traffic accident).
- Dominant in the visual field (sitting at the head of the table).[29]

One's needs and goals often dictate which stimuli are salient. For a driver whose petrol gauge shows empty, a Shell or BP sign is more salient than a McDonald's or Pizza Hut sign. The reverse would be true for a hungry driver with a full petrol tank. Moreover, research shows that people have a tendency to pay more attention to negative than to positive information. This leads to a negativity bias.[30] This bias helps explain the 'gawking factor' that slows traffic to a crawl following a car accident.

Back to our example

You begin your search for the 'right' personal finance lecturer by asking friends who have taken classes from the lecturers. You also may interview the various lecturers who teach the class in order to gather still more relevant information. Returning to Figure 4.4, all the information you obtain represents competing environmental stimuli labelled A to F. Because you are concerned about the method of instruction (e.g. line A in Figure 4.4), testing procedures (e.g. line C), and past grade distributions (e.g. line F), information in those areas is particularly salient to you. Figure 4.4 shows that these three salient pieces of information are thus perceived. You can then proceed to the second stage of information processing. Meanwhile, competing stimuli represented by lines B, D and E in Figure 4.4 fail to get your attention and are discarded from further consideration.

STAGE 2: ENCODING AND SIMPLIFICATION

Observed information is not stored in the memory in its original form. Encoding is required; raw information is interpreted or translated into mental representations. To accomplish this, perceivers assign pieces of information to **Cognitive categories**. By category we mean a number of objects that are considered equivalent. Categories are generally designated by names, such as dog, animal.[31] People, events and objects are interpreted and evaluated by comparing their characteristics with information contained in a schema (or, if plural, schemata).

Cognitive categories
mental depositories for storing information

Schemata

According to social information processing theory, a **Schema** represents a person's mental picture or summary of a particular event or type of stimulus.[32] For example, your restaurant schema probably is quite similar to the description provided in Table 4.1.

Cognitive-category labels are needed to make schemata meaningful. The next Activity illustrates this by asking you to rate the comprehensiveness of a schema both without and with its associated category label. Take a moment now to complete this exercise.

Schema
mental picture of an event or object

Encoding outcomes

We use the encoding process to interpret and evaluate our environment. Interestingly, this process can result in differing interpretations and evaluations of the same person or event. Varying interpretations of what we observe occur for many reasons. First, people possess different information in the schemata used for interpretation. For instance, male CEOs and female executives disagree in their assessment of barriers preventing women from advancing to positions of corporate leadership. Women and men also have different ideas about what types of behaviour constitute sexual harassment.[33] Second, our moods and emotions influence our focus of attention and evaluations (see Chapter 3).[34] Third, people tend to apply recently used cognitive categories during encoding. For example, you are more likely to interpret a neutral behaviour exhibited by a lecturer as positive if you were recently thinking about positive categories and events.[35] Fourth, individual differences influence encoding. Pessimistic or depressed individuals, for instance, tend to interpret their surroundings more negatively than optimistic and happy people (see Chapter 3).[36] The point is that we should not be surprised when people interpret and evaluate the same situation or event differently. Researchers are currently trying to identify the host of factors that influence the encoding process.

TABLE 4.1 RESTAURANT SCHEMA

Schema: Restaurant
Characters: Customers, hostess, waiter, chef, cashier

Scene 1: Entering
Customer goes into restaurant
Customer finds a place to sit
    He may find it himself
    He may be seated by a hostess
        He asks the hostess for a table
        She gives him permission to go to the table

Scene 2: Ordering
Customer receives a menu
Customer reads it
Customer decides what to order
Waiter takes the order
    Waiter sees the customer
    Waiter goes to the customer
    Customer orders what he wants
        Chef cooks the meal

Scene 3: Eating After some time the waiter brings the meal from the chef Customer eats the meal

Scene 4: Exiting
Customer asks the waiter for the check
Waiter gives the check to the customer
Customer leaves a tip
    The size of the tip depends on the goodness of the service
        Customer pays the cashier
        Customer leaves the restaurant

SOURCE: From D. Rumelhart, *Introduction to Human Information Processing* (New York: John Wiley & Sons, Inc., 1977). Reprinted by permission of John Wiley & Sons, Inc.

Does a schema improve the comprehension of written material?

Instructions

The purpose of this exercise is to demonstrate the role of schema in encoding. First read the passage shown below. Once done, rate the comprehensiveness of what you read using the scale provided. Next, examine the schema label presented in Reference 32 in the Notes section at the end of the chapter. With this label in mind, re-read the passage, and rate its comprehensiveness. Then think of an explanation of why your ratings changed. You will then have just experienced the impact of schema in encoding.

activity

Read this passage

The procedure is actually quite simple. First you arrange things into different groups. Of course, one pile may be sufficient depending on how much there is to do. If you have to go somewhere else due to lack of facilities, that is the next step; otherwise you are pretty well set. It is important not to overdo things. That is, it is better to do too few things at once than too many. In the short run this may not seem important but complications can easily arise. A mistake can be expensive as well. At first the whole procedure will seem complicated. Soon, however, it will become just another facet of life. It is difficult to foresee any end to the necessity for this task in the immediate future, but then one never can tell. After the procedure is completed, one arranges the materials into different groups again. Then they can be put into their appropriate places. Eventually they will be used once more, and the whole cycle will then have to be repeated. However, that is part of life.

Comprehensive scale

Very uncomprehensive		Neither					Very comprehensive
		1	2	3	4	5	

SOURCE: J. D. Bransford and M. K. Johnson, 'Contextual Prerequisite for Understanding: Some Investigations of Comprehension and Recall', *Journal of Verbal Learning and Verbal Behavior*, December 1972, p. 722. Reprinted with permission of Academic Press, Inc.

Back to our example

Having collected the relevant information about the three personal finance lecturers and their approaches, you compare this information with other details contained in the schemata. This leads you to form an impression and evaluation of what it would be like to take a course with each lecturer. In turn, the relevant information contained on paths A, C and F in Figure 4.4 are passed along to the third stage of information processing.

STAGE 3: STORAGE AND RETENTION

This phase involves storage of information in long-term memory. Long-term memory is like an apartment complex consisting of separate units connected to one another. Although different people live in each apartment, they sometimes interact. In addition, large apartment complexes have different wings (such as A, B, and C). Long-term memory similarly consists of separate but related categories. Like the individual apartments inhabited by unique residents, the connected categories contain different types of information. Information also passes between these categories. Finally, long-term memory is made up of three compartments (or wings) containing categories of information about events, semantic materials and people.[37]

Event memory

This compartment is composed of categories containing information about both specific and general events. These memories describe appropriate sequences of events in well-known situations, such as going to a restaurant (refer back to Table 4.1), going on a job interview, to a food store or to a movie.

Semantic memory

Semantic memory refers to general knowledge about the world. In doing so, it functions as a mental dictionary of concepts. Each concept contains a definition (such as a good leader) and associated traits (outgoing), emotional states (happy), physical characteristics (tall) and behaviours (works hard). Just as there are schemata for general events, concepts in semantic memory are stored as schemata.

Person memory

Categories within this compartment contain information about a single individual (your supervisor) or groups of people (managers).

Back to our example

As the time draws near for you to decide which personal finance lecturer to take, your schemata of them are stored in the three categories of long-term memory. These schemata are available for immediate comparison and/or retrieval.

STAGE 4: RETRIEVAL AND RESPONSE

People retrieve information from memory when they make judgements and decisions. Our ultimate judgements and decisions are either based on the process of drawing on, interpreting and integrating categorical information stored in long-term memory or on retrieving a summary judgement that was already made.[38]

Concluding our example, it is registration day and you have to choose which lecturer to take for personal finance. After retrieving from memory your schemata-based impressions of the three lecturers, you select a good one who uses the case method and gives essay tests (line C in Figure 4.4). In contrast, you may choose your preferred lecturer by simply recalling the decision you made two weeks ago.

Practical implications

Social cognition is the window through which we all observe, interpret and prepare our responses to people and events. A wide variety of activities, organisational processes and quality-of-life issues are thus affected by perception. Consider, for example, the following implications.

HIRING

Interviewers make hiring decisions based on their impression of how an applicant fits the perceived requirements of a job. Inaccurate impressions in either direction produce poor hiring decisions. Moreover, interviewers with racist or sexist schemata can undermine the accuracy and legality of hiring decisions. Those invalid schemata need to be confronted and improved through coaching and training. Failure to do so can lead to poor hiring decisions. For example, a study of 46 male and 66 female financial-institution professionals revealed that their hiring decisions were biased by the physical attractiveness of applicants. More attractive men and women were hired over less attractive applicants with equal qualifications.[39] On the positive side, however, a recent study demonstrated that interviewer training can reduce the use of invalid schemata. Training improved interviewers' ability to obtain high-quality, job-related information and to stay focused on the interview task. Trained interviewers provided more balanced judgements about applicants than non-trained interviewers.[40] A Belgian study of 1724 respondents of the perception of diversity in the workplace revealed that people pretended to be rarely influenced by sex differences when hiring new employees. Age played a more important role: younger people preferred younger people, older respondents opted for their contemporaries. In traditional environments people chose more traditionally: ethnic minorities and [known] homosexuals had less chance of being recruited.[41] Diversity will be discussed at the end of this chapter.

PERFORMANCE APPRAISAL

Faulty schemata about what constitutes good as opposed to poor performance can lead to inaccurate performance appraisals, which erode work motivation, commitment and loyalty (see Chapter 6). For example, a recent study of 166 production employees indicated that they had greater trust in management when they perceived that the performance appraisal process provided accurate evaluations of their performance.[42] Therefore, it is important for managers to identify accurately the behavioural characteristics and results indicative of good performance at the beginning of a performance review cycle. These characteristics can then serve as the benchmarks for evaluating employee performance.

The importance of using objective rather than subjective measures of employee performance was highlighted in a meta-analysis involving 50 studies and 8341 individuals. Results revealed that objective and subjective measures of employee performance were only moderately related. The researchers concluded that objective and subjective measures of performance are not interchangeable.[43] Professionals are thus advised to use more objectively based measures of performance – as much as possible – because subjective indicators are prone to bias and inaccuracy. In those cases where the job does not possess objective measures of performance, however, professionals should still use subjective evaluations. Furthermore, because memory of specific instances of employee performance deteriorates over time, employers need a mechanism for accurately recalling employee behaviour.[44] Research reveals that individuals can be trained to be more accurate raters of performance.[45]

Attributions

Why did the plant manager not inform us earlier about the internationalisation plans? Why were the French, German and Belgian governments against the war in Iraq, whereas Great Britain and the US were strong proponents? Why did Madonna and Britney Spears kiss each other at the 2004 MTV awards? Just like scientists, laymen try to answer why people are acting or behaving in a certain way, what the meaning is or underlying causes are of that unexpected behaviour. People want to make sense of the world by trying to find an explanation of other people's behaviour. The explanations they come up with for these 'why' questions are **Attributions**. Heider, the pioneer in attribution research, formulated attributions as the inferred causes why we behave the way we do.[46] According to Sims and Lorenzi attributions are cognitive evaluations that attempt to formulate explanations for an event, such as failure or success in an achievement-oriented task. Studying how attributions operate is important for the understanding of behaviour. Insight in the functioning of attributions is of great significance in the prediction of decision making, and especially in the context of performance appraisal, and the capability of professionals to influence employees towards future performance achievement.[47] Consequently, the inquiry how attributions work provides insight into the motivation of employees toward achievement. Two people accomplish for example the same production level; the manager evaluates person A as displaying a lack of effort, while person B achieving the same productivity is assessed as a hard worker. Henceforth, the supervisor decides to give person B a pay rise because of his proven zeal at work, while person A is reprimanded because of his lack of effort. A comprehensive attribution example is displayed below.

Types of attribution

It is possible to formulate an almost unlimited number of attributions for perceived actions, events and behaviour. Cross-cultural attribution research asking six UK and five German engineers to evaluate a culture change programme through semi-structured interviews elicited 419 attributions (see the next Snapshot).[48] Mervielde classified the plethora of attributions in a framework.[49] The proposed framework covers 'locus of causality', 'stability', 'controllability', 'generalisability', 'desirability' and 'proximity'. Gioia and Sims described the first three dimensions of this framework in organisational settings.[50]

Heider was the founding father of the locus of causality dimension. He discerned internal and external causes of behaviour. Internal causes of behaviour concern factors within the actor (**Internal factors**), while external causes are situated outside the actor (**External factors**).[51] Somebody who fails his statistics exam can attribute this deficiency to misfortune, task difficulty (both external causes) or intelligence, mood (internal causes).

According to some scholars the locus of causality classification had to be expanded with a stability dimension.[52] The stability dimension refers to whether the attribution is static or dynamic in time. A task failure resulting from a single lack of effort is an unstable factor, while a lack of capability is considered a stable factor.

The controllability dimension underscores the significance of control over the causes of behaviour: are the events situated within or outside the command of a person? Returning to the example of task failure, a lack of effort is a cause within the command of a person, while task difficulty is a less controllable cause. When a person is always facing a condition that he or she does not control and the outcome is negative, this could lead to learned helplessness (see Chapter 2).

The combination of the locus of causality, stability and controllability dimensions leads to eight categories of attributions as displayed in Table 4.2.

The fourth dimension, generalisability, covers the specific character of a cause. This attribution dimension reveals information about whether an attribution or cause is generalisable across distinct situations. The purpose of this criterion is to distinguish causes with a limited effect from causes with an effect that can emerge in disparate situations. An unsound organisational climate attributed to the CEO's behaviour will have different implications from when this negative climate is explained by the autocratic character of CEOs in general.

Compared to the previous dimensions, the desirability dimension mainly accentuates the features

Attributions
inferred causes of perceived behaviour, actions or events

Internal factors
personal characteristics that cause behaviour

External factors
environmental characteristics that cause behaviour

TABLE 4.2 ATTRIBUTION DIMENSIONS

Locus of causality	Controllable		Uncontrollable	
	Stable	Unstable	Stable	Unstable
Internal	Typical effort	Intermediate effort	Ability	Mood
External	Supervisor	Co-workers	Task difficulty	Luck

Types of attributions: locus of causality, controllability and stability.

SOURCE: Reprinted from *Organizational Behavior and Human Decision Processes*, Vol. 37, D. Gioia and H. Sims, 'Cognitive-Behavior Connections: Attribution and Verbal Behavior in Leader–Subordinate Interactions', pp. 197–229, copyright 1986, with permission from Elsevier.

of attributions without considering the subjective appreciation and thus the social desirability of attributions. This dimension is essential for interpersonal attitudes. For example, Jeff arrives at work half an hour late. The fact that he could not get out of bed is a less socially desirable attribution than being late at work because of a traffic jam.

The proximity dimension finally emphasises that behaviour can sometimes be explained by multiple causes in which different causes influence each other. For instance, job satisfaction at work is encouraged by organisational support, which in turn is influenced by the personality of organisational members. Burnout is influenced by perceived stress. However, this proximal cause of burnout is affected by optimism, a distal cause of burnout.[53]

The successfulness of a cultural change process in Germany and the UK

In the context of cross-cultural attribution research, the aim of three English scholars was to examine whether five German and six English engineers from the same multinational company responded differently to the introduction of a cultural change programme. Semi-structured interviews were conducted, which included topics such as: the engineers' involvement in the programme, how successful they perceived the programme to be, what the programme was likely to achieve, potential barriers to the programme, how the programme might influence organisational culture and so on. A total of 419 attributions were analysed from 11 interviews. The UK engineers produced proportionately more negative attributions (59.1 per cent), whereas German engineers produced proportionately more positive attributions (70.0 per cent). Both groups differed because Germans and English vary on the individualism dimension of Hofstede. This dimension covers the willingness to speak one's mind. The UK scores higher on individualism compared to Germany (see also Chapter 16). Further analysis of the negative and positive attributions demonstrated that German and UK engineers attributed similar levels of stability (40 per cent) to positive outcomes. The UK engineers perceived the positive attributions to be more global (50 per cent) than did the German engineers (35 per cent). This means that UK engineers were more likely to perceive the programme as having an influence throughout the whole company. Both German and UK engineers perceived the majority of the negative attributions to involve global causes (85 per cent). However, the Germans were more likely to attribute these negative outcomes to stable causes (58 per cent) than the UK engineers (45 per cent). This means that German engineers perceived these negative attributions to be more permanent than did their English colleagues.

SOURCE: J. Silvester, E. Ferguson, and F. Patterson, 'Comparing Spoken Attributions by German and UK Engineers: Evaluating the Success of a Culture Change Programme', *European Journal of Work and Organizational Psychology*, March 1997, pp. 103–117.

snapshot

Attribution theories

Many theories have been developed about ascribing causes to behaviour. There are three theories especially that should be examined thoroughly within the organisational behaviour framework: i.e. the correspondent inference theory of Jones and Davis,[54] the covariation theory of Kelley[55] and the work of Weiner on attribution theory and achievement motivation.[56]

CORRESPONDENT INFERENCE THEORY (JONES AND DAVIS)

Jones and Davis took Heider's naive psychology (also commonsense psychology) a step further in their correspondent inference theory.[57] In his book, *The Psychology of Interpersonal Relations*, Heider contends that naive psychology guides our interactions with other people through its influence on behaviour, leading us to form ideas about others and the use of that gathered information predicting future behaviour. Naive psychology provides us with the principles to build our picture of the social environment and guide our reactions to it.[58]

The correspondent inference theory describes how an alert perceiver infers another's intentions and personal dispositions from his or her behaviour. It is a theory of how we use other people's behaviour as a basic assumption for assessing the stability of their personalities. For example, one of your colleagues likes to help other people. Consequently you might infer that Jim has an altruistic personality because of his helpful behaviour. The chance however that a disposition is derived from a perceived slice of behaviour is dependent upon three factors: non-common effects, social desirability of effects and degree of choice.

Non-common effects tell us more about a person's disposition than expected effects. Behaviour reveals more about a person when it diverges from what is known as typical expected behaviour. For instance, people think they know more about a student when he wears a sloppy tracksuit and sneakers full of mud for his oral examinations, than when he arrives dressed in a suit and wearing leather shoes.

Socially undesirable behaviour leads to correspondent inference more than correct behaviour. A person making a noise and acting conspicuously while he or she is shopping in a grocery store reveals much information on that person's personality.

A third factor is the person's degree of free choice. Behaviour that is freely chosen holds a lot more information about personality than behaviour that is coerced. In one study, participants reading a student's speech that favoured or opposed Fidel Castro tended to assume that the speech reflected the student's true attitude (personality disposition) when the student had freely chosen to write the speech, rather than when the student was instructed to write a speech favouring or opposing Fidel Castro.[59]

COVARIATION MODEL (KELLEY)

Covariation principle
principle of attribution theory holding that people attribute behaviour to factors that are present when behaviour occurs and absent when it does not

In the correspondent inference theory behaviour is attributed to an underlying personality characteristic. However, behaviour can also be the result of situational factors. The **Covariation principle** is the central theme in Kelley's theory. The covariation principle states that for a factor to be the cause of behaviour it must be present when the behaviour occurs and absent when it does not. This theory explains whether behaviour stems from internal or external causes. In this context people make internal or external inferences after gathering three types of information. According to the covariation principle people are looking in three domains that are: the perceived stimulus object, other people who could be in a similar situation and the entire context surrounding the event (for instance, other time periods). These three types of information are also called distinctiveness, consensus and consistency.

For example Max starts laughing at the 'The Austin Powers in Goldmember' movie. When Max only laughs at this movie, the behaviour is high in distinctiveness; however, the behaviour is low in distinctiveness when he laughs at all Austin Power movies. You might also want to know what happens to Max's behaviour at another point of time. Does Max also laugh when he watches the movie a second time? If it is the case, the behaviour is highly consistent; if not, it is low on consistency. Finally, it is important to know whether other people respond in similar ways to Max when watching the movie. If others respond in a similar way to this movie, then there is high consensus; if most of the others do not respond similarly, then there is low consistency.

Thus, distinctiveness information is about whether the target person responds in the same way to other stimuli as well. Consensus information concerns whether only a few people respond in the same way as the target person. Finally, the consistency information answers the question: 'Does the target person always respond in the same way to other stimuli as well?'.

According to Baron and Byrne the combination of high consensus (others behave in the same manner in this situation), high consistency (this person behaves in the same manner on other occasions when placed in the same situation) and high distinctiveness information (this person does not behave in this manner in other situations) is likely to lead to external attributions.[60] The combination of low consensus, high distinctiveness and low consistency will probably also result in external attributions.[61] However, the chance of making internal attributions is considerable when the perceived behaviour is low on consensus (others do not behave in the same manner in this situation), high on consistency (this person behaves in the same manner on other occasions when placed in the same situation) and low on distinctiveness (this person behaves in the same manner in other situations). McArthur demonstrates that this kind of information configuration leads to internal attributions of the perceived effects in 85 per cent of cases.[62] Figure 4.5 is an overview of which combinations of covariation information lead to internal or external attributions.

FIGURE 4.5 COVARIATION INFORMATION AND INTERNAL VERSUS EXTERNAL ATTRIBUTIONS

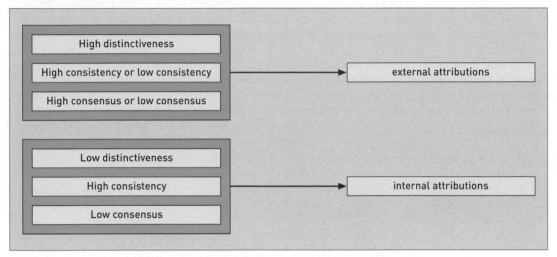

ATTRIBUTION MODEL (WEINER)

Bernard Weiner, a noted motivation theorist, developed an attribution model to explain achievement behaviour and to predict subsequent changes in motivation and performance. Figure 4.6 presents a modified version of his model. Weiner believes that the attribution process begins after an individual performs a task. A person's performance leads him or her to judge whether it was successful or unsuccessful. This evaluation then produces a causal analysis to determine if the performance was due to internal or external factors. Figure 4.6 shows that ability and effort are the primary internal causes of performance and task difficulty; luck and help from others are the key external causes. These attributions for success and failure then influence how individuals feel about themselves. It has been pointed out that high achievement motivates people to attribute their successes to their own efforts and their failures to not trying hard enough. If they fail they are likely to try again because they tend to believe that with greater effort they can succeed. These high achievement-motivated people consistently perceive their ability levels as being quite high. If they succeed it is because they tried hard and used their abilities. By contrast, those with a low need for achievement view effort as irrelevant. They attribute failure to other factors, in particular lack of ability, a condition that they believe is one of their general characteristics. Success is considered a consequence of the external factors of easy tasks and luck.[63] Hence, it is quite clear that if we are interested in motivating a person, what will work with an achievement-motivated person may be absolutely useless with a person who lacks achievement motivation (also see Chapter 5). Consequently, educational programmes attempting to bring about motivational change and development in achievement should first focus on teaching the participants that effort does make a difference and that internal causation is a key factor mediating between a task and the level of performance of that task.

A meta-analysis of 104 studies involving almost 15000 individuals showed that people who attributed failure to their lack of ability (as opposed to bad luck) experienced psychological depression.

The exact opposite attributions (good luck rather than high ability) tended to trigger depression in people experiencing positive events. In short, perceived bad luck took the sting out of a negative outcome, but perceived good luck reduced the joy associated with success.[64]

Returning to Figure 4.6, note that the psychological consequences can either increase or decrease depending on the causes of performance. For example, your self-esteem is likely to increase after achieving an 'A' in your next exam if you believe that your performance was due to your ability or effort. In contrast, this same grade can either increase or decrease your self-esteem if you believe that the test was easy. Finally, the feelings that people have about their past performance influence future performance. Figure 4.6 reveals that future performance is higher when individuals attribute success to internal causes in comparison with external attributions and lower when failure is attributed to internal causes in comparison with external factors. Future performance is more uncertain when individuals attribute either their success or failure to external causes.

In further support of Weiner's model, a study of 130 salesmen in the United Kingdom revealed that positive, internal attributions for success were associated with higher sales and performance ratings.[65] A second study examined the attribution processes of 126 employees who were made redundant by a plant closing. Practice was seen to be consistent with the model: the explanation for job loss was attributed to internal and stable causes; so the life satisfaction, self-esteem and expectations for reemployment, diminished. Furthermore, research shows that when individuals attribute their success to internal rather than external factors, they have higher expectations for future success, report a greater desire for achievement and set higher performance goals.[66]

FIGURE 4.6 A MODIFIED VERSION OF WEINER'S ATTRIBUTION MODEL

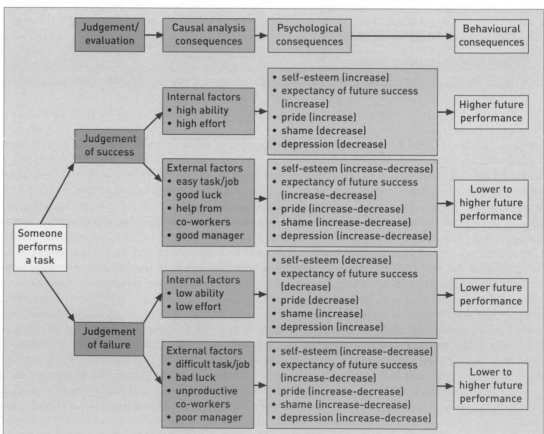

SOURCE: Based in part on B. Weiner, 'An Attributional Theory of Achievement Motivation and Emotion', *Psychological Review*, October 1985, pp. 548–73; and T. S. Bateman, G. R. Ferris and S. Strasser, 'The "Why" behind Individual Work Performance', *Management Review*, October 1984, p. 71.

Attributional biases

Several tendencies or biases distort the interpretations we make of observed behaviour. Five such biases have been identified: the fundamental error, the defensive attribution, the actor–observer effect, self-serving bias and the fundamental attribution error.[67]

The **Fundamental error** refers to the observation that attributions are more often made in terms of internal causality.[68] It is a general tendency of inferring internal causes rather than external causes of actions. Research shows that this tendency is a cultural phenomenon, a product of Western, and particularly North American, culture.[69]

The defensive attribution has its roots in the belief in a just world. This type of distortion is characterised as the tendency to blame victims for their own misfortune and is an extension of the fundamental attribution error. Believing in a just world is in fact denying 'fate'. People have the need to believe that they control their surroundings and they must be able to reduce fate as a possible cause for events.[70] They do not believe that good and bad things are randomly distributed. According to the belief in a just world an innocent victim would not be considered so innocent and would likely be ascribed responsibility for his or her condition. This is a convenient way for other people to put their minds at ease by telling themselves that such a thing cannot happen to them.[71]

The actor–observer effect concerns the fact that actors make different attributions about themselves compared to observers.[72] An actor views his or her own actions in terms of a reaction to a situation whereas an observer perceives that behaviour in terms of a personal disposition. As the behaviour itself is more important to the observer than the contextual information, the observer compares the actor's demeanour with that of other people under the same conditions and consequently makes attributions regarding the actor's personality. However, the actor assesses his or her own behaviour in comparison to his or her reactions in different situations. So, the actor does not make any comparison with other people's reactions. Hence, in the case of the actor, the context explains his or her behaviour. A special case of the actor–observer difference phenomenon is the subordinate–superior relationship. The attributions that subordinates make about themselves can differ from attributions that professionals make about them. Research shows that actors and observers often perceive the same events in a totally different way. In a situation of failure a subordinate attributes the failure to external conditions, whereas the manager is likely to ascribe the failure to internal factors. This difference often leads to conflicts between both parties.[73]

The **Self-serving bias** is the tendency to attribute our positive outcomes to internal factors and to attribute our negative outcomes to external factors. People are inclined to bear personal responsibility for successful achievements but not for failures or problematic outcomes. Consequently, in an organisational setting employees display the propensity to ascribe their successes to internal factors such as high ability and hard work, whereas failures or negative outcomes are attributed to uncontrollable external factors (tough job, bad luck, unproductive co-workers or an unsympathetic boss).[74] Three explanations are possible for this. The first is a motivational explanation and is based on self-esteem (see Chapter 2). People want to keep or enhance their self-esteem. They will be resistant to negative implications which attack their self-esteem. The second is an information-processing explanation. According to this process the self-serving bias tendency will occur because of an imbalance in the logical processing of available information. The third explanation refers to impression management. Self-serving bias will arise when individuals act to manage the impressions they make on others by taking credit for successes and denying responsibility for mistakes, errors or negative outcomes (see Chapter 13).[75] In a study on perceptions of performance appraisal by employees and supervisors it was demonstrated that supervisors used a self-serving bias in the perception of performance appraisal. Supervisors perceived that they used more participative leadership and had better conversational techniques than the subordinates perceived.[76]

The fundamental attribution error refers to the fact that desirable actions and behaviour are attributed to internal factors when it is made by in-group members and to external causes for out-group members. In the case of undesirable demeanour, this behaviour is attributed to external factors when it is made by in-group members and to internal causality for out-group members.[77] For example, a study of 1420 employees of a large utility company showed that supervisors were more inclined to make internal attributions about worker accidents than the workers themselves did.[78] Another study in which entrepreneurs' and venture capitalists' perceptions of new venture failure are compared found that the entrepreneurs attributed their failure to internal factors (58 per cent) rather than

Fundamental error tendency to attribute other's success to external factors and other's failure to internal factors

Self-serving bias tendency to attribute one's success to internal factors and one's failure to external factors

143

external factors. So, entrepreneurs do not necessarily attribute their own failures to external factors. Venture capitalists on the contrary tend to attribute their own failure to external causes (66 per cent)[79]

Attributional processes in leader–member interactions

Green and Mitchell proposed a theory of attributions in leader–member interactions.[80] This theory is a synthesis of Kelly's and Weiner's work on attributions. This theory assumes that leaders act as scientists in engaging a process of hypotheses testing by gathering information and seeking causal explanations about the behaviour and performance of their subordinates. A leader's behaviour will depend more on consistency in time (called 'consistency') and differently across situations or tasks (distinctiveness) than on information gathered on consensus information. Consequently, the leader is more likely to explain a member's performance using internal rather than external causes. By contrast, an employee will explain his or her own performance using external causes. This may result in a major source of conflict between management and subordinates. The locus of causality and stability dimension are two significant attribution dimensions mediating leader's reactions to member performance. For instance, the leader is likely to emphasise his or her actions on the member when performance is seen as the result of internal causes. However, when a member's achievement is ascribed to external causes, the leader is likely to focus his or her actions on situational factors. The leader's assessment of members is most influenced by internal and unstable attributions, such as luck. He or she will be more and less rewarding or punishing when the present performance is attributed to effort. Also, when the attributional cause of performance is stable, expectancies arise about the consistency of future performance. Another important factor associated with the actual attribution process is the level of uncertainty a leader experiences in attempting to manage subordinates. Multiple and or unstable causal attributions will surely increase the levels of insecurity felt among leaders. The relationship between the leader and his members is a very critical factor in attribution formation as well. A leader's empathy may influence the formation of favourable attributions of members. The more removed the leader is (due to great power distance), the more likely he or she is to make unfavourable causal attributions. Finally, the leader's expectations about member performance will interact with actual performance to determine leader's attributions. For example, the leader will attribute member performance to internal causes when expectations and performance are consistent, whereas external attributions are made when expectations and performance are inconsistent.

Research findings and practical implications

Attribution models can be used to explain how professionals handle poorly performing employees. One study revealed that managers gave employees more immediate, frequent and negative feedback when they attributed their performance to low effort. This reaction was even more pronounced when the manager's success was dependent on an employee's performance. A second study indicated that professionals tended to transfer employees whose poor performance was attributed to a lack of ability. These managers also decided to take no immediate action when poor performance was attributed to external factors beyond an individual's control.[81]

The preceding situations have several important implications for employers. First, employers tend to attribute behaviour disproportionately to internal causes.[82] This can result in inaccurate evaluations of performance, leading to reduced employee motivation. No one likes to be blamed for something caused by factors they perceive to be beyond their control. Further, because managers' responses to employee performance vary according to their attributions, attributional biases may lead to inappropriate actions, including promotions, transfers, lay-offs and so forth. This can weaken motivation and performance. Attributional training sessions for managers are in order. Basic attributional processes can be explained and professionals can be taught to detect and avoid attributional biases. Finally, an employee's attributions for his or her own performance can have dramatic effects on subsequent motivation, performance and personal attitudes such as self-esteem. For instance, people tend to give up, develop lower expectations for future success and experience decreased self-esteem when they attribute failure to a lack of ability (see Chapter 2). Fortunately, attributional retraining can improve both motivation and performance. Research shows that employees can be taught to attribute their failures to a lack of effort rather than to a lack of ability.[83] This attributional realignment paves the way for improved motivation and performance.

In summary, professionals need to be aware of employee attributions if they are to make full use of the motivation concepts, explained in Chapters 5 and 6.

Self-fulfilling prophecy

The historical roots of the self-fulfilling prophecy are found in Greek mythology. According to mythology, Pygmalion was a sculptor who hated women yet fell in love with an ivory statue he had carved of a beautiful woman. He became so infatuated with the statue that he prayed to the goddess Aphrodite to bring her to life. The goddess heard his prayer, granted his wish and Pygmalion's statue came to life. The essence of the **Self-fulfilling prophecy**, or Pygmalion effect, is that people's expectations or beliefs determine their behaviour and performance, thus serving to make their expectations come true. In other words, we strive to validate our perceptions of reality, no matter how faulty they may be. Thus, the self-fulfilling prophecy is an important perceptual outcome we need to understand better.

Self-fulfilling prophecy people's expectations determine behaviour and performance

Research and an explanatory model

The self-fulfilling prophecy was first demonstrated in an academic environment. After giving a bogus test of academic potential to students from grades 1 to 6, researchers informed teachers that certain students had high potential for achievement. In reality, students were randomly assigned to the 'high potential' and 'control' (normal potential) groups. Results showed that children designated as having high potential obtained significantly greater increases in both IQ scores and reading ability than the control group.[84] The teachers of the supposedly high potential group got better results because their high expectations caused them to give harder assignments, more feedback, and more recognition of achievement. Students in the normal potential group did not excel, because their teachers did not expect outstanding results.

Research has similarly shown that by raising instructors' and professionals' expectations for individuals performing a wide variety of tasks, higher levels of achievement and productivity can be obtained.[85] Subjects in these field studies included airmen at the United States Air Force Academy Preparatory School, disadvantaged people in job-training programmes, electronics assemblers, trainees in a military command course, US naval personnel and cadets in a naval officer course in the Israel Defence Forces. There is an interesting trend inherent in research supporting the Pygmalion effect. All studies exclusively involved men.

To overcome this limitation, a recent team of researchers conducted two experimental studies on samples of female and male cadets in the Israel Defence Forces. Results revealed that the Pygmalion effect was produced for both female and male cadets – but only when the leader was male. Female leaders did not produce a significant Pygmalion effect. This finding must be considered in the light of the fact that women were rated as better leaders than men in the Israel Defence Forces. The researchers concluded that the Pygmalion effect clearly works on both women and men when the leader is male but not when the leader is female.[86] Future research is obviously needed to uncover the cause of these gender-based differences.

A meta-analysis reviewed 13 studies regarding the Pygmalion effect in work organisations and had a closer look into the nature of the effect. This analysis revealed the strength of the Pygmalion effect in organisations. Seventy-nine per cent of the people in the high expectancy groups outperformed the average people in the control groups. Furthermore, the meta-analysis revealed that the Pygmalion effect varied depending on the type of organisation. The effect was stronger in military settings than in business settings. The effect was also larger for those subordinates whose initial level of performance was low in comparison to those in which whole group expectations were induced.[87]

Figure 4.7 presents a model of the self-fulfilling prophecy that helps explain these results. This model attempts to outline how supervisory expectations affect employee performance. As indicated, high supervisory expectation produces better leadership (linkage 1), which subsequently leads employees to develop higher self-expectations (linkage 2). Higher expectations motivate workers to exert more effort (linkage 3), ultimately increasing performance (linkage 4) and supervisory expectations (linkage 5). Successful performance also improves an employee's self-expectancy for achievement (linkage 6). A team of researchers recently coined the term the **Set-up-to-fail syndrome** to represent the negative side of the performance-enhancing process depicted in Figure 4.7.[88] Let us consider how it works.

Set-up-to-fail syndrome Creating and reinforcing a dynamic that essentially sets up perceived weaker performers to fail

FIGURE 4.7 A MODEL OF THE SELF-FULFILLING PROPHECY

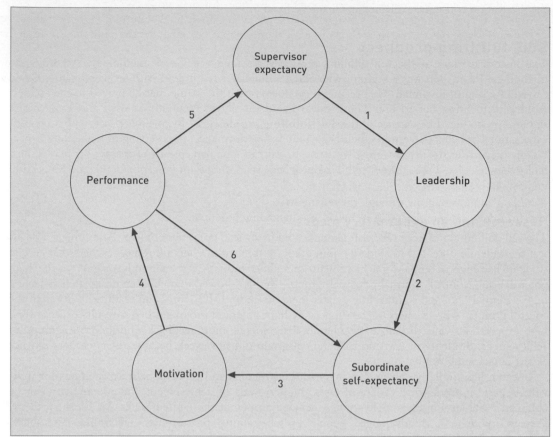

SOURCE: D. Eden, 'Self-Fulfilling Prophecy as a Management Tool: Harnessing Pygmalion', *Academy of Management Review*, January 1984, p. 67. Used with permission.

Say an employee makes a mistake, such as losing notes during a meeting or exhibits poor perform-ance on a task by turning in a report a day late. An employer then begins to wonder if this person has what it takes to be successful in the organisation. These doubts lead the employer to watch this person more carefully. The employee, of course, notices this and begins to sense a loss of trust. The suspect employee then responds in one of two ways. He or she may doubt his or her own judgement and competence. This in turn leads the individual to become more averse to taking risk and to reduce the number of ideas and suggestions for the professional's critical review. The employer notices this behaviour and interprets it as an example of low initiative. Alternatively, the employee may do the opposite and take on more and more responsibility so that he or she can demonstrate his or her com-petence and worth. This is likely to cause the employee to fail, which in turn reinforces the employer's suspicions.[89] This process results in a destructive relationship fuelled by negative expecta-tions. The self-fulfilling prophecy works in both directions. The next section discusses ideas for enhancing the Pygmalion effect and reducing the set-up-to-fail syndrome.

Self-fulfilling prophecy at work

Largely due to the Pygmalion effect, expectations have a powerful influence on employee behaviour and performance. Consequently, professionals need to harness the Pygmalion effect by building a hierarchical framework that reinforces positive performance expectations throughout the organisa-tion. This framework is based on employees' self-expectations. In turn, positive self-expectations improve interpersonal expectations by encouraging people to work toward common goals. This co-operation enhances group-level productivity and promotes positive performance expectations within the work group. At Microsoft, for example, employees routinely put in 75-hour weeks, especially when work groups are trying to meet shipment deadlines for new products. At Microsoft positive group-level expectations help to create and reinforce an organisational culture of high expectancy of success. This process then makes people enthusiastic about working for the organisation, thereby reducing turnover.[90]

As positive self-expectations are the foundation for creating an organisation-wide Pygmalion effect, let us then consider how employers can create positive performance expectations. This task may be accomplished by using various combinations of the following:

- Recognise that everyone has the potential to increase his or her performance.
- Instil confidence in your staff.
- Set high performance goals.
- Positively reinforce employees for a job well done.
- Provide constructive feedback when necessary.
- Help employees grow through the organisation.
- Introduce new employees as if they have outstanding potential.
- Become aware of your personal prejudices and any non-verbal messages that may discourage others.
- Encourage employees to visualise the successful execution of tasks.
- Help employees master key skills and tasks.[91]

Stereotypes

While it is often true that beauty is in the eye of the beholder, perception does result in some predictable outcomes. People aware of the perception process and its outcomes enjoy a competitive edge.

The Walt Disney Company, for instance, takes full advantage of perceptual tendencies to influence customers' reactions to waiting in long lines at its theme parks:

> In order to make the experience less psychologically wearing, the waiting times posted by each attraction are generously overestimated, so that one comes away mysteriously grateful for having hung around 20 minutes for a 58-second twirl in the Alice in Wonderland teacups. The lines, moreover, are always moving, even if what looks like the end is actually the start of a second set of switchbacks leading to—oh, no!—a pre-ride waiting area. Those little tricks of the theme park mean a lot.[92]

Likewise, professionals can use knowledge of perceptual outcomes to help them interact more effectively with employees. For example, Table 4.3 describes five common perceptual errors. Since these perceptual errors often distort the evaluation of job applicants and of employee performance, employers need to guard against them. This section examines one of the most important and potentially harmful perceptual outcomes associated with person perception: stereotypes. After exploring the process of stereotype formation and maintenance, we discuss sex-role stereotypes, age stereotypes, race stereotypes, and the challenge to avoid stereotypical biases.

Stereotype formation and maintenance

'A **Stereotype** is an individual's set of beliefs about the characteristics or attributes of a group.'[93] This implies people are judged on the basis of their membership of some known group. Stereotypes are not always negative. For example, the belief that engineers are good at maths is certainly part of a stereotype. Ruth Woodfield, researcher at the University of Sussex (UK), recently stated that women are most likely to be the possessors of the skills required to successfully design and develop information systems – a combination of technical and, crucially, social and communication skills. The information systems industry has however been disproportionately populated by men. Male designers, developers and vendors were often almost exclusively focused upon the technology itself, rather than on the requirements of users or the commercial viability of the technical product.[94] Stereotypes may be accurate, but very often this is not the case, as you can see in the following example:

Stereotype beliefs about the characteristics of a group

TABLE 4.3 COMMONLY FOUND PERCEPTUAL ERRORS

Perceptual error	Description	Example
Halo	A rater forms an overall impression about an object and then uses that impression to bias ratings about the object	Rating a professor high on the teaching dimensions of ability to motivate students, knowledge and communication because we like him or her
Leniency	A personal characteristic that leads an individual to consistently evaluate other people or objects in an extremely positive fashion	Rating a professor high on all dimensions of performance regardless of his or her actual performance
Central tendency	The tendency to avoid all extreme judgements and rate people and objects as average or neutral	Rating a professor average on all dimensions of performance regardless of his or her actual performance
Recency effects	The tendency to remember recent information. If the recent information is negative, the person or object is evaluated negatively	Although a professor has given good lectures for 12 to 15 weeks, he or she is evaluated negatively because lectures over the last 3 weeks were done poorly
Contrast effects	The tendency to evaluate people or objects by comparing them with characteristics of recently observed people or objects	Rating a good professor as average because you compared his or her performance with three of the best professors you have ever had in college. You are currently taking courses from the three excellent professors

> Footage of aggressive English football fans at Euro 2000 would lead us to believe that they are uniquely chubby, balding and working class. This image is not accurate because plenty of football hooligans are educated, middle-class bankers or professionals, whose comfortable, rather dull lifestyles are supplemented by the occasional excesses at the football stadium. However, today's cameramen are still instructed by their editors only to film tattooed, beer-gutted, tonsured barbarians head-butting the French or pulverising the Portuguese. This just adds to our perception that all the middle-class fans must be round the corner visiting a museum or tutting at the trouble over a cappuccino.[95]

In general, stereotypic characteristics are used to differentiate a particular group of people from other groups.[96] The previous example highlights how people use stereotypes to interpret their environment and to make judgements about others.

Unfortunately, stereotypes can lead to poor decisions and can create barriers for women, older individuals, ethnic minorities and people with disabilities. Stereotypes can undermine loyalty and job satisfaction. For example, a study of 280 minority executives revealed that 40 per cent believed that they had been denied well-deserved promotions because of discrimination. Another sample of 2958 workers indicated that women and people of ethnic minorities perceived lower chances of advancement than white people. Finally, respondents who saw little opportunity for advancement tended to be less loyal, less committed and less satisfied with their jobs.[97] Further in this chapter we will see how stereotyping can be turned into a competitive advantage thanks to managing diversity.

Stereotyping is a four-step process. It begins by categorising people into groups according to various criteria, such as gender, age, race, religion, sexual orientation and occupation. Next, we infer that all people within a particular category possess the same traits or characteristics (e.g. all women are nurturing, older people have more job-related accidents,[98] Africans are good athletes, all Muslims are fundamentalists, and all professors are absentminded). Then, we form expectations of others and interpret their behaviour according to our stereotypes. Finally, stereotypes are maintained by (1) overestimating the frequency of stereotypic behaviours exhibited by others, (2) incorrectly explaining expected and unexpected behaviours and (3) differentiating minority individuals from oneself.[99]

Although these steps are self-reinforcing, there are ways to break the chain of stereotyping. Research shows that the use of stereotypes is influenced by the amount and type of information available to an individual and his or her motivation to process information accurately.[100] People are less apt to use stereotypes to judge others when they encounter salient information that is highly inconsistent with a stereotype. For instance, you are unlikely to assign stereotypic 'professor' traits to a new professor you have this semester if he or she rides a Harley-Davidson, wears leather trousers to class, and has a pierced nose.

People also are less likely to rely on stereotypes when they are motivated to avoid using them – that is, accurate information processing requires mental effort. Stereotyping is generally viewed as a less effortful strategy of information processing. Let us now take a look at different types of stereotypes and consider additional methods for reducing their biasing effects and for welcoming 'different' people in the workplace.

Sex-Role Stereotypes

A **Sex-role stereotype** is the belief that differing traits and abilities make men and women particularly well suited to different roles. For example, gender stereotypes view women as more expressive, less independent, more emotional, less logical, less quantitatively oriented and more participative than men. Men, on the other hand, are more often perceived as lacking interpersonal sensitivity and warmth, less expressive, less apt to ask for directions, more quantitatively oriented and more autocratic and directive than women.[101]

Although research demonstrates that men and women do not systematically differ in the manner suggested by traditional stereotypes,[102] these stereotypes still persist. A study compared sex-role stereotypes held by men and women from five countries: China, Japan, Germany, the United Kingdom and the United States. Males in all five countries perceived that successful professionals possessed characteristics and traits more commonly ascribed to men in general than to women in general. Among the females, the same pattern of sex typing was found in all countries except the United States. US females perceived that males and females were equally likely to possess traits necessary for success.[103] Also of interest, research recently revealed that the old image of the 'dumb blonde' still remains entrenched. Tony Cassidy of Coventry University in the UK asked 120 students of both sexes to look at a photograph of a model and rate her intelligence, shyness, aggression, temperament, and popularity. They were given one of four photos of the same woman, identical except for the hair colour: platinum blonde, natural blonde, brown haired or red haired. The platinum blonde was rated as significantly less intelligent than the others, and this was slightly more apparent when the viewers were men.[104] Females are more often typed in terms of sexuality and sexual attractiveness according to researchers Vonk and Ashmore. Most of these sexual female types were negative (e.g. bimbo, whore, and dumb blonde). For males, they found that the types were more differentiated in terms of occupation and that the 'default' male has a job and a profession, whereas non-traditional males do not work. Because these results are consistent across multiple studies from different Western countries, we may conclude that they reflect current stereotypes of men and women in Western society.[105]

WOMEN ENTERING THE WORKFORCE

Women still have difficulties in climbing the corporate ladder. By 2010 the European Union wants 60 per cent of all women to have a job. Today female employment in the EU amounts to 55.6 per cent.[106] An improvement has, however, been noticed recently, as women constituted 42 per cent of the EU labour force in 1998. Women form 37.5 per cent of solicitors in Scotland in 2000, in comparison with 8.5 per cent in 1971; however, at a more senior level, year 2000 data show that women make up 21 per cent of advocates, 8 per cent of Queen's Counsels, 15 per cent of sheriffs and 6 per cent of judges.[107] Research at the University of Nijmegen in the Netherlands confirms that in the

Sex-role stereotype beliefs about appropriate roles for men and women

course of time, norms on traditional gender roles seem to have altered. People are more accustomed to working women, which is expressed in a decline of their support for the discrimination of women on the labour market.[108]

Despite this positive evolution and the ambitious European target, women continue to encounter the glass ceiling.[109] The **Glass ceiling** represents an invisible barrier that separates women and minorities from advancing into top management positions. It can be particularly demotivating because employees can look up and see coveted top management positions through the transparent ceiling but are unable to obtain them. In Europe, women represent hardly 3 per cent of all general managers and 17 per cent of all managers.[110]

Figures from Cranfield School of Management revealed that, although the number of female directorships in the UK was up by 20 per cent in 2003, there were still 32 companies that had no women directors at all.[111]

Historically, female employment was concentrated in relatively low-paying and low-level occupation. The gender pay gap has barely narrowed in recent years and remains high – 20 per cent on average – across Europe.[112] The top 10 per cent of women wage earners in the EU earn on average 35 per cent less than the top 10 per cent of men wage earners. This is true throughout the EU and is especially marked in France, Italy and the UK.[113] The UK has the biggest gender pay gap in Europe between the hourly rate of full-time men and part-time women. The discrepancy is 41 per cent compared with 7 per cent in The Netherlands.[114] According to recent research in France the salary gap between male and female middle managers amount up to 30 per cent.[115]

One of the reasons why women are unable to break the glass ceiling is the masculine culture typical for the highest corporate echelons. According to Marisa Silvestri, senior lecturer in Criminology at London South Bank University, there is a cult of masculinity in many organisations. She pointed to women's struggle to rise in the ranks in policing, faced with high hierarchies, transactional management styles, and linear uninterrupted career paths with little flexibility, problems with credibility in a masculine culture, and isolation from other women. In recent research from Kaisen into what men and women professionals do differently, the assessment organisation concluded that: 'in business, the things that are valued in the boardroom get valued throughout the organisation', suggesting that the qualities of mainly male boards will be seen as the qualities needed for promotion throughout the company. 'Group boundaries and group dynamics are central to people's abilities to lead', Alex Haslam, professor of psychology at Exeter University, argued. 'These are often highly gendered and masculine-defined.'[116] According to Jenny Head, professor at London University College, women at the top experience much more stress than their male counterparts. Her research revealed more female alcohol addicts in senior management than male. 'Women start drinking because they are less rewarded than their male colleagues. They have to fight harder for promotion or to stay in their top positions. They imitate their male counterparts' behaviour and start drinking', she explains.[117] Recently, however, researchers discuss whether women are not able to break the glass ceiling because of their inability to adapt to the masculine culture, which implies that only those women who have the capacity to adapt their preferences to the dominant cultural values are selected for leadership positions.

Scholars, van Vianen and Fischer, from University of Amsterdam in the Netherlands explain what they discovered in their research as to the glass ceiling:

> We propose an alternative explanation, namely that the culture preferences of women who have entered management functions were already different from those of other women at the start of their careers. From the beginning of their careers onwards, they may have felt more attracted to masculine values, resulting in career decisions that matched these preferences.[118]

In his book *The Leadership Mystique*, Manfred Kets de Vries, professor at Insead, France, states that career advancement is not easy for women'. He gives a combination of explanations. 'Very often', he says, 'they centre on the anatomy-is-destiny theme: pregnancy and childrearing throw women off the career trajectory'. Another answer given is that women are more concerned about keeping a balanced lifestyle than men and therefore not prepared to make the kind of sacrifices that top management demands. A further answer is that women are by nature more nurturing than men and therefore choose to focus on the needs of family and friends over career commitments. A more controversial answer sometimes given is that men, in their heart of hearts, are scared of women. And some are, really. Women, contrariwise, are more likely to feel comfortable with both men and women.[119]

Age stereotypes

Age stereotypes reinforce age discrimination because of their negative orientation. The activity rate of 55-to-64 year-old employees in the European Union amounted to 40.1 per cent in 2002, whereas the Union's objective is 50 per cent by 2010.[120] For example, long-standing age stereotypes depict older workers as less satisfied, not as involved with their work, less motivated, not as committed, less productive than their younger co-workers, and more apt to be absent from work. Older employees are also perceived as being more accident-prone. As with sex-role stereotypes, these age stereotypes are more fiction than fact. The business case for employing older workers seems more compelling than ever, as they are more likely to stay in their jobs for longer.[121]

THE AGEING WORKFORCE

The EU population is ageing and despite the younger age structure of acceding states, enlargement of the Union will not change this trend. By 2010 people aged 65 and over will represent 18 per cent of the total population and those below 18, 16 per cent.[122] Ageism is so widespread in the UK that there is only a five-year period in our lives when we are unlikely to be judged as too young or too old for a job. This optimum age is 35–40 years old. Figures also indicate that 40 per cent of all workers have faced discrimination at work – and age is cited as the main factor in a third of the cases. In addition, research shows that one person in five has been discouraged from applying for a job because it had an age restriction.[123] A striking example from the Netherlands:

> A fully-qualified woman applied for a job in the welfare administration. During her third interview the employer stated that she would not be selected because she was 45 years old, a mismatch with the team's average age of 30. Some weeks later she was denied another job because since that team was elderly, another 'old' person was not required.[124]

Researcher Susan Rhodes sought to determine whether age stereotypes were supported by data from 185 different studies. She discovered that as age increases so do employees' job satisfaction, job involvement, internal work motivation and organisational commitment. Moreover, older workers were not more accident-prone.[125]

Results are not as clear-cut regarding job performance. A meta-analysis of 96 studies representing 38 983 people and a cross-section of jobs revealed that age and job performance were unrelated.[126] Some researchers, however, believe that this finding does not reflect the true relationship between age and performance. They propose that the relationship between age and performance changes as people grow older.[127] This idea was tested on data obtained from 24 219 individuals. In support of this hypothesis, results revealed that age was positively related to performance for younger employees (25 to 30 years of age) and then plateaued: older employees were not less productive. Age and experience also predicted performance better for more complex jobs than other jobs, and job experience had a stronger relationship with performance than age.[128] Another recent study examined memory, reasoning, spatial relations and dual tasking for 1000 doctors, ages 25 to 92, and 600 other adults. The researchers concluded 'that a large proportion of older individuals scored as well or better on aptitude tests as those in the prime of life. We call these intellectually vigorous individuals "optimal agers"'.[129]

What about turnover and absenteeism? A meta-analysis containing 29 samples and a total of 12 356 individuals revealed that age and turnover were negatively related: that is, older employees quit less often than younger employees. Similarly, another meta-analysis of 34 studies encompassing 7772 workers indicated that age was inversely related to both voluntary (a day at the beach) and involuntary (sick day) absenteeism.[130] Contrary to stereotypes, older workers are ready and able to meet their job requirements. Moreover, results from the meta-analysis suggest professionals should focus more attention on the turnover and absenteeism among younger workers than among older workers.

THE CROSS-GENERATIONAL WORKFORCE

Recently a new form of diversity emerged in the workplace: age diversity. Never before has there been a workforce and workplace so diverse as to different generations. Four generations have to work together. Generation G, people born between 1922 and 1945, feel most comfortable with command-and-control, authority, hierarchy, all of them characteristics they grew up with. Generation B, the baby-boomers born between 1946 and 1964, are rather collaborative and co-operative and strive for consensus. This is the workaholic-generation, motivated to improve their economic and social status. Therefore, they desire more job security than the next generation, Generation X. Born between 1964 and 1977, they are less loyal to one organisation and expect less job security in return. They tend to be more motivated by workplace flexibility and the opportunity to use new technology. Generation Y, born in the decade after 1978, have a high interest in continuous learning, rather than in a lifetime job. They also expect responsibility and involvement with other people. Each generation has its own characeristics, which does however not imply they can be generalised to all people belonging to those generations. They do however imply a diverse approach if organisations want their workforce to remain motivated. As teams are the core of today's organisations it is important to stress that people do not have to have the same personalities and backgrounds to be compatible. It is important that they share the perception of each other's differences. Differences are rather a strength than a shortcoming in teams, as long as the team members have common goals and objectives (also see Chapters 9 and 10).[131]

Race stereotypes

The percentage of ethnic minority managers in Europe is not large: from 6 per cent of the population in Britain to about 1 per cent in countries such as Spain and Italy.[132] The participation of ethnic minorities on the Dutch labour market is low: 56 per cent of ethnic minorities have a job.[133] Moreover the unemployment rate among young people in the Netherlands is twice as high among ethnic minorities.[134] Antwerp, one of Belgium's major towns, can count over 150 nationalities, all of which containing people longing for a job.[135]

Research into people's attitudes towards migrants revealed that Sweden, Ireland, Norway, Finland and Denmark are most tolerant towards the entry of migrants. Hungary and Poland have the lowest score. Countries such as Spain, Slovenia, the Czech Republic and the Netherlands are in-between.[136] A bill banning headscarves and other religious symbols in state schools and regulating correct wear in the workplace was passed by the French parliament on 10 February 2004. French president Jacques Chirac said the bill also set a framework for employers to create rules about displaying the symbols at work.[137]

Unfortunately, three additional trends suggest that ethnic minorities are experiencing their own glass ceiling. First, ethnic minorities are advancing even less in the professional ranks than women. Dr Dwain Neil, who was head of recruitment and diversity at a major European oil company in the mid-1990s, says that hiring professionals often rated minority and white candidates differently, even for the same answers in job interviews. Malek Boutih of France's Association Against Racism conducted a test by sending identical résumés, one with a French name and the other with an Arab name, to a major bank. The French résumé elicited an invitation, the Arab a rejection.[138] In Belgium an increasingly number of people originating from non-European countries are changing their names under pressure from their employers. An increase by 20 per cent has been observed recently. The main reason is that a more familiar name sounds better, for example when answering the phone.[139] Second, ethnic minorities also tend to earn less. Finally, a recent study into ethnic minorities in the boardroom among the 100 largest companies in Europe revealed a concrete ceiling instead of a glass one. The researchers could not find one top company with a minority CEO, and few with even one minority officer at any senior level. A spokesperson for a German chemicals company scanned his memory for a minority board member and recalled, 'We had a Belgian once'. These findings are consistent with previous studies that indicated that ethnic minorities have more negative career experiences, lower upward mobility, lower career satisfaction, decreased job involvement and greater turnover rates than their white counterparts.[140] It is, however, remarkable to notice that ethnic minorities are faced with blatant racism and fewer opportunities than their white colleagues, even though Europe is heading towards a labour shortage in the near future.

Negative findings like these have prompted researchers to investigate whether race stereotypes actually bias performance ratings and hiring decisions. Given the increasing number of people of ethnic minorities that will enter the workforce in the near future, employers should focus on nurturing and developing ethnic minorities as well as increasing managers' sensitivities to invalid racial stereotypes.

Challenges and recommendations

The key challenge is to make decisions that are blind to gender, age, ethnical background, religion and disabilities. Organisations in the US differ very much from European ones. The United States has a common language, a fully integrated federal system and a national culture that overlays a variety of ethnic subcultures. Europe, by contrast, is an unwieldy agglomeration of countries. Even the European Union is not as homogeneous as the US. To Europeans, diversity is about national cultures and languages – and it is a reality with which they have always lived. According to Helen Bloom, consultant in the field of diversity, the most pressing challenge in diversity in Europe is extending equal opportunities to women. Minority ethnic groups are lower on the European diversity agenda, except in the United Kingdom, where minorities comprise a larger proportion of the population and are far more visible.[141]

In the next section, two approaches to deal with different groups at the workplace will be discussed: affirmative action (preventive) and managing diversity (active).

AFFIRMATIVE ACTION

Affirmative action focuses on achieving equality of opportunity in an organisation and is often mandated by national or supranational laws. The European Union has significant influence on equality law and the development of best practice. However, Great Britain, along with Sweden, has more advanced legislation on racial discrimination than other EU member states.[142] The Treaty of Amsterdam, which entered into force in May 1999, adopted an important new provision enabling the EU to propose legislation to combat discrimination based on gender, racial and ethnic origin, religion, belief, disability, age or sexual orientation. Two important directives (one on racial and one on religious belief, age and sexual orientation) were agreed in 2000.[143] Member states were required to implement legislation outlawing discrimination in the workplace on grounds of sexual orientation and religion or belief by 2 December 2003, and age and disability by 2 December 2006. Affirmative action or equal opportunities is an artificial intervention aimed at giving management a chance to correct an imbalance, an injustice, a mistake, and/or outright discrimination. In some countries the concept is well accepted in the fight against sex discrimination, but women are not the only beneficiaries: Norway's Ordinance No. 622 on the special treatment of men, adopted on 17 July 1998, provides for action to favour men in occupations where they are under-represented, such as education and child care, through training and job opportunities, together with procedural rules for enforcement. It also is important to note that under no circumstances does affirmative action require companies to hire unqualified people.

> Affirmative action focuses on achieving equality of opportunity in an organisation

MANAGING DIVERSITY

An increasing number of people and institutions now question the positive action programmes. Although it creates tremendous opportunities for women and minorities, it does not foster the type of thinking that is needed to manage diversity effectively.[144] The law can help to mould behaviour. It is particularly important as a statement of values of society but it is not enough on its own and cannot be fully effective in changing attitudes which underlie behaviour.[145] **Managing diversity** entails enabling people to perform up to their maximum potential. It focuses on changing an organisation's culture and infrastructure so that people provide the highest productivity possible. According to the British Institute for Personnel and Development, managing diversity and equal opportunities are not alternatives. They are interdependent.[146]

> Managing diversity creating organisational changes that enable all people to perform up to their maximum potential

BUILDING THE BUSINESS CASE FOR MANAGING DIVERSITY

The rationale for managing diversity goes well beyond legal, social, and moral reasons. Quite simply, the primary reason for managing diversity is the ability to grow and maintain a business in an increasingly competitive marketplace. Organisations cannot use diversity as a strategic advantage if employees fail to contribute their full talents, abilities, motivation and commitment. Thus, it is essential for an organisation to create an environment or culture that allows all employees to reach their full potential.

MANAGING DIVERSITY: A COMPETITIVE ADVANTAGE

Many organisations have learned that effectively managing diversity is a competitive advantage. This advantage stems from the process in which the management of diversity affects organisational behaviour and effectiveness. Effectively managing diversity can influence an organisation's costs and employee attitudes, recruitment of human resources, sales and market share, creativity and innovation, and group problem solving and productivity. This section explores the relationship between managing diversity and each of these outcomes:

- *Lower costs and improved employee attitudes.* Turnover and absenteeism were found to be higher for women and ethnic minorities than for whites. Dutch research noticed that turnover is higher among ethnic minorities.[147] Diversity is also related to employee attitudes. Past research revealed that people who were different from their work units in racial or ethnic background were less psychologically committed to their organisations, less satisfied with their careers and perceived less autonomy to make decisions on their jobs. Employees' mental/physical abilities and characteristics are another dimension of diversity that needs to be effectively managed. Government research has shown that disabled people in the UK are six times more likely to be unemployed than non-disabled people. And even when they have jobs, these are likely to be low-status.[148]

- *Improved recruiting efforts.* Attracting and retaining competent employees is a competitive advantage. Organisations that effectively manage diversity are more likely to meet this challenge, because women and minorities are attracted to such companies. The results of research carried out recently by the University of Amsterdam showed that women compared themselves more with female than with male targets, and saw the situation of female targets as a more likely potential future for themselves.[149] Moreover, recruiting diverse employees helps organisations to provide better customer care. Volvo, the Swedish car manufacturer, launched 'Your Concept Car' at the Geneva Motor Show 2004: a car developed exclusively by women and which is supposed to meet the requirements of female drivers.[150]

- *Increased sales, market share and corporate profits.* Workforce diversity is the mirror image of consumer diversity. It is thus important for companies to market their products so that they appeal to diverse customers and markets. Researchers are beginning to examine the effects of a top management team's (TMT's) demographic characteristics on an organisation's financial performance. For example, a study of over 1000 companies suggested that a diverse TMT can contribute to corporate profits. Results revealed that sales growth averaged 22.9 per cent, 20.2 per cent and 13 per cent for companies whose senior management team contained a majority of women, included people from ethnic minorities and consisted of a majority of white men, respectively.[151] Given these impressive results, other researchers are trying to identify the exact process or manner in which a TMT's diversity positively impacts on corporate success. The current thinking is that diversity promotes the sharing of unique ideas and a variety of perspectives, which in turn, leads to more effective decision making.[152]

- *Increased creativity and innovation.* Preliminary research supports the idea that workforce diversity promotes creativity and innovation. This occurs through the sharing of diverse ideas and perspectives. Rosabeth Moss Kanter, a management expert, was one of the first to investigate this relationship. Her results indicated that innovative companies deliberately used heterogeneous teams to solve problems, and they employed more women and ethnic minorities than less innovative companies. She also noted that innovative companies did a better job of eliminating racism, sexism and class distinction.[153] A recent summary of 40 years of diversity research supported Moss Kanter's conclusion that diversity can promote creativity and improve a team's decision making.[154] British Telecom (BT) is said to benefit from women's creativity and communication skills which are particularly well suited to the global marketplace.[155]

- *Increased group problem solving and productivity.* Because diverse groups possess a broader base of experience and perspectives from which to analyse a problem, they can potentially improve problem solving and performance. Research findings based on short-term groups that varied in terms of values, attitudes, educational backgrounds and experience supported this conclusion. Heterogeneous groups produced better-quality decisions and demonstrated higher productivity than homogeneous groups. Nevertheless, these results must be interpreted cautiously because the experimental samples, tasks, time frames and environmental situations bear very little resemblance to actual ongoing organisational settings.[156] Caution is also recommended by recent Dutch research findings. The benefits of diversity for teams process and outcomes only applied to highly outcome-interdependent (i.e. common goals) teams and teams low on longevity (i.e. short-term groups).[157]

In summary, research shows that diversity can improve creativity and innovation, but these positive benefits may not influence productivity because diverse groups generally experience more negative group dynamics. Awareness of group members' cultural and attitudinal differences can improve group effectiveness.[158]

A second lesson revolves around the fact that the group processes and performance of diverse groups are enhanced when group members share common values and norms that promote the pursuit of common goals.[159] Professionals and organisations thus are encouraged to identify ways of enhancing group members' sense of shared values and a common fate. Increasing shared values can be facilitated through an organisation's culture, which is discussed in Chapter 16, and common fate can be created by making group members accountable for group or team-level performance goals. Groups are discussed in Chapter 9 and teams in Chapter 10.

BARRIERS AND CHALLENGES TO MANAGING DIVERSITY

It is not surprising that organisations encounter significant barriers when trying to move forward with managing diversity. The following is a list of the most common barriers to implementing successful diversity programmes:[160]

- *Inaccurate stereotypes and prejudice.* This barrier manifests itself in the belief that differences are viewed as weaknesses. In turn, this promotes the view that diversity hiring will mean sacrificing competence and quality.
- *Ethnocentrism.* The ethnocentrism barrier represents the feeling that one's cultural rules and norms are superior or more appropriate than the rules and norms of another culture (also see Chapter 16).[161]
- *Poor career planning.* This barrier is associated with the lack of opportunities for diverse employees to get the type of work assignments that qualify them for senior management positions.
- *An unsupportive and hostile working environment for diverse employees.* Diverse employees are frequently excluded from social events and the friendly camaraderie that takes place in most offices.
- *Lack of political knowledge on the part of diverse employees.* Diverse employees may not get promoted because they do not know how to 'play the game' of getting along and getting ahead in an organisation. Research reveals that women and ethnic minorities are excluded from organisational networks.[162]
- *Difficulty in balancing career and family issues.* Women still assume the majority of the responsibilities associated with raising children. This makes it harder for women to work evenings and weekends or to frequently travel once they have children. Even without children in the picture, household chores take more of a woman's time than a man's time.
- *Fears of reverse discrimination.* Some employees believe that managing diversity is a smokescreen for reverse discrimination. This belief leads to very strong resistance because people feel that one person's gain is another's loss.
- *Diversity is not seen as an organisational priority.* This leads to subtle resistance that shows up in the form of complaints and negative attitudes. Employees may complain about the time, energy and resources devoted to diversity that could have been spent doing 'real work'.
- *The need to revamp the organisation's performance appraisal and reward system.* Performance appraisals and reward systems must reinforce the need to effectively manage diversity. This means that success will be based on a new set of criteria. Employees are likely to resist changes that adversely affect their promotions and financial rewards.
- *Resistance to change.* Effectively managing diversity entails significant organisational and personal change. As discussed in Chapter 17, people resist change for many different reasons.

In summary, managing diversity is a critical component of organisational success. Case studies and limited research inform us that this effort is doomed to failure unless top management is truly committed to managing diversity. The next section examines the variety of ways organisations are attempting to manage diversity.

ORGANISATIONAL PRACTICES USED TO EFFECTIVELY MANAGE DIVERSITY

Many organisations are unsure of what it takes to effectively manage diversity. This is partly due to the fact that top management only recently became aware of the combined need and importance of this issue.

So what are organisations doing to effectively manage diversity? Answering this question requires that we provide a framework for categorising organisational initiatives. Researchers and practitioners have developed relevant frameworks. One was developed by R. Roosevelt Thomas, Jr, a diversity expert. He identified eight generic action options that can be used to address any type of diversity issue. A second was proposed by another diversity expert, Ann Morrison. She empirically identified the specific diversity initiatives used by 16 organisations that successfully managed diversity. This section reviews these frameworks in order to provide you with both a broad and specific understanding about how organisations are effectively managing diversity.

R. Roosevelt Thomas, Jr's generic action options

Thomas identified eight basic responses for handling any diversity issue. After describing each action option, we discuss relationships among them.[163]

1 *Include/Exclude.* This choice is an outgrowth of affirmative action programmes. Its primary goal is to either increase or decrease the number of diverse people at all levels of the organisations. BAOBAB Catering is a Belgian organisation recruiting both Belgian employees and foreigners in the same way. Moreover, most of the foreigners are recognised refugees.[164]

2 *Deny.* People using this option deny that differences exist. Denial may manifest itself in proclamations that all decisions are colour-, gender- and age-blind and that success is solely determined by merit and performance. 'Eventually, we want the best applicant, regardless of his or her ethnic origin, gender or age', states Gust Godts, HR Director at Dupont.[165]

3 *Assimilate.* The basic premise behind this alternative is that all diverse people will learn to fit in or become like the dominant group. It only takes time and reinforcement for people to see the light. Organisations initially assimilate employees through their recruitment practices and the use of company-orientation programmes. New hires generally are put through orientation programmes that aim to provide employees with the organisation's preferred values and a set of standard operating procedures. Employees then are encouraged to refer to the policies and procedure manual when they are confused about what to do in a specific situation. These practices create homogeneity among employees. In France, for example, with its assimilationist culture all immigrants are expected to become unhyphenated French citizens.[166]

4 *Suppress.* Differences are quashed or discouraged when using this approach. This can be done by telling or reinforcing others to quit whining and complaining about issues. The old 'you've got to pay your dues' line is another frequently used way to promote the status quo.

5 *Isolate.* This option maintains the current way of doing things by setting the diverse person off to the side. In this way the individual is unable to influence organisational change. Employers can isolate people by putting them on special projects. Entire workgroups or departments are isolated by creating functionally independent entities, frequently referred to as 'silos'.

6 *Tolerate.* Toleration entails acknowledging differences but not valuing or accepting them. It represents a live-and-let-live approach that superficially allows organisations to give lip-service to the issue of managing diversity. Toleration is different from isolation in that it allows for the inclusion of diverse people. However, differences are not really valued or accepted when an organisation uses this option.

7 *Build relationships.* This approach is based on the premise that good relationships can overcome differences. It addresses diversity by fostering quality relationships – characterised by acceptance and understanding – among diverse groups.

8 *Foster mutual adaptation.* In this option, people recognise and accept differences, and most important, agree that everyone and everything is open for change. Mutual adaptation allows the greatest accommodation of diversity because it allows for change even when diversity is being effectively managed. Consider the diversity policies of the following organisations:

> Transport for London is considering replacing bank holidays with a number of 'floating' days which will allow non-Christians to work through Christmas and Easter.
>
> Unilever has a casual dress policy which permits employees to wear what they like, including clothing associated with their religion, as long as this is within the bounds of reason and safety. BT has gone a step further by attaching flexible straps to its safety helmets so that Rastafarian employees can wear them above their religiously significant hats.
>
> Some organisations offer prayer rooms. Itnet, an IT outsourcing organisation with 2500 staff, has found space in equipment storage rooms at some of its sites. Calderdale and Huddersfield NHS Trust offers prayer rooms within its chaplaincy services departments and employs a Muslim 'chaplain'.[167]

Although the action options can be used alone or in combination, some are clearly better than others. Exclusion, denial, assimilation, suppression, isolation and toleration are among the least preferred options. Inclusion, building relationships and mutual adaptation are the preferred strategies. Thomas reminds us that mutual adaptation is the only approach that unquestionably endorses the philosophy behind managing diversity. In closing this discussion, it is important to note that choosing how to best manage diversity is a dynamic process that is determined by the context of the organisation. For instance, some organisations are not ready for mutual adaptation. The best one might hope for in this case is the inclusion of diverse people.

Ann Morrison identifies specific diversity initiatives

As previously mentioned, Ann Morrison conducted a landmark study of the diversity practices used by 16 organisations that successfully managed diversity. Her results uncovered 52 different practices, 20 of which were used by the majority of the companies sampled. She classified the 52 practices into three main types: accountability, development and recruitment.[168] The top 10 practices associated with each type are shown in Table 4.4. The three types are discussed next in order of relative importance.

1 **Accountability practices** relate to professionals' responsibility to treat diverse employees fairly. Table 4.4 reveals that companies predominantly accomplish this objective by creating administrative procedures aimed at integrating diverse employees into the management ranks (practices number 3, 4, 5, 6, 8, 9 and 10). In contrast, work and family policies (practice 7) focuses on creating an environment that fosters employee commitment and productivity. The desire for a decent balance between work and personal life appears to be widespread. A Gemini Consulting survey of workers in 13 industrialised countries found it was rated more highly than a good salary everywhere but in Russia.[169]

> **Accountability practices focus on treating diverse employees fairly**

Marion Lorman, deputy director of HR at the south London health trust confirms this by the following statement: 'If we are to be able to meet our staffing needs, we are going to have to turn to a more diverse population – and that includes people who don't want traditional work patterns'.[170]

Consider the work and family practices at the following companies:

> Wendy Jeffrey's mother, Phyllis Hollyoak (87), attends Britain's first workplace eldercare day centre, or 'granny crèche', as it has been labelled. 'I can concentrate on my work because I don't have to ring to make sure she's all right', says Jeffrey, a 55-year-old pensions administrator at the Peugeot car factory in Coventry.[171]
>
> Since Amanda Bridge, operations controller at Littlewoods, returned from having a baby and nine months' career break, she started on one day a week, then two and a half, to eventually work four days a week. When she asked if starting at 7 a.m. and leaving at 3 p.m. would be a problem, they said no, as long as she agreed it with her manager and the personnel department. 'It really is a flexible firm', she says.[172]
>
> At Origin Nederland, all 6500 employees may compose their own package of working conditions. Some want more money, others prefer more holidays or simply more leisure time. An automatic simulator calculates the consequences of one's preferences in terms of one's salary.[173]
>
> In Norway each couple has one year's parental leave, four weeks of which have to be taken by the father.[174]

Development
practices
focus on
preparing diverse
employees for
greater
responsibility and
advancement

Recruitment
practices
attempts to
attract qualified,
diverse
employees at all
levels

2 The use of **Development practices** to manage diversity is relatively new compared with the historical use of accountability and recruitment practices. Development practices focus on preparing diverse employees for greater responsibility and advancement. These activities are needed because most non-traditional employees have not been exposed to the types of activity and job assignments that develop effective leadership and social networks.[175] At Ford Europe, training is introduced to enable all employees to progress to supervisory positions.[176] Table 4.4 indicates that diversity training programmes, networks and support groups, and mentoring programmes are among the most frequently used developmental practices.

3 **Recruitment practices** focus on attracting job applicants at all levels who are willing to accept challenging work assignments. This focus is critical because people learn the leadership skills needed for advancement by successfully accomplishing increasingly challenging and responsible work assignments. As shown in Table 4.4, targeted recruitment of non-professionals (practice 1) and professionals (practice 9) are commonly used to identify and recruit women and people of colour. Boeing Company relies on targeted recruiting: the Human Resources team launched a slick, advertising campaign aimed at women and ethnic minorities who feel under-utilised in their current jobs.[177]

TABLE 4.4 COMMON DIVERSITY PRACTICES

Accountability practices	Development practices	Recruitment practices
1 Top management's personal intervention	1 Diversity training programmes	1 Targeted recruitment of non-professionals
2 Internal advocacy groups	2 Networks and support groups	2 Key outside hires
3 Emphasis on employment statistics, profiles	3 Development programmes for all high-potential professionals	3 Extensive public exposure on diversity
4 Inclusion of diversity in performance evaluation goals, ratings	4 Informal networking activities	4 Corporate image as liberal, progressive, or benevolent
5 Inclusion of diversity in promotion decisions, criteria	5 Job rotation	5 Partnerships with educational institutions
6 Inclusion of diversity in management succession planning	6 Formal mentoring programme	6 Recruitment incentives such as cash supplements
7 Work and family policies	7 Informal mentoring programme	7 Internships
8 Policies against racism, sexism	8 Entry development programmes for all high-potential new hires	8 Publications or PR products that highlight diversity
9 Internal audit or attitude survey	9 Internal training (such as personal safety or language)	9 Targeted recruitment of professionals
10 Active employment committee, office	10 Recognition events, awards	10 Partnership with non-traditional groups

SOURCE: Abstracted from Tables A.10, A.11 and A.12 in A. M. Morrison, *The New Leaders: Guidelines on Leadership Diversity in America* (San Francisco, CA: Jossey-Bass, 1992).

Learning outcomes: summary of key terms

1 Recognise the antecedents influencing the perceptual process

Three groups of antecedents influence our perception. A first important group refers to the features of the perceived target. Some stimuli attract more attention than others. For instance, novelty, brightness, dominance in the visual field, unusual behaviour and functioning of the target are attention-drawing characteristics. According to the Gestaltists we perceive a target as a whole rather than the sum of its constituents. Perceptual grouping is the tendency which leads us to perceive objects as well-organised patterns rather than separate components. Four main factors determine perceptual grouping: these are, continuity, closure, proximity and similarity. A second important group of antecedents affecting the perceptual process is labelled as 'setting'. The setting in which the interaction between perceiver and perceived target takes place influences the perception. Cultural context, for example, may be of great relevance in understanding the formation of perceptions. Finally, some features associated with the perceiver are an important group of antecedents (e.g. mood, gender, personality, attitudes, etc.)

2 Describe perception in terms of the social information processing model

Perception is a mental and cognitive process that enables us to interpret and understand our surroundings. Social perception, also known as social cognition and social information processing, is a four-stage process. The four stages are selective attention/comprehension, encoding and simplification, storage and retention, and retrieval and response. During social cognition, salient stimuli are matched with schemata, assigned to cognitive categories and stored in long-term memory for events, semantic materials or people.

3 Identify and briefly explain two implications of social perception

Social perception affects hiring decisions and performance appraisals. Inaccurate or racist and sexist schemata may be used to evaluate job applicants. Similarly, faulty schemata about what constitutes good versus poor performance can lead to inaccurate performance appraisals. Invalid schemata need to be identified and replaced with appropriate schemata through coaching and training. Further, professionals are advised to use objective rather than subjective measures of performance.

4 Explain Jones and Davis' correspondent inference theory

The correspondent inference theory describes how an alert perceiver infers another's intentions and personal dispositions from his or her behaviour. This theory explains how we use other's behaviour as a cornerstone for inferring their stable dispositions. The chance that a disposition is derived from a perceived slice of behaviour is dependent upon three factors – non-common effects social desirability of effects and degree of choice.

5 Explain, according to Kelley's model, how external and internal causal attributions are formulated

Attribution theory attempts to describe how people infer causes for observed behaviour. According to Kelley's covariation model, external attributions tend to be made when consensus, consistency and distinctiveness are high or when consensus, consistency are low and distinctiveness high. Internal (personal responsibility) attributions tend to be made when consensus and distinctiveness are low and consistency is high.

6 Review Weiner's model of attribution

Weiner's model of attribution predicts achievement behaviour in terms of causal attributions. Attributions of ability, effort, task difficulty, luck and help from others affect how individuals feel about themselves. In turn, these feelings directly influence subsequent achievement-related performance.

7 Discuss how the self-fulfilling prophecy is created and how it can be used to improve individual and group productivity

The self-fulfilling prophecy, also known as the Pygmalion effect, describes how people behave so that their expectations come true. High expectations foster high employee self-expectations. These, in turn, lead to greater effort and better performance, and yet higher expectations. Conversely, the set-up-to-fail syndrome represents the negative side of the self-fulfilling prophecy. Professionals are encouraged to harness the Pygmalion effect by building a hierarchical framework that reinforces positive performance expectations throughout the organisation.

8 Discuss stereotypes and the process of stereotype formation

Stereotypes represent grossly oversimplified beliefs or expectations about groups of people. Stereotyping is a four-step process that begins by categorising people into groups according to various criteria. Next, we infer that all people within a particular group possess the same traits or characteristics. Then, we form expectations of others and interpret their behaviour according to our stereotypes. Finally, stereotypes are maintained by: overestimating the frequency of stereotypic behaviours exhibited by others, incorrectly explaining expected and unexpected behaviours and differentiating minority individuals from oneself. The use of stereotypes is influenced by the amount and type of information available to an individual and his or her motivation to accurately process information.

9 Define diversity and give five reasons why managing diversity is a competitive advantage

Diversity represents the host of individual differences that makes people different from and similar to each other. Diversity pertains to everybody. It is not simply an issue of age, race, gender, or sexual orientation. Managing diversity can: (a) lower costs and improve employee attitudes; (b) improve an organisation's recruiting efforts; (c) increase sales, market share and corporate profits; (d) increase creativity and innovation and (e) increase group problem solving and productivity.

10 Discuss the organisational practices used to effectively manage diversity

There are many different practices that organisations can use to manage diversity. R. Roosevelt Thomas, Jr, identified eight basic responses for handling any diversity issue: include/exclude, deny, assimilate, suppress, isolate, tolerate, build relationships and foster mutual adaptation. Exclusion, denial, assimilation, suppression, isolation and toleration are among the least preferred options. Inclusion, building relationships and mutual adaptation are the preferred strategies. Ann Morrison's study of diversity practices identified three main types or categories of activities. Accountability practices relate to the organisation's responsibility to treat diverse employees fairly. Development practices focus on preparing diverse employees for greater responsibility and advancement. Recruitment practices emphasise attracting job applicants at all levels who are willing to accept challenging work assignments. Table 4.4 presents a list of activities that are used to accomplish each main type.

Review questions

1 Why is it important for professionals to have a working knowledge of perception and attribution?

2 When you are sitting in your course group, what stimuli are salient? What is your schema for course group activity?

3 How would you formulate an attribution, according to Kelley's model, for the behaviour of a fellow student who starts arguing in class with your lecturer?

4 Interviewees in selection contexts use internal or external attributions as explanations for previous negative application experiences. Which of these two attribution types affect the impression on the interviewer in a positive way and why so?

5 In what situations do you tend to attribute your successes/failures to luck? How well does Weiner's attributional model in Figure 4.6 explain your answers? Explain.

6 Have you ever been stereotyped by someone else? Discuss.

7 Which type of stereotype (sex-role, age and race) do you believe is more pervasive in organisations? Why?

8 What can be done to facilitate career success of the disabled? Explain.

9 Which of the barriers to managing diversity would be most difficult to reduce? Explain.

10 Have you seen any examples that support the proposition that diversity is a competitive advantage?

Personal awareness and growth exercise

How do diversity assumptions influence team member interactions?

Objectives

1 To identify diversity assumptions.

2 To consider how diversity assumptions affect team members' interactions.

Introduction

Assumptions can be so ingrained that we do not even know that we are using them. Negative assumptions can limit our relationships with others because they influence how we perceive and respond to those we encounter in our daily lives. This exercise is designed to help identify the assumptions that you have about groups of people. Although this exercise may make you uncomfortable because it asks you to identify stereotypical assumptions, it is a positive first step to facing and examining the assumptions we make about other people. This awareness can lead to positive behavioural change.

Instructions

Complete the diversity assumptions worksheet.[178] The first column contains various dimensions of diversity. For each dimension, the second column asks you to identify the assumptions held by the general public about people with this characteristic. Use the third column to determine how each assumption might limit team members' ability to effectively interact with each other. Finally, answer the questions for discussion.

Questions for discussion

1 Where do our assumptions about others come from?

2 Is it possible to eliminate negative assumptions about others? How might this be done?

3 What most surprised you about your answers to the diversity assumption worksheet?

DIVERSITY ASSUMPTION WORKSHEET

Dimension of diversity	Assumption that might be made	Effect on team members' interactions
Age	Example: Younger people haven't had the proper experience to come up with good solutions.	Example: Input from younger employees is not solicited.
Ethnicity (e.g. Asian)		
Gender		
Race		
Physical ability (e.g. hard of hearing)		
Sexual orientation		
Marital/parental status (e.g. single parent with children)		
Religion (e.g. Muslim)		
Recreational habits (e.g. hikes on weekends)		
Educational background (e.g. college education)		
Work experience (e.g. union)		
Appearance (e.g. overweight)		
Geographic location (e.g. rural)		
Personal habits (e.g. smoking)		
Income (e.g. well-to-do)		

Group exercise

Using attribution theory to resolve performance problems

Objectives

1 To gain experience determining the causes of performance.
2 To decide on corrective action for employee performance.

Introduction

Attributions are typically made to internal and external factors. Perceivers arrive at their assessments by using various informational cues or antecedents. To determine the types of antecedents people use, we have developed a case containing various informational cues about an individual's performance. You will be asked to read the case and make attributions about the causes of performance. To assess the impact of attributions on behaviour, you will also be asked to recommend corrective action.

Instructions

Presented below is a case study that depicts the performance of Marie Martin, a computer programmer. Please read the case and then identify the causes of her behaviour by answering the question following the case. After completing this task, decide on the appropriateness of various forms of corrective action. A list of potential recommendations has been drawn up. The list is divided into four categories. Read each action, and evaluate its appropriateness by using the scale provided. Next, compute a total score for each of the four categories.

Causes of performance

To what extent was each of the following a cause of Marie's performance? Use the following scale:

	Very little				Very much
A High ability	1	2	3	4	5
B Low ability	1	2	3	4	5
C Low effort	1	2	3	4	5
D Difficult job	1	2	3	4	5
E Unproductive co-workers	1	2	3	4	5
F Bad luck	1	2	3	4	5

The Case of Marie Martin

Marie Martin, 30, received her degree in computer science from a reputable university in Europe. She also graduated with above-average grades. Marie is currently working in the computer support/analysis department as a programmer for a large organisation. During the past year, Marie has missed 10 days of work. She seems unmotivated and rarely completes her assignments on time. Marie is usually given the harder programs to work on.

Past records indicate that Marie, on average, completes programs classified as 'routine' in about 45 hours. Her co-workers, on the other hand, complete these routine programs in an average of 32 hours. Further, Marie finishes programs considered 'major problems' in about 115 hours on average. Her co-workers, however, finish these same assignments, in an average of 100 hours. When Marie has worked in programming teams, her peer performance reviews are generally average to negative. Her male peers have noted she is not creative in attacking problems and she is difficult to work with.

The computer department recently sent a questionnaire to all users of its services to evaluate the usefulness and accuracy of data received. The results indicate many departments are not using computer output because they cannot understand the reports. It was also determined that the users of output generated from Marie's programs found the output chaotic and not useful for decision making.

Appropriateness of corrective action
Evaluate the following courses of action by using the scale below:

	Very inappropriate				Very appropriate
Coercive actions					
a Reprimand Marie for her performance	1	2	3	4	5
b Threaten to fire Marie if her performance does not improve	1	2	3	4	5
Change job					
c Transfer Marie to another job	1	2	3	4	5
d Demote Marie to a less demanding job	1	2	3	4	5
Non-punitive actions					
e Work with Marie to help her do the job better	1	2	3	4	5
f Offer Marie encouragement to help her improve	1	2	3	4	5
No immediate actions					
g Do nothing	1	2	3	4	5
h Promise Marie a pay raise if she improves	1	2	3	4	5

Scoring key
Compute a score for the four categories:
Coercive actions = a + b =
Change job = c + d =
Non-punitive actions = e + f =
No immediate actions = g + h =

Questions for discussion
1 How would you evaluate Marie's performance in terms of consensus, distinctiveness and consistency?
2 Is Marie's performance due to internal or external causes?
3 What did you identify as the top two causes of Marie's performance? Are your choices consistent with Weiner's classification of internal and external factors? Explain.
4 Which of the four types of corrective action do you think is most appropriate? Explain. Can you identify any negative consequences of this choice?

Internet exercise

As mentioned earlier in this chapter affirmative action emphasises achieving equality of opportunity. This affirmative action has been the matrix for many court justice cases. Usually a case has been brought to court by a person who has been turned down for a job on grounds that legislation in force is securing equal opportunities for a specific naturally or historically disadvantaged group. The European Court of Justice has ruled both against and in favour of the complainant in these cases.

Visit our website www.mcgraw-hill.co.uk/textbooks/buelens to find suggestions of websites you can use to solve this internet exercise.

Notes

1 B. Summerskill, 'Big Brother? No, It's Just Another Day at the Office', the *Guardian*, 13 August 2000.

2 Details may be found in R. Eisenberger, P. Fasolo and V. Davis-LaMastro, 'Perceived Organizational Support and Employee Diligence, Commitment, and Innovation', *Journal of Applied Psychology*, February 1990, pp. 51–9.

3 Adapted and translated from 'Perceptie', see http://www.multiplus.nl/comm.htm.

4 M. McMahon, 'Cool Chemists', *The Times*, 14 September 2000.

5 S. S. Brehm, S. M. Kassin and S. Fein, *Social Psychology* (Boston, MA: Houghton Mifflin Company, 1999)

6 S. T. Fiske and S. E. Taylor, *Social Cognition, second edition* (Reading, MA: Addison-Wesley Publishing, 1991), pp. 1–2.

7 M. Simon, S. M. Houghton and K. Aquino, 'Cognitive Biases, Risk Perception, and Venture Formation: How Individuals Decide to Start Companies', *Journal of Business Venturing*, March 2000, pp. 113–34.

8 R. McGinty and A. Reitsch, 'Using Student Perceptions and Job Characteristics to Recruit Recent Graduates', *Review of Business*, Summer–Fall 1992, pp. 38–42.

9 J. Smithson and S. Lewis, 'Is Job Insecurity Changing the Psychological Contract?', *Personnel Review*, October 2000, pp. 680–702.

10 H. C. Koh and E. H. Y. Boo, 'The Link between Organizational Ethics and Job Satisfaction: A Study of Managers in Singapore', *Journal of Business Ethics*, February 2001, pp. 309–24.

11 J. R. Schermerhorn, J. G. Hunt and R. N. Osborn, *Organizational Behavior* (Oxford: John Wiley and Sons, 1997).

12 T. R. Alley, 'Physionomy and Social Perception', in *Social and Applied Aspects of Perceiving Faces. Resources for Ecological Psychology*, ed. T. R. Alley (Hillsdale, NJ: Lawrence Erlbaum Associates, 1988), pp. 167–86.

13 A. Vrij, 'The Existence of a Black Clothing Stereotype: The Impact of a Victim's Black Clothing on Impression Formation', *Psychology, Crime and Law*, no. 3, 1997, pp. 227–37.

14 M. Wertheimer, 'Gestalt Theory', in *The History of Psychology: Fundamental Questions*, ed. M. Munger (London: Oxford University Press, 2003), pp. 308–23; and C. V. Ehrenfels, 'On Gestalt Qualities', *Psychological Review*, 1937, pp. 521–5.

15 D. Hellriegel, J. W. Slocum, Jr, and R. W. Woodman, *Organizational Behavior* (St. Paul, MN: West Publishing Company, 1976).

16 See R. Behrens, *Design in Visual Arts* (Englewood Cliffs, NJ: Prentice-Hall, 1984), p. 49.

17 See S. S. Brehm, S. M. Kassin and S. Fein, *Social Psychology* (Boston, MA: Houghton Mifflin Company, 1999).

18 J. E. Rehfeld, 'What Working for a Japanese Company Taught Me', *Harvard Business Review*, November–December 1990, pp. 167–76.

19 F. Trompenaars and C. Hampden-Turner, *Riding the Waves of Culture* (New York: McGraw-Hill, 1998).

20 S. Penrod, *Social Psychology* (Englewood Cliffs, NJ: Prentice Hall, 1983).

21 S. Dornbush, A. H. Hastorf, S. A. Richardson, R. E. Muzzy and R. S. Vreeland, 'The Perceiver and the Perceived: The Relative Influence on the Categories of Interpersonal Cognition', *Journal of Personality and Social Psychology*, May 1965, pp. 434–40.

22 D. McBurney and V. Collings, *Introduction to Sensation/Perception* (Oxford: Prentice Hall, 1977).

23 M. Rotundo, D. H. Ngyuen and P. Sackett, 'A Meta-Analytic Review of Gender Differences in Perceptions of Sexual Harassment', *Journal of Applied Psychology*, October 2001, pp. 914–22

24 H. Ngo, S. Foley, A. Wong and R. Loi, 'Who Gets More of the Pie? Predictors of Perceived Gender Inequity at Work', *Journal of Business Ethics*, July 2003, pp. 227–41.

25 J. P. Forgas, 'Mood and Judgement: The Affect Infusion Model', *Psychological Bulletin*, January 1995, pp. 39–66.

26 C. Sedidikes and C. A. Anderson, 'Causal Perceptions of Intertrait Relations: The Glue That Holds Person Types Together', *Personality and Social Psychology Bulletin*, June 1994, pp. 294–302.

27 See S. S. Brehm, S. M. Kassin and S. Fein, *Social Psychology* (Boston, MA: Houghton Mifflin Company, 1999).

28 S. Mauno and U. Kinnunen, 'Perceived Job Insecurity Among Double Earner Couples: Do Its Antecedents Vary According to Gender, Economic Sector and the Measure Used', *Journal of Occupational and Organizational Psychology*, September 2002, pp. 295–314.

29 Adapted from discussion in S. T. Fiske and S. E. Taylor, *Social Cognition, second edition* (Reading, MA: Addison-Wesley Publishing, 1991), pp. 247–50.

30 The negativity bias was examined and supported by O. Ybarra and W. G. Stephan, 'Misanthropic Person Memory', *Journal of Personality and Social Psychology*, April 1996, pp. 691–700; and Y. Ganzach, 'Negativity (and Positivity) in Performance Evaluation: Three Field Studies', *Journal of Applied Psychology*, August 1995, pp. 491–9.

31 E. Rosch, C. B. Mervis, W. D. Gray, D. M. Johnson and P. Boyes-Braem, 'Basic Objects in Natural Categories', *Cognitive Psychology*, July 1976, p. 383.

32 Washing clothes.

33 See B. R. Ragins, B. Townsend and M. Mattis, 'Gender Gap in the Executive Suite: CEOs and Female Executives Report on Breaking the Glass Ceiling', *Academy of Management Executive*, February 1998, pp. 28–42; and P. A. Giuffre and C. L. Williams, 'Boundary Lines: Labeling Sexual Harassment in Restaurants', *Gender and Society*, September 1994, pp. 378–401.

34 See J. P. Forgas, 'On Being Happy and Mistaken: Mood Effects on the Fundamental Attribution Error', *Journal*

of Personality and Social Psychology, August 1998, pp. 318–31; and A. Varma, A. S. DeNisi and L. H. Peters, 'Interpersonal Affect and Performance Appraisal: A Field Study', *Personnel Psychology*, Summer 1996, pp. 341–60.

35 See I. Ajzen and J. Sexton, 'Depth of Processing, Belief Congruence, and Attitude-Behavior Correspondence', in *Dual-Process Theories in Social Psychology*, eds S. Chaiken and Y. Trope (New York: The Guilford Press, 1999), pp. 117–38; and A. J. Kinicki, P. W. Hom, M. R. Trost and K. J. Wade, 'Effects of Category Prototypes on Performance-Rating Accuracy', *Journal of Applied Psychology*, June 1995, pp. 354–70.

36 The relationship between depression and information processing is discussed by A. Zelli and K. A. Dodge, 'Personality Development from the Bottom Up', in *The Coherence of Personality*, eds D. Cervone and Y. Shoda (New York: The Guilford Press, 1999), pp. 94–126.

37 For a thorough discussion about the structure and organisation of memory, see L. R. Squire, B. Knowlton and G. Musen, 'The Structure and Organization of Memory', in *Annual Review of Psychology, vol. 44*, eds L. W. Porter and M. R. Rosenzweig (Palo Alto, CA: Annual Reviews, 1993), pp. 453–95.

38 A thorough discussion of the reasoning process used to make judgements and decisions is provided by S. A. Sloman, 'The Empirical Case for Two Systems of Reasoning', *Psychological Bulletin*, January 1996, pp. 3–22.

39 Results can be found in C. M. Marlowe, S. L. Schneider and C. E. Nelson, 'Gender and Attractiveness Biases in Hiring Decisions: Are More Experienced Managers Less Biased?', *Journal of Applied Psychology*, February 1996, pp. 11–21.

40 Details of this study can be found in C. K. Stevens, 'Antecedents of Interview Interactions, Interviewers' Ratings, and Applicants' Reactions', *Personnel Psychology*, Spring 1998, pp. 55–85.

41 Adapted and translated from M. Buelens, F. Debussche and K. Vanderheyden, *Mensen en verscheidenheid* (Brussels: Vacature, 1997).

42 See R. C. Mayer and J. H. Davis, 'The Effect of the Performance Appraisal System on Trust for Management: A Field Quasi-Experiment', *Journal of Applied Psychology*, February 1999, pp. 123–36.

43 Results can be found in W. H. Bommer, J. L. Johnson, G. A. Rich, P. M. Podsakoff and S. B. Mackenzie, 'On the Interchangeability of Objective and Subjective Measures of Employee Performance: A Meta-Analysis', *Personnel Psychology*, Autumn 1995, pp. 587–605.

44 See J. I. Sanchez and P. D. L. Torre, 'A Second Look at the Relationship between Rating and Behavioral Accuracy in Performance Appraisal', *Journal of Applied Psychology*, February 1996, pp. 3–10; and A. J. Kinicki, P. W. Hom, M. R. Trost and K. J. Wade, 'Effects of Category Prototypes on Performance-Rating Accuracy', *Journal of Applied Psychology*, June 1995, pp. 354–70.

45 The effectiveness of rater training was supported by D. V. Day and L. M. Sulsky, 'Effects of Frame-of-Reference Training and Information Configuration on Memory Organization and Rating Accuracy', *Journal of Applied Psychology*, February 1995, pp. 158–67.

46 F. Heider, *The Psychology of Interpersonal Relations* (New York: Wiley, 1958).

47 H. Sims, Jr, and P. Lorenzi, *The New Leadership Paradigm: Social Learning and Cognition in Organizations* (Newbury Park, CA: Sage Publications, 1992).

48 J. Silvester, E. Ferguson and F. Patterson, 'Comparing Spoken Attributions by German and UK Engineers: Evaluating the Success of a Culture Change Programme', *European Journal of Work and Organizational Psychology*, March 1997, pp. 103–17.

49 I. Mervielde, 'Attributie', in *Sociale Psychologie*, ed. I. Mervielde (Gent: Academia Press, 1999), pp. 35–75.

50 D. Gioia and H. Sims, 'Cognition-Behavior Connections: Attribution and Verbal Behaviour in Leader-Subordinate Interactions', *Organizational Behavior and Human Decision Processes*, April 1986, pp. 197–229.

51 See F. Heider, *The Psychology of Interpersonal Relations* (New York: Wiley, 1958).

52 B. Weiner, I. H. Frieze, A. Kukla, L. Reed, S. Rest and R. M. Rosenbaum, *Perceiving the Causes of Success and Failure* (Morristown, NJ: General Learning Press, 1971).

53 E. Chang, K. Rand and D. Strunk, 'Optimism and Risk for Job Burnout Among Working College Students: Stress as a Mediator', *Personality and Individual Differences*, August 2000, pp. 255–63.

54 E. E. Jones and K. E. Davis, 'From Acts to Dispositions: The Attribution Process in Person Perception', in *Advances in Experimental Social Psychology*, ed. L. Berkowitz (New York: Academic Press, 1965), pp. 219–66.

55 Kelley's model is discussed in detail in H. H. Kelley, 'The Processes of Causal Attribution', *American Psychologist*, February 1973, pp. 107–28.

56 B. Weiner, *Achievement Motivation and Attribution Theory* (Morristown, NJ: General Learning Press, 1974)

57 E. E. Jones and K. E. Davis, 'From Acts to Dispositions: The Attribution Process in Person Perception', in *Advances in Experimental Social Psychology*, ed. L. Berkowitz (New York: Academic Press, 1965), pp. 219–66.

58 See F. Heider, *The Psychology of Interpersonal Relations* (New York: Wiley, 1958).

59 E. E. Jones and V. A. Harris, 'The Attribution of Attitudes', *Journal of Experimental Social Psychology*, January 1967, pp. 1–24.

60 R. Baron and D. Byrne, *Social Psychology: Understanding Human Interaction* (Needham Heights, MA: Allyn and Bacon, 1987).

61 See H. H. Kelly, 'The Processes of Causal Attribution', *American Psychologist*, February 1973, pp. 107–28.

62 L. Z. McArthur, 'The How and What of Why: Some Determinants and Consequences of Causal Attributions', *Journal of Personality and Social Psychology*, January 1972, pp. 171–93.

63 A. Kukla, 'Attributional Determinants of Achievement Related Behavior', *Journal of Personality and Social Psychology*, August 1970, pp. 166–74.

64 See P. D. Sweeney, K. Anderson and S. Bailey, 'Attributional Style in Depression: A Meta-Analytic Review', *Journal of Personality and Social Psychology*, May 1986, pp. 974–91.

65 Results can be found in P. J. Corr and J. A. Gray, 'Attributional Style as a Personality Factor in Insurance Sales Performance in the UK', *Journal of Occupational Psychology*, March 1996, pp. 83–87.

66 Supportive results can be found in J. Silvester, N. R. Anderson and F. Patterson, 'Organizational Culture Change: An InterGroup Attributional Analysis', *Journal of Occupational and Organizational Psychology*, March 1999, pp. 1–23; J. Greenberg, 'Forgive Me, I'm New: Three Experimental Demonstrations of the Effects of Attempts to Excuse Poor Performance', *Organizational Behavior and Human Decision Processes*, May 1996, pp. 165–78; and G. E. Prussia, A. J. Kinicki and J. S. Bracker, 'Psychological and Behavioral Consequences of Job Loss: A Covariance Structure Analysis Using Weiner's (1985) Attribution Model', *Journal of Applied Psychology*, June 1993, pp. 382–94.

67 See J. C. Deschamps, 'Attributions or Explanations in Everyday Life', *European Journal of Work and Organizational Psychology*, March 1997, pp. 7–24.

68 L. Ross, 'The Intuitive Psychologist and His Shortcoming', in *Advances in Experimental Social Psychology*, ed. L. Berkowitz (New York: Academic Press, 1977).

69 R. E. Nisbett and L. Ross, *Human Inference: Strategies and Shortcomings of Social Judgement* (Englewood Cliffs, NJ: Prentice Hall, 1980).

70 M. J. Lerner, 'Le Thème de la Justice ou le Besoin de Justifier', *Bulletin de Psychologie*, January–February 1986, pp. 205–11.

71 K. G. Shaver, *An Introduction to Attribution Processes* (Cambridge, MA: Winthrop, 1975).

72 E. E. Jones and R. E. Nisbett, 'The Actor and the Observer: Divergent Perceptions of the Causes of Behaviour', in *Attribution: Perceiving Causes of Behavior*, eds E. E. Jones, D. E. Kanouse, H. H. Kelly, R. E. Nisbett, S. Valins and B. Weiner (Morristown, NJ: General Learning Press, 1972).

73 See H. Sims, Jr, and P. Lorenzi, *The New Leadership Paradigm: Social Learning and Cognition in Organizations* (Newbury Park, CA: Sage Publications, 1992).

74 C. Sedikides, W. K. Campbell, G. D. Reeder and A. J. Elliot, 'The Self-Serving Bias in Relational Context', *Journal of Personality and Social Psychology*, February 1998, pp. 378–86.

75 See H. Sims, Jr, and P. Lorenzi, *The New Leadership Paradigm: Social Learning and Cognition in Organizations* (Newbury Park, CA: Sage Publications, 1992).

76 H. Steensma and L. Otto, 'Perception of Performance Appraisal by Employees and Supervisors: Self-Serving Bias and Procedural Justice', *Journal of Collective Negotiations in the Public Sector*, no. 4, 2000, pp. 307–20.

77 T. F. Pettigrew, 'The Ultimate Attribution Error: Extending Allport's Cognitive Analysis of Prejudice', *Personality and Social Psychology Bulletin*, October 1979, pp. 461–576.

78 D. A. Hofmann and A. Stetzer, 'The Role of Safety Climate and Communication in Accident Interpretation: Implications for Learning from Negative Events', *Academy of Management Journal*, December 1998, pp. 644–57.

79 A. L. Zacharakis, D. G. Meyer and J. DeCastro, 'Differing Perceptions of New Venture Failure: A Matched Exploratory Study of Venture Capitalists and Entrepreneurs', *Journal of Small Business Management*, July 1999, pp. 1–14.

80 S. G. Green and T. R. Mitchell, 'Attributional Processes of Leaders in Leader–Member Interactions', *Organizational Behavior and Human Decision Processes*, June 1979, pp. 429–58.

81 Details may be found in S. E. Moss and M. J. Martinko, 'The Effects of Performance Attributions and Outcome Dependence on Leader Feedback Behavior Following Poor Subordinate Performance', *Journal of Organizational Behavior*, May 1998, pp. 259–74; and E. C. Pence, W. C. Pendelton, G. H. Dobbins and J. A. Sgro, 'Effects of Causal Explanations and Sex Variables on Recommendations for Corrective Actions Following Employee Failure', *Organizational Behavior and Human Performance*, April 1982, pp. 227–40.

82 See D. Konst, R. Vonk and R. V. D. Vlist, 'Inferences about Causes and Consequences of Behavior of Leaders and Subordinates', *Journal of Organizational Behavior*, March 1999, pp. 261–71.

83 See M. Miserandino, 'Attributional Retraining as a Method of Improving Athletic Performance', *Journal of Sport Behavior*, August 1998, pp. 286–97; and F. Forsterling, 'Attributional Retraining: A Review', *Psychological Bulletin*, November 1985, pp. 496–512.

84 The background and results for this study are presented in R. Rosenthal and L. Jacobson, *Pygmalion in the Classroom: Teacher Expectation and Pupils' Intellectual Development* (New York: Holt, Rinehart & Winston, 1968).

85 See D. Eden and Y. Zuk, 'Seasickness as a Self-Fulfilling Prophecy: Raising Self-Efficacy to Boost Performance at Sea', *Journal of Applied Psychology*, October 1995, pp. 628–35. For a thorough review of research on the Pygmalion effect, see D. Eden, *Pygmalion in Management: Productivity as a Self-Fulfilling Prophecy* (Lexington, MA: Lexington Books, 1990), Ch. 2.

86 This study was conducted by T. Dvir, D. Eden and M. L. Banjo, 'Self-Fulfilling Prophecy and Gender: Can Women Be Pygmalion and Galatea?', *Journal of Applied Psychology*, April 1995, pp. 253–70.

87 N. M. Kierein and M. A. Gold, 'Pygmalion in Work Organizations: A Meta-Analysis', *Journal of Organizational Behaviour*, December 2000, pp. 913–28.

167

88 See J.-F. Manzoni and J.-L. Barsoux, 'The Set-Up-to-Fail Syndrome', *Harvard Business Review*, March–April 1998, pp. 101–13.

89 This example was based on J.-F. Manzoni and J.-L. Barsoux, 'The Set-Up-to-Fail Syndrome', *Harvard Business Review*, March–April 1998, pp. 101–13; and 'Living Down to Expectations', *Training*, July 1998, p. 15.

90 The role of positive expectations at Microsoft is discussed by S. Hamm and O. Port, 'The Mother of All Software Projects', *Business Week*, 22 February 1999, pp. 69, 72.

91 These recommendations were adapted from J. Keller, 'Have Faith–In You', *Selling Power*, June 1996, pp. 84, 86; and R. W. Goddard, 'The Pygmalion Effect', *Personnel Journal*, June 1985, p. 10.

92 C. Leerhsen, 'How Disney Does It', *Newsweek*, 3 April 1989, p. 52.

93 C. M. Judd and B. Park, 'Definition and Assessment of Accuracy in Social Stereotypes', *Psychological Review*, January 1993, p. 110.

94 R. Woodfield, 'Women and Information Systems Development: Not Just A Pretty (Inter)face?', *Information Technology & People*, no. 2, 2002, pp. 199–238.

95 J. Brand, 'You Can Always Spot A Wife Beater By the Charm Offensive', the *Independent*, 2 July 2000.

96 For a thorough discussion of stereotype accuracy, see M. C. Ashton and V. M. Esses, 'Stereotype Accuracy: Estimating the Academic Performance of Ethnic Groups', *Personality and Social Psychology Bulletin*, February 1999, pp. 225–36.

97 See C. Comeau-Kirschner, 'Navigating the Roadblocks', *Management Review*, May 1999, p. 8; and S. Shellenbarger, 'Work-Force Study Finds Loyalty Is Weak, Division of Race and Gender Are Deep', *The Wall Street Journal*, 3 September 1993, pp. B1, B9.

98 D. Dupré, 'Statistics in Focus: Theme 3 – 16/2001', *Eurostat*, 2001.

99 The process of stereotype formation and maintenance is discussed by S. T. Fiske, M. Lin and S. L. Neuberg, 'The Continuum Model: Ten Years Later', in *Dual-Process Theories in Social Psychology*, eds S. Chaiken and Y. Trope (New York: The Guilford Press, 1999), pp. 231–54.

100 This discussion is based on material presented in G. V. Bodenhausen, C. N. Macrae and J. W. Sherman, 'On the Dialectics of Discrimination', in *Dual-Process Theories in Social Psychology*, eds S. Chaiken and Y. Trope (New York: The Guilford Press, 1999), pp. 271–90.

101 See A. H. Eagly, S. J. Karu and B. T. Johnson, 'Gender and Leadership Style among School Principals: A Meta-Analysis', *Educational Administration Quarterly*, February 1992, pp. 76–102; and I. K. Broverman, S. Raymond Vogel, D. M. Broverman, F. E. Clarkson and P. S. Rosenkrantz, 'Sex-Role Stereotypes: A Current Appraisal', *Journal of Social Issues*, 1972, p. 75.

102 See B. P. Allen, 'Gender Stereotypes Are Not Accurate: A Replication of Martin (1987) Using Diagnostic vs. Self-Report and Behavioral Criteria', *Sex Roles*, May 1995, pp. 583–600.

103 Results can be found in V. E. Schein, R. Mueller, T. Lituchy and J. Liu, 'Think Manager – Think Male: A Global Phenomenon?', *Journal of Organizational Behavior*, January 1996, pp. 33–41.

104 S. Bosseley, 'Gentlemen Prefer Blonde Stereotypes', the *Guardian*, 10 April 1999.

105 R. Vonk and R. D. Ashmore, 'Thinking about Gender Types: Cognitive Organization of Female and Male Types', *British Journal of Social Psychology*, June 2003, pp. 257–80.

106 Translated from 'Nog te weinig vrouwelijke managers', *Vacature*, 6 March 2004, p. 1.

107 S. C. E. Riley, 'Constructions of Equality and Discrimination in Professional Men's Talk', *British Journal of Social Psychology*, September 2002, pp. 443–61.

108 M. Gesthuizen, P. Scheepers and M. Verloo, 'Support for the Discrimination of Women on the Labour Market in the Netherlands: Individual and Contextual Characteristics,' *The Netherlands' Journal of Social Sciences*, no. 1, 2002, pp. 48–64.

109 European Commision, *Employment in Europe* (Luxembourg: Office for Official Publications of the European Communities, 1997), p. 31.

110 Translated from M. Teugels, 'Vrouwelijke Raderleden Leter', *Vacature*, 7 March 2003.

111 'Get Women on Board', /www.peoplemanagement.co.uk/, 20 November 2003.

112 'Déjà-vu? – Trade Unions', *The Economist*, 7 June 2003, p. 77.

113 'Women's Pay in Europe', *Labour Market Trends*, May 2002, p. 227.

114 J. Simms, 'Women at the Top – You've Got Male', *Accountancy*, January 2003, p. 62.

115 Translated from C. Maussion, '30%: La Différence de Salaire entre un Homme et une Femme Cadres Moyens, Selon l'INSEE', *Libération*, 6 March 2004.

116 'What Women Want', /www.peoplemanagement.co.uk/, 15 January 2004.

117 Translated from W. Nijsten, 'Vrouwen aan de top grijpen sneller naar de fles', *De Morgen*, 2 March 2004, p. 7.

118 A. E. M. van Vianen and A. H. Fischer, 'Illuminating the Glass Ceiling: The Role of Organizational Culture Preferences', *Journal of Occupational and Organizational Psychology*, September 2003, pp. 315–37.

119 M. Kets de Vries, *The Leadership Mystique* (London: Pearson Education Limited, 2001).

120 Translated from F. Latrive, '40,1%, Le Taux d'Activité des 55-64 and dans l'Union Européenne en 2002', *Libération*, 4 March 2004.

121 'Ageism Rife in UK Workplace', /www.peoplemanagement.co.uk/, 15 January 2004.

122 European Commission, *The Social Situation in the European Union* (Luxembourg: Office for Official Publications of the European Communities, 2003).

123 'Ageism Rife in UK Workplace', /www.peoplemanagement.co.uk/, 15 January 2004.

124 /www.leeftijd.nl/

125 For a complete review, see S. R. Rhodes, 'Age-Related Differences in Work Attitudes and Behavior: A Review and Conceptual Analysis', *Psychological Bulletin*, March 1983, pp. 328–67. Supporting evidence was also provided by G. Burkins, 'Work Week: A Special News Report about Life on the Job – and Trends Taking Shape There', *The Wall Street Journal*, 5 May 1996, p. A1.

126 See G. M. McEvoy, 'Cumulative Evidence of the Relationship between Employee Age and Job Performance', *Journal of Applied Psychology*, February 1989, pp. 11–17.

127 A thorough discussion of the relationship between age and performance is contained in D. A. Waldman and B. J. Avolio, 'Aging and Work Performance in Perspective: Contextual and Developmental Considerations', in *Research in Personnel and Human Resources Management, vol. 11*, ed. G. R. Ferris (Greenwich, CT: JAI Press, 1993), pp. 133–62.

128 For details, see B. J. Avolio, D. A. Waldman and M. A. McDaniel, 'Age and Work Performance in Nonmanagerial Jobs: The Effects of Experience and Occupational Type', *Academy of Management Journal*, June 1990, pp. 407–22.

129 D. H. Powell, 'Aging Baby Boomers: Stretching Your Workforce Options', *HR Magazine*, July 1998, p. 83.

130 See P. W. Hom and R. W. Griffeth, *Employee Turnover* (Cincinnati, OH: SouthWestern, 1995), pp. 35–50; and J. J. Martocchio, 'Age-Related Differences in Employee Absenteeism: A Meta-Analysis', *Psychology and Aging*, December 1989, pp. 409–14.

131 Based on R. Zemke, C. Raines and B. Filipczak, *Generations at Work. Managing the Clash of Veterans, Boomers, Xers, and Nexters in Your Workplace* (New York: AMACOM, 2000). Also see H. Karp, C. Fuller and D. Sirias, *Creating Authentic Teams for High Performance at Work* (Palo Alto, CA: Davies Black, 2002); C. A. Martin and B. Tulgan, *Managing the Generation Mix: From Collision to Collaboration* (Amherst, MA: HRD Press, 2002); J. Wallace, 'After X Comes Y', *HR Magazine*, April 2001, p. 192; C. Anderson, 'Survey: The Young: Know Future', *The Economist*, 23 December 2000, pp. S6–S9; and S. Dufour, D. Fortin and J. Hamel, 'Sociologie d'un Conflit de Jeunesses: La Génération du "baby boom" et les "baby busters"', *Cahiers Internationaux de Sociologie*, July 1994, pp. 277–300.

132 R. Foroohar, S. Theil, S. Marias, T. Pepper, H. Wiedekind and B. Nadeau, 'Race in the Boardroom,' *Newsweek*, 18 February 2002, p. 34.

133 Translated from S. de Vries, 'Waarom bevorderen organisaties de participatie van allochtonen?', *Gedrag & Organisatie*, no. 6, 2003, pp. 407–17.

134 K. I. van der Zee, 'Omgaan met culturele diversiteit in organisaties: de rol van sociale identiteit, persoonlijkheid en dreiging', *Gedrag & Organisatie*, no. 6, 2003, pp. 393–405.

135 Translated from 'Meer dan 150 nationaliteiten in Antwerpen', *De Morgen*, 17 March 2004, p. 8.

136 Translated from J. Billiet and K. Meireman, *Immigratie en asiel: de opvattingen en houdingen van Belgen in het Europeens sociaal survey. Onderzoeksverslag van het Departement Sociologie – Afdeling Dataverzameling en Analyse* (DA/2004-36), p. 25.

137 Translated from P. Roger, 'L'Assemblée A Adopté à une Large Majorité La Loi Contre Le Voile à l'Ecole', *Le Monde*, 12 February 2004.

138 R. Foroohar, S. Theil, S. Marias, T. Pepper, H. Wiedekind and B. Nadeau, 'Race in the Boardroom,' *Newsweek*, 18 February 2002, p. 34.

139 Translated from D. De Coninck, 'Mohammed wordt Michaël, en dat is precies wat de wetgever wou', *De Morgen*, 4 September 2004.

140 See Y. F. Niemann and J. F. Dovidio, 'Relationship of Solo Status, Academic Rank, and Perceived Distinctiveness to Job Satisfaction of Racial/Ethnic Minorities', *Journal of Applied Psychology*, February 1998, pp. 55–71; J. I. Sanchez and P. Brock, 'Outcomes of Perceived Discrimination among Hispanic Employees: Is Diversity Management a Luxury or a Necessity?', *Academy of Management Journal*, June 1996, pp. 704–19; and T. H. Cox, Jr, and J. A. Finley, 'An Analysis of Work Specialization and Organization Level as Dimensions of Workforce Diversity', in *Diversity in Organizations*, eds M. M. Chemers, S. Oskamp and M. A. Costanzo (Thousand Oaks, CA: Sage Publications, 1995), pp. 62–88.

141 D. Hargreaves, 'Immigration: Rocky Road from Control to Management', the *Financial Times*, 12 October 2000, p. 4.

142 'Managing Diversity. A IPD Position Paper', Institute of Personnel and Development, p. 7 (also see www.cipd.co.uk).

143 /www.cipd.co.uk/

144 See R. R. Thomas, Jr, 'From Affirmative Action to Affirming Diversity', *Harvard Business Review*, March–April 1990, pp. 107–17.

145 /www.cipd.co.uk/

146 /www.cipd.co.uk/

147 /www.soag.nl/

148 K. Hilpern, 'Disabled But Not Unfit', the *Independent*, 8 October 2000.

149 B. P. Buunk and V. van der Laan, 'Do Women Need Female Role Models? Subjective Social Status and the Effects of Same-Sex Opposite-Sex Comparisons', *Revue Internationale de Psychologie Sociale*, December 2002, pp. 129–55.

150 Translated from 'Volledig vrouwelijk', *De Morgen*, 6 March 2004, p. 17.

151 W. R. Thompson, 'Diversity among Managers Translates into Profitability', *HR Magazine*, April 1999, p. 10.

152 For research into TMT demographics, see K. Y. Williams, 'Demography and Diversity in Organisations: A Review of 100 Years of Research' in *Research in Organizational Behavior, vol. 20*, eds B. M. Staw and L. L. Cummings (Greenwich, CT: JAI Press, 1998), pp. 77–140.

153 See R. Moss Kanter, *The Change Masters* (New York: Simon and Schuster, 1983); and L. K. Larkey, 'Toward a Theory of Communicative Interactions in Culturally Diverse Workgroups', *Academy of Management Review*, April 1996, pp. 463–91.

154 See K. Y. Williams, 'Demography and Diversity in Organisations: A Review of 100 Years of Research' in *Research in Organizational Behavior, vol. 20*, eds B. M. Staw and L. L. Cummings (Greenwich, CT: JAI Press, 1998), pp. 77–140.

155 S. Liff, 'Diversity and Equal Opportunities: Room for a Constructive Compromise?', *Human Resource Management Journal*, no. 1, 1999, pp. 65–75.

156 See K. Y. Williams, 'Demography and Diversity in Organisations: A Review of 100 Years of Research' in *Research in Organizational Behavior, vol. 20*, eds B. M. Staw and L. L. Cummings (Greenwich, CT: JAI Press, 1998), pp. 77–140.

157 M. C. Schipers, D. N. Den Hartog, P. L. Koopman and J. A. Wienk, 'Diversity and Team Outcomes: The Moderating Effects of Outcome Interdependence and Group Longevity and the Mediating Effect of Reflexivity', *Journal of Organizational Behavior*, September 2003, pp. 779–802.

158 The relationship between conflict and stages of group development is discussed by D. C. Lau and J. K. Murnighan, 'Demographic Diversity and Faultlines: The Compositional Dynamics of Organizational Groups', *Academy of Management Review*, April 1998, pp. 325–40.

159 See J. A. Chatman, J. T. Polzer, S. G. Barsade and M. A. Neale, 'Being Different Yet Feeling Similar: The Influence of Demographic Composition and Organizational Culture on Work Processes and Outcomes', *Administrative Science Quarterly*, December 1998, pp. 749–80; and D. A. Harrison, K. H. Price and M. P. Bell, 'Beyond Relational Demography: Time and the Effects of Surface- and Deep-Level Diversity on Work Group Cohesion', *Academy of Management Journal*, February 1998, pp. 96–107.

160 These barriers were taken from discussions in M. Loden, *Implementing Diversity* (Chicago: Irwin, 1996); E. E. Spragins, 'Benchmark: The Diverse Work Force', *Inc.*, January 1993, p. 33; and A. M. Morrison, *The New Leaders: Guidelines on Leadership Diversity in America* (San Francisco, CA: Jossey-Bass, 1992).

161 For a discussion of ethnocentrism, see M. Kiselica, 'Confronting My Own Ethnocentrism and Racism: A Process of Pain and Growth', *Journal of Counseling & Development*, Winter 1999, pp. 14–17; and S. Perreult and R. Y. Bourhis, 'Ethnocentrism, Social Identification, and Discrimination', *Personality and Social Psychology Bulletin*, January 1999, pp. 92–103.

162 See the related discussion in G. R. Ferris, D. D. Frink, D. P. S. Bhawuk and D. C. Gilmore, 'Reactions of Diverse Groups to Politics in the Workplace', *Journal of Management*, 1996, pp. 23–44.

163 This discussion is based on R. R. Thomas, Jr, *Redefining Diversity* (New York: AMACOM, 1996).

164 'BAOBAB Catering Wins An Award for Promoting Equal Opportunities', *EU Networks on Integration of Refugees*, August 2000, pp. 12–13.

165 Adapted and translated from B. Debeuckelaere, 'Geef wat meer kleur aan Je bedrijf', *Vacature*, 14 August 1999, p. 1.

166 R. Foroohar, S. Theil, S. Marias, T. Pepper, H. Wiedekind and B. Nadeau, 'Race in the Boardroom,' *Newsweek*, 18 February 2002, p. 34.

167 /www.peoplemanagement.co.uk.

168 For complete details and results from this study, see A. M. Morrison, *The New Leaders: Guidelines on Leadership Diversity in America* (San Francisco: Jossey-Bass, 1992).

169 'Balancing Act', the *Financial Times*, 9 May 2000.

170 'NHS Trust Wins Parents at Work Award', *People Management*.

171 A. Iziren, 'Age Concerns', *People Management*, 20 May 1999, pp. 50–52.

172 R. Johnson, 'Family Values', *People Management*, 11 March 1999, p. 46.

173 B. Debeuckelaere, 'M/V biedt aan: vakantie te koop', *Vacature.com*, 3 March 2000.

174 Adapted and translated from J. Chorus, 'Wedijver boven de wieg', *NRC Handelsblad*, 17 August 1996, p. 3.

175 Empirical support is provided by H. Ibarra, 'Race, Opportunity, and Diversity of Social Circles in Managerial Networks', *Academy of Management Journal*, June 1995, pp. 673–703; and P. J. Ohlott, M. N. Ruderman and C. D. McCauley, 'Gender Differences in Managers' Developmental Job Experiences', *Academy of Management Journal*, February 1994, pp. 46–67.

176 E. Deeks, 'High-Profile Pair to Lift Diversity at Ford', *People Management*, 6 January 2000, p. 28.

177 Excerpted from M. Adams, 'Building a Rainbow, One Stripe at a Time', *HR Magazine*, August 1998, p. 73.

178 This exercise was modified from an exercise in L. Gardenwartz and A. Rowe, *Diverse Teams at Work* (New York: McGraw-Hill, 1994), p. 169.

chapter 5 content motivation theories

By Dave Bouckenooghe and Veronique Warmoes

Learning outcomes
When you have read this chapter, you should be able to:

- define the term motivation
- review the historical roots of modern motivation theories
- explain the difference between content and process approaches of motivation
- contrast Maslow's and McClelland's need theories
- describe Alderfer's theory and the frustration regression assumption
- explain the practical significance of Herzberg's distinction between motivators and hygiene factors
- describe how internal work motivation is increased by using the job characteristics model

Motivation mojo. With profits down and morale low, keeping an outside sales team at the top of its game is more important than ever

They don't report to you, they don't take orders from you, and day-in and day-out they are not interacting face-to-face with you. So, how do you get your outside sales team motivated to go out there and sell your company's products and services? The answer is not just money. Sales managers can keep outside sales reps pumped up about making the sale and closing the deal in many other ways.

Keep the options open. Everyone knows that an incentive programme can do wonders for motivating reps, but with so many different programmes out there, how do sales managers know which one will work best? The answer is variety. By giving reps a choice of rewards, employees are much more likely to find something in the offerings that will motivate them personally. 'Every sales person is motivated by something different', says Bill Fitzpatrick, president of Sales Motivation Solutions in Melbourne. 'The first step is figuring out what they want.' As the sales and the promotions manager for Network Communications, a real estate publisher, Dave Coleman is responsible for a large nationwide outside sales team. With so many personalities, notes Coleman, one option would not work to motivate the entire team. 'The incentive programme we offer has about eight different categories of prizes ranging from electronics to jewellery to vacations', Coleman says. 'And Salesdriver, the incentive house we work with, will even add custom travel options for people who do not find what they are looking for in selections.' This area of options has Coleman's team motivated to earn their share of the prizes. 'Our team really looks forward to this programme each year,' he adds. 'We even had one woman do all of her Christmas shopping from our prize catalogue with her winnings in the programme.'

case study

Give everyone a chance. Coleman uses a point system as the basis of his team's incentive programme so everyone is eligible to earn prizes. Accumulated points are redeemable for merchandise from the web-based award catalogue. 'We have designed the programme so that everyone competes against their budget for this year', Coleman says. However they indirectly compete against each other for bragging rights, which can also be a great motivator. The point system also works in the company's favour. By weighting certain products or services with more point value, Coleman can encourage his team to focus on specific areas of the market that the company wants to emphasise each quarter.

Make it simple. Always state clear-cut objectives. 'It is critical that whatever contest you offer as an incentive must be clearly defined as to what the employees need to do to qualify', Fitzpatrick says. 'There cannot be any complicated math formulas to figure out when computing the programme.' Virtual platforms are one way to ensure programme cohesion. Having programmes online enables salespeople to access the programme from anywhere – at any time of day. Adds Coleman: 'The thing the sales reps really love about the programme is the accessibility. They have the ability to go in 24 hours a day and see how they are doing.'

Open the lines of communication. With the sales team that does not spend time interacting in the office, it is often difficult to unify the group and keep them all directly in line with company goals. As general sales manager of small and medium businesses for Gateway Computers, Matt Millen is responsible for an outside sales team of 200 employees in 40 different states. 'Communication is critical in having them feel like they are a part of the team and an extension of the corporate environment', Millen says. Weekly conference calls ensure that all 200 reps are on the same page. During this time Millen spends about 20 minutes discussing what is going on in the company and providing updates about the top sellers for the week. Winners are also given time to brag a bit and discuss how they accomplished the win. The next 30 minutes of the call are open Q&A, where Millen lets any of the 200 salespeople ask him a question. By bringing every member of the team together once a week, Millen is able to easily reinforce the company's goals while at the same time showing each sales person that he is a valued member of the team.

Beef up training. One way Millen keeps his team motivated is with a method called 'Sharing the Best Practices'. This type of buddy system works on a formal and informal basis. For instance, if someone misses goals, a top seller will step in as a mentor, helping out in the areas of opportunity. Interaction is extremely beneficial for a large outside sales team like Millen's because it is not always possible for the sales manager to personally retrain each rep. 'People are usually happy in their job if they know what they are doing, and the more likely they are to represent it better to customers', Fitzpatrick says.[1]

For discussion

In what fundamental ways do Coleman and Millen differ in their vision on how to motivate employees? Which one of both visions is the most effective one to motivate people according to you? Is it possible that a combination of both strategies is even more effective?

Effective employee motivation and satisfaction has long been one of management's most difficult and important duties. Success in this endeavour is becoming more challenging in the light of organisational trends to downsize and re-engineer and the demands associated with managing a diverse workforce. Companies are using a wide range of techniques to keep their staff happy and motivated, ranging from classical measures such as stimulating compensation schemes through signs of appreciation such as tap on the back. It is said that companies do not just want their employees to like their job, they want them to love their job. 'Contented cows give better milk', write HR-specialists Richard Hadden and Bill Catlette.[2] As a result, some innovative companies nowadays increasingly experiment with alternative, creative ploys to create an overtly enthusiastic workforce. An executive cynically explains the rationale behind this trend: 'With the old techniques, we got their mind, now we've got their heart and soul too . . . .'[3] Consider the following examples:

> Some Dotcom companies in London are trying to hang on to people by introducing super-market-style reward points for good performance. These are accumulated and cashed in for benefits covering everything from paid sabbaticals to in-house yoga sessions.[4]

> At TBWA, a British advertising agency, staff can chill out in a leisure zone equipped with two Sony Playstation pods and all the latest games, video screens and a pool table.[5]

> Saloman Smith Barney has taken to providing gourmet meals, fresh underwear and free toothbrushes to staff working past 7 p.m.[6]

> Container Store rated as the second best company by Fortune Magazine provides employees free yoga classes and chair massages. Synovus, a bank holding company, offers on-site child care, and a gym, whereas American Cast Iron Pipe has an onsite clinic that offers free medical and dental care for employees for life. Supermarket chain Wegmans allows workers 'to take off to volunteer and to care for sick pets'.[7]

As we enter the twenty-first century most employees have gone through motivational changes. Researchers Ester, Halman and de Moor of the University of Tilburg in the Netherlands compared the motivation and values of modern-day workers with those of previous generations, such as their parents and grandparents. They concluded that people want significantly more than just a high salary and good career prospects. They want to express autonomy, creativity and growth in their job. They rate meeting new challenges and finding self-expression higher than accruing status.[8]

These changes and trends impose great challenges on contemporary employers who want to keep their people motivated. As addressed in Chapter 1, Douglas McGregor presented two kinds of propositions regarding human motivation. Theory X implies that employees dislike work, are lazy, dislike responsibility and must be coerced to perform. So, people are being motivated by controlling their actions, with rewards and punishments. Theory Y assumes that employees like work, are creative, seek responsibility and can exercise self-direction. So, people are motivated when they are treated as adults rather than as children. Giving responsibility and possibilities to develop self-direction and/or participation in decisions are important determinants to motivate people.[9]

Nido Qubein, a member of the board and executive committee of a Fortune 500 financial corporation and member of the board of 17 universities, companies and community organisations asserts ten principles of motivation he learned out of working together with people.[10] As an employer, manager, supervisor or CEO you need to determine what motivates people. The first principle is that all people are motivated, but the opportunity and a clear direction are needed. If you do not provide such opportunity, people will move toward their own goals rather than the organisational ones. Second, people do things for their own reasons, not for yours or mine. People have to be shown what gains and profits they can get out of following actions that benefit the organisation. This can be accomplished by providing rewards and recognition. A third principle states that people will change jobs because of dissatisfaction and pain. When the dissatisfaction or pain of staying exceeds the pain of change, people will certainly look out for a new job. The fourth principle states that a major key to effective communication is identification. According to this principle people are easier motivated when they can identify their personal goals with the organisational goals. The fifth tenet holds that the best way to get employees' attention is to pay attention to them. So employers, supervisors, managers should learn to listen instead of merely hearing employees. Listening is much more active than hearing. By listening to employees, you will learn to recognise their complaints and problems. The sixth principle is that pride is a powerful motivator. Everybody is proud of something. Thus, finding out what makes people proud can provide a very useful insight to channel people's motivation. So, building employees' self-esteem is a paramount motivator in business. The seventh principle claims that people cannot be changed, only their actions can. If you want to change employees' behaviours, change their beliefs and feelings. Eight, an employee's perception may become the executive's reality. This implies that when an employer or supervisor sends a message to employees, employees do not react to what employers or supervisors say. They respond to what the supervisor expects them to say. So, employees conclude that the behaviour they observe in the manager, supervisor or professional is the behaviour that is wanted and accepted. Thus the self-fulfilling prophecy (Chapter 4) plays an important role in the motivation process. According to the ninth tenet: 'You get the behaviours you consistently expect and reinforce.' When employees learn that certain demeanour results in lower earnings, lower bonuses, less favourable hours, they will alter their behaviour. Finally, we judge ourselves by our motives or intentions, whereas we judge others by their behaviour or actions. So, do not try to assess motives. Just emphasise behaviour because it can be difficult to change other people's motives. Behaviour is much easier to change through the mechanism of reinforcement.

The question, 'How do I motivate people to do what I want them to do?', is frequently asked by employers, and has driven the consultancy world to start up firms specialising in delivering motivation services and products. One such firm is Projectlink Motivation, one of UK's fastest growing full-service motivation houses. Projectlink Motivation delivers programmes for over 300 organisations in the UK and Ireland. Several services and products are delivered. One such product is the so-called 'Super cheque', the fastest-growing reward currency. The Super cheque is a multi-choice reward exchangeable for the widest range of retail, travel, leisure and entertainment vouchers. Super cheques work like this: 1) When you make awards to your employees, you give them Super cheques which come in a range of values; 2) The Super cheques are presented within a congratulations wallet – which doubles as a redemption mechanism; 3) Recipients simply select vouchers of their choice from the list shown on the reverse of the congratulations wallet, working in multiples of €7.25 to up the value of their Super cheque(s); 4) When the redemption request is received, the selected vouchers are despatched back to the recipient's home address within 72 hours.[11]

The purpose of this chapter and of Chapter 6, is to provide you with a foundation for understanding the complexities of employee motivation. This chapter provides a definitional and theoretical foundation for the topic of motivation so that a rich variety of motivation theories and techniques can be introduced and discussed. Coverage of employee motivation extends to Chapter 6. After explaining what motivation involves, this chapter focuses on content theories of motivation and the job characteristics model of motivation. In the next chapter, attention turns to process-related theories of motivation. To get an encompassing view on what motivation implies and which theories exist, Chapters 5 and 6 both need to be considered.

What does motivation involve?

The term 'motivation' derives from the Latin word *movere*, meaning 'to move'. No questions have been raised about the significance motivation plays in influencing performance at work.[12] However, job performance does not only depend on the motivation of employees. As displayed in Figure 5.1, two other factors often play an important role in predicting job performance. This implies that people who are motivated to carry out a task do not necessarily perform successfully. A lot depends also on the abilities and situational characteristics to perform well. For example, a motivated employee may perform weakly on a task because he did not have the necessary tools to perform well. Thus, besides the willingness or motivation, capacity and opportunity are vital dimensions in predicting work performance. The capacity to perform refers to the ability, age, health, skills and level of education that individuals have. Having the opportunity to perform is also a key factor for performance. This factor refers to the tools, equipment, materials, working conditions, leader behaviour, organisational politics, rules and procedures, time and pay. Different combinations of these dimensions underlie different performance levels. A combination of favourable opportunities, higher capacity and higher motivation leads to very high performance, whereas a combination of low levels on the three dimensions should predict very low performance.[13] An important observation is that two people may claim that they are motivated, although their motivations may differ in direction, intensity and persistence. Direction refers to choices people make between different alternatives. The first employee, for example, may prefer intrinsic rewards (autonomy, self-growth, etc.) over extrinsic rewards (like money, financial bonuses, relationship with colleagues), whereas the second one may prefer extrinsic over intrinsic rewards for equal work. The intensity component involves the strength of the response once the choice is made. Finally, persistence implies how long a person will continue to devote effort and energy.

Employers need to understand the motivation process if they are successfully to guide employees toward accomplishing organisational objectives. The study of motivation is about the question: 'Why

FIGURE 5.1 DETERMINANTS OF WORK PERFORMANCE

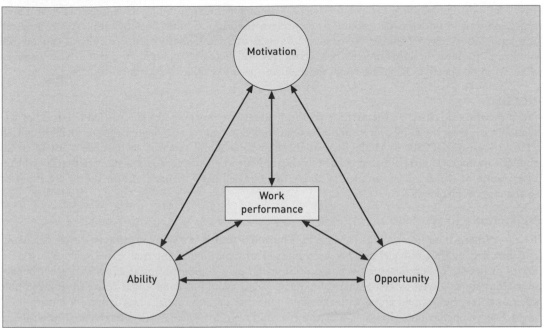

do people behave the way they do?'[14] If we want to learn about how motivation works we need at first to learn how motivation is induced. Needs can be considered as the starting point of motivations. Our needs concern something we want to attain. They refer to deficiencies individuals experience at some point in time, and function as triggers of behavioural responses. The deficiencies people might experience can have a physiological, psychological or relational nature. For example, if you are hungry while studying your history exam for tomorrow, you might interrupt your study and get something to eat out of the fridge. So needs direct behaviour to satisfy those needs. If needs stay unsatisfied or unmet they invoke more intense feelings and behavioural modifications. Thus, a need deficiency usually triggers a search for ways to reduce this deficiency and this search in its turn results in a choice of goal-directed behaviour. Hence **Motivation** can be considered as the arousal, direction and maintenance of human behaviour toward attaining some goal.[15] The assessment of this choice is dependent on whether the choice of goal-directed behaviour causes rewards or punishments. The satisfaction of a need may be experienced as a reward. However it is possible that a motivational driving force is hindered before attaining or satisfying the desired goal. The barrier to attain the desired goal can underlie constructive behaviour or cause feelings of frustration. Constructive behaviour refers to a positive reaction to the obstruction of a wanted goal. Problem solving and restructuring are two types of constructive demeanour. Problem-solving behaviour is the action emphasised at removing barriers. For instance, if you do not have the tools to do a task, you might buy or develop the necessary tools. Restructuring is about substituting an alternative goal by a goal of a lower order – for example, choosing for a higher-paid job if the work climate in the current job is bad. By contrast with constructive behaviour, frustration concerns negative responses to the blockage of a desired goal. Aggression for instance is frustration-induced behaviour.[16]

This section provides the historical roots of motivational concepts. As you will notice, a myriad of competing motivation theories exists. They all try to explain motivation. However, none of these theories explain all motivation behaviours, as no ready-made solutions or answers exist as to what motivates all people at work. The pursuit for an all-covering generalised theory of motivation is as futile as an endless quest for the Holy Grail. Therefore, an employer must be aware of the main motivational theories and judge their relevance for particular work settings before starting to apply them.

Motivation
psychological
processes that
arouse and direct
goal-directed
behaviour

Historical roots of modern motivation theories

Five methods of explaining behaviour – needs, reinforcement, cognition, job characteristics and feelings/emotions – underlie the evolution of modern theories of human motivation. As we proceed through this review, remember the objective of each alternative motivation theory is to explain and predict purposeful or goal-directed behaviour. As will become apparent, the differences between theoretical perspectives lie in the causal mechanisms used to explain behaviour.

NEEDS

Need theories are based on the premise that individuals are motivated by unsatisfied needs. Dissatisfaction with your social life, for example, should motivate you to participate in more social activities. Henry Murray, a 1930s psychologist, was the first behavioural scientist to propose a list of needs thought to underlie goal-directed behaviour. From Murray's work sprang a wide variety of need theories, some of which remain influential today. Recognised need theories of motivation are explored in the current chapter.

REINFORCEMENT

Reinforcement theorists, such as Edward L. Thorndike and B. F. Skinner, proposed that behaviour is controlled by its consequences, not by the result of hypothetical internal states such as instincts, drives or needs. This proposition is based on research data demonstrating that people repeat behaviours that are followed by favourable consequences and avoid behaviours that result in unfavourable consequences. Few would argue with the statement that organisational rewards have a motivational impact on job behaviour. However, behaviourists and cognitive theorists do disagree over the role, in motivation, of an individual's internal states and processes.

COGNITIONS

Uncomfortable with the idea that behaviour is shaped completely by environmental consequences, cognitive motivation theorists contend that behaviour is a function of beliefs, expectations, values and other mental cognitions. Behaviour is therefore viewed as the result of rational and conscious choices among alternative courses of action. In Chapter 6, we will discuss cognitive motivation theories involving equity, expectancies and goal setting.

JOB CHARACTERISTICS

This theoretical approach is based on the idea that the task itself is the key to employee motivation. Specifically, a boring and monotonous job stifles motivation to perform well, whereas a challenging job enhances motivation. Three ingredients of a more challenging job are variety, autonomy and decision-making authority. A popular way of adding variety and challenge to routine jobs is job enrichment (or job redesign). This technique is addressed at the end of this chapter.

FEELINGS/EMOTIONS

This most recent addition to the evolution of motivation theory is based on the idea that workers are 'whole people' who pursue goals other than that of becoming high performers.[17] For example, you may want to be a brilliant student, loving boyfriend or girlfriend, caring parent, good friend, responsible citizen or a happy person. Work motivation is thus thought to be a function of your feelings and emotions toward the multitude of interests and goals that you have. You are likely to study long and hard if your only interest in life is to enter graduate school and become a doctor. In contrast, a highly motivated lecturer is likely to stop lecturing and dismiss the students upon receiving a message that his or her child was seriously hurt in an accident.

Content versus process approaches of motivation

Content theories try to expound the things that actually motivate people in their job. These theories emphasise the goals to which people aspire and focus on the factors within a person that direct, energise or stop behaviour. Consequently, content theories want to identify people's needs, and the goals they want to attain in order to satisfy these needs. Whereas content theories emphasise what motivates people, process theories attempt to explain the actual process of motivation. Unlike the former theories the latter give individuals a cognitive decision-making role in selecting their goals and the

Content theories
theories regarding what motivates people

TABLE 5.1 CONTENT AND PROCESS THEORIES OF MOTIVATION

Theoretical classification	Main theories
Content theories Address the question what motivates	Maslow's hierarchy of needs model Alderfer's modified need hierarchy model McClelland's motivation theory Herzberg's two factor theory McGregor's Theory X and Y
Process theories Address the question how people get motivated	Equity theory Expectancy theory Goal-setting theory

means to achieve them. As a result **Process theories** are concerned with answering questions of how individual behaviour is energised, directed, maintained and stopped.[18] In Table 5.1 you can find the main content and process theories. The content theories, also labelled as 'need' theories are discussed in the following section. McGregor's content theory has been addressed in Chapter 1. Process theories will be addressed in Chapter 6.

Process theories theories regarding how people get motivated

Need theories of motivation

Need theories attempt to pinpoint internal factors that energise behaviour. **Needs** are physiological or psychological deficiencies that arouse behaviour. They can be strong or weak and are influenced by environmental factors. Thus, human needs vary over time and place. Three popular need theories are discussed in this section: Maslow's need hierarchy theory, Alderfer's ERG theory and McClelland's need theory.

Needs physiological or psychological deficiencies that arouse behaviour

Maslow's need hierarchy theory

In 1943 an important humanistic psychologist, Abraham Maslow, published his now-famous need hierarchy theory of motivation. Although the theory was based on clinical observation of a few neurotic individuals, it has subsequently been used to explain the entire spectrum of human behaviour. Maslow proposed that motivation is a function of five basic needs – physiological, safety, love, esteem and self-actualisation (see Figure 5.2). An advantage of this theory is that it is built upon human behaviour, whereas the reinforcement theories of motivation were inferred from lab rat experiments.

FIGURE 5.2 MASLOW'S NEED HIERARCHY

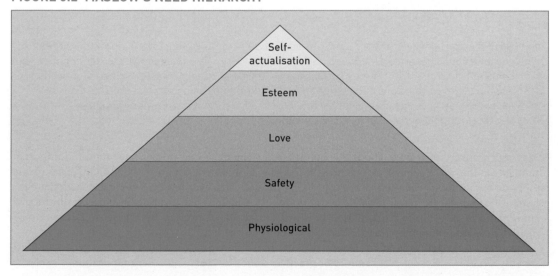

TABLE 5.2 DESCRIPTION OF FIVE BASIC NEEDS

Physiological needs	These needs are required to sustain life. In this category Maslow places chemical needs of the body such as sexual desire, hunger, sleepiness, activity needs and desired sensory satisfactions
Safety needs	Once the physiological needs are satisfied, one's needs are directed towards attaining a feeling of safety and security. It concerns the need for freedom of threat, that is, the security from threatening events or surroundings. So, people are motivated to avoid wild animals, extremes of temperature, assault, disease and the like. In this category the needs for living in a safe environment, medical insurance, job security and financial reserves are placed
Love needs	This category is used in a very comprehensive way as it includes the needs for affiliation and belongingness. It involves the need for friends, spouses, parents and group membership. Thus, typical love needs are friendship, belonging to a group, giving and receiving love
Esteem needs	This category falls into two broad categories. The first are internal esteem needs. They include desires for such feelings like power, achievement, confidence, freedom and independence. The second group refers to external esteem needs and is derived from reputation, prestige, recognition, attention and importance. Both groups of needs lead to higher self-confidence
Self-actualisation needs	These needs are the summit of the hierarchy. They refer to the desire to realise or actualise one's full potential. This category includes needs such as truth, justice, wisdom, meaning, etc.

Maslow said these five need categories are arranged in a graduated hierarchy. In other words, he believed human needs generally emerge in a predictable stair-step fashion. Accordingly, once one's physiological needs are relatively satisfied, one's safety needs emerge, and so on up the need hierarchy, one step at a time. Once a need is satisfied it activates the next higher need in the hierarchy. This process continues until the need for self-actualisation is activated.[19] A description of the five basic needs is displayed in Table 5.2.

RESEARCH FINDINGS AND PRACTICAL IMPLICATIONS

Research does not clearly support this theory because results from studies testing the need hierarchy are difficult to interpret. A well-known motivation scholar summarised the research evidence as follows:

> On balance, Maslow's theory remains very popular among employers and students of organisational behaviour, although there are still very few studies that can legitimately confirm (or refute) it . . . . It may be that the dynamics implied by Maslow's theory of needs are too complex to be put into operation and confirmed by scientific research. If this is the case, we may never be able to determine how valid the theory is or, more precisely, which aspects of the theory are valid and which not.[20]

As so much uncertainty exists about the validity of the theory, some studies have reported important findings on the management population. Managers high in the chain-of-command place greater emphasis on autonomy and self-actualisation.[21] Managers at lower levels in the organisational chain of small businesses are more satisfied with autonomy and self-actualisation in comparison to their counterparts in large firms.[22] Furthermore, it was found that American managers overseas are more satisfied with autonomy than their colleagues working in the US.[23]

A satisfied need may lose its motivational potential. Therefore, professionals are advised to motivate employees by devising programmes or practices aimed at satisfying emerging or unmet needs.

'You can't fascinate IT-professionals for very long by just offering a competitive salary', says a recruitment manager at the Real Software Group, one of Europe's leading software companies. 'You've got to beam out a certain dynamism and creativity through your company, and offer them a wide variety of future perspectives. We offer our IT'ers a technologically oriented career with four or five dimensions. They can fulfil the role of project manager, programmer, documentalist, implementator, end-users' coach, and so on. Those who had enough of a certain technology get the chance to re-educate themselves or concentrate on another technology. This is much more powerful "glue" than just offering high pay. Salary is a strong motivator on a short term base but, in the long run, we see that what drives IT-professionals the most is their love for a certain technology or scientific field.'[24]

The same recommendation applies to the context of motivating customers to purchase specific products. The Ritz-Carlton, for example, believes that customer loyalty and satisfaction are based on satisfying customer needs. The organisation attempts to motivate us to stay at its hotels by first gathering detailed information on customer preferences and needs from a variety of sources. This information is then entered into an on-line, nationwide computer system. The Ritz-Carlton then uses this information to satisfy customer needs.

When a repeat customer calls the central reservations number to book a room, the agent can retrieve the individual's preference information directly from the on-line system. This information is sent to the specific Ritz location where the room is reserved. The hotel then outputs the data in a daily guest recognition and preference report, which is circulated to all staff. With this system, hotel staff can anticipate a particular guest's breakfast habits, newspaper choices and room preferences. The Ritz's employees are well trained to ensure they are able to respond to the customers' needs. A customer management system ensures that the first employee who becomes aware of a customer complaint becomes responsible for resolving the problem quickly and completely. Each employee can reverse a transaction of up to $2000 without prior approval – if necessary – to keep a customer satisfied.[25]

Thus, it may be concluded that Maslow's theory has important implications for an organisational setting. The five needs employees may experience can be satisfied through compensation packages, company events, etc. In Table 5.3 different opportunities are shown of how the five needs can be met.[26]

TABLE 5.3 OPPORTUNITIES AND WAYS TO FULFIL THE FIVE NEEDS AT WORK

Physiological needs	Provide lunch breaks, rest breaks and wages that are sufficient to purchase the essentials of life
Safety needs	Provide a safe work environment and relative job security
Love needs	Create a feeling of acceptance, belonging and community by reinforcing team dynamics
Esteem needs	Recognise achievements, assign important projects and provide status to make employees feel appreciated and valued
Self-actualisation needs	Provide a challenging and meaningful work which enables innovation, creativity and progress according to the long term

BARRIERS TO MASLOW'S THEORY

There are some problems associated with the use of Maslow's theory in the work setting.[27]

- Employees do not always need to satisfy their needs through their work. It is possible that the higher level needs are satisfied through other life domains such as leisure.
- There is no conclusive evidence about how much time passes between the satisfaction of a lower-level need and the progress to a higher-order need.
- People value the same needs differently. Maslow's theory, however, is a universalist theory which applies to everyone. As a result this theory cannot explain differences between people and between cultures.
- Identical rewards may satisfy different needs. For instance, a high wage may satisfy the safety need and esteem need, because a high wage can be assessed as an important indicator for appraisal and recognition at work.
- Satisfaction in Maslow's theory is considered as the major motivational outcome of behaviour. However, job satisfaction does not necessarily improve work performance.
- For employees with the same needs (same level in hierarchy), the motivational factors will be different because there are many diverse ways in which people may pursue satisfaction.

Alderfer's ERG theory

Clayton Alderfer, a Yale psychology professor developed another important need-motivation theory by reworking and refining Maslow's work.[28] The ERG theory extends Maslow's needs hierarchy theory in many respects. Although Maslow's need hierarchy theory is still very popular among professionals, it lacks serious empirical evidence supporting its predictions.[29] The middle levels of Maslow's hierarchy are overlapping. Alderfer addressed this issue by reducing the five dimensions to three. The three letters of ERG-theory represent three types of needs. The first letter stands for existence needs and refers to Maslow's safety and physiological needs. This level involves the concern with basic material-existence requirements. The second group is relatedness needs and refers to the need to maintain significant relations. These relatedness needs are similar to Maslow's social and external esteem needs. Finally, the growth needs are concerned with the development of potential, and cover Maslow's self-esteem and self-actualisation needs. This third group is in fact an intrinsic desire for personal development. If you want to get an estimation of your growth need strength we invite you to complete the Activity on the next page.

Beside these similarities, there are some major differences between both theories. Contrary to the Maslow's need hierarchy model the ERG theory demonstrates that more than one need may motivate simultaneously. People can be motivated by money and self-development at the same time, according to the ERG theory. In the need hierarchy model, however, it is assumed that only one of the five needs can motivate at one point in time. For example, when someone's relatedness needs are completely satisfied, these needs cannot motivate as a higher level of esteem needs anymore. According to Alderfer the three groups of needs are more a continuum. Maslow, on the contrary, suggests that individuals progress through the hierarchy from existence needs, to relatedness needs, to growth needs, as the lower-level needs become satisfied.

A second significant difference involves that the gratification of a higher-order need being blocked, the desire to satisfy a lower-level need increases. This is also known as the **Frustration-regression hypothesis**. According to this hypothesis, individuals may also move down the hierarchy. The ERG theory acknowledges this assumption, the need hierarchy model, however, does not. Suppose, for instance, that someone's basic needs are satisfied at relatedness level and he or she is now trying to satisfy their growth needs – that is, having many friends and social relationships and now trying to learn new significant skills, so to make career advancement. However, because of a lack of opportunities to advance, those needs are unable to be satisfied. No matter how hard he or she tries, a move upward is blocked. According to the frustration-regression hypothesis, frustration of the growth needs will cause the relatedness needs to once again become dominant motivators. Henceforth, new energy will be put into making friends and building social relationships.

The ERG theory is more consistent with the knowledge of individual differences among people. This is a third major difference. Variables such as education, family background and cultural environment can alter the importance or driving force that a group of needs holds for a particular

Frustration-regression hypothesis when the gratification of a higher-order need is being blocked, the desire to satisfy a lower level need increases

Assess your own growth need strength

Instructions

People differ in the kinds of jobs they would most like to hold. The descriptions and choices in Part A give you a chance to say just what it is about a job that is most important to you. For each entry, two different kinds of jobs are briefly described. Please indicate which of the two jobs you personally would prefer if you had to make a choice between them. For each pairing, pay attention only to the characteristics listed; assume that everything else about the job is the same. After circling each answer, use the scoring key in Part B.

Part A growth need strength scale

JOB A	Strongly prefer A	Slightly prefer A	Neutral	Slightly prefer B	Strongly prefer B	JOB B
1 A job where the pay is high	1	2	3	4	5	A job where there is considerable opportunity to be creative and innovative
2 A job where you are often required to make important decisions	1	2	3	4	5	A job with many pleasant people to work with
3 A job in which greater responsibility is given to those who do the best work	1	2	3	4	5	A job in which greater responsibility is given to loyal employees who have the most seniority
4 A job in a firm that is in financial trouble and might have to close down within the year	1	2	3	4	5	A job in a firm where you are not allowed to have any say whatever in how your work is scheduled or in the procedures to be used in carrying it out
5 A very routine job	1	2	3	4	5	A job where your co-workers are not very friendly
6 A job with a supervisor who is often very critical of you and your work in front of other people	1	2	3	4	5	A job that prevents you from using a number of skills that you have worked hard to develop

activity

JOB A	Strongly prefer A	Slightly prefer A	Neutral	Slightly prefer B	Strongly prefer B	JOB B
7 A job with a supervisor who respects you and treats you fairly	1	2	3	4	5	A job that provides constant opportunities for you to learn new and interesting things
8 A job where there is a real chance you could be laid off	1	2	3	4	5	A job with very little chance to do challenging work
9 A job in which there is a real chance for you to develop new skills and advance in the organisation	1	2	3	4	5	A job that provides lots of vacation time and an excellent benefits package
10 A job with little freedom and independence to do your work in the way you best think	1	2	3	4	5	A job where working conditions conditions are poor
11 A job with very satisfying team work	1	2	3	4	5	A job that allows you to use your skills and abilities to the fullest extent
12 A job that offers little or no challenge	1	2	3	4	5	A job that requires you to be completely isolated from co-workers

Part B scoring key and norms

Step one: Write down the circled numbers for the items indicated below, and add them to determine subtotal A.

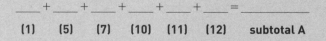

___ + ___ + ___ + ___ + ___ + ___ = _____

(1)   (5)   (7)   (10)   (11)   (12)   subtotal A

Step two: The remaining items in the growth need strength scale need to be reversed-scored. To calculate a reverse score, subtract the direct score from 6. For instance if you circled 5 in item 2, the reverse score would be 1. If you circled 2 for item 9 the reverse score would be 4. Calculate the reverse scores for items 2, 3, 4, 6, 8, 9 and write them down in the formula below. Then make the sum of the reverse scores. This sum is subtotal B.

$$\underline{\quad} + \underline{\quad} + \underline{\quad} + \underline{\quad} + \underline{\quad} + \underline{\quad} = \underline{\qquad\qquad}$$

| (2) | (3) | (4) | (6) | (8) | (9) | subtotal B |

Step three: Make the sum of subtotal A and B. A total score below 30 is an indication that you have a relative low growth need strength, whereas a score above 42 indicates relative high growth need strength.

SOURCE: See J. R. Hackman and G. Oldham, *Work Redesign* (Reading, MA: Addison Wesley, 1980), p. 275.

individual. This difference in hierarchy is not a problem for the ERG theory as it views the three groups of needs more as a continuum than a universal hierarchical level. It has been verified that Maslow's hierarchy needs model is culture bound. Research has shown that Japanese and Spanish people place social needs before their physiological requirements.[30] The hierarchy of needs in China is from low to high: physiological needs, self-actualisation through fitting in, esteem, sense of belongingness and love, safety and security.[31]

Finally, the ERG theory has demonstrated that people who are deaf are less satisfied with their relatedness need in comparison to their hearing colleagues. So, the use of the ERG theory in that study revealed some important implications and recommendations to improve the work environment. The primary area that should be worked at to improve organisations that employ the deaf is communications. These improved communications in turn should result in greater friendliness from people and increase the satisfaction level of the deaf employees with their relatedness need.[32]

According to Salancik and Pfeffer the need models of Maslow and Alderfer are so popular because they are consistent with other theories of rational choice and because they ascribe freedom to individuals.[33] The assumption that people shape their actions to satisfy unfulfilled needs gives purpose and direction to individual behaviour. Thus, the popularity of these theories is embedded in their simplicity and transparency to explain human behaviour.

McClelland's need theory

David McClelland has been studying the relationship between needs and behaviour since the late 1940s. Although he is mainly recognised for his research on the need for achievement, he also investigated the needs for affiliation and power. Before discussing each of these needs, let us consider the typical approach used to measure the strength of an individual's needs.

MEASURING STRENGTH OF NEED

The Thematic Apperception Test (TAT) is frequently used to measure an individual's motivation to satisfy various needs. In completing the TAT, people are asked to write stories about ambiguous pictures. These descriptions are then scored for the extent to which they contain achievement, power, and affiliation imagery. A meta-analysis of 105 studies demonstrated that the TAT is a valid measure of the need for achievement.[34]

Now, we would like you to examine the picture in the following Activity and then write a brief description of what you think is happening to the people in the picture, and then what you think will happen to them in the future. Once you have completed this, use the scoring guide to determine your need strength. What is your most important need?

Assess your need strength with a Thematic Apperception Test (TAT)

Instructions

The purpose of this exercise is to help you identify motivational themes expressed in the picture shown below. There are two steps. First, look at the picture briefly (10 to 20 seconds), and write the story it suggests by answering the following questions:

■ What is happening? Who are the people?
■ What past events led to this situation?

activity

- What is wanted by whom?
- What will happen? What will be done?

Next, score your story for achievement, power and affiliation motivation by using the scoring guide and scales shown below. Score the motives from 1 (low) to 5 (high). The scoring guide identifies the types of story descriptions/words that are indicative of high motives. Give yourself a low score if you fail to describe the story with words and phrases contained in the scoring guidelines. A moderate score indicates that you used some of the phrases identified in the scoring guide to describe your story. Do not read the scoring guidelines until you have written your story.

	LOW	**MODERATE**		**HIGH**
Achievement motivation	1	2	3	4	5
Power motivation	1	2	3	4	5
Affiliation motivation	1	2	3	4	5

Scoring key

Score achievement motivation high if:

- A goal, objective or standard of excellence is mentioned.
- Words such as good, better or best are used to evaluate performance.
- Someone in your story is striving for a unique accomplishment.
- Reference is made to career status or being a success in life.

Score power motivation high if:

- There is emotional concern for influencing someone else.
- Someone is actively striving to gain or keep control over others by ordering, arguing, demanding, convincing, threatening or punishing.
- Clear reference is made to a superior–subordinate relationship and the superior is taking steps to gain or keep control over the subordinate.

Score affiliation motivation high if:

- Someone is concerned about establishing or maintaining a friendly relationship with another.
- Someone expresses the desire to be liked by someone else.
- There are references to family ties, friendly discussions, visits, reunions, parties or informal get-togethers.

THE NEED FOR ACHIEVEMENT

Achievement theories propose that motivation and performance vary according to the strength of one's need for achievement. For example, a field study of 222 life insurance brokers found a positive correlation between the number of policies sold and the brokers' need for achievement. McClelland's research supported an analogous relationship for societies as a whole. His results revealed that a country's level of economic development was positively related to its overall achievement motivation.[35]

The Need for achievement is defined by the following desires:

- To accomplish something difficult.
- To master, manipulate or organise physical objects, human beings or ideas.
- To do this as rapidly and as independently as possible.
- To overcome obstacles and attain a high standard.
- To excel one's self.
- To rival and surpass others.
- To increase self-regard by the successful exercise of talent.[36]

This definition reveals that the need for achievement overlaps Maslow's higher-order needs of esteem and self-actualisation. Mr K. Y. Ho in the next Snapshot is a good example of someone with a high need for achievement:

> **Need for achievement** desire to accomplish something difficult

K. Y. Ho displays a high need for achievement

For K. Y. Ho, growing up in mainland China in the 1950s meant hunger and ragged clothes. To help out his mother, Ho, the youngest of three brothers and a sister, peddled vegetables from the family garden. His father, labouring in Hong Kong for most of Ho's childhood, sent back what he could. Later, after the family reunited in Hong Kong, life in a crammed one-room flat was scarcely better. Says Ho, 'We always worried about money, money, money.'

No longer. Now the 48-year-old Ho, living in Canada since 1983, is one of that country's most successful high-tech entrepreneurs. Today, Ho is worth about [US]$143 million, thanks to his 4.4 per cent stake in ATI Technologies Inc., which he started with two friends shortly after arriving in Canada. ATI makes graphics accelerators, the specialised 3-D chips that give popular video games such as Tomb Raider and Quake III their realistic look.

Despite his early poverty, Ho hails from a highly educated, upper-class family. His maternal grandfather was a prosperous landowner who fell on hard times after the Japanese invasion in 1937. His paternal grandfather was a book dealer and teacher. After the communists came to power in 1949, both grandparents lost most of their property. Ho's father, also a teacher, was unable to find work and left his wife and young children for a series of factory jobs in Hong Kong when Ho was still an infant. Twelve long years later, Ho and his mother joined Ho's father and an older brother. Ho's other brother and sister were forced by the government to stay behind.

Later, Ho earned a place at a top Taiwanese college, National Cheng Kung University, where he studied electrical engineering. Away from home and the watchful eyes of his parents, Ho hardly touched the books. Friends remember him as an average student. 'He spent a lot of time outside the library', recalls K. D. Au, a classmate who now owns the computerperipherals wholesaler, Althon Micro Inc., in Los Angeles, USA.

But once in the job market, Ho thrived. After graduating from university in 1974, he raced through several electronics-industry jobs at big-name corporations in Hong Kong, including Control Data Systems Inc. and Philips Electronics. Ho learned all about video games in 1981 when he went to work for Wong's Electronics Co. Ltd, a leading Hong Kong manufacturer that dealt regularly with hotshot game makers Atari and Coleco. 'He learned everything very, very fast', recalls Benedict C. M. Wong, the company's president.

Affable and quick with a smile, Ho nonetheless often disagreed with his superiors. 'He's so straightforward that he could hardly get along with the boss', recalls Patrick Hung, a classmate who later worked with Ho at Wong's. In 1983, Ho left for Canada, where many Hong Kong Chinese went looking for a fresh start. Ho's first impression: 'A lot of open space and lots of opportunity.'

SOURCE: Excerpted from J. Weber and A. Reinhardt, 'From Rags to 3-D Chips', *Business Week*, 21 June 1999, pp. 86, 90.

snapshot

Not only does Mr Ho display the need for achievement but his story highlights the point that achievement needs actually display themselves in all walks of life. One does not have to be a famous athlete, executive or personality to display high achievement. Let us now consider the characteristics of high achievers.

CHARACTERISTICS OF HIGH-ACHIEVERS

Achievement-motivated people share three common characteristics (see Figure 5.3).

FIGURE 5.3 CHARACTERISTICS OF HIGH NEED FOR ACHIEVEMENT PEOPLE

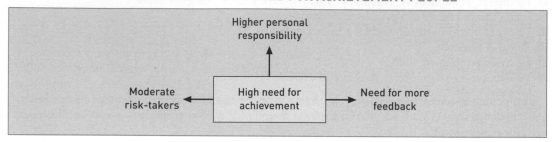

High achievers prefer to work on tasks of moderate difficulty. For example, when high achievers are asked to stand wherever they like while tossing rings at a peg on the floor, they tend to stand about 10 to 20 feet (3 to 6 metres) from the peg. This distance presents the ring tosser with a challenging but not impossible task. People with a low need for achievement, in contrast, tend to either walk up to the peg and drop the rings on or gamble on a lucky shot from far away. The high achiever's preference for moderately difficult tasks reinforces achievement behaviour by reducing the frequency of failure and increasing the satisfaction associated with successfully completing challenging tasks.

High achievers also like situations in which their performance is due to their own efforts rather than to other factors, such as luck. Personal satisfaction is derived from accomplishing the task. A third identifying characteristic of high achievers is that they desire more feedback from the outcome itself than do low achievers.[37] Feedback is a necessity, otherwise they cannot estimate failure or success in the accomplishment of their task, and derive satisfaction from their achievement.

McClelland proposed that, given these characteristics, high achievers are more likely to be successful entrepreneurs. A review of research on the 'entrepreneurial' personality supported this conclusion. Entrepreneurs were found to have a higher need for achievement than non-entrepreneurs.[38]

THE NEED FOR AFFILIATION

Researchers believe that people possess a basic desire to form and maintain a few lasting, positive and important interpersonal relationships. A recent summary of research supported this premise. In addition, the researchers noted that both psychological and physical health problems are higher among people who lack social attachments.[39] Just the same, not everyone has a high need to affiliate. People with a high **Need for affiliation** prefer to spend more time maintaining social relationships, joining groups and wanting to be loved. Individuals high in this need are not the most effective employers or leaders because they have a hard time making difficult decisions without worrying about being disliked.

THE NEED FOR POWER

The **Need for power** reflects an individual's desire to influence, coach, teach or encourage others to achieve. People with a high need for power like to work and are concerned with discipline and self-respect. There is a positive and negative side to this need. The negative face of power is characterised by an 'if I win, you lose' mentality. In contrast, people with a positive orientation to power focus on accomplishing group goals and helping employees obtain the feeling of competence. More is said about the two faces of power in Chapter 13.

Because effective employers must positively influence others, McClelland proposes that top managers should have a high need for power coupled with a low need for affiliation. He also believes that individuals with high achievement motivation are *not* best suited for top management positions. Several studies support these propositions.[40]

Need for affiliation
desire to spend time in social relationships and activities

Need for power
desire to influence, coach, teach or encourage others to achieve

RESEARCH FINDINGS AND PRACTICAL IMPLICATIONS

Given that adults can be trained to increase their achievement motivation,[41] organisations should consider the benefits of providing achievement training for employees. Moreover, the achievement, affiliation and power needs of individuals can be considered during the selection process in order to achieve better placement. For example, a study revealed that individuals' need for achievement affected their preference to work in different companies. People with a high need for achievement were more attracted to companies that had a pay-for-performance environment than were those with a low achievement motivation.[42] Finally, employers should create challenging task assignments or goals because the need for achievement is positively correlated with goal commitment, which, in turn, influences performance.[43] Moreover, challenging goals should be accompanied with a more autonomous work environment and employee empowerment to capitalise on the characteristics of high achievers. See further Chapter 6 about goals as motivators.

It is quite clear that the need for achievement as higher-level need or internal motivator is an American bias. The supposition that high achievement functions as an internal motivator underlies two cultural value dimensions: a willingness to accept moderate risks (which excludes countries with strong uncertainty avoidance) and concern with performance (which applies almost singularly to countries with strong quality-of-life characteristics). This combination is found in Anglo-American countries such as the United States, Canada and Great Britain.[44]

Herzberg's motivator-hygiene theory

The dual process theory or Herzberg's theory is a job enrichment theory of motivation as it views motivation as social influence.[45] Herzberg's theory is based on a landmark study in which 203 accountants and engineers were interviewed. These interviews sought to determine the factors responsible for job satisfaction and dissatisfaction. Herzberg found separate and distinct clusters of factors associated with job satisfaction and dissatisfaction. Job satisfaction was more frequently associated with achievement, recognition, characteristics of the work, responsibility and advancement. These factors were all related to outcomes associated with the content of the task being performed. Herzberg labelled these factors Motivators because each was associated with strong effort and good performance. These factors concern all intrinsic aspects of work. He hypothesised that motivators cause a person to move from a state of no satisfaction to satisfaction (see Figure 5.4). Therefore, Herzberg's theory predicts employers can motivate individuals by incorporating motivators into an individual's job.

> **Motivators** job characteristics associated with job satisfaction

Herzberg found job dissatisfaction to be associated primarily with factors in the work context or environment. Specifically, company policy and administration, technical supervision, salary, interpersonal relations with one's supervisor and working conditions were most frequently mentioned by employees expressing job dissatisfaction. These factors involve extrinsic aspects of work. Herzberg labelled this second cluster of factors Hygiene factors. He further proposed that they were not motivational. At best, according to Herzberg's interpretation, an individual will experience no job dissatisfaction when he or she has no grievances about hygiene factors (see Figure 5.4).[46]

> **Hygiene factors** job characteristics associated with job dissatisfaction

A recent study among older engineers clearly demonstrates that a dissatisfying job experience usually results from inadequate hygiene factors. It appears that a significant change in the hygiene factors is required to produce a small change in job attitude. Analysis of these factors leads to the conclusion that significant changes in attitude using salary increases and changes in job environment appear to be very costly and are inefficient because their effects are short in duration. Additionally the data reveal that the effects of motivators on job attitudes are much longer lasting. These motivators also have a more profound impact on job attitudes.[47]

A recent job satisfaction poll among the 100 best employers according to *Fortune Magazine*, uncovered some striking findings not supporting the motivator-hygiene theory. The most conspicuous outcome concerned the difference between what was actually important to employees and what executives assumed was important to them. According to the employees, the top five job components contributing to job satisfaction were: job security, benefits, communication between employees and management, employee flexibility to balance work and life issues, and compensation/pay. So hygiene factors like job security, benefits and salary were considered as major job components for the fulfilment of job satisfaction. The HR-professionals rated communication between employees and management, and recognition by management as the most important determinants of job satisfaction followed by relationship with immediate supervisor, job security and compensation/pay.[48]

FIGURE 5.4 HERZBERG'S MOTIVATOR HYGIENE MODEL

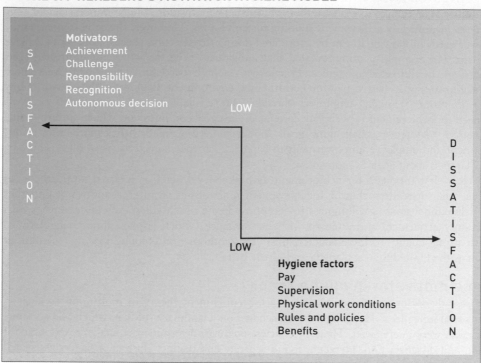

In the following Activity you can find out whether hygiene factors or motivator factors are more important to you.

The midway zero

The key to adequately understanding Herzberg's motivator-hygiene theory is to recognise that he believes that satisfaction is not the opposite of dissatisfaction. Herzberg concludes that 'the opposite of job satisfaction is not job dissatisfaction, but rather no job satisfaction; and similarly, the opposite of job dissatisfaction is not job satisfaction, but no dissatisfaction'.[49] Herzberg thus asserts that the dissatisfaction–satisfaction continuum contains a zero point, midway between dissatisfaction and satisfaction, where neither are present. Conceivably, an organisation member who has good supervision, pay and working conditions but a tedious and unchallenging task with little chance of advancement would be at the zero midpoint. That person would have no dissatisfaction (because of good hygiene factors) and no satisfaction (because of a lack of motivators). Consequently, Herzberg warns employers that it takes more than good pay and good working conditions to motivate today's employees. It takes an 'enriched job' that offers the individual opportunity for achievement and recognition, stimulation, responsibility and advancement. Unfortunately, a study of 600 managers and 900 workers indicated that organisations may not be heeding Herzberg's advice. Results revealed that only 33 per cent felt that their managers knew what motivated them, and 60 per cent concluded that they did not receive any sort of recognition or rewards for their work.[50]

Relationship of Herzberg's theory with needs

Two different needs felt by human beings underlie the observation that motivators are related to job satisfaction and hygiene factors to job dissatisfaction. The first set of needs stems from humankind's animal nature, that is the built-in drive to avoid pain from the environment, plus all the learned drives that become conditioned to the basic biological needs. For instance, hunger and thirst, basic biological drives, make it necessary to earn money, and then money becomes a specific drive. The second group of needs involves a unique human characteristic, the ability to achieve and, through achievement, to experience psychological growth. The stimuli for the growth needs are tasks that encourage growth in the work setting.[51] As a result, the motivators are situated at Maslow's

Find out whether hygiene factors or motivator factors are more important to you

Instructions

Rate the following 12 job factors presented in Part A according to how important each is to you by ticking the corresponding number. Once done so, mark your rating of each of the above factors in part A next to the corresponding numbers in part B. Add up each column in part B. If the total points in each column are equal this means that both factors are as important to you. A higher total points in one of the categories implies that you assess this category of factors as more important than the other category.

activity

Part A

	Very important	Somewhat important			Not important
	5	4	3	2	1
1 An interesting job					
2 A good boss					
3 Recognition and appreciation for the work I do					
4 The opportunity for advancement					
5 A satisfying personal life					
6 A prestigious job					
7 Job responsibility					
8 Good working conditions					
9 Sensible company rules, regulations, procedures and policies					
10 The opportunity to grow through learning new things					
11 A job I can do well and succeed at					
12 Job security					

Part B

Hygiene factors score	Motivator factors score
2 ____ 5 ____ 6 ____ 8 ____ 9 ____ 12 ____	1 ____ 3 ____ 4 ____ 7 ____ 10 ____ 11 ____
Total points:	**Total points:**

SOURCE: From *Human Relations in Organizations: A Skill Building Approach*, 2nd edn by R. Lussier. The McGraw-Hill Companies, Inc, 1993.

higher order needs, such as esteem and self-actualisation needs. These motivators are also located at the same level of McClelland's need for achievement and need for power and Alderfer's growth need. Furthermore, the hygiene factors correspond to Maslow's basic needs (physiological and safety needs), Alderfer's relatedness and existence needs, and McClelland's need for affiliation (see Table 5.4).

Applying Herzberg's model through vertical loading

Job enrichment
enriching a job through vertical loading

Job enrichment is based on the application of Herzberg's ideas. Specifically, **job enrichment** entails modifying a job in such a way that an employee has the opportunity to experience achievement, recognition, stimulating work, responsibility and advancement. These characteristics are incorporated into a job through vertical loading. Rather than giving employees additional tasks of similar difficulty (horizontal loading), vertical loading consists of giving workers more responsibility. In other words, employees take on chores normally performed by their supervisors. Employers are advised to follow seven principles when vertically loading jobs (see Table 5.5).

Evaluation of Herzberg's theory

Herzberg's theory generated a great deal of research and controversy. The controversy revolved around whether studies supporting the theory were flawed and thus invalid.[52] A motivation scholar attempted to sort out the controversy by concluding the following.

TABLE 5.4 COMPARISON OF HERZBERG'S MODEL WITH THE NEED THEORIES

Herzberg	Maslow	Alderfer	McClelland
Motivators	Self-actualisation Esteem	Growth	Achievement Power
Hygiene factors	Love Safety Physiological	Relatedness Existence	Affiliation

TABLE 5.5 PRINCIPLES OF VERTICALLY LOADING A JOB

Principle	Motivators involved
A. Removing some controls while retaining accountability	Responsibility and personal achievement
B. Increasing the accountability of individuals for their own work	Responsibility and recognition
C. Giving a person a complete natural unit of work (module, division, area and so on)	Responsibility, achievement and recognition
D. Granting additional authority to an employee in his activity; job freedom	Responsibility, achievement and recognition
E. Making periodic reports directly available to the worker himself rather than to the supervisor	Internal recognition
F. Introducing new and more difficult tasks not previously handled	Growth and learning
G. Assigning individuals specific or specialised tasks, enabling them to become experts	Responsibility, growth and advancement

SOURCE: Reprinted by permission of the *Harvard Business Review*. An exhibit from 'One More Time: How Do You Motivate Employees?' by F. Herzberg (January/February 2003). Copyright © 2003 by the President and Fellows of Harvard College; all rights reserved.

> On balance, when we combine all of the evidence with all of the allegations that the theory has been misinterpreted, and that its major concepts have not been assessed properly, one is left, more than twenty years later, not really knowing whether to take the theory seriously, let alone whether it should be put into practice in organisational settings.... There is support for many of the implications the theory has for enriching jobs to make them more motivating. But the two-factor aspect of the theory – the feature that makes it unique – is not really a necessary element in the use of the theory for designing jobs, per se.[53]

Studies that have used the same methodology as Herzberg tend to support the theory. However, this methodology (critical incident technique) has itself been criticised.[54] The descriptions of events (typical for this method) give rise to good and bad feelings. Afterwards, interviewers analyse these descriptions with an underlying risk of interviewer bias. So, the method-bound character of the theory makes its validity questionable. Another frequently mentioned critique is that the theory only applies to professionals and higher levels. The predictive power of this theory for people with unskilled jobs or repetitive work is limited. These people often are not interested in job growth-related opportunities. Furthermore, research has suggested that the model varies across cultures.[55] A recent article on the cross-cultural applicability of the motivator-hygiene theory stated that US employees are more motivated by intrinsic factors such as growth and achievement while Japanese employees ascribe more importance to work context factors such as job security, work conditions, and wages.[56] Another study covering seven countries was more supportive for the universal character of intrinsic factors in the motivator-hygiene theory. Belgium, Britain, Israel and the United States rated 'interesting work' as the most important among 11 work goals. This factor was also ranked in the top three by Japanese, Dutch and German employees.[57]

Integration of need theories

All content theories have one internal weakness: they reveal nothing about the actual motivation process. People may be motivated by the same need, but choose different actions to satisfy these needs. Therefore, more complex theories have been developed and are described in the following chapter. However, despite the criticisms of the different theories, they do a great job in telling us what motivates people. Some general conclusions can be drawn from Table 5.4:

- People seem to seek security. Consequently, employers cannot neglect the security aspect in organisations.
- People also seek social systems. Whether you call this need relatedness, need for affiliation or belongingness, this sociability aspect is an important component of effective organisations (see Chapter 17).
- People seek personal growth. Whether we call it advancement, self-actualisation, need for achievement or growth, this self-development aspect is an important element of effective organisations. This development aspect is a key characteristic for learning organisations.

Other lessons to bear in mind after having reviewed the previous need theories are:

- It is better to presume that human needs operate within a flexible hierarchy or continuum. While most people focus first on existence needs when those needs are not satisfied, it is not possible to predict which are the next most significant needs. As there is no fixed needs hierarchy, we should be cautious in predicting in which needs an employee will focus on next.
- We should also be careful not to equate motivation with satisfaction. Satisfyers may demotivate. For instance, an employee whose wage is so high that he or she can afford anything they want may not be motivated to gain a financial incentive for reaching a particular performance goal.[58]
- Always keep in mind that need theories were developed by American scholars and may be subject to cultural bias. Be aware of the literal application of these motivation theories to other cultures. For instance, Japanese or American employees are motivated by essentially the same needs, but a major difference is displayed in their conceptualisations of need satisfaction. Self-actualisation has

a totally different significance for employees from individualistic countries than for employees from collectivistic countries (see also Chapter 16). American employees strive to attain self-growth by trying to improve themselves and their positions in life, whereas Japanese employees see self-actualisation in terms of success of the group as a whole.[59]

Job characteristics model

The job characteristics theory emerged as a reaction against Taylor's movement (see Chapter 1) of job design. Taylor's scientific management movement, with its emphasis on task specialisation and its simplistic view of human motivation, is blamed for the dehumanisation of work and the development of monotonous, routine jobs. Rather than motivating people in their jobs, the Taylorist approach yielded increased levels of absenteeism and turnover. The job characteristics approach, as a direct offshoot of job enrichment, attempts to tackle the dissatisfying and demotivating character of routine jobs through the modification of these jobs, so that employees get the opportunity to experience more recognition, stimulating work and responsibility.

Overview of the job characteristics model

Two OB researchers, J. Richard Hackman and Greg Oldham, played a central role in developing the job characteristics approach. These researchers tried to determine how work can be structured so that employees are internally (or intrinsically) motivated. **Internal motivation** occurs when an individual is 'turned on to one's work because of the positive internal feelings that are generated by doing well, rather than by being dependent on external factors (such as incentive pay or compliments from the boss) for the motivation to work effectively.[60]

An example of a highly internally motivated person is Nathalie Vincke, who works at the emergency department of the Academic Hospital of Brussels.

> **Internal motivation**
> motivation caused by positive internal feelings

> 'My working days are too short!' she says. 'Some young people might have a hard time finding a job in which they feel good, but in my case it certainly wasn't so. Every day it is a pleasure to come to work, even if that means getting up really early. When I started here after I graduated from nursing school, I had the feeling that this was the moment when life really started. I have always wanted to become a nurse, ever since I was a child. I can remember a teacher in secondary school warning me that I only saw the sunny side of it and that I'd also have to do the dirty jobs but that didn't deter me. On the contrary, I am really hooked on it now. To be able to give help to the patients even more, I am continually learning new things. For example, I often visit the library to find more information on diseases. And I am studying an extra course on Thursday evenings.' Nathalie is also enthusiastic about the way new employees are introduced to the hospital. 'The hospital made great efforts to get us started', she says. 'When we arrived, there was a training course and a senior nurse was assigned to each of us as a mentor. Also, the team spirit is fantastic. If the atmosphere at work wasn't as good, nursing would sometimes seem an impossible task. But still, the feeling I get when I help a patient in a critical condition to pull through or to stabilise is indescribable.'[61]

These positive feelings power a self-perpetuating cycle of motivation. As shown in Figure 5.5, internal work motivation is determined by three psychological states. In turn, these psychological states are fostered by the presence of five core job dimensions. As you can see in Figure 5.5, the object of this approach is to promote high internal motivation by designing jobs that possess the five core job characteristics. Let us examine the major components of this model to see how it works.

CRITICAL PSYCHOLOGICAL STATES

A group of management experts described the conditions under which individuals experienced the three critical psychological states as follows:

■ **Experienced meaningfulness.** The individual must perceive the work as worthwhile or important by some system of value he or she accepts.

■ **Experienced responsibility.** He or she must believe in personal accountability for the outcomes of his or her efforts.

■ **Knowledge of results.** He or she must be able to determine, on some fairly regular basis, whether or not the outcomes of the work are satisfactory.[62]

These psychological states generate internal work motivation. Moreover, they encourage job satisfaction and perseverance because they are self-reinforcing. If one of the three psychological states is short-changed, motivation diminishes. Consider, for example, Joyce Roche's decision to quit her job as vice president of global marketing at Avon.

> " The decision to ditch a plum, top position in a major corporation where one is highly regarded might strike most people as insane. But Roche's decision grew out of her realisation that despite the great title and income (she had a very high salary with substantial bonus potential), her job did not hold the level of autonomy or responsibility she initially thought it had.[63] "

Joyce Roche's internal motivation was diminished by not feeling the psychological state of 'experienced responsibility'.

CORE JOB DIMENSIONS

In general terms, **Core job dimensions** are common characteristics found to a varying degree in all jobs. Once again, five core job characteristics elicit the three psychological states (see Figure 5.5). Three of those job characteristics – skill variety, task identity and task significance – combine to determine experienced meaningfulness of work:

■ *Skill variety.* The extent to which the job requires an individual to perform a variety of tasks that require him or her to use different skills and abilities.

Experienced meaningfulness feeling that one's job is important and worthwhile

Experienced responsibility believing that one is accountable for work outcomes

Knowledge of results feedback about work outcomes

Core job dimensions job characteristics found to various degrees in all jobs

FIGURE 5.5 THE JOB CHARACTERISTICS MODEL

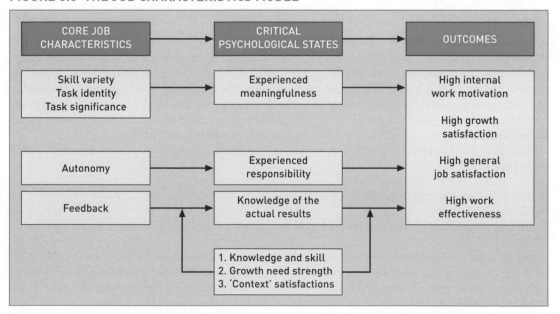

SOURCE: J. R. Hackman and G. R. Oldham, *Work Redesign*, © 1980, Addison-Wesley Publishing Co., Reading, MA, p. 90. Reprinted with permission.

- *Task identity.* The extent to which the job requires an individual to perform a whole or completely identifiable piece of work. In other words, task identity is high when a person works on a product or project from beginning to end and sees a tangible result.
- *Task significance.* The extent to which the job affects the lives of other people within or outside the organisation.

Experienced responsibility is elicited by the job characteristic of autonomy; whereas knowledge of results is fostered by the job characteristic of feedback, and these are defined as follows:

- *Autonomy*: the extent to which the job enables an individual to experience freedom, independence and discretion in both scheduling and determining the procedures used in completing the job.
- *Feedback*: the extent to which an individual receives direct and clear information about how effectively he or she is performing the job.[64]

MOTIVATING POTENTIAL OF A JOB

Motivating potential score the amount of internal work motivation associated with a specific job

Hackman and Oldham devised a tool for self-reporting in order to assess the extent to which a specific job possesses the five core job characteristics. With this tool (the Job Diagnostic Survey), it is possible to calculate a motivating potential score for a job. The **Motivating potential score** (MPS) is a summary index that represents the extent to which the job characteristics foster internal work motivation. Low scores indicate that an individual will not experience high internal work motivation from the job. Such a job is a prime candidate for job redesign. High scores reveal that the job is capable of stimulating internal motivation.

The MPS is computed as follows.

$$MPS = \frac{skill\ variety\ +\ task\ identity\ +\ task\ significance}{3} \times autonomy \times feedback$$

Judging from this equation, which core job characteristics do you think are relatively more important in determining the motivational potential of a job? Because autonomy and feedback are not divisible by another number, low amounts of autonomy and feedback have a greater chance of lowering MPS than the job characteristics of skill variety, task identity and task significance. So, jobs that are high on MPS must be high on at least one of the three factors that lead to experienced meaningfulness, and they must be high on autonomy and feedback.

DOES THE THEORY WORK FOR EVERYONE?

As previously discussed, not all people may want enriched work. Hackman and Oldham incorporated this conclusion into their model by identifying three attributes that affect how individuals respond to jobs with a high MPS. These attributes are concerned with the individual's knowledge and skill, need for strong growth (representing the desire to grow and develop as an individual), and context satisfactions (see Figure 5.5). Context satisfactions represent the extent to which employees are satisfied with various aspects of their job, such as pay, co-workers and supervision.

Hackman and Oldham proposed that people will respond positively to jobs with a high MPS when they have:

- The knowledge and skills necessary to do the job.
- High growth needs.
- An overall satisfaction with various aspects of the work context, such as pay and co-workers.

Although these recommendations make sense, several studies did not support the moderating influence of an employee's growth needs and context satisfaction.[65] The model worked equally well for employees with high and low growth needs and context satisfaction. Future research needs to examine whether an employee's knowledge and skills are an important moderator of the model's effectiveness.

Research findings and practical implications

Organisations may want to use this model to increase employee job satisfaction. Research overwhelmingly demonstrates the existence of a moderately strong relationship between job characteristics and satisfaction.[66] A recent study of 459 employees from a glass manufacturing company also indirectly supported the job characteristics model. The company redesigned the work environment by increasing employees' autonomy and participation in decision-making and then measured employees' self-efficacy in carrying out a broader and more proactive role 18 months later. Job redesign resulted in higher self-efficacy.[67]

Unfortunately, job redesign appears to reduce the quantity of output just as often as it has a positive impact. Caution and situational appropriateness are advised. For example, one study demonstrated that job redesign works better in less complex organisations (small plants or companies).[68]

Nonetheless, employers are likely to find noticeable increases in the quality of performance after a job redesign programme. Results from 21 experimental studies revealed that job redesign resulted in a median increase of 28 per cent in the quality of performance.[69] Moreover, two separate meta-analyses support the practice of using the job characteristics model to help organisations reduce absenteeism and turnover;[70] and job characteristics were found to predict absenteeism over a six-year period. This latter result is very encouraging because it suggests that job redesign can have long-lasting positive effects on employee behaviour.

An advantage of the job characteristics theory is that Hackman and Oldham developed a reliable and valid instrument (Job Diagnostic Survey) to measure the key variables of the theory.

A series of diagnostic steps and guidelines have been propounded on how to use the Job Diagnostic Survey for the implementation of job enrichment.[71] These prescriptive steps and guidelines are presented in Table 5.6.

From the five core job characteristics of the theory, several hypotheses (action principles) have been inferred on how to achieve enriched jobs (see Figure 5.6). The principles for attaining higher motivating potential scores or for enriching jobs involve:

- Combining tasks. Give employees more than one part of the work in order to increase skill variety and task identity.
- Forming natural work units in order to increase task identity and task significance.
- Establishing client relationships in order to increase skill variety, autonomy and feedback.
- Implementing Herzberg's vertical loading principles (see above) in order to increase autonomy.
- Opening feedback channels in order to increase feedback.[72]

Job characteristics research also underscores an additional implication for companies undergoing re-engineering. Re-engineering potentially leads to negative work outcomes because it increases job characteristics beyond reasonable levels. This occurs for two reasons:

- Re-engineering requires employees to use a wider variety of skills to perform their jobs.
- Re-engineering typically results in downsizing and short-term periods of understaffing.[73]

The unfortunate catch is that understaffing was found to produce lower levels of group performance, and jobs with either overly low or high levels of job characteristics were associated with higher stress.[74] Employers are advised to consider carefully the level of perceived job characteristics when implementing re-engineering initiatives.

In conclusion, professionals need to realise that job redesign is not a panacea for all their employee satisfaction and motivation problems. To enhance their chances of success with this approach, managers need to remember that a change in one job or department can create problems of perceived inequity in related areas or systems within the organisation. They need to take an open-systems perspective when implementing job redesign, as was suggested by Hackman and Oldham when they wrote the following.

TABLE 5.6 STEPS AND GUIDELINES TO FOLLOW WHEN USING JOB DIAGNOSTIC SURVEY FOR JOB ENRICHMENT

Steps	Guidelines
Step 1: Check scores in the areas of motivation and satisfaction to see if problems exist in these areas. If they do, and the job outcomes are deficient, then job enrichment may well be called for	Guide 1: Diagnose the work system in terms of some theory of work redesign before introducing any change to see what is possible and what kinds of changes are most likely to work
Step 2: Check the motivating potential scores of the jobs to see if they are low. If they are not, job enrichment is not likely to be the answer	Guide 2: Keep the focus of the change effort on the work itself, rather than the other aspects of the work context, so that real job enrichment does occur
Step 3: Check scores for the five core dimensions to see what the basic strengths and weaknesses of the present job are. In this way it is possible to identify specific areas for change	Guide 3: Prepare in advance for any possible problems and side effects, especially among employees whose jobs are not directly affected by the change; develop appropriate contingency plans
Step 4: Check to see what the growth need strength levels of job incumbents are. One can proceed with more confidence in enriching the jobs of employees with high growth needs since they are ready for the change	Guide 4: Evaluate the project on a continuing basis to see if anticipated changes actually are occurring and using as many and as objective measures as possible
Step 5: Check the scores for various aspects of job satisfaction and other information sources for roadblocks that might obstruct change or for special opportunities that might facilitate it	Guide 5: Confront difficult problems as early in the project as possible
	Guide 6: Design change processes in such a way as to fit the objectives of the job enrichment. Thus if autonomy in work is to be an objective, autonomy should be respected in designing the new jobs in the first place, in other words, be consistent with the theory in guiding the change effort throughout

FIGURE 5.6 ACTION PRINCIPLES

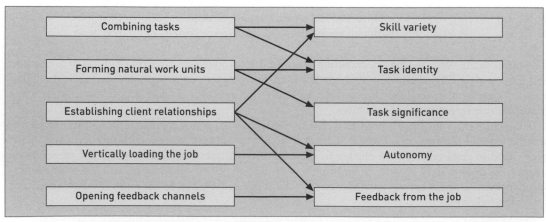

SOURCE: J. R. Hackman and G. R. Oldham, *Work Redesign*, © 1980, Addison-Wesley Publishing Co., Reading, MA, p. 90. Reprinted with permission.

> Our observations of work redesign programmes suggest that attempts to change jobs frequently run into – and sometimes get run over by – other organisational systems and practices, leading to a diminution (or even a reversal) of anticipated outcomes. . . .
>
> The 'small change' effect, for example, often develops as managers begin to realise that radical changes in work design will necessitate major changes in other organisational systems as well.[75]

Evaluation of the job characteristics theory

Considerable research has been done on the validity of the theory. Not all findings are supportive to the theory, although the positive results far outweigh the negative. Some queries exist about whether or not skill variety is redundant with autonomy, and whether or not task identity adds to the model's predictive ability.[76] Furthermore, it appears that calculating the motivating potential score by using a multiplicative relationship between core characteristics yields less optimal results. Simply adding the five scores works best.[77] Evaluation of the psychometric properties of the job diagnostic survey gives passing marks – probably even much better ones.[78] Several longitudinal studies have shown positive job enrichment effects on performance and on absenteeism.[79] The critical role of psychological states in the model has also gained support, although they may not operate in exactly the same manner vis-à-vis core characteristics and outcomes as originally hypothesised.[80] In summary, the current state of evidence supports the following statements:

- Overall analyses support the theory; people who work on enriched jobs are generally more motivated, productive and satisfied compared to those who are not.
- Job dimensions operate through the psychological states in influencing personal and work outcome variables rather than influencing them directly.
- The moderator effects of growth need strength, knowledge and context satisfactions are found to be very weak.

Learning outcomes: summary of key terms

1 Define the term motivation

Motivation is defined as those professional processes that cause the arousal, direction and persistence of voluntary, goal-oriented actions. Employers need to understand these psychological processes if they are to successfully guide employees toward accomplishing organisational objectives.

2 Review the historical roots of modern motivation theories

Five ways of explaining behaviour – needs, reinforcement, cognition, job characteristics, and feelings/emotions – underlie the evolution of modern theories of human motivation. Some theories of motivation focus on internal energisers of behaviour such as needs, satisfaction, and feelings/emotions. Other motivation theories, which deal in terms of reinforcement, cognitions, and job characteristics, focus on more complex person–environment interactions. There is no single, universally accepted theory of motivation.

3 Explain the difference between content and process approaches of motivation

The content approach of motivation addresses the question 'what motivates people'. This approach concerns the goals people want to attain, so they can satisfy unmet needs, the drivers of goal-directed behaviour. Most of the content theories are need theories (Maslow, Alderfer and McClelland). Herzberg's job enrichment theory and McGregor's theory X and Y are also classified as content theories. The process approach includes much more complex theories (equity, expectancy and goal-setting theory) and was a reaction against the content theories. These latter theories have the internal weakness of saying nothing about the actual process of motivation. The former approach as the name conveys emphasises this actual process and tries to answer the question how people become motivated. Cognitive decisions people make between several choices are the key features of these theories.

4 Contrast Maslow's and McClelland's need theories

Two well-known need theories of motivation are Maslow's need hierarchy and McClelland's need theory. Maslow's notion of a graduated hierarchy of five levels of needs has not stood up well under research. McClelland believes that motivation and performance vary according to the strength of an individual's need for achievement. High achievers prefer moderate risks and situations where they can control their own destiny. Top managers should have a high need for power coupled with a low need for affiliation.

5 Describe Alderfer's theory and the frustration regression assumption

Alderfer's need theory is in many ways a refinement of Maslow's hierarchy needs model. Clayton Alderfer determined that the middle levels in Maslow's model sometimes overlapped. He therefore reduced the five dimensions to three dimensions of needs. The existence needs refer to safety and physiological needs, whereas the relatedness needs refer to the need to maintain important relationships. Finally, the growth-related needs are concerned with the development of potential and cover Maslow's self-actualisation needs. According to the ERG theory people may regress down to a lower need level when a higher need is frustrated. For instance when people want to advance but the organisation does not give them opportunities to advance, people may become motivated by the level of pay. This is the frustration-regression assumption.

6 Explain the practical significance of Herzberg's distinction between motivators and hygiene factors

Herzberg believes job satisfaction motivates better job performance. His hygiene factors, such as policies, supervision and salary, erase sources of dissatisfaction. On the other hand, his motivators, such as achievement, responsibility and recognition, foster job satisfaction. Although Herzberg's motivator-hygiene theory of job satisfaction has been criticised on methodological grounds, it has practical significance for job enrichment.

7 Describe how internal work motivation is increased by using the job characteristics model

The psychological states of experienced meaningfulness, experienced responsibility and knowledge of results, produce internal work motivation. These psychological states are fostered by the presence of five core job characteristics. People respond positively to jobs containing these core job characteristics when they have the knowledge and skills necessary to perform the job, high growth needs and high context satisfactions.

Review questions

1 Why should the average employer be well versed in the various motivation theories?

2 Give some examples of your own experience that support or disprove Maslow's hierarchy of needs model.

3 Are you a high achiever? How can you tell? How will this help or hinder your path to top management?

4 Do you agree or disagree that the need for achievement can be learned? Do you think it is easier to learn at an early or later age in life?

5 How have hygiene factors and motivators affected your job satisfaction and perform-ance?

6 Consider Bangladesh and Bulgaria, both countries where a major part of the popu-lation is unemployed, and analyse the applicability of Maslow's and Herzberg's theories in these countries.

7 How might the job characteristics model be used to increase your internal motivation to study?

8 Certain people will say that employees are either highly motivated or not, and there is little that can be done to overcome this. What's your opinion on that?

9 What are the three most valuable lessons about employee motivation that you have learned from this chapter?

Personal awareness and growth exercise
What is your work ethic?
Objectives
1 To measure your work ethic.
2 To determine how well your work ethic score predicts your work habits.

Introduction
The work ethic reflects the extent to which an individual values work. A strong work ethic involves the belief that hard work is the key to success and happiness. In recent years, there has been concern that the work ethic is dead or dying. This worry is based on findings from observational studies and employee attitude surveys.

People differ in terms of how much they believe in the work ethic. These differences influence a variety of behavioural outcomes. What better way to gain insight into the work ethic than by measuring your own work ethic and seeing how well it predicts your everyday work habits?

Instructions
To assess your work ethic, complete the following eight-item instrument developed by a respected behavioural scientist.[81] Being honest with yourself, circle your responses on the rating scales following each of the eight items. There are no right or wrong answers. Add up your total score for the eight items, and record it in the space provided.

Following the work ethic scale is a short personal work habits questionnaire. Your responses to this questionnaire will help you determine whether your work ethic score is a good predictor of your work habits.

Work ethic scale

	Agree completely				Disagree completely				
	1	2	3	4	5				
1 When the workday is finished, people should forget their jobs and enjoy themselves.					1	2	3	4	5
2 Hard work does not make an individual a better person.					1	2	3	4	5
3 The principal purpose of a job is to provide a person with the means for enjoying his or her free time.					1	2	3	4	5
4 Wasting time is not as bad as wasting money.					1	2	3	4	5
5 Whenever possible, a person should relax and accept life as it is, rather than always striving for unreachable goals.					1	2	3	4	5
6 A person's worth should not be based on how well he or she performs a job.					1	2	3	4	5

7 People who do things the easy way are the smart ones.   1   2   3   4   5

8 If all other things are equal, it is better to have a job with
little responsibility than one with a lot of responsibility.   1   2   3   4   5

Total = _____

The higher your total score, the stronger your work ethic.

Personal work habits questionnaire

1 How many unexcused absences from classes did you have last term?
_____ absences

2 How many credit hours are you taking this term?
_____ hours

3 What is your overall grade point average?
_____ GPA

4 What percentage of your course expenses are you earning through full- or part-time employ-ment?
_____ %

5 In percentage terms, how much effort do you typically put forth into your studies and/or work?
Studies = _____ % Work = _____ %

Questions for discussion

1 How strong is your work ethic?
Weak = 8–18
Moderate = 19–29
Strong = 30–40

2 How would you rate your work habits/results?
Below average _____
Average _____
Above average _____

3 How well does your work ethic score predict your work habits or work results?
Poorly _____
Moderately well _____
Very well _____

Group exercise

Applying Maslow's hierarchy of needs model and Alderfer's ERG theory

Objectives

1 To correctly classify needs into the categories of Maslow's model and Alderfer's model.

2 To demonstrate that the use of Alderfer's theory is more straightforward and simple in comparison to Maslow's model.

Instructions

In the next exercise you will get a fragment in which the needs of the four main characters of the show Seinfeld (Elaine, George, Jerry and Kramer) are described. Read through the descriptions of the needs of the four individuals and identify the levels at which the characters would be placed on Maslow's hierarchy of needs and Alderfer's ERG theory. Also provide an explanation or rationale why you think a given level is most descriptive of an individual's dominant needs. Discuss afterwards the responses and the rationales in group.

Description

Jerry, George, Kramer and Elaine have different needs. Jerry is really dedicated to being the best stand-up comic he can, and he is very concerned about getting good reviews and being recog-nised in the entertainment industry. George just wants to be able to find a job he can hold on to so that he can move out of his parent's house into a place of his own. Kramer only cares about good food, having clothes on his back and a roof over his head. Elaine wants to have good, honest relationships with her friends, and find a stable, long-term romantic relationship.

At what level in his hierarchy of needs would Abraham Maslow place each of these four friends and why?

Please, place a cross or tick in the correct need category and explain your rationale behind that choice

Character	Maslow's need categories				
	Physiological	Safety	Love	Esteem	Self-actualisation
1. Jerry					
Rationale:					
2. George					
Rationale:					
3. Kramer					
Rationale:					
4. Elaine					
Rationale:					

How would Clayton Alderfer characterise their needs using ERG theory and why?

Please, place a cross or tick in the correct need category and explain your rationale behind that choice

Character	Alderfer's need categories		
	Existence	Relatedness	Growth
1. Jerry			
Rationale:			
2. George			
Rationale:			
3. Kramer			
Rationale:			
4. Elaine			
Rationale:			

SOURCE: C. S. Hunt, 'Must See TV: The Timelessness of Television as A Teaching Tool', *Journal of Management Education*, December 2001, pp. 631–47.

Internet exercise

This chapter discussed a variety of approaches for motivating employees. We noted that there is no 'one best theory' of motivation and that employers can use different theories to solve various types of performance problems. The purpose of this exercise is to identify motivational techniques or programmes that are being used by different companies. You will find further instructions on our website www.mcgraw-hill.co.uk/textbooks/buelens.

Notes

1 R. Gecker, 'Motivation Mojo: With Profits Down and Morale Low, Keeping An Outside Sales Team on the Top of Its Game Is More Important Than Ever', *Incentive*, September 2003, pp. 92–3.
2 Adapted and translated from G. Bollen, 'Tevreden koeien geven betere melk', *Vacature*, 25 February 2000.
3 K. Hilpern, 'Put a Little Spirit into Your work', the *Guardian*, 30 October 2000.
4 A. Chaudhuri, 'Perk Practice', the *Guardian*, 30 August 2000.
5 A. Chaudhuri, 'Perk Practice', the *Guardian*, 30 August 2000.
6 A. Chaudhuri, 'Perk Practice', the *Guardian*, 30 August 2000.
7 'Motivation Secrets of the 100 Best Employers', *HR Focus*, October 2003, pp. 10–15.
8 P. Ester, L. Halman and R. De Moor, *The Individualizing Society: Value Change in Europe and North America* (Tilburg: Tilburg University Press, 1994).
9 D. McGregor, *The Human Side of Enterprise* (New York: McGraw-Hill, 1960).
10 N. Qubein, 'Ten Principles of Motivation: Channel Energy towards Goals', *Executive Excellence*, October 2003, p. 12.
11 Adapted from 'Projectlink Motivation', *Human Resources*, September 2003, p. 59.
12 M. L. Ambrose and C. T. Kulek, 'Old Friends New Faces: Motivation Research in the 1990s', *Journal of Management*, Summer 1999, pp. 231–7. A recent number of the *Academy of Management Journal* (July 2004) is devoted to the future of work motivation theories.
13 M. Blumberg and C. D. Pringle, 'The Missing Opportunity in Organizational Research: Some Implications for a Theory of Work Performance', *Academy of Management Review*, October 1982, pp. 560–69.
14 T. R. Mitchell, 'Motivation: New Directions for Theory, Research and Practice', *Academy of Management Review*, January 1982, pp. 80–88.
15 J. Greenberg and R. A. Baron, *Behavior in Organizations: Understanding and Managing the Human Side of Work* (Englewood Cliffs, NJ: Prentice Hall, 1997).
16 L. J. Mullins, *Management and Organisational Behaviour, sixth edition* (Harlow: Prentice Hall, 2002).
17 The effects of feelings and emotions on work motivation are discussed by J. M. George and A. P. Brief, 'Motivational Agendas in the Workplace: The Effects of Feelings on Focus of Attention and Work Motivation', in *Research in Organizational Behavior, vol. 18*, eds B. M. Staw and L. L. Cummings (Greenwich, CT: JAI Press, 1996), pp. 75–109.
18 D. Buchanan and A. Huczynski, *Organizational Behaviour: An Introductory Text, fifth edition* (Harlow: Prentice Hall, 2004).
19 For a complete description of Maslow's theory, see A. H. Maslow, 'A Theory of Human Motivation', *Psychological Review*, July 1943, pp. 370–96.
20 C. C. Pinder, *Work Motivation: Theory, Issues, and Applications* (Glenview, IL: Scott, Foresman, 1984), p. 52.
21 L. W. Porter, *Organizational Patterns of Managerial Job Attitudes* (New York: American Foundation for Management Research, 1964).
22 L. W. Porter, 'Job Attitudes in Management: Perceived Deficiencies in Need Fulfillment as a Function of Size of the Company', *Journal of Applied Psychology*, December 1963, pp. 386–97.
23 J. M. Ivancevich, 'Perceived Need Satisfaction of Domestic and Overseas Managers', *Journal of Applied Psychology*, August 1969, pp. 274–8.
24 Adapted and translated from F. Van der Auwera, 'Loon is maar een magere motivator', *Vacature*, 12 July 1999.
25 Excerpted from W. Band, 'Targeting Quality Efforts to Build Customer Loyalty', *The Quality Observer*, December 1995, p. 34.
26 Retrieved from 'Maslow's Hierarchy of Needs', /www.envisionsoftware.com/articles/Maslow_Needs_Hierarchy.html/, April 2004.
27 See L. J. Mullins, *Management and Organisational Behaviour, sixth edition* (Harlow: Prentice Hall, 2002).
28 C. P. Alderfer, 'An Empirical Test of A New Theory of Human Needs', *Organizational Behavior and Human Performance*, May 1969, pp. 142–75.
29 A. K. Korman, J. H. Greenhaus, and I. J. Badin, 'Personnel Attitudes and Motivation', in *Annual Review of Psychology*, eds M. R. Rosenzweig and L. W. Porter (Palo Alto, CA: Annual Reviews, 1977), pp. 178–9.

30 M. Haire, E. E. Ghiselli and L. W. Porter, 'Cultural Patterns in the Role of the Manager', *Industrial Relations*, February 1963, pp. 95–117.

31 E. Nevis, 'Using an American Perspective in Understanding Another Culture: Toward A Hierarchy of Needs for the People's Republic of China', *Journal of Applied Behavioral Science*, no. 3, 1983, pp. 249–64.

32 R. N. Lussier, K. Say and J. Corman, 'Need Satisfaction of Deaf and Hearing Employees', *The Mid-Atlantic Journal of Business*, March 2000, pp. 47–61.

33 G. R. Salancik and J. Pfeffer, 'An Examination of Need Satisfaction Models of Job Attitudes', *Administrative Science Quarterly*, September 1977, pp. 427–56.

34 Results can be found in W. D. Spangler, 'Validity of Questionnaire and TAT Measures of Need for Achievement: Two Meta-Analyses', *Psychological Bulletin*, July 1992, pp. 140–54.

35 Results can be found in S. D. Bluen, J. Barling and W. Burns, 'Predicting Sales Performance, Job Satisfaction, and Depression by Using the Achievement Strivings and Impatience–Irritability Dimensions of Type A Behavior', *Journal of Applied Psychology*, April 1990, pp. 212–16; and D. C. McClelland, *The Achieving Society* (New York: Free Press, 1961).

36 H. A. Murray, *Explorations in Personality* (New York: John Wiley & Sons, 1983), p. 164.

37 Recent studies of achievement motivation can be found in H. Grant and C. S. Dweck, 'A Goal Analysis of Personality and Personality Coherence', in *The Coherence of Personality*, eds D. Cervone and Y. Shoda (New York: The Guilford Press, 1999), pp. 345–71; and D. Y. Dai, S. M. Moon and J. F. Feldhusen, 'Achievement Motivation and Gifted Students: A Social Cognitive Perspective', *Educational Psychologist*, Spring–Summer 1998, pp. 45–63.

38 A. Rauch and M. Frese, 'Psychological Approaches to Entrepreneurial Success: A General Model and Overview of Findings', in *International Review of Industrial and Organizational Psychology*, eds C. L. Cooper and I. T. Robertson (New York: Wiley, 2000); and K. G. Shaver, 'The Entrepreneurial Personality Myth', *Business and Economic Review*, April–June 1995, pp. 20–23.

39 Research on the affiliative motive can be found in S. C. O'Connor and L. K. Rosenblood, 'Affiliation Motivation in Everyday Experience: A Theoretical Comparison', *Journal of Personality and Social Psychology*, March 1996, pp. 513–22; and R. F. Baumeister and M. R. Leary, 'The Need to Belong: Desire for Interpersonal Attachments as a Fundamental Human Motivation', *Psychological Bulletin*, May 1995, pp. 497–529.

40 See D. K. McNeeseSmith, 'The Relationship between Managerial Motivation, Leadership, Nurse Outcomes and Patient Satisfaction', *Journal of Organizational Behavior*, March 1999, pp. 243–59; A. M. Harrell and M. J. Stahl, 'A Behavioral Decision Theory Approach for Measuring McClelland's Trichotomy of Needs', *Journal of Applied Psychology*, April 1981, pp. 242–7; and M. J. Stahl, 'Achievement, Power and Managerial Motivation: Selecting Managerial Talent with the Job Choice Exercise', *Personnel Psychology*, Winter 1983, pp. 775–89.

41 For a review of the foundation of achievement motivation training, see D. C. McClelland, 'Toward a Theory of Motive Acquisition', *American Psychologist*, May 1965, pp. 321–33. Evidence for the validity of motivation training can be found in H. Heckhausen and S. Krug, 'Motive Modification', in *Motivation and Society*, ed. A. J. Stewart (San Francisco: Jossey-Bass, 1982).

42 Results can be found in D. B. Turban and T. L. Keon, 'Organizational Attractiveness: An Interactionist Perspective', *Journal of Applied Psychology*, April 1993, pp. 184–93.

43 See D. Steele Johnson and R. Perlow, 'The Impact of Need for Achievement Components on Goal Commitment and Performance', *Journal of Applied Social Psychology*, November 1992, pp. 1711–20.

44 See S. P. Robbins, *Organizational Behavior: International Edition, tenth edition* (Harlow: Prentice Hall, 2003).

45 See F. Herzberg, B. Mausner and B. B. Snyderman, *The Motivation to Work* (New York: John Wiley & Sons, 1959).

46 Two tests of Herzberg's theory can be found in I. O. Adigun and G. M. Stephenson, 'Sources of Job Motivation and Satisfaction among British and Nigerian Employees', *Journal of Social Psychology*, June 1992, pp. 369–76; and E. A. Maidani, 'Comparative Study of Herzberg's Two-Factor Theory of Job Satisfaction Among Public and Private Sectors', *Public Personnel Management*, Winter 1991, pp. 441–8.

47 R. L. Lord, 'Traditional Motivation Theories and Older Engineers', *Engineering Management Journal*, September 2002, pp. 3–7.

48 'Motivation Secrets of the 100 Best Employers', *HR Focus*, October 2003, pp. 10–15.

49 F. Herzberg, 'One More Time: How Do You Motivate Employees?', *Harvard Business Review*, January 2003, pp. 87–96.

50 Results are presented in 'Are Your Staffers Happy? They're in the Minority', *Supervisory Management*, March 1996, p. 11.

51 See F. Herzberg, 'One More Time: How Do You Motivate Employees?', *Harvard Business Review*, January 2003, pp. 87–96.

52 Both sides of the Herzberg controversy are discussed by N. King, 'Clarification and Evaluation of the Two-Factor Theory of Job Satisfaction', *Psychological Bulletin*, July 1970, pp. 18–31; and B. Grigaliunas and Y. Weiner, 'Has the Research Challenge to Motivation–Hygiene Theory Been Conclusive? An Analysis of Critical Studies', *Human Relations*, December 1974, pp. 839–71.

53 C. C. Pinder, *Work Motivation: Theory, Issues, and Applications* (Glenview, IL: Scott, Foresman, 1984), p. 28.

54 M. D. Dunnette, J. P. Campbell and M. D. Hakel, 'Factors Contributing to Job Satisfaction and Job Dissatisfaction in Six Occupational Groups', *Organizational Behavior and Human Decision Processes*, May 1967, pp. 143–74.

55 N. J. Adler, *International Dimensions of Organizational Behaviour, fourth edition* (Cincinnati, OH: Southwestern, 2002), p. 174.

56 J. Di Cesare and G. Sadri, 'Do All Carrots Look The Same? Examining the Impact of Culture on Employee Motivation', *Management Research News*, no. 1, 2003, pp. 29–40.

57 I. Harpaz, 'The Importance of Work Goals: An International Perspective', *Journal of International Business Studies*, First Quarter 1990, pp. 75–93.

58 R. J. Aldag and L. W. Kuzuhara, *Organizational Behavior and Management: An Integrated Skills Approach* (Cincinnati, OH: Thompson Learning, 2002).

59 See J. Di Cesare and G. Sadri, 'Do All Carrots Look The Same? Examining the Impact of Culture on Employee Motivation', *Management Research News*, no. 1, 2003, pp. 29–40.

60 J. R. Hackman, G. R. Oldham, R. Janson and K. Purdy, 'A New Strategy for Job Enrichment', *California Management Review*, Summer 1975, p. 58.

61 Adapted and translated from M. Teugels, 'Mensen helpen, daar ga ik graag hard tegenaan', *Vacature*, 7 March 1998.

62 J. R. Hackman and G. Oldham, *Work Redesign* (Reading, MA: Addison Wesley, 1980), p. 58.

63 C. V. Clarke, 'Be All You Can Be!', *Black Enterprise*, February 1996, pp. 72–3.

64 Definitions of the job characteristics were adapted from J. R. Hackman and G. R. Oldham, 'Motivation through the Design of Work: Test of a Theory', *Organizational Behavior and Human Performance*, August 1976, pp. 250–79.

65 A review of this research can be found in M. L. Ambrose and C. T. Kulik, 'Old Friends, New Faces: Motivation Research in the 1990s', *Journal of Management*, Summer 1999, pp. 231–92.

66 See M. L. Ambrose and C. T. Kulik, 'Old Friends, New Faces: Motivation Research in the 1990s', *Journal of Management*, Summer 1999, pp. 231–92; C. Wong, C. Hui and K. S. Law, 'A Longitudinal Study of the Job Perception–Job Satisfaction Relationship: A Test of the Three Alternative Specifications', *Journal of Occupational and Organizational Psychology*, June 1998, pp. 127–46; and T. Loher, R. A. Noe, N. L. Moeller and M. P. Fitzgerald, 'A Meta-Analysis of the Relation of Job Characteristics to Job Satisfaction', *Journal of Applied Psychology*, May 1985, pp. 280–89.

67 Results can be found in S. K. Parker, 'Enhancing Role Breadth Self-Efficacy: The Roles of Job Enrichment and Other Organizational Interventions', *Journal of Applied Psychology*, December 1998, pp. 835–52.

68 Results can be found in M. R. Kelley, 'New Process Technology, Job Design, and Work Organization: A Contingency Model', *American Sociological Review*, April 1990, pp. 191–208.

69 Productivity studies are reviewed in R. E. Kopelman, *Managing Productivity in Organizations* (New York: McGraw-Hill, 1986).

70 Absenteeism results are discussed in Y. Fried and G. R. Ferris, 'The Validity of the Job Characteristics Model: A Review and Meta-Analysis', *Personnel Psychology*, Summer 1987, pp. 287–322; and J. R. Rentsch and R. P. Steel, 'Testing the Durability of Job Characteristics as Predictors of Absenteeism Over a Six-Year Period', *Personnel Psychology*, Spring 1998, pp. 165–90. The turnover meta-analysis was conducted by G. M. McEvoy and W. F. Cascio, 'Strategies for Reducing Turnover: A Meta-Analysis', *Journal of Applied Psychology*, May 1985, pp. 342–53.

71 J. R. Hackman and G. Oldham, *Work Redesign* (Reading, MA: Addison Wesley, 1980), p. 275.

72 J. R. Hackman and G. Oldham, *Work Redesign* (Reading, MA: Addison Wesley, 1980), p. 275.

73 A thorough discussion of re-engineering and associated outcomes can be found in J. Champy, *Reengineering Management: The Mandate for New Leadership* (New York: Harper Business, 1995); and M. Hammer and J. Champy, *Reengineering the Corporation: A Manifesto for Business Revolution* (New York: Harper Business, 1993).

74 See J. D. Jonge and W. B. Schaufeli, 'Job Characteristics and Employee Well-Being: A Test of Warr's Vitamin Model in Health Care Workers Using Structural Equation Modelling', *Journal of Organizational Behavior*, July 1998, pp. 387–407; and D. C. Ganster and D. J. Dwyer, 'The Effects of Understaffing on Individual and Group Performance in Professional and Trade Occupations', *Journal of Management*, no. 2, 1995, pp. 175–90.

75 G. R. Oldham and J. R. Hackman, 'Work Design in the Organizational Context', in *Research in Organizational Behavior*, eds B. M. Staw and L. L. Cummings (Greenwich, CT: JAI Press, 1980), pp. 248–9.

76 Y. Fried and G. R. Ferris, 'The Dimensionality of Job Characteristics: Some Neglected Issues', *Journal of Applied Psychology*, August 1986, pp. 419–26.

77 M. Hinton and M. Biderman, 'Empirically Derived Job Characteristics Measures and the Motivating Potential Score', *Journal of Business and Psychology*, Summer 1995, pp. 355–64.

78 Y. Fried, 'Meta-Analytic Comparison of the Job Diagnostic Survey and Job Characteristics Inventory as Correlates of Work Satisfaction and Performance', *Journal of Applied Behavioral Science*, October 1991, pp. 690–97; and T. D. Taber and E. Taylor, 'A Review and Evaluation of Psychometric Properties of Job Diagnostic Survey', *Personnel Psychology*, Fall 1990, pp. 467–500.

79 R. W. Griffin, 'Effects of Work Redesign on Employee Perceptions, Attitudes, and Behaviors: A Long-Term Investigation', *Academy of Management Journal*, June 1991, pp. 425–35; and J. R. Rentsch and R. P. Steel, 'Testing the Durability of Job Characteristics as Predictors of Absenteeism over a Six-Year Period', *Personnel Psychology*, Spring 1998, pp. 165–90.

80 R. W. Renn and R. J. Vandenberg, 'The Critical Psychological States: An Underrepresented Component in Job Characteristics Research', *Journal of Management*, no. 3, 1995, pp. 279–303.

81 Adapted from M. R. Blood, 'Work Values and Job Satisfaction', *Journal of Applied Psychology*, December 1969, pp. 456–9.

chapter 6 process motivation theories

By Eva Cools and Veronique Warmoes

Learning outcomes
When you finish studying the material in this chapter, you should be able to:

- ■ discuss the role of perceived inequity in employee motivation
- ■ explain Vroom's expectancy theory of motivation and Porter and Lawler's extension of the expectancy theory
- ■ explain how goal setting motivates people and identify five practical lessons to be learned from goal-setting research
- ■ discuss how the recipient's characteristics, perception and cognitive evaluation affect how people process feedback
- ■ list at least three practical lessons from feedback research
- ■ list different types of organisational rewards
- ■ describe practical recommendations to implement an organisational reward system
- ■ specify issues that should be addressed before implementing a motivational programme

Carlos Ghosn, the French CEO who turned around Japan's Nissan, put the brakes on seniority-based pay

It was in March of 1999 that I got the call from Louis Schweitzer, CEO of Renault, asking me if I would be willing to go to Tokyo to lead a turnaround at Nissan, the struggling Japanese motor giant. The two companies had just agreed to a major strategic alliance.

Our most fundamental challenge was cultural. Like other Japanese companies, Nissan paid and promoted its employees based on their tenure and age. The longer employees stuck around, the more power and money they received, regardless of their actual performance. Inevitably, that practice bred a certain degree of complacency, which undermined Nissan's competitiveness. What car buyers want, after all, is performance, performance, performance. They want well-designed, high-quality products at attractive prices, delivered on time. They don't care how the company does that or who in the company does it. It's only logical, then, to build a company's reward and incentive systems around performance, irrespective of age, gender or nationality.

So, we decided to ditch the seniority rule. Of course, that didn't mean we systematically started selecting the youngest candidates for promotion. In fact, the senior vice presidents that I've nominated over the past two years all have had long records of service, though they were usually not the most senior candidates. We looked at people's performance records, and if the highest performer was also the most senior, fine. But if the second or third or even the fifth most senior had the best track record, we did not hesitate to pass over those with longer service. As expected when changing long-standing practices, we've had some problems. When you nominate a younger person to a job in Japan, for example, he sometimes suffers from being younger – in some case, older people may not be willing to co-operate with him as fully as they might. Of course, it's also true that an experience like that can be a good test of the quality of leadership a manager brings to the job.

We also revamped our compensation system to put the focus on performance. In the traditional Japanese compensation system, managers receive no share options, and hardly any incentives are built into the manager's pay packet. If a company's average pay raise is, say, 4 per cent, then good performers can expect a 5 per cent or 6 per cent raise, and poor performers get 2 per cent or 2.5 per cent. The system extends to the upper reaches of management, which means that the people whose decisions have the greatest impact on the company have little incentive to get them right. We changed all that. High performers today can expect cash incentives that amount to more than a third of their annual pay packages, on top of which employees receive company stock options. Here, too, other Japanese companies are making similar changes.[1]

For discussion

What are the major advantages and drawbacks of using these kinds of performance-based pay systems in organisations?

As may be seen in the case study, organisations can use different approaches to motivate people. Giving people rewards, either or not related to their performance, is a widely used practice that fits in different motivation theories, as will be explained in this chapter. Another common practice to enhance people's motivation is giving people challenging, although reachable and specific goals. Striving for various goals motivates people. A long-distance runner, for example, who wants to take part in the Rotterdam Marathon will train twice as hard as he would if he were not in a competition. Even as soon as two weeks after the 2004 Olympics in Athens, many athletes started their new training routines with the 2008 Olympic games in mind. The goal-setting theory of motivation provides a good explanation for their behaviour.

This chapter explores five different aspects related to how people can be motivated and how their performance can be influenced. First, three process theories of motivation are elaborated: equity theory, expectancy theory and goal-setting theory. The distinction between content and process theories of motivation has already been elaborated in the previous chapter. As explained, content theories focus on which specific things motivate behaviour, while process theories help us explain why people behave the way they do by focusing on how people try to satisfy their needs.

Second, we focus on effective feedback and giving rewards as important tools to influence and enhance the performance of employees. Properly administered feedback and rewards can guide, teach and motivate people in the direction of positive change.

> To illustrate this, scholars of the Copenhagen Business School recently examined the outcomes of the feedback process by questioning 115 employees and their supervisors in a large Danish bank. Results showed that people who perceived that they were receiving more feedback – both positive and negative – from their supervisors, rated themselves higher in performance and self-development.[2]

To help you apply what you have learned, we end the chapter by highlighting some important aspects of successful motivational programmes.

Equity theory of motivation

Defined generally, **Equity theory** is a model of motivation that explains how people strive for fairness and justice in social exchanges or give-and-take relationships. Equity theory is based on cognitive dissonance theory, developed by social psychologist Leon Festinger in the 1950s.[3]

According to Festinger's theory, people are motivated to maintain consistency between their cognitive beliefs and their behaviour. Perceived inconsistencies create cognitive dissonance (or psychological discomfort) which, in turn, motivates corrective action (also see Chapter 3). For example, a cigarette smoker who sees a heavy-smoking relative die of lung cancer probably would be motivated to quit smoking if he or she attributed the death to smoking.

Accordingly, when victimised by unfair social exchanges, our resulting cognitive dissonance prompts us to correct the situation. Corrective action may range from a slight change in attitude or behaviour through to stealing or, in an extreme case, to trying to harm someone. For example, researchers have demonstrated that people attempt to 'get even' for perceived injustices by using either direct (e.g. theft or sabotage) or indirect (e.g. intentionally working slowly, giving a co-worker the silent treatment) retaliation.[4]

Psychologist J. Stacy Adams pioneered the application of the equity theory to the workplace.[5] Figure 6.1 illustrates the equity theory. Three elements are important in this theory:

■ Central to understanding Adams' equity theory of motivation is an awareness of key components of the individual–organisation exchange relationship: inputs and outcomes. Employees expect a fair, just or equitable return (outcome) for what they contribute to their jobs.

> Equity theory holds that motivation is a function of fairness in social exchanges

FIGURE 6.1 ADAMS' EQUITY THEORY OF MOTIVATION

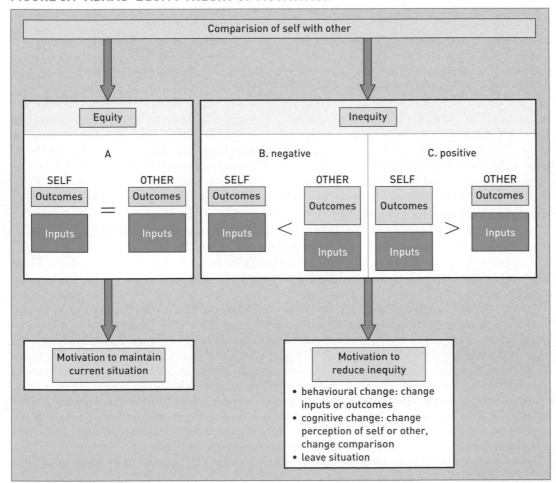

■ This relationship is pivotal in the formation of employees' perceptions of equity and inequity. Employees determine what their equitable return should be by comparing their inputs and outcomes with that of comparison others (like colleagues).

■ As a process theory of motivation, equity theory focuses on what people are motivated to do when they feel treated inequitably. Employees who perceive themselves as being in an inequitable situation try to reduce this inequity.

We focus on each of these elements.

The individual–organisation exchange relationship

Adams points out that two primary components are involved in the employee–employer exchange, inputs and outcomes. An employee's inputs, for which he or she expects a just return, include education, experience, skills and effort. On the outcome side of the exchange, the organisation provides such things as pay, fringe benefits and recognition. These outcomes vary widely, depending on one's organisation and rank. Table 6.1 presents a list of on-the-job inputs and outcomes that employees consider when making equity comparisons.

TABLE 6.1 FACTORS CONSIDERED WHEN MAKING EQUITY COMPARISONS

Inputs	Outcomes
Time	Pay/bonuses
Education/training	Fringe benefits
Experience	Challenging assignments
Skills	Job security
Creativity	Career advancement/promotions
Seniority	Status symbols
Loyalty to organisation	Pleasant/safe working environment
Age	Opportunity for personal growth/development
Personality traits	Supportive supervision
Effort expended	Recognition
Personal appearance	Participation in important decisions

SOURCE: Based in part on J. S. Adams, 'Toward an Understanding of Inequity', *Journal of Abnormal and Social Psychology*, November 1963, pp. 422–36.

Negative and positive inequity

At work, feelings of inequity revolve around a person's evaluation of whether he or she receives adequate rewards to compensate for his or her contributive inputs. People perform these evaluations by comparing the perceived fairness of their employment exchange to that of relevant others. Three different equity relationships are illustrated in Figure 6.1: equity, negative inequity and positive inequity.

Assume the two people in Figure 6.1 have equivalent backgrounds (equal education, seniority and so forth) and perform identical tasks. Only their hourly pay rates differ. Equity exists for an individual when his or her ratio of perceived outcomes to inputs is equal to the ratio of outcomes to inputs for a relevant co-worker (see part A in Figure 6.1). Since equity is based on comparing ratios of outcomes to inputs, inequity will not necessarily be perceived just because someone else receives greater rewards. If the other person's additional outcomes are due to his or her greater inputs, a sense of equity may still exist. However, if the comparison person enjoys greater outcomes for similar inputs, Negative inequity or underrewarding will be perceived (see part B in Figure 6.1). On the other hand, a person will experience Positive inequity or overrewarding when his or her outcome to input ratio is greater than that of a relevant co-worker (see part C in Figure 6.1).

Let us consider the type of inequity associated with the pay gap between chief executive officers and other workers (also see Chapter 18).

Negative inequity comparison in which another person receives greater outcomes for similar inputs

Positive inequity comparison in which another person receives lesser outcomes for similar inputs

Results of the 2003 New Earnings Survey in the UK reveal major differences between the average weekly and yearly pay of several occupations. The occupation group with the highest pay was the managers and senior officials, with an average weekly earning of £748 (an average annual pay of £42 164), followed by professionals occupations (an average weekly earning of £651 and an average annual pay of £33 741). The lowest pay was the personal service occupations group with an average weekly pay of £283 (an average annual pay of £14 146). This group includes occupations that are generally acknowledged to be low paid, like healthcare assistants, leisure and travel service occupations and hairdressers. The 2003 Survey shows that directors and chief executive officers of major organisations rank the highest among the earnings of specific occupations (with an average weekly earning of £2301), followed by the medical practitioners (with an average weekly earning of £1186). The lowest paid of all full-time adult employees were the retail desk and check-out operators, with an average weekly pay of £208.[6]

Perceived pay inequity can be devastating for one's motivation and performance at work. For example, British prisoners are said to receive inadequate health care because medical staff in the prison service are paid less than their counterparts in the National Health Services (NHS). According to Sir David Ramsbotham, former chief inspector of prisons, 'this pay inequality means that prison inmates get a worse standard of health care than they would in the community. Young offenders are particularly hard hit because they need good health if they are to develop properly and play a useful role in society on their release. But without pay levels on a par with those of the NHS, it is difficult for the prison service to attract staff with the same abilities.'[7]

Dynamics of perceived inequity

Organisations can derive practical benefits from Adams' equity theory by recognising the following two findings: on the one hand, that negative inequity is less tolerable than positive inequity and on the other that inequity can be reduced in a variety of ways. We elaborate these findings further.

THRESHOLDS OF INEQUITY

People have a lower tolerance for negative inequity than they do for positive inequity. Those who are short-changed are more powerfully motivated to correct the situation than those who are excessively rewarded. For example, if you have ever been over-worked and under-paid, you know how negative inequity can erode your job satisfaction and performance. Perhaps you put in less effort or quit the job to escape the negative inequity. Hence, it takes much more positive inequity than negative to produce the same degree of motivation.

REDUCING INEQUITY

Table 6.2 lists eight possible ways to reduce inequity. It is important to note that equity can be restored by altering one's equity ratios either behaviourally or cognitively or both. Equity theorists propose that the many possible combinations of behavioural and cognitive adjustments are influenced by the following tendencies:

■ An individual will attempt to maximise the amount of positive outcomes he or she receives.
■ People resist increasing inputs when it requires substantial effort or costs.
■ People resist behavioural or cognitive changes in inputs important to their self-concept or self-esteem.
■ Rather than changing cognitions about themselves, individuals are more likely to change cognitions about the comparison person's inputs and outcomes.
■ Leaving the field (quitting) is chosen only when severe inequity cannot be resolved through other methods.[8]

Research findings and practical implications

The comparison process underlying the equity theory was found to generalise across countries.[9] People tend to compare themselves with other individuals with whom they have close interpersonal ties (such as friends) and/or to similar others (such as people performing the same job or of the same

Measuring perceived fair interpersonal treatment

Instructions

Indicate the extent to which you agree or disagree with each of the following statements by considering what your organisation is like most of the time. Then compare your overall score with the arbitrary norms that are presented.

	Strongly disagree	Disagree	Neither	Agree	Strongly agree
1 Employees are praised for good work	1	2	3	4	5
2 Supervisors do not yell at employees	1	2	3	4	5
3 Employees are trusted	1	2	3	4	5
4 Employees' complaints are dealt with effectively	1	2	3	4	5
5 Employees are treated with respect	1	2	3	4	5
6 Employees' questions and problems are responded to quickly	1	2	3	4	5
7 Employees are treated fairly	1	2	3	4	5
8 Employees' hard work is appreciated	1	2	3	4	5
9 Employees' suggestions are used	1	2	3	4	5
10 Employees are told the truth	1	2	3	4	5

Total score = _____

Arbitrary norms

Very fair organisation = 38–50
Moderately fair organisation = 24–37
Unfair organisation = 10–23

SOURCE: Adapted in part from M. A. Donovan, F. Drasgow and L. Munson, 'The Perceptions of Fair Interpersonal Treatment Scale: Development and Validation of a Measure of Interpersonal Treatment in the Workplace', *Journal of Applied Psychology*, October 1998, pp. 683–92.

Vroom's expectancy theory

Victor Vroom formulated a mathematical model of expectancy theory in 1964 in his book *Work and Motivation*.[23] Vroom's theory has been summarised as follows.

> The strength of a tendency to act in a certain way depends on the strength of an expectancy that the act will be followed by a given consequence (or outcome) and on the value or attractiveness of that consequence (or outcome) to the actor.[24]

Motivation, according to Vroom, boils down to the decision about how much effort to exert in a specific task situation. As can be seen in Figure 6.2, this choice is based on a three-stage sequence of expectations:

■ First, motivation is affected by an individual's expectation that a certain level of effort will produce the intended performance goal. For example, if you do not believe increasing the amount of time you spend studying will significantly raise your marks in an exam, you will probably not study any harder than usual.
■ Motivation is also influenced by the individual's perceived chances of getting various outcomes as a result of accomplishing his or her performance goal. For example, when you study hard for an exam, you may expect a higher mark than when you study not that much.

FIGURE 6.2 VROOM'S EXPECTANCY MODEL

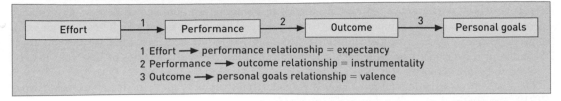

1 Effort ⟶ performance relationship = expectancy
2 Performance ⟶ outcome relationship = instrumentality
3 Outcome ⟶ personal goals relationship = valence

■ Finally, individuals are motivated to the extent that they value the outcomes received. For example, some people value a high mark as an important personal goal, while others do not.

Taken together, when we apply the whole theory to our example, this means that someone who attaches much value to having a high mark on an exam will be more motivated to put extra effort to perform well and to reach this outcome. Someone else who attaches less importance to a high mark will be less motivated to put much effort in studying the exam and so the results will be correspondingly modest. Consequently, what will happen when you study hard, put a lot of effort in your exam and receive the same mark as someone who did not put much effort in it? Will you judge your professor as being fair? How will this affect your future study efforts? The answers on these questions are self-evident.

EXPECTANCY

An **Expectancy**, according to Vroom's terminology, represents an individual's belief that a particular degree of effort will be followed by a particular level of performance. In other words, it is an effort → performance expectation. Expectancies take the form of subjective probabilities. As you may recall from a course in statistics, probabilities range from zero to one. An expectancy of zero indicates effort has no anticipated impact on performance.

> For example, suppose you do not know how to use a typewriter. No matter how much effort you exert, your perceived probability of typing 30 error-free words per minute are likely to be zero. An expectancy of 'one' suggests that performance is totally dependent on effort. If you decided to take a typing course as well as practise a couple of hours a day for a few weeks (high effort), you should be able to type 30 words per minute without any errors. In contrast, if you do not take a typing course and only practise an hour or two per week (low effort), there is a very low probability (say, a 20 per cent chance) of being able to type 30 words per minute without any errors.

The following factors influence an employee's expectancy perceptions:

■ Self-esteem.
■ Self-efficacy.
■ Previous success at the task.
■ Help received from a supervisor and subordinates.
■ Information necessary to complete the task.
■ Good materials and equipment to work with.[25]

INSTRUMENTALITY

An **Instrumentality** is a performance → outcome perception. It represents a person's belief that a particular outcome is contingent on accomplishing a specific level of performance. Performance is instrumental when it leads to something else. For example, passing exams is instrumental to graduating from college.

Instrumentalities range from −1.0 to 1.0. An instrumentality of 1.0 indicates that attainment of a particular outcome is totally dependent on task performance. An instrumentality of zero indicates that there is no relationship between performance and outcome. For example, most companies link

Expectancy
belief that effort leads to a specific level of performance

Instrumentality
belief that performance leads to a specific outcome or reward

the number of vacation days to seniority, not job performance. Finally, an instrumentality of −1.0 reveals that high performance reduces the chance of obtaining an outcome while low performance increases the chance. For example, the more time you spend studying to get a high grade on an exam (high performance), the less time you will have for enjoying leisure activities. Similarly, as you lower the amount of time spent studying (low performance), you increase the amount of time that may be devoted to leisure activities.

The concept of instrumentality is applied very clearly in the concept of performance-related pay (PRP), also referred to as **Pay-for-performance**, incentive pay or variable pay.[26] In this system, an employee's pay varies with the amount and the quality of work he or she carries out. The general idea behind pay-for-performance schemes – including, but not limited to, merit pay, bonuses and profit-sharing – is to give employees an incentive for working harder or smarter. Pay-for-performance is something extra, that is, compensation above and beyond basic wages and salaries. Advocates of this approach claim that variable pay schemes like PRP make employees understand better the connection between their performances and the rewards they receive.[27] Of course, this implies that high performance should be linked with high rewards, while low performance should be linked with low rewards. In practice, performance ratings and pay increases are often decoupled,[28] which might explain partly why organisational reward systems often fail.

Pay-for-performance
monetary incentives tied to one's results or accomplishments

VALENCE

Valence
the value of a reward or outcome

As Vroom used the term, **Valence** refers to the positive or negative value people place on outcomes. Valence mirrors our personal preferences.[29] For example, most employees have a positive valence for receiving additional money or recognition. In contrast, job stress and redundancy would be likely to prove negatively valent for most individuals. In Vroom's expectancy model, outcomes refer to different consequences that are contingent on performance, such as pay, promotions or recognition. An outcome's valence depends on an individual's needs. A study among Canadian managers also showed that money has multiple meanings for people.[30] Some perceive it as a symbol of success, for others it is something to reduce anxiety. Taking into account these different meanings when designing organisational reward systems can increase the effectiveness of the system and hence influence motivation accordingly.

The sum of the valences of all relevant outcomes has to be positive. This means, some valences may be negative, although the positive valences must outweigh the negative ones. For instance, someone with a stressful job (negative valence) may still like it and be motivated to work hard, because he or she receives a high pay and a great deal of recognition (positive valences).

One company which brought the principle of valence and personal preferences into practice is Laboratoires Boiron of Lyon, France.

> According to the company's HR manager, cash is rarely an effective employee retention tool but, when it's given to help employees achieve things they really value, it can create a powerful bond between workers and their company. Therefore, Laboratoires Boiron, a maker of homeopathic medicines, sets aside about €60 000 a year to help employees realise their personal dreams. One warehouse worker got nine months off and €4000 to help finance a voyage around the world with her husband and two children. The company also gave about €4500 to a telephone order-taker to finance a sculpture and painting studio.[31]

More commonly, many contemporary companies make use of alternative bonuses like extra holiday time. Holiday is the most popular employee incentive after cash. According to the Briton, John Fisher, who runs The Motivation Consultancy, extra holidays need not cost the company that much and it can reduce absenteeism. 'However, the most effective is an incentive scheme where employees can choose between those options they value most', Fisher says. 'For our clients, we often devise "all-in" incentive plans, including holiday time, private healthcare insurance, increased pension contributions and so on.'[32]

VROOM'S EXPECTANCY THEORY IN ACTION

Vroom's expectancy model of motivation can be used to analyse a real-life motivation programme. Consider the following performance problem described by Frederick W. Smith, founder and chief executive officer of FedEx Corporation.

> ... we were having a large problem keeping things running on time. The airplanes would come in, and everything would get backed up. We tried every kind of control mechanism that you could think of, and none of them worked. Finally, it became obvious that the underlying problem was that it was in the interest of the employees at the cargo terminal – they were college kids, mostly – to run late, because it meant that they made more money. So what we did was give them all a minimum guarantee and say, 'Look, if you get through before a certain time, just go home, and you will have beat the system.' Well, it was unbelievable. I mean, in the space of about 45 days, the place was way ahead of schedule. And I don't even think it was a conscious thing on their part.[33]

How did FedEx Corporation get its student cargo-handlers to switch from low effort to high effort? According to Vroom's model, the student workers originally exerted low effort because they were paid on the basis of time, not output. It was in their best interest to work slowly and accumulate as many hours as possible. By offering to let the student workers go home early if and when they completed their assigned duties, FedEx Corporation prompted high effort. This new arrangement created two positively valued outcomes: guaranteed pay plus the opportunity to leave early. The motivation to exert high effort became greater than the motivation to exert low effort.

Judging from the impressive results, the student workers had both high effort → performance expectancies and positive performance → outcome instrumentalities. Moreover, the guaranteed pay and early departure opportunity evidently had strongly positive valences for the student workers.

Porter and Lawler's extension

Two OB researchers, Lyman Porter and Edward Lawler III, developed an expectancy model of motivation that extended Vroom's work. This model attempted to: (1) identify the source of people's valences and expectancies; and (2) link effort with performance and job satisfaction. The model is presented in Figure 6.3.[34]

PREDICTORS OF EFFORT

Effort is a function of two elements: the perceived value of a reward (box 1 in Figure 6.3), which represents the reward's valence, and the perceived effort → reward probability (box 2, which reflects an expectancy), which means the expectation that performance will lead to reward. Employees should exhibit more effort when they believe they will receive valued rewards for task accomplishment.

FIGURE 6.3 PORTER AND LAWLER'S EXPECTANCY MODEL

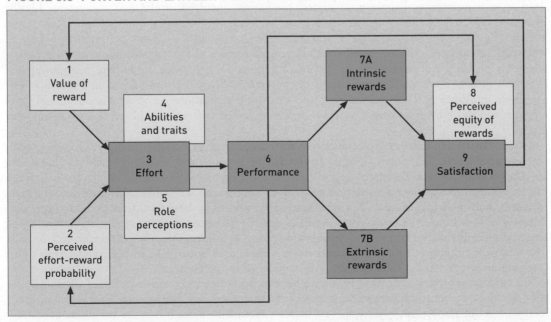

PERFORMANCE

determined by more than effort. Figure 6.3 indicates that the relationship between ormance (boxes 3 and 6) is contingent on an employee's abilities and traits (box 4) and ons (box 5). That is, employees with higher abilities attain higher performance for a of effort than employees with less ability. Similarly, effort results in higher performance mployees clearly understand, and are comfortable with, their roles. This occurs because effort nnelled into the most important job activities or tasks.

PREDICTORS OF SATISFACTION

Employees receive both intrinsic (box 7A in Figure 6.3) and extrinsic (box 7B) rewards for performance. Intrinsic rewards are self-granted and consist of intangibles such as a sense of accomplishment and achievement. Extrinsic rewards are tangible outcomes such as pay and public recognition. In turn, job satisfaction is determined by employees' perceptions of the equity of the rewards received (box 8 in Figure 6.3). Employees are more satisfied when they feel equitably rewarded. Figure 6.3 further shows that job satisfaction affects employees' subsequent valence of rewards. Finally, employees' future effort → reward probabilities are influenced by past experience with performance and rewards.

Research findings and practical implications

Many researchers have tested expectancy theory.[35] In support of the theory, a meta-analysis of 77 studies indicated that expectancy theory significantly predicted performance, effort, intentions, preferences and choice.[36] Another summary of 16 studies revealed that expectancy theory correctly predicted occupational or organisational choice 63.4 per cent of the time; this was significantly better than chance predictions.[37] Further, components of expectancy theory accurately predicted task persistence, achievement, employment status of previously unemployed people, job satisfaction, decisions to retire (80 per cent accuracy), voting behaviour in union representation elections (over 75 per cent accuracy) and the frequency of drinking alcohol.[38]

Nonetheless, expectancy theory has been criticised for a variety of reasons. For example, the theory is difficult to test, and the measures used to assess expectancy, instrumentality and valence have questionable validity.[39] However, expectancy theory has important practical implications for professionals and organisations as a whole.

The expectancy theory can be useful to create motivating working environments where people like to work and achieve high performance. It is clear that organisations cannot motivate their employees directly. Organisations can only try to establish a working environment which will lead to self-motivation. People want to feel productive, involved, useful and competent. Ideally, the personal goals people want to achieve are in line with the organisational expectations and vision. To enhance job satisfaction and motivation organisations have an important task in showing how people's efforts contribute to the organisational vision. Organisations can use various elements to enhance motivation by paying attention to the three important relationships of Vroom's theory. Some useful implications of expectancy theory are summarised in Table 6.3. The questions provided in Table 6.3 can both be used by organisations to create a motivational work climate and by individuals to get a better view to enhance self-motivation (replace 'the employee' with I).

Organisations can enhance expectancies of their employees by helping them to accomplish their performance goals. They can do this by providing support and coaching[40] and by increasing employees' self-efficacy. Research suggest that organisations have to provide employees with work that is reasonably challenging, in accordance with the employees' self-confidence, abilities, education, training, skills and experience.[41] Non-challenging work leads to boredom, frustration and low performance. Too difficult tasks, on the other hand, are rejected because they are not attainable. Paying attention to individual differences is crucial when trying to influence people's expectancies.[42] Because the expectancy theory is based on perceptions, it is also important to take into account people's own perceptions with regard to their abilities, self-confidence and self-esteem.

To enhance motivation, organisations also have to deal effectively with employees' instrumentalities. For organisations, it is, therefore, important to keep promises.[43] A promise – for instance, that a certain level of performance will lead to a bonus – cannot be broken because economic conditions

TABLE 6.3 ORGANISATIONAL IMPLICATIONS OF EXPECTANCY THEORY

Dealing with (effort–performance) expectancies
Is the employee's work reasonable, challenging, interesting and attainable?
Is the employee able to perform his/her work? Or is more education, training, experience, support or coaching needed?
Does the employee possess the necessary self-confidence and self-esteem to do his/her work? Or is time and effort needed to enhance his/her level of confidence?
Is it clear to the employee what acceptable levels of performance are? Do we agree on it? Can this performance easily be measured?
Does the work provide the employee with feelings of usefulness, involvement and competence? How can these feelings be reinforced?
Dealing with (performance–outcome) instrumentalities
Does the employee trust his/her superiors? Does the organisation keep promises made to employees? Does the organisation avoid lying to their employees?
Is the organisation fair and predictable in providing outcomes to employees? Is the organisation consistent in the application of giving rewards? While rewards may vary for different employees, are they perceived as being equitable?
Are the changes in outcomes large enough to motivate high effort?
Dealing with (outcome–personal goals) valences
Are the personal goals of the employee congruent with the organisational goals? How can a greater degree of alignment between these goals be accomplished?
Does the employee see the outcome as worth the expenditure of time and effort? What constraints on and off the job influence this employee? Do the employee and the organisation have realistic and mutual expectations?
Does the organisation reward the employee with something he/she really values? Does the organisation know which outcomes the employee values?
What kind of informal rewards can be used beside the more formal organisational rewards? How does the employee perceive these informal rewards?

SOURCE: Adapted from R. G. Isaac, W. J. Zerbe and D. C. Pitt, 'Leadership and Motivation: The Effective Application of Expectancy Theory', *Journal of Managerial Issues*, Summer 2001, p. 221.

became bad in the meanwhile. Trust and honesty are certainly important aspects of organisations that are valued by employees. Treating employees fairly with regard to outcomes is another important aspect, as was mentioned above (equity theory). Fair treatment does not mean treating everyone the same. It implies treating people in the same way (consistence) and in accordance with their needs.

Organisations also have to monitor valences for various rewards. This raises the issue of whether organisations should use monetary rewards as the primary method to reinforce performance. Although money is certainly a positively valent reward for most people, individual differences (Chapters 2 and 3) and need theories (Chapter 5) tell us that people are motivated by different rewards. Professionals should therefore focus on linking employee performance to valued rewards, regardless of the type of reward used to enhance motivation.

Motivation through goal setting

Regardless of the nature of their specific achievements, successful people tend to have one thing in common. Their lives are goal oriented. This is as true for politicians seeking votes as it is for rocket scientists probing outer space. In Lewis Carroll's delightful tale of *Alice's Adventures in Wonderland*, the smiling Cheshire cat advised the bewildered Alice, 'If you don't know where you're going, any road will take you there'. Goal-oriented professionals tend to find the right road because they know where they are going. Within the context of employee motivation, this section explores the theory, research and practice of goal setting.

Goals: definition and background

Goal
what an individual is trying to accomplish

Edwin Locke, a leading authority on goal setting, and his colleagues define a Goal as 'what an individual is trying to accomplish; it is the object or aim of an action'.[44]

The motivational impact of performance goals and goal-based reward plans has been recognised for a long time. At the turn of the century, Frederick Taylor attempted to establish scientifically how much work of a specified quality an individual should be assigned each day. He proposed that bonuses be based on accomplishing those output standards (see Chapter 1). More recently, goal setting has been promoted through a widely used technique called management by objectives (MBO).

Management by objectives
system incorporating participation in decision making, goal setting and feedback

Management by objectives is a system that incorporates participation in decision making, goal setting and objective feedback.[45] A meta-analysis of MBO programmes showed productivity gains in 68 out of 70 different organisations. Specifically, results uncovered an average gain in productivity of 56 per cent when top management commitment was high. The average gain was only 6 per cent when commitment was low. A second meta-analysis of 18 studies further demonstrated that employees' job satisfaction was significantly related to top management's commitment to an MBO implementation.[46] These impressive results highlight the positive benefits of implementing MBO and setting goals. To further understand how MBO programmes can increase both productivity and satisfaction, let us examine the process by which goal setting works.

How does goal setting work?

Despite abundant goal-setting research and practice, goal-setting theories are surprisingly scarce. An instructive model was formulated by Locke and his associates (see Figure 6.4). According to Locke's model, goal setting has four motivational mechanisms.

GOALS DIRECT ATTENTION

Goals that are personally meaningful tend to focus one's attention on what is relevant and important. If, for example, you have a term project due in a few days, your thoughts tend to revolve around

FIGURE 6.4 LOCKE'S MODEL OF GOAL SETTING

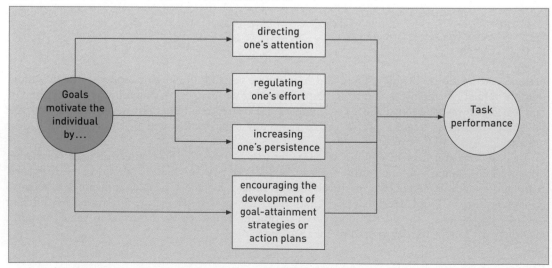

SOURCE: Adapted from *A Theory of Goal Setting and Task Performance* by E. A. Locke and G. P. Latham, © 1990. Adapted by permission of Prentice-Hall, Inc., Upper Saddle River, N.J. (Englewood Cliffs, NJ: Prentice-Hall, 1990). Reprinted by permission of Prentice-Hall, Inc.

completing that project. Similarly, the members of a home appliance sales force who are told they can win a trip to Hawaii for selling the most refrigerators will tend to steer customers toward the refrigerator display.

GOALS REGULATE EFFORT

Not only do goals make us selectively perceptive, they also motivate us to act. The lecturer's deadline for turning in your term project would prompt you to complete it, as opposed to going out with friends, watching television or studying for another course. Generally, the level of effort expended is proportionate to the difficulty of the goal. Consider the motivation of Willem Ombelet, head of a fertility clinic in Belgium.

> I want to mean something to our society, I want to make a difference to anonymous people who will never really know me. That's why I keep doing scientific work. A good scientist is like an artist. He creates, investigates and confirms. Those who haven't got this inside them, won't learn it either. For every patient, I try to find the best possible treatment. Actually, in everything I do, I'm looking for that little extra, for new things that demand from me a lot of time and effort. I have tried a bit of everything yet sometimes I have to learn things the hard way. But I keep going on. I have a feeling that I have to bring the world a message.[47]

GOALS INCREASE PERSISTENCE

Within the context of goal setting, **Persistence** represents the effort expended on a task over an extended period of time. It takes effort to run 100 metres; it takes persistence to run a 42-kilometre marathon. Persistent people tend to see obstacles as challenges to be overcome rather than as reasons to fail. A difficult goal that is important to an individual is a constant reminder to keep exerting effort in the appropriate direction. Astronaut Jim Lovell represents a great example of someone who persisted at his goals. Lovell commanded NASA's ill-fated Apollo 13 mission that almost did not return from deep space. Here's what Lovell had to say about his career in an interview.

Persistence
extent to which effort is expended on a task over time

> When you look at the end result today, it's so easy to think that it was nothing but smooth sailing all the way. But perseverance was absolutely essential to getting where I am. Not only did I fail to get into the Naval Academy the first time I tried – I barely made it as the first alternate the second time. Then to be the only one of 32 guys to flunk [fail] the physical for the Mercury Programme – you can imagine how that sets you back. But I persevered, and that's why I made it when I got the second shot. There are three traits that I think are absolutely essential to achieving success, and the first one is perseverance.[48]

GOALS FOSTER STRATEGIES AND ACTION PLANS

If you are here and your goal is out there somewhere, you face the problem of getting from here to there. For example, the person who has resolved to lose 10 kilos must develop a plan for getting from 'here' (his or her present weight) to 'there' (10 kilos lighter). Goals can help because they encourage people to develop strategies and action plans that enable them to achieve their goals.[49] By virtue of setting a weight-reduction goal, the dieter may choose a strategy of exercising more, eating less or some combination of the two.

Research findings

Research has consistently supported goal setting as a motivational technique.[50] Setting performance goals increases individual, group and organisational performance. Further, the positive effects of goal setting were not only found in the US but also elsewhere, like in Australia, Canada, the Caribbean, England and Japan. Goal setting works in different cultures, although the effects of goal specificity and goal difficulty may vary between cultures.[51] Reviews of the many goal-setting studies conducted over the last couple of decades have led to the following practical insights.

GOAL DIFFICULTY

Goal difficulty
the amount of
effort required to
meet a goal

Difficult goals lead to higher performance. **Goal difficulty** reflects the amount of effort required to meet a goal. It is more difficult to sell nine cars a month than it is to sell three a month. A meta-analysis spanning 4000 people and 65 separate studies revealed that goal difficulty was positively related to performance.[52] As illustrated in Figure 6.5, however, the positive relationship between goal difficulty and performance breaks down when goals are perceived to be impossible. Figure 6.5 reveals that performance goes up when employees are given hard goals as opposed to easy or moderate ones (section A). Performance then plateaus (section B) and drops (section C) as the difficulty of a goal goes from challenging to impossible.[53]

FIGURE 6.5 RELATIONSHIP BETWEEN GOAL DIFFICULTY AND PERFORMANCE

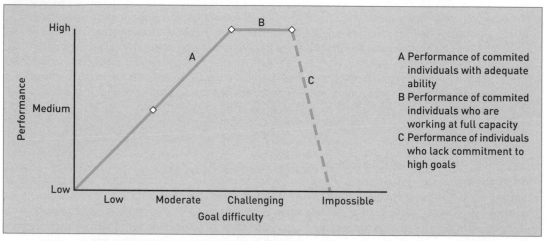

SOURCE: *A Theory of Goal Setting and Task Performance*, by E. A. Locke and G. P. Latham, © 1990. Adapted by permission of Prentice-Hall, Upper Saddle River, N.J. Reprinted by permission of Prentice-Hall, Inc., Englewood Cliffs, NJ.

Research also found the same inverted-U relationship between goal difficulty and selling effort for US salespeople. Salespeople were less inclined to increase selling effort when the goals set by their sales managers were either easy or extremely difficult than when the goals were moderately difficult.[54] However, for Chinese salespeople this relationship was not found. One explanation can be a culturally ingrained relationship between effort and performance (a social norm embedded in China's culture that you can succeed if you try harder), which encourages the Chinese salespeople to keep on trying despite their difficult goals.[55]

GOAL SPECIFICITY

Goal specificity
quantifiability of a
goal

Specific, difficult goals lead to higher performance for simple rather than complex tasks. **Goal specificity** pertains to the quantifiability of a goal, this means it refers to the extent to which a goal is specifically stated and specified. For example, a goal of selling nine cars a month is more specific than telling a salesperson to do his or her best. In an early review of goal-setting research, 99 out of 110 studies (90 per cent) found that specific, hard goals led to better performance than did either easy, medium, do-your-best goals or none. This result was confirmed in a meta-analysis of 70 studies conducted between 1966 and 1984, involving 7407 people.[56] In contrast to these positive effects, several recent studies demonstrated that setting specific, difficult goals leads to poorer performance under certain circumstances. For example, a meta-analysis of 125 studies indicated that goal-setting effects were strongest for easy tasks and weakest for complex tasks.[57] There are two explanations for this finding.

First, employees are not likely to put forth increased effort to achieve complex goals unless they 'buy-into' or support them.[58] Thus, it is important for professionals to obtain employee support for the goal-setting process. Second, novel and complex tasks take employees longer to complete. This occurs because employees spend more time thinking about how to approach and solve these tasks.

In contrast, employees do not have to spend much time thinking about solutions for easy tasks. Specific, difficult goals thus impair performance on novel, complex tasks when employees do not have clear strategies for solving these types of problems. On a positive note, however, a recent study demonstrated that goal setting led to gradual improvements in performance on complex tasks when people were encouraged explicitly to solve the problem at hand.[59]

FEEDBACK AND GOAL SETTING

Feedback plays a key role in all of our lives. For example, consider the role of feedback in bowling. Imagine going to the bowling lanes only to find that someone had hung a sheet from the ceiling to the floor in front of the pins. How likely is it that you would reach your goal score or typical bowling average? Not likely, given your inability to see the pins. Regardless of your goal, you would have to guess where to throw your second ball if you did not get a strike on your first shot. The same principles apply at work. Feedback lets people know if they are headed toward their goals or if they are off course and need to redirect their efforts. Goals plus feedback is the recommended approach.[60] Goals inform people about performance standards and expectations so that they can channel their energies accordingly. In turn, feedback provides the information needed to adjust direction, effort and strategies for goal accomplishment. Feedback enhances the effect of specific, difficult goals.

CONTINGENCY APPROACH TO GOAL SETTING

Both professionals and researchers are interested in identifying the best way to set goals. Should goals be participatively set, assigned or set by the employee him- or herself? A summary of goal-setting research indicated that no single approach was consistently more effective than others in increasing performance.[61] Participative goals, assigned goals and self-set goals are equally effective. Professionals are advised to use a contingency approach by picking a method that seems best suited to the individual and situation at hand. For example, employees' preferences for participation should be considered. Some employees desire to participate in the process of setting goals, whereas others do not. Employees are also more likely to respond positively to the opportunity to participate in goal setting when they have greater task information, higher levels of experience and training, and greater levels of task involvement. A participative approach may also help reducing employees' resistance to goal setting.

Because of individual differences (see Chapters 2 and 3), it may be necessary to establish different goals for employees performing the same job. For example, a study of 103 undergraduate business students revealed that individuals high in conscientiousness had higher motivation, greater goal commitment and obtained higher grades than students low in conscientiousness.[62]

GOAL COMMITMENT

Goal commitment affects goal-setting outcomes. Goal commitment is the extent to which an individual is personally committed to achieving a goal. Goal commitment implies both the strength of one's intention to reach a goal and the unwillingness to abandon or lower a goal over time.[63] In general, an individual is expected to persist in attempts to accomplish a goal when he or she is committed to it. Researchers believe that goal commitment moderates the relationship between the difficulty of a goal and performance. That is, difficult goals lead to higher performance only when employees are committed to their goals. Conversely, difficult goals are hypothesised to lead to lower performance when people are not committed to their goals. A meta-analysis of 21 studies based on 2360 people supported these predictions.[64] Research also found that people with a higher need for achievement have a higher goal commitment and outperform people with a low need for achievement.[65] Take a moment now to complete the goal commitment scale and the study habits questions contained in the following Activity. Is your goal commitment related to the behaviours associated with your study habits? If not, what is the cause of the discrepancy?

> **Goal commitment**
> amount of commitment to achieving a goal

Practical implications

There are three general steps to follow when implementing a goal-setting programme. Serious deficiencies in one step cannot make up for strength in the other two. The three steps need to be implemented in a systematic fashion.

activity

Is your goal commitment for this course related to your behaviour?

Instructions

Begin by identifying your performance goal (desired grade) for this course. My desired grade is
____.

Next, use the rating scale shown below to circle the answer that best represents how you feel about each of the following statements. After computing a total score for the goal-commitment items, answer the questions related to your study habits for this course.

	Strongly disagree	Disagree	Neither	Agree	Strongly agree
1 I am trying hard to reach my performance goal.	1	2	3	4	5
2 I am exerting my maximum effort (100 per cent) in pursuit of my performance goal.	1	2	3	4	5
3 I am committed to my performance goal.	1	2	3	4	5
4 I am determined to reach my performance goal.	1	2	3	4	5
5 I am enthusiastic about attempting to achieve my performance goal.	1	2	3	4	5
6 I am striving to attain my performance goal.	1	2	3	4	5

Total score =_____

Arbitrary norms

Low goal commitment = 6–15
Moderate goal commitment = 15–23
High goal commitment = 24–30

Study habits

How many hours have you spent studying for this course? ____ hours
What is your grade at this point in the course? ____
How many times have you missed lectures? ____ absences

SOURCE: Items were adapted from those presented in R. W. Renn, C. Danehower, P. M. Swiercz and M. L. Icenogle, 'Further Examination of the Measurement Properties of Leifer & McGannon's (1986) Goal Acceptance and Goal Commitment Scales', *Journal of Occupational and Organizational Psychology*, March 1999, pp. 107–13.

STEP 1: SET GOALS

A number of sources can be used as input during this goal-setting stage. Time and motion studies are one source. A second is the average past performance of employees. Third, the employee and his or her superior may set the goal participatively, through give-and-take negotiation. Fourth, goals can be set by conducting external or internal benchmarking. Benchmarking (also see Chapter 17) is used when an organisation wants to compare its performance or internal work processes with those of other organisations (external benchmarking) or other internal units, branches, departments or divisions within the organisation (internal benchmarking).[66] For example, a company might set a goal to surpass the customer service levels or profits of a benchmarked competitor. A review of trends in Human Resource Management in the UK shows an increasing interest in benchmarking as a tool to bring organisations up to best practices levels.[67] Finally, the overall strategy of a company (such as

TABLE 6.4 GUIDELINES FOR WRITING SMART GOALS

Specific	Goals should be stated in precise rather than vague terms. For example, a goal that provides for 20 hours of technical training for each employee is more specific than stating that a superior should send as many people as possible to training classes. Goals should be quantified when possible
Measurable	A measurement device is needed to assess the extent to which a goal is accomplished. Goals thus need to be measurable. It also is critical to consider the quality aspect of the goal when establishing measurement criteria. For example, if the goal is to complete a managerial study of methods to increase productivity, one must consider how to measure the quality of this effort. Goals should not be set without considering the interplay between quantity and quality of output
Attainable	Goals should be realistic, challenging and attainable. Impossible goals reduce motivation because people do not like to fail. Remember, people have different levels of ability and skill
Results oriented	Corporate goals should focus on desired end-results that support the organisation's vision. In turn, an individual's goals should directly support the accomplishment of corporate goals. Activities support the achievement of goals and are outlined in action plans. To focus goals on desired end-results, goals should start with the word 'to', followed by verbs such as complete, acquire, produce, increase or decrease. Verbs such as develop, conduct, implement or monitor imply activities and should not be used in a goal statement
Time bound	Goals specify target dates for completion

SOURCE: A. J. Kinicki, *Performance Management Systems* (Superstition Mt., AZ: Kinicki and Associates, 1992), pp. 2–9. Reprinted with permission; all rights reserved.

becoming the lowest-cost producer) may affect the goals set by employees at various levels within the organisation.

In accordance with available research evidence, goals should be 'SMART'. SMART is an acronym that stands for Specific, Measurable, Attainable, Results-oriented and Time-bound. Table 6.4 contains a set of guidelines for writing SMART goals.

When setting goals make sure not to induce some form of goal conflict. **Goal conflict** refers to degree to which people feel their multiple goals are incompatible.[68] Several types of goal conflict exist.[69] It is possible that an externally imposed goal conflicts with one's personal goal. Another type of goal conflict occurs when people have to achieve multiple outcomes when performing a single task, like meeting a quantity quota and not making mistakes. In this case, there occurs a trade-off between performance quality and quantity: people make a lot of things with many mistakes (quantity at the expense of quality) or they make few things with no mistakes (quality at the expense of quantity). A third type of goal conflict occurs when several tasks or goals have to be accomplished (for instance, selling two different products, given a limited amount of time). In this case, people handle the conflict by prioritising one task at the expense of the other. Research with 152 salespeople, who were rewarded for one type of activity while simultaneously asked to make other activities top priorities, found lower levels of commitment to a particular goal.[70]

Goal conflict degree to which people feel their multiple goals are incompatible

STEP 2: PROMOTE GOAL COMMITMENT

Obtaining goal commitment is important because employees are more motivated to pursue goals they view as reasonable, obtainable and fair. Goal commitment may be increased by using one or more of the following techniques:

- Provide an explanation for why the organisation is implementing a goal-setting programme.
- Present the corporate goals and explain how and why an individual's personal goals support them.

223

■ Have employees establish their own goals and action plans. Encourage them to set challenging, stretching goals. Goals should not be impossible.
■ Train professionals in how to conduct participative goal-setting sessions. Train employees in how to develop effective action plans.
■ Be supportive. Do not use goals to threaten employees.
■ Set goals that are under the employees' control and then provide them with the necessary resources.
■ Provide monetary incentives or other rewards for accomplishing goals.

Goal setting will not work when people are not committed to the established goals. Research shows that people have a higher goal commitment when they understand their goals, when they feel pressure from peers to perform well, when they perceive they can attain their goals and when they believe they will be recognised for their accomplishments.[71] One of the critical factors in cultivating goal commitment is demonstrating the relevance and importance of goals to individuals and organisations.[72]

STEP 3: PROVIDE SUPPORT AND FEEDBACK

Step 3 calls for providing employees with the necessary support elements or resources to get the job done. This includes ensuring that each employee has the necessary abilities and information to reach his or her goals. Appropriate goals without some degree of knowledge are not sufficient for successful performance.[73] As a pair of goal-setting experts succinctly stated, 'Motivation without knowledge is useless.'[74] Often training is required to help employees achieve difficult goals. Moreover, professionals should pay attention to employees' perceptions of effort → performance expectancies, self-efficacy and the valence of rewards (recall the elaboration of expectancy theory). This means, knowing whether employees expect the goal is attainable through effort, whether they believe they have the capacity to reach the goal and which rewards they find important when reaching the goal.[75]

Finally, employees should be provided with timely, specific feedback (knowledge of results) on how they are doing. Research shows a complicated relationship between feedback and performance. Feedback did not affect the performance level of people who where already meeting expectations, but it significantly influenced performance levels of under-achievers.[76] These findings indicate that feedback is not directly influencing performance. It rather serves as an essential condition of goal setting to work.[77] Because of the importance of feedback as a tool for reaching one's goals and for increasing motivation, we further elaborate on the feedback process.

Understanding the feedback process

Numerous surveys tell us employees have a hearty appetite for feedback.[78] So also do achievement-oriented students. Following a difficult exam, for instance, students want to know two things: how they did and how their peers did. By letting students know how their work relates to grades and competitive standards, a teacher's feedback permits the students to adjust their study habits in order to reach their goals. According to the Dutch consultant Loek van den Broek, author of the book *Feedback as an Eye-Opener*, this is a natural evolution. 'People want to know if they're doing well. It's just inherent in human nature. They also want to know what others think of them. Moreover, everybody is constantly looking for ways to improve his/her functioning. The opinion of other people is indispensable to this.'[79]

Likewise, professionals in well-run organisations follow up goal setting with a feedback programme to provide a rational basis for adjustment and improvement. It seems that more and more organisations are formally installing feedback and appraisal procedures. Consider the following two diverse feedback examples:

> " IBM's Raleigh, USA, personal computer factory: 'Every day, managers see a fresh ... number on their screens, telling them how many PCs have been shipped so far this year ... every model is broken out [detailed] so managers can see what's moving and what's not.'[80]
>
> A 55000-employee copper mine in Zambia, Africa: 'As largely uneducated workers march into the front entrance, they can't help but spot a 50-foot-high scoreboard that lists monthly and year-to-date financials, from "copper revenue" to "corporate depreciation".'[81] "

Although this sort of open-book management is becoming popular, feedback too often gets short changed. In fact, 'poor or insufficient feedback' was the leading cause of deficient performance i survey of US and European companies.[82] Although positive feedback is one of the most effe ways to reinforce good behaviour, people often feel that the only time they get feedback is when things go wrong.[83]

As the term is used here, **Feedback** is objective information about individual or collective perform-ance. Subjective assessments such as, 'You're doing a poor job', 'You're too lazy' or 'We really appre-ciate your hard work' do not qualify as objective feedback. But hard data such as units sold, days absent, amount of money saved, projects completed, customers satisfied and products rejected are all suitable for objective feedback programmes. Consultants Chip Bell and Ron Zemke offered the following perspective on feedback:

> Feedback is, quite simply, any information that answers those 'How am I doing?' ques-tions. Good feedback answers them truthfully and productively. It's information people can use either to confirm or correct their performance. Feedback comes in many forms and from a variety of sources. Some is easy to get and requires hardly any effort to understand. The charts and graphs tracking group and individual performance, that are fixtures in many workplaces, are an example of this variety. Performance feedback – the numerical type at least – is at the heart of most approaches to total quality management. Some feed-back is less accessible. It's tucked away in the heads of customers and managers. But no matter how well-hidden the feedback, if people need it to keep their performance on track, we need to get it to them – preferably while it's still fresh enough to make an impact.[84]

Experts say feedback serves two functions for those who receive it, one is instructional and the other motivational. Feedback instructs when it clarifies roles or teaches new behaviour. For example, an assistant accountant might be advised to handle a certain entry as a capital item rather than as an expense item. On the other hand, feedback motivates when it serves as a reward or promises a reward.[85] Having the boss tell you that a gruelling project you worked on earlier has just been com-pleted can be a rewarding piece of news. As documented in one study, the motivational function of feedback can be significantly enhanced by pairing specific, challenging goals with specific feedback about results.[86] We expand upon these two functions of feedback in this section by analysing a cogni-tive model of feedback and by reviewing the practical implications of recent feedback research.

A cognitive-processing model of performance feedback

Giving and receiving feedback at work are popular ideas today. Conventional wisdom says the more feedback organisational members get, the better. An underlying assumption is that feedback works automatically. Professionals simply need to be motivated to give it. According to a recent meta-analysis of 23 663 feedback incidents, however, feedback is far from automatically effective. While feedback did, in fact, have a generally positive impact on performance, performance actually declined in more than 38 per cent of the feedback incidents.[87]

These results are a stark warning for those interested in improving job performance with feedback. Subjective feedback is easily contaminated by situational factors. Moreover, if objective feedback is to work as intended, professionals need to understand the interaction between feedback recipients and their environment.[88] A more complete understanding of how employees cognitively or mentally process feedback is an important first step, as illustrated in Figure 6.6. A step-by-step exploration of the model in Figure 6.6 can help us better understand the feedback-performance relationship.

Sources of feedback

It almost goes without saying that employees receive objective feedback from others such as peers, supervisors, subordinates and outsiders. Perhaps less obvious is the fact that the task itself is a ready source of objective feedback.[89] Anyone who has spent hours on a 'quick' Internet search can appreci-ate the power of task-provided feedback. Similarly, skilled tasks such as computer programming or landing a jet provide a steady stream of feedback about how well or poorly one is doing. Although a third source of feedback is oneself, self-serving bias and other perceptual problems can contaminate

Feedback
objective information about performance

225

FIGURE 6.6 A COGNITIVE–PROCESSING MODEL OF FEEDBACK

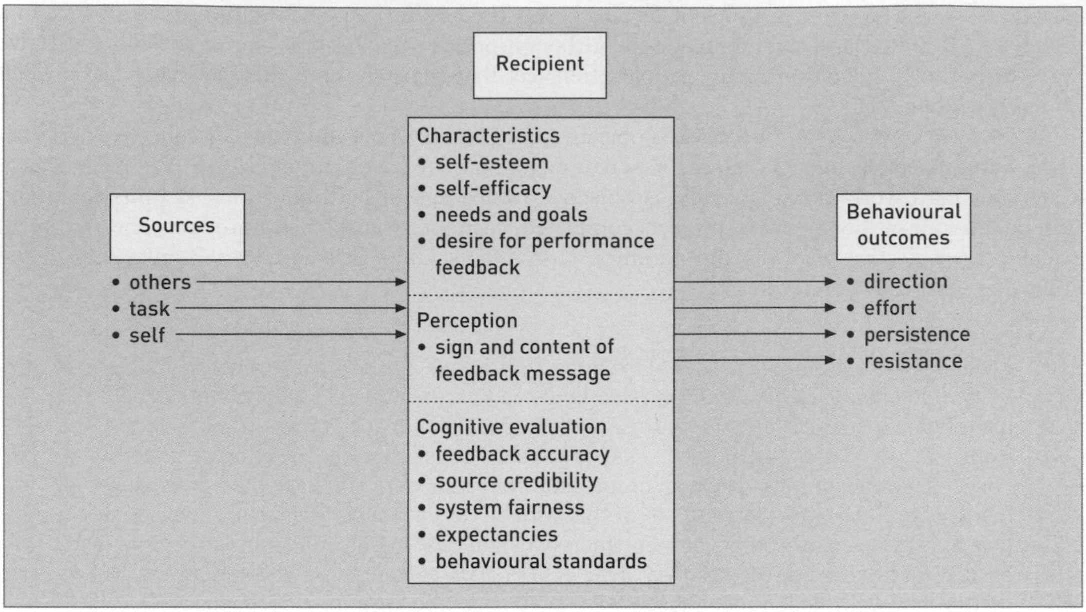

SOURCE: Based in part on discussion in M. S. Taylor, C. D. Fisher and D. R. Ilgen, 'Individuals' Reactions to Performance Feedback in Organizations: A Control Theory Perspective', in *Research in Personnel and Human Resources Management*, vol. 2, eds K. M. Rowland and G. R. Ferris (Greenwich CT: JAI Press, 1984), pp. 81–124; and A. N. Kluger and A. DeNisi, 'The Effects of Feedback Interventions on Performance: A Historic Review, a Meta-Analysis, and a Preliminary Feedback Intervention Theory', *Psychological Bulletin*, March 1996, pp. 254–84.

this source (see Chapter 4). Those high in self-confidence tend to rely on personal feedback more than those with low self-confidence. Although circumstances vary, an employee can be bombarded by feedback from all three sources simultaneously. This is where the 'gatekeeping functions' of perception and cognitive evaluation are needed to help sort things out.

The recipient of feedback
Listed in the centre portion of Figure 6.6 are three aspects of the recipient requiring our attention. They are the individual's characteristics, perception and cognitive evaluation.

THE RECIPIENT'S CHARACTERISTICS
Personality characteristics (see Chapter 2) such as self-esteem and self-efficacy can help or hinder one's readiness for feedback.[90] Those having low self-esteem and low self-efficacy generally do not actively seek feedback. Needs and goals also influence one's openness to feedback. In a laboratory study, Japanese psychology students who scored high on the need for achievement, responded more favourably to feedback than did their classmates who had a low need for achievement.[91] High self-monitors, those chameleon-like people we discussed in Chapter 2, are also more open to feedback because it helps them adapt their behaviour to the situation. Recall from Chapter 2 that high self-monitoring employees were found to be better at initiating relationships with mentors (who typically provide feedback).[92] Low self-monitoring people, in contrast, are tuned into their own internal feelings more than they are towards external cues.

THE RECIPIENT'S PERCEPTION OF FEEDBACK
The sign of feedback refers to whether it is positive or negative. Generally, people tend to perceive and recall positive feedback more accurately than they do negative feedback.[93] However, feedback with a negative sign (such as being told your performance is below average) can have a positive motivational impact. In fact, in one study, those who were told they were below average on a creativity test subsequently outperformed those who were led to believe their results were above average.

The subjects apparently took the negative feedback as a challenge and so then set and pursued higher goals. Those receiving positive feedback were apparently less motivated to do better.[94]

Nonetheless, feedback with a negative sign or threatening content needs to be administered carefully to avoid creating insecurity and defensiveness. Self-efficacy can also be damaged by negative feedback, as was discovered in a pair of experiments with business students. The researchers concluded the following: 'To facilitate the development of strong efficacy beliefs, professionals should be careful about the provision of negative feedback. Destructive criticism that attributes the cause of poor performance to internal factors, reduces both the beliefs of self-efficacy and the self-set goals of recipients.'[95]

> A recent British study into feedback at work showed that professionals think they praise people more than they actually do, whereas employees report receiving five times more criticism than praise. According to the researchers, this gap between perception and reality is partly due to it being easy to forget to praise good work, whereas bawling someone out has an urgency to it. Another reason is that much positive feedback is followed by a 'but'. To tell an employee 'that was excellent but ...' is basically a waste of praise: what is heard and remembered is the actual or implied criticism.[96]

THE RECIPIENT'S COGNITIVE EVALUATION OF FEEDBACK

Upon receiving feedback, people cognitively evaluate factors such as its accuracy, the credibility of the source, the fairness of the system (e.g. a performance-appraisal system), their performance–reward expectancies and the reasonableness of the standards. Any feedback that fails to clear one or more of these cognitive hurdles will be rejected or played down. Personal experience largely dictates how these factors are weighed. For instance, you would probably discount feedback from someone who exaggerates or from someone who performed poorly on the same task as the one you have just successfully completed. In view of the 'trust gap' (discussed in Chapter 10) credibility is an ethical matter of central importance today. Professionals who have proven untrustworthy and not credible have a hard time improving job performance through feedback.[97] Feedback from a source who apparently shows favouritism or relies on unreasonable standards behaviour would be suspect.[98] Professionals can enhance their credibility as sources of feedback by developing their expertise and creating a climate of trust. Also, as predicted by expectancy motivation theory, feedback must foster high effort → performance expectancies and performance → reward instrumentalities if it is to motivate the desired behaviour. For example, many growing children have been cheated out of the rewards of athletic competition because they were told by respected adults that they were too small, too short, too slow, too clumsy and so forth. Feedback can have a profound and lasting impact on behaviour.

Behavioural outcomes of feedback

We discussed earlier how goal setting gives behaviour direction, increases expended effort and fosters persistence. Because feedback is intimately related to the goal-setting process, it involves the same behavioural outcomes: direction, effort and persistence. However, while the fourth outcome of goal setting involves formulating goal-attainment strategies, the fourth possible outcome of feedback is resistance. Feedback schemes that either smack of manipulation or fail on one or more of the perceptual and cognitive evaluation tests just discussed, breed resistance.[99]

Research findings and practical implications

Table 6.5 lists some problems researchers identified with regard to organisational feedback systems.[100]

Keeping in mind these possible trouble signs and the following tips[101] can help professionals to build credible and effective feedback systems:

- Relate feedback to existing performance goals and clear expectations.
- Give specific and concrete feedback tied to observable behaviour or measurable results. Focus on specific behaviours. Feedback needs to be tailored to the recipient.
- Channel feedback toward key result areas.

TABLE 6.5 TROUBLE SIGNS FOR ORGANISATIONAL FEEDBACK SYSTEMS

1	Feedback is used to punish, embarrass or put down employees
2	Those receiving the feedback see it as irrelevant to their work
3	Feedback information is provided too late to do any good
4	People receiving feedback believe it relates to matters beyond their control
5	Employees complain about wasting too much time collecting and recording feedback data
6	Feedback recipients complain about feedback being too complex or difficult to understand
7	The positive acceptance of feedback is treated as a given
8	Feedback is given too infrequently

SOURCE: Based on discussions in D. R. Ilgen, C. D. Fisher and M. S. Taylor, 'Consequences of Individual Feedback on Behavior in Organizations', *Journal of Applied Psychology*, August 1979, pp. 367–8; C. O. Longenecker and D. A. Gioia, 'The Executive Appraisal Paradox', *Academy of Management Executive*, May 1992, p. 18; C. Bell and R. Zemke, 'On-Target Feedback', *Training*, June 1992, pp. 36–44; and M. L. Smith, 'Give Feedback, Not Criticism', *Supervisory Management*, February 1993, p. 4.

- Give feedback as soon as possible.[102]
- Give positive feedback for improvement, not just final results. Good feedback is future-oriented.
- Focus feedback on performance, not personalities. Feedback needs to be task-oriented and job-related instead of people-oriented.
- Base feedback on accurate and credible information.
- Keep in mind that feedback (certainly negative) is often perceived wrongly or rejected. This is especially true in cross-cultural exchanges.

Non-traditional organisational feedback processes

Traditional top-down feedback programmes have given way to some interesting variations in recent years. Two newer approaches are upward feedback and so-called 360-degree feedback. Aside from breaking away from a strict superior-to-subordinate feedback loop, these newer approaches are different because they typically involve multiple sources of feedback. Instead of simply getting feedback from one boss, often during an annual performance appraisal, more and more professionals receive structured feedback from superiors, subordinates, peers and even outsiders such as customers. Non-traditional feedback is growing in popularity for at least six reasons:

- Traditional performance-appraisal systems have created widespread dissatisfaction.
- Team-based organisation structures are replacing traditional hierarchies. This trend requires professionals to have good interpersonal skills that are best evaluated by team members.
- Systems using 'multiple-raters' are said to make for more valid feedback than single-source rating.[103]
- Advanced computer network technology (the Internet and company Intranets) now facilitates multiple-rater systems.[104]
- Bottom-up feedback meshes nicely with the trend toward participative management and employee empowerment.
- Co-workers and subordinates are said to know more about a professional's strengths and limitations than the boss.[105]

Together, these factors make a compelling case for looking at other ways to give and receive performance feedback.

UPWARD FEEDBACK

Upward feedback stands the traditional approach on its head by having subordinates provide feedback on a superior's style and performance. This type of feedback is generally anonymous. Most students are familiar with upward feedback programmes from years of filling out anonymous lecturer-evaluation surveys.

Upward feedback subordinates evaluate their boss

Superiors typically resist upward feedback programmes because they believe it erodes their authority. Other critics say anonymous upward feedback can become little more than a personality contest, or worse, the system can be manipulated by superiors making promises or threats.[106] The question of whether upward feedback should be anonymous was addressed by a study at a large insurance company. All told, 183 employees rated the skills and effectiveness of 38 superiors. Those who receive open feedback from their (named) employees viewed the process more positively than the ones who receive feedback anonymously. However, employees felt less comfortable doing this and tended to be more lenient in their assessment. This finding confirmed the criticism of the system which states that employees will tend to go easier on their boss when not protected by confidentiality.[107]

In another study, 83 supervisors were divided into three feedback groups: (a) group 1: feedback from both superiors and subordinates; (b) group 2: feedback from superiors only; and (c) group 3: feedback from subordinates only. Group 1 was most satisfied with the overall evaluation process and responded more positively to upward feedback. Group 3 expressed more concern that subordinate appraisals would undermine supervisors' authority and that supervisors would focus on pleasing subordinates.[108]

In a field study of 238 corporate managers, upward feedback had a positive impact on the performance of low to moderate performers.[109] A longitudinal study of upward feedback found that repeated upward feedback from subordinates to their bosses had a lasting positive effect on performance.[110]

These research findings suggest the practical value of anonymous upward feedback used in combination with other sources of performance feedback and evaluation. Because of a superior's resistance and potential manipulation, using upward feedback as the primary determinant for promotions and pay decisions is not recommended. Carefully collected upward feedback is useful for setting up development programmes.[111]

360-DEGREE FEEDBACK

The concept of **360-degree feedback** involves letting individuals compare their own perceived performance with that of behaviourally specific (and usually anonymous) performance information supplied by their superior, subordinates and peers. Even outsiders, like customers, may be involved in what is sometimes called 'full-circle' feedback. Research, however, indicates that, even when 360-degree feedback is implemented it is often more accurate to describe it as 270-degree feedback, because often customers are not included as a data source.[112]

The idea is to let people know how their behaviour affects others, with the goal of motivating change. The 360-degree approach recognises that little change can be expected without feedback and that different sources can provide rich and useful information to professionals to guide their behaviour. In a 360-degree feedback programme, a given professional will play different roles, including focal person, superior, subordinate and peer. Of course, the focal person role is played only once. The other roles are played in relation to other focal individuals.[113] Looking at the practice of different companies, apparently 360-degree feedback can be used for a number of purposes. Consider the various applications in the following organisations.[114]

360-degree feedback
comparison of anonymous feedback from one's superior, subordinates and peers, with one's self-perceptions

> The British Automobile Association worked out some new standards. With 360-degree feedback employees are now screened to see whether they meet these standards. Aside from their results, employees also receive a 'development guide', containing tips from supervisors, subordinates and colleagues to tackle certain weaknesses. This process is again guided by those who give the feedback. According to the company's HR manager, this system has been proven to be very effective. 'I see a lot of employees who really place a high value on their evaluations and who do things in a different way now', he says.
>
> Baxter Healthcare uses a questionnaire to check whether employees are following the ethical values outlined by the company. Each individual obtains an evaluation containing the opinions of many people within the organisation on the degree to which he or she works according to the company's ethics.
>
> Avon Rubber Company uses 360-degree feedback as a teambuilding tool. Employees are evaluated by their fellow team members on aspects such as openness and co-operation and are given some useful behavioural remarks to improve their functioning within the team.

Research findings

Rigorous research evidence of 360-degree feedback programmes is scarce. In their review article on multi-rater feedback systems, Jansen and Vloeberghs conclude that there is ample evidence concerning the individual level, but little adequate research on the organisational conditions and effects.[115]

Because upward feedback is part of 360-degree feedback programmes, the evidence reviewed earlier applies here as well. As with upward feedback, the peer- and self-evaluations that are central to 360-degree feedback programmes, are also a significant affront to tradition, but advocates insist that co-workers and superiors are appropriate performance evaluators because they are closest to the action. Generally, research builds a strong case for using peer appraisals.[116] Self-serving bias (discussed in Chapter 4) can be a problem with self-ratings. However, it might be important to train people in how to observe, judge and record other people's behaviour because peer appraisals are also not free of certain biases.[117] Some people suggest supplementing the results of a 360-degree feedback process with feedback of other 'more objective' sources, obtained for instance with assessment centre methods.[118]

A two-year study of 48 professionals given 360-degree feedback led to these somewhat promising results. According to the researchers: 'The group as a whole developed its skills but there was substantial variability among individuals in how much change occurred'.[119] Thus, as with any feedback, individuals vary in their response to 360-degree feedback. London and Smither also identified different reactions of the so-called focal person on the feedback: some employees completely neglect the feedback, others only take positive feedback into account, still others are only motivated by negative feedback or they are only interested in feedback which is given by someone who is really considered as important (e.g. the supervisor).[120]

Practical implications

Our recommendations for upward feedback, favouring anonymity[121] and discouraging linkage to pay and promotion decisions, also apply to 360-degree feedback programmes. In a follow-up survey among subordinates several months after upward feedback given to their supervisor, 24 per cent of the respondents indicated that they would have rated their boss differently if the feedback had not been anonymous. The same survey also revealed that 34 per cent of employees would have rated their bosses differently if the feedback had been used for the bosses' performance appraisal.[122] Using 360-degree feedback for appraisal or for development affects the attitudes of the subordinates and the nature of the process itself.

Developing effective 360-degree programmes is not a quick-and-easy fix, as some advocates would have us believe. It involves several interconnected steps, like describing and communicating the purpose of the 360-degree programme, developing a survey or other measuring method (survey is the most commonly used method, although alternative methods like focus groups are also used), writing a report, distributing the results and following up the improvement.[123] Table 6.6 summarises some conditions for the effective implementation of 360-degree feedback in organisations.

TABLE 6.6 ORGANISATIONAL CONDITIONS FOR 360-DEGREE FEEDBACK

1	Top management should be involved, both in the role of rater and in the role of focal person
2	Complement the results of peer- and self-appraisals with additional data from assessment centre methods
3	Involve the users in the design of the 360-degree process
4	Involve the users in the choice of peers and others who will be rating their skills, behaviour and outcomes
5	Anonymity and confidence of the feedback must be guaranteed, so the focal person remains the final owner of the data
6	Be careful in coupling multi-rater feedback systems with regular appraisal systems
7	Make sure the instrument is tested for coherence, and that it is scored, interpreted and reported following a research-based procedure

SOURCE: Adapted from P. Jansen and D. Vloeberghs, 'Multi-Rater Feedback Methods: Personal and Organizational Implications', *Journal of Managerial Psychology*, October 1999, pp. 45–7; and R. Lepsinger, D. Anntoinette and D. Lucia, *The Art and Science of 360° Feedback* (San Francisco, CA: Pfeiffer, 1997).

Organisational reward systems

Rewards are an ever-present and always controversial feature of organisational life.[124] The large changes in compensation practices, combined with other factors like increased competition for the best employees, reduced employee loyalty, increased employee pay information and enhanced variability in pay practices, make compensation and organisational reward systems a matter of great interest to organisations and employees.[125]

Some employees see their jobs as the source of a pay cheque and little else. Others derive great pleasure from their jobs and association with co-workers. Even volunteers who donate their time to charitable organisations, such as the Red Cross, walk away with rewards in the form of social recognition and the pride of having given unselfishly of their time. Hence, the subject of organisational rewards includes, but goes far beyond, monetary compensation.[126] This section examines key components of organisational reward systems. Despite the fact that reward systems vary widely, it is possible to identify and interrelate some common components. The model in Figure 6.7 focuses on four important components, which we will now examine.

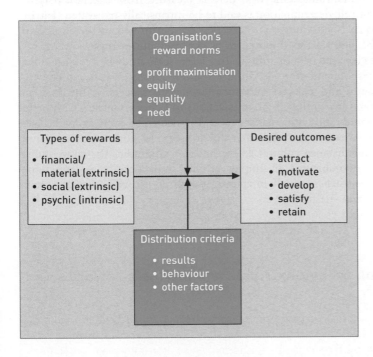

FIGURE 6.7 A GENERAL MODEL OF ORGANISATIONAL REWARD SYSTEMS

Types of reward

The variety and magnitude of organisational rewards is bewildering – from subsidised day care to education subsidies to stock options, from boxes of chocolates to golf club membership. In addition to the obvious pay and benefits, there are less obvious social and psychic rewards. Social rewards include praise and recognition from others both inside and outside the organisation. Psychic rewards come from personal feelings of self-esteem, self-satisfaction and accomplishment.

> A large-scale national study from the Chartered Institute of Personnel and Development (CIPD) on reward management (572 organisations took part, employing around 1.5 million people) revealed a wide range of rewards that are used in British companies. Most employers have some form of pension plan. The survey also finds a widespread use of variable pay (although more in the private than in the public sector). The most common way of variable pay is to link these cash amounts to an assessment of individual perform- ance, although other popular approaches include linking them to company profit or team performance. A large proportion of British employers offers access to an employee

> share-ownership scheme. This amount did not seem to be affected by three years of stock market falls. Other benefits, beside pensions, also are very important, with special attention for family-friendly benefits (like childcare vouchers, subsidised crèche facilities, enhanced maternity/paternity leave) and well-being benefits (like private healthcare, critical illness insurance, employee assistance). Another common practice is the use of flexible benefits (also known as cafeteria benefits or flex plan), which includes all kinds of arrangements that give employees a choice over the mix of cash and benefits they receive (like choosing between a car or additional cash).[127]

Extrinsic rewards
financial, material or social rewards from the environment

Intrinsic rewards
self-granted, psychic rewards

Extrinsic motivation
being motivated by extrinsic rewards

Intrinsic motivation
being motivated by intrinsic rewards

An alternative typology for organisational rewards is the distinction between extrinsic and intrinsic rewards.[128] Financial, material and social rewards qualify as **Extrinsic rewards** because they come from the environment. Psychic rewards, however, are **Intrinsic rewards** because they are self-granted. An employee who works to obtain extrinsic rewards, such as money or praise, is said to be extrinsically motivated (**Extrinsic motivation**). One who derives pleasure from the task itself or experiences a sense of competence or self-determination is said to be intrinsically motivated (**Intrinsic motivation**). Intrinsically motivated behaviours are those that are performed in the absence of any apparent external contigency.[129] The relative importance of extrinsic and intrinsic rewards is a matter of culture and personal tastes (see the next Snapshot). In a large-scale study in a multinational manufacturing company (107 292 respondents from 49 countries) a relationship was found between valuing intrinsic or extrinsic rewards and cultural and socio-economic aspects.[130] Intrinsic job characteristics were valued higher (and led to higher job satisfaction) in richer countries, with better governmental social welfare programmes and with smaller power distance and a more individualistic culture (see dimensions of Hofstede, Chapter 16), while they did not seem to work in countries with low social security and a large power distance culture. These findings contradict the conventional wisdom that intrinsic rewards are desirable for all employees. So, implementing organisational reward systems that overemphasise intrinsic rewards in countries with poor social security systems and a large power distance culture can be ineffective.

snapshot

Foreign employers rely on unique extrinsic and intrinsic rewards in China

In spite of all the complications for foreign employers, one advantage they do have is that the Chinese like working for them because it gives the workers status. As one individual reported, 'work for a joint venture and I report to a foreign boss – this is cool'. Also, it usually means that they get to practise their English and learn about life and cultures outside China. I was told of good employees quitting when they had been assigned to a local Chinese boss.

For foreign firms, the other big attraction that can keep mainland Chinese anchored to the desk for some time is the chance to travel abroad, particularly for training. Although it is not always easy to get exit permits for people, at least for any length of time, it is an increasing trend. Typically, Chinese nationals are being trained in Singapore, Australia, New Zealand and the US. The main advantage of training employees abroad is that it buys some time, and companies usually link overseas development assignments to an agreement with individuals to stay with the company for two to three years after they return.

An example of this is Johnson & Johnson's executive MBA program with the University of Singapore. Twenty of its own staff and ten from its distributors take part in a three-year program that costs upwards of $20 000 per person. This kind of investment gives foreign companies a good reputation (which means local talent will be quick to join), and in China, good news travels fast around the cadre of highly qualified personnel.

SOURCE: Excerpted from M. Johnson, 'Beyond Pay: What Rewards Work Best When Doing Business in China', *Compensation & Benefits Review*, November–December 1998, p. 54.

Organisation's reward norms

As discussed earlier (equity theory), the employer–employee linkage can be viewed as an exchange relationship. Employees exchange their time and talent for rewards. Ideally, four alternative norms dictate the nature of this exchange. In pure form, each would lead to a significantly different reward distribution system. These four norms – profit maximisation, equity, equality and need – are defined as follows.

■ *Profit maximisation*. The objective of each party is to maximise its net gain, regardless of how the other party fares. A profit-maximising company would attempt to pay the lowest level of wages for maximum effort. Conversely, a profit-maximising employee would seek maximum rewards, regardless of the organisation's financial well-being, and leave the organisation for a better deal.

■ *Equity*. According to the Reward equity norm, rewards should be allocated in proportion to contributions. Those who contribute the most should be rewarded the most. A cross-cultural study of American, Japanese and Korean college students led the researchers to conclude: 'Equity is probably a phenomenon common to most cultures, but its strength will vary'.[131] Basic principles of fairness and justice, evident in most cultures, drive the equity norm.

■ *Equality*. The Reward equality norm calls for rewarding all parties equally, regardless of their comparative contributions. Because absolute equality does not exist in today's hierarchical organisations, researchers recently explored the impact of pay inequality. They looked at pay dispersion (the pay gap between high-level and low-level employees). Result: the smaller the pay gap, the better the individual and organisational performance.[132] Thus, the outlandish compensation packages of many of today's top executives is not only a widely debated moral issue, it is a productivity issue as well (also see Chapter 18).[133]

■ *Need*. This norm calls for distributing rewards according to employees' needs rather than their contributions.[134]

> **Reward equity norm**
> rewards should be tied to contributions
>
> **Reward equality norm**
> everyone should get the same rewards

A pair of researchers concluded, in the following paragraph, that these contradictory norms are typically intertwined:

> " We propose that employer–employee exchanges are governed by the contradictory norms of profit maximisation, equity, equality and need. These norms can coexist; what varies is the extent to which the rules for correct application of a norm are clear and the relative emphasis different managements will give to certain norms in particular allocations.[135] "

Conflict and ethical debates often arise over the perceived fairness of reward allocations because of disagreement about reward norms.[136] The existence of different reward allocation norms questions the generalisability of the equity theory. Individual differences and social and political-economic contexts might explain different reactions to inequity and different preferences for reward norms.[137] Stockholders, for instance, might prefer a profit-maximisation norm, while technical specialists would like an equity norm, and unionised hourly workers would argue for a pay system based on equality. A reward norm anchored to need might prevail in a family-owned and family-operated business. Research also investigated cultural differences between reward allocation preferences, but results are not consistent and clear-cut.[138]

Effective reward systems are based on clear and consensual exchange norms. Taking into account individual preference for reward-allocation norms and social, cultural and political-economic contexts when implementing a reward system might enhance people's job satisfaction and motivation. Pay and reward systems that are effective in motivating people in one context might be met with hostility, perceptions of inequity and dissatisfaction in an environment where other values and norms predominate.[139]

Reward distribution criteria

According to one expert on organisational reward systems, there are three general criteria for the distribution of rewards:

■ Performance: results. Tangible outcomes such as individual, group or organisation performance; quantity and quality of performance.

■ Performance: actions and behaviours. For example, teamwork, co-operation, risk taking, creativity.
■ Non-performance considerations. Customary or contractual, where the type of job, nature of the work, equity, tenure, level in the hierarchy and so forth are rewarded.[140]

A review of recent studies on organisational compensation practices also revealed that factors other than individual productivity generally influence compensation decisions, such as own salary increases, performance of a whole group or organisational changes in business strategy.[141]

Desired outcomes of the reward system

As listed in Figure 6.7, a good reward system should attract talented people and motivate and satisfy them once they have joined the organisation.[142] Further, a good reward system should foster personal growth and development and keep talented people from leaving.

Despite huge investments of time and money in organisational reward systems, often the desired motivational impact is not achieved.[143] A management consultant/writer offered the following eight reasons:

■ Too much emphasis on monetary rewards.
■ Rewards lack an 'appreciation effect'.
■ Extensive benefits become entitlements.
■ Counter-productive behaviour is rewarded. (For example, a pizza delivery company related its rewards to the 'on time' performance of its drivers, only to discover that it was inadvertently rewarding reckless driving.)[144]
■ Too long a delay between performance and rewards.
■ Too many one-size-fits-all rewards.
■ Use of one-shot rewards with a short-lived motivational impact.
■ Continued use of demotivating practices such as lay-offs, across-the-board pay rises and cuts and excessive executive compensation.[145]

These stubborn problems have fostered a growing interest in more effective reward and compensation practices, like different pay-for-performance systems.[146]

Research findings

There are several issues to consider when deciding on the relative balance between monetary and non-monetary rewards. First, some research shows that employees value interesting work and recognition more than money.[147] For instance, saying 'thank you' is a significant reward to many people. Second, extrinsic rewards can lose their motivating properties over time and may undermine intrinsic motivation.[148] This conclusion, however, must be balanced by the fact that performance is related to the receipt of financial incentives, although research found mixed results concerning the performance-enhancing effect of incentives.[149] A recent meta-analysis of 39 studies involving 2773 people showed that financial incentives were positively related to performance quantity but not to performance quality. Another recent study showed that the promise of a financial reward increased children's creativity when they knew that there was an explicit positive relationship between creative performance and rewards. Another study found out that the perceived attractiveness of a task could influence the performance-pay relationship.[150] Third, monetary rewards must be large enough to generate motivation.[151] For example, Steven Kerr, chief learning officer at Goldman Sachs Group, estimates that monetary awards must be at least 12 to 15 per cent above employees' base pay to truly motivate people.[152] Unfortunately, this percentage is well above the typical salary increase received by employees.

The use of monetary incentives to motivate employees is seldom questioned. Unfortunately, recent research uncovered some negative consequences when goal achievement is linked to individual incentives. Case studies, for example, reveal that pay should not be linked to goal achievement unless the following conditions are satisfied:

■ Performance goals are under the employees' control.
■ Goals are quantitative and measurable.
■ Frequent, relatively large payments are made for performance achievement.[153]

Goal-based incentive systems are more likely to produce undesirable effects if these three conditions are not satisfied. Moreover, empirical studies demonstrated that goal-based bonus incentives produced higher commitment to easy goals and lower commitment to difficult goals. People were reluctant to commit to difficult goals that were tied to monetary incentives. People with high goal commitment also offered less help to their co-workers when they received goal-based bonus incentives to accomplish difficult individual goals. Individuals neglected aspects of the job that were not covered in the performance goals.

> For example, a sales consultant who works for a national retail store and is paid an hourly rate plus a commission tied to achieving sales goals indicates that the salespeople who make the most sales and receive the greatest commissions are those who focus on their own self-interests. Rather than engaging in behaviour that promotes outstanding customer service (such as keeping the salesfloor straightened up and clean, taking the time to ring up small cash sales, writing up sales for colleagues who are missing from the floor, following up with customers to ensure that they received their merchandise in a timely manner and sending thank-you notes), these individuals focus on maximising their personal monetary sales at the expense of customer service for the store at large.[154]

As another case in point, several studies revealed that quality suffered when employees were given quantity goals.[155] These findings underscore some of the dangers of using goal-based incentives, particularly for employees in complex, interdependent jobs requiring co-operation. Organisations need to consider the advantages, disadvantages and dilemmas of goal-based incentives prior to their implementation.[156]

Practical implications

How can employers improve the motivational impact of their current organisational reward plan? The fact is that most such plans are not pure types. They are hybrids. They combine features of several reward systems.[157] According to two experts organisational reward systems are necessarily complex, because they have to take several aspects into account. Reward systems simultaneously try to have strategic impact (this means leveraging motivation toward strategic actions) and to influence employee satisfaction and fairness.[158] Consider the case of Volvo Cars in Ghent (Belgium) as an example of a consistent organisational reward system:

> Volvo Cars considers their employees as one of four stakeholders, next to and at the same level of customers, shareholders and society. This means that giving satisfaction to employees is an important issue, not only through rewards, but in all aspects of work. How are they doing this? Through a consistent rewarding strategy Volvo Cars attempts to optimise performance and to recruit, develop and keep best talent. 'Volvo Cars Ghent, a business unit employing 3800 workers and 500 employees, focuses on consistently rewarding all employee categories', says HR-manager Hans Bogaert. 'Of course, rewards and benefits are different for workers, employees and management, but the underlying philosophy is the same. Our whole organisation at all levels is based on the teamwork principle, meaning that we attempt as much as possible to reward in a collective and consistent way. For instance, Volvo Cars globally organises a quality competition, leading to a bonus of 1000 dollars for a team member that reaches the finals. At Volvo Cars Ghent, we do not pay out this bonus individually. We save up all money, until we can give each team member €25 for a team activity. This approach did not influence motivation negatively, every edition of the Quality Award Volvo Cars Ghent has at least one team in the finals. We also consider employee satisfaction as a very important organisational goal that needs to be monitored and measured. Accordingly, we measure employee satisfaction twice yearly, including rewards and pay satisfaction. This measure usually reveals a high satisfaction for most aspects. We also have a low turnover rate at all levels, certainly at executive level.'[159]

Table 6.7 lists some practical recommendations that can help to build effective and fair organisational reward systems.

TABLE 6.7 ORGANISATIONAL PRACTICES TO STIMULATE A PERFORMANCE CULTURE

Mission and goals
- A well-articulated and clear mission and operating vision that is understood and accepted
- Organisational goals that are credible, measurable and verifiable
- Department, work unit and team goals that have a clear line of sight (connection) to the success of the organisation
- Individual goals or work measures that are intuitively related to good performance

Communication and feedback
- A pay philosophy that is clearly specified and communicated to employees
- Regular communication that keeps employees informed of performance results
- Regular feedback to employees to guide and encourage their growth and career progression
- Regular communication to recognise the importance of employee efforts and to make clear how their efforts contribute to the organisation's success

Organisational culture
- An organisational climate that encourages people to look for new and better ways to accomplish goals
- An organisational climate that stimulates people to pursue challenging goals
- An organisational climate that encourages people to tackle new problems and new tasks to accomplish organisational goals
- An organisational climate that emphasises the importance of the individual, his/her needs and aspirations
- Training and development that is seen as an investment in people
- An organisational climate where people have the opportunity to participate in the development of performance measures

Reward system
- A reward system that reinforces the importance of good performance at all levels, including both monetary and non-monetary rewards
- A reward system that is implemented in a fair and objective way, including an appeal process for people who believe they have been treated unjustly
- A reward system that encourages people to work together and co-operate, and that also creates opportunities to celebrate people's accomplishments

SOURCE: Adapted from H. Risher, 'Pay-for-Performance: The Keys to Making it Work', *Public Personnel Management*, Fall 2002, pp. 326–7; and K. M. Bartol and E. A. Locke, 'Incentives and Motivation', in *Compensation in Organizations: Current Research and Practice*, eds S. L. Rynes and B. Gerhart (San Francisco: Jossey-Bass, 2000), p. 124.

Putting motivational theories to work

It is clear from the previous and current chapter that motivating people is an important, although difficult to implement, issue for most organisations. Organisations cannot simply take one of the theories discussed in this book and apply it word for word. Dynamics within organisations interfere with applying motivation theories in 'pure' form. Moreover, although several theories exist that try to explain motivation, there are no ready-made and clear-cut solutions to deal effectively with employee motivation.[160] An all-including and ready-made motivation programme for organisations is also difficult to design. Because an all-encompassing theory of motivation does not exist (yet), organisations can try to create a stimulating and motivating work environment by implementing those aspects of existing theories that are useful and relevant for their particular work setting. We want to end the elaboration on motivation with raising some issues that need to be addressed before implementing a motivational programme. Our intent is not to discuss all relevant considerations but rather to highlight a few important ones.

The toughest job of professionals is probably to turn around people who have lost their motivation to make a positive contribution to the organisation. Professionals have an important task in creating an environment in which people can motivate themselves.[161] Contrary to a lot of popular perceptions, this does not need to be done with monetary incentives, bonuses and merit plans.[162] An important issue concerning organisational motivation is the distinction between motivation and recognition although these concepts are often mixed up.[163] Recognition through open communication, the ability to make a difference at work and a career development plan are as effective and important to motivate people.[164] Consider the example of Disneyland® Resort Paris:

> To improve motivation, morale and quality of service provided to visitors, France's Disneyland has launched 'Small World', named after one of its attractions. The whole idea is to improve motivation through a process of decentralising power, cutting down hierarchy and creating internal competition between different parts of the park – although with certain limits. The park's operations will be split into 'small world' units of 30 to 50 staff, headed by a manager. Each will be given greater responsibility and flexibility than in the past to meet three goals: to achieve management targets, to improve visitor satisfaction and to get to know and motivate staff. Small world managers will receive up to 10 per cent of their salary in bonuses linked to performance. Other staff will receive non-financial rewards, including improved promotion prospects.[165]

It is also clear from the description of several motivation theories that people are not motivated by the same aspects. Some people, for instance, attach a lot of value to money, while others are mainly motivated by growth opportunities. People also vary in their intensity and persistence of motivated behaviour. Importantly, organisations should not ignore these individual differences, because they are an important input that influences motivation and motivated behaviour. Organisations are advised to develop employees so that they have the ability and job knowledge to perform their jobs effectively. In addition, attempts should be made to nurture positive employee characteristics, such as self-esteem, self-efficacy, positive emotions, a learning goal orientation and need for achievement.

Because motivation is goal directed, the process of developing and setting goals should be consistent with our previous discussion. Moreover, the method used to evaluate performance also needs to be considered. Without a valid performance-appraisal system, it is difficult, if not impossible, to distinguish accurately good and poor performers. Organisations need to keep in mind that both equity and expectancy theory suggest that employee motivation is crushed by inaccurate performance ratings. Inaccurate ratings also make it difficult to evaluate the effectiveness of any motivational programme, so it is beneficial for organisations to assess the accuracy and validity of their appraisal systems.[166]

In keeping with expectancy theory, organisations should make rewards contingent on performance.[167] In doing so, it is important that they consider the accuracy and fairness of the reward system. The promise of increased rewards will not prompt greater effort and good performance unless those rewards are clearly tied to performance and they are large enough to gain employees' interest or attention. Moreover, equity theory tells us that motivation is influenced by employee perceptions about the fairness of reward allocations. Motivation is decreased when employees believe rewards are inequitably allocated. Rewards also need to be integrated appropriately into the appraisal system. If performance is measured at the individual level, individual achievements need to be rewarded. On the other hand, when performance is the result of group effort, rewards should be allocated to the group.

Feedback also needs to be linked to performance. Feedback provides the information and direction needed to keep employees focused on relevant tasks, activities and goals. Organisations should strive to provide specific, timely and accurate feedback to employees. Finally, an organisation's culture significantly influences employee motivation and behaviour. A positive self-enhancing culture is more likely to engender higher motivation and commitment than a culture dominated by suspicion, fault finding and blame.

Learning outcomes: Summary of key terms

1 Discuss the role of perceived inequity in employee motivation

Equity theory is a model of motivation that explains how people strive for fairness and justice in social exchanges. At work, feelings of (in)equity revolve around a person's evaluation of whether he or she receives adequate rewards to compensate for his or her contributive inputs. People perform these evaluations by comparing the perceived fairness of their employment exchange with that of relevant others. Perceived inequity creates motivation to restore equity.

2 Explain Vroom's expectancy theory of motivation and Porter and Lawler's extension of the expectancy theory

Expectancy theory assumes motivation is determined by one's perceived chances of achieving valued outcomes. Vroom's expectancy model of motivation reveals how both the effort → performance expectancies and the performance → outcome instrumentalities will influence the degree of effort expended to achieve desired (positively valent) outcomes. Porter and Lawler developed a model of expectancy that enlarged upon the theory proposed by Vroom. This model specifies (a) the source of people's valences and expectancies and (b) the relationship between performance and satisfaction.

3 Explain how goal setting motivates people and identify five practical lessons to be learned from goal-setting research

Goal-setting theory starts from the idea that people are motivated to reach goals. Goal setting provides four motivational mechanisms. It directs one's attention, regulates effort, increases persistence and encourages development of goal attainment strategies and action plans. Difficult goals lead to higher performance than easy or moderate ones. However, goals should not be impossible to achieve. Specific, difficult goals lead to higher performance for simple rather than complex tasks. Third, feedback enhances the effect of specific, difficult goals. Fourth, participative goals, assigned goals and self-set goals are equally effective. Fifth, goal commitment affects goal-setting outcomes.

4 Discuss how the recipient's characteristics, perception and cognitive evaluation affect how people process feedback

Self-esteem, self-efficacy, needs, goals and desire for feedback determine the recipient's openness to feedback. The individual's perception determines whether feedback is viewed positively or negatively. Cognitively, the recipient will tend to act on feedback that is seen as accurate, from a credible source, based on a fair system and tied to reasonable expectations and behavioural standards.

5 List at least three practical lessons from feedback research

Feedback is not automatically accepted as intended, especially negative feedback. A professional's credibility can be enhanced through expertise and a climate of trust. Feedback must neither be too frequent nor too scarce and must be tailored to the individual. Feedback accessed directly from computers is effective. Active participation in the feedback session helps people perceive feedback as more accurate.

6 List different types of organisational rewards

A wide variety of organisational rewards exist, like pension plans, pay-for-performance systems or different types of benefit (e.g. childcare vouchers, private healthcare). In addition to the obvious pay and benefits, there are less obvious social and psychic rewards. Social rewards include praise and recognition from others both inside and outside the organisation. Psychic rewards come from personal feelings of self-esteem, self-satisfaction and accomplishment. An alternative typology for organisational rewards is the distinction between extrinsic and intrinsic rewards. Financial, material and social rewards qualify as extrinsic rewards because they come from the environment. Psychic rewards, however, are intrinsic rewards because they are self-granted.

7 Describe practical recommendations to implement an organisational reward system
Organisational reward systems usually combine several types of rewards to simultaneously try to have strategic impact (this means leveraging motivation toward strategic actions) and to influence employee satisfaction and fairness. To build an effective and fair organisational reward system, it is important to: (a) make the organisational reward system an integral part of the organisation's mission and goals; (b) communicate regularly and clearly about the system to all employees; (c) stimulate a performance culture; and (d) implement the system in a fair and objective way.

8 Specify issues that should be addressed before implementing a motivational programme
Successfully designing and implementing motivational programmes is not easy. Organisations cannot simply take one of the theories discussed in this book and apply it word for word. Dynamics within organisations interfere with applying motivation theories in 'pure' form. However, organisations need to understand the motivation process if they are to successfully guide employees toward accomplishing organisational objectives. Because an all-encompassing theory of motivation does not exist (yet), organisations can try to create a stimulating and motivating work environment by implementing those aspects of existing theories that are useful and relevant for their particular work setting. Professionals have an important task in creating an environment in which people can motivate themselves, through rewards and recognition. Also important to keep in mind is that motivation is only one of several factors that influence performance and that individual differences influence motivation and motivated behaviour.

Review questions

1 Could a professional's attempt to treat his or her employees equally lead to perceptions of inequity? Explain.
2 What work outcomes (refer to Table 6.1) are most important to you? Do you think different age groups value different outcomes? What are the implications for organisations who attempt to be equitable?
3 What is your definition of studying hard? What is your expectancy for earning an A in the next exam in this course? What is the basis of this expectancy?
4 If someone who reported to you at work had a low expectancy for successful performance, what could you do to increase this?
5 Do goals play an important role in your life? Explain.
6 Goal-setting research suggests that people should be given difficult goals. How does this prescription mesh with expectancy theory? Explain.
7 How could a lecturer use equity, expectancy and goal setting theory to motivate students?
8 Relative to your course work, which of the three sources of feedback – others, task, self – has the greatest impact on your performance? If you have a job, which source of feedback is most potent in that situation?
9 Which of the four organisational reward norms do you prefer? Why?
10 What is your personal experience with failed organisational reward systems and practices?

Personal awareness and growth exercise

What kind of feedback are you getting?

Objectives

1 To provide actual examples of on-the-job feedback from three primary sources: organisation/supervisor, co-workers and self/task.

2 To provide a handy instrument for evaluating the comparative strength of positive feedback from these three sources.

Introduction

A pair of researchers from Georgia Tech developed and tested a 63-item feedback questionnaire to demonstrate the importance of both the sign and content of feedback messages.[168] Although their instrument contains both positive and negative feedback items, we have extracted 18 positive items for this self-awareness exercise.

Instructions

Thinking of your current job (or your most recent job), circle one number for each of the 18 items. Alternatively, you could ask one or more employed individuals to complete the questionnaire for you. Once the questionnaire has been completed, calculate subtotal and total scores by adding the circled numbers. Then try to answer the discussion questions.

Instrument

How frequently do you experience each of the following outcomes in your present (or past) job?

Organisational/supervisory feedback

	Rarely	Occasionally		Very frequently
1 My supervisor complimenting me on something I have done.	1	2	3	4	5
2 My supervisor increasing my responsibilities.	1	2	3	4	5
3 The company expressing pleasure with my performance.	1	2	3	4	5
4 The company giving me a pay rise.	1	2	3	4	5
5 My supervisor recommending me for a promotion or pay rise.	1	2	3	4	5
6 The company providing me with favourable data concerning my performance.	1	2	3	4	5

Subscore = _____

Co-worker feedback

	Rarely	Occasionally		Very frequently
7 My co-workers coming to me for advice.	1	2	3	4	5
8 My co-workers expressing approval of my work.	1	2	3	4	5
9 My co-workers liking to work with me.	1	2	3	4	5
10 My co-workers telling me that I am doing a good job.	1	2	3	4	5
11 My co-workers commenting favourably on something I have done.	1	2	3	4	5
12 Receiving a compliment from my co-workers.	1	2	3	4	5

Subscore = _____

Self/task feedback

		Rarely		Occasionally		Very frequently
13	Knowing that the way I go about my duties is superior to most.	1	2	3	4	5
14	Feeling I am accomplishing more than I used to.	1	2	3	4	5
15	Knowing that I can now perform or do things that previously were difficult for me.	1	2	3	4	5
16	Finding that I am satisfying my own standards for 'good work'.	1	2	3	4	5
17	Knowing that what I am doing 'feels right'.	1	2	3	4	5
18	Feeling confident of being able to handle all aspects of my job.	1	2	3	4	5

Subscore = _____

Total Score = _____

Questions for discussion

1 Which items on this questionnaire would you rate as primarily instructional in function? Are all of the remaining items primarily motivational? Explain.
2 In terms of your own feedback profile, which of the three types is the strongest (has the highest subscore)? Which is the weakest (has the lowest subscore)? How well does your feedback profile explain your job performance and/or satisfaction?
3 How does your feedback profile measure up against those of the other students? (Arbitrary norms, for comparative purposes, are: Deficient feedback = 18–42; Moderate feedback = 43–65; Abundant feedback = 66–90.)
4 Which of the three sources of feedback is most critical to your successful job performance and/or job satisfaction? Explain.

Group exercise

Rewards, rewards, rewards

Objectives

1 To tap the class's collective knowledge of organisational rewards.
2 To appreciate the vast array of potential rewards.
3 To contrast individual and group perceptions of rewards.
4 To practise your group creativity skills.

Introduction

Rewards are a centrepiece of organisational life. Both extrinsic and intrinsic rewards motivate us to join and continue contributing to organised effort. But not all rewards have the same impact on work motivation. Individuals have their own personal preferences for rewards. The best way to discover people's reward preferences is to ask them, both individually and collectively. This group brainstorming and class discussion exercise requires about 20 to 30 minutes.

Instructions

Your lecturer will divide your class randomly into teams of five to eight people. Each team will go through the following four-step process.

1 Each team will have a six-minute brainstorming session, with one person acting as recorder. The objective of this brainstorming session is to list as many different organisational rewards as the group can think of. Your team might find it helpful to think of rewards by category (such as rewards arising from the work itself, those you can spend, those you eat and drink, feel, wear, share, cannot see, etc.). Keep in mind that good brainstorming calls on you to withhold

judgements about whether ideas are good or not. Quantity is what's wanted. Building upon other people's ideas is encouraged too (see Chapter 12 for more on brainstorming).

2 Next, each individual will take four minutes to write down, in decreasing order of importance, 10 rewards they want from the job. *Note:* These are your personal preferences (your 'top 10' rewards that will motivate you to do your best).

3 Each team will then take five minutes to generate a list of 'today's 10 most powerful rewards'. List them in decreasing order of their power to motivate job performance. Voting may be necessary.

4 A general class discussion of the questions listed below will conclude the exercise.

Questions for discussion

1 How did your personal 'top 10' list compare with your group's 'top 10' list? If there is a serious mismatch, how would it affect your motivation? (To promote discussion, the lecturer may ask several volunteers to read their personal 'top 10' lists to the class.)

2 Which team had the most productive brainstorming session? (The lecturer may request each team to read its brainstormed list of potential rewards and 'top 10' list to the class.)

3 Were you surprised to hear certain rewards getting so much attention? Why?

4 How can organisations improve the incentive effect of the rewards most frequently mentioned in class?

Internet exercise

This chapter discussed how employee motivation is influenced by goal setting and the relationship between performance and rewards. We also reviewed the variety of issues that organisations should consider when implementing motivational programmes. The purpose of this exercise is for you to examine the motivational techniques used by organisations. Visit our website www.mcgraw-hill.co.uk/textbooks/buelens for suggestions of organisations and further instructions.

Notes

1 Excerpted from C. Ghosn, 'Saving the Business Without Losing the Company', *Harvard Business Review*, January 2002, pp. 39–40.

2 M. London, H. H. Larsen and L. N. Thisted, 'Relationships between Feedback and Self-Development', *Group & Organization Management*, March 1999, pp. 5–27.

3 L. Festinger, *A Theory of Cognitive Dissonance* (Stanford, CA: Stanford University Press, 1957).

4 Retaliation in response to perceived injustice was investigated by D. P. Skarlicki and R. Folger, 'Retaliation in the Workplace: The Roles of Distributive, Procedural, and Interactional Justice', *Journal of Applied Psychology*, June 1997, pp. 434–43.

5 J. S. Adams, 'Inequity in Social Exchange', in *Advances in Experimental Social Psychology, vol. 2*, ed. L. Berkowitz (New York: Academic Press, 1965), pp. 267–99.

6 For more details, see J. Bulman, 'Patterns of Pay: Results of the 2003 New Earnings Survey', *Labour Market Trends*, December 2003, pp. 601–12.

7 'Prison Health Care Failing', *BBC Online News*, 28 October 1998, www.news.bbc.co.uk. See also D. Ramsbotham, *Prisongate: The Shocking State of Britain's Prisons and The Need for Visionary Change* (New York: The Free Press, 2003).

8 Adapted from a discussion in R. L. Opsahl and M. Dunette, 'The Role of Financial Compensation in Industrial Motivation', *Psychological Bulletin*, August 1966, pp. 94–118.

9 The generalisability of the equity norm was examined by S. S. K. Lam, J. Schaubroeck and S. Aryee, 'Relationship between Organizational Justice and Employee Work Outcomes: A Cross-National Study', *Journal of Organizational Behavior*, February 2002, pp. 1–18; and J. K. Giacobbe-Miller, D. J. Miller and V. I. Victorov, 'A Comparison of Russian and US Pay Allocation Decisions, Distributive Justice Judgments, and Productivity Under Different Payment Conditions', *Personnel Psychology*, Spring 1998, pp. 137–63.

10 The choice of a comparison person is discussed by P. P. Shah, 'Who Are Employees' Social Referents? Using a

Network Perspective to Determine Referent Others', *Academy of Management Journal*, June 1998, pp. 249–68; and J. Greenberg and C. L. McCarty, 'Comparable Worth: A Matter of Justice', in *Research in Personnel and Human Resources Management, vol. 8*, eds G. R. Ferris and K. M. Rowland (Greenwich, CT: JAI Press, 1990), pp. 265–303.

11 For more details, see D. C. Feldman and H. I. Doerpinghaus, 'Patterns of Part-Time Employment', *Journal of Vocational Behavior*, December 1992, pp. 282–94. See also T. J. Thorsteinson, 'Job Attitudes of Part-Time vs. Full-Time Workers: A Meta-Analytic Review', *Journal of Occupational and Organizational Psychology*, June 2003, pp. 151–77.

12 C. Lee and J.-L. Farh, 'The Effects of Gender in Organizational Justice Perception', *Journal of Organizational Behavior*, January 1999, pp. 133–43; and L. A. Witt and L. G. Nye, 'Gender and the Relationship between Perceived Fairness of Pay or Promotion and Job Satisfaction', *Journal of Applied Psychology*, December 1992, pp. 910–17.

13 For an overview of laboratory experiments to test equity theory, see M. R. Carrell and J. E. Ditrich, 'Equity Theory: The Recent Literature, Methodological Considerations, and New Directions', *Academy of Management Review*, April 1978, pp. 202–10.

14 Results can be found in R. W. Griffeth, R. P. Vecchio and J. W. Logan, Jr, 'Equity Theory and Interpersonal Attraction', *Journal of Applied Psychology*, June 1989, pp. 394–401; and R. P. Vecchio, 'Predicting Worker Performance in Inequitable Settings', *Academy of Management Review*, January 1982, pp. 103–10.

15 J. Greenberg, 'Stealing in the Name of Justice: Informational and Interpersonal Moderators of Theft Reactions to Underpayment Inequity', *Organizational Behavior and Human Decision Process*, February 1993, pp. 81–103.

16 C. R. Wanberg, L. W. Bunce and M. B. Gavin, 'Perceived Fairness of Layoffs among Individuals Who Have Been Laid Off: A Longitudinal Study', *Personnel Psychology*, Spring 1999, pp. 59–84.

17 M. A. Korsgaard, L. Roberson and R. D. Rymph, 'What Motivates Fairness? The Role of Subordinate Assertive Behavior on Manager's Interactional Fairness', *Journal of Applied Psychology*, October 1998, pp. 731–44.

18 The role of equity in organisational change is thoroughly discussed by A. T. Cobb, R. Folger and K. Wooten, 'The Role Justice Plays in Organizational Change', *Public Administration Quarterly*, Summer 1995, pp. 135–51.

19 A comparison of individual and group perceptions of justice was conducted by E. A. Lind, L. Kray and L. Thompson, 'The Social Comparison of Injustice: Fairness Judgments in Response to Own and Others' Unfair Treatment by Authorities', *Organizational Behavior and Human Decision Processes*, July 1998, pp. 1–22.

20 The legal issues of pay equity and employment at-will are discussed by M. Adams, 'Fair and Square', *HR Magazine*, May 1999, pp. 38–44; and B. B. Dunford and D. J. Devine, 'Employment At-Will and Employee Discharge: A Justice Perspective on Legal Action Following Termination', *Personnel Psychology*, Winter 1998, pp. 903–34.

21 Results can be found in K. W. Mossholder, N. Bennett and C. L. Martin, 'A Multilevel Analysis of Procedural Justice Context', *Journal of Organizational Behavior*, March 1998, pp. 131–41.

22 The relationship between organizational justice and customer service is discussed by D. E. Bowen, S. W. Gilliland and R. Folger, 'HRM Service Fairness: How Being Fair with Employees Spills Over to Customers', *Organizational Dynamics*, Winter 1999, pp. 7–23.

23 For a complete discussion of Vroom's theory, see V. H. Vroom, *Work and Motivation* (New York: John Wiley & Sons, 1964).

24 E. E. Lawler III, *Motivation in Work Organizations* (Belmont, CA: Wadsworth, 1973), p. 45.

25 R. G. Isaac, W. J. Zerbe and D. C. Pitt, 'Leadership and Motivation: The Effective Application of Expectancy Theory', *Journal of Managerial Issues*, Summer 2001, pp. 212–26; J. Chowdhury, 'The Motivational Impact of Sales Quotas on Effort', *Journal of Marketing Research*, February 1993, pp. 28–41; and C. C. Pinder, *Work Motivation* (Glenview, IL: Scott, Foresman, 1984), Ch. 7.

26 P. S. Kim, 'Strengthening the Pay-Performance Link in Government: A Case Study of Korea', *Public Personnel Management*, Winter 2002, pp. 447–63; R. Plachy and S. Plachy, 'Rewarding Employees Who Truly Make a Difference', *Compensation & Benefits Review*, May–June 1999, pp. 34–9; R. Ganzel, 'What's Wrong with Pay for Performance?', *Training*, December 1998, pp. 34–40; R. P. Semler, 'Making a Difference: Developing Management Incentives That Drive Results', *Compensation & Benefits Review*, July–August 1998, pp. 41–8; D. Barksdale, 'Leading Employees through the Variable Pay Jungle', *HR Magazine*, July 1998, pp. 111–18; and S. T. Johnson, 'Plan Your Organization's Reward Strategy through Pay-for-Performance Dynamics', *Compensation & Benefits Review*, May–June 1998, pp. 67–72.

27 For both sides of the 'Does money motivate?' debate, see B. Ettorre, 'Is Salary a Motivator?', *Management Review*, January 1999, p. 8; N. Gupta and J. D. Shaw, 'Let the Evidence Speak: Financial Incentives Are Effective!', *Compensation & Benefits Review*, March–April 1998, pp. 26, 28–32; and A. Kohn, 'Challenging Behaviorist Dogma: Myths about Money and Motivation', *Compensation & Benefits Review*, March–April 1998, pp. 27, 33–7.

28 A. D. Smith and W. T. Rupp, 'Knowledge Workers: Exploring the Link among Performance Rating, Pay and Motivational Aspects', *Journal of Knowledge Management*, March 2003, pp. 107–24.

29 The measurement and importance of valence was investigated by N. T. Feather, 'Values, Valences, and Choice: The Influence of Values on the Perceived Attractiveness and Choice of Alternatives', *Journal of Personality and Social Psychology*, June 1995, pp. 1135–51; and A. Pecotich and G. A. Churchill, Jr, 'An Examination of the Anticipated-Satisfaction Importance Valence Controversy', *Organizational Behavior and Human Performance*, April 1981, pp. 213–26.

30 H. Das, 'The Four Faces of Pay: An Investigation into How Canadian Managers View Pay', *International Journal of Commerce & Management*, March 2002, pp. 18–40.

31 P. Nolan, 'Make a Wish', *Potentials*, October 2000.

32 S. Trelford, 'Choice Rewards', *Marketing Week*, 24 June 1999, pp. 71–4.

33 Excerpted from 'Federal Express's Fred Smith', *Inc.*, October 1986, p. 38.

34 For a thorough discussion of the model, see L. W. Porter and E. E. Lawler III, *Managerial Attitudes and Performance* (Homewood, IL: Richard D. Irwin, 1968).

35 For an overview of recent research on expectancy theory, see R. G. Isaac, W. J. Zerbe and D. C. Pitt, 'Leadership and Motivation: The Effective Application of Expectancy Theory', *Journal of Managerial Issues*, Summer 2001, pp. 212–26.

36 Results can be found in W. van Eerde and H. Thierry, 'Vroom's Expectancy Models and Work-Related Criteria: A Meta-Analysis', *Journal of Applied Psychology*, October 1996, pp. 575–86.

37 J. P. Wanous, T. L. Keon and J. C. Latack, 'Expectancy Theory and Occupational/Organizational Choices: A Review and Test', *Organizational Behavior and Human Performance*, August 1983, pp. 66–86.

38 These results are based on T. K. DeBacker and R. M. Nelson, 'Variations on an Expectancy-Value Model of Motivation in Science', *Contemporary Educational Psychology*, April 1999, pp. 71–94; R. M. Lynd-Stevenson, 'Expectancy-Value Theory and Predicting Future Employment Status in the Young Unemployed', *Journal of Occupational and Organizational Psychology*, March 1999, pp. 101–6; A. W. Stacy, K. F. Widaman and G. A. Marlatt, 'Expectancy Models of Alcohol Use', *Journal of Personality and Social Psychology*, May 1990, pp. 918–28; A. J. Kinicki, 'Predicting Occupational Role Choices for Involuntary Job Loss', *Journal of Vocational Behavior*, October 1989, pp. 204–18; E. D. Pulakos and N. Schmitt, 'A Longitudinal Study of a Valence Model Approach for the Prediction of Job Satisfaction of New Employees', *Journal of Applied Psychology*, May 1983, pp. 307–12; T. A. DeCotiis and J.-Y. LeLouarn, 'A Predictive Study of Voting Behavior in a Representation Election Using Union Instrumentality and Work Perceptions', *Organizational Behavior and Human Performance*, February 1981, pp. 103–18; P. W. Hom, 'Expectancy Prediction of Reenlistment in the National Guard', *Journal of Vocational Behavior*, April 1980, pp. 235–48; and D. F. Parker and L. Dyer, 'Expectancy Theory as a Within-Person Behavioral Choice Model: An Empirical Test of Some Conceptual and Methodological Refinements', *Organizational Behavior and Human Performance*, October 1976, pp. 97–117.

39 For reviews of the criticisms of expectancy theory, see F. J. Landy and W. S. Becker, 'Motivation Theory Reconsidered', in *Research in Organizational Behavior, vol. 9*, eds L. L. Cummings and B. M. Staw (Greenwich, CT: JAI Press, 1987), pp. 1–38; and T. R. Mitchell, 'Expectancy Models of Job Satisfaction, Occupational Preference and Effort: A Theoretical, Methodological, and Empirical Appraisal', *Psychological Bulletin*, December 1974, pp. 1053–77.

40 Components of coaching are discussed by M. Fleschner, 'The Winning Season: How Legendary Wrestling Coach Dan Gable Built Championships to Last', *Selling Power*, April 1998, pp. 14, 16; and S. R. Levine, 'Performance Coaching: Great Coaching Skills Help Build a Team of Champions', *Selling Power*, July–August 1996, p. 46.

41 R. G. Isaac, W. J. Zerbe and D. C. Pitt, 'Leadership and Motivation: The Effective Application of Expectancy Theory', *Journal of Managerial Issues*, Summer 2001, pp. 217–18.

42 For a meta-analysis on the relationship between personality and motivation, see T. A. Judge and R. Ilies, 'Relationship of Personality to Performance Motivation: A Meta-Analytic Review', *Journal of Applied Psychology*, August 2002, pp. 797–807. Also see F. Herrera, 'Demystifying and Managing Expectations', *Employment Relations Today*, Summer 2003, pp. 21–8.

43 D. Daly and B. H. Kleiner, 'How to Motivate Problem Employees', *Work Study*, February 1995, pp. 5–7; and P. Karathanos, M. D. Pettypool and M. D. Troutt, 'Sudden Lost Meaning: A Catastrophe?', *Management Decision*, January 1994, pp. 15–19.

44 E. A. Locke, K. N. Shaw, L. M. Saari and G. P. Latham, 'Goal Setting and Task Performance: 1969–1980', *Psychological Bulletin*, July 1981, p. 126.

45 A thorough discussion of MBO is provided by P. F. Drucker, *The Practice of Management* (New York: Harper, 1954); and P. F. Drucker, 'What Results Should You Expect? A User's Guide to MBO', *Public Administration Review*, January–February 1976, pp. 12–19.

46 Results from both studies can be found in R. Rodgers and J. E. Hunter, 'Impact of Management by Objectives on Organizational Productivity', *Journal of Applied Psychology*, April 1991, pp. 322–36; and R. Rodgers, J. E. Hunter and D. L. Rogers, 'Influence of Top Management Commitment on Management Program Success', *Journal of Applied Psychology*, February 1993, pp. 151–5.

47 Adapted and translated from 'De dokter', *Vacature*, 17 March 2000.

48 M. Fleschner, 'How High Can You Fly', *Selling Power*, November–December 1995, p. 15.

49 Project planning is discussed by T. D. Conkright, 'So You're Going to Manage a Project . . .', *Training*, January 1998, pp. 62–7.

50 See, for instance, E. A. Locke and G. P. Latham, *Building a Practically Useful Theory of Goal Setting and Task Motivation* (Englewood Cliffs, NJ: Prentice Hall, 2002); and J. L. Austin and J. B. Vancouver, 'Goal Constructs in Psychology: Structure, Process and Content', *Psychological Bulletin*, November 1996, pp. 338–75. For a recent extension of the goal-setting theory with the role of time, see Y. Fried and L. H. Slowik, 'Enriching the Goal-Setting Theory with Time: An Integrated Approach', *Academy of Management Review*, July 2004, pp. 404–22.

51 See, for instance, E. Fang, R. W. Palmatier and K. R. Evans, 'Goal-Setting Paradoxes? Trade-Offs between Working Hard and Working Smart: The United States versus China', *Journal of The Academy of Marketing Science*, Spring 2004, pp. 188–202.

52 Results can be found in P. M. Wright, 'Operationalization of Goal Difficulty as a Moderator of the Goal Difficulty-Performance Relationship', *Journal of Applied Psychology*, June 1990, pp. 227–34.

53 This linear relationship was not supported by P. M. Wright, J. R. Hollenbeck, S. Wolf and G. C. McMahan, 'The Effects of Varying Goal Difficulty Operationalizations on Goal Setting Outcomes and Processes', *Organizational Behavior and Human Decision Processes*, January 1995, pp. 28–43.

54 J. Chowdbury, 'The Motivational Impact of Sales Quota on Effort', *Journal of Marketing Research*, February 1993, pp. 28–41.

55 E. Fang, R. W. Palmatier and K. R. Evans, 'Goal-Setting Paradoxes? Trade-Offs between Working Hard and Working Smart: The United States versus China', *Journal of The Academy of Marketing Science*, Spring 2004, pp. 188–202.

56 E. A. Locke, K. N. Shaw, L. M. Saari and G. P. Latham, 'Goal Setting and Task Performance: 1969–1980', *Psychological Bulletin*, July 1981, pp. 125–152; and A. J. Mento, R. P. Steel and R. J. Karren, 'A Meta-Analytic Study of the Effects of Goal Setting on Task Performance: 1966–1984', *Organizational Behavior and Human Decision Processes*, February 1987, pp. 52–83.

57 Results from the meta-analysis can be found in R. E. Wood, A. J. Mento and E. A. Locke, 'Task Complexity as a Moderator of Goal Effects: A Meta-Analysis', *Journal of Applied Psychology*, August 1987, pp. 416–25.

58 See the related discussion in L. A. King, 'Personal Goals and Personal Agency: Linking Everyday Goals to Future Images of the Self', in *Personal Control in Action: Cognitive and Motivational Mechanisms*, eds M. Kofta, G. Weary and G. Sedek (New York: Plenum Press, 1998), pp. 109–28.

59 See R. P. DeShon and R. A. Alexander, 'Goal Setting Effects on Implicit and Explicit Learning of Complex Tasks', *Organizational Behavior and Human Decision Processes*, January 1996, pp. 18–36.

60 Supportive results can be found in S. C. Selden and G. A. Brewer, 'Work Motivation in the Senior Executive Service: Testing the High Performance Cycle', *Journal of Public Administration Research and Theory*, July 2000, pp. 531–50; L. A. Wilk, 'The Effects of Feedback and Goal Setting on the Productivity and Satisfaction of University Admissions Staff', *Journal of Organizational Behavior Management*, Spring 1998, pp. 45–68; and K. L. Langeland, C. M. Johnson and T. C. Mawhinney, 'Improving Staff Performance in a Community Mental Health Setting: Job Analysis, Training, Goal Setting, Feedback, and Years of Data', *Journal of Organizational Behavior Management*, Spring 1998, pp. 21–43.

61 See E. A. Locke and G. P. Latham, *A Theory of Goal Setting and Task Performance* (Englewood Cliffs, NJ: Prentice-Hall, 1990).

62 J. A. Colquitt and M. J. Simmering, 'Conscientiousness, Goal Orientation, and Motivation to Learn During the Learning Process: A Longitudinal Study', *Journal of Applied Psychology*, August 1998, pp. 654–65.

63 J. W. Slocum, Jr, W. L. Cron and S. P. Brown, 'The Effect of Goal Conflict on Performance', *Journal of Leadership and Organizational Studies*, Summer 2002, p. 77.

64 See J. J. Donovan and D. J. Radosevich, 'The Moderating Role of Goal Commitment on the Goal Difficulty-Performance Relationship: A Meta-Analytic Review and Critical Reanalysis', *Journal of Applied Psychology*, April 1998, pp. 308–15.

65 D. S. Johnson and R. Perlow, 'The Impact of Need for Achievement Components on Goal Commitment and Performance', *Journal of Applied Social Psychology*, December 1992, pp. 1711–20; and M. C. Kernan and R. G. Lord, 'Effects of Valence, Expectations, and Goal-Performance Discrepancies in Single and Multiple Goal Environments', *Journal of Applied Psychology*, April 1990, pp. 194–203.

66 The benefits of benchmarking were examined by L. Mann, D. Samson and D. Dow, 'A Field Experiment on the Effects of Benchmarking and Goal Setting on Company Sales Performance', *Journal of Management*, no. 1, 1998, pp. 73–96.

67 S. Richbell, 'Trends and Emerging Values in Human Resource Management – The UK Scene', *International Journal of Manpower*, May 2001, pp. 261–8.

68 E. A. Locke, K. G. Smith, M. Erez, D. Chuh and A. Schaffer, 'The Effect of Intra-Individual Goal Conflict on Performance', *Journal of Management*, Spring 1994, pp. 67–91.

69 Based on a discussion in J. W. Slocum, Jr, W. L. Cron and S. P. Brown, 'The Effect of Goal Conflict on Performance', *Journal of Leadership and Organizational Studies*, Summer 2002, pp. 77–89.

70 J. W. Slocum, Jr, W. L. Cron and S. P. Brown, 'The Effect of Goal Conflict on Performance', *Journal of Leadership and Organizational Studies*, Summer 2002, pp. 77–89.

71 E. A. Locke and G. P. Latham, *A Theory of Goal Setting and Task Performance* (Englewood Cliffs, NJ: Prentice-Hall, 1990).

72 G. P. Latham and T. H. Seijts, 'The Effects of Personal and Distal Goals on Performance on a Moderately Complex Task', *Journal of Organizational Behavior*, July 1999, pp. 421–9.

73 E. A. Locke, 'Motivation, Cognition, and Action: An Analysis of Studies of Task Goals and Knowledge', *Applied Psychology: An International Review*, July 2000, pp. 408–29.

74 E. A. Locke and G. P. Latham, *Goal Setting: A Motivational Technique That Works!* (Englewood Cliffs, NJ: Prentice-Hall, 1984), p. 79.

75 Interesting reviews concerning the antecedents of goal commitment are H. Klein, M. Wesson, J. Hollenbeck and B. Alge, 'Goal Commitment and the Goal-Setting Process: Conceptual Clarification and Empirical Synthesis', *Journal of Applied Psychology*, December 1999, pp. 885–96; J. C. Wofford, V. L. Goodwin and S. Premack, 'Meta-Analysis of the Antecedents of Personal Goal Level and the Antecedents and Consequences of Goal Commitment', *Journal of Management*, September 1992, pp. 595–615.

76 T. Matsui, A. Okada and R. Mizuguchi, 'Expectancy Theory Prediction of the Goal Setting Postulate: The Harder the Goal, the Higher the Performance', *Journal of Applied Psychology*, January 1983, pp. 54–8.

77 E. A. Locke and D. Henne, 'Work Motivation Theory', in *Internal Review of Industrial and Organizational Psychology*, eds C. Cooper and I. Robertson (Chichester: Wiley, 1986), pp. 1–35.

78 For instance, see 'Worker Retention Presents Challenge to U.S. Employers', *HR Magazine*, September 1998, p. 22; L. Wah, 'An Ounce of Prevention', *Management Review*, October 1998, p. 9; and S. Armour, 'Cash or Critiques: Which Is Best?', *USA Today*, 16 December 1998, p. 6B.

79 Adapted and translated from Loek Van Den Broek, '360° feedback: waarom nu?', *Gids voor Personeelsmanagement*, no. 10, 1999.

80 I. Sager, 'The Man Who's Rebooting IBM's PC Business', *Business Week*, 24 July 1995, p. 70.

81 J. A. Byrne, 'Management Meccas', *Business Week*, 18 September 1995, p. 128.

82 Data from M. Hequet, 'Giving Feedback', *Training*, September 1994, pp. 72–7.

83 P. McBride and S. Maitland, *The EI Advantage: Putting Emotional Intelligence into Practice* (London: McGraw-Hill, 2002), p. 215.

84 C. Bell and R. Zemke, 'On-Target Feedback', *Training*, June 1992, p. 36.

85 Both the definition and the functions of feedback are based on discussion in D. R. Ilgen, C. D. Fisher and M. S. Taylor, 'Consequences of Individual Feedback on Behavior in Organizations', *Journal of Applied Psychology*, August 1979, pp. 349–71; and R. E. Kopelman, *Managing Productivity in Organizations: A Practical People-Oriented Perspective* (New York: McGraw-Hill, 1986), p. 175.

86 P. C. Earley, G. B. Northcraft, C. Lee and T. R. Lituchy, 'Impact of Process and Outcome Feedback on the Relation of Goal Setting to Task Performance', *Academy of Management Journal*, March 1990, pp. 87–105.

87 Data from A. N. Kluger and A. DeNisi, 'The Effects of Feedback Interventions on Performance: A Historical Review, a Meta-Analysis, and a Preliminary Feedback Intervention Theory', *Psychological Bulletin*, March 1996, pp. 254–84.

88 D. M. Herold and D. B. Fedor, 'Individuals' Interaction with Their Feedback Environment: The Role of Domain-Specific Individual Differences', in *Research in Personnel and Human Resources Management, vol. 16*, ed. G. R. Ferris (Stanford, CT: JAI Press, 1998), pp. 215–54.

89 For relevant research, see J. S. Goodman, 'The Interactive Effects of Task and External Feedback on Practice Performance and Learning', *Organizational Behavior and Human Decision Processes*, December 1998, pp. 223–52.

90 M. R. Leary, E. S. Tambor, S. K. Terdal and D. L. Downs, 'Self-Esteem as an Interpersonal Monitor: The Sociometer Hypothesis', *Journal of Personality and Social Psychology*, June 1995, pp. 518–30; M. A. Quinones, 'Pretraining Context Effects: Training Assignment as Feedback', *Journal of Applied Psychology*, April 1995, pp. 226–38; and P. E. Levy, M. D. Albright, B. D. Cawley and J. R. Williams, 'Situational and Individual Determinants of Feedback Seeking: A Closer Look at the Process', *Organizational Behavior and Human Decision Processes*, April 1995, pp. 23–37.

91 T. Matsui, A. Okkada and T. Kakuyama, 'Influence of Achievement Need on Goal Setting, Performance, and Feedback Effectiveness', *Journal of Applied Psychology*, October 1982, pp. 645–8.

92 M. E. Burkhardt, 'Social Interaction Effects Following a Technological Change: A Longitudinal Investigation', *Academy of Management Journal*, August 1994, pp. 869–98; and D. B. Turban and T. W. Dougherty, 'Role of Protege Personality in Receipt of Mentoring and Career Success', *Academy of Management Journal*, June 1994, pp. 688–702.

93 B. D. Bannister, 'Performance Outcome Feedback and Attributional Feedback: Interactive Effects on Recipient Responses', *Journal of Applied Psychology*, May 1986, pp. 203–10.

94 S. J. Ashford and A. S. Tsui, 'Self-Regulation for Managerial Effectiveness: The Role of Active Feedback Seeking', *Academy of Management Journal*, June 1991, pp. 251–80. For complete details, see P. M. Podsakoff and J.-L. Farh, 'Effects of Feedback Sign and Credibility on Goal Setting and Task Performance', *Organizational Behavior and Human Decision Processes*, August 1989, pp. 45–67.

95 T. A. Louie, 'Decision Makers' Hindsight Bias after Receiving Favorable and Unfavorable Feedback', *Journal of Applied Psychology*, February 1999, pp. 29–41; and W. S. Silver, T. R. Mitchell and M. E. Gist, 'Responses to Successful and Unsuccessful Performance: The Moderating Effect of Self-Efficacy on the Relationship between Performance and Attributions', *Organizational Behavior and Human Decision Processes*, June 1995, p. 297.

96 I. Krechowiecka, 'Help: Why Is There Always a But?', the *Guardian*, 24 June 2000.

97 A. C. Wicks, S. L. Berman and T. M. Jones, 'The Structure of Optimal Trust: Moral and Strategic Implications', *Academy of Management Review*, January 1999, pp. 99–116; O. Harari, 'The TRUST Factor', *Management Review*, January 1999, pp. 28–31; K. van den Bos, H. A. M. Wilke and E. A. Lind, ' When Do We Need Procedural Fairness? The Role of Trust in Authority', *Journal of Personality and Social Psychology*, December 1998, pp. 1449–58; and J. McCune, 'That Elusive Thing Called Trust', *Management Review*, July–August 1998, pp. 10–16.

98 S. E. Moss and M. J. Martinko, 'The Effects of Performance Attributions and Outcome Dependence on Leader Feedback Behavior Following Poor Subordinate Performance', *Journal of Organizational Behavior*, May 1998, pp. 259–74.

99 S. H. Barr and E. J. Conlon, 'Effects of Distribution of Feedback in Work Groups', *Academy of Management Journal*, June 1994, pp. 641–55.

100 For a recent review of performance feedback in organisations, see A. M. Alvero, B. R. Bucklin and J. Austin, 'An Objective Review of the Effectiveness and Essential Characteristics of Performance Feedback in Organizational Settings (1985–1998)', *Journal of Organizational Behavior Management*, January 2001, pp. 3–29.

101 Practical tips for giving feedback can be found in M. Hequet, 'Giving Feedback', *Training*, September 1994, pp. 72–7; L. Smith, 'The Executive's New Coach', *Fortune*, 27 December 1993, pp. 126–34; T. Lammers, 'The Effective Employee-Feedback System', *Inc.*, February 1993, pp. 109–11; and E. Van Velsor and S. J. Wall, 'How to Choose a Feedback Instrument', *Training*, March 1992, pp. 47–52.

102 For supporting evidence of employees' desire for prompt feedback, see D. H. Reid and M. B. Parsons, 'A Comparison of Staff Acceptability of Immediate versus Delayed Verbal Feedback in Staff Training', *Journal of Organizational Behavior Management*, Summer 1996, pp. 35–47.

103 M. R. Edwards, A. J. Ewen and W. A. Verdini, 'Fair Performance Management and Pay Practices for Diverse Work Forces: The Promise of Multisource Assessment', *ACA Journal*, Spring 1995, pp. 50–63.

104 G. D. Huet-Cox, T. M. Nielsen and E. Sundstrom, 'Get the Most from 360-Degree Feedback: Put It on the Internet', *HR Magazine*, May 1999, pp. 92–103.

105 This list is based in part on a discussion in H. J. Bernardin, 'Subordinate Appraisal: A Valuable Source of Information about Managers', *Human Resource Management*, Fall 1986, pp. 421–39.

106 B. P. Mathews and T. Redman, 'The Attitudes of Service Industry Managers Towards Upward Appraisal', *Career Development International*, January 1997, pp. 46–53.

107 Data from D. Antonioni, 'The Effects of Feedback Accountability on Upward Appraisal Ratings', *Personnel Psychology*, Summer 1994, pp. 349–56.

108 H. J. Bernardin, S. A. Dahmus and G. Redmon, 'Attitudes of First-Line Supervisors toward Subordinate Appraisals', *Human Resource Management*, Summer–Fall 1993, p. 315.

109 Data from J. W. Smither, M. London, N. L. Vasilopoulos, R. R. Reilly, R. E. Millsap and N. Salvemini, 'An Examination of the Effects of an Upward Feedback Program Over Time', *Personnel Psychology*, Spring 1995, pp. 1–34.

110 R. R. Reilly, J. W. Smither and N. L. Vasilopoulos, 'A Longitudinal Study of Upward Feedback', *Personnel Psychology*, Fall 1996, pp. 599–612.

111 B. P. Mathews and T. Redman, 'The Attitudes of Service Industry Managers Towards Upward Appraisal', *Career Development International*, January 1997, pp. 46–53.

112 M. London and R. W. Beatty, '360-Degree Feedback as a Competitive Advantage', *Human Resource Management*, Summer 1993, p. 353.

113 For a comprehensive overview of 360-degree feedback, see W. W. Tornow and M. London, *Maximizing the Value of 360-Degree Feedback* (San Francisco: Jossey-Bass, 1998). Also see A. H. Church and D. W. Bracken, 'Advancing the State of the Art of 360-Degree Feedback: Guest Editors' Comment on the Research and Practice of Multirater Assessment Methods', *Group & Organization Management*, June 1997, pp. 149–61. For more information on 360-degree feedback, see further in this issue of *Group & Organization Management*, which is a special issue devoted to 360-degree feedback systems.

114 Adapted and translated from 'Het oordeel van iedereen rondom je', *HRM Magazine*, 1 September 1997.

115 P. Jansen and D. Vloeberghs, 'Multi-Rater Feedback Methods: Personal and Organizational Implications', *Journal of Managerial Psychology*, October 1999, pp. 45–7.

116 G. W. Cheung, 'Multifaceted Conceptions of Self-Other Ratings Disagreement', *Personnel Psychology*, Spring 1999, pp. 1–36; J. D. Makiney and P. E. Levy, 'The Influence of Self-Ratings versus Peer Ratings on Supervisors' Performance Judgments', *Organizational Behavior and Human Decision Processes*, June 1998, pp. 212–28; R. F. Martell and M. R. Borg, 'A Comparison of the Behavioral Rating Accuracy of Groups and Individuals', *Journal of Applied Psychology*, February 1993, pp. 43–50; J. R. Williams and P. E. Levy, 'The Effects of Perceived System Knowledge on the Agreement between Self-Ratings and Supervisor Ratings', *Personnel Psychology*, Winter 1992, pp. 835–47; J. Lane and P. Herriot, 'Self-Ratings, Supervisor Ratings, Positions and Performance', *Journal of Occupational Psychology*, March 1990, pp. 77–88; and M. M. Harris and J. Schaubroeck, 'A Meta-Analysis of Self-Supervisor, Self-Peer, and Peer-Supervisor Ratings', *Personnel Psychology*, Spring 1988, pp. 43–62.

117 A. H. Church, 'Do I See What I See? An Exploration of Congruence in Ratings from Multiple Perspectives', *Journal of Applied Psychology*, June 1997, pp. 983–1020; K. L. Bettenhausen and D. B. Fedor, 'Peer and Upward Appraisals: A Comparison of Their Benefits and Problems', *Group & Organization Management*, June 1997, pp. 236–63; S. Salam, J. F. Cox and H. P. Sims, Jr, 'In the Eye of the Beholder: How Leadership Relates to 360-Degree Performance Ratings', *Group & Organization Management*, June 1997, pp. 185–209; J. W. Fleenor, C. D. McCauley and S. Brutus, 'Self-Other Agreement and Leader Effectiveness', *Leadership Quarterly*, Winter 1996, pp. 487–506; L. E. Atwater, P. Roush and A. Fischtal, 'The Influence of Upward Feedback on Self and Follower-Ratings of Leadership', *Personnel Psychology*, Spring 1995, pp. 35–59; and L. E. Atwater and F. J. Yammarino, 'Does Self-Other Agreement on Leadership Perceptions Moderate the Validity of Leadership and Performance Predictions', *Personnel Psychology*, Spring 1992, pp. 141–64.

118 P. Jansen and D. Vloeberghs, 'Multi-Rater Feedback Methods: Personal and Organizational Implications', *Journal of Managerial Psychology*, October 1999, pp. 45–7; J. Francis-Smythe and P. M. Smith, 'The Psychological Impact of Assessment in a Development Center', *Human Relations*, February 1997, pp. 149–67; and A. S. Engelbrecht and A. H. Fischer, 'The Managerial Performance Implications of a Developmental Assessment Center Process', *Human Relations*, April 1995, pp. 387–404.

119 M. K. Mount, T. A. Judge, S. E. Scullen, M. R. Sytsma and S. A. Hezlett, 'Trait, Rater and Level Effects in 360-Degree Performance Ratings', *Personnel Psychology*, Autumn 1998, pp. 557–76; and J. Fisher Hazucha, S. A. Hezlett and R. J. Schneider, 'The Impact of 360-Degree Feedback on Managerial Skills Development', *Human Resource Management*, Summer 1993, p. 42.

120 M. London and J. W. Smither, 'Can Multi-Source Feedback Change Perceptions of Goal Accomplishment, Self-Evaluations, and Performance-Related Outcomes? Theory-Based Applications and Directions for Research', *Personnel Psychology*, Winter 1996, pp. 803–39.

121 Also see J. W. Westerman and J. G. Rosse, 'Reducing the Threat of Rater Non-Participation in 360-Degree Feedback Systems: An Exploratory Examination of Antecedents to Participation in Upward Ratings', *Group & Organization Management*, June 1997, pp. 288–309.

122 M. London, A. J. Wohlers and P. Gallagher, '360 Degree Feedback Surveys: A Source of Feedback to Guide Management Development', *Journal of Management Development*, November 1990, pp. 17–31.

123 M. London and R. W. Beatty, '360-Degree Feedback as a Competitive Advantage', *Human Resource Management*, Summer 1993, p. 356–7; D. W. Bracken, 'Straight Talk about Multirater Feedback', *Training & Development*, September 1994, p. 46; and D. Antonioni, 'Designing an Effective 360-Degree Appraisal Feedback Process', *Organizational Dynamics*, Autumn 1996, pp. 24–38.

124 S. Kerr, 'Risky Business: The New Pay Game', *Fortune*, 22 July 1996, pp. 94–5; and B. Filipczak, 'Can't Buy Me Love', *Training*, January 1996, pp. 29–34.

125 S. L. Rynes and B. Gerhart, *Compensation in Organizations: Current Research and Practice* (San Francisco: Jossey-Bass, 2000), p. XV.

126 Strategic models of pay and rewards are discussed in C. Joinson, 'Pay Attention to Pay Cycles', *HR Magazine*, November 1998, pp. 71–8; M. Bloom and G. T. Milkovich, 'A SHRM Perspective on International Compensation and Reward Systems', in *Research in Personnel and Human Resources Management*, ed. G. R. Ferris (Stamford, CT: JAI Press, 1999), pp. 283–303; and J. Dolmat-Connell, 'Developing a Reward Strategy That Delivers Shareholder and Employee Value', *Compensation & Benefits Review*, March–April 1999, pp. 46–53.

127 Chartered Institute of Personnel and Development, *Survey Report: Reward Management 2004. A Survey on Policy and Practice*, February 2004, /www.cipd.co.uk/.

128 B. S. Frey and M. Osterloh, *Successful Management by Motivation: Balancing Intrinsic and Extrinsic Incentives* (New York: Springer-Verlag, 2002).

129 For complete discussions, see A. P. Brief and R. J. Aldag, 'The Intrinsic-Extrinsic Dichotomy: Toward Conceptual Clarity', *Academy of Management Review*, July 1977, pp. 496–500; and E. L. Deci, *Intrinsic Motivation* (New York: Plenum Press, 1975), Ch. 2.

130 For more details on this study, see X. Huang and E. Van de Vliert, 'Where Intrinsic Job Satisfaction Fails to Work: National Moderators of Intrinsic Motivation', *Journal of Organizational Behavior*, March 2003, pp. 159–79.

131 C. C. Chen, J. R. Meindl and H. Hui, 'Deciding on Equity or Parity: A Test of Situational, Cultural, and Individual Factors', *Journal of Organizational Behavior*, March 1998, pp. 115–29; and K. I. Kim, H.-J. Park and N. Suzuki, 'Reward Allocations in the United States, Japan, and Korea: A Comparison of Individualistic and Collectivistic Cultures', *Academy of Management Journal*, March 1990, pp. 188–98.

132 Based on M. Bloom, 'The Performance Effects of Pay Dispersion on Individuals and Organizations', *Academy of Management Journal*, February 1999, pp. 25–40.

133 Good discussions can be found in A. Rappaport, 'New Thinking on How to Link Executive Pay with Performance', *Harvard Business Review*, March–April 1999, pp. 91–101; J. Kahn, 'A CEO Cuts His Own Pay', *Fortune*, 26 October 1998, pp. 56, 60, 64; and W. Grossman and R. E. Hoskisson, 'CEO Pay at the Crossroads of Wall Street and Main: Toward the Strategic Design of Executive Compensation', *Academy of Management Executive*, February 1998, pp. 43–57.

134 List adapted from J. L. Pearce and R. H. Peters, 'A Contradictory Norms View of Employer–Employee Exchange', *Journal of Management*, Spring 1985, pp. 19–30.

135 J. L. Pearce and R. H. Peters, 'A Contradictory Norms View of Employer–Employee Exchange', *Journal of Management*, Spring 1985, p. 25.

136 D. B. McFarlin and P. D. Sweeney, 'Distributive and Procedural Justice as Predictors of Satisfaction with Personal and Organizational Outcomes', *Academy of Management Journal*, August 1992, pp. 626–37.

137 S. L. Mueller and L. D. Clarke, 'Political-Economic Context and Sensitivity to Equity: Differences between the United States and the Transition Economies of Central and Eastern Europe', *Academy of Management Journal*, June 1998, pp. 319–29.

138 K. G. Wheeler, 'Cultural Values in Relation to Equity Sensitivity Within and Across Cultures', *Journal of Managerial Psychology*, October 2002, pp. 612–27; S. S. K. Lam, J. Schaubroeck and S. Aryee, 'Relationship between Organizational Justice and Employee Work Outcomes: A Cross-National Study', *Journal of Organizational Behavior*, February 2002, pp. 1–18; and S. L. Mueller and L. D. Clarke, 'Political-Economic Context and Sensi-

tivity to Equity: Differences Between the United States and the Transition Economies of Central and Eastern Europe', *Academy of Management Journal*, June 1998, pp. 319–29.

139 K. G. Wheeler, 'Cultural Values in Relation to Equity Sensitivity Within and Across Cultures', *Journal of Managerial Psychology*, October 2002, p. 612. Also see M. Brown and J. S. Heywood, *Paying for Performance: An International Comparison* (Armonk, NY: M. E. Sharpe, 2003).

140 M. Von Glinow, 'Reward Strategies for Attracting, Evaluating, and Retaining Professionals', *Human Resource Management*, Summer 1985, p. 193.

141 S. L. Rynes and J. E. Bono, 'Psychological Research on Determinants of Pay', in *Compensation in Organizations: Current Research and Practice*, eds S. L. Rynes and B. Gerhart (San Francisco: Jossey-Bass, 2000), pp. 3–31.

142 Six reward system objectives are discussed in E. E. Lawler III, 'The New Pay: A Strategic Approach', *Compensation & Benefits Review*, July–August 1995, pp. 14–22. Also see A. E. Barber and R. D. Bretz, Jr, 'Compensation, Attraction, and Retention', *Compensation in Organizations: Current Research and Practice*, eds S. L. Rynes and B. Gerhart (San Francisco: Jossey-Bass, 2000), pp. 32–60.

143 For a more extensive overview of reasons for failure of organisational reward systems and possible solutions, see A. D. Smith and W. T. Rupp, 'Knowledge Workers: Exploring the Link among Performance Rating, Pay and Motivational Aspects', *Journal of Knowledge Management*, March 2003, pp. 107–24; and J. Pfeffer and J. F. Velga, 'Putting People First for Organizational Success', *Academy of Management Executive*, May 1999, pp. 37–48.

144 D. R. Spitzer, 'Power Rewards: Rewards That Really Motivate', *Management Review*, May 1996, p. 47. Also see S. Kerr, 'An Academy Classic: On the Folly of Rewarding A, while Hoping for B', *Academy of Management Executive*, February 1995, pp. 7–14.

145 List adapted from discussion in D. R. Spitzer, 'Power Rewards: Rewards That Really Motivate', *Management Review*, May 1996, pp. 45–50. Also see R. Eisenberger and J. Cameron, 'Detrimental Effects of Reward: Reality or Myth?', *American Psychologist*, November 1996, pp. 1153–66.

146 See, for example, S. L. Rynes and B. Gerhart, *Compensation in Organizations: Current Research and Practice* (San Francisco: Jossey-Bass, 2000); and T. P. Flannery, D. A. Hofrichter and P. E. Platten, *People, Performance, and Pay: Dynamic Compensation for Changing Organizations* (New York: The Free Press, 1996).

147 Supportive results are presented in L. Morris, 'Employees Not Encouraged to Go Extra Mile', *Training & Development*, April 1996, pp. 59–60; and L. Morris, 'Crossed Wires on Employee Motivation', *Training & Development*, July 1995, pp. 59–60.

148 E. L. Deci, R. Koestner and R. M. Ryan, 'A Meta-Analytic Review of Experiments Examining the Effect of Extrinsic Rewards on Intrinsic Motivation', *Psychological Bulletin*, November 1999, pp. 627–68; D. R. Spitzer, 'Power Rewards: Rewards That Really Motivate', *Management Review*, May 1996, pp. 45–50; and A. Kohn, *Punished by Rewards: The Trouble with Gold Stars, Incentive Plans, A's, Praise, and Other Bribes* (Boston, MA: Houghton Mifflin Company, 1993).

149 See, for instance, L. W. Howard and T. W. Doughtery, 'Alternative Reward Strategies and Employee Reactions', *Compensation & Benefits Review*, January–February 2004, pp. 41–51; J. D. Shaw, N. Gupta and J. E. Delery, 'Pay Dispersion and Workforce Performance: Moderating Effects of Incentives and Interdependence', *Strategic Management Journal*, June 2002, pp. 491–512; S. E. Bonner, R. Hastie, G. B. Sprinkle and S. M. Young, 'A Review of the Effects of Financial Incentives on Performance in Laboratory Tasks: Implications for Management Accounting, *Journal of Management Accounting Research*, no. 1, 2000, pp. 19–64; C. F. Camerer and R. M. Hogarth, 'The Effects of Financial Incentives in Experiments: A Review and Capital-Labor-Production Framework, *Journal of Risk and Uncertainty*, December 1999, pp. 7–42; and M. Bloom, 'The Performance Effects of Pay Dispersion on Individuals and Organizations', *Academy of Management Journal*, February 1999, pp. 25–40.

150 Results from these studies can be found in N. J. Fessler, 'Experimental Evidence on the Links between Monetary Incentives, Task Attractiveness, and Task Performance', *Journal of Management Accounting Research*, no. 2, 2003, pp. 161–76; G. D. Jenkins, Jr, A. Mitra, N. Gupta and J. D. Shaw, 'Are Financial Incentives Related to Performance? A Meta-Analytic Review of Empirical Research', *Journal of Applied Psychology*, October 1998, pp. 777–87; and R. Eisenberger, S. Armeli and J. Pretz, 'Can the Promise of Reward Increase Creativity?', *Journal of Personality and Social Psychology*, March 1998, pp. 704–14.

151 For examples of research on pay raises, see A. Mitra, N. Gupta and G. D. Jenkins, Jr, 'A Drop in the Bucket: When is Pay Raise a Pay Raise?', *Journal of Organizational Behavior*, March 1997, pp. 117–37; and K. S. Teel, 'Are Merit Raises Really Based on Merit?', *Personnel Journal*, March 1986, pp. 88–94.

152 S. Kerr, 'Organizational Rewards: Practical, Cost-Neutral Alternatives That You May Know, But Don't Practice', *Organizational Dynamics*, Summer 1999, pp. 61–70.

153 See the related discussion in T. P. Flannery, D. A. Hofrichter and P. E. Platten, *People, Performance & Pay* (New York: The Free Press, 1996).

154 R. Ganzel, 'What's Wrong with Pay for Performance?', *Training*, December 1998, pp. 34–40; and P. M. Wright, J. M. George, S. R. Farnsworth and G. C. McMahan, 'Productivity and Extra-Role Behavior: The Effects of Goals and Incentives on Spontaneous Helping', *Journal of Applied Psychology*, June 1993, pp. 374–81.

155 Supporting results can be found in S. W. Gilliland and R. S. Landis, 'Quality and Quantity Goals in a Complex Decision Task: Strategies and Outcomes', *Journal of Applied Psychology*, October 1992, pp. 672–81.

156 Potential pitfalls of goal setting and monetary incentives as well as guidelines to effectively deal with them are discussed in P. M. Wright, 'Goal Setting and Monetary Incentives: Motivational Tools That Can Work *Too* Well', *Compensation & Benefits Review*, May–June 1994, pp. 41–9.

157 L. W. Howard and T. W. Doughtery, 'Alternative Reward Strategies and Employee Reactions', *Compensation & Benefits Review*, January–February 2004, pp. 41–51; H. Risher, 'Pay-for-Performance: The Keys to Making It Work', *Public Personnel Management*, Fall 2002, pp. 317–32; K. M. Bartol and E. A. Locke, 'Incentives and Motivation', in *Compensation in Organizations: Current Research and Practice*, eds S. L. Rynes and B. Gerhart (San Francisco: Jossey-Bass, 2000), pp. 104–47; J. Igalens and P. Roussel, 'A Study of the Relationships between Compensation Package, Work Motivation and Job Satisfaction', *Journal of Organizational Behavior*, December 1999, pp. 1003–25; and D. O'Neill, 'Blending the Best of Profit Sharing and Gainsharing', *HR Magazine*, March 1994, pp. 66–70.

158 L. W. Howard and T. W. Doughtery, 'Alternative Reward Strategies and Employee Reactions', *Compensation & Benefits Review*, January–February 2004, p. 45; and R. L. Heneman, G. E. Ledford, Jr, and M. T. Gresham, 'The Changing Nature of Work and Its Effect on Compensation Design and Delivery', in *Compensation in Organizations: Current Research and Practice*, eds S. L. Rynes and B. Gerhart (San Francisco: Jossey-Bass, 2000), pp. 195–240.

159 Adapted and translated from 'De Volvo-case: collectief en consistent belonen', *HR Square*, February 2004, p. 36.

160 A recent issue of the *Academy of Management Review* (July 2004) is devoted to the future of work motivation theory. See, for instance, R. M. Steers, R. T. Mowday and D. L. Shaprio, 'The Future of Work Motivation Theory', *Academy of Management Review*, July 2004, pp. 379–87; and E. A. Locke and G. P. Latham, 'What Should We Do about Motivation Theory? Six Recommendations for the Twenty-First Century', *Academy of Management Review*, July 2004, pp. 388–404.

161 N. Nicholson, 'How to Motivate Your Problem People', *Harvard Business Review*, January 2003, pp. 56–67; and H. Levinson, 'Management by Whose Objectives?', *Harvard Business Review*, January 2003, pp. 107–16.

162 Useful and varied examples to reward people can be found in B. Fryer, 'Moving Mountains', *Harvard Business Review*, January 2003, pp. 41–7; and B. Nelson, *1001 Ways to Reward Employees* (New York: Workman Publishing, 1994).

163 F. Hansen, M. Slith and R. B. Hansen, 'Rewards and Recognition in Employee Motivation', *Compensation & Benefits Review*, September–October 2002, pp. 64–72.

164 P. Falcone, 'Motivating Staff Without Money', *HR Magazine*, August 2002, p. 105.

165 A. Jack, 'Big Stakes in a Small World – Andrew Jack Looks at the Latest Attempt to Improve Performance at EuroDisney', the *Financial Times*, 13 January 1995, p. 12.

166 Useful articles to help develop a performance appraisal system are F. Hansen, M. Slith and R. B. Hansen, 'Rewards and Recognition in Employee Motivation', *Compensation & Benefits Review*, September–October 2002, pp. 64–72; B. G. Mani, 'Performance Appraisal Systems, Productivity, and Motivation: A Case Study', *Public Personnel Management*, Summer 2002, pp. 141–59; and C. O. Longenecker and L. S. Fink, 'Creating Effective Performance Appraisals', *Industrial Management*, September–October 1999, pp. 18–23.

167 This conclusion is consistent with research summarised in F. Luthans and A. D. Stajkovic, 'Reinforce for Performance: The Need to Go Beyond Pay and Even Rewards', *Academy of Management Executive*, May 1999, pp. 49–57.

168 This exercise is adapted from material in D. M. Herold and C. K. Parsons, 'Assessing the Feedback Environment in Work Organizations: Development of the Job Feedback Survey', *Journal of Applied Psychology*, May 1985, pp. 290–305.

chapter 7 occupational stress

By Marc Buelens and Fannie Debussche

Learning outcomes

When you finish studying the material in this chapter, you should be able to:

- define the term 'stress'
- explain why the Karasek's Job Demand-Control (JD-C) model is so important
- describe the model of occupational stress
- explain how stressful life events create stress
- review the model of burnout and highlight the solutions to reduce it
- explain the mechanisms of social support
- describe the coping process
- discuss the personality characteristic of hardiness
- discuss the Type A behaviour pattern and its practical implications
- contrast the four dominant stress-reduction techniques

It's all down to me ...

My workload is relentless – that's not an unfair description. I have peaks and troughs, but there's no such thing as a clear desk at the end of the day. I am a personal assistant to the chairman of an investment trust, who also has philanthropic, artistic and community commitments outside his main corporate job. It's all work: whether it's the dry cleaner or the executive jet, it's all down to me.

I start between 9 and 9.30 a.m. Lunch more often than not is a sandwich at my desk, and I get away between 6 and 7 p.m., sometimes taking work home because I can't find a quiet moment during the day. Trying to reconcile the credit card statements is difficult if you are constantly interrupted.

A lot of my time is spent organising things, thinking 'If he's going to be at that meeting, I need to organise this, and he'll have to go from that to the next meeting, so I need to remind him that when he does that he needs to do this.' It's about thinking things through and organising as much of his life as possible.

As a secretary, by definition it's my job to take on the stress of other people's jobs. It goes without saying that secretaries are less in control of their workloads and experience a lot of stress of their own. Some bosses may tell their secretary what needs doing, and leave them to get on with it uninterrupted. But in busy offices that's the last thing that happens. It's a constant case of 'Can you just ...'.

That's what creates most stress: not being in control of one's own day. I come in thinking, 'I must work on the New York trip', but my boss has worked on his own at home the night before and what I had planned to do is put on the back burner. And while that happens the email's going, and colleagues need things. The frustration comes from knowing that you should have planned the New York trip today and you haven't got round to it.

I have been with the company for 18 years and with my boss for 17, and life has definitely got busier in that time. I think it's just a question of pace. Thirty years ago letters came in and people dictated replies, and if you were lucky they were turned around in three or four days. Now everything has to be done very quickly. Also there's the globalisation factor: if you have the misfortune to be working in London and dealing a lot with the west coast of America or even New York, you can't ring them in the morning. You have to stay late. It's the same thing with Europe in the morning. If people know they can snatch you early they will. There's no hiding place.

I try to keep my sense of humour, and a sense of balance and perspective. You need to be able to switch off otherwise you can easily get into waking up at night thinking, 'I didn't give him that memo . . .'. I also write everything down. Post-it notes, that's what has saved us – you wonder what we did before we had them!

One of the things that adds to the stress is if you are part of a bigger team and you have to rely on others to do certain things. But you have to be flexible and understand that they have their own priorities and difficulties. The pressure starts to build up because of interruptions and this element of firefighting, rather than a quietly organised work process.'[1]

For discussion

How do you respond to an intense workload, for example, during an examination period? What do you do to cope with it?

As this case study suggests, life in the twenty-first century can be hectic and stressful. Students must cope with tests, projects and increasing competition when looking for a job after graduation. Married couples must wrestle with the demands of managing careers and a family. Single parents encounter similar pressures. Stress at work is also on the rise, as many workers today find themselves in a devastating spiral of overload, conflict, tension and burnout, or as a reporter for the *Guardian* observed

> When asking somebody 'How's it going?' he or she'll probably tell you something like this: 'Oh, you know, a bit stressed', or maybe: 'OK. Exhausted, but OK'. Stressed, manic, unbelievably busy, crazy, shattered, absolutely frantic, seconds away from meltdown – these are now standard answers to any enquiry about your well-being.[2]

According to a study from the International Labour Organization (ILO), more than 10 million Europeans become ill because of stress every year. The costs of this 'stress epidemic' are huge: it is estimated that in the European Union an average of 3 to 4 per cent of gross national product is spent on mental health problems.[3]

> For example, in the UK, a country known for its 'long-hours culture', 3 in 10 workers have mental health problems and 15 to 30 per cent suffer from anxiety and depression. In Finland, more than half of the workforce is blighted with stress-related symptoms, 7 per cent are 'severely burnt out' and the country suffers from a high suicide rate. In Germany, almost 10 per cent of early retirements are caused by depression and over 80 million working days are lost every year due to stress.[4] In Japan, a new term has been added to the dictionaries: Karoshi, meaning 'dead from overwork'.[5]

It is not surprising, therefore, that a spokesman of the ILO stated: 'Today, the workers of the world are united in just one thing, that is: record levels of stress.'[6] The biggest contributor to work stress arises from fundamental changes that have been made in many organisations. As a result of increased competition, employees are being asked to deliver a better quality and a greater quantity of work in less time with fewer resources. Second, technological advancements make it harder for employees to completely disconnect from the office. Pagers, fax machines, email and cellular phones make it easy to disrupt our free time while at home or on holiday. Third, the dynamics of modern life make it difficult to balance the demands of work and home. Research demonstrates that work stress spills over into one's personal life and vice versa.[7] Finally, motivation and stress are related. Research has demonstrated that pursuing extrinsic over intrinsic goals results in poorer well-being. Striving for extrinsic goals, such as money, status, control over others, often requires stressful ego-involved activities.[8] Motivation and rewards are discussed in Chapter 6.

This chapter looks at the sources of stress, examines stressors and burnout, highlights four moderators of occupational stress and explores a variety of stress-reduction techniques.

Sources of stress

We all experience stress on a daily basis. Although stress is caused by many factors, researchers conclude that stress triggers one of two basic reactions: active fighting or passive flight (running away from or acceptance of stressors), the so-called Fight-or-flight response.[9] Stressors are environmental factors that produce stress. Stressors are discussed in detail later in this chapter. Physiologically, this stress response is a biochemical 'top gear' involving hormonal changes that mobilise the body for extraordinary demands. Imagine how our prehistoric ancestors responded to the stress associated with a charging sabre-toothed tiger. To avoid being eaten, they could stand their ground and fight the beast or run away. In either case, their bodies would have been energised by an identical hormonal change, involving the release of adrenaline into the bloodstream.

In our contemporary society, this fight-or-flight system still has a very visible consequence in the way we handle stress. Psychotherapist Bob Vansant gives us the following explanation:

> 'In our world there are only two different types of people', he says. 'On the one hand you have the maniacs with their cellular phones and portables close at range, the so-called workaholics who are always in gear. On the other hand, you have the depressive people who can't keep up with the pace any more and try to hide themselves away as a sort of silent protest against our manic lifestyle.'[10]

In today's hectic, urbanised and industrialised society, charging beasts have been replaced by problems such as deadlines, role conflict and ambiguity, financial responsibilities, information overload, technology, traffic congestion, noise and air pollution, family problems and work overload. As with our ancestors, our response to stress may or may not trigger negative side effects, including headaches, ulcers, insomnia, heart attacks, high blood pressure and strokes. The same stress response that helped our prehistoric ancestors survive has too often become a factor that seriously impairs our daily lives. Consider the following two examples:

> At the age of 35, Carolyn Draper's life went on hold. She was in a highly stressful job, teaching in a tough inner-city secondary school in Sheffield. She dreaded going to work and every day she came home and collapsed into a chair with exhaustion. Her limbs ached, she began to get headaches and she finally succumbed to a nasty bout of flu. 'From that day on my life was never really the same', Carolyn says. 'I felt so shattered that I was going to bed really early but waking up feeling even more tired than ever. When I told my superiors, they said I was feeling depressed and that two weeks of counselling would have me feeling as right as rain. I burst into tears. I began to think I was going round the bend.'[11]

> Adrenaline surges through Christine Peters's veins. The information-systems supervisor is frazzled from her day-long battle with computer flare-ups and system crashes. Desperate for a moment of peace, Peters ducks into a washroom. She leans against the cool wall and breathes deep, trying to meditate. Her trance is shattered by a knock on the door. The computers have crashed again . . . .[12]

Fight-or-flight response
to either confront stressors or try to avoid them

Stressors
environmental factors that produce stress

Stress can be caused by socio-demographic (e.g. age, schooling), socio-economic (e.g. being under-paid) and psychological factors. A study of 420 Hungarian nurses showed that the psychosocial work environment is the most strongly associated with nurses' psychosomatic health.[13]

Defining stress

To an orchestra violinist, stress may stem from giving a solo performance before a large audience. While heat, smoke and flames may represent stress to a firefighter, delivering a speech or presenting a lecture may be stressful for those who are shy. In short, stress means different things to different people. We need a working definition.

Stress
behavioural, physical or psychological response to stressors

Formally defined, Stress is 'an adaptive response, mediated by individual characteristics and/or psychological processes, that is a consequence of any external action, situation or event that places special physical and/or psychological demands upon a person'.[14] This definition is not as difficult as it seems when we reduce it to three interrelated dimensions of stress: environmental demands, referred to as 'stressors'; those that produce an adaptive response; those that are influenced by individual differences.

Hans Selye, considered the father of the modern concept of stress, pioneered the distinction between stressors and the stress response. Moreover, Selye emphasised that both positive and negative events can trigger an identical stress response, which can be either beneficial or harmful. He referred to stress that is positive or produces a positive outcome as 'Eustress'. For example, an employee who has to make a presentation to a large audience can feel extra pressure, but the fact that he or she likes to do presentations very much will make him or her experience the pressure in a positive way – as very motivating and challenging – rather than in a negative way.[15] Selye also noted that:

Eustress
stress that is good or produces a positive outcome

- Stress is not merely nervous tension.
- Stress can have positive consequences.
- Stress is not something to be avoided.
- The complete absence of stress is death.[16]

Selye was right in pointing to the positive aspects of stress. All learning implies at least a moderate amount of stress. Regular exposure to a manageable amount of stress keeps us fit; too little stress makes us bored. On the other hand, the same employee who really loved doing presentations would soon get fed up by them when he has to work out and prepare lots of labour-intensive, time-consuming presentations over a short period. He would not have the time to recover between the presentations, and his regular tasks will keep on stacking up. If this situation continues, he might become very strained and exhausted.[17] So, although a moderate amount of stress seems to be beneficial, excessive stress proves to be very detrimental. What conditions cause excessive stress and how can it be alleviated or even eliminated?

The Karasek or Job Demand-Control (JD-C) model of job stress

The Karasek model is one of the most often quoted models on stress. It is the most influential theory on job stress in Europe, where it inspired many work environment laws. Robert Karasek developed and popularised the so-called 'job demand-control model' throughout the 1980s. The model emphasises the stress factors inherent in the work organisation, rather than the individual characteristics. He came to this idea while studying the lack of success of stop-smoking programmes. He found that job stress is one cause of smoking. Individually oriented coping strategies such as stop-smoking campaigns were not very successful, because of work environment tensions.

The complete Karasek model consists of three dimensions.[18] Central in the model is the interaction between job demands and job control. The first two dimensions define the work environment. The first dimension is the psychological demand of a job. The second dimension is the amount of autonomy, the control or 'decision latitude' permitted in deciding how to meet these demands. To what extent can workers influence the way their work is organised? Can workers use their skills and knowledge? The third dimension is social support. Examples of social support are showing sympathy for someone's situation or installing a specialised service where employees can go with specific problems. This third dimension, however, has been a late addition, not even made by the author himself.[19]

Work stress becomes apparent when psychological demand is high and decision latitude is low. This means that high psychological demands or work pressure as such do not necessarily lead to work stress. The combination of high psychological demands and low autonomy to deal with these demands is more dangerous and can easily lead to depression, burnout and stress. The negative effects of this combination are reinforced by a lack of social support.

Let us focus on a occupational stress model that more thoroughly elaborates the links between stressors, individual differences and outcomes.

A model of occupational stress

Figure 7.1 presents an instructive model of occupational stress. The model shows that four types of stressors lead to perceived stress which, in turn, produces a variety of outcomes. The model also specifies several individual differences that moderate the stressor–stress–outcome relationship. A moderator is a variable that causes the relationship between two variables – such as stress and outcomes – to be stronger for some people and weaker for others.

FIGURE 7.1 A MODEL OF OCCUPATIONAL STRESS

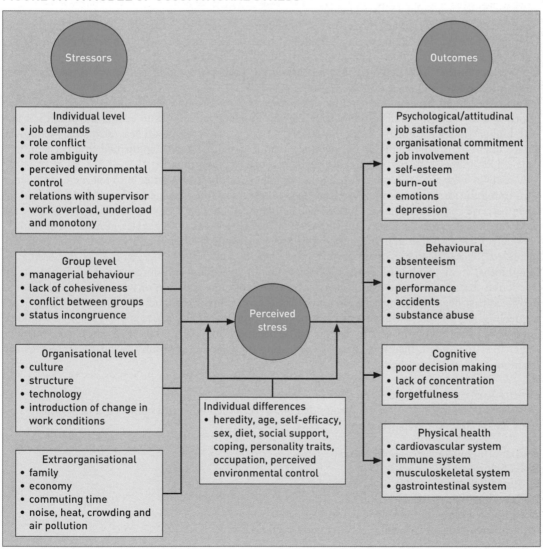

SOURCE: Adapted from M. Koslowsky, *Modeling the Stress-Strain Relationship in Work Settings* (New York: Routledge, 1998); and M. T. Matteson and J. M. Ivancevich, 'Organizational Stressors and Heart Disease: A Research Model', *Academy of Management Review*, July 1979, p. 350.

> For example, a study of 256 employees in a business office of a large retail organisation investigated whether allowing workers to use personal-stereo headsets influenced the relationship between job characteristics and a variety of work outcomes. Results revealed that employees who used stereo headsets had shown significant improvement in their performance, turnover intentions, job satisfaction and mood. Use of personal-stereo headsets moderated the effects of stress.[20]

STRESSORS

Stressors are a prerequisite for stress. Figure 7.1 shows the four major types of stressors: individual, group, organisational and those outside the organisation (extraorganisational). The most common examples of stressors are job demands, work overload, role conflict, role ambiguity, everyday hassles, perceived control over events occurring in the work environment and job characteristics.[21]

Individual-level stressors

Individual-level stressors are those directly associated with a person's work responsibilities. During the past few decades, a vast amount of research has been undertaken to determine the effect of these stressors. Some examples are listed below.

A study of 771 US workers and a total of 2642 employees from Canada, the United Kingdom and Germany revealed that the increasing amount of time people spend sending and receiving messages was a stressor at work. US workers sent and received the most messages. Forty-five per cent of the US workers further indicated that they felt hassled or bothered by interruptions at work: they were interrupted at least six times an hour.[22]

In another study, among German blue-collar workers, it was found that subjects experiencing high efforts and low reward conditions and subjects who had few possibilities to exert control in their job, had higher risks of coronary heart diseases than their counterparts in less adverse psychosocial environments.[23] A later study, among working men in Stockholm, also confirmed that decision latitude could influence the risk of coronary problems such as infarctions.[24]

A study in a Swedish telecom company showed that stressors do not differ between men and women performing the same type of job. Perceived stress however is strongly related to hierarchical level. Managers perceive more quantitative overload and home–work conflict than non-managers, who perceive more threat of downsizing, inadequate information, knowledge demands and lack of meaning at work.[25]

Finally, it is important to manage the individual-level stressor of job security as it is associated with increased job satisfaction, organisational commitment and performance, and it is decreasing. A longitudinal study in Finland, for instance, examined antecedents and outcomes of job insecurity. It was found that, if the organisation was in a negative economic situation or when the probability was perceived that negative changes would occur over the next three years and employees were experiencing feelings of low self-esteem, then it was possible to predict that worries about job losses would be felt by all. This insecurity led to higher job exhaustion and higher absentee rates later on. The researchers concluded, therefore, that by preventing the experience of job insecurity, employers can promote employees' well-being at work.[26]

Group-level stressors

Group-level stressors are caused by group dynamics (see Chapter 9) and managerial behaviour. Managers create stress for employees by:

- Exhibiting inconsistent behaviour.
- Failing to provide support.
- Showing lack of concern.
- Providing inadequate direction.
- Creating a high-productivity environment.
- Focusing on negatives while ignoring good performance.

The experience of sexual harassment (also see Chapter 9) represents another group-level stressor. Studies show that such experiences are negatively associated with work, supervision and promotion satisfaction while being positively related to ambiguity, conflict and stress.[27]

Organisational stressors

Organisational stressors also affect large numbers of employees. Organisational culture, which will be discussed in Chapter 16, is a prime example. For instance, a high-pressure environment that places chronic work demands on employees fuels the stress response.[28] A sales manager who was taken over by the competitive atmosphere and the 'dog-eat-dog' culture in his company explains the situation.

> At a given moment, I had become the sort of person who ate lunch with a fork in one hand and a phone in the other. When we got close to a deadline, I would apologise for visiting the toilet at work. Sometimes I was so afraid of going home that I left my jacket on the back of my chair, hoping the boss would think I've just nipped out for a cigarette.[29]

The increased use of information technology is another source of organisational stress (also see Chapter 8). Research provides preliminary support for the idea that participative management can reduce organisational stress.[30]

Extraorganisational stressors

Extraorganisational stressors are those caused by factors outside the organisation. A German study of 54 teleworkers and a control group showed that teleworkers suffer less from task-related stressors such as interruptions or time pressure, and more from non-job-related stressors such as noisy home, restricted material resources and conflicts with the family.[31]

Conflicts associated with balancing one's career and family life are always very stressful, as is shown in the following examples:[32]

> Londoner Matthew Wright would like to see more of his daughters – Olivia (seven) and Alexandra (four) – but work gets in the way. The 36-year-old managing director for Europe of head-hunters Russel Reynolds Associates squeezes his personal life in around long hours and foreign travel – he often spends two or three nights a week away from home. 'I only spend around 15 minutes with my children on weekdays', he admits. Even when working in London, his journey begins while the children are still asleep. Getting home at a reasonable time may well mean taking work home with him. 'I aim to get home in time to put them to bed', he says. Weekends on the other hand are 'exclusively for friends and family – apart from the odd Saturday morning flight back from the US'.

> 'I saw the opportunities and I went for them. I didn't have the time for a family', says Stephanie Murdoch, 35. She chose work over motherhood shortly after joining insurance company JLT Group Services as a claims processor. Twelve years later, she is the managing director. The most stressful part of her life, she says, is 'maintaining the balance between work and home. Left to my own devices I am the kind of person who puts everything into their job. The pressure turns me on'. She is married to a 'househusband' who stopped work when Stephanie's job took them from Worcester to London. Now he provides regular 'reality-checks' if she is in danger of letting work take over. 'We do have rows about my work. I am not the easiest person to live with', she says.

From these examples, it is clear that work often interferes with family life, but the following results from two British studies are nevertheless pretty remarkable. In a survey by *Management Today* it was found that 25 per cent of British workers find that stress continuously messes up their sex life.[33] A similar study undertaken by the company Seven Seas found that 65 per cent of those questioned in the UK claimed that their sexual performance was sometimes affected by stress, and one-third said their lives were so stressed that they had thought of work while having sex. A total of 89 per cent of men and women blamed work for not having enough time to meet the opposite sex.[34]

PERCEIVED STRESS

Perceived stress represents an individual's overall perception about how various stressors are affecting her or his life. The perception of stressors is an important component within the stress process because people interpret the same stressors differently.[35] For example, some individuals perceive unemployment as a positive, liberating experience, whereas others perceive it as a negative, debilitating one.[36]

OUTCOMES

Theorists contend that stress has psychological/attitudinal, behavioural, cognitive and physical health consequences. A large body of research supports the theory that perceived stress has a negative effect on many aspects of our lives.[37] Stress was negatively related to job satisfaction, organisational commitment, positive emotions and performance, while being positively correlated with burnout and staff turnover.[38] For example, a recent survey of 750 workers over the age of 18 revealed that one in six reported being so angered by a co-worker that he or she felt like hitting the person. The greatest amount of pent-up anger was experienced by workers under the age of 35 and those in clerical, office and sales jobs.[39] Research also provides ample evidence to support the conclusion that stress nega-tively affects our physical health. Stress contributes to the following health problems: a lowered ability to ward off illness and infection, high blood pressure, coronary heart disease, tension headaches, back pain, diarrhoea and constipation.[40]

INDIVIDUAL DIFFERENCES

People do not experience the same level of stress or exhibit similar outcomes for a given type of stressor. For example, the type of stressors experienced at work varied by occupation and gender. The stressor of low control (over one's job tasks) was higher in lower-level clerical jobs than professional occupations, while interpersonal conflict was a greater source of stress for women than men.[41] Per-ceived control was also a significant moderator of the stress process. People perceived lower levels of stress, and experienced more favourable consequences from stress, when they believed they could exert control over the stressors affecting their lives.[42]

In support of this finding, another study showed that employees had more negative physiological responses to perceived stress when they worked on an assembly line than in a more flexible work organisation.[43] Assembly-line technology allows employees much less control than other organis-ational arrangements. Finally, the personality trait of chronic hostility or cynicism was also a signifi-cant moderator of the stress process. Research demonstrated that people who were chronically angry, suspicious or mistrustful were twice as likely to have coronary artery blockages. We can all protect our hearts by learning to avoid these tendencies.[44]

In summary, even though researchers have been able to identify several important moderators, a large gap still exists in identifying relevant individual differences. For example, there are many people who never seem to get stressed, although they work very hard:

> I've never really felt under stress or overworked', says Tom Kok, a Dutch entrepreneur who has never worked less than a 60-hour-week in the past few years. `But there have been some moments when I could very easily have been. Yet I also think I know how it feels to be overstressed: you get up in the morning and at first you think 'let's get started' but a few seconds later you break down. But one way or another, these things don't affect me very much. I think I have a healthy capacity to just shrug my shoulders and say 'So what ...?' I like to put things in perspective.[45]

Important stressors and stress outcomes

As we have seen, stressors trigger stress which, in turn, leads to a variety of outcomes. This section explores an important category of extraorganisational stressors: that of stressful life events. Burnout, another especially troublesome stress-related outcome, is also examined.

Stressful life events

Events such as experiencing the death of a family member, being assaulted, moving home, ending an intimate relationship, being seriously ill or taking a big test can create stress. These events are stress-ful because they involve significant changes that require adaptation and often social readjustment. These Stressful life events, which are not work-related have been the most extensively investigated extraorganisational stressors.

Thomas Holmes and Richard Rahe conducted pioneering research on the relationship between stressful life events and subsequent illness. During their research, they developed a widely used ques-tionnaire to assess life stress.[46]

Stressful life events
life events that disrupt daily routines and social relationships

ASSESSING STRESSFUL LIFE EVENTS

The Social Readjustment Rating Scale developed by Holmes and Rahe has been the dominant method for assessing an individual's cumulative stressful life events for the past 30 years. The rating instrument was recently updated and revised by a group of researchers in order to modernise the list of stressors and to overcome some technical problems with the survey. As shown in the next Activity, the new rating scale consists of 51 life events. Each event has a corresponding value, called a life change unit, representing the degree of social readjustment necessary to cope with the event. The larger the value, the more stressful the event. These values were obtained from a national sample of 3122 people who evaluated the stressfulness of each event.[47] (Please take a moment to complete the social readjustment rating scale and to calculate your total life stress score.)

Research revealed a positive relationship between the total score on the original Social Readjustment Rating Scale and subsequent illness. The interpretative norms reveal that low scores are associated with good health, and larger scores are related to increased chances of experiencing illness. A word of caution is in order, however. If you scored over 150, don't head for a sterile cocoon. High scores on the Social Readjustment Rating Scale do not guarantee you will become ill. Rather, a high score simply increases one's statistical risk of illness.[48]

How much life stress do you experience?

Instructions

Place a tick next to each of the events you experienced within the past year. Then add the life change units associated with the various events to derive your total life stress score.

Life event	Life change unit
_____ Death of spouse/mate	87
_____ Death of close family member	79
_____ Major injury/illness to self	78
_____ Detention in prison or other institution	76
_____ Major injury/illness to close family member	72
_____ Foreclosure on loan/mortgage	71
_____ Divorce	71
_____ Being a victim of crime	70
_____ Being the victim of police brutality	69
_____ Infidelity	69
_____ Experiencing domestic violence/sexual abuse	69
_____ Separation or reconciliation with spouse/mate	66
_____ Being fired/laid-off/unemployed	64
_____ Experiencing financial problems/difficulties	62
_____ Death of close friend	61
_____ Surviving a disaster	59
_____ Becoming a single parent	59
_____ Assuming responsibility for sick or elderly loved one	56
_____ Loss of, or major reduction in, health insurance/benefits	56
_____ Self/close family member being arrested for breaking the law	56
_____ Major disagreements over child support/custody/visiting rights	53
_____ Experiencing/involved in a car accident	53
_____ Being disciplined at work/demoted	53
_____ Dealing with unwanted pregnancy	51
_____ Adult child moving in with parent/parent moving in with adult child	50
_____ Child develops behaviour or learning problem	49
_____ Experiencing employment discrimination/sexual harassment	48
_____ Attempting to modify addictive behaviour of self	47

activity

Life event	Life change unit
_____ Discovering/attempting to modify addictive behaviour of close family member	46
_____ Employer reorganisation/downsizing	45
_____ Dealing with infertility/miscarriage	44
_____ Getting married/remarried	43
_____ Changing employers/careers	43
_____ Failure to obtain/qualify for a mortgage	42
_____ Pregnancy of self/spouse/mate	41
_____ Experiencing discrimination/harassment outside the workplace	39
_____ Release from prison	39
_____ Spouse/mate begins/ceases work outside the home	38
_____ Major disagreement with boss/co-worker	37
_____ Change in residence	35
_____ Finding appropriate child care/day care	34
_____ Experiencing a large, unexpected monetary gain	33
_____ Changing positions (transfer, promotion)	33
_____ Gaining a new family member	33
_____ Changing work responsibilities	32
_____ Child leaving home	30
_____ Obtaining a home mortgage	30
_____ Obtaining a major loan other than home mortgage	30
_____ Retirement	28
_____ Beginning/ceasing formal education	26
_____ Being charged with breaking the law	22

Total score_____

Interpretation norms

Less than 150   = Odds are you will experience good health next year
150–300   = 50% chance of illness next year
Greater than 300 = 70% chance of illness next year

SOURCE: C. J. Hobson, J. Kamen, J. Szostek, C. M. Nethercut, J. W. Tiedmann and S. Wojnarowicz, 'Stressful Life Events: A Revision and Update of the Social Readjustment Rating Scale', *International Journal of Stress Management*, January 1998, pp. 7–8.

RESEARCH FINDINGS AND PRACTICAL IMPLICATIONS

Numerous studies have examined the relationship between life stress on the one hand and illness and job performance on the other. Subjects with higher scores on the Social Readjustment Rating Scale had significantly more problems with chronic headaches, sudden cardiac death, pregnancy and birth complications, tuberculosis, diabetes, anxiety, depression and a host of minor physical ailments. Meanwhile, psychosocial problems and academic and work performance declined as scores on the Social Readjustment Rating scale increased.[49]

Negative (as opposed to positive) personal life changes were associated with greater susceptibility to colds, job stress and psychological distress, and also lower levels of job satisfaction and organisational commitment.[50]

Finally, recent studies revealed that women rated the life events contained in the Social Readjustment Rating Scale as more stressful than men. Results also showed that there were no meaningful differences in life event ratings between various age groups and income levels.[51] The key implication is that employee illness and job performance are affected by extraorganisational stressors, particularly those that are negative and uncontrollable. Because employees do not leave their personal problems at the office door or factory gate, organisations need to be aware of external sources of employee stress or, as Cary Cooper argues: 'Employers have a duty of care in respect of how they manage not only their equipment or physical environment but also their people, including their workload, their hours of work and perhaps their careers'.[52]

Once identified, alternative work schedules, training programmes and counselling can be used to help employees cope with these stressors. This may not only reduce the costs associated with illnesses and absenteeism but may also lead to positive work attitudes, better job performance and reduced staff turnover. For example, consider the views of the following managers, who actively try to make sure that their policies fit the needs of their employees:

> Mireille Jacquemyn, HR-manager of the Antwerp Zoo (Belgium), is responsible for a lot of employees. She tries to find rapid and practical solutions to their day-to-day problems. For example, her employees are free to work as much and whenever they want to. Further on, she organises extra childcare for their children, an interesting option for employees who work at times when most childcare services fail, as is sometimes the case during weekends and public holidays.

> Rozemarijn Laureyssens, medical director at Dupont de Nemours, Genève, Switzerland, tries to feel for the individual needs of all employees by implementing a range of flexibility systems. For example, employees can benefit from part-time working, job-sharing, compressed workweeks, working at home, flextime, ... Moreover, all employees can take six months leave without pay for social reasons.[53]

In addition, by acknowledging that work outcomes are affected by extraorganisational stressors, professionals may avoid the trap of automatically attributing poor performance to low motivation or lack of ability. Such awareness is likely to engender positive reactions from employees and lead to resolution of problems, not just symptoms. For individuals with a high score on the Social Readjustment Rating Scale, it would be best to defer controllable stressors, such as moving or buying a new car, until things settle down.

Burnout

Burnout is a stress-induced problem common among members of 'helping' professions such as teaching, social work, human resources, nursing and law enforcement. It does not involve a specific feeling, attitude or physiological outcome anchored to a specific point in time. Rather, burnout is a condition that occurs over time. Dr Graham Lucas, psychiatrist at the Cromwell and Priory Hospitals in London, refers to the phenomenon as 'the catastrophic consequence of long-lasting, relentless stress'.[54] Consider the symptoms, causes and consequences of burnout in the following two examples:

Burnout
a condition of emotional exhaustion and negative attitudes

> Sandy Wilson, a consultant with many years of experience, felt frustrated, tense and washed-out. He was 49 years old and had the knowledge to tackle any problem but he didn't have the courage any more. He took less physical exercise, drank a lot and neglected the relationship with his son. He only saw himself doing the same exhausting work for years to come. 'I've lost my spirit. I have no more will to fight', he told his wife.[55]
>
> 'In my case, burnout came up very slowly and gradually', says A. B., who would like to remain anonymous. 'I've worked as a nurse for over twenty years. I was always prepared to engage in additional training and education, including weekend or evening-courses. And I never complained when I had to work overtime. But if you never get a pat on the back from the top, or if the management team gives very few stimuli to keep pace with recent developments, the motivation drops. In the long run there are no more challenges left.'[56]

TABLE 7.1 ATTITUDINAL CHARACTERISTICS OF BURNOUT

Attitude	Description
Fatalism	A feeling that you lack control over your work
Boredom	A lack of interest in doing your job
Discontent	A sense of being unhappy with your job
Cynicism	A tendency to undervalue the content of your job and the rewards received
Inadequacy	A feeling of not being able to meet your objectives
Failure	A tendency to discredit your performance and conclude that you are ineffective
Overwork	A feeling of having too much to do and not enough time to complete it
Nastiness	A tendency to be rude or unpleasant to your co-workers
Dissatisfaction	A feeling that you are not being justly rewarded for your efforts
Escape	A desire to give up and get away from it all

SOURCE: Adapted from D. P. Rogers, 'Helping Employees Cope with Burn-out', *Business*, October–December 1984, p. 4.

You can see that burnout has a devastating impact on employee well-being. Typical characteristics are withdrawal, fatigue and less job involvement, the latter being mainly noticed in those who are normally highly involved. If you can answer 'yes' to several of the following questions, you're probably heading for, or already suffering from, a major burnout:

- Do you experience your work as an unbearable burden?
- Are you constantly worrying about your work?
- Do you consider every assignment an awful job?
- Are you constantly feeling empty and indifferent?
- Do you have to drag yourself out of your bed every morning?
- Is 'job satisfaction' a term you've only ever heard of (not experienced)?
- Can you hardly ever laugh at work?
- Do you find your colleagues immensely irritating?[57]

Of course, everyone has a bad day from time to time, but people who suffer from burnout are constantly feeling unhappy at work.

Table 7.1 describes ten attitudinal characteristics of burnout. Experts say a substantial number of people suffer from this problem. For example, a national study of 28 000 Americans indicated that more than 50 per cent were 'burned out'.[58] A study of 1800 software professionals, from 19 German and Swiss companies, revealed a positive association between measures of burnout (especially lack of identification) with job stressors and a lack of positive features in the work situation (such as control at work, complexity at work and openness to criticism within the team). These results imply that burnout is not limited to people working in the helping professions. To promote better understanding of this important outcome of stress, we turn our attention to a model of the burnout process and highlight relevant research and techniques for its prevention.[59]

A MODEL OF BURNOUT

A model of burnout is presented in Figure 7.2. The fundamental premise underlying the model is that burnout develops in phases. The three key phases are emotional exhaustion, depersonalisation and feeling a lack of personal accomplishment.[60] As shown in Figure 7.2, emotional exhaustion is due to a combination of personal stressors and job and organisational stressors.[61] People who expect a lot from themselves and the organisations in which they work tend to create more internal stress, which, in turn, leads to emotional exhaustion. Similarly, emotional exhaustion is fuelled by having too much work to do, by role conflict and by the type of interpersonal interactions encountered at work. Frequent, intense face-to-face interactions that are emotionally charged are associated with higher levels of emotional exhaustion. Over time, emotional exhaustion leads to depersonalisation, which is a state of psychologically withdrawing from one's job. This ultimately results in a feeling of being unappreciated, ineffective or inadequate. The additive effect of these three phases is a host of negative attitudinal and behavioural outcomes. Consider the following case:

FIGURE 7.2 A MODEL OF BURNOUT

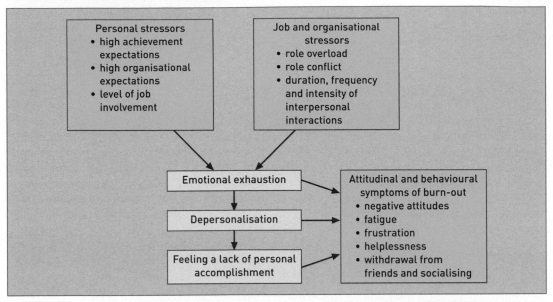

SOURCE: Based in part on C. L. Cordes and T. W. Dougherty, 'A Review and an Integration of Research on Job Burnout', *Academy of Management Review*, October 1993, p. 641.

> " A vice president of a large corporation who hadn't received an expected promotion left his company to become the head of a smaller, family-owned business, which was floundering and needed his skills. Although he had jumped at the opportunity to rescue the small company, once there he discovered an unimaginable morass of difficulties, among them continual conflicts within the family. He felt he could not leave but neither could he succeed. Trapped in a kind of psychological quicksand, he worked days, nights and weekends for months in an attempt to pull himself free. His wife protested, to no avail. Finally, he was hospitalised for exhaustion.[62] "

RESEARCH FINDINGS AND PRACTICAL IMPLICATIONS

A meta-analysis of 61 studies covering several thousand people uncovered three important conclusions.[63] First, burnout was positively related to job stressors and turnover intentions and negatively associated with the receipt of supportive resources (e.g. social support and team cohesion), job enhancement opportunities, performance-contingent rewards, organisational commitment and job satisfaction. Second, the different phases of burnout, as shown in Figure 7.2, obtained differential relationships with a variety of behavioural and attitudinal symptoms of burnout. This supports the idea that burnout develops in phases. Nonetheless, researchers do not yet agree completely on the order of these phases.[64] Finally, burnout was more strongly related to employees' work demands than it was to the resources people received at work. This suggests that organisations should be particularly sensitive to employees' workloads. The next Snapshot discusses how Zeneca Pharmaceuticals, which is located in the United Kingdom, tried to adhere to this recommendation.

Removing personal, job and organisational stressors is the most straightforward way to prevent burnout. Organisations can also reduce burnout by buffering its effects. Potential **Buffers** include extra staff or equipment at peak work periods, support from top management, increased freedom to make decisions, recognition for accomplishments, time off for personal development or rest and equitable rewards. Decreasing the quantity and increasing the quality of communications is another possible buffer. Finally, organisations can change the content of an individual's job by adding or eliminating responsibilities, increasing the amount of participation in decision making, altering the pattern of interpersonal contacts or assigning the person to a new position.[65]

Buffers
resources or administrative changes that reduce burnout

snapshot

How Zeneca helps employees manage their workloads

Zeneca's highly developed employee assistance programme is one of a small number in Britain that specifically aims to tackle stress at its source. Somewhere in the mid-1990s the pharmaceutical firm set up a specialist team to give advice and training on how to balance the needs of the workplace with the pressures of everyday life.

Zeneca's Counselling and Life Management team, shortened to CALM, runs workshops and other events where employees can pick up tips on caring for elderly relatives, coping with marital break-ups, handling financial pressures and other matters that lead to stress. An assessment of mental health is part of the employees' medical screening.

More than 5500 employees, who work either at Zeneca's UK headquarters near Macclesfield, Cheshire or at other centres around the country, can contact the CALM team by telephone or request a face-to-face meeting. Earlier an entire manufacturing team, including managers and support staff, attended a three-hour workshop on balanced living.

'What we are broadly telling people is that there are various arenas in their lives, including their family, social life, and intellectual and cultural aspects', Richard Heron, medical officer at Zeneca, explains. 'It is important that they pay attention to all of them, because they all play their part in creating the whole person.'

Zeneca has been offering employee counselling for a long time, but it is only since setting up the CALM programme that the company has made a real attempt to tackle the causes of stress at work, as well as treating the symptoms. For example, the company also decided to use its appraisal system to review workload and draft individual development plans, so that staff would have opportunities to develop knowledge and skills to match the demands of their jobs.

Pivotal to the success of these efforts to prevent excessive pressure on employees, was a letter from the company's chief executive urging managers to keep track of individual's workloads, set staff reasonable timescales and make sure that they had 'enough free time for outside pursuits'.

SOURCE: N. Merrick, 'Getting to Grips', *People Management*, 10 December 1998; and A. Arkin, 'HSE Guide Helps Stress Victims Claim Damages', *People Management*, 15 June 1996.

Both Deloitte & Touche and Ernst & Young have implemented some of these recommendations.

> Deloitte & Touche is implementing a policy on some projects that curbs their consultants' travel time. Instead of spending five days a week at a client's offices, consultants spend three nights and four days, fly home and work a fifth day in their home cities. That means 'you can plan your life and be home for a real weekend,' says Malva Rabinowitz, a Deloitte managing director. Most clients recognise it's a good thing when they see the policy in action.
>
> Similarly, Ernst & Young is involving clients on some consulting projects in setting up a 'team calendar' that integrates team members' work and personal commitments, says Bob Forbes, an Ernst partner. While client needs still come first, the calendar puts people's off-the-job lives on the radar screen. Ernst & Young has a committee monitoring accountants' workloads. It helps burnout candidates shift clients or schedule vacations.[66]

There also are two long-term strategies for reducing burnout that are increasingly being used by companies. Apple Computer, American Express, IBM, McDonald's Corporation and Intel, for instance, use sabbaticals to replenish employees' energy and desire to work. These programmes allow employees to take a designated amount of time off from work after being employed a certain number of years. Companies in Canada, Australia and Israel also use sabbaticals to prevent stress and burnout, whereas Europe does not have a sabbatical culture. In the Netherlands, the organisation Stichting Sabbatical Leave argues that a sabbatical leave should be a right for every employee. When a number of large Dutch companies such as PTT Telecom, Randstad and KLM were asked if they were planning to introduce sabbatical leaves in the future, they did not seem to be very enthusiastic.[67]

An employee retreat is the second long-term strategy. Retreats entail sending employees to an offsite location for three to five days. While there, everyone can relax, reflect or engage in team and relationship-building activities. This is precisely what PricewaterhouseCoopers is doing to help its employees cope with work stress: PricewaterhouseCoopers has a two-day stress survival clinic where participants meet with a physician, nutritionist and psychiatrist. The retreat, held in such locations as Toronto and Captiva Island, Florida, includes Mediterranean-style cuisine served in candlelit dining rooms and time to focus on coping better with pressure.[68]

Moderators of occupational stress

Moderators, as mentioned earlier, are variables that cause the relationship between stressors, perceived stress and outcomes to be weaker for some people and stronger for others. Professionals with a working knowledge of important stress moderators can confront employee stress in the following ways:

- Awareness of moderators helps identify those most likely to experience stress and its negative outcomes. Then stress-reduction programmes can be formulated for high-risk employees.
- Moderators, in and of themselves, suggest possible solutions for reducing the negative outcomes of occupational stress.

Keeping these objectives in mind, we will examine four important moderators: social support, coping, hardiness and 'Type A behaviour'.

Social support

Talking to a friend or getting together with 'mates' can be comforting during times of fear, stress or loneliness. For a variety of reasons, meaningful social relationships help people do a better job of handling stress. Social support is measured in terms of both the quantity and quality of an individual's social relationships. Figure 7.3 illustrates the mechanisms of social support.

> **Social support** amount of helpfulness derived from social relationships

A MODEL OF SOCIAL SUPPORT

As Figure 7.3 shows, one's support network must be perceived before it can be used. Support networks evolve from any or all of five sources: cultural norms, social institutions, companies, groups or individuals. For example, there is more cultural emphasis on caring for the elderly in Japan than in Europe. Japanese culture is thus a strong source of social support for older Japanese people. Alternatively, individuals may fall back on social institutions such as Social Security or the Red Cross, religious groups or family and friends for support. In turn, these various sources provide four types of support:

- Esteem support: providing information that a person is accepted and respected despite any problems or inadequacies.
- Informational support: providing help in defining, understanding and coping with problems.
- Social companionship: spending time with others in leisure and recreational activities.
- Instrumental support: providing financial aid, material resources or necessary services.[69]

If social support is perceived as available, an individual then decides whether to use it.[70] Generally, social support is used either as a global or a functional support but in some cases it is used as both. Global social support is very broad in scope, coming as it does from four sources, and is applicable to any situation at any time. Functional social support is narrower and, if relied on in the wrong situation, can be unhelpful.

For example, if you crashed your new car, a good insurance (instrumental support) would be a better buffer than sympathy from a bartender. On the other hand, social companionship would be more helpful than instrumental support in coping with loneliness. After social support is engaged for one or both of these purposes, its effectiveness can be determined. If consolation or relief is not

> **Global social support** the total amount of social support available
>
> **Functional social support** support sources that buffer stress in specific situations

FIGURE 7.3 A FLOW MODEL OF THE MECHANISMS OF SOCIAL SUPPORT

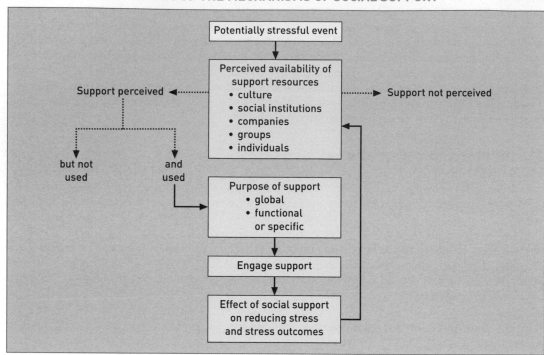

SOURCE: Portions adapted from S. Cohen and T. A. Wills, 'Stress, Social Support, and the Buffering Hypothesis', *Psychological Bulletin*, September 1985, pp. 310–57; and J. G. Bruhn and B. U. Philips, 'Measuring Social Support: A Synthesis of Current Approaches', *Journal of Behavioral Medicine*, June 1984, pp. 151–69.

experienced, it may be that the type of support was inappropriate. The feedback loop in Figure 7.3, from effect of social support back to perceived availability, reflects the need to fall back on other sources of support when necessary.

RESEARCH FINDINGS AND PRACTICAL IMPLICATIONS

Research shows that global social support is negatively related to physiological processes and mortality. In other words, people with low social support tend to have poorer cardiovascular and immune system functioning and tend to die earlier than those with strong social support networks.[71] Further, global support protects against the perception of stress, depression, psychological illness, pregnancy complications, anxiety, loneliness, high blood pressure and a variety of other ailments.

In contrast, negative social support, which amounts to someone undermining another person, negatively affects one's mental health.[72] We would all be well advised to avoid people who try to undermine us. Moreover, there is no clear pattern of results regarding the buffering effects of both global and functional social support.[73] It appears that social support sometimes serves as a buffer against stress but we do not know precisely when or why so additional research is needed. Finally, global social support is positively related to the availability of support resources; that is, people who interact with a greater number of friends, family or co-workers have a wider base of social support from which to draw during stressful periods.[74]

Coping

Coping is 'the process of managing demands (external or internal) that are appraised as taxing or exceeding the resources of the person'.[75] Because effective coping helps reduce the impact of stressors and stress, your personal life and professional skills can be enhanced by understanding this process better. Figure 7.4 depicts an instructive model of coping.

The coping process has three major components: situational and personal factors; cognitive appraisals of the stressor; and coping strategies. As shown in Figure 7.4, both situational and

Coping
process of
managing stress

FIGURE 7.4 A MODEL OF THE COPING PROCESS

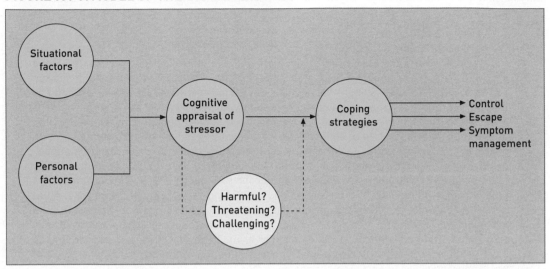

SOURCE: Based in part on R. S. Lazarus and S. Folkman, 'Coping and Adaptation', in *Handbook of Behavioral Medicine*, ed. W. D. Gentry (New York: The Guilford Press, 1984), pp. 282–325.

personal factors influence the appraisal of stressors. In turn, appraisal directly influences the choice of coping strategies. Each of the major components of this model deserves a closer look.

SITUATIONAL AND PERSONAL FACTORS

Situational factors are environmental characteristics that affect how people interpret (appraise) stressors. For example, the ambiguity of a situation – such as walking down a dark street at night in an unfamiliar area – makes it difficult to determine whether a potentially dangerous situation exists. Ambiguity creates differences in how people appraise and subsequently cope with stressors. Other situational factors are the frequency of exposure to a stressor and social support networks.

Personal factors are personality traits and personal resources that affect the appraisal of stressors. For instance, because being tired or sick can distort the interpretation of stressors, an extremely tired individual may appraise an innocent question as a threat or challenge. Traits such as locus of control, self-esteem, optimism, self-efficacy (recall our discussion in Chapters 2 and 3) and work experience were also found to affect the appraisal of stressors.[76]

COGNITIVE APPRAISAL OF STRESSORS

Cognitive appraisal reflects an individual's overall perception or evaluation of a situation or stressor. Cognitive appraisal results in a categorisation of the situation or stressor as either harmful, threatening or challenging. It is important to understand the differences between these appraisals because they influence how people cope. 'Harm (including loss) represents damage already done; threat involves the potential for harm; and challenge means the potential for significant gain under difficult odds.'[77] Coping with harm usually entails undoing or reinterpreting something that occurred in the past because the damage is already done. In contrast, threatening situations engage anticipatory coping. That is, people cope with threat by preparing for harm that may occur in the future. Challenge also activates anticipatory coping. In contrast with threat, an appraisal of challenge results in coping that focuses on what can be gained rather than what may be lost.

COPING STRATEGIES

Coping strategies are characterised by the specific behaviours and cognitions used to cope with a situation. People use a combination of three approaches to cope with stressors and stress (see Figure 7.4).

The first, called a **Control strategy**, has a 'take-charge' tone. For example, so-called 'downshifting', where someone moves to a less stressful job, is a possible coping strategy to gain more flexibility

Control strategy
coping strategy that directly confronts or solves problems

in your life. Consider the story of Krysia Devreux-Bletek, managing director of the Brussels software company Ecsem:

> We worked our brains out during the week. We drove thousands of kilometres a year. Over the weekends we were busy rebuilding, painting or wallpapering as if we wanted some kind of a palace. We bought ourselves a large freezer, a microwave and tons of vitamin tablets in order to keep going. After a while we started feeling guilty: we hardly had any time to see our kids grow up, and many friends who were in the same situation were divorced. Fortunately we worked in a super-booming sector, people admired us for what we were doing, we had lots of contacts and so we went even further and started our own business . . . . So, in addition to our relentless workload we took on an extra burden: financial risk. We never really slept well and now we know why. But the job was unbelievably fascinating and challenging, so we went all out for it. Dinners with friends or family? No time. Sport? No time. Just sitting around and do nothing for a moment? Nonsense. All at once, we finally got our senses back: our quality of life increased visibly when my husband took a sideways step and started working at home. At that time, our choice wasn't socially acceptable. Other couples faced a dilemma: her or me? They saw it as a sacrifice but to us it was an obvious decision. We've lost our feelings of guilt, the freezer is almost empty and we're enjoying playing sport together again . . . .[78]

Escape strategy
coping strategy that avoids or ignores stressors and problems

Symptom management strategy
coping strategy that focuses on reducing the symptoms of stress

An Escape strategy amounts to the opposite of tackling the problem head-on. Individuals use this strategy when they passively accept stressful situations or avoid them by failing to confront the cause of stress (an obnoxious co-worker, for instance).

Finally, a Symptom management strategy uses methods such as relaxation, meditation, medication and exercise.

RESEARCH FINDINGS AND PRACTICAL IMPLICATIONS

As suggested by the model in Figure 7.4, an individual's appraisal of a stressor correlates with the choice of a coping strategy.[79] In further support of the coping model, personal factors, appraisal and coping all significantly predicted psychological symptoms of stress. Nonetheless, research has not clearly identified which type of coping strategy – control, escape or symptom management – is most effective. It appears that the best coping strategy depends on the situation at hand.[80] Escaping stress – by going on vacation, for example – is sometimes better than confronting a stressor with a control-oriented coping strategy. Researchers are currently trying to determine these contingency relationships.

Hardiness

Hardiness
personality characteristic that neutralises stress

Suzanne Kobasa, a behavioural scientist, identified a collection of personality characteristics, referred to as Hardiness. These involve the ability to, perceptually or behaviourally, transform negative stressors into positive challenges. Hardiness embraces the personality dimensions of commitment, locus of control and challenge.[81]

PERSONALITY CHARACTERISTICS OF HARDINESS

Commitment reflects the extent to which an individual is involved in whatever he or she is doing. Committed people have a sense of purpose and do not give up under pressure because they tend to 'invest themselves' in the situation. The extent of commitment, however, is culturally determined, observes Cary Cooper: 'A UK manager who takes work home is said to be committed to his job. A German manager who does the same would be thought of as incompetent, because part of his job as a manager is to manage time'.[82]

As discussed in Chapter 2, individuals with an internal locus of control believe they can influence the events that affect their lives. People possessing this trait are more likely to foresee stressful events, thereby reducing their exposure to anxiety-producing situations. Moreover, their perception of being in control leads them to use proactive coping strategies.

Challenge is represented by the belief that change is a normal part of life. Hence, change is seen as an opportunity for growth and development rather than a threat to security.

RESEARCH FINDINGS AND PRACTICAL IMPLICATIONS

A five-year study of 259 managers from a public utility revealed that hardiness – commitment, locus of control and challenge – reduced the probability of illness following exposure to stress.[83] The three components of hardiness were also found to directly influence how 276 members of the Israeli Defence Forces appraised stressors and ultimately coped with them. Hardy individuals interpreted stressors less negatively and were more likely to use control strategies than less hardy people.[84] Furthermore, additional research demonstrated that hardy individuals displayed lower stress, burnout and psychological distress and experienced higher job satisfaction than their less hardy counterparts.[85] Finally, a study of 73 pregnant women revealed that hardy women had fewer problems during labour and more positive perceptions of their infants than less hardy women.[86]

One practical offshoot of this research is organisational training and development programmes that strengthen the characteristics of commitment, personal control and challenge. Because of cost limitations, it is necessary to target key employees or those most susceptible to stress (such as air traffic controllers). The hardiness concept also meshes nicely with job design. Enriched jobs are likely to fuel the hardiness components of commitment and challenge. Recall our discussion in Chapter 5. A final application of the hardiness concept is as a diagnostic tool. Employees getting low scores on hardiness tests would be good candidates for stress-reduction programmes.

Type A behaviour pattern

Cardiovascular disease is the leading cause of death among adults in Western industrialised countries. Because 'Type A behaviour' was linked to cardiovascular disease, researchers devoted significant effort in identifying Type A characteristics and the situations that elicit this behaviour pattern.

TYPE A BEHAVIOUR DEFINED

Meyer Friedman and Ray Rosenman, the cardiologists who isolated the **Type A behaviour syndrome** in the 1950s, gave the following explanation of the behaviour:

> Type A behaviour pattern is an action–emotion complex that can be observed in any person who is aggressively involved in a chronic, incessant struggle to achieve more and more in less and less time, and if required to do so, against the opposing efforts of other things or persons. It is not a psychosis or a complex of worries or fears or phobias or obsessions but a socially acceptable – indeed often praised – form of conflict. People possessing this pattern are also quite prone to exhibiting a free-floating but extraordinarily well-rationalised hostility. As might be expected, this behaviour pattern has degrees of intensity.[87]

Type A behaviour syndrome aggressively involved in a chronic, determined struggle to accomplish more in less time

Because Type A behaviour is a matter of degree, it is measured on a continuum. This continuum has the hurried, competitive Type A behaviour pattern at one end and the more relaxed Type B behaviour at the other. Take a moment to complete the Type A survey contained in the next Activity. This exercise will help you better understand the characteristics of the Type A behaviour pattern. Where do you fall on the Type A continuum?

TYPE A CHARACTERISTICS

While labelling Type A behaviour as 'hurry sickness', Friedman and Rosenman noted that Type A individuals frequently tend to exhibit most of the behaviour listed in Table 7.2. In high-pressure, achievement-oriented schools and work environments, Type A behaviour is unwittingly cultivated and even admired.

RESEARCH FINDINGS AND PRACTICAL IMPLICATIONS

Research findings highlight the advantages and disadvantages of being Type A.

OB research has demonstrated that Type A employees tend to be more productive than their Type B co-workers. For instance, Type A behaviour yielded a significant and positive correlation with the average grades of 766 students, the quantity and quality of 278 university lecturers' performances and the sales performance of 222 life insurance brokers.[88]

On the other hand, Type A behaviour is associated with some negative consequences. A meta-analysis of 99 studies revealed that Type A individuals had higher heart rates, diastolic blood

Where are you on the Type A–B behaviour continuum?

Instructions

For each question, indicate the extent to which each statement is true of you.

	Not at all true of me		Neither very true nor very untrue of me		Very true of me
1 I have given up before I'm absolutely sure that I'm licked (defeated).	1	2	3	4	5
2 Sometimes I feel that I shouldn't be working so hard but something drives me on.	1	2	3	4	5
3 I thrive on challenging situations. The more challenges I have, the better.	1	2	3	4	5
4 In comparison to most people I know, I'm very involved in my work.	1	2	3	4	5
5 It seems as if I need 30 hours a day to finish all the things I'm faced with.	1	2	3	4	5
6 In general, I approach my work more seriously than most people I know.	1	2	3	4	5
7 I guess there are some people who can be nonchalant about their work, but I'm not one of them.	1	2	3	4	5
8 My achievements are considered to be significantly higher than those of most people I know.	1	2	3	4	5
9 I've often been asked to be a manager of some group or groups.	1	2	3	4	5

Total score = _____

Arbitrary norms

Type B = 9–22
Balanced Type A and Type B = 23–35
Type A = 36–45

SOURCE: Taken from R. D. Caplan, S. Cobb, J. R. P. French, Jr, R. Van Harrison and S. R. Pinneau, Jr, *Job Demands and Worker Health* (New Publication No. [NIOSH] 75–160), (Washington, DC: US Department of Health, Education and Welfare, 1975), pp. 253–4.

pressure and systolic blood pressure than Type B people. Type A people also showed greater cardiovascular activity when they encountered any of the following situations:

■ Receipt of positive or negative feedback.
■ Receipt of verbal harassment or criticism.
■ Tasks requiring mental as opposed to physical work.[89]

Unfortunately for Type A individuals, these situations are frequently experienced at work. A second meta-analysis of 83 studies further demonstrated that the hard-driving and competitive aspects of Type A are related to coronary heart disease but that the speed, impatience and job involvement aspects are not. This meta-analysis also showed that feelings of anger, hostility and aggression were more strongly related to heart disease than was Type A behaviour.[90]

Researchers have now developed stress-reduction techniques to help Type A people to pace themselves more realistically and achieve better balance in their lives; they are discussed in the next section of this chapter. Management can help Type A people, however, by not overloading them with work despite their apparent eagerness to take an ever-increasing load. Coaches need to actively help, rather than unthinkingly exploit, Type A individuals.

TABLE 7.2 TYPE A CHARACTERISTICS

1	Hurried speech; explosive accentuation of key words
2	Tendency to walk, move and eat rapidly
3	Constant impatience with the rate at which most events take place (e.g. irritation with slow-moving traffic and slow-talking and slow-to-act people)
4	Strong preference for thinking of or doing two or more things at once (e.g. reading this text and doing something else at the same time)
5	Tendency to turn conversations around to personally meaningful subjects or themes
6	Tendency to interrupt while others are speaking to make your point or to complete their train of thought in your own words
7	Guilt feelings during periods of relaxation or leisure time
8	Tendency to be oblivious to surroundings during daily activities
9	Greater concern for things worth *having* than with things worth being
10	Tendency to schedule more and more in less and less time; a chronic sense of time urgency
11	Feelings of competition rather than compassion when faced with another Type A person
12	Development of nervous tics or characteristic gestures
13	A firm belief that success is due to the ability to get things done faster than the other guy
14	A tendency to view and evaluate personal activities and the activities of other people in terms of 'numbers' (e.g. number of meetings attended, telephone calls made, visitors received)

SOURCE: Adapted from M. Friedman and R. H. Rosenman, *Type A Behavior and Your Heart* (Greenwich, CT: Fawcett Publications, 1974), pp. 100–102.

Stress-reduction techniques

All told, it is estimated that almost 85 per cent of all illness and injury is the result of lifestyle choices.[91] Therefore, it is not surprising that, increasingly, organisations are implementing a variety of stress-reduction programmes to help employees cope with modern-day stress. Consider the following example of Scient, an IT-company who actively tries to create a chilled atmosphere and a play-like culture to cope with the many pressures of everyday work:

> 'Dot-com consultancy is a high stress, long-hours occupation but you would not think it from the mellow, "take-it-easy" atmosphere of this workplace', says Tony O'Connell. He is one of the two 'morale officers' in the company, charged with keeping the troops happy. 'Fun is part of our deal,' he says, 'otherwise our employees probably wouldn't last very long'. At Scient, IT-professionals whizz around on aluminium mini-scooters, riding past desks decorated with inflatable plastic aliens and Yogi Bears. Consultants hold discussion groups seated comfortably on colourful leather sofas and armchairs. Next door to the snooker room is the company snack bar, where staff can raid a chilled soft drinks cabinet and toast bagels in the microwave. Cream cheese and smoked salmon is in the fridge. Every day is dress-down Friday at Scient and in a break-out room, named after one of the staff's favourite local pubs, a group of young consultants attends a seminar on customer care. Scient is a young, fast-growing global company with a lot of blue chip clients but the key to its success in this competitive marketplace is its new take on human resources: the creation of a new post, the morale officer. 'I'm here to take the temperature, to act as a sounding board for employees with problems. I'm also a social secretary but most importantly: I'm here to spread fun. People who enjoy themselves can cope with the pressures better. That's why I ordered the mini scooters and the plastic aliens. I'm also organising a movie night and a summer picnic. And those three cans of spray hair colouring you see on my desk are left over from the England versus Germany match in Euro 2000, when live pictures were projected on to a wall at Scient's offices and there was a bet with Scient's Munich office.'[92]

TABLE 7.3 STRESS-REDUCTION TECHNIQUES

Technique	Descriptions	Assessment
Muscle relaxation	Uses slow deep breathing and systematic muscle tension reduction	Inexpensive and easy to use; may require a trained professional to implement
Biofeedback	A machine is used to train people to detect muscular tension; muscle relaxation is then used to alleviate this symptom of stress	Expensive due to costs of equipment; however, equipment can be used to evaluate effectiveness of other stress-reduction programmes
Meditation	The relaxation response is activated by redirecting one's thoughts away from oneself; a four-step procedure is used	Least expensive, simple to implement, and can be practised almost anywhere
Cognitive restructuring	Irrational or maladaptive thoughts are identified and replaced with those that are rational or logical	Expensive because it requires a trained psychologist or counsellor
Holistic wellness	A broad, interdisciplinary approach that goes beyond stress reduction by advocating that people strive for personal wellness in all aspects of their lives	Involves inexpensive but often behaviourally difficult lifestyle changes

Although this example is pretty striking, stress-prevention programmes in the UK tend to be confined to large organisations employing in excess of 500 employees. However, a number of government initiatives have been introduced within the European Union, including collaborative research programmes, new working regulations and published guidelines to help organisations reduce workplace stress and the formation of a Europe-wide Health and Safety Agency in Bilbao, Spain.[93]

Stress intervention can focus on the individual, the organisation (as in the above example) or on the interface between individual and organisation (for example, through participation).

There are many different individual stress-reduction techniques available. The most frequently used approaches are muscle relaxation, biofeedback, meditation and cognitive restructuring. Each method involves somewhat different ways of coping with stress (see Table 7.3). Most workplace stress initiatives focus on individual stress-management training and not on reducing the sources of organisational stress, for example by redesigning tasks (also see Chapter 5). The different stress reduction therapies that are available can be classified as somatic, cognitive or behavioural. Some techniques deal almost exclusive with the bodily, somatic aspects, others concentrate on cognitive restructuring, while a third group concentrates on so-called coping behaviour.

Muscle relaxation

The common denominators of the various muscle relaxation techniques are slow and deep breathing and a conscious effort to relieve muscle tension. Among the variety of techniques available, the most frequently used is probably 'progressive relaxation'. It consists of repeatedly tensing and relaxing muscles beginning at the feet and progressing to the face. Relaxation is achieved by concentrating on the warmth and calmness associated with relaxed muscles. Take a few moments now to try this technique by carrying out the following.

While sitting in a chair, start by taking slow, deep breaths. Inhale through your nose and exhale through your mouth. Continue until you feel calm. Begin progressive relaxation by pointing your toes toward the ceiling for 10 seconds. Concentrate on the tension within your calves and feet. Now return your toes to a normal position and focus on the relaxed state of your legs and feet. (Your goal is to experience this feeling all over your body.) Tense and relax your feet for 10 seconds one more time. Moving to your calves, and continuing all the way to the muscles in your face, tense one major muscle at a time for 10 seconds, and then let it relax. Do this twice for each muscle before moving to another one. You should feel totally relaxed upon completing this routine.

Biofeedback

A biofeedback machine is used to train people to detect and control stress-related symptoms such as tense muscles and elevated blood pressure. The machine translates unconscious bodily signs into a recognisable cue (flashing light or beeper). Muscle relaxation and meditative techniques are then used to alleviate the underlying stress. The person learns to recognise bodily tension without the aid of the machine. In turn, according to the advocates of biofeedback, this awareness helps the person proactively cope with stress. Research supports the positive benefits of biofeedback. Biofeedback was found to significantly improve psychological and physiological changes, including increased problem-solving abilities.[94]

Meditation

Meditation activates a relaxation response by redirecting one's thoughts away from oneself. The Relaxation response is the physiological and psychological opposite of the fight-or-flight stress response. Significantly, however, the relaxation response must be learned and consciously activated, whereas the stress response is automatically engaged. Herbert Benson, a Harvard medical doctor, analysed many meditation programmes and derived a four-step relaxation response. The four steps are:

Relaxation response state of peacefulness

- Find a quiet environment.
- Use a mental device such as a peaceful word or pleasant image to shift the mind from externally oriented thoughts.
- Disregard distracting thoughts by relying on a passive attitude.
- Assume a comfortable position, preferably sitting erect in order to avoid undue muscular tension or going to sleep.

Benson emphasises that the most important factor is a passive attitude.[95] Maximum benefits are supposedly obtained by following this procedure once or twice a day for 10 to 20 minutes, preferably just before breakfast and dinner. People following this advice experienced favourable reductions in blood pressure and anxiety levels and slept better.[96] For example, a recent study of 36 men and women between the ages of 55 and 85 showed that blood pressure significantly dropped from 145/94 to 135/88 after using transcendental meditation for three months.[97]

Cognitive restructuring

A two-step procedure is followed. First, irrational or maladaptive thought processes that create stress are identified. For example, Type A individuals may believe they must be successful at everything they do. The second step consists of replacing these irrational thoughts with more rational or reasonable ones. Perceived failure would create stress for the Type A person. Cognitive restucturing would alleviate stress by encouraging the person to adopt a more reasonable belief about the outcomes associated with failure. For instance, the person might be encouraged to adopt the belief that isolated failure does not mean he or she is a bad person or a loser. Research revealed that stress symptoms were reduced when people jointly used cognitive restructuring and meditation.[98]

Effectiveness of stress-reduction techniques

Two teams of OB researchers reviewed the research on stress-management intervention. Although much of the published research is methodologically weak, results offer preliminary support for the conclusion that muscle relaxation, biofeedback, meditation and cognitive restructuring all help employees cope with occupational stress.[99]

Some researchers advise organisations not to implement these stress-reduction programmes despite their positive outcomes. They rationalise that these techniques relieve symptoms of stress rather than eliminate the stressors themselves.[100] Thus, they conclude that organisations are using a 'Band-Aid' approach to stress reduction. A holistic approach has subsequently been offered as a more proactive and enduring solution.

A holistic wellness model

A **Holistic wellness approach** encompasses and goes beyond stress reduction by advocating that individuals strive for 'a harmonious and productive balance of physical, mental and social well-being brought about by the acceptance of one's personal responsibility for developing and adhering to a health promotion programme'.[101] Five dimensions of a holistic wellness approach are as follows:

Holistic wellness approach advocates personal responsibility for reducing stressors and stress

- *Personal responsibility.* Take responsibility for your own well-being (e.g. quit smoking, moderate your intake of alcohol, wear your seat belt). A study of 4400 people revealed that continuous smoking throughout one's life reduces life expectancy by 18 years.[102]
- *Nutritional awareness.* Because we are what we eat, try to increase your consumption of foods that are high in fibre, vitamins and nutrients – such as fresh fruit and vegetables, poultry and fish – while decreasing those high in sugar and fat.
- *Stress reduction and relaxation.* Use the techniques just discussed to relax and reduce the symptoms of stress.
- *Physical fitness.* Exercise to maintain strength, flexibility, endurance and a healthy body weight. A recent review of employee fitness programmes indicated that they were a cost-effective way of reducing medical costs, absenteeism, turnover and occupational injuries. Fitness programmes were also positively linked with job performance and job satisfaction.[103]
- *Environmental sensitivity.* Be aware of your environment and try to identify the stressors that are causing your stress. A control strategy might be useful to eliminate stressors.

Pfizer Incorporated, a research-based health care company, is a good example of a company that supports a holistic wellness approach for its employees. The company instituted a model approach called Pfizer's Programmes for Integrating Total Health (PFIT):

> Every employee is eligible to join PFIT, which is subsidised by Pfizer and requires minimal monthly payments from employees. Each new member is required to undergo a series of medical assessments: a maximal stress test, body fat analysis and a full physical exam, including blood analysis. Tests are performed at Pfizer's on-site medical facility by a registered nurse and internist/cardiologist. These assessments are used as a tool to determine cardiovascular risk factors and the current fitness levels of prospective members. The results are evaluated by the medical and fitness staff. After reviewing the tests, a fitness staff member gives the new participant an exercise orientation. During the orientation, the staff member and the participant discuss the results of the medical and nutritional assessment, identify cardiovascular risk factors, and develop a personalised exercise programme that is based on these results and the individual's goals. Members are assessed annually or biannually, depending on age and medical history . . . .
>
> The physical therapy programme employs a licensed physical therapist and certified athletic trainer. If an employee is in need of physical therapy, he or she provides Pfizer with a prescription for therapy, and the physical therapy is provided on-site. An annual health promotion calendar is designed to offer all employees (members and nonmembers) monthly programme options, which include screenings, lectures, seminars and intervention programmes. Some examples of the intervention programmes include high blood pressure and cholesterol intervention, smoking cessation, diabetes control, stress management, nutrition education and cancer screenings.[104]

Pfizer has found that PFIT is an attractive benefit for potential employees and that it has helped to retain valuable employees. In conclusion, advocates say that both your personal and professional life can be enriched by adopting a holistic approach to wellness.

Learning outcomes: Summary of key terms

1 Define the term 'stress'

Stress is an adaptive reaction to environmental demands or stressors that triggers a fight-or-flight response. This response creates hormonal changes that mobilise the body for extraordinary demands.

2 Explain why Karasek's Job Demand-Control (JD-C) model is so important

The Karasek Job Demand-Control (JD-C) model has been highly influential in many European countries. Many work environment laws have been inspired by this model. The JD-C model emphasises the stress factors inherent in the work organisation, more than it stresses the individual characteristics.

3 Describe the model of occupational stress

Perceived stress is caused by four sets of stressors: individual level, group level, organisational level and extraorganisational. In turn, perceived stress has psychological/attitudinal, behavioural, cognitive and physical health outcomes. Several individual differences moderate relationships between stressors, perceived stress and outcomes.

4 Explain how stressful life events create stress

Stressful life events are changes that disrupt an individual's lifestyle and social relationships. Holmes and Rahe developed the Social Readjustment Rating Scale to assess an individual's cumulative stressful life events. A positive relationship exists between the scores on the Social Readjustment Rating Scale and illness. Uncontrollable events that are negative create the most stress.

5 Review the model of burnout and highlight the solutions to reduce it

Burnout develops in phases. The three key phases are emotional exhaustion, depersonalisation and feeling a lack of personal accomplishment. Emotional exhaustion, the first phase, is caused by a combination of personal stressors and job and organisational stressors. The total effect of the burnout phases is a host of negative attitudinal and behavioural outcomes. Burnout can be reduced by buffering its effects. Potential buffers include extra staff or equipment, support from top management, increased freedom to make decisions, recognition of accomplishments, time off, equitable rewards and increased communication from the top. The content of an individual's job can also be changed or the person can be assigned to a new position. Sabbaticals and employee retreats are also used to reduce burnout.

6 Explain the mechanisms of social support

Social support, an important moderator of relationships between stressors, stress and outcomes, represents the amount of perceived helpfulness derived from social relationships. Cultural norms, social institutions, companies, groups and individuals are all sources of social support. These sources provide four types of support: esteem, informational, social companionship and instrumental.

7 Describe the coping process

Coping is the management of stressors and stress. Coping is directly affected by the cognitive appraisal of stressors which, in turn, is influenced by situational and personal factors. People cope by using control, escape or symptom management strategies. Because research has not identified the most effective method of coping, a contingency approach to coping is recommended.

8 Discuss the personality characteristic of hardiness

Hardiness is a collection of personality characteristics that neutralises stress. It includes the characteristics of commitment, locus of control and challenge. Research has demonstrated that hardy individuals respond less negatively to stressors and stress than less hardy people. Less hardy employees would be good candidates for stress-reduction programmes.

9 Discuss the Type A behaviour pattern and its practical implications
The Type A behaviour pattern is characterised by someone who is aggressively involved in a chronic, determined struggle to accomplish more and more in less and less time. Type B is the opposite of Type A. Although there are several positive outcomes associated with being Type A, Type A behaviour is positively correlated with coronary heart disease. Management can help Type A individuals by not overloading them with work despite their apparent eagerness to take on an ever-increasing work load.

10 Contrast the four dominant stress-reduction techniques
Muscle relaxation, biofeedback, meditation and cognitive restructuring are predominant stress-reduction techniques. Slow and deep breathing and a conscious effort to relieve muscle tension are common denominators of muscle relaxation. Biofeedback relies on a machine to train people to detect bodily signs of stress. This awareness facilitates proactive coping with stressors. Meditation activates the relaxation response by redirecting one's thoughts away from oneself. Cognitive restructuring entails identifying irrational or maladaptive thoughts and replacing them with rational or logical ones.

Review questions

1 What are the key stressors encountered by students? Which ones are under their control?

2 Describe the behavioural and physiological symptoms you have observed in others when they are under stress.

3 Why do uncontrollable events lead to more stress than controllable events?

4 Why would people in the helping professions become burned out more readily than people in other occupations?

5 Do you think your lecturers are likely to become burned out? Explain your rationale.

6 Which of the five sources of social support is most likely to provide individuals with social support? Explain.

7 Why would people have difficulty using a control strategy to cope with the aftermath of a natural disaster like an earthquake or flood?

8 How can people increase their hardiness and reduce their Type A behaviour?

9 Have you used any of the stress-reduction techniques? Evaluate their effectiveness.

Personal awareness and growth exercise

Are you burned out?

Objectives

1 To determine the extent to which you are burned out.
2 To determine if your burnout scores are predictive of burnout outcomes.
3 To identify specific stressors that affect your level of burnout.

Introduction

An OB researcher named Christina Maslach developed a self-report scale measuring burnout. This scale assesses burnout in terms of three phases: depersonalisation, personal accomplishment and emotional exhaustion. To determine if you suffer from burnout in any of these phases, we would like you to complete an abbreviated version of this scale. Moreover, because burnout has been found to influence a variety of behavioural outcomes, we also want to determine how well burnout predicts three important outcomes.

Instructions

To assess your level of burnout, complete the following 18 statements development by Maslach.[105] Each item probes how frequently you experience a particular feeling or attitude. If you are currently working, use your job as the frame of reference for responding to each statement. If you are a full-time student, use your role as a student as your frame of reference. After you have completed the 18 items, refer to the scoring key and follow its directions. Remember, there are no right or wrong answers. Indicate your answer for each statement by circling one number from the following scale.

1 = A few times a year
2 = Monthly
3 = A few times a month
4 = Every week
5 = A few times a week
6 = Every day

Burnout inventory

1	I've become more callous towards people since I took this job.	1 2 3 4 5 6
2	I worry that this job is hardening me emotionally	1 2 3 4 5 6
3	I don't really care what happens to some of the people who need my help.	1 2 3 4 5 6
4	I feel that people who need my help blame me for some of their problems.	1 2 3 4 5 6
5	I deal very effectively with the problems of those people who need my help.	1 2 3 4 5 6
6	I feel I'm positively influencing other people's lives through my work.	1 2 3 4 5 6
7	I feel very energetic.	1 2 3 4 5 6
8	I can easily create a relaxed atmosphere with those people who need my help.	1 2 3 4 5 6
9	I feel exhilarated after working closely with those who need my help.	1 2 3 4 5 6
10	I have accomplished many worthwhile things in the job.	1 2 3 4 5 6
11	In my work, I deal with emotional problems very calmly.	1 2 3 4 5 6
12	I feel emotionally drained from my work.	1 2 3 4 5 6
13	I feel used up at the end of the working day.	1 2 3 4 5 6
14	I feel fatigued when I get up in the morning.	1 2 3 4 5 6
15	I feel frustrated by my job.	1 2 3 4 5 6
16	I feel I'm working too hard at my job.	1 2 3 4 5 6
17	Working with people directly puts too much stress on me.	1 2 3 4 5 6
18	I feel like I'm at the end of my tether.	1 2 3 4 5 6

Scoring

Compute the average of those items measuring each phase of burnout.
Depersonalisation (questions 1–4) _____
Personal accomplishment (questions 5–11) _____
Emotional exhaustion (questions 12–18) _____

Assessing burnout outcomes

1 How many times were you absent from work over the last three months (indicate the number of absences from your course last term if using the student role)? _____ absences

2 How satisfied are you with your job (or role as a student)? Circle one.

Very   Very
dissatisfied   Dissatisfied   Neutral   Satisfied   satisfied

3 Do you have trouble sleeping? Circle one.
Yes   No

Questions for discussion

1 To what extent are you burned out in terms of depersonalisation and emotional exhaustion?
Low = 1–2.99; Moderate = 3–4.99; High = 5 or above

2 To what extent are you burned out in terms of personal accomplishment?
Low = 5 or above; Moderate = 3–4.99; High = 1–2.99

3 How well do your burnout scores predict your burnout outcomes?

4 Do your burnout scores suggest that burnout follows a sequence going from depersonalisation, to feeling a lack of personal accomplishment, to emotional exhaustion? Explain.

5 Which of the unique burnout stressors illustrated in Figure 7.2 are affecting your level of burnout?

Group exercise

Reducing the stressors in your environment

Objectives

1 To identify the stressors in your environment.

2 To evaluate the extent to which each stressor is a source of stress.

3 To develop a plan for reducing the impact of stressors in your environment.

Introduction

Stressors are environmental factors that produce stress. They are prerequisites to experiencing the symptoms of stress. As previously discussed in this chapter, people do not appraise stressors in the same way. For instance, having to complete a challenging assignment may be motivational for one person and threatening to another.

Instructions

Your lecturer will divide the class into groups of four to six. Once the group is assembled, the group should brainstorm and record a list of stressors that they believe exist in their environments. Use the guidelines for brainstorming discussed in Chapter 12. After recording all the brainstormed ideas on a piece of paper, remove redundancies and combine like items so that the group has a final list of unique stressors. Next, each group member should individually determine the extent to which each stressor is a source of stress in his or her life. For the purpose of this exercise, stress is defined as existing whenever you experience feelings of pressure, strain or emotional upset. The stress evaluation is done by first indicating the frequency with which each stressor is a source of stress to you. Use the six-point rating scale provided. Once everyone has completed their individual ratings, combine the numerical judgements to get an average stress score for each stressor. Next, identify the five stressors with the highest average stress ratings. Finally, the group should develop a plan for coping with each of these five stressors. Try to make your recommendations as specific as possible.

Rating scale

Answer the following question for each stressor: To what extent is the stressor a source of stress?

1 = Never
2 = Rarely
3 = Occasionally
4 = Often
5 = Usually
6 = Always

Questions for discussion

1 Are you surprised by the type of stressors that were rated as creating the most stress in your lives? Explain.
2 Did group members tend to agree or disagree when evaluating the extent to which the various stressors created stress in their lives? What is the source of the different appraisals?
3 Which form of coping did your plans include most, control or escape-oriented strategies? Explain.

 # Internet exercise

We highlighted in this chapter how people cope with stress by using a variety of control, escape and symptom management strategies. Your ability to effectively cope with perceived stress is very important because ineffective coping can make a stressful situation even worse. The purpose of this exercise is to provide you with feedback on how well you cope with perceived stress. Go to our website www.mcgraw-hill.co.uk\textbooks\buelens for further instructions.

Notes

1 Excerpted from E. Addley, 'It's All Down to Me', the *Guardian*, 8 May 2000. Reproduced with permission.
2 S. Watson, 'Of Course I'm Stressed Out – I'm Important!', the *Guardian*, 7 April 2000.
3 F. Williams, 'ILO Warns of Epidemic of Stress', the *Financial Times*, 10 October 2000, p. 8.
4 A. Osborn, 'Workplace Blues Leave Employers in the Red', the *Guardian*, 12 October 2000.
5 M. Coles, 'Managers Tired of Only Living to Work', the *Sunday Times*, 30 July 2000.
6 F. Williams, 'ILO Warns of Epidemic of Stress', the *Financial Times*, 10 October 2000, p. 8.
7 See L. Grunberg, S. Moore and E. S. Greenberg, 'Work Stress and Problem Alcohol Behavior: A Test of the Spillover Model', *Journal of Organizational Behavior*, September 1998, pp. 487–502.
8 D. Bouckenooghe, M. Buelens, J. Fontaine and K. Vanderheyden, 'The Prediction of Stress by Values and Value Conflict', *Journal of Psychology* (in press). Also see R. Knoop, 'Work Values and Job Satisfaction', *Journal of Psychology*, September 1994, pp. 683–90; and R. Knoop, 'Relieving Stress through Value Rich Work', *Journal of Psychology*, November 1994, pp. 829–36.
9 The stress response is thoroughly discussed in H. Selye, *Stress without Distress* (New York: J. B. Lippincott, 1974).
10 Adapted and translated from M. Teugels, 'Manisch levensritme leidt tot depressies', *Vacature*, 20 February 1999.
11 L. Bestic, 'Tired? Ignore It at Your Peril', the *Independent*, 24 February 2000.
12 J. Amparano, 'On-Job Stress Is Making Workers Sick', *The Arizona Republic*, 4 August 1996, pp. A1, A12.
13 B. F. Piko, 'Psychosocial Work Environment and Psychosomatic Health of Nurses in Hungary', *Work & Stress*, March 2003, pp. 93–100.

14 J. M. Ivancevich and M. T. Matteson, *Stress and Work: A Managerial Perspective* (Glenview, IL: Scott, Foresman, 1980), pp. 8–9.

15 Adapted and translated from A. Giegas, 'Dossier: Stress', *Vacature*, published online only http://www.vacature. com/scripts/indexpage.asp?headingID=1103, 2000.

16 See H. Selye, *Stress without Distress* (New York: J. B. Lippincott, 1974).

17 Adapted and translated from A. Giegas, 'Dossier: Stress', *Vacature*, published online only http://www.vacature. com/scripts/indexpage.asp?headingID=1103, 2000.

18 See R. Karasek, 'Job Demands, Job Decision Latitude and Mental Strain: Implications for Job Redesign', *Administrative Science Quarterly*, 24, 1979, pp. 285–306; and R. Karasek and T. Theorell, *Healthy Work: Stress, Productivity and the Reconstruction of Working Life* (New York: Basic Books, 1990).

19 See S. Cohen and T. Wills, 'Stress, Social Support, and the Buffering Hypothesis, *Psychological Bulletin*, September 1985, pp. 310–57; and B. J. Uchino, J. Cacioppo and J. Kiecolt-Glader, 'The Relationship between Social Support and Psychological Processes: A Review with Emphasis on Underlying Mechanisms and Implications for Health', *Psychological Bulletin*, May 1996, pp. 488–531.

20 This study was conducted by G. R. Oldham, A. Cummings, L. J. Mischel, J. M. Schmidtke and J. Zhou, 'Listen While You Work? Quasi-Experimental Relations between Personal-Stereo Headset Use and Employee Work Responses', *Journal of Applied Psychology*, October 1995, pp. 547–64.

21 See J. D. Jonge, G. J. P. Van Breikelen, J. A. Landeweerd and F. J. N. Nijhuis, 'Comparing Group and Individual Level Assessments of Job Characteristics in Testing the Job Demand Control Model: A Multilevel Approach', *Human Relations*, January 1999, pp. 95–122; and J. Schaubroeck and L. S. Fink, 'Facilitating and Inhibiting Effects of Job Control and Social Support on Stress Outcomes and Role Behavior: A Contingency Model', *Journal of Organizational Behavior*, March 1998, pp. 167–95.

22 Results from these studies are reported in C. Frankie, 'Americans Tops in Work Messages', *The Arizona Republic*, 3 October 1999, p. A29; and A. R. Karr, 'Work Week: A Special News Report About Life on the Job – And Trends Taking Shape There', the *Wall Street Journal*, 9 February 1999, p. A1.

23 H. Bosma, R. Peter and J. Siegrist, 'Two Alternative Job Stress Models and the Risk of Coronary Heart Disease', *American Journal of Public Health*, January 1998, pp. 68–74.

24 T. Theorell *et al.*, 'Decision Latitude, Job Strain and Myocardial Infarction: A Study of Working Men in Stockholm', *American Journal of Public Health*, March 1998, pp. 382–8.

25 E. Torkelson and T. Muhonen, 'Stress and Health among Women and Men in a Swedish Telecom Company', *European Journal of Work and Organizational Psychology*, June 2003, pp. 171–86.

26 U. Kinnunen, S. Mauno, S. Nutti and M. Happonen, 'Perceived Job Insecurity: A Longitudinal Study among Finnish Employees', *European Journal of Work and Organizational Psychology*, June 1999, pp. 243–60.

27 Supportive results can be found in V. J. Magley, C. L. Hulin, L. F. Fitzgerald and M. DeNardo, 'Outcomes of Self-Labeling Sexual Harassment', *Journal of Applied Psychology*, June 1999, pp. 390–402; and L. F. Fitzgerald, F. Drasgow, C. L. Hulin, M. J. Gelfand and V. J. Magley, 'Antecedents and Consequences of Sexual Harassment in Organizations: A Test of an Integrated Model', *Journal of Applied Psychology*, August 1997, pp. 578–89.

28 The relationship between chronic work demands and stress was investigated by J. Schaubroeck and D. C. Ganster, 'Chronic Demands and Responsivity to Challenge', *Journal of Applied Psychology*, February 1993, pp. 73–85. Also see E. Demerouti, A. B. Bakker, F. Nachreiner and W. B. Schaufeli, 'The Job Demands-Resources Model of Burnout', *Journal of Applied Psychology*, June 2001, pp. 499–512.

29 C. Midgley, 'Make This the Week that You Reclaim Your Life', *The Times*, 8 May 2000.

30 See J. M. Plas, *Person-Centered Leadership: An American Approach to Participatory Management* (Thousand Oaks, CA: Sage, 1996).

31 U. Konradt, G. Hertel and R. Schmook, 'Quality of Management by Objectives, Task-Related Stressors, and Non-Task-Related Stressors as Predictors of Stress and Job Satisfaction among Teleworkers', *European Journal of Work and Organizational Psychology*, March 2003, pp. 61–79.

32 E. Davis, 'Does your Life Work?', *Management Today*, August 1999, pp. 48–55.

33 Anonymous, 'Het Britse seksleven is in gevaar', *Vacature*, 3 December 1999.

34 Anonymous, 'Stress Causes One-Third to Think about Work While Having Sex', the *Guardian*, 5 November 1999.

35 See R. Lazarus, *Stress and Emotion: A New Synthesis* (New York: Springer Publishing, 1999).

36 Research on job loss is summarised by K. A. Hanisch, 'Job Loss and Unemployment Research from 1994 to 1998: A Review and Recommendations for Research and Intervention', *Journal of Vocational Behavior*, October 1999, pp. 188–220. Also see F. M. McKee-Ryan and A. J. Kinicki, 'Coping with Job Loss: A Life-Facet Perspective', in *International Review of Industrial and Organizational Psychology*, eds C. L. Cooper and I. T. Robertson (Chichester: John Wiley & Sons, 2002), pp. 1–30.

37 For reviews of this research, see K. Sparks, B. Faragher and C. L. Cooper, 'Well-Being and Occupational Health in the 21st Century Workplace', *Journal of Occupational and Organizational Psychology*, November 2001, pp. 489–509; and R. M. Ryan and E. L. Deci, 'On Happiness and Human Potentials: A Review of Research in Hedonic and Eudaimonic Well-Being', in *Annual Review of Psychology*, eds S. T. Fiske, D. L. Schacter and C.-Z. Waxler (Palo Alto, CA: Annual Reviews, 2001), pp. 141–66.

38 Supportive results can be found in A. J. Kinicki, F. M. McKee-Ryan, C. A. Schriesheim and K. P. Carson, 'Assessing the Construct Validity of the Job Descriptive Index: A Review and Meta-Analysis', *Journal of Applied*

Psychology, February 2002, pp. 14–32; A. A. Grandey and R. Cropanzano, 'The Conservation of Resources Model Applied to Work–Family Conflict and Strain', *Journal of Vocational Behavior*, April 1999, pp. 350–70; J. R. Edwards and N. P. Rothbard, 'Work and Family Stress and Well-Being: An Examination of Person–Environment Fit in the Work and Family Domains', *Organizational Behavior and Human Decision Processes*, February 1999, pp. 85–129; and A. J. Kinicki, F. M. McKee and K. J. Wade, 'Annual Review, 1991–1995: Occupational Health', *Journal of Vocational Behavior*, October 1996, pp. 190–220.

39 Results from this study were reported in 'Poll: 1 in 6 Workers Want to Hit Someone', *The Arizona Republic*, 6 September 1999, p. A11.

40 Supportive results can be found in D. C. Ganster, M. L. Fox and D. J. Dwyer, 'Explaining Employees' Health Care Costs: A Prospective Examination of Stressful Job Demands, Personal Control, and Physiological Reactivity', *Journal of Applied Pychology*, October 2001, pp. 954–64; R. S. DeFrank and J. M. Ivancevich, 'Stress on the Job: An Executive Update', *Academy of Management Executive*, August 1998, pp. 55–66; and M. Koslowsky, *Modeling the Stress–Strain Relationship in Work Settings* (New York: Routledge, 1998).

41 Results can be found in L. Narayanan, S. Menon and P. E. Spector, 'Stress in the Workplace: A Comparison of Gender and Occupations', *Journal of Organizational Behavior*, January 1999, pp. 63–73.

42 See M. E. Lachman and S. L. Weaver, 'The Sense of Control as a Moderator of Social Class Differences in Health and Well-Being', *Journal of Personality and Social Psychology*, March 1998, pp. 763–73.

43 These findings are reported in B. Melin, U. Lundberg, J. Soderlund and M. Granqvist, 'Psychological and Physiological Stress Reactions of Male and Female Assembly Workers: A Comparison between Two Different Forms of Work Organization', *Journal of Organizational Behavior*, January 1999, pp. 47–61.

44 Research on chronic hostility is discussed by 'Healthy Lives: A New View of Stress', *University of California, Berkeley Wellness Letter*, June 1990, pp. 4–5. Also see R. S. Jorgensen, B. T. Johnson, M. E. Kolodziej and G. E. Schreer, 'Elevated Blood Pressure and Personality: A Meta-Analytic Review', *Psychological Bulletin*, September 1996, pp. 293–320.

45 P. De Winter, 'Dat meldt zich maar ziek!' *Management Team*, 19 May 2000, pp. 90–101.

46 This landmark study was conducted by T. H. Holmes and R. H. Rahe, 'The Social Readjustment Rating Scale', *Journal of Psychosomatic Research*, August 1967, pp. 213–18.

47 The rating scale was revised by C. J. Hobson, J. Kamen, J. Szostek, C. M. Nethercut, J. W. Tiedmann and S. Wojnarowicz, 'Stressful Life Events: A Revision and Update of the Social Readjustment Rating Scale', *International Journal of Stress Management*, January 1998, pp. 1–23.

48 Normative predictions are discussed in O. Behling and A. L. Darrow, 'Managing Work-Related Stress', in *Modules in Management*, eds J. E. Rosenzweig and F. E. Kast (Chicago: Science Research Associates, 1984).

49 This research is discussed by K. S. Kendler, L. M. Karkowski and C. A. Prescott, 'Causal Relationship between Stressful Life Events and the Onset of Major Depression', *American Journal of Psychiatry*, June 1999, pp. 837–48; C. Segrin, 'Social Skills, Stressful Life Events, and the Development of Psychosocial Problems', *Journal of Social and Clinical Psychology*, Spring 1999, pp. 14–34; and R. S. Bhagat, 'Effects of Stressful Life Events on Individual Performance Effectiveness and Work Adjustment Processes within Organizational Settings: A Research Model', *Academy of Management Review*, October 1983, pp. 660–71.

50 See D. R. Pillow, A. J. Zautra and I. Sandler, 'Major Life Events and Minor Stressors: Identifying Mediational Links in the Stress Process', *Journal of Personality and Social Psychology*, February 1996, pp. 381–94; R. C. Barnett, S. W. Raudenbush, R. T. Brennan, J. H. Pleck and N. L. Marshall, 'Change in Job and Marital Experiences and Change in Psychological Distress: A Longitudinal Study of Dual-Earner Couples', *Journal of Personality and Social Psychology*, November 1995, pp. 839–50; and S. Cohen, D. A. J. Tyrell and A. P. Smith, 'Negative Life Events, Perceived Stress, Negative Affect, and Susceptibility to the Common Cold', *Journal of Personality and Social Psychology*, January 1993, pp. 131–40.

51 See C. J. Hobson, J. Kamen, J. Szostek, C. M. Nethercut, J. W. Tiedmann and S. Wojnarowicz, 'Stressful Life Events: A Revision and Update of the Social Readjustment Rating Scale', *International Journal of Stress Management*, January 1998, pp. 1–23; and R. H. Rahe, 'Life Changes Scaling: Other Results, Gender Differences', *International Journal of Stress Management*, October 1998, pp. 249–50.

52 S. Cartwright, 'Taking the Pulse of Executive Health in the UK', *Academy of Management Executive*, March 2000, pp. 16–24.

53 Adapted and translated from M. Teugels, 'Leg je mensen in de watten', *Vacature*, 10 October 2000.

54 A. Maitland, 'Management Burnout: Anxiety, Depression and Stress at Work Can End in Personal Catastrophe', the *Financial Times*, 20 November 1998.

55 A. Maitland, 'Management Burnout: Anxiety, Depression and Stress at Work Can End in Personal Catastrophe', the *Financial Times*, 20 November 1998.

56 Adapted and translated from M. Teugels, 'Het burnout–fenomeen', *Vacature*, 9 May 2000.

57 Adapted and translated from A. Giegas, 'Dossier burnout', *Vacature*, /http://www.vacature.com/scripts/indexpage. asp?headingID=1477/, 2000.

58 Results are presented in T. D. Schellhardt, 'Off the Track: Is Your Job Going Nowhere? That May Be Natural, But It Doesn't Have to Be Permanent', the *Wall Street Journal* (Eastern Edition), 26 February 1996, p. R4.

59 S. Sonnentag, F. C. Brodbeck, T. Heinbokel and W. Stolte, 'Stressor–Burnout Relationship on Software Development Teams', *Journal of Occupational and Organizational Psychology*, December 1994, pp. 327–41.

60 The phases are thoroughly discussed by C. Maslach, *Burnout: The Cost of Caring* (Englewood Cliffs, NJ: Prentice-Hall, 1982).

61 The discussion of the model is based on C. L. Cordes and T. W. Dougherty, 'A Review and Integration of Research on Job Burnout', *Academy of Management Review*, October 1993, pp. 621–56.

62 H. Levinson, 'When Executives Burn Out', *Harvard Business Review*, July–August 1996, p. 153.

63 Results and conclusions can be found in R. T. Lee and B. E. Ashforth, 'A Meta-Analytic Examination of the Correlates of the Three Dimensions of Burnout', *Journal of Applied Psychology*, April 1996, pp. 123–33.

64 See R. T. Lee and B. E. Ashforth, 'A Meta-Analytic Examination of the Correlates of the Three Dimensions of Burnout', *Journal of Applied Psychology*, April 1996, pp. 123–33; E. Babakus, D. W. Cravens, M. Johnston and W. C. Moncrief, 'The Role of Emotional Exhaustion in Sales Force Attitude and Behavior Relationships', *Journal of the Academy of Marketing Science*, no. 1, 1999, pp. 58–70; and R. D. Iverson, M. Olekalns and P. J. Erwin, 'Affectivity, Organizational Stressors, and Absenteeism: A Causal Model of Burnout and Its Consequences', *Journal of Vocational Behavior*, February 1998, pp. 1–23.

65 Recommendations for reducing burnout are discussed by J. E. Moore, 'Are You Burning Out Valuable Resources', *HR Magazine*, January 1999, pp. 93–7; and L. Grensing-Pophal, 'Recognizing and Conquering On-the-Job Burnout: HR, Heal Thyself', *HR Magazine*, March 1999, pp. 82–8.

66 Excerpted from S. Shellenbarger, 'Work & Family: Three Myths That Make Managers Push Staff to the Edge of Burnout', the *Wall Street Journal*, 17 March 1999, p. B1.

67 Based on and translated from E. Verdegaal, 'Sabbatical Leave: prima, maar niet in de tijd van de baas', *Management Team*, 17 November 1995, pp. 111–14.

68 S. Armour, 'Employers Urge Workers to Chill Out Before Burning Out', *USA Today*, 22 June 1999, p. 5B.

69 Types of support are discussed in S. Cohen and T. A. Wills, 'Stress, Social Support, and the Buffering Hypothesis', *Psychological Bulletin*, September 1985, pp. 310–57.

70 The perceived availability and helpfulness of social support was discussed by B. P. Buunk, J. D. Jonge, J. F. Ybema and C. J. D. Wolff, 'Psychosocial Aspects of Occupational Stress', in *Handbook of Work and Organizational Psychology, second edition*, eds P. J. D. Drenth, H. Thierry and C. J. D. Wolff (New York: Psychology Press, 1998), pp. 145–82.

71 See R. A. Clay, 'Research at the Heart of the Matter', *Monitor on Psychology*, January 2001, pp. 42–5; B. N. Uchino, J. T. Cacioppo and J. K. Kiecolt-Glaser, 'The Relationship between Social Support and Physiological Processes: A Review with Emphasis on Underlying Mechanisms and Implications for Health', *Psychological Bulletin*, May 1996, pp. 488–531; and H. Benson and M. Stark, *Timeless Healing: The Power and Biology of Belief* (New York: Scribner, 1996).

72 Supporting results can be found in L. L. Schirmer and F. G. Lopez, 'Probing the Social Support and Work Strain Relationship among Adult Workers: Contributions of Adult Attachment Orientations', *Journal of Vocational Behavior*, August 2001, pp. 17–33; C. J. Holahan, R. H. Moos, C. K. Holahan and R. C. Cronkite, 'Resource Loss, Resource Gain, and Depressive Symptoms: A 10-Year Model', *Journal of Personality and Social Psychology*, September 1999, pp. 620–29; D. S. Carlson and P. L. Perrewe, 'The Role of Social Support in the Stressor–Strain Relationship: An Examination of Work–Family Conflict', *Journal of Management*, Winter 1999, pp. 513–40; and M. H. Davis, M. M. Morris and L. A. Kraus, 'Relationship-Specific and Global Perceptions of Social Support: Associations with Well-Being and Attachment', *Journal of Personality and Social Psychology*, February 1998, pp. 468–81.

73 See S. Aryee, V. Luk, A. Leung and S. Lo, 'Role Stressors, Interrole Conflict, and Well-Being: The Moderating Influence of Spousal Support and Coping Behaviors among Employed Parents in Hong Kong', *Journal of Vocational Behavior*, April 1999, pp. 259–78; and C. Viswesvaran, J. I. Sanchez and J. Fisher, 'The Role of Social Support in the Process of Work Stress: A Meta-Analysis', *Journal of Vocational Behavior*, April 1999, pp. 314–34.

74 For details, see B. P. Buunk, B. J. Doosje, L. G. J. M. Jans and L. E. M. Hopstaken, 'Perceived Reciprocity, Social Support, and Stress at Work: The Role of Exchange and Communal Orientation', *Journal of Personality and Social Psychology*, October 1993, pp. 801–11; and C. E. Cutrona, 'Objective Determinants of Perceived Social Support', *Journal of Personality and Social Psychology*, February 1986, pp. 349–55.

75 R. S. Lazarus and S. Folkman, 'Coping and Adaptation', in *Handbook of Behavioral Medicine*, ed. W. D. Gentry (New York: The Guilford Press, 1984), p. 283.

76 The antecedents of appraisal were investigated by G. J. Fogarty, M. A. Machin, M. J. Albion, L. F. Sutherland, G. I. Lalor and S. Revitt, 'Predicting Occupational Strain and Job Satisfaction: The Role of Stress, Coping, Personality, and Affectivity Variables', *Journal of Vocational Behavior*, June 1999, pp. 429–52; E. C. Chang, 'Dispositional Optimism and Primary and Secondary Appraisal of a Stressor: Controlling Influences and Relations to Coping and Psychological and Physical Adjustment', *Journal of Personality and Social Psychology*, April 1998, pp. 1109–20; and J. C. Holder and A. Vaux, 'African American Professionals: Coping with Occupational Stress in Predominantly White Work Environments', *Journal of Vocational Behavior*, December 1988, pp. 315–33.

77 R. S. Lazarus and S. Folkman, 'Coping and Adaptation', in *Handbook of Behavioral Medicine*, ed. W. D. Gentry (New York: The Guilford Press, 1984), p. 289.

78 Adapted and translated from K. Devreux-Bletek, 'Schat, vergeet niet je multi-vitamine preparaat te nemen', *Vacature*, 4 April 2000. Reproduced with permission.

79 See C. R. Leana, D. C. Feldman and G. Y. Tan, 'Predictors of Coping Behavior after a Layoff', *Journal of Organ-*

izational Behavior, 1998, pp. 85–97; and B. Major, C. Richards, M. L. Cooper, C. Cozzarelli and J. Zubek, 'Personal Resilience, Cognitive Appraisals, and Coping: An Integrative Model of Adjustment to Abortion', *Journal of Personality and Social Psychology*, March 1998, pp. 735–52.

80 See results presented in M. A. Gowan, C. M. Riordan and R. D. Gatewood, 'Test of a Model of Coping with Involuntary Job Loss Following a Company Closing', *Journal of Applied Psychology*, February 1999, pp. 75–86; and T. M. Begley, 'Coping Strategies as Predictors of Employee Distress and Turnover after an Organizational Consolidation: A Longitudinal Analysis', *Journal of Occupational and Organizational Psychology*, December 1998, pp. 305–29.

81 This pioneering research is presented in S. C. Kobasa, 'Stressful Life Events, Personality, and Health: An Inquiry into Hardiness', *Journal of Personality and Social Psychology*, January 1979, pp. 1–11.

82 'Burning the Midnight Oil', *Management Today*, February 1995, pp. 11–12.

83 See S. C. Kobasa, S. R. Maddi and S. Kahn, 'Hardiness and Health: A Prospective Study', *Journal of Personality and Social Psychology*, January 1982, pp. 168–77.

84 Results can be found in V. Florian, M. Mikulincer and O. Taubman, 'Does Hardiness Contribute to Mental Health during a Stressful Real-Life Situation? The Roles of Appraisal and Coping', *Journal of Personality and Social Psychology*, April 1995, pp. 687–95; and K. L. Horner, 'Individuality in Vulnerability: Influences on Physical Health', *Journal of Health Psychology*, January 1998, pp. 71–85.

85 See C. Robitschek and S. Kashubeck, 'A Structural Model of Parental Alcoholism, Family Functioning, and Psychological Health: The Mediating Effects of Hardiness and Personal Growth Orientation', *Journal of Counseling Psychology*, April 1999, pp. 159–72; and Basic Behavioral Science Task Force of the National Advisory Mental Health Council, 'Basic Behavioral Science Research for Mental Health: Vulnerability and Resilience', *American Psychologist*, January 1996, pp. 22–8.

86 B. Priel, N. Gonik and B. Rabinowitz, 'Appraisals of Childbirth Experience and Newborn Characteristics: The Role of Hardiness and Affect', *Journal of Personality*, September 1993, pp. 299–315.

87 M. Friedman and R. H. Rosenman, *Type A Behavior and Your Heart* (Greenwich, CT: Fawcett Publications, 1974), p. 84.

88 See C. Lee, L. F. Jamieson and P. C. Earley, 'Beliefs and Fears and Type A Behavior: Implications for Academic Performance and Psychiatric Health Disorder Symptoms', *Journal of Organizational Behavior*, March 1996, pp. 151–77; S. D. Bluen, J. Barling and W. Burns, 'Predicting Sales Performance, Job Satisfaction, and Depression by Using the Achievement Strivings and Impatience–Irritability Dimensions of Type A Behavior', *Journal of Applied Psychology*, April 1990, pp. 212–16; and M. S. Taylor, E. A. Locke, C. Lee and M. E. Gist, 'Type A Behavior and Faculty Research Productivity: What Are the Mechanisms?', *Organizational Behavior and Human Performance*, December 1984, pp. 402–18.

89 Results from the meta-analysis are contained in S. A. Lyness, 'Predictors of Differences between Type A and B Individuals in Heart Rate and Blood Pressure Reactivity', *Psychological Bulletin*, September 1993, pp. 266–95.

90 See S. Booth-Kewley and H. S. Friedman, 'Psychological Predictors of Heart Disease: A Quantitative Review', *Psychological Bulletin*, May 1987, pp. 343–62. More recent results can be found in T. Q. Miller, T. W. Smith, C. W. Turner, M. L. Guijarro and A. J. Hallet, 'A Meta-Analytic Review of Research on Hostility and Physical Health', *Psychological Bulletin*, March 1996, pp. 322–48.

91 See J. Rothman, 'Wellness and Fitness Programs', in *Sourcebook of Occupational Rehabilitation*, ed. P. M. King (New York: Plenum Press, 1998), pp. 127–44; and S. Shellenbarger, 'Work & Family: Rising Before Dawn, Are You Getting Ahead or Just Getting Tired?', the *Wall Street Journal*, 17 February 1999, p. B1.

92 S. Hoare, 'Where Fun is Part of the Deal', *The Times*, 7 September 2000.

93 S. Cartwright, 'Taking the Pulse of Executive Health in the UK', *Academy of Management Executive*, March 2000, pp. 16–24.

94 Supportive results can be found in W. E. Holden, M. M. Deichmann and J. D. Levy, 'Empirically Supported Treatments in Pediatric Psychology: Recurrent Pediatric Headache', *Journal of Pediatric Psychology*, April 1999, pp. 91–109; and V. Barcia, P. Maria, J. Sanz and F. J. Labrador, 'Psychological Changes Accompanying and Mediating Stress–Management Training for Essential Hypertension.' *Applied Psychophysiology and Biofeedback*, September 1998, pp. 159–78.

95 See H. Benson, *The Relaxation Response* (New York: William Morrow and Co., 1975).

96 Research pertaining to meditation is discussed by A. G. Marlatt and J. L. Kristeller, 'Mindfulness and Meditation', in *Integrating Spirituality Into Treatment: Resources for Practitioners*, ed. W. R. Miller (Washington, DC: American Psychological Association, 1999), pp. 67–84; and H. Benson and M. Stark, *Timeless Healing* (New York: Scribner, 1996).

97 Results are presented in 'Your Blood Pressure: Think It Down', *Cooking Light*, October 1996, p. 24.

98 See M. W. Otto, 'Cognitive Behavioral Therapy for Social Anxiety Disorder: Model, Methods, and Outcome', *Journal of Clinical Psychiatry*, no. 1, 1999, pp. 14–19.

99 See S. Reynolds, E. Taylor and D. A. Shapiro, 'Session Impact in Stress Management Training', *Journal of Occupational Psychology*, June 1993, pp. 99–113; and J. M. Ivancevich, M. T. Matteson, S. M. Freedman and J. S. Phillips, 'Worksite Stress Management Interventions', *American Psychologist*, February 1990, pp. 252–61.

100 An evaluation of stress-reduction programmes is conducted by P. A. Landsbergis and E. Vivona-Vaughan, 'Evaluation of an Occupational Stress Intervention in a Public Agency', *Journal of Organizational Behavior*,

January 1996, pp. 29–48; and D. C. Ganster, B. T. Mayes, W. E. Sime and G. D. Tharp, 'Managing Organizational Stress: A Field Experiment', *Journal of Applied Psychology*, October 1982, pp. 533–42.

101 R. Kreitner, 'Personal Wellness: It's Just Good Business', *Business Horizons*, May–June 1982, p. 28.

102 Results are presented in 'The 18-Year Gap', *University of California, Berkeley Wellness Letter*, January 1991, p. 2.

103 A thorough review of this research is provided by D. L. Gebhardt and C. E. Crump, 'Employee Fitness and Wellness Programs in the Workplace', *American Psychologist*, February 1990, pp. 262–72. Also see A. J. Daley and G. Parfitt, 'Good Health – Is It Worth It? Mood States, Physical Well-Being, Job Satisfaction and Absenteeism in Members and Non-Members of a British Corporate Health and Fitness Club', *Journal of Occupational and Organizational Psychology*, June 1996, pp. 121–34.

104 Excerpted from Rothman, 'Wellness and Fitness Programs', in *Sourcebook of Occupational Rehabilitation*, ed. P. M. King (New York: Plenum Press, 1998), pp. 140, 141, 143.

105 Adapted from C. Maslach and S. E. Jackson, 'The Measurement of Experienced Burnout', *Journal of Occupational Behavior*, April 1981, pp. 99–113.

section

3

group and social processes

chapter 8 communication

By Eva Cools and Herman Van den Broeck

Learning outcomes
When you finish studying the material in this chapter, you should be able to:

- describe the perceptual process model of communication

- describe the process, personal, physical and semantic barriers to effective communication

- demonstrate your familiarity with effective oral, written and non-verbal communication skills

- discuss the primary sources of listener comprehension. Identify the three different listening styles and review the ten keys to effective listening

- contrast the communication styles of assertiveness, non-assertiveness and aggressiveness

- discuss the patterns of hierarchical communication and 'the grapevine'

- explain the contingency approach to media selection

- elaborate on information overload and how to deal with it effectively

case study

Get the message . . .?

'My job is all about communication', says Sophie Jeffrey, who for the past few years has worked as press and PR officer for Isle of Wight tourism. 'By phone, fax or email – it's all about getting information across.'

Jeffrey believes that the most important factor in communicating effectively is knowing why you are doing your job. 'If you want to get your message across – whatever it is – it's essential to have a clear statement of intention in your head at all times. For me, it's to promote the Isle of Wight as a quality destination and support the tourism industry, and I keep that in mind whenever I'm dealing with someone.'

One moment she may be talking to a journalist from a national newspaper, the next to a local hotelier. 'It's important to deal with everyone in a similar way,' she believes, 'to return their calls immediately, answer queries or offer help. One of the most overlooked factors in effective communicating is listening – making sure you've really heard what they want and that you are responding to their needs.'

A large part of Jeffrey's role is ensuring people know what is happening on the island, much of which is done through press releases. 'When you're writing press releases you have to ensure everything is clear. There is an emphasis these days on using plain English, keeping things simple. It's also important to proofread any document that is being sent out – if a release has mistakes or typing errors it creates a negative impression.'

There is more to successful communicating than simply making a succession of points. 'It's hugely important to have notes in front of you when you make a phone call so that you have all the information to hand, and know what points you need to make. But a call shouldn't be too formal – where possible it's good to try to form some sort of relationship with the person you're dealing with. If you are friendly and interested, people are far more receptive to what you have to say.'

A good phone manner, she believes, can make all the difference. 'I have been told that if you smile when you're on the phone people can sense it. Communicating is more than just passing on information. If you're upbeat and enthusiastic it tends to be infectious and people are generally more receptive to what you're saying.'

But things don't always go perfectly, and it's important to deal with problems or criticisms in the right way. 'If there is any negative feedback it's important to take it on board', says Jeffrey. 'Getting defensive is pointless. You have to listen to what is said, think carefully about what sort of response to offer and then come back with an explanation.'

The least effective way to communicate, she believes, is to be negative. 'Whether it's someone visiting the island, a local restaurant owner or a TV crew wanting to come and film, I always tell them I can help. Even if I can't personally deal with their query, I can usually find someone who can, and that helps keep the lines of communication open. In my business I make it my policy never to say no.'[1]

For discussion
Sophie Jeffrey is undoubtedly an excellent communicator. What makes her so effective?

'One cannot not communicate.'[2] This is probably the most cited quote concerning communication. This means that all behaviour is communication. Communication is everywhere and ever present. This makes it even more important to master good communication skills.

> Education and business leaders in the UK warn that young people face being overlooked for jobs because they are not able to speak English properly. Street slang became popular by rap music artists and the wider TV culture. A campaign, part of The Campaign for Real Education, is launched in education to provide children of all backgrounds with a basic grasp of written and spoken English. Nick Seaton, chairman of The Campaign for Real Education, says that companies even have to organise 'remedial training' for some employees because their language skills are not developed enough to give a good presentation or to write reports. 'You would expect from the education system that it provides youth with the necessary skills to speak and write correctly to function in a company, but that is no longer the case', Seaton states. Several company leaders already raised concerns about the communication skills of their employees. Not only the popularity of street slang causes the communication troubles, the increasing use of communication technologies also causes problems. Chairman Khalid Aziz of Aziz Corporation says that 'we are witnessing a decline in the overall level of communication skills, and the blame for this lies in the way technology is being used in the workplace'. A lot of spelling errors, abbreviations and informal language is used in emails, which means that communication is not running as smoothly as in the past. 'The increasing use of email and mobile phone text messages affects the employees' abilities to communicate properly with customers and colleagues.'[3]

The previous example illustrates that effective communication skills are critical for both individual and organisational success. Moreover, a study of 274 students revealed that the quality of student–faculty communication – in the teacher's office, informally on campus, or before and after class – was positively related to student motivation. Another study involving 65 savings and loan employees and 110 manufacturing employees revealed that employee satisfaction with organisational communication was positively and significantly correlated with both job satisfaction and performance.[4] Finally, a survey of 300 executives underscored the importance of communication. Results demonstrated that 71 per cent and 68 per cent of respondents, respectively, believed that written communication skills and interpersonal communication skills were critical competencies that needed enhancement via training. These executives believed the lack of communication skills had resulted in increased costs.[5]

This chapter will help you understand better how you can both improve your communication skills and design more effective communication programmes. We will discuss basic dimensions of the communication process, interpersonal communication, organisational communication patterns and the dynamics of modern communications.

Basic dimensions of the communication process

Communication interpersonal exchange of information and understanding

Communication is defined as 'the exchange of information between a sender and a receiver, and the inference (perception) of meaning between the individuals involved'.[6] Analysis of this exchange reveals that communication is a two-way process consisting of consecutively linked elements (see Figure 8.1). Professionals who understand this process can analyse their own communication patterns as well as design communication programmes that fit organisational needs. This section reviews a perceptual process model of communication and discusses various barriers that can harm effective communication.

A perceptual process model of communication

Historically, the communication process has been described in terms of a conduit model. This traditional model depicts communication as a pipeline in which information and meaning are transferred from person to person. Recently, however, communication scholars have criticised the conduit model for being based on unrealistic assumptions. For example, the conduit model assumes communication transfers intended meanings from person to person.[7] If this assumption was true, miscommunication would not exist and there would be no need to worry about being misunderstood. We could simply say or write what we want and assume the listener or reader accurately understands our intended meaning.

Perceptual model of communication consecutively linked elements within the communication process

As we all know, communicating is not that simple or clear-cut. Communication is fraught with miscommunication. In recognition of this, researchers have begun to examine communication as a form of social information processing (recall the discussion in Chapter 4) in which receivers interpret messages by cognitively processing information. This view led to the development of a **Perceptual model of communication** that depicts communication as a process in which receivers create meaning in their own minds. Let us briefly examine the elements of the perceptual process model shown in Figure 8.1.

SENDER

The sender is an individual, group or organisation that desires, or attempts, to communicate with a particular receiver. Receivers may be individuals, groups or organisations.

FIGURE 8.1 A PERCEPTUAL PROCESS MODEL OF COMMUNICATION

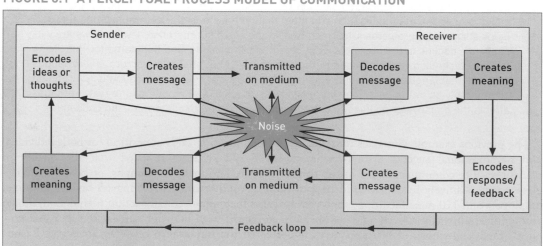

ENCODING

Communication begins when a sender encodes an idea or thought. Encoding translates mental thoughts into a code or language that can be understood by others. People typically encode using words, numbers, gestures, non-verbal cues, such as facial expressions or pictures. Moreover, different methods of encoding can be used to portray similar ideas. The following short exercise highlights this point.

On a piece of paper, draw a picture of the area currently surrounding you. Now, write a verbal description of the same area. Does the pictorial encoding portray the same basic message as the verbal description? Which mode was harder to use and which more effective? Interestingly, a growing number of management consultants recommend using visual communication, such as drawings, to analyse and improve group interaction and problem solving and to reduce stress.

THE MESSAGE

The output of encoding is a message. There are two important points to keep in mind about messages. First, they contain more than meets the eye. Messages may contain hidden agendas as well as trigger moods or emotional reactions. For example, comparisons of internal and external documents within the forest products industry, over a 10-year period, demonstrated that executives' private and public evaluative statements about events and situations were inconsistent. These executives apparently wanted to convey different messages to the public and to internal employees.[8] Duncan Green, who runs the testing department of a large Internet service provider, knows all about these kind of difficulties:

> 'Where I became the test manager I had to learn fast that your staff doesn't always tell you the whole truth', he says, 'which can make things extremely complicated. I've had a member of my team, Jack, come and complain that someone wasn't pulling their weight on a project they had been given. When I investigated, it became clear that he had complained out of feelings of resentment that he hadn't been put onto the project himself.'[9]

Second, messages need to match the medium that is used to transmit them. How would you evaluate the match between the message of letting someone know they have been laid off and the communication media used in the following examples?

> A man finds out he has been let go when a restaurant won't accept his company credit card. A woman gets the news via a note placed on her chair during lunch. Employees at a high-tech firm learn of their fate when their security codes no longer open the front door of their office building.[10]

These horrible mismatches reveal how thoughtless employers can be when they do not carefully consider the interplay between a message and the medium used to convey it.

SELECTING A MEDIUM

People can communicate through a variety of media. Potential media include face-to-face conversations, telephone calls, email, voice mail, videoconferencing, written memos or letters, photographs or drawings, meetings, bulletin boards, computer output, and charts or graphs. Choosing the appropriate medium depends on many factors, including the nature of the message, its intended purpose, the type of audience, proximity to the audience, time horizon for disseminating the message and personal preferences.

All media have advantages and disadvantages. Face-to-face conversations, for instance, are useful for communicating about sensitive or important issues and those requiring feedback and intensive interaction. Telephones are convenient, fast and private but non-verbal information is absent. Although writing memos or letters is time consuming, it is a good medium when it is difficult to meet, when formality and a written record are important, and when face-to-face interaction is not necessary to enhance understanding.

DECODING

Decoding is the receiver's version of encoding. Decoding consists of translating verbal, oral or visual aspects of a message into a form that can be interpreted. Receivers rely on social information processing to determine the meaning of a message during decoding (see Chapter 4). Decoding is a key contributor to misunderstanding in interracial and intercultural communication because decoding by the receiver is subject to social and cultural values that may not be understood by the sender (see Chapter 16). Also, the growing popularity of email has brought about what some people refer to as a new language, one which is not always easily decoded by those unfamiliar with it.

> 'It all wouldn't bother me very much if it were confined to communication between nerds [boring computer know-alls] on the net', writes a cynical reporter in the *Sunday Times*, 'but it is already creeping into our everyday language. We'll all be nerds very soon, I guess. When I asked somebody to go for a drink after work, he mailed: 'sorry. can't. I'm on 24/7'. He seemed genuinely surprised when I asked him to explain. It turned out that he meant he was too busy, working '24 hours a day, 7 days a week'. There are many more such ugly examples: if you want to invite a couple for tea these days, you might mail: 'ru2up4T?' It seems that we will breed a generation of youngsters who will routinely write 'r' instead of 'are' and '2' instead of 'to' or 'too'.[11]

CREATING MEANING

In contrast to the conduit model's assumption that meaning is directly transferred from sender to receiver, the perceptual model is based on the belief that a receiver creates the meaning of a message in his or her mind. Often, a receiver's interpretation of a message will differ from that intended by the sender. In turn, receivers act according to their own interpretations (not that of the sender). After considering this element of the communication process, a communication expert concluded the following:

> Miscommunication and unintentional communication are to be expected, for they are the norm. Organisational communicators who [were to] take these ideas seriously would realise just how difficult successful communication truly is. Presumably, they would be conscious of the constant effort needed to communicate in ways most closely approximating their intentions .... Communication is fraught with unintentionality and, thereby, great difficulty for communicators.[12]

Professionals are encouraged to rely on redundancy of communication to reduce this unintentionality. Redundant communication can be achieved by transmitting the message over multiple media. For example, a production manager might follow up a phone conversation about a critical schedule change with a memo. Certainly for the communication of change processes it can be important to keep in mind to bring your message over multiple media. This is necessary to reduce the resistance to change and to enhance acceptance of the announced changes (also see Chapter 17).

Moreover, communication is multidimensional and takes place at two separate but interrelated levels.[13] The Content level ('what') covers basically factual or cognitive information, such as ideas, places, people and objects. The Relationship level ('how') covers information on our emotional states or attitudinal reactions towards our environment. Consider the following example: 'Close the door!' and 'Would you mind closing the door, please?' On the content level, the message is the same. On the relationship level, a different kind of relationship is presupposed.[14]

Much communication is actually an attempt to control the relationship. Why does a manager change some details in the excellent report of a good employee? The report may show some mistakes, but the manager probably wants to show who is the boss. How can the furious reaction of a supervisor be explained when an employee indicates a mistake? On the content level the employee is right, but the supervisor has difficulty to accept that a subordinate corrects him. These examples also illustrate that confusion between the two levels occurs frequently. Have you ever felt resistance from a colleague when you made remarks on his or her work? Criticising a task is quite often interpreted as criticising an individual.

Content level
'what' is communicated

Relationship level
how the relationship between sender and receiver is communicated

Communication is also influenced by the context in which it takes place (e.g. the space where the communication takes place or the temporal context). Difficulties with cross-cultural communication illustrate the importance of this context (see Chapter 16).

FEEDBACK

The receiver's response to a message is the crux of the feedback loop. At this point in the communication process, the receiver becomes a sender. Specifically, the receiver encodes a response and then transmits it to the original sender. This new message is then decoded and interpreted. As you can see from this discussion, feedback is used as a comprehension check. It gives senders an idea of how accurately their message has been understood. Advice and tips on how to give effective feedback were elaborated earlier in Chapter 6.

It is clear that the distinction between sender and receiver is presented in a simple way to clarify the communication process. In real life, people are senders and receivers of messages simultaneously. When talking to someone, we are continuously looking at the effects of our words and, in doing so, receiving information from the so-called receiver. And vice versa: the receiver is reacting to the so-called sender's message while listening. The concept communicators is proposed as an alternative to the distinction between sender and receiver.[15]

The perceptual model of communication presents communication as a two-way process. Of course, not all media allow for immediate feedback. A distinction can be made between one-way and two-way communication. One-way communication does not allow for immediate feedback, like sending a report to a colleague. Two-way communication has the opportunity to ask questions and to give feedback, like in telephone calls or face-to-face conversations. Research found that one-way communication is usually faster than two-way communication. Owing to the lack of immediate feedback it is, however, often less accurate.[16]

NOISE

Noise represents anything that interferes with the transmission and understanding of a message. It affects all linkages of the communication process. Noise includes factors such as speech impairment, poor telephone connections, illegible handwriting, inaccurate statistics in a memo or report, poor hearing and eyesight and physical distance between sender and receiver. People can improve communication by reducing noise.

Noise
interference with the transmission and understanding of a message

Barriers to effective communication

Communication noise is a barrier to effective communication as it interferes with the accurate transmission and reception of a message. Awareness of these barriers is a good starting point to improve the communication process. There are four key barriers to effective communication: process, personal, physical and semantic.

PROCESS BARRIERS

Every element of the perceptual model of communication shown in Figure 8.1 is a potential process barrier. Consider the following examples:

- *Sender barrier*. A customer gets incorrect information from a customer service agent because he or she was recently hired and lacks experience.
- *Encoding barrier*. An employee for whom English is a second language has difficulty explaining why a delivery was late.
- *Message barrier*. An employee misses a meeting for which he or she never received a formal invitation.
- *Medium barrier*. A salesperson gives up trying to make a sales call when the potential customer fails to return three previous phone calls.
- *Decoding barrier*. An employee does not know how to respond to a supervisor's request to stop exhibiting 'passive aggressive' behaviour.
- *Receiver barrier*. A student who is talking to a friend during a lecture asks the professor the same question as the one that has just been answered.
- *Feedback barrier*. The non-verbal head nodding of an interviewer leads an interviewee to think that he or she is answering questions well.

Barriers in any of these process elements can distort the transfer of meaning. Reducing these barriers is essential but difficult given the current diversity of the workforce (see Chapter 4).

PERSONAL BARRIERS

There are many personal barriers to communication. We highlight eight of the more common ones:

- The ability to communicate effectively: people possess varying levels of communication skills.
- The way people process and interpret information: people use different frames of reference and experiences to interpret the world around them (Chapter 4); people selectively attend to various stimuli. These differences affect both what we say and what we think we hear.
- The level of interpersonal trust between people: this can either prevent or enable effective communication. Communication is more likely to be distorted when people do not trust each other.
- The existence of stereotypes and prejudices (Chapter 4): they can powerfully distort what we perceive about others.
- The egos of the people communicating: egos can cause political battles, turf wars and the pursuit of power, credit and resources. Egos influence how people treat each other as well as our receptivity to being influenced by others.
- The ability to listen: some people possess poor listening skills.[17]
- The natural tendency to evaluate or judge a sender's message: how would you respond to the following statement: 'I like the book you are reading'? You might say, 'I agree, it's good', or alternatively, 'I disagree, the book is boring'. We all tend to evaluate messages from our own point of view or frame of reference. Strong feelings or emotions about the issue being discussed enhance the own evaluation tendency.
- The inability to listen with understanding: listening with understanding occurs when a receiver can 'see the expressed idea and attitude from the other person's point of view, to sense how it feels to him, to achieve his frame of reference in regard to the thing he is talking about'. Listening with understanding reduces defensiveness and improves accuracy in perceiving a message.[18]

PHYSICAL BARRIERS

The distance between employees can interfere with effective communication. It is hard to understand someone who is speaking to you from 20 metres away. Work and office noise are also additional barriers. Poor telephone lines or crashed computers represent physical barriers to effective communication through modern technologies.

In spite of the general acceptance of physical barriers, they can be reduced. Walls that are distracting or inhibiting can be torn down. Making the optimum choice of medium and so reduce the physical barriers, is a way to manage these barriers.

SEMANTIC BARRIERS

Semantics is the study of words. Semantic barriers show up as encoding and decoding errors because these phases of communication involve transmitting and receiving words and symbols. These barriers occur very easily. Consider the following statement: crime is ubiquitous.

Do you understand this message? Even if you do, would it not be simpler to say that 'crime is all around us' or 'crime is everywhere'? Choosing your words more carefully is the easiest way to reduce semantic barriers. Avoiding jargon that is not familiar to the person you are talking to also helps avoiding miscommunication. This barrier can also be decreased by attentiveness to mixed messages and cultural diversity. Mixed messages occur when a person's words imply one message while his or her actions or non-verbal cues suggest something different. Obviously, understanding is enhanced when a person's actions and non-verbal cues match the verbal message.

PRACTICAL IMPLICATIONS

Two strategies may improve your communication skills. First, make sure your message is clear by using the following tips:

- *Empathy*. Put yourself in the perspective of the receiver when you encode a message.

- *Redundancy*. Repeat the major elements ('say what you are going to say, say it, and then say what you have said').
- *Effective timing*. Choose a moment when it is less likely that the receiver is distracted by noise or other messages.
- *Descriptive*. Focus on the problem instead of the person, give advice for improvement instead of blaming the receiver.
- *Feedback*. Use feedback to check whether your message has been received and reached its response.

Second, improve your understanding of what others try to communicate to you. According to Peter Honey, the British author of *Improve Your People Skills*, the easiest, but also the most neglected way to avoid misunderstanding of a message is to ask questions. Asking questions can help to gain both factual and affective information.[19]

> 'The business of testing understanding is integral to doing your job successfully', he says. 'Meetings and conversations can go on for ages and it's impossible to remember everything that's been said. It's always a good idea to ask for a recap or a summary, or for a clearer explanation. Asking questions is central to human nature but I think it gets knocked out of us in school – most of us can remember feeling foolish if we put our hand up to ask a question.'[20]

Improving your listening skills can also enhance your understanding of messages sent to you. In sum, people have to become better encoders and better decoders.

Interpersonal communication

The quality of interpersonal communication within an organisation is very important. People with good communication skills have been found to help groups make better decisions and to be promoted more frequently than individuals with less developed abilities.[21] Although there is no universally accepted definition of **Communication competence**, it is a performance-based index of an individual's ability to use effectively the appropriate communication behaviour in a given context.[22]

Communication competence is determined by three components: communication abilities and traits, situational factors and the individuals involved in the interaction (see Figure 8.2). Cross-cultural awareness, for example, is an important communication ability or trait (Chapter 16). Communication competence also implies knowing which communication medium is most suitable in a

Communication competence
ability to use the appropriate communication behaviour effectively in a given context

FIGURE 8.2 **COMMUNICATION COMPETENCE AFFECTS UPWARD MOBILITY**

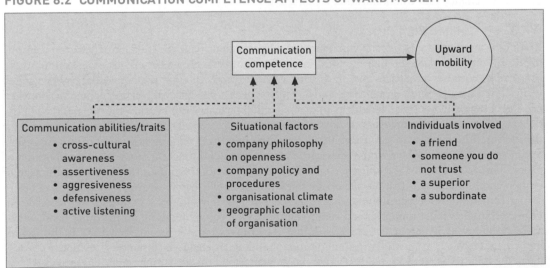

given situation. Communication competence is also influenced by the individuals involved in the interaction. For example, people are likely to withhold information and react emotionally or defensively when interacting with someone they dislike or distrust. Communication competence can be improved by controlling one's communication skills. We will discuss verbal and non-verbal communication and elaborate further on active listening and assertiveness.

Verbal and non-verbal communication

A common distinction in communication literature is the one between verbal and non-verbal communication. Verbal communication includes oral and written communication. We do not only communicate through spoken or written messages, but also convey information non-verbally. Two major differences between verbal and non-verbal communication can be indicated.

First, verbal communication is usually more conscious, while non-verbal signals are more automatic and unconscious. We rarely plan gestures and body movements during conversations, while we mostly do plan what to say or write. Second, non-verbal communication is not that clear and rule-bound as verbal communication. If your colleague looks on his watch, what does that mean? Are you boring him or does he have another appointment planned after this conversation? Consequently, non-verbal signals are more ambiguous and susceptible to misinterpretation. Communication experts estimate that non-verbal communication is responsible for up to 60 per cent of a message being communicated. So, one's non-verbal signals should be consistent with one's intended verbal messages.[23] Looking at the whole communication context might help to avoid misunderstandings. If your colleague is also leaning backwards and yawning while looking at his watch, there is a big chance you are indeed boring him.

Women, in general, are more apt to focus on non-verbal signals when communicating, which explains why they are often better listeners than men. Men usually tend to focus more on words, both in conversations and written documents. The increase of impersonal communication through emails, faxes and documents favours male-oriented communication, while the rise of videoconferencing and other personal information technologies might be an advantage for women.[24]

ORAL COMMUNICATION

Oral communication is the most frequent means of communication. Examples are diverse: presentations, group discussions, face-to-face conversations, meetings, but also informal exchanges through the grapevine (which is the unofficial communication system of the informal organisation, as will be explained further in the chapter). Oral communication is fast and allows for immediate feedback. When an oral message is conveyed, rapid feedback is possible to check whether the receiver understands the message correctly. A major disadvantage of oral communication in organisations arises when a message has to pass through various people. Every receiver interprets the message differently and in the end, the content might be changed significantly. The more people are involved, the greater the chance that communication is distorted.

WRITTEN COMMUNICATION

Writing is another way of verbal communication. Organisations typically use a lot of **Written communication**: letters, emails, meeting minutes, manuals, organisational newsletters, reports. Written communication both has advantages and drawbacks. Written communication is tangible and can be verified easily. The message can for instance be stored, which makes it possible to check the content again when necessary. It also allows later reference to an existing written message (for instance the organisational HR-policy). This implies that the message does not have to be repeated all over again. People can read it for themselves. The increase of information and communication technologies nowadays makes it possible for organisations to distribute written messages through Internet, Intranet, Extranet and email instead of paper. This has improved the efficiency of written communication significantly. Another advantage of written communication is that people usually think more carefully before writing something than before saying something. Consequently, a written message is probably clearer, logical and well considered. However, it takes more time than oral communication. Oral communication, on the other hand, allows more flexibility as it permits adaptations during the conversation. A second drawback is the lack of immediate feedback from written communication. Sending an email, for instance, does not necessarily mean the message is received and there is also no guarantee that the sender interprets it as intended.

NON-VERBAL COMMUNICATION

Non-verbal communication is 'any message, sent or received independent of the written or spoken word . . . [It] includes such factors as use of time and space, distance between persons when conversing, use of colour, dress, walking behaviour, standing, positioning, seating arrangement, office locations and furnishing'.[25] Non-verbal communication can help to complement, illustrate or emphasise what is said. Sometimes non-verbal signals and speech contradict each other, in which case we are more prone to believe what we see than what we hear.[26]

Because of the prevalence of non-verbal communication and its significant impact on organisational behaviour (including but not limited to, perceptions of others, hiring decisions, work attitudes and turnover),[27] it is important that professionals become consciously aware of the various sources of non-verbal communication.

> **Non-verbal communication** messages sent that are neither written nor spoken

Body movements and gestures

Body movements (such as leaning forwards or backwards) and gestures (such as pointing) provide additional non-verbal information that can either enhance or detract from the communication process. A recent study showed that the use of appropriate hand gestures increased listeners' practical understanding of a message.[28] Open body positions, such as leaning backward, convey immediacy, a term used to represent openness, warmth, closeness and availability for communication. Defensiveness is communicated by gestures such as folding arms, crossing hands and crossing one's legs. Judith Hall, a communication researcher, conducted a meta-analysis of gender differences in body movements and gestures. Results revealed that women nodded their heads and moved their hands more than men. Leaning forward, large body shifts and foot and leg movements were exhibited more frequently by men.[29] Although it is both easy and fun to interpret body movements and gestures, it is important to remember that body-language analysis is subjective, easily misinterpreted and highly dependent on the context and cross-cultural differences.[30] Inaccurate interpretations can create additional 'noise' in the communication process. This was also discussed in Chapter 4.

Touch

Touching is another powerful non-verbal cue. People tend to touch those they like, although it might be necessary to distinguish between different kinds of touching to correctly interpret what you see, according to the interpersonal relationship and the way and amount of touching.[31] A doctor, who is examining a patient, is touching only for professional reasons. Shaking hands is different in a work context than when meeting a friend. A meta-analysis of gender differences in touching indicated that women do more touching during conversations than men.[32] Of particular note, however, is the fact that men and women interpret touching differently. It might be possible to diminish sexual harassment claims by keeping this perceptual difference in mind. Moreover, norms for touching vary significantly around the world. Consider the example of two males walking across campus holding hands. In the Middle East, this behaviour would be quite normal for males who are friends or who have great respect for each other. In contrast, this behaviour is not commonplace in other parts of the world. More examples can be found in the next Snapshot.

Facial expressions

Facial expressions convey a wealth of information. Smiling, for instance, typically represents warmth, happiness or friendship, whereas frowning conveys dissatisfaction or anger. Do you think these interpretations apply to different cross-cultural groups? If you said yes, it supports the view that there is a universal recognition of emotions from facial expressions. If you said no, this indicates you believe the relationship between facial expressions and emotions varies across cultures. A recent summary of relevant research revealed that the association between facial expressions and emotions varies across cultures.[33] Therefore, professionals need to be careful in interpreting facial expressions among diverse groups of employees. A smile, for example, does not convey the same emotion in different countries. In some cultures, people learn to suppress or hide their emotions. In Western countries, for instance, men are not supposed to cry, while women are not supposed to express anger in public.

Eye contact

Eye contact is a strong non-verbal cue that serves four functions in communication. First, eye contact regulates the flow of communication by signalling the beginning and end of conversation. There is a tendency to look away from others when beginning to speak and to look at them when done. Second, gazing (as opposed to glaring) facilitates and monitors feedback because it reflects interest and attention. Third, eye contact conveys emotion. People tend to avoid eye contact when discussing bad news or providing negative feedback. Fourth, gazing relates to the type of relationship between communicators. As is true for body movements, gestures and facial expressions, norms for eye contact vary across cultures. Westerners are taught at an early age to look at their parents when spoken to. In contrast, Asians are taught to avoid eye contact with a parent or superior in order to show obedience and subservience.[34] Once again, professionals should be sensitive to different orientations toward maintaining eye contact with diverse employees.

snapshot

Norms for touching vary across countries

China
- Hugging or taking someone's arm is considered inappropriate.
- Winking or beckoning with one's index finger is considered rude.

The Philippines
- Handshaking and a pat on the back are common greetings.

Indonesia
- Handshaking and head nodding are customary greetings.

Japan
- Business cards are exchanged before bowing or handshaking.
- A weak handshake is common.
- Lengthy or frequent eye contact is considered impolite.

Malaysia
- It is considered impolite to touch someone casually, especially on the top of the head.
- It is best to use your right hand to eat and to touch people and things.

South Korea
- Men bow slightly and shake hands, sometimes with two hands; women refrain from shaking hands.
- It is considered polite to cover your mouth while laughing.

Thailand
- Public displays of temper or affection are frowned on.
- It is considered impolite to point at anything using your foot or to show the soles of your feet.

SOURCE: Guidelines taken from R. E. Axtell, *Gestures: The Do's and Taboos of Body Language Around the World* (New York: John Wiley & Sons, 1991).

Active listening

A study showed that listening effectiveness was positively associated with success in sales and obtaining managerial promotions.[35] Estimates suggest that people typically spend about 9 per cent of a working day reading, 16 writing, 30 talking and 45 listening.[36] A suitable saying is that 'nature gave people two ears but only one tongue, which is a gentle hint that they should listen more than they talk'.[37] Unfortunately, research evidence suggests that most people are not very good at listening. For example, communication experts estimate that people generally comprehend about 25 per cent of a typical verbal message. Interestingly, this problem is partly due to the fact that we can process information faster than most people talk. The average speaker communicates 125 words a minute while we can process 500 words a minute. Poor listeners use this information-processing gap to daydream and think about other things, thereby missing important parts of what is being communicated.[38]

Listening involves much more than hearing a message. Hearing is merely the physical component of listening. Listening is the process of *actively* decoding and interpreting verbal messages. Listening requires cognitive attention and information processing; hearing does not. With this distinction in mind, we will examine a model of listener comprehension, listening styles and some practical advice for becoming a more effective listener.

Listener comprehension represents the extent to which an individual can recall factual information and draw accurate conclusions and inferences from a verbal message. It is a function of listener, speaker, message and environmental characteristics (see Figure 8.3). Communication researchers Kittie Watson and Larry Barker conducted a global review of research into listening and arrived at the following conclusions. Listening comprehension is positively related to high mental and reading abilities, academic achievements, a large vocabulary, being 'ego-involved with the speaker', having energy, being female, having extrinsic motivation to pay attention and being able to take good notes. Speakers have a negative impact on listening comprehension when they talk too quickly or too slowly, possess disturbing accents or speech patterns, can't be seen by the audience, lack credibility or are disliked. In contrast, clear messages that are given in the active voice increase listener comprehension. The same is true for messages containing viewpoints similar to the listener's or those that disconfirm expectations. Finally, comfortable environmental characteristics and compact seating arrangements enhance listening comprehension.[39]

> **Listening**
> actively decoding and interpreting verbal messages

FIGURE 8.3 LISTENER COMPREHENSION MODEL

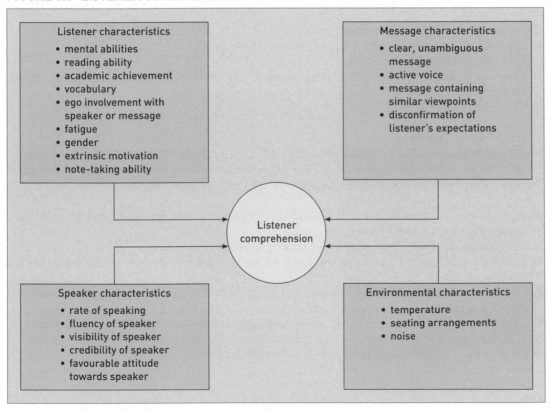

SOURCE: Adapted from discussion in K. W. Watson and L. L. Barker, 'Listening Behavior: Definition and Measurement', in *Communication Yearbook 8*, ed. R. N. Bostrom (Beverly Hills, CA: Sage Publications, 1984), pp. 178–97.

LISTENING STYLES

A pair of communication experts identified three different listening styles.[40] Their research indicated that people prefer to hear information that is suited to their own listening style. People also tend to speak in a style that is consistent with their own listening style. Because inconsistent styles represent a barrier to effective listening, it is important to understand and respond to the different listening styles.

Results-style listeners

Results-style listeners don't like any beating around the bush. They are interested in hearing the 'bottom line' or result of the communication message first and then they like to ask questions. The following examples of behaviour identify a results-style listener:

- They sound direct. Everything is explicit, so you never have to wonder. They may sound blunt or even rude sometimes.
- They are action oriented.
- They are oriented in the present.
- They love to solve problems. Because of their love of fixing things and their action orientation, they are usually good crisis managers.
- Their first interest is in the bottom line [final/financial outcome].

> **Results-style listeners** interested in hearing the bottom line or result of a message

Reasons-style listeners

Reasons-style listeners want to know the rationale for what someone is saying or proposing. They must be convinced about a point of view before accepting it. A reasons-style listener typically exhibits the following behaviour:

- They are most concerned with whether or not a solution is practical, realistic and reasonable for the situation.
- They weigh and balance everything.
- If asked a direct question, they frequently answer 'It depends'.
- They argue, out loud or internally.
- They expect people to present ideas in an organised way and have little tolerance, and no respect, for a 'disorderly' mind.
- Their first concern is 'Why?'.

> **Reasons-style listeners** interested in hearing the rationale behind a message

Process-style listeners

Process-style listeners like to discuss issues in detail. They prefer to receive background information prior to having a thorough discussion and like to know why an issue is important in the first place. You can identify process-style listeners by watching for the following behaviour:

- They are people oriented. They have a high concern for relationships, believing that people and relationships are the keys to long-term success.
- They like to know the whole story before making a decision.
- They have a high regard for quality and will hold out for a quality solution to a problem, even if it seems unrealistic to others.
- They are future oriented. They are not only concerned about the future but they predict what may happen as a result of decisions made today.
- They have ongoing conversations. They continue subjects from one conversation to the next.
- Their language and messages tend to be indirect. They imply rather than state the bottom line.
- Their primary concerns are 'How?' and 'What are the benefits?'.

> **Process-style listeners** like to discuss issues in detail

PRACTICAL IMPLICATIONS

You can improve your listening skills by avoiding the 10 habits of bad listeners while cultivating the 10 good listening habits (see Table 8.1). Stephen Covey, author of the bestseller, *The 7 Habits of Highly Effective People*, offers another good piece of advice about becoming a more effective listener. He concludes that we should 'seek first to understand, then to be understood'.[41] This means, trying to make an

TABLE 8.1 THE KEYS TO EFFECTIVE LISTENING

Keys to effective listening	The bad listener	The good listener
1 Capitalise on thought speed	Tends to daydream	Stays with the speaker, mentally summarises the speaker, weighs evidence and listens between the lines
2 Listen for ideas	Listens for facts	Listens for central or overall ideas
3 Find an area of interest	Tunes out dry speakers or subjects	Listens for any useful information
4 Judge content, not delivery	Tunes out dry or monotone speakers	Assesses content by listening to entire message before making judgements
5 Hold your fire	Gets too emotional or worked up by something said by the speaker and enters into an argument	Withholds judgement until comprehension is complete
6 Work at listening	Does not expend energy on listening	Gives the speaker full attention
7 Resist distractions	Is easily distracted	Fights distractions and concentrates on the speaker
8 Hear what is said	Shuts out or denies unfavourable information	Listens to both favourable and unfavourable information
9 Challenge yourself	Resists listening to presentations of difficult subject matter	Treats complex presentations as exercise for the mind
10 Use handouts, overheads or other visual aids	Does not take notes or pay attention to visual aids	Takes notes as required and uses visual aids to enhance understanding of the presentation

SOURCES: Derived from N. Skinner, 'Communication Skills', *Selling Power*, July/August 1999, pp. 32–4; and G. Manning, K. Curtis and S. McMillen, *Building the Human Side of Work Community* (Cincinnati, OH: Thomson Executive Press, 1996), pp. 127–54.

effort to understand the other person before putting your own viewpoint across and at the same time being prepared to consider the other person's viewpoint before trying to influence them to accept yours.[42] In conclusion, it takes awareness, effort and practice to improve one's listening comprehension.

Assertiveness, aggressiveness and non-assertiveness

The saying 'You can attract more flies with honey than with vinegar' captures the difference between using an assertive communication style and an aggressive one. Research studies indicate that assertiveness is more effective than aggressiveness in both work-related and consumer contexts.[43] An Assertive style is expressive and self-enhancing and is based on the 'ethical notion that it is not right or good to violate our own or others' basic human rights, such as the right to self-expression or the right to be treated with dignity and respect'.[44] In contrast, an Aggressive style is expressive and self-enhancing and strives to take unfair advantage of others. A Non-assertive style is characterised by timid and self-denying behaviour. Non-assertiveness is ineffective because it gives the other person an unfair advantage. Non-assertiveness aims to appease others and avoid conflict at any cost. For example, consider the assertive style of the personal assistant of Alexander van der Hooft, managing director of PinkRoccade, a company that supplies IT staff and services:

Assertive style
expressive and self-enhancing but does not take advantage of others

Aggressive style
expressive and self-enhancing but takes unfair advantage of others

Non-assertive style
timid and self-denying behaviour

'As a personal assistant, I have to fend off the queries and patter of numerous salespeople and head hunters [those actively seeking out potential staff] every day', she says. 'Everyone will try to speak to Alexander and a lot will try anything to get through to him, from saying they've spoken to him the previous day to telling me he'll be furious if I don't put them through'. She believes that knowing how to be assertive without being aggressive is essential to her work. 'Everything to do with Alexander comes through me. I have to filter what's relevant', she says. 'I often get people from within the company ringing me to see if he is available, trying to see him as soon as possible. I have to judge when is a good time and often have to be quite firm with people, telling them things exactly as they are but in a polite manner. But it's external calls that cause the most problem. I've had people hang up on me or become rude or aggressive simply because I won't let them through to Alexander. The art is then to remain calm but at the same time display some authority. One of the best techniques is simply to keep on repeating the same phrase – I always say he is out of the office and that I can't put them through. People do tend to get quite shirty [agitated] and I think it's often based on snobbery – they can't believe that a personal assistant is authorised to deal with them.'[45]

Professionals may improve their communication competence by trying to be more assertive and less aggressive or non-assertive. This can be achieved by using the appropriate non-verbal and verbal behaviour listed in Table 8.2. Remember that non-verbal and verbal behaviour should complement and reinforce each other. One should attempt to use the non-verbal behaviour of good eye contact; a

TABLE 8.2 COMMUNICATION STYLES

Communication style	Description	Non-verbal behaviour pattern	Verbal behaviour pattern
Assertive	Pushing hard without attacking; permits others to influence outcome; expressive and self-enhancing without intruding on others	Good eye contact Comfortable but firm posture Strong, steady and audible voice Facial expressions matched to message Appropriately serious tone Selective interruptions to ensure understanding	Direct and unambiguous language No attributions or evaluations of other's behaviour Use of 'I' statements and co-operative 'we' statements
Aggressive	Taking advantage of others; expressive and self-enhancing at other's expense	Glaring eye contact Moving or leaning too close Threatening gestures (pointed finger, clenched fist) Loud voice Frequent interruptions	Swear words and abusive language Attributions and evaluations of other's behaviour Sexist or racist terms Explicit threats or put-downs
Non-Assertive	Encouraging others to take advantage of us; inhibited; self-denying	Little eye contact Downward glances Slumped posture Constantly shifting weight Wringing hands Weak or whiny voice	Qualifiers ('maybe', 'kind of') Fillers ('uh', 'you know', 'well') Negaters ('It's not really that important', 'I'm not sure')

SOURCE: Adapted in part from J. A. Waters, 'Managerial Assertiveness', *Business Horizons*, September–October 1982, pp. 24–9.

strong, steady and audible voice; and selective interruptions. Avoid non-verbal behaviour such as glaring or little eye contact; threatening gestures or slumped posture; and a weak or whiny voice. Appropriate verbal behaviour includes direct and unambiguous language and the use of 'I' messages instead of 'you' statements. For example, when you say, 'Mike, I was disappointed with your report because it contained typographical errors', rather than 'Mike, you made a bad report', you reduce defensiveness. 'I' statements describe your feelings about someone's performance or behaviour instead of laying blame on the person. An alternative is the use of 'we' messages, as applied to the above example: 'Mike, we need to talk about your report, because there are some typographical errors. It is important that we deliver a good report.' 'We' messages help to convey an impression of partnership and joint responsibility for any problem to be discussed.[46]

Of course, assertiveness implies more than reacting to behaviour of others. We distinguish between giving criticism, making clear requests and saying no.

GIVING CRITICISM

To avoid confusion between the content and relationship levels of communication, it is important to give criticism in an emotionally intelligent way. Basically, this means focusing on the action and not on the person. Assertiveness implies being friendly towards the person, but being clear towards the task. The following advice can help to give criticism in an appropriate way:[47]

- Describe the situation or the behaviour of people to which you are reacting. Express your feelings and/or explain what impact the other's behaviour has on you.
- Empathise with the other person's position in the situation. Give the other person the chance to react to your criticism.
- Specify what changes you would like to see in the situation or in another person's behaviour and offer to negotiate those changes with the other person.
- Indicate, in a non-threatening way, the possible consequences if change does not occur.
- Summarise, after two-way discussion, the agreed action, making sure the other person knows what is expected.

It is also important to focus on 'the here and now': events from the past or old feelings may not influence your current interaction.

MAKING CLEAR REQUESTS

People often complain that they don't get what they want. Quite often, however, this happens because they simply do not, or not clearly, ask what they want. Making clear requests can help professionals to avoid misunderstandings that lead to criticism. How can an employee know what you expect from that report if you do not clearly communicate your expectations? Clear requests can also help to fulfil unmet needs by simply asking for it. How can your boss know you need help with your report if you do not ask for it? Some tips can help to make assertive requests:[48]

- Decide what you want. This may not always be easy or clear-cut. First state what you do not want and then arrive at what you want through an elimination process.
- Decide whom to ask. This implies thinking about who can meet your request. Also prepare what to do when that person does not want to fulfil your request. It might be helpful to consider what impact your request may have on the other person.
- Decide when to ask. Timing is important when asking requests to someone.
- Decide how to ask. Do not speak in vague or ambiguous ways, because that makes it more difficult to understand clearly what you want.

SAYING NO

Another important aspect of assertiveness implies saying no to requests by other people. We often think that refusing a question will lead to anger or that the other person will not like us any more. Or they may be hurt or think that we cannot cope with it. Accordingly, we often say yes while we want to say no, which may lead to an overload of work. We feel guilty saying no, although there is no reason for it. The following tips can help to say no in an assertive way:[49]

- Do not start to apologise. Give reasons, not excuses.
- Keep it brief and simple. Do not start giving a long list of reasons for your refusal, because this can lead to misunderstandings.
- Do not speak in ambiguous or vague terms. Be clear that you refuse the request.
- Use appropriate non-verbal behaviour, which also fits with your verbal communication.
- Make use of the 'broken record' technique. This means calmly repeating the same message over and over again, without getting angry or changing your mind. Certainly when the other person gets aggressive or does not want to listen, this technique can help.

Organisational communication patterns

Organisational communication implies both formal and informal communication, internal and external communication. Examining organisational communication patterns is a good way to identify factors contributing to effective and ineffective management. Research reveals that employees do not receive enough information from their immediate supervisors. It is therefore no surprise to learn that many employees use unofficial, informal communication systems (the grapevine) as a source of information. This section promotes a working knowledge of two important communication patterns: hierarchical communication and the grapevine. We conclude with gender differences in communication.

Hierarchical communication

Hierarchical communication is defined as 'those exchanges of information and influence between organisational members, at least one of whom has formal authority (as defined by official organisational sources) to direct and evaluate the activities of other organisational members'.[50] This communication pattern involves information exchanged downward from supervisor to employee and upward from employee to supervisor. Supervisors provide several types of information through downward communication: job instructions, job rationale, organisational procedures and practices, feedback about performances, official memos, policy statements and instillation of organisational goals. Employees, in turn, communicate information upward about themselves, co-workers and their problems, organisational practices and policies, and what needs to be done and how to do it. Timely and valid hierarchical communication can promote individual and organisational success. Research indicates, for instance, that absence of job-related information causes unnecessary stress among employees.[51] Upward communication, on the other hand, provides bosses with necessary feedback concerning current organisational issues and problems and day-to-day operations to make effective decisions. It is also a source of feedback for the effectiveness of their downward communication.[52] Organisations are encouraged to foster two-way communication among all employees.

However, there are many companies in which hierarchical communication turns out to be highly problematic.

> For instance, according to Angela Baron of the Chartered Institute of Personnel and Development (CIPD), a surprising number of organisations fail to plan how they will tell their staff about reorganising. 'If a company plans to restructure, chances are that it won't tell the workers', she says. 'Many organisations don't keep staff informed but inevitably someone picks something up and rumours – and consequently stress and low morale – become rife. Even when there isn't harmful hearsay, sudden news of restructuring, without careful planning of how it will be communicated downwards, can leave employees feeling uninvolved and undervalued.' To illustrate, Angela Baron tells the striking anecdote of the chief executive who, in an attempt to repair some of the damage that was already made by the lack of proper communication, organised an office party. 'Enjoy yourselves', he told employees during a brief speech at the start of the evening. 'And don't worry too much about the redundancies. We'll let you know about those at the next party.' To the chief's genuine surprise, his joke was met with silence.[53]

Another problem that might occur in hierarchical communication is communication distortion. **Communication distortion** occurs when an employee purposely modifies the content of a message, thereby reducing the accuracy of communication between managers and employees. Employees tend

---

Hierarchical communication exchange of information between superiors and employees

Communication distortion purposely modifying the content of a message

to engage in this practice because of workplace politics, a desire to manage impressions or fear of how a supervisor might respond to a message.[54] Communication experts point out the organisational problems caused by distortion.

> Distortion is an important problem in organisations because modifications to messages cause misdirectives to be transmitted, non-directives to be issued, incorrect information to be passed on, and a variety of other problems related to both the quantity and quality of information.[55]

Distortion tends to increase when supervisors have high upward influence or power (also see Chapter 13). Employees also tend to modify or distort information when they aspire to move upward and when they do not trust their supervisors.[56]

To assess the communication pattern between yourself and your immediate supervisor, please take a moment to complete the next Activity. Think of your current (or last) job when responding to the various items. Once this is completed, check your responses to the first three statements to see whether they suggest low or high potential for distortion. Then compare this with your responses to the last three statements, which measure three outcomes of distortion.

What is your potential for communication distortion?

Instructions
Circle your response to each question by using the following scale:
1 = Strongly disagree
2 = Disagree
3 = Neither agree nor disagree
4 = Agree
5 = Strongly agree

Supervisor's upward influence
In general, my immediate supervisor can have a big impact on my career in this organisation.   1 2 3 4 5

Aspiration for upward mobility
It is very important for me to progress upward in this organisation.   1 2 3 4 5

Supervisory trust
I feel free to discuss the problems and difficulties of my job with my immediate supervisor without jeopardising my position or having it count against me later.   1 2 3 4 5

Withholding information
I provide my immediate supervisor with a small amount of the total information I receive at work   1 2 3 4 5

Selective disclosure
When transmitting information to my immediate supervisor, I often emphasise those aspects that make me look good.   1 2 3 4 5

Satisfaction with communication
In general, I am satisfied with the pattern of communication between my supervisor and I.   1 2 3 4 5

Arbitrary norms (to be considered per statement)
Low = 1–2
Moderate = 3
High = 4–5

SOURCE: Adapted and excerpted in part from K. H. Roberts and C. A. O'Reilly III, 'Measuring Organizational Communication,' *Journal of Applied Psychology*, June 1974, p. 323.

The grapevine

Even if supervisors communicate effectively with their employees, people will make use of the **Grapevine**. The term originated from the US Civil War practice of stringing battlefield telegraph lines between trees. Today, the grapevine represents the unofficial communication system of the informal organisation.[57] Information travelling along the grapevine supplements official or formal channels of communication. Although the grapevine can be a source of inaccurate rumours, it functions positively as an early warning sign for organisational changes, a medium for creating organisational culture, a mechanism for fostering group cohesiveness and a way of informally bouncing ideas off others.[58] Evidence indicates that the grapevine is alive and well in today's workplace. The grapevine will, however, be more active in organisations where people can communicate more easily and have similar backgrounds, because the grapevine is mainly based on informal social networks.

A national survey of the readers of *Industry Week*, a professional management magazine, revealed that employees used the grapevine as their most frequent source of information.[59] Contrary to general opinion, the grapevine is not necessarily counterproductive. We can distinguish some advantages and some drawbacks. Plugging into the grapevine can help employees, managers and organisations alike to achieve desired results. The grapevine can help employees to find the necessary information, certainly when it is not available through formal channels.[60] It relieves anxiety and fulfils the need for affiliation, which explains why the grapevine is far more active in times of uncertainty and ambiguity.[61] Nevertheless, information in the grapevine is distorted by deleting the fine detail and exaggerating other aspects of a message. This may mean that messages that are communicated through the grapevine cause more uncertainty and anxiety instead of reducing it. Moreover, when organisations fail to fill the gap between the official and unofficial messages quickly and effectively, employees will feel demotivated because it seems like management is not caring for them.

> Having a brief chat when you're by the coffee machine or between meetings has always been an essential part of the daily grind [life] in any office. Now, though, employers are starting to accept that this kind of face-to-face communication is just as important as the more formal type you have with your superiors. Both go a long way to improve teambuilding, to get rid of conflict where necessary and improve staff morale.[62]

GRAPEVINE PATTERNS

Communication along the grapevine follows predictable patterns (see Figure 8.4). The most frequent pattern is not a single strand or gossip chain but a cluster.[63] Although the probability and cluster patterns look similar, the process by which information is passed is very different. People randomly gossip to others in a probability structure. For instance, Figure 8.4 shows that person A tells persons F and D a piece of information but ignores co-workers B and J. Person A may have done this simply because he or she ran into co-workers F and D in the corridor. In turn, persons F and D randomly discuss this information with others at work. In contrast, the cluster pattern is based on the idea that information is selectively passed from one person to another. People tend to communicate selectively because they know that certain individuals tend to leak or pass information to others, and they actually want the original piece of information to be spread around. For example, Figure 8.4 shows that person A selectively discusses a piece of information with three people, one of whom – person F – tells two others, and then one of those two – person B – tells another. Only certain individuals repeat what they hear when the probability or cluster patterns are operating. People who consistently pass along grapevine information to others are called **Liaison individuals** or 'gossips':

> About 10 per cent of the employees on an average grapevine will be highly active participants. They serve as liaisons with the rest of the staff members who receive information but spread it to only a few other people. Usually these liaisons are friendly, outgoing people who are in positions that allow them to cross departmental lines. For example, secretaries tend to be liaisons because they can communicate with the top executive, the janitor and everyone in-between without raising eyebrows.[64]

FIGURE 8.4 GRAPEVINE PATTERNS

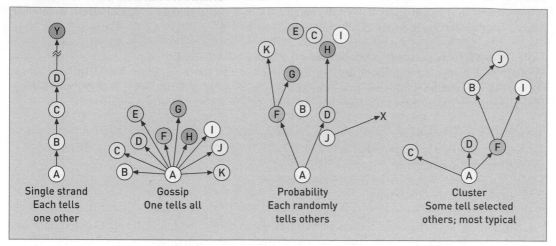

SOURCE: K. Davis and J. W. Newstrom, *Human Behavior at Work: Organizational Behavior*, 7th edn (New York: McGraw-Hill, 1985), p. 317. Used with permission. Copyright © 1985. Reproduced with permission of the McGraw-Hill Companies.

Effective professionals monitor the pulse of work groups by regularly communicating with known liaisons individuals. **Organisational moles**, however, use the grapevine for a different purpose. They obtain information, often negative, in order to enhance their power and status. They do this by secretly reporting their perceptions and hearsay about the difficulties, conflicts or failure of other employees to powerful members of management. This enables moles to divert attention away from themselves and to appear more competent than others. Organisations need to be aware of this behaviour and to try to create an open, trusting environment, since organisational moles can destroy teamwork, create conflict and impair productivity.[65]

Organisational moles use the grapevine to enhance their power and status

RESEARCH FINDINGS AND PRACTICAL IMPLICATIONS

Although research activity on this topic has slackened in recent years, past research about the grapevine has provided the following insights. The grapevine is faster than formal channels; it is about 75 per cent accurate; people rely on it when they are insecure, threatened or faced with organisational changes; and employees use the grapevine to acquire the major part of their workplace information.[66] However, these findings may no longer be representative of the grapevine in our current era of information and communication technologies. Today, people are making use of email and instant message systems to exchange informal messages besides traditional informal talks in the coffee corner of the organisation. As a consequence, the informal social network of employees has expanded significantly, making it possible to gossip to anyone and not just to your own social network. It is even possible to post messages anonymously on certain web sites so that everybody can see them. Electronic communication is, however, more often misinterpreted. There is no room for subtleties of language or intonation, which makes it more difficult to see whether someone is making a joke, being sarcastic or telling the truth.[67] It is also very easy to copy an email and send it to several other people, which makes it even faster than the traditional grapevine.

The key recommendation for organisations is to monitor and influence the grapevine rather than attempt to control it. Trying to control the grapevine is impossible, it will always exist one way or another. It is better to use it as an indicator of employee uncertainty and anxiety. The grapevine can be seen as a filter and feedback mechanism that indicates the issues that are important for employees. Effective professionals accomplish monitoring and influencing the grapevine by openly sharing relevant information with employees. For example, they can increase the amount of communication both by keeping in touch with liaison individuals and by making sure information travels to people 'isolated' from the formal communication system. Other ways of influencing and monitoring the grapevine is to provide it with advance notice of departmental or organisational changes, to listen carefully to employees' responses and to send information selectively. The finding that the grapevine is more active in times of uncertainty and changes can be a useful signal for organisations to intensify official communication in order to refute incorrect rumours.

Communication differences between men and women

Women and men have communicated differently since the dawn of time. These differences can create communication problems that undermine productivity and interpersonal communication. Research has indicated five common communication problems between men and women:

1 Men are too authoritarian.
2 Men do not take women seriously.
3 Women are too emotional.
4 Men do not accept women as co-workers or bosses.
5 Women do not speak up enough.[68]

Gender-based differences in communication are partly caused by linguistic styles commonly used by men and women. Deborah Tannen, a communication expert, defines a **Linguistic style** as follows:

Linguistic style
a person's typical speaking pattern

> Linguistic style refers to a person's characteristic speaking pattern. It includes such features as directness or indirectness, pacing and pausing, word choice, and the use of such elements as jokes, figures of speech, stories, questions and apologies. In other words, linguistic style is a set of culturally learned signals by which we not only communicate what we mean but also interpret others' meaning and evaluate one another as people.[69]

Linguistic style not only helps explain communication differences between men and women. It also influences our perceptions of others' confidence, competence and abilities. Increased awareness of linguistic styles can improve your communication accuracy and competence.

WHY DO LINGUISTIC STYLES VARY BETWEEN MEN AND WOMEN?

Researchers do not completely agree on the cause of communication differences between men and women. There are two competing explanations that involve the well-worn distinction between nature and nurture (also see Chapters 2 and 3). Some researchers believe that interpersonal differences between men and women are caused by inherited biological differences between the sexes. More specifically, this perspective, which is also called the 'Darwinian' perspective or 'evolutionary psychology', attributes gender differences in communication to drives, needs and conflict associated with reproductive strategies used by men and women. For example, proponents would say that men communicate more aggressively, interrupt others more than women and hide their emotions because they have an inherent desire to possess features attractive to women in order to compete with other men for purposes of mate selection. Although men may not be competing for mate selection during a business meeting, evolutionary psychologists propose that men cannot turn off the biologically based determinants of their behaviour.[70]

In contrast, social role theory is based on the idea that men and women learn ways of speaking as children growing up. Research shows that girls learn conversational skills and habits that focus on rapport and relationships, whereas boys learn skills and habits that focus on status and hierarchies. Accordingly, women come to view communication as a network of connections in which conversations are negotiations for closeness. This orientation leads women to seek and give confirmation and support more so than men. Men, on the other hand, see conversations as negotiations in which people try to achieve and maintain the upper hand. Accordingly, it is important for men to protect themselves from others' attempts to put them down or push them around. This perspective increases men's need to maintain independence and avoid failure.[71]

COMMUNICATION DIFFERENCES

Research demonstrates that men and women communicate differently in a number of ways.[72] Table 8.3 illustrates ten different communication patterns that vary between men and women. There are

TABLE 8.3 COMMUNICATION DIFFERENCES BETWEEN MEN AND WOMEN

Women are happy to ask for information in public situations	Men are less likely to ask for information or directions in public situations that would reveal their lack of knowledge
In decision making, women are more likely to downplay their certainty	Men are more likely to downplay their doubts
Women tend to apologise even when they have done nothing wrong	Men tend to avoid apologies as signs of weakness or concession
Women tend to accept blame as a way of smoothing awkward situations	Men tend to ignore blame and place it elsewhere
Women tend to temper criticism with positive buffers	Men tend to give criticism directly
Women tend to insert unnecessary and unwarranted 'thank-yous' in conversations	Men may avoid thanks altogether as a sign of weakness
Women tend to ask 'What do you think?' to build consensus	Men often perceive that question to be a sign of incompetence and lack of confidence
Women tend to allow men to usurp their ideas without protest	Men tend to usurp [take] ideas stated by women and claim them as their own
Women use softer voice volume to encourage persuasion and approval	Men use louder voice volume to attract attention and maintain control
Women tend to give directions in indirect ways, a technique that may be perceived as confusing, less confident or manipulative by men	

SOURCE: Excerpted from D. M. Smith, *Women at Work: Leadership from the Next Century* (Upper Saddle River, NJ: Prentice Hall, 2000), pp. 26–32.

two important issues to keep in mind about the aspects identified in Table 8.3. First, the aspects identified in the table cannot be generalised to include all men and women. Some men are less likely to boast about their achievements while some women are less likely to share the credit. The point is that there are always exceptions to the rule. Second, your linguistic style influences perceptions about your confidence, competence and authority. These judgements may, in turn, affect your future job assignments and subsequent promotability. Consider, for instance, linguistic styles displayed by John and Mary. John downplays any uncertainties he has about issues and asks very few questions. He does this even when he is unsure about an issue being discussed. In contrast, Mary is more forthright at admitting when she does not understand something and she tends to ask a lot of questions. Some people may perceive John as more competent than Mary because he displays confidence and acts as if he understands the issues being discussed.

The male way of communicating can be described as **Report talk**, while the female way of communicating can be described as **Rapport talk**.[73] Men traditionally give information in a direct and straightforward manner. They directly give advice to others and use combative language. In their effort to communicate clearly men can appear to be domineering. Advantages of 'report talk' are that it is unambiguous, gets to the point and is briefer than rapport talk. Drawbacks are that it is not inclusive, does not build relationships and ignores the response of the other person. Women traditionally communicate less directly than men do. They use a lot of small talk and try to include the other person in the conversation – for instance, by turning a statement into a question to encourage the other person to speak. In their effort to be inclusive women can seem to be indecisive. Advantages of 'rapport talk' are that it builds relationships, lightens the atmosphere and is inclusive. Drawbacks are that it appears indecisive and takes longer. So, when men and women fail to understand this difference, irritations and frustrations can arise. Men blame women for talking all the

Report talk
typical male way of communicating

Rapport talk
typical female way of communicating

time, while women say that men are not listening. This occurs, for instance, when women discuss personal experiences and problems to create rapport with the receiver. When men hear problems, they want to control the situation by offering solutions. Women become frustrated because they want to create closeness and connection, not to get advice, while men become frustrated because they don't understand that women do not appreciate their advice and keep talking.

Practical implications

Genderflex
temporarily using communication behaviours typical of the other gender

Author Judith Tingley suggests that men and women should learn to genderflex. Genderflex entails the temporary use of communication behaviours typical of the other gender in order to increase the potential for influence.[74] For example, a woman might use sports analogies to motivate a group of males. Tingley believes that this approach increases understanding and sensitivity between the sexes. Research has not yet investigated the effectiveness of this approach.

In contrast, Deborah Tannen recommends that everyone needs to become aware of how linguistic styles work and how they influence our perceptions and judgements. She believes that knowledge of linguistic styles helps to ensure that people with valuable insights or ideas get a hearing. Consider how gender-based linguistic differences affect who gets heard in a meeting:

> Those who are comfortable speaking up in groups, who need little or no silence before raising their hands, or who speak out easily without waiting to be recognised are far more likely to get heard at meetings. Those who refrain from talking until it's clear that the previous speaker is finished, who wait to be recognised, and who are inclined to link their comments to those of others will do fine at a meeting where everyone else is following the same rules, but will have a hard time getting heard in a meeting with people whose styles are more like the first pattern. Given the socialisation process typical of boys and girls, men are more likely to have learned the first style and women the second, making meetings more congenial for men than for women.[75]

Knowledge of these linguistic differences can assist professionals in devising methods to ensure everyone's ideas are heard and given fair credit both in and outside meetings. Furthermore, it is useful to consider the organisational strengths and limitations of your linguistic style. You may want to consider modifying a linguistic characteristic that is a detriment to perceptions of your confidence, competence and authority. In conclusion, communication between the sexes can be improved by remembering that men and women have different ways of saying the same thing.

Dynamics of modern communication

Effective communication is the cornerstone of survival in today's competitive business environment. This is particularly true for companies that operate or compete worldwide or those undertaking significant organisational change. Professionals who use information technology effectively are more likely to contribute to organisational success. We conclude this chapter on communication with some relevant issues for modern communication. We also elaborate a contingency approach for choosing communication media and focus on how to deal with the huge amount of information that is available to us.

Communication in the computerised information age

Just as the personal computer revolutionised the workplace throughout the 1980s and 1990s, recent developments in information and communication technology will create a new revolution in the coming decade. Organisations are increasingly using this new information and communication technology as a lever to improve productivity and customer and employee satisfaction. In turn, communication patterns at work are changing radically.[76] The workplace is no longer constrained by geography, time and organisational boundaries. Consider how Patrick Braun, vice president operations of Cisco Systems EMEA (Europe, Middle East and Africa), is using information technology to stay on top of his job:

> I'm responsible for about 200 people in over 20 countries. Without the modern technical equipment it would be impossible to communicate with them fast and regularly. Since I'm travelling for about two-thirds of my working time, some instruments such as telephonic conference calls and videoconferencing are indispensable. Every Monday I talk to my senior managers for an hour-and-a-half while we're each in different regions of Europe. If I had to fly to each meeting I would lose a terrible amount of time. I mean, a single meeting in another country would take at least a day, even with the best flight schedule. I wouldn't be without my mobile phone either. Now I'm always attainable – because now calls switch automatically between my office number, my mobile number and my voicemail. I also make use of the 'mobile office' concept: I can log in anytime and anywhere on the Cisco network, to read my mail or to get access to our Intranet. When I go to one of our offices in Norway or Switzerland, all I have to do is install my laptop. Our network is designed in a way that it recognises me immediately and gives me direct access. Also, our administration system is almost paperless: all our documentation on customers is on CD-ROM. With all these technical aids, we are capable of operating our business with a relatively small group of people. If you were to take a look at our order book, you'd say we need at least another hundred people for Benelux alone. Finally, you must now think that I communicate only via the new technologies but the opposite is true: the time that I save by using mail, teleconferencing, etc. allows me to invest more in my personal contacts.[77]

INTERNET/INTRANET/EXTRANET

The **Internet** is a public network of computer networks, whereas an **Intranet** is nothing more than an organisation's private Internet. Intranets also have firewalls that block outside Internet users from accessing internal information. This is done to protect the privacy and confidentiality of company documents. Hence, Intranet systems provide organisations with the advantage of Internet technology to disseminate organisational information and enhance communication between employees, while still maintaining system security. Organisations use the Intranet, for instance, for policy manuals, employee benefits information, job openings or standard company documents. In contrast to the internal focus of an Intranet, an **Extranet** is an extended Intranet in that it connects internal employees with selected customers, suppliers and other strategic partners. Ford Motor Company, for instance, has an Extranet that connects its dealers worldwide. Ford's Extranet was set up to help support the sales and servicing of cars and to enhance customer satisfaction.

The primary benefit of the Internet, Intranets and Extranets is that they can enhance the ability of employees to find, create, manage and distribute information. The effectiveness of these 'Nets', however, depends on how organisations set up and manage their Intranet/Extranet and how employees use the acquired information – because information by itself cannot solve nor do anything.[78] For example, communication effectiveness can actually decrease if a corporate Intranet becomes a dumping ground for disorganised information. In this case, employees will find themselves drowning in a sea of information.

Internet
a public network of computer networks

Intranet
an organisation's private Internet

Extranet
connects internal employees with selected customers, suppliers and strategic partners

ELECTRONIC MAIL

Electronic mail or email uses the Internet/Intranet to send computer-generated text and documents between people. Email is a major communication medium throughout the world because of three key benefits:[79]

Electronic mail
uses the Internet/Intranet to send computer-generated text and documents

- Email reduces the cost of distributing information to a large number of employees. It also reduces the costs and time associated with print duplication and paper distribution. Emails are quickly formed, edited and stored.
- Email is a tool for increasing teamwork. It enables employees to quickly send messages to colleagues on the next floor, in another building or even in another country. In support of this benefit, a study of 375 professionals indicated they used email for three dominant reasons: (a) to keep others informed; (b) to follow up an earlier communication; and (c) to communicate the same thing to many people.[80]
- Email fosters flexibility. This is particularly true for employees with a portable computer because they can log onto the Internet whenever and wherever they want. People can choose to read their emails when they have time to do so. It is possible to randomly access the information, by selecting messages in the order you prefer.

In spite of these positive benefits, there are three key drawbacks to consider. First, information overload is a major drawback of email. The ease of use of email seems also to be its major drawback. People now tend to send more messages than ever, and there is a lot of 'spamming' going on: sending junk mail, bad jokes or irrelevant memos (such as email copies or 'cc'). Selecting, reading and responding to all these messages can easily take an entire day. It can lead to a lot of wasted time and effort and it can distract employees from completing critical job duties.

Second, preliminary evidence suggests that people are using email to communicate when they should be using other media. This practice can result in reduced communication effectiveness. A four-year study of communication patterns within a university supported this prediction. The increased use of email was associated with decreased face-to-face interactions and with a drop in the overall amount of organisational communication. Employees also expressed a feeling of being less connected and less cohesive as a department as the amount of emails increased.[81] This interpersonal 'disconnection' may, indeed, be caused by the trend of replacing everyday face-to-face interactions by electronic messages. It is important to remember that employees' social needs are satisfied through the many different interpersonal interactions that occur at work. Steven Roberts, a British freelance copywriter, tells of his experiences in this matter:

> 'Recently', he says, 'I was working in the offices of a large television company. Nobody spoke to each other – virtually all information was communicated by email. Several times, I announced to my boss that I'd finished a job, only to be told to repeat this information by email and then to await my next instructions by email too. And my boss was sitting right next to me!'[82]

A final major drawback of using email is the lack of non-verbal and emotional content. It lacks the non-verbal signals that are present in face-to-face communication or phone calls, which means that emails are often misinterpreted. How do you, for instance, convey sarcasm through email? People currently use all kinds of symbols, called **Emoticons**, to express emotions in emails. Some examples can be found in Table 8.4. Other non-verbal solutions are, for instance, the use of all capitals or boldface, which is the non-verbal alternative of shouting or anger. Using these emoticons and other non-verbal solutions is, however, no guarantee for effectively communicating emotions and other non-verbal signals.

Emoticons
symbols used to express emotions in email

TABLE 8.4 EMOTICONS USED IN EMAILS

:-) happy	:-@ screaming	<g> grin
:-(or :-[sad	:-O yelling or surprise	<L> laughing
;-) wink	:-D surprise or shock	<Y> yawning
:-e disappointment	:'-(crying	

Companies are advised to develop policies for email and Internet use.[83] These policies can also outline writing rules, because people do not use proper spelling and grammatical rules when writing emails. Table 8.5 lists some simple rules, sometimes called **Netiquette rules**, that can improve the effectiveness and quality of communication through email.[84]

Netiquette rules
rules that attempt to improve the quality and effectiveness of communication through email

> A large-scale study among British organisations by the Chartered Institute of Personnel and Development (CIPD) reveals that 94 per cent of UK organisations have an email or Internet policy. 60 per cent of the organisations have problems with email or Internet misuse. The same study shows that nearly one third of UK organisations dismiss employees for excessive or inappropriate use of email or the Internet. Richard Goff of CIPD comments that 'email and Internet abuse remain a real concern for most organisations, particularly the legal ramifications of misuse. It is encouraging to see such a high proportion with email and Internet policies'. 'On the other side', he says, 'excessive monitoring on the part of the employer can stifle creativity and more importantly trust between employers and staff. Internet and email have become essential communication tools and there are times when using them for matters unrelated to work is necessary.'[85]

TABLE 8.5 NETIQUETTE RULES

Don't send emails you would not like to be published. There is always a risk when sending emails that they are forwarded to others or put on a web site. Emails can travel everywhere, so they must be written carefully. People often see email as private and impermanent. However, messages can be stored on servers and be made public years later.

Don't send emails when you are angry. Avoid sending emails impulsively. Sending hostile messages occurs a lot, it is also known as flaming. **Flaming** is the common term used for the kind of provocative communication that is possible in the relatively anonymous setting of the email system. Flaming happens because people communicate impersonally and at a distance, which means they use more provocative language. Flaming can create a climate of distrust, fear and anger.[86]

Respond as soon as possible to emails. If you do not have the time for an immediate response (for instance when it takes time looking up some information to formulate an answer), send an email to the other person to let him/her know when you will answer the message. The other person then knows you received the message safely and that you are working on it. Otherwise, people are left in a state of uncertainty, not knowing whether you received and understood the message correctly.

Writing emails:
Fill in the subject line of the email header with an informative description of the message.
Keep it short and to the point. A length of 25 lines seems appropriate, because this is the format of your computer screen.
Write grammatically correct, properly formatted and concise messages. Email seems an informal medium, which makes people write sloppy or quickly formulated messages.
Attach more complex or lengthy information in an appendix to your email. However, avoid too lengthy attachments, because they take too much time to download or can sometimes not be opened at all.
Do not use too many colours and different kinds of fonts in your mail. This may seem beautiful on your computer screen, but can become a mess when sent.

Flaming provocative communication due to the impersonal and anonymous setting of the email system

VIDEOCONFERENCING

Videoconferencing, also known as teleconferencing or virtual conferencing, uses video and audio links along with computers to enable people who are located at different locations to see, hear and talk to each other. This enables people from many locations to conduct a meeting without having to travel. Videoconferencing thus can significantly reduce an organisation's travel expenses. However, videoconferencing might not always lead to the anticipated effect, as you can read in the next Snapshot.

In the 1990s many organisations set up special videoconferencing rooms or booths with specially equipped television cameras. More modern equipment enables people to attach small cameras and microphones to their desks or computer monitors, which reduces the cost of videoconferencing significantly. This enables employees to conduct long-distance meetings and training classes without leaving their office. Other applications of videoconferencing are, for instance, medical specialists that diagnose and supervise surgery or lecturers that give courses to student at different locations throughout the world.

COLLABORATIVE COMPUTING

Collaborative computing entails using state-of-the-art computer software and hardware to help people work together better. They enable people to share information without the constraints of time and space. This is accomplished by using computer networks to provide a link – across a room or across the globe – between people. Collaborative applications include instant messaging and

Collaborative computing using computer software and hardware to help people work together better

311

Videoconferencing leads to increased meetings and costs in Thailand

Technology makes communication easier, especially across international borders, right? Not necessarily. Although Western companies are making major investments in technologies, designed to make their global communications more efficient, such tools are often underused and even counterproductive in cross-cultural business environments. You need to consider several factors before selecting which technology to use and in which context.

As for what can go wrong, consider the case of videoconferencing in Thailand. An American firm had invested in the installation of videoconferencing facilities in its Thailand subsidiary. In addition to enabling communication with other sites around the world, the new videoconferencing capability was intended to increase the productivity of the firm's local Thai employees. Many would have to spend an entire day travelling the crowded roads between the company's outlying factory to attend a meeting at Bangkok headquarters. It was thought that videoconferencing would make such travel unnecessary. But things didn't quite turn out as planned. The Thais had trouble getting used to the new technology. The former managing director of the Thai subsidiary, a US expatriate, remembers ruefully: 'I soon found out that the local managers were conducting the videoconference for my benefit and then arranging to have a face-to-face meeting afterwards. They still wanted to be able to meet in person to gauge the reaction of others.'

So, instead of creating greater efficiency, the new videoconferencing facility resulted in additional meetings and extra costs.

SOURCE: Excerpt from E. Gundling, 'How to Communicate', *Training and Development*, June 1999, p. 28. Copyright June 1999, *Training and Development*, American Society for Training and Development. Reprinted with permission. All rights reserved.

email systems, calendar management, videoconferencing, computer teleconferencing, electronic whiteboards and the type of computer-aided decision-making systems that will be discussed in Chapter 12.

Organisations that use fully-fledged collaborative systems have the ability to create virtual teams (see Chapter 10) or to operate as a virtual organisation (see Chapter 14). Virtual teams and organisations tend to use Internet/Intranet systems, collaborative software systems and videoconferencing systems.[87] These real-time systems enable people to communicate with anyone at any time.

It is important to keep in mind that modern-day information technology only enables people to interact virtually, it does not guarantee effective communication. Interestingly, there are a whole host of unique communication problems associated with using the information technology needed to 'operate virtually'.[88] The Royal Bank of Scotland, for instance, has used videoconferencing techniques since 1985, as face-to-face meetings have to take place every day and the participants are separated by 500 kilometres.[89]

TELECOMMUTING

Telecommuting
doing work that is generally performed in the office away from the office using different information technologies

Telecommuting, also known as teleworking, involves doing office work away from the office, using a variety of information technologies. Telecommuting involves receiving and sending work from a remote location via some form of information technology such as wireless devices, fax or a home computer that is linked via modem to an office computer. Telecommuting is more common for jobs that involve computer work, writing and phone work that require concentration and limited interruptions.[90] Since its introduction in the 1970s and 1980s, the total number of teleworkers increased to around 9 million by the end of 1999. In 2002, on average 13 per cent of employed persons in the EU practised some form of telecommuting (against 25 per cent in the US), with leading countries in Europe being the Netherlands, Denmark and Finland. At present, European countries differ greatly in their adoption of telecommuting, with a larger number of teleworkers in the Northern European than in the Southern European countries.[91]

Proposed benefits of telecommuting include:

- Reduction of capital costs.
- Increased flexibility and autonomy for workers.
- Competitive edge in recruitment.
- Increased job satisfaction and lower turnover.
- Increased productivity.
- Additional sources of workers (such as prison inmates and the homebound disabled).

Employees like telecommuting because it helps resolve work–family conflicts. A study revealed that homeworkers at British Telecom coped better with the daily stresses of working than the office-bound operators.[92] Organisations in turn may expect to receive more organisational commitment, job satisfaction and employee retention and attraction in return.[93] However, characteristics of the teleworker and the environment influence the successful implementation of telecommuting significantly. Research indicates, for instance, the strong influence of support variables on telecommuting success, such as supervisor, family and technical support.[94] Although telecommuting represents an attempt to accommodate employees' needs and desires, it requires adjustments and is not for everybody. Many people thoroughly enjoy the social camaraderie that exists within an office setting. These individuals probably would not like to telecommute. Others lack the self-motivation needed to work at home. Research shows that appropriate communication strategies towards teleworkers have an important impact on their job satisfaction: for example, clearly communicating job responsibilities, goals and objectives, deadlines and job expectations.[95] Finally, organisations must be careful to implement telecommuting in a non-discriminatory manner. Organisations can easily and unknowingly violate one of several anti-discrimination laws.[96]

Choosing media: a contingency perspective

Media selection is a key component of communication effectiveness. If an inappropriate medium is used, decisions may be based on inaccurate information, important messages may not reach the intended audience and employees may become dissatisfied and unproductive. We propose a contingency model that is designed to help people select communication media in a systematic and effective manner. Media selection in this model is based on the interaction between information richness and the complexity of the problem or situation at hand.

INFORMATION RICHNESS

Organisational theorists Richard Daft and Robert Lengel define **Information richness** in the following manner:

 Richness is defined as the potential information-carrying capacity of data. If the communication of an item of data, such as a wink, provides substantial new understanding, it would be considered rich. If the datum provides little understanding, it would be low in richness.[97]

> **Information richness** information-carrying capacity of data

Information richness refers to the information-carrying capacity of a medium, which means the volume and variety of information that can be transmitted. As this definition implies, alternative media possess levels of information richness that vary from high to low.

Information richness is determined by four factors:

- Feedback (ranging from fast to very slow).
- Channel (ranging from the combined visual and audio characteristics of a videoconference to the limited visual aspects of a computer report).
- Type of communication (ranging from personal to impersonal).
- Language source (ranging from the natural body language and speech contained in a face-to-face conversation to the numbers contained in a financial report).

Face-to-face contact is the richest form of communication. It provides immediate feedback, which serves as a comprehension check and makes it possible to customise the information exchange to the situation. Moreover, multiple communication channels, like verbal and non-verbal ones, are used simultaneously. Although high in richness, telephone and videoconferencing are not as informative as the face-to-face medium. In contrast, newsletters, computer reports and emails possess the lowest richness. Feedback for these media is very slow, the channels involving only limited visual information and the information provided being generic or impersonal.

COMPLEXITY OF THE PROBLEM OR SITUATION

Professionals face problems and situations that range from low to high in complexity. Low complexity situations are routine, predictable and are managed by using objective or standard procedures. These situations are straightforward and have a minimum of ambiguity. Calculating an employee's pay is an example of low complexity. Highly complex situations, like a corporate reorganisation, are ambiguous, unpredictable, hard to analyse and often emotion-laden. Professionals spend considerably more time analysing these situations because they rely on more sources of information during their deliberations. There are no set solutions to complex problems or situations.

CONTINGENCY RECOMMENDATIONS

The contingency model for selecting media is graphically depicted in Figure 8.5. As shown, there are three zones of communication effectiveness. Effective communication occurs when the richness of the medium is matched appropriately with the complexity of the problem or situation. Media low in richness – impersonal static or personal static – are better suited to simple problems, while media high in richness – interactive media or face-to-face – are appropriate for complex problems or situations.

Conversely, ineffective communication occurs when the medium is either too rich or insufficiently rich for the complexity of the problem or situation. For example, a district sales manager would fall into the overload zone if he or she communicated monthly sales reports through richer media. Conducting face-to-face meetings or telephoning each salesperson would provide excessive information and take more time than necessary to communicate monthly sales data. The oversimplification zone represents another ineffective choice of communication medium. In this situation, media with

FIGURE 8.5 A CONTINGENCY MODEL FOR SELECTING COMMUNICATION MEDIA

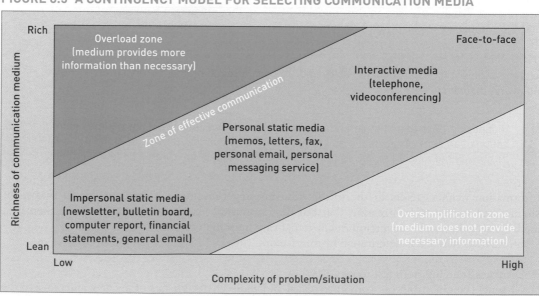

SOURCES: Adapted from R. Lengel and R. L. Daft, 'The Selection of Communication Media as an Executive Skill', *Academy of Management Executive*, August 1988, p. 226; and R. L. Daft and R. H. Lengel, 'Information Richness: A New Approach to Managerial Behavior and Organization Design', *Research in Organizational Behavior*, eds B. M. Staw and L. L. Cummings (Greenwich, CT: JAI Press, 1984) p. 199.

inadequate richness are used to communicate complicated problems. An example would be an executive who uses a letter or an email message to communicate news of a merger or a major reorganisation. This choice of medium is ineffective because employees are likely to be nervous and concerned about how a merger or reorganisation will affect their futures. Choosing the wrong medium in this situation will lead to misunderstanding and accordingly take a longer time to resolve things. Research showed that face-to-face communication was the most effective medium to announce change processes.[98] Of course, this is not possible in large organisations, but group communications with opportunities to ask questions are a valuable alternative.

Helpful questions to select the most appropriate medium to deliver your message are for instance:

■ How much information do I have to transmit?
■ Is speed of importance?
■ Is feedback needed?
■ Does the message require deeper elaboration?
■ Which media are certainly inappropriate for delivering the message?

Sometimes it can be necessary to use multiple media to convey your message effectively.

Dealing with information overload

Often, our times are called the 'Information Age', referring to the increase of information that is available to us. People, however, do not have an infinite capacity to process this information. Herbert Simon was the first to introduce the concept of bounded rationality, referring to the finding that people have limited cognitive abilities to process information (see Chapters 1 and 12).[99] When the information we have to work with exceeds our processing capacity, this results in **Information overload**. The current diversity of communication media and technologies and the pressure to compete globally means that more and more people suffer from information overload. They feel overwhelmed by too much information and are unable to respond adequately to all messages that reach them or to make adequate decisions with the available information. Modern technology was designed to empower us and set us free, but instead it has led to greater demands.[100] Consider the frustration of Steven Roberts, a British freelance copywriter, when he came back to his office after a two-week holiday:

> A man walks into a bar . . . Why blondes are stupid . . . What a woman really means when she says . . . Has anybody seen my pen? This isn't my stream of consciousness, these are just some of the 328 unread messages I found in my inbox after my two weeks off. My heart sank as I scrolled down them: inane jokes, inane responses to inane jokes, inane responses to the responses . . . . Occasionally, there was something of importance: a message from a client, a reminder that I have an appraisal next week. By the time I stored and deleted where appropriate, it was lunchtime. Then I started work, every thought interrupted by that familiar ping, as another email dropped into my inbox.[101]

RESEARCH FINDINGS

Information overload is a serious problem in many organisations, leading to a decrease in productivity. David Shenk, author of *Data Smog: Surviving the Information Glut*, uses the concept 'information obesity'. In the past, the challenge was to find enough information, while now the challenge is to find the most relevant, meaningful, contextualised information to turn it into useful knowledge and wisdom.[102] Managing information effectively within the organisation has become critically important because it provides a basis for gaining a competitive advantage.[103] A Reuters Business Information study investigated information overload in a large-scale study with 1300 managers in the UK, USA, Hong Kong and Singapore:

> The study indicated that people spend too much time looking for information. 38 per cent of the managers surveyed waste substantial amounts of time looking for information. Decisions are often delayed. 43 per cent of respondents thought that decisions were delayed and otherwise adversely affected by the existence of too much information. 47 per

Information overload
when the information we have to work with exceeds our processing capacity

cent of respondents said that information collection distracts them from their main responsibilities. They also find it difficult to develop strategies to deal with the information they retrieve. Two-thirds of respondents associated information overload with tension with colleagues and loss of job satisfaction. 42 per cent attributed ill health to this stress. 61 per cent said they had to cancel social activities as a result of information overload and 60 per cent that they are frequently too tired for leisure activities.[104]

What happens when people have to deal with too much information? They select or ignore information; they forget things or pass them over to others. The amount of information that is available makes it difficult to discriminate between useless and useful information. The consequence is that a lot of information is screened out, which means that it is not even decoded. This leads to ineffective communication, a loss of information and inadequate decisions. Research shows that the decision-making performance of individuals correlates positively with the information available, up to a certain point. If more information is provided beyond this point, performance starts to decline and the information is no longer integrated in the decision-making process. The burden of too much information available confuses the person, affects the ability to set priorities and makes prior information harder to recall.[105]

Information overload also is a common source of workplace stress (see Chapter 7). A basic condition of human well-being is that the challenges we face match our skills to handle them. If the challenges become higher (as in a situation of information overload), we feel anxious and in a situation of loss of control. Psychologist David Lewis uses the term 'Information Fatigue Syndrome', including symptoms like exhaustion, anxiety, failure of memory and shortness of attention.[106]

TABLE 8.6 DEVELOPING AN ORGANISATIONAL POLICY TO COUNTER INFORMATION OVERLOAD

Make use of an exception principle to regulate the information flow. This means that only exceptions or deviations from policies or procedures should be reported. Is it really necessary to cc everyone of the department when reporting on the status of a project? Think twice before forwarding an article, interesting website or joke to colleagues. Do they really need this?
Provide abstracts or summaries instead of entire documents if you want to inform a colleague of something. The entire document can be delivered later on when useful
Make use of human interventions, like personal assistants, to select your messages. Only those documents or messages that are essential are forwarded
Install filters to banish unwanted junk mail (called spam) from mailboxes
Make use of Intranet systems to store information that can be useful for multiple users. This will reduce the number of emails that are sent within organisations. Intranet also increases the access of employees to information
Stimulate people to use all kind of folders on their PC or files in their desk to store information that they need later on without considering it immediately. People often have the tendency to try to process all information that reaches them immediately, even if they cannot use it at that moment. This also means creating folders in their mailbox to move low priority mails to be dealt with when they have time to do so
Promote information literacy in individuals via appropriate training.[108] Information literacy refers to the ability to access, evaluate and use information of a variety of sources. The key to information management is focusing on the quality of the data you receive. Necessary steps for information literacy are: ■ To learn to articulate the information you need (this means for instance understanding your goals and priorities). ■ To develop a sourcing strategy for finding the information you need (for instance identifying potential sources, including books, articles, databases, people with expertise in that matter, and common keywords concerning the information you are looking for).

Information overload also puts us under pressure to multitask, which means doing several tasks simultaneously: for example, talking on the phone while reading and writing emails. This leads to an inability to focus and makes us easily feel frustrated.

PRACTICAL IMPLICATIONS

Solutions to deal with information overload in organisations can be introduced at the individual but also at the organisational level.[107] Some organisations, for instance, encourage their employees to send fewer emails or discourage the use of the word 'urgent' when sending mails. Solutions to solve information overload can focus on two different aspects: increasing the information-processing capacity of people or reducing the information load that reaches people. Just like the earlier mentioned, netiquette rules can help to develop an organisational policy for effective email writing and use, solutions to deal with information overload can be integrated in an organisational policy (see Table 8.6).

This also implies setting a time limit for how long you will search for information. It is easy to keep on searching and finding more and more and even more information, even if you already have enough.

Learning outcomes: Summary of key terms

1 Describe the perceptual process model of communication

Communication is a process of consecutively linked elements. Historically, this process was described in terms of a conduit model. Criticisms of this model led to the development of a perceptual process model of communication that depicts receivers as information processors who create the meaning of messages in their own mind. Because receivers' interpretations of messages often differ from those intended by senders, miscommunication is a common occurrence. Noise refers to anything that interferes with the transmission and understanding of a message. Communication occurs on two separate but interrelated levels – the content and the relationship level – and needs to be interpreted in the context wherein it takes place.

2 Describe the process, personal, physical and semantic barriers to effective communication

Every element of the perceptual model of communication is a potential process barrier. There are eight personal aspects that commonly become a barrier for effective communication: (a) the ability to communicate effectively; (b) the way people process and interpret information; (c) the level of interpersonal trust between people; (d) the existence of stereotypes and prejudice; (e) the egos of the people communicating; (f) the inability to listen; (g) the natural tendency to evaluate or judge a sender's message; and (h) the inability to listen with understanding. Physical barriers pertain to distance, physical objects, time, and work and office noise. Semantic barriers show up as encoding and decoding errors because these phases of communication involve transmitting and receiving words and symbols. Cultural diversity is a key contributor to semantic barriers.

3 Demonstrate your familiarity with effective oral, written and non-verbal communication skills

Oral communication refers to all verbal communication that is spoken. It is fast and allows for immediate feedback. Written communication refers to all kinds of verbal communication that is written. Written communication makes information distribution to a lot of people possible, it is tangible and can be verified easily. Body movements and gestures, touch, facial expressions and eye contact are important non-verbal cues. The interpretation of these non-verbal cues varies significantly across cultures.

4 Discuss the primary sources of listener comprehension. Identify the three different listening styles and review the ten keys to listen effectively

Listening is the process of actively decoding and interpreting verbal messages. Characteristics of the listener, speaker, message and environment influence listener comprehension.

Communication experts identified three unique listening styles. A results-style listener likes to hear the bottom line or result of a message at the beginning of a conversation. Reasons-style listeners want to know the rationale for what someone is saying or proposing. Process-style listeners like to discuss issues in detail. Good listeners use the following ten listening habits: (a) capitalise on thought speed by staying with the speaker and listening between the lines; (b) listen for ideas rather than facts; (c) identify areas of interest between the speaker and listener; (d) judge content and not delivery; (e) do not judge until the speaker has completed his or her message; (f) put energy and effort into listening; (g) resist distractions; (h) listen to both favourable and unfavourable information; (i) read or listen to complex material to exercise the mind; and (j) take notes when necessary and use visual aids to enhance understanding.

5 Contrast the communication styles of assertiveness, non-assertiveness and aggressiveness
An assertive style is expressive and self-enhancing but does not violate other people's basic human rights. In contrast, an aggressive style is expressive and self-enhancing but takes unfair advantage of others. A non-assertive style is characterised by timid and self-denying behaviour. An assertive communication style is more effective than either an aggressive or non-assertive style. Assertiveness is important when giving criticism, making clear requests and saying no to requests of others.

6 Discuss the patterns of hierarchical communication and 'the grapevine'
Hierarchical communication patterns describe exchanges of information between supervisors and their employees. Supervisors provide five types of downward communication: job instructions, job rationale, organisational procedures and practices, feedback about performance, and indoctrination of goals. Employees communicate information upward about themselves, co-workers and their problems, organisational practices and policies, and what needs to be done and how to do it. The grapevine is the unofficial communication system of the informal organisation. Communication along the grapevine follows four predictable patterns: single strand, gossip, probability and cluster. The cluster pattern is the most common.

7 Explain the contingency approach to media selection
Selecting media is a key component of communication effectiveness. Media selection is based on the interaction between the information richness of a medium and the complexity of the problem/situation at hand. Information richness ranges from low to high and is a function of four factors: speed of feedback, characteristics of the channel, type of communication and language source. Problems/situations range from simple to complex. Effective communication occurs when the richness of the medium matches the complexity of the problem at hand. Richer media need to be used as situations become more complex.

8 Elaborate on information overload and how to deal with it effectively
Our 'Information Age' leads to an ever-increasing amount of information. When the information exceeds our information processing capacity, this results in information overload. Information overload leads to decreased productivity, ineffective communication, loss of information, inadequate decisions and workplace stress. Solutions to deal with information overload in organisations can be introduced on the individual but also on the organisational level. These solutions can focus on two different aspects: increasing the information-processing capacity of people or reducing the information load that reaches people.

Review questions

1 Describe a situation where you had trouble decoding a message. What caused the problem?

2 What are some sources of noise that interfere with communication during a lecture, an encounter with a lecturer in his or her office, and a movie?

3 Which barrier to effective communication is most difficult to reduce? Explain.

4 Are you good at reading non-verbal communication? Give some examples.

5 Would you describe your prevailing communication style as assertive, aggressive, or non-assertive? How can you tell? Would your style help or hinder you as a professional?

6 What is your personal experience of the grapevine? Do you see it as a positive or negative factor in the workplace? Explain.

7 Have you ever experienced gender differences concerning communication? Give some examples.

8 Which of the three zones of communication in Figure 8.5 (overload, effective, over-simplification) do you think is most common in today's large organisations? What is your rationale?

9 Have you ever felt overwhelmed with information? How did you deal with it? Was it effective?

Personal awareness and growth exercise

Assessing your listening skills

Objectives

1 To assess your listening skills.

2 To develop a personal development plan aimed at increasing your listening skills.

Introduction

Listening is a critical component of effective communication. Unfortunately, research and case studies suggest that many of us are not very good at actively listening. This is particularly bad in light of the fact that people spend more time listening than they do speaking or writing. This exercise provides you with the opportunity to assess your listening skills and develop a plan for improvement.

Instructions

The following statements reflect various habits we use when listening to others. For each statement, indicate the extent to which you agree or disagree with it by selecting one number from the scale provided. Circle your response for each statement. Remember, there are no right or wrong answers. After completing the survey, add up your total score for the 17 items and record it in the space provided.

Listening skills survey

1 = Strongly disagree

2 = Disagree

3 = Neither agree nor disagree

4 = Agree

5 = Strongly agree

1	I daydream or think about other things when listening to others.	1	2	3	4	5
2	I do not mentally summarise the ideas being communicated by a speaker.	1	2	3	4	5
3	I do not use a speaker's body language or tone of voice to help interpret what he or she is saying.	1	2	3	4	5
4	I listen more for facts than overall ideas during classroom lectures.	1	2	3	4	5
5	I tune out dry speakers.	1	2	3	4	5
6	I have a hard time paying attention to boring people.	1	2	3	4	5
7	I can tell whether someone has anything useful to say before he or she finishes communicating a message.	1	2	3	4	5
8	I stop listening to a speaker when I think he or she has nothing interesting to say.	1	2	3	4	5
9	I get emotional or upset when speakers make jokes about issues or things that are important to me.	1	2	3	4	5
10	I get angry or distracted when speakers use offensive words.	1	2	3	4	5
11	I do not expend a lot of energy when listening to others.	1	2	3	4	5
12	I pretend to pay attention to others even when I'm not really listening.	1	2	3	4	5
13	I get distracted when listening to others.	1	2	3	4	5
14	I deny or ignore information and comments that go against my thoughts and feelings.	1	2	3	4	5
15	I do not seek opportunities to challenge my listening skills.	1	2	3	4	5
16	I do not pay attention to the visual aids used during lectures.	1	2	3	4	5
17	I do not take notes on handouts when they are provided.	1	2	3	4	5

Total score = _____

Preparing a personal development plan

1 Use the following norms to evaluate your listening skills:

17–34 = Good listening skills

35–53 = Moderately good listening skills

54–85 = Poor listening skills.

How would you evaluate your listening skills?

2 Do you agree with the assessment of your listening skills? Why or why not?

3 The 17-item listening skills survey was developed to assess the extent to which you use the keys to effective listening presented in Table 8.1. Use Table 8.1 and the development plan format to prepare your development plan. First, identify the five statements from the listening skills survey that received your highest ratings – high ratings represent low skills. Record the survey numbers in the space provided in the development plan. Next, compare the content of these survey items to the descriptions of bad and good listeners shown in Table 8.1. This comparison will help you identify the keys to effective listening being measured by each survey item. Write down the keys to effective listening that correspond to each of the five items you want to improve. Finally, write down specific actions or behaviours that you can undertake to improve the listening skill being considered.

Development plan

Survey items	Key to effective-listening I want to improve	Action steps required (what do you need to do to build listening skills for this listening characteristic?)

320

Group exercise

Practising different styles of communication

Objectives

1 To demonstrate the relative effectiveness of communicating assertively, aggressively and non-assertively.

2 To give you hands-on experience with different styles of communication.

Introduction

Research shows that assertive communication is more effective than either an aggressive or non-assertive style. This role-playing exercise is designed to increase your ability to communicate assertively. Your task is to use different communication styles while attempting to resolve the work-related problems of a poor performer.

Instructions

Form a group of three and read the 'Poor Performer' and 'Store Manager' roles provided here. Then decide who will play the poor performer role, who the managerial role, and who the observer. The observer will be asked to provide feedback to the manager after each role-play. When playing the managerial role, you should first attempt to resolve the problem by using an aggressive communication style. Attempt to achieve your objective by using the non-verbal and verbal behaviour patterns associated with the aggressive style shown in Table 8.2. Take about four to six minutes to act out the instructions. The observer should give feedback to the manager after completing the role-play. The observer should comment on how the employee responded to the aggressive behaviours displayed by the manager.

After feedback is provided on the first role-play, the person playing the manager should then try to resolve the problem with a non-assertive style. Observers once again should provide feedback. Finally, the manager should confront the problem with an assertive style. Once again, rely on the relevant non-verbal and verbal behaviour patterns presented in Table 8.2, and take four to six minutes to act out each scenario. Observers should try to provide detailed feedback on how effectively the manager exhibited non-verbal and verbal assertive behaviours. Be sure to provide positive and constructive feedback.

After completing these three role-plays, switch roles: manager becomes observer, observer becomes poor performer and poor performer becomes manager. When these role-plays are completed, switch roles once again.

Role: poor performer

You sell shoes full-time for a national chain of shoe stores. Over the past month, you have been absent three times without giving your manager a reason. The quality of your work has been slipping. You have a lot of creative excuses when your boss tries to talk to you about your performance.

When playing this role, feel free to invent a personal problem that you may eventually want to share with your manager. However, make the manager dig for information about this problem. Otherwise, respond to your manager's comments as you would normally.

Role: store manager

You manage a store for a national chain of shoe stores. In the privacy of your office, you are talking to one of your salespeople who has had three unexcused absences from work during the last month. (This is excessive, according to company guidelines, and must be corrected.) The quality of the person's work has been slipping. Customers have complained that this person is rude and co-workers have told you this individual isn't carrying a fair share of the work. You are fairly sure this person has some sort of personal problem. You want to identify that problem and get him or her back on course.

Questions for discussion
1 What drawbacks of the aggressive and non-assertive styles did you observe?
2 What were major advantages of the assertive style?
3 What were the most difficult aspects of trying to use an assertive style?
4 How important was non-verbal communication during the various role-plays? Explain with examples.

Internet exercise

As covered in this chapter, communication styles vary from non-assertive to aggressive. We recommended that you strive to use an assertive style while avoiding the tendencies to be non-assertive or aggressive. In trying to be assertive, however, keep in mind that too much of a good thing is bad. That is, the use of an assertive style can become an aggressive one if taken too far.

Visit our website www.mcgraw-hill.co.uk/textbooks/buelens for further instructions.

Notes

1 A. Thorpe, 'The Office Gossip', the *Guardian*, 15 May 2000. Reproduced with permission.

2 P. Watzlawick, J. Beavin and D. Jackson, *Pragmatics of Human Communication* (New York: W. W. Norton, 1967).

3 'Slang Makes Youth "Unemployable"', *BBC Online News*, 11 March 2004, /www.news.bbc.co.uk/.

4 See M. A. Jaasma and R. J. Koper, 'The Relationship of Student-Faculty Out-of-Class communication to Instructor Immediacy and Trust and to Student Motivation', *Communication Education*, January 1999, pp. 41–7; and P. G. Clampitt and C. W. Downs, 'Employee Perceptions of the Relationship between Communication and Productivity: A Field Study', *Journal of Business Communication*, 1993, pp. 5–28.

5 Results can be found in D. Fenn, 'Benchmark: What Drives the Skills Gap?', *Inc.*, May 1996, p. 111.

6 J. L. Bowditch and A. F. Buono, *A Primer on Organizational Behavior, fourth edition* (New York: John Wiley & Sons, 1997), p. 120.

7 For a review of these criticisms, see L. L. Putnam, N. Phillips and P. Chapman, 'Metaphors of Communication and Organization', in *Handbook of Organization Studies*, eds S. R. Clegg, C. Hardy and W. R. Nord (London: Sage Publications, 1996), pp. 375–408.

8 Results of this study can be found in C. M. Fiol, 'Corporate Communications: Comparing Executives' Private and Public Statements', *Academy of Management Journal*, April 1995, pp. 522–36.

9 A. Thorpe, 'How to . . . Avoid Misunderstandings', the *Guardian*, 4 November 2000.

10 L. Labich, 'How to Fire People and Still Sleep at Night', *Fortune*, 10 June 1996, p. 65.

11 J. Humphrys, 'Hell is Other People Talking Webspeak on Mobile Phones', the *Sunday Times*, 27 August 2000.

12 S. R. Axley, 'Managerial and Organizational Communication in Terms of the Conduit Metaphor', *Academy of Management Review*, July 1984, pp. 428–37.

13 P. Watzlawick, J. Beavin and D. Jackson, *Pragmatics of Human Communication* (New York: W. W. Norton, 1967).

14 O. Hargie, C. Saunders and D. Dickson, *Social Skills in Interpersonal Communication, third edition* (London: Routledge, 1994), pp. 16–18.

15 O. Hargie, C. Saunders and D. Dickson, *Social Skills in Interpersonal Communication, third edition* (London: Routledge, 1994), p. 11.

16 H. J. Leavitt, *Managerial Psychology, revised edition* (Chicago: University of Chicago Press, 1964).

17 The preceding barriers are discussed by J. P. Scully, 'People: The Imperfect Communicators', *Quality Progress*, April 1995, pp. 37–9.

18 For a thorough discussion of the seventh and eight barrier, see C. R. Rogers and F. J. Roethlisberger, 'Barriers and Gateways to Communication', *Harvard Business Review*, July–August 1952, pp. 46–52.

19 More information on asking questions can be found in O. Hargie, C. Saunders and D. Dickson, *Social Skills in Interpersonal Communication, third edition* (London: Routledge, 1994), Ch. 5 and Ch. 6.

20 A. Thorpe, 'How to . . . Avoid Misunderstandings', the *Guardian*, 4 November 2000.

21 Results can be found in B. Davenport Sypher and T. E. Zorn, Jr, 'Communication-Related Abilities and Upward Mobility: A Longitudinal Investigation', *Human Communication Research*, Spring 1986, pp. 420–31.

22 Communication competence is discussed by J. S. Hinton and M. W. Kramer, 'The Impact of Self-Directed Videotape Feedback on Students' Self-Reported Levels of Communication Competence and Apprehension', *Communication Education*, April 1998, pp. 151–61; and L. J. Carrell and S. C. Willmington, 'The Relationship between Self-Report Measures of Communication Apprehension and Trained Observers' Ratings of Communication Competence', *Communication Reports*, Winter 1998, pp. 87–95.

23 The importance of non-verbal communication is discussed by L. K. Guerrero and J. A. DeVito, *The Nonverbal Communication Reader: Classic and Contemporary Readings, second edition* (Prospect Heights, IL: Waveland Press, 1999).

24 C. Harler, 'Electronic Communication May Accentuate Sex Differences', *Communications News*, April 1996, p. 4.

25 W. D. St John, 'You Are What You Communicate', *Personnel Journal*, October 1985, p. 40.

26 S. F. Zaidel and A. Mehrabian, 'The Ability to Communicate and Infer Positive and Negative Attitudes Facially and Vocally', *Journal of Experimental Research in Personality*, September 1969, pp. 233–41.

27 The effect of non-verbal cues on hiring decisions was examined by G. E. Wright and K. D. Multon, 'Employer's Perceptions of Nonverbal Communication in Job Interviews for Persons with Physical Disabilities', *Journal of Vocational Behavior*, October 1995, pp. 214–27; and R. C. Liden, C. L. Martin and C. K. Parsons, 'Interviewer and Applicant Behaviors in Employment Interviews', *Academy of Management Journal*, April 1993, pp. 372–86.

28 Results can be found in S. D. Kelly, D. J. Barr, R. B. Church and K. Lynch, 'Offering a Hand to Pragmatic Understanding: The Role of Speech and Gesture in Comprehension and Memory', *Journal of Memory and Language*, May 1999, pp. 577–92.

29 Related research is summarised by J. A. Hall, 'Male and Female Nonverbal Behavior', in *Multichannel Integrations of Nonverbal Behavior*, eds A. W. Siegman and S. Feldstein (Hillsdale, NJ: Lawrence Erlbaum, 1985), pp. 195–226.

30 A thorough discussion of cross-cultural differences is provided by R. E. Axtell, *Gestures: The Do's and Taboos of Body Language around the World* (New York: John Wiley & Sons, 1991). Problems with body language analysis are also discussed by C. L. Karrass, 'Body Language: Beware the Hype', *Traffic Management*, January 1992, p. 27; and M. Everett and B. Wiesendanger, 'What Does Body Language Really Say?', *Sales & Marketing Management*, April 1992, p. 40.

31 L. Van Poecke, *Nonverbale communicatie* (Leuven: Garant, 1996).

32 Results can be found in J. A. Hall, 'Male and Female Nonverbal Behavior', in *Multichannel Integrations of Nonverbal Behavior*, eds A. W. Siegman and S. Feldstein (Hillsdale, NJ: Lawrence Erlbaum, 1985), pp. 195–226.

33 See J. A. Russell, 'Facial Expressions of Emotion: What Lies Beyond Minimal Universality?', *Psychological Bulletin*, November 1995, pp. 379–91.

34 Norms for cross-cultural eye contact are discussed by C. Engholm, *When Business East Meets Business West: The Guide to Practice and Protocol in the Pacific Rim* (New York: John Wiley & Sons, 1991).

35 See D. Ray, 'Are You Listening?', *Selling Power*, June 1999, pp. 28–30; and P. Meyer, 'So You Want the President's Job', *Business Horizons*, January–February 1998, pp. 2–6.

36 Estimates are provided in both J. Hart Seibert, 'Listening in the Organizational Context', in *Listening Behavior: Measurement and Application*, ed. R. N. Bostrom (New York: The Guilford Press, 1990), pp. 119–27; and D. W. Caudill and R. M. Donaldson, 'Effective Listening Tips for Managers', *Administrative Management*, September 1986, pp. 22–3.

37 Cited in K. Davis and J. W. Newstrom, *Human Behavior at Work: Organizational Behavior, seventh edition* (New York: McGraw-Hill, 1985), p. 438.

38 See C. G. Pearce, 'How Effective Are We as Listeners?', *Training & Development*, April 1993, pp. 79–80; and G. Manning, K. Curtis and S. McMillen, *Building Community: The Human Side of Work* (Cincinnati, OH: Thomson Executive Press, 1996), pp. 127–54.

39 For a summary of supporting research, see K. W. Watson and L. L. Barker, 'Listening Behavior: Definition and Measurement', in *Communication Yearbook 8*, ed. R. N. Bostrom (Beverly Hills, CA: Sage Publications, 1984); and L. B. Comer and T. Drollinger, 'Active Empathetic Listening and Selling Success: A Conceptual Framework', *Journal of Personal Selling & Sales Management*, Winter 1999, pp. 15–29.

40 For a thorough discussion of the different listening styles, see R. T. Bennett and R. V. Wood, 'Effective Communication via Listening Styles', *Business*, April–June 1989, pp. 45–8.

41 See S. R. Covey, *The 7 Habits of Highly Effective People* (New York: Simon & Schuster, 1989).

42 P. McBride and S. Maitland, *The EI Advantage: Putting Emotional Intelligence into Practice* (London: McGraw-Hill, 2002), p. 117.

43 See E. Raudsepp, 'Are You Properly Assertive?', *Supervision*, June 1992, pp. 17–18; and D. A. Infante and W. I. Gorden, 'Superiors' Argumentativeness and Verbal Aggressiveness as Predictors of Subordinates' Satisfaction', *Human Communication Research*, Fall 1985, pp. 117–25.

44 J. A. Waters, 'Managerial Assertiveness', *Business Horizons*, September–October 1982, p. 25.

45 A. Thorpe, 'The Office Gossip', the *Guardian*, 24 July 2000.

46 O. Hargie, C. Saunders and D. Dickson, *Social Skills in Interpersonal Communication, third edition* (London: Routledge, 1994), p. 275.

47 Derived from P. McBride and S. Maitland, *The EI Advantage: Putting Emotional Intelligence into Practice* (London:

McGraw-Hill, 2002), pp. 176–9; and J. A. Waters, 'Managerial Assertiveness', *Business Horizons*, September–October 1982, p. 27.

48 Based on P. McBride and S. Maitland, *The EI Advantage: Putting Emotional Intelligence into Practice* (London: McGraw-Hill, 2002), pp. 165–6.

49 Based on P. McBride and S. Maitland, *The EI Advantage: Putting Emotional Intelligence into Practice* (London: McGraw-Hill, 2002), pp. 182–3; and M. J. Smith, *When I Say No, I Feel Guilty* (New York: Bantam, 1975).

50 C. Redding, *Communication within the Organization: An Interpretive Review of Theory and Research* (New York: Industrial Communication Council, 1972).

51 J. R. Carlson and R. W. Zmud, 'Channel Expansion Theory and the Experimental Nature of Media Richness Perceptions', *Academy of Management Journal*, April 1999, pp. 153–70.

52 G. L. Kreps, *Organizational Communication* (New York: Longman, 1990), p. 203.

53 K. Hilpern, 'Hang On – That's My Job', the *Guardian*, 14 February 2000.

54 For a thorough discussion of communication distortion, see E. W. Larson and J. B. King, 'The Systematic Distortion of Information: An Ongoing Challenge to Management', *Organizational Dynamics*, Winter 1996, pp. 49–61.

55 J. Fulk and S. Mani, 'Distortion of Communication in Hierarchical Relationships', in *Communication Yearbook 9*, ed. M. L. McLaughlin (Beverly Hills, CA: Sage Publications, 1986), p. 483.

56 For a review of this research, see J. Fulk and S. Mani, 'Distortion of Communication in Hierarchical Relationships', in *Communication Yearbook 9*, ed. M. L. McLaughlin (Beverly Hills, CA: Sage Publications, 1986), pp. 483–510.

57 See, for instance, N. B. Kurland and L. H. Pelled, 'Passing the Word: Toward a Model of Gossip and Power in the Workplace', *Academy of Management Review*, April 2000, pp. 428–38; and N. Nicholson, 'The New Word on Gossip', *Psychology Today*, June 2001, pp. 41–5.

58 Organisational benefits of the grapevine are discussed by T. Galpin, 'Pruning the Grapevine', *Training & Development*, April 1995, pp. 28–32; and J. Smythe, 'Harvesting the Office Grapevine', *People Management*, September 1995, pp. 24–7.

59 Results can be found in S. J. Modic, 'Grapevine Rated Most Believable', *Industry Week*, 15 May 1989, pp. 11, 14.

60 D. Krackhardt and J. R. Hanson, 'Informal Networks: The Company Behind the Chart', *Harvard Business Review*, July–August 1993, pp. 104–11; and H. Mintzberg, *The Structuring of Organizations* (Englewood Cliffs, NJ: Prentice Hall, 1979), pp. 43–9.

61 M. Noon and R. Delbridge, 'News from Behind My Hand: Gossip in Organizations', *Organization Studies*, January–February 1993, pp. 23–36; R. L. Rosnow, 'Inside Rumor: A Personal Journey', *American Psychologist*, May 1991, pp. 484–96; and C. J. Walker and C. A. Beckerle, 'The Effect of State Anxiety on Rumor Transmission', *Journal of Social Behavior and Personality*, August 1987, pp. 353–60.

62 'Why It's Good to Talk', the *Guardian*, 12 April 1999.

63 See K. Davis, 'Management Communication and the Grapevine', *Harvard Business Review*, September–October 1953, pp. 43–9.

64 H. B. Vickery III, 'Tapping into the Employee Grapevine', *Association Management*, January 1984, pp. 59–60.

65 A thorough discussion of organisational moles is provided by J. G. Bruhn and A. P. Chesney, 'Organizational Moles: Information Control and the Acquisition of Power and Status', *Health Care Supervisor*, September 1995, pp. 24–31.

66 Earlier research is discussed by K. Davis, 'Management Communication and the Grapevine', *Harvard Business Review*, September–October 1953, pp. 43–9; and L. Festinger, D. Cartwright, K. Barber, J. Fleischl, J. Gottsdanker, A. Keysen and G. Leavitt, 'A Study of Rumor: Its Origin and Spread', *Human Relations*, September 1948, pp. 464–86. Recent research is discussed by G. Michelson and V. S. Mouly, 'You Didn't Hear it From Us But . . . Towards an Understanding of Rumour and Gossip in Organisations', *Australian Journal of Management*, September 2002, pp. 57–65; N. DiFonzo and P. Bordia, 'How Top PR Professionals Handle Hearsay: Corporate Rumors, Their Effects, and Strategies to Manage Them', *Public Relations Review*, Summer 2000, pp. 173–90; G. Michelson and S. Mouly, 'Rumor and Gossip in Organizations: A Conceptual Study', *Management Decision*, May 2000, pp. 339–46; and S. M. Crampton, J. W. Hodge and J. M. Mishra, 'The Informal Communication Network: Factors Influencing Grapevine Activity', *Public Personnel Management*, Winter 1998, pp. 569–84.

67 For more information on the grapevine and technology, see P. Bordia and R. L. Rosnow, 'Rumor Rest Stops on the Information Highway: Transmission Patterns in a Computer-Mediated Rumor Chain', *Human Communication Research*, April 1998, pp. 163–79; C. L. Harrington and D. D. Bielby, 'Where Did You Hear That? Technology and the Social Organization of Gossip', *Sociological Quarterly*, August 1995, pp. 607–28; and 'The High-Tech Grapevine', *Psychology Today*, July–August 1996, p. 47.

68 Results are presented in J. C. Tingley, *Genderflex: Men & Women Speaking Each Other's Language at Work* (New York: American Management Association, 1994).

69 D. Tannen, 'The Power of Talk: Who Gets Heard and Why', *Harvard Business Review*, September–October 1995, p. 139.

70 For a thorough review of the evolutionary explanation of gender differences in communication, see A. H. Eagly and W. Wood, 'The Origins of Sex Differences in Human Behavior', *American Psychologist*, June 1999,

pp. 408–23; and J. Archer, 'Sex Differences in Social Behavior: Are the Social Role and Evolutionary Explanations Compatible?', *American Psychologist*, September 1996, pp. 909–17.

71 See H. Fisher, *The Natural Talents of Women and How They Are Changing the World* (New York: Ballantine Books, 1999); and D. Tannen, *You Just Don't Understand: Women and Men in Conversation* (New York: Ballantine Books, 1990).

72 Research on gender differences can be found in A. Mulac, J. J. Bradac and P. Gibbons, 'Empirical Support for the Gender-as-Culture Hypothesis: An Intercultural Analysis of Male/Female Language Differences', *Human Communications Research*, January 2001, pp. 121–52; and K. Hawkins and C. B. Power, 'Gender Differences in Questions Asked during Small Decision-Making Group Discussions', *Small Group Research*, April 1999, pp. 235–56.

73 D. Tannen, *Talking from 9 to 5* (New York: Avon, 1994).

74 This definition was taken from J. C. Tingley, *Genderflex: Men & Women Speaking Each Other's Language at Work* (New York: American Management Association, 1994), p. 16.

75 D. Tannen, 'The Power of Talk: Who Gets Heard and Why', *Harvard Business Review*, September–October 1995, pp. 147–8.

76 The influence of information technology on OB is thoroughly discussed by R. P. Gephart, Jr, 'Introduction to the Brave New Workplace: Organizational Behavior in the Electronic Age', *Journal of Organizational Behavior*, June 2002, pp. 327–44.

77 Adapted and translated from F. Van der Auwera, 'Nieuwe technologie maakt managers mobiel', *Vacature*, 31 May 1997.

78 This conclusion is discussed by O. Edwards, 'Inflammation Highway', *Forbes*, 26 February 1996, p. 120.

79 The benefits of using email were derived from R. F. Federico and J. M. Bowley, 'The Great E-Mail Debate', *HR Magazine*, January 1996, pp. 67–72; and J. Hunter and M. Allen, 'Adaptation to Electronic Mail', *Journal of Applied Communication Research*, August 1992, pp. 254–74.

80 Results can be found in M. L. Markus, 'Electronic Mail as the Medium of Managerial Choice', *Organization Science*, November 1994, pp. 502–27.

81 Results can be found in M. S. Thompson and M. S. Feldman, 'Electronic Mail and Organizational Communication: Does Saying "Hi" Really Matter', *Organization Science*, November–December 1998, pp. 685–98.

82 H. Freeman, 'Caught Up in the Communication Loop', the *Guardian*, 30 September 2000.

83 See the discussion in B. Sloboda, 'Netiquette: New Rules and Policies for the Information Age', *Management Quarterly*, Winter 1999, pp. 9–32.

84 Useful sources for using email appropriately are G. Colombo, 'Polish Your E-mail Etiquette', *Sales and Marketing Management*, June 2000, p. 34; B. Sloboda, 'Netiquette: New Rules and Policies for the Information Age', *Management Quarterly*, Winter 1999, pp. 9–32; M. M. Extejt, 'Teaching Students to Correspond Effectively Electronically: Tips for Using Electronic Mail Properly', *Business Communication Quarterly*, June 1998, pp. 57–67; K. Wasch, 'Netiquette: Do's and Don'ts of E-mail Use', *Association Management*, May 1997, pp. 76–7; and V. Shea, *Netiquette* (San Francisco, CA: Albion Press, 1994).

85 'Nearly One Third of Organisations Sack Their Staff for Email Abuse', *HR Software Show*, June 2003, p. 25.

86 I. Macduff, 'Flames on the Wires: Mediating from an Electronic Cottage', *Negotiation Journal*, January 1994, pp. 5–15.

87 The types of information technology used by virtual teams is discussed by A. M. Townsend, S. M. DeMarie and A. R. Hendrickson, 'Virtual Teams: Technology and the Workplace of the Future', *Academy of Management Executive*, August 1998, pp. 17–29.

88 Challenges associated with virtual operations are discussed by S. O'Mahony and S. R. Barley, 'Do Digital Telecommunications Affect Work and Organization? The State of Our Knowledge', in *Research in Organizational Behavior, vol. 21*, eds R. I. Sutton and B. M. Staw (Stanford, CT: JAI Press, 1999), pp. 125–61; and C. Grove and W. Hallowell, 'Spinning Your Wheels? Successful Global Teams Know How to Gain Traction', *HR Magazine*, April 1998, pp. 25–8.

89 M. Demsey, 'Scottish Pace-Setter – For a Decade, the Royal Bank has Pioneered in Video', the *Financial Times*, 1 November 1995; and 'Videoconferencing Increased 185%', *Face to Face Newsletter*, /www.imcca.org/newsfacetoface_05.pdf/, 2002.

90 Excerpted from K. Kiser, 'Working on World Time', *Training*, March 1999, p. 29. More information on teleworking can be found in D. E. Bailey and N. B. Kurland, 'A Review of Telework Research: Findings, New Directions, and Lessons for the Study of Modern Work', *Journal of Organizational Behavior*, June 2002, pp. 383–400.

91 P. Peters and L. den Dulk, 'Cross-Cultural Differences in Managers' Support for Home-Based Telework: A Theoretical Elaboration', *International Journal of Cross Cultural Management*, December 2003, pp. 329–46.

92 D. Panucci, 'Remote Control', *Management Today*, April 1995, pp. 78–80.

93 D. E. Bailey and N. B. Kurland, 'A Review of Telework Research: Findings, New Directions, and Lessons for the Study of Modern Work', *Journal of Organizational Behavior*, June 2002, pp. 383–400.

94 See V. Y. Haines III, S. St Onge and M. Archambault, 'Environmental and Person Antecedents of Telecommuting Outcomes', *Journal of End User Computing*, July–September 2002, pp. 32–50.

95 See D. B. Ilozor, B. D. Ilozor and J. Carr, 'Management Communication Strategies Determine Job Satisfaction in Telecommuting', *Journal of Management Development*, May 2001, pp. 495–507.

96 Supporting evidence is presented in S. Fister, 'A Lure for Labor', *Training*, February 1999, pp. 56–62; M. Apgar, IV, 'The Alternative Workplace: Changing Where and How People Work', *Harvard Business Review*, May–June 1998, pp. 121–36; and C. Hymowitz, 'Remote Managers Find Ways to Narrow the Distance Gap', the *Wall Street Journal*, 6 April 1999, p. B1.

97 R. L. Daft and R. H. Lengel, 'Information Richness: A New Approach to Managerial Behavior and Organizational Design', in *Research in Organizational Behavior*, eds B. M. Staw and L. L. Cummings (Greenwich, CT: JAI Press, 1984), p. 196.

98 S. M. Klein, 'Communication Strategies for Successful Organizational Change', *Change Management*, January–February 1994, p. 27.

99 H. A. Simon, 'Bounded Rationality and Organizational Learning', *Organization Science*, February 1991, pp. 125–34.

100 M. M. Weil and L. D. Rosen, *TechnoStress: Coping with Technology @WORK @HOME @PLAY* (New York: John Wiley & Sons, 1998).

101 H. Freeman, 'Caught Up in the Communication Loop', the *Guardian*, 30 September 2000.

102 D. Shenk, *Data Smog: Surviving the Information Glut* (New York: HarperCollins, 1997).

103 M. J. Tippins and R. S. Sohi, 'IT Competency and Firm Performance: Is Organizational Learning a Missing Link?', *Strategic Management Journal*, August 2003, pp. 745–61.

104 Reuters, *Dying for Information? An Investigation into the Effects of Information Overload in the UK and Worldwide* (London: Reuters, 1996).

105 M. J. Eppler and J. Mengis, 'A Framework for Information Overload: Research in Organizations', September 2003, /http://www.knowledge-communication.org/wp10.pdf/.

106 D. Lewis, *Information Overload: Practical Strategies for Surviving in Today's Workplace* (London: Penguin Books, 1999).

107 For tips on dealing with information overload, see D. Lewis, *Information Overload: Practical Strategies for Surviving in Today's Workplace* (London: Penguin Books, 1999); D. Shenk, *Data Smog: Surviving the Information Glut* (New York: HarperCollins, 1997); C. W. Simpson and L. Prusak, 'Troubles with Information Overload: Moving from Quantity to Quality in Information Provision', *Journal of Information Management*, December 1995, pp. 413–25; and K. Alesandrini, *Survive Information Overload* (Homewood, IL: Business One-Irwin, 1993).

108 D. Bawden, C. Holtman and N. Courtney, 'Perspectives on Information Overload', *Aslib Proceedings*, September 1999, pp. 249–55.

chapter 9 group dynamics

By Karlien Vanderheyden, Eva Cools and Fannie Debussche

Learning outcomes

When you finish studying the material in this chapter, you should be able to:

- identify the four criteria of a group from a sociological perspective

- identify and briefly describe the five stages in Tuckman's theory of group development

- distinguish between role overload, role conflict and role ambiguity

- contrast roles and norms, and specify four reasons norms are enforced in organisations

- distinguish between task and maintenance functions in groups

- summarise the practical implications for group size and group member ability

- discuss why organisations need to handle mixed-gender task groups carefully

- describe groupthink, and identify at least four of its symptoms

- define social loafing, and explain how organisations can prevent it

A retrospective of the Challenger Space Shuttle disaster: was it groupthink?

The debate over whether to launch on 28 January 1986, unfolded as follows, according to the report of the Presidential Commission on the Space Shuttle Challenger Accident. Shortly after 1 p.m. ET on 27 January, NASA's [the National Aeronautic and Space Administration's] booster rocket manager in Cape Canaveral, Larry Wear, asks officials of rocket-maker Morton Thiokol in Utah whether cold weather on the 28th would present a problem for launch.

By 2 p.m., NASA's top managers are discussing how temperatures in the 30s at the launch pad might affect the shuttle's performance. In Utah, an hour later, Thiokol engineer Roger Boisjoly learns of the forecast for the first time.

By late afternoon, mid-level NASA managers at the Cape are on the phone with Thiokol managers, who point out that the booster's rubbery O-rings, which seal in hot gases, might be affected by cold. That concern brings in officials from NASA's Marshall Space Flight Center in Huntsville, Alabama, which buys the rockets from Thiokol and readies them for launch. Marshall managers decide that a three-way telephone conference call is needed, linking NASA and Thiokol engineers and managers in Alabama, Florida and Utah.

The first conference call begins about 5.45 p.m., and Thiokol tells NASA it believes launch should be delayed until noon or afternoon, when the weather turns warmer. It is decided a second conference call would be needed later that evening. Marshall deputy project manager Judson Lovingood tells shuttle projects manager Stan Reinartz at the Cape that if Thiokol persists, NASA should not launch. Top NASA managers at Marshall are told of Thiokol's concern.

At 8.45 p.m., the second conference call begins, involving 34 engineers and managers from NASA and Thiokol at the three sites. Thiokol engineers Boisjoly and Arnie Thompson present charts

case study

327

showing a history of leaking O-ring joints from tests and previous flights. The data show that the O-rings perform worse at lower temperatures and that the worst leak of hot gases came in January 1985, when a shuttle launched with the temperature at 11.5 °C. Thiokol managers recommend not flying Challenger at temperatures colder than that. NASA's George Hardy says he's 'appalled' at Thiokol's recommendation. Larry Mulloy, Marshall's booster rocket manager, complains that Thiokol is setting down new launch criteria and exclaims, 'My God, Thiokol, when do you want me to launch, next April?'. Thiokol Vice President Joe Kilminster asks for five minutes to talk in private. The debate continues for 30 minutes. Boisjoly, Thompson, engineer Bob Ebeling and others are overruled by Thiokol management, who decide to approve the launch.

At 11 p.m., Kilminster tells NASA that Thiokol has changed its mind. Temperature is still a concern but the data are inconclusive. He recommends launch. Thiokol's concerns that cold weather could hurt the booster joints are not passed up NASA's chain of command beyond officials at the Marshall Space Flight Center. Challenger is launched at 11.38 a.m. 28 January in a temperature of 2.2 °C.

Shortly after the launch, the Challenger was engulfed in a fiery explosion that led to the deaths of six astronauts and teacher-in-space Christa McAuliffe. As a shocked world watched great billows of smoke trail over the Atlantic, it was clear to those involved that launching Challenger in 2.2 °C weather was a catastrophic decision.

... Ten years later

Two who argued the longest and loudest against launch were Thiokol engineers Roger Boisjoly and Arnie Thompson. But their lives took widely differing paths after the accident. Boisjoly remembers the prelaunch debate this way: 'When NASA created the pressure, they all buckled.' He became known nationally as the primary whistle-blower. Thiokol removed Boisjoly from the investigation team and sent him home after he testified before a presidential commission that the company ignored evidence that the booster rocket seals would fail in cold weather. Boisjoly, 57, says he was blackballed by the industry and run out of town by Thiokol. For a time, he sought psychiatric help. 'It just became unbearable to function', says Boisjoly, who now lives with his wife and daughter in a small mountain town in Utah. He spoke on condition that the town not be named because he fears for his family's safety. Boisjoly is convinced he is a marked man because some former co-workers believe his testimony contributed to resulting layoffs at Thiokol. After the accident, he says, drivers would try to run him off the road when he was out on a walk. He got threatening phone calls. Someone tried to break into his house. 'It became so uncomfortable for me that I went out and bought a .38 revolver', he says. Now retired, Boisjoly earns $1500 for speeches to universities and business groups. He also runs his own engineering company and teaches Sunday school in the Mormon church, something he says he never would have dreamed of doing before the accident.

Says Thompson, the other voice against launch: 'There were the two of us that didn't want to fly and we were defeated. A lot of my top managers were not happy with me.' Yet, with longer ties to Thiokol than Boisjoly, Thompson was promoted to manager and stayed on through the shuttle's redesign. He retired three years ago at the end of a 25-year career. Now 66, he spends his time building a small office building in Brigham City, Utah. 'My attitude was, I wanted to stay on and redesign the bird and get back into the air', says Thompson. 'I had a personal goal to get flying again.'

Thiokol's Bob Ebeling was so sure that Challenger was doomed, he asked his daughter, Leslie, then 33, to his office to watch 'a super colossal disaster' unfold on live TV. When it exploded, 'I was in the middle of a prayer for the Lord to do his will and let all these things come to a happy ending and not let this happen', says Ebeling, who managed the rocket ignition system for Thiokol. 'We did our level best but it wasn't good enough.' The fact that he foresaw disaster and could not stop it has tortured him since.

Ebeling, 69, says that within a week of the accident he became impotent and suffered high stress and constant headaches, problems he still has today. After 40 years of engineering experience, Thiokol 'put me out to pasture on a medical' retirement, he says. Ebeling still feels 'the decision to recommend a launch was pre-ordained by others, by NASA leaning on our upper management. The deck was stacked.'

One of those who overruled Ebeling and the others was Jerry Mason, the senior Thiokol manager on the conference call. He took an early retirement from Thiokol five months after the disaster, ending a 25-year career in aerospace. 'I was basically responsible for the operation the day it happened', says Mason, 69. 'It was important to the company to put that behind them and get going on the recovery and it would be hard to do that with me sitting there. So I left.' In Mason's case, that meant going abruptly from corporate chieftain to unpaid volunteer. He helped set up a local economic development board and now chairs the Utah Wildlife Federation. 'I had a pretty successful career, and would liked to have gone out with the feeling that I really had done very well all the time instead of having to go out feeling I'd made a mistake at the end.'

For Judson Lovingood, the loss was more personal. Formerly one of NASA's deputy managers for the shuttle project, he wonders still if Challenger contributed to the breakup of his marriage. 'I think (Challenger) had an effect on my personal life', says Lovingood, 'a long-term effect'. After the accident, he went to work for Thiokol in Huntsville and retired as director of engineering in 1993. Now remarried, he spends his time puttering in the yard of his Gurley, Alabama, home. 'Sometimes when I think about the seven people (aboard the shuttle), it's pretty painful', says Lovingood.

Besides McAuliffe, on board Challenger were commander Dick Scobee, pilot Mike Smith and astronauts Ron McNair, Ellison Onizuka, Judy Resnik and Greg Jarvis. Their families settled with the government and Thiokol for more than $1.5 billion. Still, 'I think people should hold us collectively responsible as a group', Lovingood says. 'Every person in that meeting the night before the launch shared in the blame.'

Investigations of the Challenger explosion placed much of the blame on NASA's George Hardy, a senior engineering manager. By saying he was 'appalled' by Thiokol's fears of flying in cold weather, critics charged, Hardy pressured Thiokol into approving the launch. But Hardy refuses to shoulder the blame. 'If Thiokol had stuck to their position, there wasn't any way we were going to launch', he says. Hardy left NASA four months after the accident. Now 65, he runs a small aerospace consulting company in Athens, Alabama.

Whatever else the last decade brought, many of the recollections return to that pressure-packed conference call on the eve of launch.[1]

For discussion
All things considered, who in this group was to blame for finally launching the Challenger?

Because the management of organisational behaviour is above all else a social endeavour, professionals need a strong working knowledge of interpersonal behaviour. Research consistently reveals the importance of social skills for both individual and organisational success (see the next snapshot). Management involves getting things done with and through others. The job is simply too big to do it alone.

Let us begin by defining the term 'group' as a prelude to examining types of groups, functions of group members, and the group development and formation process. Our attention then turns to group roles and norms, the basic building blocks of group dynamics. Impacts of group structure and member characteristics on group outcomes are explored next. Finally, three serious threats to group effectiveness are discussed. (Teams and teamwork are discussed in Chapter 10.)

Groups: definitions, types and functions
Groups and teams are inescapable features of modern life. College students are often teamed with their peers for class projects. Parents serve on community advisory boards at their local high school. Professionals find themselves on product planning committees and productivity task forces. Productive organisations simply cannot function without gathering individuals into groups and teams.[2] But, as personal experience shows, group effort can bring out both the best and the worst in people. A marketing department meeting, where several people excitedly brainstorm and refine a creative

snapshot

Social skills lead to success

An ongoing study by the Center for Creative Leadership (involving diverse samples from Belgium, France, Germany, Italy, the United Kingdom, the United States and Spain) found four stumbling blocks that tend to derail executives' careers. According to the researchers: 'A derailed executive is one who, having reached the general manager level, finds that there is little chance of future advancement due to a misfit between job requirements and personal skills.' The four stumbling blocks, consistent across the cultures studied, are as follows:

1 Problems with interpersonal relationships
2 Failure to meet business objectives
3 Failure to build and lead a team
4 Inability to change or adapt during a transition

Notice how both the first and third career stumbling blocks involve interpersonal skills – the ability to get along and work effectively with others. Professionals with interpersonal problems were typically described as manipulative and insensitive. Interestingly, two-thirds of the derailed European professionals studied had problems with interpersonal relationships. That same problem reportedly plagued one-third of the derailed US executives.

SOURCE: Based on studies in 'Gets Along Well with Others', *Training*, August 1996, pp. 17–18;
and E. Van Velsor and J. Brittain Leslie, 'Why Executives Derail: Perspectives across Time and Cultures',
Academy of Management Executive, November 1995, pp. 62–72.

new advertising campaign, can yield results beyond the capabilities of individual contributors. Conversely, committees have become the butt of jokes (e.g. a committee is a place where they take minutes and waste hours; a camel is a horse designed by a committee) because they all are too often plagued by lack of direction and by conflict. Organisations nowadays need a solid understanding of groups and group processes to both avoid their pitfalls and tap their vast potential.

Definitions

Group
two or more freely interacting people with shared norms and goals and a common identity

Although other definitions of groups exist, we draw from the field of sociology and define a **Group** as two or more freely interacting individuals who share collective norms and goals and have a common identity.[3] Figure 9.1 illustrates how the four criteria in this definition combine to form a conceptual whole. Organisational psychologist Edgar Schein shed additional light on this concept by drawing instructive distinctions between a group, a crowd and an organisation:

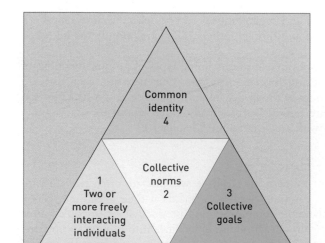

FIGURE 9.1 FOUR SOCIOLOGICAL CRITERIA OF A GROUP

> The size of a group is thus limited by the possibilities of mutual interaction and mutual awareness. Mere aggregates of people do not fit this definition because they do not interact and do not perceive themselves to be a group even if they are aware of each other as, for instance, a crowd on a street corner watching some event. A total department, a union or a whole organisation would not be a group in spite of thinking of themselves as 'we', because they generally do not all interact and are not all aware of each other. However, work teams, committees, subparts of departments, cliques and various other informal associations among organisational members would fit this definition of a group.[4]

Take a moment now to think of various groups of which you are a member. Does each of your 'groups' satisfy the four criteria in Figure 9.1?

The Hawthorne studies of Elton Mayo (elaborated in Chapter 1) were one of the first studies that discovered the importance of group dynamics in organisations. Another psychologist who worked further on the idea that groups are important in organisations is Rensis Likert.[5] According to Likert, organisations should be viewed as a collection of groups rather than individuals. Work groups are important in satisfying individuals' needs. Groups in organisations that fulfil this psychological function are more productive. In addition to Likert, several authors promote the use of small groups as basic building blocks for an organisation.[6]

Formal and informal groups

Individuals join groups, or are assigned to groups, to accomplish various purposes.

If the group is formed by a professional to help the organisation accomplish its goals (also see Chapter 14), then it qualifies as a **Formal group**. Formal groups typically wear such labels as work group, team, committee, quality circle or task force. According to the demand and processes of the organisation, different types of formal groups can be distinguished (for instance, the accounting department). A command (or functional) group is fairly permanent and is usually specified by the organisation chart. A command group is characterised by functional reporting between subordinates and their group manager. A task (or special-project) group contains employees who work together to complete a particular task. A task group is usually temporary and the group often dissolves when its task is finished. Employees mostly belong simultaneously to a command group and to one or several task groups.

An **Informal group** exists when the members' overriding purpose of getting together is friendship or common interests.[7] Informal groups are not deliberately created, but evolve naturally. Within the formal structure of organisations, there will always be an informal structure (see Figure 9.2), often referred to as the distinction between the formal and the informal organisation (also see Chapter 8 about the grapevine and Chapter 14 about co-ordination mechanisms in organisations). Two specific types of informal groups are friendship groups and interest groups. Friendship groups arise mostly

Formal group
group formed by the organisation

Informal group
group formed by friends

FIGURE 9.2 INFORMAL GROUPS EXIST WITHIN THE FORMAL STRUCTURE OF ORGANISATIONS

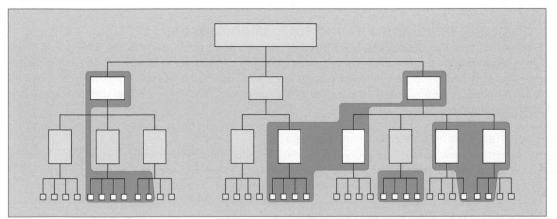

from some common characteristics of people, like their age, political beliefs or ethnic background, that lead to relationships between people that often extend to off-the-job activities. Interest groups are organised around a common interest or activity, independent of the task or command groups they belong to. People group together to accomplish some common objective, although friendship may also develop between the members.

Although formal and informal groups often overlap, such as a team of corporate auditors heading for the tennis courts after work, some employees are not friends with their co-workers. The desirability of overlapping formal and informal groups is problematic. Some managers firmly believe personal friendship fosters productive teamwork on the job while others view workplace 'gossip' as a serious threat to productivity. Both situations are common, and it is the manager's job to strike a workable balance, based on the maturity and goals of the people involved.

Functions of groups

Researchers point out that formal groups fulfil two basic functions: organisational and individual.[8] The various functions are listed in Table 9.1. Complex combinations of these functions can be found in formal groups at any given time.

TABLE 9.1 FORMAL GROUPS FULFIL ORGANISATIONAL AND INDIVIDUAL FUNCTIONS

Organisational functions	Individual functions
1 Accomplish complex, interdependent tasks that are beyond the capabilities of individuals 2 Generate new or creative ideas and solutions 3 Co-ordinate interdepartmental efforts 4 Provide a problem-solving mechanism for complex problems requiring varied information and assessments 5 Implement complex decisions 6 Socialise and train newcomers	1 Satisfy the individual's need for affiliation 2 Develop, enhance and confirm the individual's self-esteem and sense of identity 3 Give individuals an opportunity to test and share their perceptions of social reality 4 Reduce the individual's anxieties and feelings of insecurity and powerlessness 5 Provide a problem-solving mechanism for personal and interpersonal problems

SOURCE: Adapted from E. H. Schein, *Organizational Psychology, third edition* (Englewood Cliffs, NJ: Prentice Hall, 1980), pp. 149–51.

Although informal groups may to an extent serve the same functions, people also have some other reasons to be part of informal groups in their work context. As explained in Chapter 5, people want to fulfil different kind of needs. The need for social interaction (relatedness need) seems to be an important reason for people to also join informal groups. Another important theory is the social identity theory that states that we define ourselves by our social affiliations, making a distinction between the in-group and the out-group. We are motivated to belong to groups that are similar to ourselves, as this affiliation reinforces our social identity.[9]

The group development and formation process

Groups and teams in the workplace go through a maturation process, such as one would find in any life-cycle situation (e.g. humans, organisations, products). While there is general agreement among theorists that the group development process occurs in identifiable stages, they disagree about the exact number, sequence, length and nature of those stages.[10] We elaborate two different models of group development and formation.

Tuckman's group development process

An oft-cited model is the one proposed in 1965 by educational psychologist Bruce W. Tuckman. His original model involved only four stages (forming, storming, norming and performing). The five-stage model in Figure 9.3 evolved when Tuckman and a doctoral student added 'adjourning' in 1977.[11] A word of caution is in order. Somewhat akin to Maslow's need hierarchy theory (see Chapter 5), Tuckman's theory has been repeated and taught so often and for so long that many have

FIGURE 9.3 TUCKMAN'S FIVE-STAGE THEORY OF GROUP DEVELOPMENT

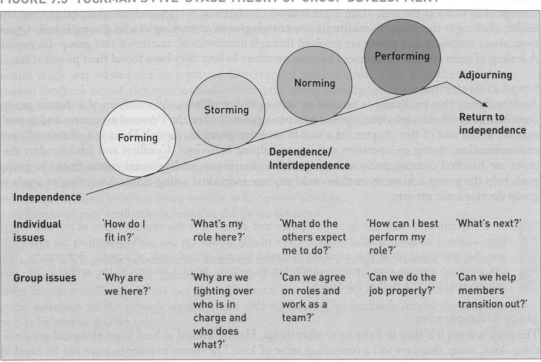

come to view it as documented fact, not merely a theory. Even today, it is good to remember Tuckman's own caution that his group development model was derived more from group therapy sessions than from natural-life groups. Still, many in the OB field like Tuckman's five-stage model of group development because of its easy-to-remember labels and commonsense appeal.[12]

FIVE STAGES

Let us briefly examine each of the five stages in Tuckman's model. Notice in Figure 9.3 how individuals give up a measure of their independence when they join and participate in a group. Also, the various stages are not necessarily of the same duration or intensity. For instance, the storming stage may be practically non-existent or painfully long, depending on the goal clarity and the commitment and maturity of the members. You can make this process come to life by relating the various stages to your own experiences with work groups, committees, athletic teams, social or religious groups or class project teams. Some group happenings that surprised you when they occurred may now make sense or strike you as inevitable when seen as part of a natural development process.

Stage 1: Forming

During this 'ice-breaking' stage, group members tend to be uncertain and anxious about such things as their roles, who is in charge and the group's goals. Mutual trust is low, and there is a good deal of holding back to see who takes charge and how. If the formal leader (e.g. a supervisor) does not assert his or her authority, an emergent leader will eventually step in to fulfil the group's need for leadership and direction. Leaders typically mistake this honeymoon period as a mandate for permanent control. But later problems may force a leadership change.

Stage 2: Storming

This is a time of testing. Individuals test the leader's policies and assumptions as they try to determine how they fit into the power structure.[13] Subgroups take shape, and subtle forms of rebellion, such as procrastination, occur. Many groups stall in stage 2 because power politics (also see Chapter 13) erupts into open rebellion.[14]

THREE LEVELS OF GROUP FORMATION

Homans' model (see Figure 9.4) consists of three different levels/systems each influencing the characteristics of a group.

FIGURE 9.4 HOMANS' MODEL OF GROUP FORMATION

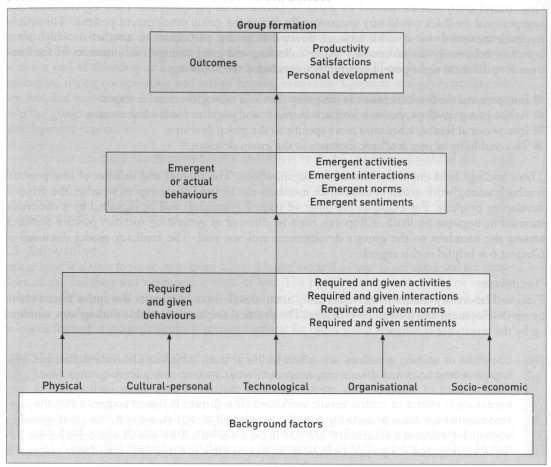

SOURCE: G. C. Homans, *The Human Group* (London: Routledge and Kegan Paul, 1951).

The background factors are the external system, providing the context in which the group activity takes place. The five background factors identified by Homans are:

1 Physical context: this refers to the organisation of physical objects and human activities (e.g. furniture, office arrangement, division of work at the assembly line).
2 Cultural-personal: this factor refers to the individuals themselves and to the norms, values and goals they share.
3 Technological context: this refers to the facilities the group will have access to.
4 Organisational context: consists of the policies, practices and rules in the company (e.g. performance appraisal system, bonus system).
5 Socio-economic context: the economic situation which may influence the functioning of the company (legislation, unemployment, etc.).

Required and given behaviours are the behaviours organisations expect of their employees. Employees have to perform certain activities, they need to have certain interactions with others, they have to respect certain norms/rules and they have to feel certain sentiments towards their work (see also emotional labour in Chapter 3). For example, waiters in restaurants have to perform certain activities like serving food and drinks to the people. They have to interact with colleagues and customers (e.g. greeting the customers). They have to respect rules like the time they have to start working. And, at last, they have to feel positive towards the employer and the customers.

Emergent or actual behaviours are the behaviours employees show in addition to, or in place of, the behaviours required by the organisation. They concern the activities, the interactions, the norms/rules and the sentiments. For example, employees develop informal relationships with colleagues they do not have to work with.

The different systems (background factors, required behaviours, emergent behaviours) influence each other. A change in one system stimulates a change in another system. For instance, when the company moves to another location (physical context), certain rules can be changed (e.g. formal communication channels). This may also influence the informal relationships between employees (emergent behaviours).

APPLICATION OF THE THEORY

Let us consider a company which stimulates creativity and innovation. Several background factors will influence the performance of the teams.

The basic values, assumptions and beliefs are enacted in established forms of behaviours and activity and are reflected as structures, policy, practices, management practices and procedures. These structures and practices have a direct impact on the creativity and innovation in the workplace: for example, the resources available to develop new ideas.[26]

The behaviour rewarded reflects an organisation's values. If creative/innovative behaviour is rewarded, employees will recognise that this should be the dominant way of behaving.[27] Many organisations want their employees to be more creative and to take risks, but they reward their employees for well-proven, trusted methods and fault-free work. In order to stimulate innovation, people should be rewarded for experimenting and developing new ideas. Also more freedom to do their work, more autonomy and better opportunities for personal/professional growth will stimulate a creative atmosphere.[28] As teams are an important part of the innovation process, it is important to reward both teams and individuals. Employees will not be motivated to put some effort in teamwork if they are only rewarded on an individual basis. There should also be a tolerance of mistakes in order to stimulate creativity and innovation. Mistakes can be ignored, covered up, used to punish someone or perceived as a learning opportunity.[29] Employees should be able to learn from their mistakes and to discuss them with colleagues openly.

The technological context is also important because it can support the innovation process. If employees have easy access to Internet and Intranet and if they are used to communicating and exchanging ideas through these media, the creativity and innovation processes can be improved.[30]

With regard to the required and emergent behaviour, work-team members should allow for diversity and individual talents to complement one another. In order to stimulate creativity, team members should be able to trust and respect each other, and to understand each other's perspectives and ways of functioning, decision making and solving problems. They also have to communicate well, to be critically constructive and to be open to new ideas.[31]

Roles and norms: building blocks for group and organisational behaviour

Work groups transform individuals into functioning organisational members through subtle yet powerful social forces. These social forces, in effect, turn 'I' into 'we' and 'me' into 'us'. Group influence weaves individuals into the organisation's social fabric by communicating and enforcing both role expectations and norms. We need to understand roles and norms if we are to effectively manage group and organisational behaviour.

Roles

Four centuries have passed since William Shakespeare had his character Jaques speak the following memorable lines in Act II of *As You Like It*: 'All the world's a stage, And all the men and women merely players: They have their exits and their entrances; And one man in his time plays many parts ....' This intriguing notion of all people as actors in a universal play was not lost on twentieth-century sociologists who developed a complex theory of human interaction based on roles. According to an OB scholar, **Roles** are sets of behaviour that people expect of occupants of a position.[32] Role theory attempts to explain how these social expectations influence employee behaviour. This section explores role theory by analysing a role episode and defining the terms 'role overload', 'role conflict', 'role ambiguity' and 'task versus maintenance' roles.

Roles
expected
behaviours for a
given position

ROLE EPISODES

A role episode, as illustrated in Figure 9.5, consists of a snapshot of the ongoing interaction between two people. In any given role episode, there is a role sender and a focal person who is expected to act out the role. Within a broader context, one may be simultaneously a role sender and a focal person. For the sake of social analysis, however, it is instructive to deal with separate role episodes.

FIGURE 9.5 A ROLE EPISODE

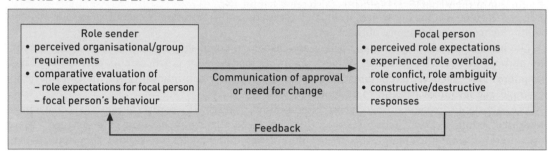

SOURCE: Adapted in part from R. L. Kohn, D. M. Wolfe, R. P. Quinn, and J. D. Snoek, *Organizational Stress: Studies in Role Conflict and Ambiguity*, 1981 edition (Malabar, FL: Robert E. Krieger Publishing, 1964), p. 26.

Role episodes begin with the role sender's perception of the relevant organisation's or group's behavioural requirements. Those requirements serve as a standard for formulating expectations for the focal person's behaviour. The role sender then cognitively evaluates the focal person's actual behaviour against those expectations. Appropriate verbal and non-verbal messages are then sent to the focal person to pressure him or her into behaving as expected.[33] Consider how Westinghouse used a carrot-and-stick approach to communicate role expectations:

> The carrot is a plan, that . . . rewarded 134 managers with options to buy 764 000 shares of stock for boosting the company's financial performance. The stick is quarterly meetings that are used to rank managers by how much their operations contribute to earnings per share. The soft-spoken . . . [chairman of the board] doesn't scold. He just charts in green the results of the sectors that have met their goals and charts the laggards in red. Peer pressure does the rest. Shame 'is a powerful tool', says one executive.[34]

On the receiving end of the role episode, the focal person accurately or inaccurately perceives the communicated role expectations. Various combinations of role overload, role conflict and role ambiguity are then experienced. (These three outcomes are defined and discussed in the following sections.) The focal person then responds constructively by engaging, for example, in problem solving or destructively because of undue tension, stress and strain.[35]

ROLE OVERLOAD

Role overload
others'
expectations
exceed one's
ability

According to organisational psychologist Edgar Schein, **Role overload** occurs when 'the sum total of what role senders expect of the focal person far exceeds what he or she is able to do'.[36] Students who attempt to handle a full course load and maintain a decent social life while working 30 or more hours a week to support themselves know full well the consequences of role overload. As the individual tries to do more and more in less and less time, stress mounts and personal effectiveness slips (also see Chapter 7 on stress).

ROLE CONFLICT

Have you ever felt like you were being torn apart by the conflicting demands of those around you? If so, you were a victim of role conflict. **Role conflict** is experienced when 'different members of the role set expect different things of the focal person'.[37] Employees often face conflicting demands between work and family, for example.[38] Interestingly, however, women experience greater role conflict between work and family than men, because women perform the majority of the household duties and child-care responsibilities.[39]

Role conflict also may be experienced when internalised values, ethics or personal standards collide with others' expectations. For instance, an otherwise ethical production supervisor may be told by a superior to 'fudge a little' on the quality control reports so an important deadline will be met. The resulting role conflict forces the supervisor to choose between being loyal but unethical or ethical but disloyal. Tough ethical choices such as this mean personal turmoil, interpersonal conflict and even resignation. Consequently, experts say business schools should do a better job of weaving ethics training into their course requirements (also see Chapter 18).

Role conflict
others have conflicting or inconsistent expectations

ROLE AMBIGUITY

Those who experience role conflict may have trouble complying with role demands, but they at least know what is expected of them. Such is not the case with **Role ambiguity**, which occurs when 'members of the role set fail to communicate to the focal person expectations they have or information needed to perform the role, either because they do not have the information or because they deliberately withhold it'.[40] In short, people experience role ambiguity when they do not know what is expected of them. Organisational newcomers often complain about unclear job descriptions and vague promotion criteria. According to role theory, prolonged role ambiguity can foster job dissatisfaction, erode self-confidence and hamper job performance. As might be expected, role ambiguity varies across cultures (see the next Snapshot).

Role ambiguity
others' expectations are unknown

Cultural differences in role ambiguity

In a recent 21-nation study, people in individualistic cultures were found to have higher role ambiguity than people in collectivist cultures. In other words, people in collectivist or 'we' cultures had a clearer idea of others' expectations. Collectivist cultures make sure everyone knows their proper place in society. People in individualistic 'me' cultures, such as Western Europe and the United States, may enjoy more individual discretion, but comparatively less input from others has its price – namely, greater role ambiguity.

SOURCE: Drawn from M. Peterson *et al.*, 'Role Conflict, Ambiguity, and Overload: A 21-Nation Study', *Academy of Management Journal*, April 1995, pp. 429–52.

snapshot

Take a moment now to complete the self-assessment exercise in the Activity. See if you can distinguish between sources of role conflict and sources of role ambiguity, as they affect your working life.

TASK VERSUS MAINTENANCE ROLES

Task roles enable the work group to define, clarify and pursue a common purpose. Meanwhile, **Maintenance roles** foster supportive and constructive interpersonal relationships. In short, task roles keep the group on track while maintenance roles keep the group together. A fraternity or sorority member is performing a task function when he or she stands at a business meeting and says, 'What is the real issue here? We don't seem to be getting anywhere.' Another individual who says, 'Let's hear from those who oppose this plan', is performing a maintenance function. Importantly, each of the various task and maintenance roles may be played in varying combinations and sequences by either the group's leader or any of its members.

As described in Table 9.2, both task and maintenance roles need to be performed if a work group is to accomplish anything.[41]

Task roles
task-oriented group behaviour

Maintenance roles
relationship-building group behaviour

Measuring role conflict and role ambiguity

Instructions

While thinking of your current (or last) job, circle one response for each of the following statements. Please consider each statement carefully because some are worded positively and some negatively.

		Very false					Very true		
1	I feel certain about how much authority I have.	7	6	5	4	3	2	1	____
2	I have to do things that should be done differently.	1	2	3	4	5	6	7	____
3	I know that I have divided my time properly.	7	6	5	4	3	2	1	____
4	I know what my responsibilities are.	7	6	5	4	3	2	1	____
5	I have to buck a rule or policy in order to carry out an assignment.	1	2	3	4	5	6	7	____
6	I feel certain how I will be evaluated for a raise or promotion.	7	6	5	4	3	2	1	____
7	I work with two or more groups who operate quite differently.	1	2	3	4	5	6	7	____
8	I know exactly what is expected of me.	7	6	5	4	3	2	1	____
9	I do things that are apt to be accepted by one person and not accepted by others.	1	2	3	4	5	6	7	____
10	I work on unnecessary things.	1	2	3	4	5	6	7	____

Role conflict score =
Role ambiguity score =

Scoring key and norms

In the space in the far right column, label each statement with either a 'C' for role conflict or an 'A' for role ambiguity. (See note 42 for a correct categorisation.)[42]

Calculate separate totals for role conflict and role ambiguity and compare them with these arbitrary norms:

 5–14 = Low;
15–25 = Moderate;
26–35 = High.

SOURCE: Adapted from J. R. Rizzo, R. J. House and S. I. Lirtzman, 'Role Conflict and Ambiguity in Complex Organizations', *Administrative Science Quarterly*, June 1970, p. 156.

The task and maintenance roles listed in Table 9.2 can serve as a handy checklist for supervisors and group leaders who wish to ensure proper group development. Roles that are not always performed when needed, such as those of co-ordinator, evaluator and gatekeeper, can be performed in a timely manner by the formal leader or assigned to other members. The task roles of initiator, orienter and energiser are especially important because they are goal-directed roles. Recent research studies on group goal setting confirm the motivational power of challenging goals. As with individual goal setting (see Chapter 6), difficult but achievable goals are associated with better group results.[43] Also in line with individual goal-setting theory and research, group goals are more effective if group members clearly understand them and are both individually and collectively committed to achieving them. Initiators, orienters and energisers can be very helpful in this regard.

International managers need to be sensitive to cultural differences regarding the relative importance of task and maintenance roles:

> In Japan, for example, cultural tradition calls for more emphasis on maintenance roles, especially the roles of harmoniser and compromiser. Courtesy requires that members not be conspicuous or disputatious in a meeting or classroom. If two or more members discover that their views differ – a fact that is tactfully taken to be unfortunate – they adjourn to find more information and to work toward a stance that all can accept. They do not press their personal opinions through strong arguments, neat logic, or rewards and threats. And they do not hesitate to shift their beliefs if doing so will preserve smooth interpersonal relations (i.e. to lose is to win).[44]

TABLE 9.2 FUNCTIONAL ROLES PERFORMED BY GROUP MEMBERS

Task roles	Description
Initiator	Suggests new goals or ideas
Information seeker/giver	Clarifies key issues
Opinion seeker/giver	Clarifies pertinent values
Elaborator	Promotes greater understanding through examples or exploration of implications
Co-ordinator	Pulls together ideas and suggestions
Orienter	Keeps group headed toward its stated goal(s)
Evaluator	Tests group's accomplishments with various criteria such as logic and practicality
Energiser	Prods group to move along or to accomplish more
Procedural technician	Performs routine duties (e.g. handing out materials or rearranging seats)
Recorder	Performs a 'group memory' function by documenting discussion and outcomes

Maintenance roles	Description
Encourager	Fosters group solidarity by accepting and praising various points of view
Harmoniser	Mediates conflict through reconciliation or humour
Compromiser	Helps resolve conflict by meeting others 'half way'
Gatekeeper	Encourages all group members to participate
Standard setter	Evaluates the quality of group processes
Commentator	Records and comments on group processes/dynamics
Follower	Serves as a passive audience

SOURCE: Adapted from discussion in K. D. Benne and P. Sheats, 'Functional Roles of Group Members', *Journal of Social Issues*, Spring 1948, pp. 41–9.

Norms

Norms are more encompassing than roles. While roles involve behavioural expectations for specific positions, norms help organisational members determine right from wrong and good from bad. According to one respected team of management consultants: 'A norm is an attitude, opinion, feeling or action – shared by two or more people – that guides their behaviour.'[45] Although norms are typically unwritten and seldom discussed openly, they have a powerful influence on group and organisational behaviour.[46]

> PepsiCo Inc., for instance, has evolved a norm that equates corporate competitiveness with physical fitness. According to observers, leanness and nimbleness are qualities that pervade the company. When Pepsi's brash young managers take a few minutes away from the office, they often head straight for the company's physical fitness center or for a jog around the museum-quality sculptures outside of PepsiCo's Purchase, New York, headquarters.[47]

At PepsiCo and elsewhere, group members positively reinforce those who adhere to current norms with friendship and acceptance. On the other hand, non-conformists experience criticism and even Ostracism, or rejection by group members. Anyone who has experienced the 'silent treatment' from a group of friends knows what a potent social weapon ostracism can be. Norms can be put into proper perspective by understanding how they develop and why they are enforced.

THE DEVELOPMENT OF GROUP NORMS

Elton Mayo during the Hawthorne experiments in the 1930s already noted the existence of group norms[48] (see Chapter 1). The employees restricted their output to conform to a group-agreed norm or standard.

Norms
shared attitudes, opinions, feelings or actions that guide social behaviour

Ostracism
rejection by other group members

In another study, Muzafer Sherif described how group norms emerged.[49] In his experiment, the autokinetic effect was created in order to test the hypothesis. In complete darkness (e.g. a closed room that is not illuminated) a single small light seems to move, and it may appear to move erratically in all directions. If you present the point of light repeatedly to a person, he may see the light appearing at different places in the room each time, especially if he does not know the distance between himself and the light. Muzafer Sherif studied the influence of the group situation on the extent and direction of the experimental movement.

When an individual is put into this stimulus situation (which is unstable and unstructured), he establishes a range and norm (a reference point) within that range. The range and norm are typical for each individual. The ranges and norms vary according to the individuals, revealing individual differences.

Every individual develops a range and a norm in the individual situation. When the individuals are put together in a group situation, the ranges and norms tend to converge (see Figure 9.6). But the convergence is not so close as when they first work in the group situation, having less opportunity to set up stable individual norms. When individuals face the same unstable, unstructured situation as members of the group for the first time, they develop a range and a norm peculiar to the group. When a member of the group faces the same situation alone subsequently, he or she perceives the situation in terms of the range and norm developed within the group. Muzafer Sherif concluded that supra-individual qualities arise in group situations.

Generally speaking, experts say norms evolve in an informal manner as the group or organisation determines what it takes to be effective. Norms develop in various combinations of the following four ways:

■ Explicit statements by supervisors or co-workers: for instance, a group leader might explicitly set norms about not drinking (alcohol) at lunch.

FIGURE 9.6 SHERIF'S STUDY OF THE EMERGENCE OF GROUP NORMS

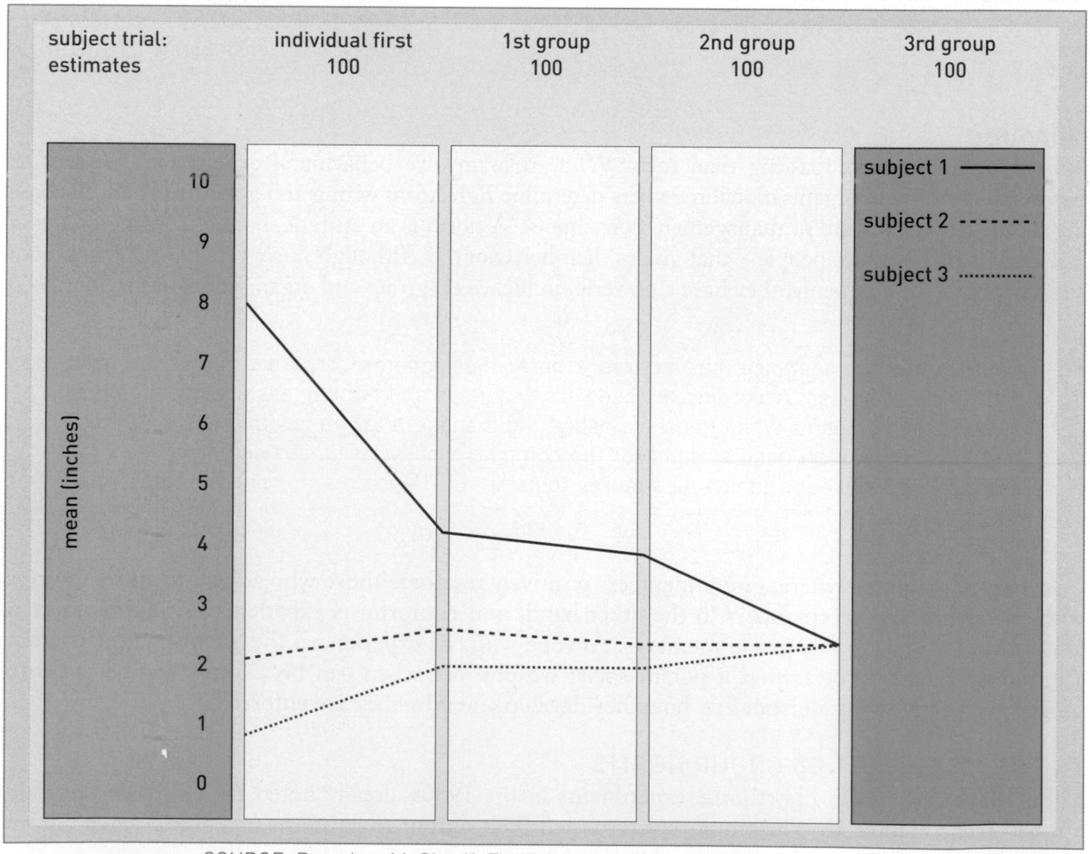

SOURCE: Based on M. Sherif, *The Psychology of Social Norms* (New York: Harper & Row, 1936).

- Critical events in the group's history: these events can establish an important precedent. For example, a key recruit may have decided to work elsewhere because a group member said too many negative things about the organisation. Hence, a norm against such 'sour grapes' behaviour might evolve.
- Primacy: the first behaviour pattern that emerges in a group often sets group expectations. If the first group meeting is marked by very formal interaction between supervisors and subordinates, then the group often expects future meetings to be conducted in the same way (see Chapter 4).
- Carryover behaviours from past situations: these behaviours from past situations can increase the predictability of group members' behaviours in new settings and facilitate task accomplishment. For instance, students and professors carry fairly constant sets of expectations from class to class.[50]

Norms can affect performance either positively or negatively.[51] We would like you to take a few moments and think about the norms that are currently in effect in your classroom. List the norms on a sheet of paper. Do these norms help or hinder your ability to learn?

WHY NORMS ARE ENFORCED
Norms tend to be enforced by group members when they:

- Help the group or organisation survive.
- Clarify or simplify behavioural expectations.
- Help individuals avoid embarrassing situations.
- Clarify the group's or organisation's central values and/or unique identity.[52]

Working examples of each of these four situations are presented in Table 9.3.

RESEARCH FINDINGS AND PRACTICAL IMPLICATIONS
Both roles and norms are studied extensively in laboratory experiments and field research. Although instruments used to measure role conflict and role ambiguity have questionable validity,[53] two

TABLE 9.3 FOUR REASONS NORMS ARE ENFORCED

Norm	Reason for enforcement	Example
Make our department look good in top management's eyes	Group/organisation survival	After vigorously defending the vital role played by the Human Resources Management Department at a divisional meeting, a staff specialist is complimented by her boss
Success comes to those who work hard and don't make waves	Clarification of behavioural expectations	A senior manager takes a young associate aside and cautions him to be a bit more patient with co-workers who see things differently
Be a team player, not a star	Avoidance of embarrassment	A project team member is ridiculed by her peers for dominating the discussion during a progress report to top management
Customer service is our top priority	Clarification of central values/unique identity	Two sales representatives are given a surprise Friday afternoon party for having received prestigious best-in-the-industry customer service awards from an industry association

separate meta-analyses indicated that role conflict and role ambiguity affected employees negatively. Specifically, role conflict and role ambiguity were associated with job dissatisfaction, tension and anxiety, lack of organisational commitment, intentions to quit and, to a lesser extent, poor job performance.[54]

The meta-analyses results hold few surprises for organisations. Generally, because of the negative association reported, it makes sense for organisations to reduce both role conflict and role ambiguity. In this endeavour, organisations can use several practices explained throughout the book, like feedback (see Chapter 6), formal rules and procedures (see Chapter 14), directive leadership (see Chapter 11), setting of specific (difficult) goals (see Chapter 6) and participation (see Chapter 12).

Regarding norms, a recent set of laboratory studies involving a total of 1504 college students as subjects has important implications for workplace diversity programmes (see Chapter 4). Subjects in groups where the norm was to express prejudices, condone discrimination and laugh at hostile jokes tended to engage in these undesirable behaviours. Conversely, subjects tended to disapprove of prejudicial and discriminatory conduct when exposed to groups with more socially acceptable norms.[55]

Group structure and composition

Work groups of varying size are made up of individuals with varying ability and motivation. Moreover, those individuals perform different roles, on either an assigned or voluntary basis. No wonder some work groups are more productive than others or that some committees are tightly knit while others wallow in conflict. In this section, we examine five important dimensions of group structure and composition: (1) liking structure, (2) group size, (3) gender composition, (4) individual ability and group effectiveness and (5) personality and roles. We conclude with some general findings with regard to the use of homogeneous versus heterogeneous groups.

Liking structure

Sociometry is a method used to indicate the feelings of acceptance or rejection of individuals in a group.[56] Individual members will like, dislike or be indifferent to each other, in varying degrees. Based on the individual preferences/rejections of individual team members, a map of the emotional relationships in a team is developed. Sociometric tests are used to map the feelings of individuals towards each other. Moreno asked team members to fill in a test like the one below (see Figure 9.7).

Based on such a sociometric assessment the feelings towards individuals can be divided into three classes: attraction (liking), rejection (disliking) and indifference (neutral feeling). Moreno calculated how many times individuals had been chosen (or not chosen at all) for a certain activity. These results were put into a sociogram, a chart which shows the liking/disliking/indifference relationships between members of a group (see Figure 9.8).

Looking at a sociogram, different types of individuals can be identified:

- Star: a person who got a large number of choices (sometimes 'over-chosen').
- Isolate: a person who makes no choices and is not chosen (there is an indifference between this person and the other individuals of the group).
- Neglectee: a person who is not chosen (although he/she makes choices).
- Rejectee: a person who is not chosen by anyone and is rejected by one or more people.
- Mutual pair or mutual trio: individuals who choose one another.

Today sociometry continues to be applied and is called 'social network analysis'. The social network approach views organisations in society as a system of objects (e.g. people, groups, organisations) joined by a variety of relationships. Not all pairs of objects are directly joined, and some are joined by multiple relationships. Social network analysis is concerned with the structure and patterning of these relationships and seeks to identify both their causes and consequences.[57]

Social network analysis is applicable to a wide range of areas.[58] For instance, at the organisational level, communication studies (see Chapter 8 about the grapevine)[59] and work on power and political processes[60] can benefit from social network analysis. Also, to study careers[61] and socialisation, a better insight into networks of information and influence can be very useful. At the interorganisational level, social network analysis can make the direct and indirect relationships between organisations more explicit.[62]

FIGURE 9.7 SOCIOMETRIC ASSESSMENT

Below are eight boxes

☐ In the column marked 'Work with – Yes', write the names of two people in your class whom you prefer to work with.

☐ In the column marked 'Work with – No', write the names of two people in your class whom you prefer not to work with.

Repeat this with the remaining boxes marked 'Study with', 'Visit' and 'Live with in proximity'

Work with	
Yes	No

Study with	
Yes	No

Visit	
Yes	No

Live with in proximity	
Yes	No

SOURCE: Based on J. L. Moreno, *Who Shall Survive?* second edition (New York: Beacon Press, 1953).

FIGURE 9.8 SOCIOGRAM

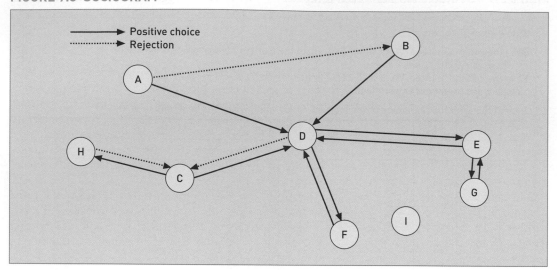

SOURCE: Based on J. L. Moreno, *Who Shall Survive?* second edition (New York: Beacon Press, 1953).

Group size

How many group members is too much? The answer to this deceptively simple question has intrigued professionals and academics for years. Folk wisdom says 'two heads are better than one' but that 'too many cooks spoil the broth'. So where should an organisation draw the line when staffing a committee? At 3? At 5 or 6? At 10 or more? Researchers have taken two different approaches to pinpointing optimum group size: mathematical modelling and laboratory simulations. Let us briefly review recent findings from these two approaches.

THE MATHEMATICAL MODELLING APPROACH

This approach involves building a mathematical model around certain desired outcomes of group action such as decision quality. Owing to differing assumptions and statistical techniques, the results of this research are inconclusive. Statistical estimates of optimum group size have ranged from 3 to 13.[63]

THE LABORATORY SIMULATION APPROACH

This stream of research is based on the assumption that group behaviour needs to be observed firsthand in controlled laboratory settings. A laboratory study by respected Australian researcher Philip Yetton and his colleague, Preston Bottger, provides useful insights about group size and performance.[64]

A total of 555 subjects (330 managers and 225 management students, of whom 20 per cent were female) were assigned to task teams ranging in size from 2 to 6. The teams worked on the National Aeronautics and Space Administration moon survival exercise. (This exercise involves the rank ordering of 15 pieces of equipment that would enable a spaceship crew on the moon to survive a 320-kilometres trip between a crash-landing site and home base.)[65] After analysing the relationships between group size and group performance, Yetton and Bottger concluded the following:

> It would be difficult, at least with respect to decision quality, to justify groups larger than five members . . . Of course, to meet needs other than high decision quality, organisations may employ groups significantly larger than four or five.[66]

More recent laboratory studies exploring the brainstorming productivity of various size groups (2 to 12 people), in face-to-face versus computer-mediated situations, proved fruitful. In the usual face-to-face brainstorming sessions (also see Chapter 12), productivity of ideas did not increase as the size of the group increased. But brainstorming productivity increased as the size of the group increased when ideas were typed into networked computers.[67] These results suggest that computer networks could help deliver on the promise of productivity improvement through modern information technology.[68]

PRACTICAL IMPLICATIONS

Within a contingency management framework, there is no hard-and-fast rule about group size. It depends on the organisation's objective for the group. If a high-quality decision is the main objective, then a three- to five-member group would be appropriate. However, if the objective is to generate creative ideas, encourage participation, socialise new members, engage in training or communicate policies, then groups much larger than five could be justified. Nonetheless, organisations need to be aware of qualitative changes that occur when group size increases. A meta-analysis of eight studies found the following relationships: as group size increased, group leaders tended to become more directive and group member satisfaction tended to decline slightly.[69]

Odd-numbered groups (e.g. three, five, seven members) are recommended if the issue is to be settled by a majority vote. Voting deadlocks (e.g. 2–2, 3–3) too often hamper effectiveness of even-numbered groups. A majority decision rule is not necessarily a good idea. One study found that better group outcomes were obtained by negotiation groups that used a unanimous as opposed to majority-decision rule. Individuals' self-interests were more effectively integrated when groups used a unanimous-decision criterion.[70]

Effects of men and women working together in groups

The demographic shift brought an increase in the number of organisational committees and teams composed of both men and women (also see Chapter 4).[71] Some profound effects on group dynamics might be expected.[72] Let us see what researchers have found in the way of group gender composition effects and what organisations can do about them.

WOMEN FACE AN UPHILL BATTLE IN MIXED-GENDER TASK GROUPS

Recent laboratory and field studies paint a picture of inequality for women working in mixed-gender groups. Both women and men need to be aware of these often subtle but powerful group dynamics so that corrective steps can be taken.

In a laboratory study of six-person task groups, a clear pattern of gender inequality was found in the way group members interrupted each other (also see Chapter 8). Men interrupted women significantly more often than they did other men. Women, who tended to interrupt less frequently and less successfully than men, interrupted men and women equally.[73] Recent studies into mixed-gender groups have indicated that female-dominated work teams will tend to be more receptive to negative feedback than male-dominated teams.[74]

A field study of mixed-gender police and nursing teams in the Netherlands found another group dynamics disadvantage for women. These two particular professions – police work and nursing – were fruitful research areas because men dominate the former while women dominate the latter. As women move into male-dominated police forces and men gain employment opportunities in the female-dominated world of nursing, who faces the greatest resistance? The answer from this study was the women police officers. As the representation of the minority gender (either female police officers or male nurses) increased in the work groups, the following changes in attitude were observed:

> The attitude of the male majority changes from neutral to resistant, whereas the attitude of the female majority changes from favorable to neutral. In other words, men increasingly want to keep their domain for themselves, while women remain willing to share their domain with men.[75]

Again, organisations are faced with the challenge of countering discriminatory tendencies in group dynamics.

According to B. A. Gutek, social sexual behaviour is influenced by social rules on male and female interactions. Hence, they are inappropriate for occupational gender interactions.[76] Research has shown that sexiness and attractiveness are female stereotypes (also see Chapter 4).[77] This explains why working women are often regarded as sex objects by colleagues and supervisors, which can give way to sexual harassment.[78] The European Commission defines sexual harassment as follows:

> Sexual harassment: where any form of unwanted verbal, non-verbal or physical conduct of a sexual nature occurs with the purpose or effect of violating the dignity of a person, in particular when creating an intimidating, hostile, degrading, humuliating or offensive environment.[79]

According to a study conducted for the European Commission, 40 to 50 per cent of women in the EU considered that they had been sexually harassed at least once in their working lives, and 10 per cent of men.[80]

PRACTICAL IMPLICATIONS

Male and female employees can and often do work well together in groups.[81] A survey of 387 male US government employees sought to determine how they were affected by the growing number of female co-workers. The researchers concluded: 'Under many circumstances, including inter-gender interaction in work groups, frequent contact leads to cooperative and supportive social relations.'[82] Still, affirmative steps are needed to ensure that the documented sexualisation of work environments does not erode into sexual harassment. Whether perpetrated against women or men, sexual harassment is demeaning, unethical and appropriately called 'work environment pollution'. A new European Union rule taking effect in October 2005 for the first time defines sexual harassment as a form of discrimination. It also requires EU countries to establish judicial or administrative bodies to enforce equal treatment in the workplace. This will probably result in a growth of the number of lawsuits charged against employers. Sex-discrimination will hence no longer be a purely US phenomenom. UK financial firms already seem to have a number of cases against them.[83]

Individual ability and group effectiveness

Imagine that you are a department head charged with making an important staffing decision amid the following circumstances. You need to form 8 three-person task teams from a pool of 24 employees. Based on each of the employee's prior work records and their scores on ability tests, you know that 12 have high ability and 12 have low ability. The crux of your problem is how to assign the 12 high-ability employees. Should you spread your best talent around by making sure there are both high- and low-ability employees on each team? Then again, you may want to concentrate your best talent by forming four high-ability teams and four low-ability teams. Or should you attempt to find a compromise between these two extremes? What is your decision? Why? One field experiment provided an instructive and interesting answer.

THE ISRAELI TANK-CREW STUDY

Aharon Tziner and Dov Eden, researchers from Tel Aviv University, systematically manipulated the composition of 208 three-man tank crews. All possible combinations of high- and low-ability personnel were studied (high-high-high; high-high-low; high-low-low; and low-low-low). Ability was a composite measure of (1) overall intelligence, (2) amount of formal education, (3) proficiency in Hebrew and (4) interview ratings. Successful operation of the tanks required the three-man crews to perform with a high degree of synchronised interdependence.[84] Tank-crew effectiveness was determined by commanding officers during military manoeuvres for the Israel Defence Forces.

As expected, the high-high-high ability tank crews performed the best and the low-low-low the worst. But the researchers discovered an important interaction effect:

> Each member's ability influenced crew performance effectiveness differently depending on the ability levels of the other two members. A high-ability member appears to achieve more in combination with other uniformly high-ability members than in combination with low-ability members.[85]

The tank crews composed of three high-ability personnel far outperformed all other ability combinations. The interaction effect also worked in a negative direction because the low-low-low ability

FIGURE 9.9 ABILITY OF ISRAELI TANK-CREW MEMBERS AND IMPROVEMENTS OF EFFECTIVENESS

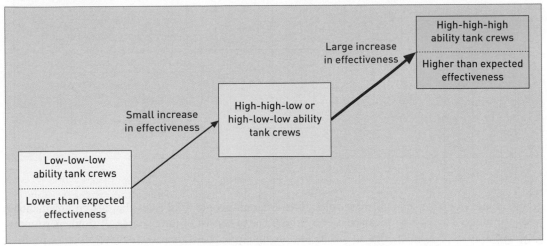

SOURCE: Adapted from B. A Gutek, A. Gross Cohen and A. M. Konrad, 'Predicting Social-Sexual Behavior at Work: A Contact Hypothesis', *Academy of Management Journal*, September 1990, p. 577.

crews performed far below expected levels. Moreover, as illustrated in Figure 9.9, significantly greater performance gains were achieved by creating high-high-high ability crews than by upgrading low-low-low ability crews with one or two high-ability members.

This returns us to the staffing problem at the beginning of this section. Tziner and Eden recommended the following solution:

> Our experimental results suggest that the most productive solution would be to allocate six highs and all 12 lows to six teams of high-low-low ability and to assign the six remaining highs to two teams of high-high-high ability. This avoids the disproportionately low productivity of the low-low-low ability combination, while leaving some of the highs for high-high-high ability teams where they are most productive .... Our results show that talent is used more effectively when concentrated than when spread around.[86]

PRACTICAL IMPLICATIONS

While the real-life aspect of the tank-crew study makes its results fairly generalisable, a qualification is in order. Specifically, modern complex organisations demand a more flexible contingency approach. Figure 9.10 shows two basic contingencies. If organisations seek to improve the performance of all groups or train novices, high-ability personnel can be spread around. This option would be appropriate in a high-volume production operation. However, if the desired outcome is to maximise performance of the best group(s), then high-ability personnel should be concentrated. This second option would be advisable in research and development departments, for example, where technological breakthroughs need to be achieved. Extraordinary achievements require clusters of extraordinary talent.[87]

Of course, ability is only one way in which people differ. In the next paragraph, groups are composed based on personality differences. In that regard, it is better to create mixed groups.

Different roles in groups: Belbin's theory

Meredith Belbin[88] developed a framework for understanding roles within a group. His framework is very popular and widely used. People are typically chosen for functional roles on the basis of experience and not personal characteristics or aptitudes. Belbin's idea is that the most consistently successful groups comprise a range of different roles (based on personal characteristics) undertaken by various members. Belbin identified nine (initially eight) different roles (see Table 9.4). In creative

349

FIGURE 9.10 A CONTINGENCY MODEL FOR STAFFING WORK GROUPS: EFFECTIVE USE OF AVAILABLE TALENT

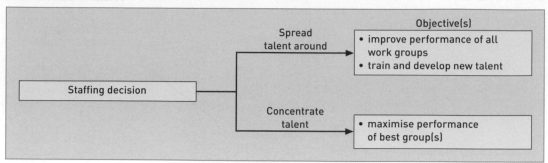

groups, there is a balance of all these roles. The different people fulfil roles that are complementary to one another. This doesn't mean that every group has to consist of nine people. A single person can play several roles. As can be seen in Table 9.4, the nine roles have their own characteristics, positive qualities and allowable weaknesses.

The nine roles can be classified into three broader categories: do-roles (the implementer, the shaper, the completer-finisher), think-roles (the specialist, the monitor-evaluator, the plant) and social roles (the resource investigator, the teamworker, the co-ordinator). It is important that at least these three basic categories in your group are represented in order to be successful.

RESEARCH FINDINGS AND PRACTICAL IMPLICATIONS

Belbin's theory has been studied a lot. Some of these studies were rather critical. There is little empirical evidence for the theory: it is difficult to find objective measures of team success that can be related to team composition. Moreover, Belbin uses a self-perception questionnaire to measure people's roles. The use of peer ratings, for instance, would be a more objective measure. Some research[89] into the reliability of the Belbin Self-Perception Inventory has concluded that internal consistency reliability is poor, raising concerns about the validity of the inventory as a selection and development tool. Swailes and McIntyre-Bhattty,[90] however, found that, for a large data set, results show that the internal consistency of item responses is better than previous research suggests and tends towards the boundary of which internal consistency is considered acceptable in social and psychological research.

Despite possible doubts about the value of Belbin's Self-Perception Inventory, it remains a popular method to examine teams and to compare the roles of individual team members. Balderson and Broderick state that in their 'experience, the very high face validity and acceptability of the measures ... suggest that the ... team roles proposed do have some validity even if aspects of their measurement may benefit from further scrutiny'.[91]

To conclude: homogeneous or heterogeneous groups?

Organisations increasingly search for selection methods to staff effective work groups and teams. Individual differences other than gender, abilities and roles are in that regard also studied in relation to group composition, like cognitive styles,[92] learning styles[93] and personality.[94]

In a laboratory study with 94 people working either in heterogeneous or homogeneous task groups (according to MBTI dimension sensing–intuiting, see Chapter 2), it was found that cognitively diverse dyads performed better than homogeneous sensing dyads when working on a complex task. The same result was, however, not found when comparing cognitively diverse dyads with homogeneous intuiting ones.[95]

A study among 182 employees of an insurance company led to the finding that in groups designed to achieve a balanced group learning process (based on the learning styles model of Honey and Mumford, see Chapter 2) the learning process model can predict group performance.[96]

A study among 298 graduate students performing in work teams for a course in 'Organisation Management', revealed that Extraversion (one of the Big Five dimensions, see Chapter 2) is especially important to understand how personality traits influence team performance.[97]

TABLE 9.4 DIFFERENT ROLES IN GROUPS

Role and its characteristics	Positive qualities	Allowable weaknesses
Do-roles **Implementer** Need for structure Predictable Efficient Dutiful Conservative	Organisational skills Common sense Self-discipline Works hard Translates decisions and strategies into well-defined and practical tasks	Inflexible Lack of open-mindedness to unproven ideas Too conservative
Shaper Firm Extravert Demanding Bursting with energy Impatient Forgiving	Shapes other people's ideas Enthusiastic Willingness to denounce inertia, inefficiency, self-satisfaction and self-deceit	Impulsive Impatient Quick-tempered Easily frustrated
Completer-Finisher Accurate Tidy Conscientious Fear of failure	Perfectionist Wants to control every detail	Incorrigible faultfinder Cannot see the wood for the trees
Think-roles **Specialist** Determined Dedicated Proud of his work	Expert in a certain field Happy to help others in his field Prefers autonomous work Inquisitive	Overlooks the overall picture Bogs down in technical details Does not like it when others enter his or her territory
Monitor-Evaluator Serious Gifted Unemotional Careful Sober	Discretion Down-to-earth Analysis and decision making Constructive criticism Judging other people's ideas	Lack of inspiration Too serious Boring Seldom shows feelings
Plant Individualistic Unorthodox Creativity New approaches	Imagination Knowledge	Pushy and uncontrolled Unrealistic ideas Dreamer
Social roles **Resource Investigator** Extravert Enthusiast Curious Communicative Catches relevant new ideas from others, but does not launch new ideas him or herself	Social skills Scans the environment for new ideas and methods Ability to cope with challenges Needs to be motivated by	Gets bored easily Little perseverance Little self-criticism Needs pressure other group members

continued

TABLE 9.4 continued

Role and its characteristics	Positive qualities	Allowable weaknesses
Social roles **Teamworker** Most sensitive group member Social Faithful to the group Mild	Sees underlying emotions in the team Good listener Empathy	Not assertive enough Not demanding Compliant Indecisive
Co-ordinator Calm Self-control	Unbiased Detects the objectives well Formulates the objectives, takes care of the agenda, establishes priorities	Does not come up with new ideas Listens to ideas of other people and then makes a decision

SOURCE: Based on R. M. Belbin, *Team Roles at Work* (London: Butterworth-Heinemann, 1993).

As these research results reveal, group heterogeneity offers both opportunities and challenges with regard to group effectiveness. Does diversity in groups enhance or detract from its effectiveness? This depends upon the diversity in question.[98]

Diversity with regard to task-related knowledge and skills is good as this implies that each group member has relevant and distinct skills that can contribute to accomplishing the task. Several studies confirm that task-related diversity can lead to greater effectiveness.[99] In Chapter 10, relevant team-work skills are elaborated further.

However, relations-oriented diversity (meaning those characteristics that can cause differentiation between ingroups and outgroups,[100] like ethnicity, gender and age) can inhibit effectiveness, although studies found for each of these concepts mixed results.[101] For instance, age diversity in groups reflects differences in values, attitudes and perspectives, which might cause stereotypes and prejudices (see also Chapter 4). Risk-taking propensity is, for instance, related to age, which can cause conflicts over the degree of risk to take to solve a certain problem. Earlier in the chapter we elaborated further on gender and group work and we pointed to some possible risks when using mixed-gender groups. Ethnocentrism (see Chapter 16) can be a problem in heterogeneous work groups.

To conclude, diversity in groups can be seen as a double-edged sword: it is needed for innovation and creative solutions, but it can cause conflict and turnover. According to Ilgen, neither extreme homogeneity or heterogeneity is likely to be optimal when a series of compromises needs to be considered as groups are composed to meet multiple objectives (which are not always compatible, like striving for efficiency and for quality). On the one hand, heterogeneity or diversity increases the knowledge pool that is important for addressing team tasks. On the other hand, people generally prefer to be with others like themselves (see earlier about social identity theory). Too much heterogeneity can also make it difficult to communicate and co-ordinate between team members.[102]

Threats to group effectiveness

Even when task groups are carefully staffed and organised, group dynamics can still go haywire. Forehand knowledge of three major threats to group effectiveness – the Asch effect, groupthink and social loafing – can help organisations take necessary preventive steps. Because the first two problems relate to blind conformity, some brief background is in order.

Very little would be accomplished in task groups and organisations without conformity to norms, role expectations, policies, and rules and regulations. After all, deadlines, commitments and product/service quality standards have to be established and adhered to if the organisation is to survive. However, as is pointed out by management consultants Robert Blake and Jane Srygley Mouton, conformity is a two-edged sword:

Social forces powerful enough to influence members to conform may influence them to perform at a very high level of quality and productivity. All too often, however, the pressure to conform stifles creativity, influencing members to cling to attitudes that may be out of touch with organisational needs and even out of kilter with the times.[103]

Moreover, excessive or blind conformity can stifle critical thinking, the last line of defence against unethical conduct. Almost daily accounts in the popular media of insider trading scandals, illegal dumping of hazardous wastes and other unethical practices make it imperative that professionals understand the mechanics of blind conformity.

The Asch effect

More than 45 years ago, social psychologist Solomon Asch conducted a series of laboratory experiments that revealed a negative side of group dynamics.[104] Under the guise of a 'perception test', Asch had groups of seven to nine volunteer college students look at 12 pairs of cards such as the ones in Figure 9.11. The object was to identify the line that was the same length as the standard line. Each individual was told to announce his or her choice to the group. Since the differences among the comparison lines were obvious, there should have been unanimous agreement during each of the 12 rounds. But that was not the case.

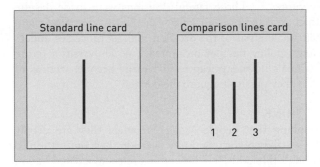

FIGURE 9.11 THE ASCH EXPERIMENT

A MINORITY OF ONE

All but one member of each group were Asch's confederates who agreed to systematically select the wrong line during seven of the rounds (the other five rounds were control rounds for comparison purposes). The remaining individual was the naive subject who was being tricked. Group pressure was created by having the naive subject in each group be among the last to announce his or her choice. Thirty-one subjects were tested. Asch's research question was: 'How often would the naive subjects conform to a majority opinion that was obviously wrong?'.

Only 20 per cent of Asch's subjects remained entirely independent; 80 per cent yielded to the pressures of group opinion at least once! Fifty-eight per cent knuckled under to the 'immoral majority' at least twice. Hence, the **Asch effect**, the distortion of individual judgment by a unanimous but incorrect opposition, was documented. (Do you ever turn your back on your better judgment by giving in to group pressure?)

Asch effect
giving in to a unanimous but wrong opposition

RESEARCH FINDINGS AND PRACTICAL IMPLICATIONS

Asch's experiment has been widely replicated with mixed results. Both high and low degrees of blind conformity have been observed with various situations and subjects. Replications in Japan and Kuwait have demonstrated that the Asch effect is not unique to the United States.[105] A cross-cultural study, using white British males and white American males showed no significant differences between them. The study confirmed the existence of the Asch effect, but remarked that the effect was significant weaker than the results Asch reported in the 1950s.[106] Internationally, collectivist countries, where the group prevails over the individual, produced higher levels of conformity than individualistic countries.[107] The point is not precisely how great the Asch effect is in a given situation or culture, but rather, professionals committed to ethical conduct need to be concerned that the Asch effect exists. Even isolated instances of blind, unthinking conformity seriously threaten the effectiveness and integrity of work groups and organisations. Functional conflict and assertiveness can help employees respond appropriately when they find themselves facing an immoral majority. Ethical codes mentioning specific practices also can provide support and guidance (see Chapter 18). For Jeffrey Skilling, the disgraced former CEO of Enron, the Asch effect was something to cultivate and nurture. Consider this organisational climate for blind obedience:

> Skilling was filling headquarters with his own troops. He was not looking for 'fuzzy skills,' a former employee recalls. His recruits talked about a socialisation process called 'Enronising'. Family time? Quality of Life? Forget it. Anybody who did not embrace the elbows-out culture 'didn't get it'. They were 'damaged goods' and 'shipwrecks', likely to be fired by their bosses at blistering annual job reviews known as rank-and-yank sessions. The culture turned paranoid: former CIA and FBI agents were hired to enforce the security. Using 'sniffer' programs, they would pounce on anyone emailing a potential competitor. The 'spooks' as the former agents were called, were known to barge into offices and confiscate computers.[108]

Groupthink

Why did President Lyndon B. Johnson and his group of intelligent White House advisers make some very unintelligent decisions that escalated the Vietnam War? How is it possible that in 1995 Robert McNamara, US Secretary of Defense under Kennedy and Johnson, reflecting on the Vietnam war, had to admit 'We were wrong, terribly wrong'.[109] Those fateful decisions were made despite obvious warning signals, including stronger than expected resistance from the North Vietnamese and dwindling support at home and abroad. Systematic analysis of the decision-making processes underlying the war in Vietnam and other US foreign policy fiascoes prompted Yale University's Irving Janis to coin the term 'groupthink'.[110] Professionals nowadays can all too easily become victims of groupthink, just like President Johnson's staff, if they passively ignore the danger.

DEFINITION AND SYMPTOMS OF GROUPTHINK

Groupthink
Janis's term for a cohesive in-group's unwillingness to realistically view alternatives

Janis defines **Groupthink** as 'a mode of thinking that people engage in when they are deeply involved in a cohesive in-group, when members' strivings for unanimity override their motivation to realistically appraise alternative courses of action'.[111] He adds, '. . . groupthink refers to a deterioration of mental efficiency, reality testing and moral judgment that results from in-group pressures'.[112] Unlike Asch's subjects, who were strangers to each other, members of groups victimised by groupthink are friendly, tightly knit and cohesive. In short, policy- and decision-making groups can become so cohesive that strong-willed executives are able to gain unanimous support for poor decisions (see Figure 9.12).[113]

FIGURE 9.12 SYMPTOMS OF GROUPTHINK LEAD TO DEFECTIVE DECISION MAKING

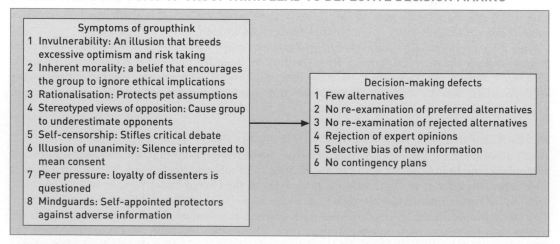

SOURCES: Symptoms adapted from I. L. Janis, *Groupthink*, second edition (Boston, MA: Houghton Mifflin, 1982), pp. 174–5. Defects excerpted from G. Moorhead, 'Groupthink Hypothesis in Need of Testing', *Group & Organization Studies*, December 1982, p. 434. Copyright © 1982 by Sage Publications. Reprinted by permission of Sage Publications, Inc.

RESEARCH FINDINGS AND PRACTICAL IMPLICATIONS

Laboratory studies using college students as subjects validate portions of Janis's groupthink concept. Specifically, it has been found that groups with a moderate amount of cohesiveness produce better decisions than low- or high-cohesive groups. Highly cohesive groups victimised by groupthink make the poorest decisions, despite high confidence in those decisions.[114] A recent review of experiments and studies of the groupthink model (between 1974 and 1998) also found partial support for the groupthink phenomenon.[115]

Janis believes prevention is better than cure when dealing with groupthink. He recommends the following preventive measures:

- Each member of the group should be assigned the role of critical evaluator. This role involves actively voicing objections and doubts.
- Top-level executives should not use policy committees to rubber-stamp decisions that have already been made.
- Different groups with different leaders should explore the same policy questions.
- Subgroup debates and outside experts should be used to introduce fresh perspectives.
- Someone should be given the role of devil's advocate when discussing major alternatives. This person tries to uncover every conceivable negative factor (see Chapter 13).
- Once a consensus has been reached, everyone should be encouraged to rethink their position to check for flaws.[116]

These anti-groupthink measures can help cohesive groups produce sound recommendations and decisions.[117] Chapter 10 focuses more in-depth on cohesiveness.

When *Business Week* recently tackled the issue of corporate governance, this was one of the recommendations:

> " The best insurance against crossing the ethical divide is a roomful of skeptics. CEOs must actively encourage dissent among senior managers by creating decision-making processes, reporting relationships and incentives that encourage opposing viewpoints. At too many companies, the performance review system encourages a 'yes-man culture' that subverts the organisation's checks and balances. By advocating dissent, top executives can create a climate where wrongdoing will not go unchallenged.[118] "

Social loafing

Is group performance less than, equal to or greater than the sum of its parts? Can three people, for example, working together accomplish less than, the same as or more than they would working separately? An interesting study conducted more than a half century ago by a French agricultural engineer named Ringelmann found the answer to be 'less than'.[119] In a rope-pulling exercise, Ringelmann reportedly found that three people pulling together could achieve only two and a half times the average individual rate. Eight pullers achieved less than four times the individual rate. This tendency for individual effort to decline as group size increases has come to be called Social loafing.[120] Let us briefly analyse this threat to group effectiveness and synergy with an eye toward avoiding it.

Social loafing decrease in individual effort as group size increases

SOCIAL LOAFING THEORY AND RESEARCH

Among the theoretical explanations for the social loafing effect are: (1) equity of effort ('Everyone else is goofing off, so why shouldn't I?'), (2) loss of personal accountability ('I'm lost in the crowd, so who cares?'), (3) motivational loss due to the sharing of rewards ('Why should I work harder than the others when everyone gets the same reward?') and (4) co-ordination loss as more people perform the task ('We're getting in each other's way').

Laboratory studies refined these theories by identifying situational factors that moderated the social loafing effect. Social loafing occurred when:

- The task was perceived to be unimportant, simple or not interesting.[121]
- Group members thought their individual output was not identifiable.[122]
- Group members expected their co-workers to loaf.[123]

But social loafing did not occur when group members in two laboratory studies expected to be evaluated.[124] Also, recent research suggests that self-reliant 'individualists' are more prone to social loafing than are group-oriented 'collectivists'. However, individualists can be made more co-operative by keeping the group small, by holding each member personally accountable for results and by fostering group cohesiveness.[125] A recent field investigation into social loafing also stresses the need to acknowledge the role that task interdependence might play in encouraging social loafing, especially given the trend in organisations toward interdependent work teams (see Chapter 10).[126]

PRACTICAL IMPLICATIONS

These findings demonstrate that social loafing is not an inevitable part of group effort. Organisations can curb this threat to group effectiveness by making sure the task is challenging and perceived as important (also see Chapters 5 and 6). Additionally, it is a good idea to hold group members person-ally accountable for identifiable portions of the group's task. One way to do this is with the step-ladder technique, a group decision-making process proven effective in recent research (see Table 9.5). Compared with conventional groups, stepladder groups produced significantly better decisions in the same amount of time. 'Furthermore, stepladder groups' decisions surpassed the quality of their best individual members' decisions 56 per cent of the time. In contrast, conventional groups' decisions surpassed the quality of their best members' decisions only 13 per cent of the time.'[127] The stepladder technique could be a useful tool for organisations relying on self-managed or total quality management (TQM) teams (see Chapter 10).

TABLE 9.5 HOW TO AVOID SOCIAL LOAFING IN GROUPS AND TEAMS: THE STEPLADDER TECHNIQUE

The stepladder technique is intended to enhance group decision making by structuring the entry of group members into a core group. Increasing or decreasing the number of group members alters the number of steps. In a four-person group, the stepladder technique has three steps. Initially, two group members (the initial core group) work together on the problem at hand. Next, a third member joins the core group and presents his or her preliminary solutions for the same problem. The entering member's presentation is followed by a three-person discussion. Finally, the fourth group member joins the core group and presents his or her preliminary solutions. This is followed by a four-person discussion, which has as its goal the rendering of a final group decision.

The stepladder technique has four requirements:

1 Each group member must be given the group's task and sufficient time to think about the problem before entering the core group.
2 The entering member must present his or her preliminary solutions before hearing the core group's preliminary solutions.
3 With the entry of each additional member to the core group, sufficient time to discuss the problem is necessary.
4 A final decision must be purposely delayed until the group has been formed in its entirety.

SOURCE: Excerpted from S. G. Rogelberg, J. L. Barnes-Farrell and C. A. Lowe, 'The Stepladder Technique: An Alternative Group Structure Facilitating Effective Group Decision Making', *Journal of Applied Psychology*, October 1992, p. 731. Copyright © 1992 by the American Psychological Association. Reprinted with permission.

Learning outcomes: Summary of key terms

1 Identify the four criteria of a group from a sociological perspective

Sociologically, a group is defined as two or more freely interacting individuals who share collective norms and goals and have a common identity.

2 Identify and briefly describe the five stages in Tuckman's theory of group development

The five stages in Tuckman's theory are forming (the group comes together), storming (members test the limits and each other), norming (questions about authority and power are resolved as the group becomes more cohesive), performing (effective communication and co-operation help the group get things done) and adjourning (group members go their own way).

3 Distinguish between role overload, role conflict and role ambiguity

Organisational roles are sets of behaviours people expect of occupants of a position. One may experience role overload (too much to do in too little time), role conflict (conflicting role expectations) or role ambiguity (unclear role expectations).

4 Contrast roles and norms, and specify four reasons norms are enforced in organisations

While roles are specific to the person's position, norms are shared attitudes that differentiate appropriate from inappropriate behaviour in a variety of situations. Norms evolve informally and are enforced because they help the group or organisation survive, clarify behavioural expectations and the group's or organisation's central values and help people avoid embarrassing situations.

5 Distinguish between task and maintenance functions in groups

Members of formal groups need to perform both task (goal-oriented) and maintenance (relationship-oriented) roles if anything is to be accomplished.

6 Summarise the practical implications for group size and group member ability

Laboratory simulation studies suggest decision-making groups should be limited to five or fewer members. Larger groups are appropriate when creativity, participation or socialisation are the main objectives. If majority votes are to be taken, odd-numbered groups are recommended to avoid deadlocks. Results of the Israeli tank-crew study prompted researchers to conclude that it is better to concentrate high-ability personnel in separate groups. Within a contingency perspective, however, there are situations in which it is advisable to spread high-ability people around.

7 Discuss why organisations need to carefully handle mixed-gender task groups

Women face special group dynamics challenges in mixed-gender task groups. Steps need to be taken to make sure increased sexualisation of work environments does not erode into illegal sexual harassment.

8 Describe groupthink, and identify at least four of its symptoms

Groupthink plagues cohesive in-groups that shortchange moral judgment while putting too much emphasis on unanimity. Symptoms of groupthink include invulnerability, inherent morality, rationalisation, stereotyped views of opposition, self-censorship, illusion of unanimity, peer pressure and mindguards. Critical evaluators, outside expertise and devil's advocates are among the preventive measures recommended by Irving Janis, who coined the term 'groupthink'.

9 Define social loafing, and explain how organisations can prevent it

Social loafing involves the tendency for individual effort to decrease as group size increases. This problem can be contained if the task is challenging and important, individuals are held accountable for results and group members expect everyone to work hard. The stepladder technique, a structured approach to group decision making, can reduce social loafing by increasing personal effort and accountability.

Review questions

1 Which of the following would qualify as a sociological group? A crowd watching a basket ball game? One of the basket ball teams? Explain.

2 What is your opinion about employees being friends with their co-workers (overlapping formal and informal groups)?

3 What is your personal experience with groups that failed to achieve stage 4 of group development? At which stage did they stall? Why?

4 Considering your current lifestyle, how many different roles are you playing? What sorts of role conflict and role ambiguity are you experiencing?

5 Which roles do you prefer to play in work groups: task or maintenance? How could you do a better job in this regard?

6 What norms do university students usually enforce in class? How are they enforced?

7 How would you respond to a manager who made the following statement: 'When it comes to the size of work groups, the bigger the better'?

8 Are women typically at a disadvantage in mixed-gender work groups? Give your rationale.

9 Have you ever been a victim of either the Asch effect or groupthink? Explain the circumstances.

10 Have you observed any social loafing recently? What were the circumstances and what could be done to correct the problem?

Personal awareness and growth exercise

Is this a mature work group or team?

Objectives

1 To increase your knowledge of group processes and dynamics.

2 To give you a tool for assessing the maturity of a work group or task team as well as a diagnostic tool for pinpointing group problems.

3 To help you become a more effective group leader or contributor.

Introduction

Group action is so common today that many of us take it for granted. But are the groups and teams to which we contribute much of our valuable time mature and hence more likely to be effective? Or do they waste our time? How can they be improved? We can and should become tough critical evaluators of group processes.

Instructions

Think of a work group or task team with which you are very familiar (preferably one you worked with in the past or are currently working with). Rate the group's maturity on each of the 20 dimensions.[128] Then add your circled responses to get your total group maturity score. The higher the score, the greater the group's maturity.

		Very false (or never)			Very true (or always)	
1	Members are clear about group goals.	1	2	3	4	5
2	Members agree with the group's goals.	1	2	3	4	5
3	Members are clear about their roles.	1	2	3	4	5
4	Members accept their roles and status.	1	2	3	4	5
5	Role assignments match member abilities.	1	2	3	4	5
6	The leadership style matches the group's developmental level.	1	2	3	4	5
7	The group has an open communication structure in which all members participate.	1	2	3	4	5
8	The group gets, gives and uses feedback about its effectiveness and productivity.	1	2	3	4	5
9	The group spends time planning how it will solve problems and make decisions.	1	2	3	4	5
10	Voluntary conformity is high.	1	2	3	4	5
11	The group norms encourage high performance and quality.	1	2	3	4	5
12	The group expects to be successful.	1	2	3	4	5
13	The group pays attention to the details of its work.	1	2	3	4	5
14	The group accepts coalition and subgroup formation.	1	2	3	4	5
15	Subgroups are integrated into the group as a whole.	1	2	3	4	5
16	The group is highly cohesive.	1	2	3	4	5
17	Interpersonal attraction among members is high.	1	2	3	4	5
18	Members are co-operative.	1	2	3	4	5
19	Periods of conflict are frequent but brief.	1	2	3	4	5
20	The group has effective conflict-management strategies.	1	2	3	4	5

Total score = _____

Discussion questions

1 Compare your total score with the following arbitrary norms:
    20–39   'When in doubt, run in circles, scream and shout!'
    40–59   A long way to go
    60–79   On the right track
    80–100   Ready for group dynamics graduate school

2 Does your evaluation help explain why the group or team was successful or not? Explain.

3 Was (or is) there anything you could have done (or can do) to increase the maturity of this group? Explain.

4 How will this evaluation instrument help you be a more effective group member or leader in the future?

Group exercise

A committee decision
Objectives
1 To give you first-hand experience with work group dynamics through a role-playing exercise.[129]
2 To develop your ability to evaluate group effectiveness.

Introduction
Please read the following case before going on.

The Johnny Rocco case

Johnny has a grim personal background. He is the third child in a family of seven. He has not seen his father for several years, and his recollection is that his father used to come home drunk and beat up every member of the family; everyone ran when his father came staggering home.

His mother, according to Johnny, wasn't much better. She was irritable and unhappy, and she always predicted that Johnny would come to no good end. Yet she worked when her health allowed her to do so in order to keep the family in food and clothing. She always decried the fact that she was not able to be the kind of mother she would like to be.

Johnny quit school in the seventh grade. He had great difficulty conforming to the school routine – he misbehaved often, was truant frequently and fought with schoolmates. On several occasions he was picked up by the police and, along with members of his group, questioned during several investigations into cases of both petty and grand larceny. The police regarded him as 'probably a bad one'.

The juvenile officer of the court saw in Johnny some good qualities that no one else seemed to sense. Mr O'Brien took it on himself to act as a 'big brother' to Johnny. He had several long conversations with Johnny, during which he managed to penetrate to some degree Johnny's defensive shell. He represented to Johnny the first semblance of personal interest in his life. Through Mr O'Brien's efforts, Johnny returned to school and obtained a high school diploma. Afterwards, Mr O'Brien helped him obtain a job.

Now 20, Johnny is a stockroom clerk in one of the laboratories where you are employed. On the whole Johnny's performance has been acceptable, but there have been glaring exceptions. One involved a clear act of insubordination on a fairly unimportant matter. In another, Johnny was accused, on circumstantial grounds, of destroying some expensive equipment. Though the investigation is still open, it now appears the destruction was accidental.

Johnny's supervisor wants to keep him on for at least a trial period, but he wants 'outside' advice as to the best way of helping Johnny grow into greater responsibility. Of course, much depends on how Johnny behaves in the next few months. Naturally, his supervisor must follow personnel policies that are accepted in the company as a whole. It is important to note that Johnny is not an attractive young man. He is rather weak and sickly, and he shows unmistakable signs of long years of social deprivation.

A committee is formed to decide the fate of Johnny Rocco. The chairperson of the meeting is Johnny's supervisor and should begin by assigning roles to the group members. These roles [shop steward (representing the union), head of production, Johnny's co-worker, director of personnel and social worker who helped Johnny in the past] represent points of view the chairperson believes should be included in this meeting. (Johnny is not to be included.) Two observers should also be assigned. Thus, each group will have eight members.

Instructions
After roles have been assigned, each role player should complete the personal preference part of the work sheet, ranking from 1 to 11 the alternatives according to their appropriateness from the vantage point of his or her role.

Once the individual preferences have been determined, the chairperson should call the meeting to order. The following rules govern the meeting: (1) The group must reach a consensus ranking of the alternatives; (2) the group cannot use a statistical aggregation, or majority vote, decision-making process; and (3) members should stay 'in character' throughout the discussion. Treat this as a committee meeting consisting of members with different backgrounds, orientation and interests who share a problem.

After the group has completed the assignment, the observers should conduct a discussion of the group process, using the Group Effectiveness Questions here as a guide. Group members should not look at these questions until after the group task has been completed.

Group effectiveness questions

1 Referring to Table 9.2, what task roles were performed? By whom?
2 What maintenance roles were performed? By whom?
3 Were any important task or maintenance roles ignored? Which?
4 Was there any evidence of the Asch effect, groupthink or social loafing? Explain.

Questions for discussion

1 Did your committee do a good job? Explain.
2 What, if anything, should have been done differently?
3 How much similarity in rankings is there among the different groups in your class? What group dynamics apparently were responsible for any variations in rankings?

Worksheet

Personal preference	Group decision	
_____	_____	Warn Johnny that at the next sign of trouble he will be fired.
_____	_____	Do nothing, as it is unclear if Johnny did anything wrong.
_____	_____	Create strict controls (do's and don'ts) for Johnny with immediate strong punishment for any misbehaviour.
_____	_____	Give Johnny a great deal of warmth and personal attention and affection (overlooking his present behaviour) so he can learn to depend on others.
_____	_____	Fire him. It's not worth the time and effort spent for such a low-level position.
_____	_____	Talk over the problem with Johnny in an understanding way so he can learn to ask others for help in solving his problems.
_____	_____	Give Johnny a well-structured schedule of daily activities with immediate and unpleasant consequences for not adhering to the schedule.
_____	_____	Do nothing now, but watch him carefully and provide immediate punishment for any future behaviour.
_____	_____	Treat Johnny the same as everyone else, but provide an orderly routine so he can learn to stand on his own two feet.
_____	_____	Call Johnny in and logically discuss the problem with him and ask what you can do to help him.
_____	_____	Do nothing now, but watch him so you can reward him the next time he does something good.

Internet exercise

The purpose of this exercise is to assess your knowledge on groups. Please return to the case study at the beginning of this chapter and read it again. Look up additonal information on NASA's website and answer the following questions. NASA's website can be found at www.mcgraw-hill. co.uk/textbooks/buelens.

Notes

1 Based on G. Kranz, *Failure Is Not an Option* (New York: Berkley Publishing Group, 2001); P. Hoversten, 'Thiokol Wavers, Then Decides to Launch', *USA Today*, 22 January 1996, p. 2A. Copyright 1996, *USA Today*. Reprinted with permission; and P. Hoversten, P. Edmonds and H. El Nasser, 'Debate Raged before Doomed Launch', *USA Today*, 22 January 1996, *USA Today*. Reprinted with permisssion.

2 For instructive research overviews, see K. L. Bettenhausen, 'Five Years of Group Research: What We Have Learned and What Needs To Be Addressed', *Journal of Management*, June 1991, pp. 345–81; R. T. Mowday and R. I. Sutton, 'Organizational Behavior: Linking Individuals and Groups to Organizational Contexts', in *Annual Review of Psychology*, vol. 44, eds L. W. Porter and M. R. Rosenzweig (Palo Alto, CA: Annual Reviews, 1993), pp. 195–229; R. A. Guzzo, 'Fundamental Considerations about Work Groups', in *Handbook of Work Group Psychology*, ed. M. A. West (Chichester: John Wiley, 1996), pp. 3–21; J. E. McGrath, 'Small Group Research, That Once and Future Field: An Interpretation of the Past With an Eye to the Future', *Group Dynamics: Theory, Research, and Practice*, no. 1, 1997, pp. 7–27; and S. G. Cohen and D. E. Baily, 'What Makes Teams Work: Group Effectiveness Research for the Shop Floor to the Executive Suite', *Journal of Management*, no. 3, 1997, pp. 239–90. A recent special issue of *Group Dynamics: Theory, Research, and Practice* (no. 1, 2000) is devoted to the history and future of group research. For instance, see E. Sundstrom, M. McIntyre, T. Halfhill and H. Richards, 'Work Groups: From the Hawthorne Studies to Work Teams of the 1990s and Beyond', *Group Dynamics: Theory, Research, and Practice*, no. 1, 2000, pp. 44–67.

3 This definition is based in part on one found in D. Horton Smith, 'A Parsimonious Definition of Group: Toward Conceptual Clarity and Scientific Utility', *Sociological Inquiry*, Spring 1967, pp. 141–67.

4 E. H. Schein, *Organizational Psychology, third edition* (Englewood Cliffs, NJ: Prentice-Hall, 1980), p. 145. For more, see L. R. Weingart, 'How Did They Do That? The Way and Means of Studying Group Processess', in *Research in Organizational Behavior*, vol. 19, eds L. L. Cummings and B. M. Staw (Greenwich, CT: JAI Press, 1997), pp. 189–239.

5 R. Likert, *New Patterns of Management* (New York: McGraw-Hill, 1961).

6 See L. G. Bolman and T. E. Deal, *Reframing Organizations* (San Francisco: Jossey-Bass, 1991), ch. 7; J. R. Katzenbach and D. K. Smith, *The Wisdom of Teams: Creating the High Performance Organization* (Boston, MA: Harvard Business School Press, 1993); and F. LaFasto and C. Larson, *When Teams Work Best: 6,000 Team Members and Leaders Tell What It Takes to Succeed* (Thousand Oaks, CA: Sage Publications, 2001).

7 See D. Krackhardt and J. R. Hanson, 'Informal Networks: The Company behind the Chart', *Harvard Business Review*, July–August 1993, pp. 104–11; E. Bonabeau, 'Predicting the Unpredictable', *Harvard Business Review*, March 2002, pp. 109–16; and R. Cross and L. Prusak, 'The People Who Make Organizations Go – or Stop', *Harvard Business Review*, June 2002, pp. 105–12.

8 E. H. Schein, *Organizational Psychology, third edition* (Englewood Cliffs, NJ: Prentice-Hall, 1980), pp. 149–53.

9 For works on the social identity theory, see M. Hogg and D. Abrams, *Social Identifications: A Social Psychology of Intergroup Relations and Group Processes* (London: Routledge, 1988); B. E. Ashforth and F. Mael, 'Social Identity Theory and the Organization', *Academy of Management Review*, January 1989, pp. 20–39; M. A. Hogg and D. J. Terry, 'Social Identity and Self-Categorization Processes in Organizational Contexts', *Academy of Management Review*, January 2000, pp. 121–40; and J. C. Turner and K. J. Reynolds, 'The Social Identity Perspective in Intergroup Relations: Theories, Themes, and Controversies', in *Blackwell Handbook of Social Psychology: Intergroup Processes*, eds R. Brown and S. Gaertner (Oxford: Blackwell Publishing, 2001), pp. 133–52.

10 For an instructive overview of five different theories of group development, see J. P. Wanous, A. E. Reichers and S. D. Malik, 'Organizational Socialization and Group Development: Toward an Integrative Perspective', *Academy of Management Review*, October 1984, pp. 670–83.

11 See B. W. Tuckman, 'Developmental Sequence in Small Groups', *Psychological Bulletin*, June 1965, pp. 384–99; and B. W. Tuckman and M. A. C. Jensen, 'Stages of Small-Group Development Revisited', *Group & Organizational Studies*, December 1977, pp. 419–27. An instructive adaptation of the Tuckman model can be found in L. Holpp, 'If Empowerment Is So Good, Why Does It Hurt?', *Training*, March 1995, p. 56.

12 Alternative group development models are discussed in L. N. Jewell and H. J. Reitz, *Group Effectiveness in Organizations* (Glenview, IL: Scott, Foresman, 1981), pp. 15–20; and R. S. Wellins, W. C. Byham and

J. M. Wilson, *Empowered Teams: Creating Self-Directed Work Groups That Improve Quality, Productivity, and Participation* (San Francisco: Jossey-Bass, 1991). Also see Y. Agazarian and S. Gantt, 'Phases of Group Development: Systems-Centered Hypotheses and Their Implications for Research and Practice', *Group Dynamics: Theory, Research, and Practice*, no. 3, 2003, pp. 238–52.

13 Practical advice on handling a dominating group member can be found in M. Finley, 'Belling the Bully', *HR Magazine*, March 1992, pp. 82–6.

14 For related research, see C. Kampmeier and B. Simon, 'Individuality and Group Formation: The Role of Independence and Differentiation', *Journal of Personality and Social Psychology*, September 2001, pp. 448–62.

15 L. N. Jewell and H. J. Reitz, *Group Effectiveness in Organizations* (Glenview, IL: Scott, Foresman, 1981), p. 19. Also see C. B. Gibson, A. E. Randel and P. C. Early, 'Understanding Group Efficacy: An Empirical Test of Multiple Assessment Methods', *Group & Organization Management*, March 2000, pp. 67–97; V. U. Druskat and S. B. Wolff, Building the Emotional Intelligence of the Group', *Harvard Business Review*, March 2001, pp. 80–90; A. Edmonson, R. Bohmer and G. Pisano, 'Speeding Up Team Learning', *Harvard Business Review*, October 2001, pp. 125–32; and S. W. Lester, B. M. Meglino and M. A. Korsgaard, 'The Antecedents and the Consequences of Group Potency: A Longitudinal Investigation of Newly Formed Work Groups', *Academy of Management Journal*, April 2002, pp. 352–68.

16 Based on J. F. McGrew, J. G. Bilotta and J. M. Deeney, 'Software Team Formation and Decay: Extending the Standard Model for Small Groups', *Small Group Research*, April 1999, pp. 209–34.

17 J. F. McGrew, J. G. Bilotta and J. M. Deeney, 'Software Team Formation and Decay: Extending the Standard Model for Small Groups', *Small Group Research*, April 1999, p. 232.

18 J. F. McGrew, J. G. Bilotta and J. M. Deeney, 'Software Team Formation and Decay: Extending the Standard Model for Small Groups', *Small Group Research*, April 1999, p. 231.

19 D. Davies and B. C. Kuypers, 'Group Development and Interpersonal Feedback', *Group & Organizational Studies*, June 1985, p. 194.

20 D. Davies and B. C. Kuypers, 'Group Development and Interpersonal Feedback', *Group & Organizational Studies*, June 1985, pp. 184–208.

21 C. J. G. Gersick, 'Marking Time: Predictable Transitions in Task Groups', *Academy of Management Journal*, June 1989, pp. 274–309.

22 See, for instance, A. Seers and S. Woodruff, 'Temporal Pacing in Task Forces: Group Development or Deadline Pressure?', *Journal of Management*, no. 2, 1997, pp. 169–87; M. J. Waller, J. M. Conte, C. B. Gibson and M. A. Carpenter, 'The Effect of Individual Perceptions of Deadlines on Team Performance', *Academy of Management Review*, October 2001, pp. 586–600; and C. M. Ford and D. M. Sullivan, 'A Time for Everything: How the Timing of Novel Contributions Influences Project Team Outcomes', *Journal of Organizational Behavior*, March 2004, pp. 279–92.

23 D. K. Carew, E. Parisi-Carew and K. H. Blanchard, 'Group Development and Situational Leadership: A Model for Managing Groups', *Training and Development Journal*, June 1986, pp. 48–9. For evidence linking leadership and group effectiveness, see G. R. Bushe and A. L. Johnson, 'Contextual and Internal Variables Affecting Task Group Outcomes in Organizations', *Group & Organization Studies*, December 1989, pp. 462–82.

24 For an excellent collection of readings on leadership, see F. Hesselbein, M. Goldsmith and R. Beckhard, *The Leader of the Future: New Visions, Strategies, and Practices for the Next Era* (San Francisco: Jossey-Bass, 1996). Also see C. Huxham and S. Vangen, 'Leadership in the Shaping and the Implementation of Collaboration Agendas: How Thing Happens in a (Not Quite) Joined-Up World', *Academy of Management Journal*, December 2000, pp. 1159–75; and N. Sivasubramaniam, W. D. Murry, B. J. Avolio and D. I. Jung, 'A Longitudinal Model of the Effects of Team Leadership and Group Potency on Group Performance', *Group & Organization Management*, March 2002, pp. 66–96.

25 G. C. Homans, *The Human Group* (London: Routledge, 1951).

26 P. E. Tesluk, J. L. Faar and S. R. Klein, 'Influences of Organizational Culture and Climate on Individual Creativity', *Journal of Creative Behavior*, January 1997, pp. 21–41.

27 S. Arad, M. A. Hanson and R. J. Schneider, 'A Framework for the Study of Relationships between Organizational Characteristics and Organizational Innovation', *Journal of Creative Behavior*, January 1997, pp. 42–58.

28 C. K. W. De Dreu and M. A. West, 'Minority Dissent and Team Innovation: The Importance of Participation in Decision Making', *Journal of Applied Psychology*, no. 6, 2001, pp. 1191–201; C. K. W. De Dreu, 'Team Innovation and Team Effectiveness: The Importance of Minority Dissent and Reflexivity', *European Journal of Work and Organizational Psychology*, no. 3, 2002, pp. 285–98; and E. C. Martins and F. Terblanche, 'Building Organizational Culture that Stimulates Creativity and Innovation', *European Journal of Innovation Management*, Winter 2003, pp. 64–74.

29 O. Brodtrick, 'Innovation as Reconciliation of Competing Values', *Optimum*, Winter 1997, pp. 1–4.

30 E. C. Martins and F. Terblanche, 'Building Organizational Culture that Stimulates Creativity and Innovation', *European Journal of Innovation Management*, Winter 2003, pp. 64–74.

31 L. A. Curral, R. H. Forrester, J. F. Dawson and M. A. West, 'It's What You Do and the Way That You Do It: Team Task, Team Size, and Innovation-Related Group Processes', *European Journal of Work and Organizational Psychology*, no. 2, 2001, pp. 187–204; E. C. Martins and F. Terblanche, 'Building Organizational Culture that

Stimulates Creativity and Innovation', *European Journal of Innovation Management*, Winter 2003, pp. 64–74; and M. A. West, G. Hirst, A. Richter and H. Shipton, 'Twelve Steps to Heaven: Successfully Managing Change through Developing Innovative Teams', *European Journal of Work and Organizational Psychology*, no. 2, 2004, pp. 269–99. A recent issue of *Journal of Organizational Behavior* (March 2004) is devoted to individual and group innovation.

32 G. Graen, 'Role-Making Processes within Complex Organizations', in *Handbook of Industrial and Organizational Psychology*, ed. M. D. Dunnette (Chicago: Rand McNally, 1976), p. 1201.

33 Other role determinants are explored in H. Ibarra 'Network Centrality, Power, and Innovation Involvement: Determinants of Technical and Administrative Roles', *Academy of Management Journal*, June 1993, pp. 471–501. Role modelling applications are covered in J. Barbian, 'A Little Help from Your Friends', *Training*, March 2002, pp. 38–41.

34 Excerpted from G. L. Miles, 'Doug Danforth's Plan to Put Westinghouse in the Winner's Circle', *Business Week*, 28 July 1986, p. 75.

35 For a review of research on the role episode model, see L. A. King and D. W. King, 'Role Conflict and Role Ambiguity: A Critical Assessment of Construct Validity', *Psychological Bulletin*, January 1990, pp. 48–64. Consequences of role perceptions are discussed in R. C. Netemeyer, S. Burton and M. W. Johnston, 'A Nested Comparison of Four Models of the Consequences of Role Perception Variables', *Organizational Behavior and Human Decision Processes*, January 1995, pp. 77–93.

36 E. H. Schein, *Organizational Psychology, third edition* (Englewood Cliffs, NJ: Prentice-Hall, 1980), p. 198. Also see E. Van De Vliert and N. W. Van Yperen, 'Why Cross-National Differences in Role Overload? Don't Overlook Ambient Temperature!', *Academy of Management Journal*, August 1996, pp. 986–1004.

37 E. H. Schein, *Organizational Psychology, third edition* (Englewood Cliffs, NJ: Prentice-Hall, 1980), p. 198. The relationship between inter-role conflict and turnover is explored in P. W. Hom and A. J. Kinicki, 'Toward a Greater Understanding of How Dissatisfaction Drives Employee Turnover', *Academy of Management Journal*, October 2001, pp. 975–87.

38 See A. S. Wharton and R. J. Erickson, 'Managing Emotions on the Job and at Home: Understanding the Consequences of Multiple Emotional Roles', *Academy of Management Review*, July 1993, pp. 457–86; and S. Shellenbarger, 'Feel Like You Need To Be Cloned? Even That Wouldn't Work', the *Wall Street Journal*, 10 July 1996, p. B1.

39 See D. Moore, 'Role Conflict: Not Only for Women? A Comparative Analysis of 5 Nations', *International Journal of Comparative Sociology*, June 1995, pp. 17–35; and S. Shellenbarger, 'More Men Move Past Incompetence Defense to Share Housework', the *Wall Street Journal*, 21 February 1996, p. B1.

40 E. H. Schein, *Organizational Psychology, third edition* (Englewood Cliffs, NJ: Prentice-Hall, 1980), p. 198. Four types of role ambiguity are discussed in M. A. Eys and A. V. Carron, 'Role Ambiguity, Task Cohesion and Self-Efficacy', *Small Group Research*, June 2001, pp. 356–73.

41 See K. D. Benne and P. Sheats, 'Functional Roles of Group Members', *Journal of Social Issues*, Spring 1948, pp. 41–9.

42 1 = A; 2 = C; 3 = A; 4 = A; 5 = C; 6 = A; 7 = C; 8 = A; 9 = C; 10 = C.

43 See H. J. Klein and P. W. Mulvey, 'Two Investigations of the Relationships among Group Goals, Goal Commitment, Cohesion, and Performance', *Organizational Behavior and Human Decision Processes*, January 1995, pp. 44–53; D. F. Crown and J. G. Rosse, 'Yours, Mine, and Ours: Facilitating Group Productivity through the Integration of Individual and Group Goals', *Organizational Behavior and Human Decision Processes*, November 1995, pp. 138–50; and A. L. Kristof-Brown and C. K. Stevens, 'Goal Congruence in Project Teams: Does the Fit Between Members' Personal Mastery and Performance Goals Matter?', *Journal of Applied Psychology*, no. 6, 2001, pp. 1083–95.

44 A. Zander, 'The Value of Belonging to a Group in Japan', *Small Group Behavior*, February 1983, pp. 7–8. Also see P. R. Harris and R. T. Moran, *Managing Cultural Differences, fourth edition* (Houston, TX: Gulf Publishing, 1996), pp. 267–76.

45 R. R. Blake and J. Srygley Mouton, 'Don't Let Group Norms Stifle Creativity', *Personnel*, August 1985, p. 28.

46 See D. Kahneman, 'Reference Points, Anchors, Norms, and Mixed Feelings', *Organizational Behavior and Human Decision Processes*, March 1992, pp. 296–312; K. L. Gammage, A. V. Carron and P. A. Estabrooks, 'Team Cohesion and Individual Productivity: The Influence of the Norm For Productivity and Identifiability of Individual Effort', *Small Group Research*, February 2001, pp. 3–18; M. M. Colman and A. V. Carron, 'The Nature of Norms in Individual Sport Teams', *Small Group Research*, April 2001, pp. 206–22; and M. C. Higgins, 'Follow the Leader? The Effects of Social Influence on Employers Choice', *Group & Organization Management*, September 2001, pp. 255–82.

47 A. Dunkin, 'Pepsi's Marketing Magic: Why Nobody Does It Better', *Business Week*, 10 February 1986, p. 52.

48 E. Mayo, *The Human Problems of an Industrial Civilization* (Cambridge, MA: Harvard University Press, 1933).

49 M. Sherif, *The Psychology of Norms* (New York: Harper & Row, 1936).

50 D. C. Feldman, 'The Development and Enforcement of Group Norms', *Academy of Management Review*, January 1984, pp. 50–52.

51 See D. M. Casperson, 'Mastering the Business Meal', *Training & Development*, March 2001, pp. 68–9; J. M. Marques, D. Abrams and R. G. Serodio, 'Being Better By Being Right: Subjective Group Dynamics and

Derogation of In-Group Deviants When Generic Norms Are Undermined', *Journal of Personality and Social Psychology*, September 2001, pp. 436–47; and T. Wildschut, C. A. Insko and L. Gaertner, 'Intragroup Social Influence and Intergroup Competition', *Journal of Personality and Social Psychology*, June 2002, pp. 975–92.

52 For more on norms, see K. L. Bettenhausen and K. J. Murnigham, 'The Development of an Intragroup Norm and the Effects of Intrapersonal and Structural Challenges', *Administrative Science Quarterly*, March 1991, pp. 20–35; R. I. Sutton, 'Maintaining Norms about Expressed Emotions; The Case of Bill Collectors', *Administrative Science Quarterly*, June 1991, pp. 245–68; R. D. Russell and C. J. Russell, 'An Examination of the Effects of Organisational Norms, Organizational Structure, and Environmental Uncertainty on Entrepreneurial Strategy', *Journal of Management*, December 1992, pp. 639–56; J. R. Hackman, 'Group Influences on Individuals in Organizations', in *Handbook of Industrial & Organizational Psychology, vol. 3, second edition*, eds M. D. Dunnette and L. M. Hough (Palo Alto, CA: Consulting Psychologists Press, 1992), pp. 235–50; and T. Postmes, R. Spears and S. Cihangir, 'Quality of Decision Making and Group Norms', *Journal of Personality and Social Psychology*, no. 6, 2001, pp. 918–30.

53 See R. G. Netemeyer, M. W. Johnston, and S. Burton, 'Analysis of Role Conflict and Role Ambiguity in a Structural Equations Framework', *Journal of Applied Psychology*, April 1990, pp. 148–57; and G. W. McGee, C. E. Ferguson, Jr, and A. Seers, 'Role Conflict and Role Ambiguity: Do the Scales Measure These Two Constructs?', *Journal of Applied Psychology*, October 1989, pp. 815–18.

54 See S. E. Jackson and R. S. Schuler, 'A Meta-Analysis and Conceptual Critique of Research on Role Ambiguity and Role Conflict in Work Settings', *Organizational Behavior and Human Decision Processes*, August 1985, pp. 16–78. Also see L. A. King and D. W. King, 'Role Conflict and Role Ambiguity: A Critical Assessment of Construct Validity', *Psychological Bulletin*, January 1990, pp. 48–64.

55 Based on C. S. Crandall, A. Eshleman and L. O'Brien, 'Social Norms and the Expresion and Suppression of Prejudice: The Struggle for Internalization', *Journal of Personality and Social Psychology*, March 2002, pp. 359–78. Also see J. A. Chatman and F. J. Flynn, 'The Influence of Demographic Heterogeneity on the Emergence and Consequences of Cooperative Norms in Work Teams', *Academy of Management Journal*, October 2001, pp. 956–74; and E. V. Hobman, P. Bordia and C. Gallois, 'Perceived Dissimilarity and Work Group Involvement: The Moderating Effects of Group Openness to Diversity', *Group & Organization Management*, October 2004, pp. 560–87.

56 J. L. Moreno, *Who Shall Survive?, second edition* (New York: Beacon Press, 1953). Also see J. L. Moreno and H. H. Jennings, *The Sociometry Reader* (Glencoe, IL: The Free Press, 1960).

57 N. M. Tichy, M. L. Tushman and C. Fombrun, 'Social Network Analysis for Organizations', *Academy of Management Review*, October 1979, pp. 507–19.

58 N. M. Tichy, M. L. Tushman and C. Fombrun, 'Social Network Analysis for Organizations', *Academy of Management Review*, October 1979, pp. 507–19.

59 L. Porter and K. Roberts, 'Communication in Organizations', in *Handbook of Industrial and Organizational Psychology*, ed. M. Dunnette (Chicago: Rand McNally, 1976); and M. L. Tushman, 'Communication Across Organizational Boundaries: Special Boundary Roles in the Innovation Process', *Administrative Science Quarterly*, 1976, pp. 587–605.

60 A. Pettigrew, 'Information Control as a Power Source', *Sociology*, 1972, pp. 187–204; and M. Zald, *Power in Organizations* (Nashville, TN: Vanderbilt University Press, 1970).

61 M. Grannovetter, *Getting a Job: A Study of Contacts and Careers* (Cambridge, MA: Harvard University Press, 1974).

62 W. M. Evan, 'The Organizational Set: Toward a Theory of Interorganizational Relations', in *Approaches to Organizational Design*, ed. J. D. Thompson (Pittsburgh: University of Pittsburgh Press, 1966); H. Aldrich and D. Whetten, 'Organization Sets, Action Sets, and Networks: Making the Most of Simplicity', in *Handbook of Organization Design, vol. 1*, eds P. Nystrom and W. Starbuck (London: Oxford University Press, 1977), pp. 385–408; and J. Pennings, *Interlocking Directorates* (Carnegie-Mellon Institute, Unpublished manuscript, 1978).

63 For example, see B. Grofman, S. L. Feld and G. Owen, 'Group Size and the Performance of a Composite Group Majority: Statistical Truths and Empirical Results', *Organizational Behavior and Human Performance*, June 1984, pp. 350–59.

64 See P. Yetton and P. Bottger, 'The Relationships among Group Size, Member Ability, Social Decision Schemes, and Performance', *Organizational Behavior and Human Performance*, October 1983, pp. 145–59.

65 This copyrighted exercise may be found in J. Hall, 'Decisions, Decisions, Decisions', *Psychology Today*, November 1971, pp. 51–4, 86, 88.

66 P. Yetton and P. Bottger, 'The Relationships among Group Size, Member Ability, Social Decision Schemes, and Performance', *Organizational Behavior and Human Performance*, October 1983, p. 158.

67 Based on R. B. Gallupe, A. R. Dennis, W. H. Cooper, J. S. Valacich, L. M. Bastianutti and J. F. Nunamaker, Jr, 'Electronic Brainstorming and Group Size', *Academy of Management Journal*, June 1992, pp. 350–69. Also see H. Barki and A. Pinsonneault, 'Small Group Brainstorming and Idea Quality: Is Electronic Brainstorming the Most Effective Approach?', *Small Group Research*, April 2001, pp. 158–205; and T. J. Kramer, G. P. Fleming and S. M. Mannis, 'Improving Face-to-Face Brainstorming through Modeling and Facilitation', *Small Group Research*, October 2001, pp. 533–57.

68 For encouraging data, see L. S. Richman, 'The Big Payoff from Computers', *Fortune*, 7 March 1994, p. 28.

69 Drawn from B. Mullen, C. Symons, L.-T. Hu and E. Salas, 'Group Size, Leadership Behavior, and Subordinate

Satisfaction', *Journal of General Psychology*, April 1989, pp. 155–69. Also see P. Oliver and G. Marwell, 'The Paradox of Group Size in Collective Action: A Theory of the Critical Mass. II', *American Sociological Review*, February 1988, pp. 1–8.

70 Details of this study are presented in L. L. Thompson, E. A. Mannix and M. H. Bazerman, 'Group Negotiation: Effects of Decision Rule, Agenda and Aspiration', *Journal of Personality and Social Psychology*, January 1988, pp. 86–95.

71 For example, see A. B. Fisher, 'Getting Comfortable with Couples in the Workplace', *Fortune*, 3 October 1994, pp. 138–44; A. P. Baridon and D. R. Eyler, 'Workplace Etiquette for Men and Women', *Training*, December 1994, pp. 31–7; J. Connelly, 'Let's Hear It for the Office', *Fortune*, 6 March 1995, pp. 221–2; and M. Hequet, 'Office Romance', *Training*, February 1996, pp. 44–50.

72 See S. G. Rogelberg and S. M. Rumery, 'Gender Diversity, Team Decision Quality, Time on Task, and Interpersonal Cohesion', *Small Group Research*, February 1996, pp. 79–90; and K. Hawkins and C. B. Power, 'Gender Differences in Questions Asked During Small Decision-Making Group Discussions', *Small Group Research*, April 1999, pp. 235–56; R. K. Shelly and P. T. Munroe, 'Do Women Engage in Less Task Behavior Than Men?', *Sociological Perspectives*, Spring 1999, pp. 49–67; and L. E. Sandelands, 'Male and Female in Organizational Behavior', *Journal of Organizational Behavior*, March 2002, pp. 149–65.

73 See L. Smith-Lovin and C. Brody, 'Interruptions in Group Discussions: The Effects of Gender and Group Composition', *American Sociological Review*, June 1989, pp. 424–35. More research on gender differences can be found in A. Mulac, J. J. Bradac and P. Gibbons, 'Empirical Support for the Gender-as-Culture Hypothesis: An Intercultural Analysis of Male/Female Language Differences', *Human Communications Research*, January 2001, pp. 121–52; K. Hawkins and C. B. Power, 'Gender Differences in Questions Asked during Small Decision-Making Group Discussions', *Small Group Research*, April 1999, pp. 235–56; and D. Tannen, 'The Power of Talk: Who Gets Heard and Why', *Harvard Business Review*, September–October 1995, pp. 147–8.

74 L. Karakowsky and D. Miller, 'Teams That Listen and Teams That Do Not', *Team Performance Management: An International Journal*, July 2002, pp. 146–56; and 'Dealing With Dynamics of Gender: How Men and Women Cope with Criticism', *Human Resource Management International Digest*, March 2003, pp. 24–6.

75 E. M. Ott, 'Effects of the Male-Female Ratio at Work', *Psychology of Women Quarterly*, March 1989, p. 53.

76 B. A. Gutek, 'Sexuality in the Workplace: Key Issues in Social Research and Organizational Practice', in *The Sexuality of Organizations*, eds J. Hearn, D. L. Sheppard, P. Tancred-Sheri and G. Burrell (London: Sage, 1989). Also see C. A. Pierce and H. Aguinis, 'A Framework for Investigating the Link between Workplace Romance and Sexual Harassment', *Group & Organization Management*, June 2001, pp. 206–29.

77 J. E. Williams and D. L. Best, *Measuring Sex Stereotypes: A Thirty Nation Study* (Beverly Hills, CA: Sage, 1982). Also see M. Rotundo, D. Nguyen and P. R. Sackett, 'A Meta-Analytic Review of Gender Differences in Perceptions of Sexual Harassment', *Journal of Applied Psychology*, October 2001, pp. 914–22.

78 C. L. Cooper and S. Lewis, 'Working Together: Men and Women in Organisations', *Leadership and Organisation Development Journal*, no. 5, 1995, pp. 29–31.

79 European Commission, 'Anna Diamantopoulou Welcomes Tough New EU Rules Against Sexual Harassment at Work', 24 April 2002, see http://europa.eu.int/comm/employment_social/news/2002/apr/092_en.html.

80 European Commission, 'Anna Diamantopoulou Welcomes Tough New EU Rules Against Sexual Harassment at Work', 24 April 2002, see http://europa.eu.int/comm/employment_social/news/2002/apr/092_en.html.

81 See S. A. Lobel, R. E. Quinn, L. St. Clair and A. Warfield, 'Love without Sex: The Impact of Psychological Intimacy between Men and Women at Work', *Organizational Dynamics*, Summer 1994, pp. 5–16.

82 S. J. South, C. M. Bonjean, W. T. Markham and J. Corder, 'Female Labor Force Participation and the Organizational Experiences of Male Workers', *The Sociological Quarterly*, Summer 1983, p. 378.

83 K. Capell, L. Cohn, R. Tiplady and J. Ewing, 'Sex-Bias Suits: The Fight Gets Ugly', *Business Week*, 6 September 2004, p. 64; G. Gomez, J. Owens and J. Morgan, 'Prohibiting Sexual Harassment in the European Union: An Unfinished Public Policy Agenda', *Employee Relations*, March 2004, p. 292; R. Hogler, J. H. Frame and G. Thornton, 'Workplace Sexual Harassment Law: An Empirical Analysis of Organizational Justice and Legal Policy', *Journal of Managerial Issues*, Summer 2002, pp. 234–50; and M. Rotundo, D.-H. Nguyen and P. R. Sacket, 'A Meta-Analytic Review of Gender differences in Perceptions of Sexual Harassment', *Journal of Applied Psychology*, October 2001, pp. 914–22.

84 A former Israeli tank commander's first-hand account of tank warfare in the desert can be found in A. Kahalani, 'Advice from a Desert Warrior', *Newsweek*, 3 September 1990, p. 32.

85 A. Tziner and D. Eden, 'Effects of Crew Composition on Crew Performance: Does the Whole Equal the Sum of Its Parts?', *Journal of Applied Psychology*, February 1985, p. 91.

86 A. Tziner and D. Eden, 'Effects of Crew Composition on Crew Performance: Does the Whole Equal the Sum of Its Parts?', *Journal of Applied Psychology*, February 1985, p. 91.

87 For related research, see R. Saavedra, C. P. Earley and L. Van Dyne, 'Complex Interdependence in Task-Performing Groups', *Journal of Applied Psychology*, February 1993, pp. 61–72; G. A. Neuman and J. Wright, 'Team Effectiveness: Beyond Skills and Cognitive Ability', *Journal of Applied Psychology*, no. 3, 1999, pp. 376–89; and J. A. LePine, 'Team Adaptation and Postchange Performance: Effects of Team Composition in Terms of Members' Cognitive Ability and Personality', *Journal of Applied Psychology*, no. 1, 2003, pp. 27–39.

88 R. M. Belbin, *Management Teams: Why They Succeed or Fail* (London: Butterworth-Heinemann, 1983);

R. M. Belbin, *Team Roles at Work* (London: Butterworth-Heinemann, 1993); and R. M. Belbin, *The Coming Shape of Organizations* (London: Butterworth-Heinemann, 1996).

89 A. Furnham, H. Steele and D. Pendleton, 'A Psychometric Assessment of the Belbin Team Role Self-Perception Inventory', *Journal of Occupational and Organizational Psychology*, September 1993, pp. 245–7; W. G. Broucek and G. A. Randall, 'An Assessment of the Construct Validity of the Belbin Self-Perception Inventory and Observer's Assessment from the Perspective of the Five-Factor Model', *Journal of Occupational and Organizational Psychology*, September 1996, pp. 389–405; S. G. Fisher, W. Macrosson and G. Sharp, 'Further Evidence Concerning the Belbin Team Role Self-Perception Inventory', *Personnel Review*, December 1996, pp. 61–7; B. Senior, 'Team Roles and Team Performance; Is There "Really" a Link?', *Journal of Organizational and Occupational Psychology*, September 1997, pp. 241–58; and S. G. Fisher, T. A. Hunter and W. D. K. Macrosson, 'A Validation Study of Belbin's Team Roles', *European Journal of Work and Organizational Psychology*, no. 2, 2001, pp. 121–44.

90 S. Swailes and T. McIntyre-Bhatty, 'Research Note: The Belbin Team Inventory: Reinterpreting Reliability Estimates', *Journal of Managerial Psychology*, June 2002, pp. 529–36.

91 S. J. Balderson and A. J. Boderick, 'Behavior in Teams: Exploring Occupational and Gender Differences', *Journal of Managerial Psychology*, no. 5, 1996, p. 33.

92 See P. K. Hammerschmidt, 'The Kirton Adaption Innovation Inventory and Group Problem Solving Success Rates', *Journal of Creative Behavior*, First Quarter 1996, pp. 61–75; R. J. Volkema and R. H. Gorman, 'The Effect of Cognitive-Based Group Composition on Decision-Making Process and Outcome', *Journal of Management Studies*, January 1998, pp. 105–21; S. G. Fisher, W. D. K. Macrosson and J. Wong, 'Cognitive Style and Team Role Preference', *Journal of Managerial Psychology*, no. 8, 1998, pp. 544–57; C. W. Allinson, S. J. Armstrong and J. Hayes, 'The Effects of Cognitive Style on Leader-Member Exchange: A Study of Manager-Subordinate Dyads', *Journal of Occupational and Organizational Psychology*, June 2001, pp. 201–20; K. W. Buffinton, K. W. Jablokow and K. A. Martin, 'Project Team Dynamics and Cognitive Style', *Engineering Management Journal*, September 2002, pp. 25–33; and M. M. Cheng, P. F. Luckett and A. K. D. Schulz, 'The Effects of Cognitive Style Diversity on Decision-Making Dyads: An Empirical Analysis in the Context of a Complex Task', *Behavioral Research in Accounting*, 2003, pp. 39–62.

93 See C. J. Jackson, 'Predicting Team Performance from a Learning Process Model', *Journal of Managerial Psychology*, no. 1/2, 2002, pp. 6–13; and D. A. Wyrick, 'Understanding Learning Styles to Be a More Effective Team Leader and Engineering Manager', *Engineering Management Journal*, March 2003, pp. 27–33.

94 See B. Barry and G. L. Stewart, 'Composition, Process, and Performance in Self-Managed Groups: The Role of Personality', *Journal of Applied Psychology*, no. 1, 1997, pp. 62–78; J. H. Bradley and F. J. Hebert, 'The Effect of Personality Type on Team Performance', *Journal of Management*, no. 5, 1997, pp. 337–65; S. L. Kichuk and W. H. Wiesner, 'Work Teams: Selecting Members for Optimal Performance', *Canadian Psychology*, no. 1/2, 1998, pp. 23–32; M. R. Barrick, G. L. Stewart, M. J. Neubert and M. K. Mount, 'Relating Member Ability and Personality to Work-Team Processes and Team Effectiveness', *Journal of Applied Psychology*, no. 3, 1998, pp. 377–91; G. A. Neuman, S. H. Wagner and N. L. Christiansen, 'The Relationship between Work-Team Personality Composition and the Job Performance of Teams', *Group & Organization Management*, March 1999, pp. 28–45; and A. E. M. van Vianen and C. K. W. De Dreu, 'Personality in Teams: Its Relationship to Social Cohesion, Task Cohesion, and Team Performance', *European Journal of Work and Organisational Psychology*, no. 2, 2001, pp. 97–120.

95 M. M. Cheng, P. F. Luckett and A. K. D. Schulz, 'The Effects of Cognitive Style Diversity on Decision-Making Dyads: An Empirical Analysis in the Context of a Complex Task', *Behavioral Research in Accounting*, 2003, pp. 39–62.

96 C. J. Jackson, 'Predicting Team Performance from a Learning Process Model', *Journal of Managerial Psychology*, no. 1/2, 2002, pp. 6–13.

97 B. Barry and G. L. Stewart, 'Composition, Process, and Performance in Self-Managed Groups: The Role of Personality', *Journal of Applied Psychology*, no. 1, 1997, pp. 62–78.

98 Based on a discussion in K. L. Unsworth and M. A. West, 'Teams: The Challenges of Cooperative Work', in *Introduction to Work and Organizational Psychology: A European Perspective*, ed. N. Chmiel (Oxford: Blackwell Publishers, 2000), pp. 327–46. Also see S. E. Jackson, K. E. May and K. Whitney, 'Understanding the Dynamics of Diversity in Decision-Making Teams', in *Team Effectiveness and Decision Making in Organizations*, eds R. A. Guzzo, E. Salas and Associates (San Francisco, CA: Jossey-Bass, 1995), pp. 204–61; S. E. Jackson, 'The Consequences of Diversity in Multidisciplinary Work Teams', in *Handbook of Work Group Psychology*, ed. M. A. West (Chichester: John Wiley, 1996), pp. 53–75; S. S. Webber and L. M. Donahue, 'Impact of Highly and Less Job-Related Diversity on Work Group Cohesion and Performance: A Meta-Analysis', *Journal of Management*, no. 2, 2001, pp. 141–62; A. Drach-Zahavy and A. Somech, 'Team Heterogeneity and Its Relationship with Team Support and Team Effectiveness', *Journal of Educational Administration*, no. 1, 2002, pp. 44–66; and S. E. Jackson, A. Joshi and N. L. Erhardt, 'Recent Research on Team and Organizational Diversity: SWOT Analysis and Implications', *Journal of Management*, no. 6, 2003, pp. 801–30.

99 See, for instance, K. A. Bantel, 'Strategic Clarity in Banking: Role of Top Management Team Demography', *Psychological Reports*, December 1993, pp. 1187–201. A recent issue of *Journal of Organizational Behavior* (September 2004) is devoted to team diversity.

100 Based on the social identity theory, see M. Hogg and D. Abrams, *Social Identifications: A Social Psychology of Intergroup Relations and Group Processes* (London: Routledge, 1988); and J. C. Turner and K. J. Reynolds, 'The Social Identity Perspective in Intergroup Relations: Theories, Themes, and Controversies', in *Blackwell Handbook of Social Psychology: Intergroup Processes*, eds R. Brown and S. Gaertner (Oxford: Blackwell Publishing, 2001), pp. 133–52.

101 See for an overview, S. E. Jackson, A. Joshi and N. L. Erhardt, 'Recent Research on Team and Organizational Diversity: SWOT Analysis and Implications', *Journal of Management*, no. 6, 2003, pp. 801–30.

102 D. R. Ilgen, 'Teams Embedded in Organizations: Some Implications', *American Psychologist*, February 1999, p. 136.

103 R. R. Blake and J. Srygley Mouton, 'Don't Let Group Norms Stifle Creativity', *Personnel*, August 1985, p. 29.

104 For additional information, see S. E. Asch, *Social Psychology* (Englewood Cliffs, NJ: Prentice-Hall, 1952), ch. 16.

105 See T. P. Williams and S. Sogon, 'Group Composition and Conforming Behavior in Japanese Students', *Japanese Psychological Research*, November 1984, pp. 231–4; and T. Amir, 'The Asch Conformity Effect: A Study in Kuwait', *Social Behavior and Personality*, July 1984, pp. 187–90.

106 N. Nicholson, S. G. Cole and T. Rocklin, 'Conformity in the Asch Situation: A Comparison Between Contemporary British and US University Students', *British Journal of Social Psychology*, February 1985, pp. 59–63.

107 Data from R. Bond and P. B. Smith, 'Culture and Conformity: A Meta-Analysis of Studies Using Asch's Line Judgment Task', *Psychological Bulletin*, January 1996, pp. 111–37.

108 J. L. Roberts and E. Thomas, 'Enron's Dirty Laundry', *Newsweek*, 11 March 2002, p. 26. Also see G. Farrell and J. O'Donnell, 'Watkins Testifies Skilling, Fastow Duped Lay, Board', *USA Today*, 15 February 2002, pp. 1B–2B; and M. Schminke, D. Wells, J. Peyrefitte and T. C. Sebora, 'Leaderships and Ethics in Work Groups: A Longitudinal Assessment', *Group & Organization Management*, June 2002, pp. 272–93.

109 R. McNamara, *In Retrospect: The Tragedy and Lessons of Vietnam* (New York: Times Books, 1995).

110 For an interesting analysis of the presence or absence of groupthink in selected US foreign policy decisions, see C. McCauley, 'The Nature of Social Influence in Groupthink: Compliance and Internalization', *Journal of Personality and Social Psychology*, August 1989, pp. 250–60. Also see G. Whyte, 'Groupthink Reconsidered', *Academy of Management Review*, January 1989, pp. 40–56.

111 I. L. Janis, *Groupthink, second edition* (Boston, MA: Houghton Mifflin, 1982), p. 9. Alternative models are discussed in K. Granstrom and D. Stwine, 'A Bipolar Model of Groupthink: An Extension of Janis's Concept', *Small Group Research*, February 1998, pp. 32–56; and A. R. Flippen, 'Understanding Groupthink from a Self-Regulatory Perspective', *Small Group Research*, April 1999, pp. 139–65.

112 I. L. Janis, *Groupthink, second edition* (Boston, MA: Houghton Mifflin, 1982), p. 9. For an alternative model, see R. J. Aldag and S. Riggs Fuller, 'Beyond Fiasco: A Reappraisal of the Groupthink Phenomenon and a New Model of Group Decision Processes', *Psychological Bulletin*, May 1993, pp. 533–52. Also see A. A. Mohamed and F. A. Wiebe, 'Toward a Process Theory of Groupthink', *Small Group Research*, August 1996, pp. 416–30.

113 For an ethical perspective, see R. R. Sims, 'Linking Groupthink to Unethical Behavior in Organizations', *Journal of Business Ethics*, September 1992, pp. 651–62.

114 Details of this study may be found in M. R. Callaway and J. K. Esser, 'Groupthink: Effects of Cohesiveness and Problem-Solving Procedures on Group Decision Making', *Social Behavior and Personality*, July 1984, pp. 157–64. Also see C. R. Leana, 'A Partial Test of Janis's Groupthink Model: Effects of Group Cohesiveness and Leader-Behavior on Defective Decision Making', *Journal of Management*, Spring 1985, pp. 5–17; G. Moorhead and J. R. Montanari, 'An Empirical Investigation of the Groupthink Phenomenon', *Human Relations*, May 1986, pp. 399–410; and J. N. Choi and M. U. Kim, 'The Organizational Application of Groupthink and its Limits in Organizations', *Journal of Applied Psychology*, April 1999, pp. 297–306.

115 W. Park, 'A Comprehensive Empirical Investigation of the Relationships among Variables of the Groupthink Model', *Journal of Organizational Behavior*, December 2001, pp. 873–87.

116 Adapted from discussion in I. L. Janis, *Groupthink, second edition* (Boston, MA: Houghton Mifflin, 1982), Ch. 11.

117 An illustrative case study is reported in C. P. Neck and G. Moorhead, 'Jury Deliberations in the Trial of US John DeLorean: A Case Analysis of Groupthink Avoidance and an Enhanced Framework', *Human Relations*, October 1992, pp. 1077–91.

118 J. A. Byrne, 'How to Fix Corporate Governance', *Business Week*, 6 May 2002, p. 78. Also see J. A. Byrne, 'Restoring Trust in Corporate America', *Business Week*, 24 June 2002, pp. 30–35.

119 Based on discussion in B. Latane, K. Williams and S. Harkins, 'Many Hand Make Light the Work: The Causes and Consequences of Social Loafing', *Journal of Personality and Social Psychology*, June 1979, pp. 822–32; and D. A. Kravitz and B. Martin, 'Ringelmann Rediscovered: The Original Article', *Journal of Personality and Social Psychology*, May 1986, pp. 936–41.

120 See J. A. Shepperd, 'Productivity Loss in Performance Groups: A Motivation Analysis', *Psychological Bulletin*, January 1993, pp. 67–81; R. E. Kidwell, Jr, and N. Bennett, 'Employee Propensity to Withhold Effort: A Conceptual Model to Intersect Three Avenues of Research', *Academy of Management Review*, July 1993, pp. 429–56; and S. J. Karau and K. D. Williams, 'Social Loafing: Meta-Analytic Review and Theoretical Integration', *Journal of Personality and Social Psychology*, October 1993, pp. 681–706.

121 See S. J. Zaccaro, 'Social Loafing: The Role of Task Attractiveness', *Personality and Social Psychology Bulletin*, March 1984, pp. 99–106; J. M. Jackson and K. D. Williams, 'Social Loafing on Difficult Tasks: Working Collec-

tively Can Improve Performance', *Journal of Personality and Social Psychology*, October 1985, pp. 937–42; and J. M. George, 'Extrinsic and Intrinsic Origins of Perceived Social Loafing in Organizations', *Academy of Management Journal*, March 1992, pp. 191–202.

122 For complete details, see K. Williams, S. Harkins and B. Latane, 'Identifiability as a Deterrent to Social Loafing: Two Cheering Experiments', *Journal of Personality and Social Psychology*, February 1981, pp. 303–11.

123 See J. M. Jackson and S. G. Harkins, 'Equity in Effort: An Explanation of the Social Loafing Effect', *Journal of Personality and Social Psychology*, November 1985, pp. 1199–206.

124 Both studies are reported in S. G. Harkins and K. Szymanski, 'Social Loafing and Group Evaluation', *Journal of Personality and Social Psychology*, June 1989, pp. 934–41.

125 Data from J. A. Wagner III, 'Studies of Individualism-Collectivism: Effects on Cooperation in Groups', *Academy of Management Journal*, February 1995, pp. 152–72. Also see P. W. Mulvey and H. J. Klein, 'The Impact of Perceived Loafing and Collective Efficacy on Group Goal Processes and Group Performance', *Organizational Behavior and Human Decision Processes*, April 1998, pp. 62–87; P. W. Mulvey, L. Bowes-Sperry and H. J. Klein, 'The Effects of Perceived Loafing and Defensive Impression Management on Group Effectiveness', *Small Group Research*, June 1998, pp. 394–415; and L. Karakowsky and K. Mcbey, 'Do My Contributions Matter? The Influence of Imputed Expertise on Member Involvement and Self-Evalutions in the Work Group', *Group & Organization Management*, March 2001, pp. 70–92.

126 R. C. Liden, S. J. Wayne, R. A. Jaworski and N. Bennett, 'Social Loafing: A Field Investigation, *Journal of Management*, June 2004, pp. 285–304.

127 S. G. Rogelberg, J. L. Barnes-Farrell and C. A. Lowe, 'The Stepladder Technique: An Alternative Group Structure Facilitating Effective Group Decision Making', *Journal of Applied Psychology*, October 1992, p. 730. Also see S. G. Rogelberg and M. S. O'Connor, 'Extending the Stepladder Technique: An Examination of Self-Paced Stepladder Groups', *Group Dynamics: Theory, Research, and Practice*, no. 2, 1998, pp. 82–91.

128 Twenty items excerpted from S. A. Wheelan and J. M. Hochberger, 'Validation Studies of the Group Development Questionnaire', *Small Group Research*, February 1996, pp. 143–70.

129 D. A. Whetten and K. S. Cameron, *Developing Management Skills* (Glenview, IL: Scott, Foresman and Company, 1984). Copyright © 1984 by Scott, Foresman and Company. Reprinted by permission of Addison Wesley Educational Publishers, Inc.

chapter 10 teams and teamwork

By Karlien Vanderheyden, Eva Cools and Fannie Debussche

Learning outcomes
When you finish studying the material in this chapter, you should be able to:

- ◼ distinguish between a 'team' and a 'group'
- ◼ identify and describe the four types of work teams
- ◼ explain the ecological model of work team effectiveness
- ◼ discuss why teams fail
- ◼ list at least three things organisations can do to build trust
- ◼ distinguish two types of cohesiveness and summarise the related research findings
- ◼ define quality circles, virtual teams and self-managed teams

Teamwork is vital in battle of the elements

'Running a business is like sailing a yacht', says Ian Gordon-Cumming of British Telecommunications. 'It epitomises all the qualities required to compete in today's global marketplace: leadership, teamwork, innovation and competitiveness.'

British Telecommunications, who organise and sponsor the BT Global Challenge, a round-the-world sailing contest, believes this initiative will prove an innovative way of wooing customers by portraying the race as a metaphor for business. Also, as many of the participants are managers, another purpose of the race is to provide an excellent occasion to enhance people skills, skills which can be transferred into the workplace.

Since 1998, every year 12 skippers sail from Southampton in southern England intent on joining the exclusive club of those who have circled the world 'the wrong way'. Each will command a 72-foot, 42-tonne yacht and a 17-strong crew. All aim to finish first after the 45 000 km course, but the race requires more than navigation skills and an understanding of the sea. Apart from the skipper, all the crew members are amateurs, most never having sailed before. To cope with the challenge, skippers will have to draw on management and communication skills. 'The 12 competing yachts are identical. Winning will therefore solely depend on commitment, team dynamics and a uniting of cultural differences', says Gordon-Cumming.

Mr Hopkinson, who manages an IT team for Granada Media, says: 'The crew is 17 and at Granada, my team is the same. In both cases, my job is to persuade them to do things to achieve a common goal and make sure they work together. This won't be the easiest thing: the crew and the skippers face 160 days at sea. They will visit five continents, encountering the toughest ocean conditions one can think of. Nights will often be short on sleep and the weather a constant foe. There is also a high risk of injury. In the race, there will be great scope for disharmony and conflict.'

The skippers agree that establishing shared goals and fostering co-operation is an essential technique to counter friction on deck. 'You have to persuade your crew to buy into your goals. Every person on board has to be geared towards achieving them', says Hopkinson. The mutiny that occurred at the end of the first leg of the BT Global Challenge, aboard a boat ironically named 'Teamwork', shows the pressures that have to be contained.

One participant says: 'The 40-knot wind is clawing at you. Icy waves are slamming over your head. Beneath your feet, the bow of the boat is surging through 60 metres or more. You feel cold, exhausted, very frightened and wish you were somewhere else. But as you struggle to change the heavy sail, you have to keep going. The rest of the crew depend on you, particularly the person at your side.'

Many of the people in the race are attracted by the thrill of adventure. Others see it as a remarkable management-development course. 'You get a new focus and stop fussing about details when the next wave might kill you. When you go for a job interview, you can certainly demonstrate something a little different that lifts you above the crowd. Ocean racing turned me from a man into a manager', says Robin Knox-Johnston, who has participated in many races. 'It also has been a great lesson in the benefits of involving colleagues. I used to run my business treating staff as a means to an end. The race helped me to take on a broader perspective', he says.

'In an era where companies stress the importance of team building, such races can be an incomparable management-forcing house', says Anthony Lane, chairman of Time Management International, the consulting firm. 'This is one of the most accelerated personal development courses you can possibly go on. Leadership and teamworking skills are right at the forefront – there is nowhere to hide. You can't get off a boat.'

Throughout the competition, representatives from 25 organisations will monitor the skippers' progress and draw management lessons from the race. There will also be business seminars at the seven ports where the challengers will dock.[1]

For discussion

Imagine that you were a participant in the BT Global Challenge. What to you are the most crucial characteristics your crew needs to succeed in the race, and how do you think these could be stimulated?

Teams and teamwork are popular terms in organisations these days. Cynics might dismiss teamwork as just another fad or quick-fix gimmick. But a closer look reveals a more profound and durable trend. Following the economic recession in the eighties, American and European companies did some introspection. Work redesign projects in work teams like Volvo in Sweden were the result. Also errors of high visibility like airline accidents revealed a lack of teamwork. Moreover, the general movement towards flatter structures of organisation and reducing the layers of middle management (see also Chapter 14), increased the empowerment of employees and stressed the importance of effective teamwork. At last teamwork was a solution to respond to the increased diversity in the marketplace.

Manfred Kets de Vries, professor at Insead France, has been searching for years for those key aspects that distinguish the best organisations from the rest. He found some common traits at the heart of the most admired companies, and teamwork turned out to be a very important dominator.

> Successful organisations are good at building teams and exploiting teamwork. People need to be able to work in teams, they need to subordinate their own agenda to the well-being of the group. Further, successful organisations foster diversity, which entails respect for the individual and makes group decision making more creative. Such organisations also empower their employees. Decision making is pushed to the lowest level at which a competent decision can be made, to the level of work groups and production teams. To foster such a process, managers should operate with minimal secrecy.[2]

The team approach becomes very important in managing organisations.[3] Teams promise to be a cornerstone of progressive management for the foreseeable future.[4] According to management expert Peter Drucker, tomorrow's organisations will be flatter, information based and organised around teams.[5] This opinion was bolstered by a survey of human resource executives in which 44 per cent called for more teamwork when asked what change employees need to make to achieve current business goals.[6] This means virtually all employees will need to polish their team skills. According to some managers, even scientists and IT specialists, who are traditionally regarded as individualists and who rely mainly on technical skills to fulfil their jobs, will have to take on a broader role in the future.

> Hardcore scientists and IT-specialists are frequently regarded as weirdos, dedicated 'lone wolfs' who are seemingly married to their research, their measuring equipment and their paradigms. 'This is probably the greatest cliche of the last few years', states an editorial article in the magazine *Science Technology*. 'In most cases, the modern scientist has become a "team-animal", who has to look beyond the limits of his own territory, otherwise his knowledge and career will fade very quickly. Renowned companies like Janssens Pharmaceuticals are now implementing cross-functional teamwork, even for their most specialised doctoral researchers.'[7]
>
> Marc Coninck, IT-manager at Belgium's KBC Insurance agrees: 'The idea that a computer scientist is primary a technological whizz-kid is completely outdated. On the contrary, we increasingly have to act like people managers. Of course, you can try to fill in your function as chief of an IT-department from a purely technical perspective, but the core of our job is undoubtedly shifting to guiding people.'[8]

Examples of the trend towards teams and teamwork abound. What are the advantages for organisations for implementing team-based working?

■ Teams enable organisations to develop and deliver products and services speedily and cost effectively, while retaining high quality.
■ Teams enable organisations to learn and keep on learning more effectively.
■ Innovation is promoted because of cross-fertilisation of ideas.
■ Teams can integrate and process information in ways that individuals cannot.
■ Teamwork can help to improve productivity.[9]

The emphasis in this chapter is on tapping the full and promising potential of teams. We will identify different types of work teams, introduce a model of team effectiveness, discuss keys to effective teamwork, explore applications of the team concept and review team-building techniques.

Work teams: types, effectiveness and stumbling blocks

Together with the shift towards the use of groups in organisations came a shift in terminology: the word 'team' became more familiar than the word 'group'. However, in literature and practice the word 'group' and 'team' are used interchangeably. Guzzo[10] states that all teams are groups but not all groups are teams, as the word 'group' is used very extensively in general social sciences to even indicate social aggregates in which there is no interdependence of members (the latter being a crucial element to define a team).[11] Jon R. Katzenbach and Douglas K. Smith, management consultants at McKinsey & Company, say it is a mistake to use the terms 'group' and 'team' interchangeably. After studying many different kinds of teams – from athletic to corporate to military – they concluded that successful teams tend to take on a life of their own. Katzenbach and Smith define a **Team** as 'a small number of people with complementary skills who are committed to a common purpose, performance goals and approach for which they hold themselves mutually accountable'.[12] Relative to Tuckman's theory of group development (see Chapter 9) – forming, storming, norming, performing and adjourning – teams are task groups that have matured to the performing stage (but not slipped into decay).

Because of conflicts over power and authority and unstable interpersonal relations, many work groups never qualify as a real team.[13] Katzenbach and Smith clarified the distinction this way: 'The

Team
small group with complementary skills who hold themselves mutually accountable for common purpose, goals and approach

TABLE 10.1 THE EVOLUTION OF A TEAM

> A work group becomes a team when
>
> 1 leadership becomes a shared activity,
> 2 accountability shifts from strictly individual to both individual and collective,
> 3 the group develops its own purpose or mission,
> 4 problem solving becomes a way of life, not a part-time activity,
> 5 effectiveness is measured by the group's collective outcomes and products.

SOURCE: Condensed and adapted from J. R. Katzenbach and D. K. Smith, *The Wisdom of Teams: Creating the High-Performance Organization* (New York: HarperBusiness, 1993), p. 214.

essence of a team is common commitment. Without it, groups perform as individuals; with it, they become a powerful unit of collective performance.'[14]

Definitions of teams generally suggest a number of conditions which must be fulfilled before a group becomes a team (see also Table 10.1):

- Members of the group have shared goals in relation to their work.
- They interact with each other to achieve those shared goals.
- All team members have well-defined and interdependent roles.
- They have an organisational identity as a team, with a defined organisational function.[15]

When Katzenbach and Smith refer to 'a small number of people' in their definition, they mean between 2 and 25 team members. Generally, they found effective teams to have fewer than ten members. This conclusion was echoed in a survey of 400 workplace team members in the United States and Canada: 'The average team consists of ten members. Eight is the most common size.'[16]

A general typology of work teams

Work teams are created for various purposes and thus face different challenges. Professionals can deal with those challenges more effectively when they understand how teams differ. A helpful way of sorting things out is to consider a typology of work teams developed by Eric Sundstrom and his colleagues.[17] Four general types of work teams listed in Table 10.2 are: advice, production, project and action teams. Each of these labels identifies a basic purpose. For instance, advice teams tend to make recommendations for managerial decisions and seldom make final decisions themselves. In contrast, production and action teams actually carry out the decisions of the management.

Four key variables in Table 10.2 deal with technical specialisation, co-ordination, work cycles and outputs. Technical specialisation is low when the team draws upon members' general experience and problem-solving ability. It is high when team members are required to apply technical skills acquired through higher education or extensive training. The degree of co-ordination with other work units is determined by the team's relative independence (low co-ordination) or interdependence (high co-ordination). Work cycles are the amount of time teams need to discharge their missions. The various outputs listed in Table 10.2 are intended to illustrate real-life effects. A closer look at each type of work team is required.[18]

ADVICE TEAMS

As their name implies, advice teams are created to broaden the information base for managerial decisions. Quality circles, discussed later, are a prime example because they facilitate suggestions for quality improvement from volunteer production or service workers. Advice teams tend to have a low degree of technical specialisation. Likewise, co-ordination is low because advice teams generally work on their own. Ad hoc committees (e.g. the annual sports event committee) have shorter life cycles than standing committees (e.g. the grievance committee).

PRODUCTION TEAMS

This second type of team is responsible for performing day-to-day operations. Minimal training for routine tasks accounts for the low degree of technical specialisation. Generally, co-ordination is high,

TABLE 10.2 FOUR GENERAL TYPES OF WORK TEAMS AND THEIR OUTPUTS

Types and examples	Degree of technical specialisation	Degree of co-ordination with other work units	Work cycles	Typical outputs
Advice Committees Review panels, boards Quality circles Employee involvement groups Advisory councils	Low	Low	Work cycles can be brief or long; one cycle can be team life span	Decisions Selections Suggestions Proposals Recommendations
Production Assembly teams Manufacturing crews Mining teams Flight attendant crews Data processing groups Maintenance crews	Low	High	Work cycles typically repeated or continuous process; cycles often briefer than team life span	Food, chemicals Components Assemblies Retail sales Customer service Equipment repairs
Project Research groups Planning teams Architect teams Engineering teams Development teams Task forces	High	Low (for traditional units) Or High (for cross functional units)	Work cycles typically differ for each new project; one cycle can be team life span	Plans, designs Investigations Presentations Prototypes Reports, findings
Action Sports team Entertainment groups Expeditions Negotiating teams Surgery teams Cockpit crews Military platoons and squads	High	High	Brief performance events, often repeated under new conditions, requiring extended training and/or preparation	Combat missions Expeditions Contracts, lawsuits Concerts Surgical operations Competitive events

SOURCE: Excerpted and adapted from E. Sundstrom, K. P. De Meuse and D. Futrell, 'Work Teams: Applications and Effectiveness', *American Psychologist*, February 1990, p. 125.

however, because work flows from one team to another. For example, track maintenance crews require fresh information from train crews about necessary repairs.

Project teams

Projects require creative problem solving, often involving the application of specialised knowledge. For example, Boeing's 777 jumbo jet was designed by project teams consisting of engineering, manufacturing, marketing, finance and customer service specialists. State-of-the-art computer modelling programmes allowed the teams to assemble three-dimensional computer models of the new aircraft. Design and assembly problems were ironed out during project team meetings before production workers started cutting any metal. Boeing's 777 design teams required a high degree of co-ordination between organisational sub-units because they were cross-functional.[19] A pharmaceutical research team of biochemists, on the other hand, would interact less with other work units because the projects are relatively self-contained.

> The creation of a project team at Blue Circle, a British company, resulted in a totally new product on the European market. When Blue Circle introduced a standardised boiler for the European market, a design team was set up comprising British, French, German and Dutch specialists. Their task was to adapt to the huge variations in the different European housing, climate and plumbing demands. The team was based in the United Kingdom. English was the working language. The team's efforts finally resulted in a condensing boiler that could be used anywhere, not just in one particular country.[20]

ACTION TEAMS

This last type of team is best exemplified by sports teams, airline cockpit crews, hospital surgery teams, mountain-climbing expeditions, film crews, management and trade union negotiating committees, and police special intervention teams among others. A unique challenge for action teams is to exhibit peak performance on demand.[21]

> For example, teams at Stage Co – a company that delivers technical stage crew to summer festivals such as Glastonbury in the UK, the Roskilde-Festival in Denmark, the Werchter festival in Belgium and 'Rock am Ring' in Germany – need to combine high specialisation with high co-ordination to ensure a good concert. Highly trained technicians build up the main stage, then they need to break it down immediately after the show, because the pieces are needed fast elsewhere, for the next festival. This requires immense speed and intense co-operation, so everybody in the crew needs to know exactly what to do. Moreover, co-ordination between the stage crew, the festival organisers, the sound engineers and the musicians has to be perfect. Also, some music groups bring their own crew along because of the specific needs of their performance, so a lot of topics have to be discussed with them too.[22]

This four-way typology of work teams is dynamic and changing, not static. Some teams evolve from one type to another. Other teams represent a combination of types.

Work team effectiveness: an ecological model

The effectiveness of athletic teams is a straightforward matter of counting the competitions you win against those you lose. Things become more complicated, however, when the focus shifts to work teams in today's organisations.[23] Figure 10.1 lists two effectiveness criteria for work teams: performance and viability. According to Sundstrom and his colleagues: 'Performance means acceptability of output to customers within or outside the organisation who receive team products, services, information, decisions or performance events (such as presentations or competitions).' While the foregoing relates to satisfying the needs and expectations of outsiders such as clients, customers and fans, another team-effectiveness criterion arises – namely, Team viability, defined as team member satisfaction and continued willingness to contribute. Are the team members better or worse off for having contributed to the team effort?[24] A work team is not truly effective if it gets the job done but self-destructs in the process or burns everyone out.

Figure 10.1 is an ecological model because it portrays work teams within their organisational environment. In keeping with the true meaning of the word ecology – the study of interactions between organisms and their environments – this model emphasises that work teams need an organisational life-support system. Six critical organisational context variables are listed in Figure 10.1. Work teams have a much greater chance of being effective if they are nurtured and helped by the organisation. The team's purpose needs to be in concert with the organisation's strategy. Similarly, team participation and autonomy require an organisational culture that values those processes. Team members also need appropriate technological tools and training. Teamwork needs to be reinforced by the organisational reward system (also see Chapter 6). Such is not the case when pay and bonuses are tied solely to individual output.

Five important factors of the internal processes of work teams are listed in Figure 10.1. Contained in Table 10.3, is an expanded list of team characteristics which can prove useful in evaluating task teams both in college and at work.[25]

Team viability team members' satisfaction and willingness to contribute

FIGURE 10.1 AN ECOLOGICAL MODEL OF WORK TEAM EFFECTIVENESS

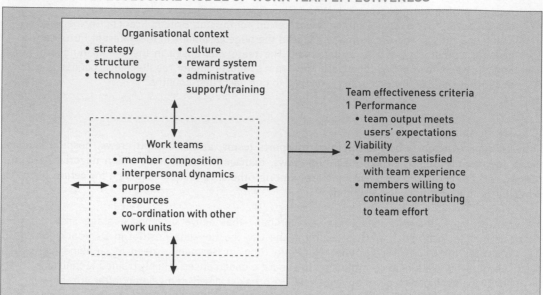

SOURCE: Adapted in part from E. Sundstrom, K. P. De Meuse and D. Futrell, 'Work Teams: Application and Effectiveness', *American Psychologist*, February 1990, pp. 120–33; and J. N. Choi, 'External Activities and Team Effectiveness: Review and Theoretical Development', *Small Group Research*, April 2002, pp. 181–208.

Why do work teams fail? pitfalls and stumbling blocks

Advocates of the team approach paint a very optimistic and bright picture. Yet there is a dark side to teams.[26] Teams have become a managerial panacea. They are used for problems where technological change, radical decisions or individual excellence would be a better solution. No wonder that at a seminar of senior managers held by Cranfield Management School, UK, two-thirds of the participants expressed their disillusionment with the results of their teamworking initiatives. Also, research at Temple University, Florida, revealed that 80 to 100 per cent of teams had difficulties achieving their goals.[27] David Butcher of Cranfield presents the following viewpoint:

> The root of the problem is that companies see teams as an end rather than a means, often setting them up where they are not required. In situations where their use is justified, their effectiveness is often stymied by managers who don't know how to handle them properly. Teams are over-hyped, overrated, but used in a wrong way. The paradox derives from the very 'diplomatic immunity' of teamwork: in many organisations it is so ingrained in management that it is impossible to attack, criticise or even discuss rationally.[28]

When implemented unwisely, teamwork can turn into an organisational nightmare. For example, reflect on what probably happened at the European headquarters of Citrix Corporation in Shaffhausen, Switzerland, where a marketing executive quoted: 'Teamwork is a lot of people doing what I say.'[29] Although these words sound extreme, teams can and often do fail. The American team specialist Richard Whitely speaks of a disease called teamitis.[30] Anyone contemplating the use of team structures in the workplace therefore needs a balanced perspective on their advantages and limitations. In their daily work with various companies the British consultants Rob Yeung and Sebastian Bailey encounter the following most frequently observed symptoms when implementing teamwork:[31]

■ Hidden agendas: a belief that certain members of the team are secretly building their own empires or furthering their own careers rather than working for the good of the organisation,

TABLE 10.3 CHARACTERISTICS OF AN EFFECTIVE TEAM

1 Clear purpose	The vision, mission, goal or task of the team has been defined and is now accepted by everyone. There is an action plan
2 Informality	The climate tends to be informal, comfortable and relaxed. There are no obvious tensions or signs of boredom
3 Participation	There is much discussion, and everyone is encouraged to participate
4 Listening	The members use effective listening techniques such as questioning, paraphrasing and summarising to get out ideas
5 Civilised disagreement	There is disagreement, but the team is comfortable with this and shows no signs of avoiding, smoothing over or suppressing conflict
6 Consensus decisions	For important decisions, the goal is substantial but not necessarily unanimous agreement through open discussion of everyone's ideas, avoidance of formal voting or easy compromises
7 Open communication	Team members feel free to express their feelings on the tasks as well as on the group's operation. There are few hidden agendas. Communication takes place outside of meetings
8 Clear roles and work assignments	There are clear expectations about the roles played by each team member. When action is taken, clear assignments are made, accepted and carried out. Work is fairly distributed among team members
9 Shared leadership	While the team has a formal leader, leadership functions shift from time to time depending on the circumstances, the needs of the group and the skills of the members. The formal leader models the appropriate behaviour and helps establish positive norms
10 External relations	The team spends time developing key outside relationships, mobilising resources and building credibility with important players in other parts of the organisation
11 Style diversity	The team has a broad spectrum of team-player types including members who emphasise attention to task, goal setting, focus on process and questions about how the team is functioning
12 Self-assessment	Periodically, the team stops to examine how well it is functioning and what may be interfering with its effectiveness

SOURCE: G. M. Parker, *Team Players and Teamwork: The New Competitive Business Strategy* (San Francisco: Jossey-Bass, 1990), p. 33. Copyright © 1990 by Jossey-Bass Inc., Publishers. Reprinted by permission of John Wiley & Sons, Inc.

> 'Whenever I try to get my top executives together to wrestle with new challenges, invariably one or more of the division presidents will argue that they're aggressively dealing with the problem in their own units', says Richard, the chief executive of a large financial services firm. 'But these problems call for companywide action, not piecemeal initiatives. Frankly, I think we're paying a big price for the autonomy we've granted senior executives. They're each running their own fiefdoms, unwilling to think about how they might disadvantage other departments. We can't get our act together.'[32]

■ Lack of understanding: misconceptions about why the team has been brought together are common when a team is first formed.

■ Lack of leadership: the team leader does not have the skills required to manage the team effectively. Sometimes, it may be that no one member is recognised by all as the leader.

■ Wrong mix of team members: for example, there are 'creative types' who love to generate ideas but cannot focus on detail, while there are 'doers' who would rather not contribute to discussions and prefer to be given tasks to do. A team that is unevenly balanced could either generate ideas but fail to implement them, or alternatively, discover that it does not have any ideas to implement (also see Chapter 9).

■ Unhealthy team environment: for example, the team is unable to cope under pressure as outlined in the following quote:

> 'The biggest pitfall in a team is not having issues raised early enough', says Gary Spellins, managing director of Lex Services, which delivers a range of outsourcing solutions to diverse companies. 'When you're working to tight deadlines, the earlier you put your hand up, the better, but very often team members are too afraid to take initiative and hope somebody else will ring the alarm bell. It's easier to add resources to fix a problem before a deadline than to rectify it after you've missed the deadline. In a team, you need to create an environment where there are no surprises.'[33]

If teams are to be effective, both management and team members must make a concerted effort to think and do things differently. Figure 10.2 presents a useful summary of various stumbling blocks and pitfalls, which managers and team members must bear in mind if they want to avoid the above problems.

According to the centre of Figure 10.2, the main threats to team effectiveness are unrealistic expectations leading to frustration. Frustration, in turn, encourages people to abandon teams. Both managers and team members can be victimised by unrealistic expectations.[34] On the left side of Figure 10.2 is a list of common management mistakes. These mistakes generally involve doing a poor job of creating a supportive environment for teams and teamwork. On the right side of Figure 10.2 is a list of common problems for team members. Contrary to critics' Theory X (Chapter 1) contention that employees lack the motivation and creativity for real teamwork, it is common for

FIGURE 10.2 WHY WORK TEAMS FAIL

Mistakes typically made by management
- teams cannot overcome weak strategies and poor business practices
- hostile environment for teams (command-and-control culture; competitive/individual reward plans; management resistance)
- teams adopted as a fad, a quick-fix; no long-term commitment
- lessons from one team not transferred to others (limited experimentation with teams)
- vague or conflicting team assignments
- inadequate team skills training
- poor staffing of teams
- lack of trust

Unrealistic expectations resulting in frustration

Problems typically experienced by team members
- team tries to do too much too soon
- conflict over differences in personal work styles (and/or personality conflicts)
- too much emphasis on results, not enough on team processes and group dynamics
- unanticipated obstacle causes team to give up
- resistance to doing things differently
- poor interpersonal skills (aggressive rather than assertive communication, destructive conflict, win-lose negotiation)
- poor interpersonal chemistry (loners, dominators, self-appointed experts do not fit in)
- lack of trust

SOURCE: Adapted from discussion in S. R. Rayner, 'Team Traps: What They Are, How to Avoid Them', *National Productivity Review*, Summer 1996, pp. 110–15; L. Holpp and R. Phillips, 'When Is a Team Its Own Worst Enemy?', *Training*, September 1995, pp. 71–82; and B. Richardson, 'Why Work Teams Flop – and What Can Be Done About It', *National Productivity Review*, Winter 1994/95, pp. 9–13.

teams to take on too much too quickly and to drive themselves too hard for fast results. Important group dynamics and team skills get lost in the rush for results. Consequently, team members' expectations need to be given a reality check by management and team members themselves. Also, teams need to be counselled against quitting when they run into an unanticipated obstacle. Failure is part of the learning process for teams, as it is elsewhere in life. Comprehensive training in interpersonal skills can prevent many common teamwork problems.

Identifying and developing good team players

Anyone who is familiar with wilderness hiking and camping knows the folly of heading for the wilds without proper gear and skills. One's life can depend on being able to conserve fluids, prevent hypothermia and avoid dangerous situations. So, too, organisations need to make sure teams are staffed with appropriately skilled people. Michael J. Stevens and Michael A. Campion developed a very useful model for assessing one's readiness for teamwork.[35] It lists the knowledge, skills and abilities (KSAs) needed for both team member and team success (see Table 10.4). Three of the KSAs are interpersonal: conflict resolution, collaborative problem solving and communication. Two KSAs involve self-management: goal setting and performance management, and planning and task co-ordination. As an integrated package, these five KSAs are a template for the team players we need today. Professionals in team-oriented organisations need to be mindful of these KSAs when recruiting, hiring, staffing and training. How do you measure up? Where do you need improvement?

However, it is clear that staffing work teams on the basis of individual-task KSAs alone is not enough. Other characteristics of individual team members also facilitate team functioning, such as people's preferences, personality and interaction styles (see Chapter 9).[36]

TABLE 10.4 GOOD TEAM PLAYERS HAVE THE RIGHT KNOWLEDGE, SKILLS AND ABILITIES

Interpersonal KSAs

1 Conflict resolution KSAs
Recognising types and sources of conflict; encouraging desirable conflict but discouraging undesirable conflict; and employing integrative (win-win) negotiation strategies rather than distributive (win-lose) strategies.

2 Collaborative problem-solving KSAs
Identifying situations requiring participative group problem solving and using the proper degree of participation; and recognising obstacles to collaborative group problem solving and implementing corrective actions.

3 Communicative KSAs
Understanding effective communication networks and using decentralised networks where possible; recognising open and supportive communication methods; maximising the consistency between non-verbal and verbal messages; recognising and interpreting the non-verbal messages of others; and engaging in and understanding the importance of small task and ritual greetings.

Self-management KSAs

4 Goal-setting and performance management KSAs
Establishing specific, challenging and accepted team goals; and monitoring, evaluating and providing feedback on both overall team performance and individual team-member performance.

5 Planning and task co-ordination KSAs
Co-ordinating and synchronising activities, information and tasks between team members, as well as aiding the team in establishing individual task and role assignments that ensure the proper balance of workload between team members.

SOURCE: L. Miller, 'Reexamining Teamwork KSAs and Team Performance', *Small Group Research*, December 2001, Table I, p. 748, as adapted from M. J. Stevens and M. A. Campion, 'The Knowledge, Skill, and Ability Requirements for Teamwork: Implications for Human Resource Management', *Journal of Management*, Summer 1994, Table I, p. 505.

Effective teamwork through co-operation, trust and cohesiveness

As competitive pressures intensify, experts say organisational success will depend increasingly on teamwork rather than individual stars. For instance, Britain's Chartered Institute of Personnel and Development (CIPD) investigated seven European companies who were in the process of changing into what the researchers called 'lean and responsive organisations'. Teamwork and co-operation turned out to be the most important factors in this change process. A principal conclusion of the study was that employees have to work together and exchange experiences in order to succeed in the transformation process.[37] If this emphasis on teamwork has a familiar ring, it is because sports champions generally say they owe their success to it. Whether in the athletic arena or the world of business, three components of teamwork receiving the greatest attention are co-operation, trust and cohesiveness. Let us explore the contributions each can make to effective teamwork.

Co-operation

Individuals are said to be co-operating when their efforts are systematically integrated to achieve a collective objective. The greater the integration, the greater the degree of co-operation.

As early as the 1940s, Morton Deutch showed how people's beliefs are related to their interdependence. When acting in co-operation with each other, they believe that goal attainment by other people will also foster their own goals. When in competition, however, people believe that goal attainment by others ('competitors') will diminish their own. 'When others fail I succeed.' Independent people see no relationship between their own results and the results of others.[38] In practice, most team members find themselves in a 'mixed motive' situation. Just think of the footballer who is in a position to score, yet sees a teammate even better placed to score the winner. John Kay – the British strategy specialist – illustrates this with the following analysis of Liverpool Football Club:

> If we where to build a model of the game of football, it would recognise that every time a player has the ball he faces the alternative of shooting for goal or passing to a better placed player. If he passes to a player of similar calibre to himself, he will score fewer goals but the team will score more. If everyone in the team plays a passing game, every member of it can expect to score more goals than if their normal instinct is to shoot. That choice is repeated every few minutes in every match the team plays and there are two equilibria – a passing game or a shooting game. Liverpool is well known for its passing game. Many of its opponents adopt a more individualistic style.
>
> Liverpool illustrates the principal ways in which architecture can form the basis of a distinctive capability. The club has created an intangible asset – the organisational knowledge of the club – which, although it is derived from the contributions of the individual members, belongs to the firm and not to the individual members and cannot be appropriated by them. There are organisational routines – complex manoeuvres, perfected through repeated trial – in which each player fulfils his own role without needing or necessarily having, a picture of the whole. And there is the 'passing game', the co-operative ethic, in which the player's instinct is to maximise the number of goals the club scores rather than the number of goals he scores. Each of these sources of sporting success has its precise business analogies.[39]

However, it is not only managers and football trainers who have seen the benefits of co-operation. Many workers on the floor are delighted too by the team systems that are increasingly being implemented by Europe's largest companies. For instance, the following quote stems from a production worker at Philips:

> Today, the work isn't harder but it's completely different. Everybody now thinks ahead. Because everybody now works together and is kept informed, the work goes faster and more fluently. In the past, the only thing we thought about was women and booze. Today, working here is fun. Everybody is responsible. Everybody works in the same direction. Nowadays people don't mind staying a little later to solve a problem because they know why they're doing it. That's important.[40]

CO-OPERATION VERSUS COMPETITION

A widely held assumption among American managers is that 'competition brings out the best in people'. From an economic viewpoint, business survival depends on staying ahead of the competition. However, from an interpersonal viewpoint, critics contend competition has been over-emphasised, primarily at the expense of co-operation.[41] Alfie Kohn is a strong advocate of greater emphasis on co-operation in our classrooms, offices and factories.

> My review of the evidence has convinced me that there are two ... important reasons for competition's failure. First, success often depends on sharing resources efficiently, and this is nearly impossible when people have to work against one another. Co-operation takes advantage of all the skills represented in a group as well as the mysterious process by which that group becomes more than the sum of its parts. By contrast, competition makes people suspicious and hostile toward one another and actively discourages this process ....
>
> Second, competition generally does not promote excellence because trying to do well and trying to beat others simply are two different things. Consider a child in class, waving his arm wildly to attract the teacher's attention, crying, 'Oooh! Oooh! Pick me!' When he is finally recognised, he seems befuddled. 'Um, what was the question again?', he finally asks. His mind is focused on beating his classmates, not on the subject matter.[42]

RESEARCH FINDINGS AND PRACTICAL IMPLICATIONS

After conducting a meta-analysis of 122 studies encompassing a wide variety of subjects and settings, one team of researchers concluded the following:

- Co-operation is superior to competition in promoting achievement and productivity.
- Co-operation is superior to individualistic efforts in promoting achievement and productivity.
- Co-operation without intergroup competition promotes higher achievement and productivity than co-operation with intergroup competition.[43]

Given the size and diversity of the research base, these findings strongly endorse co-operation in modern organisations. Co-operation can be encouraged by reward systems[44] that reinforce teamwork as well as individual achievement (see also Chapter 6). Interestingly, co-operation can be encouraged by quite literally tearing down walls, or not building them in the first place. A recent study of 299 managers and professionals employed by eight small businesses proves insightful:

> The researchers looked at the effect of private offices, shared private offices, cubicles and team-oriented open offices on productivity, and found to their initial surprise that the small team, open-office configuration (desks scattered about in a small area with no partitions) to be significantly correlated with superior performance. In addition, they found that the open-office configuration was particularly favored by the youngest employees, who believe open offices provide them greater access to their colleagues and the opportunity to learn from their more seasoned senior compatriots.[45]

There is a movement among architects and urban planners to design and build structures that encourages spontaneous interaction, co-operation and teamwork.[46] Sorry about the private office you might have had in mind!

Research suggests that organisations can enhance equal employment opportunity and diversity programmes by encouraging voluntary helping behaviour in interracial work teams.[47] Accordingly, it is reasonable to conclude that voluntary helping behaviour could build co-operation in mixed-gender teams and groups as well. Remember Chapters 4 and 9 showed that 'diversity' should include more than just racial or gender differences. The Swedish-Swiss ABB group, for example, applied this idea when composing a team responsible for the design of a new factory:

> 'I put together a seven-member design team, composed of two workers from manufacturing, three from engineering, one from finance and myself. One team member was a female and one of the males was a person of colour. Their ages ranged from 23 to 40 years. Their company service ranged from 4 months to 12 years. They held [family] positions from [that of] a single mother to a father with teenage children. In short, they were a representative cross-section of business and modern lifestyles. Each member brought something unique to the team and each got something different from the experience', says B. Randall Palef, ABB Switchgear Division's Human Resources Manager at the time of the project.[48]

Trust

These have not been good times for trust in the corporate world. Years of mergers, downsizings, layoffs and redundancies, bloated executive bonuses and broken promises have left many employees justly cynical about trusting management.[49] A survey of over 1000 employees in six British companies concluded that trust is the missing factor: only 13 per cent think that the people they work with feel valued by the company; 9 per cent think that top management has a sincere interest in the welfare of its employees and hardly 8 per cent are convinced that management gives fair deals.[50] However, as an encouraging sign, an increasing amount of managers view trust as a key factor in doing business. One of them is Eduard Kint of the Swedish furniture company Kinnarps:

> 'A truly market-oriented team drives on trust', he says. 'From their first day off, I try to give my employees the feeling I trust them. I want them to decide autonomously and take initiative. This is not a kindergarten but a company of adults. I'm not here to control them all the time. Adults are to be treated as such. One exception aside, I have never regretted this mentality. I think, if you want to be an effective team, a high amount of trust is vital. That's why working here at Kinnarps has been summarised as 'freedom with the necessary responsibility', which has led to enormous creativity and a fantastic team.[51]

In this section, we examine the concept of trust and introduce six practical guidelines for building it.

A COGNITIVE LEAP

Trust
reciprocal faith in other's intentions and behaviour

Trust is defined as reciprocal faith in others' intentions and behaviour.[52] Experts on the subject explain the reciprocal (give-and-take) aspect of trust as follows.

> When we see others acting in ways that imply that they trust us, we become more disposed to reciprocity by trusting them more. Conversely, we come to distrust those whose actions appear to violate our trust or to distrust us.[53]

Propensity to trust
a personality trait involving one's general willingness to trust others

In short, we tend to give what we get: trust begets trust; distrust begets distrust. A newer model of organisational trust includes a personality trait called Propensity to trust. The developers of the model explain it as follows.

> Propensity might be thought of as the general willingness to trust others. Propensity will influence how much trust one has for a trustee prior to data on that particular party being available. People with different developmental experiences, personality types and cultural backgrounds vary in their propensity to trust .... An example of an extreme case of this is what is commonly called blind trust. Some individuals can be observed to repeatedly trust in situations that most people would agree do not warrant trust. Conversely, others are unwilling to trust in most situations, regardless of circumstances that would support doing so.[54]

What is your propensity to trust? How did you develop that personality trait? (See the trust questionnaire in the Personal awareness and growth exercise at the end of this chapter.)

Trust involves 'a cognitive "leap" beyond the expectations that reason and experience alone would warrant'.[55] (See Figure 10.3.) For example, suppose a member of a newly formed class project team

FIGURE 10.3 INTERPERSONAL TRUST INVOLVES A COGNITIVE LEAP

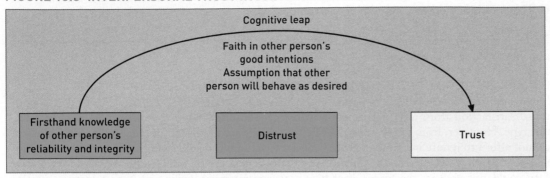

works hard, basing this on the assumption that her teammates are also working hard. That assumption, on which her trust is based, is a cognitive leap that goes beyond her actual experience with her team-mates. When you trust someone, you have faith in their good intentions. The act of trusting someone, however, carries with it the inherent risk of betrayal.[56] Progressive managers believe that the benefits of interpersonal trust far outweigh any risks of betrayed trust.

HOW TO BUILD TRUST

Management professor and consultant Fernando Bartolome offers the following six guidelines for building and maintaining trust:

■ Communication: keep team members and employees informed by explaining policies and decisions and providing accurate feedback. Be candid about your own problems and limitations. Tell the truth.[57] As an example,

> ... according to Geoff Boisi, head of investment banking at Chase in London, the best way for someone to create a trusting, candid partnership, is to abandon the word 'I' and to plump for 'we' instead. 'We have seen the light. We are never, ever going to use the first person singular again', he says. '"I" is weak ... "We" hints at consensus and reflection. "I" is shot from the hip ... "I" is asking for an argument ... "We" is begging for agreement and trust. "We" means teamwork ... "I" is a one-man band.' Boisi believes that these slight grammatical adjustments can really make a difference. 'It's simple but incredibly powerful', he says. 'I think this is an important tool that we should all incorporate in our daily lives.'[58]

■ Support: be available and approachable. Provide help, advice, coaching and support for team members' ideas.
■ Respect: delegate real decision-making authority – it is the most important expression of managerial respect. Actively listening to the ideas of others is a close second. (Empowerment is not possible without trust, as will also be explained in Chapter 13.)[59]
■ Fairness: be quick to give credit and recognition to those who deserve it. Make sure all performance appraisals and evaluations are objective and impartial (also see Chapter 6).[60]
■ Predictability: as mentioned previously, be consistent and predictable in your daily affairs. Keep both expressed and implied promises.
■ Competence: enhance your credibility by demonstrating good business sense, technical ability and professionalism.[61]

Trust needs to be earned; it cannot be demanded.

Cohesiveness

Cohesiveness is a process whereby 'a sense of "we-ness" [togetherness] emerges to transcend individual differences and motives.'[62] Members of a cohesive team stick together. They are reluctant to leave the team. Cohesive team members stick together for one or both of the following reasons:

Cohesiveness
a sense of 'we-ness' that helps groups stick together

■ They enjoy each others' company.
■ They need each other to accomplish a common goal.

Accordingly, two types of cohesiveness, identified by sociologists, are socio-emotional cohesiveness and instrumental cohesiveness.[63]

SOCIO-EMOTIONAL AND INSTRUMENTAL COHESIVENESS

Socio-emotional cohesiveness is a sense of togetherness that develops when individuals derive emotional satisfaction from team participation. Most general discussions of cohesiveness are limited to this type. However, from the standpoint of getting things accomplished in task groups and teams, we cannot afford to ignore instrumental cohesiveness. **Instrumental cohesiveness** is a sense of togetherness that develops when team members are mutually dependent on one another because they believe they could not achieve the team's goal by acting separately. A feeling of 'we' is instrumental to achieving the common goal. Team advocates generally assume both types of cohesiveness are essential to productive teamwork. But is this really true?

RESEARCH FINDINGS AND PRACTICAL IMPLICATIONS

What is the connection between team cohesiveness and performance? A landmark meta-analysis of 410 studies involving 8702 subjects provided the following insights:

■ There is a small but statistically significant cohesiveness → performance effect.
■ The cohesiveness → performance effect was stronger for smaller and 'real' teams (as opposed to contrived groups in laboratory studies).
■ The cohesiveness → performance effect becomes stronger as one moves from (real) civilian groups to military groups to sports teams.
■ Commitment to the task at hand (meaning that the individual sees the performance standards as legitimate) has the most powerful impact on the cohesiveness → performance linkage.
■ The performance → cohesiveness linkage is stronger than the cohesiveness → performance linkage. Thus, the tendency for success to bind team members together is greater than the tendency for closely knit groups to be more successful.
■ Contrary to the popular view, cohesiveness is not 'a 'lubricant' that minimises friction due to the human 'grit' in the system.[64]
■ All this evidence led the researchers to the practical conclusion that: 'Efforts to enhance group performance by fostering interpersonal attraction or "pumping up" group pride are not likely to be effective.'[65]

A second meta-analysis found no significant relationship between cohesiveness and the quality of team decisions. However, support was found for Janis's contention that groupthink (see Chapter 9) tends to afflict cohesive in-groups with strong leadership. Teams whose members liked each other a great deal tended to make poorer-quality decisions.[66]

Research tells us that cohesiveness is no 'secret weapon' in the quest for improved team performance. The trick is to keep task teams small, make sure performance standards and goals are clear and accepted, achieve some early successes and follow the tips in Table 10.5. A good example is Renault's restructured factory in Douai, France. A new production system was introduced for the construction of the Megane, based on strong employee involvement. Those who were involved in the project from the beginning were responsible for the training of 200 colleagues, who, in turn, instructed their peers. This training system enhanced employee co-operation.[67] Self-selected work teams (in which people pick their own team-mates) and social events outside working hours can stimulate socio-emotional cohesiveness.[68] The fostering of socio-emotional cohesiveness needs to be balanced with instrumental cohesiveness. The latter can be encouraged by making sure everyone in the team recognises and appreciates each member's vital contribution to the team's goal. While balancing the two types of cohesiveness, professionals need to remember that groupthink theory and research cautions against too much cohesiveness.

Socio-emotional cohesiveness sense of togetherness based on emotional satisfaction

Instrumental cohesiveness sense of togetherness based on the mutual dependency required to get the job done

TABLE 10.5 STEPS MANAGERS CAN TAKE TO ENHANCE THE TWO TYPES OF COHESIVENESS

Socio-emotional cohesiveness
Keep the team relatively small
Strive for a favourable public image to increase the status and prestige of belonging. Encourage interaction and co-operation
Emphasise members' common characteristics and interests
Point out environmental threats (e.g. competitors' achievements) to rally the team

Instrumental cohesiveness
Regularly update and clarify the team's goal(s)
Give every team member a vital 'piece of the action'
Channel each team member's special talents toward the common goal(s). Recognise and equitably reinforce every member's contributions
Frequently remind team members they need each other to get the job done

Teams in action: quality circles, virtual teams and self-managed teams

All sorts of interesting approaches to teams and teamwork can be found in the workplace today. A great deal of experimentation is taking place as organisations struggle to become more flexible and responsive. New information technologies have spurred experimentation with team formats. This section profiles three different approaches to teams: quality circles, virtual teams and self-managed teams. We have selected these particular types of team for three reasons: they have recognisable labels; they have at least some research evidence; and they range from low to high degrees of empowerment.

As indicated in Table 10.6, the three types of teams are distinct but not totally unique. Overlaps exist. For instance, computer-networked virtual teams may or may not have volunteer members and may or may not be self-managed. Another point of overlap involves the fifth variable in Table 10.6, that is, the relationship to organisation structure. Quality circles are called parallel structures because they exist outside normal channels of authority and communication.[69] Self-managed teams, on the other hand, are integrated into the basic organisational structure. Virtual teams vary in this

TABLE 10.6 BASIC DISTINCTIONS BETWEEN QUALITY CIRCLES, VIRTUAL TEAMS AND SELF-MANAGED TEAMS

	Quality circles	Virtual teams	Self-managed teams
Type of team	Advice	Advice or project (usually project)	Production, project or action
Type of empowerment	Consultation	Consultation, participation or delegation	Delegation
Members	Production/service personnel	Managers and technical specialists	Production/service, technical specialists
Basis of membership	Voluntary	Assigned (some voluntary)	Assigned
Relationship to organisation structure	Parallel	Parallel or integrated	Integrated
Amount of face-to-face communication	Strictly face-to-face	Periodic to none	Varies, depending on use of information technology

regard, although they tend to be parallel because they are made up of functional specialists (engineers, accountants, marketers, etc.) who team up on temporary projects. Keeping these basic distinctions in mind, let us explore quality circles, virtual teams and self-managed teams.

Quality circles

Quality circles are small teams of people from the same work area who voluntarily get together to identify, analyse and recommend solutions for problems related to quality, productivity and cost reduction. Some prefer the term 'quality control' circles. With an ideal size of 10 to 12 members, they typically meet for about an hour to an hour-and-a-half at a time, on a regular basis. Some companies allow meetings during work hours, others encourage quality circles to meet after work on employees' time. Once a week or twice a month are common schedules. Management facilitates the quality circle programme through skills training and listening to periodic presentations of recommendations. Monetary rewards for suggestions tend to be the exception rather than the rule. Intrinsic motivation, derived from learning new skills and meaningful participation, is the primary reward for quality circle volunteers.

THE QUALITY CIRCLE MOVEMENT

American quality control experts helped introduce the basic idea of quality circles to Japanese industry soon after the Second World War. The idea eventually returned to the United States, Britain and many other countries and became a fad during the 1970s and 1980s. Proponents made zealous claims about how quality circles were the key to higher productivity, lower costs, employee development and improved job attitudes. At its zenith, during the mid-1980s, the quality circle movement claimed millions of employee participants around the world.[70] Hundreds of companies and government agencies adopted the idea under a variety of labels.[71] The dramatic growth of quality circles has been attributed to a desire to replicate Japan's industrial success; a penchant for business fads; and the relative ease of installing quality circles without restructuring the organisation.[72] All too often, however, early enthusiasm gave way to disappointment, apathy and despair.[73] Many quality circles failed because of insufficient preparation and management support, union opposition or other difficulties.[74] But quality circles, if properly administered and supported by management, can be much more than a management fad seemingly past its prime. According to researchers Edward E. Lawler and Susan A. Mohrman, 'quality circles can be an important first step toward organisational effectiveness through employee involvement'.[75]

RESEARCH FINDINGS AND PRACTICAL IMPLICATIONS

There is a body of objective field research on quality circles. Still, much of what we know comes from testimonials and case histories from managers and consultants who have a vested interest in demonstrating the technique's success. Although documented failures are scarce, one expert concluded that quality circles have failure rates of more than 60 per cent.[76] Poor implementation is probably more at fault than the concept itself.[77]

To date, field research on quality circles has been inconclusive. Lack of standardised variables is the main problem, as is typical when comparing the results of field studies.[78] Team participation programmes of all sizes and shapes have been called quality circles. Here is what we have learned to date. A case study of military and civilian personnel found a positive relationship between quality circle participation and desire to continue working for the organisation. The observed effect on job performance was slight. A longitudinal study spanning 24 months revealed that quality circles had only a marginal impact on employee attitudes but had a positive impact on productivity. In a more recent study, utility company employees who participated in quality circles received significantly better job performance ratings and were promoted more frequently than non-participants. This suggests that quality circles live up to their billing as a good employee development technique.[79] Overall, quality circles are a promising participative management tool (also see Chapter 12), if they are carefully implemented and supported by all levels of management.

Virtual teams

Virtual teams are a product of modern times. They take their name from virtual-reality computer simulations, where 'it's almost like the real thing'. Thanks to evolving information technologies such as the Internet, email, videoconferencing, groupware and fax machines, you can be a member of a

FIGURE 10.4 CHARACTERISTICS THAT DIFFERENTIATE VIRTUAL TEAMS FROM TRADITIONAL TEAMS

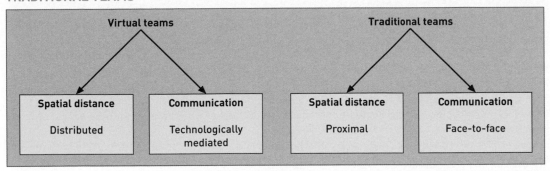

SOURCE: Adapted from B. S. Bell and S. W. J. Kozlowski, 'A Typology of Virtual Teams: Implications for Effective Leadership', *Group Organization Management*, March 2002, pp. 14–49.

work team without really being there (see Chapter 8).[80] Figure 10.4 focuses on the characteristics that differentiate between virtual teams and traditional teams: spatial distance on the one hand and information, data and personal communication on the other hand. Traditional team meetings have a specific location. Team members are either physically present or absent. Virtual teams, in contrast, convene electronically with members reporting in from different locations, different organisations, and even different time zones (see the next Snapshot).

As companies expand globally, face increasing time compression in product development, and use more foreign-based subcontracting labour, virtual teams promise the flexibility, responsiveness, lower costs, and improved resource utilisation necessary to meet ever-changing task requirements in highly turbulent and dynamic global business environments.[81]

Because virtual teams are so new, there is no consensual definition. Our working definition of a virtual team is a physically dispersed task team that conducts its business through modern information technology.[82] Advocates say virtual teams are very flexible and efficient because they are driven by information and skills, not by time and location. People with the necessary information or skills can be team members, regardless of where or when they actually do their work. On the negative side, lack of face-to-face interaction can weaken trust, communication and accountability. Other possible dysfunctions are low individual commitment, role overload, role ambiguity, absenteeism and social loafing.[83]

Remember from Chapter 8 that in face-to-face communication people rely on several cues: paraverbal (tone of voice, inflection, voice volume) and non-verbal (eye movement, facial expression, hand gestures, other body language). These cues provide feedback and help regulate the flow of conversation. These communication modalities are constrained to a varying extent in virtual teams. For example, electronic mail prevents both paraverbal and non-verbal cues, telephone conference calls allow the use of paraverbal cues (but not non-verbal cues) and videoconferencing provides both paraverbal and non-verbal cues.[84]

In virtual teams, it might be difficult to communicate contextual information (e.g. different perception of people from different organisations). Also unevenly distributed information, differences in speed of access to information, difficulty in communicating and understanding the salience of information (e.g. what is most important) and difficulty in interpreting the meaning of silence (e.g. is the other person absent or is he not eager to respond) can cause problems.[85] At last, in virtual teams it is more difficult to exchange information. As a consequence, virtual teams usually are more task-oriented and exchange less social-emotional information. The development of relational links is slowed down. However, research had demonstrated the importance of strong relational links like enhanced creativity and motivation, increased morale, better decisions and fewer process losses.[86]

TRUST IN VIRTUAL TEAMS

Trust is important for any team to function and excel, but its importance for virtual teams is even more critical.[87] So, in order to prevent geographical and organisational distances of virtual team members to become psychological distances, trust has to be established. Global virtual teams may experience 'swift' trust. 'Swift' trust is not based on strong interpersonal relationships (this is the

A virtual shell game for the seven-time-zone team

About the time the sun starts to go down in the Netherlands, Russ Conser's workday kicks into high gear. As a member of a team responsible for evaluating business opportunities for Shell Technology Ventures, a subsidiary of the oil giant Royal Dutch/Shell, Conser has been helping set up an office near The Hague. Thus far, much of his work has focused on hiring staff and figuring out the logistics of how to get the work done.

What often complicates Conser's day isn't so much the challenges that go along with opening a new office, it's keeping up with his team members – about half of whom are seven time zones away in Houston.

Conser and his colleagues rely heavily on email and videoconferences to communicate with one another. But getting the right message to the right people on both sides of the Atlantic hasn't been easy. 'We routinely find out we're miscommunicating, that we forgot to inform a person in the loop that some people had different expectations as to what's going to happen', he says.

The time difference adds another wrinkle. 'We have about a three-hour window each day when we can interact in real time', he explains. Consequently, phone conversations often extend into the night, when the Houston staff is at the office. Other times, the team members in the Netherlands have to wait until the sun comes up in Houston to get information they need. 'When they get back to us, we've lost another day on the calendar', says Conser, who has been in the Netherlands since August.

Conser isn't alone in his struggle to communicate with colleagues an ocean away. Rather, he is part of a growing community of people who work as members of 'virtual' teams, separated by time, distance, culture and organisational boundaries.

SOURCE: K. Kiser, 'Working on World Time,' *Training*, March 1999, pp. 29–30. Reprinted with permission from the March 1999 issue of *Training* magazine. Copyright © 1999, Lakewood Publications, Minneapolis, MN. All rights reserved.

traditional conceptualisation of trust) but on broad categorical social structures and, later on, action. Trust is imported into virtual teams rather than developed. Unlike face-to-face teams, where trust develops based on social bonds formed by informal chats around the water cooler, impromptu meetings or afterwork gatherings, virtual team members establish trust based on predictable performance.[88] Research results show some typical characteristics of virtual teams that started with low levels of trust: a lack of social introduction (e.g. family information), concern with technical uncertainties and a lack of enthusiasm. Teams that started with a high level of trust showed high initial enthusiasm and extensive social dialogue.

Teams that finished projects with low trust were characterised by negative leadership (e.g. complainers), lack of individual initiative and unpredictable communication (no regular pattern of communication). Teams finishing the project with a high level of trust showed predictable communication, substantive feedback, strong individual initiative and calm reaction to problems.[89]

One of the most critical roles for the e-team leader is to repair broken trust after a conflict has occurred. If a face-to-face interaction is not possible, then an e-leader should arrange for video- and audio-conferencing.[90]

RESEARCH FINDINGS AND PRACTICAL IMPLICATIONS

As one might expect with a new and ill-defined area, research evidence to date is a bit sparce. Here is what we have learned so far from recent studies of computer-mediated groups:

- Virtual teams formed over the Internet follow a group development process similar to that for face-to-face teams.[91]
- Internet chat rooms create more work and yield poorer decisions than face-to-face meetings and telephone conferences.[92]
- Successful use of groupware (software that facilitates interaction among virtual group members) requires training and hands-on experience.[93]
- Inspirational leadership has a positive impact on creativity in electronic brainstorming groups.[94]

- Face-to-face groups reported a higher degree of cohesion, were more satisfied with the decision process followed by the groups and were more satisfied with the team's outcome.[95]
- While face-to-face teams reported greater satisfaction with the group interaction process, the exchange of information was no more effective than in virtual teams.[96]
- Conflict management is particularly difficult for asynchronous virtual teams (those not interacting in real time) that have no opportunity for face-to-face interaction.[97] A proactive effort to solve problems however strengthens relationships in virtual teams.[98]

Virtual teams may be in fashion but they are not a cure-all. In fact, they may be a giant step backward for those not well versed in modern information technology. Professionals who rely on virtual teams agree on one point: meaningful face-to-face contact, especially during early phases of the group development process, is absolutely essential. Virtual team members need 'faces' in their minds to go with names and electronic messages. Roy Harrison, training and development policy adviser at Britain's Chartered Institute of Personnel and Development, states that the main question surrounding virtual teams is indeed how to encourage positive interaction without face-to-face contact. 'Technology allows people to get in touch but where do you get the "soul" from?', he says.[99] Additionally, virtual teams cannot succeed without some old-fashioned factors such as top management support, hands-on training, a clear mission and specific objectives, schedules, deadlines and effective leadership.[100] Table 10.7 lists eight recommendations for leadership in virtual teams (for more on leadership see Chapter 11).

The following guidelines may help leaders of virtual teams:[101]

- Virtual teams need a clear objective for each meeting. To ensure success the preparation is very important, e.g. the right participants, the distribution of all appropriate documents beforehand, the establishment of the role of the leader.
- The psychological profile and the personality characteristics of team members in virtual teams are very important: in order to function well, participants have to be patient, persistent and they need a certain degree of flexibility, tolerance and understanding.
- In virtual teams a clear definition of responsibilities is very important. This can prevent team members becoming confused and frustrated.
- Also helpful are clear guidelines on how often to communicate and a regular pattern of communication.
- The way conflicts are handled in virtual teams, is very important. As a team leader you should try to address discontent as quickly as possible and to focus on the concerned individual (do not involve the whole team when it is not necessary). To be most effective, team leaders need to do two things well: shift from a focus on time to a focus on results and recognise that virtual teams, instead of needing a fewer managers, require better supervisory skills among existing managers.

TABLE 10.7 RECOMMENDATIONS FOR LEADERSHIP IN VIRTUAL TEAMS

- Provide training on participation in virtual teams, rather than assuming that best practices from traditional teams will transfer seamlessly to virtual environments.
- Start with team-building exercises, using face-to-face where possible to establish a basis for relationships.
- Make certain that both task and relational roles are provided for, either through team members or through software.
- Establish standards for communicating contextual cues with each message to reduce the potential for misinterpretations.
- Structure the process through appropriate process structuring tools, but remember to build flexibility where users can adapt tools to their own needs.
- Nurture emergent leadership and self-leadership that moves the team forward by frequent communication and feedback.
- Put special and continuous emphasis on relational development.
- Anticipate unintended consequences and debrief how the team dealt with those events.

SOURCE: Reprinted from *Organizational Dynamics*, Vol. 31, I. Zigurs, 'Leadership in Virtual Teams: Oxymoron or Opportunity?', pp. 339–51. Copyright 2003, with permission from Elsevier.

Self-managed teams

Have you ever thought you could do a better job than your boss? Well, if the trend toward self-managed work teams continues to grow as predicted, you just may get your chance. Entrepreneurs and artisans often boast of not having a supervisor. The same generally cannot be said for employees working in organisational offices and factories. But things are changing. In fact, according to a British study published by the Industrial Society, 10 per cent of the 500 personnel managers polled said that most teams in their organisations were self-managed. Nearly 40 per cent declared that their company operated at least some self-managed teams.[102] Consider, for example, the following situations.

> The Body Shop experimented with an autonomous team existing of 30 full-time employees, all with equal status. Each member was paid the same salary. This group operated as a single self-managed team with the collective authority of a branch manager, rotating the four departmental teams and managerial responsibilities. Although some adjustments were carried out, the experiment was a great success.[103]

> In an assignment for the European Foundation for Quality Management, the Belgian company Bekaert-Stanwick searched for a 'best practice' model to show how companies could use autonomous teams. At Bekaert-Stanwick, employees make decisions at the lowest level, at that of the production and assembly line workers. Teams of eight to ten people work in different shifts, aiming for faster and more qualitative production. Apart from the team leader, every member of the team is responsible for production, safety, communication, personnel problems and quality. Each team formulates its own mission, preferably as clear as possible. Within teams, everybody has his own responsibility, ranging from those of quality and safety to social activities. There's also a rotation system for the function of team leader.[104]

Companies such as Asea Brown Boveri, a Swedish-Swiss firm, 3M in the United States and BP Norge in Norway successfully introduced self-managed teams. According to these companies self-managed teams speed up decision making and innovation. They also stimulate people to become self-motivated and they help employees to connect with the company's vision in a very personal way. Employees can affect important issues and they can develop their own skills like leadership skills.[105]

WHAT ARE SELF-MANAGED TEAMS?

Something much more complex is involved than this apparently simple label suggests. The term 'self-managed' does not mean simply turning workers loose to do their own thing. Indeed, as we will see, an organisation embracing self-managed teams should be prepared to undergo revolutionary changes in management philosophy, structure, staffing and training practices, and reward systems. Moreover, the traditional notions of managerial authority and control are turned on their heads. Not surprisingly, many managers strongly resist giving up the reins of power to people they view as subordinates. They see self-managed teams as a threat to their job security.[106] Texas Instruments, for instance, has constructively dealt with this problem at its Malaysian factory by making former production supervisors part of the all-important training function. Also specialists and support employees (such as engineers and HR professionals) may fear the introduction of self-managed teams. They will have to share their special knowledge with self-managed teams while this specific knowledge used to be a source of self-esteem and status.[107]

Self-managed teams
groups of employees granted administrative oversight for their work

Self-managed teams are defined as groups of workers who are given 'administrative oversight' for their task domains. Administrative oversight involves delegating activities such as planning, scheduling, monitoring and staffing. These are chores normally performed by managers. In short, employees in these unique work groups act as their own supervisor.[108] Self-managed teams are variously referred to as semiautonomous work groups, autonomous work groups, self-directed work groups or superteams.

Varying interpretations of 'self-managed' or 'self-directed' can lead to confusion and wrong steps. Essentially, the concept means that team members share or rotate leadership and hold themselves mutually responsible for a set of performance goals, an approach to their work and deliverables that reflect the company's mission, vision and business plan. The team members have a high responsibility: they decide how to organise themselves in order to get their work done and they are responsible for their own output as well as for that of others.[109]

What is the task of the former manager? Usually the former manager starts as a team leader. He makes sure that every team member has the same information, understands the business vision and has clear goals (e.g. financial targets). The former manager is also responsible for keeping the project on track.

Once the team members have more experience with working in the team, they gradually take over some decision-making and conflict-resolution responsibilities from the team leader. As the team matures, the former manager acts more as a coach/adviser but he always remains a member of the team, participating in decisions and supplying expertise, knowledge and resources. He or she has to teach the team members to cope with self-responsibility and self-accountability.

The team members must measure their progress against the agreed-upon goals and approach, as well as their skills and competencies to determine where they require development, on-the-job training and coaching.[110]

A common feature of self-managed teams, particularly among those above the shopfloor or clerical level, is **Cross-functionalism**.[111]

As indicated in Table 10.8, self-managed teams can be empowered in many different ways, producing countless variations.

Among companies with self-managed teams, the most commonly delegated tasks are work scheduling and dealing directly with outside customers. The least common team chores are hiring and firing.[112] Most of today's self-managed teams remain bunched at the shop-floor level in factory settings. Experts predict growth of the practice in the managerial ranks and in service operations.[113]

> **Cross-functionalism** team made up of technical specialists from different areas

TABLE 10.8 THERE ARE MANY WAYS TO EMPOWER SELF-MANAGED TEAMS

External leader behaviour
- Make team members responsible and accountable for the work they do
- Ask for and use team suggestions when making decisions
- Encourage team members to take control of their work
- Create an environment in which team members attempt to solve work-related problems
- Display trust and confidence in the team's abilities

Production/service responsibilities
- The team sets its own production/service goals and standards
- The team assigns jobs and tasks to its members
- Team members develop their own quality standards and measurement techniques
- Team members take on production/service learning and development opportunities
- Team members handle their own problems with internal and external customers
- The team works with a whole product or service, not just a part

Human resource management system
- The team gets paid, at least in part, as a team
- Team members are cross-trained on jobs within their team
- Team members are cross-trained on jobs in other teams
- Team members are responsible for hiring, training, punishment and firing
- Team members use peer evaluations to formally evaluate each other

Social structure
- The team gets support from other teams and departments when needed
- The team has access to and uses important and strategic information
- The team has access to and uses resources of other teams
- The team has access to and uses resources inside and outside the organisation
- The team frequently communicates with other teams
- The team makes its own rules and policies

SOURCE: B. L. Kirkman and B. Rosen, 'Powering Up Teams', *Organizational Dynamics*, Winter 2000, Exhibit 3, p. 56.

HISTORICAL AND CONCEPTUAL ROOTS OF SELF-MANAGED TEAMS

Self-managed teams are an offshoot of a combination of behavioural science and management practice.[114] Group dynamics research of variables, such as cohesiveness, initially paved the way.[115] A later stimulus was the socio-technical systems approach in which researchers tried to harmonise social and technical factors. Their goal was to increase productivity and the quality of employees' working lives simultaneously.[116] The socio-technical systems approach is an integral approach that, in the 1950s, formed the basis for the principle of team-based organisations. It is an originally British approach (introduced in the 1940s at the Tavistock Institute in the United Kingdom) that finds worldwide implementation in organisational change processes and currently has an Australian, Scandinavian, Dutch and American variant. The Dutch variant is a structure approach by definition with emphasis on the design and implementation of a team-based organisational structure. Therefore, the Dutch variant does not only imply a concept for the structure of a team-based organisation, but also concept for the change management approach to implement such a structure as well.[117]

More recently, the idea of self-managed teams has been given a strong boost by advocates of job design and participative management.[118] The job characteristics model of Hackman and Oldham, for example, outlined in Chapter 5, showed that internal motivation, satisfaction and performance can be enhanced through five core job characteristics. In relation to members of self-managed teams, we can see that of those five core factors, increased autonomy is a major benefit. Autonomy itself comprises three types: method, scheduling and criteria (see the next Activity on work team autonomy).

Members of self-managed teams score high on group autonomy. Autonomy empowers those who are ready and able to handle added responsibility. (So how did you score on the Activity?)

activity

Measuring work group autonomy

Instructions

Think of your current (or past) job and work teams. Characterise the team's situation by circling one number on the following scale for each statement. Add your responses for a total score.

Work method autonomy	Strongly disagree				Strongly agree		
1 My work team decides how to get the job done.	1	2	3	4	5	6	7
2 My work team determines what procedures to use.	1	2	3	4	5	6	7
3 My work team is free to choose its own methods when carrying out its work.	1	2	3	4	5	6	7

Work scheduling autonomy							
4 My work team controls the scheduling of its work.	1	2	3	4	5	6	7
5 My work team determines how its work is sequenced.	1	2	3	4	5	6	7
6 My work team decides when to do certain activities.	1	2	3	4	5	6	7

Work criteria autonomy							
7 My work team is allowed to modify the normal way it is evaluated so some of our activities are emphasised and some de-emphasised.	1	2	3	4	5	6	7
8 My work team is able to modify its objectives (what it is supposed to accomplish).	1	2	3	4	5	6	7
9 My work team has some control over what it is supposed to accomplish.	1	2	3	4	5	6	7

Total score =

Norms

10–26 = Low autonomy
27–45 = Moderate autonomy
46–63 = High autonomy

SOURCE: Adapted from an individual autonomy scale in J. A. Breaugh, 'The Work Autonomy Scales: Additional Validity Evidence', *Human Relations*, November 1989, pp. 1033–56.

FIGURE 10.5 THE EVOLUTION OF SELF-MANAGED WORK TEAMS

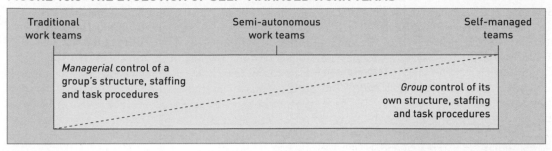

The net result of this confluence is the continuum in Figure 10.5. The traditional clear-cut distinction between manager and managed is being blurred as nonmanagerial employees are delegated greater authority and granted increased autonomy. It is important to note, however, that self-managed teams do not eliminate the need for all managerial control (see the upper right-hand corner of Figure 10.5. Semi-autonomous work teams represent a balance between managerial and group control.[119]

RESEARCH FINDINGS

As with quality circles and virtual teams, much of what we know about self-managed teams comes from testimonials and case studies. Fortunately, a body of higher-quality field research is slowly emerging. A review of three meta-analyses covering 70 individual studies concluded that self-managed teams had:

- A positive impact on productivity.
- A positive impact on specific attitudes relating to self-management (e.g. responsibility and control).
- No significant impact on general attitudes (e.g. job satisfaction and organisational commitment).
- No significant impact on absenteeism or turnover.[120]

Other recent research insights about self-managed teams include:

- Disciplinary actions should be handled by group consensus because individual team members tend to be too lenient.[121]
- Group cohesiveness is associated with higher performance ratings.[122]
- When implementing self-managed teams in multinational companies, societal values need to be taken into consideration because some cultures are more resistant to the practice than others. In fact, 'teams-related resistance is apparently greater for employees in the United States than for those in Finland or the Philippines'.[123]

Although encouraging, these results do not qualify as a sweeping endorsement of self-managed teams. Nonetheless, experts say the trend toward self-managed work teams will continue upward. Managers need to be prepared for the resulting shift in organisational administration.

The increasing use of self-managed teams in the workplace raises questions about how these teams need to be composed for best results. Little research evidence exists with regard to characteristics of successful self-managed team members. Given the specific context of laboratory studies, these results are not always generalisable to work teams in organisations. A study among 126 manufacturing and support personnel indicates that people's personality (Big Five) has an influence on their self-efficacy to participate in a self-managed team. This study's findings reveal the importance of taking into account people's personalities when deciding whether or not to implement self-managed teams and also to decide who to select to work in such teams.[124]

PRACTICAL IMPLICATIONS

Experience shows that it is better to build a new production or service facility around self-managed teams than to attempt to convert an existing one. The former approach involves so-called 'greenfield

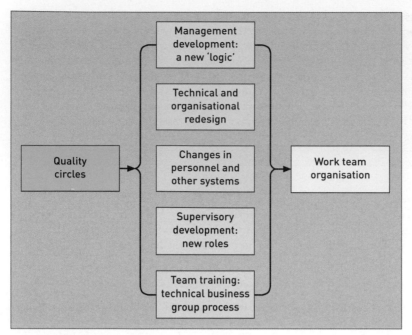

FIGURE 10.6 MAKING THE TRANSITION BETWEEN QUALITY CIRCLES AND SELF-MANAGED TEAMS

SOURCE: 'Quality Circles: After the Honeymoon', by Edward E. Lawler III, *et al.*
Reprinted, by permission of publisher, from *Organizational Dynamics*, Spring 1987
© 1987. American Management Association, New York. All Rights Reserved.

sites'. Greenfield sites give management the advantage of selecting appropriate technology and carefully screening job applicants likely to be good team players.

But the fact is, most organisations are not afforded greenfield opportunities. They must settle for introducing self-managed teams into an existing organisation structure.[125] This is where Lawler and Mohrman's transitional model is helpful (see Figure 10.6). Even though their model builds a bridge specifically from quality circles to team organisation, their recommendations apply to the transition from any sort of organisation structure to teams. As mentioned earlier, quality circles are a good stepping-stone from a nonparticipative organisation to one driven by self-managed teams.

Extensive management training and socialisation are required to deeply embed Theory Y (Chapter 1) and participative management (Chapter 13) values into the organisation's culture. It is necessary for this new logic to start with top management and filter down, otherwise, resistance among middle- and lower-level managers will block the transition to teams.[126] Some turnover can be expected among managers who refuse to adjust to broader empowerment.

Both technical and organisational redesign are necessary for the transition to self-managed teams. The new teams may require special technology. Volvo's team-based car assembly plant, for example, relies on portable assembly platforms rather than traditional assembly lines. Structural redesign of the organisation must take place because self-managed teams are an integral part of the organisation, not patched onto it as in the case of quality circles:

> For example, in one of Texas Instruments' computer chip factories a hierarchy of teams operates within the traditional structure. Four levels of teams are responsible for different domains. Reporting to the steering team that deals with strategic issues are quality-improvement, corrective-action and effectiveness teams. Texas Instruments' quality-improvement and corrective-action teams are cross-functional teams; and are made up of middle managers and functional specialists such as accountants and engineers. Production workers make up the effectiveness teams. The corrective-action teams are unique because they are formed to deal with short-term problems and are disbanded when a solution is found. All the other teams are long-term assignments.[127]

In turn, systems for personnel, goal setting and rewards will need to be adapted to encourage the new self-managed teamwork. Staffing decisions may shift from management to team members who hire their own co-workers. A study of 60 self-managing teams involving 540 employees suggests how goal setting should be reoriented. Teams with highly co-operative goals functioned more smoothly and had better results than teams with competitive goals.[128] Accordingly, individual bonuses must give way to team bonuses. Supervisory development workshops are needed to teach managers to be facilitators rather than order givers.[129] Finally, extensive team training is required to help team members learn more about technical details, the business as a whole, and how to be team players.

At BP Norge self-managed teams were successfully introduced (see Table 10.9).[130]

Team building

Team building is a catch-all term for a whole host of techniques aimed at improving the internal functioning work teams. Whether conducted by company trainers or outside consultants, team-building workshops strive for greater co-operation, better communication and less dysfunctional conflict. Experiential learning techniques such as interpersonal trust exercises, conflict-handling role play sessions and interactive games are common. For example, Germany's Opel uses Lego® blocks to teach its car workers the tight teamwork necessary for just-in-time production.[131] Meanwhile,

> **Team building**
> experiential
> learning aimed at
> better internal
> functioning of
> teams

TABLE 10.9 BP NORGE: AN EXAMPLE OF THE SUCCESSFUL IMPLEMENTATION OF SELF-MANAGED TEAMS

The development of self-managed teams took place in three overlapping phases:

- Discovery and agitation: focusing; changing old thought patterns; recognising the differences between teamwork, groups and self-managed teams; linking the 'self-managed teams' concept to the BP Norge vision and business strategy; breaking the resistance.
- Proliferation and dissemination: exploring; establishing new ways of working; identifying teams and selecting team leaders; establishing specific team work products and measurable performance goals; transferring responsibility from the hierarchy to the self-managed teams; providing just-in-time training to develop specific competencies and mental models.
- Integration and institutionalisation: having each group hold itself accountable as a team; aligning work processes, decision making, information, measurement, performance management and organisation structure with the self-managed teams and business strategy; developing and rotating leadership; removing boundaries; and practising new competencies at higher levels of proficiency.

All of these phases are necessary for long-term success of the self-managed teams. The first phase got the most attention because it is the most challenging one (e.g. overcoming resistance).

A two-day workshop was organised representing people from different levels in the organisation. First, a group of team leaders was trained to be facilitators and coaches for their own teams. Later on, other members would become team leaders.

Employees at BP Norge could decide themselves if they wanted to participate in self-managed teams. Therefore management provided full information on self-managed teams. For instance, videos about self-managed teams were shown in which the concept was outlined both from the management perspective and the employee perspective. Examples of organisations which implemented self-managed teams successfully were also demonstrated.

There was deep scepticism but participants and facilitators talked about team development and they discussed the different stages through which any change project has to progress (denial, resistance, exploration and commitment). The use of humour also helped. During dinner on the first day, participants were asked: 'What hard questions do you have for senior management about self-managed teams – questions you or others have been the most embarrassed to ask?' Participants could be honest about their feelings and have an open dialogue. This way participants learned a lot about self-managed teams and gradually they started analysing the effectiveness of their current work groups.

SOURCE: M. Moravec, O. J. Johannessen and T. A. Hjelmas, 'Thumbs Up for Self-Managed Teams', *Management Review*, July–August 1997, pp. 42–7.

Hamburg Mannheimer organised a three-day rafting in the French Alps: 15 staff who were performing well, went on an adventure survival-camp, including mountain climbing, bungee-jumping ...[132] Insurance company Axa, sends its managers to a wine chateau in Bordeaux for management training, including team-building activities in the form of role-play and simulations of business situations.[133]

Complete coverage of the many team-building techniques would require a separate book. Consequently, the scope of our current discussion is limited to the goal of team building and the day-to-day development of self-management skills. This foundation is intended to give you a basis for selecting appropriate team-building techniques from the many you are likely to encounter in the years ahead.[134]

The goal of team building: high-performance teams

Team building allows team members to wrestle with simulated or real-life problems. Outcomes are then analysed by the team to determine what team processes need improvement. Learning stems from recognising and addressing faulty team dynamics. Perhaps one sub-team withheld key information from another, thereby hampering team progress. With cross-cultural teams becoming commonplace in today's global economy, team building is more important than ever (see the next Snapshot).[135]

snapshot

This London company has turned corporate team building into a circus

Are you ready to take your corporate team to new heights? Prepare yourself, because the next department meeting may cover the flying trapeze, acrobatic balancing and tight-wire walking, that is, if the next meeting takes place at Circus Space.

Besides being one of Europe's top circus facilities, London's Circus Space offers programmes designed to help corporate groups learn the circus way when it comes to teamwork, leadership, communication and trust. While many companies claim these values, incorporating them into the workplace can be tricky.

'When an acrobatic or flying trapeze troupe works with a director on a new act for the show, they are inherently creating a successful team that trusts and relies on each other to create an end result', says Adult Programme Manager Rob Colbert. 'Likewise in business, you need a productive team that works well together.'

The tailor-made classes, which attempt to teach a different view of simple goal, have attracted a word-of-mouth-based audience with companies like UBS Warburg, Disney, Microsoft, International Distillers and Unilever. Colbert attributes Circus Space's success to its unusual method of training.

'The main criticism of other team-building workshops from our clients is that they are either too dull or competitive, and this is where the circus training has come in', Colbert says. 'Our courses offer a shared physical experience where participants can directly gain new ways of learning and a real sense of achievement, develop a mutual support and respect for each other and have the opportunity to use the skills as a powerful management metaphor.'

Colbert says just by coming to Circus Space, companies are stepping in the right direction. 'If companies employ us to be creative with their new recruits, then companies are sending a powerful message about their expectations and how they want their new employees to work', he explains. 'Whereas with managers and directors, the companies are saying: "We want you to open up and look at new possibilities, take risks and be creative".'

SOURCE: 'Training on the Tight Wire', *Training*, November 2001, p. 31.

According to Richard Beckhard, a respected authority on organisation development, the four purposes of team building are:

■ To set goals and/or priorities.
■ To analyse or allocate the way work is performed.

- To examine the way a group is working and its processes (such as norms, decision making and communication).
- To examine relationships among the people doing the work.[136]

A nationwide survey of team members from many organisations undertaken by Wilson Learning Corporation, provides a useful model or benchmark of what we should expect of teams. The researchers' question was simply: 'What is a high-performance team?'[137] The respondents were asked to describe their peak experiences in work teams. Analysis of the survey results yielded the following eight attributes of high-performance teams:

- Participative leadership: creating an interdependency by empowering, freeing up and serving others.
- Shared responsibility: establishing an environment in which all team members feel as responsible as the manager for the performance of the work unit.
- Aligned on purpose: having a sense of common purpose about why the team exists and the function it serves.
- Good communication: creating a climate of trust and open, honest communication.
- Future focused: seeing change as an opportunity for growth.
- Focused on task: keeping meetings focused on results.
- Creative talents: applying individual talents and creativity.
- Rapid response: identifying and acting on opportunities.[138]

These eight attributes effectively combine many of today's most progressive ideas on management,[139] among them being participation, empowerment, service ethic, individual responsibility and development, self-management, trust, active listening and envisioning. But patience and diligence are also required. According to a manager familiar with work teams, 'high-performance teams may take three to five years to build'.[140] Let us keep this inspiring model of high-performance teams in mind as we conclude our discussion of team building.

Developing team members' self-management skills

A promising dimension of team building has emerged in recent years. Proponents call it Self-management leadership, defined as the process of leading others to lead themselves. An underlying assumption is that self-managed teams are likely to fail if team members are not expressly taught to engage in self-management behaviours. This makes sense because it is unreasonable to expect employees who are accustomed to being managed and led to suddenly manage and lead themselves. Transition training is required, as discussed in the prior section. A key part of the transition to self-management involves current managers engaging in self-management leadership behaviours. This is team building in the fullest sense of the term.

Six aspects of self-management leadership behaviour were isolated in a field study of a manufacturing company organised around self-managed teams. The following leadership behaviour was observed:

- Encourages self-reinforcement (e.g. getting team members to praise each other for good work and results).
- Encourages self-observation/evaluation (e.g. teaching team members to judge how well they are doing).
- Encourages self-expectation (e.g. encouraging team members to expect high performance from themselves and the team).
- Encourages self-goal-setting (e.g. having the team set its own performance goals).
- Encourages rehearsal (e.g. getting team members to think about and practise new tasks).
- Encourages self-criticism (e.g. encouraging team members to be critical of their own poor performance).[141]

According to the researchers, Charles Manz and Henry Sims, this type of leadership is a dramatic departure from traditional practices such as giving orders and/or making sure everyone gets along (see Chapter 11). Empowerment, not domination, is the overriding goal (see Chapter 13).

Self-management leadership process of leading others to lead themselves

Learning outcomes: Summary of key terms

1 Distinguish between a 'team' and a 'group'

Definitions of teams generally suggest a number of conditions which must be fulfilled before a group becomes a team: members of the group have shared goals in relation to their work; they interact with each other to achieve those shared goals; all team members have well-defined and interdependent roles; and they have an organisational identity as a team, with a defined organisational function.

2 Identify and describe the four types of work teams

Four general types of work teams are advice, production, project and action teams. Each type has its characteristic degrees of specialisation and co-ordination, work cycle and outputs.

3 Explain the ecological model of work team effectiveness

According to the ecological model, two effectiveness criteria for work teams are performance and viability. The performance criterion is met if the team satisfies its clients/customers. A work team is viable if its members are satisfied and continue contributing. An ecological perspective is appropriate because work teams require an organisational life-support system. For instance, team participation is enhanced by an organisational culture that values employee empowerment.

4 Discuss why teams fail

Teams fail because unrealistic expectations cause frustration and failure. Common management mistakes include weak strategies, creating a hostile environment for teams, faddish use of teams, not learning from team experience, vague team assignments, poor team staffing, inadequate training and a lack of trust. Team members typically fail if they try too much too soon, experience conflict over differing work styles and personalities, ignore important group dynamics, resist change, exhibit poor interpersonal skills and chemistry, and display a lack of trust.

5 List at least three things oganisations can do to build trust

Six recommended ways to build trust are through communication, support, respect (especially delegation), fairness, predictability and competence.

6 Distinguish two types of cohesiveness and summarise the related research findings

Cohesive groups have a shared sense of togetherness or a 'we' feeling. Socio-emotional cohesiveness involves emotional satisfaction. Instrumental cohesiveness involves goal-directed togetherness. There is a small but significant relationship between cohesiveness and performance. The effect is stronger for smaller teams. Commitment to task among team members strengthens the cohesiveness → performance linkage. Success can build team cohesiveness. Cohesiveness is not a cure-all for team problems. Too much cohesiveness can lead to groupthink.

7 Define quality circles, virtual teams and self-managed teams

Quality circles are small teams of volunteers who meet regularly to solve quality-related problems in their work area. Virtual teams are physically dispersed work teams that conduct their business via modern information technologies such as the Internet, email and videoconferences. Self-managed teams are work teams that perform their own administrative chores such as planning, scheduling and staffing.

Review questions

1 Why bother taking an ecological perspective of work team effectiveness?

2 Which of the factors listed in Table 10.3 is most crucial to a successful team? Explain.

3 In your personal friendships, how do you come to trust someone? How fragile is that trust? Explain.

4 Why is delegation so important to building organisational trust?

5 Why should a team leader strive for both socio-emotional and instrumental cohesiveness?

6 Are virtual teams likely to be just a passing fad? Why or why not?

7 Would you like to work on a self-managed team? Explain.

8 How would you respond to a manager who said, 'Why should I teach my people to manage themselves and work myself out of a job?'

9 Have you ever been a member of a high-performing team? If so, explain the circumstances and success factors.

Personal awareness and growth exercise

How trusting are you?

Objectives

1 To introduce you to different dimensions of interpersonal trust.

2 To measure your trust in another person.

3 To discuss the managerial implications of your propensity to trust.

Introduction

The trend toward more open and empowered organisations where teamwork and self-management are vital requires heightened interpersonal trust. Customers need to be able to trust organisations producing the goods and services they buy, managers need to trust non-managers to carry out the organisation's mission, and team members need to trust each other in order to get the job done. As with any other interpersonal skill, we need to be able to measure and improve our ability to trust others. This exercise is a step in that direction.

Instructions[142]

Think of a specific individual who currently plays an important role in your life (e.g. present or future spouse, friend, supervisor, co-worker, team member, etc.), and rate his or her trustworthiness for each statement according to the following scale. Total your responses, and compare your score with the arbitrary norms provided.

Overall trust	Strongly disagree									Strongly agree
1 I can expect this person to play fair.	1	2	3	4	5	6	7	8	9	10
2 I can confide in this person and know she/he desires to listen.	1	2	3	4	5	6	7	8	9	10
3 I can expect this person to tell me the truth.	1	2	3	4	5	6	7	8	9	10
4 This person takes time to listen to my problems and worries.	1	2	3	4	5	6	7	8	9	10

fails, the deal will be condemned as one of the biggest flops in corporate history – and both men could find themselves on the wrong side of the DaimlerChrysler supervisory board.

The strange truth today is that only a German can save the American icon. Zetsche admits that a 'not-invented-here' syndrome kept Chrysler and Mercedes from sharing much in the beginning. It took a group of senior executives several months to put together what Schrempp calls the company's 'brand bible', which decrees what is sacred about both Mercedes and Chrysler. Zetsche wants to be called a 'Chrysler guy', but the fact that he worked at Daimler for 25 years makes all the difference. Few were surprised that Schrempp chose Zetsche to take on DaimlerChrysler's greatest challenge. He's fast, decisive and an experienced troubleshooter. Zetsche revived Daimler's Freightliner truck business, in Portland, Oregon, by cutting a quarter of the workforce and reducing capacity. As chief engineer at Mercedes in the early 1990s, he fought off Japanese rivals by expanding his lineup and making development more efficient. At 38, he was the youngest member ever of Daimler's management board. Later, he took over Mercedes' sales and marketing and came away with a keen understanding of the consumer side of the business.

Certainly nobody rolled out the welcome wagon when Zetsche arrived in Detroit. For resentful company veterans, Zetsche's appointment confirmed their worst fear: that Chrysler had lost what remained of its independence. Naturally, tensions were high at an early press conference when a reporter asked the question on nearly everyone's mind: 'How many more Germans are you going to bring over?' Zetsche leaned into the microphone and answered: 'Four.' A wry smile appeared through his enormous moustache. 'My wife and three kids.'

As it turned out, Zetsche has just the combination of humility and warmth to ease tensions among Chrysler's demoralised staff. He eats in the cafeteria, interrupts plant tours to talk with workers, and even promises to shave his head (he's already half-bald) if the new Dodge Ram again topped the J.D. Power & Associates quality survey. His town hall meetings are so popular that plant officials resort to a lottery to choose participants.

Along the way, the German engineer has confounded his critics in Detroit, who included almost everybody he works with, by turning out to be a decent, even likeable fellow. He has spread a lot of misery, but he has done it with such sensitivity – and often in person – that potential antagonists usually decide to co-operate instead. After so many layoffs, no one expected Zetsche to address a United Auto Workers convention in Las Vegas in March. Indeed, few CEOs have ever ventured to speak at the union's gatherings. Zetsche not only gave a speech but also mingled with the delegates for five hours.

Zetsche's decisive leadership is welcome relief for an outfit that drifted aimlessly after the merger. 'There's not an employee around here who didn't know this company was in trouble', says James D. Donlon III, senior vice-president and controller. 'They just needed somebody to get up and tell it like it is.'

In terms of product development, Zetsche wants Chrysler to balance style with thrift – an approach he calls 'disciplined pizzazz'. He is overhauling the vehicle-development process to put more focus on the earliest stages. By pulling together teams from all areas of the company – design, engineering, marketing, manufacturing and purchasing – Zetsche hopes to reduce waste and resolve nagging quality problems without diminishing Chrysler's creative instincts.[1]

For discussion

Why would a company like Daimler think that only a German can lead one of the best-known American companies?

Someone once observed that a leader is a person who finds out which way the parade is going, jumps in front of it, and yells 'Follow me!' The plain fact is that this approach of leadership has little chance of working in today's rapidly changing world. Admired leaders, such as Nelson Mandela, Mahatma Gandhi, Body Shop's Anita Roddick, John Kennedy, Charles de Gaulle and Virgin's Richard Branson, led people in bold new directions. They envisioned how things could be improved, rallied followers and refused to accept failure. In short, successful leaders are those individuals who

TABLE 11.1 WHAT THE SUCCESSFUL BUSINESS LEADER SHOULD HAVE AND WHAT HE REALLY HAS

	What he/she should have (%)	What my present CEO has (%)
Able to build effective teams	96	50
Knows how to listen	93	44
Capable of making decisions on his own	87	66
Knows how to retain good people	86	39
Energetic	85	62
Innovative	83	47
Visionary	79	45
Has high ethical standards	76	53
Strong-willed	70	65
Charismatic	54	34
Motivated by power	35	59
Motivated by money	17	40
Ruthless	10	28
Paternalistic	6	24

SOURCE: 'Leadership', *Management Centre Europe*, 1988, p. 11.

can make a noticeable difference. But how much of a difference can leaders make in modern organisations?

OB researchers have discovered that leaders can make a difference. One study, for example, tracked the relationship between net profit and leadership in 167 companies from 13 industries. It also covered a time span of 20 years. Higher net profits were earned by companies with effective leaders.[2] Successful organisational change is highly dependent upon effective leadership throughout an organisation. According to John Kotter, organisational change expert, successful organisational transformation requires 70 to 90 per cent leadership and 10 to 30 per cent management.[3] More on organisational change and on John Kotter's insights can be read in Chapter 17. In a carefully controlled study of Icelandic fishing ships, it was found that differences in skippers accounted for a third to half the catch.[4] Leadership can make a difference.

On the other hand, subordinates are generally not very pleased with their leaders, as can be found in Table 11.1.

But even the research data are not very conclusive. Peter Wright, a British OB specialist, offers the following view in his book on managerial leadership:

> Most research findings, even when significant, account for a relatively small amount of the variance in subordinates' work performance and satisfaction. Similarly, there are a great many alternative approaches to leadership theory, the different theories within any one approach often contradict each other, and none is without flaws or limitations.[5]

Leadership is culturally bound. Americans are the only people who talk so openly – sometimes obsessively – about the very notion of leadership. In America, leadership has become something of a cult concept. The French, tellingly, have no adequate word of their own for it. Germans have perfectly good words for leader and leadership; but Hitler rendered them politically incorrect. Mussolini similarly stigmatised the word *duce*.[6] The situation is even more extreme in the Netherlands or the Scandinavian countries, where leaders do not behave like leaders at all, at least not in the way described in American textbooks.[7]

An excellent example of informal leadership is the way Ingvar Kamprad managed IKEA, the world's largest home furnishing chain. The patriarchal way in which he treated his customers and staff reflected his philosophy of life. He is blessed with a genuine warmth and interest in people, which is undoubtedly one of the most important reasons for his success. Thanks to his influence, the company has an informal atmosphere which stresses simplicity. It is reflected in the neat but casual dress of the employees – jeans and sweaters – and in the relaxed office atmosphere where practically everyone sits in an open-plan office.[8]

This culturally bound phenomenon is not only restricted to charismatic leaders or to top management. The tendency to rely on supervision is clearly much stronger in English-speaking countries, especially in the US, than in other countries. Figure 11.1 gives a survey of the intensity of supervision in a number of European countries and in the US. Supervision varies from very low in Switzerland to very high in the US.

Concepts of leadership also differ between clusters of European countries. Northwestern European countries, and in particular the Nordic countries, score very highly on a dimension called 'interpersonal directness and proximity'. In these countries successful business leaders are seen as enthusiastic, encouraging, sincere, informal, trustworthy and inspirational. In countries such as Georgia, Poland, Turkey and Slovenia, successful leaders are seen as self-interested, non-participative, asocial, very administrative, well organised, face-saving and indirect. The Germanic cluster (Germany, Austria, Switzerland) and the Czech Republic score very highly on the dimension called 'autonomy': successful leaders are seen as independent, autonomous, unique and even self-sacrificing. The Latin cluster (Portugal, Spain, Italy) is situated on the other end of this dimension: middle management in those countries see successful leaders as visionary, team integrators and status conscious.[9]

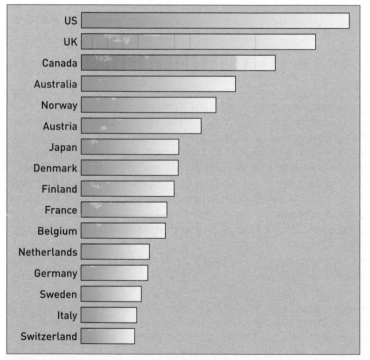

FIGURE 11.1 THE INTENSITY OF SUPERVISION IN 16 COUNTRIES

SOURCE: D. Gordon, 'Boxes of Different Stripes: A Cross National Perspective on Monitoring and Supervision', *AEA Papers and Proceedings*, May 1994, p. 376.

Leadership, and especially its most pronounced form, charismatic leadership, is a mixed blessing. Most American scholars tend to emphasise the beneficial aspects of leadership. Europeans are much more sceptical. It comes as no surprise that the most influential European writer on leadership, Manfred Kets de Vries, who teaches leadership at Insead, near Paris, has built a world reputation through his highly critical writings on the subject. He often describes leaders as neurotic and especially as narcissistic.

After formally defining the term 'leadership', this chapter focuses on the following areas: trait and behavioural approaches to leadership; alternative situational theories of leadership; charismatic leadership; and additional perspectives on leadership. Because there are so many different leadership theories within each of these areas, it is impossible to discuss them all.

What does leadership involve? ?Q~

Because the topic of leadership has fascinated people for centuries, many definitions abound. This section presents a definition of leadership and highlights the similarities and differences between leading and managing.

What is leadership?

Disagreement about the definition of leadership stems from the fact that it involves a complex interaction between the leader, followers and situation. For example, some researchers define leadership in terms of personality and physical traits, while others believe leadership is represented by a set of prescribed behaviours. In contrast, other researchers believe that leadership is a temporary role that can be filled by anyone. There is a common thread, however, among the different definitions of leadership. The common thread is social influence.

The succinct definition of **Leadership** as social influence can be elaborated, for the purpose of this chapter, to 'a social influence process in which the leader seeks the voluntary participation of subordinates in an effort to reach organisational goals.'[10] An even more formal definition is given by the GLOBE research group as: 'the ability of an individual to influence, motivate and enable others to contribute toward the effectiveness and success of organisations of which they are members'.[11]

> Leadership
> influencing
> employees to
> voluntarily
> pursue
> organisational
> goals

Note that both definitions are definitions of organisational leadership, not leadership in general As you can see from this definition, leadership clearly entails more than wielding power and exercising authority, and is exhibited on different levels. At the individual level, for example, leadership involves mentoring, coaching, inspiring and motivating. Leaders build teams, create cohesion and resolve conflicts at the group level. Finally, leaders build culture and create change at the organisational level.[12]

Figure 11.2 provides a conceptual framework for understanding leadership. It was created by integrating components of the different theories and models discussed in this chapter.

Figure 11.2 indicates that certain leader characteristics or traits are the foundation of effective leadership. In turn, these characteristics affect an individual's ability to employ managerial behaviour

FIGURE 11.2 A CONCEPTUAL FRAMEWORK FOR UNDERSTANDING LEADERSHIP

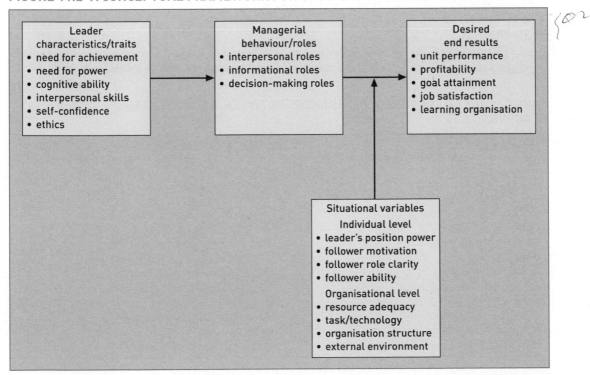

SOURCE: Adapted in part from G. Yukl, 'Managerial Leadership: A Review of Theory and Research', *Journal of Management*, June 1989, p. 274.

and roles. Effective leadership also depends on various situational variables. These variables are important components of the contingency leadership theories discussed later in this chapter. Finally, leadership is results-oriented.

Leading versus managing

It is important to appreciate the difference between leadership and management in order to fully understand what leadership is all about. Bernard Bass, a leadership expert, concluded that: 'Leaders manage and managers lead but the two activities are not synonymous.'[13] Bass tells us that although leadership and management overlap, each entails a unique set of activities or functions. Broadly speaking, managers typically perform functions associated with planning, investigating, organising and control; while leaders deal with the interpersonal aspects of a manager's job. Leaders inspire others, provide emotional support and try to get employees to rally around a common goal. Management is about coping with complexity. As Harvard-specialist John Kotter has stressed over and over again: leadership is about coping with change.[14] The most often cited difference has been formulated by management and leadership gurus like Peter Drucker and Warren Bennis: 'Management is doing things right; leadership is doing the right things.'[15]

It has become a fad to exaggerate the difference between managers and leaders. More and more observers of the world of OB will use John Kotter's words: 'Most corporations today are overly managed and underled'. Table 11.2 summarises the contrast between 'weak' managers and 'real' leaders.

The distinction between management and leadership is more or less ideological, it is very often a distinction between 'bad' and 'good', where management stands for the cold, static, bureaucratic or non-inspiring and leadership for the dynamic, future-oriented or inspiring. This distinction however, is purely artificial: there is nothing good or bad about management or leadership as such. To illustrate our point of view, take a look at Table 11.3.

Trait and behavioural theories of leadership

This section examines the two earliest approaches used to explain leadership. Trait theories focused on identifying the personal traits that differentiated leaders from followers. Behavioural theorists examined leadership from a different perspective. They tried to uncover the different kinds of leader behaviour that resulted in higher work group performance.

Trait theory

Until 1950 the prevailing belief was that leaders were born not made. Selected people were thought to possess inborn traits that made them successful leaders: hence the idea of a Leader trait.

Leader trait
personal characteristic that differentiates a leader from a follower

TABLE 11.2 THE SUPPOSED DIFFERENCES BETWEEN 'WEAK' MANAGERS AND 'REAL' LEADERS

Managers...	Leaders...
Wait until it happens	Are pro-active
Are happy with the status quo	Challenge the status quo
Are pursuing objectives	Have a vision
Are experts of the past	Are experts of the future
Do the things right	Do the right things
Follow their job description	Change their job description
Respect budgets	Create value
Avoid mistakes	Seek learning opportunities
See information as power	Share information
Are myopic	Take the broad view
Are difficult to reach	Are approachable
Adore status symbols	Want the best for all
Use reward and punishment	Inspire and motivate

SOURCE: M. Buelens, 'The Informal Organization: leading for Performance', in *Integrated Performance Management: A Guide to Strategy Implementation*, eds. K. Verweire and L. A. A. Van den Berghe, (London: Sage Publications, 2004), pp. 167–79.

TABLE 11.3 THE DIFFERENCE BETWEEN 'SICK' LEADERS AND 'DEDICATED' MANAGERS

Managers . . .	Leaders . . .
Remain humble	Are megalomaniac
Behave like a good citizen	Spend too much money on pet projects
Listen to collaborators	Listen to themselves
Keep balance	Become psychopaths
Think before they act	Have big hairy audacious goals
End with a golden watch	End in prison or mental hospitals
Remain in the background	Are on the front cover
Follow realistic strategies	Follow wish-driven strategies

SOURCE: M. Buelens, 'The Informal Organization: leading for Performance', in *Integrated Performance Management: A Guide to Strategy Implementation*, eds. K. Verweire and L. A. A. Van den Berghe, (London: Sage Publications, 2004), pp. 167–79.

Before the Second World War hundreds of studies were conducted to pinpoint the traits of successful leaders. Dozens of leadership traits were identified. During the post-war period, however, enthusiasm was replaced by widespread criticism. Studies conducted by Ralph Stogdill in 1948 and by Richard Mann in 1959, which sought to summarise the impact of traits on leadership, caused the trait approach to fall into disfavour.

STOGDILL'S AND MANN'S FINDINGS

Based on his review, Stogdill concluded that five traits tended to differentiate leaders from average followers: (1) intelligence, (2) dominance, (3) self-confidence, (4) level of energy and activity, and (5) task-relevant knowledge.[16] Jack Welch, former chief executive officer of General Electric, has been one of the most highly regarded managers in the world. Consider the leadership traits that he indicated he was looking for in his replacement during an interview with *Fortune*:

> Vision. Courage. The four E's: energy, ability to energize others, the edge to make tough decisions and execution, which is key because you can't just decide but have got to follow up in 19 ways. Judgement. The self-confidence to always hire someone who's better than you. Are they growing things? Do they add new insights to the businesses they run? Do they like to nurture small businesses?
>
> And one more: an insatiable appetite for accomplishment. Too many CEOs, Welch once said, believe that the high point comes the day they land the job. Not Welch, who says, 'I'm 63 and finally getting smart.'[17]

Although Welch was looking for some of the same traits as those identified by Ralph Stogdill, research revealed that these five traits did not accurately predict which individuals became leaders in organisations.

Mann's review was similarly disappointing for the trait theorists. Among the seven categories of personality traits he examined, Mann found intelligence was the best predictor of leadership. However, Mann warned that all observed positive relationships between traits and leadership were weak (correlations averaged about 0.15).[18]

Together, Stogdill's and Mann's findings nearly dealt a death blow to the trait approach. But now, decades later, leadership traits are once again receiving serious research attention.

CONTEMPORARY TRAIT RESEARCH

A 1986 meta-analysis by Robert Lord and his associates remedied a methodological shortcoming of previous trait data analyses. Based on a re-analysis of Mann's data and subsequent studies, Lord concluded that people have leadership prototypes that affect our perceptions of who is and who is not an effective leader. Your **Leadership prototype** is a mental representation of the traits and behaviours that you believe are possessed by leaders. We thus tend to perceive that someone is a leader when he or she exhibits traits or types of behaviour that are consistent with our prototypes.[19] Lord's research

Leadership prototype mental representation of the traits and behaviours possessed by leaders

demonstrated that people are perceived as being leaders when they exhibit the traits associated with intelligence, masculinity and dominance. A more recent study of 200 students also confirmed the idea that leadership prototypes influence leadership perceptions. Results revealed that perceptions of an individual as a leader were affected by that person's sex – males were perceived to be leaders more than females – and behavioural flexibility. People who were more behaviourally flexible were perceived to be more like a leader.[20] Recently, a study of 6052 middle-level managers from 22 European countries revealed that leadership prototypes are culturally based. In other words, leadership prototypes are influenced by national cultural values.[21]

Another pair of leadership researchers attempted to identify key leadership traits by asking the following open-ended question to more than 20 000 people around the world: 'What values (personal traits or characteristics) do you look for and admire in your superiors?' The top four traits included honesty, forward-lookingness, inspiration and competence.[22] The researchers concluded that these four traits constitute a leader's credibility. This research suggests that people want their leaders to be credible and to have a sense of direction. This conclusion is consistent with recent concerns regarding ethical and legal lapses at companies such as Enron.

> A deep cynicism has settled over the corporate world as many employees in a variety of businesses wonder how much, if at all, they can trust their bosses. In corporate America, the trigger event was the Enron scandal. But while more becomes known about the energy's trader rotten numbers, and the cheating and lying that apparently prevailed in its senior ranks, accounting problems and ethical breaches are surfacing at a growing list of other companies.[23]

In 1998 Daniel Goleman wrote an influential article in *Harvard Business Review*, in which he applied principles of emotional intelligence to leadership.[24] Since then more and more articles and books quote his (unproven) basic insights: understanding your own and other people's emotions well helps you to move people in the direction of accomplishing desired goals. In practice, this means that all leaders have to understand their emotions (self-awareness), have to control disruptive impulses and moods and understand the emotional make-up of others. In this approach the most important traits are self-knowledge, self-control, empathy and social intelligence (also see Chapter 3).

GENDER AND LEADERSHIP

The increase in the number of women in the workforce has generated much interest in understanding the similarities and differences between female and male leaders. Important issues concern whether women and men assume varying leadership roles within work groups, use different leadership styles, are more or less effective in leadership roles and whether there are situational differences that produce gender differences in leadership effectiveness. Three meta-analyses were conducted to summarise research pertaining to these issues.

The first meta-analysis demonstrated that men and women differed in the type of leadership roles they assumed within work groups. Men were seen as displaying more overall leadership and task leadership. In contrast, women were perceived as displaying more social leadership.[25] Results from the second meta-analysis revealed that leadership styles varied by gender. Women used a more democratic or participative style than men. Men employed a more autocratic and directive style than women.[26] Finally, a meta-analysis of more than 75 studies uncovered three key findings:

- Female and male leaders were rated as equally effective. This is a very positive outcome because it suggests that despite barriers and possible negative stereotypes toward female leaders, female and male leaders were equally effective.
- Men were rated as more effective leaders than women when their roles were defined in more masculine terms, and women were more effective than men in roles defined in less masculine terms.
- Gender differences in leadership effectiveness were associated with the percentage of male leaders and male subordinates. Specifically, male leaders were seen as more effective than females when there was a greater percentage of male leaders and male subordinates. Interestingly, a similar positive bias in leadership effectiveness was not found for women.[27]

Research carried out in the UK by Hay Management Consultants on 15 male and 20 female leaders and 191 male and female subordinates concluded the following. The styles that female managers use are not working as effectively with their male subordinates. The men do not see female managers doing such things as giving clear directions, explaining decisions and monitoring task performance. The authoritative style is an effective and important one. If women are not seen as using it by men, this may not only affect their team's effectiveness but could influence their visibility with colleagues and bosses.[28] In contrast to these traits, the next Snapshot outlines the relevant leadership traits of Russian leaders from the 1400s to the present day. As you can see, Russian organisations need to nurture and develop a similar but different set of leadership traits.

RUSSIAN LEADERSHIP TRAITS IN THREE ERAS

Leadership trait	Traditional Russian society (1400s to 1917)	The red executive (1917 to 1991)	The market-oriented manager (1991 to present)
Leadership motivation Power	Powerful autocrats	Centralised leadership stifled grass-roots democracy	Shared power and ownership
Responsibility	Centralisation of responsibility	Micromanagers and macropuppets	Delegation and strategic decision making
Drive Achievement motivation	Don't rock the boat	Frustrated pawns	The sky's the limit
Ambition	Equal poverty for all	Service to party and collective good	Overcoming the sin of being a winner
Initiative	Look both ways	Meticulous rule following and behind-the-scenes finessing	Let's do business
Energy	Concentrated spasms of work	8-hour day, 8-to-8, firefighting	8-day week, chasing opportunities
Tenacity	Life is a struggle	Struggling to accomplish the routine	Struggling to accomplish the new
Honesty and integrity Dual ethical standard	Deception in dealings . . . loyalty in friendships	Two sets of books, personal integrity	Wild capitalism, personal trust
Using connections	Currying favour with landowners	Greasing the wheels of the state	Greasing palms, but learning to do business straight
Self-confidence	From helplessness to bravado	From inferior quality to 'big is beautiful'	From cynicism to overpromising

SOURCE: S. M. Puffer, 'Understanding the Bear: A Portrait of Russian Business Leaders', *Academy of Management Executive*, February 1994, p. 42. Used with permission.

Behavioural styles theory

This phase of leadership research began during the Second World War as part of an effort to develop better military leaders. It was a response to the seeming inability of trait theory to explain leadership effectiveness and to the human relations movement, an offshoot of the Hawthorne Studies (in Chapter 1). The thrust of early behavioural leadership theory was to focus on leader behaviour, instead of on personality traits. It was believed that leader behaviour directly influenced the effectiveness of the work group. This led researchers to identify patterns of behaviour (called leadership styles) that enabled leaders to influence others effectively.

THE OHIO STATE STUDIES

Researchers at Ohio State University began by generating a list of the types of behaviour exhibited by leaders. At one point, the list contained 1800 statements describing nine categories. Ultimately, the Ohio State researchers concluded there were only two independent dimensions to describe the behaviour of a leader: consideration and initiating structure. Consideration, involving a focus on a concern for group members' needs and desires, is well illustrated by the leadership style of Penny Hughes, former president of Coca-Cola Company Great Britain and Ireland.

> According to a close colleague of hers: Penny is really excellent at establishing rapport with people and encouraging them to be more open, more challenging. To an unusual and refreshing degree she genuinely values people and is totally fair with them. She often walks around the office, sits on the back of a chair and shares a joke with us. There is always lots of laughter![29]

Consideration creating mutual respect and trust between leader and followers

Initiating structure is leader behaviour that organises and defines what group members should be doing to maximise output. These two dimensions of leader behaviour were oriented at right angles to yield four behavioural styles of leadership (see Figure 11.3).

Initially, it was hypothesised that a high-structure, high-consideration style would be the one best style of leadership. Over the years, the effectiveness of this style has been tested many times. Overall, results have been mixed. Researchers thus concluded that there is not one best style of leadership.[30] Rather, it is argued that effectiveness of a given leadership style depends on situational factors.

Initiating structure organising and defining what group members should be doing

UNIVERSITY OF MICHIGAN STUDIES

As in the Ohio State studies, this research sought to identify behavioural differences between effective and ineffective leaders. Researchers identified two different styles of leadership: one was centred on the employee, the other on the job. These behavioural styles parallel the consideration and initiating-structure styles identified by the Ohio State group. In summarising the results of these studies, one management expert concluded that effective leaders:

FIGURE 11.3 FOUR LEADERSHIP STYLES DERIVED FROM THE OHIO STATE STUDIES

		Initiating structure	
		Low	**High**
Consideration	**High**	Low structure, high consideration Less emphasis is placed on structuring employee tasks while the leader concentrates on satisfying employee needs and wants	High structure, high consideration The leader provides a lot of guidance about how tasks can be completed while being highly considerate of employee needs and wants
	Low	Low structure, low consideration The leader fails to provide necessary structure and demonstrates little consideration for employee needs and wants	High structure, low consideration Primary emphasis is placed on structuring employee tasks while the leader demonstrates little consideration for employee needs and wants

420

- Tend to have supportive or employee-centred relationships with employees.
- Use group rather than individual methods of supervision.
- Set high performance goals.[31]

BLAKE AND MOUTON'S MANAGERIAL/LEADERSHIP GRID® Q3

Perhaps the most widely known behavioural styles model of leadership is the Managerial Grid®. Behavioural scientists Robert Blake and Jane Srygley Mouton, developed and trademarked the highly controversial grid.[32] They use it to demonstrate that there is one best style of leadership. Blake and Mouton's Managerial Grid® (renamed the Leadership Grid® in 1991) is a matrix formed by the intersection of two dimensions of leader behaviour (see Figure 11.4). On the horizontal axis is 'concern for production'. 'Concern for people' is on the vertical axis.

Blake and Mouton point out that 'the variables of the Managerial Grid® are attitudinal and conceptual, with behaviour descriptions derived from and connected with the thinking that lies behind action'.[33] In other words, concern for production and concern for people involve attitudes and patterns of thinking, as well as specific types of behaviour. By scaling each axis of the grid from 1 to 9, Blake and Mouton were able to plot five leadership styles. Because it emphasises teamwork and

> Leadership Grid® represents four leadership styles found by crossing concern for production and concern for people

FIGURE 11.4 THE LEADERSHIP GRID

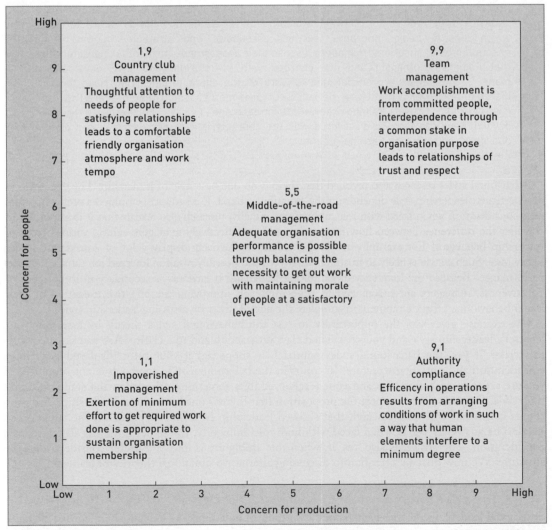

SOURCE: From *Leadership Dilemmas – Grid Solutions*, p. 29 by Robert R. Blake and Anne Adams McCanse.

interdependence, the 9,9 style is considered by Blake and Mouton to be the best, regardless of the situation.

In support of the 9,9 style, Blake and Mouton cite the results of a study in which 100 experienced managers were asked to select the best way of handling 12 managerial situations. Between 72 and 90 per cent of the managers selected the 9,9 style for each of the 12 situations.[34] Moreover, Blake and Mouton report, 'The 9,9, orientation ... leads to productivity, satisfaction, creativity and health.'[35] Critics point out that Blake and Mouton's research may be self-serving. At issue is the grid's extensive use as a training and consulting tool for diagnosing and correcting organisational problems.

BEHAVIOURAL STYLES THEORY IN PERSPECTIVE

By emphasising the behaviour of leaders, something that is learned, the behavioural style approach makes it clear that leaders are made, not born. This is the opposite of the traditional assumption of the trait theorists. Given what we know about behaviour shaping and model-based training, the behaviour of a leader can be systematically improved and developed. Consider, for example, how Steve Sitek, director of performance development and training at Ernst and Young's Finance, Technology and Administration Division, is striving to grow and develop leadership talent within the organisation.

> Sitek oversees a senior development programme that helps executives gain feedback on how they measure up against 11 critical leadership characteristics. Internal studies have shown a direct correlation between executive performance and the 11 characteristics, which include being innovative, excited, persuasive and strategic. In one-to-one encounters with superiors, managers discuss their assessments to identify characteristics that need strengthening and are charged with structuring their own development plans .... Managers are encouraged to work on the characteristics they need to grow incrementally over a multi-year period. Sitek produces specific training geared to each characteristic. 'I have a training programme for each one', he says. 'For example, the No. 1 development gap that we discovered was the characteristic of persuasiveness. I offer a one-day programme on this characteristic.'[36]

Behavioural styles research also revealed that there is no one best style of leadership. The effectiveness of a particular leadership style depends on the situation at hand. For instance, employees prefer structure over consideration when faced with role ambiguity.[37] Finally, research also reveals that it is important to consider the difference between how frequently and how effectively managers exhibit various types of leadership behaviour. For example, a manager might ineffectively display a lot of considerate leader behaviours. Such a style is likely to frustrate employees and possibly result in lowered job satisfaction and performance. Because the frequency of exhibiting leadership behaviours is secondary in importance to effectiveness, managers are encouraged to concentrate on improving the effective execution of their leader behaviours.[38] Take a moment to complete the next Activity on assessing leadership style.

The exercise gives you the opportunity to test the behavioural styles theory by assessing your lecturer's leadership style and your associated class satisfaction and role clarity. Are you satisfied with this class? If yes, the behavioural styles approach is supported if your tutor displayed both high consideration and initiating structure. In contrast, the behavioural style approach is not supported if you are satisfied with this class and your teacher exhibits something other than the standard high-high style. Do your results support the proposition that there is one best style of leadership? Are your results consistent with past research that showed leadership behaviour depends on the situation at hand? The answer is 'yes' if, when faced with high role ambiguity, you prefer initiating structure over consideration. The answer is also 'yes' if, when role ambiguity is low, you prefer consideration over structure. We now turn our attention to discussing alternative situational theories of leadership.

Situational theories propose that leader styles should match the situation at hand

Situational theories

Situational leadership theories came about as a result of an attempt to explain the inconsistent findings about traits and styles. **Situational theories** propose that the effectiveness of a particular style of leader behaviour depends on the situation. As situations change, different styles become appropriate.

Assessing the tutor's leadership style, study group satisfaction and student role clarity

Instructions

A team of researchers converted a set of leadership measures for application in a student setting. For each of the items shown here, use the following rating scale to circle the answer that best represents your feelings. Next, use the scoring key to calculate the scores for your lecturer's leadership style, your study group satisfaction and student role clarity.

1 = Strongly disagree
2 = Disagree
3 = Neither agree nor disagree
4 = Agree
5 = Strongly agree

1 My tutor behaves in a manner which is thoughtful of my personal needs.	1 2 3 4 5
2 My tutor maintains a friendly working relationship with me.	1 2 3 4 5
3 My tutor looks out for my personal welfare.	1 2 3 4 5
4 My tutor gives clear explanations of what is expected of me.	1 2 3 4 5
5 My tutor tells me the performance goals for the class.	1 2 3 4 5
6 My tutor explains the level of performance that is expected of me.	1 2 3 4 5
7 I am satisfied with the variety of study group assignments.	1 2 3 4 5
8 I am satisfied with the way my tutor handles the students.	1 2 3 4 5
9 I am satisfied with the spirit of co-operation among my fellow students.	1 2 3 4 5
10 I know exactly what my responsibilities are.	1 2 3 4 5
11 I am given clear explanations of what has to be done.	1 2 3 4 5

Scoring key

Tutor consideration (1, 2, 3) _____
Tutor initiating structure (4, 5, 6) _____
Study group satisfaction (7, 8, 9) _____
Role clarity (10, 11) _____

Arbitrary norms

Low consideration = 3–8
High consideration = 9–15
Low structure = 3–8
High structure = 9–15
Low satisfaction = 3–8
High satisfaction = 9–15
Low role clarity = 2–5
High role clarity = 6–10

SOURCE: The survey was adapted from A. J. Kinicki and C. A. Schriesheim, 'Teachers as Leaders: A Moderator Variable Approach', *Journal of Educational Psychology*, 1978, pp. 928–35.

activity

This directly challenges the idea of one best style of leadership. Let us closely examine three alternative situational theories of leadership.

Fiedler's contingency model

Fred Fiedler, an OB scholar, developed a situational model of leadership. It is the oldest and one of the most widely known models of leadership. Fiedler's model is based on the following assumption:

> The performance of a leader depends on two interrelated factors: the degree to which the situation gives the leader control and influence – that is, the likelihood that [the leader] can successfully accomplish the job; and the leader's basic motivation – that is, whether [the leader's] self-esteem depends primarily on accomplishing the task or on having close supportive relations with others.[39]

With respect to a leader's basic motivation, Fiedler believes that leaders are either task motivated or relationship motivated. These basic motivations are similar to initiating structure/concern for production and consideration/concern for people. Consider the basic leadership motivation possessed by Cynthia Danaher, general manager of Hewlett-Packard's Medical Products Group:

> Once a manager is in charge of thousands of employees, the ability to set the direction and delegate is more vital than team-building and coaching, she believes .... When Ms Danaher changed her top management team and restructured the Medical Products Group, moving out of slow-growth businesses to focus on more profitable clinical equipment, she had to relinquish her need for approval. 'Change is painful, and someone has to be the bad guy', she says. Suddenly employees she considered friends avoided her and told her she was ruining the group. 'I wasn't used to tolerating that, and I'd try to explain over and over why change had to occur', she says. Over time, she has learned to simply 'charge ahead', accepting that not everyone will follow and that some won't survive.[40]

Clearly, Danaher has used a 'task motivated' style of leadership to create organisational change within Hewlett-Packard.

Fiedler's theory is also based on the premise that leaders have one dominant leadership style that is resistant to change. He suggests that leaders must learn to manipulate or influence the leadership situation in order to create a 'match' between their leadership style and the amount of control within the situation at hand. After discussing the components of situational control and the leadership matching process, we review relevant research and some practical implications.[41]

SITUATIONAL CONTROL

Situational control refers to the amount of control and influence the leader has in her or his immediate work environment. Situational control ranges from high to low. High control implies that the leader's decisions will produce predictable results because the leader has the ability to influence work outcomes. Low control implies that the leader's decisions may not influence work outcomes because the leader has very little influence. There are three dimensions of situational control: leader–member relations, task structure and position power. These dimensions vary independently, forming eight combinations of situational control (see Figure 11.5).

The three dimensions of situational control are as follows.

Leader–member relations
extent to which leader has the support, loyalty and trust of work group

■ **Leader–member relations** is the most important component of situational control. Good leader–member relations suggest that the leader can depend on the group, thus ensuring that the work group will try to meet the leader's goals and objectives.

FIGURE 11.5 REPRESENTATION OF FIEDLER'S CONTINGENCY MODEL

Situational control	High control situations			Moderate control situations			Low control situations	
Leader–member relations	Good	Good	Good	Good	Poor	Poor	Poor	Poor
Task structure	High	High	Low	Low	High	High	Low	Low
Position power	Strong	Weak	Strong	Weak	Strong	Weak	Strong	Weak
Situation	I	II	III	IV	V	VI	VII	VIII

Optimal leadership style	Task-motivated leadership	Relationship-motivated leadership	Task-motivated leadership

SOURCE: Adapted from F. E. Fiedler, 'Situational Control and a Dynamic Theory of Leadership', in *Managerial Control and Organizational Democracy*, eds B. King, S. Streufert and F. E. Fiedler (New York: John Wiley & Sons, 1978), p. 114.

■ **Task structure** is the second most important component of situational control. A managerial job, for example, contains less structure than that of a bank teller. Because structured tasks have guidelines for how the job should be completed, the leader has more control and influence over employees performing such tasks.

■ **Position power**, the final component, covers the leader's formal power to reward, punish or otherwise obtain compliance from employees.[42]

Task structure amount of structure contained within work tasks

Position power degree to which leader has formal power

LINKING LEADERSHIP MOTIVATION AND SITUATIONAL CONTROL

Fiedler's complete contingency model is presented in Figure 11.5. The last row under the Situational control column shows that there are eight different leadership situations. Each situation represents a unique combination of leader–member relations, task structure and position power. Situations I, II, and III represent high control situations. The figure also shows that task-motivated leaders are expected to be the most effective in situations of high control. Under conditions of moderate control (situations IV, V, and VI), relationship-motivated leaders are thought to be the most effective. Finally, the results orientation of task-motivated leaders is predicted to be more effective under conditions of low control (situations VII and VIII).

RESEARCH FINDINGS AND PRACTICAL IMPLICATIONS

The overall accuracy of Fiedler's contingency model was tested by means of a meta-analysis of 35 studies containing 137 leader-style performance relations. The researchers found the following to be true:

■ The contingency theory was correctly deduced from studies on which it was based.
■ In laboratory studies testing the model, the theory was supported for all leadership situations except situation II.
■ In field studies testing the model, three of the eight situations (IV, V and VII) produced completely supportive results, while partial support was obtained for situations I, II, III, VI and VIII.

A more recent meta-analysis of data obtained from 1282 groups also provided mixed support for the contingency model.[43] These findings suggest that Fiedler's model needs theoretical refinement.[44]

The major contribution of Fiedler's model is that it prompted others to examine the contingency nature of leadership. This research, in turn, reinforced the notion that there is no one best style of leadership. Leaders are advised to alter their task and relationship orientation to fit the demands of the situation at hand.

Path–goal theory

Path–goal theory is based on the expectancy theory of motivation discussed previously in Chapter 6. Expectancy theory proposes that motivation to exert effort increases as one's effort → performance → outcome expectations improve. Path–goal theory focuses on how leaders influence followers' expectations.

According to the path–goal model, behaviour of a leader is acceptable when employees view it as a source of satisfaction or as paving the way to future satisfaction. In addition, it is motivational to the extent that it clears the obstacles to goal accomplishment, provides the guidance and support needed by employees and ties meaningful rewards to goal accomplishment. Because the model deals with pathways to goals and rewards it is called the 'path–goal' theory of leadership. House sees the leader's main job as helping employees to keep to the right paths to reach challenging goals and valued rewards. This approach has a very intuitive appeal. Leaders are always interested in changing people's behaviour so that they produce more, better or other results. This theory suggests that, in most cases, you begin better by telling them clearly what results you are looking for. Then you discuss how to get those results and you have them experience the rewards once they have obtained the results. If this experience is too far away (e.g. promotion), you visualise the way from efforts to results and from results to rewards.

LEADERSHIP STYLES

House believes leaders can exhibit more than one leadership style. This contrasts with Fiedler, who proposes that leaders have only one dominant style. The four leadership styles identified by House are as follows:

- Directive leadership. Providing guidance to employees about what should be done and how to do it, scheduling work and maintaining standards of performance.
- Supportive leadership. Showing concern for the well-being and needs of employees, being friendly and approachable, and treating workers as equals.
- Participative leadership. Consulting with employees and seriously considering their ideas when making decisions.
- Achievement-oriented leadership. Encouraging employees to perform at their highest level by setting challenging goals, emphasising excellence and demonstrating confidence in employee abilities.[45]

Research evidence supports the idea that leaders exhibit more than one leadership style.[46] Descriptions of business leaders reinforce these findings. In the 1980s and early 1990s Percy Barnevik, then CEO of the Swedish-Swiss group Asea Brown Boveri was one of the most admired business leaders in Europe. He used multiple leadership styles. When he introduced a matrix organisation and seriously reduced staff numbers, he preferred to communicate directly with the 206 000 staff members: 'You cannot hide up there in an ivory tower. You have to be out there.' Although he prefers a persuasive approach when dealing with conflicts, he had to adopt a severe approach when he was faced with stubborn unions in the 1980s. It was only by issuing an ultimatum that Barnevik achieved the cuts he wanted.[47]

CONTINGENCY FACTORS

Contingency factors *situational variables that influence the appropriateness of a leadership style*

Contingency factors affect expectancy or path–goal perceptions. Contingency factors are situational factors that cause one style of leadership to be more effective than another. This model has two groups of contingency variables. They are employee characteristics and environmental factors. Five important employee characteristics are their locus of control, task ability, need for achievement, experience, and need for clarity. Three relevant environmental factors are the employee's task, authority system and work group. All these factors have the potential for hindering or motivating employees.

VALIDITY AND REVISION OF THE PATH–GOAL MODEL

There have been about 50 studies testing various predictions derived from House's original model. Results have been mixed, with some studies supporting the theory and others not. House thus proposed a new version of his theory.[48] Among other changes he places more emphasis on the need for leaders to foster intrinsic motivation (see Chapters 5 and 6) through empowerment (see Chapter 12). The most important change deals with 'shared leadership'. An employee does not have to be a supervisor or manager to engage in leader behaviour. Leadership can be shared among many employees within an organisation.

Hersey and Blanchard's situational leadership theory

Readiness *follower's ability and willingness to complete a task*

Situational leadership theory (SLT) was developed by management writers Paul Hersey and Kenneth Blanchard.[49] According to their theory, effective leadership behaviour depends on the level of readiness on the part of a leader's followers. Readiness is defined as the extent to which a follower possesses the ability and willingness to complete a task. Willingness is a combination of confidence, commitment and motivation.

The SLT model is summarised in Figure 11.6. The appropriate leadership style is found by cross-referencing follower readiness (which varies from low to high) with one of four leadership styles. The four leadership styles represent combinations of task- and relationship-oriented leader behaviours (S1 to S4). Leaders are encouraged to use a 'telling style' (directive) for followers with low readiness. This style combines high task-oriented leader behaviours, such as providing instructions, with low relationship-oriented behaviours, such as close supervision (see Figure 11.6). As follower readiness increases, leaders are advised to gradually move from a telling to a selling style, then on to a participating and, ultimately, a delegating style. In the most recent description of this model, the four leadership styles depicted in Figure 11.6 are referred to as telling or directing (S1), persuading or coaching (S2), participating or supporting (S3), and delegating (S4).[50]

Although SLT is widely used as a training tool, it is not strongly supported by scientific research.

FIGURE 11.6 SITUATIONAL LEADERSHIP MODEL

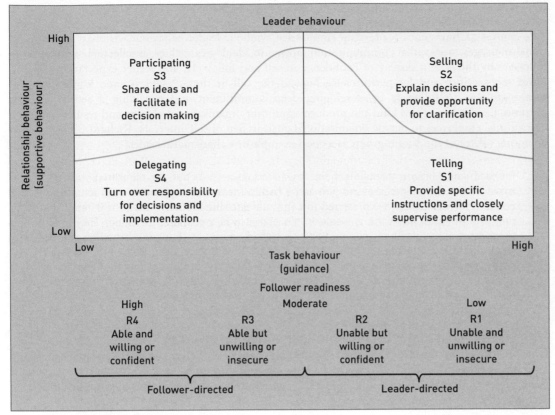

For instance, leadership effectiveness was not attributable to the predicted interaction between follower readiness and leadership style in a study of 459 salespeople.[51] Moreover, a study of 303 teachers indicated that SLT was accurate only for employees with low readiness. This finding is consistent with a survey of 57 chief nurse executives in California. These executives did not delegate in accordance with SLT.[52] Finally, researchers have concluded that the self-assessment instrument used to measure leadership style and follower readiness is inaccurate and should be used with caution.[53] In summary, managers should exercise discretion when using prescriptions from SLT.

From transactional to charismatic leadership

New perspectives of leadership theory have emerged in the past decades, variously referred to as 'charismatic', 'heroic', 'transformational' or 'visionary' leadership.[54] These competing but related perspectives have created confusion amongst researchers and practising managers. Fortunately, Robert House and Boas Shamir have given us a practical, integrated theory. It is referred to as that of 'charismatic leadership'.

This section begins by highlighting the differences between transactional and charismatic leadership. We then discuss a model of the charismatic leadership process and its implications for research and management.

What is the difference between transactional and charismatic leadership?

Most of the models and theories previously discussed earlier in this chapter represent Transactional leadership. Leaders are seen as engaging in behaviours that maintain a quality interaction between

Transactional leadership focuses on interpersonal interactions between managers and employees

427

themselves and followers. The two underlying characteristics of transactional leadership are that leaders use contingent rewards to motivate employees; and leaders exert corrective action only when subordinates fail to obtain performance goals.

In contrast, **Charismatic leadership** emphasises 'symbolic leader behaviour, visionary and inspirational messages, non-verbal communication, appeal to ideological values, intellectual stimulation of followers by the leader, display of confidence in self and followers, and leader expectations for follower self-sacrifice and for performance beyond the call of duty'.[55] Charismatic leadership gives meaningfulness to followers by developing deep commitment and providing a sense of moral purpose. Leadership of this kind can produce significant organisational change and results because it 'transforms' employees to pursue organisational goals in lieu of self-interests. Richard Branson, chief operating officer of the Virgin group, is a good example of a charismatic leader:

> Richard didn't breeze through school. It wasn't just a challenge for him, it was a nightmare. His dyslexia embarrassed him as he had to memorise and recite word for word in public. He was sure he did terribly on the standard IQ tests ... these are tests that measure abilities where he is weak. In the end, it was the tests that failed. They totally missed his ability and passion for sports. They had no means to identify ambition, the fire inside that drives people to find a path to success that zigzags around the maze of standard doors that won't open. They never identified the most important talent of all. It's the ability to connect with people, mind to mind, soul to soul. It's that rare power to energise the ambitions of others so that they, too, rise to the level of their dreams.[56]

How does charismatic leadership transform followers?

Charismatic leaders transform followers by creating changes in their goals, values, needs, beliefs and aspirations. They accomplish this transformation by appealing to followers' self-concepts – namely, their values and personal identity. Figure 11.7 presents a model of how charismatic leadership accomplishes this transformation process.

FIGURE 11.7 A CHARISMATIC MODEL OF LEADERSHIP

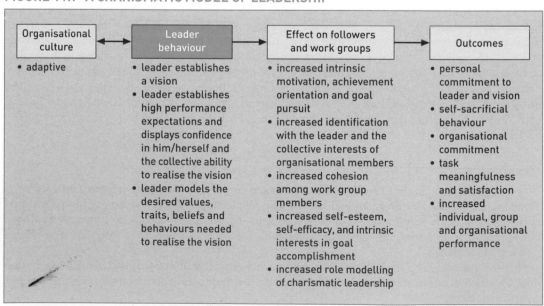

SOURCE: Based in part on D. A. Waldman and F. J. Yammarino, 'CEO Charismatic Leadership Levels-of-Management and Levels-of-Analysis Effects', *Academy of Management Review*, April 1999, pp. 266–85; and B. Shamir, R. J. House and M. B. Arthur, 'The Motivational Effects of Charismatic Leadership: A Self-Concept Based Theory', *Organization Science*, November 1993, pp. 577–94.

Figure 11.7 shows that organisational culture is a key precursor of charismatic leadership. Organisations with adaptive cultures anticipate and adapt to environmental changes and focus on leadership that emphasises the importance of service to customers, stockholders and employees. This type of management orientation involves the use of charismatic leadership. Organisational culture is discussed in Chapter 16.

Charismatic leaders first engage in three key sets of leader behaviour. If done effectively, this behaviour positively affects individual followers and their work groups. These positive effects, in turn, influence a variety of outcomes. Before discussing the model of charismatic leadership in more detail, it is important to note two general conclusions about charismatic leadership.[57] First, the two-headed arrow between organisational culture and leader behaviour in Figure 11.7 reveals that individuals with charismatic behavioural tendencies are able to influence culture. This implies that charismatic leadership reinforces the core values of an adaptive culture and helps to change the dysfunctional aspects of an organisation's culture that develop over time. Second, charismatic leadership has an effect on multiple levels within an organisation. For example, Figure 11.7 shows that charismatic leadership can positively influence individual outcomes (e.g. motivation), group outcomes (e.g. group cohesion) and organisational outcomes (e.g. financial performance). You can see that the potential for positive benefits from charismatic leadership is quite widespread.

CHARISMATIC LEADER BEHAVIOUR

The first set of charismatic leader behaviours involves establishing a common vision of the future. A vision is 'a realistic, credible, attractive future for your organisation'.[58] According to Burt Nanus, a leadership expert, the 'right' vision unleashes human potential because it serves as a beacon of hope and common purpose. It does this by attracting commitment, energising workers, creating meaning in employees' lives, establishing a standard of excellence, promoting high ideals, and bridging the gap between an organisation's present problems and its future goals and aspirations.[59] In contrast, the 'wrong' vision can be very damaging to an organisation. Consider what happened to Britain's Saatchi and Saatchi, once the world's most famous publicity agency:

> Strengthened by successive successful publicity campaigns, including Margaret Thatcher's in the eighties, Maurice Saatchi's unrestrained ambition pulled down the entire business. Thanks to a positive evolution on the stock market, he suddenly had an enormous budget at his disposal which prompted him to buy publicity agencies, marketing companies, public relations agencies and publishing houses. He was game for anything. His wild buying binge led to pure megalomania as, in 1987, he decided to takeover Hill Samuel to be followed by one of Britain's biggest banks, the Midland Bank. Mismanagement and disorganisation, followed by a crash resulted in the company's breakdown.[60]

As you can see, Maurice Saatchi's vision produced disastrous results. This highlights the fact that charismatic leaders do more than simply establish a vision. They must also gain input from others in developing an effective implementation plan. For example, Johnson & Johnson obtained input about its vision and implementation plan by carrying out a survey amongst all its 80 000 employees.[61]

Is charismatic leadership a mixed blessing?

The charismatic model of leadership presented in Figure 11.7 is strongly supported by research. For example, one often hears quoted a study of 31 presidents of the United States indicating that charisma significantly predicted presidential performance.[62] However, there are many untested gaps and some aspects have not been confirmed by research.[63]

The study of American presidents also made clear that narcissism is a common characteristic of charismatic leaders. Charisma can clearly be a source of negative outcomes. These narcissistic leaders have been described in much detail by Manfred Kets de Vries.[64] They surround themselves with uncritical subordinates. They know what is best, and do not need advice. They undertake over-ambitious, grandiose projects to glorify themselves. When the first signals are sent that the projects might not be as simple as expected, they ignore those signals, thereby missing the opportunity to correct the situation in time. When the project finally completely fails, they are the only person not to blame. They simple refuse to take any responsibility and they search for scapegoats.

Many critical studies of leadership have not only questioned the value of charisma, but even the concept of leadership itself. In the light of the many corporate scandals in the world (e.g. Enron in the United States, Ahold in the Netherlands, Swissair in Switzerland, Parmalat in Italy) many writers have warned against the 'self-serving' leader and have pointed to the dangers of 'larger than life' leaders, or have described 'the curse of the superstar'.[65] In almost all cases of corporate fraud or clear abuse of corporate resources, a 'strong' leader could be identified who was beyond control of colleagues or supervisory boards. Ethical behaviour is discussed in Chapter 18.

Additional perspectives on leadership

This section examines four additional approaches to leadership: substitutes for leadership, servant leadership, superleadership and coaching.

Substitutes for leadership

Substitutes for leadership situational variables that can substitue for, neutralise or enhance the effects of leadership

Virtually all leadership theories assume that some sort of formal leadership is necessary, whatever the circumstances. But this basic assumption is questioned by this model of leadership. Specifically, some OB scholars propose that there are a variety of situational variables that can act as **Substitutes for leadership**.[66] These substitutes can thus increase or diminish a leader's ability to influence the work group. For example, leader behaviour that initiates structure would tend to be resisted by independent-minded employees with high ability and vast experience. Consequently, such employees would be guided more by their own initiative than by managerial directives.

KERR AND JERMIER'S SUBSTITUTES FOR LEADERSHIP MODEL

According to Steven Kerr and John Jermier, the OB researchers who developed this model, the key to improving leadership effectiveness is to identify the substitutes for leadership (see Table 11.4). Characteristics of the subordinate, the task and the organisation can act as substitutes for traditional hierarchical leadership. Further, different characteristics are predicted to negate different types of leader behaviour.

For example, tasks that provide feedback concerning accomplishment, such as taking a test, tend to negate task-oriented but not relationship-oriented leader behaviour (see Table 11.4). Although the list in Table 11.4 is not all-inclusive, it shows that there are more substitutes for task-oriented leadership than for relationship-oriented leadership.

Two different approaches have been used to test this model. The first is based on the idea that substitutes for leadership are contingency variables that moderate the relationship between leader behaviour and employee attitudes and behaviour.[67] A recent summary of this research revealed that only 318 of the 3741 (9 per cent) contingency relationships tested supported the model.[68] This demonstrates that substitutes for leadership do not moderate the effect of a leader's behaviour as suggested by Steve Kerr and John Jermier. The second approach to test the substitutes model examined whether substitutes for leadership have a direct effect on employee attitudes and behaviours. A recent meta-analysis of 36 different samples revealed that the combination of substitute variables and leader behaviours significantly explained a variety of employee attitudes and behaviours. Interestingly, the substitutes for leadership were more important than leader behaviours in accounting for employee attitudes and behaviours.[69]

Servant-Leadership

Servant-leadership focuses on increased service to others rather than to oneself

Servant-leadership is more a philosophy of managing than a testable theory. The term **Servant-leadership** was coined by Robert Greenleaf in 1970. Greenleaf believes that great leaders act as servants, putting the needs of others, including employees, customers and community, as their first priority. Servant-leadership focuses on increased service to others rather than to oneself.[70] Servant-leadership is not a quick-fix approach to leadership. Rather, it is a long-term, transformational approach to life and work. Table 11.5 presents 10 characteristics possessed by servant-leaders. One can hardly go wrong by trying to adopt these characteristics.

Superleadership

Superleader someone who leads others to lead themselves

The approach to leadership of a **Superleader**, leading others to lead themselves, has already been discussed in relation to developing team members' self-management skills in Chapter 10. We briefly

TABLE 11.4 SUBSTITUTES FOR LEADERSHIP

Characteristic	Relationship-oriented or considerate leader behaviour is unnecessary	Task-oriented or initiating structure leader behaviour is unnecessary
Of the subordinate		
1 Ability, experience, training, knowledge		x
2 Need for independence	x	x
3 'Professional' orientation	x	x
4 Indifference toward organisational rewards	x	x
Of the task		
5 Unambiguous and routine		x
6 Methodologically invariant		x
7 Provides its own feedback concerning accomplishment		x
8 Intrinsically satisfying	x	
Of the organisation		
9 Formalisation (explicit plans, goals and areas of responsibility)		x
10 Inflexibility (rigid, unbending rules and procedures)		x
11 Highly specified and active advisory and staff functions		x
12 Closely knit, cohesive work groups	x	x
13 Organisational rewards not within the leader's control	x	x
14 Spatial distance between superior and subordinates	x	x

SOURCE: Adapted from S. Kerr and J. M. Jermier, 'Substitutes for Leadership: Their Meaning and Measurement', *Organizational Behavior and Human Performance*, December 1978, pp. 375–403.

highlight it again because superleadership is as relevant within teams as it is to any general leadership situation. Superleaders empower followers by acting as a teacher and coach rather than as a dictator and autocrat. The need for this form of leadership is underscored by a survey of 1046 Americans. Results demonstrated that only 38 per cent of the respondents had ever had an effective coach or mentor.[71]

Productive thinking is the cornerstone of superleadership. Specifically, managers are encouraged to teach followers how to engage in productive thinking.[72] This is expected to increase employees' feelings of personal control and intrinsic motivation. Superleadership has the potential to free up a manager's time because employees are encouraged to manage themselves. Future research is needed to test the validity of recommendations derived from this new approach to leadership.

Coaching

Modern management thinking is no longer characterised by dominant and authoritarian leadership but by coaching.[73] A good coach is able to offer commitment and support, build skills and teams, and to focus on results.

■ COMMITMENT

A manager directs from a distance, whereas a coach acts directly with his players. A coach is present on the field, to support his team. He is present at the moment of action, which he experiences actively. He is not engrossed in files or participating in long-lasting meetings. Action happens in the field. A real coach is not afraid 'to put his shoulder to the wheel' and help when it is needed. The rational, cool and distant manager has to make place for the enthusiastic coach, who

TABLE 11.5 CHARACTERISTICS OF THE SERVANT-LEADER

Servant-leadership characteristics	Description
1 Listening	Servant-leaders focus on listening to identify and clarify the needs and desires of a group
2 Empathy	Servant-leaders try to empathise with others' feelings and emotions. An individual's good intentions are assumed even when he or she performs poorly
3 Healing	Servant-leaders strive to make themselves and others whole in the face of failure or suffering
4 Awareness	Servant-leaders are very self-aware of their strengths and limitations
5 Persuasion	Servant-leaders rely more on persuasion than positional authority when making decisions and trying to influence others
6 Conceptualisation	Servant leaders take the time and effort to develop broader based conceptual thinking. Servant-leaders seek an appropriate balance between a short-term, day-to-day focus and a long-term, conceptual orientation
7 Foresight	Servant-leaders have the ability to foresee future outcomes associated with a current course of action or situation
8 Stewardship	Servant-leaders assume that they are stewards of the people and resources they manage
9 Commitment to the growth of people	Servant-leaders are committed to people beyond their immediate work role. They commit to fostering an environment that encourages personal, professional and spiritual growth
10 Building community	Servant-leaders strive to create a sense of community both within and outside the work organisation

SOURCE: These characteristics and descriptions were derived from L. C. Spears, 'Introduction: Servant-Leadership and the Greenleaf Legacy', in *Reflections on Leadership: How Robert K. Greenleaf's Theory of Servant-Leadership Influenced Today's Top Management Thinkers*, ed. L. C. Spears (New York: John Wiley & Sons, 1995), pp. 1–14.

trusts his subordinates and knows them personally. He is conscious of their weaknesses and is capable of getting the best out of them. Day after day, he tries to improve his staff's performance and possibilities.

■ SKILL BUILDING
The coach invests much effort in his or her employees' skill building. He or she is aware of the fact that they are the driving force of his organisation. He or she will see to it that they improve their professional skills, can organise their work themselves and are directed towards a common goal.

■ SUPPORT
The coach will principally support his or her team to enable it to show results.

■ TEAM BUILDER
The coach is a team builder, he brings people together with different skills, interests and backgrounds to create a solid team. A struggle for power and political conflict has to be replaced by

mutual respect. The coach is successful in transforming internal into external competition, directed towards the real competitors.

■ RESULT-ORIENTED
The coach's efforts are not aimed at creating a cosy environment, he wants to see results.

Learning outcomes: Summary of key terms

1 Define the term 'leadership', and explain the difference between leading and managing

Leadership is defined as a process of social influence in which the leader tries to obtain the voluntary participation of employees in an effort to reach organisational objectives. Leadership entails more than having authority and power. Although leadership and management overlap, each entails a unique set of activities or functions. Managers typically perform functions associated with planning, investigating, organising and control; while leaders deal with the interpersonal aspects of a manager's job.

2 Review the research on trait theory and discuss the idea of one best style of leadership, using the Ohio State studies and the Leadership Grid® as points of reference

Previous leadership research did not support the notion that effective leaders possessed unique traits to those of their followers. However, teams of researchers analysed this historical data again, this time using modern-day statistical procedures. Results revealed that individuals tend to be perceived as leaders when they possess one or more of the following traits: intelligence, dominance and masculinity. A recent study further demonstrated that employees value credible leaders. Credible leaders are honest, forward-looking, inspiring and competent. Research also examined the relationship between gender and leadership. Results demonstrated that: (a) men and women differed in the type of leadership roles they assume; (b) leadership styles varied by gender; and (c) gender differences in ratings of leadership effectiveness were associated with the percentage of male leaders and male subordinates. The Ohio State studies revealed that there were two key independent dimensions of leadership behaviour: consideration and initiating structure. Authors of the Leadership Grid® proposed that leaders should adopt a style that demonstrates high concern for production and people. Research did not support the premise that there is one best style of leadership.

3 Explain, according to Fiedler's contingency model, how leadership style interacts with situational control

Fiedler believes the effectiveness of a leader depends on an appropriate match between leadership style and situational control. Leaders are either task motivated or relationship motivated. Situation control is composed of leader–member relations, task structure and position power. Task-motivated leaders are effective under situations of both high and low control. Relationship-motivated leaders are more effective when they have moderate situational control.

4 Discuss Hersey and Blanchard's situational leadership theory

According to situational leadership theory (SLT), effective leader behaviour depends on the readiness level of a leader's followers. As follower readiness increases, leaders are advised to gradually move from a telling to a selling to a participating and, finally, to a delegating style. Research does not support SLT.

5 Define and differentiate between transactional and charismatic leadership

There is an important difference between transactional and charismatic leadership. Transactional leaders focus on the interpersonal transactions between managers and employees. Charismatic leaders motivate employees to pursue organisational goals above their own self-interests. Both forms of leadership are important for organisational success.

6 Explain how charismatic leadership transforms followers and work groups
Organisational culture is a key precursor of charismatic leadership, which is composed of three sets of leader behaviour. These sets, in turn, positively affect followers' and work groups' goals, values, beliefs, aspirations and motivation. These positive effects are then associated with a host of preferred outcomes.

7 Describe the substitutes for leadership and explain how they substitute for, neutralise, or enhance the effects of leadership
There are 14 substitutes for leadership (see Table 11.4) that can substitute for, neutralise or enhance the effects of leadership. These substitutes contain characteristics of the subordinates, the task and the organisation. Research shows that substitutes directly influence employee attitudes and performance.

8 Describe what is meant by superleadership
A superleader is someone who leads others to lead themselves. Superleaders empower followers by acting as a teacher and coach rather than a dictator and autocrat.

9 Describe servant-leadership and coaching
Servant-leadership is more a philosophy than a testable theory. It is based on the premise that great leaders act as servants, putting the needs of others, including employees, customers, and community, as their first priority. A good coach has the following characteristics: commitment, support, an ability to build skills and teams, and an ability to focus on results.

Review questions

1 Is everyone cut out to be a leader? Explain.
2 Has your education helped you to develop any of the traits that characterise leaders?
3 Should organisations change anything in response to research pertaining to gender and leadership? If yes, describe your recommendations.
4 What leadership traits and behavioural styles are possessed by your prime minister?
5 Does it make more sense to change a person's leadership style or the situation? How would Fred Fiedler and Robert House answer this question?
6 Describe how a lecturer might use House's path–goal theory to clarify student's path–goal perceptions.
7 Identify three charismatic leaders and describe their leadership traits and behavioural styles.
8 Have you ever worked for a charismatic leader? Describe how he or she transformed followers.
9 In your view, which leadership theory has the greatest practical application? Why?

Personal awareness and growth exercise

How ready are you to assume the leadership role?

Objectives

1 To assess your readiness for the leadership role.

2 To consider the implications of the gap between your career goals and your readiness to lead.

Introduction

Leaders assume multiple roles. Roles represent the expectations that others have of occupants of a position. It is important for potential leaders to consider whether they are ready for the leadership role because mismatches in expectations or skills can derail a leader's effectiveness. This exercise assesses your readiness to assume the leadership role.

Instructions

For each statement, indicate the extent to which you agree or disagree with it by selecting one number from the scale provided. Circle your response for each statement.

Remember, there are no right or wrong answers. After completing the survey, add your total score for the 20 items, then record it in the space provided.

1 = Strongly disagree

2 = Disagree

3 = Neither agree nor disagree

4 = Agree

5 = Strongly agree

1 It is enjoyable having people rely on me for ideas and suggestions.	1 2 3 4 5
2 It would be accurate to say that I have inspired other people.	1 2 3 4 5
3 It's a good practice to ask people provocative questions about their work.	1 2 3 4 5
4 It's easy for me to compliment others.	1 2 3 4 5
5 I like to cheer people up even when my own spirits are down.	1 2 3 4 5
6 What my team accomplishes is more important than my personal glory.	1 2 3 4 5
7 Many people imitate my ideas.	1 2 3 4 5
8 Building team spirit is important to me.	1 2 3 4 5
9 I would enjoy coaching other members of the team.	1 2 3 4 5
10 It is important to me to recognise others for their accomplishments.	1 2 3 4 5
11 I would enjoy entertaining visitors to my firm even if it interfered with my completing a report.	1 2 3 4 5
12 It would be fun for me to represent my team at gatherings outside our department.	1 2 3 4 5
13 The problems of my teammates are my problems too.	1 2 3 4 5
14 Resolving conflict is an activity I enjoy.	1 2 3 4 5
15 I would co-operate with another unit in the organisation even if I disagreed with the position taken by its members.	1 2 3 4 5
16 I am an idea generator on the job.	1 2 3 4 5
17 It's fun for me to bargain whenever I have the opportunity.	1 2 3 4 5
18 Team members listen to me when I speak.	1 2 3 4 5
19 People have asked me to assume the leadership of an activity several times in my life.	1 2 3 4 5
20 I've always been a convincing person.	1 2 3 4 5

Total score: _____

Norms for interpreting the total score[74]

90–100	= High readiness for the leadership role
60–89	= Moderate readiness for the leadership role
40–59	= Some uneasiness with the leadership role
39 or less	= Low readiness for the leadership role

Questions for discussion

1 Do you agree with the interpretation of your readiness to assume the leadership role? Explain why or why not.

2 If you scored below 60 and desire to become a leader, what might you do to increase your readiness to lead? To answer this question, we suggest that you study the statements carefully – particularly those with low responses – to determine how you might change either an attitude or a behaviour so that you can realistically answer more questions with a response of 'agree' or 'strongly agree'.

3 How might this evaluation instrument help you to become a more effective leader?

Group exercise

Exhibiting leadership within the context of running a meeting[75]

Objectives

1 To consider the types of problems that can occur when running a meeting.

2 To identify the types of leadership behaviour that can be used to handle problems that occur in meetings.

Introduction

Managers often find themselves playing the role of formal or informal leader when participating in a planned meeting (e.g. committees, work groups, task forces, etc.). As leaders, individuals must often handle a number of interpersonal situations that have the potential of reducing the group's productivity. For example, if an individual has important information that is not shared with the group, the meeting will be less productive. Similarly, two or more individuals who engage in conversational asides could disrupt the normal functioning of the group. Finally, the group's productivity will also be threatened by two or more individuals who argue or engage in personal attacks on one another during a meeting. This exercise is designed to help you practise some of the behaviour necessary to overcome these problems and at the same time share in the responsibility of leading a productive group.[76]

Instructions

Your tutor will divide the class into groups of four to six. Once the group is assembled, briefly summarise the types of problem that can occur when running a meeting – start with the material presented in the preceding introduction. Write your final list on a piece of paper. Next, for each problem on the group's list, the group should brainstorm a list of appropriate leader behaviours that can be used to handle the problem. Use the guidelines for brainstorming discussed in Chapter 12. Try to arrive at an agreed list.

Questions for discussion

1 What type of problems that occur during meetings is most difficult to handle? Explain.

2 Are there any particular leader behaviours that can be used to solve multiple problems during meetings? Discuss your rationale.

3 Was there a lot of agreement about which leader behaviours were useful for dealing with specific problems encountered in meetings? Explain.

Internet Exercise

The topic of leadership has been important since the dawn of time. History is filled with examples of great leaders such as Mohandas ('Mahatma') Gandhi, Martin Luther King and Winston Churchill. These leaders are most likely to have possessed some of the leadership traits discussed in this chapter, and they probably used a situational approach to lead their followers. The purpose of this exercise is for you to evaluate the leadership styles of an historical figure. Go to our website www.mcgraw-hill.co.uk/textbooks/buelens for further instructions and suggestions of historical leaders.

Notes

1 Adapted from J. Muller and C. Tierny, 'Can This Man Save Chrysler?', *Business Week*, 17 September 2001, pp. 86–9.

2 See S. Lieberson and J. F. O'Connor, 'Leadership and Organizational Performance: A Study of Large Corporations', *American Sociological Review*, April 1972, pp. 117–30.

3 The role of leadership within organisational change is discussed by O. Harari, 'Why Do Leaders Avoid Change', *Management Review*, March 1999, pp. 35–8; and J. P. Kotter, *Leading Change* (Boston, MA: Harvard Business School Press, 1996).

4 T. Thorlindson, *The Skipper Effect in Icelandic Herring Fishing* (Reykjavik: University of Iceland, 1987); and M. Smith and C. Cooper, 'Leadership and Stress', *Leadership and Organization Development Journal*, no. 2, 1994, pp. 3–7.

5 P. Wright, *Managerial Leadership* (London: Routledge, 1996).

6 'The American Survey', *The Economist*, 9 December 1995, pp. 53–4.

7 In the UK John Adair has become very popular as an expert on leadership training. See J. Adair, *Effective Leadership* (London: Pan Books, 1988).

8 Based on C. A. Bartlett and A. Nanda, 'Ingvar Kamprad and Ikea', in *Global Marketing Management: Cases and Readings*, eds R. Buzzell, J. Quelch and C. Bartlett (Reading, MA: Addison-Wesley Publishing Company, 1995), pp. 69–95; and B. Ernstrtim, 'The Well Tempered Viking', *Scanorama*, June 1989, pp. 64–72.

9 R. J. House, N. S. Wright and R. N. Aditiya, 'Cross-Cultural Research on Organizational Leadership: A Critical Analysis and a Proposed Theory', in *New Perspectives in International Industrial Organizational Psychology*, eds P. C. Earley and M. Erez (San Francisco, CA: New Lexington, 1997), pp. 535–625.

10 C. A. Schriesheim, J. M. Tolliver and O. C. Behling, 'Leadership Theory: Some Implications for Managers', *MSU Business Topics*, Summer 1978, p. 35.

11 R. J. House, N. S. Wright and R. N. Aditiya, 'Cross-Cultural Research on Organizational Leadership: A Critical Analysis and a Proposed Theory', in *New Perspectives in International Industrial Organizational Psychology*, eds P. C. Earley and M. Erez (San Francisco, CA: New Lexington, 1997), pp. 535–625.

12 The multiple levels of leadership are discussed by F. J. Yammarino, F. Dansereau and C. J. Kennedy, 'A Multi-Level Multidimensional Approach to Leadership: Viewing Leadership through an Elephant's Eye', *Organizational Dynamics*, Winter 2001, pp. 149–63. Also see H. Mintzberg, 'Covert Leadership: Notes on Managing Professionals', *Harvard Business Review*, November–December 1998, pp. 140–47.

13 B. M. Bass, *Bass & Stogdill's Handbook of Leadership: Theory, Research, and Managerial Applications*, third edition (New York: Free Press, 1990), p. 383.

14 J. P. Kotter, *A Force for Change: How Leadership Differs from Management* (New York: Free Press, 1990); J. P. Kotter, *Leading Change* (Boston, MA: Harvard Business School Press, 1996); and J. P. Kotter, *John Kotter on What Leaders Really Do* (Boston, MA: Harvard Business School Press, 1999).

15 For a thorough discussion about the differences between leading and managing, see G. Weathersby, 'Leading vs. Management', *Management Review*, March 1999, p. 5; R. J. House and R. N. Aditya, 'The Social Scientific Study of Leadership: Quo Vadis?', *Journal of Management*, no. 3, 1997, pp. 409–73; and A. Zalesnik, 'Managers and Leaders: Are They Different?' *Harvard Business Review*, May–June 1977, pp. 67–78.

16 For complete details, see R. M. Stogdill, 'Personal Factors Associated with Leadership: A Survey of the Literature', *Journal of Psychology*, 1948, pp. 35–71; and R. M. Stogdill, *Handbook of Leadership* (New York: Free Press, 1974).

17 Excerpted from T. A. Stewart, 'The Contest for Welch's Throne Begins: Who Will Run GE?', *Fortune*, 11 January 1999, p. 27.

18 See R. D. Mann, 'A Review of the Relationships between Personality and Performance in Small Groups', *Psychological Bulletin*, July 1959, pp. 241–70.

19 Perceptions of leadership were examined by R. F. Martell and A. L. DeSmet, 'A Diagnostic-Ratio Approach to

Measuring Beliefs about the Leadership Abilities of Male and Female Managers', *Journal of Applied Psychology*, December 2001, pp. 1223–31; and R. A. Baron, G. D. Markman, and A. Hirsa, 'Perceptions of Women and Men as Entrepreneurs: Evidence for Differential Effects of Attributional Augmenting', *Journal of Applied Psychology*, October 2001, pp. 923–9.

20 See R. J. Hall, J. W. Workman and C. A. Marchioro, 'Sex, Task, and Behavioral Flexibility Effects on Leadership Perceptions', *Organizational Behavior and Human Decision Processes*, April 1998, pp. 1–32; and R. G. Lord, C. L. De Vader and G. M. Alliger, 'A Meta-Analysis of the Relation between Personality Traits and Leadership Perceptions: An Application of Validity Generalization Procedures', *Journal of Applied Psychology*, August 1986, p. 407.

21 Results from this study can be found in F. C. Brodbeck *et al.*, 'Cultural Variation of Leadership Prototypes across 22 European Countries,' *Journal of Occupational and Organizational Psychology*, March 2000, pp. 1–29.

22 Results can be found in J. M. Kouzes and B. Z. Posner, *The Leadership Challenge* (San Francisco, CA: Jossey-Bass, 1995).

23 C. Hyowitz, 'In the Lead: Managers Must Respond to Employee Concerns about Honest Business', the *Wall Street Journal*, 19 February 2002, p. B1.

24 See D. Goleman, 'What Makes a Leader?', *Harvard Business Review*, November–December 1998, pp. 92–102.

25 Gender and the emergence of leaders was examined in A. H. Eagly and S. J. Karau, 'Gender and the Emergence of Leaders: A Meta-Analysis', *Journal of Personality and Social Psychology*, May 1991, pp. 685–710; and R. K. Shelly and P. T. Munroe, 'Do Women Engage in Less Task Behavior Than Men?', *Sociological Perspectives*, Spring 1999, pp. 49–67.

26 See A. H. Eagly, S. J. Karau and B. T. Johnson, 'Gender and Leadership Style among School Principals: A Meta-Analysis', *Educational Administration Quarterly*, February 1992, pp. 76–102.

27 Results can be found in A. H. Eagly, S. J. Karau and M. G. Makhijani, 'Gender and the Effectiveness of Leaders: A Meta-Analysis', *Psychological Bulletin*, January 1995, pp. 125–45.

28 Hay Management Consultants.

29 R. Tait, *Roads to the Top: Career Decisions and Development of 18 Business Leaders* (Basingstoke: Macmillan, 1995), p. 21.

30 This research is summarised and critiqued by E. A. Fleishman, 'Consideration and Structure: Another Look at Their Role in Leadership Research', in *Leadership: The Multiple-Level Approaches*, eds F. Dansereau and F. J. Yammarino (Stamford, CT: JAI Press, 1998), pp. 51–60; and B. M. Bass, *Bass & Stogdill's Handbook of Leadership: Theory, Research, and Managerial Applications, third edition* (New York: Free Press, 1990), Ch. 24.

31 See V. H. Vroom, 'Leadership', in *Handbook of Industrial and Organizational Psychology*, ed. M. D. Dunnette (Chicago: Rand McNally, 1976).

32 Even the way Blake and Mouton cite research that contradicts their theory as supportive is sometimes highly questionable.

33 R. R. Blake and J. S. Mouton, 'A Comparative Analysis of Situationalism and 9,9 Management by Principle', *Organizational Dynamics*, Spring 1982, p. 23.

34 R. R. Blake and J. S. Mouton, 'A Comparative Analysis of Situationalism and 9,9 Management by Principle', *Organizational Dynamics*, Spring 1982, pp. 28–9. Also see R. R. Blake and J. S. Mouton, 'Management by Grid Principles or Situationalism: Which?', *Group & Organization Studies*, December 1981, pp. 439–55.

35 R. R. Blake and J. S. Mouton, 'A Comparative Analysis of Situationalism and 9,9 Management by Principle', *Organizational Dynamics*, Spring 1982, p. 21.

36 Excerpted from R. J. Grossman, 'Heirs Unapparent', *HR Magazine*, February 1999, p. 39.

37 See B. M. Bass, *Bass & Stogdill's Handbook of Leadership: Theory, Research, and Managerial Applications, third edition* (New York: Free Press, 1990), Ch. 20–25.

38 The relationships between the frequency and mastery of leader behaviour and various outcomes were investigated in F. Shipper and C. S. White, 'Mastery, Frequency, and Interaction of Managerial Behaviors Relative to Subunit Effectiveness', *Human Relations*, January 1999, pp. 49–66.

39 F. E. Fiedler, 'Job Engineering for Effective Leadership: A New Approach', *Management Review*, September 1977, p. 29.

40 Excerpted from C. Hymowitz, 'In the Lead: How Cynthia Danaher Learned to Stop Sharing and Start Leading', the *Wall Street Journal*, 16 March 1999, p. B1.

41 For more on this theory, see F. E. Fiedler, 'A Contingency Model of Leadership Effectiveness', in *Advances in Experimental Social Psychology, vol. 1*, ed. L. Berkowitz (New York: Academic Press, 1964); and F. E. Fiedler, *A Theory of Leadership Effectiveness* (New York: McGraw-Hill, 1967).

42 Additional information on situational control is contained in F. E. Fiedler, 'The Leadership Situation and the Black Box in Contingency Theories', in *Leadership Theory and Research: Perspectives and Directions*, eds M. M. Chemers and R. Ayman (New York: Academic Press, 1993), pp. 2–28.

43 See L. H. Peters, D. D. Hartke and J. T. Pohlmann, 'Fiedler's Contingency Theory of Leadership: An Application of the Meta-Analyses Procedures of Schmidt and Hunter', *Psychological Bulletin*, March 1985, pp. 274–85. The meta-analysis was conducted by C. A. Schriesheim, B. J. Tepper and L. A. Tetrault, 'Least Preferred Co-Worker Score, Situational Control, and Leadership Effectiveness: A Meta-Analysis of Contingency Model Performance Predictions', *Journal of Applied Psychology*, August 1994, pp. 561–73.

44 A review of the contingency theory and suggestions for future theoretical development is provided by R. Ayman,

M. M. Chemers and F. Fiedler, 'The Contingency Model of Leadership Effectiveness: Its Levels of Analysis', in *Leadership: The Multiple-Level Approaches*, eds F. Dansereau and F. J. Yammarino (Stamford, CT: JAI Press, 1998), pp. 73–94; and R. P. Vecchio, 'Some Continuing Challenges for the Contingency Model of Leadership', in *Leadership: The Multiple-Level Approaches*, eds F. Dansereau and F. J. Yammarino (Stamford, CT: JAI Press, 1998), pp. 115–24.

45 Adapted from R. J. House and T. R. Mitchell, 'Path–Goal Theory of Leadership', *Journal of Contemporary Business*, Autumn 1974, p. 83. For more detail on this theory, see R. J. House, 'A Path–Goal Theory of Leader Effectiveness', *Administrative Science Quarterly*, September 1971, pp. 321–38.

46 See R. Hooijberg, 'A Multidirectional Approach toward Leadership: An Extension of the Concept of Behavioral Complexity', *Human Relations*, July 1996, pp. 917–46.

47 Based on A. Brown, 'Top of the Bosses', *International Management*, April 1994, pp. 26–31.

48 R. J. House, 'Path–Goal Theory of Leadership: Lessons, Legacy, and a Reformulated Theory', *Leadership Quarterly*, Autumn 1996, pp. 323–52.

49 A thorough discussion of this theory is provided by P. Hersey and K. H. Blanchard, *Management of Organizational Behavior: Utilizing Human Resources, fifth edition* (Englewood Cliffs, NJ: Prentice-Hall, 1988).

50 A comparison of the original theory and its latent version is provided by P. Hersey and K. Blanchard, 'Great Ideas Revisited', *Training & Development*, January 1996, pp. 42–7.

51 Results can be found in J. R. Goodson, G. W. McGee and J. F. Cashman, 'Situational Leadership Theory', *Group & Organization Studies*, December 1989, pp. 446–61.

52 The first study was conducted by R. P. Vecchio, 'Situational Leadership Theory: An Examination of a Prescriptive Theory', *Journal of Applied Psychology*, August 1987, pp. 444–51. Results from the study of nurse executives can be found in C. Adams, 'Leadership Behavior of Chief Nurse Executives', *Nursing Management*, August 1990, pp. 36–9.

53 See D. C. Lueder, 'Don't Be Misled by LEAD', *Journal of Applied Behavioral Science*, May 1985, pp. 143–54; and C. L. Graeff, 'The Situational Leadership Theory: A Critical View', *Academy of Management Review*, April 1983, pp. 285–91.

54 For details on these different theories, see J. McGregor Burns, *Leadership* (New York: Harper & Row, 1978); N. M. Tichy and M. A. Devanna, *The Transformational Leader* (New York: John Wiley & Sons, 1986); J. M. Kouzes and B. Z. Posner, *The Leadership Challenge: How to Get Extraordinary Things Done in Organizations* (San Francisco, CA: Jossey-Bass, 1990); B. Nanus, *Visionary Leadership* (San Francisco, CA: Jossey-Bass, 1992); B. Bass and B. J. Avolio, 'Transformational Leadership: A Response to Critiques', in *Leadership Theory and Research: Perspectives and Directions*, eds M. M. Chemers and R. Ayman (New York: Academic Press, 1993), pp. 49–80; B. Shamir, R. J. House and M. B. Arthur, 'The Motivational Effects of Charismatic Leadership: A Self-Concept Based Theory', *Organization Science*, November 1993, pp. 577–94; and H. B. Jones, 'Magic, Meaning and Leadership: Weber's Model and the Empirical Literature', *Human Relations*, June 2001, pp. 753–71.

55 B. Shamir, R. J. House and M. B. Arthur, 'The Motivational Effects of Charismatic Leadership: A Self-Concept Based Theory', *Organization Science*, November 1993, p. 578.

56 See http://www.execpc.com/~shepler/branson.

57 This discussion is based on D. A. Waldman and F. J. Yammarino, 'CEO Charismatic Leadership: Levels-of-Management and Levels-of-Analysis Effects', *Academy of Management Review*, April 1999, pp. 266–85.

58 B. Nanus, *Visionary Leadership* (San Francisco, CA: Jossey-Bass, 1992), p. 8.

59 See B. Nanus, *Visionary Leadership* (San Francisco, CA: Jossey-Bass, 1992); and W. L. Gardner and B. J. Avolio, 'The Charismatic Relationship: A Dramaturgical Perspective', *Academy of Management Review*, January 1998, pp. 32–58.

60 Based on and translated from J. Grobben, 'Tien voor twee', *Knack*, 2 February 1995, pp. 40–42.

61 See G. Fuchsberg, 'Visioning Missions Becomes Its Own Mission', the *Wall Street Journal*, 7 January 1994, p. B1.

62 Results can be found in R. J. House, W. D. Spangler and J. Woycke, 'Personality and Charisma in the US Presidency: A Psychological Theory of Leader Effectiveness', *Administrative Science Quarterly*, September 1991, pp. 364–96.

63 J. B. Miner, *Organizational Behavior: Foundations, Theories, and Analyses* (Oxford: Oxford University Press, 2002), p. 755.

64 See M. Kets de Vries, *The Leadership Mystique* (London: Financial Times–Prentice Hall, 2001).

65 See R. Khurana, 'The Curse of the Superstar CEO', *Harvard Business Review*, September 2002, pp. 60–66.

66 For an expanded discussion of this model, see S. Kerr and J. Jermier, 'Substitutes for Leadership: Their Meaning and Measurement', *Organizational Behavior and Human Performance*, December 1978, pp. 375–403.

67 See J. P. Howell, P. W. Dorfman and S. Kerr, 'Moderator Variables in Leadership Research', *Academy of Management Review*, January 1986, pp. 88–102.

68 Results can be found in P. M. Podsakoff, S. B. MacKenzie, M. Ahearne and W. H. Bommer, 'Searching for a Needle in a Haystack: Trying to Identify the Illusive Moderators of Leadership Behaviors', *Journal of Management*, no. 3, 1995, pp. 423–70.

69 For details of this study, see P. M. Podsakoff, S. B. MacKenzie and W. H. Bommer, 'Meta-Analysis of the Relationship between Kerr and Jermier's Substitutes for Leadership and Employee Job Attitudes, Role Perceptions, and Performance', *Journal of Applied Psychology*, August 1996, pp. 380–99.

70 An overall summary of servant leadership is provided by L. C. Spears, *Reflections on Leadership: How Robert K. Greenleaf's Theory of Servant-Leadership Influenced Today's Top Management Thinkers* (New York: John Wiley & Sons, 1995).

71 L. McDermott, 'Wanted: Chief Executive Coach', *Training & Development*, May 1996, pp. 67–70.

72 For a discussion of superleadership, see C. C. Manz and H. P. Sims, Jr, 'SuperLeadership: Beyond the Myth of Heroic Leadership', in *Leadership: Understanding the Dynamics of Power and Influence in Organizations*, ed. R. P. Vecchio (Notre Dame, IN: University of Notre Dame Press, 1997), pp. 411–28; and C. C. Manz and H. P. Sims, Jr, *Superleadership: Leading Others to Lead Themselves* (New York: Berkley Books, 1989).

73 Based on T. Peters and N. Austin, *A Passion for Excellence* (Glasgow: Collins, 1985); C. D. Orth, H. E. Wilkinson and R. C. Benfari, 'The Manager's Role as Coach and Mentor', *Organizational Dynamics*, Spring 1987, pp. 66–74; R. D. Evered and J. C. Selman, 'Coaching and the Art of Management', *Organizational Dynamics*, Autumn 1989, pp. 16–32.

74 The scale used to assess readiness to assume the leadership role was taken from A. J. DuBrin, *Leadership: Research Findings, Practice, and Skills* (Boston, MA: Houghton Mifflin Company, 1995), pp. 10–11.

75 This exercise was based on an exercise in L. W. Mealiea, *Skills for Managers in Organizations* (Burr Ridge, IL: Irwin, 1994), pp. 96–7.

76 The introduction was quoted from L. W. Mealiea, *Skills for Managers in Organizations* (Burr Ridge, IL: Irwin, 1994), p. 96.

chapter 12 decision making

By Marc Buelens and Dirk Van Poucke

Learning outcomes

When you finish studying the material in this chapter, you should be able to:

- compare and contrast the rational model of decision making, Simon's normative model and the 'garbage can' model
- discuss the contingency relationships that influence the three primary strategies used to select solutions
- explain the model of decision-making styles
- describe the model of escalation of commitment
- summarise the advantages and disadvantages of involving groups in the decision-making process
- explain how participative management affects performance
- compare brainstorming, the nominal group technique, the Delphi technique and computer-aided decision-making
- describe the stages of the creative process
- explain the model of organisational creativity and innovation

Flight simulators for management

Thor Sigvaldason is late. As part of a novel consulting cluster at PriceWaterhouseCoopers, he is supposed to be at an important client meeting at 10 a.m. But he has overslept for the session with a top executive of a department store.

When Sigvaldason finally arrives, 20 minutes late, his brown hair is still wet from a shower. He eases quietly into the room, watched only by his boss, K. Winslow Farrell Jr, 45, whose face doesn't hide his displeasure.

Thor brings up on a computer screen what has taken the team 1800 hours to construct. It shows awkward block-like figures roaming about a crude layout of a department store. They have created an elaborate computer model of a department store with hundreds of 'synthetic' shoppers. The idea is to simulate how real shoppers actually operate in a store. If all goes well, the actions of those 'adaptive agents' will so closely mimic human behaviour that decision makers for the first time will be able to use them to test the impact of their decisions before implementing them in the real world. Farrell sees it as the ultimate 'flight simulator' for management. The system will allow the client to make risk-free decisions such as:

- the number of salespeople needed in each store department to maximise profits,
- how to turn browsers into shoppers,
- where to locate service desks and cash registers to increase sales.

Farrell is trying to create a virtual world where executives can safely test hunches, run scenarios, and preview the impact of big and small decisions – all without major investments, public embarrassments, and competitive backfires. And if you make a wrong decision in the model, you're only dealing with a synthetic public, not the real world.

For years, management has sought to harness the power of econometrics and technology. Operations research and linear programming, however, have rarely won the attention of the CEO because they were so esoteric and difficult to grasp. Farrell's group is hoping that the ability to see decisions acted out on a computer screen will greatly help sell the idea in the executive suite. Others agree. 'Management is numerically illiterate', insists Michael Schrage, a technology consultant and author. 'Instead of selling equations, they are selling pretty pictures. Visualisation is the marriage of mathematics and marketing.'

The potential is great. For a major entertainment company, his group has created 40 000 movie-going agents – cloned from a survey of actual movie-goers – to help executives determine the best way to market and distribute films. Farrell says that the model is up and working, forecasting first week box-office receipts at accuracy rates of more than 30 per cent better than traditional forecasting methods that rely on historical records.

Like Sigvaldason, 31, whose forte is visualisation, many are unaccustomed to working in a corporate setting where they have to attend meetings on time, wear suits and keep their hair neatly trimmed. Until several women joined the group, a couple of team members would show up for work in flannel shirts, jeans and hiking boots, then strip in the lab to slip into suits for meetings.

In the windowless lab room, it is not unusual for profanity to be heard in an array of languages. The work is often long and tedious. Sometimes, team members toil until the wee hours of the morning to debug some software or meet a client deadline. Wei says his wife often scolds him for coming home late, and he wonders whether his nearly two-year-old son recognises him.

Still, it's easy to overlook things humans take for granted – and that may be the biggest hurdle Farrell faces in creating a practical management tool. In an early iteration of the model built for the entertainment company, almost all the agents rushed out to see a film in its first week. The reason: the consultants failed to account for whether the agents had enough leisure time to go to the cinema.

If Farrell's team can deliver on the promise of these new concepts, they will likely give birth to a new and powerful management tool that could change the way executives manage their companies. But they have many daunting hurdles to overcome – starting with the need to show up on time for those client presentations.[1]

For discussion

Do you think 'flight simulators for management' can improve decision making?

Decision making is one of the primary responsibilities of all employees. The quality of decisions made is important for two principal reasons. First, the quality of decisions directly affects career opportunities, rewards and job satisfaction. Second, decisions contribute to the success or failure of an organisation.

Decision making is a means to an end. It entails identifying and choosing alternative solutions that lead to a desired state of affairs. The process begins with a problem and ends when a solution has been chosen. To gain an understanding of how professionals can make better decisions, this chapter focuses on: models of decision making, the dynamics of decision making, group decision-making and creativity.

Decision making identifying and choosing solutions that lead to a desired end result

Models of decision making

There are several models of decision making. Each is based on a different set of assumptions and offers a unique insight into the decision-making process. This section reviews three key historical models of decision making. They are:

- The rational model.
- Simon's normative model.
- The 'garbage can' model.

Each successive model assumes that the decision-making process is less and less rational. Let us begin with the most orderly or rational explanation of decision making.

The rational model

The **Rational model** proposes that people use a rational, four-step sequence when making decisions – that is, they identify the problem, generate alternative solutions, select a solution, and implement and evaluate the solution. According to this model, professionals are entirely objective and possess complete information on which to make a decision. Despite criticism for being unrealistic, the rational model is instructive because it analyses the decision-making process and serves as a conceptual anchor for more recent models.[2] (Also see Chapter 6 on process theories of motivation.) Let us now consider each of these four steps in detail.

Rational model
logical four-step approach to decision making

IDENTIFYING THE PROBLEM

A **Problem** exists when the actual situation and the desired situation differ. For example, a problem exists when you have to pay rent at the end of the month but don't have enough money. Your problem is not that you have to pay rent. Your problem is obtaining the necessary funds.

Problem
gap between an actual and desired situation

> The challenge for post-communist Georgia, a nation of 5.4 million, is to turn its wine into a quality export that can compete with the table wines of Spain, Italy and France and someday yield an award-winning vintage. But as I learned on a recent three-day visit, there's a long way to go before Georgia can consistently produce the rival of a typical Chianti, much less a noble St Emilion. The problem is an economy and political culture that are still dysfunctional 10 years after Soviet rule. The banking system barely works, depriving businesses of credit, and corruption is pervasive, with widespread counterfeiting of products including wine.[3]

How do companies know when a problem exists or will emerge in the near future? One expert proposed that decision makers use one of three methods to identify problems: historical cues, planning and other people's perceptions:[4]

- Using historical cues to identify problems assumes that the recent past is the best estimate of the future. Thus, professionals rely on past experience to identify discrepancies (problems) from expected trends. For example, a sales manager may conclude that a problem exists because the first-quarter sales are less than they were a year ago. This method is prone to error because it is highly subjective.
- A planning approach is more systematic and can lead to more accurate results. This method consists of using projections or imagined events (scenarios) to estimate what is expected to occur in the future. A time period of one or more years is generally used.

  The **Scenario technique** is used to identify future states, based on a given set of circumstances ('environmental conditions'). Once different scenarios are developed, companies devise alternative strategies to survive in the various circumstances. This process helps in the creation of contingency plans for far into the future. Companies such as Royal Dutch/Shell, IBM and Pfizer are increasingly using the scenario technique as a planning tool.[5]

Scenario technique
speculative forecasting method

- A final approach to identifying problems is to rely on the perceptions of others. A restaurant manager may realise that his or her restaurant provides poor service when a large number of customers complain about how long it takes to receive food after placing an order. In other words, customers' comments signal that a problem exists. Interestingly, companies frequently compound their problems by ignoring customer complaints or feedback.

GENERATING SOLUTIONS

After identifying a problem, the next logical step is to generate alternative solutions. For repetitive and routine decisions, such as deciding when to send customers a bill, alternatives are readily available in the form of 'decision rules'. For example, a company might routinely bill customers three days after shipping a product. Where no decision rules exist, however, novel and unstructured decisions must be made. Professionals must creatively generate alternative solutions. Organisations can use a number of techniques to stimulate the necessary creativity and these are discussed later in this chapter.

SELECTING A SOLUTION

Ideally, decision makers want to choose the alternative with the greatest value. Decision theorists refer to this as maximising the expected utility of an outcome. This is no easy task. First, assigning values to alternatives is complicated and prone to error. Not only are values subjective but they also vary according to the preferences of the decision maker. Before selecting a solution people often anticipate the experience of regret of making the wrong choice (how could I have been so stupid?) and take it into account when making decisions. Dutch researchers have described a nice example of the influence of this process. In the Dutch Postcode lottery the winning numbers are based on randomly drawn postcodes. The complete postcode is shared by a group of 25 addresses in one single street. When you do not play and your postcode is drawn, you know that you would have won, had you played the lottery. Compared to the classic State Lottery, people anticipate much more post-decisional regret, which in its turn influences the decision to play. Most people think that more choice means better options and greater satisfaction. But more choice can lead to excessive choice. According to Barry Schwartz, unlimited choice can produce genuine suffering. Owing to the very strong post-decisional regret, too many options can lead to stress, anxiety and decision-making paralysis.[6]

Research demonstrates that people vary in their preferences for safety or risk when making decisions. A recent meta-analysis of 150 studies revealed that males displayed more risk taking than females.[7] The second step in selecting a solution, that of evaluating alternatives, assumes that each can be judged according to set standards or criteria. This further assumes that: valid criteria exist, each alternative can be compared against these criteria and that the decision maker actually uses the criteria. As you know from making your own key life decisions, people frequently violate these assumptions.

IMPLEMENTING AND EVALUATING THE SOLUTION

Once a solution is chosen, it needs to be implemented. Before implementing a solution, though, decision makers need to do their homework. For example, three ineffective managerial tendencies have been observed frequently during the initial stages of implementation (see Table 12.1). Skilful managers try to avoid these tendencies. Table 12.1 indicates that to promote necessary understanding, acceptance and motivation, managers should involve implementers in the choice-making step.

After the solution is implemented, the evaluation phase assesses its effectiveness. If the solution is effective, it should reduce the difference between the actual and desired states that created the problem. If the gap is not closed, the implementation was not successful, and one of the following is true: either the problem was incorrectly identified, or the solution was inappropriate. If the implementation was, indeed, unsuccessful, management can return to the first step, that of problem identification. If the problem was correctly identified, then management should consider implementing one of the previously identified but untried solutions. This process can continue until all feasible solutions have been tried or the problem has changed.[8]

SUMMARISING THE RATIONAL MODEL

Optimising
choosing the best possible solution

The rational model is based on the premise that, when professionals make decisions, they are aiming to solve problems by producing the best possible solution, which is referred to in the literature as Optimising. This assumes that managers have:

TABLE 12.1 THREE MANAGERIAL TENDENCIES REDUCE THE EFFECTIVENESS OF IMPLEMENTING SOLUTIONS

Managerial tendency	Recommended solution
The tendency not to ensure that people understand what needs to be done	Involve the implementators in the choice-making step. When this is not possible, a strong and explicit attempt should be made to identify any misunderstanding, perhaps by having the implementor explain what he or she thinks needs to be done and why
The tendency not to ensure the acceptance or motivation for what needs to be done	Once again, involve the implementators in the choice-making step. Attempts should also be made to demonstrate the payoffs for effective implementation and to show how completion of various tasks will lead to successful implementation
The tendency not to provide appropriate resources for what needs to be done	Many implementations are less effective than they could be because adequate resources, such as time, staff, or information, were not provided. In particular, the allocations of such resources across departments and tasks are assumed to be appropriate because they were appropriate for implementing the previous plan. These assumptions should be checked

SOURCE: Modified from G. P. Huber, *Managerial Decision Making* (Glenview, IL: Scott, Foresman, 1980), p. 19.

- Knowledge of all possible alternatives.
- Complete knowledge about the consequences that follow each alternative.
- A well-organised and stable set of preferences for these consequences.
- The computational ability to compare consequences and to determine which one is preferred.[9]

As noted by Herbert Simon (also see Chapter 1) 'The assumptions of perfect rationality are contrary to fact. It is not a question of approximation; they do not even remotely describe the processes that human beings use for making decisions in complex situations.'[10] Thus, the rational model is at best an instructional tool. Since decision makers do not follow these rational procedures, Simon proposed a normative model of decision making.

Simon's normative model

This model attempts to identify the process that professionals actually use when making decisions. The process is guided by a decision maker's bounded rationality. **Bounded rationality** represents the notion that decision makers are 'bounded' or restricted by a variety of constraints when making decisions. These constraints include any personal or environmental characteristics that reduce rational decision-making. Examples are the limited capacity of the human mind, problem complexity and uncertainty, amount and timeliness of information at hand, importance of the decision and time demands.[11]

In contrast to the rational model, Simon's normative model suggests that decision making is characterised by: limited information processing, the use of judgemental heuristics and a process that involves 'satisficing' with something short of ideal. Each of these characteristics is now explored.

LIMITED INFORMATION PROCESSING

Decision makers are limited by how much information they process because of bounded rationality. This results in the tendency to acquire manageable rather than optimal amounts of information (see also Chapter 8 with regard to information overload). In turn, this practice makes it difficult for

Bounded rationality **constraints that restrict decision making**

CONCEPTUAL

People with a conceptual style have a high tolerance for ambiguity and tend to focus on the people or social aspects of a work situation. They take a broad perspective to problem solving and like to consider many options and future possibilities. Conceptual types adopt a long-term perspective and rely on intuition and discussion with others to acquire information. They are willing to take risks and are good at finding creative solutions to problems. On the downside, however, a conceptual style can foster an idealistic and indecisive approach to decision making.

BEHAVIOURAL

Of the four styles, this is the one which focuses most on the people aspect of decisions. Individuals with this style work well with others and enjoy social interactions in which opinions are openly exchanged. Behavioural types are supportive, receptive to suggestions, show warmth, and prefer verbal to written information. Although they like to hold meetings, people with this style have a tendency to avoid conflict and to be too concerned about others. This can lead behavioural types to adopt a 'wishy washy' approach to decision making and to have a hard time saying no to others and to have problems making difficult decisions.

RESEARCH FINDINGS AND PRACTICAL IMPLICATIONS

Research shows that very few people have only one dominant decision-making style. Rather, most people have characteristics that fall into two or three styles. Studies also show that decision-making styles vary across occupations, job levels and countries.[28] You can use knowledge of decision-making styles in three ways.

First, knowledge of styles helps you to understand yourself. Awareness of your style assists you in identifying your strengths and weaknesses as a decision maker and facilitates the potential for self-improvement. (You can assess your decision-making style by completing the Personal awareness and growth exercise located at the end of this chapter.)

Second, you can increase your ability to influence others by being aware of styles. For example, if you are dealing with an analytical person, you should provide as much information as possible to support your ideas. This same approach is more likely to frustrate a directive type.

Finally, knowledge of styles gives you an awareness of how people can take the same information and yet arrive at different decisions by using a variety of decision-making strategies. Different decision-making styles represent one likely source of interpersonal conflict at work (conflict is discussed in Chapter 13). It is important to conclude with the caveat that there is no one ideal decision-making style applicable to all situations.

Escalation of commitment

Once a decision has been made, there can be a tendency to stick to that decision regardless. Escalation situations involve circumstances in which things have gone wrong but where the situation could possibly be turned around by investing additional time, money or effort.[29] The next Snapshot provides an example of escalation of commitment at Daewoo Motor Company.

Escalation of commitment
sticking to an ineffective course of action too long

Escalation of commitment refers to the tendency to stick to an ineffective course of action when it is unlikely that the bad situation can be reversed. Personal examples include investing more money into an old or broken car, waiting an extremely long time for a bus when you could have walked there just as easily or trying to save a disruptive personal relationship that has lasted ten years. Case studies also indicate that escalation of commitment is partially responsible for some of the worst financial losses experienced by organisations. For example, from 1966 to 1989 the Long Island Lighting Company's investment in the Shoreham nuclear power plant in the US escalated from $65 million to $5 billion, despite a steady flow of negative feedback. The plant was never opened.[30]

OB Researchers Jerry Ross and Barry Staw identified four reasons for escalation of commitment (see Figure 12.4). They involve psychological and social determinants, organisational determinants, project characteristics and contextual determinants.[31]

PSYCHOLOGICAL AND SOCIAL DETERMINANTS

Defence of one's ego and individual motivations are the key psychological contributors to escalation of commitment. Individuals continue to invest when the signs say otherwise – throw good money

snapshot

Daewoo Motor Company falls prey to escalation of commitment

Kim Woo Choong thought he had scored quite a coup in 1993. That year, his Daewoo Motor Company got the green light to assemble cars in Vietnam. Then the economy stalled, and demand for cars plunged by one-third, to just 5200 units annually. Daewoo's sales shrivelled to 423 vehicles in 1998. Undaunted, Daewoo launched a new car, the Matiz, for $8800. Sales in Vietnam may now double this year. But rivals doubt Daewoo's total $33 million investment is paying off. 'There's no way they could make money at this price', says a foreign auto executive in Hanoi.

The Vietnam quagmire helps explain why Korea's Daewoo Group is in such a mess that creditors are now trying to force its breakup – and why it is negotiating with General Motors Corp to sell pieces of its car company. From the United States to India, Chairman Kim is stumbling in his quest to build a car giant. In most places, the reasons are similar: plunging into dicey countries, selling at a loss to gain share and refusing to retreat when the cause is hopeless.

DAEWOO'S GLOBAL HEADACHES

Korea	United States	Western Europe	India	Vietnam
Car sales plunged by 56% in 1998, to 234 000 units, as Daewoo was adding capacity	The goal to sell 100 000 cars in its first year is unlikely to be met. Daewoo is offering steep rebates	Sales have risen in Britain, Germany, and Italy. But analysts don't expect the gains to last	Analysts estimate Daewoo is losing more than $30 million annually by offering $2500 discounts	Its hopes of hitting it big by arriving early have been dashed by rivals and a decline in demand

SOURCE: Excerpted from J. Veale, L. Armstrong, and J. Muller, 'How Daewoo Ran Itself Off the Road', *Business Week*, 30 August 1999, p. 48.

FIGURE 12.4 A MODEL OF ESCALATION OF COMMITMENT

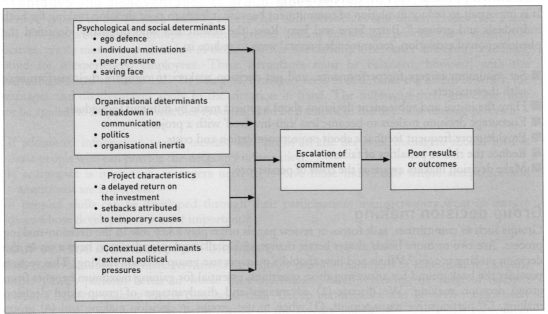

SOURCE: Based on discussion in J. Ross and B. M. Staw, 'Organizational Escalation and Exit: Lessons from the Shoreham Nuclear Power Plant', *Academy of Management Journal*, August 1993, pp. 701–32.

■ Groups were less efficient than individuals. This suggests that time constraints are an important consideration in determining whether to involve groups in decision making. Consider how long it took a team of Nokia executives to decide whether or not to license its software to other phone makers. 'Nokia executives, who prize consensus, debated the issue for nine months from mid-2000 to early 2001. At eight successive monthly meetings of the company's nine-person executive board, members raised questions and stalled the project.'[40] This example highlights that time constraints are an important consideration when determining whether to involve groups in decision making.

■ Groups were more confident about their judgements and choices than individuals. Because group confidence does not necessarily guarantee the quality of a decision, this overconfidence can fuel groupthink (see Chapter 9) and a resistance to considering alternative solutions proposed by outsiders.

■ Group size affected decision outcomes. Decision quality was negatively related to group size.[41]

■ Decision-making accuracy was higher both when groups knew a great deal about the issues at hand and group leaders possessed the ability to evaluate effectively the group members' opinions and judgements. Groups need to give more weight to relevant and accurate judgements while downplaying irrelevant or inaccurate judgements made by its members.[42]

■ The composition of a group affects its decision-making processes and ultimately performance. For example, groups of familiar people are more likely to make better decisions when members share a lot of unique information. In contrast, unacquainted group members should outperform groups of friends when most group members possess common knowledge.[43]

Additional research suggests that managers should use a contingency approach when determining whether to include others in the decision-making process. Important factors when using others in decision making are minority dissent, which means the extent to which group members feel comfortable in disagreeing with other group members, and the group's level of participation in decision making. High levels of minority dissent and participation are important for innovative groups. Take a moment to complete the next Activity. It assesses the amount of minority dissent and participation in group decision making for a group project you have completed or are currently working on in school or on the job. Is your satisfaction with the group related to minority dissent and participation in decision making? If not, what might explain this surprising result?

Let us now consider some contingency recommendations.

PRACTICAL CONTINGENCY RECOMMENDATIONS

If the decision occurs frequently, such as deciding on promotions or who qualifies for a loan, use groups, as they tend to produce more consistent decisions than do individuals. Given time constraints, let the most competent individual, rather than a group, make the decision. In the face of 'environmental threats' such as time pressure and the potentially serious effect of a decision, groups use less information and fewer communication channels. This increases the probability of a bad decision.[44] This conclusion underscores a general recommendation that managers should keep in mind, not least because the quality of communication strongly affects a group's productivity. It is essential, therefore, to devise mechanisms to enhance the effectiveness of communication when dealing with complex tasks (see Chapter 8).

Participative management

An organisation needs to maximise its workers' potential if it wants to compete successfully in the global economy. As noted by Jack Welch, the former CEO of General Electric: 'Only the most productive companies are going to win. If you can't sell a top quality product at the world's lowest price, you're going to be out of the game. In that environment, 6 per cent annual improvement in productivity may not be good enough anymore; you may need between 8 and 9 per cent.'[45] Participative management and employee empowerment (which is further discussed in Chapter 13) are highly touted methods for meeting this productivity challenge. Interestingly, employees also seem to desire or recognise the need for participative management. A survey of 2408 employees, for example, revealed that almost 66 per cent desired more influence or decision-making power in their jobs.[46]

Confusion exists about the exact meaning of **Participative management** (PM). One management

Participative management involving employees in various forms of decision making

activity

Assessing participation in group decision making

Instructions

The following survey measures minority dissent, participation in group decision making and satisfaction with a group. For each of the items, use the rating scale shown below to circle the answer that best represents your feelings based on a group project you were or currently are involved in. Next, use the scoring key to compute scores for the levels of minority dissent, participation in decision making and satisfaction with the group.

1 = Strongly disagree
2 = Disagree
3 = Neither agree nor disagree
4 = Agree
5 = Strongly agree

1 Within my team, individuals disagree with one another.	1 2 3 4 5
2 Within my team, individuals do not go along with majority opinion.	1 2 3 4 5
3 Within my team, individuals voice their disagreement of majority opinion.	1 2 3 4 5
4 Within my team, I am comfortable voicing my disagreement of the majority opinion.	1 2 3 4 5
5 Within my team, individuals do not immediately agree with one another.	1 2 3 4 5
6 As a team member, I have a real say in how work is carried out.	1 2 3 4 5
7 Within my team, most members have a chance to participate in decisions.	1 2 3 4 5
8 My team is designed so that everyone has the opportunity to participate in decisions.	1 2 3 4 5
9 I am satisfied with my group.	1 2 3 4 5
10 I would like to work with this group on another project.	1 2 3 4 5

Scoring key

Minority dissent (add scores for items 1, 2, 3, 4, 5): _____
Participation in decision making (add scores for items 6, 7, 8): _____
Satisfaction (add scores for items 9, 10): _____

Arbitrary norms

Low minority dissent = 5–15
High minority dissent = 16–25
Low participation in decision making = 3–8
High participation in decision making = 9–15
Low satisfaction = 2–5
High satisfaction = 6–10

SOURCE: The items in the survey were developed from C. K. W. De Dreu and M. A. West, 'Minority Dissent and Team Innovation: The Importance of Participation in Decision Making', *Journal of Applied Psychology*, December 2001, pp. 1192–201.

expert clarified this situation by defining participative management as the process whereby employees play a direct role in setting goals, making decisions, solving problems and making changes in the organisation. Without question, participative management entails much more than simply asking employees for their ideas or opinions.

Advocates of PM claim employee participation increases employee satisfaction, commitment and performance. To gain a greater understanding of how and when participative management works, we begin by discussing a model of participative management.

A MODEL OF PARTICIPATIVE MANAGEMENT

Consistent with both Maslow's need theory and the job characteristics model of job design (see Chapter 5), participative management is predicted to increase motivation because it helps employees fulfil three basic needs: autonomy, meaningful work and interpersonal contact. Satisfaction of these needs enhances feelings of acceptance and commitment, security, challenge and satisfaction. In turn, these positive feelings are purported to lead to increased innovation and performance.[47]

Participative management does not work in all situations. Three factors influence the effectiveness of PM: the design of work, the level of trust between management and employees, and the employees' competence and readiness to participate. With respect to the design of work, individual participation is counterproductive when employees are highly dependent on each other, as on an assembly line. The problem with individual participation in this case is that employees generally do not have a broad understanding of the entire production process. Also, participative management is less likely to succeed when employees mistrust management. Finally, PM is more effective when employees are competent, prepared and interested in participating.[48]

RESEARCH FINDINGS AND PRACTICAL IMPLICATIONS

Participative management can significantly increase employee job involvement, organisational commitment, creativity and perceptions of procedural justice and personal control.[49] Two meta-analyses provide additional support for the value of participative management. Results from a meta-analysis involving 27 studies and 6732 individuals revealed that employee participation in the performance appraisal process was positively related to an employee's satisfaction with his or her performance review perceived value of the appraisal, motivation to improve performance following a performance review and perceived fairness of the appraisal process.[50] A second meta-analysis of 86 studies involving 18 872 people further demonstrated that participation had a small but significant effect on job performance and a moderate link with job satisfaction.[51] This latter finding questions the widespread conclusion that participative management should be used to increase employee performance.

So what is a manager to do? We believe that PM is not a quick-fix solution for low productivity and motivation, as some enthusiastic supporters claim. Nonetheless, because participative management is effective in certain situations, managers can increase their chances of obtaining positive results by using, once again, a contingency approach.[52] For example, the effectiveness of participation depends on the type of interactions between managers and employees as they jointly solve problems. Effective participation requires a constructive interaction that fosters co-operation and respect, as opposed to competition and defensiveness.[53] Managers are advised not to use participative programmes when they are having destructive interactions with their employees.

Experiences of companies implementing participative management programmes suggest three additional practical recommendations. First, supervisors and middle managers tend to resist participative management because it reduces their power and authority. It is important to gain the support and commitment of employees who have managerial responsibility. Second, a longitudinal study of Fortune 1000 firms in 1987, 1990 and 1993 indicated that employee involvement was more effective when it was implemented as part of a broader total-quality-management programme.[54] Total quality management is discussed in Chapter 15. This study suggests that organisations should use participative management and employee involvement as vehicles to help them meet their strategic and operational goals as opposed to using these techniques as ends in themselves. Third, the process of implementing participative management must be monitored and managed by top management.[55]

Group problem-solving techniques

Using groups to make decisions generally requires that they reach a consensus. According to a decision-making expert, a **Consensus** 'is reached when all members can say they either agree with the decision or have had their "day in court" and were unable to convince the others of their viewpoint. In the final analysis, everyone agrees to support the outcome.'[56] This definition indicates that consensus does not require unanimous agreement because group members may still disagree with the final decision but are willing to work toward its success.

Groups can come across obstacles as they try to arrive at a consensus decision. For example, groups may not generate all the relevant alternatives to a problem because an individual dominates or

Consensus presenting opinions and gaining agreement to support a decision

intimidates other group members. This can be either overt or subtle, or indeed both. For instance, group members who possess power and authority, such as a CEO, can be intimidating, regardless of interpersonal style, simply by being present in the room. Moreover, shyness inhibits the generation of alternatives. Shy or socially anxious individuals may withhold their input for fear of embarrassment or through lack of confidence.[57] Satisficing (or sufficing) is another hurdle to effective group decision making and is the result of a group having limited time or information, or an inability to handle large amounts of information.[58] A management expert offered the following advice for successfully achieving consensus: groups should use active listening skills, involve as many members as possible, seek out the reasons behind arguments and dig for the facts. At the same time, groups should not 'horse trade' (I'll support you on this decision because you supported me on the last one), vote or agree just to avoid upsetting the process.[59] Voting is not encouraged because it can split the group into winners and losers.[60]

Decision-making experts have developed three group problem-solving techniques – brainstorming, the nominal group technique and the Delphi technique – to reduce the above obstacles. Knowledge of these techniques can help current and future professionals to use group-aided decision making more effectively. Further, the advent of computer-aided decision making enables professionals to use these techniques to solve complex problems with large groups of people.

BRAINSTORMING

Brainstorming was developed by A. F. Osborn, an advertising executive, to increase creativity.[61] **Brainstorming** is a technique used to help groups generate multiple ideas and alternatives for solving problems. It is effective because it helps reduce interference, during this early stage, from the critical and judgemental reactions of other group members.

Brainstorming
process to
generate a
quantity of ideas

When brainstorming, a group is convened, and the problem at hand is reviewed. Then individual members are asked to silently generate ideas, or alternatives, for solving the problem. Silent idea generation is recommended in preference to having group members randomly shout out their ideas because it leads to a greater number of unique ideas. Next, these ideas are solicited and written on a blackboard or flip chart. A recent study suggests that managers or team leaders may prefer to collect the brainstormed ideas anonymously. Results demonstrated that more controversial ideas and more useful ideas were generated by anonymous brainstorming groups.[62] Finally, a second session is used to check and evaluate the alternatives. Decision makers are advised to follow four rules for brainstorming:[63]

■ Stress quantity over quality. Decision makers should try to generate and write down as many ideas as possible. Encouraging quantity encourages people to think beyond their favourite (pet) ideas.
■ Freewheeling, as in 'thinking without the brakes on', should be encouraged; do not set limits. Group members are advised to offer any and all the ideas they have. The wilder and more outrageous, the better.
■ Suspend judgement. Don't criticise during the initial stage of idea generation. Phrases such as 'we've never done it that way', 'it won't work', 'it's too expensive' and 'the boss will never agree', should not be used.
■ Ignore seniority. People cannot think or suggest freely when they are trying to impress the boss or when office politics are involved. The facilitator of a brainstorming session should emphasise that everyone has the same rank. No one is given 'veto power' when brainstorming.

Brainstorming is an effective technique for generating new ideas and alternatives. It is not appropriate for evaluating alternatives or selecting solutions.

THE NOMINAL GROUP TECHNIQUE

The **Nominal group technique** (NGT) helps groups not only generate ideas but also evaluate and select solutions. NGT is a structured group meeting that adheres to the following format.[64]

**Nominal group
technique**
process to
generate ideas
and evaluate
solutions

A group is convened to discuss a particular problem or issue. After the problem is understood, individuals silently generate ideas in writing. Each individual, in turn, then offers one idea from his or her list. Ideas are recorded on a blackboard or flip chart; they are not discussed at this stage of the process. Once all ideas are elicited, the group discusses them. Anyone may criticise or defend any item. During this step, clarification is provided as well as general agreement or disagreement with the idea. The '30-second soap box' technique, which entails giving each participant a maximum of 30 seconds to argue for or against any of the ideas under consideration, can be used to facilitate this discussion.

Finally, group members vote anonymously for their top choices with weighted votes (e.g. 1st choice = 3 points; 2nd choice = 2 points; 3rd choice = 1 point). The group leader then adds the votes to determine the group's choice. Prior to making a final decision, the group may decide to discuss the top ranked items and conduct a second round of voting.

The nominal group technique reduces the obstacles to group decision making by: separating brainstorming from evaluation, promoting balanced participation between group members and incorporating mathematical voting techniques in order to reach consensus. NGT has been used successfully in many different decision-making situations.

THE DELPHI TECHNIQUE

This problem-solving method was originally developed by the Rand Corporation for technological forecasting.[65] Now it is used as a multipurpose planning tool. The **Delphi technique** is a group process that, anonymously, generates ideas or judgements from physically dispersed experts. Unlike the NGT, experts' ideas are obtained from questionnaires or via the Internet rather than by face-to-face group discussion.

A manager begins the Delphi process by identifying the issue or issues to be investigated. For example, a manager might want to inquire about customer demand, customers' future preferences or the effect of locating a plant in a certain region of the country. Next, participants are identified and a questionnaire is developed. The questionnaire is sent to participants and returned to the manager. In today's computer-networked environments, this often means that the questionnaires are emailed to participants. The manager then summarises the responses and sends feedback to the participants. At this stage, participants are asked to:

- Review the feedback.
- Prioritise the issues being considered.
- Return the survey within a specified time period.

This cycle repeats until the manager obtains the necessary information.

The Delphi technique is useful in instances when: face-to-face discussions are impractical, disagreements and conflict are likely to impair communication, certain individuals might severely dominate group discussion or groupthink is a probable outcome of the group process.[66]

COMPUTER-AIDED DECISION MAKING

The purpose of computer-aided decision making is to reduce obstacles to consensus while collecting more information in a shorter period of time. There are two types of computer-aided decision-making systems: chauffeur-driven and group-driven.[67] Chauffeur-driven systems ask participants to answer predetermined questions on electronic keypads or dials. Live television audiences on quiz shows such as *Who Wants to Be a Millionaire* are frequently polled for their answers using this system. The computer system tabulates participants' responses in a matter of seconds.

Group-driven meetings are conducted in special facilities equipped with individual computer workstations that are networked to each other. Instead of talking, participants type their input, ideas, comments, reactions or evaluations on their keyboards. The input simultaneously appears on a large projector screen at the front of the room, thereby enabling all participants to see all the input. This computer-driven process reduces obstacles to consensus as the input is anonymous, everyone gets a chance to contribute and no one can dominate the process. Research demonstrated that, for large groups of people, computer-aided decision making produces a greater quality and quantity of ideas than either traditional brainstorming or the nominal group technique. There were no significant advantages to group-aided decision making with smaller groups of four to six.[68] Moreover, a recent study demonstrated that computer-aided decision making produced relatively more ideas as group size increased from 5 to 10 members. The positive benefits of larger groups, however, were more pronounced for heterogeneous as opposed to homogeneous groups.[69]

Delphi technique group process that anonymously generates ideas from physically dispersed experts

Creativity

In the light of today's need for quick decisions, an organisation's ability to stimulate the creativity and innovation of its employees is becoming increasingly important. Some organisations believe that creativity and innovation are the seeds of success:

> An office is more than a place to house employees. These days, it's a place to seek the inspiration of an urban skyline or a peaceful sunset. Not to mention a place to shoot a few hoops, play some ping-pong, take a nap, sip an espresso – or build a little buzz. Today's small companies seek an environment that quickly communicates an image of success and creativity, one that wows potential clients, reassures investors, attracts hard-to-find recruits and helps employees forget how hard they're working. Achieving all that can mean going to extraordinary lengths. The firm of Thompson & Rose Architects pushes the process to the next level. In their architecture for the office of the future, everything is mutable. Nothing is fixed, not even the exterior skin of the office building, which changes with the weather – shading in summer, allowing more solar heating in the winter, permitting ambient light inside in all seasons.[70]

To gain further insight into managing the creative process, we begin by defining creativity and highlighting the stages underlying individual creativity. This section then presents a model of organisational creativity and innovation.

Definition and stages

Although many definitions have been proposed, **Creativity** is defined here as the process of using imagination and skill to develop a new or unique product, object, process or thought.[71] It can be as simple as locating a new place to hang your car keys to as complex as developing a pocket-size microcomputer. This definition highlights three broad types of creativity: creating something new (creation); combining or synthesising things (synthesis) and improving or changing things (modification).

Creativity process of developing something new or unique

Early approaches to explaining creativity were based on differences between the left and right hemispheres of the brain. Researchers thought the right-hand side of the brain was responsible for creativity. More recently, however, researchers have questioned this explanation:

> 'The left brain/right brain dichotomy is simplified and misleading', says Dr John C Mazziotta, a researcher at the University of California at Los Angeles School of Medicine. What scientists have found instead is that creativity is a feat of mental gymnastics engaging the conscious and subconscious parts of the brain. It draws on everything from knowledge, logic, imagination, and intuition to the ability to see connections and distinctions between ideas and things.[72]

Let us now examine the stages underlying the creativity process.

Researchers are not absolutely certain how creativity takes place. Nonetheless, we do know that creativity involves 'making remote associations' between unconnected events, ideas, physical objects or information stored in memory. Consider how remote associations led to a creative idea that ultimately increased revenue for Japan Railways (JR) East, the largest rail carrier in the world:

> While JR East was building a new bullet-train line, water began to cause problems in the tunnel being dug through Mount Tanigawa. As engineers drew up plans to drain it away, some of the workers had found a use for the water – they were drinking it. A maintenance worker, whose job was to check the safety of the tunneling equipment, thought it tasted so good that he proposed that JR East should bottle and market it as premium mineral water. This past year, 'Oshimizu' water generated some $60 million of sales for JR East.[73]

The maintenance worker obviously associated the tunnel water with bottled water, and this led to the idea of marketing the water as a commercial product. Figure 12.5 depicts five stages underlying the creative process.[74]

> Market-survey results were negative; major office-supply distributors were skeptical. So he began giving samples to 3M executives and their secretaries. Once they actually used the little pieces of adhesive paper, they were hooked. Having sold 3M on the project, Fry used the same approach with other executives throughout the United States.[81]

Notice how Fry had to influence others to try out his idea. Figure 12.6 shows that creative people have the ability to persuade and influence others.

GROUP CHARACTERISTICS

Figure 12.6 also lists six characteristics that influence the level of creativity exhibited by a work group. In general, group creativity is fuelled by a cohesive environment that supports open interaction, diverse viewpoints and playful surroundings.[82] Kodak, for example, created a 'humour room' where employees can relax and have creative brainstorming sessions. The room contains joke books, videotapes of comedians, stress-reducing toys and software for creative decision making.[83] Structured problem-solving procedures, such as those previously discussed and supportive supervision, also enhance creativity.[84]

ORGANISATIONAL CHARACTERISTICS

Research and corporate examples clearly support the importance of organisational characteristics in generating organisational creativity. Organisations such as Virgin, 3M, Microsoft, The Body Shop and DuPont are all known as innovative companies that encourage creativity via the organisational characteristics shown in Figure 12.6. DuPont, for example, created the Center for Creativity and Innovation in 1991. Its mission is to encourage creativity throughout the organisation.

> Although the center is staffed by only three full-time employees, it has the support of 10 facilitators – creativity-training 'volunteers' who hold full-time DuPont jobs outside the center. In this way, DuPont conducts creativity training in-house. This has two important advantages: first, the company has fewer security concerns; and second, training costs are lower.
>
> Top management support for the center is visible and continuous. A senior manager sponsors each creative problem-solving workshop and attends as a full participant, not just an observer. The company's support for creativity training is expressed by Edgar Woolard, Chairman: 'We intend to provide hero status to those who show us how to get products to the marketplace more promptly and more creatively.'[85]

This example illustrates the point that organisational creativity requires resources, commitment and a reinforcing organisational culture. Table 12.4 presents a number of suggestions that may be used to help create this culture.

TABLE 12.4 SUGGESTIONS FOR IMPROVING EMPLOYEE CREATIVITY

- Develop an environment that supports creative behaviour. Try to avoid using an autocratic style of leadership
- Encourage employees to be more open to new ideas and experiences
- Keep in mind that people use different strategies, like walking around or listening to music, to foster their creativity
- Provide employees with stimulating work that creates a sense of personal growth. Allow employees to have fun and play around
- Encourage an open environment that is free from defensive behaviour. Treat errors and mistakes as opportunities for learning
- Let employees occasionally try out their pet ideas. Provide a margin of error
- Avoid using a negative mind-set when an employee approaches you with a new idea. Reward creative behaviour

SOURCE: Adapted from discussion in E. Raudsepp, '101 Ways to Spark Your Employees' Creative Potential', *Office Administration and Automation*, September 1985, pp. 38, 39–43, 56.

Learning outcomes: Summary of key terms

1 Compare and contrast the rational model of decision making, Simon's normative model and the 'garbage can' model

The rational decision-making model consists of identifying the problem, generating alternative solutions, selecting a solution, and implementing and evaluating the solution. Research indicates that decision makers do not follow the series of steps outlined in the rational model. Simon's normative model is guided by a decision maker's bounded rationality. Bounded rationality means that decision makers are bounded or restricted by a variety of constraints when making decisions. The normative model suggests that decision making is characterised by (a) limited information processing, (b) the use of judgemental heuristics and (c) satisficing. The 'garbage can' model of decision making assumes that decision making does not follow an orderly series of steps. In this process, decisions result from the interaction among four independent streams of events: problems, solutions, participants and choice opportunities.

2 Discuss the contingency relationships that influence the three primary strategies used to select solutions

Decision makers use either an aided-analytic, unaided-analytic or non-analytic strategy when selecting a solution. The choice of a strategy depends on the characteristics of the decision task and the characteristics of the decision maker. In general, the greater the demands and constraints faced by a decision maker, the higher the probability that an aided-analytic approach will be used. Aided-analytic strategies are more likely to be used by competent and motivated individuals. Ultimately, decision makers must compromise between their desire to make correct decisions and the amount of time and effort they can allow for the decision-making process.

3 Explain the model of decision-making styles

The model of decision-making styles is based on the idea that styles vary along two different dimensions: value orientation and tolerance for ambiguity. When these two dimensions are combined, they form four styles of decision making: directive, analytical, conceptual and behavioural. People with a directive style have a low tolerance for ambiguity and are oriented towards the task itself and technical concerns. Analytics have a higher tolerance for ambiguity and are characterised by a tendency to overly analyse a situation. People with a conceptual style have a high threshold for ambiguity and tend to focus on the people or social aspects of a work situation. This behavioural style is the most people oriented of the four styles.

4 Describe the model of escalation of commitment

Escalation of commitment refers to the tendency to stick to an ineffective course of action despite it being unlikely that a bad situation can be reversed. Psychological and social determinants, organisational determinants, project characteristics and contextual determinants cause decision makers to exhibit this decision-making error.

5 Summarise the advantages and disadvantages of involving groups in the decision-making process

Although research shows that groups typically outperform the average individual, there are five important issues to consider when using groups to make decisions: (a) groups are less efficient than individuals, (b) a group's overconfidence can fuel groupthink, (c) decision quality is negatively related to group size, (d) groups are more accurate when they know a great deal about the issues at hand and when the leader possesses the ability to effectively evaluate the group members' opinions and judgements, (e) the composition of a group affects its decision-making processes and performance. In the final analysis, professionals are encouraged to use a contingency approach when determining whether to include others in the decision-making process.

6 Explain how participative management affects performance

Participative management reflects the extent to which employees participate in setting goals, making decisions, solving problems and making changes in the organisation. Participative management is expected to increase motivation because it helps employees fulfil three basic needs: (a) autonomy, (b) meaningful work and (c) interpersonal contact. Participative management does not work in all situations. The design of work and the level of trust between management and employees influence the effectiveness of participative management.

7 Compare brainstorming, the nominal group technique, the Delphi technique, and computer-aided decision-making

Group problem-solving techniques facilitate better decision making within groups. Brainstorming is used to help groups generate multiple ideas and alternatives for solving problems. The nominal group technique assists groups both to generate ideas and to evaluate and select solutions. The Delphi technique is a group process that anonymously generates ideas or judgements from physically dispersed experts. The purpose of computer-aided decision making is to reduce the obstacles to consensus, while collecting more information in a shorter period of time.

8 Describe the stages of the creative process

Creativity is defined as the process of using imagination and skill to develop a new or unique product, object, process or thought. It is not adequately explained by differences between the left and right hemispheres of the brain. There are five stages of the creative process: preparation, concentration, incubation, illumination and verification.

9 Explain the model of organisational creativity and innovation

Organisational creativity is directly influenced by organisational characteristics and the creative behaviour that occurs within work groups. In turn, a group's creative behaviour is influenced by group characteristics and the individual creative behaviour and performance of its members. Individual creativity is directly affected by a variety of individual characteristics. Finally, individual, group and organisational characteristics all influence each other within this process.

Review questions

1 What role do emotions play when making a decision?
2 Do you think people are rational when they make decisions? Under what circumstances would an individual tend to follow a rational process?
3 Describe a situation in which you 'satisficed' when making a decision. Why did you do this instead of optimising the decision?
4 Do you think the 'garbage can' model is a realistic representation of organisational decision making? Explain your rationale.
5 Why would decision-making styles be a source of interpersonal conflict?
6 Describe a situation in which you exhibited escalation of commitment. Why did you escalate a losing situation?
7 Do you prefer to solve problems in groups or by yourself? Why?
8 Given the intuitive appeal of participative management, why do you think it fails as often as it succeeds? Explain.
9 Do you think you are creative? Why or why not?
10 What advice would you offer a manager who was attempting to improve the creativity of his or her employees? Explain.

Personal awareness and growth exercise

What is your decision-making style?

Objectives

1 To assess your decision-making style.
2 To consider the managerial implications of your decision-making style.

Introduction

Earlier in the chapter we discussed a model of decision-making styles that is based on the idea that styles vary along the dimensions of an individual's value orientation and tolerance for ambiguity. In turn, these dimensions combine to form four styles of decision making (see Figure 12.3): directive, analytical, conceptual and behavioural. Alan Rowe, an OB researcher, developed an instrument called the Decision Style Inventory to measure these four styles. This exercise provides the opportunity for you to assess and interpret your decision-making style using this measurement device.

Instructions

The Decision Style Inventory consists of 20 questions, each with four responses.[86] You must consider each possible response to a question and then rank them according to how much you prefer each response. There are no right or wrong answers, so respond with what first comes to mind. Although many of the questions are based on how individuals make decisions at work, feel free to use your student role as a frame of reference to answer the questions. For each question, you have four responses, and each should be ranked either 1, 2, 4 or 8; with 8 being for the response that is most like you, 4 for the one moderately like you, 2 for slightly like you, and 1 for least like you. For instance, a question could be answered as follows: [8], [4], [2], [1]. Notice that each number was used only once to answer a question. Do not repeat any number when answering a given question. These numbers should be written in the blank column alongside each response.

Once all of the responses for the 20 questions have been ranked, total the scores in each of the four columns. The total score for column one represents your score for the directive style, column two your analytical style, column three your conceptual style, and column four your behavioural style.

1 My prime objective in life is to:	have a position with status	be the best in whatever I do	be recognised for my work	feel secure in my job
2 I enjoy work that:	is clear and well defined	is varied and challenging	lets me act independently	involves people
3 I expect people to be:	productive	capable	committed	responsive
4 My work lets me:	get things done	find workable approaches	apply new ideas	be truly satisfied
5 I communicate best by:	talking with others	putting things in writing	being open with others	having a group meeting
6 My planning focuses on:	current problems	how best to meet goals	future opportunities	needs of people in the organisation
7 I prefer to solve problems by:	applying rules	using careful analysis	being creative feelings	relying on my
8 I prefer information that is:	simple and direct	complete	broad and informative	easily understood
9 When I'm not sure what to do, I:	rely on my intuition	search for alternatives	try to find a compromise	avoid making a decision
10 Whenever possible, I avoid:	long debates	incomplete work	technical problems	conflict with others

11 I am really good at:	remembering details	finding answers	seeing many options	working with people	
12 When time is important, I:	decide and act quickly	apply proven approaches	look for what will work	refuse to be pressurised	
13 In social settings, I:	speak to many people	observe what others are doing	contribute to the conversation	want to be part of the discussion	
14 I always remember:	people's names	places I have been	people's faces	people's personalities	
15 I prefer jobs where I:	receive high rewards	have challenging assignments	can reach my personal goals	am accepted by the group	
16 I work best with people who are:	energetic and ambitious	very competent	open minded	polite and understanding	
17 When I am under stress, I:	speak quickly	try to concentrate on the problem	become frustrated	worry about what I should do	
18 Others consider me:	aggressive	disciplined	imaginative	supportive	
19 My decisions are generally:	realistic and direct	systematic and logical	broad and flexible	sensitive to the other's needs	
20 I dislike:	losing control	boring work	following rules	being rejected	
Total score					

SOURCE: © Alan J. Rowe, Professor Emeritus. Revised 18/12/98. Reprinted by permission.

Questions for discussion

1 In terms of your decision-making profile, which of the four styles represents your decision-making style best (i.e. has the highest score)? Which is the least reflective of your style (has the lowest score)?
2 Do you agree with this assessment? Explain.
3 How do your scores compare with the following norms: directive (75), analytical (90), conceptual (80) and behavioural (55)? What do the differences between your scores and the survey norms suggest about your decision-making style?
4 What are the advantages and disadvantages of your decision-making profile?
5 Which of the other decision-making styles is most inconsistent with your style? How would this difference affect your ability to work with someone who has this style?

Group exercise

Ethical decision making

Objectives
1 To apply the rational model of decision making
2 To examine the ethical implications of a managerial decision.

Introduction
In this chapter we learned there are four steps in the rational model of decision making. The third stage involves evaluating alternatives and selecting a solution. Part of this evaluation may entail deciding whether or not a solution is ethical. The purpose of this exercise is to examine the steps in decision making and to consider the issue of ethical decision making.

Instructions

Break into groups of five or six people and read the following case. As a group, discuss the decision made by the company and answer the questions for discussion at the end of the case. Before answering questions 4 and 5, however, brainstorm alternative decisions the managers at TELECOMPROS could have made. Finally, the entire class can reconvene and discuss the alternative solutions that were generated.

The case of Telecompros

For large cellular service providers, maintaining their own customer service call centre can be very expensive. Many have found they can save money by outsourcing their customer service calls to outside companies.

Telecompros is one such company. It specialises in cellular phone customer service. Telecompros saves large cellular companies money by eliminating overhead costs associated with building a call centre, installing additional telephone lines, and so forth. Once Telecompros is hired by large cellular service providers, Telecompros employees are trained on the cellular service providers' systems, policies, and procedures. Telecompros' income is derived from charging a per hour fee for each employee.

Six months ago, Telecompros acquired a contract with Cell2U, a large cellular service provider serving the western United States. In the beginning of the contract, Cell2U was very pleased. As a call centre, Telecompros has a computer system in place that monitors the number of calls the centre receives and how quickly the calls are answered. When Cell2U received its first report, the system showed that Telecompros was a very productive call centre and it handled the call volume very well. A month later, however, Cell2U launched a nationwide marketing campaign. Suddenly, the call volume increased and Telecompros' customer service reps were unable to keep up. The phone monitoring system showed that some customers were on hold for 45 minutes or longer, and at any given time throughout the day there were as many as 50 customers on hold. It was clear to Cell2U that the original number of customer service reps it had contracted for was not enough. It renegotiated with upper management at Telecompros and hired additional customer service reps. Telecompros was pleased because it was now receiving more money from Cell2U for the extra employees, and Cell2U was happy because the call centre volume was no longer overwhelming and its customers were happy with the attentive customer service.

Three months later though, Telecompros' customer service supervisors noticed a decrease in the number of customer service calls. It seemed that the reps had done such a good job that Cell2U customers had fewer problems. There were too many people and not enough calls. With little to do, some reps were playing computer games or surfing the Internet while waiting for calls to come in.

Knowing that if Cell2U analysed its customer service needs, it would want to decrease the reps to save money. Telecompros' upper management made a decision. Rather than decrease its staff and lose the hourly pay from Cell2U, the upper management told customer service supervisors to call the customer service line. Supervisors called in and spent enough time on the phone with reps to ensure that the computer registered the call and the time it took to 'resolve' the call. Then they would hang up and call the call centre again. Telecompros did not have to decrease its customer service reps, and Cell2U continued to pay for the allotted reps until the end of the contract.

Questions for discussion

1 Was the decision made by Telecompros an ethical one? Why or why not?

2 If you were a manager at Telecompros, what would you have done when your manager asked you to call the customer service line? What are the ramifications of your decision? Discuss.

3 Where did the decision-making process at Telecompros break down? Explain.

4 What alternative solutions to the problem at hand did you identify? What is your recommended solution? Explain why you selected this alternative.

5 How would you implement your preferred solution? Describe in detail.

Internet Exercise

There are countless brainstorming sessions conducted by individuals and groups within organisations on a daily basis. We do not expect this trend to stop. To help you successfully set up and participate in a brainstorming session, this chapter provided a set of guidelines for conducting a brainstorming session. We did not, however, discuss different techniques that can be used to enhance individual and group creativity while brainstorming. The purpose of this exercise is for you to learn two techniques that can be used to enhance creative idea generation and to complete two creativity puzzles. Go to our website www.mcgraw-hill.co.uk/textbooks/buelens for further instructions.

Notes

1 J. Byrne, 'Virtual Management: Computer Models May Give Execs Previews of How Decisions Pan Out', *Business Week*, September 1998, p. 80. Reproduced with permission.

2 For a review of research on rational decision making, see K. E. Stanovich, *Who Is Rational?* (Mahwah, NJ: Lawrence Erlbaum, 1999), pp. 1–31.

3 P. Starobin, 'A Wine Region Waiting to Ripen', *Business Week*, 19 February 2001.

4 See W. F. Pounds, 'The Process of Problem Finding', *Industrial Management Review*, Fall 1969, pp. 1–19.

5 Scenario planning is discussed by S. Schnaars and P. Ziamou, 'The Essentials of Scenario Writing', *Business Horizons*, July–August 2001, pp. 25–31.

6 See M. Zeelenberg and R. Pieters, 'Consequences of Regret Aversion in Real Life: The Case of the Dutch Post-code Lottery, *Organizational Behavior and Human Decision Processes*, March 2004, pp. 155–68; and B. Schwartz, *The Paradox of Choice* (New York: HarperCollins, 2004).

7 See B. A. Melers, A. Schwartz and A. D. J. Cooke, 'Judgment and Decision Making', in *Annual Review of Psychology*, eds J. T. Spence, J. M. Darley and D. J. Foss (Palo Alto, CA: Annual Reviews, 1998), pp. 447–77; and E. U. Webber, C. K. Hsee and J. Sokolowska, 'What Folklore Tells Us about Risk and Risk Taking: Cross-Cultural Comparisons of American, German, and Chinese Proverbs', *Organizational Behavior and Human Decision Processes*, August 1998, pp. 170–86. See also J. P. Byrnes, D. C. Miller and W. D. Schafer, 'Gender Differences in Risk Taking: A Meta-Analysis', *Psychological Bulletin*, May 1999, pp. 367–83.

8 The implementation process and its relationship to decision outcomes is discussed by S. J. Miller, D. J. Hickson and D. C. Wilson, 'Decision-Making in Organizations', in *Handbook of Organization Studies*, eds S. R. Clegg, C. Hardy and W. R. Nord (London: Sage Publications, 1996), pp. 293–312.

9 For a review of these assumptions, see H. A. Simon, 'A Behavioral Model of Rational Choice', *The Quarterly Journal of Economics*, February 1955, pp. 99–118.

10 H. A. Simon, 'Rational Decision Making in Business Organizations', *American Economic Review*, September 1979, p. 510.

11 For a complete discussion of bounded rationality, see H. A. Simon, *Administrative Behavior, second edition* (New York: Free Press, 1957); J. G. March and H. A. Simon, *Organizations* (New York: John Wiley, 1958); H. A. Simon, 'Altruism and Economics', *American Economic Review*, May 1993, pp. 156–61; and R. Nagel, 'A Survey on Experimental Beauty Contest Games: Bounded Rationality and Learning', in *Games and Human Behavior*, eds D. V. Budescu, I. Erev and R. Zwick (Mahwah, NJ: 1999), pp. 105–42. German researcher Gerd Gigerenzer has published a long list of articles on the relevance of bounded rationality, see, for instance, P. M. Todd and G. Gigerenzer, 'Bounding Rationality to the World', *Journal of Economic Psychology*, April 2003, pp. 143–65.

12 Biases associated with using shortcuts in decision making are discussed by A. Tversky and D. Kahneman, 'Judgment under Uncertainty: Heuristics and Biases', *Science*, September 1974, pp. 1124–31; and D. Stahlberg, F. Eller, A. Maass and D. Frey, 'We Knew It All Along: Hindsight Bias in Groups', *Organizational Behavior and Human Decision Processes*, July 1995, pp. 46–58.

13 For a study of the availability heuristic, see L. A. Vaughn, 'Effects of Uncertainty on Use of the Availability of Heuristic for Self-Efficacy Judgments', *European Journal of Social Psychology*, March–May 1999, pp. 407–10.

14 The model is discussed in detail in M. D. Cohen, J. G. March and J. P. Olsen, 'A Garbage Can Model of Organizational Choice', *Administrative Science Quarterly*, March 1971, pp. 1–25; and P. L. Koopman, J. W. Broekhuijsen and A. F. M. Wierdsma, 'Complex-Decision Making in Organizations', in *Handbook of Work and Organizational Psychology, second edition*, eds P. J. D. Drenth and J. Thierry (Hove: Psychology Press, 1998), pp. 357–86.

15 M. D. Cohen, J. G. March and J. P. Olsen, 'A Garbage Can Model of Organizational Choice', *Administrative Science Quarterly*, March 1971, p. 2.

16 Results can be found in B. Levitt and C. Nass, 'The Lid on the Garbage Can: Institutional Constraints on Decision Making in the Technical Core of College-Text Publishers', *Administrative Science Quarterly*, June 1989, pp. 190–207.

17 This discussion is based on material presented by J. G. March and R. Weissinger-Baylon, *Ambiguity and Command* (Marshfield, MA: Pitman Publishing, 1986), pp. 11–35.

18 Excerpted from N. Deogun, 'Burst Bubbles: Aggressive Push Abroad Dilutes Coke's Strength as Big Markets Stumble', the *Wall Street Journal*, 8 February 1999, p. A1.

19 Simulated tests of the garbage can model were conducted by M. Masuch and P. LaPotin, 'Beyond Garbage Cans: An A1 Model of Organizational Choice', *Administrative Science Quarterly*, March 1989, pp. 38–67; and M. B. Mandell, 'The Consequences of Improving Dissemination in Garbage-Can Decision Processes', *Knowledge: Creation, Diffusion, Utilization*, March 1988, pp. 343–61.

20 For a complete discussion, see L. R. Beach and T. R. Mitchell, 'A Contingency Model for the Selection of Decision Strategies', *Academy of Management Review*, July 1978, pp. 439–44.

21 See B. Azar, 'Why Experts Often Disagree', *APA Monitor*, May 1999, p. 13.

22 H. Filman, 'Manufacturing Masters its ABCs', *Business Week*, 7 August 2000.

23 Results can be found in N. Harvey, 'Why Are Judgments Less Consistent in Less Predictable Task Situations?', *Organizational Behavior and Human Decision Processes*, September 1995, pp. 247–63; and J. W. Dean, Jr, and M. P. Sharfman, 'Does Decision Process Matter? A Study of Strategic Decision-Making Effectiveness', *Academy of Management Journal*, April 1996, pp. 368–96.

24 Results from this study can be found in S. W. Gilliland, N. Schmitt and L. Wood, 'Cost-Benefit Determinants of Decision Process and Accuracy', *Organizational Behavior and Human Decision Processes*, November 1993, pp. 308–30.

25 See P. E. Johnson, S. Graziolo, K. Jamal and I. A. Zualkernan, 'Success and Failure in Expert Reasoning', *Organizational Behavior and Human Decision Processes*, November 1992, pp. 173–203.

26 This definition was derived from A. J. Rowe and R. O. Mason, *Managing with Style: A Guide to Understanding, Assessing and Improving Decision Making* (San Francisco, CA: Jossey-Bass, 1987).

27 The discussion of styles was based on material contained in A. J. Rowe and R. O. Mason, *Managing with Style: A Guide to Understanding, Assessing and Improving Decision Making* (San Francisco, CA: Jossey-Bass, 1987).

28 A. J. Rowe and R. O. Mason, *Managing with Style: A Guide to Understanding, Assessing and Improving Decision Making* (San Francisco, CA: Jossey-Bass, 1987); and M. J. Dollinger and W. Danis, 'Preferred Decision-Making Styles: A Cross-Cultural Comparison', *Psychological Reports*, June 1998, pp. 755–61.

29 A thorough discussion of escalation situations can be found in B. M. Staw and J. Ross, 'Behavior in Escalation Situations: Antecedents, Prototypes, and Solutions', in *Research in Organizational Behavior, vol. 9*, eds L. L. Cummings and B. M. Staw (Greenwich, CT: JAI Press, 1987), pp. 39–78.

30 The details of this case are discussed in J. Ross and B. M. Staw, 'Organizational Escalation and Exit: Lessons from the Shoreham Nuclear Power Plant', *Academy of Management Journal*, August 1993, pp. 701–32.

31 J. Ross and B. M. Staw, 'Organizational Escalation and Exit: Lessons from the Shoreham Nuclear Power Plant', *Academy of Management Journal*, August 1993, pp. 701–32.

32 Psychological determinants of escalation are discussed by J. H. Hammond, R. L. Keeney and H. Raiffa, 'The Hidden Traps in Decision Making', *Harvard Business Review*, September–October 1998; and J. Brockner, 'The Escalation of Commitment to a Failing Course of Action: Toward Theoretical Progress', *Academy of Management Review*, January 1992, pp. 39–61.

33 Results can be found in S. L. Kirby and M. A. Davis, 'A Study of Escalating Commitment in Principal-Agent Relationships: Effects of Monitoring and Personal Responsibility', *Journal of Applied Psychology*, April 1998, pp. 206–17.

34 See D. A. Hantula and J. L. D. Bragger, 'The Effects of Feedback Equivocality on Escalation of Commitment: An Empirical Investigation of Decision Dilemma Theory', *Journal of Applied Social Psychology*, February 1999, pp. 424–44; and H. Garland, C. A. Sandefur and A. C. Rogers, 'De-Escalation of Commitment in Oil Exploration: When Sunk Costs and Negative Feedback Coincide', *Journal of Applied Psychology*, December 1990, pp. 721–7.

35 See J. Ross and B. M. Staw, 'Organizational Escalation and Exit: Lessons from the Shoreham Nuclear Power Plant', *Academy of Management Journal*, August 1993, pp. 701–32.

36 Supportive results are provided by G. McNamara, H. Moon and P. Bromiley, 'Banking on Commitment: Intended and Unintended Consequences of an Organization's Attempt to Attenuate Escalation of Commitment', *Academy of Management Journal*, April 2002, pp. 443–52; and J. C. Edwards, 'Self-Fulfilling Prophecy and Escalating Commitment', *Journal of Applied Behavioral Science*, September 2001, pp. 343–60.

37 See B. M. Staw and J. Ross, 'Behavior in Escalation Situations: Antecedents, Prototypes, and Solutions', in *Research in Organizational Behavior, vol. 9*, eds L. L. Cummings and B. M. Staw (Greenwich, CT: JAI Press, 1987), pp. 39–78; and W. S. Silver and T. R. Mitchell, 'The Status Quo Tendency in Decision Making', *Organizational Dynamics*, Spring 1990, pp. 34–6.

38 These guidelines were derived from G. P. Huber, *Managerial Decision Making* (Glenview, IL: Scott, Foresman, 1980), p. 149.

39 G. W. Hill, 'Group versus Individual Performance: Are N + 1 Heads Better than One?', *Psychological Bulletin*, May 1982, p. 535.

40 D. Pringle, 'Finnish Line: Facing Big Threat from Microsoft, Nokia Places a Bet', the *Wall Street Journal*, 22 May 2002, p. A16.

41 These conclusions are based on studies from J. H. Davis, 'Some Compelling Intuitions about Group Consensus Decisions, Theoretical and Empirical Research, and Interpersonal Aggregation Phenomena: Selected

Examples, 1950–1990', *Organizational Behavior and Human Decision Processes*, June 1992, pp. 3–38; and J. A. Sniezek, 'Groups Under Uncertainty: An Examination of Confidence in Group Decision Making', *Organizational Behavior and Human Decision Processes*, June 1992, pp. 124–55.

42 Supporting results can be found in J. Hedlund, D. R. Ilgen and J. R. Hollenbeck, 'Decision Accuracy in Computer-Mediated versus Face-to-Face Decision-Making Teams', *Organizational Behavior and Human Decision Processes*, October 1998, pp. 30–47; and J. R. Hollenbeck, D. R. Ilgen, D. J. Sego, J. Hedlund, D. A. Major and J. Phillips, 'Multilevel Theory of Team Decision Making: Decision Performance in Teams Incorporating Distributed Expertise', *Journal of Applied Psychology*, April 1995, pp. 292–316.

43 See J. R. Winquist and J. R. Larson, Jr, 'Information Pooling: When It Impacts Group Decision Making', *Journal of Personality and Social Psychology*, February 1998, pp. 371–7; and D. H. Gruenfeld, E. A. Mannix, K. Y. Williams and M. A. Neale, 'Group Composition and Decision Making: How Member Familiarity and Information Distribution Affect Process and Performance', *Organizational Behavior and Human Decision Processes*, July 1996, pp. 1–15.

44 See D. L. Gladstein and N. P. Reilly, 'Group Decision Making under Threat: The Tycoon Game', *Academy of Management Journal*, September 1985, pp. 613–27.

45 'Jack Welch's Lessons for Success', *Fortune*, 25 January 1993, p. 86.

46 Results are presented in J. T. Delaney, 'Workplace Cooperation: Current Problems, New Approaches', *Journal of Labor Research*, Winter 1996, pp. 45–61.

47 For an extended discussion of this model, see M. Sashkin, 'Participative Management Is an Ethical Imperative', *Organizational Dynamics*, Spring 1984, pp. 4–22.

48 See G. Yukl and P. P. Fu, 'Determinants of Delegation and Consultation by Managers', *Journal of Organizational Behavior*, March 1999, pp. 219–32.

49 Supporting results can be found in J. Hunton, T. W. Hall and K. H. Price, 'The Value of Voice in Participative Decision Making', *Journal of Applied Psychology*, October 1998, pp. 788–97; C. R. Leana, R. S. Ahlbrandt and A. J. Murrell, 'The Effects of Employee Involvement Programs on Unionized Workers' Attitudes, Perceptions, and Preferences in Decision Making', *Academy of Management Journal*, October 1992, pp. 861–73; and D. Plunkett, 'The Creative Organization: An Empirical Investigation of the Importance of Participation in Decision Making', *Journal of Creative Behavior*, Second Quarter 1990, pp. 140–48.

50 Results can be found in B. D. Cawley, L. M. Keeping and P. E. Levy, 'Participation in the Performance Appraisal Process and Employee Reactions: A Meta-Analytic Review of Field Investigations', *Journal of Applied Psychology*, August 1998, pp. 615–33.

51 Results are contained in J. A. Wagner III, C. R. Leana, E. A. Locke and D. M. Schweiger, 'Cognitive and Motivational Frameworks in US Research on Participation: A Meta-Analysis of Primary Effects', *Journal of Organizational Behavior*, January 1997, pp. 49–65.

52 See E. A. Locke, D. M. Schweiger and G. R. Latham, 'Participation in Decision Making: When Should It Be Used?', *Organizational Dynamics*, Winter 1986, pp. 65–79.

53 A thorough discussion of this issue is provided by W. A. Randolph, 'Navigating the Journey to Empowerment', *Organizational Dynamics*, Spring 1995, pp. 19–32.

54 Results can be found in S. A. Mohrman, E. E. Lawler III and G. E. Ledford, Jr, 'Organizational Effectiveness and the Impact of Employee Involvement and TQM Programs: Do Employee Involvement and TQM Programs Work?', *Journal for Quality and Participation*, January–February 1996, pp. 6–10.

55 See R. Rodgers, J. E. Hunter and D. L. Rogers, 'Influence of Top Management Commitment on Management Program Success', *Journal of Applied Psychology*, February 1993, pp. 151–5.

56 G. M. Parker, *Team Players and Teamwork: The New Competitive Business Strategy* (San Francisco, CA: Jossey-Bass, 1990).

57 Results can be found in L. M. Camacho and P. B. Paulus, 'The Role of Social Anxiousness in Group Brainstorming', *Journal of Personality and Social Psychology*, June 1995, pp. 1071–80.

58 Methods for increasing group consensus were investigated by R. L. Priem, D. A. Harrison and N. K. Muir, 'Structured Conflict and Consensus Outcomes in Group Decision Making', *Journal of Management*, no. 4, 1995, pp. 691–710.

59 These recommendations were obtained from G. M. Parker, *Team Players and Teamwork: The New Competitive Business Strategy* (San Francisco, CA: Jossey-Bass, 1990).

60 Supportive results can be found in S. Mohammed and E. Ringseis, 'Cognitive Diversity and Consensus in Group Decision Making: The Role of Inputs, Processes, and Outcomes, *Organizational Behavior and Human Decision Processes*, July 2001, pp. 310–35.

61 See A. F. Osborn, *Applied Imagination: Principles and Procedures of Creative Thinking, third edition* (New York: Scribners, 1979).

62 See W. H. Cooper, R. Brent Gallupe, S. Pollard and J. Cadsby, 'Some Liberating Effects of Anonymous Electronic Brainstorming', *Small Group Research*, April 1998, pp. 147–78; and P. B. Paulus, T. S. Larey and A. H. Ortega, 'Performance and Perceptions of Brainstormers in an Organizational Setting', *Basic and Applied Social Psychology*, August 1995, pp. 249–65.

63 These recommendations were derived from C. Caggiano, 'The Right Way to Brainstorm', *Inc.*, July 1999, p. 94; and G. McGartland, 'How to Generate More Ideas in Brainstorming Sessions', *Selling Power*, July–August 1999, p. 46.

64 See J. G. Lloyd, S. Fowell and J. G. Bligh, 'The Use of the Nominal Group Technique as an Evaluative Tool in Medical Undergraduate Education', *Medical Education*, January 1999, pp. 8–13; and A. L. Delbecq, A. H. Van de Ven and D. H. Gustafson, *Group Techniques for Program Planning: A Guide to Nominal Group and Delphi Processes* (Glenview, IL: Scott, Foresman, 1975).

65 See N. C. Dalkey, D. L. Rourke, R. Lewis and D. Snyder, *Studies in the Quality of Life: Delphi and Decision Making* (Lexington, MA: Lexington Books, 1972).

66 Benefits of the Delphi technique are discussed by N. I. Whitman, 'The Committee Meeting Alternative: Using the Delphi Technique', *Journal of Nursing Administration*, July–August 1990, pp. 30–36.

67 A thorough description of computer-aided decision-making systems is provided by M. C. Er and A. C. Ng, 'The Anonymity and Proximity Factors in Group Decision Support Systems', *Decision Support Systems*, May 1995, pp. 75–83; and A. LaPlante, 'Brainstorming', *Forbes*, 25 October 1993, pp. 45–61.

68 Supportive results can be found in S. S. Lam and J. Schaubroeck, 'Improving Group Decisions by Better Pooling Information: A Comparative Advantage of Group Decision Support Systems', *Journal of Applied Psychology*, August 2000, pp. 565–73; and I. Benbasat and J. Lim, 'Information Technology Support for Debiasing Group Judgments: An Empirical Evaluation', *Organizational Behaviour and Human Decision Processes*, September 2000, pp. 167–83.

69 This study was conducted by J. S. Valacich, B. C. Wheeler, B. E. Mennecke and R. Wachter, 'The Effects of Numerical and Logical Group Size on Computer-Mediated Idea Generation', *Organizational Behavior and Human Decision Processes*, June 1995, pp. 318–29.

70 P. Schinzler, 'Offices That Spark Creativity', *Business Week*, 28 August 2000.

71 This definition was adapted from one provided by R. K. Scott, 'Creative Employees: A Challenge to Managers', *Journal of Creative Behavior*, First Quarter 1995, pp. 64–71.

72 E. T. Smith, 'Are You Creative?', *Business Week*, 30 September 1985, pp. 81–2. For a review of research about the left and right hemispheres of the brain, see T. Hines, 'Left Brain/Right Brain Mythology and Implications for Management and Training', *Academy of Management* Review, October 1987, pp. 600–6.

73 Excerpted from S. Stern, 'How Companies Can Be More Creative', *HR Magazine*, April 1998, p. 59.

74 These stages are thoroughly discussed by E. Glassman, 'Creative Problem Solving', *Supervisory Management*, January 1989, pp. 21–6.

75 Details of this study can be found in M. Basadur, 'Managing Creativity: A Japanese Model', *Academy of Management Executive*, May 1992, pp. 29–42.

76 M. Basadur, 'Managing Creativity: A Japanese Model', *Academy of Management Executive*, May 1992, pp. 29–42.

77 'Caring Enough', *Selling Power*, June 1999, p. 18.

78 This discussion is based on research reviewed in M. A. Collins and T. M. Amabile, 'Motivation and Creativity', in *Handbook of Creativity*, eds R. J. Sternberg (Cambridge, UK: Cambridge University Press, 1999), pp. 297–311; G. J. Feist, 'A Meta-Analysis of Personality in Scientific and Artistic Creativity', *Personality and Social Psychology Review*, no. 4, 1998, pp. 290–309; and R. W. Woodman, J. E. Sawyer and R. W. Griffin, 'Toward a Theory of Organizational Creativity', *Academy of Management Review*, April 1993, pp. 292–321.

79 T. A. Matherly and R. E. Goldsmith, 'The Two Faces of Creativity', *Business Horizons*, September–October 1985, p. 9.

80 Personality and creativity were investigated by S. Taggar, 'Individual Creativity and Group Ability to Utilize Individual Creative Resources: A Multilevel Model,' *Academy of Management Journal*, April 2002, pp. 315–30; and J. M. George and J. Zhou, 'When Openness to Experience and Conscientiousness Are Related to Creative Behavior: An Interactional Approach,' *Journal of Applied Psychology*, June 2001, pp. 513–24.

81 J. M. Higgins, 'Innovate or Evaporate: Seven Secrets of Innovative Corporations', *The Futurist*, September–October 1995, p. 46.

82 See the related discussion in T. M. Amabile, 'How to Kill Creativity', *Harvard Business Review*, September–October 1998, pp. 77–87.

83 See S. Caudron, 'Humor Is Healthy in the Workplace', *Personnel Journal*, June 1992, pp. 63–6.

84 See T. DeSalvo, 'Unleash the Creativity in Your Organization', *HR Magazine*, June 1999, pp. 154–64; and G. R. Oldham and A. Cummings, 'Employee Creativity: Personal and Contextual Factors at Work', *Academy of Management Journal*, June 1996, pp. 607–34.

85 L. K. Gundry, J. R. Kickul and C. W. Prather, 'Building the Creative Organization', *Organizational Dynamics*, Spring 1994, p. 32.

86 The survey and detailed sources can be found in A. J. Rowe and R. O. Mason, Managing with Style: A Guide to Understanding, Assessing, and Improving Decision Making (San Francisco, CA: Jossey-Bass, 1987).

chapter 13 power, politics and conflict

By Steven Mestdagh, Dirk Van Poucke and Eva Cools

Learning outcomes
When you finish studying the material in this chapter, you should be able to:

- explain the concept of mutuality of interest

- name at least three 'soft' and two 'hard' influence tactics, and summarise the practical lessons from influence research

- identify and briefly describe French and Raven's five bases of power, and discuss the responsible use of power

- explain why delegation is the highest form of empowerment, and discuss the link with delegation, trust and personal initiative

- define organisational politics, and how it is triggered

- distinguish between favourable and unfavourable impression management tactics

- explain how to manage organisational politics

- define the term 'conflict', distinguish between functional and dysfunctional conflict, and identify three desired conflict outcomes

- explain how professionals can stimulate functional conflict and identify the five conflict-handling styles

- explain the difference between distributive and integrative negotiation, and discuss the concept of added-value negotiation

case study

Negotiating your career path requires a little give and take

It's one of the most prized skills in the workplace, and it can get you what you want and more, but most of us have no idea how to negotiate. Yet as working practices change, the ability to broker agreements is becoming a key part of office life.

'We no longer live in a world where people do things because of the authority of the person who is instructing them', says David Thomas, chief executive of the Careers Research and Advisory Centre (CRAC).

'People in authority need to put their point across persuasively. It is not enough to have the title of manager, you must be able to make your case. It is the challenge of a working life where there is a lack of certainty about hierarchy and how tasks should be approached.'

Two very public examples illustrate this point: many people were unconvinced by Tony Blair's arguments in favour of a war with Iraq. In effect, he failed to negotiate with the electorate. Similarly, Andy Gilchrist, leader of the Fire Brigades Union (FBU), took a hard negotiating position and demanded a 40 per cent pay rise for his members. Yet it is debatable whether industrial action will secure a better deal.

Gerald Atkinson teaches negotiation to executives at Henley Management College. He says: 'In the firefighters' dispute both sides made appalling errors in negotiation. The FBU's demand fell into the extreme category and Gilchrist was playing a confrontational game from the start. On the other hand, the employers had no common objective and there were so many different agendas that it was difficult for them to draw up a coherent strategy for negotiation. This illustrates one of the most important points in negotiation: be clear about what you want and have a strategy and be prepared.

'Negotiation is a game of moves, counter moves and surprise tactics. Not everyone knows how to, or wants to, play it. There is one type of personality who will never negotiate – they are too trusting and co-operative when they need to be hard-nosed.'

Since most organisations run team projects, being able to negotiate with co-workers is essential, says Thomas. 'You need negotiating skills in the office because you have to be able to get people to understand your point of view. You also need to interpret and appreciate the views of others. Younger people have taken this on board; older workers must think about the way work has changed. Just because you are in a position of authority, your staff may not do as you ask unless they agree with it.'

Negotiating also ensures you don't get bullied. 'You need an insight into when someone is bluffing and when you can apply pressure to secure a deal', says Atkinson. 'Some people are tough and direct while others are sales-orientated.'

Before you start, draw up a proposal, but be prepared to scale it back to a more realistic position, and have a worst-case scenario so you know when to walk away.

If you are negotiating with a co-worker, you need to understand the psychology of persuasion to avoid conflict. When you are dealing with your boss, you need to take a non-confrontational approach and ensure you illustrate your point of view.

One of the most difficult parts is being able to handle conflict and rejection, says Atkinson. It's not just how you react when you are turned down, but how others react if you do the same to them. 'Sometimes you have to be prepared for the other party to lash out.'

It helps to be clear about who you are negotiating with and how much power they hold. 'The more Machiavellian type of person will needle you to get a reaction, and it's important to stay calm', says Atkinson. 'The mark of a successful negotiator is self-confidence.'[1]

For discussion

Negotiation is just one way to solve conflicts in the workplace. What other methods of conflict resolution can be used in organisations?

At the very heart of interpersonal dealings in today's work organisations is a constant struggle between individual and collective interests. For example, Björn wants a raise, but his company does not make enough money to both grant raises and pay minimum stockholder dividends. Pre-occupation with self-interest is understandable. After all, each of us was born, not as a co-operating organisation member, but as an individual with instincts for self-preservation. It took socialisation in family, school, religious, sports, recreation and employment settings to introduce us to the notion of mutuality of interest. Basically, **Mutuality of interest** involves win-win situations in which one's self-interest is served by co-operating actively and creatively with potential adversaries. A pair of organisation development consultants offered this perspective of mutuality of interest:

Mutuality of interest balancing individual and organisational interests through win-win co-operation

> " Nothing is more important than this sense of mutuality to the effectiveness and quality of an organisation's products and services. Management must strive to stimulate a strong sense of shared ownership in every employee, because otherwise an organisation cannot do its best in the long run. Employees who identify their own personal self-interest with the quality of their organisation's output understand mutuality and strive to maintain it in their jobs and work relations.[2] "

Figure 13.1 graphically portrays the constant dilemma between employees' self-interest and the organisation's need for mutuality of interest. It also shows the linkage between this chapter and other key topics in this book. Professionals need a complete tool kit of techniques to guide diverse individuals, who are often powerfully motivated to put their own self-interests first, to pursue common objectives. At stake in this tug-of-war between individual and collective interests is no less than the ultimate survival of the organisation.

FIGURE 13.1 THE CONSTANT TUG-OF-WAR BETWEEN SELF-INTEREST AND MUTUALITY OF INTEREST REQUIRES MANAGERIAL ACTION

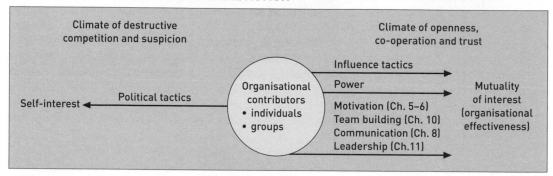

Organisational influence tactics: getting one's way at work

How do you get others to carry out your wishes? Do you simply tell them what to do? Or do you prefer a less direct approach, such as promising to return the favour? Whatever approach you use, the crux of the issue is social influence. A large measure of interpersonal interaction involves attempts to influence others, including parents, bosses, co-workers, spouses, teachers, friends and children. Even if superiors do not expect to get such dramatic results, they need to sharpen their influence skills. A good starting point is familiarity with the following research insights.

Nine generic influence tactics

A particularly fruitful stream of research, initiated by David Kipnis and his colleagues in 1980, reveals how people influence each other in organisations. The Kipnis methodology involved asking employees how they managed to get either their bosses, co-workers or subordinates to do what they wanted them to do.[3] Statistical refinements and replications by other researchers over a 13-year period eventually yielded nine influence tactics. The nine tactics, ranked in diminishing order of use in the workplace are listed in Table 13.1.

These approaches can be considered generic influence tactics because they characterise social influence in all directions. Researchers have found this ranking to be fairly consistent regardless of whether the direction of influence is downward, upward or lateral.[4]

Some call the first five influence tactics 'soft' tactics because they are friendlier and not as coercive as the last four tactics. The latter tactics accordingly are called 'hard' tactics because they involve more overt pressure.

Three possible influence outcomes

Put yourself in this familiar situation. It's Wednesday and a big project you've been working on for your project team is due Friday. You're behind on the preparation of your computer graphics for your final report and presentation. You catch a friend who is great at computer graphics as he heads out of

TABLE 13.1 NINE GENERIC INFLUENCE TACTICS

1 Rational persuasion	Trying to convince someone with reason, logic or facts
2 Inspirational appeals	Trying to build enthusiasm by appealing to others' emotions, ideals or values
3 Consultation	Getting others to participate in planning, making decisions and changes
4 Ingratiation	Getting someone in a good mood prior to making a request; being friendly, helpful and using praise or flattery
5 Personal appeals	Referring to friendship and loyalty when making a request
6 Exchange	Making express or implied promises and trading favours
7 Coalition tactics	Getting others to support your effort to persuade someone
8 Pressure	Demanding compliance or using intimidation or threats
9 Legitimating tactics	Basing a request on one's authority or right, organisational rules or policies, or express or implied support from superiors

SOURCE: Based on Table 1 in G. Yukl, C. M. Falbe and J. Y. Youn, 'Patterns of Influence Behavior for Managers', *Group & Organization Management*, March 1993, pp. 5–28.

the office at quitting time. You try this exchange tactic to get your friend to help you out: 'I'm way behind. I need your help. If you could come back in for two to three hours tonight and help me with these graphics, I'll complete those spreadsheets you've been complaining about'. According to researchers, your friend will engage in one of three possible influence outcomes:

- Commitment. Your friend enthusiastically agrees and will demonstrate initiative and persistence while completing the assignment.
- Compliance. Your friend grudgingly complies and will need prodding to satisfy minimum requirements.
- Resistance. Your friend will say no, make excuses, stall or put up an argument.[5]

The best outcome is commitment because the target person's intrinsic motivation will energise good performance. However, professionals often have to settle for compliance in today's hectic workplace. Resistance means a failed influence attempt.

Research findings and practical implications
Laboratory and field studies have taught us useful lessons about the relative effectiveness of influence tactics along with other instructive insights:

- Commitment is more likely when people rely on consultation, strong rational persuasion and inspirational appeals and do not rely on pressure and coalition tactics.[6] Interestingly, in one study, supervisors were not very effective at downward influence. They relied most heavily on inspiration (an effective tactic), ingratiation (a moderately effective tactic) and pressure (an ineffective tactic).[7]
- A meta-analysis of 69 studies suggests ingratiation (making the boss feel good) can slightly improve your performance appraisal results and make your boss like you significantly more.[8]
- Commitment is more likely when the influence attempt involves something important and enjoyable and is based on a friendly relationship.[9]
- In a survey, 214 employed MBA students (55 per cent female) tended to perceive their superiors' 'soft' influence tactics as fair and 'hard' influence tactics as unfair. Unfair influence tactics were associated with greater resistance among employees.[10]
- Another study probed male–female differences in influencing work group members. Many studies have found women to be perceived as less competent and less influential in work groups than men. The researchers had male and female work group leaders engage in either task behaviour

FIVE BASES OF POWER

A popular classification scheme for social power traces back 40 years to the work of John French and Bertram Raven. They proposed that power arises from five different bases: reward power, coercive power, legitimate power, expert power and referent power. Many researchers have studied these five power bases and searched for others. For the most part, French and Raven's list remains intact.[19] Each power base involves a different approach to influencing others:

Reward power
obtaining compliance with promised or actual rewards

Coercive power
obtaining compliance through threatened or actual punishment

Legitimate power
obtaining compliance through formal authority

Expert power
obtaining compliance through one's knowledge or information

Referent power
obtaining compliance through charisma or personal attraction

■ *Reward power.* A manager has Reward power to the extent that he or she obtains compliance by promising or granting rewards.

■ *Coercive power.* Threats of punishment and actual punishment give an individual Coercive power. A sales manager who threatens to fire any salesperson who uses a company car for family vacations is relying on coercive power.

■ *Legitimate power.* This base of power is anchored to one's formal position or authority. Thus, individuals who obtain compliance primarily because of their formal authority to make decisions have Legitimate power. Legitimate power may express itself in either a positive or negative manner in managing people. Positive legitimate power focuses constructively on job performance. Negative legitimate power tends to be threatening and demeaning to those being influenced. Its main purpose is to build the power holder's ego.

■ *Expert power.* Valued knowledge or information gives an individual Expert power over those who need such knowledge or information. The power of supervisors is enhanced because they know about work schedules and assignments before their employees do. Skilful use of expert power played a key role in the effectiveness of team leaders in a recent study of three physician medical diagnosis teams.[20] Knowledge is power in today's high-tech workplaces (see Chapter 17).

■ *Referent power.* Also called 'charisma', Referent power comes into play when one's personality becomes the reason for compliance. Role models have referent power over those who identify closely with them.[21] From Martin Luther King to Bill Gates, almost every well-known leader used or uses referent power to influence his or her followers.

> Shipley and Egan investigated the relationship between brewers and their tenants in the UK. They concluded that brewers apply the wrong types of power in the wrong way and consequently these brewers generate too little channel co-operation and too much conflict.
>
> Most tenants are small independent business persons contracted for a short period (three years). These short-tenancy contracts give brewers substantial power to apply coercive power by threatening non-renewal. Conversely, tenants have little or no countervailing power. The results showed that tenants are not well motivated and it's concluded that this is because brewers use coercive power excessively and reward power insufficiently.[22]

To enhance your understanding of these five bases of power and to assess your self-perceived power, please take a moment to complete the next Activity. Think of your present job or your most recent job when responding to the various items. What is your power profile? Finally, as power is strongly linked to leadership, we also suggest you to take look at Chapter 11 to find out more about this topic.

RESEARCH FINDINGS AND PRACTICAL IMPLICATIONS

In one study a sample of 94 male and 84 female non-managerial and professional employees completed TAT tests. The researchers found that the male and female employees had similar needs for power and personalised power. But the women had a significantly higher need for socialised power than did their male counterparts.[23] This bodes well for today's work organisations where women are playing an ever greater administrative role. Unfortunately, as women gain power in the workplace, greater tension between men and women has been observed. *Training Magazine* offered this perspective:

What is your self-perceived power?

Instructions

Score your various bases of power for your current (or former) job, using the following scale:

1 = Strongly disagree
2 = Disagree
3 = Slightly agree
4 = Agree
5 = Strongly agree

Reward power

1 I can reward individuals at lower levels.   1 2 3 4 5
2 My review actions affect the rewards gained at lower levels.   1 2 3 4 5
3 Based on my decisions, lower level personnel may receive a bonus.   1 2 3 4 5
Score _____

Coercive power

1 I can punish employees at lower levels.   1 2 3 4 5
2 My work is a check on lower level employees.   1 2 3 4 5
3 My diligence reduces error.   1 2 3 4 5
Score _____

Legitimate power

1 My position gives me a great deal of authority.   1 2 3 4 5
2 The decisions made at my level are of critical importance.   1 2 3 4 5
3 Employees look to me for guidance.   1 2 3 4 5
Score _____

Expert power

1 I am an expert in this job.   1 2 3 4 5
2 My ability gives me an advantage in this job.   1 2 3 4 5
3 Given some time, I could improve the methods used on this job.   1 2 3 4 5
Score _____

Referent power

1 I attempt to set a good example for other employees.   1 2 3 4 5
2 My personality allows me to work well in this job.   1 2 3 4 5
3 My fellow employees look to me as their informal leader.   1 2 3 4 5
Score _____

Scoring key and norms

Arbitrary norms for each of the five bases of power are:

3–6 = Weak power base
7–11 = Moderate power base
12–15 = Strong power base

SOURCE: Adapted and excerpted in part from D. L. Dieterly and B. Schneider, 'The Effect of Organizational Environment on Perceived Power and Climate: A Laboratory Study', *Organizational Behavior and Human Performance*, June 1974, pp. 316–37.

> ... observers view the tension between women and men in the workplace as a natural outcome of power inequities between the genders. Their argument is that men still have most of the power and are resisting any change as a way to protect their power base. [Consultant Susan L] Webb asserts that sexual harassment has far more to do with exercising power in an unhealthy way than with sexual attraction. Likewise, the glass ceiling, a metaphor for the barriers women face in climbing the corporate ladder to management and executive positions, is about power and access to power.[24]

In the same context, a recent Swedish survey revealed that gender-differentiated access to power in organisations is essential in explaining women's relatively low wages. Moreover, women who work in organisations in which relatively many of the supervisors are men have lower pay than do those women with similar qualifications and job demands who work in organisations with a stronger female representation in the power structure. According to the researchers, 'power relations are of crucial importance for understanding how gender inequalities in financial rewards are generated and sustained in the labour market'.[25] Gender inequality is also discussed in Chapters 4 and 8.

A reanalysis of 18 field studies that measured French and Raven's five bases of power uncovered 'severe methodological shortcomings'.[26] After correcting for these problems, the researchers identified the following relationships between power bases and work outcomes such as job performance, job satisfaction and turnover:

- Expert and referent power had a generally positive impact.
- Reward and legitimate power had a slightly positive impact.
- Coercive power had a slightly negative impact.

The same researcher, in a 1990 follow-up study involving 251 employed business seniors, looked at the relationship between influence styles and bases of power. This was a bottom-up study. In other words, employee perceptions of managerial influence and power were examined. Rational persuasion was found to be a highly acceptable managerial influence tactic. Why? Because employees perceived it to be associated with the three bases of power they viewed positively: legitimate, expert and referent.[27]

In summary, expert and referent power appear to get the best combination of results and favourable reactions from lower-level employees.[28]

Responsible and ethical use of power through empowerment

If leaders are to use their various bases of power effectively and ethically, they need to strive for commitment rather than mere compliance and understand the difference between power sharing and power distribution.

FROM COMPLIANCE TO COMMITMENT

Responsible leaders strive for socialised power while avoiding personalised power. In fact, in a recent survey, organisational commitment (see Chapter 3) was higher among executives whose superiors exercised socialised power than among colleagues with 'power-hungry' bosses. The researchers used the appropriate terms uplifting power versus dominating power.[29]

How does this relate to the five bases of power? As with influence tactics, managerial power has three possible outcomes: commitment, compliance or resistance. Reward, coercive and negative legitimate power tend to produce compliance (and sometimes, resistance). On the other hand, positive legitimate, expert and referent power tend to foster commitment. Once again, commitment is superior to compliance because it is driven by internal or intrinsic motivation (see Chapters 5 and 6).[30]

Employees who merely comply require frequent 'jolts' of power from the boss to keep them headed in a productive direction. Committed employees tend to be self-starters who do not require close supervision – a key success factor in today's flatter, team-oriented organisations (see Chapter 14).

According to research cited earlier, expert and referent power have the greatest potential for improving job performance and satisfaction and reducing turnover. Formal education, training and self-development can build a manager's expert power. At the same time, one's referent power base can be strengthened by forming and developing strategic alliances.

EMPOWERMENT: FROM POWER SHARING TO POWER DISTRIBUTION

An exciting trend in today's organisations focuses on giving employees a greater say in the workplace. This trend wears various labels, including 'participative management' and 'open-book management' (also see chapter 12). Regardless of the label one prefers, it is all about empowerment. Management consultant and writer W. Alan Randolph offers this definition: 'Empowerment is recognising and releasing into the organisation the power that people already have in their wealth of useful knowledge, experience and internal motivation'.[31] A core component of this process is pushing decision-making authority down to progressively lower levels.

Engelbert Breuker, director of Penta Scope, a Dutch consulting agency, explains why his company became an 'empowered organisation':

> Since 1997, Penta Scope has the form of a networked organisation where empowerment is the basic philosophy. Most of our people were, as line managers, the victims of massive IT-changes occuring halfway the nineties. Everybody thinks that changes are the result of technology, but it is in fact mostly people that take an important place in these processes. Empowerment then, supplies people with power, strength and energy to tackle these changes. In my vision, the most important thing is not human resource management, but human talent. As an employee in our organisation, you are your own boss, your ambitions lie within the network and can be realised there. Those who have an idea, those who want to do something, must also be able to bring it into practice. Formerly, one person used to decide for everyone, now everyone can decide for themselves. In fact we turned our personnel management completely upside down.[32]

Empowerment sharing varying degrees of power with lower-level employees to tap their full potential

NO INFORMATION SHARING, NO EMPOWERMENT

Open-book management breaks down the traditional organisational caste system made up of information 'haves' and information 'have-nots'. Superiors historically were afraid to tell their employees about innovations, company finances and strategic plans for fear of giving the advantage to unions and competitors. To varying extents, those threats persist today. Nonetheless, in the larger scheme of things, organisations with unified and adequately informed employees have a significant competitive advantage.

> One organisation that makes extensive use of information sharing initiatives as a basis to empowerment is British Petroleum. BP has a sustained effort under way to increase communication and 'knowledge flow' across the company. Group executives seek extensive employee input before decisions are made. To enhance things, a dedicated Intranet site provides employees with business information. Furthermore, a flat organisational structure – there is nothing between the 92 business units and the nine-member executive group to whom they report – makes it possible to engage more staff members.[33]

The problematic question then becomes: how much information sharing is enough (or too much)? As demonstrated in the large- and small-company case studies in Table 13.3, there is no exact answer. Empowering managers need to learn from experience, be careful in what they share and let employees know when certain information requires secrecy. Make no mistake, however, empowerment through open-book management carries some risk of betrayal, like any act of trust (also see Chapter 10). Advocates of empowerment believe the rewards (more teamwork and greater competitiveness) outweigh the risks.

A MATTER OF DEGREE

The concept of empowerment requires some adjustments in traditional thinking. First, power is not a zero-sum situation where one person's gain is another's loss. Social power is unlimited. This requires win-win thinking. 'The more power you give away, the more you have', it is said.[34] Authoritarian managers who view employee empowerment as a threat to their personal power are missing the point because of their win-lose thinking.[35]

The second adjustment to traditional thinking involves seeing empowerment as a matter of degree not as an either-or proposition.[36] Figure 13.2 illustrates how power can be shifted to the hands of

TABLE 13.3 HOW MUCH INFORMATION SHOULD BE SHARED? TWO CASES

Large company

When Ron Ferner first joined Campbell's Soup, in the 1960s, none of the company's executives believed in sharing any kind of information with anybody. By the time he retired, in 1996, Ferner and his colleagues had started sharing everything – goals, financials, product news – with employees.

'At first I was very sceptical about sharing information with employees, but now I'm a believer. I saw the power of the thing. But we always drew the line at salaries. And if we had a supersecret project that we were not sure we would actually launch, we may not have told. But everything else was fair game. Even with the hourly employees that ran the filling machines, putting soup in the cans, we shared the financials.

'At one point Campbell's had a philosophy of meeting with all employees every quarter. I had 1800 people in my plant. It took three days to hold the meetings. It was quite a chore, but worth it. The employees got very comfortable. It was a real change from the old days, when we would stand behind a post and peek out to watch them work.

'That approach doesn't work overnight. If you don't talk to employees for 10 years and then show up and say that today we start talking, you'll be really disappointed. You have to pick where to draw the line very carefully. You're building trust and don't want to backtrack. It took us years to talk to employees and make them comfortable. Once they were, we started getting their ideas and finding out what the real problems were. A lot of things amazed us.

'One time a packaging team in Sacramento was having problems with boxes breaking. Some of us managers started talking to them about what the problems were and realised they really had a good handle on what was wrong. So we said 'Why don't you guys call the supplier?' Then we called the supplier to tell them they would be hearing from our crew, and they said, 'Why not have them talk directly to our hourly employees?'

'If the managers alone had tried to solve this problem, it would have gone on forever. Instead, we rented a van, sent our people over, and solved the whole thing. Afterward, we had a party. It gave the workers great confidence. That never would have happened in the days when Campbell's had a policy of not telling anybody anything that wasn't written down for them.'

Small company

Adjacency CEO Andrew Sather and his partner, Chris DeVore, figured that for their four-year-old [Internet service] company to become a powerhouse, they would have to tap into the entrepreneurial instincts of every staffer. That meant treating all employees as if they were partners. All were given equity stakes. 'I tried to set up the kind of company where I'd like to work', Sather says.

Last year Sather and DeVore gathered their 25 workers together every week to discuss the most intimate details of their company, including cash flow and potential customers. The partners could tell that workers appreciated the honest communication. At meetings, employees would pepper the partners with loads of questions. But it quickly became apparent that there were some things employees would rather not know. For instance, they didn't want to hear about Adjacency's close calls with missing payroll – not an uncommon syndrome in the entrepreneurial world, but one that employees find quite unnerving. 'We overestimated our employees' desire to be entrepreneurs, and sometimes we scared them', Sather says.

Sather and DeVore also overestimated their staff's ability to keep secrets. Last summer they told employees about a huge, potentially lucrative deal with a hot new client. One worker left the meeting so pumped that he bragged to a friend at a competing company. Bad move. The 'friend' relayed the news to his bosses, who promptly tried to persuade the coveted customer to dump Adjacency and go with them. 'We almost lost the client', DeVore says. 'The client was livid, and rightfully so'.

The partners considered shutting down the flow of sales information but decided against it. Now they are careful to identify what information is top secret.

'We've learned to get a lot more explicit about how information can be used', Sather says. In fact, the partners still divulge just as much confidential information as they did before the incident, conveying to employees that they trust them more than ever. There is one topic though, that Sather and DeVore are careful to avoid: the nitty-gritty details of cash flow. 'We've learned to filter some information that employees find disconcerting', Sather admits.

[Now that Adjacency has fully integrated its business with Sapient, an innovative E-services consultancy, it will be interesting to observe how much of its open-book management style persists.]

SOURCES: Thea Singer, 'Share It All with Employees, Soup to Nuts', *Inc.*, Tech 1999, No. 1, p. 48; and S. Greco and M. Ballon, 'Too Hot To Handle', *Inc.*, February 1999, p. 52.

FIGURE 13.2 THE EVOLUTION OF POWER: FROM DOMINATION TO DELEGATION

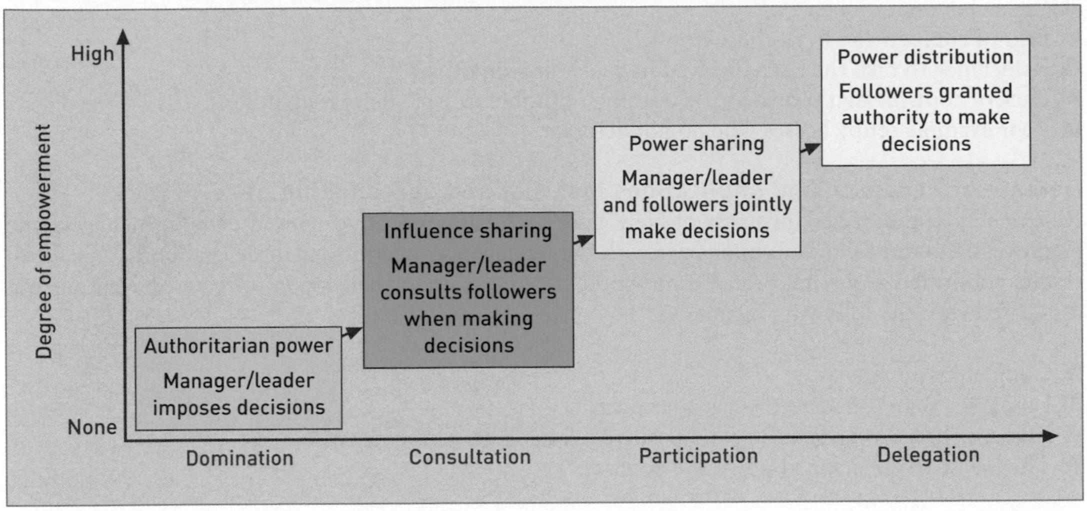

non-managers step by step. The overriding goal is to increase productivity and competitiveness in leaner organisations. Each step in this evolution increases the power of organisational contributors who traditionally had little or no legitimate power.

Delegation

The highest degree of empowerment is Delegation, the process of granting decision-making authority to lower-level employees. This amounts to power distribution. Delegation has long been the recommended way to lighten the busy manager's load while at the same time developing employees' abilities. Importantly, delegation gives non-managerial employees more than simply a voice in decisions. It empowers them to make their own decisions. A prime example of an entrepreneur that has discovered the benefits of delegation is Paul Bishop, founder of the British training company Winning Moves:

> 'I used to be a genuine control freak. I was working from 5 a.m. and getting back home after my children had gone to bed – but I still had to examine every letter that left the office, and change something, even if the letter was perfect', Bishop tells. His company had grown rapidly, passing the 1 million turnover mark within three years. His diary was crammed, his desk overflowing, and there were never enough hours in the day to complete the many projects he started. He only realised there was a problem when his employees criticised communication within the company in a staff survey. 'I knew we wouldn't grow further unless I relaxed my grip on others', he says. 'I had to learn to empower the people around me.' Bishop acted fast. He forced himself to 'butt out' of group meetings where he was answering questions on behalf of others. He evolved a system whereby top-line goals for the company were set collectively but responsibility for how best to achieve them was delegated to the individuals involved. It worked. Bishop is now getting home to see his kids and he is clearly pleased that his employees are keen to take on more responsibility and improve their skills and that they appear more motivated.[37]

Barriers to delegation

Delegation is easy to talk about, but many superiors find it hard to actually do. A concerted effort to overcome the following common barriers to delegation needs to be made:

■ Belief in the fallacy 'if you want it done right, do it yourself'.
■ Lack of confidence and trust in lower-level employees.
■ Low self-confidence.

Delegation
granting decision-making authority to people at lower levels

■ Fear of being called lazy.
■ Vague job definition.
■ Fear of competition from those below.
■ Reluctance to take the risks involved in depending on others.
■ Lack of controls that provide early warning of problems with delegated duties.
■ Poor example set by bosses who do not delegate.[38]

Delegation research and implications for trust and personal initiative

Researchers at the State University of New York at Albany recently surveyed pairs of managers and employees and did follow-up interviews with the managers concerning their delegation habits. Their results confirmed some important commonsense notions about delegation. Greater delegation was associated with the following factors:

■ Competent employees.
■ Employee shared manager's task objectives.
■ Manager had a long-standing and positive relationship with employee.
■ The lower-level person also was a supervisor.[39]

This delegation scenario boils down to one pivotal factor, trust.[40]

Superiors prefer to delegate important tasks and decisions to the people they trust. As discussed in Chapters 9 and 10, it takes time and favourable experience to build trust. Of course, trust is fragile; it can be destroyed by a single remark, act or omission. Ironically, superiors cannot learn to trust someone without, initially at least, running the risk of betrayal. This is where empowerment in Figure 13.2 evolves towards trust: from consultation, over participation to delegation. In other words, superiors need to start small and work up the empowerment ladder. They need to delegate small tasks and decisions and scale up as competence, confidence and trust grow. Employees need to work on their side of the trust equation as well. One of the best ways to earn a superior's trust is to show initiative (see Figure 13.3). Researchers in the area offer this instructive definition and characterisation:

FIGURE 13.3 PERSONAL INITIATIVE: THE OTHER SIDE OF DELEGATION

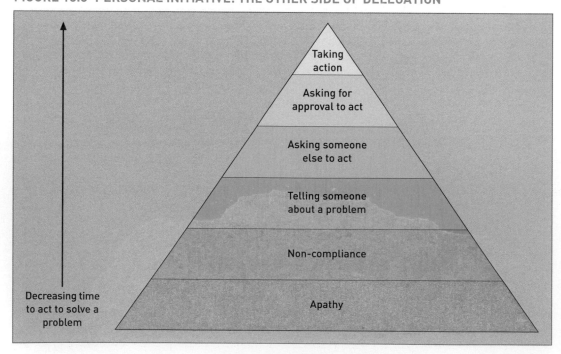

Personal initiative is a behaviour syndrome resulting in an individual's taking an active and self-starting approach to work and going beyond what is formally required in a given job. More specifically, personal initiative is characterised by the following aspects: it (1) is consistent with the organisation's mission, (2) has a long-term focus, (3) is goal-directed and action-oriented, (4) is persistent in the face of barriers and setbacks, and (5) is self-starting and proactive.[41]

> **Personal initiative** going beyond formal job requirements and being an active self-starter

RESEARCH FINDINGS AND PRACTICAL IMPLICATIONS

Like other widely heralded techniques – such as TQM (Chapter 15), 360-degree feedback (Chapter 6), teams (Chapter 10) and learning organisations (Chapter 17) – empowerment has its fair share of critics and suffers from unrealistic expectations.[42] Research results to date are mixed, with a recent positive uptrend:

- According to a field study of 26 insurance claims supervisors, employees who enjoyed a greater degree of delegation processed more insurance claims at lower cost.[43]
- A study of 297 service employees led the researchers to conclude: 'Empowerment may contribute to an employee's job satisfaction, but not as profoundly shape work effort and performance.'[44]
- A study of 24 growing companies by Centre Entreprise at Cambridge University, UK, showed that delegation is fundamental in order to expand a company. While the leaders of the companies examined were all highly motivated and ambitious, some achieved much faster and more consistent growth than others. These high achievers were characterised by their ability to recruit a team of senior managers at an early stage and by their willingness to cede a high degree of control and responsibility to them.[45]
- When the job performance of 81 empowered employees at the home office of a Canadian life insurance company was compared with a control group of 90 employees, the researchers found 'minimal support' for empowerment.[46]
- Factors associated with perceived empowerment were studied at a US hospital. Among 612 nurses, skilled professionals and administrators (21 per cent male), higher perceived empowerment was associated with higher rank, longer tenure with the organisation, approachable leaders, effective and worthwhile task groups, higher job satisfaction and lower propensity to quit. No gender or race effects were found.[47]

We believe empowerment has good promise if superiors go about it properly. Empowerment is a sweeping concept with many different definitions. Consequently, researchers use inconsistent measurements, and cause–effect relationships are fuzzy. Managers committed to the idea of employee empowerment need to follow the path of continuous improvement, learning from their successes and failures. Eight years of research with 10 'empowered' companies led consultant W. Alan Randolph to formulate the three-pronged empowerment plan in Figure 13.4. Notice how open-book management and active information sharing are needed to build the necessary foundation of trust. Beyond that, clear goals and lots of relevant training are needed. While noting that the empowerment process can take several years to unfold, Randolph offered this perspective:

> While the keys to empowerment may be easy to understand, they are hard to implement. It takes tremendous courage to start sharing sensitive information. It takes true strength to build more structure just at the point when people want more freedom of action. It takes real growth to allow teams to take over the management decision-making process. And above all, it takes perseverance to complete the empowerment process.[48]

Organisational politics and impression management

Most students of OB find the study of organisational politics intriguing. Perhaps this topic owes its appeal to the antics of certain movies, picturing corporate villains who get their way by stepping on anyone and everyone. As we will see, however, organisational politics includes, but is not limited to, dirty dealing. Organisational politics is an ever-present and sometimes annoying feature of modern work life. For example, a recent survey showed that internal office politics are holding back the

FIGURE 13.4 RANDOLPH'S EMPOWERMENT MODEL

The empowerment plan
Share information • share company performance information • help people understand the business • build trust through sharing sensitive information • create self-monitoring possibilities

| **Create autonomy through structure**
• create a clear vision and clarify the little pictures
• clarify goals and roles collaboratively
• create new decision-making rules that support empowerment
• establish new empowering performance management processes
• use heavy doses of training | **Let teams become the hierarchy**
• provide direction and training for new skills
• provide encouragement and support for change
• gradually have managers let go of control
• work through the leadership vacuum stage
• acknowledge the fear factor |

Remember: Empowerment is not magic;
it consists of a few simple steps and a lot of persistence.

SOURCE: 'Navigating the Journey to Empowerment', by W. Alan Randolph. Reprinted from *Organizational Dynamics*, Spring 1995. © 1995 American Management Association International. Reprinted by permission of the American Management Association International, New York, NY. All rights reserved. http://www.amanet.org.

growth of the UK's electronic economy. It was found that 25 per cent of IT directors believe politics is to blame for the brakes being put on e-business projects.[49] On the other hand, organisational politics is often a positive force in modern work organisations. Skilful and well-timed politics can help you get your point across, neutralise resistance to a key project or get a choice job assignment. David Butcher, who leads executive seminars on organisational politics at Cranfield Management School, UK, puts things in perspective by observing the following:

> The idea that business and politics don't mix is one of management's most deeply ingrained myths. When people say of a corporation or a hospital that 'it's a very political organisation', it's not meant as a compliment. In the same way, 'he or she plays politics' is a damning assessment of a person. But the ideal of a company as a politics-free zone is getting harder and harder to sustain. It was born of an era where rationality and control were the paramount values, and hierarchy and bureaucracy the logical management expression of them. Unfortunately the world is no longer predictable and stable, but chaotic and volatile, so the simplistic vision of management as an exercise in machine-like rationality doesn't wash any more. [...] Large organisations are hotbeds of political intrigue. Senior managers have competing agendas. It was ever thus. Management works that way. If you ask managers what they do, they say that politics is part of their job. It's a purely notional view that says otherwise. It's time we recognise that fact. Once you accept that a company is a political system, you can begin to make things happen.[50]

We explore this important and interesting area by: (1) defining the term organisational politics, (2) identifying three levels of political action, (3) discussing eight specific political tactics, (4) considering a related area called impression management and (5) examining relevant research and practical implications.

Definition and domain of organisational politics

Organisational politics | intentional enhancement of self-interest

'Organisational politics involves intentional acts of influence to enhance or protect the self-interest of individuals or groups.'[51] An emphasis on self-interest distinguishes this form of social influence. Managers are endlessly challenged to achieve a workable balance between employees' self-interests and organisational interests, as discussed at the beginning of this chapter. When a proper balance exists, the pursuit of self-interest may serve the organisation's interests.

Political behaviour becomes a negative force when self-interests erode or defeat organisational interests. For example, researchers have documented the political tactic of filtering and distorting information flowing up to the boss. This self-serving practice put the reporting employees in the best possible light.[52]

UNCERTAINTY TRIGGERS POLITICAL BEHAVIOUR

Political manoeuvring is triggered primarily by uncertainty. Five common sources of uncertainty within organisations are:

- Unclear objectives.
- Vague performance measures.
- Ill-defined decision processes.
- Strong individual or group competition.[53]
- Any type of change.

Regarding this last source of uncertainty, organisation development specialist Anthony Raia noted: 'Whatever we attempt to change, the political subsystem becomes active. Vested interests are almost always at stake and the distribution of power is challenged'.[54]

Thus, we would expect a field sales representative, striving to achieve an assigned quota, to be less political than a management trainee working on a variety of projects. While some management trainees stake their career success on hard work, competence and a bit of luck, many do not. These people attempt to gain a competitive edge through some combination of the political tactics discussed below. Meanwhile, the salesperson's performance is measured in actual sales, not in terms of being friends with the boss or taking credit for others' work. Thus, the management trainee would tend to be more political than the field salesperson because of greater uncertainty about management's expectations. Because employees generally experience greater uncertainty during the earlier stages of their careers, it has also been found that junior employees are more political than more senior ones.[55]

THREE LEVELS OF POLITICAL ACTION

Although much political manoeuvring occurs at the individual level, it can also involve group or collective action. Figure 13.5 illustrates three different levels of political action: the individual level, the coalition level and the network level.[56] Each level has its distinguishing characteristics. At the individual level, personal self-interests are pursued by the individual. The political aspects of coalitions and networks are not so obvious, however.

People with a common interest can become a political Coalition by fitting the following definition. In an organisational context, a coalition is an informal group bound together by the active pursuit of a single issue. Coalitions may or may not coincide with formal group membership (also see Chapter 9). When the target issue is resolved (a sexually harassing supervisor is fired, for

Coalition temporary groupings of people who actively pursue a single issue

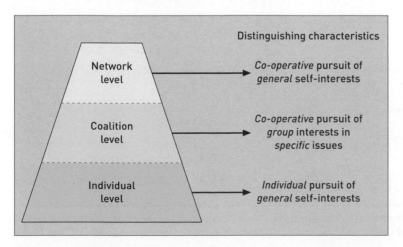

FIGURE 13.5 LEVELS OF POLITICAL ACTION IN ORGANISATIONS

Distinguishing characteristics

Network level → *Co-operative* pursuit of *general* self-interests

Coalition level → *Co-operative* pursuit of *group* interests in *specific* issues

Individual level → *Individual* pursuit of *general* self-interests

example), the coalition disbands. Experts note that political coalitions have 'fuzzy boundaries'. meaning they are fluid in membership, flexible in structure and temporary in duration.[57]

A third level of political action involves networks.[58] Unlike coalitions, which pivot on specific issues, networks are loose associations of individuals seeking social support for their general self-interests. Politically, networks are people-oriented, while coalitions are issue-oriented. Networks have broader and longer-term agendas than do coalitions.

POLITICAL TACTICS

Anyone who has worked in an organisation has first-hand knowledge of blatant politicking. Blaming someone else for your mistake is an obvious political ploy. But other political tactics are more subtle. Researchers have identified a range of political behaviour.

One landmark study, involving in-depth interviews with 87 managers from 30 electronics companies, identified eight political tactics. Top-, middle- and low-level managers were represented about equally in the sample. According to the researchers: 'Respondents were asked to describe organisational political tactics and personal characteristics of effective political actors based upon their accumulated experience in all organisations in which they had worked'.[59] The eight political tactics that emerged are listed in descending order in the first column of Table 13.4.

TABLE 13.4 EIGHT COMMON POLITICAL TACTICS IN ORGANISATIONS

Political tactic	Percentage of managers mentioning tactic	Brief description of tactic
1 Attacking or blaming others	54%	Used to avoid or minimise association with failure. Reactive when scapegoating is involved. Proactive when goal is to reduce competition for limited resources
2 Using information as a political tool	54%	Involves the purposeful withholding or distortion of information. Obscuring an unfavourable situation by overwhelming superiors with information
3 Creating a favourable image (impression management)	53%	Dressing/grooming for success. Adhering to organisational norms and drawing attention to one's successes and influence. Taking credit for others' accomplishments
4 Developing a base of support	37%	Getting prior support for a decision. Building others' commitment to a decision through participation
5 Praising others (ingratiation)	25%	Making influential people feel good ('apple polishing')
6 Forming power coalitions with strong allies	25%	Teaming up with powerful people who can get results
7 Associating with influential people	24%	Building a support network both inside and outside the organisation
8 Creating obligations (reciprocity)	13%	Creating social debts ('I did you a favour, so you owe me a favour')

SOURCE: Adapted from R. W. Allen, D. L. Madison, L. W. Porter, P. A. Renwick and B. T. Mayes, 'Organizational Politics: Tactics and Characteristics of Its Actors', *California Management Review*, Fall 1979, pp. 77–83.

Column 3 describes these political tactics and column 4 indicates how often each reportedly was used by the interviewed managers.

The researchers distinguished between reactive and proactive political tactics. Some of the tactics, such as scapegoating, are reactive because the intent is to defend one's self-interest. Other tactics, such as developing a base of support, are proactive because they seek to promote the individual's self-interest.

What is your attitude toward organisational politics? How often do you rely on the various tactics in Table 13.4? You can get a general indication of your political tendencies by comparing your behaviour with the characteristics in Table 13.5. Would you characterise yourself as politically naive, politically sensible or a political shark? How do you think others view your political actions? What are the career, friendship and ethical implications of your political tendencies?[61]

Impression management

Impression management is defined as 'the process by which people attempt to control or manipulate the reactions of others to images of themselves or their ideas.'[62] This encompasses how one talks, behaves and looks. Most impression management attempts are directed at making a good impression on relevant others. But, as we will see, some employees strive to make a bad impression. For purposes of conceptual clarity, we will focus on upward impression management (trying to impress one's immediate supervisor) because it is most relevant for managers. Still, it is good to remember that anyone can be the intended target of impression management. Parents, teachers, peers, employees and customers are all fair game when it comes to managing the impressions of others. At an organisational level impression management can be used as a tool to differentiate the organisation's image for competitor companies. This is discussed in Chapter 18.

> **Impression management** getting others to see us in a certain manner

A CONCEPTUAL CROSSROADS

Impression management is an interesting conceptual crossroads involving self-monitoring, attribution theory and organisational politics.[63] Perhaps this explains why impression management has won active research attention in recent years. Remember that high self-monitoring employees ('chameleons' who adjust to their surroundings) are likely to be more inclined to engage in impression management than low self-monitors (see Chapter 2). Impression management also involves the systematic manipulation of attributions (see Chapter 4). For example, a bank president will look

TABLE 13.5 ARE YOU POLITICALLY NAIVE, POLITICALLY SENSIBLE OR A POLITICAL SHARK?

Characteristics	Naive	Sensible	Shark
Underlying attitude	Politics is unpleasant	Politics is necessary	Politics is an opportunity
Intent	Avoid at all costs	Further departmental goals	Self-serving and predatory
Techniques	Tell it like it is	Network; expand connections; use system to give and receive favours	Manipulate; use fraud and deceit when necessary
Favourite tactics	None – the truth will win out	Negotiate, bargain	Bully; misuse information; cultivate and use 'friends' and other contacts

SOURCE: Reprinted with permission from J. K. Pinto and O. P. Kharbanda, 'Lessons for an Accidental Profession', *Business Horizons*, March–April 1995, p. 45. Copyright © 1998 by the Indiana University Board of Trustees at Indiana University, Kelley School of Business.

good if the board of directors is encouraged to attribute organisational successes to his or her efforts and attribute problems and failures to factors beyond his or her control. Impression management definitely fits into the realm of organisational politics because of an overriding focus on furthering one's self-interests.

MAKING A GOOD IMPRESSION

If you 'dress for success', project an upbeat attitude at all times and avoid offending others, you are engaging in favourable impression management – particularly so if your motive is to improve your chances of getting what you want in life.[64] Former British Airways chairman, Lord King, admitted he had underestimated his casually dressed rival (Richard Branson, Virgin chairman). 'If Branson had worn a pair of steelrimmed shoes, a double-breasted suit and shaved off his beard, I would have taken him seriously. As it was, I couldn't. I underestimated him.'[65] On the lighter side, the trends towards more casual dress codes has working men and women rethinking what it means to dress for success. *Newsweek* recently framed the irony this way:

> Guys, it's your turn. As women are liberated from some of the meaner dictates of dress, men are losing a certain brand of fashion freedom. Sure, you may no longer have to wear a suit and tie to work. But there's the rub. With so many offices gone 'casual', the corporate uniform is gone. You have to consider not only when to dress up or down, but a whole new vocabulary of texture, pattern and fabric. And that mandate dreaded by some females of the species now applies to you too: accessorise! Can I wear a silk-crepe tie with denim? Bucks with dress pants?[66]

No one ever said that impression management was easy!

A statistical factor analysis of the influence attempts reported by a sample of 84 bank employees (including 74 women) identified three categories of favourable upward impression management tactics.[67] As labelled in the next Activity, favourable upward impression management tactics can be job-focused (manipulating information about one's job performance), supervisor-focused (praising and doing favours for one's supervisor) and self-focused (presenting oneself as a polite and nice person). Take a short break from your studying to complete the Activity. How did you do?

A moderate amount of upward impression management is a necessity for the average employee today. Too little, and busy managers are liable to overlook some of your valuable contributions when they make job assignment, pay and promotion decisions. Too much, and you run the risk of being branded a 'schmoozer', a 'phony' and other unflattering things by your co-workers.[68] Excessive flattery and ingratiation can backfire by embarrassing the target person and damaging one's credibility. Also, the risk of unintended insult is very high when impression management tactics cross gender, racial, ethnic and cultural lines.[69] International management experts warn:

> The impression management tactic is only as effective as its correlation to accepted norms about behavioural presentation. In other words, slapping a Japanese subordinate on the back with a rousing 'Good work, Hiro!' will not create the desired impression in Hiro's mind that the expatriate intended. In fact, the behaviour will likely create the opposite impression.[70]

MAKING A POOR IMPRESSION

At first glance, the idea of consciously trying to make a bad impression in the workplace seems absurd. But an interesting new line of impression management research has uncovered both motives and tactics for making oneself look bad. In a survey of the work experiences of business students at a large northwestern US university, more than half 'reported witnessing a case of someone intentionally looking bad at work'.[71] Why?

Four motives came out of the study:

■ Avoidance: employee seeks to avoid additional work, stress, burnout or an unwanted transfer or promotion.

activity

How much do you rely on upward impression management tactics?

Instructions

Rate yourself on each item according to how you behave on your current (or most recent) job. Add your circled responses to calculate a total score. Compare your score with our arbitrary norms.

Job-focused tactics	Rarely			Very often	
1 I exaggerate the value of my positive work results and make my supervisor aware of them.	1	2	3	4	5
2 I try to make my work appear better than it is.	1	2	3	4	5
3 I try to take responsibility for positive results, even when I'm not solely responsible for achieving them.	1	2	3	4	5
4 I try to make my negative results less severe than they initially appear, when informing my supervisor.	1	2	3	4	5
5 I arrive at work early and/or work late to show my supervisor I am a hard worker.	1	2	3	4	5

Supervisor-focused tactics					
6 I show an interest in my supervisor's personal life.	1	2	3	4	5
7 I praise my supervisor about his/her accomplishments.	1	2	3	4	5
8 I do personal favours for my supervisor that I'm not required to do.	1	2	3	4	5
9 I compliment my supervisor on her/his dress or appearance.	1	2	3	4	5
10 I agree with my supervisor's major suggestions and ideas.	1	2	3	4	5

Self-focused tactics					
11 I am very friendly and polite in the presence of my supervisor.	1	2	3	4	5
12 I try to act as a model employee in the presence of my supervisor.	1	2	3	4	5
13 I work harder when I know my supervisor will see the results.	1	2	3	4	5

Total score = _____

Arbitrary norms

13–26 Free agent
27–51 Better safe than sorry
52–65 Hello, Hollywood!

SOURCE: Adapted from S. J. Wayne and G. R. Ferris, 'Influence Tactics, Affect, and Exchange Quality in Supervisor-Subordinate Interactions: A Laboratory Experiment and Field Study', *Journal of Applied Psychology*, October 1990, pp. 487–99.

- Obtain concrete rewards: employee seeks to obtain a pay raise or a desired transfer, promotion or demotion.
- Exit: employee seeks to get laid off, fired or suspended, and perhaps also to collect unemployment or workers' compensation.
- Power: employee seeks to control, manipulate or intimidate others, get revenge, or make someone else look bad.[72]

Within the context of these motives, unfavourable upward-impression management makes sense. Five unfavourable upward impression-management tactics identified by the researchers are as follows:

- Decreasing performance: restricting productivity, making more mistakes than usual, lowering quality, neglecting tasks.
- Not working to potential: pretending ignorance, having unused capabilities.
- Withdrawing: being tardy, taking excessive breaks, faking illness.

■ Displaying a bad attitude: complaining, getting upset and angry, acting strangely, not getting along with co-workers.

■ Broadcasting limitations: letting co-workers know about one's physical problems and mistakes (both verbally and non-verbally).[73]

Recommended ways to manage employees who try to make a bad impression can be found throughout this book. They include, for instance, more challenging work, greater autonomy, better feedback, supportive leadership, clear and reasonable goals, and a less stressful work setting.[74]

Research findings and practical implications

Recent field research involving employees in real organisations rather than students in contrived laboratory settings has yielded these useful insights.

In a study of 514 non-academic university employees in the southwestern United States, white men had a greater understanding of organisational politics than racial and ethnic minorities and white women. The researchers endorsed the practice of using mentors to help women and minorities develop their political skills.[75]

Another study of 68 women and 84 men employed by five different service and industrial companies in the United States uncovered significant gender-based insights about organisational politics. In what might be termed the battle of the sexes,

. . . it was found that political behaviour was perceived more favourably when it was performed against a target of the opposite gender . . . . Thus subjects of both sexes tend to relate to gender as a meaningful affiliation group. This finding presents a different picture from the one suggesting that women tend to accept male superiority at work and generally agree with sex stereotypes which are commonly discriminatory in nature.[76]

Impression management attempts can either positively or negatively impact one's performance appraisal results.[77] The researchers in one study of 67 manager–employee pairs concluded: 'Subordinates who were friendly and reasonable were perceived as amiable and favourably evaluated.'[78] However, subordinates who relied on ingratiation (making the boss feel good) did not get better performance appraisals.[79]

Organisational politics cannot be eliminated. A manager would be naive to expect such an outcome. But political manoeuvring can and should be managed to keep it constructive and within reasonable bounds. Harvard's Abraham Zaleznik put the issue this way: 'People can focus their attention on only so many things. The more it lands on politics, the less energy – emotional and intellectual – is available to attend to the problems that fall under the heading of real work.'[80]

An individual's degree of 'politicalness' is a matter of personal values, ethics and temperament. People who are either strictly non-political or highly political generally pay a price for their behaviour. The former may experience slow promotions and feel left out, while the latter may run the risk of being called self-serving and lose their credibility. People at both ends of the political spectrum may be considered poor team players. A moderate amount of prudent political behaviour generally is considered a survival tool in complex organisations. Experts remind us that:

. . . political behaviour has earned a bad name only because of its association with politicians. On its own, the use of power and other resources to obtain your objectives is not inherently unethical. It all depends on what the preferred objectives are.[81]

With this perspective in mind, the practical steps in Table 13.6 are recommended. How many of the Enron- and Ahold-type scandals could have been prevented with this approach? Measurable objectives are management's first line of defence against negative expressions of organisational politics.[82]

TABLE 13.6 HOW TO KEEP ORGANISATIONAL POLITICS WITHIN REASONABLE BOUNDS

- Screen out overly political individuals at hiring time
- Create an open-book management system
- Make sure every employee knows how the business works and has a personal line of sight to key results with corresponding measureable objectives for individual accountability
- Have non-financial people interpret periodic financial and accounting statements for all employees
- Establish formal conflict resolution and grievance processes
- As an ethics filter, do only what you would feel comfortable doing on national television
- Publicly recognise and reward people who get real results without political games

SOURCE: Adapted in part from discussion in L. B. MacGregor Server, *The End of Office Politics as Usual* (New York: American Management Association, 2002), pp. 184–99.

Managing interpersonal and intergroup conflict

Mention the term 'conflict' and most people envision fights, riots or war. But these extreme situations represent only the most overt and violent expressions of conflict. During the typical work day, people in organisations encounter more subtle and non-violent expressions of conflict. Conflict, like power and organisational politics, is an inevitable and sometimes positive force in modern work organisations. Dean Tjosvold, from Hong Kong's Lingnan University, notes that 'change begets conflict, conflict begets change'[83] and challenges us to do better with this sobering global perspective:

> Learning to manage conflict is a critical investment in improving how we, our families and our organisations adapt and take advantage of change. Managing conflicts well does not insulate us from change, nor does it mean that we will always come out on top or get all that we want. However, effective conflict management helps us keep in touch with new developments and create solutions appropriate for new threats and opportunities.
>
> Much evidence shows we have often failed to manage our conflicts and respond to change effectively. High divorce rates, disheartening examples of sexual and physical abuse of children, the expensive failures of international joint ventures and bloody ethnic violence have convinced many people that we do not have the abilities to cope with our complex interpersonal, organisational and global conflicts.[84]

Defining conflict

A comprehensive review of the conflict literature yielded this consensus definition: '**Conflict** is a process in which one party perceives that its interests are being opposed or negatively affected by another party'.[85] The word 'perceives' reminds us that sources of conflict and issues can be real or imagined. The resulting conflict is the same. Conflict can escalate (strengthen) or de-escalate (weaken) over time. 'The conflict process unfolds in a context, and whenever conflict, escalated or not, occurs the disputants or third parties can attempt to manage it in some manner.'[86] Consequently, employees need to understand the dynamics of conflict and know how to handle it effectively (both as disputants and as third parties).

Conflict
one party perceives its interests are being opposed or set back by another party

A CONFLICT CONTINUUM

Ideas about managing conflict underwent an interesting evolution during the twentieth century. Initially, scientific management experts such as Frederick Taylor believed all conflict ultimately threatened management's authority and thus had to be avoided or quickly resolved. Later, human relationists recognised the inevitability of conflict and advised managers to learn to live with it. Taylor's approach and the human relations view are thoroughly discussed in Chapter 1. Emphasis remained on resolving conflict whenever possible, however. Beginning in the 1970s, OB specialists realised conflict had both positive and negative outcomes, depending on its nature and intensity. This perspective introduced the revolutionary idea that organisations could suffer from too little conflict. Figure 13.6 illustrates the relationship between conflict intensity and outcomes.

FIGURE 13.6 THE RELATIONSHIP BETWEEN CONFLICT INTENSITY AND OUTCOMES

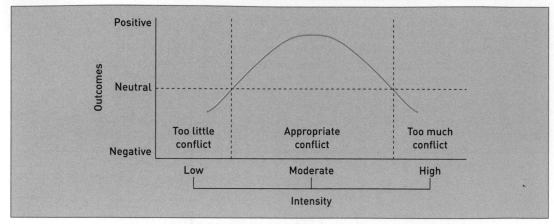

SOURCE: L. D. Brown, *Managing Conflict of Organizational Interfaces*, © 1986, Addison-Wesley Publishing Co., Inc., Reading, MA. Figure 1.1 on page 8. Reprinted with permission.

Work groups, departments or organisations that experience too little conflict tend to be plagued by apathy, lack of creativity, indecision and missed deadlines. Excessive conflict, on the other hand, can erode organisational performance because of political infighting, dissatisfaction, lack of teamwork and turnover. Workplace aggression and violence can be manifestations of excessive conflict (see Chapter 3).[87] Appropriate types and levels of conflict energise people in constructive directions.[88]

FUNCTIONAL VERSUS DYSFUNCTIONAL CONFLICT

Functional conflict serves organisation's interests

Dysfunctional conflict threatens organisation's interests

The distinction between **Functional conflict** and **Dysfunctional conflict** pivots on whether the organisation's interests are served. According to one conflict expert:

> Some [types of conflict] support the goals of the organisation and improve performance; these are functional, constructive forms of conflict. They benefit or support the main purposes of the organisation. Additionally, there are those types of conflict that hinder organisational performance; these are dysfunctional or destructive forms. They are undesirable and the manager should seek their eradication.[89]

Functional conflict is commonly referred to in management circles as 'constructive' or 'co-operative' conflict.[90]

> Helmut Werner's performance is naturally of keen interest to his boss, Daimler-Benz chief Jurgen E. Schrempp. Daimler needs big profits from Mercedes as Schrempp expensively unwinds a failed diversification policy. But German business and auto magazines regularly report stories of rows and back-stabbing that read like TV soap operas. Allegedly, Schrempp was leery of the Smart project and objected to building the A-Class in Brazil. Wrong, says Werner: There was lively debate about Smart, but Schrempp is on board. By another account, marketing czar Zetsche is Schrempp's spy to keep tabs on Werner. In reality, Werner got Zetsche his first big career break. Says an exasperated Werner: 'Nothing that is written about personal bitterness is true'. But he admits: 'We have controversial discussions. It is a very constructive conflict'.[91]

ANTECEDENTS OF CONFLICT

Certain situations produce more conflict than others. By knowing the antecedents of conflict, organisations are better able to anticipate conflict and take steps to resolve it if it becomes dysfunctional. Among the situations that tend to produce either functional or dysfunctional conflict are:

■ Incompatible personalities or value systems.
■ Overlapping or unclear job boundaries.

- Competition for limited resources.
- Interdepartment/intergroup competition.
- Inadequate communication.
- Interdependent tasks (e.g. one person cannot complete his or her assignment until others have completed their work).
- Organisational complexity (conflict tends to increase as the number of hierarchical layers and specialised tasks increase).
- Unreasonable or unclear policies, standards or rules.
- Unreasonable deadlines or extreme time pressure.
- Collective decision making (the greater the number of people participating in a decision, the greater the potential for conflict).
- Decision making by consensus.
- Unmet expectations (employees who have unrealistic expectations about job assignments, pay or promotions are more prone to conflict).
- Unresolved or suppressed conflicts.[92]

Proactive people carefully read these early warnings and take appropriate action. For example, group conflict can be reduced by making decisions on the basis of a majority vote rather than seeking a consensus.

DESIRED CONFLICT OUTCOMES

Within organisations, conflict management is more than simply a quest for agreement. If progress is to be made and dysfunctional conflict minimised, a broader agenda is in order. Tjosvold's co-operative conflict model calls for three desired outcomes:

- Agreement: but at what cost? Equitable and fair agreements are best. An agreement that leaves one party feeling exploited or defeated will tend to breed resentment and subsequent conflict.
- Stronger relationships: good agreements enable conflicting parties to build bridges of goodwill and trust for future use. Moreover, conflicting parties who trust each other are more likely to keep their end of the bargain.
- Learning: functional conflict can promote greater self-awareness and creative problem solving. Like the practice of management itself, successful conflict handling is learned primarily by doing. Knowledge of the concepts and techniques in this chapter is a necessary first step, but there is no substitute for hands-on practice. In a contentious world, there are plenty of opportunities to practice conflict management.[93]

Intergroup conflict

Conflict among work groups, teams and departments is a common threat to organisational competitiveness.

> Siemens has also taken radical measures to force managers to adapt to the market's stern demands. The company called in its blue-ribbon customers. Engineers and managers alike were humbled as Opel, Ford and Sony gave them an earful at three-day gripe sessions at Siemens' Bavarian hideaway. Alan Burton, Ford's European telecom manager, shocked one group by disclosing he had received competing bids from three Siemens divisions for the same tender.[94]

People who understand the mechanics of intergroup conflict are better equipped to face this sort of challenge.

IN-GROUP THINKING: THE SEEDS OF INTERGROUP CONFLICT

As we discussed in previous chapters, cohesiveness − a 'we-feeling' binding group members together − can be a good or bad thing (see Chapters 9 and 10). A certain amount of cohesiveness can turn a group of individuals into a smooth-running team. Too much cohesiveness, however, can breed groupthink because a desire to get along pushes aside critical thinking. The study of in-groups by small group researchers has revealed a whole package of changes associated with increased group cohesiveness. Specifically:

- Members of in-groups view themselves as a collection of unique individuals, while they stereotype members of other groups as being 'all alike'.
- In-group members see themselves positively and as morally correct, while they view members of other groups negatively and as immoral.
- In-groups view outsiders as a threat.
- In-group members exaggerate the differences between their group and other groups. This typically involves a distorted perception of reality.[95]

Avid sports fans who simply cannot imagine how someone would support the opposing team exemplify one form of in-group thinking. Also, this pattern of behaviour is a form of ethnocentrism (see Chapter 16). Reflect for a moment on evidence of in-group behaviour in your life. Does your circle of friends make fun of others because of their ethnic origin, gender, nationality, sexual preference, diploma or occupation?

In-group thinking is one more fact of organisational life that virtually guarantees conflict. Professionals cannot eliminate in-group thinking, but they certainly should not ignore it when handling intergroup conflicts.

RESEARCH FINDINGS AND PRACTICAL IMPLICATIONS

Sociologists have long recommended the contact hypothesis for reducing intergroup conflict. According to the contact hypothesis, the more the members of different groups interact, the less intergroup conflict they will experience. Those interested in improving race, international and union–management relations typically encourage cross-group interaction. The hope is that any type of interaction, short of actual conflict, will reduce stereotyping and combat in-group thinking. But recent research has shown this approach to be naive and limited. For example, one recent study of 83 health centre employees (83 per cent female) probed the specific nature of intergroup relations and concluded:

 The number of negative relationships was significantly related to higher perceptions of intergroup conflict. Thus, it seems that negative relationships have a salience that overwhelms any possible positive effects from friendship links across groups.[96]

Intergroup friendships are still desirable, as documented in many studies,[97] but they are readily overpowered by negative intergroup interactions. Thus, priority number one for people faced with intergroup conflict is to identify and root out specific negative linkages among groups. A single personality conflict, for instance, may contaminate the entire intergroup experience. The same goes for an employee who voices negative opinions or spreads negative rumours about another group. Our updated contact model in Figure 13.7 is based on this and other recent research insights, such as the need to foster positive attitudes toward other groups.[98] Also, notice how conflict within the group and negative gossip from third parties are threats that need to be neutralised if intergroup conflict is to be minimised.

As demonstrated by British Airways in the next Snapshot, the quest for good intergroup relations needs to be creative, systematic and relentless.

Managing conflict

As we have seen, conflict has many faces and is a constant challenge for managers who are responsible for reaching organisational goals. Our attention now turns to the active management of both functional and dysfunctional conflict. We discuss how to stimulate functional and dysfunctional conflict. Relevant research lessons are also examined.

STIMULATING FUNCTIONAL CONFLICT

Sometimes committees and decision-making groups become so bogged down in details and procedures that nothing substantive is accomplished. Carefully monitored functional conflict can help

FIGURE 13.7 AN UPDATED CONTACT MODEL FOR MINIMISING INTERGROUP CONFLICT

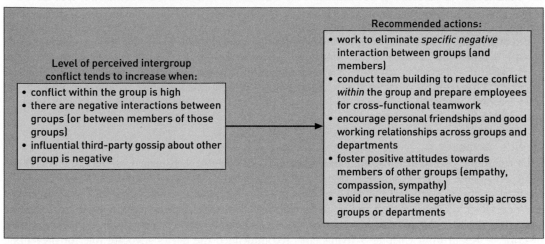

SOURCE: Based on research evidence in G. Labianca, D. J. Brass and B. Gray, 'Social Networks and Perceptions of Intergroup Conflict: The Role of Negative Relationships and Third Parties', *Academy of Management Journal*, February 1998, pp. 55–67; C. D. Batson *et al.*, 'Empathy and Attitudes: Can Feeling for a Member of a Stigmatized Group Improve Feelings Toward the Group?', *Journal of Personality and Social Psychology*, January 1997, pp. 105–18; and S. C. Wright *et al.*, 'The Extended Contact Effect: Knowledge of Cross-Group Friendships and Prejudice', *Journal of Personality and Social Psychology*, July 1997, pp. 73–90.

Breaking barriers at British Airways

Who? Marcia Bradley, 45, marketing manager, culture-change projects, British Airways.

What's your problem? 'We're quality fanatics. There's a "BA way", and there's a wrong way. But sometimes we go outside the company for ideas. How do I turn outsiders into insiders without compromising their ideas? How do I convince insiders to give outsiders a chance?'

Tell me about it. 'I'm part of a major initiative to rethink the experience of being at an airport. I work with lots of vendors and consultants. But we have such a strong way of doing things at BA that there's a tendency to keep outsiders at arm's length. We risk creating great proposals that collect dust – or rolling out initiatives that don't meet expectations. I need to show my BA colleagues and my outside colleagues what they can learn from each other.'

What's your solution? 'Total immersion. Before we even think about a proposal, we might spend three months introducing our partners to BA, and vice versa. We make sure that the consultants experience our product. We arrange for them to fly BA to meetings – both in Club Class (first class) and in World Traveller (economy class). We ask for their impressions: How comfortable were the seats? How long did you wait at the counter? We open a dialogue about the company.'

'Partners also meet key BA players – in structured get-to-know-you gatherings as well as for brainstorming. We even ask these partners to spend time with people with whom they won't be working. They visit departments; they drop in on meetings.'

'Finally, they get a formal education in BA's values and in our brand integrity. It's part history lesson, part "rules of the road" orientation. We cover everything from our principles of customer service to the choice of colours on our aircraft.'

'The pay-off is huge. When it's time to sign off on budgets or to approve designs, we do it faster and more confidently.'

SOURCE: C. Olofson, 'Let Outsiders In, Turn Your Insiders Out', *Fast Company*, March 1999, p. 46.

snapshot

get the creative juices flowing once again. People in organisations basically have two options. They can fan the fires of naturally occurring conflict – but this approach can be unreliable and slow. Alternatively, they can resort to programmed conflict.

Experts in the field define **Programmed conflict** as 'conflict that raises different opinions regardless of the personal feelings of the managers'.[99] The trick is to get contributors to either defend or criticise ideas based on relevant facts rather than on the basis of personal preference or political interests. This requires disciplined role playing. Two programmed conflict techniques with proven track records are devil's advocacy and the dialectic method. Let us explore these two ways of stimulating functional conflict.

> **Programmed conflict** encourages different opinions without protecting management's personal feelings

Devil's advocacy

This technique gets its name from a traditional practice within the Roman Catholic Church. When someone's name came before the College of Cardinals for elevation to sainthood, it was absolutely essential to ensure that he or she had a spotless record. Consequently, one individual was assigned the role of devil's advocate to uncover and air all possible objections to the person's canonisation. In accordance with this practice, **Devil's advocacy** in today's organisations involves assigning someone the role of critic.[100] Recall from Chapter 9 Irving Janis recommended the devil's advocate role for preventing groupthink.

> **Devil's advocacy** assigning someone the role of critic

FIGURE 13.8 TECHNIQUES FOR STIMULATING FUNCTIONAL CONFLICT: DEVIL'S ADVOCACY AND THE DIALECTIC METHOD

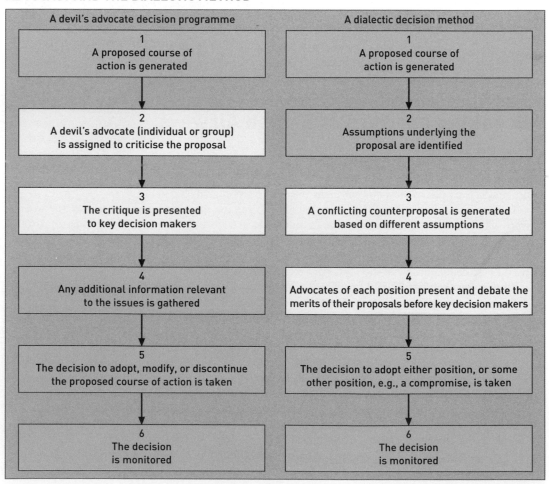

A devil's advocate decision programme	A dialectic decision method
1 A proposed course of action is generated	**1** A proposed course of action is generated
2 A devil's advocate (individual or group) is assigned to criticise the proposal	**2** Assumptions underlying the proposal are identified
3 The critique is presented to key decision makers	**3** A conflicting counterproposal is generated based on different assumptions
4 Any additional information relevant to the issues is gathered	**4** Advocates of each position present and debate the merits of their proposals before key decision makers
5 The decision to adopt, modify, or discontinue the proposed course of action is taken	**5** The decision to adopt either position, or some other position, e.g., a compromise, is taken
6 The decision is monitored	**6** The decision is monitored

SOURCE: R. A. Coslier and C. R. Schwenk, 'Agreement and Thinking Alike: Ingredients for Poor Decisions', *Academy of Management Executive*, February 1990, pp. 72–3. Used with permission.

In the left half of Figure 13.8, note how devil's advocacy alters the usual decision-making process in steps 2 and 3. This approach to programmed conflict is intended to generate critical thinking and reality testing.[101] It is a good idea to rotate the job of devil's advocate so not one person or group develops a strictly negative reputation. Moreover, periodic devil's advocacy role-playing is good training for developing analytical and communication skills.

The dialectic method

Like devil's advocacy, the dialectic method is a time-honoured practice. This particular approach to programmed conflict dates back to the dialectic school of philosophy in ancient Greece. Plato and his followers attempted to synthesise truths by exploring opposite positions (called thesis and antithesis). Court systems in the United States and elsewhere rely on directly opposing points of view for determining guilt or innocence. Accordingly, today's **Dialectic method** calls for professionals to foster a structured debate of opposing viewpoints prior to making a decision.[102] Steps 3 and 4 in the right half of Figure 13.8 set the dialectic approach apart from the normal decision-making process.

A major drawback of the dialectic method is that 'winning the debate' may overshadow the issue at hand. Also, the dialectic method requires more skill training than does devil's advocacy. Regarding the comparative effectiveness of these two approaches to stimulating functional conflict, however, a laboratory study ended in a tie. Compared with groups that strived to reach a consensus, decision-making groups using either devil's advocacy or the dialectic method yielded equally higher-quality decisions.[103] However, in a more recent laboratory study, groups using devil's advocacy produced more potential solutions and made better recommendations for a case problem than groups using the dialectic method.[104] In light of this mixed evidence, professionals have some latitude in using either devil's advocacy or the dialectic method for pumping creative life back into stalled deliberations. Personal preference and the role players' experience may well be the deciding factors in choosing one approach over the other. The important thing is to actively stimulate functional conflict when necessary (for example, when the risk of blind conformity or groupthink is high).

Dialectic method fostering a debate of opposing viewpoints to better understand an issue

ALTERNATIVE STYLES FOR HANDLING DYSFUNCTIONAL CONFLICT

People tend to handle negative conflict in patterned ways referred to as 'styles'. Several conflict styles have been categorised over the years. According to conflict specialist Afzalur Rahim's model, five different conflict-handling styles can be plotted on a 2×2 grid. High to low concern for self is found on the horizontal axis of the grid while low to high concern for others forms the vertical axis (see Figure 13.9). Various combinations of these variables produce the five different conflict-handling styles: integrating, obliging, dominating, avoiding and compromising.[105] There is no single best style; each has strengths and limitations and is subject to situational constraints.

FIGURE 13.9 FIVE CONFLICT-HANDLING STYLES

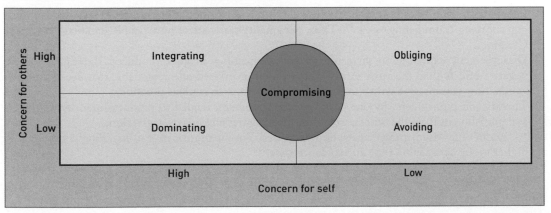

SOURCE: M. A. Rahim, 'A Strategy for Managing Conflict in Complex Organizations, *Human Relations*, January 1985, p. 84. Used with permission of Plenum Publishing.

Integrating (problem solving)

In this style, interested parties confront the issue and co-operatively identify the problem, generate and weigh alternative solutions and select a solution. Integrating is appropriate for complex issues plagued by misunderstanding. Its primary strength is its longer-lasting impact because it deals with the underlying problem rather than merely with symptoms. The primary weakness of this style is that it is very time-consuming.

Obliging (smoothing)

'An obliging person neglects his or her own concern to satisfy the concern of the other party.'[106] This style, often called 'smoothing', involves playing down differences while emphasising commonalities. Obliging may be an appropriate conflict-handling strategy when it is possible eventually to get something in return. But it is inappropriate for complex or worsening problems. Its primary strength is that it encourages co-operation. Its main weakness is that it is a temporary fix that fails to confront the underlying problem.

Dominating (forcing)

High concern for self and low concern for others encourages 'I win, you lose' tactics. The other party's needs are largely ignored. This style is often called 'forcing' because it relies on formal authority to force compliance. Dominating is appropriate when an unpopular solution must be implemented, the issue is minor or a deadline is near. It is inappropriate in an open and participative climate. Speed is its primary strength. The primary weakness of this domineering style is that it often breeds resentment.

Avoiding

This tactic may involve either passive withdrawal from the problem or active suppression of the issue. Avoidance is appropriate for trivial issues or when the costs of confrontation outweigh the benefits of resolving the conflict. It is inappropriate for difficult and worsening problems. The main strength of this style is that it buys time in unfolding or ambiguous situations. The primary weakness is that the tactic provides a temporary fix that sidesteps the underlying problem.

Compromising

This is a give-and-take approach involving moderate concern for both self and others. Compromise is appropriate when parties have opposite goals or possess equal power. But compromise is inappropriate when overuse would lead to inconclusive action (e.g. failure to meet production deadlines). The primary strength of this tactic is that the democratic process has no losers, but it is a temporary fix that can stifle creative problem solving.

Research findings and practical implications

Laboratory studies, relying on college students as subjects, uncovered the following insights about organisational conflict:

- People with a high need for affiliation tended to rely on a smoothing (obliging) style while avoiding a forcing (dominating) style.[107] Thus, personality traits affect how people handle conflict (see Chapter 2).
- Disagreement expressed in an arrogant and demeaning manner produced significantly more negative effects than the same sort of disagreement expressed in a reasonable manner.[108] In other words, how you disagree with someone is very important in conflict situations.
- Threats and punishment, by one party in a disagreement, tended to produce intensifying threats and punishment from the other party.[109] In short, aggression breeds aggression.
- As conflict increased, group satisfaction decreased. An integrative style of handling conflict led to higher group satisfaction than an avoidance style.[110]

Field studies involving managers and real organisations have given us the following insights:

- Both intradepartmental and interdepartmental conflict decreased as goal difficulty and goal clarity increased. Thus, challenging and clear goals can defuse conflict. Goal setting is discussed in Chapter 5.

- Higher levels of conflict tended to erode job satisfaction and internal work motivation.[111]
- Men and women at the same managerial level tended to handle conflict similarly. In short, there was no gender effect.[112]
- Conflict tended to move around the organisation.[113] Thus, managers need to be alerted to the fact that conflict often originates in one area or level and becomes evident somewhere else. Conflict needs to be traced back to its source if there is to be lasting improvement.
- Samples of Japanese, German and American managers who were presented with the same conflict scenario preferred different resolution techniques. Japanese and German managers did not share the Americans' enthusiasm for integrating the interests of all parties. The Japanese tended to look upward to management for direction, whereas the Germans were more bound by rules and regulations. In cross-cultural conflict resolution, there is no one best approach. Cultural-specific preferences need to be taken into consideration prior to beginning the conflict-resolution process.[114] Cross-cultural issues are discussed in Chapter 16.

Three realities dictate how organisational conflict should be managed. First, various types of conflict are inevitable because they are triggered by a wide variety of antecedents. Second, too little conflict may be as counterproductive as too much. Third, there is no single best way of avoiding or resolving conflict. Consequently, conflict specialists recommend a contingency approach to managing conflict. Antecedents of conflict and actual conflict need to be monitored. If signs of too little conflict such as apathy or lack of creativity appear, then functional conflict needs to be stimulated. This can be done by nurturing appropriate antecedents of conflict and/or programming conflict with techniques such as devil's advocacy and the dialectic method. On the other hand, when conflict becomes dysfunctional, the appropriate conflict-handling style needs to be enacted. Realistic training involving role playing can prepare managers to try alternative conflict styles.

Professionals can keep from getting too deeply embroiled in conflict by applying four lessons from recent research: (1) establish challenging and clear goals, (2) disagree in a constructive and reasonable manner, (3) do not get caught up in conflict triangles and (4) refuse to get caught in the aggression-breeds-aggression spiral.

Handling intergroup conflict with negotiation and third-party intervention

Although the conflict-handling styles just discussed can be used for all types of conflict, the model primarily targets interpersonal conflict. But what about intergroup conflict that is increasingly common in today's team- and project-oriented organisations? And about interorganisational conflict often encountered in today's world of organisational alliances and partnerships? Negotiation and third-party intervention can be helpful in these areas.

Negotiation

Formally defined, **Negotiation** is a give-and-take decision-making process involving interdependent parties with different preferences.[115] Common examples include labour–management negotiations over wages, hours and working conditions and negotiations between supply-chain specialists and vendors involving price, delivery schedules and credit terms. Self-managed work teams (Chapter 10) with overlapping task boundaries also need to rely on negotiated agreements.[116] Negotiating skills are more important than ever today.[117]

Negotiation give-and-take process between conflicting interdependent parties

TWO BASIC TYPES OF NEGOTIATION

Negotiation experts distinguish between two types of negotiation – distributive and integrative. Understanding the difference requires a change in traditional 'fixed-pie' thinking:

> A distributive negotiation usually involves a single issue – a 'fixed pie' – in which one person gains at the expense of the other. For example, haggling over the price of a rug in a bazaar is a distributive negotiation. In most conflicts, however, more than one issue is at stake, and each party values the issues differently. The outcomes available are no longer a

fixed pie divided among all parties. An agreement can be found that is better for both parties than what they would have reached through distributive negotiation. This is an integrative negotiation.

However, parties in a negotiation often do not find these beneficial trade-offs because each assumes its interests directly conflict with those of the other party. 'What is good for the other side must be bad for us' is a common and unfortunate perspective that most people have. This is the mind-set we call the mythical 'fixed pie'.[118]

Distributive negotiation involves traditional win–lose thinking. Integrative negotiation calls for a progressive win–win strategy,[119] such as the one in Figure 13.10. In a laboratory study of joint-venture negotiations, teams trained in integrative tactics achieved better outcomes for both sides than untrained teams.[120] However, another study involving 700 employees from 11 cultures discovered that the integrative (or problem-solving) approach to negotiation was not equally effective across cultures.[121] North American negotiators generally are too short-term oriented and poor relationship builders when negotiating in Asia, Latin America and the Middle East.[122]

FIGURE 13.10 AN INTEGRATIVE APPROACH: ADDED-VALUE NEGOTIATION

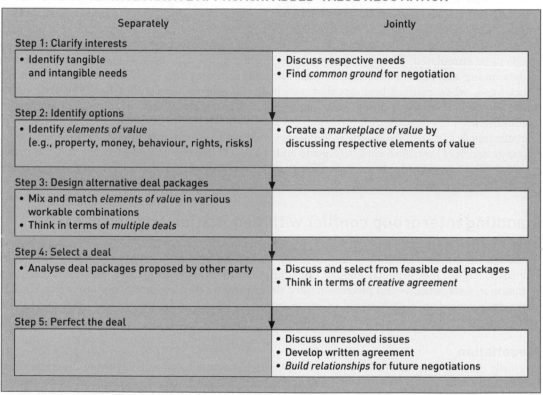

Separately	Jointly
Step 1: Clarify interests	
• Identify tangible and intangible needs	• Discuss respective needs • Find *common ground* for negotiation
Step 2: Identify options	
• Identify *elements of value* (e.g., property, money, behaviour, rights, risks)	• Create a *marketplace of value* by discussing respective elements of value
Step 3: Design alternative deal packages	
• Mix and match *elements of value* in various workable combinations • Think in terms of *multiple deals*	
Step 4: Select a deal	
• Analyse deal packages proposed by other party	• Discuss and select from feasible deal packages • Think in terms of *creative agreement*
Step 5: Perfect the deal	
	• Discuss unresolved issues • Develop written agreement • *Build relationships* for future negotiations

SOURCE: Adapted from K. Albrecht and S. Albrecht, 'Added Value Negotiation', *Training*, April 1993, pp. 26–9.

ETHICAL PITFALLS IN NEGOTIATION

The success of integrative negotiation, such as added-value negotiation, hinges to a large extent on the quality of information exchanged, as researchers have recently documented.[123] Telling lies, hiding key facts and engaging in the other potentially unethical tactics listed in Table 13.7 erode trust and goodwill, both vital in win–win negotiations.[124] An awareness of these dirty tricks can keep good faith bargainers from being unfairly exploited.[125] Unethical negotiating tactics need to be factored into organisational codes of ethics (also see Chapter 18).

RESEARCH FINDINGS AND PRACTICAL IMPLICATIONS

Recent laboratory and field studies have yielded these insights:

TABLE 13.7 QUESTIONABLE/UNETHICAL TACTICS IN NEGOTIATION

Tactic	Description/clarification/range
Lies	Subject matter for lies can include limits, alternatives, the negotiator's intent, authority to bargain, other commitments, acceptability of the opponent's offers, time pressures and available resources
Puffery	Among the items that can be puffed up are the value of one's payoffs to the opponent, the negotiator's own alternatives, the costs of what one is giving up or is prepared to yield, importance of issues and attributes of the products or services
Deception	Acts and statements may include promises or threats, excessive initial demands, careless misstatements of facts or asking for concessions not wanted
Weakening the opponent	The negotiator here may cut off or eliminate some of the opponent's alternatives, blame the opponent for his own actions, use personally abrasive statements to or about the opponent or undermine the opponent's alliances
Strengthening one's own position	This tactic includes building one's own resources, including expertise, finances and alliances. It also includes presentations of persuasive rationales to the opponent or third parties (e.g. the public, the media) or getting mandates for one's position
Non-disclosure	Includes partial disclosure of facts, failure to disclose a hidden fact, failure to correct the opponents' misperceptions or ignorance and concealment of the negotiator's own position or circumstances
Information exploitation	Information provided by the opponent can be used to exploit his weaknesses, close off his alternatives, generate demands against him or weaken his alliances
Change of mind	Includes accepting offers one had claimed one would not accept, changing demands, withdrawing promised offers and making threats one promised would not be made. Also includes the failure to behave as predicted
Distraction	These acts or statements can be as simple as providing excessive information to the opponent, asking many questions, evading questions or burying the issue. Or they can be more complex, such as feigning weakness in one area so that the opponent concentrates on it and ignores another
Maximisation	Includes demanding the opponent make concessions that result in the negotiator's gain and the opponent's equal or greater loss. Also entails converting a win-win situation into win-lose

SOURCE: H. J. Reitz, J. A. Wall, Jr, and M. S. Love, 'Ethics in Negotiation: Oil and Water or Good Lubrication?' Reprinted with the permission of *Business Horizons*, May–June 1998, p. 6. Copyright © 1998 by the Board of Trustees at Indiana University, Kelley School of Business.

- Negotiators with fixed-pie expectations produced poor joint outcomes because they restricted and mismanaged information.[126]
- A meta-analysis of 62 studies found a slight tendency for women to negotiate more co-operatively than men. However, when faced with a 'tit-for-tat' bargaining strategy (equivalent countermoves), women were significantly more competitive than men.[127]
- Personality characteristics can affect negotiating success. Negotiators who scored high on the Big Five personality dimensions of extraversion and agreeableness (see Chapter 2) tended to do poorly with distributive (fixed-pie; win-lose) negotiations.[128]

■ Good and bad moods can have positive and negative effects, respectively, on negotiators' plans and outcomes.[129] So wait until both you and your boss are in a good mood before you ask for a raise (see Chapter 3).

■ Studies of negotiations between Japanese, between Americans, and between Japanese and Americans found less productive joint outcomes across cultures than within cultures.[130] Less understanding of the other party makes cross-cultural negotiation more difficult than negotiations at home.

Third-party intervention

Third-party interventions are necessary when conflicting parties are unwilling and/or unable to engage in conflict resolution or integrative negotiation. Integrative or added-value negotiation is most appropriate for intergroup and interorganisational conflict. The key is to get the conflicting parties to abandon traditional fixed-pie thinking and their win-lose expectations.

Too often, disputes between employees, between employees and their employer and between companies end up in lengthy and costly court battles. A more constructive, less expensive approach called 'alternative dispute resolution' has enjoyed enthusiastic growth in recent years.[131] **Alternative dispute resolution** (ADR), according to a pair of Canadian labour lawyers, 'uses faster, more user-friendly methods of dispute resolution, instead of traditional, adversarial approaches (such as unilateral decision making or litigation)'.[132] The following ADR techniques represent a progression of steps third parties can take to resolve organisational conflicts.[133] They are ranked from easiest and least expensive to most difficult and costly. A growing number of organisations have formal ADR policies involving an established sequence of various combinations of these techniques:

■ *Facilitation.* A third party, usually a manager, informally urges disputing parties to deal directly with each other in a positive and constructive way.

■ *Conciliation.* A neutral third party informally acts as a communication conduit between disputing parties. This is appropriate when conflicting parties refuse to meet face-to-face. The immediate goal is to establish direct communication, with the broader aim of finding a common ground and constructive solution.

■ *Peer review.* A panel of trustworthy co-workers, selected for their ability to remain objective, hears both sides of the dispute in an informal and confidential meeting. Any decision by the review panel may or may not be binding, depending on the company's ADR policy. Membership on the peer review panel often is rotated among employees.

■ *Ombuds(wo)man.* Someone who works for the organisation, and is widely respected and trusted by his or her co-workers, hears grievances on a confidential basis and attempts to arrange a solution. This approach, which is more common in European than in North American companies, permits someone to get help from above without relying on the formal hierarchy chain.

■ *Mediation.* 'The mediator – a trained, third-party neutral – actively guides the disputing parties in exploring innovative solutions to the conflict. Although some companies have in-house mediators who have received ADR training, most also use external mediators who have no ties to the company.'[134] Unlike an arbitrator, a mediator does not render a decision. It is up to the disputants to reach a mutually acceptable decision.

■ *Arbitration.* Disputing parties agree ahead of time to accept the decision of a neutral arbitrator in a formal courtlike setting, often complete with evidence and witnesses. Participation in this form of ADR can be voluntary or mandatory, depending upon company policy or union contracts.[135] Statements are confidential. Decisions are based on legal merits

Alternative dispute resolution avoiding costly lawsuits by resolving conflicts informally or through mediation or arbitration

Learning outcomes: Summary of key terms

1 Explain the concept of mutuality of interest

Managers are constantly challenged to foster mutuality of interest (a win-win situation) between individual and organisational interests. Organisation members need to actively co-operate with actual and potential adversaries for the common good.

2 Name at least three 'soft' and two 'hard' influence tactics, and summarise the practical lessons from influence research

Five soft influence tactics are rational persuasion, inspirational appeals, consultation, ingratiation and personal appeals. They are more friendly and less coercive than the four hard influence tactics: exchange, coalition tactics, pressure and legitimating tactics. According to research, soft tactics are better for generating commitment and are perceived as more fair than hard tactics. Ingratiation – making the boss feel good through compliments and being helpful – can slightly improve performance appraisal results and make the boss like you a lot more. Influence through domination is a poor strategy for both men and women. Influence is a complicated and situational process that needs to be undertaken with care, especially across cultures.

3 Identify and briefly describe French and Raven's five bases of power, and discuss the responsible use of power

French and Raven's five bases of power are reward power (rewarding compliance), coercive power (punishing non-compliance), legitimate power (relying on formal authority), expert power (providing needed information) and referent power (relying on personal attraction). Responsible and ethical managers strive to use socialised power (primary concern is for others) rather than personalised power (primary concern for self). Research found higher organisational commitment among employees with bosses who used uplifting power than among those with power-hungry bosses who relied on dominating power.

4 Explain why delegation is the highest form of empowerment, and discuss the link with delegation, trust and personal initiative

Delegation gives employees more than a participatory role in decision making. It allows them to make their own work-related decisions. Managers tend to delegate to employees they trust. Employees can get managers to trust them by demonstrating personal initiative (going beyond formal job requirements and being self-starters).

5 Define organisational politics, and how it is triggered

Organisational politics is defined as intentional acts of influence to enhance or protect the self-interests of individuals or groups. Uncertainty triggers most politicking in organisations. Political action occurs at individual, coalition and network levels. Coalitions are informal, temporary and single-issue alliances.

6 Distinguish between favourable and unfavourable impression management tactics

Favourable upward impression management can be job-focused (manipulating information about one's job performance), supervisor-focused (praising or doing favours for the boss) or self-focused (being polite and nice). Unfavourable upward-impression management tactics include decreasing performance, not working to potential, withdrawing, displaying a bad attitude, and broadcasting one's limitations.

7 Explain how to manage organisational politics

Since organisational politics cannot be eliminated, managers need to learn to deal with it. Uncertainty can be reduced by evaluating performance and linking rewards to performance. Measurable objectives are key. Participative management also helps.

8 Define the term 'conflict', distinguish between functional and dysfunctional conflict and identify three desired conflict outcomes

Conflict is a process in which one party perceives that its interests are being opposed or negatively affected by another party. It is inevitable and not necessarily destructive. Too little conflict, as evidenced by apathy or lack of creativity, can be as great a problem as too much conflict. Functional conflict enhances organisational interests while dysfunctional conflict is counter-productive. Three desired conflict outcomes are agreement, stronger relationships and learning.

9 Explain how professionals can stimulate functional conflict, and identify the five conflict-handling styles

There are many antecedents of conflict – including incompatible personalities, competition for limited resources and unrealised expectations – that need to be monitored. Functional conflict can be stimulated by permitting antecedents of conflict to persist and/or programming conflict during decision making with devil's advocates or the dialectic method. The five conflict-handling styles are integrating (problem solving), obliging (smoothing), dominating (forcing), avoiding and compromising. There is no single best style.

10 Explain the difference between distributive and integrative negotiation, and discuss the concept of added-value negotiation

Distributive negotiation involves fixed-pie and win-lose thinking. Integrative negotiation is a win-win approach to better results for both parties. The five steps in added value negotiation are as follows: Step 1, clarify interests; Step 2, identify options; Step 3, design alternative deal packages; Step 4, select a deal; and Step 5, perfect the deal. Elements of value, multiple deals and creative agreement are central to this approach.

Review questions

1 Of the nine generic influence tactics, which do you use the most when dealing with friends, parents, your boss or your professors? Would other tactics be more effective?

2 Will empowerment turn out to be just another management fad? Explain your rationale.

3 What are the main advantages and drawbacks of the trend toward increased delegation?

4 Why do you think organisational politics is triggered primarily by uncertainty?

5 How much impression management do you see in your classroom and/or workplace today? Citing specific examples, are those tactics effective?

6 What examples of functional and dysfunctional conflict have you observed lately?

7 Which of the antecedents of conflict do you think are most common (or most troublesome) in today's workplaces?

8 Which of the five conflict-handling styles is your strongest (your weakest)? How can you improve your ability to handle conflict?

9 Has your concept of negotiation, prior to reading this chapter, been restricted to 'fixed-pie' thinking? Explain.

Personal awareness and growth exercise

What is your primary conflict-handling style?

Objectives

1 To continue building your self-awareness.

2 To assess your approach to conflict.

3 To provide a springboard for handling conflicts more effectively.

Introduction

Professor Afzalur Rahim, developer of the five-style conflict model in Figure 13.9, created an assessment instruction upon which the one in this exercise is based. The original instrument was validated through a factor analysis of responses from 1219 managers from across the United States.[136]

Instructions

For each of the 15 items, indicate how often you rely on that tactic by circling the appropriate number. After you have responded to all 15 items, complete the scoring key below.

Conflict-handling tactics	Rarely				Always
1 I argue my case with my colleagues to show the merits of my position.	1	2	3	4	5
2 I negotiate with my colleagues so that a compromise can be reached.	1	2	3	4	5
3 I try to satisfy the expectations of my colleagues.	1	2	3	4	5
4 I try to investigate an issue with my colleagues to find a solution acceptable to us.	1	2	3	4	5
5 I am firm in pursuing my side of the issue.	1	2	3	4	5
6 I attempt to avoid being 'put on the spot' and try to keep my conflict with my colleagues to myself.	1	2	3	4	5
7 I hold on to my solution to a problem.	1	2	3	4	5
8 I use 'give and take' so that a compromise can be made.	1	2	3	4	5
9 I exchange accurate information with my colleagues to solve a problem together.	1	2	3	4	5
10 I avoid open discussion of my differences with my colleagues.	1	2	3	4	5
11 I accommodate the wishes of my colleagues.	1	2	3	4	5
12 I try to bring all our concerns out in the open so that the issues can be resolved in the best possible way.	1	2	3	4	5
13 I propose a middle ground for breaking deadlocks.	1	2	3	4	5
14 I go along with the suggestions of my colleagues.	1	2	3	4	5
15 I try to keep my disagreements with my colleagues to myself in order to avoid hard feelings.	1	2	3	4	5

Scoring key

Integrating		Obliging		Dominating		Avoiding		Compromising	
Item	score	Item	score	Item	score	Item	score	Item	score
4	___	3	___	1	___	6	___	2	___
9	___	11	___	5	___	10	___	8	___
12	___	14	___	7	___	15	___	13	___
Total = ___		Total = ___		Total = ___		Total = ___		Total = ___	

Your primary conflict-handling style is: _____
(The category with the highest total.)
Your back-up conflict-handling style is: _____
(The category with the second highest total.)

Questions for discussion

1 Are the results what you expected? Explain.
2 Is there a clear gap between your primary and back-up styles or did they score about the same? If they are about the same, does this suggest indecision about handling conflict on your part? Explain.
3 Will your primary conflict-handling style carry over well to many different situations? Explain.
4 What is your personal learning agenda for becoming a more effective conflict handler?

Group exercise

Bangkok blowup (a role-playing exercise)

Objectives

1 To further your knowledge of interpersonal conflict and conflict-handling styles.
2 To give you a first-hand opportunity to try the various styles of handling conflict.

Introduction

This is a role-playing exercise intended to develop your ability to handle conflict. There is no single best way to resolve the conflict in this exercise. One style might work for one person, while another gets the job done for someone else.

Instructions

Read the following short case, 'Can Larry fit in?' Pair up with someone else and decide which of you will play the role of Larry and which will play the role of Melissa, the office manager. Pick up the action from where the case leaves off. Try to be realistic and true to the characters in the case. The manager is primarily responsible for resolving this conflict situation. Whoever plays Larry should resist any unreasonable requests or demands and co-operate with any personally workable solution. *Note:* To conserve time, try to resolve this situation in less than 15 minutes.

Case: 'Can Larry fit in?'[137]
Melissa, Office Manager

You are the manager of an auditing team sent to Bangkok, Thailand, to represent a major international accounting firm headquartered in New York. You and Larry, one of your auditors, were sent to Bangkok to set up an auditing operation. Larry is about seven years older than you and has had five more years with the firm. Your relationship has become very strained since you were recently appointed as the office manager. You feel you were given the promotion because you have established an excellent working relationship with the Thai staff as well as a broad range of international clients. In contrast, Larry has told other members of the staff that your promotion simply reflects the firm's heavy emphasis on affirmative action. He has tried to isolate you from the all-male accounting staff by focusing discussions on sports, local night spots and so forth.

You are sitting in your office reading some complicated new reporting procedures that have just arrived from the home office. Your concentration is suddenly interrupted by a loud knock on your door. Without waiting for an invitation to enter, Larry bursts into your office. He is obviously very upset, and it is not difficult for you to surmise why he is in such a nasty mood.

You recently posted the audit assignments for the coming month, and you scheduled Larry for a job you knew he wouldn't like. Larry is one of your senior auditors, and the company norm is that they get the choice assignments. This particular job will require him to spend two weeks away from Bangkok in a remote town, working with a company whose records are notoriously messy.

Unfortunately, you have had to assign several of these less desirable audits to Larry recently because you are short of personnel. But that's not the only reason. You have received several complaints from the junior staff (all Thais) recently that Larry treats them in a condescending manner. They feel he is always looking for an opportunity to boss them around, as if he were their supervisor instead of an experienced, supportive mentor. As a result, your whole operation works more smoothly when you can send Larry out of town on a solo project for several days. It keeps him from coming into your office and telling you how to do your job, and the morale of the rest of the auditing staff is significantly higher.

Larry slams the door and proceeds to express his anger over this assignment.

Larry, Senior Auditor

You are really annoyed! Melissa is deliberately trying to undermine your status in the office. She knows that the company norm is that senior auditors get the better jobs. You've paid your dues and now expect to be treated with respect. And this isn't the first time this has happened. Since she was made the office manager, she has tried to keep you out of the office as much as possible. It's as if she doesn't want her rival for leadership around the office. When you were asked to go to Bangkok, you assumed that you would be made the office manager because of your seniority in the firm. You are certain that the decision to pick Melissa is yet another indication of reverse discrimination against white males.

In staff meetings, Melissa has talked about the need to be sensitive to the feelings of the office staff as well as the clients in this multicultural setting. 'Who is she to preach about sensitivity! What about my feelings, for heaven's sake?', you wonder. This is nothing more than a straightforward power play. She is probably feeling insecure about being the only female accountant in the office and being promoted over someone with more experience. 'Sending me out of town', you decide, 'is a clear case of "out of sight, out of mind".' Well, it's not going to happen that easily. You are not going to let her treat you unfairly. It's time for a showdown. If she doesn't agree to change this assignment and apologise for the way she's been treating you, you're going to register a formal complaint with her boss in the New York office. You are prepared to submit your resignation if the situation doesn't improve.

Questions for discussion

1 What antecedents of conflict appear to be present in this situation? What can be done about them?
2 Having heard how others handled this conflict, did one particular style seem to work better than the others?

Internet exercise

Influence and political tactics are an inescapable part of modern organisation life, as discussed in his chapter. The purpose of this exercise is to broaden your understanding of organisational influence and politics and help you to deal with them effectively. Go to our website at www.mcgraw-hill.co.uk/textbooks/buelens for further instructions.

Notes

1 M. Curphey, 'Negotiating Your Career Path Requires a Little Give and Take', the *Observer*, 18 May 2003.
2 H. Malcolm and C. Sokoloff, 'Values, Human Relations, and Organization Development', in *The Emerging Practice of Organizational Development*, eds W. Sikes, A. Drexler and J. Gant (San Diego, CA: University Associates, 1989), p. 64.
3 See D. Kipnis, S. M. Schmidt and I. Wilkinson, 'Intraorganizational Influence Tactics: Explorations in Getting One's Way', *Journal of Applied Psychology*, August 1980, pp. 440–52; C. A. Schriesheim and T. R. Hinkin, 'Influence Tactics Used by Subordinates: A Theoretical and Empirical Analysis and Refinement of the Kipnis, Schmidt and Wilkinson Subscales', *Journal of Applied Psychology*, June 1990, pp. 246–57; and G. Yukl and C. M. Falbe, 'Influence Tactics and Objectives in Upward, Downward and Lateral Influence Attempts', *Journal of Applied Psychology*, April 1990, pp. 132–40.
4 For related reading, see M. Lippitt, 'How to Influence Leaders', *Training & Development*, March 1999, pp. 18–22; and L. Schlesinger, 'I've Got Three Words for You: Suck It Up', *Fast Company*, April 1999, p. 104.
5 Based on discussion in G. Yukl, H. Kim and C. M. Falbe, 'Antecedents of Influence Outcomes', *Journal of Applied Psychology*, June 1996, pp. 309–17.
6 Data from G. Yukl, H. Kim and C. M. Falbe, 'Antecedents of Influence Outcomes', *Journal of Applied Psychology*, June 1996, pp. 309–17.
7 Data from G. Yukl and J. B. Tracey, 'Consequences of Influence Tactics Used with Subordinates, Peers, and the Boss', *Journal of Applied Psychology*, August 1992, pp. 525–35. Also see C. M. Falbe and G. Yukl, 'Consequences for Managers of Using Single Influence Tactics and Combinations of Tactics', *Academy of Management Journal*, August 1992, pp. 638–52; C. A. Higgins, T. A. Judge, and G. R. Ferris, 'Influence Tactics and Work Outcomes: A Meta-Analysis', *Journal of Organizational Behavior*, February 2003, pp. 89–106; and D. M. Cable

and T. A. Judge, 'Managers' Upward Influence Tactic Strategies: The Role of Manager Personality and Supervisor Leadership Style', *Journal of Organizational Behavior*, March 2003, pp. 197–214.

8   Data from R. A. Gordon, 'Impact of Ingratiation on Judgments and Evaluations: A Meta-Analytic Investigation', *Journal of Personality and Social Psychology*, July 1996, pp. 54–70. Also see S. J. Wayne, R. C. Liden and R. T. Sparrowe, 'Developing Leader-Member Exchanges', *American Behavioral Scientist*, March 1994, pp. 697–714; A. Oldenburg, 'These Days, Hostile Is Fitting for Takeovers Only', *USA Today*, 22 July 1996, pp. 8B, 10B; and J. H. Dulebohn and G. R. Ferris, 'The Role of Influence Tactics in Perceptions of Performance Evaluations' Fairness', *Academy of Management Journal*, June 1999, pp. 288–303.

9   Data from G. Yukl, H. Kim and C. M. Falbe, 'Antecedents of Influence Outcomes', *Journal of Applied Psychology*, June 1996, pp. 309–17.

10 Data from B. J. Tepper, R. J. Eisenbach, S. L. Kirby and P. W. Potter, 'Test of a Justice-Based Model of Subordinates' Resistance to Downward Influence Attempts', *Group & Organization Management*, June 1998, pp. 144–60. Also see A. Somech and A. Drach-Zahavy, 'Relative Power and Influence Strategy: The Effects of Agent/Target Organizational Power on Superiors' Choices of Influence Strategies', *Journal of Organizational Behavior*, March 2002, pp. 167–79.

11 J. E. Driskell, B. Olmstead and E. Salas, 'Task Cues, Dominance Cues, and Influence in Task Groups', *Journal of Applied Psychology*, February 1993, p. 51. No gender bias was found in H. Aguinis and S. K. R. Adams, 'Social-Role versus Structural Models of Gender and Influence Use in Organizations: A Strong Inference Approach', *Group & Organization Management*, December 1998, pp. 414–46.

12 Adapted from R. B. Cialdini, 'Harnessing the Science of Persuasion', *Harvard Business Review*, October 2001, pp. 72–9. Also see J. A. Conger, 'The Necessary Art of Persuasion', *Harvard Business Review*, May 1998, pp. 84–95; M. Watkins, 'Principles of Persuasion', *Negotiation Journal*, April 2001, pp. 115–37; and G. A. Williams and R. B. Miller, 'Change the Way You Persuade', *Harvard Business Review*, May 2002, pp. 64–73.

13 D. Tjosvold, 'The Dynamics of Positive Power', *Training and Development Journal*, June 1984, p. 72. Also see T. A. Stewart, 'Get with the New Power Game', *Fortune*, 13 January 1997, pp. 58–62; and 'The Exercise of Power', *Harvard Business Review*, May 2002, p. 136.

14 M. W. McCall, Jr, *Power, Influence, and Authority: The Hazards Carrying a Sword*, Technical Report No. 10 (Greensboro, NC: Center for Creative Leadership, 1978), p. 5. For an excellent update on power, see E. P. Hollander and L. R. Offermann, 'Power and Leadership in Organizations', *American Psychologist*, February 1990, pp. 179–89. Also see R. Greene, *The 48 Laws of Power* (New York: Viking, 1998); and N. B. Kurland and L. H. Pelled, 'Passing the Word: Toward a Model of Gossip and Power in the Workplace', *Academy of Management Review*, April 2002, pp. 428–38.

15 Based on and translated from M. Hensen, 'De polonaise van het grote geld', *De Standaard*, 20–21 January 1996.

16 L. H. Chusmir, 'Personalized versus Socialized Power Needs among Working Women and Men', *Human Relations*, February 1986, p. 149.

17 See B. Lloyd, 'The Paradox of Power', *The Futurist*, May–June 1996, p. 60; and R. Lubit, 'The Long-Term Organizational Impact of Destructively Narcissistic Managers', *Academy of Management Executive*, April 2001, pp. 127–38.

18 D. W. Cantor and T. Bernay, *Women in Power: The Secrets of Leadership* (Boston, MA: Houghton Mifflin, 1992), p. 40; and K. Morris, 'Trouble in Toyland', *Business Week*, 15 March 1999, p. 40.

19 See J. R. P. French and B. Raven, 'The Bases of Social Power', in *Studies in Social Power*, ed. D. Cartwright (Ann Arbor, MI: University of Michigan Press, 1959), pp. 150–67. Also see P. Podsakoff and C. Schreisheim, 'Field Studies of French and Raven's Bases of Power: Critique, Analysis, and Suggestions for Future Research', *Psychological Bulletin*, May 1985, pp. 387–411; B. H. Raven, 'A Power/Interaction Model of Interpersonal Influence: French and Raven Thirty Years Later', *Journal of Social Behavior and Personality*, no. 2, 1992, pp. 217–44; B. J. Raven, 'The Bases of Power: Origins and Recent Developments', *Journal of Social Issues*, no. 4, 1993, pp. 227–51; P. P. Carson and K. D. Carson, 'Social Power Bases: A Meta-Analytic Examination of Interrelationships and Outcomes', *Journal of Applied Social Psychology*, July 1993, pp. 1150–69; J. M. Whitmeyer, 'Interest-Network Structures in Exchange Networks', *Sociological Perspectives*, Spring 1999, pp. 23–47; and C. M. Fiol, E. J. O'Connor and H. Anguinis, 'All for One and One for All? The Development and Transfer of Power across Organizational Levels', *Academy of Management Review*, April 2001, pp. 224–42.

20 Data from J. R. Larson, Jr, C. Christensen, A. S. Abbott and T. M. Franz, 'Diagnosing Groups: Charting the Flow of Information in Medical Decision-Making Teams', *Journal of Personality and Social Psychology*, August 1996, pp. 315–30.

21 See D. A. Morand, 'Forms of Address and Status Leveling in Organizations', *Business Horizons*, November–December 1995, pp. 34–9; and H. Lancaster, 'A Father's Character, Not His Success, Shapes Kids' Careers', the *Wall Street Journal*, 27 February 1996, p. B1.

22 D. Shipley and C. Egan, 'Power, Conflict and Co-operation in Brewer-Tenant Distribution Channels', *International Journal of Service Industry Management*, no. 4, 1992, pp. 44–62.

23 Details may be found in L. H. Chusmir, 'Personalized versus Socialized Power Needs among Working Women and Men', *Human Relations*, February 1986, pp. 149–59. For a review of research on individual differences in the need for power, see R. J. House, 'Power and Personality in Complex Organizations', in *Research in Organizational Behavior*, eds B. M. Staw and L. L. Cummings (Greenwich, CT: JAI Press, 1988), pp. 305–57.

24 B. Filipczak, 'Is It Getting Chilly in Here?', *Training*, February 1994, p. 27.

25 M. Hultin and R. Szulkin, 'Wages and Unequal Access to Organizational Power: An Empirical Test of Gender Discrimination', *Administrative Science Quarterly*, September 1999, pp. 453–72.

26 P. M. Podsakoff and C. A. Schriesheim, 'Field Studies of French and Raven's Bases of Power: Critique, Reanalysis, and Suggestions for Future Research', *Psychological Bulletin*, May 1985, p. 388. Also see D. Tjosvold, 'Power and Social Context in Superior-Subordinate Interaction', *Organizational Behavior and Human Decision Processes*, June 1985, pp. 281–93; M. A. Rahim and G. F. Buntzman, 'Supervisory Power Bases, Styles of Handling Conflict with Subordinates, and Subordinate Compliance and Satisfaction', *Journal of Psychology*, March 1989, pp. 195–210; and C. A. Schriesheim, T. R. Hinkin and P. M. Podsakoff, 'Can Ipsative and Single-Item Measures Produce Erroneous Results in Field Studies of French and Raven's (1950) Five Bases of Power? An Empirical Investigation', *Journal of Applied Psychology*, February 1991, pp. 106–14.

27 See T. R. Hinkin and C. A. Schriesheim, 'Relationships between Subordinate Perceptions and Supervisor Influence Tactics and Attributed Bases of Supervisory Power', *Human Relations*, March 1990, pp. 221–37. Also see D. J. Brass and M. E. Burkhardt, 'Potential Power and Power Use: An Investigation of Structure and Behavior', *Academy of Management Journal*, June 1993, pp. 441–70; and K. W. Mossholder, N. Bennett, E. R. Kemery and M. A. Wesolowski, 'Relationships between Bases of Power and Work Reactions: The Mediational Role of Procedural Justice', *Journal of Management*, no. 4, 1998, pp. 533–52.

28 See H. E. Baker III, '"Wax On – Wax Off": French and Raven at the Movies', *Journal of Management Education*, November 1993, pp. 517–19.

29 Based on P. A. Wilson, 'The Effects of Politics and Power on the Organizational Commitment of Federal Executives', *Journal of Management*, Spring 1995, pp. 101–18. For related research, see J. B. Arthur, 'Effects of Human Resource Systems on Manufacturing Performance and Turnover', *Academy of Management Journal*, June 1994, pp. 670–87.

30 For related research, see L. G. Pelletier and R. J. Vallerand, 'Supervisors' Beliefs and Subordinates' Intrinsic Motivation: A Behavioral Confirmation Analysis', *Journal of Personality and Social Psychology*, August 1996, pp. 331–40.

31 As quoted in W. A. Randolph and M. Sashkin, 'Can Organizational Empowerment Work in Multinational Settings?', *Academy of Management Executive*, February 2002, p. 104. Also see R. C. Liden and S. Arad, 'A Power Perspective of Empowerment and Work Groups: Implications for Human Resources Management Research', in *Research in Personnel and Human Resources Management, vol. 14*, ed. G. R. Ferris (Greenwich, CT: JAI Press, 1996), pp. 205–51.

32 Adapted and translated from M. Knapen, 'Het nieuwe delegeren', *Management Team*, 11 September 1998.

33 S. Caudron, 'The Only Way to Stay Ahead', *Industry Week*, 17 August 1998.

34 L. Shaper Walters, 'A Leader Redefines Management', *The Christian Science Monitor*, 22 September 1992, p. 14.

35 For related discussion, see M. M. Broadwell, 'Why Command & Control Won't Go Away', *Training*, September 1995, pp. 62–8; R. E. Quinn and G. M. Spreitzer, 'The Road to Empowerment: Seven Questions Every Leader Should Consider', *Organizational Dynamics*, Autumn 1997, pp. 37–49; and I. Cunningham and L. Honold, 'Everyone Can Be a Coach', *HR Magazine*, June 1998, pp. 63–6.

36 See R. C. Ford and M. D. Fottler, 'Empowerment: A Matter of Degree', *Academy of Management Executive*, August 1995, pp. 21–31.

37 S. Gracie, 'Delegate, Don't Abdicate', *Management Today*, March 1999. For more on delegation, see L. Bossidy, 'The Job No CEO Should Delegate', *Harvard Business Review*, March 2001, pp. 46–9; and S. Gazda, 'The Art of Delegating', *HR Magazine*, January 2002, pp. 75–8.

38 R. Kreitner, *Management, eighth edition* (Boston, MA: Houghton Mifflin, 2001), p. 315. Also see K. Dover, 'Avoiding Empowerment Traps', *Management Review*, January 1999, pp. 51–5; and C. A. Walker, 'Saving Your Rookie Managers from Themselves', *Harvard Business Review*, April 2002, pp. 97–102.

39 Drawn from G. Yukl and P. P. Fu, 'Determinants of Delegation and Consultation by Managers', *Journal of Organizational Behavior*, March 1999, pp. 219–32. Also see C. A. Schriesheim, L. L. Neider and T. A. Scandura, 'Delegation and Leader-Member Exchange: Main Effects, Moderators, and Measurement Issues', *Academy of Management Journal*, June 1998, pp. 298–318.

40 See G. M. Spreitzer and A. K. Mishra, 'Giving Up without Losing Control: Trust and Its Substitutes' Effects on Managers' Involving Employees in Decision Making', *Group & Organization Management*, June 1999, pp. 155–87.

41 M. Frese, W. Kring, A. Soose and J. Zempel, 'Personal Initiative at Work: Differences between East and West Germany', *Academy of Management Journal*, February 1996, p. 38. For comprehensive updates, see D. J. Campbell, 'The Proactive Employee: Managing Workplace Initiative', *Academy of Management Executive*, August 2000, pp. 52–66; and M. Frese and D. Fay, 'Personal Initiative: An Active Performance Concept for Work in the 21st Century', in *Research in Organizational Behavior, vol. 23*, eds B. M. Staw and R. I. Sutton (New York: JAI Press, 2001), pp. 133–87.

42 See J. A. Belasco and R. C. Stayer, 'Why Empowerment Doesn't Empower: The Bankruptcy of Current Paradigms', *Business Horizons*, March–April 1994, pp. 29–41; and W. A. Randolph, 'Re-Thinking Empowerment: Why Is It So Hard to Achieve?', *Organizational Dynamics*, Fall 2000, pp. 94–107.

43 For complete details, see C. R. Leana, 'Power Relinquishment versus Power Sharing: Theoretical Clarification and Empirical Comparison of Delegation and Participation', *Journal of Applied Psychology*, May 1987, pp. 228–33.

44 M. D. Fulford and C. A. Enz, 'The Impact of Empowerment on Service Employees', *Journal of Managerial Issues*, Summer 1995, p. 172.

45 M. Jansen, 'Delegation Is the Key to Effective Growth', *The Times*, 26 October 1999.

46 Data from A. J. H. Thorlakson and R. P. Murray, 'An Empirical Study of Empowerment in the Workplace', *Group & Organization Management*, March 1996, pp. 67–83.

47 Data from C. S. Koberg, R. W. Boss, J. C. Senjem and E. A. Goodman, 'Antecedents and Outcomes of Empowerment: Empirical Evidence from the Health Care Industry', *Group & Organization Management*, March 1999, pp. 71–91. Also see K. Aquino, S. L. Grover, M. Bradfield and D. G. Allen, 'The Effects of Negative Affectivity, Hierarchical Status, and Self-Determination on Workplace Victimization', *Academy of Management Journal*, June 1999, pp. 260–72; and J. P. Guthrie, 'High-Involvement Work Practices, Turnover, and Productivity: Evidence from New Zealand', *Academy of Management Journal*, February 2001, pp. 180–90.

48 W. A. Randolph, 'Navigating the Journey to Empowerment', *Organizational Dynamics*, Spring 1995, p. 31.

49 C. Hirst, 'Boardroom Battles Slow E-Business Advance', the *Independent*, 3 December 2000.

50 Adapted from S. Caulkin, 'Political? Be Proud of It', the *Observer*, 3 September 2000; and D. Dearlove, 'Power Games Play Off', *The Times*, 11 November 1999.

51 R. W. Allen, D. L. Madison, L. W. Porter, P. A. Renwick and B. T. Mayes, 'Organizational Politics: Tactics and Characteristics of Its Actors', *California Management Review*, Fall 1979, p. 77. A comprehensive update can be found in K. M. Kacmar and R. A. Baron, 'Organizational Politics: The State of the Field, Links to Related Processes, and an Agenda for Future Research', in *Research in Personnel and Human Resources Management*, vol. 17, ed. G. R. Ferris (Stamford, CT: JAI Press, 1999), pp. 1–39. Also see K. M. Kacmar and G. R. Ferris, 'Politics at Work: Sharpening the Focus of Political Behavior in Organizations', *Business Horizons*, July–August 1993, pp. 70–74; and M. C. Andrews and K. M. Kacmar, 'Discriminating among Organizational Politics, Justice, and Support', *Journal of Organizational Behavior*, June 2001, pp. 347–66.

52 See P. M. Fandt and G. R. Ferris, 'The Management of Information and Impressions: When Employees Behave Opportunistically', *Organizational Behavior and Human Decision Processes*, February 1990, pp. 140–58.

53 First four based on discussion in D. R. Beeman and T. W. Sharkey, 'The Use and Abuse of Corporate Politics', *Business Horizons*, March–April 1987, pp. 26–30.

54 A. Raia, 'Power, Politics, and the Human Resource Professional', *Human Resource Planning*, no. 4, 1985, p. 203.

55 A. J. DuBrin, 'Career Maturity, Organizational Rank, and Political Behavioral Tendencies: A Correlational Analysis of Organizational Politics and Career Experience', *Psychological Reports*, October 1988, p. 535.

56 This three-level distinction comes from A. T. Cobb, 'Political Diagnosis: Applications in Organizational Development', *Academy of Management Review*, July 1986, pp. 482–96.

57 An excellent historical and theoretical perspective of coalitions can be found in W. B. Stevenson, J. L. Pearce and L. W. Porter, 'The Concept of "Coalition" in Organization Theory and Research', *Academy of Management Review*, April 1985, pp. 256–68.

58 See K. G. Provan and J. G. Sebastian, 'Networks within Networks: Service Link Overlap, Organizational Cliques, and Network Effectiveness', *Academy of Management Journal*, August 1998, pp. 453–63.

59 R. W. Allen, D. L. Madison, L. W. Porter, P. A. Renwick and B. T. Mayes, 'Organizational Politics: Tactics and Characteristics of Its Actors', *California Management Review*, Fall 1979, p. 77.

60 See W. L. Gardner III, 'Lessons in Organizational Dramaturgy: The Art of Impression Management', *Organizational Dynamics*, Summer 1992, pp. 33–46.

61 For more on political behaviour, see A. Nierenberg, 'Masterful Networking', *Training & Development*, February 1999, pp. 51–3; J. Barbian, 'It's Who You Know', *Training*, December 2001, p. 22; and S. Bing, 'Throwing the Elephant: Zen and the Art of Managing Up', *Fortune*, 18 March 2002, pp. 115–16.

62 A. Rao, S. M. Schmidt and L. H. Murray, 'Upward Impression Management: Goals, Influence Strategies, and Consequences', *Human Relations*, February 1995, p. 147.

63 See P. M. Fandt and G. R. Ferris, 'The Management of Information and Impressions: When Employees Behave Opportunistically', *Organizational Behavior and Human Decision Processes*, February 1990, pp. 140–58; W. L. Gardner and B. J. Avolio, 'The Charismatic Relationship: A Dramaturgical Perspective', *Academy of Management Review*, January 1998, pp. 32–58; L. Wah, 'Managing – Manipulating? – Your Reputation', *Management Review*, October 1998, pp. 46–50; M. C. Bolino, 'Citizenship and Impression Management: Good Soldiers or Good Actors?', *Academy of Management Review*, January 1999, pp. 82–98; and W. H. Turnley and M. C. Bolino, 'Achieving Desired Images While Avoiding Undesired Images: Exploring the Role of Self-Monitoring in Impression Management', *Journal of Applied Psychology*, April 2001, pp. 351–60.

64 For related research, see M. G. Pratt and A. Rafaeli, 'Organizational Dress as a Symbol of Multilayered Social Identities', *Academy of Management Journal*, August 1997, pp. 862–98.

65 A. Arkin, 'Tailoring Clothes to Suit the Image', *People Management*, 24 August 1995.

66 J. Solomon, 'Why Worry about Pleat Pull and Sloppy Socks?', *Newsweek*, 30 September 1996.

67 See S. J. Wayne and G. R. Ferris, 'Influence Tactics, Affect, and Exchange Quality in Supervisor-Subordinate Interactions: A Laboratory Experiment and Field Study', *Journal of Applied Psychology*, October 1990, pp. 487–99. For another version, see Table 1 (p. 246) in S. J. Wayne and R. C. Liden, 'Effects of Impression Management on Performance Ratings: A Longitudinal Study', *Academy of Management Journal*, February 1995, pp. 232–60.

68 See R. Vonk, 'The Slime Effect: Suspicion and Dislike of Likeable Behavior toward Superiors', *Journal of*

Personality and Social Psychology, April 1998, pp. 849–64; and M. Wells, 'How to Schmooze Like the Best of Them', *USA Today*, 18 May 1999, p. 14E.

69 See P. Rosenfeld, R. A. Giacalone and C. A. Riordan, 'Impression Management Theory and Diversity: Lessons for Organizational Behavior', *American Behavioral Scientist*, March 1994, pp. 601–04; R. A. Giacalone and J. W. Beard, 'Impression Management, Diversity, and International Management', *American Behavioral Scientist*, March 1994, pp. 621–36; and A. Montagliani and R. A. Giacalone, 'Impression Management and Cross-Cultural Adaptation', the *Journal of Social Psychology*, October 1998, pp. 598–608.

70 M. E. Mendenhall and C. Wiley, 'Strangers in a Strange Land: The Relationship between Expatriate Adjustment and Impression Management', *American Behavioral Scientist*, March 1994, pp. 605–20.

71 T. E. Becker and S. L. Martin, 'Trying to Look Bad at Work: Methods and Motives for Managing Poor Impressions in Organizations', *Academy of Management Journal*, February 1995, p. 191.

72 T. E. Becker and S. L. Martin, 'Trying to Look Bad at Work: Methods and Motives for Managing Poor Impressions in Organizations', *Academy of Management Journal*, February 1995, p. 181. Also see M. K. Duffy, D. C. Ganster and M. Pagon, 'Social Undermining in the Workplace', *Academy of Management Journal*, April 2002, pp. 331–51.

73 Adapted from T. E. Becker and S. L. Martin, 'Trying to Look Bad at Work: Methods and Motives for Managing Poor Impressions in Organizations', *Academy of Management Journal*, February 1995, pp. 180–81.

74 Based on discussion in T. E. Becker and S. L. Martin, 'Trying to Look Bad at Work: Methods and Motives for Managing Poor Impressions in Organizations', *Academy of Management Journal*, February 1995, pp. 192–3.

75 Data from G. R. Ferris, D. D. Frink, D. P. S. Bhawuk, J. Zhou and D. C. Gilmore, 'Reactions of Diverse Groups to Politics in the Workplace', *Journal of Management*, no. 1, 1996, pp. 23–44. For other findings from the same database, see G. R. Ferris, D. D. Frink, M. C. Galang, J. Zhou, K. M. Kacmar and J. L. Howard, 'Perceptions of Organizational Politics: Prediction, Stress-Related Implications, and Outcomes', *Human Relations*, February 1996, pp. 233–66.

76 A. Drory and D. Beaty, 'Gender Differences in the Perception of Organizational Influence Tactics', *Journal of Organizational Behavior*, May 1991, pp. 256–7. Also see L. A. Rudman, 'Self-Promotion as a Risk Factor for Women: The Costs and Benefits of Counterstereotypical Impression Management', *Journal of Personality and Social Psychology*, March 1998, pp. 629–45; and J. Tata, 'The Influence of Gender on the Use and Effectiveness of Managerial Accounts', *Group & Organization Management*, September 1998, pp. 267–88.

77 See S. J. Wayne and R. C. Liden, 'Effects of Impression Management on Performance Ratings: A Longitudinal Study', *Academy of Management Journal*, February 1995, pp. 232–60. Also see M. L. Randall, R. Cropanzano, C. A. Bormann and A. Birjulin, 'Organizational Politics and Organizational Support as Predictors of Work Attitudes, Job Performance, and Organizational Citizenship Behavior', *Journal of Organizational Behavior*, March 1999, pp. 159–74.

78 A. Rao, S. M. Schmidt and L. H. Murray, 'Upward Impression Management: Goals, Influence Strategies, and Consequences', *Human Relations*, February 1995, p. 165.

79 Also see A. Tziner, G. P. Latham, B. S. Price and R. Haccoun, 'Development and Validation of a Questionnaire for Measuring Perceived Political Considerations in Performance Appraisal', *Journal of Organizational Behavior*, March 1996, pp. 179–90.

80 A. Zaleznik, 'Real Work', *Harvard Business Review*, January–February 1989, p. 60.

81 C. M. Koen, Jr, and S. M. Crow, 'Human Relations and Political Skills', *HR Focus*, December 1995, p. 11.

82 See L. A. Witt, 'Enhancing Organizational Goal Congruence: A Solution to Organizational Politics', *Journal of Applied Psychology*, August 1998, pp. 666–74.

83 D. Tjosvold, *Learning to Manage Conflict: Getting People to Work Together Productively* (New York: Lexington Books, 1993), p. xi.

84 D. Tjosvold, *Learning to Manage Conflict: Getting People to Work Together Productively* (New York: Lexington Books, 1993), pp. xi–xii.

85 J. A. Wall, Jr, and R. Robert Callister, 'Conflict and Its Management', *Journal of Management*, no. 3, 1995, p. 517.

86 J. A. Wall, Jr, and R. Robert Callister, 'Conflict and Its Management', *Journal of Management*, no. 3, 1995, p. 544.

87 See A. M. O'Leary-Kelly, R. W. Griffin and D. J. Glew, 'Organization-Motivated Aggression: A Research Framework', *Academy of Management Review*, January 1996, pp. 225–53; D. Bencivenga, 'Dealing with the Dark Side', *HR Magazine*, January 1999, pp. 50–58; K. Dobbs, 'The Lucrative Menace of Workplace Violence', *Training*, March 2000, pp. 54–62; S. C. Douglas and M. J. Martinko, 'Exploring the Role of Individual Differences in the Prediction of Workplace Aggression', *Journal of Applied Psychology*, August 2001, pp. 547–59; and K. Tyler, 'Afraid to Fly, and It Shows', *HR Magazine*, September 2001, pp. 64–74.

88 See S. Alper, D. Tjosvold and K. S. Law, 'Interdependence and Controversy in Group Decision Making: Antecedents to Effective Self-Managing Teams', *Organizational Behavior and Human Decision Processes*, April 1998, pp. 33–52.

89 S. P. Robbins, '"Conflict Management" and "Conflict Resolution" Are Not Synonymous Terms', *California Management Review*, Winter 1978, p. 70.

90 Co-operative conflict is discussed in D. Tjosvold, *Learning to Manage Conflict: Getting People to Work Together*

Productively (New York: Lexington Books, 1993). Also see A. C. Amason, 'Distinguishing the Effects of Functional and Dysfunctional Conflict on Strategic Decision Making: Resolving a Paradox for Top Management Teams', *Academy of Management Journal*, February 1996, pp. 123–48.

91 Adapted from J. Templeman, B. Vlasic and C. Power, 'The New Mercedes', *Business Week*, 26 August 1996.

92 Adapted in part from discussion in A. C. Filley, *Interpersonal Conflict Resolution* (Glenview, IL: Scott, Foresman, 1975), pp. 9–12; and B. Fortado, 'The Accumulation of Grievance Conflict', *Journal of Management Inquiry*, December 1992, pp. 288–303. Also see D. Tjosvold and M. Poon, 'Dealing with Scarce Resources: Open-Minded Interaction for Resolving Budget Conflicts', *Group & Organization Management*, September 1998, pp. 237–55.

93 Adapted from discussion in D. Tjosvold, *Learning to Manage Conflict: Getting People to Work Together Productively* (New York: Lexington Books, 1993), pp. 12–13.

94 P. Schinzler, 'Offices that Spark Creativity', *Business Week*, 28 August 2000.

95 Based on discussion in G. Labianca, D. J. Brass and B. Gray, 'Social Networks and Perceptions of Intergroup Conflict: The Role of Negative Relationships and Third Parties', *Academy of Management Journal*, February 1998, pp. 55–67. Also see C. Gomez, B. L. Kirkman and D. L. Shapiro, 'The Impact of Collectivism and In-Group/Out-Group Membership on the Evaluation Generosity of Team Members', *Academy of Management Journal*, December 2000, pp. 1097–106; J. M. Twenge, R. F. Baumeister, D. M. Tice and T. S. Stucke, 'If You Can't Join Them, Beat Them: Effects of Social Exclusion of Aggressive Behavior', *Journal of Personality and Social Psychology*, December 2001, pp. 1058–69; T. Kessler and A. Mummendey, 'Is There Any Scapegoat Around? Determinants of Intergroup Conflicts at Different Categorization Levels', *Journal of Personality and Social Psychology*, December 2001, pp. 1090–102; and T. Kessler and A. Mummendey, 'Sequential or Parallel? A Longitudinal Field Study Concerning Determinants of Identity-Management Strategies', *Journal of Personality and Social Psychology*, January 2002, pp. 75–88.

96 G. Labianca, D. J. Brass and B. Gray, 'Social Networks and Perceptions of Intergroup Conflict: The Role of Negative Relationships and Third Parties', *Academy of Management Journal*, February 1998, p. 63.

97 For example, see S. C. Wright, A. Aron, T. McLaughlin-Volpe and S. A. Ropp, 'The Extended Contact Effect: Knowledge of Cross-Group Friendships and Prejudice', *Journal of Personality and Social Psychology*, July 1997, pp. 73–90.

98 See C. D. Batson, M. P. Polycarpou, E. Harmon-Jones, H. J. Imhoff, E. C. Mitchener, L. L. Bednar, T. R. Klein and L. Highberger, 'Empathy and Attitudes: Can Feeling for a Member of a Stigmatized Group Improve Feelings Toward the Group?', *Journal of Personality and Social Psychology*, January 1997, pp. 105–18. Evidence that it pays to ignore interpersonal conflicts in teams is reported in C. K. W. De Dreu and A. E. M. Vianen, 'Managing Relationship Conflict and the Effectiveness of Organizational Teams', *Journal of Organizational Behavior*, May 2001, pp. 309–28.

99 R. A. Cosier and C. R. Schwenk, 'Agreement and Thinking Alike: Ingredients for Poor Decisions', *Academy of Management Executive*, February 1990, p. 71. Also see J. P. Kotter, 'Kill Complacency', *Fortune*, 5 August 1996, pp. 168–70; and S. Caudron, 'Keeping Team Conflict Alive', *Training & Development*, September 1998, pp. 48–52.

100 For example, see 'Facilitators as Devil's Advocates', *Training*, September 1993, p. 10. Also see K. L. Woodward, 'Sainthood for a Pope?', *Newsweek*, 21 June 1999, p. 65.

101 Good background reading on devil's advocacy can be found in C. R. Schwenk, 'Devil's Advocacy in Managerial Decision Making', *Journal of Management Studies*, April 1984, pp. 153–68.

102 See G. Katzenstein, 'The Debate on Structured Debate: Toward a Unified Theory', *Organizational Behavior and Human Decision Processes*, June 1996, pp. 316–32.

103 See D. M. Schweiger, W. R. Sandberg and P. L. Rechner, 'Experiential Effects of Dialectical Inquiry, Devil's Advocacy, and Consensus Approaches to Strategic Decision Making', *Academy of Management Journal*, December 1989, pp. 745–72.

104 See J. S. Valacich and C. Schwenk, 'Devil's Advocacy and Dialectical Inquiry Effects on Face-to-Face and Computer-Mediated Group Decision Making', *Organizational Behavior and Human Decision Processes*, August 1995, pp. 158–73. Other techniques are presented in K. Cloke and J. Goldsmith, *Resolving Conflicts at Work: A Complete Guide for Everyone on the Job* (San Francisco, CA: Jossey-Bass, 2000), pp. 229–35.

105 A recent statistical validation for this model can be found in M. A. Rahim and N. R. Magner, 'Confirmatory Factor Analysis of the Styles of Handling Interpersonal Conflict: First-Order Factor Model and Its Invariance Across Groups', *Journal of Applied Psychology*, February 1995, pp. 122–32. Also see C. K. W. De Dreu, A. Evers, B. Beersma, E. S. Kluwer and A. Nauta, 'A Theory-Based Measure of Conflict Management Strategies in the Workplace', *Journal of Organizational Behavior*, September 2001, pp. 645–68; and M. A. Rahim, *Managing Conflict in Organizations* (Westport, CT: Greenwood Publishing Group, 2001).

106 M. A. Rahim, 'A Strategy for Managing Conflict in Complex Organizations', *Human Relations*, January 1985, p. 84.

107 See R. E. Jones and B. H. Melcher, 'Personality and the Preference for Modes of Conflict Resolution', *Human Relations*, August 1982, pp. 649–58.

108 See R. A. Baron, 'Reducing Organizational Conflict: An Incompatible Response Approach', *Journal of Applied Psychology*, May 1984, pp. 272–9.

109 See G. A. Youngs, Jr, 'Patterns of Threat and Punishment Reciprocity in a Conflict Setting', *Journal of Personality and Social Psychology*, September 1986, pp. 541–6.

110 For more details, see V. D. Wall, Jr, and L. L. Nolan, 'Small Group Conflict: A Look at Equity, Satisfaction and Styles of Conflict Management', *Small Group Behavior*, May 1987, pp. 188–211. Also see S. M. Farmer and J. Roth, 'Conflict-Handling Behavior in Work Groups: Effects of Group Structure, Decision Processes, and Time', *Small Group Research*, December 1998, pp. 669–713.

111 See M. E. Schnake and D. S. Cochran, 'Effect of Two Goal-Setting Dimensions on Perceived Intraorganizational Conflict', *Group & Organization Studies*, June 1985, pp. 168–83. Also see O. Janssen, E. Van De Vliert, and C. Veenstra, 'How Task and Person Conflict Shape the Role of Positive Interdependence in Management Teams', *Journal of Management*, no. 2, 1999, pp. 117–42.

112 Drawn from L. H. Chusmir and J. Mills, 'Gender Differences in Conflict Resolution Styles of Managers: At Work and at Home', *Sex Roles*, February 1989, pp. 149–63.

113 See K. K. Smith, 'The Movement of Conflict in Organizations: The Joint Dynamics of Splitting and Triangulation', *Administrative Science Quarterly*, March 1989, pp. 1–20. Also see J. B. Olson-Buchanan, F. Drasgow, P. J. Moberg, A. D. Mead, P. A. Keenan and M. A. Donovan, 'Interactive Video Assessment of Conflict Resolution Skills', *Personnel Psychology*, Spring 1998, pp. 1–24; and D. E. Conlon and D. P. Sullivan, 'Examining the Actions of Organizations in Conflict: Evidence from the Delaware Court of Chancery', *Academy of Management Journal*, June 1999, pp. 319–29.

114 Based on C. Tinsley, 'Models of Conflict Resolution in Japanese, German, and American Cultures', *Journal of Applied Psychology*, April 1998, pp. 316–23; and S. M. Adams, 'Settling Cross-Cultural Disagreements Begins with "Where" Not "How"', *Academy of Management Executive*, February 1999, pp. 109–10. Also see K. Ohbuchi, O. Fukushima and J. T. Tedeschi, 'Cultural Values in Conflict Management: Goal Orientation, Goal Attainment, and Tactical Decision', *Journal of Cross-Cultural Psychology*, January 1999, pp. 51–71; and R. Cropanzano, H. Aguinis, M. Schminke and D. L. Denham, 'Disputant Reactions to Managerial Conflict Resolution Tactics: A Comparison among Argentina, The Dominican Republic, Mexico, and the United States', *Group & Organization Management*, June 1999, pp. 124–54.

115 Based on a definition in M. A. Neale and M. H. Bazerman, 'Negotiating Rationally: The Power and Impact of the Negotiator's Frame', *Academy of Management Executive*, August 1992, pp. 42–51.

116 See L. Thompson, E. Peterson and S. E. Brodt, 'Team Negotiation: An Examination of Integrative and Distributive Bargaining', *Journal of Personality and Social Psychology*, January 1996, pp. 66–78.

117 See D. A. Whetten and K. S. Cameron, *Developing Management Skills, third edition* (New York: HarperCollins, 1995), pp. 425–30. Also see C. Joinson, 'Talking Dollars: How to Negotiate Salaries with New Hires', *HR Magazine*, July 1998, pp. 73–8; 'Negotiation Is Not War', *Fortune*, 12 October 1998, pp. 160–64; A. Davis, 'For Dueling Lawyers, the Internet Is Unlikely Referee', the *Wall Street Journal*, 12 May 1999, pp. B1, B4; R. Shell, 'Negotiator, Know Thyself', *Inc.*, May 1999, pp. 106–7; and J. K. Sebenius, 'Six Habits of Merely Effective Negotiators', *Harvard Business Review*, April 2001, pp. 87–95.

118 M. H. Bazerman and M. A. Neale, *Negotiating Rationally* (New York: The Free Press, 1992), p. 16. Also see J. F. Brett, G. B. Northcraft and R. L. Pinkley, 'Stairways to Heaven: An Interlocking Self-Regulation Model of Negotiation', *Academy of Management Review*, July 1999, pp. 435–51.

119 Good win-win negotiation strategies can be found in R. Fisher and W. Ury, *Getting to YES: Negotiating Agreement without Giving In* (Boston, MA: Houghton Mifflin, 1981); R. R. Reck and B. G. Long, *The Win-Win Negotiator: How to Negotiate Favorable Agreements That Last* (New York: Pocket Books, 1987); and R. Fisher and D. Ertel, *Getting Ready to Negotiate: The Getting to YES Workbook* (New York: Penguin Books, 1995). Also see D. M. Kolb and J. Williams, 'Breakthrough Bargaining', *Harvard Business Review*, February 2001, pp. 88–97; and K. A. Wade-Benzoni, A. J. Hoffman, L. L. Thompson, D. A. Moore, J. J. Gillespie and M. H. Bazerman, 'Barriers to Resolution in Ideologically Based Negotiations: The Role of Values and Institutions', *Academy of Management Review*, January 2002, pp. 41–57.

120 See L. R. Weingart, E. B. Hyder and M. J. Prietula, 'Knowledge Matters: The Effect of Tactical Descriptions on Negotiation Behavior and Outcome', *Journal of Personality and Social Psychology*, June 1996, pp. 1205–17.

121 Data from J. L. Graham, A. T. Mintu and W. Rodgers, 'Explorations of Negotiation Behaviors in Ten Foreign Cultures Using a Model Developed in the United States', *Management Science*, January 1994, pp. 72–95.

122 For practical advice, see K. Kelley Reardon and R. E. Spekman, 'Starting Out Right: Negotiation Lessons for Domestic and Cross-Cultural Business Alliances', *Business Horizons*, January–February 1994, pp. 71–9. For more, see C. H. Tinsley, 'How Negotiatiors Get to Yes: Predicting the Constellation of Strategies Used across Cultures to Negotiate Conflict', *Journal of Applied Psychology*, August 2001, pp. 583–93; and P. Ghauri and T. Fang, 'Negotiating with the Chinese: A Socio-Cultural Analysis', *Journal of World Business*, Fall 2001, pp. 303–25.

123 For supporting evidence, see J. K. Butler, Jr, 'Trust Expectations, Information Sharing, Climate of Trust, and Negotiation Effectiveness and Efficiency', *Group & Organization Management*, June 1999, pp. 217–38.

124 See H. J. Reitz, J. A. Wall, Jr, and M. S. Love, 'Ethics in Negotiation: Oil and Water or Good Lubrication?', *Business Horizons*, May–June 1998, pp. 5–14; M. E. Schweitzer and J. L. Kerr, 'Bargaining under the Influence: The Role of Alcohol in Negotiations', *Academy of Management Executive*, May 2000, pp. 47–57; and A. M. Burr, 'Ethics in Negotiation: Does Getting to Yes Require Candor?', *Dispute Resolution Journal*, May–July 2001, pp. 8–15.

125 For related research, see A. E. Tenbrunsel, 'Misrepresentation and Expectations of Misrepresentation in an Ethical Dilemma: The Role of Incentives and Temptation', *Academy of Management Journal*, June 1998, pp. 330–39.

126 Based on R. L. Pinkley, T. L. Griffith and G. B. Northcraft, '"Fixed Pie" a la Mode: Information Availability, Information Processing, and the Negotiation of Suboptimal Agreements', *Organizational Behavior and Human Decision Processes*, April 1995, pp. 101–12.

127 Based on A. E. Walters, A. F. Stuhlmacher and L. L. Meyer, 'Gender and Negotiator Competitiveness: A Meta-Analysis', *Organizational Behavior and Human Decision Processes*, October 1998, pp. 1–29.

128 Based on B. Barry and R. A. Friedman, 'Bargainer Characteristics in Distributive and Integrative Negotiation', *Journal of Personality and Social Psychology*, February 1998, pp. 345–59. Also see C. K. W. De Dreu, E. Giebels and E. Van de Vliert, 'Social Motives and Trust in Integrative Negotiation: The Disruptive Effects of Punitive Capability', *Journal of Applied Psychology*, June 1998, pp. 408–22.

129 For more, see J. P. Forgas, 'On Feeling Good and Getting Your Way: Mood Effects on Negotiator Cognition and Bargaining Strategies', *Journal of Personality and Social Psychology*, March 1998, pp. 565–77.

130 Drawn from J. M. Brett and T. Okumura, 'Inter- and Intracultural Negotiation: US and Japanese Negotiators', *Academy of Management Journal*, October 1998, pp. 495–510. Also see W. L. Adair, T. Okumura and J. M. Brett, 'Negotiation Behavior when Cultures Collide: The United States and Japan', *Journal of Applied Psychology*, June 2001, pp. 371–85. For more negotiation research findings, see G. B. Northcraft, J. N. Preston, M. A. Neale, P. H. Kim and M. C. Thomas-Hunt, 'NonLinear Preference Functions and Negotiated Outcomes', *Organizational Behavior and Human Decision Processes*, January 1998, pp. 54–75; J. T. Polzer, E. A. Mannix and M. A. Neale, 'Interest Alignment and Coalitions in Multiparty Negotiation', *Academy of Management Journal*, February 1998, pp. 42–54; J. M. Brett, D. L. Shapiro and A. L. Lytle, 'Breaking the Bonds of Reciprocity in Negotiations', *Academy of Management Journal*, August 1998, pp. 410–24; W. P. Bottom, 'Negotiator Risk: Sources of Uncertainty and the Impact of Reference Points on Negotiated Agreements', *Organizational Behavior and Human Decision Processes*, November 1998, pp. 89–112; D. A. Moore, T. R. Kurtzberg and L. L. Thompson, 'Long and Short Routes to Success in Electronically Mediated Negotiations: Group Affiliations and Good Vibrations', *Organizational Behavior and Human Decision Processes*, January 1999, pp. 22–43; and A. D. Galinsky and T. Mussweiler, 'First Offers as Anchors: The Role of Perspective-Taking and Negotiator Focus', *Journal of Personality and Social Psychology*, October 2001, pp. 657–69.

131 For background, see D. L. Jacobs, 'First, Fire All the Lawyers', *Inc.*, January 1999, pp. 84–5; and P. S. Nugent, 'Managing Conflict: Third-Party Interventions for Managers', *Academy of Management Executive*, February 2002, pp. 139–54.

132 B. Morrow and L. M. Bernardi, 'Resolving Workplace Disputes', *Canadian Manager*, Spring 1999, p. 17.

133 Adapted from discussion in K. O. Wilburn, 'Employment Disputes: Solving Them Out of Court', *Management Review*, March 1998, pp. 17–21; B. Morrow and L. M. Bernardi, 'Resolving Workplace Disputes', *Canadian Manager*, Spring 1999, pp. 17–19, 27. Also see W. H. Ross and D. E. Conlon, 'Hybrid Forms of Third-Party Dispute Resolution: Theoretical Implications of Combining Mediation and Arbitration', *Academy of Management Review*, April 2000, pp. 416–27.

134 K. O. Wilburn, 'Employment Disputes: Solving Them Out of Court', *Management Review*, March 1998, p. 19. Also see B. P. Sunoo, 'Hot Disputes Cool Down in Online Mediation', *Workforce*, January 2001, pp. 48–52.

135 For background on this contentious issue, see T. J. Heinsz, 'The Revised Uniform Arbitration Act: An Overview', *Dispute Resolution Journal*, May–July 2001, pp. 28–39; C. Hirschman, 'Order in the Hearing!', *HR Magazine*, July 2001, pp. 58–64; and J. D. Wetchler, 'Agreements to Arbitrate', *HR Magazine*, August 2001, pp. 127–34.

136 The complete instrument may be found in M. A. Rahim, 'A Measure of Styles of Handling Interpersonal Conflict', *Academy of Management Journal*, June 1983, pp. 368–76. A validation study of Rahim's instrument may be found in E. Van De Vliert and B. Kabanoff, 'Toward Theory-Based Measures of Conflict Management', *Academy of Management Journal*, March 1990, pp. 199–209.

137 D. A. Whetten and K. S. Cameron, *Developing Management Skills* (Glenview, IL: Scott, Foresman and Company, 1984).

section
4

organisational processes

chapter 14 organisation structure and types

By Annick Willem, Marc Buelens and Geert Devos

Learning outcomes
When you finish studying the material in this chapter, you should be able to:

- describe the four characteristics common to all organisations

- describe the relationship between differentiation and integration in organisations

- describe the organisation's parts and the way tasks can be grouped

- explain the different co-ordination mechanisms an organisation can use

- define and briefly explain the practical significance of centralisation and decentralisation

- discuss the bureaucratic organisation

- discuss Burns and Stalker's findings regarding mechanistic and organic organisations

- describe the seven organisation types of Mintzberg and discuss how they differ in the structural elements

- describe why new organisational forms developed and what the main differences are with the classical forms

- describe horizontal, hourglass and virtual organisations

case study

The British Airways story

Even by the standards of modern management myths the British Airways (BA) transformation was impressive. In the late 1970s and early 1980s BA was performing disastrously against almost every indicator. An old fleet made for uncomfortable journeys and contributed significantly to the airline's record of unpunctuality, its productivity was considerably below that of its main overseas competitors, it was beset by industrial disputes – and it was recording substantial financial losses £140 million (€202 million) or some £200 (€289) a minute in 1981. It seemed that staff discontent was more than matched by customer dissatisfaction, and in 1980 a survey by the International Airline Passengers' Association put BA at the top of a list of airlines to be avoided at all costs. By 1996 this picture was reversed. Not only had BA become the world's most profitable carrier, it was also voted the company that most graduates would like to work for; by the year 2000, another survey declared it the second most admired company in Europe.

Cultural changes

It is certainly true that a great deal of effort and energy went into shaping BA's culture. At the heart of this was the 'putting people first' (PPF) training programme launched by Colin Marshall, the company's new chief executive, in December 1983. Originally intended for staff who had direct contact with customers, it was, in fact, attended by all 40 000 employees by 1986 and it aimed to revolutionise their attitudes. In a direct challenge to the hierarchical and militaristic culture that existed in BA at the time, staff were instructed not to attend in uniform and, once on the course, put into cross-functional and cross-grade groups.

The most impressive aspect of BA's culture change, however, is not so much the sophistication of the PPF training programme itself, nor the commitment of executive time, but the extent to which other employment policies and practices were changed to fit the 'new' culture and the continued emphasis on these practices and programmes throughout the 1980s and 1990s. Three-quarters of the 100 Customer First Teams, formed to propagate the message of PPF, survived into the 1990s. Not only were team briefings and team working introduced but these were developed and refined with TQM, autonomous team working and multi-skilling introduced in many areas. Direct contact with all staff was considered so important that 'down route' briefings were developed to ensure that mobile and isolated staff were not neglected and in March 1996 BA became the first company to make daily TV broadcasts to its staff.

In addition to this, emotions were increasingly emphasised in the work process. The way cabin crew were rostered was changed, creating 'families' of staff to work the same shift patterns. These were intended to provide mutual support, make cabin crew feel happier about their work environments and, as a result, facilitate the production of emotional labour. A new role of 'Passenger group co-ordinator' was introduced and staff appointed entirely on the basis of personal qualities. The importance of emotional processes was also reflected in the new appraisal and reward systems in which work was judged on the way it was performed as well as against harder targets. Managerial bonuses could be as much as 20 per cent of salary and were calculated on a straight 50:50 split between exhibiting desired behaviours and achieving quantitative goals.

Structural reasons for BA's success

Yet the existence of cultural factors does not negate the effects of more material ones, and there were certainly structural reasons for BA's success. Colin Marshall's emphasis on putting people first and caring for one another had been preceded by a rule of fear. BA's first response to its problems had been a massive series of redundancies, the largest in British history at the time, with staff numbers reduced 40 per cent between 1981 and 1983 (albeit with generous severance). Senior staff were not exempt from this process, with 161 being 'removed' overnight on one memorable occasion in 1983.

So, to re-cast our fairy-tale in rather more prosaic terms, BA, while clearly putting a great deal of effort into encouraging (or 'designing') certain staff behaviours, did not base its employment policies and practices around the new culture in the way that many accounts suggest. Their array of 'soft' human resource management techniques was certainly impressive but not everyone benefited from them, and those employed in partner, associated, merged or taken-over firms often experienced very different terms and conditions from the core BA staff.

The 1997 dispute: change or continuity?

By the end of the 1990s many of the structural factors that had provided the basis for the company's success were under threat. The newly emerged low-cost carriers such as Easyjet and Ryanair were undercutting BA's prices and, elsewhere, alliances between rivals Lufthansa and United Airlines ensured that cross-national traffic would be less likely to transfer to BA. BA sought its own alliance with American Airlines, which proposed £1 billion of cost savings from within the organisation. Much of this was to come from staff savings including 5000 voluntary redundancies with staff to be replaced by newly hired employees on lower pay. This policy of reducing labour costs was also extended to 'core' BA staff. In early 1997 BA attempted to change the structure of payments to cabin crew. It was proposed that the existing employees would be 'bought out' of their series of allowances (petrol, overnight stay, etc.) by receiving a higher basic wage. BA offered a three-year guarantee that no crew member would earn less under the new system but nothing beyond that.

The subsequent strike ballot had an 80 per cent turnout with 73 per cent of employees voting in favour of strike action. The strike was costly. Airline seats are a particularly perishable form of customer good and aircraft scheduling is easily disrupted. The union promised to save £42 million over three years. Catering was sold off but existing staff kept earning and BA staff discounts, while sanctions against strikers were withdrawn and the union increased its membership by 50 per cent to over 10 000. Moreover, the agreement itself fostered further dissent. By the end of 1997 4000 staff had left but 4500 more were recruited including 2000 in 1998. By the terms of the agreement, these new staff were employed on different contracts from existing employees. As a result, cabin crew working the same shifts on the same aircraft were (increasingly) on different pay scales. The impact of this on both labour relations and BA's much prized team-working was problematic and problems were fuelled by suggestions that BA favoured employees on new contracts for promotion to purser (first line manager).

Conclusion

Employees do not 'react' to the management of culture in isolation, nor does a 'positive' cultural rhetoric negate problematic experiences of job design, disempowerment, payment systems or control mechanisms. Rather responses will be influenced by a person's experience of work as a whole, and employees are more capable of noting discrepancies between managerial promises and organisational practice.[1]

For discussion

Explain how people co-operated before 1981, between 1983 and 1996 and after 1997. How can BA regain its employees' trust and commitment? Can you suggest any changes in the structural and material factors to increase BA's productivity?

Virtually every aspect of life is affected at least indirectly by some type of organisation.[2] We look to organisations to feed, clothe, house, educate and employ us. Organisations attend to our needs for entertainment, police and fire protection, insurance, recreation, national security, transportation, news and information, legal assistance and health care. Many of these organisations seek a profit, others do not. Some are extremely large, others are tiny, family-run operations. Despite this mind-boggling diversity, modern organisations have one basic thing in common. They are the primary context for organisational behaviour. In a manner of speaking, organisations are the chessboard upon which the game of organisational behaviour is played. Therefore, present professionals need a working knowledge of modern organisations to improve their chances of making the right moves when managing people at work.

This chapter explores the structural features and different types of traditional and new organisations. We begin by defining the term 'organisation'. Our attention then turns to the main elements of organisation structure, namely division of labour, hierarchy of authority and co-ordination of efforts. Next, we discuss how these different elements result in several organisation types. We conclude with a review of modern organisation types.

Defining and charting organisations

Organisation
system of consciously co-ordinated activities of two or more people

As a necessary springboard for this chapter we need to formally define the term 'organisation' and clarify the meaning of organisation charts.

What is an organisation?

According to Chester Barnard's classic definition (see the work of Barnard in Chapter 1), an **Organisation** is 'a system of consciously co-ordinated activities or forces of two or more persons'.[3] Embodied

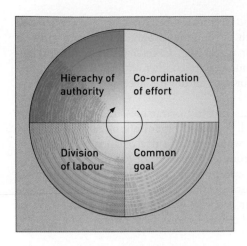

FIGURE 14.1 FOUR CHARACTERISTICS COMMON TO ALL ORGANISATIONS

in the conscious co-ordination aspect of this definition are four factors common to all organisations: division of labour, hierarchy of authority, co-ordination of effort and common goal (see Figure 14.1).[4] We will elaborate further on the first three later in this chapter. Effectively reaching common goals will be discussed in Chapter 15. Organisation theorists refer to these factors as the organisation 'structure'[5] and these factors are the major features determining the characteristics of the organisation types. Of course, depending on the size of an organisation these factors can play another role in determining the organisation structure.

Organisations are subject to norms of rationality,[6] meaning that organisations have goals and structures to achieve them. Common goals are what unite the individuals and provide the organisation with a raison d'être. The goals are constantly evolving and organisations continue to reach for them. A few organisations have clear finite goals, such as the construction of a subway network in a city. Once the construction is finished, the common organisational goal is reached and the organisation can dissolve. Other organisations never cease to exist because their goals are infinite. For instance, organisations with 'providing punctual, fast and cheap transportation to city inhabitants' as their goal exist as long as there are inhabitants in the city. In Chapter 15 we pay more attention to the different kinds of goals that organisations can have and their relatedness to organisational effectiveness and effectiveness criteria.

Differentiation and integration

Organisations are depicted by several common structural elements. These issues all deal with the fundamental premise of organisation structure: work division and co-ordination of the divided work. The structure of organisation is therefore in simple terms described as 'the sum total of the ways in which the organisation divides its labour into distinct tasks and then achieves co-ordination among them'.[7] Consider the following example:

> European bank and insurance companies divide their labour into back office and front office. The latter are close to the customers, while the former do not have customer contacts but prepare and administrate the work of the front office. This deviation allows the banks to hire employees with different skills for front and back offices. Many of the back-office tasks are IT-related. The Boston Consulting Group wrote a report with the Indian employers organisation in which they state that India will take care of the IT-related back-office jobs for European financial organisations, because India has a surplus of IT skilled people, while Europe has a deficit of such people. The deficit in Europe is estimated at 5 million people by 2020. Modern communication technology has proven to be able to deal with the co-ordination of the most geographically dispersed work.[8]

In their classic text, *Organization and Environment*, Harvard researchers Paul Lawrence and Jay Lorsch explained how two structural forces simultaneously fragment the organisation and bind it together. They cautioned that an imbalance between these two forces – labelled 'differentiation' and 'integration' – could hinder organisational effectiveness.

Differentiation
division of labour and specialisation that cause people to think and act differently

Integration
co-operation among specialists to achieve common goals

Differentiation occurs through division of labour and technical specialisation. A behavioural outcome of differentiation is that technical specialists, such as computer programmers, tend to think and act differently from specialists in, say, accounting or marketing. Excessive differentiation can cause the organisation to become entrenched in miscommunication, conflict and politics. Thus, differentiation needs to be offset by an opposing structural force to ensure the necessary co-ordination. This is where **Integration** enters the picture.

When Lawrence and Lorsch studied successful and unsuccessful companies in three industries, they concluded that as environmental complexity increased, successful organisations exhibited higher degrees of both differentiation and integration. In other words, an effective balance was achieved. Unsuccessful organisations, in contrast, tended to suffer from an imbalance of too much differentiation and not enough offsetting integration. Professionals need to fight this tendency if their growing and increasingly differentiated organisations are to be co-ordinated. They also discovered that 'the more differentiated an organisation, the more difficult it is to achieve integration'.[9] Managers of today's complex organisations need to strive constantly and creatively to achieve greater integration.[10]

> For example, how does 3M Company, with its dozens of autonomous divisions and more than 60 000 products, maintain its competitive edge in technology? Among other things, 3M makes sure its technical specialists interact with one another frequently so that cross-fertilisation of ideas takes place. Art Fry, credited with inventing the now popular Post-it Notes (also see Chapter 12), actually owes much of his success to colleague Spencer Silver, an engineer down the hall who created an apparently useless semi-adhesive. If Fry and Silver had worked in a company without a strong commitment to integration, we probably would not have Post-it Notes. 3M does not leave this sort of cross-fertilisation to chance. It organises for integration with such things as a Technology Council that regularly convenes researchers from various divisions and an annual science fair at which 3M scientists enthusiastically hawk their new ideas, not to customers, but to each other![11]

Vertical specialisation
determines who takes responsibility and who has decision-making power in the organisation

Herbert Simon (also see in Chapter 1) distinguishes between task specialisation and division of authority or vertical specialisation.[12] **Vertical specialisation** determines who takes responsibility and who has decision-making power in the organisation. Vertical specialisation thus divides the decision-making tasks and establishes an authority structure but is also a means of co-ordination, as will become clear further in the chapter. The organisation seeks to reach its goal by designing an organisation structure based on differentiation and integration. Differentiation is reflected in the division of labour and the hierarchy of authority; while integration is reflected in the co-ordination of efforts. Each of these aspects will be discussed further in the chapter.

Organisation charts

Organisation chart
graphic illustration of boxes and lines showing chain of formal authority and division of labour

An **Organisation chart** is a graphic representation of formal authority and division of labour relationships. To the casual observer, the term organisation chart means the family-tree-like pattern of boxes and lines posted on workplace walls. Within each box one usually finds the names and titles of current position holders. To organisation theorists, however, organisation charts reveal much more. The partial organisation chart in Figure 14.2 reveals several of the structural dimensions discussed in the next paragraphs, such as: hierarchy of authority, division of labour, departmentalisation, spans of control, and line and staff positions. However, organisation charts simplify the complexity of organisation structure, often running the risk of providing a partial view on the structure or even a misleading view. Organisation charts are a helping tool for understanding the organisation structure, but we need to dig deeper to fully understand the organisational processes and effectiveness.

Elements of organisation structure

We will now look at three important factors of organisation structure: division of labour, hierarchy of authority and co-ordination of effort.

Division of labour and responsibility

Organisations realise objectives and perform activities far beyond the possibilities of a single person. The construction of the Eurotunnel required the work of 15 000 people and lasted for seven years.[13]

FIGURE 14.2 SAMPLE ORGANISATION CHART FOR A HOSPITAL (EXECUTIVE AND DIRECTOR LEVELS ONLY)

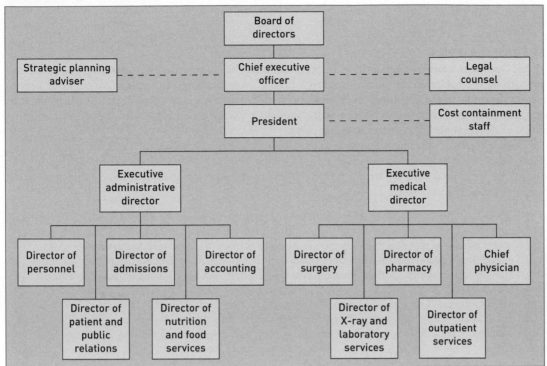

Each worker had its own task and responsibility for a very small part of the tunnel building. Effective allocation of tasks or **Division of labour** requires:

- Clarification of the objective of the organisation.
- Decomposing the objective in a cascade of sub-elements and accompanying tasks.
- Allocating people to the tasks.
- Determining which people are responsible for the tasks and sub-elements.

Hence, people in the organisation not only need to know what they are supposed to do but also for what part of the process they have decision-making authority. In organisations, the term 'function' is used to indicate one's bundle of tasks and responsibilities. Let us focus on some aspects of how organisations divide their functions and tasks.

Division of labour the allocation of tasks and responsibilities to the members of the organisation

LINE AND STAFF FUNCTIONS

There are two main kinds of tasks: line and staff functions. **Line managers** such as the president, the two executive directors, and the various directors in Figure 14.2 occupy formal decision-making positions within the organisation and have responsibilities for major parts of the organisation's activity. Line personnel execute operational tasks. Line positions are usually connected by solid lines on organisation charts. Dotted lines indicate staff relationships. **Staff personnel** provides research, advice and recommendations to their line managers, who have the authority to make decisions. For example, the cost-containment specialists in the sample organisation chart merely advise the president on relevant matters. They have no line authority over other organisational members, apart from supervising the work of their own staff assistants. Line and staff functions can also be distinguished by their capacity to earn income for the organisation.[14] Line functions earn the organisation's income directly, while staff functions provide the support for earning that income. A consequence is that line functions are the core functions of the organisation. Failure in staff functions is less threatening to the business than failure in line functions. The former can also be more easily outsourced. Modern trends, such as cross-functional teams (Chapter 10) and re-engineering, are blurring the distinction between line and staff positions.

Line managers have authority to make organisational decisions

Staff personnel provide research, advice and recommendations to line managers

According to a study of 207 police officers in Israel, line personnel exhibited greater job commitment than their staff counterparts.[15] This result was anticipated because the line managers' decision-making authority empowered them and gave them comparatively more control over their work situations (see Chapter 13).

SPECIALISATION

Work deviation leads to specialisation in organisations. People repeatedly performing the same task grow to be specialised in the execution of that task. However, the level of specialisation in an organisation depends on the extent to which work is divided. High levels of specialisation exist when each one only performs a limited number of tasks; while in a low specialisation situation, people perform a range of different and frequently changing tasks.

Extreme forms of splitting up tasks exist on assembly lines in factories, such as a car manufacturing plant, where each employee is responsible for fastening one particle to the car. Frederick Taylor[16] was one of the first promoters of strong task deviation to increase rationalisation and efficiency of the work, as explained in Chapter 1.

> Specialisation in car manufacturing plants has changed a lot since then. In particular, the Japanese production scheme seems to differ from the European and American ones and gives Japanese manufacturers a competitive advantage. The lean production system, also called the Toyota-system and developed in the mid-1970s in Japan, is based on less specialisation which allows more flexibility, greater product variability, decentralised authority and more lateral communication across functional boundaries. In Europe car manufacturers experimented with the lean production system in the 1980s and 1990s by introducing more teamwork, flexibility and self-regulating work groups, with differing success rates. The possibilities of implementing lean production, involving lower specialisation, depends on the support of top management, the approval of labour unions and compliance with governmental regulations.[16]

GROUPING OF PEOPLE AND DEPARTMENTALISATION

Organisations divide their major activities into numerous parts, split between all organisational members and also regroup tasks and people. Organisations consist of units or departments in which related tasks and specialists are grouped. **Departmentalisation** is necessary to organise the tasks and people and to establish authority and co-ordination. The matrix form of departmentalisation requires special attention because of its clear benefits and drawbacks making this kind of departmentalisation difficult to manage.

Departmentalisation the grouping of people based on common characteristics

DEPARTMENTALISATION

The criteria used to form departments are similar resources, similar expertise, products, markets, geographical regions or customers. Four major kinds of grouping are commonly used, namely functional, product, geographical and matrix departmentalisation. Figure 14.3 (on page 529) illustrates each of the four.

Functional **departmentalisation** grouping people based on function

Product-based **departmentalisation** grouping people based on product, service on customer

Functional departmentalisation groups people and their tasks by the function in the same way – as finance and marketing specialists or production personnel. **Product-based departmentalisation** groups people and tasks related to the different types of products or services, in the same way as specialists in loans, savings, mortages and insurance in a bank. **Product-based departmentalisation** is also customer-based, since different types of products or services might be used by different groups of customers. When the organisation has no specific groups of customers or products, projects become the grouping criteria. As projects are limited in time, project groups are composed and dissolved at the start and the end of the project.

> Product, functional and project structures can be found in one company. In Brussels, a major construction project is executed by Denys for the construction of 6.7 km pipelines under Brussels' roads and channels to collect water for the new wastewater treatment plant. Denys has a functional structure as top structure. One of the functional divisions is 'the projects' which is further divided in 5 product-based divisions. Each of these product divisions holds several major project groups working in Belgium or in the rest of the world on a major construction project. Such projects can take a few months or several years. The project in Brussels will take about 3.5 years.[17]

Geographical departmentalisation is based on the different regions where the organisations operate and is of particular interest for multinational organisations or organisations that need to provide goods or services close to the customer, such as local shops or restaurants.

Organisations can choose which one of the departmentalisation types best fits their goals:

> British Telecom for instance changed its structure from geographical to product-based in 2000. This change was necessary to allow a better view of the growth potential of the different product lines. This also allows the organisation to develop products within a separate legal entity. The Yellow Pages product of BT became a separate entity, Yell, and is listed separately on the stock exchange. Other divisions are BT Retail – serving UK fixed-line customers; BT Wholesale – running the UK network; BT Global Services – a data-centric broadband IP business focused on corporate and wholesale markets; BT Openworld – a mass-market Internet access business focused increasingly on broadband services and BT Wireless – an international mobile business emphasising mobile data and next generation services. A year later BT Wireless also became a separate company. The current structure combines the strength of the BT Group as a whole with the speed and responsiveness of the individual business units, each of which has specialised knowledge of the markets in which it operates and of the customers it serves.[18]

A **Matrix form of departmentalisation** combines two of the above-mentioned departmentalisations. Each kind of departmentalisation emphasises only one aspect of the people's tasks – for example, functional characteristics or different groups of customers. A sales representative working in a structure with functional departmentalisation will be a member of the sales department that emphasises the importance of selling but ignores the production of the goods sold. When the same sales representative works in a product-based departmentalisation structure, he will be a member of a specific product department. Emphasis will be on all characteristics of that product, including its production, but the sales aspect will be ignored. This kind of organisation departmentalisation is usually represented in a matrix structure.

Benefits and drawbacks of the matrix structure

The matrix form is an attempt to balance two kinds of departmentalisation simultaneously. It was originally pictured as the solution to combining functional and product departmentalisation and having the best of both worlds. As a consequence, the unity of command (see further) is eliminated, risking conflicts between the two authority lines.[19] This is seen as the most important disadvantage of the matrix structure. Moreover, in addition to conflicting decisions in the dual line of command, the balance between the two lines of attention may give way to problems as well. People in a unit with both a product and marketing focus will need a marketing and a product mindset. There is a real risk that one of the two will predominate. People might begin to focus too much on the specific features of the product, becoming highly specialised in that aspect, but neglecting the marketing aspects and their role in the overall marketing strategy of the company, or vice versa. Table 14.1 gives an overview of the advantages and disadvantage of the matrix structure.

TABLE 14.1 ADVANTAGES AND DISADVANTAGES OF THE MATRIX STRUCTURE

Advantages of the matrix structure	Disadvantages of the matrix structure
Combining the efficiency of the functional structure with the flexibility of the divisional (product) structure	Conflict due to dual lines of authority
Combining functional expertise with product (or project) expertise	Impossibility to combine the dual attention for functional and product/project demands
Dual attention for functional goals and product goals	Difficult allocation of functional experts over the different product groups
Flexibility to extend the number of products or to regroup	Imbalance between the two interests; resulting in the domination of one of the two and losing the advantages of the matrix
Maximising the value and use of individual experts	Confusion about responsibilities
	Costly co-ordination caused by the more complex structure

Geographical departmentalisation grouping people based on region

Matrix form of departmentalisation grouping people based on function and product simultaneously

The Swedish company ABB (Asea Brown Boveri) is considered to be the main promoter and successful implementor of the matrix structure. However, ABB abandoned the perfect balanced matrix structure a few years ago. Matrix structures are still found in many companies but in an imbalanced form with one of the two entries of the matrix dominating. The British researchers Goold and Campbell studied several large multinationals over four years and suggest that there is nothing fundamentally wrong with the matrix, as long as the cells in the matrix operate as semi-independent business units with a large degree of autonomy in decision making and are combined with a hierarchy and processes that integrate these units and stipulate the horizontal co-ordination needs. [20]

Hierarchy of authority

As stated in the definition of an organisation above, a second important element of organisation structure is hierarchy of authority. Hierarchy of authority determines the vertical division of responsibility and decision making. As Figure 14.2 illustrates, there is an unmistakable hierarchy of authority.[21] The ten directors report to the two executive directors who report to the president who reports to the chief executive officer. Ultimately, the chief executive officer answers to the hospital's board of directors. A formal hierarchy of authority also delineates the official communication network (Chapter 8). Hence, authority defines who has the responsibility and decision-making power. Hierarchy of authority not only makes the supreme authority responsible for the subordinating units but gives the supreme authority the power to direct and control the people in those units.

Unity of command
each employee should report to a single manager

The chart in Figure 14.2 shows also strict unity of command up and down the line. Unity of command indicates that each employee should report to only one manager. Otherwise, the argument goes, inefficiency would prevail because of conflicting orders and lack of personal accountability.[22] (Indeed, these are problems in today's more fluid and flexible organisations based on innovations such as cross-functional and self-managed teams, see Chapter 10.) The duality of command depicted in the matrix with the resulting potential conflicts is a situation that some organisations cannot afford. The army, for instance, maintains strict unity of command with a clear system of command and control. In a battle situation there is no time to discuss conflicting commands.[23]

Span of control
the number of people reporting directly to a given manager

Related to the hierarchy of authority is the span of control. The Span of control refers to the number of people reporting directly to a certain manager.[24] Spans of control can range from narrow to wide. For example, the president in Figure 14.2 has a narrow span of control of two. (Usually, staff assistants are not included in a manager's span of control.) The executive administrative director in Figure 14.3 has a wider span of control of five. Spans of control exceeding 30 can be found in assembly-line operations where machine-paced and repetitive work substitutes for close supervision. Historically, spans of five to six were considered best. Generally, the narrower the span of control, the closer the supervision and the higher the administrative costs as a result of a higher manager-to-worker ratio. The recent emphasis on leanness and administrative efficiency dictates spans of control should be as wide as possible while guarding against inadequate supervision and lack of co-ordination. Wider spans also complement the trend toward greater worker autonomy and empowerment (see Chapter 13).

CENTRALISATION

Centralisation
the concentration of decision-making power at the level of the top management team

Decentralisation
the dispersion of decision-making power in the organisation

Centralisation and Decentralisation are two ends of a continuum referring to the extent to which the decision-making power is concentrated at the top or dispersed in the organisation. In a fully centralised organisation the top management team takes all the decisions. The larger the organisation becomes, the more difficult it will be to concentrate all power at the top because of the limited capacity of this top management team to make every decision.

> In 2001, Procter and Gamble choose to change its structure from horizontal to vertical with more centralisation and less autonomy for the different local business units. This was necessary to unroll innovations faster world wide and to lower operational costs. Local business units in Europe became global business units or market development units. In the latter case, those units are only responsible for introducing a product in a local market. The global business units are responsible for all aspects of a product and brand world wide. Hence, the European divisions of Procter and Gamble cannot develop new products for the European market only. All product development is centralised and must serve the world market.[25]

FIGURE 14.3 FOUR KINDS OF DEPARTMENTALISATION

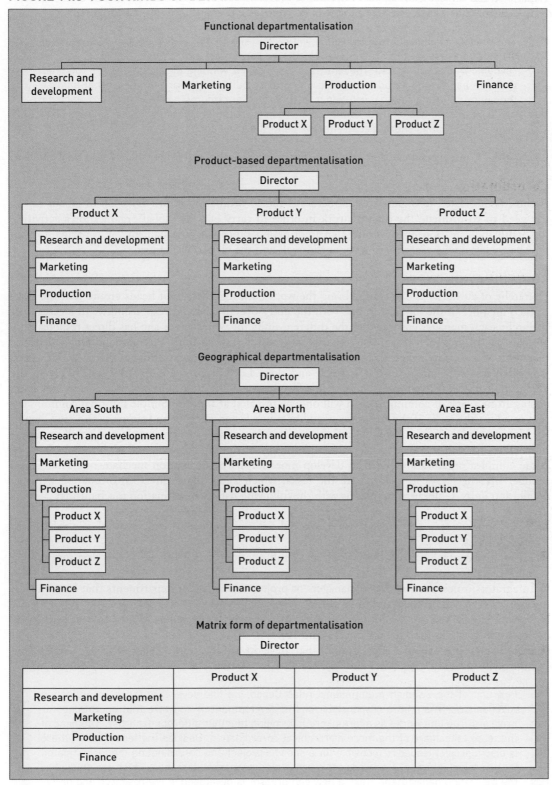

Experts on the subject warn against extremes of centralisation or decentralisation. The challenge is to achieve a workable balance between the two. A management consultant put it as follows:

> The modern organisation in transition will recognise the pull of two polarities: a need for greater centralisation to create low-cost shared resources; and, a need to improve market responsiveness with greater decentralisation. Today's winning organisations are the ones that can handle the paradox and tensions of both pulls. These are the firms that analyse the optimum organisational solution in each particular circumstance, without prejudice for one type of organisation over another. The result is, almost invariably, a messy mixture of decentralised units sharing cost-effective centralised resources.[26]

Centralisation and decentralisation are not an either–or proposition; they are an and–also balancing act.

Co-ordination

A third issue related to organisation structure is the co-ordination effort. Division of labour brings the need to co-ordinate the divided work in order to carry out the global organisation's activities. Galbraith indicates **Co-ordination** as an information-processing mechanism.[27] Co-ordination can only be achieved when information about the goals and the tasks is exchanged.

Co-ordination tuning the activities to reach a common goal by exchanging information

CO-ORDINATION TYPES

Hierarchy of authority is one way to bring the work back together. Unit heads ensure that the tasks of each member in the unit are in line with the unit's overall goal and responsibility. In a cascade of hierarchy each manager ensures that the different units for which he or she has direct responsibility are working in line with the goals. The directive power and the unity of command embedded in a hierarchy of authority make hierarchy a strong and effective way to co-ordinate the tasks. However, it is often less efficient because it is costly and slow. Look back at Figure 14.2 specifically to the accounting unit and the surgery unit. A conflict between the two units about incorrect invoicing arising from a lack of communication will only be revealed at the top. Simple informal communication to adjust the tasks of the two units would be much faster, cheaper and simpler (also see Chapter 8). However, such informal mutual adjustment is only possible in very simple and small organisations allowing each member to keep a complete view of the organisation and each member's tasks. More complex organisations need to develop more formal co-ordination mechanisms. There are a number of other ways to co-ordinate the tasks, which allow more direct co-ordination between people and units. Galbraith provides us with the following list of co-ordination mechanisms[28]:

- Rules, programmes and procedures: fixing and determining each member's duties in relation to other's duties.
- Hierarchy: controlling tasks by gathering all information in one function with decision-making authority.
- Integrators: roles, such as brand managers or project managers, or departments that have the co-ordination of certain tasks and units as their responsibility.
- Formal groups: teams, task groups or project groups, which are groups formed to deal with inter-departmental tasks (also see Chapters 9 and 10).
- Informal groups: spontaneous groups that develop to solve interdepartmental co-ordination informally (also see Chapters 9 and 10).

> In a unit of the Swedish multinational Atlas Copco, we find several of these co-ordination mechanisms. The unit is responsible for the development of software that operates compressors. The unit works as a formal group bringing together different expertise. The head of the team takes care of the more hierarchical co-ordination. Besides the team leader, there is also a project leader responsible for a specific project and co-ordinating the tasks related to the project laterally. A new project is based on new market demands, which are studied by the marketing department. Next, a new compressor is developed in the research and development department. Finally, the electronics department of which this unit is part gets the order to develop new software. This is a procedure taking care of the co-ordination and relationships between the responsibilities of each of these departments.[29]

The need for co-ordination can also be minimised through clear goal setting (see Chapter 6) in combination with delegation of authority (Chapter 13).[30] The reasoning is that in the presence of clear goals and sub-goals, the tasks are naturally co-ordinated when each member of the organisation directs their work towards those goals.

STANDARDISATION AS CO-ORDINATION
Different forms of standardisation are another way to co-ordinate tasks without additional information exchange. Henri Mintzberg identified four types of standardisation as co-ordination mechanisms.[31] Table 14.2 describes each of the four types.

TABLE 14.2 FOUR TYPES OF STANDARDISATION

Standardisation of work	This implies exactly specifying and programming the tasks in such a way that tasks are streamlined, without any deviation from the programme. This is especially possible when the tasks are routine, simple and easy to describe, such as the tasks in an assembly line
Standardisation of output	The results of the tasks are specified: what needs to be reached, and not how. This is of interest when the way tasks are performed does not affect other units of the organisation or the overall objectives. The output is mostly determined by the number of pieces to be produced, number of customers to be visited or turnover to be realised
Standardisation of skills	By hiring people with the same skills, standardisation in the tasks is obtained, in a similar way to lawyers in law firms or doctors in hospitals. Standardisation of skills is also possible by making all employees go through the same training
Standardisation of norms	Hiring, training or influencing people to have them share the same norms. Those norms determine how they carry out the tasks. This way of achieving co-ordination is used widely in religious or radical organisations.

SOURCE: Based on H. Mintzberg, *Mintzberg on Management* (New York: The Free Press, 1989), p. 101.

FORMALISATION
Finally, the level of formalisation is also related to co-ordination choices. Formalisation indicates the level at which the rights and duties of the members of the organisation are fixed. The larger the organisation the more formalisation is used to keep control. The greater the use of informal groups and the lesser the use of hierarchy, rules, procedures and standardisation of work, the lower the formalisation. In small organisations the director is able to control and correct unacceptable behaviour directly. Formalisation covers not only the fixing of what and how one should perform one's tasks but can be extended to all kinds of behaviour in the organisation, such as dress code, working hours, smoking regulations, use of office equipment or Internet.

Formalisation the extent to which rights and duties of organisational members are determined

Organisation types
The following organisation types are based on the composition of previously elaborated structural elements: division of labour, hierarchy of authority and co-ordination. Although all types co-exist, there is a clear evolution in the organisation types, an evolution that parallels business reality. The first large companies at the beginning of the twentieth century focused on efficiency and control, therefore, developing mechanistic and bureaucratic organisation types (also see Chapter 1). Later the shortcomings of very mechanistic organisations in terms of flexibility were realised and the organic organisation type was a proposed alternative. More organisation types appeared,

operating in particular environments, such as in professional services or those combining a diversified range of activities. In the last quarter of the twentieth century globalisation, high-speed technological evolution and the World Wide Web affected the development of new organisation types.

Furthermore, organisations can be categorised as do-organisations and think-organisations. The traditional organisation types were very much oriented towards acting or the pragmatic execution of the tasks with the emphasis on efficiency and effectiveness. Modern organisations often find themselves in more complex environments requiring an emphasis on 'thinking' or analysing the environment, seeking for opportunities and adapting to environmental changes through learning. The major classic and new organisation types will be described in the following paragraphs. Some organisation types will probably remind you of Morgan's organisational metaphors in Chapter 1. Keep in mind that the types described in this chapter are 'pure' types. In real life, such pure types are rarely found because many companies are a mixture, such as bureaucratic staff parts combined with a different kind of production core, for example, professional or organic.

Bureaucratic organisations

Bureaucracy
Max Weber's idea of the most rationally efficient form of organisation

Weber's (1947) description of Bureaucracy as the ideal organisation form inspired many organisation design theorists.[32] He patterned his ideal organisation after the much-vaunted Prussian army and called it 'bureaucracy'. Weber recognised three types of organisations depending on the use of authority and power. One organisation has a charismatic leader dominating the organisation; in another, standing, precedents and habits determine power and authority; a third (ideal) type bases authority and power on objective criteria: the bureaucratic organisation. Rules and procedures based on rationality and not on personality, habits or dominant leaders determine the bureaucratic organisation. In bureaucratic organisations the roles are very clearly defined and are focused on maximising efficiency. An organisation is not a group of people but a combination of roles and tasks. Power only originates from a certain role. Decision making is fully rational. Such an organisation requires a huge number of rules, procedures and control mechanisms resulting in complexity, inefficiency and inflexibility. Human beings seem to find it difficult to operate in a perfect rational machine structure and start to 'use' the system. The latter gave Weber's bureaucracy a fairly poor reputation although it was originally described as an ideal type that would solve irrational behaviour in many existing organisations.

According to Weber's theory, the following four factors should make bureaucracies the epitome of efficiency:

- Division of labour: people become proficient when they perform standardised tasks over and over again.
- A hierarchy of authority: a formal chain of command ensures co-ordination and accountability.
- Framework of rules: carefully formulated and strictly enforced rules ensure predictable behaviour.
- Administrative impersonality: personnel decisions such as hiring and promoting should be based on competence not favouritism.

All organisations possess varying degrees of the four characteristics listed above. Thus, every organisation is a bureaucracy to some extent, although very small organisations will only have a limited number of these elements, if any at all. Bureaucracies are typically associated with very large organisations. In terms of the ideal metaphor, a bureaucracy should run like a well-oiled machine and its members should perform with the precision of a polished military unit. But practical and ethical problems arise when bureaucratic characteristics become extreme or dysfunctional. For example, extreme expressions of specialisation, rule following and impersonality can cause a bureaucrat to treat a client as a number rather than as a person.[33]

Weber would probably be surprised and dismayed that his model of rational efficiency has become a synonym for inefficiency.[34] Today, bureaucracy stands for being put on hold, waiting in queues and getting shuffled from one office to the next (see the next Snapshot). This irony can be explained largely by the fact that organisations with excessive or dysfunctional bureaucratic tendencies become rigid, inflexible and resistant to environmental demands and influences. Jack Welch, General

Electric's former legendary CEO and voted in the US as number one manager of the century, told *Fortune* magazine about his 'tough love' approach to battling bureaucracy:

> Giving people self-confidence is by far the most important thing that I can do. Because then they will act. I tell people, if this place is stifling you, shake it, shake it, break it. Check the system, because it wants to be a bureaucracy. And if it doesn't work, get the hell out. If GE can't give you what you want, go get it somewhere else.[35]

The Mugama: Egypt's bureaucratic legacy is a nice example of bureaucracy

Cairo – in Egypt the bureaucracy is not just an engine of policy or even a state of mind. It is a semicircular concrete behemoth in the centre of this city's central square.

In this towering edifice – the Mugama ('Uniting') Central Government Complex – office opens on to office, crumbling stairway on to stairway, and the circular corridors that wheel 14 stories high around a dusky inner courtyard seem to have no end.

The Mugama holds 20 000 public employees in 1400 rooms. It is headquarters to 14 government departments. So deep is its reach into the everyday life of Cairenes that most adult city dwellers will find themselves forced to visit it several times a year. Upward of 45 000 people pass through its portals each day.

Perhaps unrivalled anywhere in the world as a symbol of governmental dithering and public despair, it is at once the most feared and hated structure in Egypt and the evolutionary product of millennia of bureaucracy on the shores of the Nile.

Twelve hapless clients of the Mugama have hurled themselves from its broken windows or from the soaring circular balconies that ring the central lobby up to the thirteenth floor dome. A generation of Arab social engineers, who threw off a monarchy and seized Egypt in the name of its poor and unrepresented, planted their dreams in the Mugama's corridors and largely watched them die there.

'The Mugama is to Egypt generally a symbol of 4000 years of bureaucracy and for the average Egyptian, it means all that is negative about the bureaucracy routine, slow paperwork, complicated paperwork, a lot of signatures, impersonality. It is a Kafka building', said political sociologist Saad Eddin Ibrahim.

'You enter there, you can get the job done – the same job – in five minutes, in five days, in five months or five years', Ibrahim said. 'You can never predict what might happen to you in that building. Anybody who has dealt with that building for whatever reason knows the uncertainty of his affairs there.'

In Egypt, the legacy of bureaucracy dates back to the time of the pharaohs. Temple walls and statues depict countless scribes, papyrus and pen in hand, taking down for the files of posterity everything from the deeds of the Pharaoh to the tax man's inventory. Subsequent French, Turkish and British occupiers refined Egyptian red tape to a fine art.

Today, it takes 11 different permits for a foreign resident to buy an apartment in downtown Cairo. A bride wishing to join her husband working abroad in the Persian Gulf region must get stamps and signatures from the Foreign Ministry, the Ministry of Justice, the prosecutor general, the local court in her district, and the regional court, a process that one Cairo newspaper referred to as 'legalised torture'.

One young physician recently left the Mugama in tears after three days of trying to resign from her government job. 'They told me finally it would be easier if I just took a long sick leave', she said with a sigh. 'But I'm leaving the country for a year!'

SOURCE: Kimberly Murphy, 'Woe Awaits in Tower of Babble', *Los Angeles Times*, 24 May 1993.

snapshot

Mechanistic versus organic organisations

A landmark study on organisation types was reported by a pair of British behavioural scientists, Tom Burns and G. M. Stalker. In the course of their research they drew a very instructive distinction between what they called 'mechanistic' and 'organic' organisations. **Mechanistic organisations** are rigid bureaucracies with strict rules, narrowly defined tasks and top-down communication. For example, when *Business Week* correspondent Kathleen Deveny spent a day working in a McDonald's restaurant, she found a very mechanistic organisation:

Mechanistic organisations rigid, command-and-control bureaucracies

> Here every job is broken down into the smallest of steps, and the whole process is auto-mated . . . .
>
> Anyone could do this, I think. But McDonald's restaurants operate like Swiss watches, and the minute I step behind the counter I am a loose part in the works . . . .
>
> I bag French fries for a few minutes, but I'm much too slow. Worse, I can't seem to keep my station clean enough. Failing at French fries is a fluke, I tell myself . . . .
>
> I try to move faster, but my co-workers are playing at 45 rpm, and I'm stuck at $33\frac{1}{3}$.[36]

This sort of mechanistic structure is necessary at McDonald's because of the competitive need for uniform product quality, speedy service and cleanliness. In contrast, organic organisations are flexible networks of multitalented individuals who perform a variety of tasks.[37] Consider the next example:

> Ubizen is providing security software to large corporations worldwide. It was established in 1995 in Belgium as a spin-off from a university.[38] The company was young, flexible, fast growing with a lot of young highly-skilled engineers and organic, almost chaotic, just like many other software and Internet companies that were established in the Internet hype of the nineties. The lack of control in their very organic structure and fast growth made many of these companies go off the rails. Ubizen faced problems as well, among others caused by its very organic structure.[38]

Organic organisations fluid and flexible network of multi-talented people

There tends to be centralised decision making in mechanistic organisations and decentralised decision making in **Organic organisations**. Generally, centralised organisations are more tightly controlled while decentralised organisations are more adaptive to changing situations.[39] Each has its appropriate use.

A MATTER OF DEGREE

It is important to note, as illustrated in Table 14.3, that each of the mechanistic–organic characteristics is a matter of degree. Organisations tend to be relatively mechanistic or relatively organic. Pure types are rare because divisions, departments or units in the same organisation may be more or less mechanistic or organic.

RESEARCH FINDINGS

When they classified a sample of actual companies as either mechanistic or organic, Burns and Stalker discovered one type was not superior to the other. Each type had its appropriate place, depending on the environment. When the environment was relatively stable and certain, the successful organisations tended to be mechanistic. Organic organisations tended to be the successful ones when the environment was unstable and uncertain.[40]

In a more recent study of 103 department managers from eight manufacturing firms and two aerospace organisations, managerial skill was found to have a greater impact, on an overall measure of department effectiveness, in organic departments than in mechanistic departments. This led the researchers to recommend the following contingencies for management staffing and training:

> If we have two units, one organic and one mechanistic, and two potential applicants differing in overall managerial ability, we might want to assign the more competent to the organic unit since in that situation there are few structural aids available to the manager in performing required responsibilities. It is also possible that managerial training is especially needed by managers being groomed to take over units that are more organic in structure.[41]

TABLE 14.3 CHARACTERISTICS OF MECHANISTIC AND ORGANIC ORGANISATIONS

Characteristic	Mechanistic organisation	Organic organisation
1 Task definition and knowledge required	Narrow; technical	→ Broad; general
2 Linkage between individual's contribution and organisation's purpose	Vague or indirect	→ Clear or direct
3 Task flexibility	Rigid; routine	→ Flexible; varied
4 Specification of techniques, obligations, and rights	Specific	→ General
5 Degree of hierarchical control	High	→ Low (self-control emphasised)
6 Primary communication pattern	Top-down	→ Lateral (between peers)
7 Primary decision-making style	Authoritarian	→ Democratic; participative
8 Emphasis on obedience and loyalty	High	→ Low

SOURCE: Adapted from discussion in T. Burns and G. M. Stalker, *The Management of Innovation* (London: Tavistock, 1961), pp. 119–25.

Another interesting finding comes from a study of 42 voluntary church organisations. As the organisations became more mechanistic (more bureaucratic) the intrinsic motivation of their members decreased. Mechanistic organisations apparently undermined the volunteers' sense of freedom and self-determination. Additionally, the researchers believe their findings help to explain why bureaucracy tends to feed on itself: 'A mechanistic organisational structure may breed the need for a more extremely mechanistic system because of the reduction in intrinsically motivated behaviour.'[42] Thus, bureaucracy begets greater bureaucracy.

Most recently, field research in two factories, one mechanistic and the other organic, found expected communication patterns. Command-and-control (downward) communication characterised the mechanistic factory. Consultative or participative (two-way) communication prevailed in the organic factory.[43]

BOTH MECHANISTIC AND ORGANIC STRUCTURES ARE NEEDED

Although most students and practitioners typically express a distaste for mechanistic organisations, not all organisations or subunits can or should be organic. For example, as mentioned earlier, McDonald's could not achieve its admired quality and service standards without extremely mechanistic restaurant operations. Imagine the food and service you would get if McDonald's employees used their own favourite way of doing things and worked at their own pace! On the other hand, mechanistic structure alienates some employees because it erodes their sense of self-control.

We mentioned in the beginning of this chapter that organisations are behaving rationally by determining and trying to achieve a common goal through developing a structure that divides and co-ordinates the tasks to make this goal achievement possible. Extreme organic organisations are losing sight of the rationality norm. The goals are adapting fast, while tasks might not adapt that fast, resulting in a discrepancy between the tasks of the very autonomous working experts in the organic organisation and the organisation's goals (if the latter are clear at all). The tasks are very broadly defined and hardly controlled. There is lateral informal co-ordination, self-regulation and self-control but no monitoring of where the organisation as a whole is heading. The next Actvitity will help you to determine whether you prefer an organic or mechanistic organisation.

Mintzberg's organisation types

A well-known overview of organisation types can be found in Mintzberg's work *Mintzberg on Management* in which he describes seven organisation types.[44] These are configurations of co-ordination mechanisms, division of labour and hierarchy of authority, discussed earlier. We have already

activity

Do you prefer a mechanistic or an organic organisation?

This Activity is designed to help you determine which organisation type you prefer. For example, you might prefer an organisation with clearly defined rules or no rules at all. You might prefer an organisation where almost any employee can make important decisions, or where important decisions are screened by senior executives.

Instruction
I would like to be in an organisation where

	Strongly agree	Agree	Neutral	Disagree	Strongly disagree
1 A person's career ladder has several steps toward higher status and responsibility	5	4	3	2	1
2 Employees perform their work with few rules to limit their discretion	1	2	3	4	5
3 Responsibility is pushed down to employees who perform the work	1	2	3	4	5
4 Supervisors have few employees, so they work closely with each person	1	2	3	4	5
5 Senior executives make most decisions to ensure that the company is consistent in its actions	5	4	3	2	1
6 Jobs are clearly defined so there is no confusion over who is responsible for various tasks	5	4	3	2	1
7 Employees have their say on issues, but senior executives make most of the decisions	5	4	3	2	1
8 Job descriptions are broadly stated or non-existent	1	2	3	4	5
9 Everyone's work is tightly synchronised around top management operating plans	5	4	3	2	1
10 Most work is performed in teams with close supervision	5	4	3	2	1
11 Work gets done through informal discussion with co-workers rather than through formal rules	1	2	3	4	5
12 Supervisors have so many employees that they cannot watch anyone closely	5	4	3	2	1
13 Everyone has clearly understood goals, expectations and job duties	5	4	3	2	1
14 Senior executives assign overall goals, but leave daily decisions to frontline teams	1	2	3	4	5
15 Even in a large company, the CEO is only three or four levels above the lowest position	1	2	3	4	5

Scoring key and norms
Add up your scores now. Scores range in a continuum from 15 to 75 with 15 representing the maximum preference for an organic structure and 75 representing the maximum presence for a maximum mechanistic structure.

The statements are grouped under three factors.

Tall hierarchy: 1-4-10-12-15

Formalisation: 2-6-8-11-13

Centralisation: 2-5-7-9-14.

SOURCE: Adapted from S. L. McShane and M. A. Von Glinow, *Organizational Behavior* (New York: McGraw-Hill, 2003), pp. 535–6.

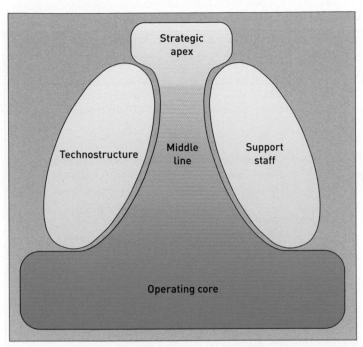

FIGURE 14.4 FIVE BASIC
PARTS OF ORGANISATIONS

SOURCE: H. Mintzberg, *Structuring of Organizations*, 1st edition,
© 1979. Reprinted by permission of Pearson Education, Inc.,
Upper Saddle River, NJ.

mentioned Mintzberg's emphasis on standardisation as co-ordination mechanism (see Table 14.2) apart from informal mutual adjustment and direct supervision. Mintzberg, however, also emphasises that there are five parts in each organisation reflecting five types of tasks. These organisation parts are (see Figure 14.4):

■ Strategic apex – managers and directors.
■ Middle line – middle line managers having responsibility for sub-elements of the organisation's activity and authority over line personnel.
■ Operating core – line personnel responsible for the core tasks of the organisation.
■ Technostructure – staff personnel analysing and taking care of the administration of the work of the line personnel, such as accountants, control functions, human resource functions and planning functions.
■ Support staff – staff functions who are not dealing with core tasks but who provide necessary support to allow the execution of the operational tasks, such as research and development, marketing, communication functions or the company's IT functions.

Each of Mintzberg's generic organisation types differs in the co-ordination mechanism that dominates and in the organisation part that is most important and most influential in the organisation. In Table 14.4, the seven types and their main features are listed.

THE ENTREPRENEURIAL ORGANISATION

The Entrepreneurial organisation is a very simple organisation type. Its small size allows informality and the company leader is able to co-ordinate, control and manage the organisation on its own. Such type is often found with start-ups, small local firms, such as the local grocery store or companies led by owner-managers. The owner-managers try to maintain control of the organisation as long as possible even when the company is growing beyond the management limits of the owner-manager. Entrepreneurial organisations are often founded to introduce a new idea or product.

Entrepreneurial organisation
a simple organisation strongly building on and driven by a leader

TABLE 14.4 MINTZBERG'S ORGANISATION TYPES

	Division of labour and key part of the organisation	Co-ordination	Hierarchy of authority
Entrepreneurial	Small, limited specialisation Strategic apex	Informal Direct supervision	Autocratic leader Centralisation
Machine	Strong specialisation Functional grouping Technostructure	Very formal Bureaucratic Rules and procedures as co-ordination – standardisation of processes	Centralised and hierarchic decision making with unity of command
Diversified	Large, product-based structure Middle line	Formal Can be bureaucratic Full range of co-ordination mechanisms but emphasis on standardisation of output	Decentralised divisions, but centralisation and hierarchy at headquarters and divisions possible
Professional	Highly specialised with very autonomous workers Operating core	Bureaucratic Standardisation of skills in combination with a few rules as co-ordination mechanisms	Low hierarchy, decision-making power resides with the professionals Decentralised
Innovative	Lower specialisation through change but with experts able to innovate Operating core	Flexible and organic Co-ordination in formal and informal teams and through liaison personnel. Informally – mutual adjustment	Decentralised with low levels of hierarchy Unity of command is violated
Missionary	Loosely organised small units, tasks and roles are clear and focused through the clarity of the mission	Co-ordination by standardisation of values and norms and often also strict explicit rules	Centralisation through charismatic leader and central mission but decentralisation in daily operations
Political	Different work deviations are possible but the choice will be political	Formal and mainly informal co-ordination by power	Decentralisation through politicking Enforcing or destroying hierarchy of authority

SOURCE: Based on H. Mintzberg, *Mintzberg on Management* (New York: The Free Press, 1989).

A British biological firm from Surrey came up with an environmentally friendly way to produce paper based on straw. Sue Riddlestone, a former nurse and mother of three children, founded seven years ago BioRegional MiniMills. 'By now, we have founded an ecological village where we produce our own environmental friendly charcoal and where we concentrate on our environmental friendly production of paper', explains Sue. Worldwide, there are about 9000 paper and cardboard producers and the demand for paper is still increasing yearly. Most of these producers are multinationals, leaving no space for the small companies. The new production method will allow small independent paper producers to compete with the big guys in the market.[45]

THE MACHINE ORGANISATION

The **Machine organisation** described by Mintzberg equals the mechanic organisation type of Burns and Stalker. It is a type found in larger organisations, often active in mass production. Control is the key word in this organisation and efficiency dominates effectiveness.

Recent research in the Netherlands on the structure of small and medium-sized Dutch companies indicated to what extent hierarchy, departmentalisation, specialisation, centralisation, standardisation and the different co-ordination types were used in these small companies with less than 100 employees.[46] There was quite some variation in the levels of each of these structural elements, allowing the researchers to identify nine different types of small companies. A majority of these companies were similar to or small variations of Mintzberg's entrepreneurial type, but only a small part are real simple organisation forms. Furthermore, 40 per cent of these small companies were machine bureaucracies although less complex than the larger firms where machine organisations are mostly found.

> **Machine organisation** well-structured, often bureaucratic organisation oriented towards efficiency

THE DIVERSIFIED ORGANISATION

The **Diversified organisation** type or also called divisionalised organisation arose because of companies that expanded their business through take-overs, exploiting new markets and products, acting globally or multinationally. These companies are always large with a diverse range of products or markets often unrelated. The size and diversification makes it hardly possible to integrate the business fully. Therefore, the organisation is divided in different semi-autonomous business units based on product, market or geography. The divisions are often large companies that can exist independently. This organisation distinguishes itself from other organisation types by the existence of headquarters that control business units and take over some divisions' support functions. Headquarters are heavily occupied in developing control structures for the divisions. The divisions themselves have generally few contacts with each other.

> **Diversified organisation** large organisations with headquarters and semi-autonomous units

> " The European company Agfa Gevaert, active in the image and photo business, is an example of a divisionalised company. The operational divisions are: Graphic systems, HealthCare, Consumer Imaging and Speciality products. There are four regional sales divisions. Although the divisions are distinctive in products and customers, this divisionalised organisation can gain synergies through sales and research and development. However, the CEO, Ludo Verhoeven, explains that within the sales divisions there were too many national support units. 'Therefore, we have centralised some of these, such as IT which is now grouped for each sales division instead of for each country in these divisions.'[47] Typical for divisionalised organisations is that they are often restructuring their portfolio of businesses. New business are sold, acquired, integrated with existing businesses or split off. The company acquired Lastra recently. Lastra is an Italian manufacturer of plates, related chemicals and equipment for the offset printing industry. 'Lastra is a perfect fit for Agfa', said Albert Follens, member of the Board of Management and General Manager Graphic Systems. 'The combination of the Lastra and Agfa strengths will result in tangible benefits for all the customers of both companies. The envisioned strategy is to keep the Lastra Group's brands and its dealer network in place. In addition, this acquisition will strengthen our cost leadership in printing plates, generating important revenue and cost synergies.'[48] "

THE PROFESSIONAL ORGANISATION

Universities are an example of **Professional organisations**. The professionals work in a functional structure but independently and with large decision-making power. Paradoxically, this does not lead to an informal flexible structure but to a kind of bureaucratic organisation with strict rules and procedures developed by the professionals themselves to control the highly skilled and complex tasks. Flexibility is low but the tasks are stable and even often routine, allowing standardisation. There is very low co-operation and integration among the different groups of professionals. This leads to lack of innovation and a blinkered outlook when it comes to interprofessional work. The difficulty in realising interdisciplinary research in universities is a consequence of the lack of integration in these kind of structures. A report of the UK research council in May 2000 based on visits to 13 UK universities indicated the need for, but also the barriers against, interdisciplinary research. The barriers mentioned are: being too busy to meet new collaborators, an absence of mechanisms for finding collaborators in home university or elsewhere; the need to learn a 'new language' to work across

> **Professional organisation** decentralised organisation with professionals doing highly skilled work

disciplines; strong preconceptions about another discipline; concern about the ability to find a suitably qualified RA; concern about not being given recognition by either discipline, which would hinder career progression; and, pressure to publish not allowing time to establish collaborations or learn a new language.[49]

THE INNOVATIVE ORGANISATION

Innovative organisation
often young and flexible organisation oriented towards innovation

The **Innovative organisation** is organic and therefore opposite to the more bureaucratic forms just mentioned. Young R&D firms are characterised by this organisation type. The decentralisation, teamwork, limited authority, often matrix structure, limited rules, procedures and standardisation and the bottom-up decision making provide this organisation with the necessary flexibility and open character to be innovative and highly adaptable. However, efficiency is low and it is hard to keep control of the organisation.

THE MISSIONARY ORGANISATION

Missionary organisation
an organisation bound together by a clear mission and strong shared values among its members

A **Missionary organisation** type is characterised by its very clear and strong mission in which the organisational members have strong beliefs. Médecins Sans Frontières is one example, but missionary organisations do also exist in the profit sector. However, this organisation type in the profit sector is often combined with other types, such as entrepreneurial or machine type. The values, norms and mission rule the organisation, enforced by a charismatic leader who keeps the mission and stories alive.

Missionary organisations are decentralised in their operations but there is strong centralisation through the values and leadership that binds the members of the organisation and make sure tasks are co-ordinated. Many missionary organisations are not-for profit often with religious or ideological goals.

> The Animal Liberation Front (ALF) has all the characteristics of a missionary organisation. The mission (liberating all animals) is clear and binds the worldwide branches. It is a loosely coupled network of sympathisers and sometimes violent commandos. Many of the people calling themselves members of ALF do not know each other and there is no formal system to bring them in contact, but when an action has to take place their common mission seems to bring them together in temporary teams. The only formal communication network is the Internet making it easy for people with the same mission to form one group. Although the ALF is a loose network, it has headquarters in London. In the early years of the organisation (mid 1960s and 1970s) a few activists became heroes by their actions and often arrests followed. Hero stories are an important way to achieve integration in these kinds of organisations.[50]

THE POLITICAL ORGANISATION

Political organisation
an organisation in which power is illegitimate resulting in disintegration and conflict

A **Political organisation** is dominated by power and organisational politics (see also Chapter 13). Organisational politics can be so dominant that it rules out all other structural features. Political manoeuvring will then also become the only co-ordination mechanism. The same goes for decision making, as the hierarchical power is undermined by playing politics. Some organisations, however, can be politicised without being fully dominated by organisational politics. Thus, the political organisation is often found in combination with one of the other organisation types, such as the machine organisation. Political intrigue thus destabilises the working of these organisation types.

New organisation types

Over the past decades several new organisation types have arisen. All of the more recent forms are less hierarchical than the classic forms and try to achieve more flexibility in their structures. In the 1990s there were voices in the management literature whispering that small lean and mean innovative firms can easily beat the big multinational corporations.[51] Large corporations try to prevent this from happening by creating divisions or subsidiaries which were smaller, leaner and more innovative. Alternatives to make the whole organisation leaner are: more decentralisation, focus on core competencies and products only, strategic alliances and network forms to create more flexibility. Flexibility can focus on many dimensions in the organisation, such as in the number of employees, divisions, products, markets, wages, costs, ability to quickly redefine tasks and functions, flexibility in production and the organisational form. The latter refers to new ways of grouping units and new kinds of alliances and co-operation between organisations. In these new forms, work division and co-ordination will require new mechanisms and is generally harder to achieve in a flexible organisation form. The relentless process of disembedding and recombining social relations and interactions in space and time makes the difference between the new organisations and their traditional counterparts.[52] However, flexibility is a threat to the integration of the organisation.[53] Strong integration cannot be combined with leanness.

New organisation types are also being developed because of a need to deal with more complexity. The classic organisation types are fairly simple and often unable to capture the complexity of business practices.[54] Choices between different organisational forms or between centralisation and decentralisation are not that straightforward in a complex business environment. However, more complex forms, such as the matrix structure, seem to complicate the working of the organisation even more.

Research findings and practical implications

A group of European researchers worked on a research project 'Organizing for the 21st Century' to see whether new forms of competition and rapid change lead to new forms of organising.[55] Research was done in the UK, Spain, France, Switzerland, the Netherlands, Sweden, Germany and Italy. Traditional forms are based on division and differentiation, while new forms are based on combination and integration – for example, by integrating line and staff functions, combining strategy formulation and implementation, downsizing and delayering structures and the use of multifunctional teams and open communication across hierarchical levels. In general, new forms use more horizontal co-ordination mechanisms and flexible work assignments leading to decision making at lower levels in the organisation. Furthermore, norms, trust, reputation, self-discipline and even friendship are new integration mechanisms.

Several Dutch researchers studied new organisation forms.[56] They also found horizontal networking, flexibility and dynamism as the new ways to organise. Van den Bosch stresses that organisational forms co-evolve with the environment and the combinative capabilities. The latter consist of systems capabilities (systems, procedures), social capabilities (norms, values and internal social relationships) and co-ordination capabilities (co-ordination mechanisms).

There is an evolution in organisational forms. This evolution is also caused by fashion in management beliefs.[57] Innovations in organisational forms emerge in one company and, when successful, spread to other companies. However, variation in the specific organisational contexts, sectors, markets and countries ensures that not all companies adapt the same form and this contextual variation is a continuous source of evolution in organisational forms.

New-style versus old-style organisations

Organisation theorists Jay R. Galbraith and Edward E. Lawler III have called for a 'new logic of organising'.[58] They recommend a whole new set of adjectives to describe organisations (see Table 14.5).

TABLE 14.5 PROFILES OF NEW-STYLE AND OLD-STYLE ORGANISATIONS

New	Old
Dynamic, learning	Stable
Information rich	Information is scarce
Global	Local
Small and large	Large
Product/customer oriented	Functional
Skills oriented	Job oriented
Team oriented	Individual oriented
Involvement oriented	Command/control oriented
Lateral/networked	Hierarchical
Customer oriented	Job requirements oriented

SOURCE: J. R. Galbraith and E. E. Lawler III, 'Effective Organizations: Using the New Logic of Organizing', p. 298 in *Organizing for the Future: The New Logic for Managing Complex Organizations*, eds J. R. Galbraith, E. E. Lawler III and Associates. Copyright 1993 Jossey-Bass Inc. Publishers. Reprinted by permission of Jossey-Bass, Inc., a subsidiary of John Wiley & Sons, Inc.

FIGURE 14.5 THE SHAPE OF TOMORROW'S ORGANISATIONS

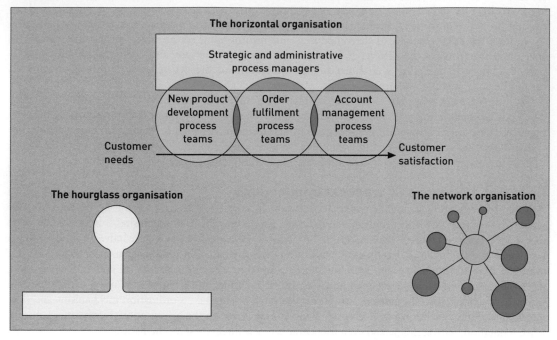

Traditional pyramid-shaped (or strongly hierarchical) organisations, conforming to the old-style pattern, tend to be too slow and inflexible today. Leaner, more organic organisations are needed to accommodate today's strategic balancing act between cost, quality and speed. They are customer focused, dedicated to continuous improvement and learning, and structured around teams. These qualities, along with computerised information technology, will, it is hoped, enable big organisations to mimic the speed and flexibility of small organisations.

The shape of the newest organisation types

Figure 14.5 illustrates three radical departures from the traditional pyramid-shaped organisation. Each is the logical result of various trends that are evident today. Three other types are the virtual organisation, the project organisation and the platform organisation. We have exaggerated these new organisations for instructional purposes. Combinations of these new organisation types with classic more hierarchical forms are more likely to be found in our existing organisations. Let us look at some of the newest organisations types. (Please note that these characterisations are not intended to be final answers. We simply seek to stimulate thoughtful debate.)

HORIZONTAL ORGANISATIONS

Despite the fact that re-engineering became synonymous with huge redundancies and has been called a passing fad, it is likely to have a lasting effect on organisation design. Namely, it helped refine the concept of a horizontally oriented organisation. Unlike traditional, vertically oriented organisations with functional units such as production, marketing and finance, **Horizontal organisations** are flat and built around core processes aimed at satisfying customers.

    Rather than focusing single-mindedly on financial objectives or functional goals, the horizontal organisation emphasises customer satisfaction. Work is simplified and hierarchy flattened by combining related tasks – for example, an account-management process that subsumes the sales, billing and service functions – and eliminating work that does not add value. Information zips along an internal superhighway: The knowledge worker analyses it, and technology moves it quickly across the corporation instead of up and down, speeding up and improving decision-making.

    Okay, so some of this is derivative; the obsession with process, for example, dates back to Total Quality Management. Part of the beauty of the horizontal corporation is that it distils much of what

Horizontal organisation organisations with few hierarchical levels, built around core processes

we know about what works in managing today. Its advocates call it an actionable model – jargon for a plan you can work with – that allows companies to use ideas like teams, supplier–customer integration, and empowerment in ways that reinforce each other. A key virtue is that the horizontal corporation is the kind of company a customer would design. In most cases, a horizontal organisation requires some employees to be organised functionally where their expertise is considered critical, as in human resources or finance. But those departments are often pared down and judiciously melded into a design where the real authority runs along process lines.[59]

What is it like to work in a horizontal organisation?[60] It is a lot more interesting than traditional bureaucracies with their functional ghettos. Most employees are close to the customer (both internal and external) – asking questions, getting feedback, and jointly solving problems. Constant challenges come from being on cross-functional teams where co-workers with different technical specialties work side-by-side on projects. Sometimes people will find themselves dividing their time between several projects. Blurred and conflicting lines of authority break the traditional unity-of-command principle. Project goals and deadlines tend to replace the traditional supervisor role. Training in both technical and teamwork skills are a top priority. Multiskilled employees at all levels will find themselves working on different teams and various projects during the year. Paradoxically, self-starters and team players will thrive. Because of the flatness of the organisation, lateral transfers are more common than traditional vertical promotions. This might be a source of discontent for many of those who want to move upward. Constant change will take its toll in terms of interpersonal conflict, personal stress and burnout. Furthermore skill-based pay complements pay-for-performance (see Chapter 6).

> OgilvyOne, the biggest world wide direct-marketing companies, changed its structure to be more horizontal. The company was very fragmented with autonomous divisions and characterised by internal competition, making it hard to issue world-wide campaigns. The need for internal world-wide co-operation to serve large customers, demanded the changes. This integration was not achieved by large centralisation but by a horizontal structure where integration is obtained through a common knowledge database, which was a powerful source of information on end-customer behaviour. Their knowledge system was called Truffles, referring to pigs looking for truffles, like OgilvyOne looks for knowledge. The knowledge base was accompanied with the creation of a very co-operative culture where friendship is most important. OgilvyOne also likes to compare oneself with a jazz band instead of an orchestra, because the company needs to be lean and flexible, able to improvise and react on its audience. [61]

HOURGLASS ORGANISATIONS

The **Hourglass organisation** gets its name from the organisation's pinched middle. Thanks to modern information technology, a relatively small executive group is able to co-ordinate the efforts of numerous operating personnel who make goods or render services.[62] Multiple and broad layers of middle managers who served as conduits for information in old-style organisations are unnecessary in hourglass organisations. Competition for promotions among operating personnel is intense because of the restricted hierarchy. Lateral transfers are more common. Management will compensate for the lack of promotion opportunities with job rotation, skill training and pay-for-performance.

What few middle managers there are will be cross-functional problem-solvers who also possess a number of technical skills. The potential for alienation between the executive elite and those at the base of the hourglass is great, thus giving trade unions an excellent growth opportunity.

NETWORK ORGANISATIONS

A **Network organisation** is similar to horizontal organisations in being very flat. The linkages among the groups in the organisation are reciprocal communication patterns instead of hierarchical authority relationships (see Chapter 8).[63] The networks are formed around similar interests, tasks, products, know-how or any other goal to work together.

Hourglass organisation
an organisation with a very limited number of middle managers

Network organisation
an organisation structured around reciprocal communication patterns between groups of people

> Visa, the world-wide electronic payment company, is a clear example of a network organisation. The company is jointly owned by 21000 member financial institutions, which are also its intermediate customers selling the cards to their customers. Visa, thus, creates a network that bounds the financial institutions world-wide.[64]

There exist informal networks in all types of organisations, even in the very bureaucratic ones, but a real network organisation is typified by the absence of unidirectional authority relationships and the presence of a complex web of relationships allowing direct, fast and flexible communication. In such network organisation the boundaries of the organisation become vague. The people involved in the internal organisational networks are also involved in networks with customers, suppliers, profession related networks, non-professional private networks and networks with other (even competing) companies. The networks cross the traditional organisation boundaries, allowing more intense and flexible inter-organisational co-operation. The groups in the network organisation are loosely coupled instead of tied in a formal structure. However, there is no anarchy in the network organisation. There is self-organisation, self-control and self-responsibility in the network. In the network organisation, trust and social control exist as forms of informal integration of the tasks. Some people take a facilitating role in the network and safeguard the integration of the tasks. Burt[65] mentions structural holes to indicate the people that have a boundary spanning role between networks. Structural holes exist when two networks which are not related are nevertheless connected by one member who plays a brokerage role in connecting two separate networks. Burt uses the concept 'structural holes' to explain the power and advantage that brokers have when they can link two separate networks. Take for example a manager who changes from one company to another, allowing that manager to link his previous network developed as manager of the first company with his newly developed network as manager in the second company. By bridging the two networks, a 'structural hole' exists and the manager can benefit from opportunities generated through linking the two networks.

VIRTUAL ORGANISATIONS

Virtual organisations geographically dispersed people accomplishing tasks together thanks to modern information technology

Like virtual teams, discussed in Chapter 10, modern information technology allows people in **Virtual organisations** to accomplish something despite being geographically dispersed.[66] Instead of relying heavily on face-to-face meetings, as before, members of virtual organisations send email and voicemail messages, exchange project information over the Internet, and convene videoconferences with far-flung participants. In addition, cellular phones have made the dream of 'doing business from the beach' a reality!

This disconnection between work and location is causing managers to question traditional assumptions about centralised offices and factories. Why keep offices for people who are never there because they are out finding and helping customers? Why have a factory when it is less expensive to contract out the work? Indeed, many so-called virtual organisations are really a network of several individuals or organisations hooked together contractually and electronically. A prime example is the Australian company OnLine English:[67]

> How does an academic from a non-English speaking background, wishing to publish in an English language international journal, find a service to edit his or her English? Ideally, they would have immediate access to a native speaker specialist editor with high level qualifications in their particular field. OnLine English (OLE) was designed as a virtual organisation to address this need. Now, researchers based anywhere on the globe have immediate access to a team of specialist editors.
>
> Highly skilled editors with PhDs, who are keen to work at short notice with rapid turn-around times, are rare. Using the Internet, OLE has been able to recruit from the whole of Australia to form a lively network of 30+ such individuals. Running a highly responsive service 24 hours a day, 365 days a year, once required large infrastructure costs. OLE has minimised such costs by creating a virtual infrastructure, co-ordinated from several home offices. Delivering a service with every document team-checked plus quality control and negotiation with the client once required considerable time and face-to-face meetings. OLE has developed online protocols with feedback procedures and quality control that enable consultants living thousands of kilometres apart to collaborate closely and rapidly. On any job, each team member sees exactly what other team members are contributing.

> Constant improvement and common standards are achieved through every job being incrementally checked and improved. These outcomes are jointly managed. The team operates within a clear framework. All communication is moderated by the manager. There is no off-task chatter. OLE believes that it has maximized the efficiency of the input of high level skills by team members. Those who like to work flexibly and intensively find this an attractive work environment. The outcome is that the customer benefits from having his or her manuscript rapidly edited into English ready for international publication. The fact that the service was delivered by an editing team in another part of the world, with most of the team never meeting face-to-face, is irrelevant. What is important to the client is the quality of the service delivery and of the product.[67]

Here is how we envision life in the emerging virtual organisations and organisational networks. Things are very interesting and profitable for the elite core of entrepreneurs and engineers who hit on the right business formula. Turnover among the financial and information 'have nots' – data entry, customer service, and production employees – are high because of glaring inequities and limited opportunities for personal fulfilment and growth. Telecommuters who work from home feel liberated and empowered (and sometimes lonely) (see Chapter 8).

Commitment, trust and loyalty could erode badly if managers do not heed this caution by Charles Handy, the British management expert. According to Handy: 'A shared commitment still requires personal contact to make the commitment feel real. Paradoxically, the more virtual an organisation becomes the more its people need to meet in person.'[68]

Independent contractors, both individuals and organisations, participate in many different organisational networks and thus have diluted loyalty to any single one. Substandard working conditions and low pay at some smaller contractors make them little more than Internet-age sweat shops. Companies living from one contract to another offer little in the way of job security and benefits. Opportunities to start new businesses are numerous but prolonged success could prove elusive at Internet speed.

The only certainty about these organisations is they produce a lot of surprises. Only flexible, adaptable people who see problems as opportunities, are self-starters capable of teamwork, and are committed to life-long learning are able to handle whatever comes their way.

PROJECT ORGANISATIONS

Some organisations have very particular activities that make the previously mentioned organisation types unsuitable. Organisations that have a few major large tasks, such as construction firms building bridges over motorways, need to adopt a project-organisation type. All organisational resources are grouped around the few projects. Each time a project stops or starts, the resources, such as the workers, need to be regrouped. There are project leaders and support staff for the administration of the projects. Traditional hierarchical layers and fixed structures would block the flexibility needed to do the project. The projects are often also executed at the site of the customer or the final destination of the goods produced. Hence, temporary offices (mostly office containers) are placed on the construction sites where engineers find their temporary bases. Teamwork in a project organisation is not only a way to co-ordinate interfunctionally but dominates the working of the organisation, hence, also the work deviation and decision making. In **Project organisations** the project groups work semi-autonomously resulting in a decentralised form of decision making. The different project groups are loosely coupled and form a network of project groups.

Parts of organisations often have a project structure while the rest of the company has a more functional one. The development departments of large companies mostly have this project structure, such as in Volvo, the Swedish car manufacturer. After failed attempts to merge or strongly co-operate with Renault, Volvo urgently needed to redesign one of its old car models. A project team was assigned to this task:

Project organisation
an organisation consisting of temporarily semi-autonomous project groups

> A project manager responsible for the technical part said:
> 'In a project like this, the network of contacts is very important, if not the most important thing. The pure design issues were not very complicated, what was important was to know what to design, and to understand how it would work in the system.'

> " A manager of a sub-project indicated: 'It's all about organisation and communication and to get people see what's happening in production. Designers are good at many things but not on aspects related to the production process. Everyone thinks their part is working well but it's all about verification. This means that we need to constantly discuss possible alternatives of action. For instance, which parts to change is dependent on the lead-time of each part. Whether a certain part is considered verified is thus very much a question of what other teams have done.'[69] "

PLATFORM ORGANISATION TYPE

Platform organisation combines the new flexible types with the more classic organisation types

Finally, the **Platform organisation** combines the new flexible types with the more classic organisation types.[70] It is a structure typically used in Japanese organisations with a hierarchical authority top structure, combined with flexible teams and a strong middle management that plays an important role in the integration of the organisation and combining the vertical and horizontal structure. Teams and autonomy should be complemented with hierarchical layers who co-ordinate the more routinely and stable parts of the activities in the organisation. The teams are then more loosely coupled and flexible in their tasks and composition. Systems and hierarchy are used to exploit efficiently innovations and new knowledge, developed in these teams. Furthermore, hierarchy needs to set the rules and boundaries for the teamwork. Another precaution in the use of only horizontal organisations and self-regulation is based on the fact that middle management plays an important role in the organisation. This role is not substituted with an alternative in horizontal organisations. Middle managers translate goals in practical objectives, coach employees, communicate between units, take ad hoc decisions, solve conflicts, co-ordinate and plan tasks, measure output and provide expertise.[71] Providing expertise can be important in organisations where middle managers are former workers of the departments they are managing. Hierarchy should serve the organisation by transmitting information and knowledge in the organisation.

Learning outcomes: Summary of key terms

1 Describe the four characteristics common to all organisations

They are co-ordination of effort (achieved through policies and rules, but also through standardisation and lateral mechanisms), a common goal (a collective purpose), division of labour (people performing separate but related tasks, choosing the right kind of departmentalisation) and a hierarchy of authority (the chain of command).

2 Describe the relationship between differentiation and integration in organisations

Harvard researchers Lawrence and Lorsch found that successful organisations achieved a proper balance between the two opposing structural forces of differentiation and integration. Differentiation forces the organisation apart. Through a variety of mechanisms – including hierarchy, rules, teams and liaisons – integration draws the organisation together.

3 Describe the organisation's parts and the way tasks can be grouped

Mintzberg identified five parts that can be found in all kind of organisations (strategic apex, middle line, operating core, technostructure, support staff). To group different tasks, organisations can choose between functional, product, market or project-based grouping, geographical groups and the matrix form.

4 Explain the different co-ordination mechanisms an organisation can use

Galbraith and Mintzberg identified a range of integration mechanisms which can be horizontal (integrators and formal groups), vertical (hierarchy, rules and procedures), informal (informal groups) or based on standardisation (standardisation of work, skills, output and norms).

5 Define and briefly explain the practical significance of centralisation and decentralisation

Because key decisions are made at the top of centralised organisations, they tend to be tightly controlled. In decentralised organisations, employees at lower levels are empowered to make important decisions. Contingency design calls for a proper balance.

6 Discuss the bureaucratic organisation

Weber proposed bureaucratic and mechanically working structures as the ideal way to create an efficient organisation. The extreme use of rules and procedures and the impersonal character of these rules conflict human nature resulting in dysfunctional behaviour. This might make a bureaucratic organisation highly inefficient.

7 Discuss Burns and Stalker's findings regarding mechanistic and organic organisations

British researchers Burns and Stalker found that mechanistic (bureaucratic, centralised) organisations tended to be effective in stable situations. In unstable situations, organic (flexible, decentralised) organisations were more effective. These findings underscored the need for a contingency approach to organisation design.

8 Describe the seven organisation types of Mintzberg and discuss how they differ in the structural elements

The seven types are: entrepreneurial, machine, diversified, professional, innovative, missionary and political. These types differ in the kind of departmentalisation and the level of specialisation. They also differ in the co-ordination mechanisms used and the extent to which they have bureaucratic characteristics. The level of centralisation and decentralisation is another element that differentiates Mintzberg's seven types.

9 Discuss why new organisational forms developed and what the main differences are with the classic forms

There is a need for more flexibility, use of lateral co-ordination and organisations that can adapt very fast. The classic organisation types are too hierarchical, inflexible and seem to be able to operate only in stable environments requiring hardly any changing of the tasks and way of working.

10 Describe horizontal, hourglass, and virtual organisations

Horizontal organisations are flat structures built around core processes aimed at identifying and satisfying customer needs. Cross-functional teams and empowerment are central to horizontal organisations. Hourglass organisations have a small executive level, a short and narrow middle-management level (because information technology links the top and bottom levels), and a broad base of operating personnel. Virtual organisations are normally families of interdependent companies. They are contractual and fluid in nature.

Review questions

1 How many organisations directly affect your life today? List as many as you can.
2 What would an organisation chart of your current (or last) place of employment look like? Does the chart you have drawn reveal the hierarchy (chain of command), division of labour, span of control, and line–staff distinctions? Does it reveal anything else? Explain.
3 What is wrong with an organisation having too much differentiation and too little integration?
4 What are the advantages and disadvantages of more horizontal instead of vertical co-ordination?

5 How can an organisation be efficient and well organised without the pitfalls of the bureaucratic organisation?

6 If organic organisations are popular with most employees, *why* can't all organisations be structured in an organic fashion?

7 Can you recognise the different parts in your organisation (Mintzberg's organisation parts)?

8 Think of an existing example for each of Mintzberg's organisation types.

9 What are the disadvantages of many of the new organisational forms?

10 Which of the new organisational forms is most used in real business life today? Why?

Personal awareness and growth exercise

Organisation design field study

Objectives

1 To get out into the field and talk to a practising manager about organisational structure.

2 To increase your understanding of the important distinction between mechanistic and organic organisations.

3 To broaden your knowledge of the differences between organisational forms and the evolution in those forms.

Introduction

A good *way* to test the validity of what you have just read about organisation design is to interview a practising manager. (*Note:* If you are a manager, simply complete the questionnaire yourself.)

Instructions

Your objective is to interview a manager about aspects of organisational structure, environmental uncertainty and organisational effectiveness. A manager is defined as anyone who supervises other people in an organisational setting. The organisation may be small or large and for-profit or not-for profit. Higher-level managers are preferred but middle managers and first-line supervisors are acceptable. If you interview a lower-level manager, be sure to remind him or her that you want a description of the overall organisation, not just an isolated subunit. Your interview will centre on the adaptation of Table 14.3, as discussed below.

When conducting your interview, be sure to explain to the manager what you are trying to accomplish. But assure the manager that his or her name will not be mentioned in lecture or group discussions or any written projects. Try to take brief notes during the interview for later reference.

Questionnaire

The following questionnaire, adapted from Table 14.3, will help you determine if the manager's organisation is relatively mechanistic or relatively organic in structure. *Note:* For items 1 and 2 on the following questionnaire, ask the manager to respond in terms of the average non-managerial employee. (Circle one number for each item.)

Characteristics

1	Task definition and knowledge required	Narrow; technical	1	2	3	4	5	6	7	Broad; general
2	Link between individual's contribution and organisation purpose	Vague or indirect	1	2	3	4	5	6	7	Clear or direct
3	Task flexibility	Rigid; routine	1	2	3	4	5	6	7	Flexible; varied

			1 2 3 4 5 6 7	
4	Specification of techniques, obligations and rights	Specific	1 2 3 4 5 6 7	General
5	Degree of hierarchical control	High	1 2 3 4 5 6 7	Low (self-control emphasised)
6	Primary communication pattern	Top-down	1 2 3 4 5 6 7	Lateral (between peers)
7	Primary decision-making style	Authoritarian	1 2 3 4 5 6 7	Democratic; participative
8	Emphasis on obedience and loyalty	High	1 2 3 4 5 6 7	Low

Total score = _____

Questions for discussion

1 Using the following norms, was the manager's organisation relatively mechanistic or organic?

8–24 = Relatively mechanistic

25–39 = Mixed

40–56 = Relatively organic

2 Which of all organisational forms discussed in this chapter comes closest to the manager's organisation?

Group exercise

Analysing a professional organisation

Objectives

1 To continue developing your group interaction and teamwork skills.

2 To understand better how the abstract structural elements and organisational forms are used in a real situation.

3 To conduct an audit of an existing organisation and understand how hard the choices related to organisation structure are.

4 To establish priorities, deal with conflicting demands and consider trade-offs for modern managers.

Introduction

Choices about division of labour, co-ordination and hierarchy are much more complex in real life, even when the common goals are very clear. This exercise shows you how hard it is to apply this theory into practice.

It requires a team meeting of about one hour, several interviews, another meeting to bring the results together and a general class discussion for one hour. Total time required for this exercise is about one day.

Instructions

Your lecturer will randomly assign you to teams with about three members each. There needs to be at least four teams. In case there are more teams, the task of each team can be further split up.

1 Select your college or university as the case setting, but determine in advance which part you will audit. You might want to study the whole university or only the management department. It is most realistic to limit the exercise to one department if this exercise needs to be accomplished in one day.

2 Discuss with your instructor who you can interview. It might be necessary that your lecturer informs a few people in the organisation about the fact that students will bring them a short visit and ask some questions about the structure of their organisation.

It is the purpose to know for each of the topics discussed in this chapter how they are in the university or college. Start with a team brainstorming session to decide who will ask the questions and what questions you need to ask to obtain the required information. Each interview can be very brief, about 15 minutes. You can ask any employee in the organisation but you will need to interview several people (between 3 and 10, depending on the size of the organisation) to have a good view on the working of the organisation. Some interviewed might give you conflicting answers. Try to find out why and try to come to a consensus about each of the elements that you analyse.

The topics for the groups are:

Group 1: Identify the different groups in the organisation (i.e. management, middle managers, operating line personnel, supporting staff and technostructure staff) and the level of specialisation

Group 2: Determine the division in decision-making tasks (i.e. hierarchy of authority, unity of command, span of control, level of centralisation)

Group 3: How do people work together to execute common tasks (i.e. which co-ordination mechanisms are used) and what is the level of formalisation?

Group 4: Look at Table 14.5 and try to discover whether the organisation is more the old or the new type. Ask whether the organisation has enough flexibility.

For each group: Ask if they are happy with the current state of these structural elements and why? Would they like to change anything?

Each group discusses its results and summarises the answers. Next, all groups bring their answers together by briefly presenting it to the other groups in the classroom. Finally, during the general class discussion, try to label the organisation using Mintzberg's types. Discuss also if this organisation has a good structure or if things can or should be changed.

Internet exercise

This chapter discusses elements of structure, such as departmentalisation, hierarchy, organisation charts, etc. These elements can be recognised in many of today's organisations. Organisations tend to describe and make their structure public so that the public knows who is doing what tasks in the organisation and who one should contact in the organisation for information. Take for example a university website. Surf to www.mcgraw-hill.co.uk/textbooks/buelens for suggestions and further instructions.

Notes

1 Excerpted from I. Grugulis and A. Wilkinson, 'Managing Culture at British Airways: Hype, Hope and Reality', *Long Range Planning*, April 2002, pp. 179–94.

2 See P. F. Drucker, 'The New Society of Organizations', *Harvard Business Review*, September–October 1992, pp. 95–104; J. R. Galbraith, E. E. Lawler III, and Associates, *Organizing for the Future: The New Logic for Managing Complex Organizations* (San Francisco, CA: Jossey-Bass, 1993); and R. W. Oliver, *The Shape of Things to Come: Seven Imperatives for Winning in the New World of Business* (New York: McGraw-Hill, 1999).

3 C. I. Barnard, *The Functions of the Executive* (Cambridge, MA: Harvard University Press, 1938), p. 73. Also see M. C. Suchman, 'Managing Legitimacy: Strategic and Institutional Approaches', *Academy of Management Review*, July 1995, pp. 571–610.

4 Drawn from E. H. Schein, *Organizational Psychology, third edition* (Englewood Cliffs, NJ: Prentice-Hall, 1980), pp. 12–15.

5 For interesting and instructive insights about organisation structure, see G. Morgan, *Images of Organization* (Newbury Park, CA: Sage, 1986); G. Morgan, *Creative Organization Theory: A Resource Book* (Newbury Park, CA: Sage, 1989); G. Hofstede, 'An American in Paris: The Influence of Nationality on Organization Theories', *Organization Studies*, no. 3, 1996, pp. 525–37; and J. G. March, 'Continuity and Change in Theories of Organizational Action', *Administrative Science Quarterly*, June 1996, pp. 278–87.

6 W. R. Scott, *Institutions and Organizations, second edition* (Englewood Cliffs, NJ: Prentice-Hall, 1987).

7 H. Mintzberg, *The Structuring of Organizations* (Englewood Cliffs, NJ: Prentice Hall, 1979), p. 2.

8 Translated from J. Bohets, 'India wil komend arbeidstekort in hoogontwikkelde landen verhelpen', *De Standaard*, 18 March 2004, p. 54.

9 P. R. Lawrence and J. W. Lorsch, *Organization and Environment* (Homewood, IL: Richard D. Irwin, 1967), p. 157.

10 Pooled, sequential and reciprocal integration are discussed in J. W. Lorsch, 'Organization Design: A Situational Perspective', *Organizational Dynamics*, Autumn 1977, pp. 2–14. Also see J. E. Ettlie and E. M. Reza, 'Organizational Integration and Process Innovation', *Academy of Management Journal*, October 1992, pp. 795–827; and A. L. Patti and J. P. Gilbert, 'Collocating New Product Development Teams: Why, When, Where, and How?', *Business Horizons*, November–December 1997, pp. 59–64.

11 See B. Dumaine, 'Ability to Innovate', *Fortune*, 29 January 1990, pp. 43, 46. For good readings on innovation and technology, see O. Port, 'Getting to "Eureka!"', *Business Week*, 10 November 1997, pp. 72–5; J. W. Gurley, 'Got a Good Idea? Better Think Twice', *Fortune*, 7 December 1998, pp. 215–16; J. C. McCune, 'The Technology Treadmill', *Management Review*, December 1998, pp. 10–12; and L. Yates and P. Skarzynski, 'How Do Companies Get to the Future First?', *Management Review*, January 1999, pp. 16–22.

12 H. Simon, *Administrative Behavior* (New York: The Free Press, 1945), p. 368.

13 http://www.nationmaster.com/encyclopedia/Chunnel

14 J. Brogan, 'Distinguishing Functions', *Industrial Engineer*, April 2003, pp. 32–5.

15 M. Koslowsky, 'Staff/Line Distinctions in Job and Organizational Commitment', *Journal of Occupational Psychology*, June 1990, pp. 167–73.

16 See T. A. Kochan, R. D. Lansbury and J. P. MacDuffie, *After Lean Production: Evolving Employment Practices in the World Auto Industry* (Ithaca, NY: Cornell University Press, 1997), p. 349.

17 See http://www.denys.be for explanations about their organisation and projects.

18 See http://www.btplc.com/Thegroup/Companyprofile/Groupbusinesses/Principalactivities.htm and translated from 'Reorganisatie BT toont buitenwereld groeikansen', *De Tijd*, 14 April 2000.

19 See S. M. Davis and P. R. Lawrence, 'Problems of Matrix Organizations', *Harvard Business Review*, May–June 1978; S. M. Davis and P. R. Lawrence, *Matrix* (Reading, MA: Addison-Wesley, 1977); and M. Goold and A. Campbell, 'Structured Networks: Towards the Well-Designed Matrix', *Long Range Planning*, October 2003, pp. 427–39.

20 M. Goold and A. Campbell, 'Structured Networks: Towards the Well-Designed Matrix', *Long Range Planning*, October 2003, pp. 427–39.

21 For an interesting historical perspective of hierarchy, see P. Miller and T. O'Leary, 'Hierarchies and American Ideals, 1900–1940', *Academy of Management Review*, April 1989, pp. 250–65.

22 For related research, see S. Finkelstein and R. A. D'Aveni, 'CEO Duality as a Double-Edged Sword: How Boards of Directors Balance Entrenchment Avoidance and Unity of Command', *Academy of Management Journal*, October 1994, pp. 1079–1108.

23 Translated from H. Fischer, 'Die Artillerietruppe im Heer der Zukunft', *Bundesheer, Österreichische Militärische Zeitschrift*, 2/2004.

24 For an excellent overview of the span of control concept, see D. D. Van Fleet and A. G. Bedeian, 'A History of the Span of Management', *Academy of Management Review*, July 1977, pp. 356–72. Also see E. E. Lawler III and J. R. Galbraith, 'New Roles for the Staff: Strategic Support and Service', in *Organizing for the Future: The New Logic for Managing Complex Organizations*, eds J. R. Galbraith, E. E. Lawler III, and Associates (San Francisco, CA: Jossey-Bass, 1993), pp. 65–83.

25 Translated from G. Ackaert, 'Uitvinders bij P&G moeten binnen de lijnen kleuren', *De Tijd*, 19 May 2001, p. 13.

26 P. Kaestle, 'A New Rationale for Organizational Structure', *Planning Review*, July–August 1990, p. 22.

27 J. R. Galbraith, *Organization Design* (Reading, MA: Addison-Wesley Publishing Company, 1977).

28 J. R. Galbraith, *Organization Design* (Reading, MA: Addison-Wesley Publishing Company, 1977).

29 Translated from T. Slock, 'Teamspirit: Het CTE-team Atlas Copco zorgt voor interne klanten', *jobat.be*, 11 November 2003.

30 J. R. Galbraith, *Organization Design* (Reading, MA: Addison-Wesley Publishing Company, 1977).

31 H. Mintzberg, *Mintzberg on Management* (New York: Free Press, 1989).

32 Based on M. Weber, *The Theory of Social and Economic Organization*, translated by A. M. Henderson and T. Parsons (New York: Oxford University Press, 1947). An instructive analysis of the mistranslation of Weber's work may be found in R. M. Weiss, 'Weber on Bureaucracy: Management Consultant or Political Theorist?', *Academy of Management Review*, April 1983, pp. 242–8.

33 For a critical appraisal of bureaucracy, see R. P. Hummel, *The Bureaucratic Experience, third edition* (New York:

St. Martin's Press, 1987). The positive side of bureaucracy is presented in C. T. Goodsell, *The Case for Bureaucracy: A Public Administration Polemic* (Chatham, NJ: Chatham House Publishers, 1983).

34 See G. Pinchot and E. Pinchot, 'Beyond Bureaucracy', *Business Ethics*, March–April 1994, pp. 26–9; and O. Harari, 'Let the Computers Be the Bureaucrats', *Management Review*, September 1996, pp. 57–60.

35 J. Huey and G. Colvin, 'The Jack and Herb Show', *Fortune*, 11 January 1999, p. 164.

36 K. Deveny, 'Bag Those Fries, Squirt That Ketchup, Fry Those Fish', *Business Week*, 13 October 1986, p. 86.

37 See D. A. Morand, 'The Role of Behavioral Formality and Informality in the Enactment of Bureaucratic versus Organic Organizations', *Academy of Management Review*, October 1995, pp. 831–72.

38 See http://www.ubizen.be/c_about_us/1_company/c111.html for the history of the company.

39 See G. P. Huber, C. C. Miller and W. H. Glick, 'Developing More Encompassing Theories about Organizations: The Centralization–Effectiveness Relationship as an Example', *Organization Science*, no. 1, 1990, pp. 11–40; and C. Handy, 'Balancing Corporate Power: A New Federalist Paper', *Harvard Business Review*, November–December 1992, pp. 59–72. Also see W. R. Pape, 'Divide and Conquer', *Inc. Technology*, no. 2, 1996, pp. 25–7; and J. Schmidt, 'Breaking Down Fiefdoms', *Management Review*, January 1997, pp. 45–9.

40 Details of this study can be found in T. Burns and G. M. Stalker, *The Management of Innovation* (London: Tavistock, 1961).

41 D. J. Gillen and S. J. Carroll, 'Relationship of Managerial Ability to Unit Effectiveness in More Organic versus More Mechanistic Departments', *Journal of Management Studies*, November 1985, pp. 674–5.

42 J. D. Sherman and H. L. Smith, 'The Influence of Organizational Structure on Intrinsic versus Extrinsic Motivation', *Academy of Management Journal*, December 1984, p. 883.

43 See J. A. Courtright, G. T. Fairhurst and L. E. Rogers, 'Interaction Patterns in Organic and Mechanistic Systems', *Academy of Management Journal*, December 1989, pp. 773–802.

44 See H. Mintzberg, *Mintzberg on Management* (New York: Free Press, 1989); and H. Mintzberg, *The Structuring of Organizations* (Englewood Cliffs: Prentice Hall, 1979).

45 See T. Dierckens, 'Stroo als grondstof voor papier', *De Morgen*, 7 March 2003.

46 Translated from M. Mosselman, J. Meijaard and M. J. Brand, 'De mythe ontrafeld', *Management en Organisatie*, 6 December 2003, pp. 37–53.

47 Translated from J. Reyns 'Agfa Gevaert is met 40% stijging de sterkste stijger binnen de BEL20 in 2002 en hoort tot europese toppers: het begin van een lange 'outperformance'?', *Trends*, 9 January 2003, pp. 17–18.

48 See further in the press release of Agfa Gevaert at http://news.agfa.com/corporate/news.nsf/news/.

49 Research Councils UK, 'Promoting Interdisciplinary Research and Training', *Report of the Joint Research Council Visits to 13 UK Universities*, February–May 2000, /http://www.rcuk.ac.uk/researchforum/univisit.doc/.

50 Based on the translation of J. Van Dyck, 'Huis met vele deuren', *Gazet Van Antwerpen*, 13 August 1999; and on S. Best and A. J. Nocella II, 'Behind the Mask: Uncovering the Animal Liberation Front', 2004, available on http://www.animalliberationfront.com/.

51 A reflection of the discussion going on in the 1990s can be found in D. M. Gordon, *Fat and Mean: The Corporate Squeeze of Working Americans and the Myth of Managerial "Downsizing"* (New York: Free Press, 1996); and B. Harrison, *Lean and Mean: The Changing Landscape of Corporate Power in the Age of Flexibility* (New York: Basic Books, 1994).

52 H. Tsoukas, 'Re-Viewing Organization', *Human Relations*, January 2001, p. 7.

53 H. Kaufman, *Time, Change, and Organizations* (Chatman, NJ: Chatam House, 1985).

54 For research on organisational complexity, see S. L. Brown and K. M. Eisenhardt, 'The Art of Continuous Change: Linking Complexity Theory and Time-Paced Evolution in Relentlessly Shifting Organizations', *Administrative Science Quarterly*, no. 1, 1997, pp. 1–35; and J. Mathews, 'Holonic Organisational Architectures', *Human Systems Management*, no. 1, 1996, pp. 27–54.

55 See A. Pettigrew and E. Fenton, *Innovating New Forms of Organizing* (Newbury Park, CA: Sage Publications, 2000); and A. Pettigrew, W. Ruigrok, A. M. Pettigrew, R. Whittington, L. Melin, C. Sanchez-Runde and F. A. J. Van den Bosch, *Innovative Form of Organizing: International Perspective* (Newbury Park, CA: Sage Publications, 2003).

56 J. E. van Aken and M. Weggeman, 'Managing Learning in Informal Innovation Networks: Overcoming the Daphne-Dilemma', *R&D Management*, April 2000, pp. 139–49; J. M. Ulijn, D. O'Hair, M. Weggeman, G. Ledlow and T. Hall, 'Innovation, Culture and Communication of Corporate Strategy: What is the Mission for International Business Communication?', *Journal of Business Communication*, no. 3, 2000, pp. 293–315; M. de Boer, F. A. J. Van den Bosch and H. W. Volberda, 'Managing Organizational Knowledge Integration in the Emerging Multimedia Complex', *Journal of Management Studies*, May 1999, pp. 379–98; F. A. J. Van den Bosch, H. W. Volberda and M. de Boer, 'Co-Evolution of Firm Absorptive Capacity and Knowledge Environment: Organizational Forms and Combinative Capabilities', *Organization Science*, September–October 1999, pp. 551–68; H. W. Volberda, *Building the Flexible Firm: How to Remain Competitive* (New York: Oxford University Press, 1998); and M. S. Dijksterhuis, F. A. J. Van den Bosch and H. W. Volberda, 'Where Do New Organizational Forms Come From? Management Logics As A Source of Co-Evolution', *Organization Science*, September–October 1999, pp. 569–82.

57 M. S. Dijksterhuis, F. A. J. Van den Bosch and H. W. Volberda, 'Where Do New Organizational Forms Come from? Management Logics As Source of Co-Evolution', *Organization Science*, September–October 1999, pp. 569–82.

58 See J. R. Galbraith and E. E. Lawler III, 'Effective Organizations: Using the New Logic of Organizing', in *Organizing for the Future: The New Logic for Managing Complex Organizations*, eds J. R. Galbraith, E. E. Lawler III, and Associates (San Francisco, CA: Jossey-Bass, 1993), pp. 285–99.

59 R. Jacob, 'The Struggle to Create an Organization for the 21st Century', *Fortune*, 3 April 1995, pp. 91–2.

60 See S. Sonnesyn Brooks, 'Managing a Horizontal Revolution', *HR Magazine*, June 1995, pp. 52–8; and M. Hequet, 'Flat and Happy', *Training*, April 1995, pp. 29–34.

61 S. Ghoshal and L. Gratton, 'Integrating the Entreprise' *MIT Sloan Management Review*, Fall 2002, p. 31.

62 For related discussion, see B. Filipczak, 'The Ripple Effect of Computer Networking', *Training*, March 1994, pp. 40–47.

63 See the work of A. Grandori and G. Soda, 'Inter-Firm Networks: Antecedents, Mechanisms and Forms', *Organization studies*, no. 2, 1995, pp. 183–214; C. Hastings, *The New Organization: Growing the Culture of Organisational Networking* (London: McGraw-Hill, 1993); and W. W. Powell, 'Neither Market nor Hierarchy: Network Forms of Organization', in *Research in Organizational Behavior*, eds L. L. Cummings and B. M. Staw (Greenwich, CT: JAI Press, 1990), pp. 295–336.

64 See on Visa's webpages: http://www.corporate.visa.com/av/main.shtml.

65 R. S. Burt, *Structural Holes: The Social Structure of Competition* (Cambridge, MA: Harvard University Press, 1992).

66 See O. Harari, 'Transform Your Organization into a Web of Relationships', *Management Review*, January 1998, pp. 21–4; R. J. Alford, 'Going Virtual, Getting Real', *Training & Development*, January 1999, pp. 34–44; S. Greco, 'Go Right to the Outsource', *Inc.*, February 1999, p. 39; M. Minehan, 'Forecasting Future Trends for the Workplace', *HR Magazine*, February 1999, p. 176; and W. B. Werther, Jr, 'Structure-Driven Strategy and Virtual Organization Design', *Business Horizons*, March–April 1999, pp. 13–18.

67 www.oleng.com.au

68 Adapted from personal communication.

69 J. Söderlund, 'Managing Complex Development Projects: Arenas, Knowledge Processes and Time', *R&D Management*, no. 5, 2002, pp. 425–6.

70 I. Nonaka and H. Takeuchi, *The Knowledge-Creating Company* (Oxford: Oxford University Press, 1995).

71 D. Keuning, T. H. Maas, et al. *Delayering Organizations* (London: Pitman, 1994), p. 221.

chapter 15 organisation design and effectiveness

By Annick Willem, Marc Buelens and Geert Devos

Learning outcomes

When you finish studying the material in this chapter, you should be able to:

■ describe the three general views on organisational fit: open systems, chaos theory and systems theory

■ explain the contingency approach to organisations, including the benefits and shortcomings of such approach

■ describe the impact of environmental uncertainty on the organisation

■ describe major strategy types and the relationship with organisation structure

■ explain the role of size in the contingency view

■ define technology as organisational element

■ explain the effect of technology on the organisation structure and the four major studies that have explored the relationship between technology and structure

■ describe the four generic organisational effectiveness criteria

■ describe the resource-based view on organisations

■ explain how professionals can prevent organisational decline

Inside Dell's lean machine

The company may not use the jargon, but it is clear that lean thinking is the foundation of Dell's hugely successful business model. Michael Dell pioneered his company's direct model when he founded the business just over 18 years ago in Texas. Dell is famous for cutting out dealers and distributors and selling directly to organisations and the public, whether by phone, through catalogues or on the Internet.

But Michael Dell's ideas have also made a significant impact on the way computers, and indeed other high-tech and electronic goods, are made. Unlike many of its competitors, Dell makes all its own computers; the company is also a significant player in the contract manufacturing industry. In addition, despite the cut-throat margins in the PC business, Dell Computer manufactures in the US and Europe, at Limerick in Ireland, as well as in Asia, China and South America. Each plant serves its regional markets; even in high-wage economies such as the US and (increasingly) Ireland, Dell believes controlling its own production makes sense.

Dell executives rarely make reference to manufacturing terminology such as lean or kaizen, but a walk through the company's European plant makes it is clear that both philosophies are applied with some rigour. Dell's build-to-order model means that the company holds no stock, and few components. At the Limerick plant there are no warehouses as such. The factory is built on an east-to-west axis. Lorries with parts come in to the factory's north, and built computers and servers leave the south. This creates a linear flow from components to complete machines and lets the company make the most of its just-in-time deliveries.

Productive

Dell says that its Limerick plant, known as the European Manufacturing Facility 3, is its most productive manufacturing operation. The plant uses cellular techniques, with each cell responsible for assembly and testing; an experienced operator can build more than 100 computers a day.

There is ample evidence of another part of the Dell approach at Limerick. A team building a new production line includes workers from the company's Malaysian plant at Penang, which has the company's most recent assembly lines. Each time Dell builds a new line or facility, as it is doing in Ireland, it brings in a team with experience of the next most recent build so they can pass on the lessons they have learned.

This way, Dell believes, each production line will be more efficient than the last, and best practice is spread throughout the company; with six production plants, the company can foster 'healthy competition' to be the best in the group.

He suggests that his company's cost structure 'is less than half that of our competitors', and this has enabled Dell to make money in markets where other companies, using less advanced techniques, fail to be profitable.

He attributes this to the leanness of Dell's operation, its responsiveness to customer demands, and the speed at which the business operates. 'It is about reducing the time from order to cash, reducing the time in the supply chain', he says.

Quality

The other characteristic of the Dell business model is the attention to detail and the belief in continuous improvement. Dell's manufacturing techniques are a margin ahead of its competitors, but Michael Dell is aware that they will aim to catch up.

A key part of the quality equation is the people Dell employs. Dell can trace each component in a computer back to its manufacturer and each assembled machine back to its manufacturing cell. Experience in Ireland, where PC production has switched to a cellular structure, shows that employees take greater pride in the quality of their work when they are also responsible for testing what they make.

Dell has a highly skilled workforce and the company puts a strong emphasis on education. As a result, many of the suggestions for manufacturing improvements come from the factory floor. 'Employees can drive process improvements', says Libert. 'Despite our world class operation, these guys on the production floor are smart enough to point out where it could be even better.'

For Michael Dell, manufacturing is one of the core differentiators of his business. And there is nothing in his manner that suggests he would be happy to be just average.[1]

For discussion
Is Dell Computer likely to be an effective company 10 years from now? Why or why not?

In the previous chapter, we mentioned that organisations attempt to achieve their goals by division of labour, hierarchy of authority and co-ordination. Different combinations of these three structural features lead to different organisation types. Organisations have some freedom in choosing their form but this freedom is limited. To be an effective organisation, the elements of structure need to be in line with the contextual factors. Many European countries evolve to an information society. This is also the case for Finland, where new IT service firms arise. The context of these organisations is more turbulent than in traditional sectors.

Telenor, a seller of Internet-based business catalogues, has a turbulent environment. The work is hectic, but the employees learn a lot. All company operations are divided into eight teams to cope with this context. There is competition between the teams, but teams are used more as a tool to reach organisational efficiency. It is clear that structure, in this case a team-based structure, should be adapted to cope with such a turbulent environment.[2]

First, we explain why the contextual factors are important and discuss the different views on a fit between contextual and structural factors. Then, we look at the different contextual factors and their effect on the organisation structure. Next, the issue of organisational effectiveness and effectiveness criteria are described. We end the chapter by focusing on the threat of organisational decline.

Organisational fit

A first important theory in the fit approach towards organisations and their contexts was the distinction between open and closed systems. Chaos theory and systems theory are two theories based on the open-systems view. Around the same period (in the 1950s and 1960s), organisation theorists started to develop fit models based on a contingency view of organisations. Both views indicate that structure should be a function of the different contextual variables. We will first discuss the open-systems view and the two theories based on it, before looking at the contingency theory.

Closed versus open systems

The distinction between a **Closed system** and an **Open system** is a matter of degree. Because every worldly system is partly closed and partly open, the key question is: how great a role does the environment play in the functioning of the system? For instance, a battery-powered clock is a relatively closed system. Once the battery is inserted, the clock performs its time-keeping function hour after hour until the battery goes dead. The human body, on the other hand, is a highly open system because it requires a constant supply of life-sustaining oxygen from the environment. Nutrients are also imported from the environment. Open systems are capable of self-correction, adaptation and growth, thanks to characteristics such as homeostasis and feedback control.

Organisations depend on the environment for their resources but are also influenced in several ways by their environment. There are no organisations that are fully closed but some depend more on their environment. The traditional mechanistic organisation discussed in the previous chapter is seen as a closed-system model because it largely ignores environmental influences. It gives the impression that organisations are self-sufficient entities. Conversely, the more organic and the newer organisation types emphasise interaction between organisations and their environments. These newer models are based on open-system assumptions. Open and closed systems are important to illustrate how organisation theorists look at organisations. Organisations can be seen either as primarily closed – operating in a particular given environment, in which the organisation adapts to this environment and creates a stable harmony with the environment – or as primarily open, which implies continuous interaction with the environment is preferred over stable harmony.

Chaos theory

Based on findings in physics, **Chaos theory** was applied to organisations.[3] This theory states that we live in an extremely uncertain world where small changes can have huge impact. The world's complexity prevents us from influencing or even predicting changes. Hence, the world looks like chaos, but underneath this chaos there are non-linear relationships and patterns. Chaos theory is illustrated by the butterfly effect, a popular but rather exaggerated view of the world's complexity. The flapping of a butterfly's wings can cause changes in air circulation that can affect the weather on the other side of the world. Small insignificant changes can inconspicuously influence the future of organisations. Chaos theory thus blurs cause-and-effect relationships. However, this does not mean that organisations should not try to control their internal and external environment. Many external effects on organisations can be anticipated.

> In our complex global world the effect of a medical problem in one region of the world can have unexpected effects on organisations in other areas. The SARS epidemic, a recent virulent disease that spread in Asia in the first half of 2003 and which has resulted in many deaths, has had huge effects on organisations in the rest of the world. Tourist organisations specialising in tours throughout Asia had a huge drop in sales in that period.

Closed system
a relatively self-sufficient entity

Open system
organism that must constantly interact with its environment to survive

Chaos theory
the environment is extremely uncertain and turbulent resulting in high complexity and disorder but patterns of order are still recognisable in the chaos

Singapore Airlines had to dismiss 414 employees. Although the number of victims was not as high as was expected (812 did not survive the epidemic, 32 of the victims were in Singapore), the world was plunged into fear for almost a year. The SARS effect was concentrated in Asia, the fastest-growing region in the world and the one area keeping the global economy afloat. This meant that the economic effects were much larger than could have been expected. The media spread the fear. HSBC economists estimated that every 1 per cent drop in GDP growth in Asia outside Japan trims export growth by 0.2 per cent in the US. However, the effects of the disease were unpredictable. While some companies almost went bankrupt, others profited. A Chinese Internet company, Sohu.com, has made extra profits because people in fear of contamination stayed at home, and ordered goods via the Internet.[4]

The greatest creativity occurs at the boundaries of chaos. Organisations that thrive on self-organising, innovation and creativity are in a state of chaos. The organisation is kept together with just a few core values, which create some order in the disorder. More and more organisations will be facing turbulent environments and will find themselves in a state of chaos and frequent transformations. Even governmental organisations that are traditionally organised in a more mechanistic way cannot reach their objectives any more with fixed stable roles and rules. They also have to apply principles of chaos as well and prepare for frequent changes that can bring temporary states of disorder.[5]

Systems theory

The **Systems theory** approach states that each element, for instance an individual, belongs as a subsystem to a system of higher order, for instance the organisation.[6] The concept originally emerged from biology and was initiated in an article of Ludwig Von Bertalanffy in 1951.[7] The existence of a hierarchy in a systems' elements is crucial to the systems theory. The functioning of the subsystem is determined by the functioning of the higher-order system. Boulding, for instance, identifies nine subsystems to explain our world, starting from labels and classification systems as the lowest system to transcendental beings as the most complex systems. A hierarchy of systems goes from simplest to most complex and the working of the complex systems is based on the working of the lower subsystems. Applying this to organisations gives us the following subsystems: the organisation itself as open system in interaction with its environment, the departments of the organisation as subsystems and the individuals in these departments also as a kind of subsystem with the procedures and control mechanisms as yet another kind of subsystem of a lower order. The systems theory of organisations emerged from field studies by the London Tavistock Institute in the 1950s.[8] The systems theory in organisation theory is inspired by the general systems theory but focuses less on the organisation as a subsystem of the environment than on the development of general abstract relations among organisational elements. Systems theory is important for analysing organisations, as it stresses the embeddedness of the different elements. Similar to the open-systems view, it emphasises that all elements are influencing each other and that the whole system should be taken into account when we try to build effective organisations.

> **Systems theory**
> every element is a subsystem of a larger system and every system is composed of subsystems, depending on each other and on the whole

The contingency approach to organisation design

Fit approaches to organisations do not offer a deterministic logic on how organisations must be designed but instead a systematic way to look at variations in organisation structures. The contingency approach, however, takes a normative view to organisational fit. According to the **Contingency approach to organisation design**, organisations tend to be more effective when they are structured to fit the demands of the situation.[9] The typical contingency variables are technology, environment, strategy, size, culture and structure.[10] A contingency theory thus seeks for a balanced fit among these variables (also see Chapter 1).[11] According to the contingency view of organisations, organisational problems are caused by a lack of such a fit. Contingency should not be misunderstood as predicting one best way for organising, but is merely concerned with finding the right balance in combining organisational elements, called 'contingency factors'.[12] A bad fit will lead to performance losses. Several of the contingency factors can be influenced or changed by management. The environment, however, is harder to influence. Hence, a contingency approach merely results in organisations adapting to their environment.[13]

> **Contingency approach to organisation design**
> creating an effective organisation-environment fit

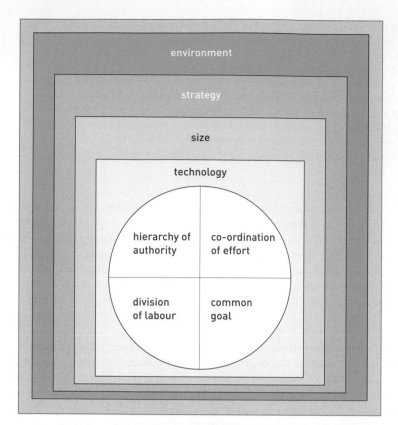

**FIGURE 15.1
CONTINGENCY FACTORS
AND ORGANISATIONAL
ELEMENTS**

A study comparing companies with and without bad fits in a sample of 224 Danish small and medium-sized firms confirmed this performance loss. Any kind of bad fit could generate lower financial performance. However, more varieties of bad fits did not lead to greater losses. Hence, only the firms with no bad fits at all did better than companies suffering from one or more bad fits.[14] Another study of small firms in the US, indicated only very weak relationships between structural fit and performance. In fact, the researcher could not confirm that bad fits led to performance losses.[15] Mintzberg's models of ideal structures (discussed in the previous chapter) are examples of structures that have a perfect fit among the internal elements and the environment. However, a study categorising firms according to Mintzberg's typology does not reveal that firms which do not fit well in one of the ideal structures perform worse.[16] Nonetheless, the studies are all too limited in scope to fully reject the idea that organisations need a contingency fit to be successful.

We will take a look at the different contingency factors in the next paragraphs. Figure 15.1 extends Figure 14.1.

Assessing environmental uncertainty

The environment is a source of uncertainty. Most organisations are facing a range of influences from their environment, which they cannot control. Influences can come from changes in regulations from governments, changes in labour supply because of changes in the number of students that followed a certain technical education, changes in customer preferences, etc. A whole range of groups influence the organisation. We will see further in this chapter that every organisation has many stakeholders (i.e. groups of people with an interest in the organisation), which can influence the organisation and are a source of uncertainty. Hence, the organisation also tries to keep peace with its stakeholders by taking into account their interests and needs. The organisation is thus in interaction with its environment and can reduce uncertainty through this interaction. However, only very large organisations are able to reduce environmental uncertainty by having control of the environment instead of the environment having control of the organisation.

Most commercial organisations need to make sufficient revenue and profit to survive. However, some organisations can make their environment pay for their losses. Governments in particular are willing to help companies survive through financial support if they create jobs for many people.

> The French government made attempts to save Alstom, a failing engineering giant, through buying shares in Alstom. However, the European Commission did not allow such help. This forced the French government to seek for an alternative, which was to lend money instead of buying shares. The French finance minister used his influence to convince Mr Mario Monti, the European competition commissioner, to allow state help for Alstrom. Hence, it is clear that Alstom can influence its environment.[17]

DIMENSIONS OF ENVIRONMENTAL UNCERTAINTY

Environmental uncertainty is caused by the fact that we cannot predict changes and that we cannot understand the complexity in that environment. Lawrence and Lorsch described uncertainty as the lack of clarity in information, causal relationships and the time lag in information about the environment.[18] They mainly focus on the unpredictability aspect in environmental uncertainty. Different parts of the organisation can face different levels of uncertainty because they are influenced by different parts of the environment and have different levels of interaction with that environment. The sales department will interact more heavily with the environment than the accounting department.[19] Robert Duncan proposed a two-dimensional model for classifying environmental demands on the organisation (see Table 15.1). The horizontal axis is the simple→complex dimension. This dimension 'focuses on whether the factors in the environment considered for decision making are few in number and similar or many in number and different'.[20] On the vertical axis of Duncan's model is the static→dynamic dimension. 'The static–dynamic dimension of the environment depicts the factors of the environment that remain the same over time or change.'[21] When combined, these two dimensions characterise four situations that represent increasing uncertainty for organisations. According to Duncan, the complex–dynamic situation of highest uncertainty is the most common organisational environment today.

TABLE 15.1 A FOUR-WAY CLASSIFICATION OF ORGANISATIONAL ENVIRONMENTS

	Simple	Complex
Static	**Low perceived uncertainty** ■ Small number of factors and components in the environment ■ Factors and components are somewhat similar to one another ■ Factors and components remain the same and are not changing ■ Example: Soft drink industry 1	**Moderately low perceived uncertainty** ■ Large number of factors and components in the environment ■ Factors and components are not similar to one another ■ Factors and components remain basically the same ■ Example: Food products 2
Dynamic	3 **Moderately high perceived uncertainty** ■ Small number of factors and components in the environment ■ Factors and components are somewhat similar to one another ■ Factors and components of the environment are in continual process of change ■ Example: Fast-food industry	4 **High perceived uncertainty** ■ Large numbers of factors and components in the environment ■ Factors and components are not similar to one another ■ Factors and components of environment are in a continual process of change ■ Examples: Commercial airline industry Telephone Communications

SOURCE: R. Duncan, 'What Is the Right Organization Structure? Decision Tree Analysis Provides the Answer', *Organizational Dynamics*, Winter 1979, pp. 59–80.

> Amid these fast-paced times, nothing stands still, not even in the simple–static quadrant. For example, during the first 94 years of the history of the Coca-Cola Company (to 1980), only one soft drink bore the company's name. Just six years later, Coke had its famous name on seven soft drinks, including Coca-Cola Classic, Coke and Cherry Coke. Despite operating in an environment characterised as simple and static, the Coca-Cola Company has had to become a more risk-taking, entrepreneurial company.[22]

The example of Coca-Cola illustrates that organisations facing moderate to high uncertainty (quadrants 3 and 4 in Table 15.1) have to be highly flexible, responsive and adaptive today.[23] Contingency organisation design is more important than ever because it helps managers to structure their organisations to fit the key structural elements discussed in the previous chapter.

Several later studies have focused on the environment itself as a contingency variable as well. Daft and Lengel for instance use the concepts environmental uncertainty and equivocality. The latter concept refers to uncertainty about cause and effect, and about multiple and conflicting interpretations of the environment, which cause confusion.[24]

Bourgeois and Eisenhardt discuss environmental velocity to indicate organisations that are in an extremely volatile environment.[25] Information on such changes is inadequate, is received far too late and is mostly not available. Organisations have then no other choice than to react very quickly to the changes that occur and to take decisions based on limited information.

> The British Broadcasting Corporation (BBC) has long been an organisation in a stable environment able to control part of its environment, especially the government that provides the licence fee and money collected from households in the UK. This shelters the BBC from competition with commercial broadcasters. However, even the BBC faces a changing environment with less control on that environment as a consequence. New technology, such as satellites, larger broadband capacity and digitalisation have lowered production costs and made the development of traditional TV programmes easy. Many commercial broadcasters have taken over the broadcasting role of the BBC. Hence, BBC which is funded by the British public will need to change and offer new kinds of services to the public, such as providing information through the Internet. However, for the time being, the BBC is still operating in a protected environment, allowing it to stick to classic ways of information spreading.[26]

Besides the dimension complex and dynamic, Mintzberg also added environmental diversity and hostility.[27] Organisational diversity exists when an organisation is active in many different products or markets. The more an organisation is specialised, the narrower its environment becomes. Reducing environmental diversity is a means to reduce complexity. Hostility exists when organisations have stakeholders who are not in co-operative relationships with the organisation. A polluting company will be in a hostile environment because government and a number of pressure groups will try to force the company to change its activities. Many companies also face hostility through heavy competition in their markets.

> The extreme competition in the airline sector provides a clear example of a hostile environment. This hostile environment results in losses for most of the airline companies. In Europe, Virgin Express experienced losses through severe competition and having too many flights for the number of potential customers. Ryanair in particular competes keenly on price and even gives away free seats when there is spare capacity. Even when the number of airline passengers increases, profits still decrease in such hostile environment. Organisations can try to cope with the hostility by aiming for more co-operation and partnerships.[28]

ENVIRONMENTAL UNCERTAINTY AND STRUCTURE

The structure of organisations is influenced by the above-mentioned characteristics. This means that certain structures are more or less effective and efficient under certain environmental conditions.[29] Table 15.2 shows which structural factors relate to the two main dimensions of environmental

TABLE 15.2 STRUCTURE FITTING THE ENVIRONMENTAL CHARACTERISTICS

	Simple environment	Complex environment
Stable environment	**High formalisation** ■ Limited use of co-ordination mechanisms (mainly: rules and procedures) ■ Simple structure (mostly functional) ■ Low differentiation ■ Centralisation	**High formalisation** ■ Limited use of co-ordination mechanisms (mainly: standardisation of procedures and skills) ■ Mechanic ■ Divisional ■ Large specialisation
Dynamic environment	**Low formalisation** ■ A need for many flexible co-ordination mechanisms (such as direct horizontal communication and direct supervision) ■ Organic ■ Large need for information about the environment ■ Simple structure (such as geographic) ■ Despecialisation	**Low formalisation** ■ A need for many flexible co-ordination mechanisms (such as direct horizontal communication, teams and integrators) ■ Organic ■ Large need for information about the environment ■ Divisional ■ Large differentiation ■ Decentralised

SOURCE: Based on T. Burns and G. M. Stalker, *The Management of Innovation* (London: Tavistock, 1961); P. R. Lawrence and J. W. Lorsch, *Organization and Environment* (Boston, MA: Harvard University Press, 1967); R. B. Duncan, 'Characteristics of Organizational Environments and Perceived Environmental Uncertainty', *Administrative Science Quarterly*, September 1972, pp. 313–27; and H. Mintzberg, *The Structuring of Organizations* (Englewood Cliffs, NJ: Prentice Hall, 1979).

uncertainty. High diversity and large equivocality will increase the complexity of the environment. Hostile environments mostly cause instability. To cope with a hostile environment all forces need to be concentrated within the organisation through centralisation.[30]

Population ecology theory also seeks to explain the organisation in its environment but focuses on groups of similar organisations, active in similar markets or offering similar products and services. This theory explains the birth, development and death of organisations in terms of their adaptiveness to their environment. Organisations that are able to adapt and consistently acquire crucial resources have the best chance to survive. Hence, the population ecology theory also emphasises the need for organisations to 'fit' their environment.[31]

The contingency theory and the open systems-view have one important thing in common. They are based on an 'environmental imperative', meaning that the environment is said to be the primary determinant of effective organisational structure. Other organisation theorists disagree. They contend that factors such as the organisation's corporate strategy, size and core technology hold the key to organisational structure. The next sections examine the significance of these three additional contingency variables.

Strategy and organisation structure

Strategy is also a contingency variable. We have mentioned in the previous chapter that organisations develop task allocation and co-ordination to help them to achieve their goals. What those goals may be will be discussed in the section on organisational effectiveness. Strategy refers to the processes developed in the organisation to create value, seek for opportunities and to achieve its goals. Hence, strategy refers to the decision-making process to manage the organisation's relationships with its environment.

Chandler introduced the now famous phrase 'structure follows strategy'[32] indicating that structure is determined by the strategy of the organisation. Chandler based his statement on a study of about 100 large American companies. However, later researchers have found that structure can also affect strategy. Factors such as complexity, centralisation and formalisation have an impact on the decision-making process in the organisation and, hence, on the strategy that will emerge.[33] The kind of structure will also make the organisation more or less flexible, allowing more or less potential to see and grasp opportunities in the market. Although structure and strategy mutually influence each other, we can nevertheless make some statements about the kind of structure best fitting a particular strategy.

STRATEGY TYPES

Michael Porter identified three generic strategies which will allow organisations to develop a competitive advantage over other organisations that are competing in the same markets.[34] These three strategies are 'cost leadership' (i.e. products offered at low prices based on efficient low-cost production), 'differentiation' (i.e. products offered at a premium price based on the uniqueness or image of the product) and 'focus' (i.e. selecting a niche in the market where competition is low or even absent). The first strategy requires a more efficient organisation structure, while the other two strategies require a structure that allows close contact with the customers and the processing of information about the market.

Miles and Snow developed another four-category typology of strategy.[35] The first category consists of the 'defenders', organisations that have few products or markets but are efficient in serving these markets. Organisations with this strategy rarely make changes to their products, structure and operational goals. The second category refers to organisations with an 'analysers' strategy. Such organisations have their major business in a stable environment where they can emphasise efficiency and do not need to change their structure and products. However, they also have more turbulent products or areas in which they seek for innovation and change, especially when they see that competitors are making important changes. In fact this is a 'defenders' strategy but with an eye on the environment so as to be ready to change when this is necessary. The third category, the 'prospectors', refers to organisations which are very innovative and continually seeking change in their products, markets, structure and processes so as to be ahead of competition or to follow early trends in the environment. Efficiency is not a priority in this type of organisation. Finally, there is the category of 'reactors', organisations that are forced by their environment to change and to respond. However, their reactive character means that they only change when forced to, resulting in a poor fit between structure and strategy.

An organisation with an innovative or prospectors strategy will require low formalisation, decentralisation and extensive use of lateral co-ordination mechanisms, such as teams and task forces. An organisation that focuses on differentiation towards different markets, or fits in the analysers category, will need a structure that allows it to capture a lot of customer information and should be moderately formalised and decentralised. Strategies that are stable over the long term, such as the defenders and cost leadership, allow high levels of formalisation and centralisation, in particular to achieve efficiency and cost control, which are the major objectives.[36]

> Kimberly-Clark, a US paper products group, can be categorised as a company with a differentiation and an analysers strategy. The company has in line with its strategy a divisionalised structure. Competition has become harder especially from the main competitor Procter & Gamble. In such a situation centralisation is required to concentrate all efforts. Kimberly-Clark is bringing its North American and European personal product and consumer tissues business under a single North Atlantic management team to create a more unified global organisation.[37]

> Novartis, a Swiss company and one of the largest pharmaceutical companies in the world, has a more prospector strategy. Innovation is very important for the company and it is putting a large emphasis on the development of the skills of its employees. *Financial Times* readers have chosen the chairman of Novartis, Daniel Vasella, as the most influential European business leader over the last quarter of a century. Novartis is not only innovative but has built a strong market position with strong brands and a diverse product portfolio. Hence, the strategy is also diversified. Novartis claims that mergers and alliances are necessary to achieve scale benefits, also in research and innovation. Innovation is thus not only a strategy for small and new companies. Although size helped, their clearly innovative strategy is the basis of Novartis' success.[38]

A STRATEGIC CHOICE MODEL

In 1972 British sociologist John Child rejected the imperative approach to organisational structure in favour of an emerging alternative. He proposed a strategic choice model based on behavioural rather than rational economic principles. Child believed structure resulted from a political process involving organisational power holders.[39] According to the strategic choice model that has evolved from Child's work,[40] an organisation's structure is determined largely by a dominant coalition of top-management strategists.[41]

As Figure 15.2 illustrates, specific strategic choices or decisions reflect how the dominant coalition perceives environmental constraints and the organisation's objectives. These strategic choices are tempered by the decision makers' personal beliefs, attitudes, values and ethics (see Chapters 2 and 3).[42] For example, consider this unusual relationship between top management's ethics (see Chapter 18) and corporate strategy, as reported in the following extract from *Business Ethics* magazine:

> As a manufacturer and retailer of outdoor clothing and equipment, it's natural for Patagonia to be concerned about the environment. But as a for-profit business, it's also natural for the company to feel a need to look at its bottom line. Patagonia has found a way to do both, and to turn upside down traditional concepts of how companies grow in the bargain. The company first warned its customers of the impending change in its [1992] fall/winter catalogue .... 'We are limiting Patagonia's growth with the eventual goal of halting growth altogether. We dropped 30 per cent of our clothing line .... What does this mean to you? Well, last fall you had a choice of five ski pants; now you may choose between two. Two styles of ski pants are all anyone needs.' And ... [the 1993] catalogue featured the following message: 'At Patagonia, as a company, and as individuals, we sometimes find the array of choices dizzying. But the choices must be faced, resolved soberly, and judicious action taken. To fully include environmental concerns in our ordinary work is to give something back to the planet that sustains us, and that we have taxed so heavily. It's a complex process, but the simplest of gifts.' To that end, say Patagonia spokespeople Lu Setnicksa and Mike Harrelson, the company has embarked on an aggressive effort to examine everything from the materials it uses to produce its products, to which products it actually makes, to what kind of paper it uses in its copying machines.[43]

So far, a more efficient Patagonia has enjoyed increased profits, despite a decrease in sales revenue. Directing our attention once again to Figure 15.2, the organisation is structured to accommodate its mix of strategies. Ultimately, corrective action is taken if organisational effectiveness criteria are not met.

FIGURE 15.2 THE RELATIONSHIP BETWEEN STRATEGIC CHOICE AND ORGANISATIONAL STRUCTURE

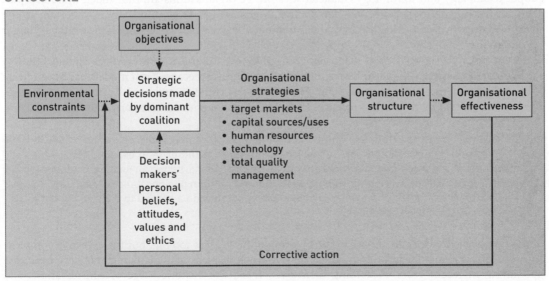

RESEARCH FINDINGS AND PRACTICAL IMPLICATIONS

In a study of 97 small and mid-sized companies in Quebec, Canada, strategy and organisational structure were found to be highly interdependent. Strategy influenced structure and structure influenced strategy. This was particularly true for larger, more innovative and more successful firms.[44]

Strategic choice theory and research teaches professionals at least two practical lessons. First, the environment is just one of many determinants of structure. Second, like any other administrative process, organisation design is subject to the interplays of personal power and politics (see Chapter 13).

Organisational size

Another contingency variable is organisational size. It is an important structural variable subject to two schools of thought. Economists belonging to the first school, have long extolled the virtues of economies of scale. This approach, often called the 'bigger is better' model, assumes the per-unit cost of production decreases as the organisation grows. In effect, bigger is said to be more efficient. For example, on an annual basis, Daimler-Chrysler can supposedly produce its 100 000th car less expensively than its 10th.

The second school of thought hinges on the law of diminishing returns. Called the 'small is beautiful' model,[45] this approach contends that oversized organisations and subunits tend to be plagued by costly behavioural problems. Large and impersonal organisations are said to breed apathy and alienation, with resulting problems such as staff turnover and absenteeism. Two strong advocates of this second approach are the authors Peters and Waterman of the popular book *In Search of Excellence*:

> In the excellent companies, small in almost every case is beautiful. The small facility turns out to be the most efficient; its turned-on, motivated, highly productive worker, in communication (and competition) with his peers, outproduces the worker in the big facilities time and again. It holds for plants, for project teams, for divisions – for the entire company.[46]

In the contingency literature size is especially important because it affects the fit between the other structural and contingency elements. A group of researchers from the Tavistock Institute in London did contingency based research on the design of organisations on a large sample of British companies in the 1960s and 1970s. Their studies and findings are bundled in the Aston studies. The Aston studies investigated the relationship between specialisation, standardisation and formalisation as characteristics of the structure, automatisation and integration of the technology and the size of the organisation. The researchers found several relationships between the technology and structural variables but these relationships where all overruled by the size variable. Size has a major impact on the structure of organisations. Larger organisations have many large departments, each of which has its proper technology and technology characteristics. Large organisations are thus much more complex than smaller organisations with only one dominant technology. This complexity is important to the design of organisations. The use of standardisation, for example, is of importance only in larger organisations.[47]

Recent research suggests that, when designing their organisations, professionals should follow a middle ground between 'bigger is better' and 'small is beautiful' because both models have been oversold. Indeed, a newer perspective says complexity, not size, is the central issue.[48] British management teacher and writer Charles Handy recently offered the following instructive perspective:

> Growth does not have to mean more of the same. It can mean better rather than bigger. It can mean leaner or deeper, both of which might improve rather than expand the current position. Businesses can grow more profitable by becoming better, or leaner, or deeper, more concentrated, without growing bigger. Bigness, in both business and life, can lead to a lack of focus, too much complexity and, in the end, too wide a spread to control. We have to know when big is big enough.[49]

We do not have a definite answer to the question of how big is too big, but the excessive complexity argument is compelling. This argument may also help explain why many mergers have been disappointing in recent years. According to *Business Week*, the 'historic surge of consolidations and combinations is occurring in the face of strong evidence that mergers and acquisitions, at least over the past 35 years or so, have hurt more than helped companies and shareholders'.[50]

Some organisations become so large that top management loses sight of what is happening in the organisation. Large organisations need a structure that allows top management to receive all the crucial information about the workings of the organisation. Royal Dutch Shell suffered from the consequences of such a faulty information system. In December 2003 it turned out that a claimed reserve of 2.3 billion barrels of oil did not exist at all, which amounted to an enormous financial setback for the company. At the top of the company are two executive boards, one with the directors of the former Dutch oil company (Royal Dutch oil) and one with the directors representing the former British company (Shell). The duality in the top decision-making structure contributed to poor supervision and is probably also the underlying cause of the long-term underperformance of the company.[51]

The effect of technology on structure

Finally, technology is another contingency variable. Several of the classic organisation theorists have studied the relationship between technology and structure. Technology includes all the processes, means and instruments that are available in the organisation to allow the organisation to perform the tasks and reach its goals – such as, procedures, skills, engineering techniques and working methods.

> **Technology**
> collective instruments used to do the work in organisations

WOODWARD'S STUDY

Joan Woodward proposed a technological imperative in 1965 after studying 100 small manufacturing firms in southern England. She found distinctly different structural patterns for effective and ineffective companies based on technologies. There are three levels of complexity based on the type of production, namely (in order of complexity):

1 Single-piece production or small amounts.
2 Mass production.
3 Continuous or flow production.

The higher the complexity, the more specialisation and the more need for overhead functions. Co-ordination in single-piece production is based on autonomy and direct horizontal communication. In mass production, rules and procedures predominate. Finally, the flow production requires direct supervision and direct contact with short communication lines. In this type of production there is also an extreme need for control requiring intensive use of diverse co-ordination mechanisms, such as hierarchy and rules. Effective organisations based on a technology of medium complexity tend to have a mechanistic structure (see Chapter 14). Effective organisations with either low- or high-complexity technology tend to have an organic structure. However, the focus on production is a limitation to the generalisation of Woodward's findings. Her contribution is nevertheless of great importance because she was one of the first to prove the relationship between technology, structure and performance empirically. Woodward concluded that technology was the overriding determinant of organisational structure.[52]

THOMPSON'S TECHNOLOGY TYPES

Thompson also relates technology to organisation design. He identifies different types of interdependencies between units and tasks based on different technology in the organisation. The types of interdependencies are:

- Sequential (i.e. task 2 follows task 1 or output of task 1 is input for task 2).
- Reciprocal (i.e. task 2 depends on task 1 and task 1 also depends on task 2 or both tasks use each other's output as input).
- Pooled (i.e. tasks depend on and contribute to the 'whole' of other activities in the organisation or tasks are independent but all contribute to the organisation's goals).
- Intensive interdependency (i.e. complex bundles of independent tasks that need strong integration to allow a common output).[53]

The last type is a more complex form of pooled interdependency requiring closer and more intensive co-ordination. Contrary to Woodward, Thompson also discusses service organisations. His four types differ in the level of interdependency between the units but also in the level of standardisation of input, processes and output, and in the intensity of co-operation. When integrating these three criteria we can derive the following statements based on Thompson's work:

- In sequential and reciprocal technology, input, processes and output are fully standardised, while these are less standardised in the other two types.
- In pooled technology, there is only standardisation of processes.
- In intense technology, there is no standardisation possible. Therefore, co-ordination depends on the level of interdependency and standardisation.

Each type of technology is best organised by specific co-ordination mechanisms. Sequential technology needs rules and procedures. Pooled technology requires few co-ordination efforts and only a few rules, because there is no pressing need to integrate the tasks. Intense technology requires a lot of integration and, hence, the use of direct communication lines and continuous mutual adjustment. In this latter case integration must go so far that one unit becomes to a certain extent integrated in the other unit or organisation, even when the two parties are legally speaking not part of one organisation. A parallel example is the student who becomes a member of the school during the period of education.

PERROW'S TECHNOLOGY TYPES

Perrow is a third organisation design theorist to take a contingency view of organisations and to try to explain the structure of organisations by means of technology characteristics. He developed a theory closely related to the standardisation of Thompson and production technologies of Woodward. Perrow, however, has a more fine-tuned description of complexity. He measures complexity along two dimensions, namely the level of change (or exceptions in the technology) and the level of analysability of the technology (or comprehensibility). Analysable technology can be divided into

TABLE 15.3 TECHNOLOGY AND STRUCTURE

		Changes in the technology	
		Rarely	Very frequent
Complexity of the technology	Low	■ Analysable and understandable technology which is routine ■ Centralisation and formalisation ■ Standardisation, rules and procedures as co-ordination mechanisms ■ Mass production and sequential technology ■ Large span of control ■ Example: Car factory	■ Analysable and understandable technology but with many exceptions ■ Standardisation of skills, rules and processes but low formalisation ■ Engineering-based production ■ Example: Software developing firms
	High	■ Low analysability but routine ■ Low standardisation ■ Formalisation ■ Decentralisation ■ Continuous production flow ■ Non-routine production ■ Example: Nuclear plant	■ Low analysability with many exceptions ■ Decentralisation ■ Low standardisation, except for standardisation of skills and low formalisation ■ Low span of control ■ Intense technology ■ Single-piece production ■ Example: Architect firm

SOURCE: Based on C. Perrow, *Organizational Analysis: A Sociological View* (London: Tavistock Publications, 1970); J. D. Thompson, *Organizations in Action* (New York: McGraw-Hill, 1967); and J. Woodward, *Industrial Organization: Theory and Practice* (London: Oxford University Press, 1965).

subtasks, which can then be automated or made more routine by standardised rules and procedures. Table 15.3 summarises these relationships between technology and structure.

The two technology dimensions can be combined to develop four categories of technology that each have particular characteristics and co-ordination needs:

- Few changes and high analysability result in routine technology with standard operating procedures.
- Many changes and low analysability allow no standardisation but require direct ad hoc communication.
- Many changes but also highly analysability is known as 'engineering technology' and can be standardised with specific rules and standards but not with routine procedures.
- Few changes but no analysability, is to be found in crafts work and does not allow procedures either.[54]

GALBRAITH'S VIEW OF TECHNOLOGY UNCERTAINTY

Finally, Galbraith is one of the organisation design authors who has paid most attention to the role of information in organisational structuring. The central idea in his work *Designing Complex Organizations* is that information can reduce uncertainty caused by the variability in the technology. The larger the technological uncertainty, the more information needs to be shared among decision makers during the task execution in order be able to co-ordinate the tasks in the organisation. Each mechanism for co-ordinating and structuring the organisation is different in the amount and type of information that can be shared. Galbraith mentions several co-ordination mechanisms which can help to share information. The greater the need for information, the greater the variety of co-ordination mechanisms required. When, after all co-ordination mechanisms have been applied, an information need still exists, the information need itself can be reduced or the information processing capacity can be extended through other mechanisms than co-ordination ones. These mechanisms are vertical information systems and related laterally, and are in fact also forms of co-ordination. Rules, programmes and procedures specify the activities in advance and minimise communication and information sharing. Hierarchy allows the co-ordination of more complex tasks by gathering all required information into one function. When this results in an information overload (see Chapter 8) for the information-processing roles (the managers), more decision rights are given to the employees (delegation of decision making). The information sharing of this latter co-ordination mechanism is reduced to communicating the targets and boundaries of individual behaviour. Hence, Galbraith considers goal setting combined with delegation of decision making to the place where the information is gathered and the actions occur as an alternative mechanism when planning and authority are insufficient.[55]

Research findings

Many studies of the relationship between technology and structure have been conducted since these authors' landmark publications. Unfortunately, disagreement and confusion have prevailed. For example, a comprehensive review of 50 studies conducted between 1965 and 1980 found six technology concepts and 140 technology-structure relationships.[56] A statistical analysis of those studies prompted the following conclusions:

- The more the technology requires interdependence between individuals and/or groups, the greater the need for integration (co-ordination).
- 'As technology moves from routine to non-routine, subunits adopt less formalised and [less] centralised structures.'[57]

Additional insights can be expected in this area as researchers co-ordinate their definitions of technology and refine their methodologies.[58]

NEW TECHNOLOGY

Some organisation theorists pay special attention to new technology and in particular to information technology (IT) in relation to the structure of organisations (also see Chapter 8).[59] These theorists believe that IT has dramatically changed our way of working in organisations. On the one hand, IT allows organisations to routinise their processes. On the other, IT also allows more flexibility and complexity in the processes. Furthermore, IT has been very supportive to information processing, communication, co-ordination and decision making in organisations.

The benefits of the new technology can be summarised as:

■ New opportunities for workers.
■ New roles and communication lines cutting across traditional functional and vertical boundaries.
■ New ways of horizontal co-operation.
■ More communication, allowing more teamwork.

The negative aspects are:

■ Dependency on technology and personal alienation.
■ IT used by managers to reinforce their hierarchical power.
■ Workers more extensively controlled and monitored, resulting in a climate of distrust.

Information technology has a much larger impact than other technological innovations because it not only automates our work but also 'informates' it. This has led to a major shift in the skills people need to do their job and in who has the power in organisations. Furthermore, IT has reduced personal interaction and rationalised and objectified work.[60]

Information technology is thus not only used in operations or to collect data but also to help in decision making and managing the organisation. CRM (customer relationship management) is one such IT-based management tool that is increasingly receiving attention. CRM goes further than merely collecting sales figures; it also analyses the data which is then ready for management to take decisions based on the CRM analyses.[61]

Organisational diagnosis

Organisational diagnosis takes a very normative view of organisation design and applies contingency principles very rigorously. It determines how the organisation should be designed on the basis of the main principles of organisation theory, taking into account the needs of the organisation, its environment and the other contingency elements.[62] The effectiveness criteria are the assessment criteria used to judge the organisational design. First, the 'fit' between the different contingency elements, namely goals and strategy, environment, technology and size is assessed. Next, the fit between those elements and organisation design and culture is analysed. The configurations of the structural elements discussed in the previous chapter are investigated to see whether certain elements do not fit with the contingency elements. In such assessments, an open-systems view is taken.[63] In a systems view, as explained at the beginning of this chapter, each change in a subcomponent is considered to have an effect on the other subcomponents, which have to alter as well. Accordingly, in organisational diagnosis, a great deal of attention is paid to the interdependencies between the subcomponents. The final step in each diagnosis process is to look for gaps in the working of the organisation and to alter the design to bring the organisation again into a situation of overall compliance between the elements or into a state of equilibrium. However, this systematic diagnostic approach to organisations pays only minor attention to organisational behaviour. Organisational behaviour is just one of the elements that needs to fit with the other elements. The complexity of organisational behaviour is reduced to a few generic cultural types and results in an under-socialisation view of organisations (i.e. neglecting the importance of socialisation, social identity and values in the organisation) (see also Chapter 16).

Richard Burton and Borge Obel have continued research into the organisational diagnosis field and clarified many of the relationships between the different elements from the often contradictory and fuzzy literature on organisation structure.[64] However, most of the literature they are referring to dates from the 1960s and 1970s. There are still studies published taking a contingency view or dealing with designing organisations, but studies which try to explain full fit models of organisation design with very deterministic causal relationships between the organisational elements are rare. Therefore, we are still without solid evidence on many of the relationships mentioned in this chapter. Insight into how the different elements interplay is not provided by the new trends in organisation theory either.[65]

Organisational diagnosis
a normative approach to the design of organisations based on strict-fit relationships between the elements of the organisation

Critics of the contingency approach

Criticisms of the contingency and fit approaches of organisation design are based on the fact that organisations consist of processes and not of stable structural elements. Moreover, those processes are continually evolving.[66] Critics point out that neither the organisation nor its processes or the environment remain stable. Therefore, it is almost impossible to determine an optimal fit between the elements. We also need insight into the processes that lead to obtaining and maintaining fit and that enable us to explain the dynamism in organisations.[67]

Another criticism involves environmental determinism.[68] Environmental determinism states that organisations are shaped by their environment and have limited potential to influence that environment. The contingency approach, however, very much takes the same view. Criticism of this view is based on the resource-dependency perspective and in the 'enacted' view of organisations.

The resource-dependency perspective states that organisations depend on other organisations for acquiring their resources, which creates a natural source of uncertainty.[69] Outsourcing increases the dependency on others for resources, while vertical integration (i.e. taking over the organisation supplying one of the resources) puts more resources under the control of the organisation and therefore reduces uncertainty. However, the organisation is not completely dependent on the resource providers but can negotiate with them as well. Most organisations also have several alternative providers for each of their resources. The organisation will identify its most crucial resources and try to minimise the risk by obtaining a stable supply of the critical resources that are absolutely necessary to make the organisation able to achieve its goals.

Karel Weick introduced the concept of the enacted environment to explain that we 'enact' or perceive our environment in a very personal and subjective way.[70] Key individuals in organisations, mostly the managers, construct their environment and then react to it. Consequently, two managers can view the same environment as being very complex or fairly simple and will therefore react differently. The idea of an enacted view fits in with a larger sociological view of the world. The interpretative view claims there is no world out there that we can observe. Instead, we only see the things we want to see from our very personal viewpoint. The enacted view also includes that we filter information based on our presuppositions about the world (see also symbolic interactionism in Chapter 1 and perception in Chapter 4).

However, Drazin and Van de Ven[71] mention that although contingency theory is criticised, it is still useful. We need to make assumptions about relationships in organisations, knowing that the world is much more complex and that every assumption only holds good within certain boundaries. Thus, contingency theory offers a useful systematic way to study organisation structures.[72]

Organisational effectiveness

We mentioned the need to define an organisational goal to give the members of the organisation their common goal and to allow the development of an organisation structure that supports the achievement of that goal. Organisational effectiveness refers to the degree that organisations are able to accomplish their goals. However, if someone asked you 'How effective are you?', you might find it difficult to answer. You might want to know if they were referring to your average marks, annual income, actual accomplishments, ability to get along with others, public service or perhaps something else entirely. The same goes for modern organisations. Effectiveness criteria abound. Even when the overall organisational goal is clear, its remains difficult to determine what criteria will be used to measure if the organisation is realising or moving towards its goal.

Assessing organisational effectiveness is an important topic for professionals, stockholders, government agencies and OB specialists. The purpose of this section is to introduce a widely applicable and useful model of organisational effectiveness.

Generic organisational effectiveness criteria

A good way to understand this complex subject better is to consider four generic approaches to assessing organisational effectiveness (see Figure 15.3). These effectiveness criteria apply equally well to large or small and profit or not-for-profit organisations. Moreover, as denoted by the overlapping circles in Figure 15.3, the four effectiveness criteria can be used in various combinations. The key thing to remember is that 'no single approach to the evaluation of effectiveness is appropriate in

FIGURE 15.3 FOUR WAYS TO ASSESS ORGANISATIONAL EFFECTIVENESS

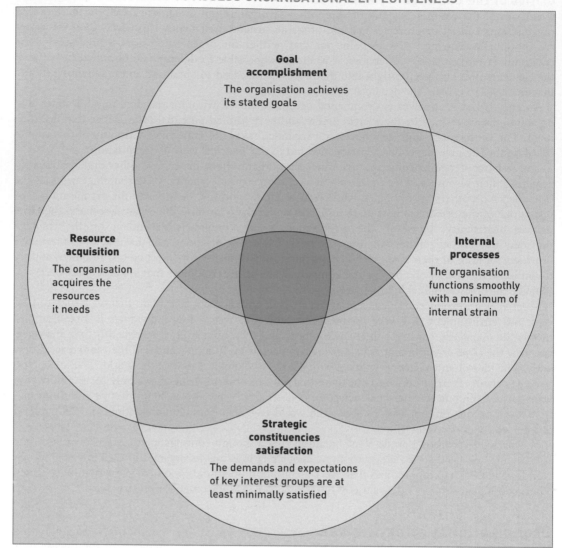

SOURCE: Adapted from discussion in K. Cameron, 'Critical Questions in Assessing Organizational Effectiveness', *Organizational Dynamics*, Autumn 1980, pp. 66–80; and K. S. Cameron, 'Effectiveness as Paradox: Consensus and Conflict in Conceptions of Organizational Effectiveness', *Management Science*, May 1986, pp. 539–53

all circumstances or for all organisation types'.[73] What do Coca-Cola and France Télécom, for example, have in common, other than being large profit-seeking corporations? Because a multidimensional approach is required, we need to look more closely at each of the four generic effectiveness criteria.

GOAL ACCOMPLISHMENT

Goal accomplishment is the most widely used effectiveness criterion for organisations. Key organisational results or outputs are compared with previously stated goals or objectives. Deviations, either plus or minus, require corrective action. This is simply an organisational variation of the personal goal-setting process discussed in Chapter 6. Effectiveness, relative to the criterion of goal accomplishment, is gauged by how well the organisation meets or exceeds its goals.[74]

Productivity improvement, involving the relationship between inputs and outputs, is a common organisation-level goal.[75] Additionally, goals may be set for organisational efforts such as minority recruiting, pollution prevention and quality improvement. Given today's competitive pressures and e-commerce revolution, innovation and speed are very important organisational goals worthy of measurement and monitoring.[76] Toyota gave us a powerful indicator of where things are going in this regard. The Japanese auto maker announced it could custom-build a car in just five days! A customer's new Toyota would roll off the Ontario, Canada, assembly line just five days after the order was placed. A 30-day lag was the industry standard at that time.[77]

RESOURCE ACQUISITION

This second criterion relates to inputs rather than outputs. An organisation is deemed effective in this regard if it acquires the necessary factors of production such as raw materials, labour, capital and managerial and technical expertise. Organisations such as Médecins Sans Frontières also have to judge their effectiveness in terms of how much money they raise from donations.

The **Resource view** takes a different approach towards organisational effectiveness by emphasising the resources of the organisation.[78] The resources are all instruments, machines, processes, knowledge, information, systems, skills or any kind of tangible and intangible assets that the organisation possesses or can make use of. Unique and scarce resources can give some organisations an advantage over others. For organisations operating in a competitive environment, such advantages are very important. An organisation can thus be evaluated in terms of the scarce resources it has or can control. According to the resource-based view, the success and effectiveness of an organisation is based on the ability to develop and safeguard strategic valuable (scarce) resources. Strategic valuable resources can create value for the organisation by preventing the threat of decline or by allowing the exploitation of opportunities. They may also be scarce and hard to imitate or have no alternative that can replace the resource.[79]

On the basis of the resource-based view, several researchers have thoroughly studied the kind of organisational resources and introduced the terms 'capabilities' and 'competences' to indicate strategic valuable resources that help organisations to be competitive and to create wealth. Capabilities are repeatable patterns of action in the use of assets to create, produce and/or offer products to a market.[80] A competence is the ability to sustain the co-ordinated deployment of assets in a way that helps a firm achieve its goals.[81] Organisations can create competitive advantages based on their competences and capabilities (see the next Snapshot). In other words, competitive advantages are based on the distinctive processes in organisations (among others based on co-ordination and task allocation), the portfolio of unique and difficult-to-trade assets and the evolution path (including previous investments and choices, learning and adaptation).[82]

INTERNAL PROCESSES

Some refer to this third effectiveness criterion as the 'healthy systems' approach. An organisation is said to be a healthy system if information flows smoothly and if employee loyalty, commitment, job satisfaction and trust prevail. It also means a harmonious balance of the structural features discussed in the previous chapter and a well-fit organisation type. Structure and behaviour are equally

> **Resource view** growth and competitive advantages of organisations are based on the presence of rare and immobile resources under control of the organisation

---

Diversification at Coca-Cola Company

Coca-Cola has without doubt an enormously strong brand and popular product, but the growth in the consumption of soft drinks declined at the end of the 1990s. Coca-Cola made use of one of its strategic resources to cope with this decline. It used its immense distribution system to push other kinds of soft drinks (especially diet drinks), sport drinks and mineral waters in the market. Especially in the US, the unique distribution network is the key to the success of Coca-Cola's new products. The distribution network in Europe is weaker and therefore it is expected that these weaker resources will make it harder for Coca-Cola to take in the European mineral water market.

SOURCE: Translated from P. Van Maldegem and R. Cambré, 'Diversificatie loont voor frisdrankenproducenten', *De Tijd*, 24 July 2003, p. 5.

snapshot

important and goals may be set for any of the structural and behavioural internal processes. Healthy systems, from a behavioural view, tend to have a minimum of dysfunctional conflict and destructive political manoeuvring. M. Scott Peck, the physician who wrote the highly regarded book, *The Road Less Travelled*, characterises healthy organisations in ethical terms (also see Chapter 18):

> A healthy organisation, Peck says, is one that has a genuine sense of community: It's a place where people are emotionally present with one another, and aren't afraid to talk about fears and disappointments – because that's what allows us to care for one another. It's a place where there is authentic communication, a willingness to be vulnerable, a commitment to speaking frankly and respectfully – and a commitment not to walk away when the going gets tough.[83]

Efficiency and productivity

Efficiency
realising a certain output with a minimum amount of input

Productivity
realising the highest possible output with a specific amount of input

Criteria often used to evaluate the structural side of organisational processes are efficiency and productivity. **Efficiency** is achieved when a certain output is realised with the lowest costs; while costs can be monetary value but also resources and time. The larger the efficiency the more potential profit a profit-oriented organisation can make or the more a non-profit-oriented organisation can do with the same amount of money. Efficiency will require the absence of dysfunctionality in the organisation structure, such as unnecessary co-ordination of tasks or employees' time wasted due to the delayed delivery of raw material. **Productivity** indicates the amount of output created with a given amount of input and is thus closely related to efficiency. Low productivity is caused by inefficient use of input.

> The public administration of the UK government located in London were evaluated on the efficiency criteria. The study revealed that efficiency can be increased by moving staff out of London to local areas and by increasing local staff while decreasing the staff in the departments' headquarters (in the next 15 years, up to 60000). Current departments are too large, the co-operation with regional services is too low and, especially, the wages in London are a lot higher than in the rest of the UK. Staff turnover is much higher in London as well. Big savings can be gained when functions such as human resources, accounting, purchasing and IT are shared between departments, councils and other parts of the public sector. However, before the efficiency gains can be obtained, large upfront cuts need to be made.[84]

However, not all organisations have efficiency as an effectiveness criterion. An emphasis on efficiency competes with other criteria, such as quality, flexibility or innovation. The most efficient and productive way of operating does not always mean the most qualitative way or the most innovative way. Often, quality, flexibility and innovativeness can only be reached at higher costs. These criteria are becoming more and more important for organisations in turbulent and dynamic environments.

Total Quality Management

Total quality management
An organisational culture dedicated to training, continuous improvement and customer satisfaction

Experts on the subject offer the following definition of **Total quality management**:

> Total Quality Management (TQM) means that the organisation's culture is defined by, and supports the attainment of customer satisfaction through an integrated system of tools, techniques and training. This involves the continuous improvement of organisational processes, resulting in high-quality products and services.[85]

Quality consultant Richard J. Schonberger sums up TQM as 'continuous, customer-centred, employee-driven improvement'.[86] TQM is necessarily employee-driven because product/service quality cannot be continually improved without the active learning and participation of every employee. Thus, in successful quality-improvement programmes, TQM principles are embedded in the organisation's culture (also see Chapter 16).[87] Despite variations in the language and scope of TQM programmes, it is possible to identify four common TQM principles. TQM is firmly established today thanks in large part to the pioneering work of W. Edwards Deming. Deming's influence is clearly evident in this list:[88]

■ Do it right the first time to eliminate costly rework.
■ Listen to, and learn from, customers and employees.
■ Make continuous improvement an everyday matter.
■ Build teamwork, trust and mutual respect.[89]

Quality is a difficult criterion to assess because it depends on the expectation of a product or service. Organisations who choose radically for quality of their output apply Total Quality Management. TQM exists when the needs of the customers of the organisation are heard and the organisation tries to meet and communicate about these needs with its customers. Furthermore, all departments in the organisation need to aim for high quality, the back-office departments included. Finally, quality is a continuous improvement project because quality can always be improved and it also depends on customer needs, which are frequently changing.[90]

EFQM

In 1988 fourteen major European companies founded the European Foundation for Quality Management (EFQM) with the endorsement of the European Commission, in order to stimulate quality in European companies by rewarding prizes and recognition for high-level quality management. Figure 15.4 shows the EFQM Excellence Model used to assess the quality and excellence in organisations. The foundation presents the European Quality Award each year. By making companies compete for the EFQM award, quality is stimulated. Companies can also become a member of EFQM when they are striving for excellence and want to use the EFQM model as their assessment tool. It is estimated that over 20 000 European companies use the EFQM model as assessment tool. In summary the model says that: 'Excellent results with respect to performance, customers, people and society are achieved through leadership driving policy and strategy that is delivered through people partnerships and resources, and processes.' Each of the labels in the boxes in Figure 15.4 has a clear definition and a number of assessment criteria. Each criterion has a list of guidance points that can help organisations to improve the quality of their services and manufacturing. The 'results' indicate what the company has achieved and is achieving; the 'enablers' indicate how those results are being achieved. In 2002 Dexia-Sofaxis, an operational unit of Bosch, the customs and tax region Aarhus, Banc International d'Andorra, I Banca Mora and three other SMEs won EFQM prizes.[91]

FIGURE 15.4 THE EFQM EXCELLENCE MODEL

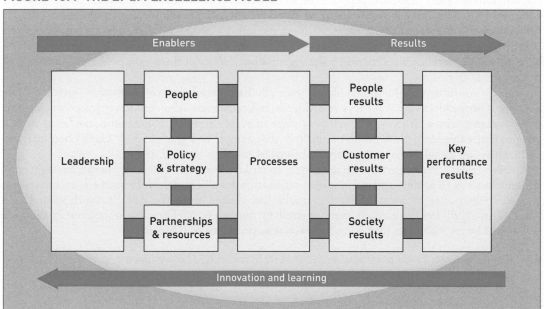

SOURCE: http://www.efqm.org/model_awards/model/excellence_model.htm

RESEARCH FINDINGS AND PRACTICAL IMPLICATIONS

Boldwijn and Kumpe visited and analysed several different European manufacturing companies to study the goals of these companies. They found that there has been an evolution in the goals of European manufacturers. In the 1960s companies needed to achieve maximum efficiency. Later, in the 1970s, attention shifted towards quality and low cost. There was large global competition, but at the same time customers became more demanding. In the next phase, around the 1980s, flexibility became an additional goal. Competition was still large and customers were still demanding but the pace of technological renewal and the search by companies to innovate in order to deal with the increasing competition forced every production company to become more flexible. They needed to be able to cope with change and especially to be able to change fast. Manufacturing companies are now still in a similar situation. Hence, Boldwijn and Kumpe claim that companies can only survive when they are able to combine different goals, which are hard to combine and might even be conflicting. However, those companies which are able to deal with the paradox of efficiency and flexibility while keeping high quality are the really superior ones. The authors give examples of Philips, Fiat, DAF and several other European manufacturers that have been able to survive for a very long period in highly competitive markets. Reaching these three goals demands an integrative approach with close co-operation between the R&D and production departments and a flexible organisation structure, including short information loops, flat and decentralised structures. People should not be too specialised in their tasks, but should be able to work at different workstations in the factory to allow the flexible allocation of tasks.[92]

> Telecom operators, such as AT&T, have been busy with product innovation and large marketing campaigns to gain market share but now it is time again to pay attention to efficiency. The large telecom operators are now worried about their billing support systems. The big market share means nothing when vital tasks such as service activation, billing and customer care are not working efficiently. Billing is, however, complex with ten new services introduced yearly. Billing needs to be reliable and flexible but not too complex for customers.[93]

STRATEGIC CONSTITUENCIES SATISFACTION

Organisations both depend on people and affect the lives of people. Consequently, many consider the satisfaction of key interested parties to be an important criterion of organisational effectiveness.

A **Strategic constituency** is any group of individuals who have some stake in the organisation – for example, resource providers, users of the organisation's products or services, producers of the organisation's output, groups whose co-operation is essential for the organisation's survival or those whose lives are significantly affected by the organisation.[94] We call these groups the 'stakeholders' of the organisation.

Strategic constituencies (or stakeholders) generally have competing or conflicting interests.[95] For instance, shareholders who want higher dividends and consumers who seek lower prices would most likely disagree with a union's demand for a wage increase. Strategic constituents can be identified systematically through a **Stakeholder audit** (see the example in Figure 15.5).[96] Conflicting interests and relative satisfaction among the listed stakeholders can then be dealt with.

A never-ending challenge for management is to strike a workable balance between strategic constituencies so as to achieve at least minimal satisfaction on all fronts. McDonald's is an interesting and compelling case in point. After the smoke had cleared from the riots in south central Los Angeles in April 1992, observers were amazed to find every McDonald's restaurant in the area untouched by arsonists. But that outcome was not surprising to McDonald's:

> For Edward H. Rensi, president and CEO of McDonald's USA, the explanation of what happened, or didn't happen, in South Central LA was simple: 'Our businesses there are owned by African-American entrepreneurs who hired African-American managers who hired African-American employees who served everybody in the community, whether they be Korean, African American or Caucasian.'[97]

Strategic constituency any group of people with a stake in the organisation's operation or success

Stakeholder audit systematic identification of all parties likely to be affected by the organisation

FIGURE 15.5 A SAMPLE US STAKEHOLDER AUDIT IDENTIFYING STRATEGIC CONSTITUENCIES

SOURCE: 'The Stakeholder Audit Goes Public', by N. C. Roberts *et al*, *Organizational Dynamics*, Winter 1989 © 1989, American Management Association International, New York. Reprinted by permission of the American Management Association International, New York, NY. All rights reserved. http://www.amanet.org.

Multiple effectiveness criteria: practical implications

Experts on the subject recommend a multidimensional approach to assessing the effectiveness of modern organisations. This means no single criterion is appropriate for all stages of the organisation's life cycle, nor will a single criterion satisfy competing stakeholders. Well-managed organisations mix and match effectiveness criteria to fit the unique requirements of the situation.[98]

> The Body Shop, originally a small entrepreneurial company from the south coast of England, but now a large international company has many different objectives and effectiveness criteria. The Body Shop is known for its campaign against animal testing and its ecologically friendly products but The Body Shop is also a commercial organisation with investors, employees, franchisees and shareholders among its many stakeholders and a turnover of £381 million in 2003. The following criteria are all mentioned as being important. The complete list of effectiveness criteria is even longer and more diverse:
>
> - Sales growth in every country.
> - Higher product quality.
> - Tight control of the costs within the business.
> - Work towards partnerships with key suppliers based on mutual trust and respect.
> - Innovation but in a most cost-effective way by utilising supplier expertise and capabilities.
> - Ensuring that the business is ecologically sustainable.
> - Campaigning for the protection of the environment, human and civil rights.
> - Balancing financial and human needs of the stakeholders: employees, customers, franchisees, suppliers and shareholders.[99]

Organisational leaders need to identify and seek input from strategic constituencies. This information, when merged with the organisation's stated mission and philosophy, enables management to derive an appropriate combination of effectiveness criteria. The following guidelines are helpful in this regard:

■ The goal accomplishment approach is appropriate when 'goals are clear, consensual, time-bounded, measurable'.[100]

■ The resource acquisition approach is appropriate when inputs have a traceable effect on results or output. For example, the amount of money the Red Cross receives through donations dictates the level of services provided.

■ The internal processes approach is appropriate when organisational performance is strongly influenced by specific processes (e.g. cross-functional teamwork).

■ The strategic constituencies approach is appropriate when powerful stakeholders can significantly benefit or harm the organisation.[101]

The relationship between effectiveness and organisational culture is discussed in Chapter 16 (Table 16.1, based on research by Cameron and Quinn).

The next Activity wants to stimulate your reflection on organisational effectiveness criteria.

activity

What do you see as organisational effectiveness criteria?

There is no single way to measure organisational effectiveness, as discussed in this chapter. Different stakeholders want organisations to do different and often conflicting things. The purpose of this exercise is to introduce alternative effectiveness criteria and to assess real companies with them.

Each year, *Fortune* magazine publishes a ranking of the Global Most Admired Companies. Some might pass this off as simply a corporate-image popularity contest. But we view it as much more. *Fortune* applies a set of eight attributes that could arguably be called effectiveness criteria. These criteria are:

■ Revenues.
■ Profits.
■ Assets (as indicated on the financial balance sheets).
■ Stockholders' equity (sum of all capital stock and reserves on the balance sheets).
■ Market value (based on share price).
■ Earnings per share (based on the earnings indicated on the income sheets).
■ Total return to investors (based on prices appreciation and dividend yield).
■ Medians (position of the company based on the median of the seven financial criteria in the full list of companies).

In 2003, the following ten companies were ranked as the most globally admired companies:

■ Wal-Mart stores.
■ General Motors.
■ Exxon Motors.
■ Royal Dutch Shell Group.
■ BP.
■ Ford Motor Co.
■ DaimlerChrysler.
■ Toyota Motors.
■ General Electric.
■ Mitsubishi.

Questions

1 Do you agree that the eight attributes are really organisational effectiveness criteria? Explain. What other criteria would you add to the list? Which would you remove from the list?
2 Are you surprised by the top-ranked company (or companies) in the top ten list? Explain.

Keeping these basic concepts of organisational effectiveness in mind, we turn our attention to preventing organisational decline in the next section.

The ever-present threat of organisational decline

If you think failure is scary, try success. Time after time, big companies such as Fiat, Apple Computers, Marks & Spencer, C&A, IBM and Boeing have stumbled badly after periods of great success. Donald N. Sull, a strategy professor at the London Business School, recently framed the situation as follows.

> One of the most common business phenomena is also one of the most perplexing: when successful companies face big changes in their environment, they often fail to respond effectively. Unable to defend themselves against competitors armed with new products, technologies or strategies, they watch their sales and profits erode, their best people leave and their stock valuations tumble. Some ultimately manage to recover – usually after painful rounds of downsizing and restructuring – but many don't.[102]

Researchers call this downward spiral **Organisational decline** and define it as 'a decrease in an organisation's resource base'.[103] The term 'resource' is used very broadly in this context, encompassing money, talent, customers, and innovative ideas and products. Professionals seeking to maintain organisational effectiveness need to be alert to the problem because experts tell us 'decline is almost unavoidable unless deliberate steps are taken to prevent it'.[104] The first key step is to recognise the early warning signs of organisational decline.

> **Organisational decline** decrease in organisation's resource base (money, customers, talent, innovations)

> The legendary Danish toys company, Lego, is now facing a serious organisational decline. Sales decreased by 25 per cent last year, market share shrank, the CEO had to leave, as well as hundreds of other employees. The decline went on for several years and was caused by several wrong strategic and marketing decisions made to keep up with the new trends, but the changes failed to meet customers' needs. The toys market changed, became more competitive and more dependent on temporary trends. Lego wanted to follow that change but focused so much on following the new trends that it lost sight of its core strengths, namely simple Lego blocks for little children. Lego's culture has to change as well. For many years they were so successful that they forgot to listen to their customers. They were not accustomed to thinking of marketing and product development, but in the current environment with many more kinds of toys in the market, Lego is not in such a comfortable position any more.[105]

Early-warning signs of decline

Professionals who monitor the early warning signs of organisational decline are better able to reorganise in a timely and effective manner.[106] Table 15.4 provides a list of the most important early warning signs of organisational decline. However, recent research has uncovered a troublesome tendency towards inaccurate perception among entrenched top management teams. In companies where there has been little if any turnover among top executives, there is a tendency to attribute organisational problems to external causes (such as competition, the government, technology shifts); by contrast, internal attributions tend to be made by top management teams which include many new members (see also Chapter 4). Thus, proverbial 'new blood' at the top appears to be a good insurance policy against inaccurately perceiving the early-warning signs of organisational decline.[107]

Preventing organisational decline

The time to start doing something about organisational decline is when everything is going right. For it is during periods of high success that the seeds of decline are sown.[108] Complacency is the number one threat because it breeds overconfidence and inattentiveness.[109]

TABLE 15.4 THE EARLY WARNING SIGNS OF ORGANISATIONAL DECLINE

- Excess personnel
- Tolerance of incompetence
- Cumbersome administrative procedures
- Disproportionate staff power (e.g. technical staff specialists politically overpowering line managers, whom they view as unsophisticated and too conventional)
- Replacement of substance with form (e.g. the planning process becomes more important than the results achieved)
- Scarcity of clear goals and decision benchmarks

- Fear of embarrassment and conflict (e.g. formerly successful executives may resist new ideas for fear of revealing past mistakes)
- Loss of effective communication
- Outdated organisational structure
- Increased scapegoating by leaders
- Resistance to change
- Low morale
- Special interest groups are more vocal
- Decreased innovation

SOURCE: K. S. Cameron, D. A. Whetten and M. U. Kim, 'Organizational Dysfunctions of Decline', *Academy of Management Journal*, March 1987, pp. 126–38; D. K. Hurst, *Crisis and Renewal: Meeting the Challenge of Organizational Change* (Boston, MA: Harvard Business School Press, 1995); and V. L. Barker III and P. W. Patterson, Jr, 'Top Management Team Tenure and Top Manager Causal Attributions at Declining Firms Attempting Turnarounds', *Group & Organization Management*, September 1996, pp. 304–36.

On a mild fall day in Paris Alcatel Chairman Serge Tchuruk received a shrill wake-up call from Silicon Valley. Tchuruk had been busy selling money-losing divisions of the giant phone-gear manufacturer and carving out layers of bureaucracy – turning Alcatel around the old-fashioned way. But in its long-standing history, Alcatel had never faced a New World phenomenon like Cisco Systems Inc. The Silicon Valley hotshot had been racing around the Continent, gobbling up contracts at Alcatel's expense – and was so successful that on that September afternoon, Tchuruk had to issue a warning that earnings would not meet expectations. Investors, led by American fund managers, responded with a vengeance, driving Alcatel shares down by 38 per cent.

That hurt. But it also helped shake things up at Alcatel. After the plunge, Tchuruk kick-started an effort to remodel Alcatel after the Silicon Valley rivals that were stealing its business. Over the next 18 months, he went on a high-tech buying spree, gobbling up a half-dozen North American companies for $11.3 billion. He shifted entire divisions across the Atlantic, and named the American head of his US unit, Krish Prabhu, president and heir to Alcatel's top job. He even instituted stock options, long taboo in egalitarian France. Afterwards Tchuruk mused: 'We're not really a French company any more.'[110]

Learning outcomes: Summary of key terms

1 Describe the three general views on organisational fit: open systems, chaos theory and systems theory

Closed systems, such as a battery-powered clock, are relatively self-sufficient. Open systems, such as the human body, are highly dependent on the environment for survival. Organisations are said to be open systems. Chaos theory sees organisations as operating in a highly turbulent environment creating disorder and unanticipated changes for the organisation. According to the systems theory the organisation is part of a large system, while at the same time the organisation itself consists of many interrelated subsystems.

2 Explain the contingency approach to organisations, including the benefits and shortcomings of such approach

The contingency approach to organisation design calls for fitting the organisation to the demands of the situation. Contingency factors are: environment, technology, structure, strategy and size. The major benefit is the creation of a harmonious balance in the organisational elements and contingency factors to create an organisation design that is best fitted to the particular environment. One drawback of this view is that it pays little attention to organisational processes, change and environmental determinism. The latter questions the unidirectional impact of the environment on the organisation.

3 Describe the impact of environmental uncertainty on the organisation

Environmental uncertainty can be mainly assessed in terms of various combinations of two dimensions: (a) simple or complex and (b) static or dynamic. Uncertainty can also be caused by equivocality, diversity and hostility. Depending on the uncertainty in the environment, the organisation needs to be structured differently.

4 Describe major strategy types and the relationship with organisation structure

Porter differentiates between cost leadership, differentiation and focus. Miles and Snow categorise organisations based on their strategies as defenders, analysers, prospectors and reactors. The more defensive the strategy, the more the structure needs to be oriented towards efficiency. The more innovative the strategy, the more flexible the organisation structure needs to be.

5 Explain the role of size in the contingency view

Size is a source of complexity. The larger the size, the more complexity and the more advanced co-ordination mechanisms need to be used and the more differences are observed in the contingency factors of each department. The complexity can cause problems by counterbalancing the economics of scale advantage due to the larger scale. Regarding the optimum size for organisations, the challenge for today's managers is to achieve smallness within bigness by keeping sub-units at a manageable size.

6 Define technology as organisational element

Technology encompasses all means used in the organisation to achieve the organisational goals, such as procedures, work methods, skills, tools and knowledge. Information technology is seen as an important new kind of technology that has both positive and negative effects on working in the organisation.

7 Explain the effect of technology on the organisation structure and the four major studies that have explored the relationship between technology and structure

Woodward explained how mass, piece and flow production lead to different levels of complexity and therefore require different co-ordination mechanisms to deal with the complexity. Thompson identifies four kinds of interdependencies between tasks and the kind of co-ordination best suited for each of these interdependencies. Perrow describes the complexity of tasks in terms of level of analysability of technology and level of change in relation to different types of work and possibilities for standardisation. Galbraith explains that the complexity of the technology refers to the information needed to co-ordinate the tasks.

8 Describe the four generic organisational effectiveness criteria

They are goal accomplishment (satisfying stated objectives), resource acquisition (gathering the necessary productive inputs), internal processes (building and maintaining healthy organisational systems which try to achieve the difficult combination of efficiency, quality, productivity, flexibility and innovativeness) and strategic constituencies satisfaction (achieving at least minimal satisfaction for all key stakeholders).

9 Describe the resource-based view of organisations

Organisation success is based on control over unique and hard-to-imitate resources. The effectiveness of organisations is evaluated on the basis of the possession of such resources and how these resources can be applied to create unique competences and capabilities which in turn generate a competitive advantage.

10 Explain how professionals can prevent organisational decline
Because complacency is the leading cause of organisational decline, managers need to create a culture of continuous improvement. Decline automatically follows periods of great success, so prevention is needed to avoid the erosion of organisational resources (money, customers, talent and innovative ideas).

Review questions

1 Explain why your university or school is a system and why it is an open system.
2 Why is a fit in the organisational elements necessary and what are the dangers of an organisation that is not adapted to its environment? Can you give an example of an organisation that fits the environment well and one that does not?
3 Think of an organisation you know well and describe its environment. Do the same for the technology, size and strategy. Is there a fit among the different contingency factors and the organisation structure?
4 Is there an evolution in the environments organisations have to deal with now compared to 20 years ago?
5 How can you tell if an organisation (or subunit) is too big?
6 Is information technology changing the contingency relationships, in particular the effect of size, technology and environment on the design of organisations?
7 How would you respond to a manager who claimed the only way to measure a business's effectiveness is in terms of how much profit it makes?
8 Can organisations cope with different effectiveness criteria at the same time and how?
9 What are the stakeholders of an university and how does the organisation satisfy the needs of these stakeholders?
10 Why is it important to focus on the role of complacency in organisational decline?

Personal awareness and growth exercise

Organisation design field study

Objectives
1 To get out into the field and talk to a practising manager about organisational structure.
2 To broaden your knowledge of contingency design, in terms of organisation–environment fit.
3 To make you understand the different effectiveness criteria.

Introduction
A good way to test the validity of what you have just read about organisation design is to interview a practising manager. (Note: If you are a manager, simply complete the questionnaire yourself.)

Instructions
Your objective is to interview a manager about aspects of organisational structure, environmental uncertainty and organisational effectiveness. A manager is defined as anyone who supervises other people in an organisational setting. The organisation may be small or large and for-profit or not-for-profit. Higher-level managers are preferred but middle managers and first-line supervisors are acceptable. If you interview a lower-level manager, be sure to remind him or her that you want a description of the overall organisation, not just an isolated subunit. Your interview will centre on the question described below.

When conducting your interview, be sure to explain to the manager what you are trying to accomplish. But assure the manager that his or her name will not be mentioned in lecture or group discussions or any written projects. Try to take brief notes during the interview for later reference.

Questionnaire

The following questionnaire will help you determine the contingency factors of the manager's organisation. (Circle one number for each item.)

Characteristics of technology, size, structure and strategy

1 Technology changes:	Rarely	1	2	3	4	5	6	7		Very frequent
2 Technology is very:	Simple	1	2	3	4	5	6	7		Complex
3 Task flexibility is	Rigid; routine	1	2	3	4	5	6	7		Flexible; varied
4 The organisation is compared to others in the industry	Small	1	2	3	4	5	6	7		Large
5 Degree of hierarchical control	High	1	2	3	4	5	6	7		Low (self-control emphasised)
6 Primary communication pattern	Top-down	1	2	3	4	5	6	7		Lateral (between peers)
7 Primary decision-making style	Authoritarian	1	2	3	4	5	6	7		Democratic; participative
8 The organisation can be described as very:	Formalised	1	2	3	4	5	6	7		Non-formalised
9 Decision-making power is:	Centralised	1	2	3	4	5	6	7		Decentralised

Question about the organisation's environment

This organisation faces an environment that is (circle one number):

Stable and certain	1	2	3	4	5	6	7	8	9	10		Unstable and uncertain

Question about the organisation's strategy

This organisation has a strategy that can be described as (circle one number):

Stable	1	2	3	4	5	6	7	8	9	10		Innovative
Cost leadership	1	2	3	4	5	6	7	8	9	10		Differentiation or focus

Additional questions about the organisation's effectiveness

1 Profitability (if a profit-seeking business):

Low	1	2	3	4	5	6	7	8	9	10		High

2 Degree of organisation goal accomplishment:

Low	1	2	3	4	5	6	7	8	9	10		High

3 Customer or client satisfaction:

Low	1	2	3	4	5	6	7	8	9	10		High

4 Employee satisfaction:

Low	1	2	3	4	5	6	7	8	9	10		High

Based on the scores on the technology questions (first 3 questions), the size question (question 4), the structure questions (from 5 to 9) and the three other groups of questions, describe the fit factors of this organisation.

Questions for discussion

1 Compare the different fit factors and discuss whether there is a fit among the factors.
2 Is the organisation adapted to its environment?
3 Does the organisation's degree of effectiveness reflect how well it fits its environment? Explain.

Group exercise

Stakeholder audit team

Objectives

1 To continue developing your group interaction and teamwork skills.

2 To engage in open-system thinking.

3 To conduct a stakeholder audit and thus more fully appreciate the competing demands placed on today's managers.

4 To establish priorities and consider trade-offs for modern managers.

Introduction

According to open-system models of organisations, environmental factors – social, political, legal, technological and economic – greatly affect what managers can and cannot do. This exercise gives you an opportunity to engage in open-system thinking within a team setting. It requires a team meeting of about 20 to 25 minutes followed by a general class discussion for 10 to 15 minutes. Total time required for this exercise is about 30 to 40 minutes.

Instructions

Your lecturer will randomly assign you to teams with five to eight members each. Choose one team member to act as record keeper and spokesperson.

Identify an organisation that is familiar to everyone in your team (it can be a local business, your college or university, or a well-known organisation such as McDonald's, Royal Dutch Shell or British Airways).

Next do a stakeholder audit for the organisation in question. This will require a team brainstorming session followed by brief discussion. Your team will need to make reasonable assumptions about the circumstances surrounding your target organisation.

Finally, your team should select the three (or more) high-priority stakeholders on your team's list. Rank them number one, number two, and so on. (Tip: A top-priority stakeholder is one with the greatest short-term impact on the success or failure of your target organisation.) Be prepared to explain to the entire class your rationale for selecting each high-priority stakeholder.

Questions for discussion

1 How does this exercise foster open-system thinking? Give examples.

2 Did this exercise broaden your awareness of the complexity of modern organisational environments? Explain.

3 Why do managers need clear priorities when it comes to dealing with organisational stakeholders?

4 How many trade-offs (meaning one party gains at another's expense) can you detect in your team's list of stakeholders? Specify them.

5 How difficult was it for your team to complete this assignment? Explain.

Internet exercise

Fortune's ranking of the Global Most Admired Companies can be viewed as a measurement of organisation effectiveness, as described in the Activity on organisational effectiveness criteria. Now surf to our website www.mcgraw-hill.co.uk/textbooks/buelens for instructions on an internet exercise on an organisation in your home country.

Notes

1 Excerpted from S. Pritchard, 'Inside Dell's Lean Machine', *Works Management*, December 2002, pp. 14–17.

2 R. Blom and H. Melin, 'Information Society and the Transformation of Organizations in Finland', *Work and Occupations*, May 2003, pp. 176–93.

3 See for more information on this new theory J. Gleick, *Chaos: Making a New Science* (New York: Penguin Books, 1987); R. D. Stacey, *Managing the Unknowable: Strategic Boundaries between Order and Chaos in Organizations* (San Francisco, CA: Jossey-Bass, 1992); and R. A. Thiétart and B. Forgues, 'Chaos Theory and Organization', *Organization Science*, January–February 1995, pp. 19–31.

4 Based on the articles 'Asia in Sars Isolation Ward', the *Observer*, 27 April 2003; and translated from 'Sars haalt Singapore onderuit', *De Standaard*, 14 July 2003.

5 See A. Farazmand, 'Chaos and Transformation Theories: A Theoretical Analysis with Implications for Organization Theory and Public Management', *Public Organization Review*, December 2003, p. 339; and S. L. Dolan, S. Garcia and A. Auerbach, 'Understanding and Managing Chaos in Organisations', *International Journal of Management*, March 2003, pp. 23–36.

6 K. E. Boulding, 'General Systems Theory: The Skeleton of Science', *Management Science*, April 1956, pp. 197–208.

7 L. Von Bertalanffy, 'Problems of General Systems Theory: A New Approach to the Unity of Science', *Human Biology*, no. 4, 1951, pp. 58–9.

8 S. R. Barley and G. Kunda, 'Bringing Work Back In', *Organization Science*, January–February 2001, pp. 76–95.

9 For updates, see J. M. Pennings, 'Structural Contingency Theory: A Reappraisal', in *Research in Organizational Behavior, vol. 14* (Greenwich, CT: JAI Press, 1992), pp. 267–309; A. D. Meyer, A. S. Tsui and C. R. Hinings, 'Configurational Approaches to Organizational Analysis', *Academy of Management Journal*, December 1993, pp. 1175–95; and D. H. Doty, W. H. Glick and G. P. Huber, 'Fit, Equifinality, and Organizational Effectiveness: A Test of Two Configurational Theories', *Academy of Management Journal*, December 1993, pp. 1196–1250.

10 See for the main authors that developed the contingency theory: T. Burns and G. M. Stalker, *The Management of Innovation* (London: Tavistock, 1961); A. D. Chandler, *Strategy and Structure* (Cambridge, MA: MIT Press, 1962); J. Woodward, *Industrial Organization: Theory and Practice* (London: Oxford University Press, 1965); J. D. Thompson, *Organizations in Action* (New York: McGraw-Hill, 1967); P. R. Lawrence and J. W. Lorsch, *Organization and Environment* (Boston, MA: Harvard University Press, 1967); D. S. Pugh and C. R. Hinings, *Organizational Structure: Extensions and Replications* (Westmead: Saxon House, 1976); J. R. Galbraith, *Organization Design* (Reading, MA: Addison-Wesley Publishing Company, 1977); and P. N. Khandwalla, *Design of Organizations* (New York: Harcourt Brace Jovanovich, 1977).

11 R. Burton and B. Obel, *Strategic Organizational Diagnosis and Design: Developing Theory for Application* (Boston, MA: Kluwer Academic, 1995).

12 S. R. Barley and G. Kunda, 'Bringing Work Back In', *Organization Science*, January–February 2001, pp. 76–95. An interesting distinction between three types of environmental uncertainty can also be found in F. J. Milliken, 'Three Types of Perceived Uncertainty about the Environment: State, Effect, and Response Uncertainty', *Academy of Management Review*, January 1987, pp. 133–43.

13 J. Birkinshaw, R. Nobel and J. Ridderstrale, 'Knowledge As a Contingency Variable: Do the Characteristics of Knowledge Predict Organization Structure?', *Organization Science*, May–June 2002, pp. 274–89.

14 R. M. Burton, J. Lauridson and B. Obel, 'Return on Assets Loss from Situational and Contingency Misfits', *Management Science*, November 2002, pp. 1461–86.

15 H. Barth, 'Fit Among Competitive Strategy, Administrative Mechanisms, and Performance: A Comparative Study of Small Firms in Mature and New Industries', *Journal of Small Business Management*, April 2003, pp. 133–48.

16 W. A. Drago, 'Mintzberg's "Pentagon" and Organization Positioning', *Management Research News*, no. 4/5, 1998, pp. 30–41.

17 D. Dombey, 'Alstom Case Revives Debate on State Aid', *Financial Times*, 26 April 2004.

18 P. R. Lawrence and J. W. Lorsch, *Organization and Environment* (Boston, MA: Harvard University Press, 1967).

19 P. R. Lawrence and J. W. Lorsch, *Organization and Environment* (Boston, MA: Harvard University Press, 1967).

20 R. Duncan, 'What Is the Right Organization Structure?', *Organizational Dynamics*, Winter 1979, p. 63.

21 R. Duncan, 'What Is the Right Organization Structure?', *Organizational Dynamics*, Winter 1979, p. 63.

22 See P. Sellers, 'Crunch Time for Coke', *Fortune*, 19 July 1999, pp. 72–8.

23 See T. J. Tetenbaum, 'Shifting Paradigms: From Newton to Chaos', *Organizational Dynamics*, Spring 1998, pp. 21–32; W. Miller, 'Building the Ultimate Resource', *Management Review*, January 1999, pp. 42–5; D. P. Ellerman, 'Global Institutions: Transforming International Development Agencies into Learning Organizations', *Academy of Management Executive*, February 1999, pp. 25–35; and K. Maani and C. Benton, 'Rapid Team Learning: Lessons from Team New Zealand America's Cup Campaign', *Organizational Dynamics*, Spring 1999, pp. 48–62.

24 R. L. Daft and R. H. Lengel, 'Organizational Information Requirements, Media Richness and Structural Design', *Management Science*, May 1986, pp. 554–71.

25 J. Bourgeois and K. Eisenhardt, 'Strategic Decision Processes in High Velocity Environments: Four Cases in the Microcomputer Industry', *Management Science*, July 1988, pp. 816–35.

26 A. Azhar 'Move On', the *Observer*, 6 February 2004.

27 H. Mintzberg, *The Structuring of Organizations* (Englewood Cliffs, NJ: Prentice Hall, 1979).

28 Translated from G. Meeusen, 'Virgin Express zakt diep in het rood', *De Tijd*, 31 March 2004.

29 T. Burns and G. M. Stalker, The *Management of Innovation* (London: Tavistock, 1961); P. R. Lawrence and J. W. Lorsch, *Organization and Environment* (Boston, MA: Harvard University Press, 1967); R. B. Duncan, 'Characteristics of Organizational Environments and Perceived Environmental Uncertainty', *Administrative Science Quarterly*, September 1972, pp. 313–27; and H. Mintzberg, *The Structuring of Organizations* (Englewood Cliffs, NJ: Prentice Hall, 1979).

30 H. Mintzberg, *The Structuring of Organizations* (Englewood Cliffs, NJ: Prentice Hall, 1979).

31 For more information on the population ecology theory, see M. T. Hannan and J. H. Freeman, 'The Population Ecology of Organizations', *American Journal of Sociology*, March 1977, pp. 929–64; H. Aldrich, *Organizations and Environment* (Englewood Cliffs, NJ: Prentice Hall, 1979); and H. Kaufman, *Time, Change and Organizations* (Chatham, NJ: Chatham House, 1985).

32 A. D. Chandler, *Strategy and Structure* (Cambridge, MA: MIT Press, 1962).

33 J. W. Frederickson, 'The Strategic Decision Process and Organization Structure', *Academy of Management Review*, no. 2, 1986, pp. 280–97.

34 M. Porter, *Competitive Advantage: Creating and Sustaining Superior Performance* (New York: Free Press, 1985).

35 R. E. Miles and C. C. Snow, *Organizational Strategy, Structure and Process* (New York: McGraw-Hill, 1978).

36 For authors who further developed the Miles and Snow categories, see D. Miller, 'The Structural and Environmental Correlates of Business Strategy', *Strategic Management Review*, no 1, 1987, pp. 55–76; and N. Nicholson, A. Rees and A. Brooks-Rooney, 'Strategy, Innovation and Performance', *Journal of Management Studies*, no. 5, 1990, pp. 511–34.

37 S. Jones, 'Kimberly-Clark Unveils Operations Revamp', *Financial Times*, 19 January 2004.

38 Based on D. Bradshaw, 'Swiss Group at Top of Learning Tree', *Financial Times*, 22 March 2004; and G. Dyer, 'Most Influential Business Figure: Daniel Vasella – The Medicine Man', *Financial Times*, 22 March 2004.

39 See J. Child, 'Organizational Structure, Environment and Performance: The Role of Strategic Choice', *Sociology*, January 1972, pp. 1–22.

40 See J. Galbraith, *Organization Design* (Reading, MA: Addison-Wesley Publishing, 1977); J. R. Montanari, 'Managerial Discretion: An Expanded Model of Organization Choice', *Academy of Management Review*, April 1978, pp. 231–41; and H. R. Bobbitt, Jr, and J. D. Ford, 'Decision-Maker Choice as A Determinant of Organizational Structure', *Academy of Management Review*, January 1980, pp. 13–23.

41 For an alternative model of strategy making, see S. L. Hart, 'An Integrative Framework for Strategy-Making Processes', *Academy of Management Review*, April 1992, pp. 327–51. Also see F. E. Harrison and M. A. Pelletier, 'A Typology of Strategic Choice', *Technological Forecasting and Social Change*, November 1993, pp. 245–63; H. Mintzberg, 'The Rise and Fall of Strategic Planning', *Harvard Business Review*, January–February 1994, pp. 107–14; M. Valle, 'Buy High, Sell Low: Why CEOs Kiss Toads, and How Shareholders Get Warts', *Academy of Management Executive*, May 1998, pp. 97–8; G. R. Weaver, L. K. Trevino and P. L. Cochran, 'Corporate Ethics Programs as Control Systems: Influences of Executive Commitment and Environmental Factors', *Academy of Management Journal*, February 1999, pp. 41–57; and C. McDermott and K. K. Boyer, 'Strategic Consensus: Marching to the Beat of a Different Drummer?', *Business Horizons*, July–August 1999, pp. 21–8.

42 See A. Bhide, 'How Entrepreneurs Craft Strategies That Work', *Harvard Business Review*, March–April 1994, pp. 150–61; and J. W. Dean, Jr, and M. P. Sharfman, 'Does Decision Process Matter? A Study of Strategic Decision-Making Effectiveness', *Academy of Management Journal*, April 1996, pp. 368–96; R. L. Osborne, 'Strategic Values: The Corporate Performance Engine', *Business Horizons*, September–October 1996, pp. 41–7; and B. Ettorre, 'When Patience Is a Corporate Virtue', *Management Review*, November 1996, pp. 28–32.

43 S. Perlstein, 'Less Is More', *Business Ethics*, September–October 1993, p. 15.

44 Details may be found in D. Miller, 'Strategy Making and Structure: Analysis and Implications for Performance', *Academy of Management Journal*, March 1987, pp. 7–32. For more, see T. L. Amburgey and T. Dacin, 'As the Left Foot Follows the Right? The Dynamics of Strategic and Structural Change', *Academy of Management Journal*, December 1994, pp. 1427–52; and M. W. Peng and P. S. Heath, 'The Growth of the Firm in Planned Economies in Transition: Institutions, Organizations, and Strategic Choice', *Academy of Management Review*, April 1996, pp. 492–528.

45 The phrase 'small is beautiful' was coined by the late British economist E. F. Schumacher, *Small Is Beautiful: Economics As If People Mattered* (New York: Harper & Row, 1973).

46 T. J. Peters and R. H. Waterman, Jr, *In Search of Excellence* (New York: Harper & Row, 1982), p. 321. Also see T. Peters, 'Rethinking Scale', *California Management Review*, Fall 1992, pp. 7–29.

47 D. S. Pugh and D. J. Hickson, *Organizational Structure in Its Context, The Aston Programme I, second edition* (Westmead: Saxon House, Teakfield Limited, 1976); D. S. Pugh and C. R. Hinings, *Organizational Structure: Extensions and Replications – The Aston programme II, first edition* (Westmead: Saxon House, Teakfield Limited, 1976); and D. S. Pugh and R. L. Payne, *Organizational Behaviour in Its Context – The Aston Programme III, first edition* (Westmead: Saxon House, Teakfield Limited, 1977).

48 See, for example, W. McKinley, 'Decreasing Organizational Size: To Untangle or Not to Untangle?', *Academy of Management Review*, January 1992, pp. 112–23; W. Zellner, 'Go-Go Goliaths', *Business Week*, 13 February 1995,

pp. 64–70; T. Brown, 'Manage "BIG!"', *Management Review*, May 1996, pp. 12–17; and E. Shapiro, 'Power, Not Size, Counts', *Management Review*, September 1996, p. 61.

49 C. Handy, *The Hungry Spirit* (New York: Broadway Books, 1998), pp. 107–8. Also see C. Handy, 'The Doctrine of Enough', *Management Review*, June 1998, pp. 52–4.

50 P. L. Zweig, 'The Case against Mergers', *Business Week*, 30 October 1995, p. 122. Also see O. Harari, 'Too Big for Your Own Good?', *Management Review*, November 1998, pp. 30–32; G. Colvin, 'The Year of the Mega Merger', *Fortune*, 11 January 1999, pp. 62–4; A. Taylor III, 'More Mergers. Dumb Idea', *Fortune*, 15 February 1999, pp. 26–7; P. Troiano, 'Mergers: Good or Bad?' *Management Review*, April 1999, p. 9; and R. J. Grossman, 'Irreconcilable Differences', *HR Magazine*, April 1999, pp. 42–8.

51 M. Dickson, 'Companies UK: Icon of Inefficiency', *Financial Times*, 27 April 2004.

52 See J. Woodward, *Industrial Organization: Theory and Practice* (London: Oxford University Press, 1965); and P. D. Collins and F. Hull, 'Technology and Span of Control: Woodward Revisited', *Journal of Management Studies*, March 1986, pp. 143–64.

53 J. D. Thompson, *Organizations in Action* (New York: McGraw-Hill, 1976).

54 C. Perrow, *Organizational Analysis: A Sociological View* (London: Tavistock Publications, 1970).

55 J. R. Galbraith, *Designing Complex Organizations* (Reading, MA: Addison-Wesley Publishing Company, 1973).

56 See L. W. Fry, 'Technology-Structure Research: Three Critical Issues', *Academy of Management Journal*, September 1982, pp. 532–52.

57 L. W. Fry, 'Technology-Structure Research: Three Critical Issues', *Academy of Management Journal*, September 1982, p. 548. Also see R. Reese, 'Redesigning for Dial Tone: A Socio-Technical Systems Case Study', *Organizational Dynamics*, Autumn 1995, pp. 80–90.

58 For example, see C. C. Miller, W. H. Glick, Y.-D. Wang and G. P. Huber, 'Understanding Technology-Structure Relationships: Theory Development and Meta-Analytic Theory Testing', *Academy of Management Journal*, June 1991, pp. 370–99; and K. H. Roberts and M. Grabowski, 'Organizations, Technology and Structuring', in *Handbook of Organization Studies*, eds S. R. Clegg, C. Hardy and W. R. Nord (Thousand Oaks, CA: Sage Publications, 1996), pp. 409–23.

59 In particular, see H. Scarbrough and M. Corbett, *Technology and Organization: Power, Meaning and Design* (London: Routledge, 1992), p. 178; J. Fulk and G. DeSanctis, 'Electronic Communication and Changing Organizational Forms', *Organization Science*, July–August 1995, pp. 337–49; and H. Kolodny, M. Lin, B. Srymne and H. Denis, 'New Technology and the Emerging Organizational Paradigm, *Human Relations*, December 1996, pp. 1457–87.

60 S. Zuboff, *The Age of the Smart Machine* (New York: Basic Books, 1984).

61 G. Nairn, 'Vendors Are Gearing Up for Next Phase CRM', *Financial Times*, 3 March 2004.

62 R. M. Burton and B. Obel, *Strategic Organizational Diagnosis and Design* (Boston, MA: Kluwer Academic Publishers, 1998), p. 478.

63 M. Harrison and A. Shiron, *Organizational Diagnosis and Assessment* (Thousand Oaks, CA: Sage Publications, 1999), p. 486.

64 R. M. Burton and B. Obel, *Strategic Organizational Diagnosis and Design* (Boston, MA: Kluwer Academic Publishers, 1998), p. 478.

65 L. Donaldson, *Defence of Organization Theory: A Reply to the Critics* (Cambridge: Cambridge University Press, 1990); and L. Donaldson, *American Anti-Management Theories of Organization: A Critique of Paradigm Proliferation* (Cambridge: Cambridge University Press, 1995).

66 For critics on the contingency approach, see R. B. Duncan and A. Weiss, 'Organizational Learning: Implications for Organizational Design', in *Research in Organizational Behavior, vol. 1*, ed. B. Staw (Greenwich, CT: JAI Press, 1979), pp. 75–123; B. C. Schoonhoven, 'Problems with Contingency Theory: Testing Assumptions Hidden within the Language of Contingency Theory', *Administrative Science Quarterly*, March 1981, pp. 349–77; C. Gresov, 'Exploring Fit and Misfit with Multiple Contingencies', *Administrative Science Quarterly*, September 1989, pp. 431–53; and S. R. Barley and G. Kunda, 'Bringing Work Back In', *Organization Science*, January–February 2001, pp. 76–95.

67 R. B. Duncan and A. Weiss, 'Organizational Learning: Implications for Organizational Design', in *Research in Organizational Behavior, vol. 1*, ed. B. Staw (Greenwich, CT: JAI Press, 1979), pp. 75–123.

68 W. G. Astley and A. H. Van de Ven, 'Central Perspectives and Debates in Organization Theory', *Administrative Science Quarterly*, March 1983, pp. 245–73.

69 See J. Pfeffer and G. R. Salancik, *The External Control of Organizations: A Resource Dependency Perspective* (New York: Harper and Row, 1978).

70 See K. Weick, *The Social Psychology of Organizing* (Reading, MA: Addison-Wesley Publishing Company, 1969), p. 121; and L. Smircich and C. Stubbart, 'Strategic Management in An Enacted World', *Academy of Management Review*, no. 1, 1985, pp. 8–15.

71 R. Drazin and A. H. Van De Ven, 'Alternative Forms of Fit in Contingency Theory', *Administrative Science Quarterly*, September 1985, pp. 514–39.

72 J. Birkinshaw, R. Nobel and J. Ridderstrale, 'Knowledge as a Contingency Variable: Do the Characteristics of Knowledge Predict Organization Structure?', *Organization Science*, May–June 2002, pp. 274–89.

73 K. Cameron, 'Critical Questions in Assessing Organizational Effectiveness', *Organizational Dynamics*, Autumn

1980, p. 70. Also see J. Pfeffer, 'When It Comes to "Best Practices" – Why Do Smart Organizations Occasionally Do Dumb Things?', *Organizational Dynamics*, Summer 1996, pp. 33–44; G. N. Powell, 'Reinforcing and Extending Today's Organizations: The Simultaneous Pursuit of Person–Organization Fit and Diversity', *Organizational Dynamics*, Winter 1998, pp. 50–61; R. C. Vergin and M. W. Qoronfleh, 'Corporate Reputation and the Stock Market', *Business Horizons*, January–February 1998, pp. 19–26; K. Gawande and T. Wheeler, 'Measures of Effectiveness for Governmental Organizations', *Management Science*, January 1999, pp. 42–58; and E. V. McIntyre, 'Accounting Choices and EVA', *Business Horizons*, January–February 1999, pp. 66–72.

74 See B. Wysocki Jr, 'Rethinking a Quaint Idea: Profits', the *Wall Street Journal*, 19 May 1999, pp. B1, B6; and J. Collins, 'Turning Goals into Results: The Power of Catalytic Mechanisms', *Harvard Business Review*, July–August 1999, pp. 71–82.

75 See, for example, R. O. Brinkerhoff and D. E. Dressler, *Productivity Measurement: A Guide for Managers and Evaluators* (Newbury Park, CA: Sage Publications, 1990); J. McCune, 'The Productivity Paradox', *Management Review*, March 1998, pp. 38–40; and R. J. Samuelson, 'Cheerleaders vs. The Grumps', *Newsweek*, 26 July 1999, p. 78.

76 See A. Reinhardt, 'Log On, Link Up, Save Big', *Business Week*, 22 June 1998, pp. 132–8; and R. W. Oliver, 'Happy 150th Birthday, Electronic Commerce!', *Management Review*, July–August 1999, pp. 12–13.

77 Data from M. Maynard, 'Toyota Promises Custom Order in 5 Days', *USA Today*, 6 August 1999, p. 1B.

78 Main articles on the resource based view are E. Penrose, *The Theory of the Growth of The Firm* (Oxford: Blackwell Publishing, 1959); J. B. Barney, 'Organization Culture: Can It Be A Source of Sustained Competitive Advantages?', *Academy of Management Review*, no. 3, 1986, pp. 656–65; J. B. Barney, 'Firm Resources and Sustained Competitive Advantages', *Journal of Management*, no 1, 1991, pp. 99–120; and J. T. Mahoney, 'A Resource-Based Theory of Sustainable Rents', *Journal of Management*, no. 6, 2001, pp. 651–60.

79 J. B. Barney, 'Firm Resources and Sustained Competitive Advantages', *Journal of Management*, no. 1, 1991, pp. 99–120.

80 R. Sanchez, A. Heene and H. Thomas, 'Introduction: Towards the Theory and Practice of Competence-Based Competition', in *Dynamics of Competence-Based Competition: Theory and Practice in the New Strategic Management*, eds R. Sanchez, A. Heene and H. Thomas (Oxford: Pergamon, 1996), p. 7.

81 R. Sanchez, A. Heene and H. Thomas, 'Introduction: Towards the Theory and Practice of Competence-Based Competition', in *Dynamics of Competence-Based Competition: Theory and Practice in the New Strategic Management*, eds R. Sanchez, A. Heene and H. Thomas (Oxford: Pergamon, 1996), p. 8.

82 D. J. Teece, G. Pisano and A. Shuen, 'Dynamic Capabilities and Strategic Management', *Strategic Management Journal*, August 1997, pp. 509–33.

83 'Interview: M. Scott Peck', *Business Ethics*, March–April 1994, p. 17.

84 N. Timmins, 'Whitehall Could Lose 7,000 Jobs in Efficiency Drive', *Financial Times*, 16 March 2004.

85 M. Sashkin and K. J. Kiser, *Putting Total Quality Management to Work* (San Francisco, CA: Berret-Koehler, 1993).

86 R. J. Schonberger, 'Total Quality Management Cuts a Broad Swath – Through Manufacturing and Beyond', *Organizational Dynamics*, Spring 1992, p. 18. Also see K. Y. Kim, J. G. Miller and J. Heineke, 'Mastering the Quality Staircase, Step by Step', *Business Horizons*, January–February 1997, pp. 17–21; R. Bell and B. Keys, 'A Conversation with Curt W. Reimann on the Background and Future of the Baldrige Award', *Organizational Dynamics*, Spring 1998, pp. 51–61; and B. Kasanoff, 'Are You Ready for Mass Customization?', *Training*, May 1998, pp. 70–78.

87 See R. K. Reger, L. T. Gustafson, S. M. Demarie and J. V. Mullane, 'Reframing the Organization: Why Implementing Total Quality Is Easier Said than Done', *Academy of Management Review*, July 1994, pp. 565–84.

88 See T. F. Rienzo, 'Planning Deming Management for Service Organizations', *Business Horizons*, May–June 1993, pp. 19–29. Also see M. R. Yilmaz and S. Chatterjee, 'Deming and the Quality of Software Development', *Business Horizons*, November–December 1997, pp. 51–8. Deming's landmark work is W. E. Deming, *Out of the Crisis* (Cambridge, MA: MIT Press, 1986).

89 Adapted from D. E. Bowen and E. E. Lawler III, 'Total Quality-Oriented Human Resources Management', *Organizational Dynamics*, Spring 1992, pp. 29–41.

90 J. R. Evans and J. W. Dean, *Total Quality: Management, Organization and Strategy, second edition* (Cincinnati, OH: South-Western Publishing, 2000), p. 376; and B. Dale, *Managing Quality* (Malden, MA: Blackwell Publishing, 1999), p. 471.

91 See the EFQM website for all details: http://www.efqm.org.

92 P. T. Bolwijn and T. Kumpe, 'The Success of Flexible, Low-Cost, Quality Competitors: A European Perspective', *European Management Journal*, no 2, 1991, pp. 135–45; and P. T. Bolwijn and T. Kumpe, 'Manufacturing in the 1990s – Productivity, Flexibility and Innovation', *Long Range Planning*, August 1990, pp. 44–58.

93 G. Nairn, 'Operators Make More Out of Less Legacy Systems', *Financial Times*, 14 April 2004.

94 K. Cameron, 'Critical Questions in Assessing Organizational Effectiveness', *Organizational Dynamics*, Autumn 1980, p. 67. Also see W. Buxton, 'Growth from Top to Bottom', *Management Review*, July–August 1999, p. 11.

95 See R. K. Mitchell, B. R. Agle and D. J. Wood, 'Toward a Theory of Stakeholder Identification and Salience: Defining the Principle of Who and What Really Counts', *Academy of Management Review*, October 1997, pp. 853–96; W. Beaver, 'Is the Stakeholder Model Dead?', *Business Horizons*, March–April 1999, pp. 8–12;

J. Frooman, 'Stakeholder Influence Strategies', *Academy of Management Review*, April 1999, pp. 191–205; and T. M. Jones and A. C. Wicks, 'Convergent Stakeholder Theory', *Academy of Management Review*, April 1999, pp. 206–21.

96 See N. C. Roberts and P. J. King, 'The Stakeholder Audit Goes Public', *Organizational Dynamics*, Winter 1989, pp. 63–79; and I. Henriques and P. Sadorsky, 'The Relationship between Environmental Commitment and Managerial Perceptions of Stakeholder Importance', *Academy of Management Journal*, February 1999, pp. 87–99.

97 E. M. Reingold, 'America's Hamburger Helper', *Time*, 29 June 1992, p. 66.

98 See C. Ostroff and N. Schmitt, 'Configurations of Organizational Effectiveness and Efficiency', *Academy of Management Journal*, December 1993, pp. 1345–61.

99 See website of The Body Shop International: http://www.thebodyshop.com.

100 K. S. Cameron, 'Effectiveness as Paradox: Consensus and Conflict in Conceptions of Organizational Effectiveness', *Management Science*, May 1986, p. 542.

101 Alternative effectiveness criteria are discussed in M. Keeley, 'Impartiality and Participant-Interest Theories of Organizational Effectiveness', *Administrative Science Quarterly*, March 1984, pp. 1–25; K. S. Cameron, 'Effectiveness as Paradox: Consensus and Conflict in Conceptions of Organizational Effectiveness', *Management Science*, May 1986, p. 542; and A. G. Bedeian, 'Organization Theory: Current Controversies, Issues, and Directions', in *International Review of Industrial and Organizational Psychology*, eds C. L. Cooper and I. T. Robertson (New York: John Wiley, 1987), pp. 1–33.

102 D. N. Sull, 'Why Good Companies Go Bad', *Harvard Business Review*, July–August 1999, pp. 42–52. Also see H. B. Cohen, 'The Performance Paradox', *Academy of Management Executive*, August 1998, pp. 30–40.

103 M. A. Mone, W. McKinley and V. L. Barker III, 'Organizational Decline and Innovation: A Contingency Framework', *Academy of Management Review*, January 1998, p. 117.

104 P. Lorange and R. T. Nelson, 'How to Recognize – and Avoid – Organizational Decline', *Sloan Management Review*, Spring 1987, p. 47.

105 C. Brown-Humes, 'After the Crash: Lego Picks up the Pieces', *Financial Times*, 2 April 2004; and 'Trouble in Toyland', *The Economist*, 23 October 2004, pp. 62–3.

106 Excerpted from P. Lorange and R. T. Nelson, 'How to Recognize – and Avoid – Organizational Decline', *Sloan Management Review*, Spring 1987, pp. 43–5. Also see E. E. Lawler III and J. R. Galbraith, 'Avoiding the Corporate Dinosaur Syndrome', *Organizational Dynamics*, Autumn 1994, pp. 5–17; and K. Labich, 'Why Companies Fail', *Fortune*, 14 November 1994, pp. 52–68.

107 For details, see K. S. Cameron, M. U. Kim and D. A. Whetten, 'Organizational Effects of Decline and Turbulence', *Administrative Science Quarterly*, June 1987, pp. 222–40. Also see A. G. Bedeian and A. A. Armenakis, 'The Cesspool Syndrome: How Dreck Floats to the Top of Declining Organizations', *Academy of Management Executive*, February 1998, pp. 58–63.

108 For related reading, see C. R. Eitel, 'The Ten Disciplines of Business Turnaround', *Management Review*, December 1998, p. 13; J. R. Morris, W. F. Cascio and C. E. Young, 'Downsizing After All These Years: Questions and Answers about Who Did It, How Many Did It, and Who Benefited from It', *Organizational Dynamics*, Winter 1999, pp. 78–87; and S. Kuczynski, 'Help! I Shrunk the Company!', *HR Magazine*, June 1999, pp. 40–45.

109 A culture of 'entitlement' also hastens organisational decline. See J. M. Bardwick, *Danger in the Comfort Zone: From Boardroom to Mailroom – How to Break the Entitlement Habit That's Killing American Business* (New York: AMACOM, 1991). Also see D. W. Organ, 'Argue with Success', *Business Horizons*, November–December 1995, pp. 1–2; and J. P. Kotter, 'Kill Complacency', *Fortune*, 5 August 1996, pp. 168–70.

110 S. Baker, 'Silicon D-Day: To Survive in the Internet Era, Europe's Tech Titans Are Learning to Do Business Valley-Style', *Business Week*, 23 October 2000.

chapter 16 organisational and international culture

By Marc Buelens and Fannie Debussche

Learning outcomes

When you finish studying the material in this chapter, you should be able to:

- discuss the difference between espoused and enacted values
- explain the typology of organisational values
- describe the manifestations of an organisation's culture and the four functions of organisational culture
- discuss the four general types of organisational culture
- summarise the methods used by organisations to embed their cultures
- describe the practical lessons from the Hofstede-Bond stream of research
- discuss the importance of cross-cultural training relative to the foreign assignment cycle

Manifestations of organisational culture at Heineken

History stares Heineken boss Anthony Ruys in the face every morning when he shows up for work. The Dutch brewer's chief executive sits in a dark-panelled office surrounded by stern portraits of three generations of Heineken ancestors. The corporate offices in Amsterdam extend from the building that once served as the family manse. And if Ruys were ever to forget that he was the guardian of a company that traces its roots back more than 400 years, he would have to reckon with his main shareholder: Charlene de Carvalho-Heineken, a descendant of the company's founder. 'There's a long tradition', says Ruys with typical Dutch understatement.

Starched white collars are no longer the order of the day at 21 Tweede Weteringplantsoen, but Heineken headquarters is still a pretty buttoned-down place. True, the vending machines in the corridors are stocked with – what else? – Heineken. But they're programmed not to dispense the brew until after 4 p.m. 'Not much has changed since Charlene's father, Alfred H. "Freddy" Heineken, ran the company', says Ruys, a 56-year-old former Unilever executive who was elevated to the top job ten years after joining the company, a relatively short tenure by Heineken standards. Freddy, a legendary bon vivant with a hard nose for business, passed away last year. And while no one from Ruys on down would dare dishonour his memory by claiming that anything as radical as a revolution is in the making at Heineken, there's an unmistakable whiff of change in the air.

Heineken, one of the first European brewers to realise the value of cross-border deals, now risks falling behind more aggressive rivals. To overcome these challenges, Ruys is pushing Heineken to break out of its play-it-safe corporate culture. Heineken's future success will depend on preserving Freddy's spirit – while meeting challenges that Freddy never anticipated.

That success is no longer guaranteed. The convergence of a weak global economy, an unusually rainy summer in the US and SARS, which emptied watering holes across Asia, will break a six-year streak of double-digit profit growth. Then there's the strong euro, which is crimping earnings from the US, a market that accounts for more than a quarter of all profits. Top management in Amsterdam is not quite panicked, but there's definitely a sense of urgency seeping into the ranks. Heineken's boss is resorting to tough tactics to stir the troops out of their complacency. A video produced for staff viewing only features a young Italian man saying: 'I hate beer'. The message: Heineken needs to win over consumers who haven't yet developed a strong loyalty to a particular beverage. That's why Ruys and his top lieutenants have been travelling to places like Madrid and Shanghai to down a cold one with groups of randomly selected young people.

It's a tough balancing act – reaching out to younger customers without alienating the middle-aged beer drinkers who are Heineken's core customers. 'Heineken seems to be an obsolete brand to me', says Véronique dos Santos, a 29-year-old human-resources assistant in Paris who favours Mexican import Corona or Desperados, a tequila-flavoured concoction. To spice up the image of its namesake brand, Heineken is giving marketing a makeover. It has arranged tie-ins with big-budget youth films, such as *The Matrix: Reloaded*, and sponsored events such as a sweepstakes where winners got to attend a Heineken house party in Jamaica.[1]

For discussion
What are the critical success factors in changing Heineken's corporate culture?

Much has been written and said about organisational culture, values and ethics in recent years. As long as people are not confronted with other cultures, they take their own world for granted and simply do not realise that a different culture might be valuable. A fish is always the last to find out it is swimming in water. In a 'credibly shrinking world' however, we always meet different cultures. Cultural differences between countries have shown us the way to other cultural differences: cultural differences between professionals, between men and women, between industrial sectors, etc. In this chapter, we will focus on two important differences: differences in organisational cultures and differences between countries and regions, as reflected in the so-called 'intercultural differences'. We will discuss culture and organisational behaviour, differences in organisational culture, socialisation and intercultural differences.

Culture and organisational behaviour
At around the year 2000 the academic study of the concept had reached a stalemate. Organisational culture seemed to be overcharged: it was the concept explaining the link between the workplace and outcomes such as satisfaction, commitment and productivity.[2] In many cases the success of a so-called 'cultural change' is a direct result of reducing autonomy, close monitoring and threat of sanctions.[3] Many academics looked at culture as a pure management fad. Exactly at the same moment, the numerous and highly visible corporate scandals were explained by 'the tone at the top', the corporate culture. There was an outcry for 'cultures of responsibilities'. The results of some 25 years of researching corporate culture can be arranged on a continuum of academic rigour. At the low end of the continuum are simplistic typologies and exaggerated claims about the benefits of imitating successful corporate cultures and values. At the other end of the continuum is a growing body of theory and research with valuable insights, but one plagued by definitional and measurement inconsistencies.[4] Despite a general lack of agreement among academics, practitioners are strongly attracted by the subject. Almost all companies are interested in planning a cultural change: becoming more quality oriented or customer focused or introducing a 'culture of accountability'.

Culture socially derived, taken-for-granted assumptions about how to think and act

Culture is complex and multilayered
While noting that cultures exist in social units of all sizes (from civilisations through to countries to ethnic groups, organisations and work groups), Edgar Schein defined **Culture** as follows:

> A pattern of basic assumptions – invented, discovered or developed by a given group as it learns to cope with its problems of external adaptation and internal integration – that has worked well enough to be considered valid and, therefore, to be taught to new members as the correct way to perceive, think and feel in relation to those problems.[5]

The word 'taught' needs to be interpreted carefully because it implies formal education or training. While cultural lessons may indeed be taught in schools, religious settings and in the workplace, formal inculcation is secondary. Most cultural lessons are learned by observing and imitating role models as they go about their daily affairs, or from those observed in the media.[6]

Culture is difficult to grasp because it is multilayered. International experts, Fons Trompenaars (from the Netherlands) and Charles Hampden-Turner (from Britain), offer the following instructive analogy in their landmark book, *Riding the Waves of Culture*:

> Culture comes in layers, like an onion. To understand it you have to unpeel it layer by layer. On the outer layer are the products of culture, like the soaring skyscrapers of Manhattan, pillars of private power, with congested public streets between them. These are expressions of deeper values and norms, in a society, that are not directly visible (values such as upward mobility, 'the more-the-better', status, material success). The layers of values and norms are deeper within the 'onion', and are more difficult to identify.[7]

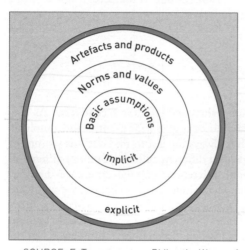

FIGURE 16.1 A MODEL OF CULTURE

SOURCE: F. Trompenaars, *Riding the Waves of Culture* (London: Nicholas Brealey Publishing, 1994), p. 23.

Culture is a subtle but pervasive force

Culture generally remains below the threshold of conscious awareness because it involves taken-for-granted assumptions about how one should perceive, think, act and feel. Cultural anthropologist Edward T. Hall put it the following way:

> Since much of culture operates outside our awareness, frequently we don't even know what we know. We pick [expectations and assumptions] up in the cradle. We unconsciously learn what to notice and what not to notice, how to divide time and space, how to walk and talk and use our bodies, how to behave as men or women, how to relate to other people, how to handle responsibility, whether experience is seen as whole or fragmented. This applies to all people. The Chinese, Japanese or Arabs are each as unaware of their assumptions as we are of our own. We each assume that they're part of human nature. What we think of as 'mind' is really internalised culture.[8]

In sum, it has been said that, 'you are your culture and your culture is you'. As part of the growing sophistication of marketing practices in the global economy, companies are realising that from this perspective, consumers from different countries need to be approached differently. Recent research suggests that the way Europeans shop is very much a reflection of where they live as it is of their organisational skills. The findings revealed major differences between countries: whereas in the Netherlands, 80 per cent of decisions are made in the store, in Italy only 42 per cent are made in that way. In the UK, France and Denmark, shoppers appear to be making more than 75 per cent of brand purchasing decisions in the store, while in Germany the figure is only 50 per cent. With all the variety, designing advertising campaigns becomes a cultural minefield.[9] Broadcast platforms and kids' lifestyles differ from country to country, which largely influences entertainment and character licensing. France has a stronger comic book culture and children are more likely to read than in the UK, where TV dominates.[10] Expanding operations to countries with different cultural values from one's own, without adapting to these differences, can lead to serious losses, researchers from Spain and the Netherlands conclude.[11]

A model of societal and organisational cultures

As illustrated in Figure 16.2, culture influences organisational behaviour in two ways. Employees bring their societal culture to work with them in the form of customs and language. Organisational culture, a by-product of societal culture, in turn affects the individual's values and ethics, attitudes, assumptions and expectations.[12]

FIGURE 16.2 CULTURAL INFLUENCES ON ORGANISATIONAL BEHAVIOUR

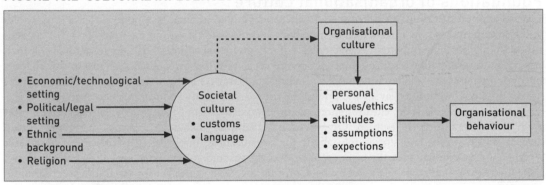

SOURCE: Adapted in part from B. J. Punnett and S. Withane, 'Hofstede's Value Survey Module: To Embrace or Abandon?', in *Advances in International Comparative Management*, vol. 5, ed. S. B. Prasad (Greenwich, CT: JAI Press, 1990), pp. 69–89.

The term 'societal culture' is used here instead of national culture because the boundaries of many modern nation-states were not drawn along cultural lines. Once inside the organisation's sphere of influence, the individual is further affected by the organisation's culture, which will be explained in the next section. Mixings of societal and organisational cultures can produce interesting dynamics in multinational companies. For example, with French and American employees working side by side at General Electric's medical imaging production facility in Waukesha, Wisconsin, unit head Claude Benchimol has witnessed some culture shock:

> The French are surprised that the American parking lots empty out as early as 5 p.m.; the Americans are surprised the French don't start work at 8 a.m. Benchimol feels the French are more talkative and candid. Americans have more of a sense of hierarchy and are less likely to criticise. But they may be growing closer to the French. Says Benchimol, 'It's taken a year to get across the idea that we are all entitled to say what we don't like, to become more productive and to work better.'[13]

Same company, same company culture, yet GE's French and American co-workers have different attitudes about time, hierarchy and communication. They are the products of different societal cultures.[14]

When managing people at work, the individual's societal culture, the organisational culture and any interaction between the two need to be taken into consideration. Eastman Kodak had launched a very successful change programme in the US, and after launching the formula in Europe, the internal consultant cried on their shoulders:

> These French and Germans are unbelievably inflexible. I have done a whole round in Europe and within each of the countries many seemed very much supporting our vision. Okay, the Germans had some problems with the process. They wanted to know all the details of the procedures and how they were connected to the envisioned change. The French, in turn, were so much worried about the unions and how to keep their people motivated. But good, we as internal consultants and management have left with the idea that we agreed on the approach. When I came back some three months later to check how the implementation was going, I noticed in France and Germany nothing had started yet. Nothing! What a disappointment![15]

Influencing people's cultural backgrounds is very difficult as is confirmed by recent research results from 15 countries. The studies showed that the unique traditions of each country have been maintained in their institutions like families, schools and forms of government and they are also conserved in differences in national cultures in the sense of 'software for the mind': patterns of thinking, feeling and acting that differentiate one country from another and continue to be transferred from generation to generation.[16] Organisational culture will be discussed hereafter. The influence of societal culture will be elaborated on in the section of intercultural differences at the end of this chapter.

Foundations of organisational culture

Organisational culture
shared values and beliefs that underlie a company's identity

Organisational culture is 'the set of shared, taken-for-granted implicit assumptions that a group holds and that determines how it perceives, thinks about and reacts to its various environments'.[17] This definition highlights three important characteristics of organisational culture. First, organisational culture is passed on to new employees through the process of socialisation, a topic discussed later in this chapter. Second, organisational culture influences our behaviour at work. Finally, organisational culture operates at two different levels. Each level varies in terms of outward visibility and resistance to change.[18]

At the more visible level, culture represents artefacts. Artefacts consist of the physical manifestation of an organisation's culture. Organisational examples include acronyms, manner of dress, awards, titles, myths and stories told about the organisation, published lists of values, observable rituals and ceremonies, special parking spaces, decorations and so on. This level also includes visible behaviours exhibited by people and groups. Consider the various artefacts in the following examples:

> Bosses in high-tech, Internet and consultancy firms no longer want to be known as the chief executives. Everyone who is in the vanguard of the new economy wants a wacky or futuristic job title. One British firm that has given its staff funky job titles is The Fourth Room, a consulting agency. There, Piers Schmidt, who would otherwise be called chief executive is called 'The Pacesetter'. Another example is to be found in the telecommunications company Orange, where Kurt Hirschhorn has the title 'Director of Strategy, Imagineering and Futurology' on his business card. 'A lot of people see my business card and they say "now there's a title". They're not sure what it means, but they know it's something different', Hirschhorn says. His team members range from 'Ambassadors of Knowledge' to 'Senior Imagineers'. 'With these titles, I knowingly try to express our vision of innovativeness and our culture', he adds. Similarly, the London law firm Mishcon de Reya appointed a 'Manager of Mischief' to emphasise their customer-oriented culture. Although this trend is becoming more common in Europe, the strangest job titles are nevertheless still found in the USA: for example, the boss of AC-Television is called 'The Keeper of the Magic', the Internet company, Encoding, has a 'Minister of Order and Reason' in its rungs and even Bill Gates, formerly known as the chairman of Microsoft changed his name to 'Chief Software Architect'.[19]

> At DHL, the international courier service company, a number of activities are organised to create a feeling of togetherness among its employees. Although mostly organised on a regional basis, this also happens on a national and international basis: for instance, every year Eurosoccer is held, where the different parts of DHL worldwide play against each other. In total, 48 DHL teams from over the world gather together for a two-day period during the soccer tournament. It is said that these matches really bring out the spirit of DHL.[20]

Artefacts are easier to change than the less visible aspects of organisational culture. At the less visible level, culture reflects the values and beliefs shared by organisational members. These values tend to persist over time and are more resistant to change. Each level of culture influences the other. For example, if a company truly values providing high-quality service, employees are more likely to adopt the behaviour of responding faster to customer complaints. Similarly, causality can flow in the other direction. Employees can come to value high-quality service based on their experiences with customers.

To gain a better understanding of how organisational culture is formed and used by employees, this section begins by discussing organisational values – the foundation of organisational culture. It then reviews the manifestations of organisational culture, a model for interpreting organisational culture, the four functions of organisational culture and research on the subject.

Organisational values

Organisational values and beliefs constitute the foundation of an organisation's culture. They also play a key role in influencing ethical behaviour (see Chapter 15). Remember from Chapter 3 that values possess five key components, which:

- Are concepts or beliefs.
- Pertain to desirable results or behaviours.
- Transcend situations.
- Guide selection or evaluation of behaviour and events.
- Are ordered by relative importance.[21]

It is important to distinguish between values that are espoused versus those that are enacted.[22]

Espoused values represent the explicitly stated values and norms that are preferred by an organisation. Often they are referred to as 'corporate glue'. They are generally established by the founder of a new or small company or by the top management team in a larger organisation. For example, Nokia, the Finnish telecom giant states four worldwide core values, named 'customer satisfaction', 'respect for the individual', 'achievement' and 'continuous learning'. Folke Rosengard, the Nokia Networks director explains.

> Respect for the individual is about openness and honesty and goes against the rigid structures and the slavish 'yes sir' mentality that often kills contemporary companies: it destroys innovativeness and development. We need creative, 'almost-anarchists' as, without them, we would be back where we started producing toilet paper. Openness is necessary when, for instance, we set up new offices elsewhere in the world: if there are problems, they have to be communicated to headquarters. If not, we in Helsinki become isolated from the rest of the world. Here in Helsinki, the creative heart of the company beats and people from all over the world come together. It often takes me more than half an hour just to walk through the canteen, simply because you know everybody. But I'd like to emphasise that it's not our philosophy to print our values on every wall, coffee mug or mouse pad in the company. Of course they are useful in interviews and recruitment conversations, but the most important thing is that our people develop a feeling of what it's all about. We walk the talk.[23]

Enacted values, on the other hand, represent the values and norms that actually are exhibited or converted into employee behaviour. Let us consider the difference between these two types of value. A company might embrace the value of integrity. If employees display integrity by following through on their commitments, then the espoused value is enacted and individual behaviour is influenced by the value of integrity. In contrast, if employees do not follow through on their commitments, then the value of integrity is simply a 'stated' aspiration that does not influence behaviour. Gareth Jones, a professor of organisation development at Britain's Henley Management College, warns that many companies exert lots of efforts to make explicit their values in all kinds of ways, but very often they remain dead letter:

Espoused values
the stated values and norms preferred by an organisation

Enacted values
the values and norms that are exhibited by employees

593

> In most cases, some analysis and plenty of workshops follow as the company goes in search of its soul. It draws up a document specifying the right values, and the chief executive delivers an exciting speech to rally the troops, ending with the exhortation, 'Now we know what we stand for, let's go for it.' And very often, that's the end of it. The values wall chart gathers dust along with the other culture-change literature. Managers may pay lots of lip service to new values, without ever really practising them or demonstrating how they can benefit the organisation. You know, there's an established technical term for values that look good on the wall but don't add value to the business. That term is bullshit.[24]

The gap between espoused and enacted values is important because it can significantly influence an organisation's culture and employee attitudes. A study of 312 British Rail train drivers, supervisors and senior managers revealed that the creation of a safety culture was negatively affected by large gaps between senior management's espoused and enacted values. Employees were more cynical about safety when they believed that senior managers' behaviours were inconsistent with the stated values regarding safety.[25]

If we look back at the Nokia example, there this enactment seems to work out pretty well. For example, the British Lynn Rutten, who has been working at the Nokia headquarters in Helsinki (called Nokia House) for about three years, states: 'They do exert a lot of effort to make sure everybody walks the line. Me, personally, I have become a Nokiasaurus'.[26]

Katharina Balazs studied the leadership, the culture and the managerial attitude in some 20 French Michelin three-star restaurants (there are only some 30 Michelin three-stars in the world!). She found that the chefs have both a very strong respect for the traditional values of their craft and are very open to new and unusual foods, cooking styles and eating habits.[27]

It also is important to consider how an organisation's value system influences organisational culture, because companies subscribe to multiple values. An **Organisation's value system** reflects the patterns of conflict and compatibility between values, not the relative importance of each.[28] This definition highlights the point that organisations endorse a constellation of values that contain both conflicting and compatible values. For example, management scholars believe that organisations have two fundamental value systems that naturally conflict with each other. One system relates to the manner in which tasks are accomplished; the other includes values related to maintaining internal cohesion and solidarity. The central issue underlying this value conflict revolves around identifying the main goal being pursued by an organisation. Is the organisation predominantly interested in financial performance, relationships or a combination of the two?[29] To help you understand how organisational values influence organisational culture, we present a typology of organisational values and review some relevant research.

Organisation's value system patterns of conflict and compatibility between organisation's values

A TYPOLOGY OF ORGANISATIONAL VALUES

Figure 16.3 presents a typology of organisational values that is based on crossing organisational reward norms and organisation power structures.[30] Organisational reward norms reflect a company's fundamental belief about how rewards should be allocated (see Chapter 6). According to the equitable reward norm, they should be proportionate to contributions. In contrast, an egalitarian-oriented value system calls for rewarding all employees' equally, regardless of their comparative contributions. Organisation power structures reflect a company's basic belief about how power and authority should be shared and distributed (see Chapter 13). These beliefs range from the extreme of being completely unequal or centralised, to equal or completely decentralised.

Figure 16.3 identifies four types of value systems: elite, meritocratic, leadership and collegial. Each type of value system contains a positive and a negative set of responses to values: some values are reinforced or endorsed by the system while others are seen as inconsistent or discouraged. For example, an elite value system endorses values related to acceptance of authority, high performance and equitable rewards. This value system, however, does not encourage values related to teamwork, participation, commitment or affiliation. In contrast, a collegial value system supports values associated with teamwork, participation, commitment and affiliation whilst discouraging values of authority, high performance and equitable rewards.

FIGURE 16.3 A TYPOLOGY OF ORGANISATIONAL VALUES

	Organisation power structure			
	Unequal or centralised power		Equal or decentralised power	
	Elite		**Meritocratic**	
	Endorsed values	Discouraged values	Endorsed values	Discouraged values
Equitable	Authority Performance rewards	Teamwork Participation Commitment Affiliation	Performance rewards Teamwork Participation Commitment Affiliation	Authority
	Leadership		**Collegial**	
	Endorsed values	Discouraged values	Endorsed values	Discouraged values
Egalitarian	Authority Performance rewards Teamwork Commitment Affiliation	Participation	Teamwork Participation Commitment Affiliation	Authority Performance rewards

(Left axis label: Organisational reward norms)

SOURCE: Adapted from B. Kabanoff and J. Holt, 'Changes in the Espoused Values of Australian Organizations 1986–1990', *Journal of Organizational Behavior*, May 1996, pp. 201–19.

RESEARCH FINDINGS AND PRACTICAL IMPLICATIONS

Organisations subscribe to a constellation of values rather than to simply one and can be profiled according to their values.[31] This, in turn, enables professionals to determine whether an organisation's values are consistent and supportive of its corporate goals and initiatives. Organisational change is unlikely to succeed if it is based on a set of values that is highly inconsistent with employees' individual values (see Chapter 17).[32] Finally, a longitudinal study of 85 Australian organisations revealed four interesting trends about the typology of organisational values, presented in Figure 16.3:[33]

■ Organisational values were quite stable over four years. This result supports the contention that values are relatively stable and resistant to change.

■ There was not a universal movement to one type of value system. The 85 organisations represented all four value systems. This finding reinforces the earlier conclusion that there is no 'one best' organisational culture or value system.

■ Organisations with elite value systems experienced the greatest amount of change over the four-year period. Elite organisations tended to become more collegial.

■ There was an overall increase in the number of organisations that endorsed the individual value of employee commitment. This trend is consistent with the notion that organisational success is partly dependent on the extent to which employees are committed to their organisations (see Chapter 3).

Manifestations of organisational culture

When is an organisation's culture most apparent? In addition to the physical artifacts of organisational culture that were previously discussed, cultural assumptions assert themselves through socialisation of new employees, subculture clashes and top management behaviour. Consider these three situations, for example:

■ A newcomer who shows up late for an important meeting is told a story about someone who was fired for repeated tardiness.

■ Conflict between product design engineers who emphasise a product's function and marketing specialists who demand a more stylish product reveals an underlying clash of subculture values.

■ Top managers, through the behaviour they model and the administrative and reward systems they create, prompt a significant improvement in the quality of a company's products.

A model for interpreting organisational culture

A useful model for observing and interpreting organisational culture was developed by Vijay Sathe, a Harvard University researcher (see Figure 16.4). The four general manifestations or evidence of organisational culture in his model are shared things (objects), shared sayings (talk), shared doings (behaviour) and shared feelings (emotion). One can begin collecting cultural information within the organisation by asking, observing, reading and feeling.

Four functions of organisational culture

As illustrated in Figure 16.5, an organisation's culture fulfils four functions.[34] To help bring these four functions to life, let us consider how each of them has taken shape in the US-based 3M Corporation. 3M is a particularly instructive example because it has a long history of being an innovative company.

GIVE MEMBERS AN ORGANISATIONAL IDENTITY

3M is known as being an innovative company that relentlessly pursues new product development. One way of promoting innovation is to encourage the research and development of new products and services. For example, 3M regularly sets future sales targets based on the percentage of sales that must come from new products. In one year, the senior management decreed that 30 per cent of its sales must come from products introduced within the past four years. The old standard was 25 per cent in five years. This identity is reinforced by creating rewards that reinforce innovation. For example, 'The 3M Corporation has its version of a Nobel Prize for innovative employees. The prize is the Golden Step award, whose trophy is a winged foot. Several Golden Steps are given out each year to employees whose new products have reached significant revenue and profit levels.'[35]

FIGURE 16.4 A MODEL FOR OBSERVING AND INTERPRETING GENERAL MANIFESTATIONS OF ORGANISATIONAL CULTURE

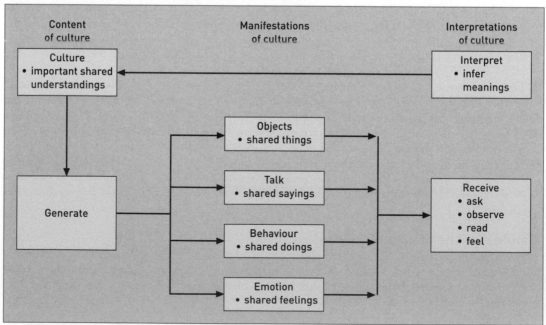

FIGURE 16.5 FOUR FUNCTIONS OF ORGANISATIONAL CULTURE

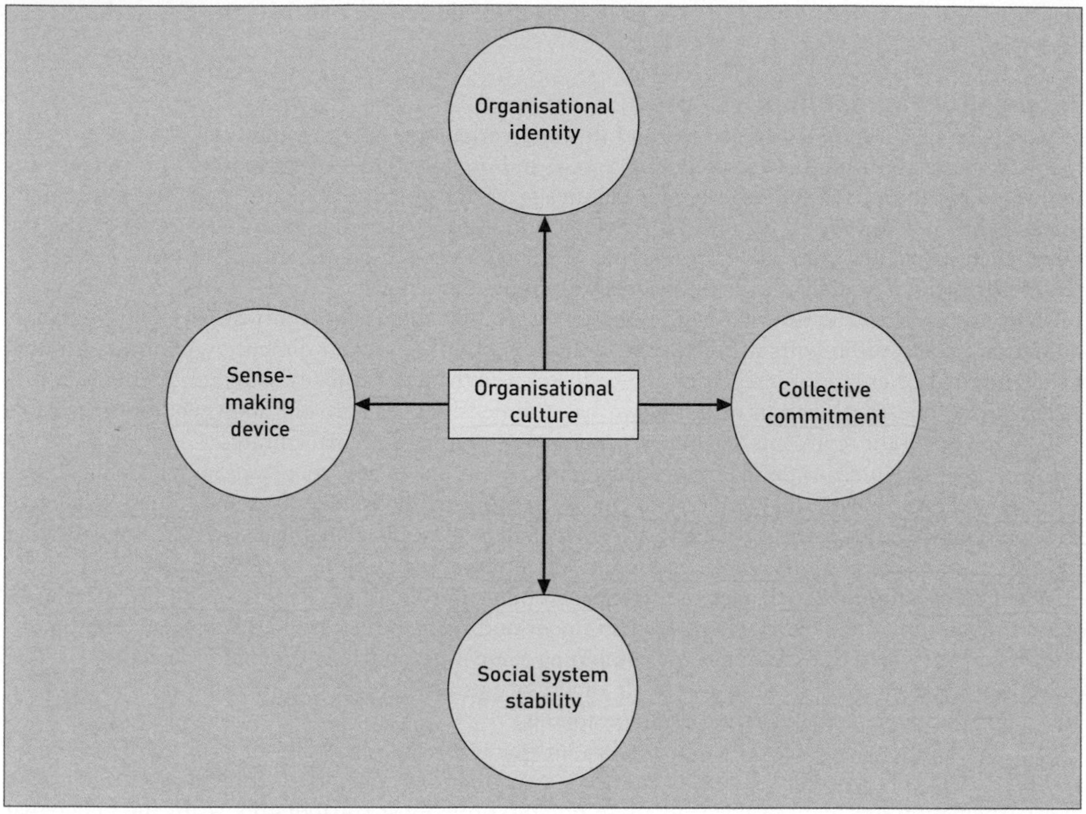

SOURCE: Adapted from discussion in L. Smircich, 'Concepts of Culture and Organizational Analysis', *Administrative Science Quarterly*, September 1983, pp. 339–58. Reproduced by permission of John Wiley & Sons, Limited.

FACILITATE COLLECTIVE COMMITMENT

One of 3M's corporate values is to be 'a company that employees are proud to be a part of'. People who like 3M's culture tend to stay employed there for long periods of time. Approximately 24 000 of its employees have more than 15 years of tenure with the company while 19 600 have stayed more than 20 years. Consider the commitment and pride expressed by Kathleen Stanislawski, a staffing manager. 'I'm a 27-year 3Mer because, quite frankly, there's no reason to leave. I've had great opportunities to do different jobs and to grow a career. It's just a great company.'[36]

PROMOTE SOCIAL SYSTEM STABILITY

Social system stability reflects the extent to which the work environment is perceived as positive and reinforcing and conflict and change are managed effectively. Consider how 3M dealt with its financial problems in 1998. 'Even in tough times, which have now arrived because of the upheavals in Asia, 3M hasn't become a mean, miserly or miserable place to work. It's shedding about 4500 jobs, but slowly and mostly by attrition.'[37] This strategy helped to maintain a positive work environment in the face of adversity. The company also attempts to promote stability through a promote-from-within culture, a strategic hiring policy that ensures that capable college graduates are hired in a timely manner and a redundancy policy that provides displaced workers with six months to find another job at 3M before their employment there is terminated.

SHAPE BEHAVIOUR BY HELPING MEMBERS MAKE SENSE OF THEIR SURROUNDINGS

This function of culture helps employees understand why the organisation does what it does and how it intends to accomplish its long-term goals. 3M sets expectations for innovation in a variety of ways. For example, the company employs an 'internship and co-op programme'. 3M also shapes expectations and behaviour by providing detailed career feedback to its employees. Fresh recruits are measured and evaluated against a career growth standard during their first six months to three years of employment.

Types of organisational culture

Researchers have attempted to identify and measure various types of organisational culture in order to study the relationship between types of culture and organisational effectiveness. This pursuit was motivated by the possibility that certain cultures were more effective than others. Unfortunately, research has not uncovered a universal typology of cultural styles that everyone accepts.[38] Just the same, there is value in providing an example of various types of organisational culture. Table 16.1 represents such an example, based on the work of influential scholars.

Many researchers identify two basic dimensions. A first dimension contrasts flexibility, change, discretion and freedom with stability, control and direction. A second dimension contrasts internal focus, internal orientation, integration, co-ordination with external focus, external orientation, differentiation. The combination of those two basic dimensions leads to the four quadrants in Table 16.1. Each quadrant represents a 'pure' or 'generic' type of organisational culture.

In an organisation characterised by an adaptability culture, the organisation constantly redefines itself. The organisation shows a high capacity to change its work methods, objectives and reward systems in response to changing external conditions. Creativity and innovation are highly valued. The organisation rapidly reacts to new needs. It is quick to capture and interpret signals from its environment.

When an organisation is characterised by an external control culture, its focus is on the market. In those organisations market share, goal achievement and competition are highly valued. The organisation has formulated a clear mission combining economic and non-economic objectives. Those objectives motivate, inspire and direct all organisational members. 'Beating the competition' or 'realising our dream' is the inspiring common theme.

In a development culture, the emphasis lies on involvement. There is a high sense of belonging and psychological ownership. Levels of morale are very high. Teamwork, mentorship, staff cohesion and participation are highly valued. In those organisations most collaborators share the belief that the best minute is the minute they invest in other people.

In an internal consistency culture, the organisation is oriented towards efficiency and smooth functioning of the organisation. The ideal organisation is a 'machine organisation' (see Chapter 14) where everything is well planned ahead and is completely under control. Consistency, respect for hierarchy and rules are highly valued. The best minute is the minute people invest in preparation of better systems.

Although an organisation may predominately represent one cultural type, it can still manifest normative beliefs and characteristics from the others. **Normative beliefs** represent an individual's thoughts and beliefs about how members of a particular group or organisation are expected to approach their work and interact with others. Research demonstrates that organisations can have functional subcultures, hierarchical subcultures based on one's level in the organisation, geographical subcultures, occupational subcultures based on one's title or position, social subcultures derived from social activities like a tennis or a reading club.

> **Normative beliefs**
> thoughts and beliefs about expected behaviour and modes of conduct

DO STRONG CORPORATE CULTURES IMPROVE FIRM PERFORMANCE?

An organisation's culture may be strong or weak, depending on variables such as cohesiveness, value consensus and individual commitment to collective goals. Contrary to what one might suspect, a

TABLE 16.1 TYPES OF ORGANISATIONAL CULTURES

	Change and flexibility	Stability and direction
External focus (differentiation)	Adaptability	External control
Internal focus (integration)	Development	Internal consistency

SOURCE: K. S. Cameron and R. E. Quinn, *Diagnosing and Changing Organizational Culture: Based on the Competing Values Framework* (Englewood Cliffs, NJ: Prentice Hall, 1999); and D. R. Denison and A. K. Mishr, 'Toward a Theory of Organizational Culture and Effectiveness', *Organization Science*, March–April 1995, pp. 204–23.

strong culture is not necessarily a good thing. The nature of the culture's central values is more important than its strength. For example, a strong but change-resistant culture may be worse, from the standpoint of profitability and competitiveness, than a weak but innovative culture. Systematic research on the link between the strength of a corporate culture and the reliability of a firm's performance has shown that a strong culture can be a mixed blessing. As long as the environment is relatively stable, strong-culture firms show superior and more reliable results. In volatile environments, however, the strong culture might hinder the dynamic learning processes that are required to adapt to the new and ever-changing environments.[39]

Studies of mergers indicated that they frequently failed due to strong cultures which proved to be incompatible.[40] Because of the increasing number of corporate mergers around the world and the conclusion that seven out of ten mergers and acquisitions failed to meet their financial promise, managers within merged companies would be well advised to consider the role of organisational culture in creating a new organisation.[41] The following Snapshot provides an example of how the management structure and culture at Deutsche Bank changed after the company merged with Bankers Trust. Once you have read the example, consider how you think the employees at Deutsche Bank will respond to Mr Breuer's proposed changes.

The merger between Deutsche Bank and Bankers Trust requires cultural and structural change

snapshot

Deutsche Bank is now run by a managing board, or Vorstand, in which a handful of executives make all the decisions by consensus. Responsibility is shared, and assigning blame is difficult. Deutsche Bank Chairman Rolf Breuer says that won't work following the merger with Bankers Trust. Instead, he is implementing what he calls 'a virtual holding company' approach, meaning a structure where different divisions are run almost like separate entities, with their own bottom lines and management boards.

'I have said that there is now an end to the Soviet Union behaviour of the central committee, where everyone is present but no-one is accountable', he says.

SOURCE: Excerpted from J. L. Hiday, A. Raghavan and J. Sapsford, 'Sizing Up: BNP Bid Raises Issue of How Large a Bank Can Get, or Should', the *Wall Street Journal*, 11 March 1999, p. A6.

HOW CULTURES ARE EMBEDDED IN ORGANISATIONS

An organisation's initial culture is an outgrowth of the founder's philosophy. For example, an achievement culture is likely to develop if the founder is an achievement-oriented individual driven by success. Over time, the original culture is either embedded as is or modified to fit the current environmental situation. Johnson & Johnson, for example, has formally documented its cherished corporate values and ideals, as conceived over four decades ago by the founder's son. The resulting Credo has helped J&J become a role model for corporate ethics.[42] Edgar Schein, a well-known OB scholar, notes that embedding a culture involves a teaching process: that is, organisational members teach each other about the organisation's preferred values, beliefs, expectations and behaviours. This is accomplished by using one or more of the following mechanisms:[43]

■ Formal statements of organisational philosophy, mission, vision, values and materials used for recruiting, selection and socialisation. Philips, for example, published a list of five corporate values, listed together with some practical ideas on how to put them into everyday practice. The five values are: delight customers, value people as our greatest resources, deliver quality and excellence in all actions, achieve premium returns on equity and encourage entrepreneurial behaviour at all levels.[44]

■ The design of physical space, work environments and buildings. Consider the use of a new alternative workplace design called 'hotelling'. As in other shared-office options, 'hotel' work spaces are furnished, equipped and supported with typical office services. Employees may have mobile cubbies, file cabinets or lockers for personal storage; and a computer system routes phone calls and email as necessary. But 'hotel' work spaces are reserved by the hour, by the day or by the week instead of being permanently assigned. In addition, a 'concierge' may provide employees with travel and logistic support. At its most advanced, 'hotel' work space is customised with the individuals' personal photos and memorabilia, which are stored electronically, retrieved and 'placed' on the occupants' desktops just before they arrive and then removed as soon as they leave.[45]

■ Slogans, language, acronyms and sayings. Philips, for example, emphasises its concern for delivering top-quality products through the slogan 'Let's make things better'. Employees are encouraged to continuously innovate to design products that are among the best and that can improve the quality of our lives. Philips's invention of the CD-player is a good illustration of this mentality. Also slogans used in job advertisements reflect the corporate culture. For instance, the Disney Corporation offers you 'dreams and imagination' and IKEA promises you 'innovation and simplicity'.[46]

■ Deliberate role modelling, training programmes, teaching and coaching by managers and supervisors.

■ Explicit rewards (see Chapter 6), status symbols (such as titles) and promotion criteria. Consider the following reward system: over a period of 31 years, Heiko H. Berle, a bodywork painter at Opel in Wanne-Eickel, Germany, was granted €25 000 as a result of 150 recommendations for innovations he introduced.[47]

■ Stories, legends and myths about key people and events. The stories in the following Snapshot, for instance, are used within Tesco plc, a leading food retailer in England, Scotland and Wales, to embed the value of providing outstanding customer service.

■ The organisational activities, processes or outcomes that leaders pay attention to, measure and control. Employees are much more likely to pay attention to the amount of on-time deliveries when senior management uses on-time deliveries as a measure of quality or customer service.

■ Leader reactions to critical incidents and organisational crises.

■ The workflow and organisational structure. Hierarchical structures are more likely to embed an orientation toward control and authority than a flatter organisation (see Chapter 14).

■ Organisational systems and procedures. An organisation can promote achievement and competition through the use of sales contests.

■ Organisational goals and the associated criteria used for employee recruitment, selection, development, promotion, layoffs and retirement of people.

Stories of outstanding customer service at Tesco plc

There was somebody who got hold of one of our assistant managers in one of our stores on a Sunday, and said, 'You've got the *Sunday Times* but you haven't got the Customer Service supplement.' They went through all the *Sunday Times* and there was no Customer Service supplement. So they said, 'No problem, we'll get hold of one and get it to you.' She said 'Well I don't live that nearby and I am going out.' They took her name and address and promised to sort it out.

They rang around a few stores and eventually found one. Sure enough, when this person came in that night, there were two copies of the *Sunday Times* sitting on her doormat. She wrote to the chairman and said this was fantastic service!

SOURCE: Excerpted from T. Mason, 'The Best Shopping Trip? How Tesco Keeps the Customer Satisfied', *Journal of the Market Research Society*, January 1998, p. 10.

The organisational socialisation process

Organisational socialisation is defined as 'the process by which a person learns the values, norms and required behaviours which permit him to participate as a member of the organisation'.[48] As previously discussed, organisation socialisation is a key mechanism used by organisations to embed their organisational cultures. In short, organisational socialisation turns outsiders into fully functioning insiders by promoting and reinforcing the organisation's core values and beliefs. For example, at IKEA, seminars are organised to explain the company's roots and values and where the name IKEA comes from. To enhance involvement, trips are organised to the founder's birthplace in Sweden, where everything began.[49] IKEA is proud of its so-called Swedish culture: informality, cost consciousness and a very humble and 'down to earth' approach.[50] Consider the following example of the socialisation process at AZG, the Academic Hospital of Groningen in the Netherlands:

Organisational socialisation process by which employees learn the organisation's values, norms and required behaviours

> " Every month, an average of 45 'freshmen' began a new job at the Academic Hospital. From the first day, every new employee is seen as a potential 'carrier of culture' of the AZG. An introduction programme makes them fully aware of what that means in practice. On the 'introduction day', the new employee is made aware of what is expected of him and taught important aspects of the hospital's culture, for example how patients are dealt with and how communication between doctors and nurses takes place. The hospital's main behavioural rules are outlined in the form of four principles: co-operation, customer orientation, initiative and effort. Furthermore, this introduction provides a certain amount of confidence, in that it tries to eliminate existing fears and uncertainties in the new employees. Also, it tries to create an immediate involvement with the organisation: for example, a large part of the day is dedicated to making new people feel immediately at home and to know that they are welcome. Finally, this introduction day is an ideal moment for new employees to get to know each other.[51] "

This section introduces a three-phase model of organisational socialisation and examines the practical application of socialisation research.

A three-phase model of organisational socialisation

One's first year in a complex organisation can be confusing. There is a constant swirl of new faces, strange jargon, conflicting expectations and apparently unrelated events. Some organisations treat new members in a rather haphazard, sink-or-swim manner. More typically, though, the socialisation process is characterised by a sequence of identifiable steps.[52]

Organisational behaviour researcher, Daniel Feldman, has proposed a three-phase model of organisational socialisation that promotes deeper understanding of this important process. As illustrated in Figure 16.6, the three phases are:

- Anticipatory socialisation.
- Encounter.
- Change and acquisition.

Each phase has its associated perceptual and social processes. Feldman's model also specifies behavioural and affective outcomes that can be used to judge how well an individual has been socialised. The entire three-phase sequence may take from a few weeks to a year to complete, depending on individual differences and the complexity of the situation.

PHASE 1: ANTICIPATORY SOCIALISATION

Organisational socialisation begins before the individual actually joins the organisation. Anticipatory socialisation information comes from many sources. Widely circulated stories about IBM being the 'white shirt' company probably deter from applying those people who would prefer to work in jeans.

All of this information – whether formal or informal, accurate or inaccurate – helps the individual anticipate organisational realities. Unrealistic expectations about the nature of the work, pay and promotions are often formulated during Phase 1. Because employees with unrealistic expectations are more likely to quit their jobs in the future, organisations may want to use realistic job previews.

FIGURE 16.6 A MODEL OF ORGANISATIONAL SOCIALISATION

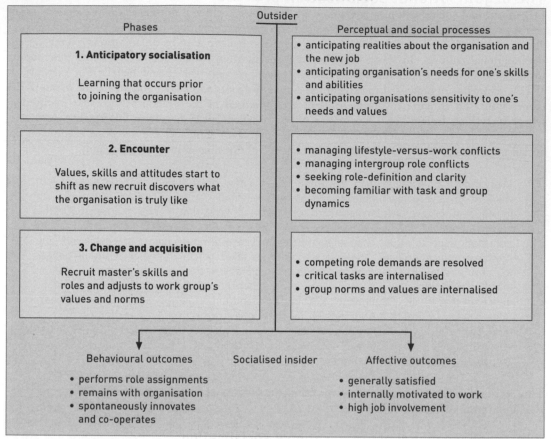

SOURCE: Adapted from material in D. C. Feldman, 'The Multiple Socialization of Organization Members', *Academy of Management Review*, April 1981, pp. 309–18.

Realistic job preview presents both positive and negative aspects of a job

A **Realistic job preview** (RJP) involves giving recruits a realistic idea of what lies ahead by presenting both positive and negative aspects of the job. RJPs may be verbal, in booklet form, audiovisual or hands-on. Research supports the practical benefits of using RJPs. A recent meta-analysis of 40 studies revealed that RJPs were related to higher performance and to lower attrition from the recruitment process. Results also demonstrated that RJPs lowered the initial expectations of job applicants and led to lower turnover among those who were hired.[53]

A modern trend used in many large organisations to seduce young, recently graduated people is to organise all kinds of flashy events. At these events, the company displays its mastery in its field, but at the same time, potential job applicants get a glimpse of the corporate culture. Consider the example of Barco Displays, a member of the Belgian Barco Group, manufacturing television and cinema screens:

> To attract new engineers, Barco invited 500 final-year students to their own in-house movie halls. The students were shown a live show, where a famous national television presenter, complete with a microphone and a camera team, jogged through the various departments and offices of the company, shooting pictures of people at work and giving short interviews with unsuspecting employees. To convince the students that everything was live, some were given a cellular phone by which they could directly ask questions to the interviewed employees. This way, Barco could show off its technical expertise and products, but the students also got a glimpse of the company's culture. 'With this initiative, Barco has proven that its innovativeness goes way beyond the technological aspect', says the company's HR-manager. 'Also, I often hear from students that they don't really know what we're doing here. With this event, we tried to fill that gap and at the same time show them what being a Barco-employee is all about.'[54]

PHASE 2: ENCOUNTER

This second phase begins once the employment contract has been signed. It is a time of surprises as the newcomer tries to make sense of unfamiliar territory. Behavioural scientists warn that **Reality shock** can occur during the encounter phase.

Reality shock a newcomer's feeling of surprise after experiencing unexpected situations or events

Becoming a member of an organisation will upset the everyday order of even the most well-informed newcomer. Matters concerning such aspects as friendships, time, purpose, demeanour, competence and the expectations the person holds of the immediate and distant future are suddenly made problematic. The newcomer's most pressing task is to build a set of guidelines and interpretations to explain and make meaningful the myriad of activities observed in the organisation.[55]

During the encounter phase, the individual is challenged to resolve any conflicts between the job and outside interests. If the hours prove too long, for example, family duties may require the individual to quit and find a more suitable work schedule. Also, as indicated in Figure 16.6, role conflict stemming from competing demands of different groups needs to be confronted and resolved (also see Chapter 10).

PHASE 3: CHANGE AND ACQUISITION

Mastery of important tasks and resolution of role conflict signals the beginning of this final phase of the socialisation process. Those who do not make the transition to phase 3 leave voluntarily or involuntarily or become isolated from social networks within the organisation. Senior executives frequently play a direct role in the change and acquisition phase.

Research findings and practical implications

Past research suggests five practical guidelines for managing organisational socialisation.[56]

Professionals should avoid a haphazard, sink-or-swim approach to organisational socialisation because formalised socialisation tactics positively influence new recruits. Formalised socialisation enhanced the manner in which newcomers adjusted to their jobs over a 10-month period and reduced role ambiguity, role conflict, stress symptoms and intentions to quit while simultaneously increasing job satisfaction and organisational commitment for a sample of 295 recently graduated students.[57]

The encounter phase of socialisation is particularly important. Studies of newly hired accountants demonstrated that the frequency and type of information obtained during their first six months of employment significantly affected their job performance, their role clarity, their understanding of the organisational culture and the extent to which they were socially integrated.[58] Managers play a key role during the encounter phase. A recent study of 205 new college graduates further revealed that their manager's task- and relationship-oriented input during the socialisation process significantly helped them to adjust to their new jobs.[59] In summary, managers need to help new recruits to become integrated in the organisational culture.

Support for stage models is mixed. Although there are different stages of socialisation, they are not identical in order, length or content for all people or jobs.[60] Organisations are advised to use a contingency approach toward organisational socialisation. In other words, different techniques are appropriate for different people at different times.

The organisation can benefit by training new employees to use proactive socialisation behaviours. A study of 154 entry-level professionals showed that effectively using proactive socialisation behaviours influenced the newcomers' general anxiety and stress during the first month of employment and their motivation and anxiety six months later.[61]

Organisations should pay attention to the socialisation of diverse employees. Research demonstrated that diverse employees, particularly those with disabilities, experienced different socialisation activities than other newcomers. In turn, these different experiences affected their long-term success and job satisfaction.[62]

Intercultural differences

As mentioned at the beginning of this chapter, the globalising world obliges us to take into account differences between countries and regions, in addition to differences in organisational cultures. It is becoming more frequently recognised that mergers or acquisitions that go beyond national borders multiply the chance of failure. Researchers Fons Trompenaars and Peter Woolliams state in a recent article on managing change across cultures that:

> ... it is striking how the Anglo-Saxon model of change has dominated the world of change management. It is based too often on a task-oriented culture and the idea that traditions need to be forgotten as soon as possible.[63]

In case of cross-national mergers or acquisitions not only organisational cultures can clash, but societal cultures get involved as well. How would you interpret the following situations?

- An Asian executive for a multinational company, transferred from Taiwan to the US, appears aloof and autocratic to his peers.[64]
- In Saudi Arabia, an invitation kindly asked that dogs and women be kept at home.[65]
- In Germany, an employee only wants to stay and work overtime if it's paid for and if a deadline is to be met.[66]

If you attribute the behaviour in these situations to personalities, three descriptions come to mind: arrogant, unfriendly and disloyal to the company. These are reasonable conclusions. Unfortunately, they are probably wrong, being based more on prejudice and stereotypes than on actual fact (also see Chapter 4). However, if you attribute the behavioural outcomes to cultural differences, you stand a better chance of making the following more valid interpretations. As it turns out:

- Asian culture encourages a more distant management style.[67]
- In some Muslim countries, women going out are seen as prostitutes.[68]
- In Germany overtime is exceptional as the company is seen as having no right to interfere with your private time.[69]

One cannot afford to overlook relevant cultural contexts when trying to understand organisational behaviour. In this section we will look into the following intercultural aspects the future professional will undoubtedly need in this globalising world: ethnocentrism, high-context and low-context societal culture, the Hofstede-Bond studies, Trompenaars' insights, time, interpersonal space and foreign assignments.

Ethnocentrism: a cultural roadblock in the global economy

Ethnocentrism, the belief that one's native country, culture, language and modes of behaviour are superior to all others, has its roots in the dawn of civilisation. First identified as a behavioural science concept in 1906, involving the tendency of groups to reject outsiders,[70] the term Ethnocentrism generally has a more encompassing (national or societal) meaning today. Worldwide evidence of ethnocentrism is plentiful. For example, ethnocentrism led to deadly 'ethnic cleansing' in Bosnia and Kosovo and genocide in the African nations of Rwanda and Burundi. Less dramatic, but still troublesome, is ethnocentrism within organisational contexts. Experts on the subject framed the problem in the following way;

Ethnocentrism belief that one's native country, culture, language and behaviour are superior

> Ethnocentric people have a preference for putting home-country people in key positions anywhere in the world and rewarding them more handsomely for work, along with a tendency to feel that this group is more intelligent, more capable or more reliable .... Ethnocentrism is often not attributable to prejudice as much as to inexperience or lack of knowledge about foreign persons and situations. This is not too surprising, since most professionals know far more about employees from their home environments. As one professional put it, 'At least I understand why our own people make mistakes. With our foreigners, I never know. The foreign people may be better. But if I can't trust a person, should I hire him or her just to prove we're multinational?'[71]

Also, many of today's top leaders are becoming increasingly careful with their international contacts, in order to avoid ethnocentrism. Ethnocentrism can be effectively dealt with through education, greater cross-cultural awareness, a conscious effort to value cultural diversity and, of course, international experience. 'You go to America or Asia and you simply learn a whole lot of things you would only read about if you stayed here', says Alison Clarke, head of an Asian division of Shandwick, a British public relations group. 'We like to think that we're the centre of the universe in Britain, but we're not. I find a lot of my colleagues here are way behind in their thinking. The trouble is that they don't realise it.'[72]

High-context and low-context societal cultures

Cultural anthropologists believe interesting and valuable lessons can be learned by comparing one culture with another. Many models have been proposed for distinguishing between the world's rich variety of cultures. One general distinction contrasts high-context and low-context cultures (see Figure 16.7 and Table 16.2).[73] Professionals in multicultural settings need to know the difference if they are to communicate and interact effectively.

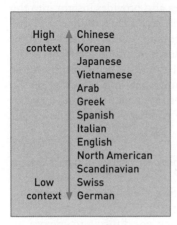

FIGURE 16.7 CONTRASTING HIGH-CONTEXT AND LOW-CONTEXT CULTURES

TABLE 16.2 CHARACTERISTICS OF HIGH-CONTEXT AND LOW-CONTEXT CULTURES

High-context culture	Low-context culture
Establish social trust first	Get down to business first
Value personal relations and goodwill	Value expertise and performance
Agreement by general trust	Agreement by specific, legalistic contract
Negotiations slow and ritualistic	Negotiations as efficient as possible

READING BETWEEN THE LINES IN HIGH-CONTEXT CULTURES

People from **High-context cultures** rely heavily on situational cues for meaning, when perceiving and communicating with another person. Non-verbal cues such as one's official position or status conveys messages more powerfully than spoken words. Thus, we come to understand better the ritual of exchanging and reading business cards in Japan. Japanese culture is relatively high-context. One's business card, listing employer and official position, conveys vital silent messages to members of Japan's homogeneous society. An intercultural communications authority explains:

> Nearly all communication in Japan takes place within an elaborate and vertically organised social structure. Everyone has a distinct place within this framework. Rarely do people converse without knowing, or determining, who is above and who is below them. Associates are always older or younger, male or female, subordinate or superior. And these distinctions all carry implications for the form of address, choice of words, physical distance and demeanour. As a result, conversation tends to reflect this formal hierarchy.[74]

Verbal and written communication in high-context cultures such as China, Korea and Japan are secondary to taken-for-granted cultural assumptions about other people.[75] In eastern Europe, business practices are more formal and decision making more hierarchical and lengthy. Titles and honorifics are important. Letters are answered late, if at all.[76]

High-context cultures primary meaning derived from non-verbal situational cues

605

READING THE FINE PRINT IN LOW-CONTEXT CULTURES

Low-context cultures primary meaning derived from written and spoken words

In **Low-context cultures**, written and spoken words carry the burden of shared meaning. True, people in low-context cultures read non-verbal messages from body language, dress, status and belongings. However, they tend to double-check their perceptions and assumptions verbally. To do so in China or Japan would be to gravely insult the other person, thus causing them to 'lose face'.[77] Their positions in Figure 16.7 indicate the German preoccupation with written rules for even the finest details of behaviour and the North American preoccupation with precise legal documents.[78] In high-context cultures agreements tend to be made on the basis of someone's word or a handshake, after a rather prolonged trust-building period. European-Americans, who have been taught from birth not to take anything for granted, see the handshake as a prelude to demanding a signature on a detailed, lawyer-approved, iron-clad contract.

For example, this distinction between high- and low-context cultures also provides insight into the mechanisms that make negotiations between Western and Asian people so difficult and for us Europeans, often unnecessarily long-winded and boring. The Western negotiator will try to seek a rather fast agreement on the basis of an impersonal set of promises written down in a contract, whereas the Asian party would prefer to explore more fully the nature of the relationship, being distrustful of legalistic approaches to complex problems, before agreeing to commit time and resources to the venture. The Asian will rely more on the trust that grows over time so that mutual confidence can also grow.[79] A good indicator as to whether a country is high or low context is to check how their meetings are held:[80]

- France: detailed agenda, briefing and co-ordination, interaction between the members through the boss, 15 minutes delay is acceptable.
- Germany: very formal, agenda and minutes, co-ordination and briefing, communication through a senior person, it is very important to be punctual.
- Italy: unstructured and informal, people may come and people may go, difficult to impose an agenda, free for all opinions, delay is accepted.
- The Netherlands: informality of manner but nevertheless keep to the basic protocols of keeping an agenda, speaking through the chairman.
- Spain: no meetings culture, only to communicate instructions, delay is endemic.
- The United Kingdom: most important and time-consuming tool, very serious, unpunctuality is the rule!

Aside from being high-context or low-context, cultures stand apart in other ways as well. In the following sections we will discuss the Hofstede-Bond stream of research, Trompenaars' forms of relating to other people, time, interpersonal space and communication.

The Hofstede–Bond stream of research

Instructive insights surfaced in the mid-1980s when the results of two very different cross-cultural management studies were merged. The first study was conducted under the guidance of Dutch researcher, Geert Hofstede. The tremendous impact his research had on contemporary cultural thinking is reflected by the fact that Hofstede is currently the world's most cited living author in the entire area of the social sciences. Canadian Michael Harris Bond, at the Chinese University of Hong Kong, was a key researcher in the second study. What follows is a brief overview of each study, a discussion of the combined results and a summary of important practical implications.

THE TWO STUDIES

Hofstede's study is a classic in the annals of cross-cultural management research.[81] He drew his data for the study from a collection of 116 000 attitude surveys administered to IBM employees worldwide between 1967 and 1973. Respondents to the attitude survey, which also asked questions on cultural values and beliefs, included IBM employees from 72 countries. Fifty-three cultures were eventually analysed and contrasted according to four cultural dimensions. Hofstede's database was unique, not only because of its large size, but also because it allowed him to isolate cultural effects. If his subjects had not performed similar jobs in different countries for the same company, no such control would have been possible. Cross-cultural comparisons were made along the first four dimensions listed in Table 16.3, power distance, individualism–collectivism, masculinity–femininity and uncertainty avoidance.

Bond's study was much smaller, involving a survey of 100 students (50 per cent women) from 22 countries and 5 continents. The survey instrument was the Chinese Value Survey (CVS), based on the Rokeach Value Survey (see Chapter 3).[82] The CVS also tapped four cultural dimensions. Three corresponded with Hofstede's first three in Table 16.3. Hofstede's fourth cultural dimension, uncertainty avoidance, was not measured by the CVS. Instead, Bond's study isolated the fifth cultural dimension in Table 16.3. It was eventually renamed 'long-term versus short-term orientation' to reflect how strongly a person believes in the long-term thinking promoted by the teachings of the Chinese philosopher Confucius (551–479 BC). According to an update by Hofstede, 'On the long-term side one finds values oriented towards the future, like thrift (saving) and persistence. On the short-term side one finds values rather more oriented towards the past and present, like respect for tradition and fulfilling social obligations.'[83] Interestingly, one may embrace Confucian long-term values without knowing a thing about Confucius.[84]

TABLE 16.3 KEY CULTURAL DIMENSIONS IN THE HOFSTEDE–BOND STUDIES

Power distance	How much do people expect inequality in social institutions (e.g. family, work organisations, government)?
Individualism–collectivism	How loose or tight is the bond between individuals and societal groups?
Masculinity–femininity	To what extent do people embrace competitive masculine traits (e.g. success, assertiveness and performance) or nurturing feminine traits (e.g. solidarity, personal relationships, service, quality of life)?
Uncertainty avoidance	To what extent do people prefer structured versus unstructured situations?
Long-term versus short-term orientation (Confucian values)	To what extent are people oriented toward the future by saving and being persistent versus being oriented toward the present and past by respecting tradition and meeting social obligations?

SOURCE: Adapted from discussion in G. Hofstede, 'Cultural Constraints in Management Theories', *Academy of Management Executive*, February 1993, pp. 81–94.

EAST MEETS WEST

By merging the two studies, a serious flaw in each was corrected. Namely, Hofstede's study had an inherent Anglo-European bias and Bond's study had a built-in Asian bias. How would cultures compare if viewed through the overlapping lenses of the two studies? Hofstede and Bond were able to answer that question because 18 countries in Bond's study overlapped the 53 countries in Hofstede's sample.[85] Table 16.4 lists the countries scoring highest on each of the five cultural dimensions. (Countries earning between 67 and 100 points on a 0 to 100 relative ranking scale, qualified as 'high' for Table 16.4.) The United States, for example, scored the highest in individualism, moderate in power distance, masculinity and uncertainty avoidance and low in long-term orientation.

In view of their inclusion in an enlarged European Union on 1 May 2004, Geert Hofstede's dimensions were measured in four Central European countries (the Czech Republic, Hungary, Poland and Slovakia). The findings show that there are important differences between the value orientations in Western Europe and Central Europe. Furthermore, there are substantial differences among the four Central European countries. Slovakia shows the largest power distance and Poland the smallest, while all four countries exhibit a relatively large power distance if compared with Western European countries. In Poland, the power distance is markedly smaller than in the other three countries. The Czech Republic stands out as the most individualistic country, while Slovakia is most collectivistic. As far as uncertainty avoidance is concerned, Slovakia again differs sharply from the other four countries. All four countries incline to the masculine pole, but Hungary and Slovakia

TABLE 16.4 COUNTRIES SCORING THE HIGHEST IN THE HOFSTEDE–BOND STUDIES

High power distance	High individualism	High masculinity	High uncertainty avoidance	High long-term orientation*
Philippines India Singapore Brazil Hong Kong***	United States Australia Great Britain Netherlands Canada New Zealand Sweden Germany**	Japan	Japan Korea Brazil Pakistan Taiwan	Hong Kong*** Taiwan Japan Korea

*Originally called Confucian Dynamism.
**Former West Germany.
***Reunited with China.

SOURCE: Adapted from Exhibit 2 in G. Hofstede and M. H. Bond, 'The Confucius Connection: From Cultural Roots to Economic Growth', *Organizational Dynamics*, Spring 1988, pp. 12–13.

do so extremely. As far as long versus short-term orientation is concerned, the Czech Republic inclines to the short-term pole, while the other countries have more intermediate positions.[86]

PRACTICAL IMPLICATIONS

Individually and together, the Hofstede and Bond studies yielded the following useful lessons for international collaboration:

■ Due to varying cultural values, theories and practices need to be adapted to the local culture. This is particularly true for made-in-America theories (such as Maslow's need hierarchy theory, see Chapter 5) and Japanese practices.[87] There is no 'one best way' to lead people across cultures.
■ High long-term orientation was the only one of the five cultural dimensions to correlate positively with national economic growth.
■ Industrious cultural values are a necessary but insufficient condition for economic growth. Markets and a supportive political climate are also required to create the right mix.[88]
■ Cultural arrogance is a luxury individuals and nations can no longer afford in a global economy.

Trompenaars' forms of relating to other people

In his study of cultural differences between 28 countries, Fons Trompenaars has developed five relevant dimensions:[89] universalism–particularism, individualism–collectivism, neutral–emotional, specific–diffuse and achievement–ascription.

UNIVERSALISM–PARTICULARISM

Universalism implies that what is good and right can be applied everywhere (abstract societal codes). Typical rule-based cultures are, for example, Anglo-Saxon and Scandinavian countries like the Netherlands, Germany and Switzerland. Particularist cultures, on the other hand, are more friendship-based. What counts here are relationships and unique circumstances. 'I must protect the people around me, no matter what the rules say.' Typical particularist countries are, for example, Russia, Spain and France. In practice, we will need both judgements. For example, sometimes universalist rules have no answers to particularist problems. Hence, co-operation between people from both cultures will sometimes cause serious problems: universalists will, for example, accuse particularists of corruption when they 'help' a friend or a family member, whereas universalists will be said to be selfish if they refuse to help an acquaintance. A very detailed contract, drawn by a universalist specifying every legal detail, is seen by the particularist as if 'he does not trust me as a business partner'. The particularist will first build a relationship with his business partner. Once mutual trust is established, a particularist considers it is not necessary to draw up a detailed contract: the relationship itself is the guarantee (see Table 16.5).

TABLE 16.5 BUSINESS AREAS AFFECTED BY UNIVERSALISM/PARTICULARISM

Universalism	Particularism
Focus is more on rules than on relationships Legal contracts are readily drawn up A trustworthy person is one who honours his or her 'word' or contract There is only one truth or reality, that which has been agreed to A deal is a deal	Focus is more on relationships than on rules Legal contracts are readily modified A trustworthy person is the one who honours changing circumstances There are several perspectives on reality relative to each participant Relationships evolve

INDIVIDUALISM–COLLECTIVISM

Individualist countries, such as the Netherlands and Sweden, are oriented towards one's self. Collectivist countries are fairly group-oriented. Think about the typical family-minded Frenchman.

Regarding oneself as an individual or as part of a group has serious influences on negotiations, on decision making and on motivation. Pay-for-performance, for example, is welcomed in the USA, the Netherlands and the UK. More collectivist cultures, such as France, most parts of Asia and Germany, are very reluctant to follow the Anglo-Saxon pay-for-performance systems (see Chapter 6). They take offence at the idea that one's performance is related to another's deficiencies. In negotiations and decision making collectivists will take no decision without prior and elaborate discussions with the home front. Individualists, however, will usually take a decision on their own without the prior consent of their colleagues or bosses. A Chinese–Dutch study showed that people in collective cultures had more constructive reactions after they had received feedback from their supervisors, compared to people from individualist cultures.[90]

TABLE 16.6 BUSINESS AREAS AFFECTED BY INDIVIDUALISM/COLLECTIVISM

Individualism	Collectivism
More frequent use of 'I' and 'me' In negotiations, decisions typically made on the spot by a representative People ideally achieve alone and assume personal responsibility Holidays taken in pairs, or even alone	More frequent use of 'we' Decisions typically referred back by delegate to the organisation People ideally achieve in groups which assume joint responsibility Holidays taken in organised groups or extended family

NEUTRAL–EMOTIONAL

Showing or not showing our emotions is culturally embedded. People from countries such as North America, Europe and Japan will hardly express their feelings in a first business contact, whereas people from southern countries like Italy and France are very affective and open. Business contacts between the cultures may frequently result in misunderstandings. Neutral people are considered as having no feelings, emotional people are considered as being out of control (see Table 16.7).

TABLE 16.7 BUSINESS AREAS AFFECTED BY NEUTRAL/AFFECTIVE RELATIONSHIPS

Neutral	Emotional
Opaque emotional state Do not readily express what they think or feel Embarrassed or awkward at public displays of emotions Discomfort with physical contact outside 'private' circle Subtle in verbal and non-verbal expressions	Show immediate reactions either verbally or non-verbally Express face and body signals At ease with physical contact Raise voice readily

SPECIFIC–DIFFUSE

In specific cultures home and business are strictly separated, contacts are on a contractual basis. In more diffuse cultures both worlds are interrelated, the entire person is involved. In specific-oriented cultures, the relationship you have with a person depends on the common ground you have with that person at that moment. If you are specialised in a certain area you will have 'the advantage' in that subject. If, on the other hand, the other person has more knowledge in another area, the roles will be reversed. In diffuse countries, like France, one's authority permeates each area of life. In such cultures, everything is connected to everything. In negotiations, for example, your business partner may ask for your personal background (see Table 16.8).

TABLE 16.8 BUSINESS AREAS AFFECTED BY SPECIFIC/DIFFUSE RELATIONSHIPS

Specific	Diffuse
More 'open' public space, more closed 'private' space	More 'closed' public space but, once in, more 'open' private space
Appears direct, open and extravert	Appears indirect, closed and introvert
'To the point' and often appears abrasive	Often evades issues and 'beats about the bush'
Highly mobile	Low mobility
Separates work and private life	Work and private life are closely linked
Varies approach to fit circumstances especially with use of titles (e.g. Herr Doktor Muller at work is Hans in social environments or in certain business meetings)	Consistent in approach, especially with use of titles (e.g. Herr Doktor Muller remains Herr Doktor Muller in any setting)

ACHIEVEMENT–ASCRIPTION

In achievement-oriented cultures, such as France, emphasis is put on what you have accomplished; in ascription-oriented cultures, your personality counts. Different countries confer status on individuals in different ways. Anglo-Saxons, for example, will ascribe status to reasons for achievement.

The following situation illustrates the way in which cultural differences can lead to serious misunderstandings in business. A Danish paint manufacturing company wanted a large English firm to represent it in Britain. Having received encouraging signals on a first visit, the Danish managers came over a second time and were surprised by the complete lack of interest. Yet they were still not turned down. The British 'no' was finally received in a telex of three lines after a total of three visits and much wasted advance planning from the Danish end. Why didn't the English say 'no' at the start?[91]

Cultural perceptions of time

In North American and northern European cultures time seems to be a simple matter. It is linear, relentlessly marching forward, never backward, in standardised chunks. To the German who received a watch for his or her third birthday, time is like money. It is spent, saved or wasted.[92] Americans are taught to show up ten minutes early for appointments. When working across cultures, however, time becomes a very complex matter.[93] Imagine a Swiss person's chagrin when left in a waiting room for 45 minutes, only to find a Latin-American government official then deals with him and three other people all at once. The Swiss person resents the lack of prompt and undivided attention. The Latin-American official resents the Swiss person's impatience and apparent self-centredness.[94] This vicious cycle of resentment can be explained by the distinction between **Monochromic time** and **Polychronic time**:

> The former is revealed in the ordered, precise, schedule-driven use of public time that typifies and even caricatures efficient northern Europeans and North Americans. The latter is seen in the multiple and cyclical activities and concurrent involvement with different people in the Mediterranean, Latin American and especially Arab cultures.[95]

Monochronic time preference for doing one thing at a time because time is limited, precisely segmented and schedule driven

Polychronic time preference for doing more than one thing at a time because time is flexible and multidimensional

A MATTER OF DEGREE

Monochronic and polychronic are relative rather than absolute concepts. Generally, the more things a person tends to do at once, the more polychronic that person is.[96] Thanks to computers and advanced telecommunications systems, highly polychronic managers can engage in 'multitasking'.[97] For instance, it is possible to talk on the telephone, read and respond to email messages (also see Chapter 8), print a report, check a pager message and eat a stale sandwich all at the same time. Unfortunately, this extreme polychronic behaviour is too often not as efficient as hoped and can be very stressful.

In a European context, we can say that, using our categories, Latins are polychronic whereas Germanics are monochronic. In other words, the first are schedule independent and the latter schedule dependent. In Italy, for example, if something intervenes to make you late – a meeting running overtime, a surprise meeting with someone important or an unexpected telephone call – then it is understandable. While it is impolite to arrive late for a meeting, it is even more impolite to break off the previous one because it is overrunning.[98]

Monochronic people prefer to do one thing at a time. What is your attitude towards time? (You can find out by completing the Polychronic Attitude Index in the next Activity.)

What is your attitude towards time?

Please consider how you feel about the following statements. Circle your choice on the scale provided, showing whether you: strongly disagree, disagree, are neutral, agree or strongly agree.

	Strongly disagree	Disagree	Neutral	Agree	Strongly agree
I do not like to juggle several activities at the same time.	5	4	3	2	1
People should not try to do many things at once.	5	4	3	2	1
When I sit down at my desk, I work on one project at a time.	5	4	3	2	1
I am not comfortable doing several things at the same time.	5	4	3	2	1

Add up your points, and divide the total by 4. Then plot your score on the scale below.

1.0	1.5	2.0	2.5	3.0	3.5	4.0	4.5	5.0
Monochronic								Polychronic

The lower your score (below 3.0), the more monochronic your orientation; and the higher your score (above 3.0), the more polychronic.

SOURCE: A. C. Bluedorn, C. F. Kaufman and P. M. Lane, 'How Many Things Do You Like to Do at Once? An Introduction to Monochronic and Polychronic Time', *Academy of Management Executive*, November 1992, Exhibit 2, p. 20.

RESEARCH FINDINGS AND PRACTICAL IMPLICATIONS

Low-context cultures, such as those of Northern America and northern Europe, tend to run on monochronic time while high-context cultures, such as those of Latin America and southern Europe, tend to run on polychronic time. People in polychronic cultures view time as flexible, fluid and multidimensional. The Germans and Swiss have made an exact science of monochronic time. In fact, a new radio-controlled watch made by a German company, Junghans, is 'guaranteed to lose no more than one second in 1 million years'.[99] Many a visitor has been a minute late for a Swiss train, only to see its tail lights leaving the station. Time is more elastic in polychronic cultures. During the Islamic holy month of Ramadan in the Middle East, for example, the faithful fast during daylight hours and the general pace of things slows markedly. Professionals need to reset their mental clocks when doing business across cultures. The way a working day is organised clearly shows a culture's

TABLE 16.9 TIPS FOR SUCCESSFUL INTERCULTURAL DEALING

Time concept	Advice for successful intercultural dealing
Punctuality	Find the basic unit of time: Is it 5 minutes, 15 or 30?
Polychronic or monochronic time	In some cultures, the business lunch is devoted to socialising with business partners. It may be hard to figure out what activities can be combined and what cannot
Fast and slow paces of life	A fast pace can lead to stress-related health problems. Social support can lessen these problems
Time as symbol	Time is not money in some cultures and treating it in monetary terms may be considered vulgar
Time efficiency	Speed is not always a virtue. Multicultural teams need more time to achieve their peak performance level; however, they may be more effective after they become comfortable working with each other for some time

SOURCE: Adapted from W. Brislin and E. S. Kim, 'Cultural Diversity in People's Understanding and Uses of Time', *Applied Psychology: An International Review*, June 2003, p. 380.

perception of time. Generally speaking, one can say that in southern Europe a working day starts early in the morning and ends at lunch time, whereas a working day in northern Europe starts between 8 and 9 a.m. and end between 5 and 6 p.m. Table 16.9 gives advice on the use of time across the world.

Interpersonal space

Anthropologist Edward T. Hall noticed a connection between culture and preferred interpersonal distance. People from high-context cultures were observed standing close when talking to someone. Low-context cultures appeared to dictate a greater amount of interpersonal space. Hall applied the term **Proxemics** to the study of cultural expectations about interpersonal space.[100] He specified four interpersonal distance zones. Some call them space bubbles. These distances are referred to as:

> **Proxemics**
> Hall's term for the cultural expectations about interpersonal space

- intimate,
- personal,
- social,
- public.

Ranges for the four interpersonal distance zones are illustrated in Figure 16.8, along with selected cultural differences.

In North America or northern Europe, business conversations are normally conducted at about a metre (three to four foot) distance, within the personal zone in Figure 16.8. A range of approximately a third of a metre (one foot) is common in Latin American and Asian cultures, which is uncomfortably close for northern Europeans and North Americans. Arabs like to get even closer. Mismatches in culturally dictated interpersonal space zones can prove very distracting for the unprepared. Hall explains:

> Arabs tend to get very close and breathe on you. It's part of the high sensory involvement of a high-context culture. The Briton on the receiving end can't identify all the sources of his discomfort but feels that the Arab is pushy. The Arab comes close, the Brit backs away. The Arab follows, because he can only interact at certain distances. Once the Briton learns that Arabs handle space differently and that breathing on people is a form of communication, the situation can sometimes be redefined so the Briton relaxes.[101]

Asian and Middle-Eastern hosts grow weary of seemingly having to chase their low-context guests around at social gatherings to maintain what they feel is proper conversational range. Backing away

612

FIGURE 16.8 INTERPERSONAL DISTANCE ZONES FOR BUSINESS CONVERSATIONS VARY FROM CULTURE TO CULTURE

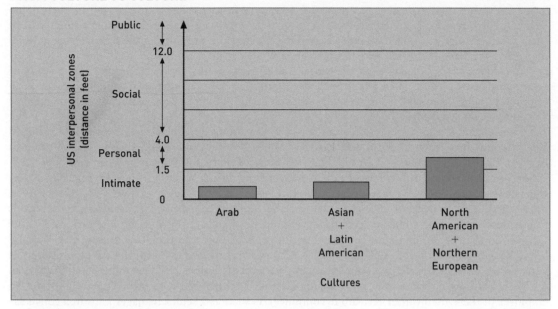

all evening to keep conversational partners at a proper distance is an awkward experience as well. Awareness of cultural differences, along with skillful accommodation, are essential to productive intercultural business dealings.

Norwegians, by comparison, can be very jealous of their bubbles of space – to an extent that they even astonished an American visitor. 'One of the first things I noticed when I moved to Norway was that Norwegians need a lot of personal space', he remarked to an interviewer. 'Once I went into someone's office for an informal chat and sat down on the edge of his desk, some two metres from him! I had the direct impression that I was on his territory. Also, I have found that if one reaches out to another during a conversation, there will almost immediately be a recoil from the listener.'[102]

Cross-cultural communication

Those attempting to communicate across cultures have three options:

- Stick to their own language.
- Rely on translators.
- Learn the local language.

The first option, preferred by those who insist English has become the language of global business, are at a serious competitive disadvantage. Ignorance of the local language means missing subtle yet crucial meanings, risking unintended insult and jeopardising the business transaction. For example, according to one well-travelled business writer, 'In Asia, a "yes" answer to a question simply means the question is understood. It's the beginning of negotiations. In the Middle East, the response will probably be some version of "God willing".'[103] Live translations, translations of written documents and advertisements, and computer email translations are helpful but plagued by accuracy problems.[104]

Bad translations might often be amusing, but they are potentially damaging to business. In *Management Today*, Jonah Bloom gives this example from a hotel brochure advertising holidays in the French Alps: 'The hotel has a heated of course swimming pool. Thus even by thunder weather dare to dive in and in case of likely congestion, the barmaid owning proper diplomas will help.' All very funny, until it's your brochure being read.

In business a lack of linguistic ability can be fatal, Bloom continues, 'the most poignant story involves a UK manufacturer that went bust. When the official receivers looked through the paperwork, they found a letter in a filing cabinet, written in German. No-one at the firm had understood it, so it had been filed away with other miscellaneous correspondence. It turned out to be a purchase big enough to have saved the firm from insolvency.'[105]

Successful international managers, especially the ones from smaller countries, tell us there is no adequate substitute for knowing the local language. However, language skills account for only part of their success: linguistic skills, although important, are not the only skill needed by a cross-cultural manager. 'We have had some people from the UK who go to a continental subsidiary with hardly any knowledge of the language, but who manage to communicate', says Nicole Huyghens, a Belgian-born manager who works in Marks & Spencer's Paris office. 'It is an attitude of mind. Humility is an important quality', she says. 'You have to accept you are not going to be as confident or competent as you are in your own environment.'[106]

Very often, communication difficulties arise in the numerous 'marriages' between Dutch and British companies, such as Reed and Elsevier, Shell, P&O Nedlloyd and so on. The discussions between British Airways and KLM, the Dutch airways, came to nothing partly because of communication problems. The Britons have a rather indirect style during meetings: they are reluctant to say things in a negative way, because this would mean loss of face for the other side. The Dutch, on the other hand, have some kind of a 'you're an idiot but don't take it personally' attitude; their style is more direct. They want to make decisions during meetings and transform them into actions; but the English do that before and after the meetings, in private. To avoid problems arising from cultural differences, the Air France–KLM merger was accompanied by research into the cultural differences between the two carriers. As to communication patterns, Air France clearly is more hierarchical than KLM. 'We are much more informal and are on familiar terms with each other very soon', states an employee of the Dutch carrier KLM. He continues 'As soon as a senior manager joins in a conversation in France, the atmosphere changes'.[107]

'That's why diplomatic missions at Shell were always assigned to the English. For the tougher business part, the Dutch were engaged', says cross-cultural expert Fons Trompenaars. 'Britons and the Dutch have a radically different style of communicating. It's the English stiff upper lip versus the Dutch openness. At Shell, this caused enormous problems during meetings.'[108]

The global manager

About 80 per cent of all medium-size and large organisations transfer employees to another country.[109] Foreign experience has become a necessary stepping stone in one's career development. As the reach of global companies continues to grow, many opportunities for living and working in foreign countries will arise. For example, one company which, in striving to become a worldwide force, makes increasing use of international assignments, is British Airways.'We knew we had to globalise our company and that centred entirely on how we develop people in the business', says Fran Spencer, former HR manager at the airline. 'We will know when we have got there: a third of graduate recruits will be from outside the UK, a quarter of the board will be non-UK nationals; and our own top 100 managers will have spent at least half a year of their working life outside the country.'[110]

FAILURE IN FOREIGN ASSIGNMENTS

Expatriate
anyone living or
working in a
foreign country

Expatriate refers to anyone living or working outside their home country. Hence, they are said to be expatriated when transferred to another country and repatriated when transferred back home. A recent article described European expatriates strikingly well as 'Euronomads'. According to Kevin Martin, a Scot working in Brussels, 'Euronomads are like mercenaries. They don't have a fixed spot to live, all they need is a decent laptop, the will to wander and a schedule of the Eurostar.'[111]

As an example, David Best, who works for the pan-European company Motor Care, does business all over Europe. He's been everywhere, to Sweden, Ireland, Germany and France. He has more international than national conversations – has six retirement plans running. He noticed that he's not so much appreciated for his knowledge and his managerial skills as his ability to adapt readily to different European cultures. 'There's a difference between talking French and acting French', he explains. 'The boss needs me, sometimes to play interpreter, sometimes just to inform him about specific sensitivities in certain cultures.'[112]

However, expatriate managers are usually characterised as culturally inept and prone to failure on international assignments. Sadly, research supports this view. A pair of international management experts recently offered the following assessment.

> Over the past decade, we have studied the management of expatriates at about 750 US, European and Japanese companies. We asked both the expatriates themselves, and the executives who sent them abroad, to evaluate their experiences. In addition, we looked at what happened after expatriates returned home. Overall, the results of our research were alarming. We found that between 10 and 20 per cent of all managers sent abroad returned early because of job dissatisfaction or difficulties in adjusting to a foreign country. Of those who stayed for the duration, nearly a third did not perform up to the expectations of their superiors. And perhaps most problematic, a fourth of those who completed an assignment left their company, often to join a competitor, within a year of repatriation. That turnover rate is double that of managers who did not go abroad.[113]

Because of the high cost of sending employees and their families to foreign countries for extended periods, significant improvement is needed. Research has uncovered specific reasons for the failure of expatriates. Listed in decreasing order of frequency, are the following seven most common reasons.

1 The expatriate's spouse cannot adjust to new physical or cultural surroundings.
2 The expatriate cannot adapt to new physical or cultural surroundings.
3 The expatriate has family problems.
4 The expatriate is emotionally immature.
5 The expatriate cannot cope with foreign duties.
6 The expatriate is not technically competent.
7 The expatriate lacks the proper motivation for a foreign assignment.[114]

Collectively, family and personal adjustment problems, not technical competence, provide the main stumbling block for people working in foreign countries. This conclusion is reinforced by the results of a survey that asked 72 Human Resource managers, at multinational corporations, to identify the most important success factor in a foreign assignment. 'Nearly 35 per cent said cultural adaptability, patience, flexibility and tolerance for others' beliefs. Only 22 per cent of them listed technical and management skills.'[115] Consider what happened to Gabrielle Rosenbaum:

> In the beginning, she was thrilled with the idea of her husband's foreign assignment with Philips. As for many Dutch men and women, a foreign assignment was equal to exotic resorts, sunshine, swimming pools, parties and recreation. The good life was in store for her and her family, until she, her husband and their three sons left for their first foreign assignment in Pakistan, where they were confronted with the everyday life of an Islamic culture. Others' habits, norms and values led to serious misunderstandings. How could she reprimand her children in a public place like a restaurant? Her three sons were a gift from God, weren't they? In their next assignment, the impoverished metropolis of Bombay, misunderstanding after misunderstanding again occurred. At home, in the Netherlands, she had treated people equally, regardless of their position. Why hadn't she realised how confusing such an attitude could be in India, where society is based on castes and contrasts? 'In Bombay in particular I realised how badly I had been prepared for this assignment. For my husband it was an enormous challenge to go abroad. He had his job to do, whereas I was left on my own, nobody had cared about how I would manage with the three children.'[116]

ANTICIPATING FAILURE IN EXPATRIATE ASSIGNMENTS

Finding the right person (usually along with a supportive and adventurous family) for a foreign position is a complex, time-consuming and costly process.[117] Even long before an eventual future expatriate assignment comes up, an assessment can draw a picture of someone's international career planning. Such an assessment can either fuel or extinguish one's international ambitions.[118] This assessment should pay more attention than is the case today to personality traits such as openness to new experiences and friendliness (also see Chapter 2). Both personality traits have proved to be helpful in building relationships with locals, which is important for expatriates' success.[119] Moreover, better selection methods would reduce the enormous costs resulting from failed foreign

FIGURE 16.9 THE FOREIGN ASSIGNMENT CYCLE

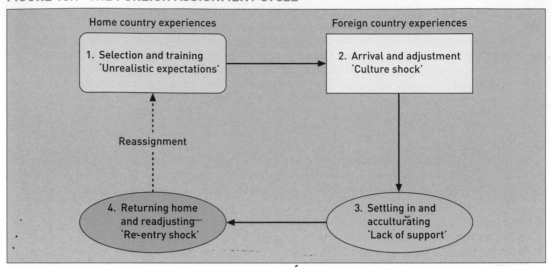

assignments.[120] In the four-stage process illustrated in Figure 16.9, the first and last stages occur at home. The middle two stages occur in the foreign or host country.

Avoiding unrealistic expectations with cross-cultural training

Realistic job previews (RJPs), as predicted earlier, have proved effective at bringing people's unrealistic expectations about a pending job assignment down to earth by providing a realistic balance of good and bad news. People with realistic expectations tend to quit less often and be more satisfied than those with unrealistic expectations. RJPs are a must for future expatriates. In addition, cross-cultural training is required.

Cross-cultural training is any type of structured experience designed to help departing employees adjust to a foreign culture. The trend is toward more such training. Although it is costly, companies wanting to help people adjust believe cross-cultural training is less expensive than failed foreign assignments. Programmes vary widely in type and in rigour.[121] Of course, the greater the difficulty, the greater the time and expense:

- Easiest: pre-departure training is limited to informational materials, including books, lectures, films, videos and Internet searches.
- Moderately difficult: experiential training is conducted through case studies, role playing, assimilators (simulated intercultural incidents) and introductory language instruction.
- Most difficult: departing employees are given some combination of the preceding methods plus comprehensive language instruction and field experience in the target culture.[122]

As an example, when a Dutch manager was assigned to start up a new Philips plant in Skierniewice, Poland, he and his wife went through an intensive 'country information programme'. Some managers who had formerly worked in Poland, such as the head of Unilever's eastern Europe division, were invited. At first the couple could ask them some simple practical questions, such as: 'What do I have to do with a drunk employee? Where can I find an interpreter? Why are the rents in Warschau that high? Is it safe to drink tap water?' Then they were taught some basic aspects of behaviour in Poland, such as the do's and don'ts of conversations, meetings and so on and an introduction to the Polish language.[123]

Recent research underscores the critical role of spouses' cross-cultural adjustment during international assignments and suggests that companies need to pay closer attention to these issues when selecting and preparing so send expatriates with spouses to another country. At the very least, both expatriates and spouses need to be included in predeparture training and training on-site.[124] These research findings can only be confirmed by the fact that adjustment problems suffered by the expatriates' spouse are the principal reason for failed expatriate assignments.

Cross-cultural training structured experiences to help people adjust to a new culture or country

616

Avoiding culture shock

Have you ever been in a totally unfamiliar situation and felt disoriented and perhaps a bit frightened? If so, you already know something about culture shock. According to anthropologists, **Culture shock** involves anxiety and doubt caused by an overload of unfamiliar expectations and social cues.[125] First-year students often experience a variation of culture shock. An expatriate manager or family member may be thrown off-balance by an avalanche of strange sights, sounds and behaviours. Among them may be unreadable road signs, strange-tasting food, not being allowed to use your left hand for social activities (in Islamic countries, the left hand is the toilet hand) or failure to get a laugh with your sure-fire joke. For the expatriate manager trying to concentrate on the fine details of a business negotiation, culture shock is more than an embarrassing inconvenience. It is a disaster! Like the confused first-year student who quits and goes home, culture-shocked employees often panic and go home early.

Even people moving to a country where they speak the same language sometimes have trouble adapting, as this British woman working in Kentucky, USA, describes: 'You never know when culture shock will bite. There you are, thinking you've got the measure of a country, you're turning out of side roads onto the proper side of the main one, you've mastered the use of 'y'all' and learned not to fear doggy bags and suddenly some tiny detail turns everything on its head, reminds you that you are, after all, a stranger in a foreign country.'[126]

The best defence against culture shock is comprehensive cross-cultural training, including intensive language study. Once again, the only way to pick up subtle – yet important – social cues is via the local language.

> Culture shock
> anxiety and doubt caused by an overload of new expectations and cues

Support during the foreign assignment

Especially during the first six months, when everything is so new to the expatriate, a support system needs to be in place.[127] The role local people can play in successful expatriate assignments has long been ignored. Researchers and expatriates along now argue for both local and expatriate support. Experts Regina Hechanova, Terry Beehr and Neil Christiansen concluded that:

> Although the social support received from other expatriates will certainly be helpful, host nationals are best equipped to provide information that will reduce uncertainty and facilitate adjustment to the host culture.[128]

Insights resulting from Dutch research among 427 expatriates from 26 countries and posted in 52 countries teach us that close relationships with other expatriates have less influence on expatriates' adaptation than close relationships with locals.[129]

Consider the advice of Philippe de Neve, Alcatel's vice-president R&D Competences, who has had foreign assignments in Shanghai, Peking, Tanzania, Tibet, Stalingrad, Siberia, St Petersburg, Madras and Paris.

> An expatriate assignment broadens one's culture and one's worldview. You take up with other nationalities or other colours of skin. I can only advise expatriates working for an international company not to confine themselves to building relationships with other expatriates. Contacts with the local population is a must.[130]

In a foreign country, where even the smallest errand can turn into an utterly exhausting production, a network of expatriates is indispensable as well. Host-country sponsors assigned to individual expatriates and their families can get things done quickly because they know the cultural and geographical territory.

> Royal Dutch Shell founded two organisations which are charged with providing practical information on the living conditions abroad: a network of Shell-families for Shell-families. There is Outpost, which tries to introduce new expats to existing expats in the same area. A Spouse Employment Consultant provides information on the working conditions, recognition of degrees, work permits and so forth.[131]

The local staff members who report to the expatriates can also make a large contribution to the expatriates' successful functioning. In many cases the local staff have a perfect understanding of cross-cultural issues and are well able to point out what training their expatriate bosses need.[132]

Avoiding re-entry shock

Strange as it may seem, many otherwise successful expatriate managers encounter their first major difficulty only after their foreign assignment is over. Why? Returning to one's native culture is taken for granted because it seems so routine and ordinary. However, having adjusted to another country's way of doing things for an extended period of time can result in putting one's own culture and surroundings in a strange new light. Three areas for potential re-entry shock are work, social activities and general environment (such as politics, climate, transportation, food).

A recent study among female European executives illustrates that many European multinationals continue to have a low sense of awareness of the need for repatriation programmes. Some testimonies:[133]

> The problem is that when one comes back from an international assignment it may happen that there is no position for the person to return to. Sometimes it is necessary to be a supplementary person in a department and one has to wait for a job. That is not very nice to come back to. (Bank Manager, Belgium)

> Expatriation policies in our organisations are very strong, but the repatriation policies are not. The company assumes that when one is returning one can slot in again. But, I believe that it is the time when one needs far more support from one's organisation. (Senior Engineer, Manufacturing Company, Ireland)

> Coming back is as bad if not worse. Going abroad is difficult in that one doesn't know what they are going to, whereas one is coming back they have a fair idea of what they are coming back to. After about six months one settles down again. One's personal life with one's family and friends is also disrupted. (Civil Servant, Ireland)

Lance Richards, senior director of international HR for Kelly Services states that repatriation must start well before the assignee 'has ever darkened the door of a Boeing 747'. Anyone considering moving their family overseas should ask: 'What happens next?' 'It's amazing how many companies don't have the answer to this simple question. Even worse, sometimes they know the answer, but won't tell the assignee', Richards says.[134]

Overall, the key to a successful foreign assignment is making it a well-integrated link in a career chain rather than treating it as an isolated adventure.

Learning outcomes: Summary of key terms

1 Discuss the difference between espoused and enacted values

Espoused values represent the explicitly stated values and norms that are preferred by an organisation. Enacted values, in contrast, reflect the values and norms that are actually exhibited or converted into employee behaviour. Employees become cynical when management espouses one set of values and norms and then behaves in an inconsistent fashion.

2 Explain the typology of organisational values

The typology of organisational values identifies four types of organisational value systems. It is based on crossing organisational reward norms and organisation power structures. The types of value systems include elite, meritocratic, leadership and collegial. Each type of value system contains a set of values that are both consistent and inconsistent with the underlying value system.

3 Describe the manifestations of an organisation's culture and the four functions of organisational culture

General manifestations of an organisation's culture are shared objects, talk, behaviour and emotion. Four functions of organisational culture are organisational identity, collective commitment, social-system stability and sensemaking devices.

4 Discuss the four general types of organisational culture

Four general types of organisational culture are the result of combining two dimensions. The first dimension contrasts flexibility with stability; the second dimension contrasts internal with external focus. In adaptability culture creativity and innovation are highly valued. In an external control culture goal achievement and competition are the most important values. In a development culture teamwork and participation are highly appreciated. In an internal consistency culture respect for hierarchy and rules are highly valued.

5 Summarise the methods used by organisations to embed their cultures

Embedding a culture amounts to teaching employees about the organisation's preferred values, beliefs, expectations and behaviours. This is accomplished by using one or more of the following 11 mechanisms: (a) formal statements of organisational philosophy, mission, vision, values and materials used for recruiting, selection and socialisation; (b) the design of physical space, work environments and buildings; (c) slogans, language, acronyms and sayings; (d) deliberate role modelling, training programmes, teaching and coaching by managers and supervisors; (e) explicit rewards, status symbols and promotion criteria; (f) stories, legends and myths about key people and events; (g) the organisational activities, processes or outcomes that leaders pay attention to, measure and control; (h) leader reactions to critical incidents and organisational crises; (i) the workflow and organisational structure; (j) organisational systems and procedures; and (k) organisational goals and the associated criteria used for employer recruitment, selection, development, promotion, layoffs and retirement.

6 Describe the practical lessons from the Hofstede–Bond stream of research

According to the Hofstede–Bond cross-cultural management studies, caution needs to be exercised when transplanting management theories and practices from one culture to another. Also, long-term orientation was the only one of five cultural dimensions in the Hofstede–Bond studies to correlate positively with national economic growth.

7 Discuss the importance of cross-cultural training relative to the foreign assignment cycle

The foreign assignment cycle has four stages: selection and training, arrival and adjustment, settling in and acculturating and returning home and adjusting. Cross-cultural training, preferably combining informational and experiential lessons before departure, can help expatriates avoid two OB trouble spots: unrealistic expectations and culture shock. There are no adequate substitutes for knowing the local language and culture.

Review questions

1 How would you respond to someone who made the following statement: 'Organisational cultures are not important as far as business is concerned'?

2 What type of value system exists within your study group? Provide examples to support your evaluation.

3 Why is socialisation essential to organisational success?

4 Regarding your cultural awareness, how would you describe the prevailing culture in your country to a stranger from another country?

5 Culturally speaking, are you individualistic or collectivist? How does that cultural orientation affect how you run your personal/business affairs?

Personal awareness and growth exercise

How does your current employer socialise employees?

Objectives

1 To promote deeper understanding of organisational socialisation processes.

2 To provide you with a useful tool for analysing and comparing organisations.

Introduction

Employees are socialised in many different ways in today's organisations. Some organisations, such as IBM, have made an exact science out of organisational socialisation. Others leave things to chance in the hope that collective goals will somehow be achieved. The questionnaire in this exercise is designed to help you gauge how widespread and systematic the socialisation process is in a particular organisation.

Instructions

If you are presently employed and have a good working knowledge of your organisation, you can complete this questionnaire yourself. If not, identify a manager or professional (such as a corporate lawyer, engineer or nurse) and have that individual complete the questionnaire for his or her organisation.

Respond to the items below as they apply to the handling of professional employees (including managers). Upon completion, compute the total score by adding up your responses. For comparison, scores for a number of strong, intermediate and weak culture firms are provided.

	Not true of this company				Very true of this company
1 Recruiters receive at least one week of intensive training.	1	2	3	4	5
2 Recruitment forms identify several key traits deemed crucial to the firm's success; traits are defined in concrete terms and the interviewer records specific evidence of each trait.	1	2	3	4	5
3 Recruits are subjected to at least four in-depth interviews	1	2	3	4	5
4 Company actively facilitates the selection during the recruiting process by revealing minuses as well as pluses.	1	2	3	4	5
5 New recruits work long hours, are exposed to intensive training of considerable difficulty and/or perform relatively menial tasks in the first months.	1	2	3	4	5
6 The intensity of entry-level experience builds cohesiveness among peers in each entering class.	1	2	3	4	5
7 All professional employees in a particular discipline begin in entry-level positions regardless of experience or advanced degrees.	1	2	3	4	5
8 Reward systems and promotion criteria require mastery of a core discipline as a precondition of advancement.	1	2	3	4	5
9 The career path for professional employees is relatively consistent over the first 6 to 10 years with the company.	1	2	3	4	5

10	Reward systems, performance incentives, promotion criteria and other primary measures of success reflect a high degree of congruence.	1	2	3	4	5
11	Virtually all professional employees can identify and articulate the firm's shared values (i.e. the purpose or mission that ties the firm to society, the customer or its employees).	1	2	3	4	5
12	There are very few instances when the actions of management appear to violate the firm's espoused values.	1	2	3	4	5
13	Employees frequently make personal sacrifices for the firm out of commitment to the firm's shared values.	1	2	3	4	5
14	When confronted with trade-offs between systems measuring short-term results and doing what's best for the company in the long term, the firm usually decides in favour of the long term.	1	2	3	4	5
15	This organisation fosters mentor–protégé(e) relationships.	1	2	3	4	5
16	There is considerable similarity among high potential candidates in each particular discipline.	1	2	3	4	5

Total score = _____

Comparative norms
55 and 80 = strongly socialised organisation
26 and 54 = moderately socialised organisation
Below 25 = weakly socialised organisation

Questions for discussion
1 How strongly socialised is the organisation in question? What implications does this degree of socialisation have for satisfaction, commitment and turnover?
2 In examining the 16 items in the preceding questionnaire, what evidence of realistic job previews and behaviour modelling can you find? Explain.
3 What does this questionnaire say about how organisational norms are established and enforced? Frame your answer in terms of specific items in the questionnaire.
4 Using this questionnaire as a gauge, would you rather work for a strongly, moderately or weakly socialised organisation?

Group exercise

Assessing the organisational culture at your school
Objectives
1 To provide you with a framework for assessing organisational culture.
2 To conduct an evaluation of the organisational culture at your school.
3 To consider the relationship between organisational culture and organisational effectiveness.

Introduction
Academics and consultants do not agree about the best way to measure an organisation's culture. Some people measure culture with surveys, while others use direct observation or information obtained in interviews/workshops with employees. This exercise uses an informal, group-based approach to assess the three levels of organisational culture discussed in this chapter. This approach has successfully been used to measure organisational culture at a variety of organisations.[135]

Instructions
Your lecturer will divide the class into groups of four to six people. Each group member should then complete the cultural assessment worksheet by him- or herself. It asks you to identify the

artefacts, espoused values and basic assumptions that are present at your current school. When everyone is done, meet as a group and share the information contained on your individual worksheets and discuss what type of culture your school possesses. Strive to reach a consensus. Finally, the group should answer the discussion questions.

Cultural assessment worksheet

Artefacts (physical or visible manifestations of culture; they include jargon, heroes, stories, language, ritual, dress, material objects, mascots, physical arrangements, symbols, traditions, and so forth)	Espoused values (the stated values and norms preferred by the organisation)	Basic assumptions (taken-for-granted beliefs about the organisation that exist on an unconscious level)

Questions for discussion

1 What are the group's consensus artefacts, espoused values and basis assumptions? Are you surprised by anything on this list? Explain.

2 What type of culture does your school possess? Do you like the organisational culture? Discuss why or why not.

3 Do you think the organisational culture identified in question 2 is best suited for maximising your learning? Explain your rationale.

4 Is your school in need of any cultural change? If yes, discuss why and recommend how the school's leaders might create this change.

Internet exercise

Thanks to the power of the Internet, you can take a trip to a far-flung corner of the world without ever leaving your chair. The purpose of this exercise is to enhance your cross-cultural awareness by using the Internet to learn about a foreign country of your choice.

Visit our website www.mcgraw-hill.co.uk/textbooks/buelens to find suggestions of websites you can use to solve this exercise.

Notes

1 J. Ewing and G. Khermouch, 'Waking Up Heineken. Earnings Are Flat. Beer Drinking Is Down. Can It Get Growth Flowing?', *Business Week*, 8 September 2004, p. 68.

2 T. Hallett, 'Symbolic Power and Organizational Culture', *Sociological Theory*, June 2003, pp. 128–49.

3 E. Ogbonna and B. Wilkinson, 'The False Promise of Organizational Culture Change: A Case Study of Middle Managers in Grocery Retailing', *Journal of Management Studies*, July 2003, pp. 1151–78.

4 For a comprehensive review of recent research, see D. R. Denison, 'What IS the Difference between Organizational Culture and Organizational Climate? A Native's Point of View on a Decade of Paradigm Wars', *Academy of Management Review*, July 1996, pp. 619–54.

5 E. H. Schein, *Organizational Culture and Leadership* (San Francisco, CA: Jossey-Bass, 1985), p. 9. Also see H. H. Baligh, 'Components of Culture: Nature, Interconnections, and Relevance to the Decisions on the Organization Structure', *Management Science*, January 1994, pp. 14–27.

6 For instructive discussion, see J. S. Black, H. B. Gregersen and M. E. Mendenhall, *Global Assignments: Successfully Expatriating and Repatriating International Managers* (San Francisco, CA: Jossey-Bass, 1992), Ch. 2.

7 F. Trompenaars and C. Hampden-Turner, *Riding the Waves of Culture: Understanding Cultural Diversity in Global Business, second edition* (New York: McGraw-Hill, 1998), pp. 6–7.

8 'How Cultures Collide', *Psychology Today*, July 1976, p. 69.

9 S. Rayner, 'Magasins sans Frontières', *Marketing Week*, 27 March 2003, p. 37.

10 A. Beswick, 'What Worked, and Where', *Promotions & Incentives*, May 2003, p. 23.

11 M. de Mooij and G. Hofstede, 'Convergence and Divergence in Consumer Behavior: Implications for International Retailing', *Journal of Retailing*, Spring 2002, pp. 61–9.

12 See M. Mendenhall, 'A Painless Approach to Integrating "International" into OB, HRM, and Management Courses', *Organizational Behavior Teaching Review*, no. 3, 1988–9, pp. 23–7.

13 J. Main, 'How to Go Global – And Why', *Fortune*, 28 August 1989, p. 73.

14 An excellent contrast between French and American values can be found in C. Gouttefarde, 'American Values in the French Workplace', *Business Horizons*, March–April 1996, pp. 60–69.

15 F. Trompenaars and P. Woolliams, 'A New Framework for Managing Change Across Cultures,' *Journal of Change Management*, May 2003, p. 368.

16 G. Hofstede, C. A. Van Deusen, C. B. Mueller and T. A. Charles, 'What Goals Do Business Leaders Pursue? A Study in Fifteen Countries', *Journal of International Business Studies*, December 2002, pp. 785–803. Also see G. Hofstede, *Software of the Mind* (New York: McGraw-Hill, 1997).

17 E. H. Schein, 'Culture: The Missing Concept in Organization Studies', *Administrative Science Quarterly*, June 1996, p. 236.

18 This discussion is based on E. H. Schein, *Organizational Culture and Leadership, second edition* (San Francisco, CA: Jossey-Bass, 1992), pp. 16–48.

19 P. Freedman, 'Don't Call Me Sir, I'm Chief Lizard Wrangler', the *Sunday Times*, 19 March 2000.

20 Adapted and translated from K. Weytjens, 'Koerier als visitekaartje', *Vacature*, 24 October 1998.

21 S. H. Schwartz, 'Universals in the Content and Structure of Values: Theoretical Advances and Empirical Tests in 20 Countries', in *Advances in Experimental Social Psychology*, ed. M. P. Zanna (New York: Academic Press, 1992), p. 4.

22 The discussion between espoused and enacted values is based on E. H. Schein, *Organizational Culture and Leadership* (San Francisco, CA: Jossey-Bass, 1985).

23 Adapted and translated from J. Schuddinck, 'Finse finesse', *Vacature*, 3 November 2000; and A. Nelissen and K. Bosmans, 'Wie kan spreken is een potentiële klant, *Vacature*, 25 February 2000.

24 G. Jones, 'Look After Your Heart', *People Management*, 29 July 1999, p. 27.

25 Results can be found in S. Clarke, 'Perceptions of Organizational Safety: Implications for the Development of Safety Culture', *Journal of Organizational Behavior*, March 1999, pp. 185–98.

26 J. Schuddinck, 'Finse finesse', *Vacature*, 3 November 2000.

27 K. Balazs, 'Some Like It Haute: Leadership Lessons from France's Great Chefs', *Organizational Dynamics*, Fall 2001, pp. 134–48.

28 See S. H. Schwartz, 'Universals in the Content and Structure of Values: Theoretical Advances and Empirical Tests in 20 Countries', in *Advances in Experimental Social Psychology*, ed. M. P. Zanna (New York: Academic Press, 1992).

29 Excerpted from S. L. Payne, 'Recognizing and Reducing Transcultural Ethical Tension', *Academy of Management Executive*, August 1998, p. 84.

30 This typology and related discussion was derived from B. Kabanoff and J. Holt, 'Changes in the Espoused Values of Australian Organizations 1986–1990', *Journal of Organizational Behavior*, May 1996, pp. 201–19.

31 For an example of profiling organisational values, see T. J. Kalliath, A. C. Bluedorn and D. F. Gillespie, 'A Confirmatory Factor Analyses of the Competing Values Instrument', *Educational and Psychological Measurement*, February 1999, pp. 143–58.

32 See the discussion in J. R. Detert, R. G. Schroeder and J. J. Mauriel, 'A Framework for Linking Culture and Improvement Initiatives in Organizations', *Academy of Management* Review, October 2000, pp. 850–63. Also see T. J. Galpin, *The Human Side of Change* (San Francisco, CA: Jossey-Bass, 1996); and J. Kotter, *Leading Change* (Boston, MA: Harvard Business School Press, 1996).

33 Results can be found in B. Kabanoff and J. Holt, 'Changes in the Espoused Values of Australian Organizations 1986–1990', *Journal of Organizational Behavior*, May 1996, pp. 201–19.

34 Adapted from L. Smircich, 'Concepts of Culture and Organizational Analysis', *Administrative Science Quarterly*, September 1983, pp. 339–58.

35 J. M. Higgins, 'Innovate or Evaporate: Seven Secrets of Innovative Corporations', *The Futurist*, September–October 1995, p. 45.

36 D. Anfuso, '3M's Staffing Strategy Promotes Productivity and Pride', *Personnel* Journal, February 1995, pp. 28–34.

37 S. Branch, 'The 100 Best Companies to Work for in America', *Fortune*, 11 January 1999, pp. 118–31.

38 See A. Xenikou and A. Furnham, 'A Correlated and Factor Analytic Study of Four Questionnaire Measures of Organizational Culture', *Human Relations*, March 1996, pp. 349–71; and D. R. Denison, 'What IS the Difference between Organizational Culture and Organizational Climate? A Native's Point of View on a Decade of Paradigm Wars', *Academy of Management Review*, July 1996, pp. 619–54.

39 J. B. Sonrensen, 'The Strength of Corporate Culture and the Reliability of Firm Performance', *Administrative Science Quarterly*, March 2002, pp. 70–91.

40 See S. Tully, 'Northwest and KLM: The Alliance from Hell', *Fortune*, 24 June 1996, pp. 64–72; and J. Marren, *Mergers & Acquisitions: A Valuation Handbook* (Homewood, IL: Irwin, 1993).

41 The success rate of mergers is discussed in R. J. Grossman, 'Irreconcilable Differences', *HR Magazine*, April 1999, pp. 42–8.

42 B. Domaine, 'Corporate Citizenship', *Fortune*, 29 January 1990, pp. 50–54.

43 The mechanisms were based on material contained in E. H. Schein, 'The Role of the Founder in Creating Organizational Culture', *Organizational Dynamics*, Summer 1983, pp. 13–28.

44 *The Philips Way. Our Values.*

45 Excerpted from M. Apgar IV, 'The Alternative Workplace: Changing Where and How People Work', *Harvard Business Review*, May–June 1998, p. 123. More examples in D. F. Kuratko, R. D. Ireland, and J. S. Hornsby, 'Improving Firm Performance Through Entrepreneurial Actions: Acordia's Corporate Entrepreneurship Strategy', *Academy of Management Executive*, November 2001, p. 67.

46 G. Jones, 'Look After Your Heart', *People Management*, 29 July 1999, p. 27.

47 Adapted and translated from 'Goede ideeën brengen op', *Talent*, 20 September 1996, pp. 1–3.

48 J. Van Maanen, 'Breaking In: Socialization to Work', in *Handbook of Work, Organization, and Society*, ed. R. Dubin (Chicago, IL: Rand-McNally, 1976), p. 67.

49 L. Adent Hoecklin, *Managing Cultural Changes for Competitive Advantage* (London: The Economist Intelligence Unit, 1993).

50 K. Kling and I. Goteamn, 'IKEA CEO Anders Dahlvig on International Growth and IKEA's Unique Corporate Culture and Brand Identity', *Academy of Management Executive*, February 2003, pp. 31–7.

51 Adapted and translated from 'Meer dan klaarstomen voor gebruik', *Gids voor Personeelsmanagement*, May 2000.

52 For an instructive capsule summary of the five different organisational socialisation models, see J. P. Wanous, A. E. Reichers and S. D. Malik, 'Organizational Socialization and Group Development: Toward an Integrative Perspective', *Academy of Management Review*, October 1984, pp. 670–83, Table 1. Also see D. C. Feldman, *Managing Careers in Organizations* (Glenview, IL: Scott, Foresman, 1988), Ch. 5.

53 Supportive evidence is provided by R. W. Griffeth and P. W. Hom, *Retaining Valued Employees* (Thousand Oaks, CA: Sage Publications, 2001), pp. 46–65. Also see P. W. Hom, R. W. Griffeth, L. E. Palich and J. S. Bracker, 'Revisiting Met Expectations As a Reason Why Realistic Job Previews Work', *Personnel Psychology*, Spring 1999, pp. 97–112.

54 Adapted and translated from J. Schuddinck, 'Hightechbedrijf op de versiertoer', *Vacature*, 3 March 2000. Reproduced with permission.

55 J. Van Maanen, 'People Processing: Strategies of Organizational Socialization', *Organizational Dynamics*, Summer 1978, p. 21.

56 For a thorough review of socialisation research, see B. E. Ashforth, *Role Transitions in Organizational Life: An Identity-Based Perspective* (Mahwah, NJ: Lawrence Erlbaum Associates, 2001), pp. 87–108.

57 Results can be found in H. Klein and N. Weaver, 'The Effectiveness of Organizational-Level Orientation Training Program in Socialization of New Hires', *Personnel Psychology*, Spring 2000, pp. 47–66.

58 See D. Cable and C. Parsons, 'Socialization Tactics and Person-Organization Fit', *Personnel Psychology*, Spring 2001, pp. 1–23.

59 See T. N. Bauer and S. G. Green, 'Testing the Combined Effects of Newcomer Information Seeking and Manager Behavior on Socialization', *Journal of Applied Psychology*, February 1998, pp. 72–83.

60 T. N. Bauer and S. G. Green, 'Testing the Combined Effects of Newcomer Information Seeking and Manager Behavior on Socialization', *Journal of Applied Psychology*, February 1998, pp. 72–83.

61 See A. M. Saks and B. E. Ashforth, 'Proactive Socialization and Behavioral Self-Management', *Journal of Vocational Behavior*, June 1996, pp. 301–23.

62 For a thorough review of research on the socialisation of diverse employees with disabilities, see A. Colella, 'Organizational Socialization of Newcomers with Disabilities: A Framework for Future Research', in *Research in Personnel and Human Resources Management*, ed. G. R. Ferris (Greenwich, CT: JAI Press, 1996), pp. 351–417.

63 F. Trompenaars and P. Woolliams, 'A New Framework for Managing Change Across Cultures,' *Journal of Change Management*, May 2003, p. 368.

64 Based on M. Mabry, 'Pin a Label on a Manager – And Watch What Happens', *Newsweek*, 14 May 1990, p. 43.

65 Adapted and translated from F. Vuga, 'In een moskee trek je je schoenen uit', *Knack*, 16 December 1987, pp. 41–4.

66 Adapted from J. Mole, *Mind Your Manners* (London: Nicholas Brealey Publishing, 1995).

67 M. Mabry, 'Pin a Label on a Manager – And Watch What Happens', *Newsweek*, 14 May 1990, p. 43.

68 F. Vuga, 'In een moskee trek je je schoenen uit', *Knack*, 16 December 1987, pp. 41–4.

69 J. Mole, *Mind Your Manners* (London: Nicholas Brealey Publishing, 1995).

70 See G. A. Sumner, *Folkways* (New York: Ginn, 1906). Also see J. G. Weber, 'The Nature of Ethnocentric Attribution Bias: Ingroup Protection or Enhancement?', *Journal of Experimental Social Psychology*, September 1994, pp. 482–504.

71 D. A. Heenan and H. V. Perlmutter, *Multinational Organization Development* (Reading, MA: Addison-Wesley, 1979), p. 17.

72 J. Fenby, 'Make That Foreign Posting Your Ticket to the Boardroom', *Management Today*, July 2000, pp. 48–53.

73 See 'How Cultures Collide', *Psychology Today*, July 1976, pp. 66–74, 97; and M. Munter, 'Cross-Cultural Communication for Managers', *Business Horizons*, May–June 1993, pp. 69–78.

74 D. C. Barnlund, 'Public and Private Self in Communicating with Japan', *Business Horizons*, March–April 1989, p. 38.

75 See E. W. K. Tsang, 'Can *Guanxi* Be a Source of Sustained Competitive Advantage for Doing Business in China?', *Academy of Management Executive*, May 1998, pp. 64–73.

76 Y. Richmond, *From Da to Yes. Understanding the Europeans* (Yarmouth: Intercultural Press, 1995).

77 The concept of 'face' and good tips on saving face in Far East Asia are presented in J. A. Reeder, 'When West Meets East: Cultural Aspects of Doing Business in Asia', *Business Horizons*, January–February 1987, pp. 69–74. Also see B. Stout 'Interviewing in Japan', *HR Magazine*, June 1998, pp. 71–7; and J. A. Quelch and C. M. Dinh-Tan, 'Country Managers in Transitional Economies: The Case of Vietnam', *Business Horizons*, July–August 1998, pp. 34–40.

78 The German management style is discussed in R. Stewart, 'German Management: A Challenge to Anglo-American Managerial Assumptions', *Business Horizons*, May–June 1996, pp. 52–4.

79 M. Cleasby, 'Managing Global Contact', *British Journal of Administrative Management*, March/April 2000, pp. 4–6.

80 Based on J. Mole, *Mind Your Manners* (London: Nicholas Brealey Publishing, 1995).

81 For complete details, see G. Hofstede, 'The Interaction between National and Organizational Value Systems', *Journal of Management Studies*, July 1985, pp. 347–57; G. Hofstede, 'Management Scientists Are Human', *Management Science*, January 1994, pp. 4–13; and G. Hofstede, *Culture's Consequences: Comparing Values, Behaviors, Institutions, and Organizations Across Nations*, second edition (Thousand Oaks, CA: Sage Publications, 2001). Also see V. J. Shackleton and A. H. Ali, 'Work-Related Values of Managers: A Test of the Hofstede Model', *Journal of Cross-Cultural Psychology*, March 1990, pp. 109–18; R. Hodgetts, 'A Conversation with Geert Hofstede', *Organizational Dynamics*, Spring 1993, pp. 53–61; and P. B. Smith, S. Dugan and F. Trompenaars, 'National Culture and the Values of Organizational Employees: A Dimensional Analysis Across 43 Nations', *Journal of Cross-Cultural Psychology*, March 1996, pp. 231–64.

82 See G. Hofstede and M. H. Bond, 'Hofstede's Culture Dimensions: An Independent Validation Using Rokeach's Value Survey', *Journal of Cross-Cultural Psychology*, December 1984, pp. 417–33. Another study using the Chinese Value Survey (CVS) is reported in D. A. Ralston, D. J. Gustafson, P. M. Elsass, F. Cheung and R. H. Terpstra, 'Eastern Values: A Comparison of Managers in the United States, Hong Kong, and the People's Republic of China', *Journal of Applied Psychology*, October 1992, pp. 664–71.

83 G. Hofstede, 'Cultural Constraints in Management Theories', *Academy of Management Executive*, February 1993, p. 90.

84 See Y. Paik and J. H. D. Sohn, 'Confucius in Mexico: Korean MNCs and the Maquiladoras', *Business Horizons*, November–December 1998, pp. 25–33.

85 For complete details, see G. Hofstede and M. H. Bond, 'The Confucius Connection: From Cultural Roots to Economic Growth', *Organizational Dynamics*, Spring 1988, pp. 4–21.

86 L. Kolman, N. Noorderhaven, G. Hofstede and E. Dienes, 'Cross-Cultural Differences in Central Europe', *Journal of Managerial Psychology*, February 2003, pp. 76–88.

87 See P. M. Rosenzweig, 'When Can Management Science Research Be Generalized Internationally?', *Management Science*, January 1994, pp. 28–39.

88 A follow-up study is J. P. Johnson and T. Lenartowicz, 'Culture, Freedom and Economic Growth: Do Cultural Values Explain Economic Growth?', *Journal of World Business*, Winter 1998, pp. 332–56.

89 Based on F. Trompenaars, *Riding the Waves of Culture* (London: Economist Books, 1994). Also see F. Trompenaars, *Did the Pedestrian Die?* (London: Capstone Publishing, 2003).

90 E. van der Vliert, K. Sanders, K. Shi, Y. Wang and X. Huang, 'Interpretation and Effects of Supervisory Feedback in China and The Netherlands', *Gedrag & Organisatie*, December 2003, pp. 125–39.

91 S. Brittan, 'Economic Viewpoint: The Follies of the Macho Manager', the *Financial Times*, 22 December 1994, p. 14.

92 See, for example, N. R. Mack, 'Taking Apart the Ticking of Time', the *Christian Science Monitor*, 29 August 1991, p. 17.

93 For a comprehensive treatment of time, see J. E. McGrath and J. R. Kelly, *Time and Human Interaction: Toward a Social Psychology of Time* (New York: The Guilford Press, 1986). Also see L. A. Manrai and A. K. Manrai, 'Effects of Cultural-Context, Gender, and Acculturation on Perceptions of Work versus Social/Leisure Time Usage', *Journal of Business Research*, February 1995, pp. 115–28.

94 A good discussion of doing business in Mexico is G. K. Stephens and C. R. Greer, 'Doing Business in Mexico: Understanding Cultural Differences', *Organizational Dynamics*, Summer 1995, pp. 39–55.

95 R. W. Moore, 'Time, Culture, and Comparative Management: A Review and Future Direction', in *Advances in International Comparative Management, vol. 5*, ed. S. B. Prasad (Greenwich, CT: JAI Press, 1990), pp. 7–8.

96 See A. C. Bluedorn, C. F. Kaufman and P. M. Lane, 'How Many Things Do You Like to Do at Once? An Introduction to Monochronic and Polychronic Time', *Academy of Management Executive*, November 1992, pp. 17–26. Also see F. Trompenaars, *Did the Pedestrian Die?* (London: Capstone Publishing, 2003).

97 'Multitasking' term drawn from S. McCartney, 'The Breaking Point: Multitasking Technology Can Raise Stress and Cripple Productivity', *The Arizona Republic*, 21 May 1995, p. D10.

98 See R. Hill, *We Europeans* (Brussels: Europublications, 1995); and also J. Mole, *Mind Your Manners* (London: Nicholas Brealey Publishing, 1995), p. 59

99 Port, 'You May Have To Reset This Watch – In a Million Years', *Business Week*, 30 August 1993, p. 65.

100 See E. T. Hall, *The Hidden Dimension* (Garden City, NY: Doubleday, 1966).

101 Adapted from 'How Cultures Collide', *Psychology Today*, July 1976, p. 72.

102 R. Hill, *We Europeans* (Brussels: Europublications, 1995), p. 53.

103 G. A. Michaelson, 'Global Gold', *Success*, March 1996, p. 16.

104 Translation services are discussed in D. Pianko, 'Smooth Translations', *Management Review*, July 1996, p. 10; and R. Ganzel, 'Universal Translator? Not Quite', *Training*, April 1999, pp. 22–4.

105 Based on J. Bloom, 'Mind Your Language', *Management Today*, August 1998, pp. 72–4.

106 V. Houlder, 'Culture Shock for Executives', the *Financial Times*, 5 April 1995, p. 19.

107 Translated and adapted from 'Na de financiën, de cultuur', *De Standaard*, 5 May 2004, p. 49.

108 Adapted and translated from F. Bieckman, 'NL-GB liefdeslessen: Britten en Nederlanders werken veel maar moeizaam samen', *Management Team*, 26 February 1999, pp. 21–4.

109 P. R. Harris and R. T. Moran, *Managing Cultural Differences, fourth edition* (Houston, TX: Gulf Publishing Company, 1996), p. 23.

110 R. Takeuchi, S. Yun and P. E. Tesluk, 'An Examination of Crossover and Spillover Effects of Spousal and Expatriate Cross-Cultural Adjustment on Expatriate Outcomes', *Journal of Applied Psychology*, August 2002, pp. 655–66.

111 Adapted and translated from G. Bollen and B. Debeuckelare, 'De euronomaden: Europese elite maakt carrière over de grenzen heen', *Vacature*, 3 December 1999.

112 G. Bollen and B. Debeuckelare, 'De euronomaden: Europese elite maakt carrière over de grenzen heen', *Vacature*, 3 December 1999.

113 J. S. Black and H. B. Gregersen, 'The Right Way to Manage Expats', *Harvard Business Review*, March–April 1999, p. 53. A more optimistic picture is presented in R. L. Tung, 'American Expatriates Abroad: From Neophytes to Cosmopolitans', *Journal of World Business*, Summer 1998, pp. 125–44.

114 Adapted from R. L. Tung, 'Expatriate Assignments: Enhancing Success and Minimizing Failure', *Academy of Management Executive*, May 1987, pp. 117–26.

115 S. Dallas, 'Rule No. 1: Don't Diss the Locals', *Business Week*, 15 May 1995, p. 8.

116 Translated from S. Jacobus, 'Femme Globale', *Management Team*, 22 September 1995, pp. 111–14.

117 An excellent reference book in this area is J. S. Black, H. B. Gregersen, and M. E. Mendenhall, *Global Assignments: Successfully Expatriating and Repatriating International Managers* (San Francisco, CA: Jossey-Bass, 1992). Also see K. Roberts, E. E. Kossek and C. Ozeki, 'Managing the Global Workforce: Challenges and Strategies', *Academy of Management Executive*, November 1998, pp. 93–106.

118 M. Derksen and A. E. M. van Vianen, 'Aspire to an Expatriate Position: Factors Contributing to International Mobility', *Gedrag & Organisatie*, December 2003, pp. 370–84.

119 I. E. de Pater, A. E. M. van Vianen and M. Derksen, 'Close Relationships and Cross-Cultural Adaptation of Expatriates: The Role of Personality and Attachment Style', *Gedrag & Organisatie*, December 2003, pp. 89–107.

120 S. T. Mol, 'Prediction of Expatriate Success as an Industrial/Organizational Psychological Phenomenon: A Theoretical Discourse', *Gedrag & Organisatie*, December 2003, pp. 385–92.

121 J. S. Black, H. B. Gregersen, and M. E. Mendenhall, *Global Assignments: Successfully Expatriating and Repatriating International Managers* (San Francisco, CA: Jossey-Bass, 1992), p. 97.

122 J. S. Lublin, 'Younger Managers Learn Global Skills', the *Wall Street Journal*, 31 March 1992, p. B1.

123 Adapted and translated from J. Kroon, 'Leven in het land van de handkus', *NRC Handelsblad*, 18 February 1999.

124 R. Takeuchi, S. Yun and P. E. Tesluk, 'An Examination of Crossover and Spillover Effects of Spousal and Expatriate Cross-Cultural Adjustment on Expatriate Outcomes', *Journal of Applied Psychology*, August 2002, pp. 655–66.

125 See P. R. Harris and R. T. Moran, *Managing Cultural Differences, fourth edition* (Houston, TX: Gulf Publishing

Company, 1996), pp. 223–8; M. Shilling, 'Avoid Expatriate Culture Shock', *HR Magazine*, July 1993, pp. 58–63; and D. Stamps, 'Welcome to America: Watch Out for Culture Shock', *Training*, November 1996, pp. 22–30.

126 S. Mackesy, 'I'm Greedy Therefore I Am', the *Independent*, 10 September 2000.

127 See H. H. Nguyen, L. A. Messe and G. E. Stollak, 'Toward a More Complex Understanding of Acculturation and Adjustment', *Journal of Cross-Cultural Psychology*, January 1999, pp. 5–31.

128 R. Hechanova, T. A. Beehr and N. D. Christiansen, 'Antecedents and Consequences of Employees' Adjustment to Overseas Assignment: A Meta-analytic Review', *Applied Psychology: An International Review*, June 2003, pp. 213–36.

129 I. E. de Pater, A. E. M. van Vianen and M. Derksen, 'Close Relationships and Cross-Cultural Adaptation of Expatriates: The Role of Personality and Attachment Style', *Gedrag & Organisatie*, December 2003, pp. 89–107.

130 Translated from E. Adams, 'Voorkom culturele blunders', *Vacature*, 18 October 2003, p. 8.

131 Adapted and translated from M. Haenen, 'Duimendraaien onder een palmboom', *NRC Handelsblad*, 7 September 1996, p. 3.

132 P. Prud'homme and F. Trompenaars, 'Invited Reaction: Developing Expatriates for the Asia-Pacific Region', *Human Resource Development Quarterly*, Fall 2000, pp. 237–43.

133 M. Linehan and H. Scullion, 'Repatriation of Female Executives: Empirical Evidence from Europe', *Women in Management Review*, April 2002, pp. 80–88; M. Linehan, 'Senior Female International Managers: Empirical Evidence from Western Europe', *International Journal of Human Resource Management*, August 2002, pp. 802–14; and M. Linehan and H. Scullion, 'The Repatriation of Female International Managers. An Empirical Study', *International Journal of Manpower*, October 2002, pp. 649–75.

134 L. Richards, 'Plan Ahead to Ensure Repatriation Success', *Personnel Today*, 3 February 2004, p. 1

135 See E. H. Schein, *The Corporate Culture Survival Guide* (San Francisco, CA: Jossey-Bass, 1999).

chapter 17 change, learning and knowledge management

By Geert Devos and Annick Willem

Learning outcomes

When you finish studying the material in this chapter, you should be able to:

- discuss the external and internal forces that create the need for organisational change
- describe Lewin's change model
- discuss Theory E and O in the six dimensions of change
- demonstrate your familiarity with the four identifying characteristics of organisation development (OD)
- discuss the ten reasons employees resist change
- identify alternative strategies for overcoming resistance to change
- explain the concepts learning organisation and knowledge management
- discuss the process by which organisations build their learning capabilities
- review the reasons organisations naturally resist learning and knowledge sharing
- discuss the role of leadership in creating a learning organisation

case study

How Gerhard Schulmeyer changed the culture at Siemens Nixdorf

In 1994 Siemens Nixdorf Informations Systeme (SNI) was a serious loss-maker. It is now the largest European player in data processing and the continent's number two in software, services and mainframes, with global sales of €7.7 billion. The programme, which put the company into profit within its initial two-year time-frame, is now in its fourth and their ongoing stage, in which employees take responsibility for improving their business processes, effectively implementing their own re-engineering, and share their knowledge and ideas on the corporate Intranet.

When Schulmeyer came to SNI late in the summer of 1994, after a career spent largely in the USA with Motorola and ABB, he found a demoralised PC-to-IT services group. The merger of Siemens and Nixdorf had left a divided culture and mounting losses despite a restructuring pro-gramme which had slashed the workforce from 52 000 to 39 000, and had made several attempts to improve the company's alignment with its customers. Schulmeyer set out to introduce a fast-moving, entrepreneurial, Silicon Valley culture into what he calls the 'hard-wired, bolted-to-the-floor' values of German industry. The company would be rebuilt around customer-focused processes and quickly: what would normally take a year would be accomplished in a quarter of the time.

Schulmeyer knew that if processes were re-engineered before a thorough change of culture, the programme often withered at the roots. So he put the culture change first and this meant 'mobilising' all the employees behind it, a process to which he allocated six months. In the three months before officially taking over at SNI and launching the change initiative in October 1994, Schulmeyer had spent most of his time meeting employees – around 9000 of them, plus key customers – and discussing frankly the measures that were needed to dig the company out of its loss-making hole and the behavioural changes required to accomplish it.

Changing values and behaviour patterns

The first priority was to get people behaving in new ways. Schulmeyer understood that it is easier for people to act their way into a new culture and, in an interview in 1995 reviewing the first year's progress, said: 'What numerous attempts that have gone wrong have shown us is that it is not possible to change the processes in an organisation without first changing and evolving ... the underlying values behind all of the actions and the resulting behaviour patterns.'

The dynamic behind Schulmeyer's programme undeniably sprang from the huge voluntary creative and emotional support he managed to generate despite the financial plight of the company and worries over job security. People responded immediately with analyses of what had gone wrong – lack of communication was a leading candidate – and ideas for change.

'Usually 80 per cent of the problems of a company are known to the people who work there but they don't have the chance to do anything about them', Schulmeyer observed during the first year.

He was rarely seen without a sheaf of charts in his hands and for those early meetings with employees he carried with him the Schedule for Change, which was divided into quarters for the first year, running to the end of 1995. Two were allocated to culture change, one of which overlapped with 'base lining' – a critical exercise in which lines of business outlined their core competencies and options for future business. The third was devoted to SNI 'visioning' and partly to re-aligning and the fourth to budgeting and restructuring. 'People usually talk about time spans of five years for a culture change', he remarked early in the process. 'It may take us five years but we have to gain the feeling that time is so valuable that we have to work and measure ourselves in much shorter slots.' The Schedule for Change was posted up all over the company to impart a sense of urgency.

Identifying change agents and opinion leaders

Schulmeyer began the process of mobilisation with just three managers – from Human Resources, Corporate Communications and Corporate Strategy – tasking them to recruit like-minded change agents. The three soon turned into 30, who spent three intensive days discussing feedback from the new CEO's talks and identifying an agenda for action.

This agenda produced a 19-point programme for action in three main categories:

- Behavioural changes among managers and employees to achieve dramatic performance improvements.
- Changing work systems to engender a culture of operational excellence.
- Changing processes to focus on, and interface with, the customer and to ensure a culture of customer excellence.

The number one problem perceived by employees was communication, with managers often keen to present a better picture to their senior managers than reality justified. The task of communicating the agenda to 36 000 employees around the world was a severe logistical challenge. The mechanism chosen was a series of large, corporate-wide, four-day events built around interactive workshops. They all took place in Hanover, each addressing a particular set of issues representing milestones in the transformation process, and became known as Hanover One, Two, Three and Four.

To lead the issues debate at Hanover One, which took place in December 1994 and represented 'the voice of the employee', the core change activators identified 300 further 'opinion leaders' who were considered highly motivated and capable of leading change in the workplace. They were joined at Hanover by 75 top managers and 30 workshop facilitators.

Out of the 19-point agenda came 60 agreed issues for action, which were carried back into the business. Project leaders built teams which started small but grew and developed their own databases. A striking example was the four-person team tasked with developing an inventory of corporate best practice in software and services. This originally consisted of four people of four nationalities: on its return from Hanover it acquired six more people. Within three months it had developed a PC-based database, and was working with all 25 SNI regional managers to harvest best-practice information and share it with employees throughout the world.

The action teams displayed their achievements on exhibition stalls at a Results Fair in May 1995, held in Munich. More than 12000 attended the two-day event. One notable result was the work of a team in SNI Greece which had taken on the task of re-engineering SNI's order-to-cash process and managed to slash its cycle time by half. About ten of the 60 actions resulted in company-wide initiatives, while 40 produced local business benefits. Only ten had no effect other than providing experience in culture-change projects.[1]

For discussion
Which were the most important contributions to successful change at SNI?

Increased competition and startling breakthroughs in information technology are forcing companies to change the way they do business. Customers are demanding greater value and lower prices. The rate of organisational and societal change is clearly accelerating. For example, a survey of 750 corporations revealed that all of them were involved in at least one organisational change programme. Another survey of 259 executives indicated that 84 per cent had one change initiative under way, while nearly 50 per cent were implementing three or more change programmes.[2]

A large consultancy firm, A. T. Kearny, asked senior executives in 294 medium and large European companies to rate their change programmes: 20 per cent were considered a success, 63 per cent had made some temporary improvement but failed to sustain it and 17 per cent had achieved no improvement at all.[3]

Companies no longer have a choice – they must change to survive. Unfortunately, it is not easy to successfully implement organisational change. People frequently resist organisational change even when it is occurring for good reasons. Many changes ultimately fail because companies do not properly understand that what is happening underneath, in the ways of working, is more important than the gains in short-term productivity. Management Consultant Peter Scott-Morgan calls these 'the unwritten rules'. These rules are in themselves logical and only by understanding their logic will companies be able to confront deep-seated resistance to change. Deep behavioural change is needed to create a culture of ongoing change.[4] Peter Senge, a well-known expert on the topic of organisational change, made the following comment about organisational change during an interview with *Fast Company* magazine:

When I look at efforts to create change in big companies over the past 10 years, I have to say that there's enough evidence of success to say that change is possible – and enough evidence of failure to say that it isn't likely.[5]

If Senge is correct, then it is all the more important for professionals to learn how they can successfully implement organisational change. This chapter was written to help navigate the journey of change.

Specifically, we discuss the forces that create the need for organisation change, models of planned change, challenges for understanding change, resistance to change and how to create a 'learning organisation'.

Forces of change

How do organisations know when they should change? What cues should an organisation look for? Although there are no clear-cut answers to these questions, the 'cues' that signal the need for change are found by monitoring the forces for change.

Organisations encounter many different forces for change. These forces come from sources outside the organisation and from internal sources. This section examines the forces that create the need for change. Awareness of these forces can help professionals determine when they should consider implementing an organisational change. The external and internal forces for change are presented in Figure 17.1.

FIGURE 17.1 EXTERNAL AND INTERNAL FORCES FOR CHANGE

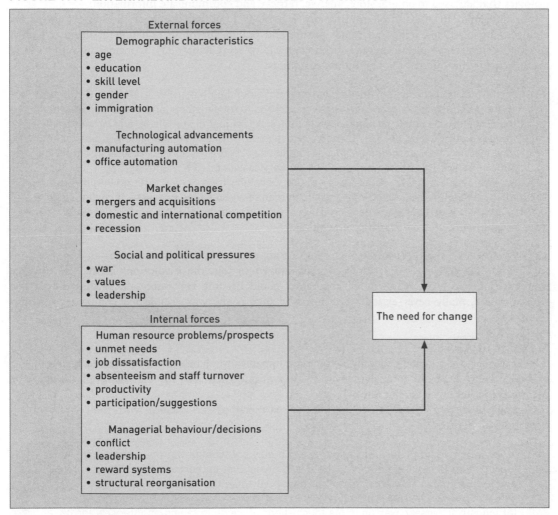

External forces

As **External forces for change** have global effects, they may cause an organisation to question the essence of what business it is in and the process by which products and services are produced. There are four key external forces for change: demographic characteristics, technological advancements, market changes, and social and political pressures. Each is now discussed.

External forces for change originate outside the organisation

DEMOGRAPHIC CHARACTERISTICS

Chapter 4 provided a detailed discussion of the demographic changes occurring in the European workforce. Two key trends identified in this discussion were that: the workforce is more diverse; and there is a business imperative to manage diversity effectively. Organisations need to manage diversity effectively if they are to receive maximum contribution and commitment from employees.

TECHNOLOGICAL ADVANCEMENTS

Both manufacturing and service organisations are increasingly using technology as a means to improve productivity and market competitiveness. Manufacturing companies, for instance, have automated their operations with robotics; computerised numerical control (CNC), which is used for metal cutting operations, and computer-aided design (CAD). CAD is a computerised process for draughting and designing the engineering of products. Companies also use computer-integrated manufacturing (CIM). This highly technical process attempts to integrate product design with product planning, control and operations. In contrast to these manufacturing technologies, the service sector is using office automation. Office automation consists of a host of computerised technologies that are used to obtain, store, analyse, retrieve and communicate information.

The development and use of information technology is probably one of the biggest forces for change. Organisations, large and small, private and public, for profit and not-for-profit, all must adapt to using a host of information technologies (also see Chapter 15). Consider how the Virgin group is using the Internet to obtain more customers:

> Richard C. N. Branson has made a career of confounding his critics. His Virgin Group Ltd spans 170 businesses, from airlines and railroads to music stores and condoms. So, when the British tycoon moves online, one shouldn't expect just digital music and virtual airline reservations. Try some 5500 London households paying gas and electric bills online through Virgin's Website since July. An additional 2000 Brits tooling around in cars they bought on the Net, thanks to a new Virgin service launched a month earlier. Then there are the nearly 2 million people in the country booking train tickets through Virgin – and 1 million using the Web to tap Virgin's help in managing $4 billion in assets, including insurance, mortgage and investment funds. And don't forget the $58 000 worth of wine they're buying online from Branson each week.[6]

Experts believe that e-business will continue to create evolutionary changes in organisations throughout the world. Organisations are encouraged to join the e-volution! Most experts agree that the dot.com hype, where small companies could become very successful within only a few short months, really never existed. The major change is the way established companies use new technology.

MARKET CHANGES

The emergence of a global economy is forcing companies to change the way they do business. For example, many Japanese companies have to discontinue their jobs-for-life philosophy because of increased international competition.

Companies all over the world are forging new partnerships and alliances with their suppliers and potential competitors.

> It was almost like the dramatic final act of a play but without the main character. As the top brass of General Motors Corp and Turin-based Fiat gathered in the Italian company's auditorium to announce their broad strategic alliance, the key player who signed off the deal wasn't even there. Gianni Agnelli, the 79-year-old patriarch of Europe's most powerful industrial dynasty, was up in his fourth-floor office suite taping an interview for Italian television. He would leave it to others to announce the fate of the car company his grandfather and namesake had founded 101 years ago.[7]

This example highlights how organisations must learn how to create collaborative win-win relationships with other organisations if they are to survive in the worldwide restructuring of alliances and partnerships.

SOCIAL AND POLITICAL PRESSURES

These forces are created by social and political events. For example, tobacco companies are experiencing a lot of pressure to alter the way they market their products. This pressure is being exerted through legislative bodies. Political events can create substantial change. For instance, the collapse of the Berlin Wall and communism in Russia created many new business opportunities. Although it is difficult for organisations to predict changes in political forces, many organisations hire lobbyists and consultants to help them detect and respond to social and political changes.

Internal forces

Internal forces for change may be subtle, such as low job satisfaction, or they can manifest themselves in outward signs, such as low productivity and conflict. Internal forces for change come from human resource problems and from managerial behaviour and decisions.

Internal forces for change originate inside the organisation

HUMAN RESOURCE PROBLEMS AND PROSPECTS

These problems stem from employee perceptions of how they are treated at work and the match between individual and organisation needs and desires. Chapter 3 highlighted the relationship between an employee's unmet needs and job dissatisfaction. Dissatisfaction is a symptom of an underlying employee problem that should be addressed. Unusual or high levels of absenteeism and staff turnover also represent forces for change. Organisations might respond to these problems by reducing employees' role conflict, overload and ambiguity (see Chapter 10) and also by removing the different stressors discussed in Chapter 7. Prospects for positive change stem from employee participation and suggestions.

MANAGERIAL BEHAVIOUR AND DECISIONS

Excessive interpersonal conflict between managers and their subordinates is a sign that change is needed. Both the manager and the employee may need interpersonal skills training or the two individuals may simply need to be separated. For example, one of the parties might be transferred to a new department. Inappropriate behaviour shown by leaders, such as inadequate direction or support, may require a change in the response to these human resource problems. As discussed in Chapter 11, leadership training is one potential solution for this problem. Inequitable reward systems – recall our discussion in Chapter 6 – and structural reorganisations are additional forces for change.

Models and dynamics of planned change

Western managers are criticised for emphasising short-term, quick-fix solutions to organisational problems. When applied to organisational change, this approach is doomed from the start. Quick-fix solutions do not really solve underlying problems, nor do they have much staying power. Therefore, researchers and managers alike have tried to identify effective ways to manage the change process. This section sheds light on their insights. After discussing Lewin's change model, we review different types of organisational change and Kotter's eight stages for leading organisational change.

Lewin's change model

Most theories of organisational change originated from the landmark work of social psychologist Kurt Lewin. Lewin developed a three-stage model of planned change which explained how to initiate, manage and stabilise the change process.[8] The three stages are unfreezing, changing and refreezing. (Unfreezing is the accepted term for this OB process, instead of the more usual terms for unfreezing, i.e. thawing or defrosting.) Before reviewing each stage, it is important to highlight the assumptions that underlie this model:[9]

- The change process involves learning something new, as well as discontinuing some current attitudes, behaviour and organisational practices.
- Change will not occur unless there is motivation to change. This is often the most difficult part of the change process.

- People are the hub of all organisational changes. Any change, whether in terms of structure, group process, reward systems or job design, requires individuals to change.
- Resistance to change is found even when the goals of change are highly desirable.
- Effective change requires reinforcing new types of behaviour, attitudes and organisational practices.

Let us now consider the three stages of change.

UNFREEZING

The focus of this stage is to create the motivation to change. In so doing, individuals are encouraged to replace old behaviours and attitudes with those desired by management. Professionals can begin the unfreezing process by disconfirming the usefulness or appropriateness of employees' present behaviours or attitudes. In other words, employees need to become dissatisfied with the old way of doing things.

Benchmarking
process by which
a company
compares its
performance with
that of high-
performing
organisations

Benchmarking is a technique that can be used to help 'unfreeze' an organisation. Benchmarking describes the overall process by which a company compares its performance with that of other companies, then learns by the strongest-performing process how companies achieve their results.[10] For example, one company discovered through its benchmarking that their costs to develop a computer system were twice as high compared to the best companies in the industry, and the time it took to get a new product to market was four times longer than the benchmarked organisations. These data about performing organisations were ultimately used to unfreeze employees' attitudes and motivate people to change the organisation's internal processes in order to remain competitive.[11] Organisations also need to devise ways to reduce the barriers to change during this stage.

CHANGING

Because change involves learning, this stage entails providing employees with new information, new behavioural models or new ways of looking at things. The purpose is to help employees learn new concepts or points of view. Role models, mentors, experts, benchmarking results and training are all useful mechanisms to facilitate change. Experts recommend that it is best to convey the idea that change is a continuous learning process rather than a one-off event.

REFREEZING

Change is stabilised during refreezing by helping employees to integrate the changed behaviour or attitude into their normal way of doing things. This is accomplished by first giving employees the chance to exhibit the new types of behaviour or attitudes. Once exhibited, positive reinforcement is used. Additional coaching and modelling are used at this point to reinforce the stability of the change.[12]

Types of change

Several models have been developed to classify different types of change. We discuss two of these models.

COMPLEXITY, COST AND UNCERTAINTY

A useful three-way typology of change is displayed in Figure 17.2.[13] This typology is generic because it relates to all sorts of change, including both administrative and technological changes. Adaptive change is lowest in complexity, cost and uncertainty. It involves repeating the implementation of a change in the same organisational unit later on or imitating a change that was implemented by a different unit. For example, an adaptive change for a department store would be to rely on 12-hour days during the annual inventory week. The store's accounting department could imitate the same change in work hours during end-of year-accounting. Adaptive changes are not particularly threatening to employees because they are familiar.

Innovative changes fall midway on the continuum of complexity, cost and uncertainty. An experiment with flexible work schedules by a farm supply warehouse qualifies as an innovative change if it entails modifying the way other firms in the industry already use it. Unfamiliarity, greater uncertainty, makes fear of change a problem with innovative changes.

FIGURE 17.2 A GENERIC TYPOLOGY OF ORGANISATIONAL CHANGE

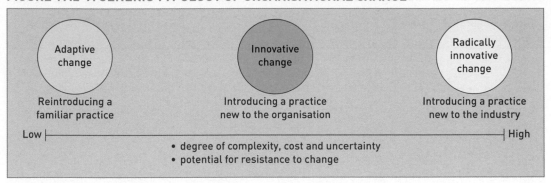

At the high end of the continuum of complexity, cost and uncertainty are the radically innovative changes. Changes of this sort are the most difficult to implement and tend to be the most threatening to managerial trust and employee job security. They can tear the fabric of an organisation's culture. Resistance to change tends to increase as changes go from adaptive to innovative to radically innovative.

DIMENSIONS OF CHANGE

Another way of distinguishing different types of change is to consider how change methods are implemented. Beer and Nohria call these different approaches Theory E and Theory O of change.[14] These approaches are guided by very different assumptions about the purpose of and means for change. Theory E stands for economic value. The creation of economic value is the main purpose. The focus of theory E is on formal structure and systems. Change is driven from the top and consultants play a major role in the process. Financial incentives are important. Change is planned and programmatic.

In Theory O change is based on organisational capability. The goal is to develop corporate culture through individual and organisational learning. Its focus is on the development of a high-commitment culture. Consultants and financial incentives are not important in the change. The process is not planned, but emergent.

Table 17.1 summarises the E and O approaches to organisational change. Theory E and O differ from each other according to six dimensions: goals, leadership, focus, process, reward system and use of consultants. Beer and Nohria argue that both theories have validity, but that they also have costs, often unintended. Theory E is more able to capture attention and focus the change on a single direction. It is usually aligned with the distribution of power in the organisation.[15] It can be fast and therefore, it is appropriate in times of crisis. Theory E has however several liabilities. One of the most important disadvantages is that top management is ignorant of key contingencies and capabilities at the front line. It often creates large short-term losses that are difficult to recover.

Theory O is more sensitive to local contingencies. It is suitable for online experimentation and learning. It is more likely to satisfy needs for autonomy and control. A major cost of Theory O is the slowness of the implementation process. The pre-existing culture and technology may limit the implementation process as well. Theory O is not well suited for strategic or corporate change. It can be insufficiently bold or visionary.

As Theory E and O both have their advantages and liabilities, it is the challenge to resolve the tension between E and O in a way the benefits are optimised and the liabilities limited (see Table 17.1: Theories E and O combined).

One company that exemplifies the reconciliation of the hard and soft approaches is ASDA, the UK grocery chain that CEO Archie Norman took over in 1991, when the retailer was nearly bankrupt. Norman laid off employees, flattened the organisation, and sold losing businesses. Yet during his tenure, ASDA also became famous for its atmosphere of trust and openness. Consider the way in which Norman dealt with the tension between E and O for two of the six dimensions of change:

TABLE 17.1 DIMENSIONS OF CHANGE

Dimensions of change	Theory E	Theory O	Theories E and O combined
Goals	Maximise shareholder value	Develop organisational capabilities	Explicitly confront the tension between economic value and organisational capability
Leadership	Manage change from the top-down	Encourage participation from the bottom-up	Set direction from the top and engage people below
Focus	Emphasise structure and systems	Build up corporate culture: employees' behaviour and attitudes	Focus simultaneously on the hard (structures and systems) and the soft (corporate culture)
Process	Plan and establish programmes	Experiment and evolve	Plan for spontaneity
Reward system	Motivate through financial incentives	Motivate through commitment – use pay as fair exchange	Use incentives to reinforce change but not drive it
Use of consultants	Consultants analyse problems and shape solutions	Consultants support management in shaping their own solutions	Consultants are expert resources who empower employees

SOURCE: Reprinted by permission of *Harvard Business Review*. [Excerpt/Exhibit] from 'Cracking the Code of Change', by M. Beer and N. Nohria, May–June 2000, Copyright © 2000 by the Harvard Business School Publishing Corporation; all rights reserved.

Leadership. From day one, Norman set strategy without expecting any participation from below. He said ASDA would adopt an every-low-pricing strategy, and Norman unilaterally determined that change begin by having two experimental store formats up and running within six months. He decided to shift power from the headquarters to the stores, declaring: 'I want everyone to be close to the stores. We must love the stores to death; that is our business.' But even from the start, there was an O quality to Norman's leadership style. As he put in his first speech: 'First, I am forthright, and I like to argue. Second, I want to discuss issues as colleagues. I am looking for your advice and your agreement.' Norman encouraged dialogue with employees and customers through colleague and customer circles. He set up a 'Tell Archie' programme so that people could voice their concerns and ideas.

Making way for opposite leadership styles was also an essential ingredient to Norman's – and ASDA's – success. This was most clear in Norman's willingness to hire Allan Leighton shortly after he took over. Leighton eventually became deputy chief executive. Norman and Leighton shared the same E and O values, but they had completely different personalities and styles. Norman, cool and reserved, impressed people with the power of his mind – his intelligence and business acumen. Leighton, who is warmer and more people-oriented, worked on employees' emotions with the power of his personality. As one employee told us, 'People respect Archie, but they love Allan.' Norman was the first to credit Leighton with having helped to create emotional commitment to the new ASDA. While it might be possible for a single individual to embrace opposite leadership styles, accepting an equal partner with a very different personality makes it easier to capitalise on those styles. Leighton certainly helped Norman reach out to the organisation. Together they held quarterly meetings with store managers to hear their ideas, and they supplemented those meetings with impromptu talks.

Focus. Norman's immediate actions followed both the E goal of increasing economic value and the O goal of transforming culture. On the E side, Norman focused on structure.

> He removed layers of hierarchy at the top of the organisation, fired the financial officer who had been part of ASDA's disastrous policies, and decreed a wage freeze for everyone – management and workers alike. But from the start, the O strategy was an equal part of Norman's plan. He bought time for all this change by warning the markets that financial recovery would take three years. Norman later said he spent 75 per cent of his early months at ASDA as the company's human resource director, making the organisation less hierarchical, more egalitarian and more transparent. Both Norman and Leighton were keenly aware that they had to win hearts and minds. As Norman put it to workers: 'We need to make ASDA a great place for everyone to work.'[16]

DESIGN AND DEVELOPMENT APPROACH

The typology of Theory E and O resembles the distinction between the design approach and the organisation development approach. Management methods such as business process re-engineering, Total Quality Management (Chapter 15), lean production and Balanced Score Card are typical design methods.[17] They are driven top-down; they are based on a clear-cut model that is implemented according to plan. Organisation development methods, like teamwork and participative management focus on a bottom-up approach. Members of the organisation are involved in the change process. There are no standardised solutions. Several perspectives are possible and the direction of the change evolves along the change process.

Kotter's design approach for leading organisational change

John Kotter, an expert in leadership and change management, believes that organisational change typically fails because senior management commit one or more of the following errors:[18]

■ Failure to establish a sense of urgency about the need for change.
■ Failure to create a powerful-enough guiding coalition that is responsible for leading and managing the change process.
■ Failure to establish a vision that guides the change process.
■ Failure to effectively communicate the new vision.
■ Failure to remove obstacles that impede the accomplishment of the new vision.
■ Failure to systematically plan for and create short-term wins. Short-term wins represent the achievement of important results or goals.
■ Declaration of victory too soon. This derails the long-term changes in infrastructure that are frequently needed to achieve a vision.
■ Failure to anchor the changes in the organisation's culture. It takes years for long-term changes to become embedded within an organisation's culture.

Kotter recommends that organisations should follow eight sequential steps to overcome these problems (see Table 17.2).

Each of the steps shown in Table 17.2 is associated with one of the fundamental errors just discussed. These steps also subsume Lewin's model of change. The first four steps represent Lewin's 'unfreezing' stage. Steps 5, 6 and 7 represent 'changing' and step 8 corresponds to 'refreezing'. Kotter's research underscores that it is ineffective to skip steps and that successful organisational change is 70 to 90 per cent leadership and only 10 to 30 per cent management. Senior managers are thus advised to focus on leading rather than managing change (also see Chapter 11).[19]

The presentation of Kotter's eight steps gives the impression that change is always a logical, step-by-step process that can be managed with a rational programme. This approach is based on assumptions that are very similar to the design approach of change or the theory E perspective. Change is not always a simple and linear process. It is often messy, going through periods of ebb and flow that repeat themselves.[20] Organisational politics often interfere and can disturb the change profoundly (see Chapter 13). Therefore, the stepwise approach of J. P. Kotter oversimplifies the complex nature of change. Professionals must realise that:

■ Change can be emergent, evolving through a series of ongoing adaptations and alterations. Without deliberate dramatic interventions, the accommodations and experiments can result, over time, in striking organisational changes.

TABLE 17.2 SEQUENTIAL STEPS TO LEADING ORGANISATIONAL CHANGE

Step	Description
1 Establish a sense of urgency	Unfreeze the organisation by creating a compelling reason for why change is needed
2 Create the guiding coalition	Create a cross-functional, cross-level group of people with enough power to lead the change
3 Develop a vision and strategy	Create a vision and strategic plan to guide the change process
4 Communicate the change vision	Create and implement a communication strategy that consistently communicates the new vision and strategic plan
5 Empower broad-based action	Eliminate barriers to change and use target elements of change to transform the organisation. Encourage risk taking and creative problem solving
6 Generate short-term wins	Plan for and create short-term 'wins' or improvements. Recognise and reward people who contribute to the wins
7 Consolidate gains and produce more change	The guiding coalition uses credibility from short-term wins to create more change. Additional people are brought into the change process as change cascades throughout the organisation. Attempts are made to reinvigorate the change process
8 Anchor new approaches in the culture	Reinforce the changes by highlighting connections between new behaviours and processes and organisational success. Develop methods to ensure leadership development and succession

SOURCE: The steps were developed by J. P. Kotter, *Leading Change* (Boston, MA: Harvard Business School Press, 1996).

■ Even when change takes place according to a deliberate, top-driven orchestration like the design approach or Theory E, change can still be iterative, politicised, going backwards and forward. Every change is different and every organisation has its own idiosyncrasies.

Nevertheless, Kotter's eight-step approach is based on a multitude of typical design-oriented organisational changes. It provides a useful set of points of attention that professionals can take into account when they introduce a top-driven change.

Organisation development

Organisation development (OD) is an applied field of study and practice. A pair of OD experts defined **Organisation development** as follows:

> Organisation development is concerned with helping managers to plan change in organising and managing people that will develop the requisite commitment, co-ordination and competence. Its purpose is to enhance both the effectiveness of organisations and the well-being of their members through planned interventions in the organisation's human processes, structures and systems, using knowledge of behavioural science and its intervention methods.[21]

Organisation development
a set of techniques or tools that are used to implement organisational change

Many other experts have given their own definition of OD. There have been many statements in OD literature to suggest that the field is uncertain of its direction and identity. In an attempt to identify the key dependent variables of OD, seven experienced OD experts reviewed 27 definitions of OD.[22] The experts reached consensus in describing the following categories as representative of ten key dependent variables of OD:

- Advance organisational renewal.
- Engage organisation culture change.
- Enhance profitability and competitiveness.
- Ensure health and well-being of organisations and employees.
- Facilitate learning and development.
- Improve problem solving.
- Increase effectiveness.
- Initiate and/or manage change.
- Strengthen system and process improvement.
- Support adaptation to change.

In this section, we briefly review the four identifying characteristics of OD and its research and practical implications.[23]

OD involves profound change

Change agents using OD generally desire deep and long-lasting improvement. OD consultant Warner Burke, for example, who strives for fundamental cultural change, wrote: 'By fundamental change, as opposed to fixing a problem or improving a procedure, I mean that some significant aspect of an organisation's culture will never be the same.'[24]

OD is value-loaded

Owing to the fact that OD is partly rooted in humanistic psychology, many OD consultants carry certain values or biases into the client organisation. They prefer co-operation over conflict, self-control over institutional control, and democratic and participative management over autocratic management. In addition to OD being driven by a consultant's values, some OD practitioners now believe that there is a broader 'value perspective' that should underlie any organisational change. Specifically, OD should always be customer focused. This approach implies that organisational interventions should be aimed at helping to satisfy customers' needs and thereby provide enhanced value to an organisation's products and services. Consider the case of B&O:

> On 29 October 1993, the chairman of the board of Bang & Olufsen (B&O) could, for the first time after years of losses, predict a profit of €17 million for the financial year 1993–94. The company's share price had risen spectacularly, from €43 million in 1990–91 to €1450 in 1994–95. These figures indicated a dramatic turnaround of a long-tottering company.
>
> B&O was the crown jewel of Danish industry, the exclusive producer of high-tech, high-fidelity audio-visual systems and other related products. Since its beginning, the company had been at the forefront of design innovation, a philosophy promoted by the two founders of the company. However, that original philosophy stressing product design – which had earned the company much acclaim – carried within it the seeds of failure. The sanctity of the design function came to reign over everything else, particularly cost and customer considerations. Saying 'no' to a new product from the design department was taboo, an action that would not even occur to anyone hoping to stay for long in the organisation. Unfortunately, even though the company won one design prize after another, financially it was anything but a winner. The balance sheet had been tottering in and out of the red for 22 years, an unheard-of period of time. As the present CEO, Anders Knutsen, said during a presentation to a group of his key people, while recalling the situation, 'Bang & Olufsen was not interested in making money; it was interested only in winning prizes.'
>
> Despite the dismal financial figures, not many at B&O seemed to be seriously worried. Most employees were used to the fact that the company was not making a profit, but they never had serious doubts about its survival. Employment security had always been an implicit part of their contract. If ever a doubt surfaced in anybody's mind about the company's future, top management's strong and confident statements reassured them. In the words of the present CEO, 'Every year when we had some problems, it was not our fault. It was the outside world that was so evil to poor Bang & Olufsen.'
>
> Finally, when it became clear that the accounting period of 1990–91 would bring a deficit of €18.25 million, the company's dismal situation could no longer be ignored. The

Supervisory Board decided to pull the plug, replacing the CEO who for 10 years had been allowed to run the company at his own discretion, with Anders Knutsen. Knutsen had learned the business of B&O by starting out as a brand manager and working his way through different positions in production and product development until finally ending up as technical director.

His first step was an analysis of the company's cultural values, prepared by B&O's top executives, which centred on an intensive evaluation of the company's critical situation. In particular, the way in which the process of new-product acceptance was treated as sacrosanct was placed under the microscope.

What followed was, as one B&O employee described it, 'an atmosphere of chaos and upheaval'. People were shocked and disoriented, uncertain how the future – theirs and the company's – would look. The shock therapy seemed to achieve the desired effect, however. Participants, trying to impose order on the prevailing chaos, threw themselves whole-heartedly into the activities of the seminar. Despite the risks, they experienced for the first time the power to do something about their own company. They were asked to engage in a strategic dialogue with top management to help restructure and refocus the company. Participating in the design for the future made for motivation, commitment and a sense of ownership. No longer was job security the main pillar of the contract. Instead, that pillar had become accountability and performance.

The distance between top management and the shop floor was cut by reducing the overall number of executives and by slashing two management layers entirely; a total of 712 people were dismissed. As accountability was pushed deep down the lines, employees were expected to develop a sense of ownership and personal responsibility for the company.

To internationalise the company, a new International Sales and Marketing Head Office was opened in Brussels. Product acceptance – the old Achilles' heel of the company (previously almost everything submitted by product design was accepted) – became much more selective. This proved to be the most disturbing 'culture shock' experienced during the transformation, as it clearly signalled management's intent to change the company.

After a 2-year period, B&O moved from a deficit that seriously threatened the existence of the company to a surplus that exceeded all expectations. The first part of the change process had come to a successful end.[25]

OD is a cycle of diagnosis and prescription

OD theorists and practitioners have long adhered to a medical model of organisation. Like medical doctors, internal and external OD consultants approach the 'sick' organisation, 'diagnose' its ills, 'prescribe' and implement an intervention and 'monitor' progress.[26]

OD is process-oriented

Ideally, OD consultants focus on the form and not the content of behavioural and administrative dealings. For example, product design engineers and market researchers might be coached on how to communicate more effectively with one another without the consultant knowing the technical details of their conversations. In addition to communication, OD specialists focus on other processes, including those of solving problems, making decisions, handling conflict, trust, sharing power and developing careers.

Research findings and practical implications

Before discussing OD research, it is important to note that many of the topics contained in this book are used during OD interventions. For example, teambuilding is commonly used to improve the functioning of work teams and was reviewed in Chapter 10. OD research, therefore, has practical implications for a variety of OB applications. OD-related interventions produced the following insights:

■ A meta-analysis of 18 studies indicated that employee satisfaction with change was higher when top management was highly committed to the change effort.[27]

- A meta-analysis of 52 studies provided support for a systems model of organisational change. Specifically, varying one target element of change created changes in other target elements. Also, there was a positive relationship between individual behaviour change and organisational-level change.[28]
- A meta-analysis of 126 studies demonstrated that multifaceted interventions, using more than one OD technique, were more effective in changing job attitudes and work attitudes than interventions that relied on only one human-process or technostructural approach.[29]

There are three practical implications to be derived from this research. First, planned organisation change works. However, management and change agents are advised to rely on multifaceted interventions. As indicated elsewhere in this book, goal setting, feedback, recognition and rewards, training, participation, and challenging job design have good track records for improving performance and satisfaction. Second, change programmes are more successful when they are geared toward meeting both short and long-term results. Professionals should not engage in organisational change for the sake of it. Change efforts should produce positive results.[30] Finally, organisational change is more likely to succeed when top management is truly committed to the change process and the desired goals of the change programme. This is particularly true when organisations pursue large-scale transformation.[31]

Challenges for understanding organisational change

The study of change involves more than the different approaches of organisational change, like the design approach or organisation development methods. The field of organisational change is far from mature in understanding dynamics and effects of process, content and context. Many organisational studies often analyse change from one of these perspectives, which gives only a partial view of the complex processes that organisational change involves.[32] Because of the complex nature and dynamic of change generalisations are hard to sustain over time. Pettigrew, Woodman and Cameron[33] discern several interconnected analytical issues in which the study of organisational change remains underdeveloped.

The examination of multiple contexts and levels of analysis in studying organisational change

To understand the nature of change it is important to notice the context in which the change takes place. Innovations in the ICT sector may be much faster than the rate and trajectory of change in health care. Change also involves different levels of analysis. These range from the individual level, through group and organisational level (the inner context) to the sector, nation states and the global competition level (the outer context). The different types of change that were discussed earlier in this chapter are typical approaches to the process of change. To understand fully those processes it is important to investigate the terrain around the stream that shapes these processes, and that is in turn shaped by these processes. The culture of an organisation (see Chapter 16) and its competitive environment are but two of the many important contextual characteristics that influence the way in which change processes are implemented.

The inclusion of time, history, process and action

Organisational changes should also be studied on a longitudinal basis. Recommendations on how to manage change depend partly on the change history of an organisation. Mergers and acquisitions can have important effects on the way in which future changes are perceived by the remaining employees. Successful or unsuccessful track records can influence the implementation of new changes. Historical investigation of industrial or institutional change can provide valuable information about evolutions in industrial sectors and organisational settings.

The link between change processes and organisational performance outcomes

Although many studies have tried to answer what makes change successful, the link between change capacity and organisational performance is rarely made. It is not because a change is successful that it contributes substantially to the performance of the organisation. Measuring organisational performance is also a tricky enterprise. The business literature's tendency to focus on an atemporal, small sample of high performers is a dangerous way of looking at performance. What is a successful company today, can be a failing organisation tomorrow. One of the rare studies that have attempted to link change practices to firm performance is a European study by Pettigrew and Whipp[34] that examined the process of managing strategic and operational change in four mature industry and service sectors of the UK economy. The scholars chose a pair of firms in each of the four sectors. Each pair was made up of a higher and a lower performer in the same market. From a 30-year time series study Pettigrew and Whipp were able to identify in what way the high performers were different from the lesser performers. The high performers:

- Conducted environmental assessment more intensely.
- Led change.
- Linked strategic and operational change.
- Managed their human resources as assets and liabilities.
- Managed coherence in the overall process of competition and change.

The study of receptivity, customisation, sequencing, pace and episodic versus continuous change processes

There are a number of important but difficult questions related to the temporal character of change. Where does a change agent begin a given change initiative? What pace of change is appropriate in different settings to meet local objectives? How can you keep the organisation receptive to change, knowing that transformations demand a lot of energy and often result in change fatigue? The answer to these questions is important in order to contribute to the theory and practice of change receptivity, customisation, sequencing and pacing.

In addition, the difference between episodic and continuous change is important.[35] **Episodic change** refers to change initiatives that are infrequent, discontinuous and intentional. Change is an occasional interruption or divergence from equilibrium. It is seen as a failure of the organisation to adapt its deep structure to a changing environment. This is the classic approach of many change studies. But there is another important type of change, **Continuous change**. In this perspective organisations are emergent and self-organising. Change is constant, evolving and cumulative. Change is a pattern of endless modifications in work processes and social practice. Numerous small accommodations cumulate and amplify. Continuous change is studied far less than episodic change. The study of continuous change is difficult and time-consuming. However, continuous change is a major phenomenon in transformations that needs our intention as much as episodic change. Sometimes it is argued that an ideal form of change is a combination of episodic and continuous change.

Finally, Pettigrew, Woodman and Cameron also refer to the investigation of international and cross-cultural comparisons in research on organisational change and to the engagement between academics and practitioners as important challenges for future research in organisational change.

It is clear that the complexity of organisational change is too high to summarise the essentials in one or two typologies of change or a few how-to-do checklists. There still remain a large number of questions to be answered as to the nature, the context and the generalisibility of change patterns. The challenges discussed in this paragraph map the guidelines of which scholars and practitioners alike should be aware of when they address change issues.

Understanding and managing resistance to change

We are all creatures of habit. It is difficult for people to try new ways of doing things. It is precisely because of this basic human characteristic that most employees do not have enthusiasm for change in the workplace. Rare is the professional who does not have several stories about carefully cultivated changes that 'died on the vine' because of resistance to change. It is important for organisations to learn to manage resistance because failed change efforts are costly. Costs include decreased employee loyalty, lowered probability of achieving corporate goals, a waste of money and resources and difficulty in fixing the failed change effort. This section examines employee resistance to change, relevant research and practical ways of dealing with the problem.

> **Episodic change** refers to change initiatives that are infrequent, discontinuous and intentional
>
> **Continuous change** perceives change as constant, evolving and cumulative

Why people resist change in the workplace

No matter how technically or administratively perfect a proposed change may be, people make or break it. Individual and group behaviour following an organisational change can take many forms (see Figure 17.3). The extremes range from acceptance to active **Resistance to change**. Many targets or victims of change are cynical about its motives, relevance and processes. Cynicism about organisational change combines pessimism about the likelihood of successful change with blame; with those responsible for change being seen as incompetent, uncaring or simply lazy.[36] A change-management programme in a large Spanish savings bank was intended to facilitate changes in managers' values, competences and practices by providing them with relevant feedback from subordinates. However, the change programme was perceived as political and part of a power game, causing negative emotional reactions such as fear, suspicion and discomfort.[37]

Figure 17.3 shows that resistance can be as subtle as passive resignation and as overt as deliberate sabotage. Professionals need to learn to recognise the manifestations of resistance, both in themselves and others, if they want to be more effective in creating and supporting change. For example, organisations can use the list in Figure 17.3 to prepare answers and tactics to combat the various forms of resistance.

Now that we have examined the manifestations of resistance to change, let us consider the reasons employees resist change in the first place. Ten of the leading reasons are elaborated here.[38]

> **Resistance to change** emotional/behavioural response to real or imagined work changes

AN INDIVIDUAL'S PREDISPOSITION TOWARD CHANGE

This predisposition is highly personal and deeply ingrained. It is an offshoot of how one learns to handle change and ambiguity as a child. Consider the hypothetical examples of Sandy and Carl.

FIGURE 17.3 THE CONTINUUM OF RESISTANCE TO CHANGE

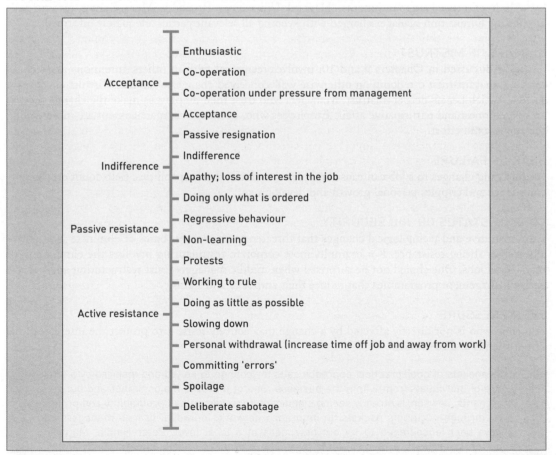

SOURCE: A. S. Judson, *Changing Behavior in Organizations: Minimizing Resistance to Change* (Cambridge, MA: Basil Blackwell, Inc., 1991), p. 48. Used with permission.

Sandy's parents were patient, flexible and understanding. From the time Sandy was weaned, she was taught that there were positive compensations for the loss of immediate gratification. She learned that love and approval were associated with making changes. In contrast, Carl's parents were unreasonable, unyielding and forced him to comply with their wishes. They forced him to take piano lessons even though he hated them. Changes were demands for compliance. This taught Carl to be distrustful and suspicious of change. These learned predispositions ultimately affect how Sandy and Carl handle change as adults.[39] Dell Computer Corporation recognises how important an individual's predisposition toward change can be and tries to hire people with positive predispositions:

> ... Dell actively seeks and cultivates a certain type of employee mindset. For example, potential employees are told early on that their former titles may not correlate exactly with positions at Dell because the company structure is relatively flat. 'We have to strip the paradigm that titles and levels mean anything', says Price [Steve Price is vice president of human resources for Dell's Public and Americas International Group]. 'People have to park their egos at the door.' Furthermore, Dell's employees have to move away from the paradigm that more means better. 'It's just the reverse', says Price. 'When we take half of what you have away from you and tell you to go rebuild it, that's a sign of success.' ... 'We typically attract people for whom change is not a problem', says Koster [Jim Koster is director of human resources for customer service].[40]

SURPRISE AND FEAR OF THE UNKNOWN
When innovative or radically different changes are introduced without warning, affected employees become fearful of the implications. Rumours from the grapevine (see Chapter 8) fill the void created by a lack of official announcements. Harvard University's Rosabeth Moss Kanter recommends appointing a transition manager charged with keeping all relevant parties adequately informed.[41]

CLIMATE OF MISTRUST
Trust, as discussed in Chapters 9 and 10, involves reciprocal faith in others' intentions and behaviour. Mutual mistrust can doom an otherwise well-conceived change to failure. Mistrust encourages secrecy, which begets deeper mistrust. Managers who trust their employees make the change process an open, honest and participative affair. Employees who, in turn, trust management are more willing to expend extra effort.

FEAR OF FAILURE
Intimidating changes to a job can cause employees to doubt their capabilities. Self-doubt erodes self-confidence and cripples personal growth and development.

LOSS OF STATUS OR JOB SECURITY
Administrative and technological changes that threaten to alter power bases or eliminate jobs generally trigger strong resistance. For example, most corporate restructuring involves the elimination of managerial jobs. One should not be surprised when middle managers resist restructuring and participative management programmes that reduce their authority and status.

PEER PRESSURE
Someone who is not directly affected by a change may actively resist it to protect the interests of his or her friends and co-workers.

> The 'pockets of good practice' approach calls for change to be led and inspired by a small cadre of individuals from within the business. One of the UK's major timber and builder's merchants, Jewson, is already seeing significant improvements in profitability and productivity through nurturing 'pockets' in its branch network. Individual branch managers had always been encouraged to try out new ideas at a local level. Peter Hindle, Managing Director, Operations, explains: 'When I visited our branches I saw different ideas and different aspects of good practice but no one was talking to each other. I found myself like the Pied Piper, spending all my time telling branch managers about the good things that

> I'd seen going on in other places.' Peter's vision was to create a pocket made up of the most successful branch managers, who would learn from each other and share ideas. From this he hopes that a model of best practice for branch management would emerge. He started the initiative by getting the top 30 branch managers together for two days every month. The meetings were, deliberately, set up not as traditional training sessions but as forums for stimulating new ideas and sharing experiences. Flexible working, annualised-hours contracts, better product training and improved transport efficiency are just some of the benefits that have resulted.[42]

DISRUPTION OF CULTURAL TRADITIONS OR GROUP RELATIONSHIPS

Whenever individuals are transferred, promoted or reassigned, cultural and group dynamics are thrown into disequilibrium.

PERSONALITY CONFLICTS

Just as a friend can get away with telling us something we would resent hearing from an adversary, the personalities of change agents can breed resistance (see Chapter 2).

LACK OF TACT OR POOR TIMING

Undue resistance can occur because changes are introduced in an insensitive manner or at an awkward time.

NON-REINFORCING REWARD SYSTEMS

Individuals resist when they do not foresee positive rewards for changing (see Chapter 6). For example, an employee is unlikely to support a change that is perceived as requiring him or her to work longer and under more pressure.

Research findings and practical implications

In a recent survey among 90 British managers (almost half of whom were working in the public sector), the following themes emerged:

- Continuing change is much higher on the agenda than managing discrete projects.
- There is evidence of 'initiative fatigue' (most people want to see the pace of change relaxed for a while), information overload and even cynicism.
- Major concerns exist over the lack of effective stress management (see Chapter 7).
- Negotiating, persuading and influencing skills are critical (see Chapter 13).
- Fear of the unknown is a major source of resistance to change but commitment to communication is instrumental rather than value-driven.
- A third of the managers enjoy the politics game, a third do not and a third are neutral.[43]

The classic study of resistance to change was reported in 1948 by Lester Coch and John R. P. French. They observed the introduction of a new work procedure in a garment factory. The change was introduced in three different ways to separate groups of workers. In the 'no participation' group, the garment makers were simply told about the new procedure. Members of a second group, called the 'representative' group, were introduced to the change by a trained co-worker. Employees in the 'total participation' group learned of the new work procedure through a graphic presentation of its cost-saving potential. Mixed results were recorded for the representative group. The 'no participation' and 'total participation' groups, meanwhile, went in opposite directions. Output dropped sharply for the 'no participation' group, while grievances and staff turnover climbed. After a small dip in performance, the 'total participation' group achieved record-high output levels while experiencing no staff turnover.[44] Since the Coch and French study, participation has been the recommended approach for overcoming resistance to change.[45]

Empirical research uncovered five additional personal characteristics related to resistance to change. A recent study of 514 employees from six organisations headquartered in four different continents (North America, Europe, Asia and Australia) revealed that personal dispositions pertaining to having a 'positive self-concept' and 'tolerance for risk' were positively related to coping with change. That is, people with a positive self-concept and a tolerance for risk handled organisational change better than those without these dispositions.[46]

A second study also found that high self-efficacy and an internal locus of control were negatively associated with resistance to change.[47] Finally, a study of 305 college students and 15 university staff members revealed that attitudes toward a specific change were positively related to the respondents' general attitudes toward change and content within their 'change schema' (you may recall from Chapter 4 that a change schema relates to various perceptions, thoughts and feelings that people have when they encounter organisational change).[48]

The preceding research is based on the assumption that individuals directly or consciously resist change. Some experts contend that this is not the case. Rather, there is a growing belief that resistance to change represents, instead, the employees' responses to obstacles in the organisation that prevent them from changing.[49] For example, John Kotter, the researcher who developed the eight steps for leading organisational change discussed earlier in this chapter, studied more than 100 companies and concluded that employees generally wanted to change but were unable to do so because of obstacles that prevented execution. He noted that obstacles in the organisation structure or in a 'performance appraisal system [that] makes people choose between the new vision and their own self-interests' impeded change more than an individual's direct resistance.[50] This new perspective implies that a systems model should be used to determine the causes of failed change. Such an approach would most likely reveal that ineffective organisational change is due to faulty organisational processes and systems rather than to employees' direct resistance.[51] In conclusion, a systems perspective suggests that people do not resist change, per se, but rather that individuals' 'anti-change' behaviour and attitudes are caused by obstacles within the work environment.

Alternative strategies for overcoming resistance to change

Before recommending specific approaches for overcoming resistance, there are four key conclusions that should be kept in mind. First, an organisation must be ready for change.

> Boehringer Ingelheim, a German pharmaceuticals manufacturer of more than 100 years' standing, is one of the few remaining privately owned companies in the pharmaceutical industry. Until the 1980s, its culture reflected a traditional, hierarchical management structure and a strong paternalistic value system. At its UK subsidiary, management identified some of the natural risk-takers who could become role models for other employees. After looking for volunteers they ended up with a network comprising one change agent for every 50 employees. This network provided the crucial element of bottom-up and sideways-driven change facilitation to complement the more traditional top-down directives.[52]

Just as a table must be set before you can eat, so must an organisation be ready for change before it can be effective.[53] The next Activity contains a survey that assesses an organisation's readiness for change. Use the survey to evaluate a company that you worked for or are familiar with that undertook to change. To what extent was the company ready for change and how did this relate, in turn, to the success of the effort to change?

A Dutch study of more than 600 managers from both the profit and non-profit sectors indicated that the readiness to change of managers is influenced in order of importance by the emotions the change arouses with the manager, the experience with previous changes and the consequences of the change for the manager's future work.[54] The emotional evaluation is of more importance than the cognitive evaluation for the attitude of a manager towards a change.

Second, organisational change is less successful when top management fails to keep employees informed about the process of change. Third, do not assume that people are resisting change consciously. Managers are encouraged to use a systems model of change, in which transforming one element of change creates changes in other elements, to identify the obstacles that are affecting the implementation process. Fourth, employees' perceptions or interpretations of a change affect resistance significantly. Employees are less likely to resist when they perceive that the benefits of a change overshadow the personal costs. As a minimum therefore, managers are advised to:

- Provide as much information as possible to employees about the change.
- Inform employees about the reasons/rationale for the change.
- Conduct meetings to address employees' questions regarding the change.
- Provide employees with the opportunity to discuss how the proposed change might affect them.[55]

Assessing an organisation's readiness for change

Instructions

Circle the number that best represents your opinions about the company being evaluated.

3 = Yes

2 = Somewhat

1 = No

1 Is the change effort being sponsored by a senior-level executive (MD, CEO, COO)?	3	2	1
2 Are all levels of management committed to the change?	3	2	1
3 Does the organisation culture encourage risk taking?	3	2	1
4 Does the organisation culture encourage and reward continuous improvement?	3	2	1
5 Has senior management clearly articulated the need for change?	3	2	1
6 Has senior management presented a clear vision of a positive future?	3	2	1
7 Does the organisation use specific measures to assess business performance?	3	2	1
8 Does the change effort support other major activities going on in the organisation?	3	2	1
9 Has the organisation benchmarked itself against world-class companies?	3	2	1
10 Do all employees understand the customers' needs?	3	2	1
11 Does the organisation reward individuals and/or teams for being innovative and for looking for root causes of organisational problems?	3	2	1
12 Is the organisation flexible and co-operative?	3	2	1
13 Does management effectively communicate with all levels of the organisation?	3	2	1
14 Has the organisation successfully implemented other change programmes?	3	2	1
15 Do employees take personal responsibility for their behaviour?	3	2	1
16 Does the organisation make decisions quickly?	3	2	1

Total score = _____

Arbitrary norms

40–48 = High readiness for change

24–39 = Moderate readiness for change

16–23 = Low readiness for change

SOURCE: Based on the discussion contained in T. A. Stewart, 'Rate Your Readiness to Change', *Fortune*, 7 February 1994, pp. 106–10.

activity

These recommendations underscore the importance of communicating with employees throughout the process of change.

In addition to communication, employee participation in the change process is another generic approach for reducing resistance. Consider how George Bauer, president of the US affiliate of Mercedes-Benz Credit Corp., used participation and employee involvement to re-engineer operations and downsize the workforce.

> The first step is delegating re-engineering efforts to those who know best where to cut: the people actually doing the work. The second step is comforting them with a guarantee: anyone bold enough to eliminate his own job will receive a new job – and probably a better one – helping to create new growth.
>
> So to the shock (and scepticism) of his superiors in Stuttgart, Mr Bauer delegated the problem of streamlining to groups of employees and managers, partly in the cold calculation that a grassroots effort would help workers 'buy in' and partly in the sincere belief that the best ideas would come from outside the executive suite.
>
> The outcome shook the operation to its core. Managers proposed reducing or even wiping out their own departments through automation or restructuring. Four entire layers of management vanished. Employees were assigned to functional teams with almost complete authority to execute decisions.[56]

Bauer's radical approach to change management resulted in a 31 per cent increase in assets between 1992 and 1995 and a 19 per cent increase in staff. JD Power & Associates also rated Mercedes-Benz Credit as number one for customer satisfaction among all the import captive-finance companies in 1995.[57] In spite of positive results like those found by Bauer, organisational change experts have nonetheless criticised the tendency to treat participation as a cure-all for resistance to change. They prefer a contingency approach because resistance can take many forms and, furthermore, because situational factors vary (see Table 17.3). Participation + Involvement does, as shown in Table 17.3, have its place, but it takes time that is not always available. Also indicated is how each of the other five methods has its own situational niche, advantages and drawbacks. In short, there is no universal strategy for overcoming resistance to change. Professionals need a complete repertoire of change strategies.[58]

TABLE 17.3 SIX STRATEGIES FOR OVERCOMING RESISTANCE TO CHANGE

Approach	Commonly used in situations	Advantages	Drawbacks
Education + communication	Where there is a lack of information or inaccurate information and analysis	Once persuaded, people will often help with the implementation of the change	Can be very time-consuming if lots of people are involved
Participation + involvement	Where the initiators do not have all the information they need to design the change and where others have considerable power to resist	People who participate will be committed to implementing change, and any relevant information they have will be integrated into the change plan	Can be very time-consuming if participators design an inappropriate change
Facilitation + support	Where people are resisting because of adjustment problems	No other approach works as well with adjustment problems	Can be time-consuming, expensive and still fail
Negotiation + agreement	Where someone or some group will clearly lose out in a change and where that group has considerable power to resist	Sometimes it is a relatively easy way to avoid major resistance	Can be too expensive in many cases if it alerts others to negotiate for compliance
Manipulation + co-optation	Where other tactics will not work or are too expensive	It can be a relatively quick and inexpensive solution to resistance problems	Can lead to future problems if people feel manipulated
Explicit + implicit coercion	Where speed is essential and where the change initiators possess considerable power	It is speedy and can overcome any kind of resistance	Can be risky if it leaves people annoyed with the initiators

SOURCE: Reprinted by permission of the *Harvard Business Review*. An exhibit from 'Choosing Strategies for Change' by J. P. Kotter and L. A. Schlesinger (March/April 1979). Copyright © 1979 by the President and Fellows of Harvard College; all rights reserved.

Creating a learning organisation

Organisations are finding that yesterday's competitive advantage is becoming the minimum entrance requirement for staying in business. This puts tremendous pressure on organisations to learn how best to improve and stay ahead of competitors. It is generally recognised that an organisation's ability to learn is a key strategic weapon.[59] In the past two decades, researchers have focused their attention more towards the creation and sharing of knowledge within and between organisations rather than on the concepts of the learning organisation. They emphasised a range of activities that are all part of knowledge management. However, many of the concepts and principles of the learning organisation and knowledge management are closely related. Both can also be seen as forms of organisational change. An organisation can only become a learning organisation when it is able to develop continuous change.

The creation of a learning organisation or successfully managing knowledge in organisations is not an easy matter. To help clarify what this process entails, this section begins by defining a learning organisation and different concepts related to knowledge management. Figure 17.4 shows the many interrelated concepts. We then present how to build an organisation that is able to make optimal use of its knowledge and has a high learning capability. Both learning and knowledge management are facing very similar natural resistance, which we will discuss in a following paragraph. The chapter concludes by reviewing new roles and skills required of leaders aiming to manage knowledge and learning.

FIGURE 17.4 THE INTERRELATEDNESS BETWEEN KNOWLEDGE AND LEARNING

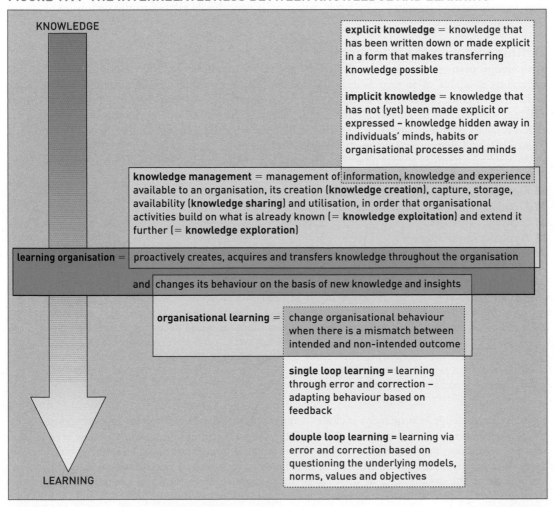

Defining a learning organisation

Peter Senge, a professor at the Massachusetts Institute of Technology, popularised the term 'learning organisation' in his best-selling book entitled *The Fifth Discipline*. He described a learning organisation in very broad terms as 'a group of people working together to collectively enhance their capacities to create results that they truly care about'.[60] Learning is in its simplest form 'a process of retention of response patterns for subsequent use' but it can also be an active process of experimenting and understanding the reasons behind events.[61] According to Argyris,[62] organisational learning occurs when two conditions are fulfilled, namely 'when an organisation achieves what it intended and when a mismatch between intentions and outcomes is identified and it is corrected'. Individual learning and organisational learning have many similarities.[63] Individuals learn through stimuli and responses during acting (see Chapter 2), which is similar with organisations learning through interaction with their environment. Organisations store and retain behavioural patterns in routines, norms and all kind of memory systems, which again parallels the retention of knowledge and behavioural patterns in individuals' brains.[64] Individuals and organisations are both filtering knowledge and feedback from their environment via their mental models and memory.[65] However, the major difference between individual and organisational learning is the collective aspect. Organisational learning requires the institutionalisation and acceptance of knowledge by the 'collective', to allow such knowledge to become collective knowledge spread again among the members through socialisation (see Chapter 16).[66] Hence, the organisation needs 'tools' for this institutionalisation process, such as communication channels, storage systems, knowledge sharing processes, storytelling, etc.

A practical interpretation results in the following definition. A **Learning organisation** is one that proactively creates, acquires, and transfers knowledge and that changes its behaviour on the basis of new knowledge and insights.[67] The latter definition is very closely related to the definition of knowledge management.

Defining knowledge management

Knowledge management can be described as the 'management of information, knowledge and experience available to an organisation, its creation, capture, storage, availability and utilisation, in order that organisational activities build on what is already known and extend it further'.[68] A more HR approach taken to knowledge management results in the following description: 'encouraging individuals to communicate their knowledge by creating environments and systems for capturing, organising, and sharing knowledge throughout the company'.[69]

Weggeman identifies several phases in the knowledge management process,[70] namely:

- Stocktaking of the knowledge available.
- Developing or buying knowledge to fill knowledge gaps.
- Sharing knowledge.
- Applying knowledge.
- Evaluating the process to keep up with changing demands.

> Ford Motor Company has developed a learning network to create lasting impact on the company's results. About 175 000 of the 350 000 employees worldwide of Ford have access to the Ford Learning Network, which includes all kinds of information from e-learning, seminars to books and articles. However, it is more than just an information database. It also includes: detecting competence gaps for each employee, monitoring the use of information, and monitoring each one's learning process in order to see whether the different units learned something and applied the new knowledge into their work processes. Questionnaires are used for such evaluations.[71]

Hence, knowledge management includes a range of management activities applied to knowledge as an organisational asset. The main difference between a learning organisation and an organisation that pays attention to knowledge management is situated in organisational adaptation.[72] A learning organisation refers more to the creation of new knowledge as part of organisational learning and the adaptation of the organisation as a whole to meet changed environmental conditions. Knowledge management is more focused on internal knowledge creation and sharing processes and on finding a

Learning organisation proactively creates, acquires and transfers knowledge throughout the organisation and changes its behaviour on the basis of new knowledge and insights

Knowledge management management of information, knowledge and experience available to an organisation, its creation, capture, storage, availability and utilisation, in order that organisational activities build on what is already known and extend it further

balance between knowledge exploration and exploitation. **Knowledge exploitation** is the use and in-depth development of knowledge existing in the organisation, while **Knowledge exploration** is the creation of new knowledge to expand the breadth of knowledge and to reconfigure existing knowledge.[73]

> The European and Middle East division of Oracle started with knowledge management in 1999. The aim was to improve collaboration and communication to increase especially knowledge sharing. This was achieved by communities of practice (formal networks), communities of interest (informal networks) and more standardisation of tools and processes making co-operation easier. Later this was completed with a network of people responsible for stimulating and following up innovations in the organisation. A complete knowledge management programme demands also the identification and completion of knowledge gaps. Hence, learning programmes were developed in management, sales and customer issues. Those educational services are delivered by Oracle University.[74]

Both knowledge management and developing a learning organisation build on the same conditions:[75]

- New ideas are a prerequisite for learning. Learning organisations actively try to infuse their organisations with new ideas and information. They do this by constantly scanning their external environments, hiring new talent and expertise when needed and devoting significant resources to training and developing their employees.
- New knowledge must be shared in the organisation. Learning organisations strive to reduce structural, process and interpersonal barriers to the sharing of information, ideas and knowledge among organisational members.
- Behaviour must change as a result of new knowledge. Learning organisations are results oriented. They foster an environment in which employees are encouraged to use new types of behaviour and operational processes to achieve corporate goals.

Single and double loop learning

The two types of learning generally accepted in the organisational learning literature are both examples of a change in knowledge stocks. The first type, ordinary learning or **Single loop learning**, which is the most frequently applied type of learning, is about reacting to responses, negative or positive feedback, from the environment. It is adapting one's behaviour to the impulses from others or to the results of one's actions. An employee who improves his or her work processes through his daily work experiences is achieving single loop learning. The second type, **Double loop learning** goes much further by questioning the underlying models, norms, objectives and habits of the action or decision.[76] By questioning these underlying models real innovation and structural changes can occur. Double loop learning thus occurs, for instance, when processes are not just improved but reconsidered, questioning whether the processes still fit the organisational goals or whether a new way of working is preferable. The latter type of learning is most difficult and therefore rarer. The first type of learning can be negative when it reinforces existing behaviour and leads the company back to the status quo.[77] This type just adds knowledge to the existing knowledge stock, while the second type questions the value and use of the existing knowledge stock. The main difference between learning and knowledge sharing is in the fact that the former is concerned with adaptation while the latter is concerned with getting more value out of existing knowledge and avoiding reinventing the wheel. The difference between learning and knowledge creation is smaller. Knowledge creation also changes knowledge stocks but is also considered more as a process of acquiring new knowledge, recombining knowledge and applying it.[78]

Knowledge creation

This brings us to another important aspect of knowledge management, namely the creation of knowledge. Nonaka and Takeuchi are among the pioneers in the knowledge-management area and introduced the concept of knowledge creation. Their knowledge-creation model (SECI) is based on the distinction between individually and organisationally held knowledge and between explicit and implicit knowledge. **Explicit knowledge** is knowledge that has been written down or made explicit

---

Knowledge exploitation creating economies of scale based on the optimal use of knowledge available to the organisation

Knowledge exploration creating new knowledge for the organisation to achieve innovation in processes and products

Single loop learning learning through error and correction – adapting behaviour based on feedback

Double loop learning learning via error and correction based on questioning the underlying models, norms, values and objectives

Explicit knowledge knowledge that has been written down or made explicit in a form that makes transferring knowledge possible

Implicit knowledge
knowledge that has not (yet) been made explicit or expressed but that is hidden away in individuals' minds, habits or organisational processes and minds

Knowledge sharing
the exchange of knowledge between at least two parties to make the knowledge available and useful for both parties, requiring a process of understanding, reconfiguring and sensemaking

Knowledge creation
a process of acquiring new knowledge, recombining knowledge and applying it in order to extend an individual's, group's or organisation's knowledge stock

Learning capabilities
the set of core competencies and internal processes that enable an organisation to adapt to its environment

in a form that makes transferring knowledge possible. **Implicit knowledge** is the opposite and can best be described as knowledge that has not (yet) been made explicit or expressed. There is a continuum from explicit to implicit knowledge, depending on how strongly the knowledge is codified. At one extreme, knowledge is codified in computerised digits, while at the other it is hardly possible to be aware of its existence.

Nonaka and Takeuchi explain that knowledge shifts between different forms (implicit and explicit) and different levels (individual and organisational). The creation of knowledge is according to their model based on **Knowledge sharing** and these shifts in form and level. This leads to four phases in the **Knowledge creation** process, namely socialisation, externalisation, internalisation and combination; abbreviated as SECI (see Figure 17.5). The process starts at the individual level, where knowledge is created, which is then shared in teams. This is knowledge shared among individuals in a socialisation process (also see Chapter 16). The next step is the transformation of this shared knowledge into explicit knowledge (externalisation). Such knowledge can be combined and incorporated into documents or databases (combination). Finally, there is a transformation of explicit knowledge into implicit knowledge by the creation of culture and vision (internalisation). Nonaka and Takeuchi view these four types of knowledge exchange as phases in a continuous knowledge-transformation process resulting in the creation of new knowledge for the members and the organisation. Hence, organisational knowledge is constructed through the socialisation of knowledge among the members of the organisation or through the externalisation of individual knowledge. Organisational knowledge also influences individual knowledge through the internalisation process. To illustrate their SECI model, Nonaka and Takeuchi use the by now famous example of Matsushita Home Bakery, the bread-making machine from Matsushita Electric Industrial (see next Snapshot).

Building an organisation's learning capability

There are several authors who have tried to explain what a learning organisation should look like.[79] McGill and Slocum, for instance, write about the 'smarter organisation'. Such organisation is able to learn to change and to learn from change. Smarter organisations actively manage the learning process to ensure that it occurs by design rather than by chance. Such organisations are able to process their experiences – with customers, competitors, partners, and suppliers – in ways that allow them to create environments in which they can be successful. Organisations need to be permeable and flexible to allow learning. Furthermore, intensive individual and organisational knowledge creation and information gathering are necessary for such learning organisations to be created.

Figure 17.6 presents a model of how organisations build and enhance their learning capability. **Learning capabilities** represent the set of core competencies, which are defined as the special

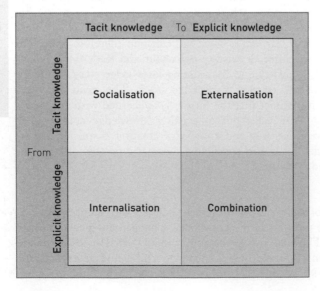

FIGURE 17.5 FOUR MODES OF KNOWLEDGE CONVERSION

SOURCE: Adaptation from pp. 62–9, from *The Knowledge Creating Company: How Japanese Companies Create the Dynamics of Innovation* by Ikujiro Nonaka and Hirotaka Takeuchi, copyright © 1995 by Oxford University Press, Inc. Used by permission of Oxford University Press, Inc.

snapshot

Matsushita Electric creates breadmaker by combining tacit and explicit knowledge

In Japan, Matsushita Electric used to be known as *maneshita*, which means 'copycat'. Big and successful but not an innovator. That changed dramatically with the introduction of the Home Bakery, the first automatic breadmaker. A software engineer, a woman named Tanaka, recognised that with Westernisation, the time had come for a breadmaker in Japan. But she knew almost nothing about baking. So she apprenticed herself to a master baker. He had all the knowledge at his fingertips, but it was very hard for him to verbalise. After watching him for two or three weeks, she went back to Matsushita to write up a set of specifications for the machine, translating his tacit knowledge into something explicit.

They made a prototype, but the bread tasted terrible. So Tanaka brought a group of her peers to observe the baker again. Finally, they realised that what the machine lacked was the twisting motion the baker used when kneading his dough. Incorporating that understanding enabled them to develop a hugely successful product.

The breadmaker changed the corporate culture at Matsushita. People in other divisions said, 'Why can't we do that?'

SOURCE: S. Sherman, 'Hot Products from Hot Tubs, or How Middle Managers Innovate', *Fortune*, 29 April 1996, pp. 165–6. © 1996 Time Inc. All rights reserved.

FIGURE 17.6 BUILDING AN ORGANISATION'S LEARNING CAPABILITY

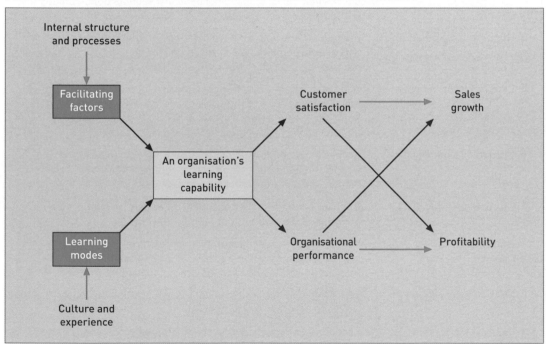

knowledge, skills and technological know-how that distinguish an organisation from its competitors, and processes that enable an organisation to adapt to its environment.[80] The general idea underlying Figure 17.6 is that learning capabilities are the fuel for organisational success. Just as petrol enables a car's engine to perform, learning capabilities equip an organisation to perform – to foresee and respond to internal and external changes. This ability, in turn, increases the chances of satisfying customers and boosting sales and profitability.[81] Let us now consider the two major contributors to an organisation's learning capability: facilitating factors and learning mode.

FACILITATING FACTORS FOR LEARNING AND KNOWLEDGE SHARING

Facilitating factors represent 'the internal structure and processes that affect how easy or hard it is for learning to occur and the amount of effective learning that takes place'.[82] Table 17.4 contains a list of ten key facilitating factors. Keep in mind as you read them that these factors can either enable or impede an organisation's ability to respond to its environment. Consider, for example, the 'concern for measurement' factor. A survey of 203 executives compared companies that did and did not focus on measurement-management. Results revealed that those companies who focused on measurement-management were identified as industry leaders, had financial performance that put them in the top third of their industry and were more successful at implementing and managing major change initiatives.[83] This study suggests that concern for measurement enhanced these organisations' learning capabilities.

Ernst & Young is a good example of a company that used several of the listed facilitating factors to increase its learning capability:

TABLE 17.4 FACTORS THAT FACILITATE ORGANISATIONAL LEARNING CAPABILITIES

1 Scanning imperative	Interest in external happenings and in the nature of one's environment. Valuing the processes of awareness and data generation. Curious about what is 'out there' as opposed to 'in here'
2 Performance gap	Shared perception of a gap between actual and desired state of performance. Disconfirming feedback interrupts a string of successes. Performance shortfalls are seen as opportunities for learning
3 Concern for measurement	Spend considerable effort in defining and measuring key factors when venturing into new areas; strive for specific, quantifiable measures; discourse over metrics is seen as a learning activity
4 Experimental mindset	Support for trying new things; curiosity about how things work; ability to 'play' with things. Small failures are encouraged, not punished. See changes in work processes, policies, and structures as a continuous series of graded tryouts
5 Climate of openness	Accessibility of information; relatively open boundaries. Opportunities to observe others; problems/errors are shared, not hidden; debate and conflict are acceptable
6 Continuous education	Ongoing commitment to education at all levels; support for growth and development of members
7 Operational variety	Variety exists in response modes, procedures, systems; significant diversity in personnel. Pluralistic rather than monolithic definition of valued internal capabilities
8 Multiple advocates	Top-down and bottom-up initiatives are possible; multiple advocates and gatekeepers exist
9 Involved leadership	Leadership at significant levels articulates vision and is very actively engaged in its actualisation; takes ongoing steps to implement vision; 'hands-on' involvement in educational and other implementation steps
10 Systems perspective	Strong focus on how parts of the organisation are interdependent; seek optimisation of organisational goals at the highest levels; see problems and solutions in terms of systemic relationships

SOURCE: Reprinted by permission of Sage Publications Ltd from B. Moingeon and A. Edmondson, in *Organizational Learning and Competitive Advantage* (Thousand Oaks, CA: Sage, © 1996), p. 43.

> Ernst & Young figures that its knowledge falls into three categories of 'content'. The first is benchmark data – studies, surveys, industry facts and figures. 'Each year we buy about $30 million of this stuff in the United States alone, so that's valuable right there', says Peetz [John Peetz is the chief knowledge officer]. 'The second content is point-to-point knowledge, which is people sharing what they know. And finally, we've got expert knowledge, or the best people in a given area who know how to solve specific problems.' To tie this together, Ernest & Young created 'power packs', or databases on specific business areas that employees load into laptops. These packs also contain contact information for the firm's network of subject experts. If a consultant runs into a glitch in a supply-chain management proposal, for example, he or she can instantly find and get help from Ernst & Young's most experienced supply-chain master.[84]

The literature on knowledge management focuses on the facilitating and impeding factor for knowledge sharing. Nonaka and Takeuchi mention the following conditions for knowledge sharing and creation:[85]

- Intention: clear goals and intention to evaluate the value of one's knowledge and to stimulate the creation of knowledge to achieve the goals (this is clearly a role for leaders and managers).
- Autonomy: freedom for individuals in the organisation to develop new knowledge, to experiment and to motivate employees.
- Fluctuation and creative chaos: making sure that there is enough change, interruptions in routines to make people work together and think of new solutions.
- Redundancy: excess information and duplication of information to allow people to understand the knowledge of others.
- Requisite variety: an internal structure that reflects the structure, variety and complexity of the environment.

LEARNING MODES

Learning modes, as shown in Figure 17.6, are directly influenced by an organisation's culture and experience or past history. Consider how the culture at Siemens Power Transmission and Distribution affected its learning modes:

Learning modes the various ways in which organisations attempt to create and maximise their learning

> Concerned that the company cafeteria was becoming a place for inappropriate socialising, management had walled off part of the room, believing that decreasing the cafeteria's size would make it less convenient for workers to linger there. 'It was exactly the wrong thing to do', says the training director. As it turned out, workers were using the cafeteria as a de facto meeting place where they could gather in a corner to discuss work issues (along with all the other things managers assumed they were talking about – cars, families, sports, etc.) .... 'By shrinking the size of the cafeteria, we're taking important space and time away from an informal learning opportunity.' Ironically, the company used the walled-off space for a conference room – one where meetings had to be scheduled in advance.[86]

This example illustrates at least two things: first, how Siemens' suspicious and low-trust culture detracted from the spontaneous learning that is critical within learning organisations, and second, when we reflect on the case study at the beginning of the chapter, how difficult it is for a large organisation to share best practices.

OB researcher, Danny Miller, reviewed the literature on organisational learning and identified six dominant modes of learning.[87] These are listed in Table 17.5.

Researchers suspect there is some type of optimal matching between the facilitating factors and learning modes that affects learning capability.[88] For example, the facilitating factor of an 'experimental mindset' should enhance the learning capability of a company that predominately uses the 'experimental learning' mode. In contrast, the inconsistency between an 'experimental mindset' and a 'structural learning' mode would be more likely to impede organisational learning. Consider once more the example of Ernst & Young:

TABLE 17.5 DOMINANT LEARNING MODES

1 Analytic learning	Learning occurs through systematic gathering of internal and external information. Information tends to be quantitative and analysed by means of formal systems. The emphasis is on using deductive logic to analyse objective data numerically
2 Synthetic learning	Synthetic learning is more intuitive and generic than the analytic mode. It emphasises the synthesis of large amounts of complex information by using systems thinking. That is, employees try to identify interrelationships between issues, problems and opportunities
3 Experimental learning	This mode is a rational methodological approach that is based on conducting small experiments and monitoring the results
4 Interactive learning	This mode involves learning-by-doing. Rather than using systematic methodological procedures, learning occurs primarily through the exchange of information. Learning is more intuitive and inductive
5 Structural learning	This mode is a methodological approach that is based on the use of organisational routines. These organisational routines represent standardised processes and procedures that specify how to carry out tasks and roles. People learn from routines because they direct attention, institutionalise standards and create consistent vocabularies
6 Institutional learning	This mode represents an inductive process by which organisations share model values, beliefs and practices either from their external environments or from senior executives. Employees learn by observing environmental examples or senior executives. Socialisation and mentoring play a significant role in institutional learning

> Some firms are learning. Among them is Ernst & Young, which has taken a lesson from the higher groves of academe. Like Oxbridge and Ivy League professors, its senior people are offered sabbaticals. Mark Jenner, a learning and development manager in the consultancy-services division, says: 'We compete on ideas, so we need to allow people creative white space. A sabbatical allows them to recharge their batteries, top up their knowledge and generate intellectual capital that we can use. It is also a way of retaining people. Consultants tell us that working on a long-term engagement is quite tough, and at the end many think, 'Do I stay for the next one or leave?'
>
> Andrew Holmes, a managing consultant, was chosen for a six-week sabbatical at Henley Management College, to work on his theory that sales could be improved if the firms' backgrounds and culture were taken into account more. He says: 'I have seen things go fundamentally wrong so many times because people behave in a way that is at odds with a company's culture.'[89]

The learning modes also determine to what extent knowledge sharing is possible. Cohen and Levinthal, for instance, were the first to study the importance of prior related knowledge for absorbing new knowledge. The receiving party needs prior related knowledge, including skills, shared language and specific knowledge.[90] Several other authors have emphasised the need for the two types of common knowledge. A common language is also very important in knowledge sharing.[91] Robert Grant recognises five conditions to make knowledge integration possible, most of which refer to the need for related knowledge.[92] These conditions are: common language, common symbols, a minimum of shared specific knowledge, shared meaning and knowledge about the content of each other's knowledge stock. However, probably the most important enabler for knowledge sharing is a culture of trust and spontaneous co-operation. People can be intrinsically or extrinsically motivated to co-operate and share their knowledge (see also Chapters 5 and 6). In the latter situation, financial or other material rewards are given to stimulate knowledge sharing. However, intrinsic motivation based on people identifying with the group or organisation, trust and a collaborative environment are much more effective in stimulating knowledge sharing.[93] A study by Karl-Erik Sveiby emphasised the importance of a collaborative climate for effective knowledge processes. Such climate was more readily found in private than in public organisations.[94]

In a study of knowledge enablers supporting the four phases of the SECI model, two researchers found that different organisational elements enabled different aspects of the model. The sharing of implicit knowledge (socialisation) is enabled by a culture of trust and strong collaboration, the availability of learning possibilities through training and job assignments and decentralisation allowing freedom for the employees. Trust, collaboration and decentralisation are also important for the externalisation of implicit knowledge. The combination of explicitly available knowledge also requires trust and an information technology structure to support the exchange of knowledge. Finally, the internalisation of explicit knowledge requires again collaboration and trust. Redundant information and knowledge to understand other's knowledge was of no importance in the SECI-knowledge model.[95] In another study, trust, job rotation, cultural integration between different groups and compatible information systems supporting communication were found as facilitating factors.[96]

> SCA Packaging, a European packaging company originating from Sweden, initiated a programme to share best production practices throughout West-Europe. A study of this best practice programme indicates that some transfers were less successful due to different aspects of motivation. First, the measurement of the effectiveness of knowledge sharing was misinterpreted as another control and performance measurement of management. Second, in less successful plants there were other priorities. Furthermore, the programme was initiated as a kind of competition between teams, which reduced motivation, again especially among the already weaker performing plants. Those plants were also less motivated to make their implicit knowledge explicit to share it with the other plants. Less motivated plants paid in general less attention to the sharing programme and involved fewer people in it. They were also less communicating about it.[97]

Organisations naturally resist learning and knowledge sharing

You may be wondering why any rational person or organisation would resist learning and knowledge sharing. It just does not make sense. Well, organisations do not consciously resist learning. They do it because of three fundamental problems that plague society at large: focusing on fragmentation rather than systems, emphasising competition over collaboration and a tendency to be reactive rather than proactive.[98] Neither do organisations deliberately create conditions that impede knowledge sharing. Overcoming these problems requires a fundamental shift in how we view the world.

FOCUSING ON FRAGMENTATION RATHER THAN SYSTEMS

Fragmentation involves the tendency to break down a problem, project or process into smaller pieces. For example, as students you are taught to memorise isolated facts, study abstract theories and learn ideas and concepts that bear no resemblance to your personal life experiences. This reinforces the use of an analytic strategy that entails solving complex problems by studying the components rather than the whole. Unfortunately, modern-day problems such as runaway healthcare costs and crime prevention cannot be solved with piecemeal linear approaches.

In organisations, fragmentation creates functional 'walls' or 'silos' that separate people into independent groups. This, in turn, creates specialists who work within specific functional areas. It also generates internal fiefdoms that battle over power, resources and control. Learning, sharing, co-operation, and collaboration are ultimately lost on the battlefield.

EMPHASISING COMPETITION OVER COLLABORATION

Competition is the dominant way of viewing our Western world and the way we work in organisations. Although nothing is intrinsically wrong with competition, it entails employees competing with the very people with whom they need to collaborate for success. Moreover, it creates an overemphasis on looking good rather than being good, which prohibits learning, because people become reluctant to admit when they do not know something. This is especially true of leaders. In turn, employees hesitate to accept tasks or assignments that they are not good at. Finally, competition produces a fixation on short-term measurable results rather than on long-term solutions to the root causes of problems. This competition is also a source of distrust. Trust is identified by many researchers as crucial in any kind of co-operation, hence, also in co-operation resulting in the creation of a learning organisation and the sharing, use and development of knowledge.[99]

BEING REACTIVE RATHER THAN CREATIVE AND PROACTIVE

People are accustomed to changing only when they need to, because life is less stressful and frustrating when we stay within our comfort zones. This contrasts with the fundamental catalyst of real learning. The drive to learn is fuelled by personal interest, curiosity, aspiration, imagination, experimentation and risk taking. The problem is that all of us have been conditioned to respond and react to others' directions and approval. This undermines the intrinsic drive to learn. When this tendency is coupled with management by fear, intimidation and crisis, people not only resist learning, they become paralysed by the fear of taking risks.

Leadership and culture are the key elements

There is hope! Effective leadership chisels away at these natural tendencies and paves the way for organisational learning and knowledge sharing (also see Chapter 11). Leaders can create an organisational culture that promotes systems thinking over fragmentation, collaboration and co-operation over competition and innovation and proaction over reactivity. Leaders must, however, adopt new roles and associated activities to create a learning organisation. They can have an impact on the existence of a collaborative culture facilitating learning and knowledge management processes. They are also crucial for

TABLE 17.6 LEADERSHIP ROLES AND ACTIVITIES FOR BUILDING A LEARNING ORGANISATION

Leadership activities	Role 1: Build a commitment to learning	Role 2: Work to generate ideas with impact	Role 3: Work to generalise ideas with impact
Make learning a component of the vision and strategic objectives	x		
Invest in learning	x		
Publicly promote the value of learning	x		
Measure, benchmark and track learning	x		
Create rewards and symbols of learning	x		
Implement continuous improvement programmes		x	
Increase employee competence through training, or buy talent from outside the organisation		x	
Experiment with new ideas, processes and structural arrangements		x	
Go outside the organisation to identify world-class ideas and processes		x	
Identify mental models of organisational processes		x	
Instil systems thinking throughout the organisation		x	
Create an infrastructure that moves ideas across organisational boundaries			x
Rotate employees across functional and divisional boundaries			x

SOURCE: Based in part on D. Ulrich, T. Jick and M. Von Glinow, 'High-Impact Learning: Building and Diffusing Learning Capability', *Organizational Dynamics*, Autumn 1993, pp. 52–66.

making those processes a priority in the organisation, clarifying the goals and directions, and for display-ing exemplary behaviour. Knowledge sharing can be part of the culture or can go against the existing culture. Culture is hard to change and only changes slowly (also see Chapter 16), but leaders are able to enhance a cultural changing process.

Specifically, leaders perform three key functions in building a learning organisation: building a commitment to learning, working to generate ideas with impact and working to generalise ideas with impact.[100] Table 17.6 contains a list of leadership activities needed to support each role.

BUILDING A COMMITMENT TO LEARNING

Leaders need to instil an intellectual and emotional commitment to learning by using the ideas shown in Table 17.6. For example, Harley Davidson has identified 'intellectual curiosity' as one of its core corporate values. Leaders can promote the value of learning by modelling the desired attitudes and behaviours. They can attend seminars as presenters or participants, share effective managerial practices with peers and disseminate readings, videos and other educational materials. Leaders also need to invest the financial resources needed to create a learning infrastructure. Consider the experience of the World Bank:

> The World Bank devotes approximately 4 per cent of its administrative budget to knowledge management. According to Stephen Denning, the former programme director of knowledge management at the World Bank, this percentage is at the lower end of corporate spending but represents a significant amount for his non-profit organisation. Senior leaders lend support to the initiative and provide the resources each of the bank's 20 sectors need to form local partnerships, provide ad hoc advice and disseminate knowledge.[101]

WORKING TO GENERATE IDEAS WITH IMPACT

Ideas with impact are those that add value to one or more of an organisation's three key stakeholders: employees, customers and shareholders. The leadership activities shown in Table 17.6 reveal six ways to generate ideas with impact.

WORKING TO GENERALISE IDEAS WITH IMPACT

Leaders must make a concerted effort to reduce interpersonal, group and organisational barriers to learning. This can be done by creating a learning infrastructure. This is a large-scale effort that includes the following activities:

- Measuring and rewarding learning.
- Increasing open and honest dialogue between organisational members.
- Reducing conflict.
- Increasing horizontal and vertical communication.
- Promoting teamwork.
- Rewarding risk taking and innovation.
- Reducing the fear of failure.
- Increasing the sharing of successes, failures and best practices across organisational members.
- Reducing stressors and frustration.
- Reducing internal competition.
- Increasing co-operation and collaboration.
- Creating a psychologically safe and comforting environment.[102]

UNLEARNING THE ORGANISATION

In addition to implementing the ideas listed in Table 17.6, organisations must concurrently 'forget' or 'unlearn' organisational practices and paradigms that made them successful. Quite simply, traditional organisations and the associated organisational behaviours they created have outlived their usefulness. Management must seriously question and challenge the ways of thinking that worked in the past if they want to create a learning organisation.[103] For example, the old management paradigm of plan-ning, organising and controlling might be replaced with one of vision, values and empowerment. The time has come for management and employees to think as owners, not as 'us' and 'them' adversaries.

Learning outcomes: Summary of key terms

1 Discuss the external and internal forces that create the need for organisational change

Organisations encounter both external and internal forces for change. There are four key external forces for change: demographic characteristics, technological advancements, market changes, and social and political pressures. Internal forces for change come from both human resource problems and managerial behaviour/decisions.

2 Describe Lewin's change model

Lewin developed a three-stage model of planned change that explained how to initiate, manage and stabilise the change process. The three states were unfreezing, which entails creating the motivation to change, changing and stabilising change through refreezing.

3 Discuss Theory E and O in the six dimensions of change

Theory E is oriented towards maximising shareholder value. It is a top-driven approach that focuses on the organisational structures and systems. At the beginning of the change, plans are drawn up to direct the change in a specific way. Change is motivated through financial incentives and consultants play a major role in analysing the problems. The goal of Theory O is to develop organisational capabilities. It encourages participation from the bottom-up and it is focused at employees' behaviour and attitudes. Financial incentives are an unimportant driver of the change and the consultants' contribution is limited to supporting management in shaping their own solutions.

4 Demonstrate your familiarity with the four identifying characteristics of organisation development (OD)

The identifying characteristics of OD are that it: involves profound change, is value loaded, is a cycle of diagnosis and prescription and is process oriented.

5 Discuss the ten reasons employees resist change

Resistance to change is an emotional/behavioural response to real or imagined threats to an established work routine. Ten reasons employees resist change are (a) an individual's predisposition toward change, (b) surprise and fear of the unknown, (c) climate of mistrust, (d) fear of failure, (e) loss of status or job security, (f) peer pressure, (g) disruption of cultural traditions and/or group relationships, (h) personality conflicts, (i) lack of tact or poor timing and (j) nonreinforcing reward systems.

6 Identify alternative strategies for overcoming resistance to change

Organisations must be ready for change. Assuming an organisation is ready for change, the alternative strategies for overcoming resistance to change are education + communication, participation + involvement, facilitation + support, negotiation + agreement, manipulation + co-optation and explicit + implicit coercion. Each has its situational appropriateness, advantages and drawbacks.

7 Explain the concepts learning organisation and knowledge management

A learning organisation is one that proactively creates, acquires and transfers knowledge and changes its behaviour on the basis of new knowledge and insights. Knowledge management is the management of information, knowledge and experience available to an organisation, its creation, capture, storage, availability and utilisation, so that organisational activities build on what is already known and extend it further. The two concepts are interrelated. Knowledge management supports the creation of a learning organisation oriented towards adaptation to the environment.

8 Discuss the process by which organisations build their learning capabilities

Learning capabilities represent the set of core competencies and processes that enable an organisation to adapt to its environment. Learning capabilities are directly affected by organisa-

tional facilitating factors and l
ture and processes that either
modes represent the various wa
learning. Researchers believe th
ing factors and learning modes th

9 Review the reasons organisatic
There are three underlying reasor
rather than systems. Fragmentatio
process into smaller pieces. It rein
rather than the whole. A dominant
collaboration is the second reason.
that people have a tendency to be r
stems from the fact that all of us hav
tions and approval.

10 Discuss the role of leadership in cre
Leaders perform three key functions in l
to learning, working to generate ideas w
There are 13 different leadership activities

section 4 organisational processes

Instructions
First, think of a time in which a previous or c
that required you to learn something new c
practice. Next, evaluate survey it
agree with the following survey ite
behavioural support for the chan

1 = Strongly disagree
2 = Disagree agree n
3 = Neither agree n
4 = Agree
5 = Strongly a

1 I beli
2 Th
3

Review questions

1 Which of the external forces for cha   .ie greatest
  change between now and the year 2020

2 Have you worked in an organisation wh ..ernal forces created change? Describe
  the situation and the resulting change.

3 How would you respond to a manager who made the following statement: 'Unfreezing is not important, employees will follow my directives'?

4 What are some useful methods that can be used to refreeze an organisational change?

5 Give examples of the way in which Theory E and O can be combined for each of the
  six dimensions of change.

6 Have you ever resisted a change at work? Explain the circumstances and your thinking at the time.

7 Which source of resistance to change do you think is the most common? Which is the
  most difficult for management to deal with?

8 Does the company you work for act like a learning organisation? Explain your rationale.

9 Which of the three reasons for organisations' natural resistance to learning is the
  most powerful? Explain.

Personal awareness and growth exercise

Does your commitment to a change initiative predict your behavioural support for the change?

Objectives

A recent series of studies showed that an employee's commitment to change was a significant and positive predictor of behavioural support for a change initiative. In order to bring this concept to life, we would like you to complete a shortened version of a commitment to change instrument.[104]

...rrent employer was undergoing a change initiative
... to discontinue an attitude, behaviour or organisational
... to this change effort by indicating the extent to which you
... ms (use the rating scale shown below). Finally, assess your
... ge.

... disagree

... agree

...ve in the value of this change.	1	2	3	4	5
...is change serves an important purpose.	1	2	3	4	5
This change is a good strategy for the organisation.	1	2	3	4	5
4 I have no choice than to go along with this change.	1	2	3	4	5
5 It would be risky to speak out against this change.	1	2	3	4	5
6 It would be too costly for me to resist this change.	1	2	3	4	5
7 I feel a sense of duty to work toward this change.	1	2	3	4	5
8 It would be irresponsible of me to resist this change.	1	2	3	4	5
9 I feel obliged to support this change.	1	2	3	4	5

Total Score = _____

Arbitrary norms
9–18 = Low commitment
19–35 = Moderate commitment
36–45 = High commitment

Behavioural support for the change
Overall, I modified my attitudes and behaviour in line with what management
was trying to accomplish.   1 2 3 4 5

Questions for discussion
1 Were you committed to the change? Why or why not?
2 Did this level of commitment affect your behavioural support for what management was trying to
accomplish?

Group exercise

Creating personal change through a force-field analysis
Objectives
1 To apply force-field analysis to a behaviour or situation you would like to change.
2 To receive feedback on your strategies for bringing about change.

Introduction
The theory of force-field analysis is based on the premise that people resist change because of
counteracting positive and negative forces. Positive forces for change are called *thrusters*. They
propel people to accept change and modify their behaviour. In contrast, *counterthrusters* or *resistors*
are negative forces that motivate an individual to maintain the status quo. People frequently fail to
change because they experience equal amounts of positive and negative forces to change.

Force-field analysis is a technique used to facilitate change by first identifying the thrusters
and resistors that exist in a specific situation. To minimise resistance to change, it is generally

recommended to first reduce or remove the negative forces to change. Removing counterthrusters should create increased pressure for an individual to change in the desired direction. Managers can also further increase motivation to change by following up the reduction of resistors with an increase in the number of positive thrusters of change.

Instructions

Your lecturer will pair you up with another student. The two of you will serve as a team that evaluates the completeness of each other's force-field analysis and recommendations. Once the team is assembled, each individual should independently complete the force-field analysis form below. Once both of you complete this activity, one team member should present results from steps 2 to 5 from the five-step Force-Field Analysis Form. The partner should then evaluate the results by considering the following questions with his or her team member.

1 Are there any additional thrusters and counterthrusters that should be listed? Add them to the list.
2 Do you agree with the 'strength' evaluations of thrusters and counterthrusters in step 4? Ask your partner to share his or her rationale for the ratings. Modify the ratings as needed.
3 Examine the specific recommendations for change listed in step 5, and evaluate whether you think they will produce the desired changes. Be sure to consider whether the focal person has the ability to eliminate, reduce or increase each thruster and counterthruster that forms the basis of a specific recommendation. Are there any alternative strategies you can think of?
4 What is your overall evaluation of your partner's intervention strategy?

Force-field analysis form[105]

Step 1
In the space provided, please identify a number of personal problems you would like to solve or aspects of your life you would like to change. Be as imaginative as possible. You are not limited to academic situations. For example, you may want to consider your work environment if you are currently employed, family situation, interpersonal relationships, club situations and so forth. It is important that you select some aspects of your life that you would like to change but until now have made no effort to.

Step 2
Review in your mind the problems or aspects listed in step 1. Now select one that you would really like to change and which you believe lends itself easily to force-field analysis. Select one that you will feel comfortable talking about to other people.

Step 3
On the form following step 4, indicate existing forces that are pushing you in the direction of change. Thrusters may be forces internal to you (pride, regret, fear) or they may be external to yourself (friends, the boss, a lecturer). Also list existing forces that are preventing you from changing. Again, the counterthruster may be internal to yourself (uncertainty, fear) or external (poor instruction, limited resources, lack of support mechanisms).

Step 4
In the space to the right of your list of thrusters and counterthrusters indicate their relative strength. For consistency, use a scale of 1 to 10, with 1 indicating a weak force and 10 indicating a high force.

Thrusters	Strength
_____	_____
_____	_____
_____	_____
_____	_____
_____	_____
_____	_____
_____	_____

Counterthrusters	Strength
_____	_____
_____	_____
_____	_____
_____	_____
_____	_____

Step 5

Analyse your thrusters and counterthrusters, and develop a strategy for bringing about the desired change. Remember that it is possible to produce the desired result by strengthening existing thrusters, introducing new thrusters, weakening or removing counterthrusters, or some combination of these. Consider the impact of your change strategy on the system's internal stress (i.e. on yourself and others), the likelihood of success, the availability of resources, and the long-term consequences of planned changes. Be prepared to discuss your recommendations with the partner in your group.

Questions for discussion

1 What was your reaction to doing a force-field analysis? Was it insightful and helpful?
2 Was it valuable to receive feedback about your force-field analysis from a partner? Explain.
3 How would you assess the probability of effectively implementing your recommendations?

Internet exercise

In this chapter we reviewed several models of organisational change. Because these models are based on different sets of assumptions, each one offers managers a unique set of recommendations for how organisational change should be implemented. We also discussed a variety of recommendations for how managers might better implement organisational change. The purpose of this exercise is for you to expand your knowledge about how organisations should implement organisational change. Go to our website www.mcgraw-hill.co.uk/textbooks/buelens for further instructions.

Notes

1 C. Kennedy, 'The Roadmap to Success: How Gerard Schulmeyer Changed the Culture at Siemens Nixdorf', *Long Range Planning*, April 1998, pp. 262–71. © 1998, with permission from Elsevier Science.
2 These statistics were taken from J. A. Lopez, 'Corporate Change: You Can Count on It', *The Arizona Republic*, 3 March 1996, pp. D1, D3; and J. J. Laabs, 'Expert Advice on How to Move Forward with Change', *Personnel Journal*, July 1996, pp. 54–63.
3 M. Coles, 'Consultants Learn to Achieve Results', the *Sunday Times*, 6 August 2000.
4 P. Scott Morgan, *The Unwritten Rules of the Game* (New York: McGraw-Hill, 1994).
5 A. M. Webber, 'Learning for a Change', *Fast Company*, May 1999, p. 180.
6 K. Capell, 'Virgin Takes E-wing', *Business Week*, 22 January 2001.
7 J. Rossant, 'Fiat-GM: The Agnellis Face Reality', *Business Week*, 27 March 2000.
8 For a thorough discussion of the model, see K. Lewin, *Field Theory in Social Science* (New York: Harper & Row, 1951).
9 These assumptions are discussed in E. H. Schein, *Organizational Psychology, third edition* (Englewood Cliffs, NJ: Prentice-Hall, 1980).
10 C. Goldwasser, 'Benchmarking: People Make the Process', *Management Review*, June 1995, p. 40.
11 Benchmark data for 'America's Best Plants' can be found in J. H. Sheridan, 'Lessons from the Best', *Industry Week*, February 1996, pp. 13–20.
12 Top management's role in implementing change according to Lewin's model is discussed by E. H. Schein, 'The Role of the CEO in the Management of Change: The Case of Information Technology', in *Transforming Organizations*, eds T. A. Kochan and M. Useem (New York: Oxford University Press, 1992), pp. 80–95.

13 This three-way typology of change was adapted from discussion in P. C. Nutt, 'Tactics of Implementation', *Academy of Management Journal*, June 1986, pp. 230–61.

14 M. Beer and N. Nohria, *Breaking the Code of Change* (Boston, MA: Harvard Business School Press, 2000).

15 K. Weick, 'Emergent Change as a Universal in Organisations', in *Breaking the Code of Change*, eds M. Beer and N. Nohria (Boston, MA: Harvard Business School Press, 2000).

16 Exerpted from M. Beer and N. Nohria, 'Cracking the Code of Change', *Harvard Business Review*, May–June 2000, pp. 133–41.

17 J. J. Boonstra, *Lopen over water* (Amsterdam: Vossiuspers AUP, 2000).

18 These errors are discussed by J. P. Kotter, 'Leading Change: The Eight Steps to Transformation', in *The Leader's Change Handbook*, eds J. A. Conger, G. M. Spreitzer and E. E. Lawler III (San Francisco, CA: Jossey-Bass Business and Management Series 1999), pp. 87–99.

19 The type of leadership needed during organisational change is discussed by J. P. Kotter, *Leading Change* (Boston, MA: Harvard Business School Press, 1996); and B. Ettorre, 'Making Change', *Management Review*, January 1996, pp. 13–18.

20 K. Weick, 'Emergent Change as a Universal in Organizations', in *Breaking the Code of Change*, eds M. Beer and N. Nohria (Boston, MA: Harvard Business School Press, 2000).

21 M. Beer and E. Walton, 'Developing the Competitive Organization: Interventions and Strategies', *American Psychologist*, February 1990, p. 154.

22 T. M. Egan, 'Organization Development: An Examination of Definitions and Dependent Variables', *Organization Development Journal*, Summer 2002, pp. 59–69.

23 An historical overview of the field of OD can be found in N. A. M. Worren, K. Ruddle and K. Moore, 'From Organisational Development to Change Management', *Journal of Applied Behavioral Science*, September 1999, pp. 273–86; and A. H. Church, J. Wazclawski and W. Siegal, 'Will the Real OD Practitioner Please Stand Up? A Call for Change in the Field', *Organization Development Journal*, Summer 1999, pp. 49–59.

24 W. W. Burke, *Organization Development: A Normative View* (Reading, MA: Addison-Wesley Publishing, 1987), p. 9.

25 M. F. Kets De Vries and K. Balazs, 'Transforming the Mind-Set of the Organization: A Clinical Perspective', *Administration & Society*, January 1999, pp. 640–75.

26 An example of using employee surveys to conduct OD is provided by B. Schneider, S. D. Ashworth, A. C. Higgs and L. Carr, 'Design, Validity, and Use of Strategically Focused Employee Attitude Surveys', *Personnel Psychology*, Autumn 1996, pp. 695–705.

27 See R. Rodgers, J. E. Hunter and D. L. Rogers, 'Influence of Top Management Commitment on Management Program Success', *Journal of Applied Psychology*, February 1993, pp. 151–5.

28 Results can be found in P. J. Robertson, D. R. Roberts and J. I. Porras, 'Dynamics of Planned Organizational Change: Assessing Empirical Support for a Theoretical Model', *Academy of Management Journal*, June 1993, pp. 619–34.

29 Results from the meta-analysis can be found in G. A. Neuman, J. E. Edwards and N. S. Raju, 'Organizational Development Interventions: A Meta-Analysis of Their Effects on Satisfaction and Other Attitudes', *Personnel Psychology*, Autumn 1989, pp. 461–90.

30 The importance of results-oriented change efforts is discussed by R. J. Schaffer and H. A. Thomson, 'Successful Change Programs Begin with Results', *Harvard Business Review*, January–February 1992, pp. 80–89.

31 See the related discussion in D. M. Schneider and C. Goldwasser, 'Be a Model Leader of Change: Here's How to Get the Results You Want from the Change You're Leading', *Management Review*, March 1998, pp. 41–5.

32 A. A. Armenakis and A. G. Bedeian, 'Organizational Change: A Review of Theory and Research in the 1990s', *Journal of Management*, no. 3, 1999, pp. 293–315.

33 A. M. Pettigrew, R. W. Woodman and K. S. Cameron, 'Studying Organizational Change and Development: Challenges for Future Research', *Academy of Management Journal*, August 2001, pp. 697–713.

34 A. M. Pettigrew and R. Whipp, *Managing Change for Competitive Success* (Oxford: Blackwell Publishing, 1999).

35 K. E. Weick and R. E. Quinn, 'Organizational Change and Development', in *Annual Review of Psychology*, eds J. T. Spence, J. M. Darley and D. J. Foss (Palo Alto, CA: Annual Reviews, 1999), pp. 361–86.

36 J. P. Wanous, A. E. Reichers and J. T. Austin, 'Cynicism about Organizational Change. Measurements, Antecedents and Correlates', *Group & Organization Management*, June 2000, pp. 132–53.

37 J. M. Peiro, V. Gonzalez-Roma and J. Canero, 'Survey Feedback as a Tool Changing Managerial Culture: Focusing on Users' Interpretations – A Case Study', *European Journal of Work and Organizational Psychology*, no. 4, 1999, pp. 537–50.

38 Adapted in part from B. W. Armentrout, 'Have Your Plans for Change Had a Change of Plan?' *HR FOCUS*, January 1996, p. 19; and A. S. Judson, *Changing Behavior in Organizations: Minimizing Resistance to Change* (Oxford: Blackwell Publishing, 1991).

39 See Basic Behavioral Science Task Force of the National Advisory Mental Health Council, 'Basic Behavioral Science Research for Mental Health: Vulnerability and Resilience', *American Psychologist*, January 1996, pp. 22–8.

40 Excerpted from C. Joinson, 'Moving at the Speed of Dell', *HR Magazine*, April 1999, p. 52.

41 See R. Moss Kanter, 'Managing Traumatic Change: Avoiding the "Unlucky 13"', *Management Review*, May 1987, pp. 23–4.

42 D. Butcher and S. Atkinson, 'Upwardly Mobilized', *People Management*, 14 January 1999.

43 D. Buchanan, T. Claydon and M. Doyle, 'Organization Development and Change: The Legacy of the Nineties', *Human Resource Management Journal*, no. 2, 1999, pp. 20–38.

44 See L. Coch and J. R. P. French, Jr, 'Overcoming Resistance to Change', *Human Relations*, 1948, pp. 512–32.

45 For a thorough review of the role of participation in organisational change, see W. A. Pasmore and M. R. Fagans, 'Participation, Individual Development, and Organizational Change: A Review and Synthesis', *Journal of Management*, June 1992, pp. 375–97.

46 Results from this study can be found in T. A. Judge, C. J. Thoresen, V. Pucik and T. W. Welbourne, 'Managerial Coping with Organisational Change: A Dispositional Perspective', *Journal of Applied Psychology*, February 1999, pp. 107–22.

47 L. Morris, 'Research Capsules', *Training & Development*, April 1992, pp. 74–6; and T. Hill, N. D. Smith and M. F. Mann, 'Role of Efficacy Expectations in Predicting the Decision to Use Advanced Technologies: The Case of Computers', *Journal of Applied Psychology*, May 1987, pp. 307–14.

48 Results can be found in C.-M. Lau and R. W. Woodman, 'Understanding Organizational Change: A Schematic Perspective', *Academy of Management Journal*, April 1995, pp. 537–54.

49 See the related discussion in E. B. Dent and S. G. Goldberg, 'Challenging "Resistance to Change"', *Journal of Applied Behavioral Science*, March 1999, pp. 25–41.

50 J. P. Kotter, 'Leading Change: Why Transformation Efforts Fail', *Harvard Business Review*, 1995, p. 64.

51 See E. B. Dent and S. G. Goldberg, 'Challenging "Resistance to Change"', *Journal of Applied Behavioral Science*, March 1999, pp. 25–41, J. Krantz, 'Comment on "Challenging Resistance to Change"', *Journal of Applied Behavioral Science*, March 1999, pp. 42–4; and E. B. Dent and S. G. Goldberg, '"Resistance to Change": A Limiting Perspective', *Journal of Applied Behavioral Science*, March 1999, pp. 45–7.

52 G. Tregunno, 'Changing Routes at Boehringer Ingelheim', *People Management*, 8 April 1999.

53 Readiness for change is discussed by B. Trahant and W. W. Burke, 'Traveling through Transitions', *Training & Development*, February 1996, pp. 37–41.

54 E. E. Metselaar, *Assessing the Willingness to Change; Construction and Validation of the DINAMO* (Amsterdam: Vrije Universiteit Amsterdam, 1997).

55 For a discussion of how managers can reduce resistance to change by providing different explanations for an organisational change, see D. M. Rousseau and S. A. Tijoriwala, 'What's a Good Reason to Change? Motivated Reasoning and Social Accounts in Promoting Organizational Change', *Journal of Applied Psychology*, August 1999, pp. 514–28.

56 T. Petzinger, Jr, 'The Front Lines: Georg Bauer Put Burden of Downsizing into Employees' Hands', the *Wall Street Journal*, 10 May 1996, p. B1.

57 T. Petzinger, Jr, 'The Front Lines: Georg Bauer Put Burden of Downsizing into Employees' Hands', the *Wall Street Journal*, 10 May 1996, p. B1.

58 Additional strategies for managing resistance are discussed by T. J. Galpin, *The Human Side of Change: A Practical Guide to Organizational Redesign* (San Francisco, CA: Jossey-Bass, 1996); and D. May and M. Kettelhut, 'Managing Human Issues in Reengineering Projects', *Journal of Systems Management*, January–February 1996, pp. 4–11.

59 See L. Baird, P. Holland and S. Deacon, 'Learning from Action: Imbedding More Learning into the Performance Fast Enough to Make a Difference', *Organizational Dynamics*, Spring 1999, pp. 19–32; and K. Kuwada, 'Strategic Learning: The Continuous Side of Discontinuous Strategic Change', *Organization Science*, November–December 1998, pp. 719–36.

60 R. M. Fulmer and J. B. Keys, 'A Conversation with Peter Senge: New Development in Organisational Learning', *Organizational Dynamics*, Autumn 1998, p. 35.

61 B. Hedberg, 'How Organizations Learn and Unlearn', in *Handbook of Organizational Design*, eds P. C. Nystrom and W. H. Starbuck (New York: Oxford University Press, 1981), pp. 3–27.

62 C. Argyris and D. A. Schon, 'Organizational Learning II', in *Organizational Development Series*, eds E. D. Schein and R. Beckhardt (Reading, MA: Addison-Wesley Publishing Company, 1996).

63 B. Elkjaer, 'Social Learning Theory: Learning as Participation in Social Processes', in *Handbook of Organisational Learning and Knowledge Management*, eds M. Easterby-Smith and M. Lyles (Oxford: Blackwell Publishing, 2003), pp. 38–53.

64 B. Hedberg, 'How Organisations Learn and Unlearn', in *Handbook of Organizational Design*, eds P. C. Nystrom and W. H. Starbuck (New York: Oxford University Press, 1981), pp. 3–27.

65 D. H. Kim, 'The Link between Individual and Organizational Learning', *Sloan Management Review*, Fall 1993, pp. 37–50.

66 Translated from M. Huysman and R. van der Vlist, 'Naar een "Organizational Learning" – benadering van de lerende organisatie', *Gedrag & Organisatie*, no. 11, 1989, pp. 219–31.

67 This definition was based on D. A. Garvin, 'Building a Learning Organization', *Harvard Business Review*, July–August 1993, pp. 78–91.

68 A. Mayo, 'Memory Bankers', *People Management*, January 1989, pp. 34–8.

69 M. N. Martinez, 'The Collective Power of Employee Knowledge', *HR Magazine*, February 1998, pp. 88–94; and M. N. Martinez, 'The Collective Power of Employee Knowledge', in *The Knowledge Management Yearbook 1999–2000*, eds J. W. Contada and J. A. Woods (Boston, MA: Butterworth-Heinemann, 1999), pp. 319–25.

70 Translated from M. Weggeman, *Kennismanagement: Inrichting en besturing van kennisintensieve organisaties*, *second edition* (Tielt: Uitgeverij Lannoo, 1989).

71 E. Sketch, 'Learning with Lasting Impact at Ford', *Knowledge Management Review*, March–April 2003, pp. 20–23.

72 For an in-depth analysis of the differences and similarities between knowledge management, learning organisation and organisational learning, see D. Vera and M. Crossan, 'Organisational Learning and Knowledge Management: Towards an Integrative Framework', in *Handbook of Organisational Learning and Knowledge Management*, eds M. Easterby-Smith and M. J. Lyles (Oxford: Blackwell Publishing, 2003), pp. 122–41.

73 D. A. Levinthal and J. G. March, 'The Myopia of Learning', *Strategic Management Journal*, January 1993, pp. 95–112; and J. G. March, 'Exploration and Exploitation in Organization Learning', *Organization Science*, March–April 1991, pp. 71–87.

74 I. Gogus, 'Becoming a Learning Organization at Oracle', *Knowledge Management Review*, September–October 2003, pp. 12–15.

75 Organisational learning is discussed by A. Edmondson and B. Moingeon, 'From Organizational Learning to the Learning Organization', *Management Learning*, no. 1, 1998, pp. 5–20; and K. Maani and C. Benton, 'Rapid Team Learning: Lessons from Team New Zealand America's Cup Campaign', *Organizational Dynamics*, Spring 1999, pp. 48–62. Knowledge management conditions are outlined in T. H. Davenport and L. Prusak, *Working Knowledge* (Boston, MA: Harvard Business School Press, 1989); K. Wiig, *Knowledge Management Foundation: Thinking about Thinking* (Arlington, TX: Schema Press, 1993); K. E. Sveiby, *Kennis als bedrijfskapitaal* (Amsterdam: Contact, 1998); and H. Scarbrough, 'Why Your Employees Don't Share What They Know', *Knowledge Management Review*, May–June 2003, pp. 16–19.

76 N. Argyres and D. A. Schön, *Organizational Learning: A Theory of Action Perspective* (Reading, MA: Addison-Wesley, 1978).

77 Translated from M. Huysman and R. van der Vlist, 'Naar een "Organisational Learning" – benadering van de lerende organisatie', *Gedrag & Organisatie*, no. 11, 1989, pp. 219–31.

78 I. Nonaka and H. Takeuchi, *The Knowledge-Creating Company* (Oxford: Oxford University Press, 1995).

79 Such as A. De Geus, *The Living Company* (London: Nicholas Brealey Publishing, 1997); and M. E. McGill and J. W. Slocum, *The Smarter Organization* (New York: John Wiley, 1994).

80 A discussion of learning capabilities and core competencies is provided by W. Miller, 'Building the Ultimate Resource', *Management Review*, January 1999, pp. 42–5; and C. Long and M. Vickers-Koch, 'Using Core Capabilities to Create Competitive Advantage', *Organizational Dynamics*, Summer 1995, pp. 7–22.

81 The relationship between organisational learning and various effectiveness criteria is discussed by S. F. Slater and J. C. Narver, 'Market Orientation and the Learning Organization', *Journal of Marketing*, July 1995, pp. 63–74.

82 A. J. DiBella, E. C. Nevis and J. M. Gould, 'Organizational Learning Style as a Core Capability', in *Organisational Learning and Competitive Advantage*, eds B. Moingeon and A. Edmondson (Thousand Oaks, CA: Sage, 1996), pp. 41–2.

83 Details of this study can be found in J. H. Lingle and W. A. Schiemann, 'From Balanced Scorecard to Strategic Gauges: Is Measurement Worth It?', *American Management Association*, March 1996, pp. 56–61.

84 Excerpted from J. Stuller, 'Chief of Corporate Smarts', *Training*, April 1998, p. 32.

85 I. Nonaka and H. Takeuchi, *The Knowledge-Creating Company* (Oxford: Oxford University Press, 1995).

86 Excerpted from D. Stamps, 'Learning Ecologies', *Training*, January 1998, p. 35.

87 This discussion and definitions are based on D. Miller, 'A Preliminary Typology of Organisational Learning: Synthesizing the Literature', *Journal of Management*, Fall 1996, pp. 485–505.

88 See the related discussion in A. J. DiBella, E. C. Nevis and J. M. Gould, 'Organizational Learning Style as a Core Capability', in *Organizational Learning and Competitive Advantage*, eds B. Moingeon and A. Edmondson (Thousand Oaks, CA: Sage, 1996), pp. 41–2.

89 M. Coles, 'Creativity Breaks Refresh Executives', the *Sunday Times*, 12 March 2000.

90 D. Cohen and D. A. Levinthal, 'Absorptive Capacity: A New Perspective on Learning and Innovation', *Administrative Science Quarterly*, March 1990, pp. 129–52.

91 G. von Krogh, J. Roos and K. Slocum, 'An Essay on Corporate Epistemology', *Strategic Management Journal*, Summer 1994, pp. 53–71.

92 R. M. Grant, 'Prospering in Dynamically-Competitive Environments: Organizational Capability as Knowledge Integration', *Organization Science*, no. 4, 1996, pp. 375–87.

93 For more on intrinsic motivation for knowledge sharing, see P. A. W. Käser and R. E. Miles, 'Understanding Knowledge Activists' Success and Failure?', *Long Range Planning*, February 2002, pp. 9–28; A. Cabrera and E. F. Cabrera, 'Knowledge-Sharing Dilemmas', *Organization Studies*, September–October 2002, pp. 687–710; and M. Osterloh and B. S. Frey, 'Motivation, Knowledge Transfer, and Organizational Forms', *Organization Science*, September–October 2000, pp. 538–50.

94 K.-E. Sveiby and R. Simons, 'Collaborative Climate and Effectiveness of Knowledge Work: An Empirical Study', *Journal of Knowledge Management*, July 2002, pp. 420–33.

95 Heeseok Lee and Byounggu Choi, 'Knowledge Management Enablers, Processes, and Organizational Performance: An Integrative View and Empirical Examination', *Journal of Management Information Systems*, Summer 2003, pp. 1179–228.

His company became one of Europe's most respected, lauded in a 1998 book called *ABB, The Dancing Giant*. Management experts said ABB showed how big corporations could cope with the complexities of global operations while keeping close ties to local markets.

For some time, Percy Barnevik has used his status as Europe's most admired manager to preach the gospel of good corporate governance. That's why his many admirers were so shocked when Mr Barnevik was tripped up by independent-minded outside directors of ABB Ltd., the Zurich-based industrial giant that he dominated for more than a decade. Led by one combative director, the board mounted an investigation and learned how a private agreement with a former co-chairman had allowed Mr Barnevik to pocket a tax-free, lump-sum pension worth $87 million when he stepped down as chief executive in 1996. The payout, while not extraordinary for a top US executive these days, was huge by European standards. But what angered directors most was that the payment came without their knowledge and that Mr Barnevik had dodged their questions about it while he continued to serve as chairman.

Faced with dwindling support on the board, Mr Barnevik resigned as ABB's chairman in November. The reasons for the abrupt departure became clear when ABB disclosed the dispute over his pension. At a stroke, the news destroyed the 61-year-old Mr Barnevik's long-standing reputation as a visionary executive who was Europe's version of Jack Welch.

The basis for Mr Barnevik's pension was a 1992 letter signed by Peter Wallenberg, who at the time was an ABB co-chairman. The letter laid out a general guideline for calculating Mr Barnevik's retirement pay, pegging his annual pension at 50 per cent of his base salary and bonuses. The bonus level had no cap, ABB officials say, and several good years in the mid-1990s drove up the payout. Mr Barnevik chose to receive a lump-sum payment rather than annual ones. He moved to London after retirement, with the result that neither Switzerland nor Britain taxed the payment. ABB directors fault Mr Barnevik for not presenting his pension package to the board for approval, especially given its huge size. They argue that such approval is part of the system of checks and balances that are normal for a major corporation. They also say he should have asked the board to review the pension of Mr Lindahl, his successor as CEO. At the end of a board meeting on 4 and 5 October 2001 Mr Barnevik gave full details of Mr Lindahl's package, totalling 85 million Swiss francs, or $50 million. 'It hit like a bombshell', says one person who attended the meeting. 'Nobody expected that much.' Then, at an emergency ABB board meeting on 21 November 2001 Mr Barnevik stood before fellow directors to say that he bore part of the responsibility for ABB's weak performance in recent years. He resigned and walked out the door. At that same meeting, directors got a report on Mr Barnevik's pension. They were shocked by the amount and considered informing shareholders immediately, but ultimately decided to get a legal expert to review the case first. On 13 February 2002, Mr Barnevik's birthday, the company made the dispute public. A news release disclosed Mr Barnevik's and Mr Lindahl's giant pension packages. The terse statement said ABB's board had determined that approval procedures for them had been unsatisfactory, and that ABB would 'seek restitution of amounts paid in excess of its obligations'. Lawyers for all sides are negotiating, and a settlement may be reached soon. Meanwhile, Swiss tax authorities are investigating, focusing on whether all of the money the executives received really qualified as pension, or whether some should be considered taxable income. People inside the sprawling industrial company were incredulous. To many executives and employees Mr Barnevik was an almost godlike figure whose integrity was unquestionable. 'I worked with the guy for 23 years', says Mr Centerman, whom Mr Barnevik had picked as chief executive after Mr Lindahl left. 'I'm just flabbergasted.' Former co-workers still marvel at the charismatic Mr Barnevik's intellect and his knack for managing people, listening to their ideas and motivating them to achieve tough goals. 'He was very effective', says Thord Widin, a senior official in a union representing white-collar workers at ABB in Sweden. 'He works very hard and for us in the union he was very good to talk to. He wanted to know what we thought of his ideas.' Now, his admirers will find it hard to repair his reputation, even if he ends up returning part of the pension. 'He's had 20 years to be a very successful manager,' says Mr Widin, 'and then to leave the arena in this way, it's very sad, I must say. Because this is the way Percy will be remembered.'

Shortly after he resigned, Mr Barnevik spoke with the Swedish daily *Dagens Nyheter*, and said his greatest regret about his pension arrangement – in which there are no allegations of any illegality – was that it wasn't detailed in ABB's annual report. 'I know that I did an honest and straightforward job and I followed the contract … so I have my pride intact', he said. He described his retirement deal as 'an American payment system in a European environment'.[1]

For discussion
Should CEO's from large companies disclose their wage and pension pay to company stakeholders?

The personal greed of many CEOs like Percy Barnevik, Jack Welch (General Electric, USA), Jean-Marie Messier (Vivendi Universal, France), Jo Lernout and Paul Hauspie (Lernout & Hauspie, Belgium), and many others has led to a feeling of disbelief in the business community. A survey conducted by *Business Week* among CEOs displayed the excessive paychecks top executives received in 2003.[2] The top earner was Reuben Mark from Colgate-Palmolive earning 141.1 million US dollars, followed at large distance by Steven Jobs (Apple Computer) and George David (United Technologies) earning respectively the considerable amount of $74.8 million and $70.5 million.

The scandal at the Texan energy giant Enron was the lift-off for asking questions about the integrity and trustworthiness of the business world at large.[3] It is almost impossible to believe that the four core values constituting the mission statement of Enron were respect, integrity, communication and excellence. However, it should be mentioned that the firm succeeded in fulfilling one core value: to excel in incomprehensible accountancy practices. Shortly after the Enron debacle, scandals at Worldcom, General Electric, Lernout & Hauspie, Swissair, etc. originated in the business landscape and shook the corporate world to its foundations.

Consequently, this major shock in the corporate world and especially in America was the signal to think about the ethics and values on which businesses were founded. *Business Week* said that companies were scrambling aboard the reform bandwagon. This need for reform was highlighted at the Malcolm Baldrige National Quality Award 2001 ceremony, when President Bush called for a renewed sense of corporate responsibility. He asserted: 'The whole design of free market capitalism depends on free people acting responsibly …. Managers should respect workers. A firm should be loyal to the community, mindful of the environment.'[4] As a result the interest and enthusiasm for corporate social responsibility (CSR), stakeholder management, corporate governance, and business ethics has increased recently. The concept of CSR is not new, since it is characterised by a long history.[5]

The increased interest in the CSR topic has conceived several initiatives for commitment to CSR with 'openness' and 'transparency' as keywords. One such initiative is the Global Reporting Initiative (GRI), a UN-funded group set up in 1999 to promote the clear reporting of social and environmental issues. To establish a CSR performance indicator in the UK for 2003, GRI has approached about 30 major companies, with global annual revenues of €65.5 billion over the past 18 months to ascertain the extent to which they were complying with the GRI sustainability reporting guidelines on economic, environmental and social performance, and the costs involved. The study found that Shell incurred the highest costs at €2.75 billion.[6]

In the Netherlands, concerns about corporate social responsibility have led to the launching of NIDO (National Initiative for Sustainable Development). NIDO was established in 1999 and is financed through special funds provided by the Dutch government. The objective of NIDO's 'from financial to sustainable profit' programme was to initiate and support change processes among companies that were seeking to create a link between their financial performance and their record on environmental and social matters.[7] Nineteen companies participated in the programme. Several lessons can be drawn from the programme.

Lesson one concerns CSR as a potential source of opportunities. Companies view it as an opportunity to strengthen their reputation. The companies involved in the programme anticipated increases in innovative power and staff motivation and enhanced possibilities for long-term survival. However, it should be cautioned that not seizing these potential opportunities could in turn have an opposite effect leading to demotivation of staff and a weakened position in the market.

671

A second lesson is that CSR can lead to added value. An illustration of competitive added value originating from engaging in CSR is Pizza Corner, an Indian fast food restaurant that successfully opened seven restaurants in the city of Bangalore, where the competition from multinationals like Domino's and Pizza Hut is huge. In an industry where product differentiation is not really a critical factor – as the quality and taste are taken for granted – one of the key factors that has led Pizza Corner, as an Indian brand, to stand up and take the competition head-on, has been the way it has been perceived as a company with a heart. Pizza Corner has earned this reputation because it engaged in a charity programme for creating a future for street children in Bangalore through financial support in education.[8]

A third important lesson is that pursuing CSR automatically involves several types of decisions. For instance, how can a company find a balance between environment, people and profits? Which normative standards should be used to weigh environment, people and profits against each other? Once these standards are chosen, a company should make decisions on what management systems or what planning and organisational systems will be adopted for the implementation of CSR. Finally, which criteria will measure the success of engaging in CSR?

Lesson four is that social corporate responsibility is not new but different. Companies have already concerned themselves with environmental issues, personnel policies, accountancy systems and financial results. The difference is that many companies are now beginning to embed CSR in their organisational strategy.

Lesson five refers to CSR's six activities:

1 List the expectations and demands of stakeholders.
2 Formulate a vision and mission regarding CSR.
3 Develop a short-term and long-term strategy with regard to corporate social responsibility.
4 Set up a monitoring and reporting system.
5 Integrate the process into the company's management systems.
6 Ensure open communication (internally and externally).

Lesson six states that a CSR programme can only be successful if it is tailored to the specific features of each organisation. The programme for Shell will differ dramatically from a small business settled in Quito.

Lesson seven teaches us that the pace at which the implementation of the process is introduced depends on several factors. For instance, a company in a strong economic position in the market has financial room to invest in such programmes. The topic becomes of less concern to organisations during economic recessions. The power and position of stakeholders can also have a certain influence as they might expect a better performance on CSR in the short run.

A number of international institutions are engaged in supporting corporate social responsibility. One such institution is the OECD (Organisation for Economic Co-operation and Development). This institution defined six Corporate Governance Principles (see Table 18.1). These principles are intended to assist OECD and non-OECD governments with their efforts to evaluate and improve the legal, institutional and regulatory framework for corporate governance in their countries, and to provide guidance and suggestions for stock exchanges, investors, corporations and other parties that have a role in the process of developing good corporate governance.

We will address the following topics: the history of corporate social responsibility, Carroll's three-dimensional model of corporate social performance, the relationship between corporate social responsibility and financial performance, corporate social responsibility communication, ethical behaviour and ethical decision making.

The evolution of corporate social responsibility

The concept of corporate social responsibility has been given different labels by academics and practitioners over the past fifty years. For instance, some will speak of corporate social responsiveness or corporate governance, others talk about business ethics, sustainable development, corporate citizenship or stakeholder management. We define Corporate social responsibility as those responsibilities and obligations organisations attempt to pursue, so they can respond to economic, societal and environmental needs in a harmonious manner.

Corporate social responsibility those responsibilities and obligations organisations attempt to pursue, so they can respond to economic, societal and environmental needs in a harmonious manner

TABLE 18.1 OECD GUIDELINES FOR CORPORATE GOVERNANCE

Principle	Content
1 Ensuring the basis for an effective corporate governance framework	The corporate governance framework should promote transparent and efficient markets, be consistent with the rule of law and clearly articulate the division of responsibilities among different supervisory, regulatory and enforcement authorities
2 The rights of shareholders and key ownership functions	The corporate governance framework should protect and facilitate the exercise of shareholders' rights
3 Equitable treatment of shareholders	The corporate governance framework should ensure the equitable treatment of all shareholders, including minority and foreign shareholders. All shareholders should have the opportunity to obtain effective redress for violation of their rights
4 The role of stakeholders in corporate governance	The corporate governance framework should recognise the rights of stakeholders established by law or through mutual agreements and encourage active co-operation between corporations and stakeholders in creating wealth, jobs, and the sustainability of financially sound entreprises
5 Disclosure and transparency	The corporate governance framework should ensure that timely and accurate disclosure is made on all material matters regarding the corporation, including the financial situation, performance, ownership and governance of the company
6 The responsibilities of the board	The corporate performance framework should ensure the strategic guidance of the company, the effective monitoring of management by the board and the board's accountability to the company and the shareholders

SOURCE: Retrieved and adapted from www.oecd.org.

The 1950s

The modern era of corporate social responsibility can be situated in the early years of 1950. Bowen's *Social Responsibilities of Businessmen* (1953) is considered by many to be the first definitive book on the subject.[9] Bowen's work was based on the belief that large businesses were institutions characterised by a concentration of power and decision making, and that their actions influenced the lives of citizens in many respects. Bowen was the first to give an initial, albeit broad, definition of the social responsibilities of businessmen. Social responsibility refers to the obligations of businessmen to pursue those policies, to make those decisions or to follow those lines of action which are desirable in terms of the objectives and values of our society.[10]

The 1960s

While the 1950s were characterised by a shortage of definitions on the topic (with the exception of Bowen), the 1960s were marked by a serious growth in the formalisation of the topic. One of the key authors from that decade is Keith Davis who viewed social responsibility as the businessmen's decisions and actions taken for reasons at least partly beyond the firm's direct economic or technical interest.[11] Davis was also famous for his **Iron law of responsibility**. This law asserts that in the long run those who do not use power in a manner which society considers responsible will tend to lose it. He took the position that, if social responsibility and power are to be relatively equal, then the avoidance of social responsibility leads to the gradual erosion of social power. This law implies that if a CEO or top manager abuses his or her power, in time this will undoubtedly lead to a loss of power. That is one of the reasons why so many CEOs have already become fallen gods.[12] Another

Iron law of responsibility those who do not use their power in a way that adheres to the values, beliefs and obligations of the society will tend to lose it

673

prominent writer during that period is Joseph McGuire. In his book *Business and Society* he stated that business must act justly, as a proper citizen should.[13]

The 1970s

During the 1970s the definitions of corporate social responsibility became more specific. Also, during this decade alternative constructs like corporate social responsiveness and corporate social performance were launched.[14] An important author during that time was Harold Johnson, who presented four views of CSR.

The first view is conventional wisdom. He defined it as follows: 'A socially responsible firm is one whose managerial staff balances a multiplicity of interests. Instead of striving only for larger profits for its stockholders, a responsible enterprise also takes into account employees, suppliers, dealers, local communities and the nation.'

The second view of CSR is the long-run profit maximisation in which is asserted that businesses carry out social programmes to add profits to their organisation.

The third view is labelled as the 'utility maximisation' view. According to this it is assumed that the prime motivation of the business firm is utility maximisation, in which the enterprise seeks multiple goals rather than only maximum profits.

Finally, the fourth approach is known as the 'lexicographic' view of social responsibility. According to this perspective profit-motivated firms may engage in socially responsible behaviour. Once they attain their profit targets, they act as if social responsibility were an important goal – even though it isn't.[15]

Another formalisation was proposed by the Committee for Economic Development in 1971. Their definition consists of three concentric circles. The inner circle includes the clear-cut basic responsibilities for the efficient execution of the economic function – products, jobs and economic growth. This responsibility is concerned with making profit. The intermediate circle encompasses a responsibility to exercise this economic function with sensitive awareness of changing social values and priorities: for example, with respect to environmental conservation, hiring, and relations with employees. These responsibilities imply the co-ordination of corporate actions to prevailing social norms, values and beliefs. The outer circle outlines newly emerging and still amorphous responsibilities that business should assume in order to become more broadly involved in actively improving the social environment.[16] This outer circle is about actions aimed at improving major social problems such as poverty and urban blight.

Prakash Sethi, another heavyweight in the CSR literature, discussed three ways in which organisations should adapt their actions to social needs. The first way is called social obligation and involves corporate behaviour in response to market forces for legal constraints. The second way is social responsibility and implies bringing corporate behaviour to a level where it is congruent with the prevailing social norms, values and expectations. Finally social responsiveness suggests that what is important is not how corporations should respond to social pressures, but what should be their long-run role in a dynamic social system.[17]

At the end of the 1970s Archie Carroll proposed a three-dimensional model of social corporate performance, which will be addressed in detail in the following section of this chapter.

The 1980s and 1990s

During the 1980s and 1990s new alternatives emerged for corporate social responsibility. Alternative concepts were introduced such as **Business ethics theory**, corporate citizenship and stakeholder theory.[18] According to Ferrel, Fraedrich and Ferrel, business ethics differs from corporate social responsibility in the sense that business ethics is about carefully thought-out rules of business organisational conduct that guide decision making while social responsibility concerns the social obligation or contract with society.[19] The concept **Corporate citizenship** underscores the fact that organisations are a members of society.[20] According to Dawkins, corporate citizenship is a synonym of corporate social performance.[21] Finally, the **Stakeholder theory** was introduced to divert attention from the term 'stockholders', and consequently divert attention from profit maximisation.[22] The stakeholder theory stresses the responsibilities companies have toward their stakeholders.[23] The stakeholder perspective depicts the firm as an aggregation of groups or individuals who affect or are affected by the firm's activities.[24] According to this theory organisational performance will depend on the collaboration between stakeholders (also see Chapter 15).

Business ethics theory is about carefully thought-out rules of business organisational conduct that guide decision making

Corporate citizenship considers organisations as members of the society

Stakeholder theory stresses the responsibilities companies have toward their stakeholders

Carroll's three-dimensional model of corporate social performance

In the different views of social responsibilities that have been suggested in the past, three issues always reappear:

- Some definitions are concerned with the social responsibilities for which an organisation is responsible.
- Other definitions address the social issues (product safety, environmental pollution, etc.) for which business carries responsibility.
- A third group of definitions is concerned with how organisations will respond to their responsibilities.

These three aspects are interrelated and form Carroll's corporate performance model.[25]

Dimension 1: Responsibilities

The entire range of responsibilities businesses have toward society can be organised into a pyramid consisting of four layers (see Figure 18.1).

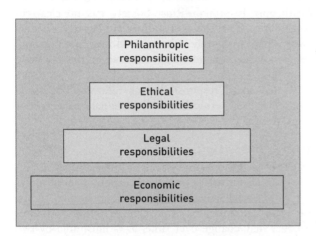

FIGURE 18.1 THE RESPONSIBILITIES PYRAMID

The first layer is **Economic responsibilities**. The foremost social responsibility for business has an economic foundation. Because organisations are the basic economic unit of a society, they carry the responsibility for producing goods and services in response to society's needs. To create wealth they have to sell these goods and products at a profit. By contributing to economic performance, businesses create jobs and as such generate welfare by reducing unemployment. Economic responsibilities are put at the bottom of the pyramid because all other business roles are predicated on the fulfilment of this dimension. For instance, when a firm ceases to exist because the economic responsibility was not fulfilled, philanthropic contributions such as the provision of day-care centres for working mothers become impossible.

The second layer involves **Legal responsibilities** and refers to the laws and regulations under which a firm is supposed to operate. For instance the Belgian airport managing company Biac proposed the creation of 10 000 new jobs at Brussels airport. This was an employment opportunity for the Belgian air company Sabena after its bankruptcy. However, the problem was that these new jobs were conditional on the number of air flights increasing. As the maximum number of flights has been regulated by law and has reached its maximum capacity, it has become very difficult to begin creating these new jobs.[26]

The third layer includes **Ethical responsibilities** and involves additional behaviours and activities that are not necessarily codified into law but nevertheless are expected by society.

Economic responsibilities organisations are the basic economic unit for a society and they carry the responsibility to produce goods and services in response to society's needs

Legal responsibilities the laws and regulations under which a firm is supposed to operate

Ethical responsibilities additional behaviours and activities that are not necessarily codified into law but are nevertheless expected by society members

> The Belgian non-governmental organisation Netwerk Vlaanderen published a report about existing financial relations between the financial institutions KBC, ING and several producers of controversial weapons. The report revealed that these financial institutions invested €1.2 billion in companies responsible for the production of nuclear weapons, cluster ammunition, etc. During the 2004 annual shareholder meeting ING-chairman Ewald Kist proclaimed that ING would withdraw from these investment activities. KBC chairman Willy Breesch however was far less accommodating. The chairman reacted to the allegations of investing in sordid arms dealing as follows: 'Concerning the commotion that has emerged since the Netwerk Vlaanderen report, I would like to state that there are no laws or legal regulations that prohibit financial institutions fromn investing in companies producing weapons.'

Indeed, the chairman had a point that there are no legal restrictions or regulations prohibiting the KBC investment. However, society and peacekeeping activists, in particular, labelled these investment activities as immoral and considered it a huge ethical problem. Ethical responsibilities to be carried out can only be expected. If there are no legal grounds for taking action against unethical or immoral business practices, publicity about unethical practices through the mass media is often the only way to put these organisations under pressure to explain the morality or immorality of their actions.

Philanthropic responsibilities those responsibilities about which the society has no clear-cut message for business

The fourth and final layer refers to **Philanthropic responsibilities**. Society has no clear-cut message for business about philanthropic responsibilities. These responsibilities are left to individual judgement and choice. The roles associated with them are purely voluntary. However, companies taking up such responsibilities can reap benefits as is demonstrated in the case of the fast-food restaurant Pizza Corner.

On the basis of these four layers Carroll defined social responsibility as follows: 'The social responsibility of business encompasses the economic, legal, ethical and discretionary expectations that society has of organisations at a given point in time'.[28]

Dimension 2: Social issues

Carroll asserted that, in addition to the assessment of an organisation's social responsibilities, determining an organisation's corporate social performance also involves the identification of social topics to which these responsibilities are tied. Examples of social issues are child labour, human rights, environment pollution, consumerism, etc. These issues are dynamic as they change in time and differ for different industries and countries.[29] Social issues may change over time, as is illustrated by two North American studies, one conducted in the 1970s and the other in the 1990s.[30]

The 1970 study set out the following major social issues: disclosure of information to shareholders, naming board members, monopolistic behaviour, equality of treatment for minorities, profit sharing, environmental protection, ethics in advertising and the social impact of technology.

The 1990 study encompassed such areas as environmental protection (e.g. reduction of emissions and waste, recycling of materials), philanthropy (donating to charities, etc.), involvement in social causes (involving anything from human rights to AIDS education), urban investment (working with local government to regenerate small businesses and the inner city environment) and employee schemes (higher standards of occupational health and safety, good standard of staff treatment, job-sharing, flexitime, etc.).

UN Global Compact, an international framework for CSR founded by UN secretary-general Kofi Annan, pays special attention to three social areas:

■ Human rights (e.g. businesses should make sure that they are not complicit in human rights abuses).
■ Labour issues (e.g. businesses should eliminate all forms of forced and compulsory labour, child labour etc.).
■ Environmental issues (pollution and destruction of the environment).[31]

Dimension 3: Response action

The response philosophy undertaken by companies for addressing the social issues and social responsibilities completes the social performance model. Thus, corporate social responsiveness is about action. William Frederick defined corporate social responsiveness as '... the capacity of a corporation to respond to social pressures. The literal act of responding, or of achieving a generally responsive posture, to society is the focus .... One searches the organisation for mechanisms, procedures, arrangements and behavioural patterns that, taken collectively, would mark the organisation as more or less capable of responding to social pressures.'[32]

The response categories are reaction, defence, accommodation and proaction.

PRACTICAL IMPLICATIONS

The corporate social performance model assists organisations' social assessment and the action taken to work out its social engagements. Remember the reaction of the KBC chairman discussed earlier in this section. The investment of KBC in nuclear weapon plants covers human rights and welfare, which fits in the layer of ethical responsibilities (see Figure 18.1). This ethical issue, however, could become a legal issue as a result of the growing protest against such activities (layer 2). Furthermore, it could even become an economic issue, as the reputation of the bank is damaged by the defensive and stubborn response to dealing with the problem (layer 1). By not handling the social issue carefully, KBC could be depicted as an unethical organisation by society, resulting in KBC clients changing to what are perceived as more ethical financial institutions. Less damaging for the company's reputation would have been a more accommodating response such as withdrawing all investments from weapon-producing companies.

In summary, the model could be used as a planning tool and as a diagnostic problem-solving tool, since it assists professionals to conceptualise the key issues in social performance, to systematise thinking about social issues and to improve planning and diagnosis in the area of social performance.[33]

The relationship between corporate social responsibility and financial performance

The relationship between corporate social responsibility and financial performance can be viewed from the perspective of practitioners, theorists and researchers.

Perspective of practitioners

According to a recent survey, some 86 per cent of European institutional investors link corporate social responsibility to long-term performance, and 30 per cent believe such policies improve short-term market value. Putting their money where their mouths are, over 50 per cent of fund managers said they would pay a premium for socially responsible companies, and 37 per cent of analysts said they would favour them in their reports, as the CSR Europe/Euronext survey of 300 fund managers and analysts found.[34] On a one-day conference entitled 'Business Performance and Corporate Social Responsibility' at Middlesex University Business School, the definite link between social and financial performance was highlighted. It was stated that CSR should be formulated as a corporate strategy in the pursuit of business success.[35]

Perspective of theorists

Although the corporate world may perceive the existence of a positive association between CSR and financial performance, some queries remain whether research corroborates this strong belief. According to some economists the definition of responsibility involved (1) reduced marginal returns, (2) purely voluntary activity, and (3) actual corporate expenditure rather than a conduit for individual philanthropy. As a result, corporate social responsibility will eventually incur costs.[36] Milton Friedman's view was that the sole responsibility of business is profit seeking. He even stated that CSR is a danger to economic progress.[37] He argued that the corporation is an economic institution and thus should confine itself to the economic sphere. Socially responsible behaviour will be rectified by the market through profits. According to Friedman, business has only one social responsibility and that is to maximise the profits of its owners. Organisations are purely legal entities incapable of value decisions. A manager who uses a firm's resources for non-profit social purposes is thought to be diverting economic efficiency and levying an illegal tax on the organisation.[38] Other scholars followed Friedman's ideas and became opponents of stakeholder theorising (the recognition that a business's responsibilities involve multiple stakeholders). These opponents of stakeholder theory stressed owner property rights. They argued that, because the owner organised or purchased the firm, he is entitled to the profit and fruits of this financial investment. In effect they depicted stakeholder theorising as theft of the extant property rights of owners.[39]

More recently, Abagail McWilliams and Donald Siegel raised two related questions: (1) Do socially responsible firms outperform or underperform other companies that do not meet the same social criteria? (2) Precisely how much should a firm spend on CSR? In addressing these questions they used a supply-and-demand theory of the firm framework and came to the conclusion that investment in CSR can lead to maximising profits, while at the same time satisfying the demands of stakeholders (customers, suppliers, employees, community groups, some stockholders, etc.) on CSR. According to these economists, and in contrast to opponents of the stakeholder theory, it is possible that firms may maximise their profits even when they take the needs of stakeholders into account. According to them the level of investment in CSR that will lead to maximum profits can be derived from a cost–benefit analysis. Their model indicates that, although firms investing in CSR will have higher costs than firms not providing CSR, both will have the same rate of profit. The rationale behind that is that the organisations exhibiting a CSR attribute will have higher costs but also higher revenues, whereas the firm that exhibits no CSR attributes will have lower costs but also lower revenues. Hence, the conclusion that profits will be equal for firms investing or not investing in CSR underscores the idea that there exists a neutral relationship between CSR activity and financial performance.[40]

Research findings

As these theories are of interest in explaining or predicting relationships, the empirical search for a link between corporate social performance and corporate financial performance is of even greater interest to business practitioners. The work of examining this relationship began about 30 years ago and has not yet concluded.[41]

In 1972 Milton Moskowitz was the first to corroborate empirically that socially responsible firms were good investment risks. He observed that the most socially responsible firms had a stock price increase of 7.28 per cent six months after they had been awarded the title 'most socially responsible firms', in contrast to the average 4.4 per cent rise for Dow-Jones, and a 5.1 per cent increase on the New York Stock Exchange during that time.[42]

Thirteen years after Moskowitz's research in 241 American firms displayed no statistically significant relationship between a strong orientation toward social responsibility or concern for society and financial performance. It made no difference whether short-term or long-term return on assets (ROA) were used, nor did it matter if that indicator was adjusted or not adjusted for risk. The study supported neither a positive nor a negative relationship between profitability and an orientation toward corporate social responsibility.[43] In a more recent study the relationship between CSR and the economic performance of 56 large UK organisations was investigated. The results supported the relationship between economic performance and CSR. A positive relationship was found between a company's economic performance and its philanthropic activities.[44]

A meta-analysis of 52 studies into the relationship between financial performance and corporate social performance, published between 1972 and 1997, revealed the following:

- 33 studies suggest a positive relationship between corporate social performance and corporate financial performance.
- 14 studies found no effect or were inconclusive.
- 5 studies found a negative relationship between corporate social performance and corporate financial performance.

In summary, empirical research supports the decision of many managers to invest in corporate social responsibility, because most indicate a positive relationship (33/52) between corporate social performance and corporate financial performance.[45]

An argument in favour of the positive relationship is that a firm perceived as high in social responsibility may face relatively few labour problems or perhaps find that customers may be more favourably disposed to its products. Alternatively, CSR activities might improve a firm's reputation and relationship with bankers, investors and government officials. Improved relationships might well be translated into economic benefits. A firm's CSR behaviour seems to be a factor that influences banks and other institutional investors' investment decisions. A high CSR profile may improve a firm's access to sources of capital.[46]

Corporate social responsibility communication

In the light of recent business scandals, a more explicit emphasis is growing on what organisations communicate and do with regard to important stakeholders and societal issues. Corporate social reporting has become a self-representation tool used by organisations to ensure that different stakeholders are satisfied with their public behaviour.[47]

Corporate social reporting: an important impression management tool

From a utilitarian vantage point, advertising and communicating CSR can be viewed as an important impression-management technique to help achieve performance objectives in terms of profitability, return on investment or sales volume. It can be viewed as a strategy to distinguish the company's image from competitors. It can be an important instrument to win consumers' hearts. For example, Imagequity+™, Asia's first impression-management company, supports its clients in improving their company's reputation by communicating their social responsibility initiatives.[48] Support of CSR creates a reputation for reliability and honesty. Consumers typically assume that the products of a reliable and honest firm will be of high quality. Advertisements that provide information about CSR attributes can be used to build, improve or sustain a reputation for quality, reliability or honesty. For instance, Heinz advertises its Starkist brand tuna as being dolphin-free. This provides the consumer with information that the product has CSR attributes and that the company is trustworthy. The product will hence be perceived of high quality.[49]

Swanson distinguishes three main types of motivation. The first type emphasises the utilitarian perspective. Seen from this angle, CSR is considered an important instrument for maximising profitability, return on investment or sales volume. This type of motivation is called 'performance-driven' CSR.

The second type is based on the negative duty approach. Businesses are accordingly compelled to adopt social responsibility initiatives in order to conform to stakeholder norms defining appropriate behaviour. This type of motivation is known as 'stakeholder-driven' CSR.

Finally, the positive-duty vantage point asserts that businesses may be self-motivated to have a positive impact regardless of social pressures calling for CSR initiatives. Because this approach expresses values considered by organisational members as central and enduring core values within the firm, this type of motivation is called 'value-driven' CSR.[50]

Cultural differences in corporate social reporting

Many companies have started using the World Wide Web as a social reporting tool. A recent inquiry analysed the content of what firms are communicating to various stakeholders on their commitment to socially responsible behaviours.[51] In this inquiry *Forbes*' top 50 US companies and top 50 multinational firms of non-US origin were analysed. A first important finding in this study is that US and non-US companies focus their attention to a similar set of stakeholders and approximately the same CSR topics. Three specific stakeholder groupings are considered as essential to the ultimate success of companies: customers, employees and owners.

CORPORATE SOCIAL REPORTING TOWARDS CUSTOMERS

Current and prospective customers receive messages that emphasise the value of goods and services. Such value creation is predicated upon a partnership that emphasises the understanding and the satisfaction of customers' needs. For instance, since 1999 the Belgian fast-food chain Quick uses New Zealand hoki for their King Fish burger. The company proudly displayed the awarded MSC-certificate (Marine Stewardship Council), an ecolabel for sustainable fishing. Quick restaurants are the first restaurant chain in mainland Europe to receive this certificate. Out of 100 burgers sold at Quick, 18 are fish burgers, compared with only a marginal 2 or 3 per cent in other fast-food chains.[52]

CORPORATE SOCIAL REPORTING TOWARDS EMPLOYEES

CSR messages for employees concentrate on skill development and career enhancement for the improvement of workers as well as corporations. This is nicely demonstrated by Siemens:

> Learning is the key to continuous improvement. It keeps our employees fit for their present and future activities. And it keeps Siemens fit for competition. By making sure our people are equipped to adapt to today's and tomorrow's rapidly changing work environment, we protect not only their career opportunities, but also our ability to compete effectively as a company. Our professional training staff continually updates training programmes and materials. The focus is on innovative learning methods and technology including autonomous learning with multimedia computer support and teletutoring, workshops and computer networks for virtual teamwork in business-oriented projects.

CORPORATE SOCIAL REPORTING TOWARDS OWNERS

Finally, stockholder messages discuss the importance of trust gained through the use of honest, inclusive and timely communications. For example, Credit Suisse emphasises the need to establish trust with their owners through clearly articulated and timely pronouncements:

> We believe investors should know they can depend on our reporting publications, and trust us to explain clearly our company's performance, our strategy and the reasoning behind it. We are also committed to prompt disclosure of any facts which might affect your investment in our company.[53]

RESEARCH FINDINGS

In a recent study a comparison was made between four countries (France, the Netherlands, the UK and the US) into their success in communicating CSR.[54] The aim of this study was to evaluate (1) the extent to which businesses attempt to project the image of a socially responsible firm and (2) the nature of CSR motivations and processes. The results revealed that UK and US firms were much more likely to discuss any dimension of CSR principles and motivations than French and Dutch firms. CSR did not receive the same level of attention across the four countries. The US and UK businesses appeared to be much more eager to be perceived as good citizens than French and Dutch firms. Additionally, no clear patterns of industries were found. Across the four countries the businesses surveyed were found to use different motivating principles (see Table 18.2). The three main types of motivations suggested by Swanson were used to analyse the motivating principles behind engagement with CSR practices.[55] Results indicated that firms in the US, UK, France and the Netherlands used different motivating principles to justify their involvement in CSR practices. The use of a value-driven approach was dominant in the US. The performance-driven approach, sometimes in combination with the stakeholder-driven one, was prevalent in the UK. The set of motivations used to justify CSR practices showed a less-transparent pattern for French and Dutch firms.

Besides the fact that countries differed in CSR principles, they also favoured different CSR processes to put their motivational principles into practice (see Table 18.3). By and large French and Dutch businesses attempted to build a socially responsible image by mentioning a number of practices that were closely linked to production practices and traditional promotions (e.g. limiting the environmental impact of their operations, quality management and sponsorship). On the

TABLE 18.2 PROFILES OF MOTIVATING PRINCIPLES BY COUNTRY

	France (%)	United Kingdom (%)	Netherlands (%)	United States (%)
Performance-driven	21	51	29	20
Stakeholder-driven	37	9	29	2
Value-driven	21	13	6	61
Performance- and stakeholder-driven	21	23	18	2
Performance- and value-driven	0	4	6	5
Stakeholder- and value-driven	0	0	6	10
Performance-, stakeholder- and value-driven	0	0	6	0

TABLE 18.3 PROFILES OF CSR PROCESSES BY COUNTRY

	France (%)	United Kingdom (%)	Netherlands (%)	United States (%)
Philanthropic programmes	18	28	25	43
Sponsorships	12	22	18	9
Volunteerism	0	14	0	20
Code of ethics	6	7	8	8
Quality programmes	26	7	5	2
Health and safety programmes	3	8	10	5
Management of environmental impacts	35	14	33	13

other hand, US firms focused on their engagement in initiatives like philanthropic programmes and volunteerism. Finally, UK firms employed (1) traditional production-and-promotion-oriented activities and (2) initiatives such as involvement in philanthropic programmes.

Ethical behaviour

Unethical behaviour is a relevant issue for all employees. It occurs at all levels of the organisation from the bottom to the top. For example, a survey of 1000 senior-level executives revealed that as many as one-third lied on their CVs.[56] This result should not be surprising as lying seems to have many benefits, such as negotiating a higher salary and stock options, and beating the fierce competition for senior management positions.

Origins of (un)ethical behaviour

Ethical and unethical conduct is the product of a complex combination of influences. The individual decision maker is at the centre of the process of ethical decision making. Moral issues are embedded in almost every decision a professional makes. Accordingly, people working in organisations are continually challenged to make the right decisions. The concept of ethical decision making will be discussed in more detail hereafter.

Three major sources influence an individual's role expectations. People play many roles in life, including those of employee or manager. Their expectations of how those roles should be played are shaped by cultural, organisational and general environmental factors. These role expectations shape an individual's moral principles, values, etc. These individual characteristics in turn influence a person's ethical actions. Examples of cultural factors that form role expectations are family, education, religion and media/entertainment. Organisational factors influencing role expectations are ethical codes, organisation culture, role models, perceived pressure for results and reward/punishment systems. Finally, general environmental factors include political/legal/economic issues. Take a moment now to complete the next Activity. As you will see in the scoring norms, people in different countries have a different attitude towards certain ethical behaviour. This illustrates that ethicality is also influenced by the external environment. What is your attitude towards these behaviours?

Many studies have found a tendency among middle- and lower-level managers to act unethically in the face of perceived pressure for results. By fostering a pressure-cooker atmosphere for results, managers can unwittingly set the stage for unethical shortcuts by employees who seek to please and be loyal to the company. Downsizing, business process re-engineering and empowerment may all be necessary steps towards creating the lean, mean organisation of the new millennium. But according to accountants at KPMG these management-inspired change programmes also heighten the risk of financial fraud.[57]

Thus, an organisation's reward/punishment system can compound the problem of pressure for results. Worse yet, according to a study of 385 managers, those supervisors who were considered by their subordinates to be consistently ethical tended to have lower salaries than their less ethical peers.[58]

In summary, ethical or unethical behaviour is the result of person–environment interactions.

How to improve the organisation's ethical climate

A team of management researchers recommended the following actions to improve ethics at work (Table 18.4).[59]

How ethical are these behaviours?

Instructions

Evaluate the extent to which you believe the following behaviours are ethical. Circle your responses on the rating scales provided. Compute your average score and compare it to the norms.

	Very unethical	Unethical	Neither ethical nor unethical	Ethical	Very ethical
1 Accepting gifts/favours in exchange for preferential treatment	1	2	3	4	5
2 Giving gifts/favours in exchange for preferential treatment	1	2	3	4	5
3 Divulging confidential information	1	2	3	4	5
4 Calling in sick to take a day off	1	2	3	4	5
5 Using the organisation's materials and supplies for personal use	1	2	3	4	5
6 Doing personal business on work time	1	2	3	4	5
7 Taking extra personal time (breaks, etc.)	1	2	3	4	5
8 Using organisational services for personal use	1	2	3	4	5
9 Passing blame for errors to an innocent co-worker	1	2	3	4	5
10 Claiming credit for someone else's work	1	2	3	4	5
11 Not reporting others' violations of organisational policies	1	2	3	4	5
12 Concealing one's errors	1	2	3	4	5

Average score = _____

Norms (average scores by country)

United States = 1.49
Great Britain = 1.70
Australia = 1.44
France = 1.66
China = 1.46
Average of all 10 countries = 1.67

SOURCE: The survey behaviours were taken from T. Jackson, 'Cultural Values and Management Ethics: A 10-Nation Study', *Human Relations*, October 2001, pp. 1287–8.

In the context of supporting and creating an ethical behaviour climate in organisations, executives fulfil a major role. Employees in an organisation led by an ethical leader will imitate their leader's behaviour and will become more ethical themselves. So, leaders are role models and set standards for moral behaviour. Being perceived as an ethical leader among employees involves building a reputation for ethical leadership (also see Chapter 11). Developing such a reputation depends on two aspects (see Figure 18.2).

The first aspect concerns being perceived as a moral person. Being viewed as an ethical person means that people think of you as having certain traits, engaging in certain kinds of behaviours and making decisions based upon ethical principles. Traits that are associated with ethical leadership are integrity, trustworthiness, honesty and sincerity. Typical behaviours of ethical leaders involve doing the right thing, showing concern for people and being open.

In developing a reputation of ethical leadership, a second aspect involves being perceived as a moral manager. A manager can create this perception by role modelling with visible action, communicating about ethics and values, and using a rewards and discipline system that sends signals about desirable and undesirable conduct.[62]

TABLE 18.4 GUIDELINES TO IMPROVE ETHICS AT WORK

1	Behave ethically yourself	Managers are potent role models whose habits and actual behaviour send clear signals about the importance of ethical conduct. Ethical behaviour is a top-to-bottom proposition
2	Screen potential employees	Surprisingly, employers are generally taking things too easily when it comes to checking references, credentials, transcripts and other information on applicant résumés. More diligent action in this area can screen out those given to fraud and misrepresentation. Integrity testing is fairly valid but is no panacea[60]
3	Develop a meaningful code of ethics	Codes of ethics can have a positive impact if they satisfy the following four criteria: ■ They are distributed to every employee. ■ They are firmly supported by top management. ■ They refer to specific practices and ethical dilemmas likely to be encountered by target employees (such as salespersons paying kickbacks, purchasing agents receiving pay-offs, laboratory scientists doctoring data or accountants 'cooking the books'). ■ Their enforcement is balanced, with rewards for compliance and strict penalties for non-compliance.
4	Provide ethics training	Employees can be trained to identify and deal with ethical issues during orientation and through seminar and video training sessions.
5	Reinforce ethical behaviour	Behaviour that is reinforced tends to be repeated, whereas behaviour that is not reinforced tends to disappear. Too often, ethical conduct is punished while unethical behaviour is rewarded
6	Provide mechanisms to deal with ethics	Ethics needs to be an everyday affair, not a one-time announcement of a new ethical code that gets filed away and forgotten. The Body Shop and US-based Ben & Jerry's both use social or ethical audits to assess how well the company is living up to its ethical standards. Organisational changes are then made on the basis of the audit results[61]

FIGURE 18.2 DEVELOPING A REPUTATION AS ETHICAL LEADER

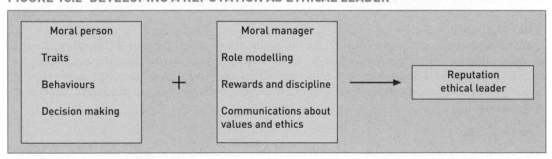

Ethical decision making

Although CSR is commonly explained in terms of the strategic commercial interest of the organisation (image and reputation management), key individuals in the organisation like managers can influence the formulation, adoption and implementation of CSR policies. Managers' personal values can act as drivers for corporate social responsibility.[63]

As managers are key individuals in the formulation, steering and execution of companies' decisions, they are often confronted with a moral dimension in decision making. Moral issues are often involved in the decision making of managers, entrepreneurs and professionals. Wherever choices affect the utilities of others, a moral decision must be made. For instance, a decision whether or not to give a pay rise to employees involves a moral decision as it affects the utilities of others.[64] Giving a pay increase or other benefits to employees reduces a company's profits and harms share-holders' interests. Giving this raise even when the business isn't doing that well could in time affect a company's employment, since higher labour costs may reduce a company's effectiveness and lead to job loss. Not giving this increase could, however, lead to dissatisfaction and turnover among employees, who may prefer to go and work for competitors.

Although ethical conduct and moral decision making is proclaimed in almost every organisation, some cases demonstrate that people attempting to perform their jobs ethically are disadvantaged because of such behaviour. Consider the following examples.

> 'This was a lily-white organisation when I joined it', he says. 'The only diversity was in the lower-end jobs. I brought in two minority managers and, shortly thereafter, started receiving some pressure from the board along some stereotypical lines: "We don't hire people like that. You're not from here. You don't understand." They wanted me to fire them. I refused, and it ultimately cost me my job.'
>
> Another HR professional lost her job ... because, she says, she refused to sit back and do things she considered wrong. What kind of things? Allowing a pay inequality to persist between a male employee whose salary was more than double that of two female colleagues; testing new applicants for HIV and basing hiring decisions on the results; screening out female applicants in their 30s based on the boss's fear that they would miss a lot of work due to child-care issues.[65]

Many decisions made within organisations are portrayed as driven by consideration of costs and benefits. As a result, the rational choice theory (RCT) of decision making has become the most successful and dominant model in explaining professionals' decision making. However, a closer examination of decision making reveals that it is not always grounded in pure rationality, but is often a reflection of culture,[66] power,[67] conflict,[68] politics and tradition[69] or symbolism (also see Chapter 12).[70] A recent paper on decision making and business ethics pinpoints the fact that the RCT does not include non-consequential principles and therefore limits the moral justification capacity of the theory.[71] To make moral just decisions it is required to have some notion of the most important philosophical, normative and ethical theories before further evaluating the RCT. Therefore we will have a look at some important ethical theories.[72]

Influential ethical theories
In this section we consider utilitarianism, Kantianism and ethical relativism.

UTILITARIANISM

Utilitarianism
considering
certain principles
and balancing the
consequences

Utilitarianism is a consequential theory. According to consequential theories the moral rightness of an action can be determined by looking at its consequences. An act or decision is considered as ethical when it produces the maximum utility (good) for everyone. In utilitarianism people consider certain principles (costs involved, how to minimise unhappiness) and balance the likely consequences of the action.

KANTIANISM

Kantianism
considering
principles like
fairness and
existing ideas of
best practice

Kantianism is a non-consequential theory. Whereas consequential theories argue that the consequences of an action should be considered in evaluating its morality, non-consequential theories claim that the act itself ought to be considered. Non-consequential theories are sometimes labelled 'deontological' theories. One such deontological theory is Kantianism. Kant's ethical theory stands as the premier illustration of a purely deontological theory, one that attempts to exclude the consideration of consequences in ethical decision making. This theory considers principles like fairness and existing ideas of best practice. In making decisions we should reflect on how others affected by the decisions would feel.

ETHICAL RELATIVISM

A third stream of ethical theories is known as **ethical relativism**. The major implication of ethical relativism is that all moral norms are relative to particular cultures. The rules of conduct that are applicable in one society do not apply to the actions of people in another society. Each community has its own norms, and morality is entirely a matter of conforming to the standards and rules accepted in one's own culture. To put it simply: what is right is what my society approves; what is wrong is what my society disapproves. The following Snapshot is a nice illustration of different cultures (China versus the West) holding different standards of ethical acceptable behaviour and decision making.

> **Ethical relativism** all moral norms are culture-bound

Comparing Chinese and Western thinking on ethical matters

By Western standards, China is a secular society; most Chinese do not 'belong' to a faith in the sense of being a Christian, Jew or Muslim. Little thought is given to supreme beings, other than venerated ancestors, or to such matters as holiness or life after death. There is a dearth of universal ethical principles or moral absolutes other than maintaining the security and well-being of the family and living up to one's Confucian obligations. These remain the primary normative prescriptions for correct behaviour. Because maintaining social harmony and order is the highest ideal, minimisation of conflict is essential and absolutes are seen as sources of conflict ... Confucianism makes no pretence to be a religion. Rather, it is a system of values that govern interpersonal behaviour with an eye toward building a civil society. It does not speak to humanity's relationship with any supreme being ... Chinese religion has evolved in ways that support and advance the maintenance of social harmony. In contrast, Judaism and Christianity (and Islam as well) prescribe behavioural and ethical standards intended to allow the faithful an opportunity to please and prove their worthiness to their Creator and Supreme Being. While banning behaviour detrimental to maintaining a civil society (though perhaps one not quite as well-mannered as China's), these religions also prescribe how the Supreme Being should be worshipped and require followers to hold certain beliefs, make certain expressions of faith and participate in various rituals. Secular authorities in the West, particularly the Romans building on the precedent set by the ancient Greeks, extended ecclesiastical law into a natural law that dealt with practices, abstract principles and beliefs beyond the spiritual domain. From natural law, greatly elaborated during the Enlightenment, were derived such notions as liberty, justice, equity, fairness, the binding contract, and ultimately, the social contract between people and their governments. These important social and political virtues, binding governments as well as citizens, acquired the force of principle as important to many – and perhaps more so to some – as the tenets of sacred scripture. Though Westerners might disagree on what is 'fair' in any set of circumstances, few would argue against the worth of 'fairness'. The Chinese, like most human beings, will recognise the evil of a wanton crime, but they will have trouble responding to the invocation of abstractions such as 'fair trade'. What is fair to the Chinese is whatever works, whatever action or manner of speech is necessary to execute a transaction satisfactorily for both parties. Westerners are taught to place the principle of honesty above the nicety of harmony; for them, constructive criticism is the 'right' thing to do, even if painful. For the Chinese, this threat to harmony is antisocial. Likewise, most Westerners would be appalled that a manager could be so unprincipled as to show favoritism in hiring a relative. A Chinese would be equally appalled by any reluctance to do so.

SOURCE: Excerpt from J. Scarborough, 'Comparing Chinese and Western cultural roots: Why East is East and ...', *Business Horizons*, November–December 1998, pp. 19–20.

The image theory as a theory of moral decision making

Having explained a number of ethical theories, let us have a look at which of these is associated with the prevalent RCT in decision making. The **rational choice theory** is only associated with the consequential theory (utilitarianism). In RCT, the decision maker is concerned with maximising utility, and therefore the theory is closely linked to utilitarianism.[73] However, many empirical observations have indicated that decision makers do not follow the kinds of processes suggested by RCT.[74]

> **Rational choice theory** maximisation of utility in decision making

TABLE 18.5 THE MAGNIFICENT SEVEN

1 Dignity of human life: The lives of people are to be respected	Human beings, by the fact of their existence, have value and dignity. We may not act in ways that directly intend to harm or kill an innocent person. Human beings have a right to live; we have an obligation to respect that right to life. Human life is to be preserved and treated as sacred
2 Autonomy: All persons are intrinsically valuable and have the right to self-determination	We should act in ways that demonstrate each person's worth, dignity and right to free choice. We have a right to act in ways that assert our own worth and legitimate needs. We should not use others as mere 'things' or only as means to an end. Each person has an equal right to basic human liberty, compatible with a similar liberty for others
3 Honesty: The truth should be told to those who have a right to know it	Honesty is also known as integrity, truth telling and honour. One should speak and act so as to reflect the reality of the situation. Speaking and acting should mirror the way things really are. There are times when others have the right to hear the truth from us; there are times when they do not
4 Loyalty: Promises, contracts and commitments should be honoured	Loyalty includes fidelity, keeping promises, keeping the public trust, good citizenship, excellence in quality of work, reliability, commitment, honouring just laws, rules and policies
5 Fairness: People should be treated justly	One has the right to be treated fairly, impartially and equitably. One has the obligation to treat others fairly and justly. All have the right to the necessities of life – especially those in deep need and the helpless. Justice includes equal, impartial, unbiased treatment. Fairness is the toleration of diversity and acceptance of differences in people and their ideas
6 Humaneness. There are two parts: (1) Our actions ought to accomplish good, and (2) we should avoid doing evil	We should do good to others and to ourselves. We should have concern for the well-being of others; usually, we show this concern in the form of compassion, giving, kindness, serving and caring
7 The common good: Actions should accomplish the 'greatest good for the greatest number' of people	One should act and speak in ways that benefit the welfare of the largest number of people, while trying to protect the rights of individuals

SOURCE: *A Rock and a Hard Place: How to Make Ethical Business Decisions When the Choices Are Tough*, © 1992 Kent Hodgson, pp. 69–73. Published by AMACOM, a division of the American Management Association. Used with permission.

Therefore, a more naturalistic theory of decision making, the image theory, was introduced. This is a theory of moral decision making, since it places principles at the heart of the process. Kent Hodgson has defined seven general moral principles on which decision makers can rely when making decisions (see Table 18.5).

According to **Image theory**, the execution of a decision depends on whether the decision maker feels that the decision fits his or her personal values, goals and strategies. These cognitive structures are called images. Therefore, the theory is known as 'image theory'. According to this theory the first stage in decision making is screening potential choices. Most of these choices are rejected. However, when an option survives the first stage, the decision maker tests the option against his personal set of values, goals and strategies (images) in the second stage. If there is a fit between the option and the internal images, the decision is accepted. If more than one option survives the screening process, the most compatible or profitable option is selected. The image theory is consistent with consequential and non-consequential ethics.

The image theory can be compatible with the utilitarian accounts of decisions, as long as one's

Image theory an alternative theory on decision making, which places principles and values at the heart of decision making

principles are based on utilitarian ideas. According to Morell the image theory is also consistent with Kantian ethics. In that case the principles used by the decision maker are most of the time legal considerations which set the boundaries of reasonable behaviour.[75]

Research findings on moral decision making

In a recent Finnish study managers' responses to a moral dilemma were examined.[76] The dilemma was described as follows:

> " A company will receive a big order from abroad if the managing director agrees to charge excess price for an order and transfer, through an intermediate, this amount back to a Swiss bank account indicated by the customer. When the matter is looked at, the managing director concludes that the risk of getting caught is non-existent. The order would guarantee half a year's work for the company. The managing director decides to agree with the arrangement. "

The managers' answers were divided into two groups according to whether they simply responded with agree/disagree toward the dilemma or included a more detailed explanation. In those responses which agreed, an explanation was offered more often than in those that did not, but almost all undecided responses included a more detailed explanation. Therefore, it seems that when managers are uncertain about their decisions they ponder it in more detail.

The mechanism of cognitive dissonance (see Chapter 3) could be an explanation for this finding. If managers have doubts about their decision, they will attempt to find a reason to justify it, because otherwise cognitive dissonance may occur. It can be argued that the manager in this dilemma is acting immorally and, if the respondent is willing to accept this kind of action, she or he is also willing to act in a way that goes against the commonly held understanding about what is good business practice. When managers are ready to act in this way, they feel they have to explain themselves, so they can minimise the emergence of cognitive dissonance.

Additionally, in the agreeing and undecided responses, deontological thinking was used far less often compared with the disagreeing responses, and the content of the agreeing and undecided responses also differed from the disagreeing deontological responses. In the agreeing responses, deontological thinking was reflected in references to following the letter of law rather than the spirit, and in undecided responses by asserting that there are some rules that cannot be broken, whereas the analysis of the disagreeing responses shows that deontological thinking was present in the form of acting according to laws and norms, individualism and 'moralising' speech.

Furthermore, the response analysis pointed out that consequential thinking in the disagreeing responses emphasised the company's long-term interest and sustainable business, whereas, in the agreeing responses, closing the deal reflected the company's short-term interests. The agreeing responses stressed work for the company as did the undecided responses, also reflecting utilitarian or consequential thinking.

Finally, relativistic thinking appeared most in the agreeing and undecided responses. The content of these responses displayed mainly reasoning according to cultural relativism – that one should act according to the norms of a particular culture. In the disagreeing responses relativistic thinking was reflected by asking others and by appealing to publicity.

In a study of 234 white marketing students and 255 black marketing students, two scenarios involving ethical issues within the retailing context were presented. Both groups were asked to judge both scenarios on 32 philosophy scales. In the hope of corroborating previous findings, the researchers believed that people brought up in different cultures hold different values and ethical beliefs. So, business practices considered as ethical by the white majority culture in the US are not viewed as such by different cultures. The results obtained from the comparison of the white sample with the black one did not confirm this assumption. The ethical beliefs of respondents raised in the white culture were very similar to the ethical beliefs of respondents raised in the black culture. In addition, the results indicated that individuals in different cultures use similar processes to evaluate ethical situations.[77]

Research on gender effects in ethical decision making has conflicting results. Some studies assert that men are more prone to unethical behaviour than women.[78] Other studies demonstrated that men and women display similar ethical behaviour.[79] A recent study examined the hypothesis that women will be more likely than men to favour ethical over unethical decision choices, regardless of the moral pressure of the situation. As predicted, the results revealed that females have a higher sensitivity toward ethical issues and a greater tendency to take action, when they perceive a questionable business practice. This became evident in two scenarios, where the ethical implications were not as clear. The male study participants tended to make more unethical decisions (economic choice) compared to the ethical choice behaviour of their female counterparts.[80]

Learning outcomes: Summary of key terms

1 Define and summarise the evolution of corporate social responsibility (CSR)

The concept of corporate social responsibility has yielded a plethora of definitions over the past fifty years. The basic definition of CSR was propounded by Bowen in the 1950s. His work is considered as the start of the modern era of CSR. According to Bowen social responsibility refers to the obligations of businessmen to pursue those policies, to make those decisions or to follow those lines of action which are desirable in terms of the objectives and values of our society. During the 1960s a serious boost to the formalisation of the topic appeared. However, the definitions that emerged during the 1960s were less specific compared with the produced conceptualisations in the 1970s. During that decade (1970s) an important model of corporate social performance was proposed. Finally, during the 1980s and 1990s new alternatives were introduced for corporate social responsibility such as stakeholder theory, business ethics theory and corporate citizenship.

2 Describe the range of responsibilities organisations have toward the society according to Carroll's three-dimensional model

The responsibilities businesses have toward society can be summarised in a pyramid consisting of four layers. At the foot of the pyramid, economic responsibilities are situated. The second layer involves legal responsibilities. The third layer is about ethical responsibilities and involves additional behaviour and activities that are not codified by law but are expected by society. Finally, the fourth layer refers to philanthropic responsibilities.

3 Explain the three issues that consistently reappear in CSR literature and that form the core of Carroll's three-dimensional model

The different perspectives that have emanated from literature on social responsibilities share three issues: (1) some definitions are concerned with the social reponsibilities that are part of a firm's responsibility (dimension 1: social responsibilities); (2) other definitions address social issues like product safety or environmental pollution, for which business has a responsibility to take (dimension 2: social issues); (3) A third group of definitions covers the way organisations will respond to their responsibilities (dimension 3: response action).

4 Describe the relationship between CSR and economic performance

According to a recent European survey the majority of investors link CSR with long-term performance. Although the corporate world may perceive such a positive link, empirical research and theoretical reasoning on the topic is far less unanimous.

5 Summarise the motivating principles organisations use to engage in CSR practices

Three main types of motivations have been identified. The first type is the performance-driven approach. According to this perspective CSR is considered as an important instrument for maximising profitability. The second type is stakeholder-driven CSR. Following this principle, businesses are compelled to adopt social responsibility initiatives in order to conform to stakeholder norms defining appropriate behaviour. Finally, there is value-driven CSR. This type asserts that businesses may be self-motivated to have a positive impact regardless of the social pressures calling for social initiatives.

6 Describe six actions professionals can rely on to improve an organisation's ethical climate

The following six actions are recommended to improve a firm's corporate social responsibility: (1) managers are role models for ethical conduct; (2) screen references, credentials and transcripts of potential employees; (3) develop a code of ethics; (4) provide training in ethics; (5) reinforce ethical behaviour; and (6) provide mechanisms to deal with ethics.

7 Describe three important streams in ethics

The first group of theories is labelled 'consequential theories'. According to these consequential theories the moral rightness of an action/decision can be determined by looking at its consequences. An example of consequential theories is utilitarianism. In utilitarianism people consider certain principles and weigh up the likely consequences of the action. The second stream of theories are non-consequential theories. Non-consequential theories assert that the act itself ought to be considered in evaluating its morality. Kantianism is a perfect illustration of a non-consequential theory. In making decisions or taking actions we should reflect on how others affected by the decisions would feel. The third stream of moral theories is known as 'ethical relativism'. Ethical relativism argues that all moral norms are relative to particular cultures. The rules of conduct that apply in one society do not apply to the actions of people in another society.

8 Explain which of the three ethical theories are associated with the rational choice theory of decision making and the image theory of decision making

The rational choice therapy (RCT) is only associated with the consequential theories (Utilitarianism). In RCT, the decision maker emphasises the maximisation of utility. The image theory, on the other hand, is consistent with consequential and non-consequential ethics.

Review questions

1 What's your opinion on the business community in general after the recent corporate scandals?

2 Does the World Bank improve global welfare?

3 Can NGOs make a difference? Are they influential enough to add pressure to companies, so that organisations will seek higher standards of social responsibilities in the future?

4 Consider the following case: 'Because of the company's financial situation, the CEO needs to dismiss an elderly long-time employee, three years from retirement. Since there are no other easy saving targets, the CEO decides to dismiss the employee.' Is this action morally justifiable?

5 In many cases, CSR practices are used to improve an organisation's reputation and profitability. Engaging in CSR practices, however, requires a lot of money. Large organisations in comparison to SMEs have greater resources at their disposal to implement such practices. So, large companies will become more powerful compared to SMEs since the former can invest more resources into CSR. In summary, CSR can have detrimental effects for SMEs. What's your opinion on that?

6 Are you an ethical person? Do you really feel the same way toward Europeans as you do toward Africans? How about women versus men? Or older people versus younger ones? Think twice before you take a bet.

7 Is the start-up of factories in low-wage countries in exchange for closing firms in expensive Western countries morally justifiable?

Personal awareness and growth exercise

Investigating the difference in moral reasoning between men and women

Objectives

1 To determine if men and women resolve moral/ethical problems differently.

2 To improve your understanding about the moral reasoning used by men and women.

Introduction

Men and women view moral problems and situations dissimilarly. This is one reason why men and women solve identical moral or ethical problems differently. Researchers believe that men rely on a justice perspective to solve moral problems whereas women are expected to use a care perspective. This exercise presents two scenarios that possess a moral/ethical issue. You will be asked to solve each problem and to explain the logic behind your decision.

Instructions

First read scenario one and then make a decision about what to do. Once this is done, use the space provided to outline the rationale for your decision to this scenario. Next, read scenario two and follow the same procedure: make a decision and explain your rationale.

Scenario one

You are the manager of a local toy store. The hottest Christmas toy of the year is the new 'Peter Panda' stuffed animal. The toy is in great demand and almost impossible to find. You have received your one and only shipment of 12, and they are all promised to people who previously stopped in to place a deposit and reserved one. A woman comes by the store and pleads with you, saying that her six-year-old daughter is in the hospital very ill, and that 'Peter Panda' is the one toy she has her heart set on. Would you sell her one, knowing that you will have to break your promise and refund the deposit to one of the other customers? (There is no way you will be able to get an extra toy in time.)

Your decision

WOULD SELL   WOULD NOT SELL   UNSURE

Rationale for your decision

Scenario two

You sell corporate financial products, such as pension plans and group health insurance. You are currently negotiating with Paul Scott, treasurer of a multinational firm, for a sale that could be in the millions of euros. You feel you are in a strong position to make the sale, but two competitors are also negotiating with Scott, and it could go either way. You have become friendly with Scott, and over lunch one day told you that he has recently been under treatment for manic depression. It so happens that in your office there is a staff psychologist who does employee counselling. The thought has occurred to you that such a trained professional might be able to coach you on how to act with and relate to a personality such as Scott's, so as to persuade and influence him most effectively. Would you consult the psychologist?

Your decision

WOULD CONSULT   WOULD NOT CONSULT   UNSURE

Rationale for your decision

Questions

1 Compare your decisions in response to both scenarios with the percentages for men and women displayed in note 81.[81]

2 What useful lessons did you learn from this exercise?

Group exercise

Applying the three-dimensional model of corporate social performance

Objective

1 Being capable of applying the three-dimensional model of Carroll to a real-life case.

Instructions

In the next exercise you will get the case of Anheuser-Bush. Read through the short case very carefully. Afterwards, try to answer the following questions individually. Then compare the responses in group and discuss possible controversies.

Questions

1 What is the central social issue in this case (dimension 2 of the corporate social performance model)?

2 What is the type of social responsibility the social issue is linked to (dimension 1)? Is it possible that the responsibilities change in time? In which direction can they change?

3 What was the reaction of the company toward the responsibilities (dimension 3)?

Anheuser-Bush Case

Some time ago (end of 1970s), Anheuser Bush test-marketed a new adult drink called Chelsea. Because the beverage contained more alcohol than the average soft drinks, consumer groups protested by calling the beverage 'kiddie beer' and claiming that the company was being socially irresponsible in making such a drink available to youth. Anheuser-Busch's first reaction was to try to claim that the beer was not dangerous and would not lead youngsters to stronger drink. The company's later response was to withdraw the beverage from the marketplace and refor-mulate it so that it would be viewed as safe. The company concluded this was the social responsible action to take given the criticism.

 # Internet exercise

As we have discussed throughout this chapter, organisations can use different motivation principles and processes to engage in CSR. Let us now consider Royal Dutch Shell, a global group of energy and petrochemical companies. This company has suffered adverse publicity since their plan in 1995 to dump the Brent Spar oil platform at sea. This adverse publicity resulted in up to a 50 per cent decline in sales in some of their markets. Criticisms of Shell by environmentalist and human rights activists were said to be the key contributors to a fundamental transformation in the company's efforts to meet its social and ethical responsibilities. Visit our website at www.mcgraw-hill.co.uk/textbooks/buelens for further instructions.

Notes

1 D. Woodruff and C. Goldsmith, 'Sour Sign-Off: A Final Pension Move Soils High Standing of Top European CEO – ABB's Barnevik Collected $87 million, Then Ducked Questions from the Board – Spur to Corporate Openness', *Wall Street Journal*, 8 March 2002, p. A1.

2 L. Lavelle, J. Hempel and D. Brady, 'Executive Pay: Top CEO Paychecks in 2003 Were, As Usual, Off-the-Charts Amazing, But the Pace of Overall Raises for Execs Slowed Considerably', *Business Week*, 19 April 2004, p. 106.

3 J. A. Petrick and R. F. Sherer, 'The Enron Scandal and the Neglect of Management Integrity Capacity', *Mid-American Journal of Business*, Spring 2003, pp. 37–49.

4 D. Leonard and R. McAdam, 'Corporate Social Responsibility', *Quality Progress*, October 2003, pp. 27–32.

5 A. B. Carroll, 'Corporate Social Responsibility', *Business and Society*, September 1999, pp. 268–95; and

D. Windsor, 'The Future of Corporate Social Responsibility', *International Journal of Organizational Analysis*, July 2001, pp. 225–56.

6 C. Evans, 'News Analysis: Corporate Social Responsibility – Sustainability: The Bottom Line', *Accountancy*, January 2003, p. 16.

7 J. Cramer, 'Corporate Social Responsibility: Lessons Learned', *Environmental Quality Management*, Winter 2003, pp. 59–66.

8 V. Anand, 'Building Blocks of Corporate Reputation – Social Responsibility Initiatives', *Corporate Reputation Review*, Spring 2002, pp. 71–4.

9 H. R. Bowen, *Social Responsibilities of the Businessman* (New York: Harper & Row, 1953).

10 H. R. Bowen, *Social Responsibilities of the Businessman* (New York: Harper & Row, 1953), p. 6

11 K. Davis, 'Can Business Afford to Ignore Social Responsibilities?', *California Management Review*, Spring 1960, pp. 70–76.

12 'Leaders: Fallen Idols: CEO's', *The Economist*, 4 May 2002, p. 11.

13 J. W. McGuire, *Business and Society* (New York: McGraw-Hill, 1963).

14 A. B. Carroll, 'Corporate Social Responsibility', *Business and Society*, September 1999, pp. 268–95; and D. Windsor, 'The Future of Corporate Social Responsibility', *International Journal of Organizational Analysis*, July 2001, pp. 225–56.

15 H. L. Johnson, *Business in Contemporary Society: Framework and Issues* (Belmont, CA: Wadsworth, 1971).

16 Committee for Economic Development, *Social Responsibilities of Business Corporations* (New York: Author, 1971).

17 S. P. Sethi, 'Dimensions of Corporate Social Performance: An Analytic Framework', *California Management Review*, Spring 1975, pp. 58–64.

18 A. B. Carroll, 'Corporate Social Responsibility', *Business and Society*, September 1999, pp. 268–95; and D. Windsor, 'The Future of Corporate Social Responsibility', *International Journal of Organizational Analysis*, July 2001, pp. 225–56.

19 O. C. Ferrell, J. Fraedrich and L. Ferrell, *Business Ethics: Ethical Decision Making and Cases* (Boston, MA: Houghton Mifflin Company, 2002).

20 S. A. Waddock, *Leading Corporate Citizens: Vision, Values, Value Added* (Boston, MA: McGraw-Hill, 2002).

21 C. E. Dawkins, 'Corporate Welfare, Corporate Citizenship, and the Question of Accountability', *Business and Society*, September 2002, pp. 269–91.

22 N. A. Dentchev, *To What Extent Is Business and Society Literature Idealistic?* (Unpublished Manuscript, 6 April 2004).

23 J. Andriof, S. A. Waddock, S. S. Rahman and B. Husted, 'Introduction: JCC The Issue: Stakeholder Responsibility', *Journal of Corporate Citizenship*, Summer 2002, pp. 16–18.

24 E. R. Freeman, *Strategic Management: A Stakeholder Approach* (Boston, MA: Pitman, 1984).

25 A. B. Carroll, 'A Three-Dimensional Model of Corporate Performance', *Academy of Management Review*, October 1979, pp. 497–505.

26 H. Hermans, 'Luchthaven: nieuwe banen of nachtrust?', *Vacature*, 9 May 2003, retrieved from http://www.vacature.com/scripts/ArtZoeker/.

27 K. Vidal, 'Vredesactivisten willen weten of KBC blijft investeren in smerige wapens?', *De Morgen*, 30 April 2004.

28 A. B. Carroll, 'Corporate Social Responsibility', *Business and Society*, September 1999, pp. 268–95; and D. Windsor, 'The Future of Corporate Social Responsibility', *International Journal of Organizational Analysis*, July 2001, pp. 225–56.

29 S. A. Waddock and M. E. Boyle, 'The Dynamics of Change in Corporate Community Relations', *California Management Review*, Summer 1995, pp. 125–40.

30 G. Balabnis, H. C. Phillips and J. Lyall, 'Corporate Social Responsibility and Economic Performance in the Top British Companies: Are They Linked?', *European Business Review*, March 1998, pp. 25–45.

31 Retrieved and adapted from http://www.globalcompact.org.

32 W. C. Frederick, *From CSR1 to CSR2: The Maturing of Business and Society Thought – Working paper No. 279* (Pittsburgh, PA: University of Pittsburgh, 1978).

33 A. B. Carroll, 'Corporate Social Responsibility', *Business and Society*, September 1999, pp. 268–95; and D. Windsor, 'The Future of Corporate Social Responsibility', *International Journal of Organizational Analysis*, July 2001, pp. 225–56.

34 H. Stock, 'Euro Funds Bank on Social Metrics: IRO's Seize Opportunity as Investor Factor in Corporate Responsibility', *Investor Relations Business*, 20 April 2003, p. 1.

35 A. Stainer, 'Business Performance and Corporate Social Responsibility: A Report on the One Day Conference', *Management Services*, July 2002, pp. 36–7.

36 H. G. Manne and H. C. Wallich, *The Modern Corporation and Social Responsibility* (Washington, DC: American Enterprise Institute for Public Policy Research, 1972).

37 M. Friedman, *Capitalism and Freedom* (Chicago, IL: University of Chicago Press, 1962); M. Friedman, 'The Social Responsibility of Business is to Increase Its Profits', *New York Times Magazine*, 13 September 1970, pp. 32–3.

38 See G. Balabnis, H. C. Phillips and J. Lyall, 'Corporate Social Responsibility and Economic Performance in the Top British Companies: Are They Linked?', *European Business Review*, March 1998, pp. 25–45.

39 E. Sternberg, 'The Stakeholder Concept: A Mistaken Doctrine', retrieved from http://papers.ssm.com/paper.taf?abstract_id=263144.

40 A. McWilliams and D. Siegel, 'Corporate Social Responsibility: A Theory of the Firm Perspective, *Academy of Management Review*, January 2001, pp. 117–27.

41 R. M. Roman, S. Hayibor and B. R. Agle, 'The Relationship between Social and Financial Performance', *Business and Society*, March 1999, pp. 109–25.

42 M. Moskowitz, 'Choosing Socially Responsible Stocks', *Business and Society Review*, Spring 1972, pp. 72–5.

43 K. E. Aupperle, A. B. Carroll and J. D. Hatfield, 'An Empirical Examination of the Relationship between Corporate Social Responsibility and Profitability', *Academy of Management Journal*, June 1985, pp. 446–63.

44 See G. Balabnis, H. C. Phillips and J. Lyall, 'Corporate Social Responsibility and Economic Performance in the Top British Companies: Are They Linked?', *European Business Review*, March 1998, pp. 25–45.

45 See R. M. Roman, S. Hayibor and B. R. Agle, 'The Relationship between Social and Financial Performance', *Business and Society*, March 1999, pp. 109–25.

46 See G. Balabnis, H. C. Phillips and J. Lyall, 'Corporate Social Responsibility and Economic Performance in the Top British Companies: Are They Linked?', *European Business Review*, March 1998, pp. 25–45.

47 R. Hooghiemstra, 'Corporate Communication and Impression Management: New Perspectives Why Companies Engage in Corporate Social Reporting', *Journal of Business Ethics*, September 2000, pp. 55–68.

48 See V. Anand, 'Building Blocks of Corporate Reputation – Social Responsibility Initiatives', *Corporate Reputation Review*, Spring 2002, pp. 71–4.

49 See A. McWilliams and D. Siegel, 'Corporate Social Responsibility: A Theory of the Firm Perspective, *Academy of Management Review*, January 2001, p. 117–27.

50 D. L. Swanson, 'Addressing a Theoretical Problem by Reorienting the Corporate Social Performance Model', *Academy of Management Review*, January 1995, pp. 43–64.

51 J. Snider, R. P. Hill and D. Martin, 'Corporate Social Responsibility in the 21st Century: A View from the World's Most Successful Firms', *Journal of Business Ethics*, December 2003, pp. 175–87.

52 A. Goyvaerts, 'Quick krijgt ecolabel voor zijn vis', *De Morgen*, 30 April 2004.

53 J. Snider, R. P. Hill and D. Martin, 'Corporate Social Responsibility in the 21st Century: A View from the World's Most Successful Firms', *Journal of Business Ethics*, December 2003, pp. 175–87.

54 I. Maignan and D. A. Ralston, 'Corporate Social Responsibility in Europe and the US: Insights from Business' Self-Presentations', *Journal of International Business Studies*, Third Quarter 2002, pp. 497–514.

55 See D. L. Swanson, 'Addressing a Theoretical Problem by Reorienting the Corporate Social Performance Model', *Academy of Management Review*, January 1995, pp. 43–64.

56 L. Wah, 'Lies in the Executive Wing', *Management Review*, May 1999, p. 9.

57 T. Dickson, 'Management: Crime Busters on the Board – Spotting Financial Fraud is Part of the Non-Executive's Role', the *Financial Times*, 17 May 1995, p. 15.

58 R. B. Morgan, 'Self- and Co-worker Perceptions of Ethics and Their Relationship to Leadership and Salary', *Academy of Management Journal*, February 1993, pp. 200–14.

59 L. K. Trevino, L. P. Hartman and M. Brown, 'Moral Person and Moral Manager: How Executives Develop A Reputation for Ethical Leadership', *California Management Review*, Summer 2000, pp. 128–42.

60 W. E. Stead, D. L. Worell and J. Garner Stead, 'An Integrative Model for Understanding and Managing Ethical Behaviour in Business Organizations', *Journal of Business Ethics*, March 1990, pp. 233–42.

61 D. S. Ones and C. Viswesvaran, 'Integrity Testing in Organizations', in *Dysfunctional Behavior in Organizations: Violent and Deviant Behavior*, ed. R. W. Griffin (Stanford, CT: JAI Press, 1998), pp. 243–76.

62 'Open Business is Good for Business', *People Management*, January 1996, pp. 24–7.

63 C. A. Hemingway and P. W. MacLagan, 'Managers' Personal Values as Drivers of Corporate Social Responsibility', *Journal of Business Ethics*, March 2004, pp. 33–44.

64 J. Baron, *Thinking and Deciding, third edition* (New York: Cambridge University Press, 2001).

65 L. Grensing-Pophal, 'Walking the Tightrope, Balancing Risks and Gains', *HR Magazine*, October 1998, p. 112.

66 R. P. Vecchio, *Organizational Behavior, fourth edition* (London: University of Chicago Press, 2001).

67 R. M. Kanter, 'Power Failure in Management Circuits', *Harvard Business Review*, July–August 1979, pp. 65–75.

68 C. Camerer and M. Knez, 'Co-ordination in Organizations: A Game-Theoretic Perspective', in *Organizational Decision Making*, ed. Z. Shapira (New York: Cambridge University Press, 1997), pp. 158–88.

69 G. R. Salancik and M. C. Brindle, 'The Social Ideologies of Power in Organizational Decisions', in *Organizational Decision Making*, ed. Z. Shapira (New York: Cambridge University Press, 1997), pp. 111–32.

70 E. J. Zajac and J. D. Westphal, 'Managerial Incentives in Organisations: Economic, Political and Symbolic Perspectives', in *Organizational Decision Making*, ed. Z. Shapira (New York: Cambridge University Press, 1997), pp. 133–57.

71 K. Morrell, 'Decision Making and Business Ethics: The Implications of Using Image Theory in Preference to Rational Choice', *Journal of Business Ethics*, March 2004, pp. 239–52.

72 J. Tsalikis and O. Nwachukwu, 'Cross-Cultural Business Ethics: Ethical Beliefs Difference between Blacks and Whites', *Journal of Business Ethics*, October 1988, pp. 745–54.

73 See K. Morrell, 'Decision Making and Business Ethics: The Implications of Using Image Theory in Preference to Rational Choice', *Journal of Business Ethics*, March 2004, pp. 239–52.

74 M. Zey, *Decision Making: Alternatives to Rational Choice Models* (London: Sage, 1992).

75 See K. Morrell, 'Decision Making and Business Ethics: The Implications of Using Image Theory in Preference to Rational Choice', *Journal of Business Ethics*, March 2004, pp. 239–52.

76 J. Kujala, 'Understanding Manager's Moral Decision-Making', *International Journal of Value-Based Management*, no. 1, 2003, pp. 37–52.

77 See J. Tsalikis and O. Nwachukwu, 'Cross-Cultural Business Ethics: Ethical Beliefs Difference between Blacks and Whites', *Journal of Business Ethics*, October 1988, pp. 745–54.

78 N. Betz, M. O'Connell and J. Shepard, 'Gender Differences in Proclivity for Unethical Behaviour', *Journal of Business Ethics*, May 1989, pp. 321–4; J. Kidwell, R. Stevens and A. Bethke, 'Differences in Ethical Perceptions between Male and Female Managers: Myth or Reality?', *Journal of Business Ethics*, August 1987, pp. 489–93; C. McNichols and T. Zimmerer, 'Situational Ethics: An Empirical Study of Differentiators of Student Attitudes', *Journal of Business Ethics*, June 1985, pp. 175–80; and R. Beltramini, R. Peterson and G. Kozmetsky, 'Concerns of College Students Regarding Business Ethics', *Journal of Business Ethics*, October 1984, pp. 195–200.

79 L. Chonko and S. Hunt, 'Ethics and Marketing Management: An Empirical Examination', *Journal of Business Research*, August 1985, pp. 339–59; D. Ruegger and E. King, 'A Study of the Effect of Age and Gender upon Student Business Ethics', *Journal of Business Ethics*, March 1992, pp. 179–86; P. Serwinck, 'Demographic and Related Differences in Ethical Views Among Small Businesses', *Journal of Business Ethics*, March 1992, pp. 555–66.

80 S. H. Glover, M. A. Bumpus, G. F. Sharp and G. A. Munchus, 'Gender Differences in Ethical Decision Making', *Women in Management Review*, no. 5/6, 2002, pp. 217–27.

81 These scenarios were excerpted from L. M. Dawson, 'Women and Men, Morality and Ethics', *Business Horizons*, July 1995, pp. 62, 65. Comparative norms were also obtained from Dawson, 'Women and Men, Morality and Ethics'. Scenario 1: would sell (28% males, 57% females); would not sell (66% males, 28% females); unsure (6% males, 15% females). Scenario 2: would consult (84% males, 32% females); would not consult (12% males, 62% females); unsure (4% males, 6% females).

Glossary of key terms

Ability
Stable characteristic responsible for a person's maximum physical or mental performance.

Accommodator
Learning style preferring learning through doing and feeling.

Accountability practices
Focus on treating diverse employees fairly.

Activist
Learning style preferring learning by concrete experience.

Adaptor
Cognitive style characterised by doing things better.

Affective component of an attitude
Feelings, moods and emotions a person has about something or someone.

Affirmative action
Focuses on achieving equality of opportunity in an organisation.

Aggressive style
Expressive and self-enhancing but takes unfair advantage of others.

Agreeableness
Personality dimension referring to a person's ability to get along with others.

Aided-analytic
Using tools to make decisions.

Alternative dispute resolution
Avoiding costly lawsuits by resolving conflicts informally or through mediation or arbitration.

Analytic
Cognitive style characterised by processing information into its component parts.

Asch effect
Giving in to a unanimous but wrong opposition.

Assertive style
Expressive and self-enhancing but does not take advantage of others.

Assimilator
Learning style preferring learning through watching and thinking.

Attention
Being consciously aware of something or someone.

Attitude
Beliefs and feelings people have about specific ideas, situations and people, which influence their behaviour.

Attributions
Inferred causes of perceived behaviour, actions or events.

Availability heuristic
Tendency to base decisions on information readily available in memory.

Behavioural component of an attitude
How a person intends or expects to act towards something or someone.

Benchmarking
Process by which a company compares its performance with that of high-performing organisations.

Big Five
Five dimensions largely representing human personality.

Bounded rationality
Constraints that restrict decision making.

Brainstorming
Process to generate a quantity of ideas.

Buffers
Resources or administrative changes that reduce burnout.

Bureaucracy
Max Weber's idea of the most rationally efficient form of organisation.

Burnout
A condition of emotional exhaustion and negative attitudes.

Business ethics theory
Is about carefully thought-out rules of business organisational conduct that guide decision making.

Case study
In-depth study of a single person, group or organisation.

Centralisation
The concentration of decision-making power at the level of the top management team.

Chaos theory
The environment is extremely uncertain and turbulent resulting in high complexity and disorder but patterns of order are still recognisable in the chaos.

695

Charismatic leadership
Transforms employees to pursue organisational goals over self-interests.

Closed system
A relatively self-sufficient entity.

Closure
Tendency to perceive objects as a constant overall form.

Coalition
Temporary groupings of people who actively pursue a single issue.

Coercive power
Obtaining compliance through threatened or actual punishment.

Cognitions
A person's knowledge, opinions or beliefs.

Cognitive categories
Mental depositories for storing information.

Cognitive component of an attitude
Beliefs, opinions, cognitions and knowledge someone has about a certain object, situation or person.

Cognitive dissonance
Refers to situations of incompatibility between different attitudes or between attitudes and behaviour.

Cognitive style
An individual's preferred way of processing information.

Cohesiveness
A sense of 'we-ness' that helps groups to stick together.

Collaborative computing
Using computer software and hardware to help people work together better.

Communication competence
Ability to use the appropriate communication behaviour effectively in a given context.

Communication distortion
Purposely modifying the content of a message.

Communication
Interpersonal exchange of information and understanding.

Competence
Any individual characteristic that is related to effective and superior performance.

Confirmation bias tendency
Tendency to seek and interpret information that verifies existing beliefs.

Conflict theory
Social structures and relationships in organisations are based on conflicts between groups and social classes.

Conflict
One party perceives its interests are being opposed or set back by another party.

Conscientiousness
Personality dimension referring to the extent a person is organised, careful, responsible and self-disciplined.

Consensus
Presenting opinions and gaining agreement to support a decision.

Consideration
Creating mutual respect and trust between leader and followers.

Content level
'What' is communicated.

Content theories
Theories regarding what motivates people.

Contingency approach to organisation design
Creating an effective organisation–environment fit.

Contingency approach
Using tools and techniques in a situationally appropriate manner; avoiding the one-best-way mentality.

Contingency factors
Situational variables that influence the appropriateness of a leadership style.

Continuity
Tendency to perceive objects as continuous patterns.

Continuous change
Perceives change as constant, evolving and cumulative.

Contrast effect
Tendency to perceive stimuli that differ from expectations as being even more different than they really are.

Control strategy
Coping strategy that directly confronts or solves problems.

Converger
Learning style preferring learning through thinking and doing.

Co-ordination
Tuning the activities to reach a common goal by exchanging information.

Coping
Process of managing stress.

Core job dimensions
Job characteristics found to various degrees in all jobs.

Corporate citizenship
Considers organisations as members of the society.

Corporate social responsibility
Those responsibilities and obligations organisations attempt to pursue, so they can respond to economic, societal and environmental needs in a harmonious manner.

Covariation principle
Principle of attribution theory holding that people attribute behaviour to factors that are present when a behaviour occurs and absent when it does not.

Creativity
Process of developing something new or unique.

Critical theory
Criticism of the rational, functionalistic, managerial and capitalistic views on organisations.

Cross-cultural training
Structured experiences to help people adjust to a new culture or country.

Cross-functionalism
Team made up of technical specialists from different areas.

Culture shock
Anxiety and doubt caused by an overload of new expectations and cues.

Culture
Socially derived, taken-for-granted assumptions about how to think and act.

Decentralisation
The dispersion of decision-making power in the organisation.

Decision making
Identifying and choosing solutions that lead to a desired end result.

Decision-making style
A combination of how individuals perceive and respond to information.

Delegation
Granting decision-making authority to people at lower levels.

Delphi technique
Group process that anonymously generates ideas from physically dispersed experts.

Departmentalisation
The grouping of people based on common characteristics.

Development practices
Focus on preparing diverse employees for greater responsibility and advancement.

Devil's advocacy
Assigning someone the role of critic.

Dialectic method
Fostering a debate of opposing viewpoints to better understand an issue.

Differentiation
Division of labour and specialisation that cause people to think and act differently.

Displayed emotion
Organisationally desirable and appropriate emotion in a given job or situation.

Diverger
Learning style preferring learning through feeling and watching.

Diversified organisation
Large organisation with headquarters and semi-autonomous units.

Division of labour
The allocation of tasks and responsibilities to the members of the organisation.

Double loop learning
Learning via error and correction based on questioning the underlying models, norms, values and objectives.

Dysfunctional conflict
Threatens organisation's interests.

Economic responsibilities
Organisations are the basic economic unit for a society and they carry the responsibility to produce goods and services in response to society's needs.

High-context cultures
Primary meaning derived from non-verbal situational cues.

Holistic wellness approach
Advocates personal responsibility for reducing stressors and stress.

Horizontal organisation
Organisations with few hierarchical levels, built around core processes.

Hourglass organisation
An organisation with a very limited number of middle managers.

Hygiene factors
Job characteristics associated with job dissatisfaction.

Image theory
An alternative theory on decision making, which places principles and values at the heart of decision making.

Imager
Cognitive style characterised by representing information in mental pictures.

Implicit knowledge
Knowledge that has not (yet) been made explicit or expressed but that is hidden away in individuals' minds, habits or organisational processes and minds.

Implicit personality theories
Network of assumptions that we hold about relationships among various types of people, traits and behaviours.

Impression management
Getting others to see us in a certain manner.

Informal group
Group formed by friends.

Information overload
When the information we have to work with exceeds our processing capacity.

Information richness
Information-carrying capacity of data.

Initiating structure
Organising and defining what group members should be doing.

Innovative organisation
Often young and flexible organisation oriented towards innovation.

Innovator
Cognitive style characterised by doing things differently.

Instrumental cohesiveness
Sense of togetherness based on the mutual dependency required to get the job done.

Instrumental values
Represent desirable ways or modes of conduct to achieve one's terminal goals.

Instrumentality
Belief that performance leads to a specific outcome or reward.

Integration
Co-operation among specialists to achieve common goals.

Intelligence
Capacity for constructive thinking, reasoning and problem solving.

Internal factors
Personal characteristics that cause behaviour.

Internal forces for change
Originate inside the organisation.

Internal locus of control
Attributing outcomes to one's own actions.

Internal motivation
Motivation caused by positive internal feelings.

Internet
A public network of computer networks.

Intranet
An organisation's private Internet.

Intrinsic motivation
Being motivated by intrinsic rewards.

Intrinsic rewards
Self-granted, psychic rewards.

Introvert
Preference for basing perception and judgement upon ideas.

Intuiting
Preference for perceiving indirectly through the unconscious.

Iron law of responsibility
Those who do not use their power in a way that strokes with the values, beliefs and obligations of the society will tend to lose it.

Job enrichment
Enriching a job through vertical loading.

Job involvement
The extent to which one is personally involved with his or her work role.

Job satisfaction
General attitude one has towards his or her job.

Judgemental heuristic
Rules-of-thumb or shortcuts that people use to reduce information-processing demands.

Judging
Preference for making quick decisions.

Kantianism
Considering principles like fairness and existing ideas of best-practice.

Knowledge creation
A process of acquiring new knowledge, recombining knowledge and applying it in order to extend an individual's, group or organisation's knowledge stock.

Knowledge exploitation
Creating economies of scale based on the optimal use of knowledge available to the organisation.

Knowledge exploration
Creating new knowledge for the organisation to achieve innovation in processes and products.

Knowledge management
Management of information, knowledge and experience available to an organisation, its creation, capture, storage, availability and utilisation, in order that organisational activities build on what is already known and extend it further.

Knowledge of results
Feedback about work outcomes.

Knowledge sharing
The exchange of knowledge between at least two parties to make the knowledge available and useful for both parties, requiring a process of understanding, reconfiguring and sense making.

Laboratory study
Manipulation and measurement of variables in contrived situations.

Leader trait
Personal characteristic that differentiates a leader from a follower.

Leader–member relations
Extent to which leader has the support, loyalty and trust of work group.

Leadership Grid®
Represents four leadership styles found by crossing concern for production and concern for people.

Leadership prototype
Mental representation of the traits and behaviours possessed by leaders.

Leadership
Influencing employees to voluntarily pursue organisational goals.

Learned helplessness
Debilitating lack of faith in one's ability to control the situation.

Learning capabilities
The set of core competencies and internal processes that enable an organisation to adapt to its environment.

Learning modes
The various ways in which organisations attempt to create and maximise their learning.

Learning organisation
Proactively creates, acquires and transfers knowledge throughout the organisation and changes its behaviour on the basis of new knowledge and insights.

Learning style
An individual's preferred use of learning abilities.

Legal responsibilities
The laws and regulations under which a firm is supposed to operate.

Legitimate power
Obtaining compliance through formal authority.

Liaison individuals
Consistently pass grapevine information along to others.

Line managers
Have authority to make organisational decisions.

Linguistic style
A person's typical speaking pattern.

Listening
Actively decoding and interpreting verbal messages.

Locus of control
Degree to which a person takes responsibility for his/her behaviour and its consequences.

Low-context cultures
Primary meaning derived from written and spoken words.

Machine organisation
Well-structured, often bureaucratic organisation oriented towards efficiency.

Maintenance roles
Relationship-building group behaviour.

Management by objectives
Management system incorporating participation in decision making, goal setting and feedback.

Managing diversity
Creating organisational changes that enable all people to perform up to their maximum potential.

Matrix form of departmentalisation
Grouping people based on function and product simultaneously.

MBTI
Measure to identify a person's personality typology based on four dimensions.

Mechanistic organisations
Rigid, command-and-control bureaucracies.

Meta-analysis
Pools the results of many studies through statistical procedure.

Missionary organisation
An organisation bound together by a clear mission and strong shared values among its members.

Monochronic time
Preference for doing one thing at a time because time is limited, precisely segmented and schedule driven.

Motivating potential score
The amount of internal work motivation associated with a specific job.

Motivation
Psychological processes that arouse and direct goal-directed behaviour.

Motivators
Job characteristics associated with job satisfaction.

Mutuality of interest
Balancing individual and organisational interests through win-win co-operation.

Need for achievement
Desire to accomplish something difficult.

Need for affiliation
Desire to spend time in social relationships and activities.

Need for power
Desire to influence, coach, teach or encourage others to achieve.

Needs
Physiological or psychological deficiencies that arouse behaviour.

Negative affectivity
Tendency to experience negative emotional states.

Negative inequity
Comparison in which another person receives greater outcomes for similar inputs.

Negotiation
Give-and-take process between conflicting interdependent parties.

Netiquette rules
Rules that attempt to improve the quality and effectiveness of communication through email.

Network organisation
An organisation structured around reciprocal communication patterns between groups of people.

Noise
Interference with the transmission and understanding of a message.

Nominal group technique
Process to generate ideas and evaluate solutions.

Non-analytic
Using rules, formulated beforehand, to make decisions.

Non-assertive style
Timid and self-denying behaviour.

Non-verbal communication
Messages sent that are neither written nor spoken.

Normative beliefs
Thoughts and beliefs about expected behaviour and modes of conduct.

Norms
Shared attitudes, opinions, feelings or actions that guide social behaviour.

Open system
Organism that must constantly interact with its environment to survive.

Openness to experience
Personality dimension referring to the extent a person is open for new experiences.

Optimising
Choosing the best possible solution.

Oral communication
Verbal communication that is spoken.

Organic organisations
Fluid and flexible network of multi-talented people.

Organisation chart
Graphic illustration of boxes and lines showing chain of formal authority and division of labour.

Organisation development
A set of techniques or tools that are used to implement organisational change.

Organisation
System of consciously co-ordinated activities of two or more people.

Organisation's value system
Patterns of conflict and compatibility between organisation's values.

Organisational behaviour
Interdisciplinary field dedicated to better understanding of management of people at work.

Organisational commitment
The extent to which one identifies oneself with an organisation and is committed to its goals.

Organisational culture
Shared values and beliefs that underlie a company's identity.

Organisational decline
Decrease in organisation's resource base (money, customers, talent, innovations).

Organisational diagnosis
A normative approach to the design of organisations based on strict fit relationships between the elements of the organisation.

Organisational moles
Use the grapevine to enhance their power and status.

Organisational politics
Intentional enhancement of self-interest.

Organisational socialisation
Process by which employees learn the organisation's values, norms and required behaviours.

Ostracism
Rejection by other group members.

Participative management
Involving employees in various forms of decision making.

Pay-for-performance
Monetary incentives tied to one's results or accomplishments.

Perceiving
Preference for gathering a lot of information before making decisions.

Perception
Cognitive process that enables us to interpret and understand our environment.

Perceptual grouping
Cognitive process to form individual stimuli into meaningful patterns.

Perceptual model of communication
Consecutively linked elements within the communication process.

Persistence
Extent to which effort is expended on a task over time.

Personal initiative
Going beyond formal job requirements and being an active self-starter.

Personalised power
Directed at helping oneself.

Personality type
Personality description based on common patterns of characteristics of people.

Personality
Stable physical and mental characteristics responsible for a person's identity.

Philanthropic responsibilities
Those responsibilities about which the society has no clear-cut message for business.

Platform organisation
Combines the new flexible types with the more classic organisation types.

Political organisation
An organisation in which power is illegitimate, resulting in disintegration and conflict.

Polychronic time
Preference for doing more than one thing at a time because time is flexible and multidimensional.

Position power
Degree to which leader has formal power.

Positive affectivity
Tendency to experience positive emotional states.

Positive inequity
Comparison in which another person receives lesser outcomes for similar inputs.

Postmodernism
A very subjective and situational view on the world around us making it impossible to develop general applicable theories of this world.

Pragmatist
Learning style preferring learning by active experimentation.

Prevalence (or representativeness) heuristic
Tendency to assess the likelihood of an event occurring based on impressions about similar occurrences.

Primacy effect
Effect by which the information first received often continues to colour later perceptions of individuals.

Problem
Gap between an actual and desired situation.

Process theories
Theories regarding how people get motivated.

Process-style listeners
Like to discuss issues in detail.

Product-based departmentalisation
Grouping people based on product, service or customer.

Productivity
Realising the highest possible output with a specific amount of input.

Professional organisation
Decentralised organisation with professionals doing highly skilled work.

Programmed conflict
Encourages different opinions without protecting management's personal feelings.

Project organisation
An organisation consisting of temporarily semi-autonomous project groups.

Propensity to trust
A personality trait involving one's general willingness to trust others.

Proxemics
Hall's term for the cultural expectations about interpersonal space.

Proximity
Tendency to group elements based upon their nearness.

Quality circles
Small teams of volunteers who strive to solve quality-related problems.

Rapport talk
Typical female way of communicating.

Rational choice theory
Maximisation of utility in decision making.

Rational model
Logical four-step approach to decision-making.

Readiness
Follower's ability and willingness to complete a task.

Realistic job preview
Presents both positive and negative aspects of a job.

Reality shock
A newcomer's feeling of surprise after experiencing unexpected situations or events.

Reasons-style listeners
Interested in hearing the rationale behind a message.

Recruitment practices
Attempts to attract qualified, diverse employees at all levels.

Referent power
Obtaining compliance through charisma or personal attraction.

Reflector
Learning style preferring learning by reflective observation.

Relationship level
How the relationship between sender and receiver is communicated.

Relaxation response
State of peacefulness.

Report talk
Typical male way of communicating.

Resistance to change
Emotional/behavioural response to real or imagined work changes.

Resource view
Growth and competitive advantages of organisations are based on the presence of rare and immobile resources under control of the organisation.

Results-style listeners
Interested in hearing the bottom line or result of a message.

Reward equality norm
Everyone should get the same rewards.

Reward equity norm
Rewards should be tied to contributions.

Reward power
Obtaining compliance with promised or actual rewards.

Role ambiguity
Others' expectations are unknown.

Role conflict
Others have conflicting or inconsistent expectations.

Role overload
Others' expectations exceed one's ability.

Roles
Expected behaviours for a given position.

Sample survey
Questionnaire responses from a sample of people.

Satisficing
Choosing a solution that meets a minimum standard of acceptance.

Scenario technique
Speculative forecasting method.

Schema
Mental picture of an event or object.

Scientific management
A scientific approach to management in which all tasks in organisations are in-depth analysed, routinised, divided and standardised, instead of using rules-of-thumb.

Self-concept
A person's self-perception as a physical, social, spiritual being.

Self-efficacy
Belief in one's ability to accomplish a task successfully.

Self-esteem
Belief about one's own self-worth based on overall self-evaluation.

Self-fulfilling prophecy
People's expectations determine behaviour and performance.

Self-managed teams
Groups of employees granted administrative oversight for their work.

Self-management leadership
Process of leading others to lead themselves.

Self-monitoring
The extent to which a person adapts his/her behaviour to the situation.

Self-serving bias
Tendency to attribute one's success to internal factors and one's failure to external factors.

Sensing
Preference for perceiving directly through the five senses.

Servant-leadership
Focuses on increased service to others rather than to oneself.

Set-up-to-fail syndrome
Creating and reinforcing a dynamic that essentially sets up perceived weaker performers to fail.

Sex-role stereotype
Beliefs about appropriate roles for men and women.

Similarity
Tendency to group objects, people and events that look alike.

Single loop learning
Learning through error and correction – adapting behaviour based on feedback.

Situational theories
Propose that leader styles should match the situation at hand.

Skill
Specific capacity to manipulate objects.

Social loafing
Decrease in individual effort as group size increases.

Social perception
Process by which people come to understand one another.

Social power
Ability to get things done using human, informational and material resources.

Social support
Amount of helpfulness derived from social relationships.

Socialised power
Directed at helping others.

Socio-emotional cohesiveness
Sense of togetherness based on emotional satisfaction.

Span of control
The number of people reporting directly to a given manager.

Staff personnel
Provide research, advice and recommendations to line managers.

Stakeholder audit
Systematic identification of all parties likely to be affected by the organisation.

Stakeholder theory
Stresses the responsibilities companies have toward their stakeholders.

Stereotype
Beliefs about the characteristics of a group.

Strategic constituency
Any group of people with a stake in the organisation's operation or success.

Stress
Behavioural, physical or psychological response to stressors.

Stressful life events
Life events that disrupt daily routines and social relationships.

Stressors
Environmental factors that produce stress.

Style
A preferred way or habitual pattern of doing something.

Substitutes for leadership
Situational variables that can substitute for, neutralise or enhance the effects of leadership.

Superleader
Someone who leads others to lead themselves.

Symbolic interactionism
Subjective interpretation of the world around us through interacting in this world.

Symptom management strategy
Coping strategy that focuses on reducing the symptoms of stress.

Systems theory
Every element is a subsystem of a larger system and every system is composed of subsystems, depending on each other and on the whole.

Task roles
Task-oriented group behaviour.

Task structure
Amount of structure contained within work tasks.

Team building
Experiential learning aimed at better internal functioning of teams.

Team viability
Team members' satisfaction and willingness to contribute.

Team
Small group with complementary skills who hold themselves mutually accountable for common purpose, goals and approach.

Technology
Collective instruments used to do the work in organisations.

Telecommuting
Doing work that is generally performed in the office away from the office using different information technologies.

Terminal values
Represent desirable goals or end-states of existence a person wants to reach during his/her life.

Theorist
Learning style preferring learning by abstract conceptualisation.

Theory Y
McGregor's modern and positive assumptions about employees being responsible and creative.

Theory
A story defining key terms, providing a conceptual framework and explaining why something occurs.

Thinking
Preference for judging based on a logical, objective and impersonal process.

Total quality management
An organisational culture dedicated to training, continuous improvement and customer satisfaction.

Transactional leadership
Focuses on interpersonal interactions between managers and employees.

Trust
Reciprocal faith in other's intentions and behaviour.

Type A behaviour syndrome
Aggressively involved in a chronic, determined struggle to accomplish more in less time.

Unaided-analytic
Analysis is limited to processing information in one's mind.

Unity of command
Each employee should report to a single manager.

Upward feedback
Subordinates evaluate their boss.

Utilitarianism
Considering certain principles and balancing the consequences.

Valence
The value of a reward or outcome.

Value system
A ranking of a person's values according to their intensity or importance.

Values
Standards or criteria for choosing goals and guiding actions that are relatively enduring and stable over time.

Verbaliser
Cognitive style characterised by representing information through verbal thinking.

Vertical specialisation
Determines who takes responsibility and who has decision-making power in the organisation.

Virtual organisation
Geographically dispersed people accomplishing tasks together thanks to modern information technology.

Virtual team
Information technology allows team members in different locations to conduct business.

Wholist
Cognitive style characterised by processing information in a whole.

Withdrawal cognitions
Overall thoughts and feelings about quitting a job.

Work values
Refer to what a person wants out of work in general.

Written communication
Verbal communication that is written.

16 PF model
16 traits or factors representing personality according to Cattell.

360-degree feedback
Comparison of anonymous feedback from one's superior, subordinates and peers, with one's self-perceptions.

Index

Page numbers for figures have suffix **f**, those for tables have suffix **t**